POLITICS
IN AMERICA

POLITICS IN AMERICA

FOURTH EDITION

THOMAS R. DYE

FLORIDA STATE UNIVERSITY

BASIC VERSION

Prentice
Hall

Upper Saddle River, New Jersey 07458

Library of Congress Cataloging-in-Publication Data

DYE, THOMAS R.
  Politics in America/Thomas R. Dye.—4th ed., basic version
    p. cm.
  Includes bibliographical references and index.
  ISBN 0-13-042018-2
  1. United States—Politics and government. I. Title.
JK271.D94 2001
320.473—dc21   00-055761

VP, Editorial Director: Laura Pearson
AVP, Director of Production and Manufacturing: Barbara Kittle
Editorial/Production Supervision: Rob DeGeorge
Copyeditor: Barbara Christenberry
Editorial Assistant: Jessica Drew
Prepress and Manufacturing Manager: Nick Sklitsis
Prepress and Manufacturing Buyer: Ben Smith
Director of Marketing: Beth Gillet Mejia
Creative Design Director: Leslie Osher
Interior and Cover Design: Thomas Nery
Art Director: Anne Bonanno Nieglos
Electronic Art Creation: Mirella Signoretto
Manager, Art and Formatting: Guy Ruggiero
Director, Image Resource Center: Melinda Reo
Interior Image Specialist: Beth Boyd
Manager, Rights and Permissions: Kay Dellosa
Photo Researcher: Diana P. Gongora
Permissions Coordinator: Anthony Arabia
Cover Coordinator: Karen Sanatar
Cover Photo: Barry Rosenthal/FPG International

This book was set in 12/13 Perpetua by Rob DeGeorge
and was printed and bound by Courier Companies, Inc.
The cover was printed by Phoenix Color Corp.

 © 2001, 1999, 1997, 1994 by Prentice-Hall, Inc.
A Pearson Education Company
Upper Saddle River, New Jersey 07458

All rights reserved. No part of this book may be
reproduced, in any form or by any means,
without permission in writing from the publisher.

Printed in the United States of America

10 9 8 7 6 5 4 3 2 1

ISBN 0-13-042018-2

PRENTICE-HALL INTERNATIONAL (UK) LIMITED, *London*
PRENTICE-HALL OF AUSTRALIA PTY. LIMITED, *Sydney*
PRENTICE-HALL CANADA INC., *Toronto*
PRENTICE-HALL HISPANOAMERICANA, S.A., *Mexico*
PRENTICE-HALL OF INDIA PRIVATE LIMITED, *New Delhi*
PRENTICE-HALL OF JAPAN, INC., *Tokyo*
PEARSON EDUCATION ASIA PTE. LTD., *Singapore*
EDITORA PRENTICE-HALL DO BRASIL, LTDA., *Rio de Janeiro*

Brief Contents

Contents

PART I   POLITICS

The study of politics is the study of influence and the influential. . . .
The influential are those who get the most of what there is to get.
Those who get the most are elite; the rest are mass.

Harold Lasswell

 1 POLITICS: WHO GETS WHAT, WHEN, AND HOW   1

 2 POLITICAL CULTURE: IDEAS IN CONFLICT   24

PART II   CONSTITUTION

The ascendancy of any elite depends upon the success of the
practices it adopts...The Constitution, written and unwritten,
embodies the practices which are deemed most fundamental to the
governmental and social order.

Harold Lasswell

 3 THE CONSTITUTION: LIMITING GOVERNMENTAL POWER   54

PART III PARTICIPANTS

People strive for power—to get the most of what there is to get.
Harold Lasswell

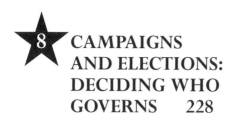

8 CAMPAIGNS AND ELECTIONS: DECIDING WHO GOVERNS 228

9 INTEREST GROUPS: GETTING THEIR SHARE AND MORE 278

PART IV INSTITUTIONS

Authority is the expected and legitimate possession of power.

Harold Lasswell

10 CONGRESS: POLITICS ON CAPITOL HILL 316

11 THE PRESIDENT: WHITE HOUSE POLITICS 374

PART V   OUTCOMES

*That political science concentrates upon the influential does not
imply the neglect of the total distribution of values throughout
the community.... The emphasis upon the probability that the few
(elite) will get the most does not imply that the many (mass) do
not profit from some political changes.*

Harold Lasswell

APPENDIX

Box Features

ACROSS THE USA

LOOKING AHEAD

Preface

Politics is an activity by which people try to get more of whatever there is to get. It is not about the pursuit of liberty as much as it is about the struggle over the allocation of values in society. Simply put, it is about "who gets what, when, and how."

By using Lasswell's classic definition of politics as the unifying framework, *Politics in America, Fourth Edition*, strives to present a clear, concise, and stimulating introduction to the American political system. Without the conflicts that arise from disagreement over who should get what, when, and how, our government would not reflect the diverse concerns of the nation. Politics consists of all of the activities—reasonable discussion, impassioned oratory, campaigning, balloting, fund raising, advertising, lobbying, demonstrating, rioting, street fighting, and waging war—by which conflict is carried on. Managing conflict is the principle function of the political system and power is the ultimate goal.

By examining the struggle for power—the participants, the stakes, the processes, and the institutional arenas—*Politics in America, Fourth Edition*, introduces students to the politics that is the basis for our democracy.

WHY *POLITICS IN AMERICA*?

Recent market research indicates that 76 percent of instructors teaching the Introductory American Government course find engaging their students to be the most difficult task facing them. *Politics in America, Fourth Edition*, is written to be lively and absorbing, reflecting the teaching philosophy that stimulating students' interest in politics and public affairs is the most important goal of an introductory course. Interesting examples and controversial debates spark students' interest and keep them connected to the material. The struggle for power in society is not a dull topic, and textbooks should not make it so.

Politics in America, Fourth Edition, strives for a balanced presentation, but "balanced" does not mean boring. It does not mean the avoidance of controversy. Liberal and conservative arguments are set forth clearly and forcefully. Race and gender are given particular attention, not because it is currently fashionable to do so,

but because American politics has long been driven by these factors. As in previous editions, the trademark of this book continues to be its desire to pull students into the debate that is our political system.

ORGANIZATION

Part I, "Politics," begins with Lasswell's classic definition of politics and proceeds to describe the nature and functions of government and the meaning of democracy. It poses the question: How democratic is the American political system? It describes the American political culture: its contradictions between liberty and conformity, political equality and economic inequality, equality of opportunity and inequality of results, thus laying the groundwork for understanding the struggle over who gets what.

Part II, "Constitution," describes the politics of constitution making—deciding how to decide. It describes how the struggle over the U.S. Constitution reflected the distribution of power in the new nation. It focuses on the classic arguments of the Founders for limiting and dividing governmental power and the structural arrangements designed to accomplish this end.

Part III, "Participants," begins by examining individual participation in politics—the way people acquire and hold political opinions and act on them through voting and protest activity. It examines the influences of family, school, gender, race, and the role of media in shaping political opinion. It describes how organization concentrates power—to win public office in the case of party organizations, and to influence policy in the case of interest groups. It assesses the role of personal ambition in politics and the role of money.

Part IV, "Institutions," describes the various governmental arenas in which the struggle for power takes place—the Congress, the presidency, the bureaucracy, the courts. More important, it evaluates the power that comes with control of each of these institutions.

Part V, "Outcomes," deals with public policies—the result of the struggle over the allocation of values. It is especially concerned with the two fundamental values of American society—liberty and equality.

INSTRUCTIONAL FEATURES

Interactive Chapter Opening Survey Each chapter opens with a brief poll called "Ask Yourself about Politics" that alerts students to the crucial issues the chapter covers and the impact of those issues on their lives. This tool can be used to get students thinking about how and why politics is important to them as individuals and as members of a community. In the Fourth Edition, we are excited to offer this survey as an interactive exercise on the accompanying Web site (www.prenhall.com/dye). Now students can compare their answers with students from across the country.

Text and Features The body of each chapter is divided into text and features. The text provides the framework of understanding American politics. Each chapter begins with a brief discussion of power in relation to the subject matter of the chapter: for example, limiting governmental power (Chapter 3, "The Constitution"), dividing governmental power (Chapter 4, "Federalism"), and the power of the media (Chapter 6, "Mass Media"). By focusing the beginning of each chapter on questions of power, students can more easily set the chapter content in the context of Lasswell's definition of politics.

The features in each chapter provide timeliness, relevance, stimulation, and perspective. Each boxed feature in the Fourth Edition of *Politics in America* is designed to encourage students to voice their opinions and explore those of others. If the key to learning is active involvement, students should be encouraged to read and respond whenever possible.

- *"What Do You Think?"* These features pose controversial questions to students and provide national opinion survey data. They cover a wide range of interests designed to stimulate classroom discussion. Examples include: "Can You Trust the Government?" "Is American Government 'Of, By and For the People'?" "Are you a Liberal or a Conservative?" "Does Money Buy Influence in Washington?" "How Would You Rate the Presidents?" "Should We Judge Presidents on Private Character or Performance in Office?" "How Much Money Does the Government Waste?" "What Constitutes Sexual Harassment?"

- *"A Conflicting View"* These features challenge students to rethink conventional notions about American politics. They are designed to be contro-

versial and to start students thinking about the push and pull that is politics. "Politics as Violence," for example, briefly summarizes the view that much of American political development has been accompanied by violence. Other "Conflicting View" features include: "An Economic Interpretation of the Constitution," "Objections to the Constitution by an Anti-Federalist," "Let the People Vote on National Issues," "The War on Drugs Threatens Individual Liberty," "The Constitution Should Be Color-Blind."

- *"Compared to What?"* These features provide students with global context by comparing the United States with other nations. Discussions include "Freedom and Democracy around the World," as well as such topics as the size of government, voter turnout, political parties, television culture, and the earnings gap between men and women.

- *"People in Politics"* These features are designed to personalize politics for students, to illustrate to them that the participants in the struggle for power are real people. They discuss where prominent people in politics went to school, how they got started in politics, how their careers developed, and how much power they came to possess. Both historical—John Locke and James Madison—and current figures, such as Jeb Bush, Ralph Nader, Colin Powell, Elizabeth Dole, Ted Kennedy, and Jesse "the body" Ventura.

- *"Up Close"* These features illustrate the struggle over who gets what. They range over a wide variety of current political conflicts, such as "Sex, Lies, and Impeachment," "Abortion, the 'Hot Button' Issue," "Dirty Politics," "AARP: The Nation's Most Powerful Interest Group," "The Christian Coalition: Organizing the Faithful," "Political Correctness vs. Free Speech on Campus," "The Cash Constituents of Congress." A special feature, "How to Run for Office," provides practical advice on how to get into electoral politics.

- *"Across the USA"* These features provide maps that summarize important statistical and demographic information relevant to American politics.

- *"What's Ahead? Twenty-First Century Directions"* Each chapter ends with provocative speculation about future American politics—what is likely to change for the better or for worse. The author presents his personal forecasts about upward and downward trends on such topics as trust in government; the influence of money in politics; the amount of sex, scandal, and violence in news coverage; the weakening of the presidency; the growth of bureaucratic regulation; racial and ethnic conflict; reliance on federal courts rather than the president or Congress to decide policy issues.

Currency   The Fourth Edition of *Politics in America* brings students up-to-date coverage of recent important political events and issues—from Bill Clinton's battles against impeachment, to an analysis of the results of the 2000 presidential election. It describes the strategies of candidates George W. Bush and Al Gore and tracks their campaigns throughout the election years from the early primaries to the general election. It focuses special attention on the role of cash in both presidential and congressional elections. Discussions about "How Much Does It Cost to Get Elected?" "Raising Campaign Cash," "What Do Contributors 'Buy'?" are both frank and perhaps disquieting to readers. Yet another special focus of the Fourth Edition is the growing importance of Hispanic Americans in the political life of the nation. And, as in previous editions, it gives special attention to racial issues in American politics. The Fourth Edition deals directly with growing anti-affirmative action politics and political and judicial attacks on racial and gender preferences.

Learning Aids   Each chapter contains a running glossary in the margin to help students master important concepts, a chapter outline, a summary, and a list of annotated suggested readings.

SUPPLEMENTS AVAILABLE FOR THE INSTRUCTOR

- **Instructor's Manual** (ISBN 0-13-027160-8) For each chapter, a summary, review of concepts, lecture suggestions and topic outlines, and additional resource materials—including a guide to media resources—are provided.
- **Test Item File** (ISBN 0-13-027175-6) Thoroughly reviewed and revised to ensure the highest level of quality and accuracy, this file offers over

1800 questions in multiple choice, true/false, and essay format with page references to the text.
- **Prentice Hall Custom Test**   A computerized test bank contains the items from the Test Item File. The program allows full editing of questions and the addition of instructor-generated items. Available in Windows (ISBN 0-13-027171-3) and Macintosh (ISBN 0-13-027174-8) versions.
- **Telephone Test Preparation Service**   With one call to our toll-free 800 number, you can have Prentice Hall prepare tests with up to 200 questions chosen from the Test Item File. Within 48 hours of your request, you will receive a personalized exam with answer key.
- **American Government Transparencies, Series VI** (ISBN 0-13-011764-1)   This set of over 100 four-color transparency acetates reproduces illustrations, charts, and maps from the text as well as from additional sources. An instructor's guide is also available.
- **Prentice Hall Custom Video:** *How A Bill Becomes a Law*   This 25-minute video chronicles an environmental law in Massachusetts— from it's start as one citizen's concern to its passage in Washington, D.C. Students see step-by-step the process of how a bill becomes a law complete through narrative and graphics. Call your local Prentice Hall representative for details.
- **Strategies for Teaching American Government: A Guide for the New Instructor** (0-13-339003-9)   This unique guide offers a wealth of practical advice and information to help new instructors face the challenges of teaching American government. This guide is also available on www.prenhall.com/dye under the faculty resources section.

SUPPLEMENTS AVAILABLE FOR THE STUDENT

- **Study Guide** (ISBN 0-13-027176-4)   Includes chapter outlines, study notes, a glossary, and practice tests designed to reinforce information in the text and help students develop a greater understanding of American government and politics.
- **The Write Stuff: Writing as a Performing and Political Art, 2nd Ed.** (0-13-364746-3)

This brief, humorous booklet by Thomas E. Cronin provides ideas and suggestions on writing in political science and is available free to students using *Politics in America, Fourth Edition*. This booklet is also available on the *Politics in America* Web site.

TECHNOLOGY INITIATIVES

With the development of new technologies, we have discovered more and more ways of helping students and instructors to further understand and analyze information. In this edition, we have made every effort to give both instructors and students a large array of multimedia tools to help with both the presentation and the learning of the material.

- **Companion Website** (www.prenhall.com/dye) Students can now take full advantage of the World Wide Web to enrich the study of American government through the *Politics in America* Web site. Created by Dave Garson of North Carolina State University, the site features interactive practice tests, chapter objectives and overviews, additional graphs and charts, and over 150 primary-source documents that are covered in the text. Interactive Web exercises guide students to do research with a series of questions and links. Students can also tap into information on the results of the 2000 presidential election and the settling in of the new administration, writing in political science, career opportunities, and internship information. Instructors can also find a special section for them that includes an update section for the latest news and how to tie it to lectures, teaching strategies for the new instructor, tables, photos and graphs from the book available for downloading in Power Point slides, additional Web links.

- **Political Science on the Internet 2001: Evaluating Online Resources** (ISBN 0-13-027758-4) This timely supplement provides an introduction to the Internet and the numerous political sites on the World Wide Web. It describes e-mail, list servers, browsers, and how to document sources. It also includes Web addresses for the most current and useful political Web sites. This 96-page supplementary book is free to students when shrink-wrapped to the text.

- **Distance Learning Solutions** For instructors interested in distance learning, Prentice Hall offers fully customizable, on-line courses in both WebCT and Blackboard platforms. See your local Prentice Hall representative or visit our special Demonstration Web site at www.prenhall.com/cms for more information.

ACKNOWLEDGMENTS

Politics in America, *Fourth Edition*, reflects the influence of many splendid teachers, students, and colleagues who have helped me over the years. I am grateful for the early guidance of Frank Sorauf, my undergraduate student adviser at Pennsylvania State University, and James G. Coke, my Ph.D. dissertation director at the University of Pennsylvania. Georgia Parthemos at the University of Georgia and Malcolm Parsons at Florida State University gave me my first teaching posts. But my students over the years contributed most to my education—notably Susan MacManus, Kent Portney, Ed Benton, James Ammons, Aubrey Jewitt, and especially John Robey. Several of my colleagues gave advice on various parts of this book: Glen Parker (on Congress), Suzanne Parker (on public opinion), James Gwartney (on economics), Robert Lichter (on the mass media), Charles Barrioux (on Bureaucracy), and especially Harmon Zeigler, whose knowledge of politics is unbounded.

At Florida State University, I am indebted to the timely research assistance provided by R. Thomas Dye, Ph.D. (History), and Christopher Stream, Ph.D. (Public Administration). And I am deeply grateful to Harriet Crawford of the Policy Sciences Center, who turned my scratchings into a manuscript.

At Prentice Hall I am indebted to Beth Gillett Mejia and Laura Pearson for their confidence in the project, Rob DeGeorge for guiding the book smoothly through production with professional competence, John Jordan for his work on the Web site and distance learning packages, and Brian Prybella and Beth Murtha for their work on the supplements package.

Finally, I would like to thank the many reviewers who evaluated the text and contributed invaluable advice:

Danny Adkinson, Oklahoma State University
Weston Agor, University of Texas at El Paso
Angela Burger, UWC–Marathon Company
Frank Colon, Lehigh University

Roy Dawes, University of Southwestern Louisiana

John Ellis, San Antonio College

Larry Elowitz, University of Southwestern Louisiana

Edward Fox, Eastern Washington University

Marilyn A. W. Garr, Johnson County Community College

Henry Glick, Florida State University

John Green, University of Akron

Dale Herspring, Kansas State University

Fred Kramer, University of Massachusetts at Amherst

Dale Krane, University of Nebraska at Omaha

Nancy McGlen, Niagara University

John McGlennon, College of William and Mary

James Meader, Augustana College

Jo Anne Myers, Marist College

Max Neiman, University of California–Riverside

Christopher Petras, Central Michigan University

Bruce Rogers, American River College

Bill Rutherford, Odessa University

John Shea, West Chester University

Robert Small, Massosoit County College

Henry Steck, SUNY–Cortland

Gerald Strom, University of Illinois at Chicago

Morris M. Wilhelm, Indiana University Southeast

Al Waite, Central Texas College

About the Author

Thomas R. Dye, formerly Professor of Government at Florida State University, is President of the Lincoln Center for Public Service. He regularly taught large introductory classes in American politics and was University Teacher of the Year in 1987. He received his B.A. and M.A. degrees from Pennsylvania State University and his Ph.D. degree from the University of Pennsylvania. He is the author of numerous books and articles on American government and public policy, including *The Irony of Democracy*; *Politics in States and Communities*; *Understanding Public Policy*; *Who's Running America*; *American Politics in the Media Age*; *Power in Society*; *Politics, Economics, and the Public*; and *American Federalism: Competition Among Governments*. His books have been translated into many languages, including Russian and Chinese, and published abroad. He has served as president of the Southern Political Science Association, president of the Policy Studies Organization, and secretary of the American Political Science Association. He has taught at the University of Pennsylvania, the University of Wisconsin, and the University of Georgia, and served as a visiting scholar at Bar-Ilan University, Israel, the Brookings Institution in Washington, D.C., and elsewhere. He is a member of Phi Beta Kappa, Omicron Delta Kappa, and Phi Kappa Phi, and is listed in most major biographical directories.

Florida State University Teacher of the Year.

POLITICS
IN AMERICA

Politics

Who Gets What, When, and How

ASK YOURSELF ABOUT POLITICS

1 Can you trust the government to do what is right most of the time?
Yes ● No ●

2 Should any group other than the government have the right to use force?
Yes ● No ●

3 Is violence ever justified as a means of bringing about political change?
Yes ● No ●

4 Is it ever right to disobey the law?
Yes ● No ●

5 Should important decisions in a democracy be submitted to voters rather than decided by Congress?
Yes ● No ●

6 Has government in the United States grown too big?
Yes ● No ●

7 In a democracy should "majority rule" be able to limit the rights of members of an unpopular or dangerous minority?
Yes ● No ●

8 Is government trying to do too many things that should be left to individuals?
Yes ● No ●

9 In your opinion, do we have a government today that is "of, by and for the people"?
Yes ● No ●

Who has power and how they use it are the basis of all these questions. Issues of power underlie everything we call politics and the study of political science.

POLITICS AND POLITICAL SCIENCE

Politics is deciding "who gets what, when, and how." It is an activity by which people try to get more of whatever there is to get—money, prestige, jobs, respect, sex, even power itself. Politics occurs in many different settings. We talk about office politics, student politics, union politics, church politics, and so forth. But political science usually limits its attention to *politics in government*.

Political science is the study of politics, or the study of who gets what, when, and how. The *who* are the participants in politics—voters, special-interest groups, political parties, television and the press, corporations and labor unions, lawyers and lobbyists, foundations and think tanks, and both elected and appointed government officials, including members of Congress, the president and vice-president, judges, prosecutors, and bureaucrats. The *what* of politics are public policies—the decisions that governments make concerning social welfare, health care, education, national defense, law enforcement, the environment, taxation, and thousands of other issues that come before governments. The *when* and *how* are the political process—campaigns and elections, political reporting in the news media, television debates, fund raising, lobbying, decision making in the White House and executive agencies, and decision making in the courts.

Political science is generally concerned with three questions: *Who governs? For what ends? By what means?* Throughout this book, we are concerned with who participates in politics, how

Conflict exists in all political activities as participants struggle over who gets what, when, and how. From the streets to the Congress to the White House, participants in the political process compete to further their goals and ambitions.

government decisions are made, who benefits most from those decisions, and who bears their greatest costs (see Figure 1-1).

Politics would be simple if everyone agreed on who should govern, who should get what, who should pay for it, and how and when it should be done. But conflict arises from disagreements over these questions, and sometimes the question of confidence in the government itself underlies the conflict (see *What Do You Think?* "Can You Trust the Government?"). Politics arises out of conflict, and it consists of all the activities—reasonable discussion, impassioned oratory, balloting, campaigning, lobbying, parading, rioting, street fighting, and waging war—by which conflict is carried on.

POLITICS AND GOVERNMENT

What distinguishes governmental politics from politics in other institutions in society? After all, parents, teachers, unions, banks, corporations, and many other organizations make decisions about who gets what in society. The answer is that only **government** decisions can *extend to the whole society*, and only government can

politics   Deciding who gets what, when, and how.

political science   The study of politics: who governs, for what ends, and by what means.

government   Organization extending to the whole society that can legitimately use force to carry out its decisions.

Who Governs: Participants

Governmental

President and White House staff
Executive Office of the President,
   including Office of Management and Budget
Cabinet officers and executive
   agency heads
Bureaucrats

Congress members
Congressional staff

Supreme Court justices
Federal appellate and district judges

Nongovernmental

Voters
Campaign contributors
Interest-group leaders and
   members
Party leaders and party
   identifiers in the electorate
Corporate and union leaders
Media leaders, including press
   and television anchors and
   reporters
Lawyers and lobbyists
Think tanks and foundation
   personnel

When and How: Institutions and Processes

Institutions

Constitution
   Separation of powers
   Checks and balances
   Federalism
   Judicial review
   Amendment procedures
   Electoral system

Presidency
Congress
   Senate
   House of Representatives

Courts
   Supreme Court
   Appellate Court
   District Court

Parties
   National committees
   Conventions
   State and local organizations

Press and television

Processes

Socialization and learning
Opinion formation
Party identification
Voting
Contributing
Joining organizations
Talking politics

Running for office
Campaigning
Polling
Fund raising
Parading and demonstrating
Nonviolent direct action
Violence

Agenda setting
Lobbying
Logrolling
Deciding
Budgeting
Implementing and evaluating
Adjudicating

What Outcomes: Public Policies

Civil liberties
Civil rights
Equality
Criminal justice
Welfare
Social Security
Health
Education

Energy
Environmental protection
Economic development
Economic stability
Taxation
Government spending and deficits
National defense
Foreign affairs

FIGURE 1-1 Who Gets What, When, and How

Political science is the study of politics. The study of politics includes the questions "Who governs?" (that is, who are the participants in politics, both within and outside of government?); "When and how are political decisions made?" (that is, how do the institutions and processes of politics function?); and "What outcomes are produced?" (that is, what public policies are adopted?). Shown here are some of the topics of concern to political science.

legitimately use force. Other institutions encompass only a part of society: for example, students and faculty in a college, members of a church or union, employees or customers of a corporation. And individuals have a legal right to voluntarily withdraw from nongovernmental organizations. But governments make decisions affecting everyone, and no one can voluntarily withdraw from government's authority

Can You Trust the Government?

Americans are suspicious of big government. Many do not trust the government in Washington to "do what is right." Although commentators often bemoan Americans' lack of confidence in government, this attitude may be a blessing in disguise. After all, if people are too trusting of government, always ready to believe that what the government does is right, they are vulnerable to bad government. A little suspicion of government may be good protection for a free people.

Confidence in government has varied over the years, as measured by polls asking, "How much of the time do you think you can trust the government in Washington to do what is right? Just about always? Most of the time? Some of the time? None of the time?" During the early years of the Johnson Administration (and even earlier, during the Kennedy and Eisenhower presidencies), public confidence in government was high. But defeat and humiliation in Vietnam appeared to diminish public confidence. On the heels of the Vietnam experience came the Watergate scandal and President Richard Nixon's forced resignation—the first resignation of a president in U.S. history—which caused public confidence in government to fall further. Presidents Gerald Ford and Jimmy Carter were unable to halt the downward slump, and the Iranian hostage crisis in 1980 caused public confidence in government to slide even lower.

Throughout the long years of decline in public confidence in government, television has broadcast many negative images of government and public policy. Television producers seldom consider good news as "news" but instead focus on violence, scandal, corruption, and incompetence. Bad news drives out the good on television. People heavily exposed to negative television reporting gradually lose their trust in government. So the explanation for the decline in public confidence in government in the past three decades may be a product of (1) a series of disturbing events (the Vietnam War, the Watergate scandal, and the Iranian hostage crisis) and/or (2) television reporting of these events and negative television reporting in general.

Public confidence in government grew during the Reagan presidency. Ronald Reagan himself, paradoxically, was publicly critical of government. In his Inaugural Address in 1981, he said, "Government is not the solution to our problem. Government is the problem." Perhaps President Reagan's personal popularity was part of the reason that popular confidence in government rose.

Economic recessions erode public confidence in government. People expect the president and Congress to lead them out of "hard times." The recession of 1990–92 was not particularly deep by historical standards, but it was one of the nation's longest periods of slowed economic progress. George Bush's Gulf War success raised public confidence only temporarily; the perceived failure of his administra-

(without leaving the country, and thus becoming subject to some other government's authority). Some individuals and organizations—muggers, gangs, crime families—occasionally use physical force to get what they want. In fact, the history of the United States has been punctuated by examples of violence used for political ends (see *A Conflicting View:* "American Politics as Violence"). But only governments can use force legitimately—that is, people generally believe it is acceptable for the government to use force if necessary to uphold its laws, but they do not extend this right to other institutions or individuals.

Most people would say that they obey the law in order to avoid fines and stay out of prison. But if large numbers of people all decided to disobey the law at the same time, the government would not have enough police or jails to hold them all. The government can rely on force only against relatively small numbers of offenders. Most of us, most of the time, obey laws out of habit—the habit of compliance. We

Public Confidence That the Federal Government Can Be Trusted to "Do What Is Right Most of the Time"

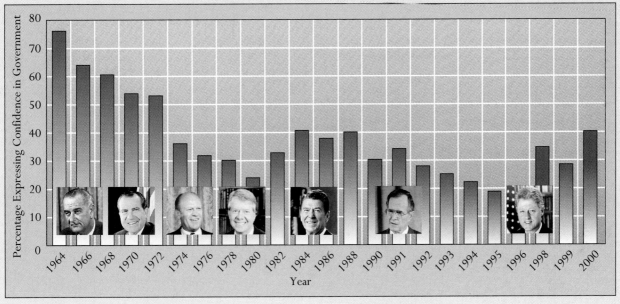

Source: Gallup Opinion Polls; see also Arthur H. Miller, "Confidence in Government during the 1980's," *American Politics Quarterly 19* (April 1991):147–73.

tion to act decisively to restore the nation's economic health helped to send public confidence in government back down to historic lows. Public trust in government fell to a new low early in the Clinton presidency. Indeed, Clinton attributed the failure of Congress to enact a national health care program to popular distrust of government. But sustained growth in the economy under President Clinton improved public trust in government somewhat.

have been taught to believe that law and order are necessary and that government is right to punish those who disobey its laws.

Government thus enjoys **legitimacy**, or rightfulness, in its use of force.[1] A democratic government has a special claim to legitimacy because it is based on the consent of its people, who participate in the selection of its leaders and the making of its laws. Those who disagree with a law have the option of working for its change by speaking out, petitioning, demonstrating, forming interest groups or parties, voting against unpopular leaders, or running for office themselves. Since people living in a democracy can effect change by "working within the system," they have a greater moral obligation to obey the law than people living under regimes in which they have no voice. However, there may be some occasions when "civil disobedience" even in a democracy may be morally justified (see *A Conflicting View:* "Sometimes It's Right to Disobey the Law").

legitimacy Widespread acceptance of something as necessary, rightful, and legally binding.

American Politics as Violence

We think of one of the central functions of government, especially democratic government, as the peaceful management of conflict in society and the protection of individual safety. Yet political violence has played a prominent role in American history. The United States was founded in armed revolution, and violence has been both a source of power and a stimulus to social change ever since. Despite their pious pronouncements against it, Americans have frequently employed violence, even in their most idealistic endeavors.

The longest and most brutal violence in American history—that between whites and Native Americans—began when the first settlers arrived in 1607. The "Indian Wars" continued with only temporary truces for nearly 300 years, until the final battle at Wounded Knee, South Dakota, in 1890. Early colonial experience in a rugged frontier country gave rise to the tradition of an armed civilian militia, which was used successfully in the Revolutionary War against British rule.

After the Revolutionary War, many armed farmers and debtors resorted to violence to assert their economic interests. The most serious rebellion broke out in 1786 in Massachusetts, when a band of insurgents, composed of farmers and laborers and led by Bunker Hill veteran Daniel Shays, captured several courthouses. Shays's Rebellion was put down by a small mercenary army paid for by well-to-do citizens who feared that a wholesale attack on property rights was imminent. The growing violence in the states contributed to the momentum leading to the Constitutional Convention of 1787, where a new central government was established with the power to "insure domestic Tranquility."

Ratification of the Constitution did not stop violence, however. Vigilantism (taking the law into one's own hands) arose in response to a perennial American problem: the absence of effective law and order in the frontier region. Practically every state and territory west of the Appalachians had at one time or another a well-organized vigilante movement, frequently backed by prominent citizens.

The ultimate turning of citizen on citizen—the Civil War—was the bloodiest war Americans ever fought. Total battle deaths of the northern and southern armies exceeded American battle deaths in World War II, even though the U.S. population at the time of the Civil War was only one-quarter that of the World War II period. Violence was also a prime ingredient of the early labor movement in the United States. Both management and workers resorted to violence in the struggles accompanying the Industrial Revolution. The last great spasm of violence in the history of American labor came in the 1930s, with the strikes and plant takeovers that accompanied the successful drive to unionize the automobile, steel, and other mass-production industries.

A long history of racial violence continues to plague the United States. Slavery itself was accompanied by untold violence. An estimated one-third to one-half of the Africans captured in slave raids never survived the ordeal of initiation into slavery. After the Civil War, racial strife and Ku Klux Klan activity became routine in the old Confederacy, and the white supremacy movement employed violence to reestablish white rule in the southern social system. Racial violence directed against blacks—whipping, torture, and lynching—was fairly common from the 1870s to the 1930s. During World War II, serious racial violence erupted in Detroit, where black and white mobs battled each other in 1943. More than 150 major riots involving race were reported in American cities from 1965 to 1968, and the rioting, burning, and looting in south-central Los Angeles in 1992 reminded the nation that racial violence—and the conditions that foment it—are continuing threats to society.

Today self-styled citizen "militias" in various parts of the country believe that they must be armed and trained in military tactics in order to ensure that federal agencies, or perhaps even the United Nations, do not threaten American freedom. More than seventy people died near Waco, Texas, in 1993, when federal agents attempted to disarm one such group. And Timothy McVeigh was convicted of the nation's single most destructive act of domestic violence in the Oklahoma City federal office building bombing in 1995 that killed 265 people.

Americans think of democratic politics as stable, with the authority to govern transferred peacefully from one administration to the next according to the preferences of the electorate. Yet political assassinations have taken the lives of four presidents: Abraham Lincoln in 1865, James A. Garfield in 1881, William McKinley in 1901, and John F. Kennedy in 1963. Several other presidents have been the targets of assassination attempts, and the assassination of Dr. Martin Luther King, Jr., in 1968, ended an era of progress in civil rights in America.

THE PURPOSES OF GOVERNMENT

All governments tax, penalize, punish, restrict, and regulate their people. Governments in the United States—the federal government in Washington, the 50 state governments, and the more than 86,000 local governments—take nearly 40 cents out of every dollar Americans earn. Each year, the Congress enacts about 500 laws; federal bureaucracies publish about 19,000 rules and regulations; the state legislatures enact about 25,000 laws; and cities, counties, school districts, and other local governments enact countless local ordinances. Each of these laws restricts our freedom in some way. Each dollar taken out of our wages or profits reduces our freedom to choose what to do with our money.

Why do people put up with governments? An answer to this question can be found in the words of the Preamble to the Constitution of the United States:

> We the people of the United States, in Order to form a more perfect Union, establish Justice, insure domestic Tranquility, provide for the common defense, promote the general Welfare, and secure the Blessings of Liberty to ourselves and our Posterity, do ordain and establish this Constitution for the United States of America.

To Establish Justice and Insure Domestic Tranquility   Government manages conflict and maintains order. We might think of government as a **social contract** among people who agree to allow themselves to be regulated and taxed in exchange for protection of their lives and property. No society can allow individuals or groups to settle their conflicts by street fighting, murder, kidnapping, rioting, bombing, or terrorism. Whenever government fails to control such violence, we describe it as "a breakdown in law and order." Without the protection of government, human lives and property are endangered, and only those skilled with fists and weapons have much of a chance of survival. The seventeenth-century English political philosopher Thomas Hobbes described life without government as "a war where every man is enemy to every man," where people live in "continual fear and danger of violent death."[2]

To Provide for the Common Defense   Many anthropologists link the origins of government to warfare—to the need of early communities to protect themselves from raids by outsiders and to organize raids against others. Since the Revolutionary War, the U.S. government has been responsible for the country's defense, but today, with a diminished threat to national security from the states of the former Soviet Union, national defense absorbs about 15 percent of the *federal* government's budget and less than 8 percent of *all* government spending—federal, state, and local combined. Nevertheless, national defense remains a primary responsibility of the U.S. government.

To Promote the General Welfare   Government promotes the general welfare in a number of ways. It provides **public goods**—goods and services that private markets cannot readily furnish either because they are too expensive for individuals to buy for themselves (for example, a national park, a highway, or a sewage disposal plant) or because if one person bought them, everyone else would "free-ride," or use them without paying (for example, clean air, police protection, or national defense).

social contract   Idea that government originates as an implied contract among individuals who agree to obey laws in exchange for protection of their rights.

public goods   Goods and services that cannot readily be provided by markets, either because they are too expensive for a single individual to buy or because if one person bought them, everyone else would use them without paying.

Sometimes It's Right to Disobey the Law

Civil disobedience is the nonviolent violation of laws that people believe to be unjust. Civil disobedience denies the *legitimacy*, or rightfulness, of a law and implies that a higher moral authority takes precedence over unjust laws. It is frequently a political tactic of minorities. (Majorities can more easily change laws through conventional political activity.) Civil disobedience is also an attractive tactic for groups that wish to change the status quo.

Why resort to civil disobedience in a democracy? Why not work within the democratic system to change unjust laws? In 1963 a group of Alabama clergy posed these questions to Martin Luther King, Jr., and asked him to call off mass demonstrations in Birmingham, Alabama. King, who had been arrested in the demonstrations, replied in his now-famous "Letter from Birmingham City Jail":

Dr. Martin Luther King, Jr., shown here marching in Mississippi with his wife, Coretta Scott King, and others, used civil disobedience to advance the rights of African Americans during the 1950s and 1960s.

> You may well ask, "Why direct action? Why sit-ins, marches, etc.?" . . . Nonviolent direct action seeks to create such a crisis and establish such creative tension that a community that has constantly refused to negotiate is forced to confront the issue. It seeks to so dramatize the issue that it can no longer be ignored. . . . One may well ask, "How can you advocate breaking some laws and obeying others?" The answer is found in the fact that there are unjust laws. I would be the first to advocate obeying just laws. One has not only a legal but a moral responsibility to obey just laws. Conversely, one has a moral responsibility to disobey unjust laws.

King argued that *nonviolent direct action* was a vital aspect of democratic politics. The political purpose of civil disobedience is to call attention or "to bear witness" to the existence of injustices. Only laws regarded as unjust are broken, and they are broken openly, without hatred or violence. Punishment is actively sought rather than avoided, since punishment will further emphasize the injustice of the laws.

The objective of nonviolent civil disobedience is to stir the conscience of an apathetic majority and to win support for measures that will eliminate the injustices. By accepting punishment for the violation of an unjust law, persons practicing civil disobedience demonstrate

their sincerity. They hope to shame the majority and to make it ask itself how far it is willing to go to protect the status quo. Thus, according to King's teachings, civil disobedience is clearly differentiated from hatred and violence:

> In no sense do I advocate evading or defying the law as the rabid segregationist would do. This would lead to anarchy. One who breaks an unjust law must do it openly, lovingly (not hatefully as the white mothers did in New Orleans when they were seen on television screaming "nigger, nigger, nigger") and with a willingness to accept the penalty. I submit that an individual who breaks a law that conscience tells him is unjust, and willingly accepts the penalty by staying in jail to arouse the conscience of the community over its injustice, is in reality expressing the very highest respect for law.

In 1964 Martin Luther King, Jr., received the Nobel Peace Prize in recognition of his extraordinary contributions to the development of nonviolent methods of social change.

Source: Martin Luther King, Jr., "Letter from Birmingham City Jail," April 16, 1963.

Nevertheless, Americans acquire most of their goods and services on the **free market**, through voluntary exchange among individuals, firms, and corporations. The **gross domestic product (GDP)**—the dollar sum of all the goods and services produced in the United States in a year—amounts to nearly $10 trillion. Government spending in the United States—federal, state, and local governments combined—amounts to about $3 trillion, or about 30 percent of the gross domestic product (see *Up Close:* "How Big Is Government and What Does It Do?").

Governments also regulate society. Free markets cannot function effectively if individuals and firms engage in fraud, deception, or unfair competition, or if contracts cannot be enforced. Moreover, many economic activities impose costs on persons who are not direct participants in these activities. Economists refer to such costs as **externalities**. A factory that produces air pollution or wastewater imposes external costs on community residents who would otherwise enjoy cleaner air or water. A junkyard that creates an eyesore makes life less pleasant for neighbors and passersby. Many government regulations are designed to reduce these external costs.

To promote general welfare, governments also use **income transfers** from taxpayers to people who are regarded as deserving. Government agencies and programs provide support and care for individuals who cannot supply these things for themselves through the private job market, for example, ill, elderly, and disabled people, and dependent children who cannot usually be expected to find productive employment. However, it is important to realize that payments to the poor are less than one-fifth of all government transfer payments to individuals. The largest income transfer programs are Social Security and Medicare, which are paid to the elderly regardless of their personal wealth. Other large transfer payments go to farmers, veterans, and the unemployed, as well as to a wide variety of businesses. As we shall see, the struggle of individuals and groups to obtain direct government payments is a major motivator of political activity.

To Secure the Blessings of Liberty All governments must maintain order, protect national security, provide public goods, regulate society, and care for those unable to fend for themselves. But *democratic* governments have a special added responsibility—to protect individual liberty by ensuring that all people are treated equally before the law. No one is above the law. The president must obey the Constitution and laws of the United States, and so must members of Congress, governors, judges, and the police. A democratic government must protect people's freedom to speak and write what they please, to practice their religion, to petition, to form groups and parties, to enjoy personal privacy, and to exercise their rights if accused of a crime.

The concentration of government power can be a threat to freedom. If a democratic government acquires great power in order to maintain order, protect national security, or provide many collective goods and services, it runs the risk of becoming too powerful for the preservation of freedom. The question is how to keep government from becoming so pervasive it threatens the individual liberty it was established to protect.

THE MEANING OF DEMOCRACY

Throughout the centuries, thinkers in many different cultures contributed to the development of democratic government. Early Greek philosophers contributed the word **democracy**, which means "rule by the many." But there is no single definition

free market Free competition for voluntary exchange among individuals, firms, and corporations.

gross domestic product (GDP) The dollar sum of all the goods and services produced in a nation in a year.

externalities Costs imposed on people who are not direct participants in an activity.

income transfers Government transfers of income from taxpayers to persons regarded as deserving.

democracy Governing system in which the people govern themselves; from the Greek term meaning "rule by the many."

How Big Is Government and What Does It Do?

Government in the United States grew enormously throughout most of the twentieth century, both in absolute terms and in relation to the size of the national economy. The size of the economy is usually measured by the gross domestic product (GDP), the dollar sum of all the goods and services produced in the United States in a year. Governments accounted for only about 8 percent of the GDP at the beginning of the century, and most governmental activities were carried out by state and local governments. Two world wars, the New Deal programs devised during the Great Depression of the 1930s, and the growth of the Great Society programs of the 1960s and 1970s all greatly expanded the size of government, particularly the federal government. The rise in government growth relative to the economy leveled off during the Reagan presidency (1981–89), and no large new programs were undertaken in the Bush and Clinton years. An economic boom in the 1990s caused the GDP to grow rapidly, while government spending grew only moderately. The result has been a modest *decline* in governmental size in relation to the economy. Today, federal expenditures amount to about 20 percent of GDP, and total governmental expenditures are about 30 percent of GDP (see Graph A).

Not everything that government does is reflected in governmental expenditures. *Regulatory activity*, for example, especially environmental regulations,

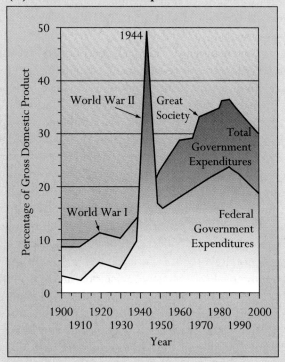

(A) What Government Spends

Source: *Budget of the United States Government, 2000.*

imposes significant costs on individuals and businesses; these costs are not shown in government budgets. Nevertheless, government spending is a common indicator of governmental functions and priorities. For example, Graph B indicates that the *federal government* spends more on senior citizens—in Social Security and

of *democracy*, nor is there a tightly organized system of democratic thought. It is better, perhaps, to speak of democratic traditions than of a single democratic ideology.

Unfortunately, the looseness of the term *democracy* allows it to be perverted by *anti*democratic governments. Hardly a nation in the world exists that does not *claim* to be "democratic." Governments that outlaw political opposition, suppress dissent, discourage religion, and deny fundamental freedoms of speech and press still claim to be "democracies," "democratic republics," or "people's republics" (for example, the Democratic People's Republic of Korea is the official name of Communist North Korea). These governments defend their use of the term *democracy* by claiming that their policies reflect the true interests of their people. But they are unwilling to allow political freedoms or to hold free elections in order to find out whether their people really agree with their policies. In effect, they use the term as a political slogan rather than a true description of their government.[3]

(B) What Federal Government Does

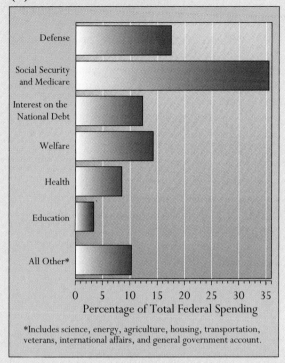

Percentage of Total Federal Spending

*Includes science, energy, agriculture, housing, transportation, veterans, international affairs, and general government account.

Source: *Budget of the United States Government, 2000.*

(C) What State and Local Governments Do

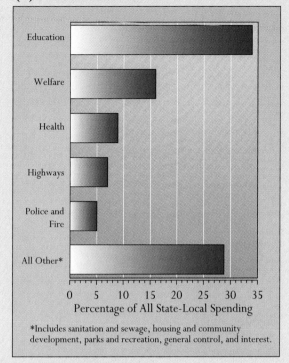

Percentage of All State-Local Spending

*Includes sanitation and sewage, housing and community development, parks and recreation, general control, and interest.

Source: *Statistical Abstract of the United States, 1999.*

Medicare outlays—than on any *other* function, including national defense. Interest payments on the national debt consume 12 percent of all federal spending. Federal welfare and health programs account for substantial budget outlays, but federal financial support of education is very modest.

State and local governments in the United States bear the major burden of public education. Welfare and health functions consume larger shares of their budgets than highways and law enforcement do (see Graph C).

The actual existence of **democratic ideals** varies considerably from country to country, regardless of their names (see *Compared to What?* "Freedom and Democracy in the World"). A meaningful definition of democracy must include the following ideals: recognition of the dignity of every individual; equal protection under the law for every individual; opportunity for everyone to participate in public decisions; and decision making by majority rule, with one person having one vote.

Individual Dignity   The underlying value of democracy is the dignity of the individual. Human beings are entitled to life and liberty, personal property, and equal protection under the law. These liberties are *not* granted by governments; they belong to every person born into the world. The English political philosopher John Locke (1632–1704) argued that a higher "natural law" guaranteed liberty to every person and that this natural law was morally superior to all human laws and

democratic ideals Individual dignity, equality before the law, widespread participation in public decisions, and public decisions by majority rule, with one person having one vote.

Freedom and Democracy around the World

Worldwide progress toward freedom and democracy has been evident over the past decade, not only in the collapse of communism in Eastern Europe and the Soviet Union but also in the movements toward democracy in such nations as South Africa, South Korea, Taiwan, and Nicaragua. Nevertheless, more than half the world's people live under governments that can hardly be called democracies.

One way to assess the degree of democracy in a governmental system is to consider its record in ensuring political freedoms—enabling citizens to participate meaningfully in government—and individual liberties. A checklist for political freedoms might include whether the chief executive and national legislature are elected; whether elections are generally fair, with open campaigning and honest tabulation of votes; and whether multiple candidates and parties participate. A checklist for individual liberties might include whether the press and broadcasting are free and independent of the government; whether people are free to assemble, protest, and form opposition parties; whether religious institutions, labor unions, business organizations, and other groups are free and independent of the government; and whether individuals are free to own property, travel, and move their residence.

The Freedom House, a New York–based think tank that regularly surveys political conditions around the world, ranks nations according to the amount of political freedom and individual liberty they allow. The categories are "Free," "Partly Free," and "Not Free," based on each nation's combined average score on political freedom and individual liberty.

The Map of Freedom

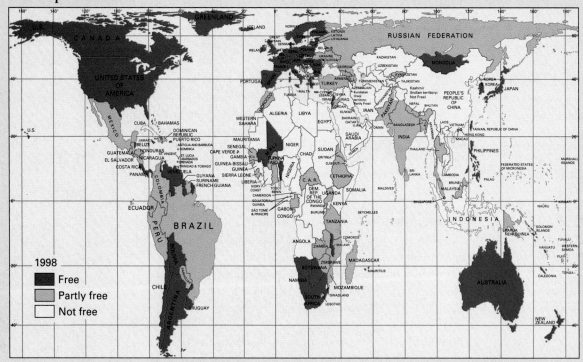

Source: Freedom House, 1998.

Democracy, Legitimacy, and Election 2000

Elections are designed to confer legitimacy on democratic governments. That is to say, the actions of democratic governments are generally considered "rightful" by citizens because they have been offered a role in the selection of government officials. Elections help to bind citizens to their government, to inspire respect for governmental authority, and to morally oblige citizens to obey the laws that elected officials have enacted.

But George W. Bush was not the choice of voters for president of the United States on election day, 2000. Al Gore received about 500,000 more popular votes nationwide than Bush. Yet George W. Bush was sworn in as president on January 20, 2001, as prescribed by the U.S. Constitution.

Democracy versus the Electoral College The nation's Founders—the 55 delegates to the 1787 Constitutional Convention—never intended that the president be elected by popular vote. They envisioned a Republic—where decisions were to be made by *representatives* of the people, not by the people themselves. They wrote a Constitution in which the president was to be chosen by a majority of "Electors," not by direct popular vote. "Each State shall appoint, in such Manner as the Legislature thereof may direct, a Number of Electors equal to the whole Number of Senators and Representatives to which the State shall be entitled in the Congress . . ." (Art. II).

As political parties emerged in the early 1800's, the states chose to hold popular elections for slates of "Electors" pledged to one or another of the presidential candidates. In other words, popular voting for presidential electors in the states came about later by custom, not because the Founders wanted a popularly-elected president (see *Up Close:* "Should We Scrap the Electoral College?" in Chapter 8).

The electoral college system has always included the possibility that the winner of the nationwide popular vote might not win a majority of state electors. But the last time this occurred was in 1888, when Republican Benjamin Harrison won 235 electoral votes to incumbent Democratic president Grover Cleveland's 168, even though Cleveland won more popular votes nationwide. Not until 112 years later—in the 2000 presidential election—did the electoral college again fail to reflect the nationwide popular vote.

Legitimacy and the Contested Election 2000
The electoral vote in 2000 was the closest in American history, 271 to 267. The switch of any state from Bush to Gore would have resulted in the election of Al Gore as president. The popular vote was very close in several states but none was closer than Florida, with its 25 electoral votes. The official Bush lead in Florida was declared to be 537 votes out of more than six million cast. Early in the evening on election night the television networks "called" the state for Gore, almost assuring his election as president. But shortly thereafter they yanked Florida back into the "too close to call" category. Later they declared Bush the winner of Florida and pronounced him the next president of the United States. But by early morning the next day Florida was again "too close to call." The virtual tie in the state resulted in the first post-election presidential contest in over a century.

Most states, including Florida, provide for recounts when the margin of victory is less than 1/2 of 1 percent. The Florida Secretary of State, after a machine recount and the counting of absentee ballots, declared Bush the winner. But armies of lawyers had already descended on Florida and initiated scores of lawsuits contesting the election.

The stakes were high—the presidency of the United States. Each side called on their legal and political heavyweights. The Bush campaign sent a team of attorneys headed by former Secretary of State James Baker, and the Gore campaign sent a team headed by former Secretary of State Warren Christopher. The battle of the ballots would consume over a month.

Several issues were involved, issues that had never been directly addressed by courts in the past. The Gore campaign demanded *hand* recounts of the votes in the state's three most populous and most Democratic counties—Miami-Dade, Broward (Fort Lauderdale), and Palm Beach. They argued that the Palm Beach "butterfly" ballot confused voters. (The Gore/Lieberman punch hole was placed third rather than second under the Bush/Cheney hole, with Buchanan's punch hole positioned in between.) They also argued that partially detached "chads" (small perforated squares in the punch cards that should fall out when the voter punches the ballot), as well as "dimpled" chads (ballots with indentations), should be examined by hand to determine the "intent" of the voter. In Miami-Dade County alone they claimed that there were 10,700 "uncounted" ballots that did not register any vote for president on the machines.

(*continued*)

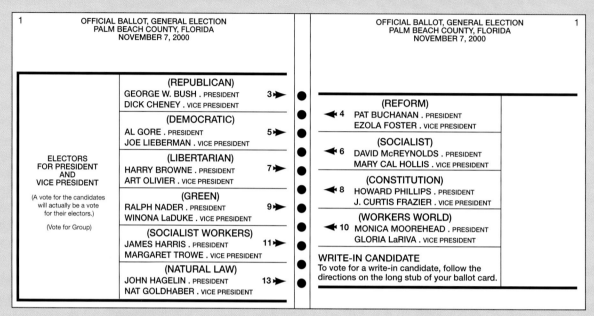

| 1 | **OFFICIAL BALLOT, GENERAL ELECTION**
PALM BEACH COUNTY, FLORIDA
NOVEMBER 7, 2000 |

The Palm Beach "Butterfly" Ballot

("Undervotes"—ballots that have no choice marked for an office—are common even in presidential elections; the average undervote throughout the nation was about 1.9 percent; the undervotes in Miami-Dade amounted to 1.7 percent of the votes in that county.) Gore's attorneys asked the Florida courts to extend the legislature's statutory deadline for counting votes.

Bush's attorneys argued that hand counts were subjective, unreliable, and open to partisan bias. They also argued that hand counting votes in only three counties discriminated against voters in all of the state's other counties. And they argued that the courts had no authority to change the deadline enacted by the state Legislature. Indeed, they cited the phrase in Article II of the U.S. Constitution (cited above) that specifically gave "the Legislature" the power to determine how presidential electors are to be chosen.

The Florida Supreme Court sided with Gore's attorneys. (All seven of its members had been appointed by Democratic governors.) It ordered that hand counts could be undertaken by the counties and that the Legislature's deadline for the receipt of votes from the counties was to be set back by more than a week. But Bush's attorneys quickly appealed to the U.S. Supreme Court, arguing that the Florida Court had erred in interpreting the mandate of the U.S. Constitution that only the Legislature of a state can determine "the Manner" of choosing presidential electors.

The Supreme Court Chooses a President The Supreme Court of the United States had never before been called upon in effect to decide a presidential election. Indeed, the Court had historically avoided "political questions" and had deferred to state courts in the interpretation of state laws, including election laws. So it came as a surprise to most observers when the Supreme Court ordered that hand counting be discontinued. After hearing oral arguments on December 10, the Court issued its historic decision, *Bush v. Gore*, on December 12.

In *Bush v. Gore* the Supreme Court of the United States chose the president. While the Court's decision rested on constitutional issues, the 5–4 division of the Court in the case raised the question of the Court's political impartiality. Indeed, an apparently embittered Justice Stevens in his dissenting opinion charged the majority with lending credence to the most cynical appraisal of the work of judges. "Although we may never know with complete certainty the winner of this year's presidential election, the identity of the loser is perfectly clear. It is the nation's confidence in the judge as an impartial guardian of the rule of law."

But the majority of the Supreme Court expressed concern that "the use of standardless manual recounts violates the Equal Protection and Due Process Clauses." And three justices in the majority held that the Florida Supreme Court "plainly departed from the legislative scheme" and therefore violated Article II of the U.S. Constitution. (See excerpts from *Bush v. Gore*)

FOCUS: Bush v. Gore *in the U.S. Supreme Court*

From the Majority Opinion:

On December 8, 2000, the Supreme Court of Florida ordered that the Circuit Court of Leon County tabulate by hand 9,000 ballots in Miami-Dade County . . . . The Court further held that relief would require manual recounts in all Florida counties where so-called "undervotes" had not been subject to manual tabulation. The court ordered all manual recounts to begin at once . . . .

The [Bush] petition presents the following questions: whether the Florida Supreme Court established new standards for resolving Presidential election contests, thereby violating Art. II, Section 1, cl. 2, of the United States Constitution and failing to comply with 3 U.S.C. Section 5, and whether the use of standardless manual recounts violates the Equal Protection and Due Process Clauses.

With respect to the equal protection question, we find a violation of the Equal Protection Clause . . . .

Much of the controversy seems to revolve around ballot cards designed to be perforated by a stylus but which, either through error or deliberate omission, have not been perforated with sufficient precision for a machine to count them.

In some cases a piece of the card—a chad—is hanging, say by two corners. In other cases there is no separation at all, just an indentation. The Florida Supreme Court has ordered that the intent of the voter be discerned from such ballots . . . .

The recount mechanisms implemented in response to the decisions of the Florida Supreme Court do not satisfy the minimum requirement for non-arbitrary treatment of voters necessary to secure the fundamental right (of equal protection). Florida's basic command for the count of legally cast votes is to consider the "intent of the voter." . . . This is unobjectionable as an abstract proposition and a starting principle. The problem inheres in the absence of specific standards to ensure its equal application.

From Justices Rehnquist, Scalia, and Thomas, concurring with the majority:

Moreover, the court's interpretation of "legal vote," and hence its decision to order a contest-period recount, plainly departed from the legislative scheme. Florida statutory law cannot reasonably be thought to require the counting of improperly marked ballots. Each Florida precinct before election day provides instructions on how properly to cast a vote; each polling place on election day contains a working model of the voting machine it uses; and each voting booth contains a sample ballot. In precincts using punch-card ballots, voters are instructed to punch out the ballot cleanly:

After voting, check your ballot card to be sure your voting selections are clearly and cleanly punched and there are no chips left hanging on the back of the card.

No reasonable person would call it "an error in the vote tabulation," or a "rejection of legal votes," when electronic or electromechanical equipment performs precisely in the manner designed, and fails to count those ballots that are not marked in the manner that these voting instructions explicitly and prominently specify.

From Dissenting Opinions, Justice Stevens:

What must underlie petitioners' entire federal assault on the Florida election procedures is an unstated lack of confidence in the impartiality and capacity of the state judges who would make the critical decisions if the vote count were to proceed. Otherwise, their position is wholly without merit. The endorsement of that position by the majority of this Court can only lend credence to the most cynical appraisal of the work of judges throughout the land. It is confidence in the men and women who administer the judicial system that is the true backbone of the rule of law. Time will one day heal the wound to that confidence that will be inflicted by today's decision. One thing, however, is certain. Although we may never know with complete certainty the identity of the winner of this year's presidential election, the identity of the loser is perfectly clear. It is the nation's confidence in the judge as an impartial guardian of the rule of law.

From Dissenting Opinions, Justice Breyer:

Halting the manual recount, and thus ensuring that the uncounted legal votes will not be counted under any

(*continued*)

standard, this Court crafts a remedy out of proportion to the asserted harm. And that remedy harms the very fairness interests the Court is attempting to protect. The manual recount would itself redress a problem of unequal treatment of ballots . . . I fear that in order to bring this agonizingly long election process to a definitive conclusion, we have not adequately attended to that necessary "check upon our own exercise of power," "our own sense of self-restraint."

The ideological division of the Supreme Court was very clear. The five justices in the majority included the three generally acknowledged conservatives (Rehnquist, Scalia, and Thomas) together with Justices O'Conner and Kennedy. The minority included the three acknowledged liberals (Stevens, Breyer, and Ginsburg) plus Souter (see Table 13–4, "Liberal and Conservative Voting Blocs on the Supreme Court"). This division encouraged critics to label the decision as partisan.

Legitimacy and the 2000 Election   George W. Bush was accepted as the legitimate president of the United States almost immediately after the Supreme Court rendered its historic decision. The vast majority of Americans appeared to recognize that the nationwide popular vote for Al Gore was secondary in importance to the Constitution of the United States and its provision for the choosing of the president by state electoral votes. There was no real constitutional crisis.

The Supreme Court possesses sufficient legitimacy in the minds of most Americans that they were prepared to accept as legitimate the Court's decision about who would be the president. The Gallup poll, conducted before the Court's decision, showed that 73 percent of Americans said they would accept the Court's decision as a "legitimate outcome no matter which candidate it favors." Americans also believed that it would be far better for the U.S. Supreme Court to decide the issue (61%) than the U.S. Congress (17%), the Florida State Supreme Court (9%), or the Florida Legislature (7%). (The Florida Legislature called a special session with the intent of certifying its own presidential Electors in the event that the issue was not resolved by the U.S. Supreme Court prior to the date of the electoral college vote; the Legislature adjourned after the Court's decision.)

In 2000 Americans were evenly divided but not deeply divided. The Constitution of the United States, as interpreted by the U.S. Supreme Court, remained the nation's source of political unity.

governments. Each individual possesses "certain inalienable Rights, among these are Life, Liberty, and Property"[4] (see *People in Politics:* "John Locke and the Justification of Revolution").

Individual dignity requires personal freedom. People who are directed by governments in every aspect of their lives, people who are "collectivized" and made into workers for the state, people who are enslaved—all are denied the personal dignity to which all human beings are entitled. Democratic governments try to minimize the role of government in the lives of citizens.

Equality   True democracy requires equal protection of the law for every individual. Democratic governments cannot discriminate between blacks and whites, or men and women, or rich and poor, or any groups of people in applying the law. Not only must a democratic government refrain from discrimination itself, but it must also work to prevent discrimination in society generally. Today our notion of equality extends to equality of opportunity—the obligation of government to ensure that all Americans have an opportunity to develop their full potential.

Participation in Decision Making   Democracy means individual participation in the decisions that affect individuals' lives. People should be free to choose for themselves how they want to live. Individual participation in government is necessary for individual dignity. People in a democracy should not have decisions made *for* them but *by* them. Even if they make mistakes, it is better that they be permitted to do so than to take away their rights to make their own decisions. The true democrat would reject even a wise and benevolent dictatorship because it would threaten the individual's character, self-reliance, and dignity. The argument for democracy is not that the people will always choose wise policies for themselves but that people who cannot choose for themselves are not really free.

Majority Rule: One Person, One Vote   Collective decision making in democracies must be by majority rule with each person having one vote. That is, each person's vote must be equal to every other person's, regardless of status, money, or fame. Whenever any individual is denied political equality because of race, sex, or wealth, then the government is not truly democratic. Majorities are not always right. But majority *rule* means that all persons have an equal say in decisions affecting them. If people are truly equal, their votes must count equally, and a majority vote must decide the issue, even if the majority decides foolishly.

THE PARADOX OF DEMOCRACY

What if a *majority* of the people decide to attack the rights of some unpopular individuals or minority groups? What if hate, prejudice, or racism infects a majority of people and they vote for leaders who promise to "get rid of the Jews" or "put blacks in their place" or "bash a few gays"? What if a majority of people vote to take away the property of wealthy people and distribute it among themselves?[5] Do we abide by the principle of majority rule and allow the majority to do what it wants? Or do we defend the principle of individual liberty and limit the majority's power? If we enshrine the principle of majority rule, we are placing all our confidence in the wisdom and righteousness of the majority of the people. Yet we know that democracy means more than majority rule, that it also means freedom and dignity for the

John Locke and the Justification of Revolution

The most important single voice influencing the thought of the nation's Founders was that of English philosopher John Locke (1632–1704). Locke's writings, especially his *Second Treatise on Government* (1690), inspired the American Revolution, the Declaration of Independence, and the Constitution of the United States.

Like Thomas Hobbes, Locke was an aristocrat who was forced to flee during England's civil war. Yet despite living in fear of political persecution, he never adopted Hobbes's pessimistic view of human nature. Rather, he held that people are basically decent, orderly, social minded, and capable of self-government.

In his *Treatise on Civil Government* (1688), Locke argued that "all men are by nature free, equal, and independent" and all enjoy "the rights to life, liberty, and property." These laws of nature are "self-evident" to those who "make use of reason." People "consent" to enter into a social contract and "accept the bonds of government" in order to better protect their rights. People "unite in a commonwealth" especially for "the preservation of their property." Government is based on the consent of the people. An "absolute monarch" is "inconsistent with civil society" because people retain the ability to judge for themselves whether their rights are truly being protected by government. The only justification for government is its ability to protect life, liberty, and property.

It follows that any government that "transgresses" on these rights, "either by ambition, fear, folly, or corruption," breaches the social contract and "forfeits the power the people had put into its hands." The people then have the right to "resume their original liberty," dissolve their bonds with the government, and create a new government "such as they think fit." Thus Locke endorsed the right of revolution—the moral right of a people to dissolve a government that violates their fundamental rights. But he advised that people should not undertake such an action unless confronted with a long list of serious grievances and many "fruitless attempts" to redress them. And he reassured rulers that a good government has nothing to fear from acceptance of his theory of the right of revolution.

When Thomas Jefferson wrote his eloquent defense of the American Revolution in the Declaration of Independence for the Continental Congress in Philadelphia in 1776, he borrowed heavily from Locke (perhaps even to the point of plagiarism):

> We hold these Truths to be self-evident, that all Men are created equal, that they are endowed by their Creator with certain unalienable Rights, that among these are Life, Liberty, and the Pursuit of Happiness—That to secure these Rights, Governments are instituted among Men, deriving their just Powers from the Consent of the Governed, that whenever any Form of Government becomes destructive of these Ends, it is the Right of the People to alter or to abolish it. . . . But when a long Train of Abuses and Usurpations, pursuing invariably the same Object, evinces a Design to reduce them under absolute Despotism, it is their Right, it is their Duty, to throw off such Government. . . . The History of the present King of Great Britain is a History of repeated Injuries and Usurpations, all having in direct Object the Establishment of an absolute Tyranny over these States. . . .
>
> We, therefore, the Representatives of the UNITED STATES OF AMERICA, in General Congress, Assembled, appealing to the Supreme Judge of the World for the Rectitude of our Intentions, do, in the Name, and by Authority of the good People of these Colonies, solemnly Publish and Declare, That these United Colonies are, and of Right ought to be, Free and Independent States.

The paradox of democracy balances the principle of majority rule against the principle of individual liberty. When the German people voted Adolf Hitler and the Nazi Party into power, did majority rule give the Nazis free rein to restrict the individual liberties of the people? Or did those who abhorred the trespasses of their government have the right to fight against its power?

individual. How do we resolve this **paradox of democracy**—the potential for conflict between majority rule and individual freedom?

Limiting the Power of Majorities The Founders of the American nation were not sure that freedom would be safe in the hands of the majority. In *The Federalist Papers* in 1787, James Madison warned against a direct democracy: "Pure democracy . . . can admit of no cure for the mischiefs of faction. . . . There is nothing to check the inducements to sacrifice the weaker party, or an obnoxious individual."[6] So the Founders wrote a Constitution and adopted a Bill of Rights that limited the power of government over the individual, that placed some personal liberties beyond the reach of majorities. They established the principle of **limited government**—a government that is itself restrained by law. Under a limited government, even if a majority of voters wanted to, they could not prohibit communists or atheists or racists from speaking or writing. Nor could they ban certain religions, set aside the rights of criminal defendants to a fair trial, or prohibit people from moving or quitting their jobs. These rights belong to individuals, not to majorities or governments.

Totalitarianism: Unlimited Government Power No government can be truly democratic if it directs every aspect of its citizens' lives. Individuals must be free to shape their own lives, free from the dictates of governments or even majorities of their fellow citizens. Indeed, we call a government with *unlimited* power over its citizens totalitarian. Under **totalitarianism**, the individual possesses no personal liberty. Totalitarian governments decide what people can say or write; what unions, churches, or parties they can join, if any; where people must live; what work they must do; what goods they can find in stores and what they will be allowed to buy and sell; whether citizens will be allowed to travel outside of their country; and so on. Under a totalitarian government, the total life of the individual is subject to government control.

paradox of democracy Potential for conflict between individual freedom and majority rule.

limited government Principle that government power over the individual is limited, that there are some personal liberties that even a majority cannot regulate, and that government itself is restrained by law.

totalitarianism Rule by an elite that exercises unlimited power over individuals in all aspects of life.

Political sociologists have observed that the military in totalitarian societies has a distinct body language. Soldiers in Nazi Germany and, as seen here, the former Soviet Union used a "goose step" when on parade—a march in which the knee is unbent and the foot, encased in a heavy boot, is stamped on the ground, providing a powerful image of authority and force. In democratic societies, the goose step is not employed; indeed, it is regarded as somewhat ridiculous.

Constitutional Government Constitutions, written or unwritten, are the principal means by which governmental powers are limited. Constitutions set forth the liberties of individuals and restrain governments from interfering with these liberties. Consider, for example, the opening words of the First Amendment to the U.S. Constitution: "Congress shall make no law respecting an establishment of religion, or prohibiting the free exercise thereof." This amendment places religious belief beyond the reach of the government. The government itself is restrained by law. It cannot, even by majority vote, interfere with the personal liberty to worship as one chooses. In addition, armed with the power of judicial review, the courts can declare unconstitutional laws passed by majority vote of Congress or state legislatures (see "Judicial Power" in Chapter 13).

Throughout this book we examine how well limited constitutional government succeeds in preserving individual liberty in the United States. We examine free speech and press, the mass media, religious freedom, the freedom to protest and demonstrate, and the freedom to support political candidates and interest groups of all kinds. We examine how well the U.S. Constitution protects individuals from discrimination and inequality. And we examine how far government can go in regulating work, homes, business, and the marketplace without destroying individual liberty.

DIRECT VERSUS REPRESENTATIVE DEMOCRACY

In the Gettysburg Address, Abraham Lincoln spoke about "a government of the people, by the people, for the people," and his ringing phrase remains an American ideal. But can we take this phrase literally? (see *What Do You Think?* "Is the American

Direct democracy still lives in many New England towns, where citizens come together periodically to pass laws, elect officials, and make decisions about such matters as taxation and land use.

Government 'Of, By and For the People'?"). More than 275 million Americans are spread over 4 million square miles. If we brought everyone together, standing shoulder to shoulder, they would occupy 66 square miles. One round of five-minute speeches by everyone would take nearly 5,000 years. "People could be born, grow old, and die while they waited for the assembly to make one decision."[7]

Direct democracy (also called pure or participatory democracy), where everyone actively participates in every decision, is rare. The closest approximation to direct democracy in American government may be the traditional New England town meeting, where all of the citizens come together face to face to decide about town affairs. But today most New England towns vest authority in a board of officials elected by the townspeople to make policy decisions between town meetings, and professional administrators are appointed to supervise the day-to-day town services. The town meeting is rapidly vanishing because citizens cannot spend so much of their time and energy in community decision making.

Representative democracy recognizes that it is impossible to expect millions of people to come together and decide every issue. Instead, representatives of the people are elected by the people to decide issues on behalf of the people. Elections must be open to competition so that the people can choose representatives who reflect their own views. And elections must take place in an environment of free speech and press, so that both candidates and voters can freely express their views. Finally, elections must be held periodically so that representatives can be thrown out of office if they no longer reflect the views of the majority of the people.

No government can claim to be a representative democracy, then, unless

1. Representatives are selected by vote of all the people.
2. Elections are open to competition.
3. Candidates and voters can freely express themselves.
4. Representatives are selected periodically.

So when we hear of "elections" in which only one party is permitted to run candidates, candidates are not free to express their views, or leaders are elected "for life," then we know that these governments are not really democracies, regardless of what they may call themselves.

direct democracy Governing system in which every person participates actively in every public decision, rather than delegating decision making to representatives.

representative democracy Governing system in which public decision making is delegated to representatives of the people chosen by popular vote in free, open, and periodic election.

Is the American Government "Of, By and For the People"?

Do you think of the government in Washington as OUR government or as THE government? If a democratic government is truly "of, by and for the people," we would expect that the people would think of it as their own. But national opinion polls indicate the majority of Americans do *not* believe that the government belongs to them:

Q. *When you think and talk about government, do you tend to think of it more as THE government or as OUR government?*

THE government	55%
OUR government	42
Not sure	3

Indeed, a majority do *not* believe that we have a government today that is "of, by and for the people."

Q. *One goal that Americans have traditionally consid-*

ered important is to have a government that is "of, by and for the people"—meaning that it involves people and represents them. In your opinion, do we have a government today that is "of, by and for the people"?

Yes	39%
No	54
Not sure	7

Earlier we observed that over two-thirds of Americans today do not trust the government "to do what is right."

Moreover, most people think that we have "too much government":

Q. *In America today, do we have too much government, not enough government, or about the right amount of government?*

Too much government	59%
Not enough government	7
About the right amount	30
Not sure	4

Throughout this book, as we examine how well representative democracy works in the United States, we consider such issues as participation in elections—why some people vote and others do not—whether parties and candidates offer the voters real alternatives, whether modern political campaigning informs voters or only confuses them, and whether elected representatives are responsive to the wishes of voters. These are the kinds of issues that concern political science.

WHO REALLY GOVERNS?

Democracy is an inspiring ideal. But is democratic government really possible? Is it possible for millions of people to govern themselves, with every voice having equal influence? Or will a small number of people inevitably acquire more power than others? To what extent is democracy attainable in *any* society, and how democratic is the American political system? That is, who really governs?

elitism Theory that all societies, even democracies, are divided into the few who govern and the many who do not.

The Elitist Perspective "Government is always government by the few, whether in the name of the few, the one, or the many."[8] This quotation from political scientists Harold Lasswell and Daniel Lerner expresses the basic idea of **elitism**. All societies, including democracies, divide themselves into the few who have power and

Overall, Americans generally believe that the government is "trying to do too many things that should be left to individuals and businesses:

Q. *Some people think the government is trying to do too many things that should be left to individuals and businesses. Others think that government should do more to solve our country's problems. Which comes closer to your own view?*

Doing too much   58%
Should do more   33
Mixed/no opinion   9

Yet on the other hand, when asked about the major responsibilities that government currently undertakes—Social Security, Medicare, national defense, etc.—most Americans say that they support these activities as a "good use" of their tax dollars.

Q. *For each of the following federal programs, how much do you personally support this as a good use of your tax dollars. Do you support [name of program] a great deal, a fair amount, just a little, or not all?*

Percentage expressing "A Great Deal" of support:

Social Security	69%
Armed services	64
Medicare	64
Workplace safety	63
Discrimination	61
Public schools	61
Food, drug safety	60
College loans	56
Minimum wage	56
Environment	55

In short, Americans appear to be ambivalent about their government. On the one hand, they express general distrust and alienation from government, believe that it tries to do too much, and doubt that has much of a positive effect on their lives. Yet when asked about specific services that the national government provides, Americans express strong approval for most of them.

Sources: The Polling Report, February 10, 1997; February 24, 1997; July 19, 1999; *Rasmussen Research*, April 15, 1999.

the many who do not. In every society, there is a division of labor. Only a few people are directly involved in governing a nation; most people are content to let others undertake the tasks of government. The *elite* are the few who have power; the *masses* are the many who do not. This theory holds that an elite is inevitable in any social organization. We cannot form a club, a church, a business, or a government without selecting some people to provide leadership. And leaders will always have a perspective on the organization different from that of its members.

In any large, complex society, then, whether or not it is a democracy, decisions are made by tiny minorities. Out of more than 275 million Americans, only a few thousand individuals at most participate directly in decisions about war and peace, wages and prices, employment and production, law and justice, taxes and benefits, health and welfare.

Elitism does *not* mean that leaders always exploit or oppress members. On the contrary, elites may be very concerned for the welfare of the masses. Elite status may be open to ambitious, talented, or educated individuals from the masses or may be closed to all except the wealthy. Elites may be very responsive to public opinion, or they may ignore the usually apathetic and ill-informed masses. But whether elites are self-seeking or public spirited, open or closed, responsive or unresponsive, it is they and not the masses who actually make the decisions.

Contemporary elite theory argues that power in America is concentrated in a small *institutional* elite. Sociologist C. Wright Mills popularized the term *power elite* in arguing that leaders of corporations, the military establishment, and the national government come together at the top of a giant pyramid of power.[9] Other social scientists have found that more than half of the nation's total assets are concentrated in the 100 largest corporations and 50 largest banks; that the officers and directors of these corporations and banks interact frequently with leaders of government, the mass media, foundations, and universities; and that these leaders are drawn disproportionately from wealthy, educated, upper-class, white, male, Anglo-Saxon Protestant groups in American society.[10]

Most people do not regularly concern themselves with decision making in Washington. They are more concerned with their jobs, family, sports, and recreation than they are with politics. They are not well informed about tax laws, foreign policy, or even who represents them in Congress. Since the "masses" are largely apathetic and ill informed about policy questions, their views are likely to be influenced more by what they see and hear on television than by their own experience. Most communication flows downward from elites to masses. Elitism argues that the masses have at best only an indirect influence on the decisions of elites.

Opinion polls indicate that many Americans agree with the elitist contention that government is run by "a few big interests" (see Figure 1-2).

The Pluralist Perspective   No one seriously argues that all Americans participate in *all* of the decisions that shape their lives; that majority preferences *always* prevail; that the values of life, liberty, and property are *never* sacrificed; or that every American enjoys equality of opportunity. Nevertheless, most American political scientists argue that the American system of government, which they describe as "pluralist," is the best possible approximation of the democratic ideal in a large, complex society. Pluralism is designed to make the theory of democracy "more realistic."[11]

Pluralism is the belief that democracy can be achieved in a large, complex society by competition, bargaining, and compromise among organized groups and that individuals can participate in decision making through membership in these groups and by choosing among parties and candidates in elections.

Pluralists recognize that the individual acting alone is no match for giant government bureaucracies, big corporations and banks, the television networks, labor unions, or

pluralism   Theory that democracy can be achieved through competition among multiple organized groups and that individuals can participate in politics through group memberships and elections.

FIGURE 1-2   **Public Opinion about Who Runs the Country**

Would you say the government is pretty much run by a few big interests looking out for themselves or that it is run for the benefit of all the people?
Source: The Gallup Poll, April 17–19, 1995.

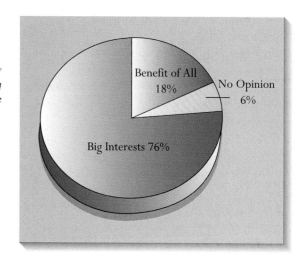

Benefit of All 18%

No Opinion 6%

Big Interests 76%

other powerful interest groups. Instead, pluralists rely on *competition* among these organizations to protect the interests of individuals. They hope that countervailing centers of power—big business, big labor, big government—will check one another and prevent any single group from abusing its power and oppressing individual Americans.

Individuals in a pluralist democracy may not participate directly in decision making, but they can join and support *interest groups* whose leaders bargain on their behalf in the political arena. People are more effective in organized groups—for example, the Sierra Club for environmentalists, the American Civil Liberties Union (ACLU) for civil rights advocates, the National Association for the Advancement of Colored People (NAACP) or the Urban League for African Americans, the American Legion or Veterans of Foreign Wars for veterans, and the National Rifle Association (NRA) for opponents of gun control.

According to the pluralist view, the Democratic and Republican parties are really coalitions of groups: the national Democratic Party is a coalition of union members, big-city residents, blacks, Catholics, Jews, and, until recently, southerners; the national Republican Party is a coalition of business and professional people, suburbanites, farmers, and white Protestants. When voters choose candidates and parties, they are helping to determine which interest groups will enjoy a better reception in government.

Pluralists contend that there are multiple leadership groups in society (hence the term *pluralism*). They contend that power is widely dispersed among these groups; that no one group, not even the wealthy upper class, dominates decision making; and that groups which are influential in one area of decision making are not necessarily the same groups that are influential in other areas of decision making. Different groups of leaders make decisions in different issue areas.

Pluralism recognizes that public policy does not always coincide with majority preferences. Instead, public policy is the "equilibrium" reached in the conflict among group interests. It is the balance of competing interest groups, and therefore, say the pluralists, it is a reasonable approximation of society's preferences.

DEMOCRACY IN AMERICA

Is democracy alive and well in America today? Elitism raises serious questions about the possibility of achieving true democracy in any large, complex society. Pluralism is more comforting; it offers a way of reaffirming democratic values and providing some practical solutions to the problem of individual participation in a modern society.

There is no doubt about the strength of democratic ideals in American society. These ideals—individual dignity, equality, popular participation in government, and majority rule—are the standards by which we judge the performance of the American political system. But we are still faced with the task of describing the reality of American politics.

This book explores who gets what, when, and how in the American political system; who participates in politics; what policies are decided upon; and when and how these decisions are made. In so doing, it raises many controversial questions about the realities of democracy, elitism, and pluralism in American life. But this book does not supply the answers; as a responsible citizen, you have to provide your own answers. At the completion of your studies, you will have to decide for yourself whether the American political system is truly democratic. Your studies will help inform your judgment, but, in the end, you yourself must make that judgment. That is the burden of freedom.

Twenty-First Century Directions

Politics is here to stay. People will always try to get more of what there is to get. James Madison explained that "the causes of faction are sewn in the nature of man"; political conflict cannot be resolved "by giving to every citizen in the same opinions, the same passions, and the same interests." More importantly, he argued that taking away the *liberty* to express differences of opinion, passion, and interest would be a remedy "worse than the disease."

⬇ ***Attitudes toward Government*** The American national government is likely to seem ever more distant from the American people. People want services that the government provides, but they do not really trust the government "to do what is right." It is not likely that attitudes toward government in general will become any more favorable in the foreseeable future.

⬆ ***Functions of Government*** Yet people will continue to ask for more and more services from the national government. For example, government health insurance will likely expand beyond Medicare for the aged and Medicaid for the poor, to include all children and perhaps eventually all Americans. Health care costs will increase as a percentage of federal, state, and local government spending.

⬇ ***Individual Rights*** The classic paradox of democracy—the conflict between majority preferences and individual rights—will never be fully resolved. But the pendulum appears to be swinging away from individual rights toward social responsibilities as defined by majorities. People appear to be increasingly willing to accept restrictions in their personal lives—police stops and searches, long prison terms for drug violations, metal detectors at airports, schools, and public buildings, bans on smoking, codes restricting "hate" speech, prohibitions on sexual harassment, etc.—in order to insure their personal safety and bring about greater conformity to social norms.

SUMMARY NOTES

- Politics is deciding who gets what, when, and how. It occurs in many different settings, but political science focuses on politics in government.
- Political science focuses on three central questions:
  Who governs?
  For what ends?
  By what means?
- Government is distinguished from other social organizations in that it
  Extends to the whole society
  Can legitimately use force
- The purposes of government are to
  Maintain order in society
  Provide for national defense

  Provide "public goods"
  Regulate society
  Transfer income
  Protect individual liberty
- The ideals of democracy include
  Recognition of individual dignity and personal freedom
  Equality before the law
  Widespread participation in decision making
  Majority rule, with one person equaling one vote
- The principles of democracy pose a paradox: How can we resolve conflicts between our belief in majority rule and our belief in individual freedom?
- Limited government places individual liberty beyond

the reach of majorities. Constitutions are the principal means of limiting government power.

- Direct democracy, in which everyone participates in every public decision, is very rare. Representative democracy means that public decisions are made by representatives elected by the people, in elections held periodically and open to competition, in which candidates and voters freely express themselves.

- Who really governs? The elitist perspective on American democracy focuses on the small number of leaders who actually decide national issues, compared to the mass of citizens who are apathetic and ill informed about politics. A pluralist perspective focuses on competition among organized groups in society, with individuals participating through group membership and voting for parties and candidates in elections.

- How democratic is American government today? Democratic ideals are widely shared in our society. But you must make your own informed judgment about the realities of American politics.

KEY TERMS

politics   2

political science   2

government   2

legitimacy   5

social contract   7

public goods   7

free market   9

gross domestic product (GDP)   9

externalities   9

income transfers   9

democracy   9

democratic ideals   11

paradox of democracy   15

limited government   15

totalitarianism   15

direct democracy   17

representative democracy   17

elitism   18

pluralism   20

SELECTED READINGS

BARKER, LUCIUS J., MACK H. JONES, AND KATHERINE TATE. *African-Americans and the American Political System*. Upper Saddle River, N.J.: Prentice Hall, 1999. A dynamic analysis of how African Americans fare within the prevailing theoretical, structural, and functioning patterns of the American political system.

CRONIN, THOMAS J. *Direct Democracy*. Cambridge, Mass.: Harvard University Press, 1989. A thoughtful discussion of direct versus representative democracy, as well as a review of initiative, referendum, and recall devices.

DAHL, ROBERT A. *Democracy and Its Critics*. New Haven, Conn.: Yale University Press, 1989. A defense of modern democracy from the pluralist perspective.

DYE, THOMAS R., AND HARMON ZEIGLER. *The Irony of Democracy*. Millennial Edition. New York: Harcourt Brace, 2000. An interpretation of American politics from the elitist perspective.

FUKUYAMA, FRANCIS. *Trust*. New York: Free Press, 1995. Argues that the breakdown of trust in America—not only in the government but at a person-to-person level—is burdening the nation with formal rules and regulations, lengthy contracts, bureaucracy, lawyers, and lawsuits.

LASSWELL, HAROLD. Politics: *Who Gets What, When, and How*. New York: McGraw-Hill, 1936. Classic description of the nature of politics and the study of political science by America's foremost political scientist of the twentieth century.

MILLS, C. WRIGHT. *The Power Elite*. New York: Oxford University Press, 1956. Classic Marxist critique of elitism in American society, setting forth the argument that "corporate chieftains," "military warlords," and a "political directorate" come together to form the nation's power elite.

NEIMAN, MAX. *Defending Government: Why Big Government Works*. Upper Saddle River, N.J.: Prentice Hall, 2000. A spirited defense of how big government can improve lives of people.

PAGE, BENJAMIN I., AND ROBERT Y. SHAPIRO. *The Rational Public*. Chicago: University of Chicago Press, 1992. An examination of fifty years of public opinion polls convinces these authors that American government is generally responsive to the views of the majority.

Political Culture
Ideas in Conflict

Political Culture

Individual Liberty

Dilemmas of Equality

Inequality of Income and Wealth

Social Mobility

Race, Ethnicity,
and Immigration

Ideologies: Liberalism
and Conservatism

Dissent in the United States

**ASK YOURSELF
ABOUT POLITICS**

1 Do you consider yourself
politically conservative,
moderate, or liberal?
Conservative ⬭
Moderate ⬭
Liberal ⬭

2 Are income differences
in America widening?
Yes ⬭ No ⬭

3 Is it the government's
responsibility to reduce
income differences
between people?
Yes ⬭ No ⬭

4 If incomes were made
more equal, would
people still be motivated
to work hard?
Yes ⬭ No ⬭

5 Do Americans today still
have the opportunity to
significantly improve
their condition in life?
Yes ⬭ No ⬭

6 Should the U.S. govern-
ment curtail immigration
to America?
Yes ⬭ No ⬭

7 Should illegal immi-
grants be denied welfare
benefits?
Yes ⬭ No ⬭

8 Is American culture
racist and sexist?
Yes ⬭ No ⬭

Ask yourself if your answers to
these question are widely shared
by most citizens of the United
States. Your answers probably
reflect not only your own beliefs
and values but also those of the
political culture to which you
belong.

POLITICAL CULTURE

Ideas have power. We are all influenced by ideas—beliefs, values, symbols—more than we realize. Ideas provide us with rationalizations for ways of life, with guides for determining right and wrong, and with emotional impulses to action. Political institutions are shaped by ideas, and political leaders are constrained by them.

The term **political culture** refers to widely shared ideas about who should govern, for what ends, and by what means. **Values** are shared ideas about what is good and desirable. Values provide standards for judging what is right or wrong. **Beliefs** are shared ideas about what is true. Values and beliefs are often related. For example, if we believe that human beings are endowed by God with rights to life, liberty, and property, then we will value the protection of these rights. Thus beliefs can justify values.

Cultural descriptions are generalizations about the values and beliefs of many people in society, but these generalizations do not apply to everyone. Important variations in values and beliefs may exist within a society; these variations are frequently referred to as **subcultures** and may arise from such diverse bases as religion, racial or ethnic identity, or political group membership.

Contradictions between Values and Conditions Agreement over values in a political culture is no guarantee that there will not be contradictions between these values and actual conditions. People both in and out of politics frequently act contrary to their professed values. No doubt the most grievous contradiction between professed national beliefs and actual conditions in America is found in the long history of slavery, segregation, and racial discrimination. The contradiction between the words of the Declaration of Independence that "all men are created equal" and the practices of slavery and segregation became the "American dilemma."[1] But this contradiction does not mean that professed values are worthless; the very existence of the gap between values and behavior becomes a motivation for change. The history of the civil rights movement might be viewed as an effort to "bear witness" to the contradiction between the belief in equality and the existence of segregation and discrimination.[2] Whatever the obstacles to racial equality in America, these obstacles would be even greater if the nation's political culture did *not* include a professed belief in equality.

Inconsistent Applications   A political culture does not mean that shared principles are always applied in every circumstance. For example, people may truly believe in the principle of "free speech for all, no matter what their views might be," and yet when asked whether racists should be allowed to speak on a college campus, many people will say no. Thus general agreement with abstract principles of freedom of speech, freedom of the press, and academic freedom does not always ensure their application to specific individuals or groups.[3] Americans are frequently willing to restrict the freedoms of particularly obnoxious groups. A generation ago it was alleged communists and atheists whose freedoms were questioned. Over time these groups have become less threatening, but today people are still willing to restrict the liberties of racists, pro-abortion or anti-abortion groups, homosexuals, and neo-Nazis.

Conflict   The idea of political culture does not mean an absence of conflict over values and beliefs. Indeed, much of politics involves conflict over very fundamental values. The American nation has experienced a bloody civil war, political assassinations, rioting and burning of cities, the forced resignation of a president, and other direct challenges to its political foundations. Indeed, much of this book deals with serious political conflict. Yet Americans do share many common ways of thinking about politics.

INDIVIDUAL LIBERTY

No political value has been more widely held in the United States than individual liberty. The very beginnings of our history as a nation were shaped by **classical liberalism**, which asserts the worth and dignity of the individual. This political philosophy emphasizes the rational ability of human beings to determine their own destinies, and it rejects ideas, practices, and institutions that submerge individuals into a larger whole and thus deprive them of their dignity. The only restriction on the individual is not to interfere with the liberties of others.

Political Liberty   Classical liberalism grew out of the eighteenth-century Enlightenment, the Age of Reason in which great philosophers such as Voltaire, John Locke, Jean-Jacques Rousseau, Adam Smith, and Thomas Jefferson affirmed their faith in reason, virtue, and common sense. Classical liberalism originated as an attack on the hereditary prerogatives and distinctions of a feudal society, the monarchy, the privileged aristocracy, and the state-established church.

political culture   Widely shared views about who should govern, for what ends, and by what means.

values   Shared ideas about what is good and desirable.

beliefs   Shared ideas about what is true.

subcultures   Variations on the prevailing values and beliefs in a society.

classical liberalism   Political philosophy asserting the worth and dignity of the individual and emphasizing the rational ability of human beings to determine their own destinies.

Proposition 187, a ballot initiative in California denying state services to illegal immigrants, exposed a clash of cultures in Los Angeles.

Classical liberalism motivated America's Founders to declare their independence from England, to write the U.S. Constitution, and to establish the Republic. It rationalized their actions and provided ideological legitimacy for the new nation. Locke, as we saw in Chapter 1, argued that a natural law, or moral principle, guaranteed every person "certain inalienable Rights," among them "Life, Liberty, and Property," and that human beings form a social contract with one another to establish a government to help protect their rights. Implicit in the social contract and the liberal notion of freedom is the belief that governmental activity and restrictions on the individual should be kept to a minimum.

Economic Freedom   Classical liberalism as a political idea is closely related to capitalism as an *economic* idea. **Capitalism** asserts the individual's right to own private property and to buy, sell, rent, and trade that property in a free market. The economic version of freedom is the freedom to make contracts, to bargain for one's services, to move from job to job, to join labor unions, to start one's own business. Capitalism stresses individual rationality in economic matters—freedom of choice in working, producing, buying, and selling—and limited governmental intervention in economic affairs. Classical liberalism emphasizes individual rationality in voter choice—freedom of speech, press, and political activity—and limitations on governmental power over individual liberty. In classical liberal politics, individuals are free to speak out, to form political parties, and to vote as they please—to pursue their political interests as they think best. In classical liberal economics, individuals are free to find work, to start businesses, and to spend their money as they please—to pursue their economic interests as they think best. The role of government is restricted to protecting private property, enforcing contracts, and performing only those functions and services that cannot be performed by the private market.

The value of liberty in these political and economic spheres has been paramount throughout our history. Only equality competes with liberty as the most honored value in the American political culture.

capitalism   Economic system asserting the individual's right to own private property and to buy, sell, rent, and trade that property in a free market.

DILEMMAS OF EQUALITY

Since the bold assertion of the Declaration of Independence that "all men are created equal," Americans have generally believed that no person has greater worth than any other person. The principle of equal worth and dignity was a radical idea in 1776, when much of the world was dominated by hereditary monarchies, titled nobilities, and rigid caste and class systems. Belief in equality drove the expansion of voting rights in the early 1800s and ultimately destroyed the institution of slavery. Abraham Lincoln understood that equality was not so much a description of reality as an ideal to be aspired to: "a standard maxim for a free society which should be familiar to all, and revered by all; constantly looked to, constantly labored for, and even though never perfectly attained, constantly approximated and thereby augmenting the happiness and value of life to all people of all colors everywhere."[4] The millions who immigrated to the United States viewed this country as a land not only of opportunity but of *equal* opportunity, where everyone, regardless of birth, could rise in wealth and status based on hard work, natural talents, and perhaps good luck.

Today, most Americans agree that no one is intrinsically "better" than anyone else. This belief in equality, then, is fundamental to Americans, but a closer examination shows that throughout our history it has been tested, as beliefs and values so often are, by political realities.

Political Equality   The nation's Founders shared the belief that the law should apply equally to all—that birth, status, or wealth do not justify differential application of the laws. But *legal equality* did not necessarily mean **political equality**, at least not in 1787 when the U.S. Constitution was written. The Constitution left the issue of voter qualifications to the states to decide for themselves. At that time, all states imposed either property or taxpayer qualifications for voting. Neither women nor slaves could vote anywhere. The expansion of voting rights to universal suffrage required many bitter battles over the course of two centuries. The long history of the struggle over voting rights illustrates the contradictions between values and practices (see "Securing the Right to Vote" in Chapter 5). Yet in the absence of the *value* of equality, voting rights might have remained restricted.

Equality of Opportunity   The American ideal of equality extends to **equality of opportunity**—the elimination of artificial barriers to success in life. The term *equality of opportunity* refers to the ability to make of oneself what one can, to develop one's talents and abilities, and to be rewarded for one's work, initiative, and achievement. Equality of opportunity means that everyone comes to the same starting line in life, with the same chance of success, and that whatever differences develop over time do so as a result of abilities, talents, initiative, hard work, and perhaps good luck.

Americans do not generally resent the fact that physicians, engineers, airline pilots, and others who have spent time and energy acquiring particular skills make more money than those whose jobs require fewer skills and less training. Neither do most Americans resent the fact that people who risk their own time and money to build a business, bring new or better products to market, and create jobs for others make more money than their employees. Nor do many Americans begrudge multimillion-dollar incomes to sports figures, rock stars, and movie stars whose talents entertain the public. And few Americans object when someone wins a

political equality   Belief that the law should apply equally to all and that every person's vote counts equally.

equality of opportunity   Elimination of artificial barriers to success in life and the opportunity for everyone to strive for success.

million-dollar lottery, as long as everyone who entered the lottery had an equal chance at winning. Americans are generally willing to have government act to ensure equality of opportunity—to ensure that everyone has an equal chance at getting an education, landing a job, and buying a home, and that no barriers of race, sex, religion, or ethnicity bar individual advancement. Differences arise over whether special efforts such as *affirmative action* should be undertaken to overcome the effects of past discriminatory barriers (see "Affirmative Action in the Courts" in Chapter 15). But the ideal of equality of opportunity is widely shared.

Equality of Results **Equality of results** refers to the equal sharing of income and material rewards. Equality of results means that everyone starts *and finishes* the race together, regardless of ability, talent, initiative, or work. Those who argue on behalf of this notion of equality say that if individuals are truly equal, then everyone should enjoy generally equal conditions in life. According to this belief, we should appreciate an individual's skills, work, knowledge, and contributions to society without creating inequalities of wealth and income. Government should act to *transfer* wealth and income from the rich to the poor to increase the total happiness of all members of society.

But equality of results, or absolute equality, is not a widely shared value in the United States. This notion of equality was referred to as "leveling" by Thomas Jefferson and generally has been denounced by the nation's political leadership—and by most Americans—then and now:

> To take from one, because it is thought his own industry and that of his fathers has acquired too much, in order to spare to others who have not exercised equal industry and skill, is to violate arbitrarily . . . the guarantee to everyone the free exercise of his industry and the fruits acquired by it.[5]

The taking of private property from those who acquired it legitimately, for no other reason than to equalize wealth or income, is widely viewed as morally wrong. Moreover, many people believe that society generally would suffer if incomes were equalized. Absolute equality, in this view, would remove incentives for people to work, save, or produce. Everyone would slack off, production would decline, goods would be in short supply, and everyone would end up poorer than ever. So some inequality may be essential for the well-being of society.

Thus Americans believe strongly in equality of opportunity but not necessarily equality of results (see Figure 2-1 on page 30). Americans seek fairness rather than equality of wealth and income.

Fairness Americans value "fairness" even though they do not always agree on what is fair. Most Americans support a "floor" on income and material well-being—a level that no one, regardless of his or her condition, should be permitted to fall below—even though they differ over how high that floor should be. Indeed, the belief in a floor is consistent with the belief in equality of opportunity; extreme poverty would deny people, especially children, the opportunity to compete in life.[6] But very few Americans want to place a "ceiling" on income or wealth. This unwillingness to limit top income extends to nearly all groups in the United States, the poor as well as the rich. Generally, Americans want people who cannot provide for themselves to be well cared for, especially children, the elderly, the ill, and the disabled. They are often willing to "soak the rich" when searching

equality of results Equal sharing of income and material goods regardless of one's efforts in life.

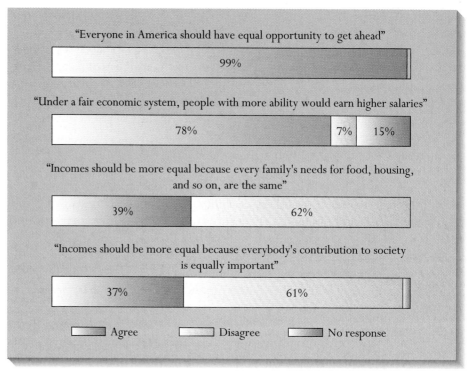

"Everyone in America should have equal opportunity to get ahead"

99%

"Under a fair economic system, people with more ability would earn higher salaries"

78%   7%   15%

"Incomes should be more equal because every family's needs for food, housing, and so on, are the same"

39%   62%

"Incomes should be more equal because everybody's contribution to society is equally important"

37%   61%

Agree   Disagree   No response

FIGURE 2-1 Beliefs about Equality

Source: Questions 1–2 based on Herbert McClosky and John Zaller, *The American Ethos: Public Attitudes toward Capitalism and Democracy* (Cambridge, Mass.: Harvard University Press, 1984), pp. 83–84; questions 3–4 based on James R. Kluegel and Eliot R. Smith, *Beliefs about Inequality: Americans' Views of What Is and What Ought to Be* (New York: Aldine de Gruyter, 1986).

for new tax sources, believing that the rich can easily afford to bear the burdens of government. But, unlike citizens in other Western democracies, Americans generally do *not* believe that government should equalize incomes (see *Compared to What?* "Should Government Equalize Incomes?").

Equality in Politics versus Economics Americans make a clear distinction between the *private economic* sphere of life and the *public political* sphere.[7] In the private economic sphere, they value the principle of "earned desserts," meaning that individuals are entitled to what they achieve through hard work, skill, talent, risk, and even good luck. They are willing to tolerate inequalities of result in economics. Self-interested behavior in the marketplace is seen as appropriate and even beneficial, if properly constrained by rules that apply equally to everyone. But in the public political sphere, Americans value absolute equality—one person, one vote. They condemn disparities of power and influence among individuals. Self-interested behavior in politics is seen as corrupt.

As long as the economic and political spheres of life are perceived as separate, then economic inequalities and political equalities can exist side by side in a society.

INEQUALITY OF INCOME AND WEALTH

Conflict in society is generated more often by inequalities among people than by hardship or deprivation. Material well-being and standards of living are usually expressed in aggregate measures for a whole society—for example, gross domes-

Should Government Equalize Incomes?

Whereas American political culture emphasizes equality of *opportunity*, the political culture in the Western Europe democracies is much more inclined toward equality of *results*. Americans generally believe that government should provide a "floor," or safety net, to protect people against true hardship; but they are generally unwilling to place a "ceiling" on incomes, or to give government the task of equalizing income differences among people. In contrast, majorities in most other Western democracies agree with this statement: "It is government's responsibility to reduce income differences between people."

Source: U.S. News and World Report, August 7, 1989, p. 25, reporting data gathered by Gallup International Research Institute, International Research Associates, National Opinion Research Center, and International Social Survey Program, 1987–88.

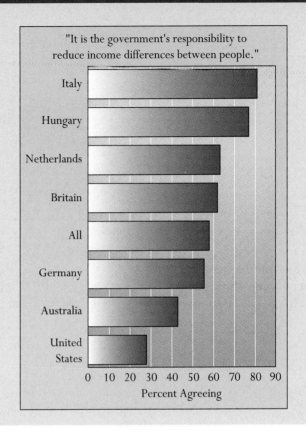

"It is the government's responsibility to reduce income differences between people."

tic product per capita, income per capita, average life expectancy, infant mortality rate. These measures of societal well-being are vitally important to a nation and its people, but *political* conflict is more likely to occur over the *distribution* of well-being *within* a society. Unequal distributions can generate conflict even in a very affluent society with high levels of income and a high standard of living.

Inequality of Income   Let us examine inequality of income in the United States systematically. Figure 2-2 (on page 32) divides all American households into two groups, the lowest one-fifth in income and the highest one-fifth—and shows the shares (percentage) of total household income received by each of these groups over the years. (If perfect income equality existed, each fifth of American households would receive 20 percent of all personal income.) The poorest one-fifth received only 3.5 percent of all household income in 1929; today, this group does a little better, at 4.2 percent of household income. The highest one-fifth received 54.4 percent of all household income in 1929; today, its percentage stands at 46.2. This was the only income group to lose in relation to other income groups.

However, while income differences in the United States have declined over the long run, inequality has actually *increased* in recent years. The income of the poorest households declined from 4.8 to 3.6 percent of total income between 1960 and

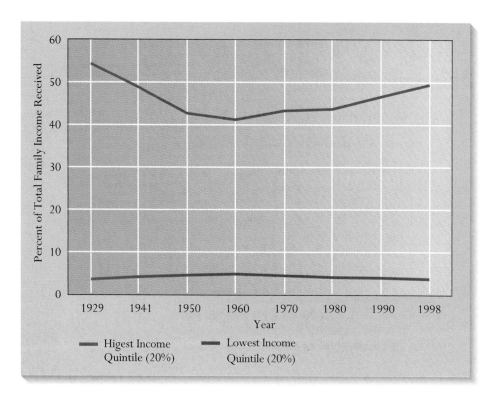

FIGURE 2-2 Shares of Total Household Income Received by Highest and Lowest Income Groups

1998; the income of the highest quintile rose from 40.9 to 46.9 percent of total income. This reversal of historical trends has generated both political rhetoric and serious scholarly inquiry about its causes.

Explaining Recent Increases in Income Inequality Recent increases in income inequality in the United States are a product of several social and economic trends: (1) the decline of the manufacturing sector of the economy (and the loss of many relatively high-paying blue-collar jobs) and the ascendancy of the communications, information, and service sectors of the economy (with a combination

As income and wealth differences between the "haves" and the "have-nots" increased in America during the 1980s and the early 1990s, more people fell through the cracks in the system and joined the ranks of the impoverished and homeless.

of high-paying and low-paying jobs); (2) the rise in the number of two-wage families, making single-wage, female-headed households relatively less affluent; (3) demographic trends, which include larger proportions of aged and larger proportions of female-headed families; and (4) global competition, which restrains wages in unskilled and semiskilled jobs while rewarding people in high-technology, high-productivity occupations.

Inequality of Wealth   Inequalities of wealth in the United States are even greater than inequalities of income. *Wealth* is the total value of a family's assets—bank accounts, stocks, bonds, mutual funds, business equity, houses, cars, and major appliances—minus outstanding debts, such as credit card balances, mortgages, and other loans. The top 1 percent of families in the United States owns almost 40 percent of all family wealth (see Figure 2-3). Inequality of wealth appeared to be diminishing until the mid-1970s, but in recent years it has surged sharply. Not surprisingly, age is the key determinant of family wealth; persons age fifty to sixty-five are by far the wealthiest, with persons over sixty-five close behind; young families generally have less than one-third of the assets of retirees.

SOCIAL MOBILITY

Political conflict over inequality might be greater in the United States if it were not for the prospect of **social mobility**. All societies are stratified, or layered, but societies differ greatly in the extent to which people move upward or downward in income and status over a lifetime or over generations. When there is social mobility, people have a good opportunity to get ahead if they study or work long and hard, save and invest wisely, or display initiative and enterprise in business affairs (however, see *A Conflicting View:* "Success Is Determined by the Bell Curve"). Fairly steep inequalities may be tolerated politically if people have a reasonable expectation of moving up over time, or at least of seeing their children do so.

social mobility   Extent to which people move upward or downward in income and status over a lifetime or generations.

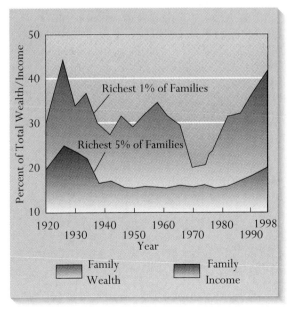

FIGURE 2-3 Inequality of Wealth and Income

Source: U.S. Bureau of the Census, *Current Population Reports,* 1998; see also Edward N. Wolff, *Top Heavy* (New York: Twentieth Century Fund, 1995), p. 28.

Success Is Determined by the Bell Curve

Most Americans believe in social mobility—the idea that anyone who studies or works hard, saves and invests wisely, and makes good use of his or her talents, initiative, and enterprise can get ahead. But a controversial book, *The Bell Curve* by Richard J. Herrnstein and Charles Murray, sets forth the argument that general intelligence largely determines success in life. General intelligence, the authors contend, is distributed among the population in a bell-shaped curve, with most people clustered around the median, smaller numbers with higher intelligence (a "cognitive elite") at one end, and an unfortunate few trailing behind at the other end (see graph). Over time, say Herrnstein and Murray, intelligence is becoming ever more necessary for the performance of key jobs in the "information society." The result will be the continuing enhancement of the power and wealth of the cognitive elite and the further erosion of the lifestyle of the less intelligent.

Even more controversial than the authors' claim that general intelligence determines success is their contention that general intelligence is mostly (60 percent) genetic. Because intelligence is mostly inherited, programs to assist the underprivileged are useless or even counterproductive.

The cognitive elite, the authors predict, will continue to distance themselves from the masses in knowledge, skills, technical competence, income, and power while social problems will be concentrated among the "dullest." Indeed, they amass statistics showing that educational deficiencies, emotional problems, welfare reliance, early childbirth, and even criminal behavior are disproportionately concentrated in low-intelligence groups (see table).

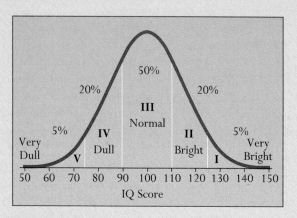

Population Distribution of IQ Scores

Source: Adapted with permission of The Free Press, a division of Simon & Schuster, from *The Bell Curve: Intelligence and Class Structure in American Life* by Richard J. Herrnstein and Charles Murray. Copyright © 1994 by Richard J. Herrnstein and Charles Murray.

But critics of *The Bell Curve* point out the lack of consensus on the role of genetics in intelligence. Indeed, recent research on infant development indicates that brain activity and the interconnections among brain cells are greatly affected by early human interaction. Infants in a stimulating environment—who are frequently coddled, spoken to, and sung to, for example—exhibit more brain activity than those with little environmental stimuli. Moreover, the implication of the bell curve thesis is that social classes and elitism are both natural and inevitable—and therefore that most efforts to ensure equality of opportunity are useless. This thesis might be seen as a justification for widening inequality in society. Finally, a racial dimension Herrnstein and Murray add to their argument is unnecessary to their thesis. Although they claim that the differences between African Americans, whites, and Asians on IQ tests should not matter if every individual were judged separately on IQ, clearly their argument reinforces racial stereotypes.

Cognitive Class		High School Dropout	Women on Welfare Assistance	Mean Age at First Childbearing	Criminal Convictions (young white males)
I	Very Bright	0%	0%	27.2 years	3%
II	Bright	0	2	25.5	7
III	Normal	6	8	23.4	15
IV	Dull	35	17	21.0	21
V	Very Dull	55	31	19.8	14

Source: Table adapted from various chapters in Herrnstein and Murray, *The Bell Curve* (1994)

How Much Mobility?   The United States describes itself as the land of opportunity. The really important political question may be how much real opportunity exists for individual Americans to improve their conditions in life relative to others. The impression given by Figure 2-2 is one of a static distribution system, with families permanently placed in upper or lower fifths of income earners. But there is considerable evidence of both upward and downward movement by people among income groupings.[8] About a third of the families in the poorest one-fifth will move upward within a decade, and about a third of families in the richest one-fifth will fall out of this top category. However, there appears to have been some slowing of this mobility in recent years; one's chances of escaping the bottom have diminished somewhat. Thus the nation is currently experiencing not only an increase in inequality but also a slowing of social mobility.

Mobility, Class Conflict, and Class Consciousness   Social mobility and the expectation of mobility, over a lifetime or over generations, may be the key to understanding why **class conflict**—conflict over wealth and power among social classes—is not as widespread or as intense in America as it is in many other nations. The *belief* in social mobility reduces the potential for class conflict because it diminishes **class consciousness**, the awareness of one's class position and the feeling of political solidarity with others in the same class in opposition to other classes. If class lines were impermeable and no one had any reasonable expectation of moving up or seeing his or her children move up, then class consciousness would rise and political conflict among classes would intensify.

Most Americans describe themselves as "middle class" rather than "rich" or "poor" or "lower class" or "upper class." There are no widely accepted income definitions of "middle class." The federal government officially defines a "poverty level" each year based on the annual cash income required to maintain a decent standard of living ($16,530 in 1998 for a family of four). Roughly 14 percent of the U.S. population lives with annual cash incomes below this poverty line. (For more discussion, see "Poverty in the United States" in Chapter 17.) This is the only income group in which a majority of people describe themselves as poor.[9] Large majorities in every other income group identify themselves as middle class. So it is no surprise that presidents, politicians, and political parties regularly claim to be defenders of America's "middle class"!

RACE, ETHNICITY, AND IMMIGRATION

America has always been an ethnically and racially pluralist society. All groups were expected to adopt the American political culture—including individual liberty, economic freedom, political equality, and equality of opportunity—and to learn American history and the English language. The nation's motto "E Pluribus Unum" (from many, one) is inscribed on its coins. Yet each of America's racial and ethnic groups brings its own traditions and values to the American political culture.

African Americans   Historically African Americans constituted the nation's largest minority. Blacks composed about 20 percent of the population at the time the U.S. Constitution was written in 1787 (although as we shall see in Chapter 3 an enslaved African American was to be counted as only 3/5ths of a person in the original Constitution). Heavy European immigration in the late nineteenth century

class conflict   Conflict between upper and lower social classes over wealth and power.

class consciousness   Awareness of one's class position and a feeling of political solidarity with others within the same class in opposition to other classes.

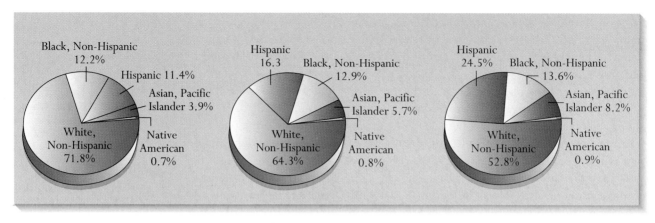

FIGURE 2-4 Racial and Ethnic Composition of the United States 2000, 2020, 2050
Source: U.S. Bureau of the Census (Middle Series).

diluted the black population to roughly 12 percent of the nation's total. As late as 1900, most African American (90 percent) were still concentrated in the Southern states. But World Wars I and II provided job opportunities in large cities of the Northeast and Midwest. Blacks could not cast ballots in most Southern counties, but they could "vote with their feet." The migration of African Americans from the rural South to the urban North was one of the largest internal migrations in our history. Today only about half of the nation's African Americans live in the South—still more than in any other region but less of a concentration than earlier in American history. Today the nation's 35 million African Americans comprise 12.1 percent of the total population of the United States (see Figure 2-4). "African-American Politics in Historical Perspective" is discussed in Chapter 15, as well as the long struggle against slavery, segregation, and discrimination. This struggle has given African Americans a somewhat different perspective on American politics (see "Race and Opinion" in Chapter 5).

Hispanic Americans   The term *Hispanic* generally refers to persons of Spanish-speaking ancestry and culture; it includes Mexican Americans, Cuban Americans, and Puerto Ricans. Today there are an estimated 31 million Hispanics in the United States, or 11.4 percent of the total population. The largest subgroup is Mexican Americans, some of whom are descendants of citizens living in Mexican territory that was annexed to the United States in 1848, but most of whom have come to the United States in accelerating numbers in recent years. The largest Mexican American populations are found in Texas, Arizona, New Mexico, and California. The second-largest subgroup is Puerto Ricans, many of whom move back and forth from the island to the mainland, especially New York City. The third-largest subgroup is Cubans, most of whom have fled from Castro's Cuba. They live mainly in the Miami metropolitan area. The politics of each of these Hispanic groups differs somewhat (see "Hispanic Politics" in Chapter 15). Hispanics will soon become the nation's largest minority (see Figure 2-4).

A Nation of Immigrants   The United States is a nation of immigrants, from the first "boat people" (Pilgrims) to the latest Haitian refugees and Cuban *balseros* ("rafters"). Historically, most of the people who came to settle in this country did so because they believed their lives would be better here, and American political

Immigration places responsibility on public schools to provide for the needs of children from different cultures. Here, Latino pupils assemble in Santa Ana, California.

culture today has been greatly affected by the beliefs and values they brought with them. Americans are proud of their immigrant heritage and the freedom and opportunity the nation has extended to generations of "huddled masses yearning to be free"—words emblazoned on the Statue of Liberty in New York's harbor. Today about 8 percent of the U.S. population is foreign-born.

Immigration policy is a responsibility of the national government. It was not until 1882 that Congress passed the first legislation restricting entry into the United States of persons alleged to be "undesirable" and virtually all Asians. After World War I, Congress passed the comprehensive Immigration Act of 1921, which established maximum numbers of new immigrants each year and set a quota for immi-

The U.S. Coast Guard may intercept boats at sea and return their occupants to their country of origin. But once immigrants reach the U.S. shore, they are entitled to a hearing in any deportation proceedings.

grants for each foreign country at 3 percent of the number of that nation's foreign-born who were living in the United States in 1910, later reduced to 2 percent of the number living here in 1890. These restrictions reflected anti-immigration feelings that were generally directed at the large wave of Southern and Eastern European Catholic and Jewish immigrants (from Poland, Russia, Hungary, Italy, and Greece) entering the United States prior to World War I (see Figure 2-5). It was not until the Immigration and Nationality Act of 1965 that national origin quotas were abolished, replaced by preference categories for close relatives of U.S. citizens or permanent resident aliens, professionals, and skilled workers.

Immigration "reform" was the announced goal of Congress in the Immigration Reform and Control Act of 1986, also known as the Simpson-Mazzoli Act. It sought to control immigration by placing principal responsibility on employers; it set fines for knowingly hiring an illegal alien. However, it allowed employers to accept many different forms of easily forged documentation and at the same time subjected them to penalties for discriminating against legal foreign-born residents. To win political support, the act granted amnesty to illegal aliens who had lived in the United States since 1982. But the act failed to reduce the flow of either legal or illegal immigrants.

Today, roughly a million people per year are admitted *legally* to the United States as "lawful permanent residents" (persons who have needed job skills or who have relatives who are U.S. citizens) or as "political refugees" (persons with "a well-founded fear of persecution" in their country of origin). In addition, each year more than 25 million people are awarded temporary visas to enter the United States for study, business, or pleasure.

FIGURE 2-5   Immigration to the United States by Decades

Source: Statistical Abstract of the United States, 1995, p. 10.

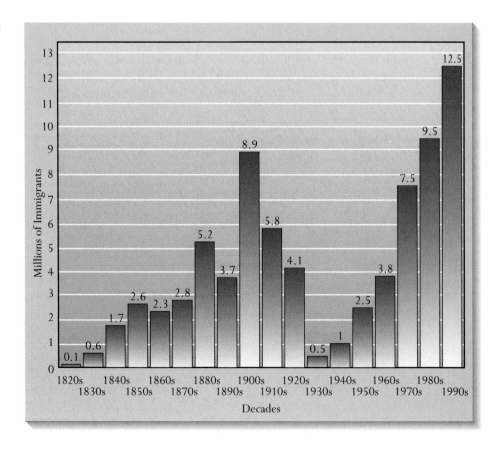

Illegal Immigration   The United States is a free and prosperous society with more than 5,000 miles of borders (2,000 with Mexico) and hundreds of international air and sea ports. In theory, a sovereign nation should be able to maintain secure borders, but in practice the United States has been unwilling and unable to do so. Estimates of illegal immigration vary widely, from the official U.S. Immigration and Naturalization Service (INS) estimate of 400,000 per year (about 45 percent of the legal immigration) to unofficial estimates ranging up to 3 million per year. The INS estimates that about 4 million illegal immigrants currently reside in the United States; unofficial estimates range up to 10 million or more. Many illegal immigrants slip across U.S. borders or enter ports with false documentation; many more overstay tourist, worker, or student visas (and are not counted by the INS as illegal immigrants).[10]

Source: Steve Kelley.

As a free society, the United States is not prepared to undertake massive roundups and summary deportations of millions of illegal residents. The Fifth and Fourteenth Amendments to the U.S. Constitution require that every *person* (not just citizen) be afforded "due process of law." The INS may turn back persons at the border or even hold them in detention camps. The Coast Guard may intercept boats at sea and return persons to their country of origin.[11] Aliens have no constitutional right to come to the United States. However, once in the United States, whether legally or illegally, every person is entitled to due process of law and equal protection of the laws. People are thus entitled to a fair hearing prior to any government attempt to deport them. Aliens are entitled to apply for asylum and present evidence at a hearing of their "well-founded fear of prosecution" if returned to their country. Experience has shown that the only way to reduce the flow of illegal immigration is to control it at the border, an expensive and difficult but not impossible task. Localized experiments in border enforcement have indicated that, with significant increases in INS personnel and technology, illegal immigration can be reduced by half or more.

Citizenship   Persons born in the United States are U.S. citizens. People who have been lawfully admitted into the United States and granted permanent residence, and who have resided in the United States for at least five years and in their home state for the last six months, are eligible for naturalization as U.S. citizens. Federal district courts as well as offices of the U.S. Immigration and Naturalization Service (INS) may grant applications for citizenship. By law, the applicant must be over age eighteen, be able to read, write, and speak English, possess good moral character, and understand and demonstrate an attachment to the history, principles, and form of government of the United States (see *What Do You Think*: "Could You Pass the Citizenship Test? on page 40").

IDEOLOGIES: LIBERALISM AND CONSERVATISM

An **ideology** is a consistent and integrated system of ideas, values, and beliefs. A political ideology tells us who *should* get what, when, and how; that is, it tells us who *ought* to govern and what goals they *ought* to pursue. When we use ideological terms such as *liberalism* and *conservatism*, we imply reasonably integrated sets of values and beliefs. And when we pin ideological labels on people, we imply that those people are fairly consistent in the application of these values and beliefs in public affairs. In reality, neither political leaders nor citizens always display integrated or consistent

ideology   Consistent and integrated system of ideas, values, and beliefs.

Could You Pass the Citizenship Test?

To ensure that new citizens "understand" the history, principles, and form of government of the United States, the INS administers a citizenship test. Could you pass it today?

Answer correctly at least 18 of 30 questions to pass:

1. How many stars are there on our flag?
2. What do the stars on the flag mean?
3. What color are the stripes?
4. What do the stripes on the flag mean?
5. What is the date of Independence Day?
6. Independence from whom?
7. What do we call a change to the Constitution?
8. How many branches are there in our government?
9. How many full terms can a president serve?
10. Who nominates judges of the Supreme Court?
11. How many Supreme Court justices are there?
12. Who was the main writer of the Declaration of Independence?
13. What holiday was celebrated for the first time by American colonists?
14. Who wrote the Star-Spangled Banner?
15. What is the minimum voting age in the U.S.?
16. Who was president during the Civil War?
17. Which president is called the "Father of our Country"?
18. What is the 50th state of the Union?
19. What is the name of the ship that brought the Pilgrims to America?
20. Who has the power to declare war?
21. What were the 13 original states of the U.S. called?
22. In what year was the Constitution written?
23. What is the introduction to the Constitution called?
24. Which president was the first Commander-in-Chief of the U.S. Army and Navy?
25. In what month do we vote for the president?
26. How many times may a senator be re-elected?
27. Who signs bills into law?
28. Who elects the president of the U.S.?
29. How many states are there in the U.S.?
30. Who becomes president if both the president and V.P. die?

Answers: 1. 50; 2. One for each state in the Union; 3. Red and white; 4. They represent the 13 original states; 5. July 4; 6. England; 7. Amendments; 8. 3; 9. 2; 10. The president; 11. 9; 12. Thomas Jefferson; 13. Thanksgiving; 14. Francis Scott Key; 15. 18; 16. Abraham Lincoln; 17. George Washington; 18. Hawaii; 19. *The Mayflower*; 20. The Congress; 21. Colonies; 22. 1787; 23. The Preamble; 24. George Washington; 25. November; 26. There is no limit at the present time; 27. The president; 28. The Electoral College; 29. 50; 30. Speaker of the House of Representatives.

Source: U.S. Immigration and Naturalization Service.

opinions; many hold conservative views on some issues and liberal views on others.[12] Many Americans avoid ideological labeling, either by describing themselves as "moderate" or "middle-of-the-road" or by simply declining to place themselves on an ideological scale. But as Figure 2-6 shows, among those who choose an ideological label to describe their politics, conservatives consistently outnumber liberals. (See also *Across the USA:* "Liberalism and Conservatism" on page 42.)

Despite inconsistencies in opinion and avoidance of labeling, ideology plays an important role in American politics. Political *elites*—elected and appointed officeholders; journalists, editors, and commentators; party officials and interest-group leaders; and others active in politics—are generally more consistent in their political views than nonelites and are more likely to use ideological terms in describing politics.[13]

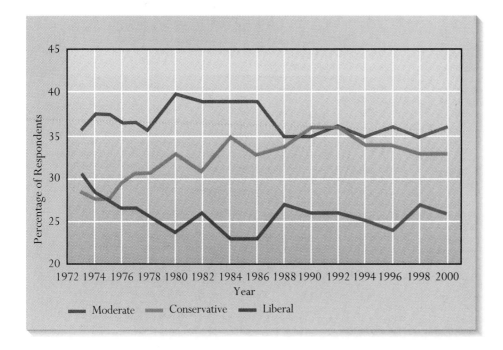

FIGURE 2-6 Americans: Liberal, Moderate, Conservative

Source: General Social Surveys, National Opinion Research Center, University of Chicago; updated from *The American Enterprise,* January/February 2000.

Modern Conservatism: Individualism plus Traditional Values   Modern **conservatism** combines a belief in free markets, limited government, and individual self-reliance in economic affairs with a belief in the value of tradition, law, and morality in social affairs. Conservatives wish to retain our historical commitments to individual freedom from governmental controls; reliance on individual initiative and effort for self-development; a free-enterprise economy with a minimum of governmental intervention; and rewards for initiative, skill, risk, and hard work. These views are consistent with the early classical liberalism of Locke, Jefferson, and the nation's Founders, discussed at the beginning of this chapter. The result is a confusion of ideological labels: modern conservatives claim to be the true inheritors of the (classical) liberal tradition.

Modern conservatism does indeed incorporate many classical liberal ideals, but it also has a distinct ideological tradition of its own. Conservatism is less optimistic about human nature. Traditionally, conservatives have recognized that human nature includes elements of irrationality, ignorance, hatred, and violence. Thus they have been more likely to place their faith in *law* and *traditional values* than in popular fads, trends, or emotions. To conservatives, the absence of law does not mean freedom but, rather, exposure to the tyranny of terrorism and violence. They believe that without the guidance of traditional values, people would soon come to grief through the unruliness of their passions, destroying both themselves and others. Conservatives argue that strong institutions—family, church, and community—are needed to control individuals' selfish and immoral impulses and to foster civilized ways of life.

It is important to note that conservatism in America incorporates different views of the role of government in economic versus social affairs. Conservatives generally prefer *limited noninterventionist government in economic affairs*—a government that relies on free markets to provide and distribute goods and services; minimizes its regulatory activity; limits social welfare programs to the "truly needy"; keeps taxes low; and rejects schemes to equalize income or wealth. On the other hand, conservatives would *strengthen government's power to regulate social conduct.* They support

conservatism   Belief in the value of free markets, limited government, and individual self-reliance in economic affairs, combined with a belief in the value of tradition, law, and morality in social affairs.

Liberalism and Conservatism

States might be classified in terms of their voters' self-identification in opinion surveys as liberal, moderate, or conservative. The most conservative state is Utah (45 percent conservative, 37 percent moderate, 13 percent liberal), followed by Indiana (42 percent conservative, 39 percent moderate, 13 percent liberal). The most liberal states are Massachusetts (26 percent conservative, 42 percent moderate, 26 percent liberal); New York (29 percent conservative, 39 percent moderate, 26 percent liberal); and New Jersey (28 percent conservative, 40 percent moderate, 26 percent liberal).

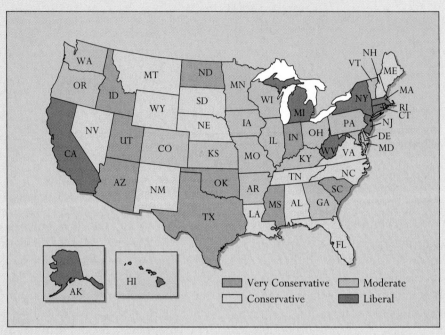

Source: Gerald C. Wright, Robert S. Erikson, and John P. McIver, "Public Opinion and Policy Liberalism in the American States," *American Journal of Political Science* 31 (November 1987): 980–1001. Reprinted by permission of the University of Wisconsin Press.

restrictions on abortion; endorse school prayer; favor a war on drugs and pornography; oppose the legitimizing of homosexuality; support the death penalty; and advocate tougher criminal penalties.

Modern Liberalism: Governmental Power to "Do Good"   Modern **liberalism** combines a belief in a strong government to provide economic security and protection for civil rights with a belief in freedom from government intervention in social conduct. Modern liberalism retains the classical liberalism commitment to individual dignity, but it emphasizes the importance of social and economic security for the whole population. In contrast to classical liberalism which looked at governmental power as a potential threat to personal freedom, modern liberalism looks on the power of government as a positive force for eliminating social and economic conditions that adversely affect people's lives and impede their self-development. The modern liberal approves of the use of governmental power to correct the perceived ills of society (see *People in Politics:* "Barbara Boxer, Defending Liberalism" on page 45).

Today's liberals believe that government can change people's lives by working to end racial and sexual discrimination, abolish poverty, eliminate slums, create jobs,

liberalism   Belief in the value of strong government to provide economic security and protection for civil rights, combined with a belief in personal freedom from government intervention in social conduct.

P. J. O'Rourke, Conservative with a Sense of Humor

"Giving money and power to government is like giving whiskey and car keys to teenage boys," according to political humorist P. J. O'Rourke. Two of his books—*Parliament of Whores: A Lone Humorist Attempts to Explain the Entire U.S. Government* (1991), dealing with the American political system, and *Give War a Chance: Eyewitness Accounts of Mankind's Struggle against Tyranny, Injustice, and Alcohol-Free Beer* (1992), describing international politics—have topped the best-seller lists. Describing himself as a "cigar-smoking conservative," O'Rourke actually bashes Republicans as well as Democrats:

> When you look at the Republicans you see the scum off the top of business. When you look at the Democrats you see the scum off the top of politics. Personally, I prefer business. A businessman will steal from you directly instead of getting the IRS to do it for him. And when Republicans ruin the environment, destroy the supply of affordable housing, and wreck the industrial infrastructure, at least they make a buck off it. The Democrats just do these things for fun.

O'Rourke describes his life as a youth growing up in Toledo, Ohio:

> My own family was poor when I was a kid, though I didn't know it; I just thought we were broke. My father died, and my mother married a drunken bum who shortly thereafter died himself. . . . But I honestly didn't know we were poor until just now, when I was researching poverty levels.

He counts himself lucky, because no one coddled him or sympathized with his family's distress. His mother never went on welfare. In the "bad old days," he was simply expected to shut up, behave, and work hard. O'Rourke started out as a Republican but joined the counterculture of the 1960s. Yet he says he was never a Democrat: "I went from being a Republican, to being a Maoist, then back to being a Republican again." He won a scholarship to Miami University of Ohio and later Johns Hopkins. In 1972 he went to work for *National Lampoon*, and on the strength of his irreverent articles he was elevated to editor-in-chief in 1978. Later he moved to Hollywood to write movie scripts, including Rodney Dangerfield films, then returned to New York to become an editor of *Rolling Stone*.

A frequent speaker on university campuses, O'Rourke reflects a distinctly conservative view of government: "A little government and a little luck are necessary in life but only a fool trusts either of them. . . . The whole idea of government is: if enough people get together and act in concert, they can take something and not pay for it." His book, *Age and Guile Beat Youth, Innocence, and a Bad Haircut: Twenty-five Years of P. J. O'Rourke* (1995), describes his ideological journey from youthful radicalism to his current mature (?) conservatism: "I was once younger than anyone ever has been. And on drugs. At least I hope I was on drugs. I'd hate to think that those were my sober and well-considered thoughts."

Source: P. J. O'Rourke, *Parliament of Whores: A Lone Humorist Attempts to Explain the Entire U.S. Government* (New York: Atlantic Monthly Press, 1991); and *Age and Guile Beat Youth, Innocence, and a Bad Haircut: Twenty-five Years of P. J. O'Rourke* (New York: Atlantic Monthly Press, 1995).

uplift the poor, provide medical care for all, educate the masses, protect the environment, and instill humanitarian values in everyone. The prevailing impulse is to "do good," to perform public services, and to assist the least fortunate in society, particularly the poor and minorities. Modern liberalism is impatient with what it sees as the slow progress of individual initiative and private enterprise toward solving socioeconomic problems, so it seeks to use the power of the national government to find solutions to society's troubles.

Liberals' concern about efforts to curtail social welfare programs reflects their support of strong government, whereas conservatives' demands for tax cuts reflect their preference for government that encourages self-reliance and individual initiative.

Modern liberalism defines equality somewhat differently from the way classical liberalism does. Classical liberalism stresses the value of equality of opportunity. Individuals should be free to make the most of their talents and skills, but differences in wealth or power that are a product of differences in talent, initiative, risk taking, and skill are accepted as natural. In contrast, modern liberalism contends that individual dignity and equality of opportunity depend in some measure on *reduction of absolute inequality* in society. Modern liberals believe that true equality of opportunity cannot be achieved where significant numbers of people are suffering from homelessness, hunger, treatable illness, or poverty. Thus modern liberalism supports government efforts to reduce inequalities in society.

FIGURE 2-7 Ideology on Campus

Source: (left) *American Enterprise,* vol. 2, July/August 1991; (right) *The Chronicle of Higher Education,* September 3, 1999.

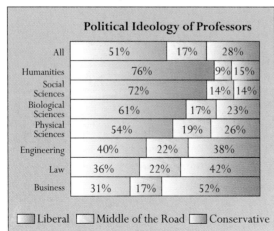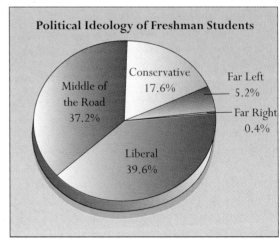

Barbara Boxer, Defending Liberalism

Perhaps no one has been more successful in defending liberal causes in Congress than California's outspoken U.S. senator, Barbara Boxer. Her political résumé boasts awards and honors from such organizations as Planned Parenthood (family planning, reproductive health, and abortion rights), the Sierra Club (environmental causes), Mobilization against AIDS, Anti-Defamation League (civil rights), and Public Citizen (consumer affairs).

A graduate of Brooklyn College with a B.A. in economics, Boxer worked briefly as a stockbroker before moving to San Francisco, where she became a journalist and later a campaign aide to a local congressional representative. Her political career is based in Marin County, a trendy, upper-class, liberal community north of San Francisco, where she first won elected office as member of the County Board of Supervisors. She was elected to the U.S. House of Representatives from her Marin County district in 1982 and quickly won a reputation as one of the most liberal members of the House. Appointed to the House Armed Services Committee, she became a leading critic of defense spending and virtually every weapon requested by the military.

When her state's liberal Democratic senator, Alan Cranston, announced he would not seek reelection to the Senate in the wake of his censure in the Keating Five affair, Boxer sought the open seat. Her opponent, conservative Republican radio and TV commentator Bruce Herschensohn, hammered at Boxer's 143 overdrafts at the House bank, her frequent absenteeism, and her extensive use of congressional perks. But with the help of Clinton's 1992 landslide (47 to 32 percent) victory over George Bush in California, Boxer eked out a 48 to 45 percent victory over Herschensohn. Her victory, together with that of Dianne Feinstein, gave California a historical first—two women U.S. senators.

Boxer quickly emerged as a powerful force in the U.S. Senate on behalf of abortion rights. She led the Senate fight for a federal law protecting abortion clinics from obstruction by demonstrators. On the Environmental and Public Works Committee she helped block efforts to relax federal environmental regulations. She led the movement to oust Republican senator Bob Packwood from the Senate on charges of sexually harassing staff members. She helped lead the fight for the Family Medical Leave Act, passed in the early days of the Clinton administration, as well as the Freedom of Access to [Abortion] Clinics Act. She was reelected by a wide margin in 1998.

Liberals also have different views of the role of government in economic versus social affairs. Liberals Liberals generally prefer an active, powerful government in economic affairs—a government that provides a broad range of public services; regulates business; protects civil rights; protects consumers and the environment; provides generous unemployment, welfare, and Social Security benefits; and reduces economic inequality. But many of these same liberals would limit the government's power to regulate social conduct. They oppose restrictions on abortion; oppose school prayer; favor "decriminalizing" marijuana use and "victimless" offenses like public intoxication and vagrancy; support gay rights and tolerance toward alternative lifestyles; oppose government restrictions on speech, press, and protest; oppose the death penalty; and strive to protect the rights of criminal defendants. Liberalism is the prevailing ideology among college professors (see Figure 2-7).

Are You a Liberal or a Conservative?

Not everyone consistently takes a liberal or a conservative position on every issue. But if you find that you agree with more positions under one of the following "liberal" or "conservative" lists, you are probably ready to label yourself ideologically.

	You Are *Liberal* if You Agree That	You Are *Conservative* if You Agree That
Economic policy	Government should regulate business to protect the public interest. The rich should pay higher taxes to support public services for all. Government spending for social welfare is a good investment in people.	Free-market competition is better at protecting the public than government regulation. Taxes should be kept as low as possible. Government welfare programs destroy incentives to work.
Crime	Government should place primary emphasis on alleviating the social conditions (such as poverty and joblessness) that cause crime.	Government should place primary emphasis on providing more police and prisons and stop courts from coddling criminals.
Social policy	Government should protect the right of women to choose abortion and fund abortions for poor women. Government should pursue affirmative action programs on behalf of minorities and women in employment, education, and so on. Government should keep religious prayers and ceremonies out of schools and public places.	Government should restrict abortion and not use taxpayer money for abortions. Government should not grant preferences to anyone based on race or sex. Government should allow prayers and religious observances in schools and public places.
National security policy	Government should support "human rights" throughout the world. Military spending should be reduced now that the cold war is over.	Government should pursue the "national interest" of the United States. Military spending must reflect a variety of new dangers in this post–cold war period.
You generally describe yourself as	"caring" "compassionate" "progressive"	"responsible" "moderate" "sensible"
and you describe your political opponents as	"extremists" "right-wing radicals" "reactionaries"	"knee jerks" "bleeding hearts" "left-wing radicals"

DISSENT IN THE UNITED STATES

Dissent from the principal elements of American political culture—individualism, free enterprise, democracy, and equality of opportunity—has arisen over the years from both the *left* and the *right*. The **left** generally refers to socialists and communists, but it is sometimes used to brand liberals. The **right** generally refers to fascists and extreme nationalists, although it is sometimes used to stamp conservatives. Despite their professed hostility toward each other, **radicals** on the left and right share many characteristics. Both are **extremist**. They reject democratic politics, compromise, and coalition building as immoral, and they assert the supremacy of the "people" over laws, institutions, and individual rights. Extremists view politics with hostility, although they may make cynical use of democratic politics as a short-term tactical means to their goals.

Conspiracy theories are popular among extremists. For example, the left sees a conspiracy among high government, corporate, and military chieftains to profit from war; the right sees a conspiracy among communists, intellectuals, the United Nations, and Wall Street bankers to subordinate the United States to a world government. The historian Richard Hofstadter has referred to this tendency as "the paranoid style of politics."[14] Both the left and right are intolerant of the opinions of others and are willing to disrupt and intimidate those with whom they disagree. Whether shouting down speakers or disrupting meetings or burning crosses and parading in hoods, the impulse to violence is often present in those who subscribe to radical politics.

Antidemocratic Ideologies   Dissent in the United States has historical roots in antidemocratic movements that originated primarily outside its borders. These movements have spanned the political spectrum from the far right to the far left.

At the far-right end of this spectrum lies **fascism**, an ideology that asserts the supremacy of the state or race over individuals. The goal of fascism is unity of people, nation, and leadership—in the words of Adolf Hitler: "*Ein Volk, Ein Reich, Ein Führer*" (One People, One Nation, One Leader). Every individual, every interest, and every class are to be submerged for the good of the nation. Against the rights of liberty or equality, fascism asserts the duties of service, devotion, and discipline. Its goal is to develop a superior type of human being, with qualities of bravery, courage, genius, and strength. The World War II defeat of the two leading fascist regimes in history—Adolf Hitler's Nazi Germany and Benito Mussolini's fascist Italy—did not extinguish fascist ideas. Elements of fascist thought are found today in extremist movements in both the United States and Europe.

Marxism arose out of the turmoil of the Industrial Revolution as a protest against social evils and economic inequalities. Karl Marx (1818–83), its founder, was not an impoverished worker but rather an upper-middle-class intellectual unable to find an academic position. Benefiting from the financial support of his wealthy colleague Frederick Engels (1820–95), Marx spent years writing *Das Kapital* (1867), a lengthy work describing the evils of capitalism, especially the oppression of factory workers (the proletariat) and the inevitability of revolution. The two men collaborated on a popular pamphlet entitled *The Communist Manifesto* (1848), which called for a workers' revolution: "Workers of the world, unite. You have nothing to lose but your chains."

left   A reference to the liberal, progressive, and/or socialist side of the political spectrum.

right   A reference to the conservative, traditional, anticommunist side of the political spectrum.

radicalism   Advocacy of immediate and drastic changes in society, including the complete restructuring of institutions, values, and beliefs. Radicals may exist on either the extreme left or extreme right.

extremism   Rejection of democratic politics and the assertion of the supremacy of the "people" over laws, institutions, and individual rights.

fascism   Political ideology in which the state and/or race is assumed to be supreme over individuals.

Marxism   The theories of Karl Marx, among them that capitalists oppress workers and that worldwide revolution and the emergence of a classless society are inevitable.

Mapping the Ideological Battleground

If Americans aligned themselves along a single liberal-conservative dimension, politics in the United States would be easier to describe but far less interesting. We might define the liberal-conservative dimension as generally referring to the role of government in society, with liberals favoring an active, powerful government and conservatives favoring a more limited, noninterventionist government. But many Americans make a distinction between *social conduct* and *economic affairs* in their views of the proper role of government. So it is possible to map ideology in the United States in a two-dimensional framework based (1) on whether people prefer more or less government (2) in either social or economic affairs. The result is the identification of four possible ideological types: liberals, conservatives, populists, and libertarians (see Figure).

Neither liberals nor conservatives in the United States take a consistent view toward the role of government. Most liberals today would expand government power in economic affairs and civil rights yet limit its power to regulate many areas of social conduct. Most conservatives would restrict government power in economic affairs and civil rights yet expand its power to regulate social conduct.

The term *populist* is frequently used to describe people who are liberal on economic affairs but conservative on social matters. These people are really very consistent in their view toward the role of government. They favor a strong government to regulate business and provide economic security, and they also favor a strong government to control social conduct. They believe strongly in tradition, law, and morality in social affairs. Occasionally the term *populist* is also used to describe people who are generally resentful of government and national leadership. Although few people use the term to describe themselves, populists may actually make up a large portion of the electorate. Liberal politicians can appeal for their votes by stressing economic issues, and conservative politicians can appeal to them by stressing social issues. And all politi-

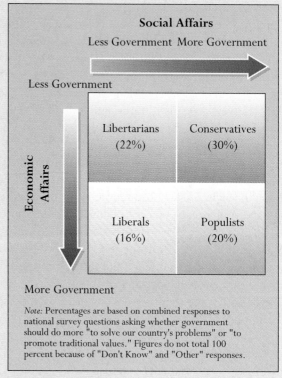

Mapping Ideologies: Opinions on the Role of Government

Source: American Enterprise 5 (May/June 1994): 91.

cians can appeal to their antigovernment bias by attacking "the fat cats," "the elitist snobs," or "the Washington power-holders."

The term *libertarian* is often used to describe people who are consistent in their preference for minimal government intervention in both economic and social affairs. They oppose government interference both in the marketplace and in the private lives of citizens. Libertarians are against most environmental regulations, consumer protection laws, antidrug laws, and government restrictions on abortion. They favor a small government with limited functions, privatization of many government services, minimal welfare benefits, and low taxes. Libertarians also oppose defense spending, foreign aid, and U.S. involvement in world affairs.

It fell to Vladimir Lenin (1870–1924) to implement Marx and Engels's revolutionary ideology in the Russian Revolution in 1917. According to **Leninism**, the key to a successful revolution is the organization of small, disciplined, hard-core groups of professional revolutionaries into a centralized totalitarian party. To explain why Marx's predictions about the ever-worsening conditions of the masses under capitalism proved untrue (workers' standards of living in Western democracies rose rapidly in the twentieth century), Lenin devised the theory of imperialism: advanced capitalist countries turned to war and colonialism, exploiting the Third World, in order to make their own workers relatively prosperous.

Communism is the outgrowth of Marxist-Leninist ideas about the necessity of class warfare, the inevitability of a worldwide proletarian revolution, and the concentration of all power in the "vanguard of the proletariat"—the Communist Party. Communism justifies violence as a means to attain power by arguing that the bourgeoisie (the capitalistic middle class) will never voluntarily give up its control over "the means of production" (the economy). Democracy is only "window dressing" to disguise capitalist exploitation. The Communist Party justifies authoritarian single-party rule as the "dictatorship of the proletariat." In theory, after a period of rule by the Communist Party, all property will be owned by the government, and a "classless" society of true communism will emerge.

Socialism   **Socialism** shares with communism a condemnation of capitalist profit making as exploitative of the working classes. Communists and socialists agree on the "evils" of industrial capitalism: the concentration of wealth, the insensitivity of the profit motive to human needs, the insecurities and suffering brought on by the business cycle, the conflict of class interests, and the tendency of capitalist nations to involve themselves in imperialist wars. However, socialists are committed to the democratic process as a means of replacing capitalism with collective ownership of economic enterprise. Socialists generally reject the notion of violent revolution as a way to replace capitalism and instead advocate peaceful, constitutional roads to bring about change. Moreover, many socialists are prepared to govern in a free society under democratic principles, including freedom of speech and press and the right to organize political parties and oppose government policy. Socialism is egalitarian, seeking to reduce or eliminate inequalities in the distribution of wealth. It attempts to achieve equality of results, rather than mere equality of opportunity.

The End of History?   Much of the history of the twentieth century has been the struggle between democratic capitalism and totalitarian communism. Thus the collapse of communism in Eastern Europe and the Soviet Union, symbolized by the tearing down of the Berlin Wall in 1989, as well as the worldwide movement toward free markets and democracy at the end of the twentieth century, has been labeled the **end of history**.[15] Democratic revolutions were largely inspired by the realization that free-market capitalism provided much higher standards of living than communism. The economies of Eastern Europe were falling further and further behind the economies of the capitalist nations of the West. Similar comparative observations of the successful economies of the Asian capitalist "Four Tigers"—South Korea, Taiwan, Singapore, and Hong Kong—even inspired China's communist leadership to experiment with market reforms. Communism destroyed the individual's incentive to work, produce, innovate, save, and invest in the future. Under communism, production for government goals (principally a strong military) came first; production for individual needs came last. The result was long

Leninism   The theories of Vladimir Lenin, among them that advanced capitalist countries turned toward war and colonialism to make their own workers relatively prosperous.

communism   System of government in which a single totalitarian party controls all means of production and distribution of goods and services.

socialism   System of government involving collective or government ownership of economic enterprise, with the goal being equality of results, not merely equality of opportunity.

end of history   The collapse of communism and the worldwide movement toward free markets and political democracy.

Political extremists of the left and right often have more in common than they would like to admit. Although decidedly different in their political philosophies, both members of right-wing American neo-Nazi groups and members of left-wing communist groups reject democratic politics and assert the supremacy of the "people" over laws, institutions, and individual rights. Gregory Johnson (left) was the catalyst for the flag burning controversy that is still raging in Congress today. Buford O'Neal Furrow, Jr. (right) was arrested for opening fire on children in a Jewish day care center in California. Several children died in this attack.

lines at stores, shoddy products, and frequent bribery of bureaucrats to obtain necessary consumer items. More important, perhaps, the concentration of both economic and political power in the hands of a central bureaucracy proved to be incompatible with democracy. Communism relies on central direction, force, and repression. Communist systems curtail individual freedom and prohibit the development of separate parties and interest groups outside of government.

Capitalism does not *ensure* democracy; some capitalist nations are authoritarian. But economic freedom inspires demands for political freedom. Thus market reforms, initiated by communist leaders to increase productivity, led to democracy movements, and those movements eventually dismantled the communist system in Eastern Europe and the old Soviet Union.

Academic Radicalism   Marxism survives on campuses today largely as an academic critique of the functioning of capitalism.[16] It provides some disaffected academics with ideas and language to attack everything that disturbs them about the United States—from poverty, racism, and environmental hazards to junk food, athletic scholarships, and obnoxious television advertising—conveniently blaming the "profit motive" for many of the ills of American society.

Contemporary radicals argue that the institutions of capitalism have conditioned people to be materialistic, competitive, and even violent. The individual has been transformed into a one-dimensional person in whom genuine humanistic values are repressed.[17] Profitability, rather than humanistic values, remains the primary crite-

Twenty-First Century Directions

The values of liberty and equality have guided the American nation throughout its history—from the Declaration of Independence in the 18th Century, through the Civil War and the abolition of slavery in the 19th Century, to the Civil Rights movement of the 20th Century. These values will continue to define the nation's aspirations for the future, even while their practical meaning will continue to be disputed.

↓ *Income Equality*   The global economy and technological change will create even greater income inequalities in the 21st Century. America's unskilled and semi-skilled workers will be competing with very low-wage workers in developing nations around the world. In contrast, America's highly skilled workers, entrepreneurs, multinational corporate executives, and investors, will reap dramatic gains. The result will be that inequality will worsen even though the aggregate income of nation will rise.

↑ *Social Mobility*   Social mobility, based on education, technical know-how, initiative and innovation, will continue to create new avenues to wealth. This mobility may be limited to a "cognitive elite," but the promise of upward movement will continue to inspire widespread popular support for the nation's social and economic system.

↑ *Cultural Diversity*   Continued high levels of immigration to America will dramatically change the ethnic composition of the nation. Hispanics will become nation's largest minority and a powerful force in the nation's politics. Both the Democratic and Republican parties will vie for their support. By mid-century, white, non-Hispanics will comprise only about one-half of the nation's population.

←→ *Liberalism and Conservatism*   Most Americans will continue to think of themselves as "moderate" and "middle-of-the-road." They will lean toward liberal programs for maintaining economic security and improving health care. Yet they will continue to echo conservative rhetoric about keeping government small and taxes low. The prudent politician will give conservative-sounding speeches while supporting liberal spending programs.

---

rion for decision making in the capitalist economy, and thus profitability is the reason for poverty and misery despite material abundance. Without capitalist institutions, life would be giving, cooperative, and compassionate. Only a *radical restructuring* of social and economic institutions will succeed in liberating people from these institutions to lead humanistic, cooperative lives.

To American radicals, the problem of social change is truly monumental, because capitalist values and institutions are deeply rooted in this country. Since most people are not aware that they are oppressed and victimized, the first step toward social change is consciousness raising—that is, making people aware of their misery.

The agenda of academic radicalism has been labeled **politically correct (PC)** thinking. Politically correct thinking views American society as racist, sexist, and homophobic. Overt bigotry is not the real issue, but rather Western institutions, language, and culture, which systematically oppress and victimize women, people of color, gays, and others.

Academic radicalism "includes the assumption that Western values are inherently oppressive, that the chief purpose of education is political transformation, and that

politically correct (PC)
Repression of attitudes, speech, and writings that are deemed racist, sexist, homophobic (anti-homosexual), or otherwise "insensitive."

all standards are arbitrary."[18] In PC thinking, "everything is political." Therefore curriculum, courses, and lectures—even language and demeanor—are judged according to whether they are politically correct or not. Universities have always been centers for the critical examination of institutions, values, and culture, but PC thinking does not really tolerate open discussion or debate. Opposition is denounced as "insensitive," racist, sexist, or worse, and intimidation is not infrequent (see "Political Correctness versus Free Speech on Campus" in Chapter 14).

SUMMARY NOTES

- Ideas are sources of power. They provide people with guides for determining right and wrong and with rationales for political action. Political institutions are shaped by the values and beliefs of the political culture, and political leaders are restrained in their exercise of power by these ideas.

- The American political culture is a set of widely shared values and beliefs about who should govern, for what ends, and by what means.

- Americans share many common ways of thinking about politics. Nevertheless, there are often contradictions between professed values and actual conditions, problems in applying abstract beliefs to concrete situations, and even occasional conflict over fundamental values.

- Individual liberty is a fundamental value in American life. The classical liberal tradition that inspired the nation's Founders included both political liberties and economic freedoms.

- Equality is another fundamental American value. The nation's Founders believed in equality before the law; yet political equality, in the form of universal voting rights, required nearly two centuries to bring about.

- Equality of opportunity is a widely shared value; most Americans are opposed to artificial barriers of race, sex, religion, or ethnicity barring individual advancement. But equality of results is not a widely shared value; most Americans support a "floor" on income and well-being for their fellow citizens but oppose placing a "ceiling" on income or wealth.

- Income inequality has increased in recent years primarily as a result of economic and demographic changes. Most Americans believe that opportunities for individual advancement are still available, and this belief diminishes the potential for class conflict.

- Liberal and conservative ideologies in American politics present somewhat different sets of values and beliefs, even though they share a common commitment to individual dignity and private property. Generally, liberals favor an active, powerful government to provide economic security and protection for civil rights but oppose government restrictions on social conduct. Generally, conservatives favor minimal government intervention in economic affairs and civil rights but support many government restrictions on social conduct.

- Many Americans who identify themselves as liberals or conservatives are not always consistent in applying their professed views. Populists are liberal on economic issues but conservative in their views on social issues. Libertarians are conservative on economic issues but liberal in their social views.

- Liberal and conservative ideas evolve over time in response to new challenges and changing conditions. Neo-conservatives share the historical classical liberal concerns about the nation's social problems but no longer believe that solutions can be found in large-scale, costly bureaucratic government programs. Neo-liberals retain their faith in the power of government but focus their attention on efforts to promote economic growth as a prerequisite to solving social problems.

- The collapse of communism in Eastern Europe and the former Soviet Union and the worldwide movement toward free markets and democracy have undermined support for socialism throughout the world. Yet Marxism survives in academic circles as a critique of the functioning of capitalism.

KEY TERMS

political culture   26

values   26

beliefs   26

subcultures   26

classical liberalism   26

capitalism   27

political equality   28

equality of
   opportunity   28

equality of results   29

social mobility   33

class conflict   35

class consciousness   35

ideology   39

conservatism   41

liberalism   42

left   47

right   47

radicalism   47

extremism   47

fascism   47

Marxism   47

Leninism   49

communism   49

socialism   49

end of history   49

politically correct (PC)   51

SELECTED READINGS

EBENSTEIN, ALAN, WILLIAM EBENSTEIN, AND EDWIN FOGELMAN. *Today's Isms: Communism, Fascism, Capitalism, Socialism.* 11th ed. Upper Saddle River, N.J.: Prentice Hall, 2000. A concise description and history of the major isms.

GREYER, GEORGIE ANNE. *Americans No More.* New York: Atlantic Monthly Press, 1996. An argument that unchecked immigration, combined with emphases on multiculturalism and multilingualism, is undermining national unity.

HENRY, WILLIAM A., III. *In Defense of Elitism.* New York: Doubleday, 1994. A humorous as well as persuasive attack on the "myths" that everyone is alike (or should be), that a just society will produce equal success for everyone, and that "the common man" is always right.

HERRNSTEIN, RICHARD J., AND CHARLES MURRAY. *The Bell Curve: Intelligence and Class Structure in American Life.* New York: Free Press, 1994. A controversial argument that success in life is mainly a result of inherited intelligence and that a very bright "cognitive elite" will continue to distance themselves from the duller masses.

HUNTINGTON, SAMUEL P. *American Politics: The Promise of Disharmony.* Cambridge, Mass.: Harvard University Press, 1981. An examination of the gaps between the promise of the American ideals of liberty and equality and the performance of the American political system.

RYSCAVAGE, PAUL. *Income Inequality in America.* Armonk, N.Y.: M.E. Sharpe, 1999. A careful analysis of current trends toward income inequality in the U.S.

WATTENBERG, BEN J. *Values Matter Most.* New York: Free Press, 1995. An argument that sound values rather than economic concerns will drive American politics in the future.

WOLFF, EDWARD N. *Top Heavy.* New York: Twentieth Century Fund, 1995. A fact-filled report on the increasing inequality of wealth in America, together with a proposal to tax wealth as well as income.

The Constitution
Limiting Governmental Power

1 Was the original Constitution of 1787 a truly democratic document?
Yes ⬤ No ⬤

2 Should citizens be able to vote directly on national policies such as prayer in public schools or doctor-assisted suicides?
Yes ⬤ No ⬤

3 Should a large state like California, with 32 million people, elect more U.S. senators than a small state like Wyoming, with only half a million people?
Yes ⬤ No ⬤

4 Should federal laws always supersede state laws?
Yes ⬤ No ⬤

5 In which do you have the most trust and confidence?
President ⬤
Congress ⬤
Supreme Court ⬤

6 Should the Constitution be amended to require Congress to pass only balanced budgets?
Yes ⬤ No ⬤

7 Should the Constitution be amended to guarantee that equal rights shall not be denied based on sex?
Yes ⬤ No ⬤

CONSTITUTIONAL GOVERNMENT

Constitutions govern government. **Constitutionalism**—a government of laws, not of people—means that those who exercise governmental power are restricted in their use of it by a higher law. If individual freedoms are to be placed beyond the reach of government and beyond the reach of majorities, then a constitution must truly limit the exercise of authority by government. It does so by setting forth individual liberties that the government—even with majority support—cannot violate.

A **constitution** legally establishes government authority. It sets up governmental bodies (such as the House of Representatives, the Senate, the presidency, and the Supreme Court in the United States). It grants them powers. It determines how their members are to be chosen. And it prescribes the rules by which they make decisions.

Constitutional decision making is deciding how to decide; that is, it is deciding on the rules for policy making. It is not policy making itself. Policies will be decided later, according to the rules set forth in the constitution.

A constitution cannot be changed by the ordinary acts of governmental bodies; change can come only through a process of general popular consent.[1] The U.S. Constitution, then, is superior to ordinary laws of Congress, orders of the president, decisions of the courts, acts of the state legislatures, and regulations of the bureaucracies. Indeed, the Constitution is "the supreme law of the land."

In a democracy "of the people, by the people, and for the people," who really has the power to govern? Are strong national government and personal liberty compatible? Can majorities limit individual rights? America's Founders struggled with such questions, and in resolving them established the oldest existing constitutional government.

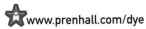 www.prenhall.com/dye

To be effective in protecting the individual from government, a constitution must be respected—by both the people and the government. Government officials must believe that they are in fact limited by the constitution, and private citizens must believe that they are in fact protected by it. The constitution must be taken seriously if it is to be effective in limiting government and protecting the liberties of individuals.

THE CONSTITUTIONAL TRADITION

Americans are strongly committed to the idea of a written constitution to establish government and limit its powers. In fact, the Constitutional Convention of 1787 had many important antecedents.

The Magna Carta, 1215   English lords, traditionally required to finance the kings' wars, forced King John to sign the Magna Carta, a document guaranteeing their feudal rights and setting the precedent of a limited government and monarchy.

The Mayflower Compact, 1620   Puritan colonists, while still aboard the Mayflower, signed a compact establishing a "civil body politic . . . to enact just and equal laws . . . for the general good of the colony; unto which we promise all due submission and obedience." After the Puritans landed at Plymouth, in what is today Massachusetts, they formed a colony based on the Mayflower Compact, thus setting a precedent of a government established by contract with the governed.

The Colonial Charters, 1624–1732   The charters that authorized settlement of the colonies in America were granted by royal action. For some of the colonies, the British king granted official proprietary rights to an individual, as in Maryland (granted to Lord Baltimore), Pennsylvania (to William Penn), and Delaware (also to Penn). For other colonies, the king granted royal commissions to companies to establish governments, as in Virginia, Massachusetts, New Hampshire, New York, New Jersey, Georgia, and North and South Carolina. Royal charters were granted directly to the colonists themselves only in Connecticut and Rhode Island. These colonists drew up their charters and presented them to the king, setting a precedent in America for written contracts defining governmental power.

The "Charter Oak Affair" of 1685–88 began when King James II became displeased with his Connecticut subjects and issued an order for the repeal of the Connecticut Charter. In 1687 Sir Edmund Andros went to Hartford, dissolved the colonial government, and demanded that the charter be returned. But Captain John Wadsworth hid it in an oak tree. After the so-called Glorious Revolution in England in 1688, the charter was taken out and used again as the fundamental law of the colony. Subsequent British monarchs silently acquiesced in this restoration of rights, and the affair strengthened the notion of loyalty to the constitution rather than to the king.

The Declaration of Independence, 1776   The First Continental Congress, a convention of delegates from twelve of the thirteen original colonies, came together in 1774 to protest British interference in American affairs. But the Revolutionary War did not begin until April 19, 1775. The evening before, British regular troops marched out from Boston to seize arms stored by citizens in Lexington and Concord, Massachusetts. At dawn the next morning, the Minutemen—armed citizens organized for the protection of their towns—engaged the British regulars

constitutionalism A government of laws, not people, operating on the principle that governmental power must be limited and government officials should be restrained in their exercise of power over individuals.

constitution The legal structure of a political system, establishing governmental bodies, granting their powers, determining how their members are selected, and prescribing the rules by which they make their decisions. Considered basic or fundamental, a constitution cannot be changed by ordinary acts of governmental bodies.

After numerous drafts by Thomas Jefferson, including such changes as the deletion of a clause condemning the slave trade that offended North Carolina and Georgia, the Declaration of Independence was accepted by the majority of the Continental Congress on July 4, 1776. The document then became "the unanimous declaration of the thirteen United States of America" on July 19, and was signed by all members of the Continental Congress on August 2. Shown in this painting are (left to right) Benjamin Franklin, Thomas Jefferson, Robert Livingston, John Adams, and Roger Sherman.

in brief battles, then harassed them all the way back to Boston. In June of that year, the Second Continental Congress appointed George Washington Commander-in-Chief of American forces and sent him to Boston to take command of the American militia surrounding the city. Still, popular support for the Revolution remained limited, and even many members of the Continental Congress hoped only to force changes—not to split off from Britain.

As this hope died, however, members of the Continental Congress came to view a formal Declaration of Independence as necessary to give legitimacy to their cause and establish the basis for a new nation. Accordingly, on July 2, 1776, the Continental Congress "Resolved, that these United Colonies are, and, of right, ought to be free and independent States." Thomas Jefferson had been commissioned to write a justification for the action, which he presented to the Congress on July 4, 1776. In writing the Declaration of Independence, Jefferson lifted several phrases directly from the English political philosopher John Locke (see Chapter 1) asserting the rights of individuals, the contract theory of government, and the right of revolution. The declaration was signed first by the president of the Continental Congress, John Hancock.

The Revolutionary War ended when British General Charles Cornwallis surrendered at Yorktown, Virginia, in October 1781. But even as the war was being waged, the new nation was creating the framework of its government.

The Articles of Confederation, 1781–1789   Although Richard Henry Lee, a Virginia delegate to the Continental Congress, first proposed that the newly independent states form a confederation on July 6, 1776, the Continental Congress did not approve the Articles of Confederation until November 15, 1777, and the last state to sign them, Maryland, did not do so until March 1, 1781. Under the Articles, Congress was a single house in which each state had two to seven members but only one vote. Congress itself created and appointed executives, judges, and military officers. It also had the power to make war and peace, conduct foreign affairs, and borrow and print money. But Congress could *not* collect taxes or enforce laws directly; it had to rely on the states to provide money and enforce its laws. The United States under the Articles was really a confederation of nations. Within this "firm league of friendship" (Article III of the Articles of Confederation), the national government was thought of as an alliance of independent states, not as a government "of the people."

TROUBLES CONFRONTING A NEW NATION

Two hundred years ago the United States was struggling to achieve nationhood. The new U.S. government achieved enormous successes under the Articles of Confederation: It won independence from Great Britain, the world's most powerful colonial nation at the time; it defeated vastly superior forces in a prolonged war for independence; it established a viable peace and won powerful allies (such as France) in the international community; it created an effective army and navy, established a postal system, and laid the foundations for national unity. But despite these successes in war and diplomacy, the political arrangements under the Articles were unsatisfactory to many influential groups—notably, bankers and investors who held U.S. government bonds, plantation owners, real estate developers, and merchants and shippers.

Financial Difficulties   Under the Articles of Confederation, Congress had no power to tax the people directly. Instead, Congress had to ask the states for money to pay its expenses, particularly the expenses of fighting the long and costly War of Independence with Great Britain. There was no way to force the states to make their payments to the national government. In fact, about 90 percent of the funds requisitioned by Congress from the states was never paid, so Congress had to borrow money from wealthy patriot investors to fight the war. Without the power to tax, however, Congress could not pay off these debts. Indeed, the value of U.S. governmental bonds fell to about 10 cents for every dollar's worth because few people believed the bonds would ever be paid off. Congress even stopped making interest payments on these bonds.

Commercial Obstacles   Under the Articles of Confederation, states were free to tax the goods of other states. Without the power to regulate interstate commerce, the national government was unable to protect merchants from heavy tariffs imposed on shipments from state to state. Southern planters could not ship their agricultural products to northern cities without paying state-imposed tariffs, and northern merchants could not ship manufactured products from state to state without interference. Merchants, manufacturers, shippers, and planters all wanted to develop national markets and prevent the states from imposing tariffs or restrictions on interstate trade. States competed with one another by passing low tariffs on foreign goods (to encourage the shipment of goods through their own ports) and high tariffs against one another's goods (to protect their own markets). The result was a great deal of confusion and bad feeling—as well as a great deal of smuggling.

Currency Problems   Under the Articles, the states themselves had the power to issue their own currency, regulate its value, and require that it be accepted in payment of debts. States had their own "legal tender" laws, which required creditors to accept state money if "tendered" in payment of debt. As a result, many forms of money were circulating: Virginia dollars, Rhode Island dollars, Pennsylvania dollars, and so on. Some states (Rhode Island, for example) printed a great deal of money, creating inflation in their currency and alienating banks and investors whose loans were being paid off in this cheap currency. If creditors refused payment in a particular state's currency, the debt could be abolished in that state. So finances throughout the states were very unstable, and banks and creditors were threatened by cheap paper money.

Civil Disorder   In several states, debtors openly revolted against tax collectors and sheriffs attempting to repossess farms on behalf of creditors who held unpaid mortgages. The most serious rebellion broke out in the summer of 1786 in western Massachusetts, where a band of 2,000 insurgent farmers captured the courthouses in several counties and briefly held the city of Springfield. Led by Daniel Shays, a veteran of the Revolutionary War battle at Bunker Hill, the insurgent army posed a direct threat to investors, bankers, creditors, and tax collectors by burning deeds, mortgages, and tax records to wipe out proof of the farmers' debts. Shays's Rebellion, as it was called, was finally put down by a small mercenary army, paid for by well-to-do citizens of Boston.

Reports of Shays's Rebellion filled the newspapers of the large eastern cities. George Washington, Alexander Hamilton, James Madison, and many other prominent Americans wrote their friends about it. The event galvanized property owners to support the creation of a strong central government capable of dealing with "radicalism." Only a strong central government, they wrote one another, could "insure domestic tranquility," guarantee "a republican form of government," and protect property "against domestic violence." It is no accident that all of these phrases appear in the Constitution of 1787.

In an attempt to prevent the foreclosure of farms by creditors, Revolutionary War veteran Daniel Shays led an armed mass of citizens in a march on a western Massachusetts courthouse. This uprising, which came to be known as Shays's Rebellion, exposed the Confederation's military weakness and increased support for a strong central government.

The Road to the Constitutional Convention   In the spring of 1785, some wealthy merchants from Virginia and Maryland met at Alexandria, Virginia, to try to resolve a conflict between the two states over commerce and navigation on the Potomac River and Chesapeake Bay. George Washington, the new nation's most prominent citizen, took a personal interest in the meeting. As a wealthy plantation owner and a land speculator who owned more than 30,000 acres of land upstream on the Potomac, Washington was keenly interested in commercial problems under the Articles of Confederation. He lent his great prestige to the Alexandria meeting by inviting the participants to his house at Mount Vernon. Out of this conference came the idea for a general economic conference for all of the states, to be held in Annapolis, Maryland, in September 1786.

The Annapolis Convention turned out to be a key stepping-stone to the Constitutional Convention of 1787. Instead of concentrating on commerce and navigation between the states, the delegates at Annapolis, including Alexander Hamilton and James Madison, called for a general constitutional convention to suggest remedies to what they saw as defects in the Articles of Confederation.

On February 21, 1787, the Congress called for a convention to meet in Philadelphia for the "sole and express purpose" of revising the Articles of Confederation and reporting to the Congress and the state legislatures "such alterations and provisions therein as shall, when agreed to in Congress and confirmed by the states, to render the federal Constitution adequate to the exigencies of government and the preservation of the union." Notice that Congress did not authorize the convention to write a new constitution or to call constitutional conventions in the states to ratify a new constitution. State legislatures sent delegates to Philadelphia expecting that their task would be limited to *revising* the Articles and that revisions would be sent back to Congress and state legislatures for their approval. But that is not what happened.

The Nation's Founders   The fifty-five delegates to the Constitutional Convention, which met in Philadelphia in the summer of 1787, quickly discarded the congressional mandate to merely "revise" the Articles of Confederation. The Virginia delegation, led by James Madison, arrived before a quorum of seven states had assembled and used the time to draw up an entirely new constitutional document. After the first formal session opened on May 25 and George Washington was elected president of the convention, the Virginia Plan became the basis of discussion. Thus, at the very beginning of the convention, the decision was made to scrap the Articles of Confederation altogether, write a new constitution, and form a new national government.[2]

The Founders were very confident of their powers and abilities. They had been selected by their state legislatures (only Rhode Island, dominated by small farmers, refused to send a delegation). When Thomas Jefferson, then serving in the critical post of ambassador to France (the nation's military ally in the Revolutionary War), first saw the list of delegates, he exclaimed, "It is really an assembly of demigods." Indeed, among the nation's notables, only Jefferson and John Adams (then serving as ambassador to England) were absent. The eventual success of the convention, and the ratification of the new Constitution, resulted in part from the enormous prestige, experience, and achievements of the delegates themselves.

Above all, the delegates at Philadelphia were cosmopolitan. They approached political, economic, and military issues from a "continental" point of view. Unlike most Americans in 1787, their loyalties extended beyond their states. They were truly nationalists.[3]

CONSENSUS IN PHILADELPHIA

The Founders shared many ideas about government. We often focus our attention on *conflict* in the Convention of 1787 and the compromises reached by the participants, but the really important story of the Constitution is the *consensus* that was shared by these men of influence.

Liberty and Property   The Founders had read John Locke and absorbed his idea that the purpose of government is to protect individual liberty and property. They believed in a natural law, superior to any human-made laws, that endowed each person with certain inalienable rights—the rights to life, liberty, and property. They believed that all people were equally entitled to these rights. Most of them, including slave owners George Washington and Thomas Jefferson, understood that the belief in personal liberty conflicted with the practice of slavery and found the inconsistency troubling.

Social Contract   The Founders believed that government originated in an implied contract among people. People agreed to establish government, obey laws, and pay taxes in exchange for protection of their natural rights. This social contract gave government its legitimacy—a legitimacy that rested on the consent of the governed, not with gods or kings or force. If a government violated individual liberty, it broke the social contract and thus lost its legitimacy.

Representative Government   Although most of the world's governments in 1787 were hereditary monarchies, the Founders believed the people should have a voice in choosing their own representatives in government. They opposed hereditary aristocracy and titled nobility. Instead, they sought to forge a republic. **Republicanism** meant government by representatives of the people. The Founders expected the masses to consent to be governed by their leaders—men of principle and property with ability, education, and a stake in the preservation of liberty. The Founders believed the people should have only a limited role in directly selecting their representatives: they should vote for members of the House of Representatives, but senators, the president, and members of the Supreme Court should be selected by others more qualified to judge their ability.

Limited Government   The Founders believed unlimited power was corrupting and a concentration of power was dangerous. They believed in a written constitution that limited the scope of governmental power. They also believed in dividing power within government by creating separate bodies able to check and balance one another's powers.

Nationalism   Most important, the Founders shared a belief in **nationalism**—a strong and independent national (federal) government with power to govern directly, rather than through state governments. They sought to establish a government that would be recognized around the world as representing "We the people of the United States." Not everyone in America shared this enthusiasm for a strong federal government; indeed, opposition forces, calling themselves Anti-Federalists, almost succeeded in defeating the new Constitution. But the leaders meeting in

republicanism   Government by representatives of the people rather than directly by the people themselves.

nationalism   Belief that shared cultural, historical, linguistic, and social characteristics of a people justify the creation of a government encompassing all of them; the resulting nation-state should be independent and legally equal to all other nation-states.

George Washington, Founder of a Nation

From the time he took command of the American Revolutionary forces in 1775 until he gave his Farewell Address to the nation in 1796 and returned to his Mount Vernon plantation, George Washington (1732–99) was, indeed, "First in war, first in peace, first in the hearts of his countrymen." His military success, combined with his diplomacy and practical political acumen, gave him overwhelming moral authority, which he used to inspire the Constitutional Convention, to secure the ratification of the Constitution, and then to guide the new nation through its first years.

Washington was raised on a Virginia plantation and inherited substantial landholdings, including his Mount Vernon plantation on the Potomac River. He began his career as a surveyor. His work took him deep into the wilderness of America's frontier. This experience later served him well when, at age twenty-one, he was commissioned by the governor of Virginia to explore "the Forks of the Ohio" (now Pittsburgh, Pennsylvania) and extend British claims against French interests west of the Allegheny Mountains. In 1753 Washington's application for a regular commission in the British army was rejected, but he was appointed a major and later promoted to lieutenant colonel in the Virginia militia.

In 1754 he led a small force toward the French Fort Duquesne, but after a brief battle at makeshift "Fort Necessity," he was obliged to retreat. In 1755 British Major General Edward Braddock asked the young militia officer to accompany his heavy regiments on a campaign to dislodge the French from Fort Duquesne. Braddock disregarded Washington's warnings about concealed ways of fighting in the New World; Braddock's parading redcoat forces were ambushed by the French and Indians near Pittsburgh, and the general was killed. Washington rallied what remained of the British forces and led them in a successful retreat back to Virginia.

Washington was viewed by Virginians as a hero, and at age twenty-two he was appointed by the Virginia Assembly "Colonel of the Virginia Regiment and Commander in Chief of all Virginia Forces." But regular British officers ridiculed the militia forces and asserted their authority over Washington. British General John Forbes occupied Fort Duquesne, renamed it Fort Pitt, and gave Washington's men the task of garrisoning it.

In 1759, having completed his service in the French and Indian Wars, Washington left his military post and returned to plantation life. He married a wealthy widow, Martha Custis, expanded his plantation holdings, and prospered in western land speculation.

The Virginia legislature elected Washington to attend the First Continental Congress in September 1774. Washington was the most celebrated veteran of the French and Indian Wars who was still young enough (forty-two) to lead military forces in a new struggle. John Adams of Massachusetts was anxious to unite the continent in the coming contest, and he persuaded the Second Continental Congress to give the Virginian command of the American revolutionary forces surrounding the British army in Boston. Upon accepting command in 1775, Washington declined a salary

Philadelphia in the summer of 1787 were convinced of the need for a strong central government that would share power with the states.

CONFLICT IN PHILADELPHIA

Consensus on basic principles of government was essential to the success of the Philadelphia convention. But conflict over the implementation of these principles not only tied up the convention for an entire summer but later threatened to prevent the states from ratifying, or voting to approve, the document the convention produced.

and modestly suggested that his experience "may not be equal to the task."

Washington faced what appeared to be insurmountable odds in his campaigns against the British army. His ragtag soldiers were no match for the well-trained and better equipped British troops. In addition, America's citizen-soldiers were only obligated to brief periods of enlistment, which, combined with a high rate of desertion, nearly resulted in the collapse of Washington's army on several occasions. Through it all Washington persevered by employing many of the tactics later defined as the principles of guerrilla warfare. By retreating deep into Pennsylvania's Valley Forge, Washington avoided defeat and saved his army. His bold Christmas night attack against Hessian troops at Trenton, New Jersey, encouraged French intervention on America's behalf. Slowly Washington was able to wear down the British resolve to fight. In the end, he succeeded in trapping a British army at Yorktown, Virginia. Assisted by a French naval blockade, he accepted the surrender of Lord Cornwallis and 8,000 of his men on October 19, 1781. As a result, peace negotiations were opened in Paris.

Perhaps Washington's greatest contribution to democratic government occurred in 1783 in Newburgh, New York, near West Point, where the veterans of his Continental Army were encamped. Despite their hardships and ultimate victory in the Revolutionary War, these soldiers remained unpaid by Congress. Indeed, Congress ignored a series of letters, known as the Newburgh Addresses, that threatened military force if Congress continued to deny benefits to the veterans. Washington was invited to Newburgh by officers who hoped he would agree to lead a military coup against the Congress. But when Washington mounted the platform he denounced the use of force and the "infamous propositions" contained in their earlier addresses to Congress. There is little doubt that he could have chosen to march on the Congress with his veteran army and install himself as military dictator. World history is filled with revolutionary army leaders who did so. But Washington chose to preserve representative government.

One of the few noncontroversial decisions of the Constitutional Convention in 1787 was the selection of George Washington to preside over the meetings. He took little part in the debates; however, his enormous prestige helped to hold the convention together and later to win support for the new Constitution.

When the first Electoral College voted on the presidential candidates, Washington received all sixty-nine votes. John Adams was elected vice president. Washington steered a steady course for the new nation by maintaining a strict neutrality toward warring Europe; in his Farewell Address, he warned against foreign entanglements as well as the formation of political parties and party spirit, which, he said, "agitates the community with ill-founded jealousies."

George Washington died on December 14, 1799, in his home at Mount Vernon. During Washington's war service, the highest rank granted him by Congress was that of lieutenant-general. In 1976 Congress granted Washington the nation's highest military rank, General of the Armies, and confirmed him forever as the senior officer on U.S. Army rolls.

Source: George Washington, Farewell Address, September 17, 1796, in Documents of American History (10th ed.), eds. Henry Steele Commager and Milton Cantor (Upper Saddle River, N.J.: Prentice Hall, 1988), 1:172.

Representation   Representation was the most controversial issue in Philadelphia. Following the election of George Washington as president of the convention, Governor Edmund Randolph of Virginia rose to present a draft of a new constitution. This Virginia Plan called for a legislature with two houses: a lower house chosen by the people of the states, with representation according to population; and an upper house to be chosen by the lower house (see Table 3-1 on page 64). Congress was to have the broad power to "legislate in all cases to which the separate States are incompetent, or in which the harmony of the United States may be interrupted." Congress was to have the power to nullify state laws that it believed violated the Constitution, thus ensuring the national government's

Table 3-1	**Constitutional Compromise**	
The Virginia Plan	**The New Jersey Plan**	**The Connecticut Compromise** **The Constitution of 1787**
Two-house legislature, with the lower house directly elected based on state population and the upper house elected by the lower.	One-house legislature, with equal state representation, regardless of population.	Two-house legislature, with the House directly elected based on state population and the Senate selected by the state legislatures; two senators per state, regardless of population.
Legislature with broad power, including veto power over laws passed by the state legislatures.	Legislature with the same power as under the Articles of Confederation, plus the power to levy some taxes and to regulate commerce.	Legislature with broad power, including the power to tax and to regulate commerce.
President and cabinet elected by the legislature.	Separate multiperson executive, elected by the legislature, removable by petition from a majority of the state governors.	President chosen by an Electoral College.
National judiciary elected by the legislature.	National Judiciary appointed by the executive.	National judiciary appointed by the president and confirmed by the Senate.
"Council of Revision" with the power to veto laws of the legislature.	National Supremacy Clause similar to that found in Article VI of the 1787 Constitution.	National Supremacy Clause: the Constitution is "the supreme Law of the Land."

supremacy over the states. The Virginia Plan also proposed a *parliamentary* form of government, in which the legislature (Congress) chose the principal executive officers of the government as well as federal judges. Finally, the Virginia Plan included a curious "council of revision," with the power to veto acts of Congress.

Delegates from New Jersey and Delaware objected strongly to the great power given to the national government in the Virginia Plan, the larger representation it proposed for the more populous states, and the plan's failure to recognize the role of the states in the composition of the new government. After several weeks of debate, William Paterson of New Jersey submitted a counterproposal. The New Jersey Plan called for a single-chamber Congress in which each state, regardless of its population, had one vote, just as under the Articles of Confederation. But unlike the Articles, the New Jersey Plan proposed separate executive and judicial branches of government and the expansion of the powers of Congress to include levying taxes and regulating commerce. Moreover, the New Jersey Plan included a National Supremacy Clause, declaring that the Constitution and federal laws would supersede state constitutions and laws.

Debate over representation in Congress raged into July 1787. At one point, the convention actually voted for the Virginia Plan, 7 votes to 3, but without New York, New Jersey, and Delaware, the new nation would not have been viable. Eventually, Roger Sherman of Connecticut came forward with a compromise. This Connecticut Compromise—sometimes called the Great Compromise—established two houses of Congress: in the upper house, the Senate, each state would have two members regardless of its size; in the lower body, the House of Representatives, each state would be represented according to population. Members of the House would be directly elected by the people; members of the Senate would be selected by their state legislatures. Legislation would have to pass both houses to be enacted. This compromise was approved by the convention on July 16.

Slavery Another conflict absorbing the attention of the delegates was slavery. In 1787 slavery was legal everywhere except in Massachusetts. Nevertheless, the delegates were too embarrassed to use the word *slave* or *slavery* in their debates or in the Constitution itself. Instead, they referred to "other persons" and "persons held to service or labour."

Delegates from the southern states, where slaves were a large proportion of the population, believed slaves should be counted in representation afforded the states, especially if taxes were to be levied on a population basis (which meant counting slaves as persons). Delegates from the northern states, with small slave populations, believed that "the people" counted for representation purposes should include only free persons. The Connecticut Plan included the now-infamous Three-fifths Compromise: three-fifths of the slaves of each state would be counted for purposes both of representation in the House of Representatives and for apportionment for direct taxes.

Slave owners also sought protection for their human "property" in the Constitution itself. They were particularly concerned about slaves running away to other states and claiming their freedom. So they succeeded in writing into the Constitution (Article IV, Section 2) a specific guarantee: "No person held to Service or Labour in one State . . . escaping into another, shall . . . be discharged from such Service or Labour, but shall be delivered up on Claim of the Party to whom such Service or Labour may be due."

Yet another compromise dealt with the slave trade. The capture, transportation, and "breaking in" of African slaves was considered a nasty business, even by southern planters. Many wealthy Maryland and Virginia plantations were already well supplied with slaves and thus could afford the luxury of conscience to call for an end to slave importation. But other planters from the less-developed southern

Although hotly debated, the issue of slave-holding was not resolved by the Founders in either the Declaration of Independence or the Constitution. As a result, the practice of buying and selling slaves—and the debate over this practice—continued for years to come, until political conflict exploded in the Civil War.

states, particularly South Carolina and Georgia, wanted additional slave labor. The final compromise prohibited the slave trade—but not before the year 1808, thereby giving the planters twenty years to import all the slaves they needed before the slave trade ended.

Voter Qualifications   Another important conflict centered on qualifications for voting and holding office in the new government. Most of the delegates believed that voters as well as officeholders should be men of property. (Only Benjamin Franklin went so far as to propose universal *male* suffrage.) But delegates argued over the specific wording of property qualifications, their views on the subject reflecting the source of their own wealth. Merchants, bankers, and manufacturers objected to making the ownership of a certain amount of land a qualification for officeholding. James Madison, a plantation owner himself, was forced to admit that "landed possessions were no certain evidence of real wealth. Many enjoyed them who were more in debt than they were worth."

After much debate, the convention approved a constitution without any expressed property qualifications for voting or holding office, except those that the states might impose themselves: "The Electors in each State shall have the Qualifications requisite for Electors of the most numerous Branch of the State Legislature." At the time, every state had property qualifications for voting, and women were not permitted to vote or hold office. (The New Jersey Constitution of 1776 enfranchised women as well as men who owned property, but in 1787, a new state law limited the vote to "free white male citizens.")

RESOLVING THE ECONOMIC ISSUES

The Founders were just as concerned with "who gets what, when, and how" as today's politicians are. Important economic interests were at stake in the Constitution. Historian Charles A. Beard pointed out that the delegates to the Constitutional Convention were men of wealth: planters, slaveholders, merchants, manufacturers, shippers, bankers and investors, and land speculators. Moreover, most of the delegates owned Revolutionary War bonds that were now worthless and would remain so unless the national government could obtain the tax revenues to pay them off[4] (see *A Conflicting View:* "An Economic Interpretation of the Constitution"). But it is certainly not true that the Founders acted only out of personal interest. Wealthy delegates were found on both sides of constitutional debates, arguing principles as well as economic interests.[5]

Levying Taxes   A central purpose of the Constitution was to enable the national government to levy its own **taxes**, so that it could end its dependence on state contributions and achieve financial credibility. The very first power given to Congress in Article I, Section 8, is the power to tax: "The Congress shall have Power To lay and collect Taxes, Duties, Imposts and Excises, to pay the Debts and provide for the common Defence and general Welfare."

The financial credit of the United States and the interests of Revolutionary War bondholders were guaranteed by Article VI in the Constitution, which specifically declared that the new government would be obligated to pay the debts of the old government. Indeed, the nation's first secretary of the treasury, Alexander Hamilton, made repayment of the national debt the first priority of the Washington Administration.

taxes   Compulsory payments to the government.

An Economic Interpretation of the Constitution

Charles Beard, historian and political scientist, provided the most controversial historical interpretation of the origin of American national government in his landmark book *An Economic Interpretation of the Constitution of the United States* (1913). Not all historians agree with Beard's economic interpretation, but all concede that it is a milestone in understanding the U.S. Constitution. Beard closely studied unpublished financial records of the U.S. Treasury Department and the personal letters and financial accounts of the fifty-five delegates to the Philadelphia convention. He concluded that they represented the following five economic interest groups, each of which benefited from specific provisions of the Constitution:

- *Public security interests* (persons holding U.S. bonds from the Revolutionary War: 37 of the 55 delegates). The taxing power was of great benefit to the holders of public securities, particularly when it was combined with the provision in Article VI that "all Debts contracted and Engagements entered into, before the Adoption of this Constitution, shall be as valid against the United States under this Constitution, as under the Confederation." That is, the national government would be obliged to pay off all those investors who held U.S. bonds, and the taxing power would give the national government the ability to do so on its own.
- *Merchants and manufacturers* (persons engaged in shipping and trade: 11 of the 55 delegates). The Interstate Commerce Clause, which eliminated state control over commerce, and the provision in Article I, Section 9, which prohibited the states from taxing exports, created a free-trade area, or "common market," among the thirteen states.
- *Bankers and investors* (24 of 55 delegates). Congress was given the power to make bankruptcy laws, to coin money and regulate its value, to fix standards of weights and measures, to punish counterfeiting, to establish post offices and post roads, to pass copyright and patent laws

to protect authors and inventors, and to punish piracies and felonies committed on the high seas. Each of these powers is a specific asset to bankers and investors as well as merchants, authors, inventors, and shippers.
- *Western land speculators* (persons who purchased large tracts of land west of the Appalachian Mountains: 14 of the 55 delegates). If western settlers were to be protected from the Indians, and if the British were to be persuaded to give up their forts in Ohio and open the way to American westward expansion, the national government could not rely on state militias but must have an army of its own. Western land speculators welcomed the creation of a national army that would be employed primarily as an Indian-fighting force over the next century.
- *Slave owners* (15 of the 55 delegates). Protection against domestic insurrection also appealed to the southern slaveholders' deep-seated fear of a slave revolt. The Constitution permitted Congress to outlaw the *import of slaves* after the year 1808. But most southern planters were more interested in protecting their existing property and slaves than they were in extending the slave trade, and the Constitution provided an explicit advantage to slaveholders in Article IV, Section 2 (later revoked by the Thirteenth Amendment, which abolished slavery) by specifically requiring the forced return of slaves who might escape to free states.

Beard argued that the members of the Philadelphia convention who drafted the Constitution were, with a few exceptions, immediately, directly, and personally interested in, and derived economic advantages from, the establishment of the new system. But many historians disagree with Beard's emphasis on the economic motives of the Founders. The Constitution, they point out, was adopted in a society that was fundamentally democratic, and it was adopted by people who were primarily middle-class property owners, especially farmers, rather than owners of businesses. The Constitution was not just an economic document, although economic factors were certainly important. Since most of the people were middle class and owned private property, practically all Americans were interested in the protection of property.

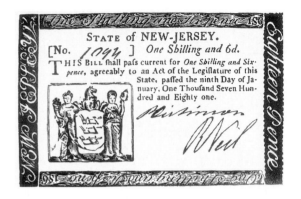

Under the Articles of Confederation, each state issued its own currency. Differences in currency regulation from state to state led to financial uncertainty and inflation. By creating a national currency and putting the national government in charge of the money supply, the Founders hoped to restore stability and control inflation.

The original Constitution placed most of the tax burden on consumers in the form of **tariffs** on goods imported into the United States. For more than a century, these tariffs provided the national government with its principal source of revenue. Tariffs were generally favored by American manufacturers, who wished to raise the price paid for foreign goods to make their home-produced goods more competitive. No taxes were permitted on *exports*, a protection for southern planters, who exported most of their tobacco and, later, cotton. Direct taxes on individuals were prohibited (Article I, Section 2) except in proportion to *population*. This provision prevented the national government from levying direct taxes in proportion to income until the Sixteenth Amendment (income tax) was ratified in 1913.

The power to tax and spend was given to Congress, not to the president or executive agencies. Instead, the Constitution was very specific: "No Money shall be drawn from the Treasury, but in Consequence of Appropriations made by Law." This is the constitutional basis of Congress's "power of the purse."

Regulating Commerce The new Constitution gave Congress the power to "regulate Commerce with foreign Nations, and among the several States" (Article I, Section 8), and it prohibited the states from imposing tariffs on goods shipped across state lines (Article I, Section 10). This power created what we call today a **common market**; it protected merchants against state-imposed tariffs and stimulated trade among the states. States were also prohibited from "impairing the Obligation of Contracts"—that is, passing any laws that would allow debtors to avoid their obligations to banks and other lenders.

Protecting Money The Constitution also ensured that the new national government would control the money supply. Congress was given the power to coin money and regulate its value. More important, the states were prohibited from issuing their own paper money, thus protecting bankers and creditors from the repayment of debts in cheap state currencies. (No one wanted to be paid for goods or labor in Rhode Island's inflated dollars.) If only the national government could issue money, the Founders hoped, inflation could be minimized.

PROTECTING NATIONAL SECURITY

At the start of the Revolutionary War, the Continental Congress had given George Washington command of a small regular army—"Continentals"—paid for by Congress and also had authorized him to take command of state militia units. During the entire war,

tariff Tax imposed on imported products (also called a custom's duty).

common market Unified trade area in which all goods and services can be sold or exchanged free from customs or tariffs.

The president rather than Congress dominates U.S. foreign policy. President Clinton tried to broker a Mideast peace agreement between Israeli Prime Minister Ehud Barak (left) and Syrian Foreign Minister Farouk al-Sharaa.

most of Washington's troops had been state militia. (The "militia" in those days was composed of every free adult male; each was expected to bring his own gun.) Washington himself had frequently decried the militia units as undisciplined, untrained, and unwilling to follow his orders. He wanted the new United States to have a *regular* army and navy, paid for by the Congress with its new taxing power, to back up the state militia units.

War and the Military Forces   Congress was authorized to "declare War," to raise and support a regular army and navy, and to make rules regulating these forces. It was also authorized to call up the militia, as it had done in the Revolution, in order to "execute the Laws of the Union, suppress Insurrections and repel Invasions." When the militia are called into national service, they come under the rule of Congress and the command of the president.

The United States relied primarily on militia—citizen-soldiers organized in state units—until World War I. The regular U.S. Army, stationed in coastal and frontier forts, directed most of its actions against Native Americans. The major actions in America's nineteenth-century wars—the War of 1812 against the British, the Mexican War of 1846–48, the Civil War in 1861–65, and the Spanish-American War in 1898—were fought largely by citizen-soldiers from these state units.

Commander-in-Chief   Following the precedent set in the Revolutionary War, the new president, who everyone expected to be George Washington, was made "Commander-in-Chief of the Army and Navy of the United States, and of the Militia of the several States, when called into the actual Service of the United States." Clearly, there is some overlap in responsibility for national defense: Congress has the power to declare war, but the president is Commander-in-Chief. During the next two centuries, the president would order U.S. forces into 200 or more military actions, but Congress would declare war only five times. Conflict between the president and Congress over war-making powers continues to this day (see "Commander-in-Chief" in Chapter 11).

Foreign Affairs   The national government also assumed full power over foreign affairs and prohibited the states from entering into any "Treaty, Alliance, or

Confederation." The Constitution gave the president, not Congress, the power to "make Treaties" and "appoint Ambassadors." However, the Constitution stipulated that the president could do these things only "by and with the Advice and Consent of the Senate," indicating an unwillingness to allow the president to act autonomously in these matters. The Senate's power to "advise and consent" to treaties and appointments, together with the congressional power over appropriations, gives the Congress important influence in foreign affairs. Nevertheless, the president remains the dominant figure in this arena.

THE STRUCTURE OF THE GOVERNMENT

The Constitution that emerged from the Philadelphia convention on September 17, 1787, founded a new government with a unique structure. That structure was designed to implement the Founders' beliefs in nationalism, limited government, republicanism, the social contract, and the protection of liberty and property. The Founders were realists; they did not have any romantic notions about the wisdom and virtue of "the people." James Madison wrote, "A dependence on the people is, no doubt, the primary control on the government; but experience has taught mankind the necessity of auxiliary precautions." The key structural arrangements in the Constitution—national supremacy, federalism, republicanism, separation of powers, checks and balances, and judicial review—all reflect the Founders' desire to create a strong national government while at the same time ensuring that it would not become a threat to liberty or property.

National Supremacy   The heart of the Constitution is the National Supremacy Clause of Article VI:

> This Constitution, and the Laws of the United States which shall be made in Pursuance thereof; and all Treaties made, or which shall be made, under the Authority of the United States, shall be the supreme Law of the Land; and the Judges in every State shall be bound thereby, any Thing in the Constitution or Laws of any State to the Contrary notwithstanding.

This sentence ensures that the Constitution itself is the supreme law of the land and that laws passed by Congress supersede state laws. This National Supremacy Clause establishes the authority of the Constitution and the U.S. government.

Federalism   The Constitution *divides power* between the nation and the states (see Chapter 4). It recognizes that both the national government and the state governments have independent legal authority over their own citizens: both can pass their own laws, levy their own taxes, and maintain their own courts. The states have an important role in the selection of national officeholders—in the apportionment of congressional seats and in the allocation of electoral votes for president. Most important, perhaps, both the Congress and three-quarters of the states must consent to changes in the Constitution itself.

Republicanism   To the Founders, a *republican* government meant the delegation of powers by the people to a small number of gifted individuals "whose wisdom may best discern the true interest of their country, and whose patriotism and love of justice, will be least likely to sacrifice it to temporary or partial considerations."[6] The Founders believed that enlightened leaders of principle and property with ability, education, and a stake in the preservation of liberty could govern the people better than the people could govern themselves. So they gave the voters only a limited voice in the selection of government leaders.

The Constitution of 1787 created *four* decision-making bodies, each with separate numbers, terms of office, and selection processes (see Table 3-2). Note that in the *original* Constitution only one of these four bodies—the House of Representatives—was to be directly elected by the people. The other three were removed from direct popular control: state legislatures selected U.S. senators; "electors" (chosen at the discretion of the state legislatures) selected the president; the president appointed Supreme Court and other federal judges.

Democracy? The Founders believed that government rests ultimately on "the consent of the governed." But their notion of republicanism envisioned decision making by *representatives* of the people, not the people themselves (see *A Conflicting View:* "Let the People Vote on National Issues" on page 76). The U.S. Constitution does not provide for *direct* voting by the people on national questions; that is, unlike many state constitutions today, it does *not* provide for national **referenda**. Moreover, as noted earlier, only the House of Representatives (sometimes referred to even today as "the people's house") was to be elected directly by voters in the states.

These republican arrangements may appear "undemocratic" from our perspective today, but in 1787 the U.S. Constitution was more democratic than any other governing system in the world. Although other nations were governed by monarchs, emperors, chieftains, and hereditary aristocracies, the Founders recognized that government depended on the *consent of the governed*. Later democratic impulses in America greatly altered the original Constitution (see "Constitutional Change" later in this chapter) and reshaped it into a much more democratic document.

referenda Proposed laws or constitutional amendments submitted to the voters for their direct approval or rejection; found in state constitutions but not in the U.S. Constitution.

Table 3-2	Decision-Making Bodies in the Constitution of 1787		
House of Representatives	**Senate**	**President**	**Supreme Court**
Members alloted to each state "according to their respective numbers," but each state guaranteed at least one member.	"Two senators from each state."	Single executive.	No size specified in the Constitution, but by recent tradition, nine.
Two-year term.	Six-year term.	Four-year term (later limited to two terms by the Twenty-second Amendment in 1951).	Life term.
Directly elected by "the People of the several States."	Selected by the state legislatures (later changed to direct election by the Seventeenth Amendment in 1913).	Selected by "Electors," appointed in each state "in such Manner as the Legislature thereof may direct" and equal to the total number of U.S. senators and House members to which the state is entitled in Congress.	Appointed by the president, "by and with the Advice and Consent of the Senate."

SEPARATION OF POWERS AND CHECKS AND BALANCES

The Founders believed that unlimited power was corrupting and that the concentration of power was dangerous. James Madison wrote, "Ambition must be made to counteract ambition." The **separation of powers** within the national government—the creation of separate legislative, executive, and judicial branches in Articles I, II, and III of the Constitution—was designed to place internal controls on governmental power. Power is not only apportioned among three branches of government, but, perhaps more important, each branch is given important **checks and balances** over the actions of the others (see Figure 3-1). According to Madison, "The constant aim is to divide and arrange the several offices in such a manner as that each may be a check on the other." No bill can become a law without the approval of both the House and the Senate. The president shares legislative power through the power to sign or to veto laws of Congress, although Congress may override a presidential veto with a two-thirds vote in each house. The president may also suggest legislation, "give to the Congress Information of the State of the Union, and recommend to their Consideration such Measures as he shall judge necessary and expedient." The president may also convene special sessions of Congress.

However, the president's power of appointment is shared by the Senate, which confirms cabinet and ambassadorial appointments. The president must also secure the advice and consent of the Senate for any treaty. The president must execute the laws, but it is Congress that provides the money to do so. The president and the rest of the executive branch may not spend money that has not been appropriated by Congress. Congress must also authorize the creation of executive departments and agencies. Finally, Congress may impeach and remove the president from office for "Treason, Bribery, or other High Crimes and Misdemeanors."

Members of the Supreme Court are appointed by the president and confirmed by the Senate. Traditionally, this court has nine members, but Congress may determine the number of justices. More important, Congress must create lower federal district courts as well as courts of appeal. Congress must also determine the number of these judgeships and determine the jurisdiction of federal courts. But the most important check of all is the Supreme Court's power of judicial review.

Judicial review, which is not specifically mentioned in the Constitution itself, is the power of the judiciary to overturn laws of Congress and the states and actions of the president that the courts believe violate the Constitution (see "Judicial Power" in Chapter 13). Judicial review, in short, ensures compliance with the Constitution.

Many Federalists, including Alexander Hamilton, believed the Constitution of 1787 clearly implied that the Supreme Court could invalidate any laws of Congress or presidential actions it believed to be unconstitutional. Hamilton wrote in 1787, "[Limited government] . . . can be preserved in no other way than through the medium of courts of justice, whose duty it is to declare all acts contrary to the manifest tenor of the Constitution void."[7] But it was not until *Marbury v. Madison* in 1803 that Chief Justice John Marshall asserted a Supreme Court ruling that the Supreme Court possessed the power of judicial review over laws of Congress. (See *People in Politics:* "John Marshall and Early Supreme Court Politics" in Chapter 13.) Today the American people express more trust and confidence in the Supreme Court than in either the President or the Congress (see Figure 3-2 on page 74).

separation of powers
Constitutional division of powers among the three branches of the national government—legislative, executive, and judicial.

checks and balances
Constitutional provisions giving each branch of the national government certain checks over the actions of other branches.

judicial review Power of the U.S. Supreme Court and federal judiciary to declare laws of Congress and the states and actions of the president unconstitutional and therefore legally invalid.

FIGURE 3-1 The Separation of Powers and Checks and Balances

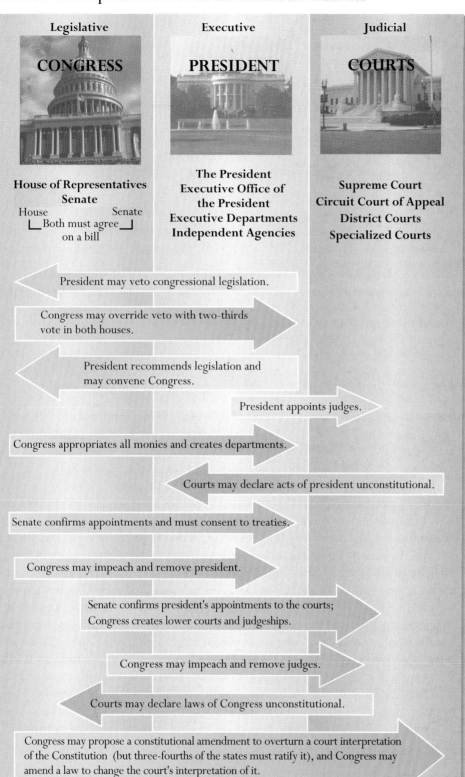

Legislative

CONGRESS

House of Representatives
Senate

House   Senate
└ Both must agree ┘
on a bill

Executive

PRESIDENT

The President
Executive Office of
the President
Executive Departments
Independent Agencies

Judicial

COURTS

Supreme Court
Circuit Court of Appeal
District Courts
Specialized Courts

President may veto congressional legislation.

Congress may override veto with two-thirds vote in both houses.

President recommends legislation and may convene Congress.

President appoints judges.

Congress appropriates all monies and creates departments.

Courts may declare acts of president unconstitutional.

Senate confirms appointments and must consent to treaties.

Congress may impeach and remove president.

Senate confirms president's appointments to the courts; Congress creates lower courts and judgeships.

Congress may impeach and remove judges.

Courts may declare laws of Congress unconstitutional.

Congress may propose a constitutional amendment to overturn a court interpretation of the Constitution (but three-fourths of the states must ratify it), and Congress may amend a law to change the court's interpretation of it.

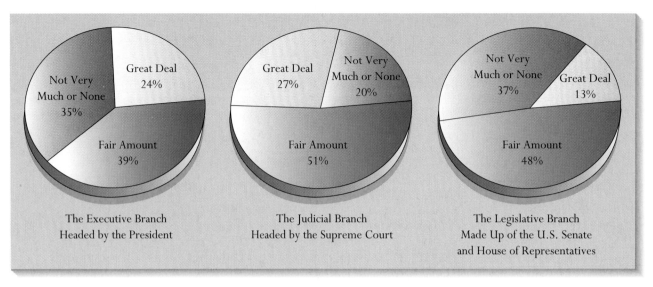

FIGURE 3-2 **Trust and Confidence in the Three Branches Of Government**

As you know, the federal government is made up of three branches: an Executive branch, headed by the President; a Judicial branch, headed by the U.S. Supreme Court; and a Legislative branch, made up of the U.S. Senate and House of Representatives. How much trust and confidence do you have at this time in [A,B,C]—a great deal, a fair amount, not very much, or none at all?

CONFLICT OVER RATIFICATION

Today the U.S. Constitution is a revered document, but in the winter of 1787–88, the Founders had real doubts about whether they could get it accepted as "the supreme Law of the Land." Indeed, the Constitution was ratified by only the narrowest of margins in the key states of Massachusetts, Virginia, and New York.

The Founders adopted a **ratification** procedure that was designed to enhance chances for acceptance of the Constitution. The ratification procedure written into the new Constitution was a complete departure from what was then supposed to be the law of the land, the Articles of Confederation, in two major ways. First, the Articles of Confederation required that amendments be approved by *all* of the states. But since Rhode Island was firmly in the hands of small farmers, the Founders knew that unanimous approval was unlikely. So they simply wrote into their new Constitution that approval required only nine of the states. Second, the Founders called for special ratifying conventions in the states rather than risk submitting the Constitution to the state legislatures. Because the Constitution placed many prohibitions on the powers of states, the Founders believed that special constitutional ratifying conventions would be more likely to approve the document than would state legislatures.

The Founders enjoyed some important tactical advantages over the opposition. First, the Constitutional Convention was held in secret; potential opponents did not know what was coming out of it. Second, the Founders called for ratifying conventions to be held as quickly as possible so that the opposition could not get itself organized. Many state conventions met during the winter months, so it was difficult for some rural opponents of the Constitution to get to their county seats in order to vote (see Figure 3-3).

The Founders also waged a very professional (for 1787–88) media campaign in support of the Constitution. James Madison, Alexander Hamilton, and John Jay issued a series of eighty-five press releases, signed simply "Publius," on behalf of the Constitution. Major newspapers ran these essays, which were later collected and published

ratification   Power of a legislature to approve or reject decisions made by other bodies. State legislators or state conventions must ratify constitutional amendments submitted by Congress. The U.S. Senate must ratify treaties made by the president.

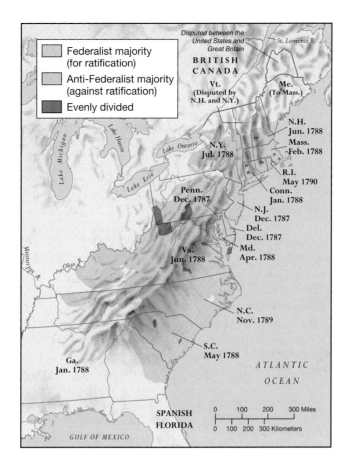

FIGURE 3-3 The Fight over Ratification

Source: Richard B. Morris, ed., *Encyclopedia of American History* (New York: Harper & Row, 1965), p. 118.

as *The Federalist Papers*. The essays provide an excellent description and explanation of the Constitution by three of its writers and even today serve as a principal reference for political scientists and judges faced with constitutional ambiguities (see *People in Politics:* "James Madison and the Control of 'Faction'" on page 80). Two of the most important *Federalist Papers* are reprinted in the Appendix to this textbook.

Nevertheless, opponents of the Constitution—the Anti-Federalists—almost succeeded in defeating the document in New York and Virginia. They charged that the new Constitution would create an "aristocratic tyranny" and pose a threat to the "spirit of republicanism." They argued that the new Senate would be an aristocratic upper house and the new president a ruling monarch. They complained that neither the Senate nor the president were directly elected by the people. They also argued that the new national government would trample state governments and deny the people of the states the opportunity to handle their own political and economic affairs. Virginia patriot Patrick Henry urged the defeat of the Constitution "to preserve the poor Commonwealth of Virginia." Finally, their most effective argument was that the new Constitution lacked a bill of rights to protect individual liberty from government abuse (see *A Conflicting View:* "Objections to the Constitution by an Anti-Federalist" on page 80).

A BILL OF RIGHTS

It may be hard to imagine today, but the original Constitution had no **Bill of Rights**. This was a particularly glaring deficiency because many of the new state constitutions proudly displayed these written guarantees of individual liberty.

Bill of Rights Written guarantees of basic individual liberties; the first ten amendments to the U.S. Constitution.

Let the People Vote on National Issues

"Direct democracy" means that the people themselves can initiate and decide policy questions by popular vote. The Founders were profoundly skeptical of this form of democracy. They had read about direct democracy in the ancient Greek city-state of Athens, and they believed the "follies" of direct democracy far outweighed any virtues it might possess. It was not until more than 100 years after the U.S. Constitution was written that widespread support developed in the American states for direct voter participation in policy making. Direct democracy developed in states and communities, and it is to be found today *only* in state and local government.

Why not extend our notion of democracy to include nationwide referenda voting on key public issues? Perhaps Congress should be authorized to place particularly controversial issues on a national ballot. Perhaps a petition signed by at least 1 million voters should also result in a question being placed on a national ballot.

Proponents of direct voting on national issues argue that national referenda would

- Enhance government responsiveness and accountability to the people.
- Stimulate national debate over policy questions.
- Increase voter interest and turnout on election day.

- Increase trust in government and diminish feelings of alienation from Washington.
- Give voters a direct role in policy making.

Opponents of direct democracy, from our nation's Founders to the present, argue that national referenda voting would

- Encourage majorities to sacrifice the rights of individuals and minorities.
- Lead to the adoption of unwise and unsound policies because voters are not sufficiently informed to cast intelligent ballots on many complex issues.
- Prevent consideration of alternative policies or modifications or amendments to the proposition set forth on the ballot. (In contrast, legislators devote a great deal of attention to writing, rewriting, and amending bills, as well as seeking out compromises among interests.)
- Enable special interests to mount expensive referendum campaigns; the outcomes of referenda would be heavily influenced by paid television advertising.

How would voters' decisions in national referenda differ from current government policies? A national poll on twenty-seven key policy issues produced the results shown here. The asterisks indicate issues in which *current public policy differs from popular preference*—almost half of the issues polled!

The Founders certainly believed in limited government and individual liberty, and they did write a few liberties into the body of the Constitution, including protection against ex post facto laws, a limited definition of treason, a guarantee of the writ of habeas corpus, and a guarantee of trial by jury (see Chapter 14).

The Federalists argued that there was really no need for a bill of rights because (1) the national government was one of **enumerated powers** only, meaning it could not exercise any power not expressly enumerated, or granted, in the Constitution; (2) the power to limit free speech or press, establish a religion, or otherwise restrain individual liberty was not among the enumerated powers; (3) therefore it was not necessary to specifically deny these powers to the new government. But the Anti-Federalists were unwilling to rest fundamental freedoms on a thin thread of

enumerated powers
Powers specifically mentioned in the Constitution as belonging to the national government.

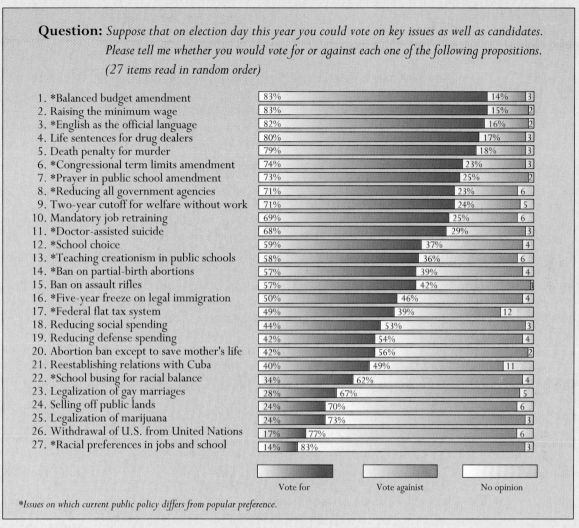

Question: *Suppose that on election day this year you could vote on key issues as well as candidates. Please tell me whether you would vote for or against each one of the following propositions. (27 items read in random order)*

	Vote for	Vote against	No opinion
1. *Balanced budget amendment	83%	14%	3
2. Raising the minimum wage	83%	15%	2
3. *English as the official language	82%	16%	2
4. Life sentences for drug dealers	80%	17%	3
5. Death penalty for murder	79%	18%	3
6. *Congressional term limits amendment	74%	23%	3
7. *Prayer in public school amendment	73%	25%	2
8. *Reducing all government agencies	71%	23%	6
9. Two-year cutoff for welfare without work	71%	24%	5
10. Mandatory job retraining	69%	25%	6
11. *Doctor-assisted suicide	68%	29%	3
12. *School choice	59%	37%	4
13. *Teaching creationism in public schools	58%	36%	6
14. *Ban on partial-birth abortions	57%	39%	4
15. Ban on assault rifles	57%	42%	1
16. *Five-year freeze on legal immigration	50%	46%	4
17. *Federal flat tax system	49%	39%	12
18. Reducing social spending	44%	53%	3
19. Reducing defense spending	42%	54%	4
20. Abortion ban except to save mother's life	42%	56%	2
21. Reestablishing relations with Cuba	40%	49%	11
22. *School busing for racial balance	34%	62%	4
23. Legalization of gay marriages	28%	67%	5
24. Selling off public lands	24%	70%	6
25. Legalization of marijuana	24%	73%	3
26. Withdrawal of U.S. from United Nations	17%	77%	6
27. *Racial preferences in jobs and school	14%	83%	3

Issues on which current public policy differs from popular preference.

Source: The Gallup Poll Monthly, May 1996.

logical inference from the notion of enumerated powers. They wanted specific written guarantees that the new national government would not interfere with the rights of individuals or the powers of the states. So Federalists at the New York, Massachusetts, and Virginia ratifying conventions promised to support the addition of a bill of rights to the Constitution in the very first Congress.

A young member of the new House of Representatives, James Madison, rose in 1789 and presented a bill of rights that he had drawn up after reviewing more than 200 recommendations sent from the states. Interestingly, the new Congress was so busy debating new tax laws that Madison had a difficult time attracting attention to his bill. Eventually, in September 1789, Congress approved a Bill of Rights as ten **amendments**, or formal changes, to the Constitution and sent them to the states.

amendment Formal change in a bill, law, or constitution.

James Madison and the Control of "Faction"

The most important contributions to American democracy by James Madison (1751–1836) were his work in helping to write the Constitution and his insightful and scholarly defense of it during the ratification struggle. Indeed, Madison is more highly regarded by political scientists and historians as a *political theorist* than as the fourth president of the United States.

Madison's family owned a large plantation, Montpelier, near present-day Orange, Virginia. Private tutors and preparatory schools provided him with a thorough background in history, science, philosophy, and law. He graduated from the College of New Jersey (now Princeton University) at eighteen and assumed a number of elected and appointed positions in Virginia's colonial government. In 1776 Madison drafted a new Virginia Constitution. While serving in Virginia's Revolutionary

assembly, he met Thomas Jefferson; the two became lifetime political allies and friends. In 1787 Madison represented Virginia at the Constitutional Convention and took a leading role in its debates over the form of a new federal government. Many of the ideas in his Virginia Plan were incorporated into the Constitution.

Madison's political insights are revealed in *The Federalist Papers*, a series of eighty-five essays published in major newspapers in 1787–88, all signed simply "Publius." Alexander Hamilton and John Jay contributed some of them, but Madison wrote the two most important essays: Number 10, which explains the nature of political conflict (faction) and how it can be "controlled"; and Number 51, which explains the system of separation of powers and checks and balances (both reprinted in the Appendix of this textbook). According to Madison, "controlling faction" was the principal task of government.

What creates faction? According to Madison, conflict is part of human nature. In all societies, we find "a zeal for different opinions concerning religion, concerning government, and many other points," as well as "an attachment to different leaders ambitiously contending for preeminence and power." Even when there are no serious differences among people, these

(Congress actually passed twelve amendments. One was never ratified; another, dealing with pay raises for Congress, was not ratified by the necessary three-quarters of the states until 1992.) The states promptly ratified the first ten amendments to the Constitution (see Table 3-3 on page 81), and these changes took effect in 1791.

The Bill of Rights was originally designed to limit the powers of the new *national* government. The Bill of Rights begins with the command "Congress shall make no law. . . ." It was not until after the Civil War that the Constitution was amended to also prohibit states from violating individual liberties. The Fourteenth Amendment, ratified in 1868, includes the command "No State shall. . . ." It prohibits the states from depriving any person of "life, liberty or property, without due process of law," or abridging "the privileges or immunities of citizens of the United States," or denying any person "equal protection of the laws." Today virtually all of the liberties guaranteed in the Constitution protect individuals not only from the national government but also from state governments.

CONSTITUTIONAL CHANGE

The purpose of a constitution is to govern government—to place limits on governmental power. Thus government itself must not be able to alter or amend a constitution easily. Yet the U.S. Constitution has changed over time, sometimes by formal

"frivolous and fanciful distinctions" will inspire "unfriendly passions" and "violent conflicts."

Clearly, Madison believed conflict could arise over just about any matter. Yet "the most common and durable source of factions, has been the various and unequal distribution of property." That is, economic conflicts between rich and poor and between people with different kinds of wealth and sources of income are the most serious conflicts confronting society.

Madison argued that factions could best be controlled in a republican government extending over a large society with a "variety of parties and interests." He defended republicanism (representative democracy) over "pure democracy," which he believed "incompatible with personal security, or the rights of property." And he argued that protection against "factious combinations" can be achieved by including a great variety of competing interests in the political system so that no one interest will be able to "outnumber and oppress the rest." Modern pluralist political theory (see Chapter 1) claims Madison as a forerunner.

Madison served in the House of Representatives from 1789 to 1797 and was largely responsible for writing the first ten amendments to the Constitution—the Bill of Rights. While in the House, Madison became concerned over the expanding power of the national government led by Hamilton and his Federalist Party. Once a proponent of a strong central government, Madison shifted to a more moderate position and split with the Federalists. Frustrated with politics, he retired to his estate in 1797 until Thomas Jefferson appointed him secretary of state in 1801. He negotiated the Louisiana Purchase and was Jefferson's handpicked successor to the presidency in 1809.

As president, Madison unfortunately allowed the nation to become embroiled in Europe's Napoleonic Wars. Conflict with the British over shipping rights and the impressment of American sailors led to a declaration of war against Great Britain in 1812. The war went badly for the United States; in 1814 Madison and the government were forced to flee Washington as the British burned the Capitol. After achieving an uneasy peace with Britain in 1815, Madison retired from politics, again following the footsteps of Thomas Jefferson by becoming president of the University of Virginia in 1826. Madison died at Montpelier on June 28, 1836.

amendment and other times by judicial interpretation, presidential and congressional action, and general custom and practice.

Amendments A constitutional amendment must first be proposed, and then it must be ratified. The Constitution allows two methods of *proposing* a constitutional amendment: (1) by passage in the House and the Senate with a two-thirds vote, or (2) by passage in a national convention called by Congress in response to petitions by two-thirds of the state legislatures. Congress then chooses the method of *ratification*, which can be either (1) by vote in the legislatures of three-fourths of the states, or (2) by vote in conventions called for that purpose in three-fourths of the states (see Figure 3-4 on page 82).

Of the four possible combinations of proposal and ratification, the method involving proposal by a two-thirds vote of Congress and ratification by three-quarters of the legislatures has been used for all the amendments except one. Only for the Twenty-first Amendment's repeal of Prohibition did Congress call for state ratifying conventions (principally because Congress feared that southern Bible Belt state legislatures would vote against repeal). The method of proposal by national convention has never been used.

In addition to the Bill of Rights, most of the constitutional amendments ratified over the nation's 200 years have expanded our notion of democracy. Today the

Objections to the Constitution by an Anti-Federalist

Virginia's George Mason was a delegate to the Constitutional Convention of 1787, but he refused to sign the final document and became a leading opponent of the new Constitution. Mason was a wealthy plantation owner and a heavy speculator in western (Ohio) lands. He was a friend of George Washington's, but he considered most other political figures of his day to be "babblers" and he generally avoided public office. However, in 1776 he authored Virginia's Declaration of Rights, which was widely copied in other state constitutions and later became the basis for the Bill of Rights. Although an ardent supporter of states' rights, he attended the Constitutional Convention of 1787 and, according to James Madison's notes on the proceedings, was an influential force in shaping the new national government. His refusal to sign the Constitution and his subsequent leadership of the opposition to its ratification made him the recognized early leader of the Anti-Federalists.

Mason's first objection to the Constitution was that it included no Bill of Rights. But he also objected to the powers given to the Senate, which was not directly elected by the people in the original document; to the federal courts; and to the president. He was wary of the Necessary and Proper Clause, which granted Congress the power to "make all laws which shall be necessary and proper" for carrying out the enumerated powers—those specifically mentioned in the Constitution. Mason correctly predicting that this clause would be used to preempt the powers of the states.

In his "objections to the Constitution" Mason wrote,

There is no declaration of rights; and the laws of the general government being paramount to the laws and constitutions of the several States, the declaration of rights in the separate States are no security.

The Senate has the power of altering all money-bills, and of originating appropriations of money, and the salaries of the officers of their own appointment in conjunction with the President of the United States; although they are not the representatives of the people, or amenable to them.

The judiciary of the United States is so constructed and extended as to absorb and destroy the judiciaries of the several States; thereby rendering law as tedious, intricate and expensive, and justice as unattainable by a great part of the community, as in England, and enabling the rich to oppress and ruin the poor.

Under their own construction of the general clause at the end of the enumerated powers, the Congress may grant monopolies in trade and commerce, constitute new crimes, inflict unusual and severe punishments, and extend their power as far as they shall think proper; so that the State Legislatures have no security for the powers now presumed to remain to them; or the people for their rights.

Note that virtually all of Mason's objections to the original Constitution had to be remedied at a later date. The Bill of Rights was added as the first ten amendments. Eventually (1913) the Seventeenth Amendment provided for the direct election of U.S. senators. And Mason correctly predicted that the federal judiciary would eventually render the law "tedious, intricate, and expensive" and that the Necessary and Proper Clause, which he refers to as "the general clause at the end of the enumerated powers," would be used to expand congressional powers at the expense of the states.

Constitution includes 27 amendments, which means that only 17 (out of more than 10,000) proposed amendments have been ratified since the passage of the Bill of Rights. It is possible to classify the amendments that have been ratified into the broad categories of constitutional processes, Prohibition, income tax, individual liberty, and voting rights (see Table 3-4 on page 83).

Amending the U.S. Constitution requires not only a two-thirds vote in both houses of Congress, reflecting *national* support, but also ratification by three-fourths

Table 3-3   The Bill of Rights

Guaranteeing Freedom of Expression

First Amendment prohibits the government from abridging freedom of speech, press, assembly, and petition.

Guaranteeing Religious Freedom

First Amendment prohibits the government from establishing a religion or interfering with the free exercise of religion.

Affirming the Right to Bear Arms and Protecting Citizens from Quartering Troops

Second Amendment guarantees the right to bear arms.

Third Amendment prohibits troops from occupying citizens' home in peacetime.

Protecting the Rights of Accused Persons

Fourth Amendment protects against unreasonable searches and seizures.

Fifth Amendment requires an indictment by a grand jury for serious crimes; prohibits the government from trying a person twice for the same crime; prohibits the government from taking life, liberty, or property without due process of law; and prohibits the government from taking private property for public use without fair compensation to the owner.

Sixth Amendment guarantees a speedy and public jury trial, the right to confront witnesses in court, and the right to legal counsel for defense.

Seventh Amendment guarantees the right to a jury trial in civil cases.

Eighth Amendment prohibits the government from setting excessive bail or fines or inflicting cruel and unusual punishment.

Protecting the Rights of People and States

Ninth Amendment protects all other unspecified rights of the people.

Tenth Amendment reserves to the states or to the people those powers neither granted to the federal government nor prohibited to the states in the Constitution.

---

of the states, reflecting widespread support within the states. The fate of the **Equal Rights Amendment**, popularly known as the ERA, illustrates the need for nationwide consensus in order to amend the Constitution. The Equal Rights Amendment is a simple statement to which the vast majority of Americans agree, according to public opinion polls: "Equality of rights under the law shall not be denied or abridged by the United States or any state on account of sex." Congress passed the ERA in 1972 with far more than the necessary two-thirds vote; both Republicans and Democrats supported the ERA, and it was endorsed by Presidents Nixon, Ford, and Carter as well as most other national political leaders and organizations. By 1978, thirty-five state legislatures had ratified the amendment—three states short of the necessary thirty-eight (three-quarters). (Five states subsequently voted to rescind, or cancel, their earlier ratification. However, because there is no language in the Constitution regarding rescission, there is some disagreement about the

Equal Rights Amendment (ERA) Proposed amendment to the Constitution guaranteeing that equal rights under the law shall not be denied or abridged on account of sex. Passed by Congress in 1972, the amendment failed to win ratification by three of the necessary three-fourths of the states.

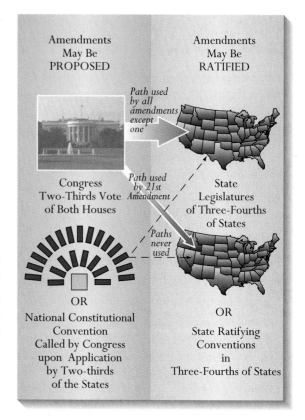

FIGURE 3-4 Constitutional Amendment Process

The Constitution set up two alternative routes for proposing amendments and two for ratifying them. One of the four possible combinations has actually been used for all except one (the Twenty-first) amendment. However, in our time there have been persistent calls for a constitutional convention to propose new amendments permitting school prayer, making abortion illegal, and requiring a balanced national budget.

Amendments
May Be
PROPOSED

Amendments
May Be
RATIFIED

Path used by all amendments except one

Congress
Two-Thirds Vote
of Both Houses

Path used by 21st Amendment

State
Legislatures
of Three-Fourths
of States

Paths never used

OR
National Constitutional
Convention
Called by Congress
upon Application
by Two-thirds
of the States

OR
State Ratifying
Conventions
in
Three-Fourths of States

constitutionality of this action.) Promising that the "ERA won't go away," proponents of the amendment have continued to press their case. But to date Congress has not acted to resubmit the ERA to the states.

Judicial Interpretations   Some of the greatest changes in the Constitution have come about not by formal amendment but by interpretations of the document by courts, Congresses, and presidents.

Through judicial review, the U.S. Supreme Court has come to play the major role in interpreting the meaning of the Constitution. This power is itself largely an interpretation of the Constitution (see "Judicial Power" in Chapter 13) because it is not specifically mentioned in the document. Over the years, the federal courts have been much more likely to strike down laws of the states than laws of Congress.

Supreme Court interpretations of the Constitution have given specific meaning to many of our most important constitutional phrases. Among the most important examples of constitutional change through judicial interpretation are the important meanings given to the Fourteenth Amendment, particularly its provisions that "No State shall . . . deprive any person of life, liberty, or property, without due process of law; nor deny to any person within its jurisdiction the equal protection of the laws":

- Deciding that "equal protection of the laws" requires an end to segregation of the races (*Brown v. Board of Education of Topeka*, 1954, and subsequent decisions).

- Deciding that "liberty" includes a woman's right to choose an abortion, and that the term *person* does not include the unborn fetus (*Roe v. Wade*, 1973, and subsequent decisions).

Table 3-4   Amendments to the Constitution since the Bill of Rights

Perfecting Constitutional Processes

Eleventh Amendment (1798) forbids federal lawsuits against a state by citizens of another state or nation.

Twelfth Amendment (1804) provides separate ballots for president and vice president in the Electoral College to prevent confusion.

Twentieth Amendment (1933) determines the dates for the beginning of the terms of Congress (January 3) and the president (January 20).

Twenty-second Amendment (1951) limits the president to two terms.

Twenty-fifth Amendment (1967) provides for presidential disability.

Twenty-seventh Amendment (1992) prevents Congress from raising its own pay in a single session.

The Experiment with Prohibition

Eighteenth Amendment (1919) prohibits the manufacture, sale, or transportation of intoxicating liquors.

Twenty-first Amendment (1933) repeals the Eighteenth Amendment.

The Income Tax

Sixteenth Amendment (1913) allows Congress to tax incomes.

Expanding Liberty

Thirteenth Amendment (1865) abolishes slavery.

Fourteenth Amendment (1868) protects life, liberty, and property and the privileges and immunities of citizenship and provides equal protection of the law.

Expanding Voting Rights

Fifteenth Amendment (1870) guarantees that the right to vote shall not be denied because of race.

Seventeenth Amendment (1913) provides for the election of senators by the people of each state.

Nineteenth Amendment (1920) guarantees that the right to vote shall not be denied because of sex.

Twenty-third Amendment (1961) gives the District of Columbia electoral votes for presidential elections.

Twenty-fourth Amendment (1964) guarantees that the right to vote shall not be denied because of failure to pay a poll tax or other tax.

Twenty-sixth Amendment (1971) guarantees that the right to vote shall not be denied to persons eighteen years of age or older.

- Deciding that "equal protection of the laws" requires that every person's vote should be weighed equally in apportionment and districting plans for the House of Representatives, state legislatures, city councils, and so on (*Baker v. Carr*, 1964, and subsequent decisions).

Presidential and Congressional Action   Congress and the president have also undertaken to interpret the Constitution. Nearly every president, for example, has argued that the phrase "executive Power" in Article II includes more than

Twenty-First Century Directions

The U.S. Constitution is the oldest written constitution in the world. It has been amended only twenty-seven times in over two hundred years, and the first ten amendments—the Bill of Rights—was part of the original ratification process. The durability of the U.S. Constitution, and the legitimacy given it by the American people, insures its continued viability in the twenty-first century.

⬇ **Formal Amendments** Despite widespread popular support for various proposals to amend the Constitution—for example, to require balanced federal budgets, to impose term limits on members of Congress, to allow prayer in public schools—no formal amendments are likely to be adopted in the foreseeable future. The constitutional amendment process requires not only widespread *popular* support both nationwide and across the states, but also the strong support of national *leadership*—in both houses of Congress and the White House. Constitutional amendments that limit the power of government are seldom popular with government officials. And the American people have developed a reverence for the Constitution that precludes tinkering with it.

⬆ **The Supreme Court and Judicial Revision** But the meaning of the Constitution will continue to evolve, primarily through judicial interpretation of the document by the U.S. Supreme Court. Indeed, it is the vagueness of

constitutional language—for example, the phrases "no establishment of religion" (First Amendment), "freedom of speech" (First Amendment), "life, liberty or property" (Fifth and Fourteenth Amendments), "due process of law" (Fifth and Fourteenth Amendments), "equal protection of the law" (Fourteenth Amendment)—that allows the Constitution to evolve over time. Later (Chapter 13) we will discuss whether the courts should shape constitutional meaning to fit their own views of the current needs of society, or whether the courts should exercise restraint and interpret the Constitution according to the original intent of the Founders.

⬅➡ **Checks and Balances, The President and Congress** The writers of the Constitution envisioned a continuing checking and balancing of power between the branches of government. Throughout most of the twentieth century the pendulum of power swung in the direction of the President and away from Congress. The American people turned for leadership to the President during periods of national crises—World War I, the Great Depression, World War II, the Cold War. But in recent years Congress has attempted to regain some of its power relative to the President. The Congress is *constitutionally* positioned as the first branch of government, but *politically*, especially in times of crises, the President prevails. This struggle for power will continue throughout the twenty-first century. In the absence of a crisis, Congress will gradually accumulate power at the expense of a weakening Presidency.

the specific powers mentioned afterward. Thomas Jefferson purchased the Louisiana Territory from France in 1803 even though there is no constitutional authorization for the president, or even the national government, to acquire new territory. Presidents from George Washington to Richard Nixon have argued that Congress cannot force the executive branch to turn over documents it does not wish to disclose (see Chapter 11).

Congress by law has tried to restrict the president's power as commander-in-chief of the armed forces by requiring the president to notify Congress when U.S.

troops are sent to "situations where imminent involvement in hostilities is clearly indicated" and limiting their stay to sixty days unless Congress authorizes an extension. This War Powers Act (1973), passed by Congress over President Richard Nixon's veto in the immediate aftermath of the Vietnam War, has been ignored by every president to date (see Chapter 11). Yet it indicates that Congress has its own ideas about interpreting the Constitution.

Custom and Practice   Finally, the Constitution changes over time as a result of generally accepted customs and practice. It is interesting to note, for example, that the Constitution never mentions political parties. (Many of the Founders disapproved of parties because they caused "faction" among the people.) But soon after Thomas Jefferson resigned as President Washington's first secretary of state (in part because he resented the influence of Secretary of the Treasury Alexander Hamilton), the Virginian attracted the support of Anti-Federalists, who believed the national government was too strong. When Washington retired from office, most Federalists supported John Adams as his successor. But many Anti-Federalists ran for posts as presidential electors, promising to be "Jefferson's men." Adams won the presidential election of 1796, but the Anti-Federalists organized themselves into a political party, the Democratic-Republicans, to oppose Adams in the election of 1800. The party secured pledges from candidates for presidential elector to cast their electoral vote for Jefferson if they won their post; then the party helped win support for its slate of electors. In this way the Electoral College was transformed from a deliberative body where leading citizens from each state came together to decide for themselves who should be president into a ceremonial body where pledged electors simply cast their presidential vote for the candidate who had carried their state in the presidential election. (For a full discussion of the current operation of the Electoral College, see *Up Close:* "Understanding the Electoral College" in Chapter 8.)

SUMMARY NOTES

- The true meaning of constitutionalism is the limitation of governmental power. Constitutions govern governments; they are designed to restrict those who exercise governmental power. Constitutions not only establish governmental bodies and prescribe the rules by which they make their decisions, but, more important, they also limit the powers of government.

- The American tradition of written constitutions extends back through the Articles of Confederation, the colonial charters, and the Mayflower Compact to the thirteenth-century English Magna Carta. The Second Continental Congress in 1776 adopted a written Declaration of Independence to justify the colonies' separation from Great Britain. All of these documents strengthened the idea of a written contract defining governmental power.

- The movement for a Constitutional Convention in 1787 was inspired by the new government's inability to levy taxes under the Articles of Confederation, its inability to fund the Revolutionary War debt, obstacles to interstate commerce, monetary problems, and civil disorders, including Shays's Rebellion.

- The nation's Founders—fifty-five delegates to the Constitutional Convention in Philadelphia in 1787—shared a broad consensus on liberty and property, the social contract, republicanism, limited government, and the need for a national government.

- The Founders compromised their differences over representation by creating two co-equal houses in the Congress: the House of Representatives, with members apportioned to the states on the basis of population and directly elected by the people for two-year terms, and the Senate, with two members allotted to each state regardless of its population and originally selected by state legislatures for six-year terms.

- The infamous slavery provisions in the Constitution—counting each slave as three-fifths of a person for purposes of taxation and representation, guaranteeing the return of escaped slaves, and postponing the end of the slave trade for twenty years—were also compromises. Voter qualifications in national elections were left to the states to determine.

- The structure of the national government reflects the Founders' beliefs in national supremacy, federalism, republicanism, separation of powers, checks and balances, and judicial review.

- The original Constitution gave the people very little influence on their government: only members of the House of Representatives were directly elected; senators were elected by state legislatures; the president was elected indirectly by "electors" chosen in each state; and members of the Supreme Court and federal judiciary were appointed for life by the president and confirmed by the Senate. Over time, the national government became more democratic through the expansion of voting rights, the direct election of senators, the emergence of political parties, and the practice of voting for presidential electors pledged to cast their vote for the candidates of one party.

- The separation of powers and checks and balances written into the Constitution was designed, in Madison's words, "to divide and arrange the several offices in such a manner as that each may be a check on the other." Judicial review was not specifically described in the original Constitution, but the Supreme Court soon asserted its power to overturn laws of Congress and the states, as well as presidential actions, that the Court determined to be in conflict with the Constitution.

- Opposition to the new Constitution was strong. Anti-Federalists argued that it created a national government that was aristocratic, undemocratic, and a threat to the rights of the states and the people. Their concerns resulted in the Bill of Rights: ten amendments added to the original Constitution, all designed to limit the power of the national government and protect the rights of individuals and states.

- Over time, constitutional changes have come about as a result of formal amendments, judicial interpretations, presidential and congressional actions, and changes in custom and practice. The most common method of constitutional amendment has been proposal by two-thirds vote of both houses of Congress followed by ratification by three-fourths of the state legislatures.

KEY TERMS

constitutionalism 56	tariff 66	checks and balances 72	enumerated powers 75
constitution 56	common market 68	judicial review 72	amendment 76
republicanism 61	referenda 68	ratification 72	Equal Rights Amendment
taxes 61	separation of powers 71	Bill of Rights 74	(ERA) 77

SELECTED READINGS

BEARD, CHARLES. *An Economic Interpretation of the Constitution.* New York: Macmillan, 1913. A classic work setting forth the argument that economic self-interest inspired the Founders in writing the Constitution.

MADISON, JAMES, ALEXANDER HAMILTON, AND JOHN JAY. *The Federalist Papers.* New York: Modern Library, 1937. These eighty-five collected essays written in 1787–88 in support

of ratification of the Constitution remain the most important commentary on that document. Numbers 10 and 51 (reprinted in the Appendix) ought to be required reading for all students of American government.

MANSBRIDGE, JANE J. *Why We Lost the ERA.* Chicago: University of Chicago Press, 1986. An account of the politics of the lost ratification battle for the Equal Rights Amendment. Public opinion polls demonstrated strong national support for the ERA, but the constitutional requirement for ratification by three-fourths of the states allowed a minority to exercise a veto.

MCDONALD, FORREST B. *Novus Ordo Seculorum*. Lawrence: University Press of Kansas, 1986. A description of the intellectual origins of the Constitution and the "new secular order" that it represented.

PELTASON, J. W. *Understanding the Constitution*. 15th ed. New York: Harcourt Brace, 2000. Of the many books that explain the Constitution, this is one of the best. It contains explanations of the Declaration of Independence, the Articles of Confederation, and the Constitution. The book is written clearly and well suited for undergraduates.

ROSSITER, CLINTON L. *1787, The Grand Convention*. New York: Macmillan, 1960. A very readable account of the people and events surrounding the Constitutional Convention in 1787, with many insights into the conflicts and compromises that took place there.

STORING, HERBERT J. *What the Anti-Federalists Were For*. Chicago: University of Chicago Press, 1981. An examination of the arguments of the Anti-Federalists in opposition to the ratification of the Constitution.

TRIBE, LAURENCE H., AND MICHAEL C. DORF. *On Reading the Constitution*. Cambridge, Mass.: Harvard University Press, 1991. An argument that the Constitution was a compromise charter that incorporated contending visions of government. Therefore, no single interpretation can explain the document; its meaning must emerge from continuous debate among citizens and leaders.

WOOD, GORDON S. *The Creation of the American Republic, 1776–1787*. New York: Norton, 1993. A study of the political conflicts in the new nation that led to the Constitutional Convention.

The Constitution of the United States

THE PREAMBLE

We the People of the United States, in Order to form a more perfect Union, establish Justice, insure domestic Tranquility, provide for the common defense, promote the general Welfare, and secure the Blessings of Liberty to ourselves and our Posterity, do ordain and establish this Constitution for the United States of America.

ARTICLE I—THE LEGISLATIVE ARTICLE

Legislative Power

Section 1   All legislative Powers herein granted shall be vested in a Congress of the United States, which shall consist of a Senate and House of Representatives.

House of Representatives: Composition; Qualifications; Apportionment; Impeachment Power

Section 2   The House of Representatives shall be composed of Members chosen every second Year by the People of the several States, and the Electors in each State shall have the Qualifications requisite for Electors of the most numerous Branch of the State Legislature.

No Person shall be a Representative who shall not have attained to the Age of twenty five Years, and been seven Years a Citizen of the United States, and who shall not, when elected, be an Inhabitant of that State in which he shall be chosen.

Representatives and direct Taxes[1] shall be apportioned among the several States which may be included within this Union, according to their respective Numbers, *which shall be determined by adding to the whole Number of free Persons, including those bound to Service for a Term of Years, and excluding Indians not taxed, three fifths of all other Persons.*[2] The actual Enumeration shall be made within three Years after the first Meeting of the Congress of the United States, and within every subsequent Term of ten Years, in such Manner as they shall by Law direct. The Number of Representatives shall not exceed one for every thirty Thousand, but each State shall have at least one Representative; and until each enumeration shall be made, the State of New Hampshire shall be entitled to chuse three, Massachusetts eight, Rhode-Island and Providence Plantations one, Connecticut five, New-York six, New Jersey four, Pennsylvania eight, Delaware one, Maryland six, Virginia ten, North Carolina five, South Carolina five, and Georgia three.

When vacancies happen in the Representation from any State, the Executive Authority thereof shall issue Writs of Election to fill such Vacancies.

The House of Representatives shall chuse their Speaker and other Officers; and shall have the sole Power of Impeachment.

Senate Composition: Qualifications, Impeachment Trials

Section 3   The Senate of the United States shall be composed of two Senators from each State, *chosen by the Legislature thereof,*[3] for six Years; and each Senator shall have one Vote.

Immediately after they shall be assembled in Consequence of the first Election, they shall be divided as equally as may be into three Classes. The Seats of the Senators of the first Class shall be vacated at the Expiration of the second Year, of the second Class at the Expiration of the fourth Year, and of the third Class at the Expiration of the sixth Year, so that one third may be chosen every second Year; *and if Vacancies happen by Resignation, or otherwise, during the Recess of the Legislature of any State, the Executive thereof may make temporary Appointments until the next Meeting of the Legislature, which shall then fill such Vacancies.*[4]

No person shall be a Senator who shall not have attained to the Age of thirty Years, and been nine Years a Citizen of the United States, and who shall not, when elected, be an inhabitant of that State for which he shall be chosen.

The Vice President of the United States shall be President of the Senate, but shall have no Vote, unless they be equally divided.

The Senate shall chuse their other Officers, and also a President pro tempore, in the Absence of the Vice President, or when he shall exercise the Office of President of the United States.

The Senate shall have the sole Power to try all Impeachments. When sitting for that Purpose, they shall be on Oath or Affirmation. When the President of the United States is tried, the Chief Justice shall preside: And no Person shall be convicted without the Concurrence of two thirds of the Members present.

Judgment in Cases of Impeachment shall not extend further than to removal from Office, and disqualification to hold and enjoy any Office of honor, Trust or Profit under the United States; but the Party convicted shall nevertheless be liable and subject to Indictment, Trial, Judgment and Punishment, according to law.

Congressional Elections: Times, Places, Manner

Section 4   The Times, Places and Manner of holding Elections for Senators and Representatives, shall be prescribed in each State by the Legislature thereof; but the Congress may at any time by Law make or alter such Regulations, except as to the Places of chusing Senators.

---

[1]Modified by the 16th Amendment
[2]Replaced by Section 2, 14th Amendment
[3]Repealed by the 17th Amendment
[4]Modified by the 17th Amendment

The Congress shall assemble at least once in every Year, *and such Meeting shall be on the first Monday in December, unless they shall by Law appoint a different Day.*[5]

Powers and Duties of the Houses

Section 5   Each House shall be the Judge of the Elections, Returns and Qualifications of its own Members, and a Majority of each shall constitute a Quorum to do Business; but a smaller Number may adjourn from day to day, and may be authorized to compel the Attendance of absent Members, in such Manner, and under the Penalties as each House may provide.

Each House may determine the Rules of its Proceedings, punish its Members for disorderly Behaviour, and, with the Concurrence of two thirds, expel a Member.

Each House shall keep a Journal of its Proceedings, and from time to time publish the same, excepting such Parts as may in their Judgment require Secrecy; and the Yeas and Nays of the Members of either House on any question shall, at the Desire of one fifth of those Present, be entered on the Journal.

Neither House, during the Session of Congress, shall, without the Consent of the other, adjourn for more than three days, nor to any other place than that in which the two Houses shall be sitting.

Rights of Members

Section 6   The Senators and Representatives shall receive a Compensation for their Services, to be ascertained by Law, and paid out of the Treasury of the United States. They shall in all Cases, except Treason, Felony and Breach of the Peace, be privileged from Arrest during their Attendance at the Session of their respective Houses, and in going to and returning from the same; and for any Speech or Debate in either House, they shall not be questioned in any other Place.

No Senator or Representative, shall, during the time for which he was elected, be appointed to any civil Office under the authority of the United States, which shall have been created, or the Emoluments whereof shall have been encreased during such time; and no Person holding any Office under the United States, shall be a Member of either House during his Continuance in Office.

Legislative Powers: Bills and Resolutions

Section 7   All Bills for raising Revenue shall originate in the House of Representatives; but the Senate may propose or concur with Amendments as on other Bills.

Every Bill which shall have passed the House of Representatives and the Senate, shall, before it becomes a Law, be presented to the President of the United States; if he approve he shall sign it, but if not he shall return it, with his Objections to that House in which it shall have originated, who shall enter the Objections at large on their Journal, and proceed to reconsider it. If after such Reconsideration two thirds of that House shall agree to pass the Bill, it shall be sent, together with the Objections, to the other House, by which it shall likewise be reconsidered, and if approved by two thirds of that House, it shall become a Law. But in all such Cases the Votes of both Houses shall be determined by Yeas and Nays, and the Names of the Persons voting for and against the Bill shall be entered on the Journal of each House respectively. If any Bill shall not be returned by the President within ten Days (Sundays excepted) after it shall have been presented to him, the Same shall be a Law, in like Manner as if he had signed it, unless the Congress by their Adjournment prevent its Return, in which Case it shall not be a Law.

Every Order, Resolution, or Vote to which the Concurrence of the Senate and House of Representatives may be necessary (except on a question

of Adjournment) shall be presented to the President of the United States; and before the Same shall take Effect, shall be approved by him, or being disapproved by him, shall be repassed by two thirds of the Senate and House of Representatives, according to the Rules and Limitations prescribed in the Case of a Bill.

Powers of Congress

Section 8   The Congress shall have Power To lay and collect Taxes, Duties, Imposts and Excises, to pay the Debts and provide for the common Defence and general Welfare of the United States; but all Duties, Imposts and Excises shall be uniform throughout the United States.

To borrow Money on the Credit of the United States;

To regulate Commerce with foreign Nations, and among the several States, and with the Indian Tribes;

To establish an uniform Rule of Naturalization, and uniform Laws on the subject of Bankruptcies throughout the United States;

To coin Money, regulate the Value thereof, and of foreign Coin, and fix the Standard of Weights and Measures;

To provide for the Punishment of counterfeiting the Securities and current Coin of the United States;

To establish Post Offices and post Roads;

To promote the Progress of Science and useful Arts, by securing for limited Times to Authors and Inventors the exclusive Right to their respective Writings and Discoveries;

To constitute Tribunals inferior to the supreme Court,

To define and punish Piracies and Felonies committed on the high Seas, and Offences against the Law of Nations;

To declare War, grant Letters of Marque and Reprisal, and make Rules concerning Captures on Land and Water;

To raise and support Armies, but no Appropriation of Money to that Use shall be for a longer Term than two Years;

To provide and maintain a Navy;

To make Rules for the Government and Regulation of the land and naval Forces;

To provide for calling for the Militia to execute the Laws of the Union, suppress Insurrections and repel Invasions;

To provide for organizing, arming, and disciplining, the Militia, and for governing such Part of them as may be employed in the Service of the United States, reserving to the States respectively, the Appointment of the Officers, and the Authority of training the Militia according to the discipline prescribed by Congress;

To exercise exclusive Legislation in all Cases whatsoever, over such District (not exceeding ten Miles square) as may, by Cession of particular States, and the Acceptance of Congress, become the Seat of the Government of the United States, and to exercise like Authority over all Places purchased by the Consent of the Legislature of the State in which the Same shall be, for the Erection of Forts, Magazines, Arsenals, dock-Yards, and other needful Buildings;—And

To make all Laws which shall be necessary and proper for carrying into Execution the foregoing Powers, and all other Powers vested by this Constitution in the Government of the United States, or in any Department or Officer thereof.

Powers Denied to Congress

Section 9   The Migration or Importation of such Persons as any of the States now existing shall think proper to admit, shall not be prohibited by the Congress prior to the Year one thousand eight hundred and eight, but a Tax or Duty may be imposed on such Importation, not exceeding ten dollars for each Person.

---

[5]Changed by the 20th Amendment

The privilege of the Writ of Habeas Corpus shall not be suspended, unless when in Cases of Rebellion or Invasion the public Safety may require it.

No Bill of Attainder or ex post facto Laws shall be passed.

No Capitation, or other direct, Tax shall be laid, unless in Proportion to the Census or Enumeration herein before directed to be taken.[6]

No Tax or Duty shall be laid on Articles exported from any State.

No Preference shall be given by any Regulation of Commerce or Revenue to the Ports of one State over those of another; nor shall Vessels bound to, or from, one State, be obliged to enter, clear, or pay Duties in another.

No Money shall be drawn from the Treasury, but in Consequence of Appropriations made by Law; and a regular Statement and Account of the Receipts and Expenditures of all public Money shall be published from time to time.

No Title of Nobility shall be granted by the United States; And no Person holding any Office of Profit or Trust under them, shall, without the Consent of Congress, accept of any present, Emolument, Office, or Title, of any kind whatever, from any King, Prince, or foreign State.

Powers Denied to the States

Section 10   No State shall enter into any Treaty, Alliance, or Confederation; grant Letters of Marque and Reprisal; coin Money; emit Bills of Credit; make any Thing but gold and silver Coin a Tender in Payment of Debts; pass any Bill of Attainder, ex post facto Law, or Law impairing the Obligation of Contracts, or grant any Title of Nobility.

No State shall, without the Consent of the Congress, lay any Imposts or Duties on Imports or Exports, except what may be absolutely necessary for executing its inspection Laws: and the net Produce of all Duties and Imposts, laid by any State on Imports or Exports, shall be for the Use of the Treasury of the United States; and all such Laws shall be subject to the Revision and Controul of the Congress.

No State shall, without the Consent of Congress, lay any Duty of Tonnage, keep Troops, or Ships of War in time of Peace, enter into any Agreement or Compact with another State, or with a foreign Power, or engage in War, unless actually invaded, or in such imminent Danger as will not admit of Delay.

Article II—The Executive Article

Nature and Scope of Presidential Power

Section 1   The executive Power shall be vested in a President of the United States of America. He shall hold his Office during the Term of four Years and, together with the Vice President, chosen for the same Term, be elected as follows:

Each State shall appoint, in such Manner as the Legislature thereof may direct, a Number of Electors, equal to the whole Number of Senators and Representatives to which the State may be entitled in the Congress: but no Senator or Representative, or Person holding an Office of Trust or Profit under the United States, shall be appointed an Elector.

The Electors shall meet in their respective States, and vote by Ballot for two Persons, of whom one at least shall not be an Inhabitant of the same State with themselves. And they shall make a List of all the Persons voted for, and of the Number of Votes for each; which List they shall sign and certify, and transmit sealed to the Seat of the Government of the United States, directed to the President of the Senate. The President of the Senate shall, in the Presence of the Senate and House of Representatives, open all the Certificates, and the Votes shall then be counted. The Person having the greatest Number of Votes shall be the President, if such Number be a Majority of the whole Number of Electors appointed; and if there be more

than one who have such Majority and have an equal Number of Votes, then the House of Representatives shall immediately chuse by Ballot one of them for President; and if no person have a Majority, then from the five highest on the List the said House shall in like Manner chuse the President. But in chusing the President, the Votes shall be taken by States, the Representation from each State having one Vote; A quorum for this Purpose shall consist of a Member or Members from two thirds of the States, and a Majority of all the States shall be necessary to a Choice. In every Case, after the Choice of the President, the person having the greatest Number of Votes of the Electors shall be the Vice President. But if there should remain two or more who have equal Vote, the Senate shall chuse from them by Ballot the Vice President.[7]

The Congress may determine the Time of chusing the Electors, and the Day on which they shall give their Votes; which Day shall be the same throughout the United States.

No Person except a natural born Citizen, or a Citizen of the United States, at the time of the Adoption of this Constitution, shall be eligible to the Office of President; neither shall any Person be eligible to that Office who shall not have attained to the Age of thirty five Years, and been fourteen Years a Resident within the United States.

In Case of the Removal of the President from Office, or of his Death, Resignation, or Inability to discharge the Powers and Duties of the said Office, the same shall devolve on the Vice President, and the Congress may by Law provide for the Case of Removal, Death, Resignation, or Inability, both of the President and Vice President, declaring what Officer shall then act as President, and such Officer shall act accordingly, until the Disability be removed, or a President shall be elected.[8]

The President shall, at stated Times, receive for his Services, a Compensation, which shall neither be encreased nor diminished during the Period of which he shall have been elected, and he shall not receive within that Period any other Emolument from the United States, or any of them.

Before he enter on the Execution of his Office, he shall take the following Oath or Affirmation:—"I do solemnly swear (or affirm) that I will faithfully execute the Office of President of the United States, and will to the best of my Ability, preserve, protect and defend the Constitution of the United States."

Powers and Duties of the President

Section 2   The President shall be the Commander in Chief of the Army and Navy of the United States, and of the Militia of the several States, when called into the actual Service of the United States, he may require the Opinion, in writing, of the principal Officer in each of the executive Departments, upon any Subject relating to the Duties of their respective Offices, and he shall have the Power to grant Reprieves and Pardons for Offences against the United States, except in Cases of Impeachment.

He shall have Power, by and with the Advice and Consent of the Senate to make Treaties, provided two thirds of the Senators present concur; and he shall nominate, and by and with the Advice and Consent of the Senate, shall appoint Ambassadors, other public Ministers and Consuls, Judges of the supreme Court, and all other Officers of the United States, whose Appointments are not herein otherwise provided for, and which shall be established by Law: but the Congress may by Law vest the Appointment of such inferior Officers, as they think proper, in the President alone, in the Courts of Law, or in the Heads of Departments.

The President shall have Power to fill up all Vacancies that may happen during the Recess of the Senate, by granting Commissions which shall expire at the End of their next Session.

Section 3   He shall from time to time give to the Congress Information of the State of the Union, and recommend to their Consideration such

---

[6]Modified by the 16th Amendment

[7]Changed by the 12th and 20th Amendments

[8]Modified by the 25th Amendment

Measures as he shall judge necessary and expedient; he may, on extraordinary Occasions, convene both Houses, or either of them, and in Case of Disagreement between them, with Respect to the Time of Adjournment, he may adjourn them to such Time as he shall think proper; he shall receive Ambassadors and other public Ministers; he shall take Care that the Laws be faithfully executed, and shall Commission all the Officers of the United States.

Section 4 The President, Vice President and all civil Officers of the United States, shall be removed from Office on Impeachment for, and Conviction of, Treason, Bribery, or other High Crimes and Misdemeanors.

ARTICLE III—THE JUDICIAL ARTICLE

Judicial Power, Courts, Judges

Section 1 The judicial Power of the United States, shall be vested in one supreme Court, and in such inferior Courts as the Congress may from time to time ordain and establish. The Judges, both the supreme and inferior Courts, shall hold their Offices during good Behaviour, and shall, at stated Times, receive for their Services, a Compensation, which shall not be diminished during their Continuance in Office.

Jurisdiction

Section 2 The judicial Power shall extend to all Cases, in Law and Equity, arising under this Constitution, the Laws of the United States, and Treaties made, or which shall be made, under their Authority;—to all Cases affecting Ambassadors, other public Ministers and Consuls;—to all Cases of admiralty and maritime Jurisdiction;—to Controversies to which the United States shall be a Party;—to Controversies between two or more States; *between a State and Citizens of another State;*[9]—between Citizens of different States;—between Citizens of the same State claiming Lands under Grants of different States, and between a State, or the Citizens thereof, and foreign States, Citizens, or Subjects.

In all Cases affecting Ambassadors, other public Ministers and Consuls, and those in which a State shall be Party, the supreme Court shall have original Jurisdiction. In all the other Cases before mentioned, the supreme Court shall have appellate Jurisdiction, both as to Law and Fact, with such Exceptions, and under such Regulations as Congress shall make.

The Trial of all Crimes, except in Cases of Impeachment, shall be by Jury; and such Trial shall be held in the State where the said Crimes shall have been committed; but when not committed within any State, the Trial shall be at such Place or Places as the Congress may by Law have directed.

Treason

Section 3 Treason against the United States, shall consist only in levying War against them, or in adhering to their Enemies, giving them Aid and Comfort. No Persons shall be convicted of Treason unless on the Testimony of two Witnesses to the same overt Act, or on Confession in open Court.

The Congress shall have Power to declare the Punishment of Treason, but no Attainder of Treason shall work Corruption of Blood, or Forfeiture except during the Life of the Person attainted.

ARTICLE IV—INTERSTATE RELATIONS

Full Faith and Credit Clause

Section 1 Full Faith and Credit shall be given in each State to the public Acts, Records, and judicial Proceedings of every other State. And the Congress may by general Laws prescribe the Manner in which such Acts, Records and Proceedings shall be proved, and the Effect thereof.

Privileges and Immunities; Interstate Extradition

Section 2 The Citizens of each State shall be entitled to all Privileges and Immunities of Citizens in the several States.

A person charged in any State with Treason, Felony or other Crime, who shall flee from Justice, and be found in another State, shall on Demand of the executive Authority of the State from which he fled, be delivered up to be removed to the State having jurisdiction of the Crime.

No person held to Service or Labour in one State, under the Laws thereof, escaping into another, shall, in Consequence of any Law or Regulation therein, be discharged from such Service or Labour, but shall be delivered up on Claim of the Party to whom such Service or Labour may be due.[10]

Admission of States

Section 3 New States may be admitted by the Congress into this Union; but no new State shall be formed or erected within the Jurisdiction of any other State; nor any State to be formed by the Junction of two or more States, or Parts of States, without the Consent of the Legislatures of the States concerned as well as of the Congress.

The Congress shall have Power to dispose of and make all needful Rules and Regulations respecting the Territory or other Property belonging to the United States; and nothing in this Constitution shall be so construed as to Prejudice any Claims of the United States, or of any particular State.

Republican Form of Government

Section 4 The United States shall guarantee to every State in this Union a Republican Form of Government, and shall protect each of them against Invasion; and on Application of the Legislature, or of the Executive (when the Legislature cannot be convened) against domestic Violence.

ARTICLE V—THE AMENDING POWER

The Congress, whenever two thirds of both Houses shall deem it necessary, shall propose Amendments to this Constitution, or, on the Application of the Legislatures of two thirds of several States, shall call a Convention for proposing Amendments, which, in either Case, shall be valid to all Intents and Purposes, as Part of this Constitution, when ratified by the Legislatures of three fourths of the several States, or by Conventions in three fourths thereof, as the one or the other Mode of Ratification may be proposed by the Congress; Provided that no Amendment which may be made prior to the Year One thousand eight hundred and eight shall in any Manner affect the first and fourth Clauses in the Ninth Section of the first Article; and that no State, without its Consent, shall be deprived of its equal Suffrage in the Senate.

ARTICLE VI—THE SUPREMACY ACT

All Debts contracted and Engagements entered into, before the Adoption of this Constitution, shall be as valid against the United States under the Constitution, as under the Confederation.

This Constitution, and the Laws of the United States which shall be made in Pursuance thereof; and all Treaties made, or which shall be made, under the Authority of the United States, shall be the supreme Law of the Land; and the Judges in every State shall be bound thereby, any Thing in the Constitution or Laws of any State to the Contrary notwithstanding.

The Senators and Representative before mentioned, and the Members of the several State Legislatures, and all executive and judicial Officers, both of the United States and of the several States, shall be bound by Oath or Affir-

---

[9]Modified by the 11th Amendment

[10]Repealed by the 13th Amendment

mation, to support this Constitution; but no religious Test shall ever be required as a Qualification to any Office or public Trust under the United States.

ARTICLE VII—RATIFICATION

The Ratification of the Conventions of nine States, shall be sufficient for the Establishment of this Constitution between the States so ratifying the Same.

Done in Convention by the Unanimous Consent of the States present the Seventeenth Day of September in the Year of our Lord one thousand seven hundred and Eighty seven and of the Independence of the United States of America the Twelfth. *In Witness whereof We have hereunto subscribed our Names.*

AMENDMENTS

[The first ten amendments were ratified on December 15, 1791, and form what is known as the "Bill of Rights."]

AMENDMENT 1—RELIGION, SPEECH, ASSEMBLY, AND POLITICS

Congress shall make no law respecting an establishment of religion, or prohibiting the free exercise thereof; or abridging the freedom of speech, or of the press; or the right of the people peaceably to assemble, and to petition the government for a redress of grievances.

AMENDMENT 2—MILITIA AND THE RIGHT TO BEAR ARMS

A well regulated Milita, being necessary to the security of a free State, the right of the people to keep and bear Arms, shall not be infringed.

AMENDMENT 3—QUARTERING OF SOLDIERS

No Soldier shall, in time of peace be quartered in any house, without the consent of the Owner, nor in time of war, but in manner to be prescribed by law.

AMENDMENT 4—SEARCHES AND SEIZURES

The right of the people to be secure in their persons, houses, papers, and effects, against unreasonable searches and seizures, shall not be violated, and no Warrants shall issue, but upon probable cause, supported by Oath or affirmation, and particularly describing the place to be searched, and the persons or things to be seized.

AMENDMENT 5—GRAND JURIES, SELF-INCRIMINATION, DOUBLE JEOPARDY, DUE PROCESS, AND EMINENT DOMAIN

No person shall be held to answer for a capital, or otherwise infamous crime, unless on a presentment or indictment of a Grand jury, except in cases arising in the land or naval forces, or in the Milita, when in actual service in time of War or public danger; nor shall any person be subject for the same offence to be twice put in jeopardy of life or limb; nor shall be compelled in any criminal case to be a witness against himself, nor be deprived of life, liberty, or property, without due process of law; nor shall private property be taken for public use, without just compensation.

AMENDMENT 6—CRIMINAL COURT PROCEDURES

In all criminal prosecutions, the accused shall enjoy the right to a speedy and public trial, by an impartial jury of the State and district wherein the crime shall have been committed, which district shall have been previously ascertained by law, and to be informed of the nature and cause of the accusation; to be confronted with the witnesses against him; to have compulsory process for obtaining Witnesses in his favor, and to have the Assistance of Counsel for his defense.

AMENDMENT 7—TRIAL BY JURY IN COMMON LAW CASES

In Suits at common law, where the value in controversy shall exceed twenty dollars, the right of trial by jury shall be preserved, and no fact tried by a jury shall be otherwise re-examined in any Court of the United States, than according to the rules of the common law.

AMENDMENT 8—BAIL, CRUEL AND UNUSUAL PUNISHMENT

Excessive bail shall not be required, nor excessive fines imposed, nor cruel and unusual punishments inflicted.

AMENDMENT 9—RIGHTS RETAINED BY THE PEOPLE

The enumeration in the Constitution, of certain rights, shall not be construed to deny or disparage others retained by the people.

AMENDMENT 10—RESERVED POWERS OF THE STATES

The powers not delegated to the United States by the Constitution, nor prohibited by it to the States, are reserved to the States respectively, or to the people.

AMENDMENT 11—SUITS AGAINST THE STATES

[Ratified February 7, 1795]

The Judicial power of the United States shall not be construed to extend to any suit in law or equity, commenced or prosecuted against one of the United States by Citizens of another State, or by Citizens or Subjects of any Foreign State.

AMENDMENT 12—ELECTION OF THE PRESIDENT

[Ratified July 27, 1804]

The Electors shall meet in their respective states, and vote by ballot for President and Vice-President, one of whom, at least, shall not be an inhabitant of the same state with themselves; they shall name in their ballots the person voted for as President, and in distinct ballots the person voted for as Vice-President, and they shall make distinct lists of all persons voted for as President, and of all persons voted for as Vice-President, and of the number of votes for each, which lists they shall sign and certify, and transmit sealed to the seat of the government of the United States, directed to the President of the Senate;—The President of the Senate shall, in presence of the Senate and House of Representatives, open all the certificates and the votes shall then be counted;—The person having the greatest number of votes for President, shall be the President, if such number be a majority of the whole number of Electors appointed; and if no person have such majority, then from the persons having the highest numbers not exceeding three on the list of those voted for as President, the House of Representatives shall choose immediately, by ballot, the President. But in choosing the President, the votes shall be taken by states, the representation from each state having one vote; a quorum for this purpose shall consist of a member or members from two-thirds of the states, and a majority of all states shall be necessary to a choice. And if the House of Representatives shall not choose a President whenever the right of choice shall devolve upon them, *before the fourth day of March next following*, then the Vice-President shall act as President, as in the case of the death or other constitutional disability of the President.[11] The person having the greatest number of votes as Vice-President, shall be the Vice-President, if such a number be a majority of the whole numbers of Electors appointed, and if no person have a majority, then from the two highest numbers on the list, the Senate shall choose the Vice-President; a quorum for the purpose shall consist of two-thirds of the whole number of Senators, and a majority of the whole number shall be necessary to a choice. But no person constitutionally ineligible to the office of President shall be eligible to that of Vice-President of the United States.

AMENDMENT 13—PROHIBITION OF SLAVERY

[Ratified December 6, 1865]

Section 1   Neither slavery nor involuntary servitude, except as a punishment for crime whereof the party shall have been duly convicted, shall exist within the United States, or any place subject to their jurisdiction.

Section 2   Congress shall have power to enforce this article by appropriate legislation.

AMENDMENT 14—CITIZENSHIP, DUE PROCESS, AND EQUAL PROTECTION OF THE LAWS

[Ratified July 9, 1868]

Section 1   All persons born or naturalized in the United States, and subject to the jurisdiction thereof, are citizens of the United States and of the State wherein they reside. No State shall make or enforce any law which shall abridge the privileges or immunities of citizens of the United States; nor shall any State deprive any person of life, liberty, or property, without due process of law; nor deny to any person within its jurisdiction the equal protection of the laws.

Section 2   Representatives shall be apportioned among the several States according to their respective numbers, counting the whole number of persons in each State, excluding Indians not taxed. But when the right to vote at any election for the choice of electors for President and Vice President of the United States, Representatives in Congress, the Executive and Judicial officers of a State, or the members of the Legislature thereof, is denied to any of the male inhabitants of such State, being twenty-one[12] years of age, and citizens of the United States, or in any way abridged, except for participation in rebellion, or other crime, the basis of representation therein shall be reduced in the proportion which the number of such male citizens shall bear to the whole number of male citizens twenty-one years of age in such State.

Section 3   No person shall be a Senator or Representative in Congress, or elector of President and Vice President, or hold any office, civil or military, under the United States, or under any State, who, having previously taken an oath, as a member of Congress, or as an officer of the United States, or as a member of any State legislature, or as an executive or judicial officer of any State, to support the Constitution of the United States, shall have engaged in insurrection or rebellion against the same, or given aid or comfort to the enemies thereof. But Congress may by a vote of two-thirds of each House, remove such disability.

Section 4   The validity of the public debt of the United States, authorized by law, including debts incurred for payment of pensions and bounties for services in suppressing insurrection or rebellion, shall not be questioned. But neither the United States nor any State shall assume or pay any debt or obligation incurred in aid of insurrection or rebellion against the United States, or any claim for the loss or emancipation of any slave; but all such debts, obligations and claims shall be held illegal and void.

Section 5   The Congress shall have power to enforce, by appropriate legislation, the provisions of this article.

AMENDMENT 15—THE RIGHT TO VOTE

[Ratified February 3, 1870]

Section 1   The right of citizens of the United States to vote shall not be denied or abridged by the United States or by any State on account of race, color, or previous condition of servitude.

Section 2   The Congress shall have power to enforce this article by appropriate legislation.

AMENDMENT 16—INCOME TAXES

[Ratified February 3, 1913]

The Congress shall have power to lay and collect taxes on incomes, from whatever source derived, without apportionment among the several States, and without regard to any census or enumeration.

AMENDMENT 17—DIRECT ELECTION OF SENATORS

[Ratified April 8, 1913]

The Senate of the United States shall be composed of two Senators from each State, elected by the people thereof, for six years; and each Senator shall have one vote. The electors in each State shall have the qualifications requisite for electors of the most numerous branch of the State legislatures.

When vacancies happen in the representation of any State in the Senate, the executive authority of such State shall issue writs of election to fill such vacancies: *Provided*, That the Legislature of any State may empower the executive thereof to make temporary appointment until the people fill the vacancies by election as the legislature may direct.

This amendment shall not be so construed as to affect the election or term of any Senator chosen before it becomes valid as part of the Constitution.

AMENDMENT 18—PROHIBITION

[Ratified January 16, 1919 Repealed December 5, 1933 by Amendment 21]

Section 1   After one year from the ratification of this article the manufacture, sale, or transportation of intoxicating liquors within, the importation thereof into, or the exportation thereof from the United States and all territory subject to the jurisdiction thereof for beverage purposes is hereby prohibited.

Section 2   The Congress and the several states shall have concurrent power to enforce this article by appropriate legislation.

Section 3   This article shall be inoperative unless it shall have been ratified as an amendment to the Constitution by the legislatures of the several states, as provided in the Constitution, within seven years from the date of the submission hereof to the States by the Congress.[13]

---

[11]Changed by the 20th Amendment
[12]Changed by the 26th Amendment

[13]Repealed by the 21st Amendment

AMENDMENT 19—FOR WOMEN'S SUFFRAGE

[Ratified August 18, 1920]

The right of the citizens of the United States to vote shall not be denied or abridged by the United States or by any State on account of sex.

Congress shall have power, by appropriate legislation, to enforce the provision of this article.

AMENDMENT 20—THE LAME DUCK AMENDMENT

[Ratified January 23, 1933]

Section 1 The terms of the President and Vice President shall end at noon on the 20th day of January, and the terms of the Senators and Representatives at noon on the 3rd day of January, of the years in which such terms would have ended if this article had not been ratified; and the terms of their successors shall then begin.

Section 2 The Congress shall assemble at least once in every year, and such meeting shall begin at noon on the 3rd day of January, unless they shall by law appoint a different day.

Section 3 If, at the time fixed for the beginning of the term of the President, the President elect shall have died, the Vice President elect shall become President. If a President shall not have been chosen before the time fixed for the beginning of his term, or if the President elect shall have failed to qualify, then the Vice President elect shall act as President until a President shall have qualified; and the Congress may by law provide for the case wherein neither a President elect nor a Vice President elect shall have qualified, declaring who shall then act as President, or the manner in which one who is to act shall be selected, and such person shall act accordingly until a President or Vice President shall have qualified.

Section 4 The Congress may by law provide for the case of the death of any of the persons from whom the House of Representatives may choose a President whenever the right of choice shall have developed upon them, and for the case of the death of any of the persons from whom the Senate may choose a Vice President whenever the right of choice shall have devolved upon them.

Section 5 Sections 1 and 2 shall take effect on the 15th day of October following the ratification of this article.

Section 6 This article shall be inoperative unless it shall have been ratified as an amendment to the Constitution by the legislatures of three-fourths of the several States within seven years from the date of its submission.

AMENDMENT 21—REPEAL OF PROHIBITION

[Ratified December 5, 1933]

Section 1 The eighteenth article of amendment to the Constitution of the United States is hereby repealed.

Section 2 The transportation or importation into any State, Territory, or Possession of the United States for delivery or use therein of intoxicating liquors, in violation of the laws thereof, is hereby prohibited.

Section 3 This article shall be inoperative unless it shall have been ratified as an amendment to the Constitution by conventions in the several States, as provided in the Constitution, within seven years from the date of the submission hereof to the States by the Congress.

AMENDMENT 22—NUMBER OF PRESIDENTIAL TERMS

[Ratified February 27, 1951]

Section 1 No person shall be elected to the office of the President more than twice, and no person who has held the office of President, or acted as Presi-

dent, for more than two years of a term to which some other person was elected President shall be elected to the Office of the President more than once. But this Article shall not apply to any person holding the office of President when this article was proposed by the Congress, and shall not prevent any person who may be holding the office of President, or acting as President, during the term within which this Article becomes operative from holding the office of President or acting as President during the remainder of such term.

Section 2 This Article shall be inoperative unless it shall have been ratified as an amendment to the Constitution by the legislatures of three-fourths of the several states within seven years from the date of its submission to the States by the Congress.

AMENDMENT 23—PRESIDENTIAL ELECTORS FOR THE DISTRICT OF COLUMBIA

[Ratified March 29, 1961]

Section 1 The District constituting the seat of Government of the United States shall appoint in such manner as the Congress may direct:

A number of electors of President and Vice President equal to the whole number of Senators and Representatives in Congress to which the District would be entitled if it were a State, but in no event more than the least populous State; they shall be in addition to those appointed by the States, but they shall be considered, for the purposes of the election of President and Vice President, to be electors appointed by a State; and they shall meet in the District and perform such duties as provided by the twelfth article of amendment.

Section 2 The Congress shall have power to enforce this article by appropriate legislation.

AMENDMENT 24—THE ANTI-POLL TAX AMENDMENT

[Ratified January 23, 1964]

Section 1 The right of citizens of the United States to vote in any primary or other election for President or Vice President, for electors for President or Vice President, or for Senator or Representative in Congress, shall not be denied or abridged by the United States or any State by reason of failure to pay any poll tax or other tax.

Section 2 The Congress shall have power to enforce this article by appropriate legislation.

AMENDMENT 25—PRESIDENTIAL DISABILITY, VICE PRESIDENTIAL VACANCIES

[Ratified February 10, 1967]

Section 1 In case of the removal of the President from office or his death or resignation, the Vice President shall become President.

Section 2 Whenever there is a vacancy in the office of the Vice President, the President shall nominate a Vice President who shall take the office upon confirmation by a majority vote of both houses of Congress.

Section 3 Whenever the President transmits to the President pro tempore of the Senate and the Speaker of the House of Representatives his written declaration that he is unable to discharge the powers and duties of his office, and until he transmits to them a written declaration to the contrary, such powers and duties shall be discharged by the Vice President as Acting President.

Section 4 Whenever the Vice-President and a majority of either the principal officers of the executive departments, or of such other body as Congress may by law provide, transmit to the President pro tempore of the Senate and the Speaker of the House of Representatives their written declaration that the President is unable to discharge the powers and duties of his office, the Vice President shall immediately assume the powers and duties of the office as Acting President.

Thereafter, when the President transmits to the President pro tempore of the Senate and the Speaker of the House of Representatives his written declaration that no inability exists, he shall resume the powers and duties of his office unless the Vice President and a majority of either the principal officers of the executive departments, or of such other body as Congress may by law provide, transmit within four days to the President pro tempore of the Senate and the Speaker of the House of Representatives their written declaration that the President is unable to discharge the powers and duties of his office. Thereupon Congress shall decide the issue, assembling within 48 hours for that purpose if not in session. If the Congress, within 21 days after receipt of the latter written declaration, or, if Congress is not in session, within 21 days after Congress is required to assemble, determines by two-thirds vote of both houses that the President is unable to discharge the powers and duties of his office, the Vice President shall continue to discharge the same as Acting President; otherwise, the President shall resume the powers and duties of his office.

AMENDMENT 26—EIGHTEEN-YEAR-OLD VOTE

[Ratified July 1, 1971]

Section 1   The right of citizens of the United States, who are eighteen years of age, or older, to vote shall not be denied or abridged by the United States or by any State on account of age.

Section 2   The Congress shall have power to enforce this article by appropriate legislation.

AMENDMENT 27—CONGRESSIONAL SALARIES

[Ratified May 7, 1992]

No law, varying the compensation for the services of the Senators and Representatives, shall take effect, until an election of Representative shall be intervened.

CHAPTER
4

Federalism
Dividing Governmental Power

Indestructible Union,
Indestructible States

Why Federalism? The Argument
for a "Compound Republic"

The Original Design
of Federalism

The Evolution of American
Federalism

Federalism Revived?

Money and Power Flow
to Washington

Coercive Federalism:
Preemptions and Mandates

A Devolution Revolution?

ASK YOURSELF
ABOUT POLITICS

1 Which level of govern-
ment deals best with
the problems it faces?
Federal ● State ●
Local ●

2 In which level of government do you have the
most confidence?
Federal ● State ●
Local

3 Should the national
government be able to
prosecute a high school
student for bringing a
gun to school?
Yes ● No ●

4 Should welfare benefits
be the same in all
states?
Yes ● No ●

5 Should each state determine its own minimum
age for drinking alcohol?
Yes ● No ●

6 Should each state determine its own maximum
highway speed limit?
Yes ● No ●

7 When the federal
government requires
states to provide safe
drinking water, clean air,
or access for the handi-
capped, should it
provide funds to carry
out these mandates?
Yes ● No ●

**What should be the relationship
between the national government
and the states? Questions like
these lie at the heart of the issue
of who gets what, when, and how.
They affect employment, transportation, health, education, the
very air we breathe. And when
there has been disagreement, the
nation has been plunged into
conflict at best and the bloodiest
war in its history at worst.**

INDESTRUCTIBLE UNION, INDESTRUCTIBLE STATES

In December 1860 South Carolina seceded from the Union and in April 1861 authorized its state militia to expel U.S. troops from Fort Sumter in Charleston harbor. Although there is no provision in the Constitution for states leaving the Union, eleven southern states—South Carolina, Mississippi, Florida, Alabama, Georgia, Louisiana, Texas, Virginia, Arkansas, Tennessee, and North Carolina, in that order—argued that the Union was a voluntary association and they were entitled to withdraw.[1] President Abraham Lincoln declared these states to be in armed rebellion and sent federal troops to crush the "rebels." The result was the nation's bloodiest war: more than 250,000 battle deaths and another 250,000 deaths from disease and privation, out of a total population of less than 30 million.

Following the Civil War, Chief Justice Salmon P. Chase confirmed what had been decided on the battlefield: "The Constitution, in all its provisions, looks to an indestructible union, composed of indestructible states."[2]

Federalism divides power between two separate authorities—the nation and the states—each of which enforces its own laws directly on its citizens. Both the nation and the states pass laws, impose taxes, spend money, and maintain their own courts. Neither the nation nor the states can dissolve the Union or amend the Constitution without the consent of the other. The Constitution itself is the only legal source of authority for both the states and the nation; the states do not get

federalism A constitutional arrangement whereby power is divided between national and subnational governments, each of which enforces its own laws directly on its citizens and neither of which can alter the arrangement without the consent of the other.

unitary system Constitutional arrangement whereby authority rests with the national government; subnational governments have only those powers given to them by the national government.

confederation Constitutional arrangement whereby the national government is created by and relies on subnational governments for its authority.

home rule Power of local government to pass laws affecting local affairs, so long as those laws do not conflict with state or federal laws.

intergovernmental relations Network of political, financial, and administrative relationships between units of the federal government and those of state and local governments.

their power from the national government, and the national government does not get its power from the states. Both national and state governments derive their power directly from the people.

American federalism differs from a **unitary system** of government, in which formal authority rests with the national government, and whatever powers are exercised by states, provinces, or subdivisions are given to those governments by the national government. Most of the world's governments—including France and Britain—are unitary. Federalism also differs from a **confederation** of states, in which the national government relies on the states for its authority, not the people (see Figure 4-1). Under the Articles of Confederation of 1781, the United States was a confederation. The national government could not even levy taxes; it had to ask the states for revenue. Like the United States, a number of other countries were confederations before establishing federal systems, and today new types of confederations with limited functions are being formed (see *Compared to What?* "Governmental Unions around the World" on page 92).

People in the United States often think of the *federal government* when the word *government* comes up. In fact, today there are more than 87,000 American governments. These state and local governments are as important in American life as the federal government, for they provide such essential day-to-day services as schools, water, and police and fire departments (see Table 4-1). However, the U.S. Constitution, the supreme law of the land, recognizes the existence of only the national government and the states. Local governments have no guarantees of power—or even existence—under the U.S. Constitution. Whatever powers they have are given to them by the state government. States can create or abolish local governments, grant or withhold their powers, or change their boundaries without their consent. Some local governments have powers guaranteed in *state* constitutions, and some are even given **home rule**—the power to pass laws affecting local affairs, so long as those laws do not conflict with state or federal laws. About 60,000 of these 87,000 governments have the power to levy taxes to support activities authorized by state law.

In short, the American federal system is large and complex, with three levels of government—national, state, and local—sharing power. Indeed, the numbers and complexity of governments in the United States make **intergovernmental relations**—all of the interactions among these governments and their officials—a major concern of political scientists and policy makers.

Table 4-1	How Many American Governments?
U.S. government	1
States	50
Counties	3,043
Municipalities	19,372
Townships	16,629
Special districts	34,683
School districts	13,726
All governments	**87,504**

Source: Statistical Abstract of the United States, 1999, p. 309.

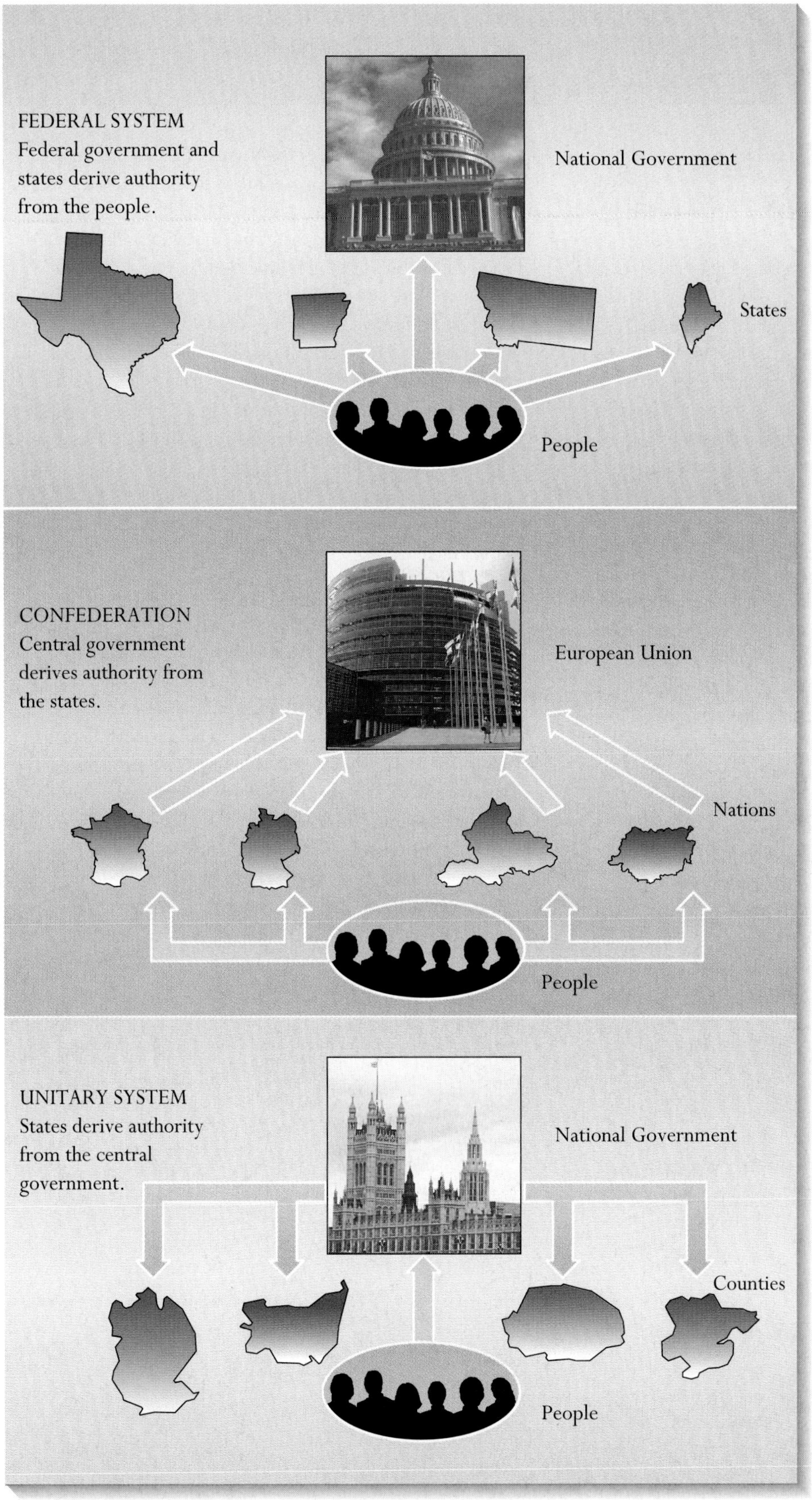

FEDERAL SYSTEM
Federal government and states derive authority from the people.
National Government
States
People
CONFEDERATION
Central government derives authority from the states.
European Union
Nations
People
UNITARY SYSTEM
States derive authority from the central government.
National Government
Counties
People

FIGURE 4-1 The Federal, Confederation, and Unitary Systems of Government

Governmental Unions around the World

Confederations have played important historical roles as societies moved toward nationhood. The case of the United States, in which the Articles of Confederation preceded the creation of a truly national government, is not unique. For example, the eighteenth-century German confederation predated the modern German nation, and the Helvetic confederation was transformed into the modern federal system of Switzerland.

The European Union   Today the most important political confederation is the European Union. The EU includes fifteen member nations—Austria, Belgium, Denmark, Finland, France, Germany, Greece, Ireland, Italy, Luxembourg, Netherlands, Portugal, Spain, Sweden, and the United Kingdom—and embraces well over 300 million people. The EU is a union with very specific functions granted by its members. It has a European Parliament; a Council of Ministers of member nations: a European Commission that serves as a bureaucracy to administer policy decisions, with a president rotating among the nations; and a European Court of Justice to adjudicate disputes among members.

The Commonwealth of Independent States
Currently, republics of the former Union of Soviet Socialist Republics—Armenia, Azerbaijan, Byelorussia, Estonia, Georgia, Kazakhstan, Kyrgyzstan, Latvia, Lithuania,

Moldavia, Russia, Tajikistan, Turkmenistan, Ukraine, and Uzbekistan—are struggling to find an acceptable form of union. The central government of the USSR ceased to exist after December 31, 1991. The president of the new Russian Federated Republic, Boris Yeltsin, opened negotiations with other republics to create a Commonwealth of Independent States along lines that would resemble a confederacy. The Russian Federated Republic is itself a formal federation, and some of its states have demanded independence from Moscow. Rebellion in Chechnya was countered by a bloody military campaign in which Russian troops inflicted heavy damages on the capital city, Grozny. Russia's new president, Vladimir Putin, has pledged to oppose with force any further movement toward independence.

Federal Systems   The formal constitutions of many governments describe a federal form of government. These include Argentina, Australia, Brazil, Canada, the Federal Republic of Germany, India, Malaysia, Mexico, Nigeria, Pakistan, Switzerland, the United Arab Emirates, the United States, and Venezuela. Yugoslavia was a federal system prior to its civil war and disintegration into ethnic enclaves of Serbia, Croatia, Macedonia, Montenegro, and war-torn Bosnia and Kosovo. Czechoslovakia was also a federal system with two republics prior to its peaceful division into two nations: Slovakia and the Czech Republic. However, despite a federal constitution, many of these governments are highly centralized, with the national government exercising a dominant role in the economic, social, and political life of the nation.

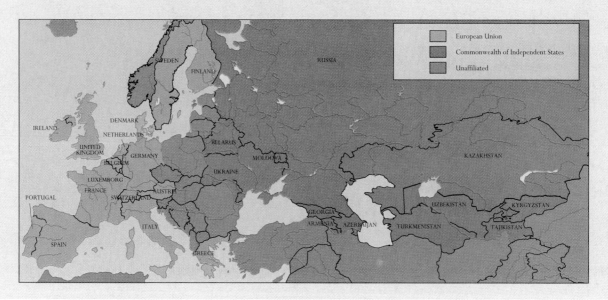

WHY FEDERALISM? THE ARGUMENT FOR A "COMPOUND REPUBLIC"

The nation's Founders believed that "republican principles" would help make government responsible to the people, but they also argued that "auxiliary precautions" were necessary to protect the liberties of minorities and individuals. They believed that majority rule in a democratic government made it particularly important to devise ways to protect minorities and individuals from "unjust" and "interested" *majorities*. They believed that federalism would better protect liberty, disperse power, and manage "faction" (conflict).

Protecting Liberty Constitutional guarantees of individual liberty do not enforce themselves. The Founders argued that to guarantee liberty, government should be structured to encourage "opposite and rival" centers of power *within* and *among* governments. So they settled on both *federalism*—dividing powers between the national and state governments—and *separation of powers*—the dispersal of power among branches within the national government.

> In the compound republic of America, the power surrendered by the people is first divided between two distinct governments, and then the portion allotted to each is subdivided among distinct and separate departments. Hence a double security arises to the rights of the people. The different governments will control each other, at the same time that each will be controlled by itself.[3]

Thus the Founders deliberately tried to create *competition* within and among governmental units as a means of protecting liberty. Rather than rely on the "better motives" of leaders, the Founders sought to construct a system in which governments and government officials would be constrained by competition with other governments and other government officials: "Ambition must be made to counteract ambition."[4]

Dispersing Power Federalism distributes power widely among different sets of leaders, national as well as state and local officeholders. The Founders believed that multiple leadership groups offered more protection against tyranny than a single set of all-powerful leaders. State and local government offices also provide a political base for the opposition party when it has lost a national election. In this way, state and local governments contribute to party competition in the United States by helping to tide over the losing party after electoral defeat at the national level so that it can remain strong enough to challenge incumbents at the next election. And finally, state and local governments often provide a training ground for national political leaders. National leaders can be drawn from a pool of leaders experienced in state and local government.

Increasing Participation Federalism allows more people to participate in the political system. With more than 87,000 governments in the United States—state, county, municipality, township, special district, and school district—nearly a million people hold some kind of public office.

Improving Efficiency Federalism also makes government more manageable and efficient. Imagine the bureaucracy, red tape, and confusion if every governmental activity—police, schools, roads, fire fighting, garbage collection, sewage disposal, and

Which Government Does the Best Job?

Americans generally favor governments closer to home. Most surveys show that Americans have greater confidence in their state and local governments than in the federal government. But Americans are divided over whether they want the federal government or state and local governments to run programs in many *specific* policy areas.

CONFIDENCE
How much confidence do you have in these institutions?

THE FEDERAL GOVERNMENT
A great deal — 4%
Quite a lot — 11%
Some — 47%
Very little — 37%

YOUR STATE GOVERNMENT
A great deal — 6%
Quite a lot — 17%
Some — 53%
Very little — 23%

YOUR LOCAL GOVERNMENT
A great deal — 11%
Quite a lot — 20%
Some — 46%
Very little — 21%

POWER
Where should power be concentrated?

State government — 64%
Federal government — 26%

BEST JOB
Which level of government does the best job of dealing with the problems it faces?

Federal — 14%
State — 34%
Local — 41%

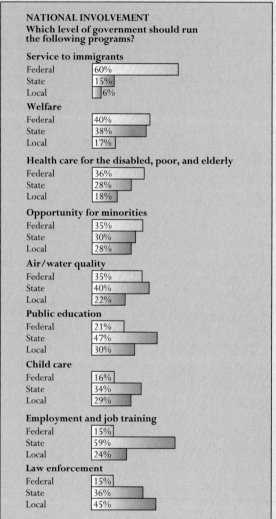

NATIONAL INVOLVEMENT
Which level of government should run the following programs?

Service to immigrants
Federal — 60%
State — 15%
Local — 6%

Welfare
Federal — 40%
State — 38%
Local — 17%

Health care for the disabled, poor, and elderly
Federal — 36%
State — 28%
Local — 18%

Opportunity for minorities
Federal — 35%
State — 30%
Local — 28%

Air/water quality
Federal — 35%
State — 40%
Local — 22%

Public education
Federal — 21%
State — 47%
Local — 30%

Child care
Federal — 16%
State — 34%
Local — 29%

Employment and job training
Federal — 15%
State — 59%
Local — 24%

Law enforcement
Federal — 15%
State — 36%
Local — 45%

Note: All figures are percentages of the U.S. public in national opinion surveys. Responses of "No opinion" and "Don't know" are not shown.

Source: General responses on confidence, power, and the running of specific programs from *Hart and Teeter for the Council for Excellence in Government, State Legislatures* (July/August 1995); responses on best job from Gallup/CNN/USA Today Poll reported in *The Polling Report* (February 10, 1997).

so forth—in every local community in the nation were controlled by a centralized administration in Washington. Government can become arbitrary when a bureaucracy far from the scene directs local officials. Thus decentralization often softens the rigidity of law. (See *What Do You Think?* "Which Government Does the Best Job?")

Ensuring Policy Responsiveness   Federalism encourages policy responsiveness. The existence of multiple governments offering different packages of benefits and costs allows a better match between citizen preferences and public policy. Americans are very mobile. People and businesses can "vote with their feet" by relocating to those states and communities that most closely conform to their own policy preferences. This mobility not only facilitates a better match between citizen preferences and public policy but also encourages competition between states and communities to offer improved services at lower costs.[5]

Encouraging Policy Innovation   The Founders hoped that federalism would encourage policy experimentation and innovation. Today federalism may seem like a "conservative" idea, but it was once the instrument of liberal reformers. Federal programs as diverse as the income tax, unemployment compensation, Social Security, wage and hour legislation, bank deposit insurance, and food stamps were all state programs before becoming national undertakings. Today much of the current "liberal" policy agenda—mandatory health insurance for workers, child-care programs, notification of plant closings, government support of industrial research and development—has been embraced by various states. The phrase *laboratories of democracies* is generally attributed to the great progressive jurist Supreme Court Justice Louis D. Brandeis, who used it in defense of state experimentation with new solutions to social and economic problems.[6]

Managing Conflict   Federalism allows different peoples to come together in a nation without engendering irresolvable conflict. Conflicts between geographically separate groups in America are resolved by allowing each to pursue its own policies within its separate state or community instead of battling over a single national policy to be applied uniformly throughout the land.

Some Important Reservations   Despite the strengths of federalism, it has its problems. First of all, federalism can obstruct action on national issues. Although decentralization may reduce conflict at the national level, it may do so at the price of "sweeping under the rug" very serious national injustices (see *A Conflicting View:* "The Dark Side of Federalism" on page 97). Federalism also permits local leaders and citizens to frustrate national policy, to sacrifice national interest to local interests. Decentralized government provides an opportunity for local NIMBYs (people who subscribe to the motto "*Not In My Back Yard*") to obstruct airports, highways, waste disposal plants, public housing, drug rehabilitation centers, and many other projects that would be in the national interest.

Finally, federalism permits the benefits and costs of government to be spread unevenly across the nation. For example, some states spend more than twice as much on the education of each child in the public schools as other states do. Taxes in some states are more than twice as high per capita as they are in other states. Welfare benefits in some states are more than twice as high as in other states. Competition among states may keep welfare benefits low in states that want to discourage poor people from moving there. Thus federalism obstructs uniformity in policy.

THE ORIGINAL DESIGN OF FEDERALISM

delegated, or **enumerated, powers**   Powers specifically mentioned in the Constitution as belonging to the national government.

Necessary and Proper Clause   Clause in Article I, Section 8, of the U.S. Constitution granting Congress the power to enact all laws that are "necessary and proper" for carrying out those responsibilities specifically delegated to it. Also referred to as the Implied Powers Clause.

implied powers   Powers not mentioned specifically in the Constitution as belonging to Congress but inferred as necessary and proper for carrying out the enumerated powers.

National Supremacy Clause   Clause in Article VI of the U.S. Constitution declaring the constitution and laws of the national government "the supreme law of the law" superior to the constitutions and laws of the states.

concurrent powers   Powers exercised by both the national government and state governments in the American federal system.

reserved powers   Powers not granted to the national government or specifically denied to the states in the Constitution that are recognized by the Tenth Amendment as belonging to the state governments. This guarantee, known as the Reserved Powers Clause, embodies the principle of American federalism.

The U.S. Constitution *originally* defined American federalism in terms of (1) the powers expressly delegated to the national government plus the powers implied by those that are specifically granted, (2) the concurrent powers exercised by both states and the national government, (3) the powers reserved to the states, (4) the powers denied by the Constitution to both the national government and the states, and (5) the constitutional provisions giving the states a role in the composition of the national government (see Figure 4-2 on page 98).

Delegated Powers   The U.S. Constitution lists seventeen specific grants of power to Congress, in Article I, Section 8. These are usually referred to as the **delegated**, or **enumerated, powers**. They include authority over war and foreign affairs, authority over the economy ("interstate commerce"), control over the money supply, and the power to tax and spend "to pay the debts and provide for the common defence and general welfare." After these specific grants of power comes the power "to make all laws which shall be necessary and proper for carrying into execution the foregoing powers, and all other powers vested by this Constitution in the government of the United States or in any department or officer thereof." This statement is generally known as the **Necessary and Proper Clause**, and it is the principal source of the national government's **implied powers**—powers not specifically listed in the Constitution but inferred from those that are.

National Supremacy   The delegated and implied powers, when coupled with the assertion of "national supremacy" (in Article VI), ensure a powerful national government. The **National Supremacy Clause** is very specific in asserting the supremacy of federal laws over state and local laws:

> This Constitution, and the laws of the United States which shall be made in pursuance thereof; and all treaties made, or which shall be made, under the authority of the United States, shall be the supreme law of the land; and the Judges in every state shall be bound thereby, any thing in the constitution or laws of any state to the contrary notwithstanding.

Concurrent and Reserved Powers   Despite broad grants of power to the national government, the states retain considerable governing power. **Concurrent powers** are those recognized in the Constitution as belonging to *both* the national and state governments, including the power to tax and spend, make and enforce laws, and establish courts of justice. The Tenth Amendment reassured the states that "the powers not delegated to the United States . . . are reserved to the States respectively, or to the people." Through these **reserved powers**, the states generally retain control over property and contract law; criminal law; marriage and divorce; and the provision of education, highways, and social welfare activities. (But for a discussion of increasing federal involvement in crime fighting, traditionally a "reserved" power of the states, see *A Conflicting View:* "Don't Make Everything A Federal Crime!" on page 100) The states control the organization and powers of their own local governments. Finally, the states, like the federal government, retain the power to tax and spend for the general welfare.

The Dark Side of Federalism

Segregationists once regularly used the argument of "states' rights" to deny equal protection of the law to African Americans. Indeed, *states' rights* become a code word for opposition to federal civil rights laws. In 1963 Governor George Wallace invoked the states' rights argument when he stood in the doorway at the University of Alabama to prevent the execution of a federal court order that the university admit two African American students and integrate. U.S. assistant attorney general Nicholas Katzenbach and federal marshals were on hand to enforce the order, and Wallace only temporarily delayed them. Shortly after his dramatic stand in front of the television cameras, he retreated to his office. Later in his career, Wallace sought African American votes, declaring, "I was wrong. Those days are over."

Federalism in America remains tainted by its historical association with slavery, segregation, and discrimination. In the Virginia and Kentucky Resolutions of 1798, Thomas Jefferson and James Madison asserted the doctrine of "nullification," claiming that states could nullify unconstitutional laws of Congress. Although the original intent of this doctrine was to counter congressional attacks on a free press under the Alien and Sedition Acts of 1798, it was later revived to defend slavery. John C. Calhoun of South Carolina argued forcefully in the years before the Civil War that slavery was an issue for the states to decide and the Constitution gave Congress no power to interfere with slavery in the southern states or in the new western territories.

In the years immediately following the Civil War, the issues of slavery, racial inequality, and African American voting rights were *nationalized*. Nationalizing these issues meant removing them from the jurisdiction of the states and placing them in the hands of the national government. The Thirteenth, Fourteenth, and Fifteenth Amendments to the Constitution were enforced by federal troops in the southern states during the post–Civil War Reconstruction era. But after the Compromise of 1876 led to the withdrawal of federal troops from the southern states, legal and social segregation of African Americans became a "way of life" in the region. Segregation was *denationalized*, which reduced national conflict over race but exacted a high price from the nation's African American population. Segregationists asserted the states' rights argument so often in defense of racial discrimination that it became a code phrase for racism. Not until the 1950s and 1960s were questions of segregation and equality again made into national issues. The civil rights movement asserted the supremacy of national law and in 1954 won a landmark decision in the case of *Brown v. Board of Education of Topeka*, when the U.S. Supreme Court ruled that segregation enforced by state (or local) officials violated the Fourteenth Amendment's guarantee that no state could deny any person the equal protection of the law. Later the *national* Civil Rights Act of 1964 outlawed discrimination in private employment and businesses serving the public.

Only now that national constitutional and legal guarantees of equal protection of the law are in place is it possible to reassess the true worth of federalism. Having established that federalism will not mean racial inequality, Americans are now free to explore the values of decentralized government.

In an attempt to block the admission of two African American students to the University of Alabama in 1963, Governor George Wallace barred the door with his body in the face of U.S. federal marshals. The tactic did not succeed, and the two students were admitted.

FIGURE 4-2 Original Constitutional Distribution of Powers

Under the Constitution of 1787, certain powers were delegated to the national government, other powers were shared by the national and state governments, and still other powers were reserved for state governments alone. Similarly, certain powers were denied by the Constitution to the national government, other powers were denied to both the national and state governments, and still other powers were denied only to state governments. Later amendments especially protected individual liberties.

POWERS GRANTED BY THE CONSTITUTION

NATIONAL GOVERNMENT
Delegated Powers

Military Affairs and Defense
- Provide for the common defense (I-8).
- Declare war (I-8).
- Raise and support armies(I-8).
- Provide and maintain a navy (I-8).
- Define and punish piracies (I-8).
- Define and punish offenses against the law of nations (I-8).
- Provide for calling forth the militia to execute laws, suppress insurrections, and repel invasions (I-8).
- Provide for organizing, arming, and disciplining the militia (I-8).
- Declare the punishment of treason (III-3).

Economic Affairs
- Regulate commerce with foreign nations, among the several states, and with Indian tribes (I-8).
- Establish uniform laws on bankruptcy (I-8).
- Coin money and regulate its value (I-8).
- Fix standards of weights and measures (I-8).
- Provide for patents and copyrights (I-8).
- Establish post offices and post roads (I-8).

Governmental Organization
- Constitute tribunals inferior to the Supreme Court (I-8, III-1).
- Exercise exclusive legislative power over the seat of government and over certain military installations (I-8).
- Admit new states (IV-3).
- Dispose of and regulate territory or property of the United States (IV-3).

"Implied" Powers
- Make laws necessary and proper for carrying the expressed powers into execution (I-8).

NATIONAL AND STATE GOVERNMENTS
Concurrent Powers

- Levy taxes (I-8).
- Borrow money (I-8).
- Contract and pay debts (I-8).
- Charter banks and corporations (I-8).
- Make and enforce laws (I-8).
- Establish courts (I-8).
- Provide for the general welfare (I-8).

STATE GOVERNMENTS
Reserved to the States

- Regulate intrastate commerce.
- Conduct elections.
- Provide for public health, safety, and morals.
- Establish local government.
- Maintain the militia (National Guard).
- Ratify amendments to the federal Constitution (V).
- Determine voter qualifications (I-2).

"Reserved" Powers

- Powers not delegated to national government nor denied to the States by the Constitution (X).

POWERS DENIED BY THE CONSTITUTION

NATIONAL GOVERNMENT

- Give preference to the ports of any state (I-9).
- Impose a tax or duty on articles exported from any state (I-9).
- Directly tax except by apportionment among the states on a population basis (I-9), now superseded as to income tax (Amendment XVI).
- Draw money from the Treasury except by appropriation (I-9).

NATIONAL AND STATE GOVERNMENTS

- Grant titles of nobility (I-9).
- Limit the suspension of habeas corpus (I-9).
- Issue bills of attainder (I-10).
- Make ex post facto laws (I-10).
- Establish a religion or prohibit the free exercise of religion (Amendment I).
- Abridge freedom of speech, press, assembly, or right of petition (Amendment I).
- Deny the right to bear arms protected (Amendment II).
- Restrict quartering of soldiers in private homes (Amendment III).
- Conduct unreasonable searches or seizures. (Amendment IV).
- Deny guarantees of fair trials (Amendment V, Amendment VI, and Amendment VII).
- Impose excessive bail or unusual punishments (Amendment VII).
- Take life, liberty, or property without due process (Amendment V).
- Permit slavery (Amendment XIII).
- Deny life, liberty, or property without due process of law (Amendment XIV).
- Deny voting because of race, color, previous servitude (Amendment XV), sex (Amendment XIX), or age if 18 or over (Amendment XXVI).
- Deny voting because of nonpayment of any tax (Amendment XXIV).

STATE GOVERNMENTS

Economic Affairs
- Use legal tender other than gold or silver coin (I-10).
- Issue separate state coinage (I-10).
- Impair the obligation of contracts (I-10).
- Emit bills of credit (I-10).
- Levy import or export duties, except reasonable inspection fees, without the consent of Congress (I-10).
- Abridge the privileges and immunities of national citizenship (Amendment XIV)
- Make any law that violates federal law (Amendment VI).
- Pay for rebellion against the United States or for emancipated slaves (Amendment XIV)

Foreign Affairs
- Enter into treaties, alliances, or confederations (I-10).
- Make compact with a foreign state, except by congressional consent (I-10).

Military Affairs
- Issue letters of marque and reprisal (I-10).
- Maintain standing military forces in peace without congressional consent (I-10).
- Engage in war, without congressional consent, except in imminent danger or when invaded (I-10).

Powers Denied to the States The Constitution denies the states some powers in order to safeguard national unity. States are specifically denied the power to coin money, enter into treaties with foreign nations, interfere with the "obligation of contracts," levy taxes on imports or exports, or engage in war.

Powers Denied to the Nation and the States The Constitution denies some powers to both national and state government—namely, the powers to abridge individual rights. The Bill of Rights originally applied only to the national government, but the Fourteenth Amendment, passed by Congress in 1866 and ratified by 1868, provided that the states must also adhere to fundamental guarantees of individual liberty.

State Role in National Government The states are basic units in the organizational scheme of the national government. The House of Representatives apportions members to the states by population, and state legislatures draw up the districts that elect representatives. Every state has at least one member in the House of Representatives, regardless of its population. Each state elects two U.S. senators, regardless of its population. The president is chosen by the electoral votes of the states, with each state having as many electoral votes as it has senators and representatives combined. Finally, three-fourths of the states must ratify amendments to the U.S. Constitution.

"Look, the American people don't want to be bossed around by federal bureaucrats. They want to be bossed around by state bureaucrats."

Source: ©1999 Robert Mankoff from cartoonbank.com. All Rights Reserved.

THE EVOLUTION OF AMERICAN FEDERALISM

American federalism has evolved over 200 years from a state-centered division of power to a national-centered system of government. Although the original constitutional wordings have remained in place, power has flowed toward the national government since the earliest days of the Republic. American federalism has been forged in the fires of political conflicts between states and nation, conflicts that have usually been resolved in favor of the national government. (See *Up Close:* "Historical Markers in the Development of American Federalism" on page 102). Generalizing about the evolution of American federalism is no easy task. But let us try to describe broadly some major periods in the evolution of federalism, then look at five specific historical developments that had far-reaching impact on that evolution.

State-Centered Federalism, 1787–1868 From the adoption of the Constitution of 1787 to the end of the Civil War, the states were the most important units in the American federal system. It is true that during this period the legal foundation for the expansion of national power was being laid, but people looked to the states for resolving most policy questions and providing most public services. Even the issue of slavery was decided by state governments. The supremacy of the national government was frequently questioned, first by the Anti-Federalists (including Thomas Jefferson) and later by John C. Calhoun and other defenders of slavery.

Dual Federalism, 1868–1913 The supremacy of the national government was decided on the battlefields of the Civil War. Yet for nearly a half-century after that conflict, the national government narrowly interpreted its delegated powers, and the states continued to decide most domestic policy issues. The resulting pattern has been described as **dual federalism**. Under this pattern, the states and the nation divided most governmental functions. The national government concentrated its attention on the "delegated" powers—national defense, foreign affairs, tariffs, interstate commerce,

dual federalism Early concept of federalism in which national and state powers were clearly distinguished and functionally separate.

Don't Make Everything a Federal Crime!

Political office holders in Washington are continually pressured to make "a federal crime" out of virtually every offense in society. Neither Democrats nor Republicans, liberals nor conservatives, are willing to risk their political futures by telling their constituents that crime fighting is a state and local responsibility. So Washington lawmakers continue to add common offenses to the ever lengthening list of federal crimes.

Traditionally, federal crimes were limited to a relatively narrow range of offenses, including counterfeiting and currency violations; tax evasion, including alcohol, tobacco, and firearm taxes; fraud and embezzlement; robbery of federally insured banks; murder or assault of a federal official; and violations of customs and immigrations laws. While some federal criminal laws overlapped state laws, most criminal activity—murder, rape, robbery, assault, burglary, theft, auto theft, gambling, sex offenses, and so on—fell under state jurisdiction. Indeed, the *police power* was believed to be one of the "reserved" powers states referred to in the Tenth Amendment.

But over time Congress has made more and more offenses *federal* crimes. Today federal crimes range from drive-by shootings and violence against women to obstructing sidewalks in front of abortion clinics. Any violent offense motivated by racial, religious, or ethnic animosity is a "hate crime" subject to federal investigation and prosecution. "Racketeering" and "conspiracy" (organizing and communicating with others about the intent to commit a crime) is a federal crime. The greatest impact of federal involvement in law enforcement is found in drug-related crime. Drug offenders may be tried in either federal or state courts or both. Federal drug laws, including those prohibiting possession, carry heavier penalties than those of most states.

The effect of federalizing crime is to subject citizens to the possibility of being tried twice for the same crime—in federal court and in state court for an offense that violates both federal and state criminal codes. The U.S. Supreme Court has held that such multiple prosecution does *not* violate the Double Jeopardy Clause of the Fifth Amendment, "nor shall any person be subject for the same offense to be twice put in jeopardy of life or limb." *Heath vs. Alabama*, 474 U.S. 82 (1985). In the well-publicized Rodney King case, a California state jury acquitted police officers of beating King, but a federal court jury later convicted them of violating King's civil rights.

Another effect of federalizing crime is to further fragment an already fragmented law-enforcement

---

the coinage of money, standard weights and measures, post office and post roads, and the admission of new states. State governments decided the important domestic policy issues—education, welfare, health, and criminal justice. The separation of policy responsibilities was once compared to a layer cake, with local governments at the base, state governments in the middle, and the national government at the top.[7]

Cooperative Federalism, 1913–1964   The distinction between national and state responsibilities gradually eroded in the first half of the twentieth century. American federalism was transformed by the Industrial Revolution and the development of a national economy; by the federal income tax in 1913, which shifted financial resources to the national government; and by the challenges of two world wars and the Great Depression. In response to the Great Depression of the 1930s, state governors welcomed massive federal public works projects under President Franklin D. Roosevelt's New Deal program. In addition, the federal government intervened directly in economic affairs, labor relations, business practices, and agriculture. Through its grants of money, the national government cooperated with the states in public assistance, employment services, child welfare, public housing, urban renewal, highway building, and vocational education.

structure in United States. The federal government's principal investigative agencies are the Federal Bureau of Investigation (FBI) and the Drug Enforcement Administration (DEA), both units of the Department of Justice; the Bureau of Alcohol, Tobacco, and Firearms (ATF), and the Internal Revenue Service (IRS) in the Treasury Department; and the Customs Bureau and Immigration and Naturalization Service (INS) in the State Department. Efforts to combine these law-enforcement agencies have consistently foundered in bureaucratic battles. It is not uncommon at a major crime scene to see FBI, DEA, and ATF agents mingling with officers from state-level agencies, County Sheriff's departments, and local police forces.

Yet despite growing federalization of crime, state and local governments in America continue to bear the major burden of law-enforcement (see Table). Over 10 million people are arrested and charged with offenses from misdemeanors to felonies in the United States today. But only about 50,000 people are prosecuted for crime by federal authorities in federal courts.

Criminal Justice Activity by Level of Government

	Federal	State and Local
Full-time Personnel (in thousands)		
Law Enforcement	74	922
Prisons		
Number of facilities	125	1,375
Prisoners		
Number (in thousands) sentenced	81.9	1,162.4
to more than one year (excludes local		
jails and juvenile detention centers)		

Source: Statistical Abstract of the United States, 1999, pp. 226, 231.

This new pattern of federal-state relations was labeled **cooperative federalism**. Both the nation and the states exercised responsibilities for welfare, health, highways, education, and criminal justice. This merging of policy responsibilities was compared to a marble cake: "As the colors are mixed in a marble cake, so functions are mixed in the American federal system."[8] Yet even in this period of shared national-state responsibility, the national government emphasized cooperation in achieving common national and state goals. Congress generally acknowledged that it had no direct constitutional authority to regulate public health, safety, or welfare. Instead, it relied primarily on its powers to tax and spend for the general welfare, providing financial assistance to state and local governments to achieve shared goals. Congress did not usually legislate directly on local matters.

Centralized Federalism, 1964–1980   Over the years, it became increasingly difficult to maintain the fiction that the national government was merely assisting the states to perform their domestic responsibilities. By the time President Lyndon B. Johnson launched the Great Society program in 1964, the federal government clearly had its own *national* goals. Virtually all problems confronting American society—from solid-waste disposal and water and air pollution to consumer safety,

cooperative federalism
Model of federalism in which national, state, and local governments work together exercising common policy responsibilities.

Historical Markers in the Development of American Federalism

Among the most important events in the development of American federalism: (1) the Supreme Court's decision in *McCulloch v. Maryland* in 1819 giving a broad interpretation of the Necessary and Proper Clause; (2) the victory of the national government in the Civil War 1861–1865; (3) the establishment of national system of civil rights based on the Fourteenth Amendment culminating in the Supreme Court's desegregation decision in *Brown vs. Board of Education*; (4) the expansion of the national government's power under the Interstate Commerce Clause during the Great Depression of the 1930s; and (5) the growth of federal revenues after the passage of the Sixteenth (income tax) Amendment in 1913.

McCulloch v. Maryland and the Necessary and Proper Clause

Political conflict over the scope of national power is as old as the nation itself. In 1790 Secretary of the Treasury Alexander Hamilton proposed the establishment of a national bank. Congress acted on Hamilton's suggestion in 1791, establishing a national bank to serve as a depository for federal money and to aid the federal government in borrowing funds. Jeffersonians believed the national bank was a dangerous centralization of government. They objected that the power to establish the bank was nowhere to be found in the enumerated powers of Congress.

Hamilton replied that Congress could derive the power to establish a bank from grants of authority in the Constitution relating to money, in combination with the clause authorizing Congress "to make all laws which shall be necessary and proper for carrying into execution the foregoing powers."

The question finally reached the Supreme Court in 1819, when the State of Maryland levied a tax on the national bank and the bank refused to pay it. In the case of *McCulloch v. Maryland*, Chief Justice Marshall accepted the broader Hamiltonian version of the Necessary and Proper Clause: "Let the end be legitimate, let it be within the scope of the Constitution, and all means which are appropriate, which are plainly adopted to that end, which are not prohibited but consistent with the letter and the spirit of the Constitution, are constitutional."*

The *McCulloch* case firmly established the principle that the Necessary and Proper Clause gives Congress the right to choose its means in carrying out the enumerated powers of the national government. Because of this broad interpretation of the Necessary and Proper Clause, today Congress can devise programs, create agencies, and establish national laws on the basis of long chains of reasoning from the most meager phrases of the constitutional text.

Secession and Civil War

The Civil War was the greatest crisis of the American federal system. Did a state have the right to oppose national law to the point of secession that is, withdrawing from the federal Union? The question of secession was decided on Civil War battlefields between 1861 and 1865. Yet the states' rights doctrine and political disputes over the character of American federalism did not disappear with General Robert E. Lee's surrender at Appomattox. In addition to establishing that states cannot secede from the federal union, the Civil War led to three constitutional amendments clearly aimed at limiting state power in the interests of individual freedom. The Thirteenth Amendment eliminated slavery in the states; the Fifteenth Amendment prevented states from denying the vote on the basis of race, color, or previous enslavement; and the Fourteenth Amendment declared,

> No State shall make or enforce any law which shall abridge the privileges or immunities of citizens of the United States; nor shall any state deprive any person of life, liberty, or property, without due process of law; nor deny to any person within its jurisdiction the equal protection of the laws.

During the post–Civil War Reconstruction era (1866–77), Congress passed several laws designed to enforce these amendments—laws guaranteeing the right to vote, providing remedies for the denial of rights by any person acting under "the color of law" (any public official), and prohibiting discrimination in public accommodation.† But after 1877, Congress gave up its efforts to reconstruct southern society, and the Supreme Court also failed to uphold these Reconstruction laws.

National Guarantees of Civil Rights However, in the twentieth century, the Supreme Court began to build a national system of civil rights based on the Fourteenth Amendment. First, the Court held that the Fourteenth Amendment prevented states from interfering with free speech, free press, or religious practices. But it was not until 1954, in the desegregation decision in *Brown v. Board of Education of Topeka*, that the Court begin to call for the full assertion of national authority on behalf of civil rights.[‡] When it decided that the Fourteenth Amendment prohibited the states from segregating the races in public schools, the Court was asserting national authority over longstanding practices in many of the states.

But in the years following *Brown*, some state officials tried to prevent the enforcement of a national law. Governor Orval Faubus called out the Arkansas National Guard to prevent a federal court from desegregating Little Rock Central High School in 1957. President Dwight D. Eisenhower responded by ordering the Arkansas National Guard removed and sent units of the U.S. Army to enforce national authority. This presidential action reinforced the principle of national supremacy in the American political system.

The Expansion of Interstate Commerce The growth of national power under the Interstate Commerce Clause of the Constitution is another important development in the evolution of American federalism. For many years, the U.S. Supreme Court narrowly defined *interstate commerce* to mean only the movement of goods and services across state lines. Until the late 1930s, it insisted that agriculture, mining, manufacturing, and labor relations were outside the reach of the delegated powers of the national government. However, when confronted with the Great Depression of the 1930s and Franklin Roosevelt's threat to add enough members to the Supreme Court to win favorable rulings, the Court yielded. It redefined *interstate commerce* to include any activity that "substantially affects" the national economy.[§] Indeed, the Court frequently approved of congressional restrictions on economic activities that had only very indirect effects on interstate commerce.[||]

The Income Tax and Federal Grants In the famous Northwest Ordinance of 1787, which provided for the governing of the territories west of the Appalachian Mountains, Congress made grants of land for the establishment of public schools. Then in the Morrill Land Grant Act of 1862, Congress provided grants of land to the states to promote higher education, especially agricultural and mechanical studies. Federal support for "A and M" or "land grant" universities continues today.

With the money provided to Washington by the passage of the Sixteenth (income tax) Amendment in 1913, Congress embarked on cash grants to the states. Among the earliest cash grant programs were the Federal Highway Act of 1916 and the Smith-Hughes Act of 1917 (vocational education). With federal money came federal direction. For example, states that wanted federal money for highways after 1916 had to accept uniform standards of construction and even a uniform road-numbering system (U.S. 1, U.S. 30, and so on). Shortly after these programs began, the U.S. Supreme Court considered the claim that these federal grants were unconstitutional intrusions into areas "reserved" for the states. But the Court upheld grants as a legitimate exercise of Congress's power to tax and spend for the general welfare.[¶]

In a long bloody war to establish national supremacy, the North's ultimate victory served to prove once and for all that the federal union cannot be dissolved.

McCulloch v. Maryland, 4 Wheaten 316 (1819).

[†]Civil Rights Acts of 1866, 1872, and 1875.

[‡]*Brown v. Board of Education of Topeka, Kansas*, 347 U.S. 483 (1954).

[§]*National Labor Relations Board v. Jones & Laughlin Steel Corporation* 301 U.S. 1 (1937).

[||]*Wickard v. Filburn* 317 U.S. 128 (1938).

[¶]*Massachusetts v. Mellon, Framingham v. Mellon* 262 U.S. 447 (1923).

home insulation, noise abatement, and even "highway beautification"—were declared to be national problems. Congress legislated directly on any matter it chose, without regard to its *enumerated powers* and without pretending to render only financial assistance. The Supreme Court no longer concerned itself with the reserved powers of the states, and the Tenth Amendment lost most of its meaning. The pattern of national-state relations became **centralized federalism**. As for the cake analogies, one commentator observed, "The frosting had moved to the top, something like a pineapple upside-down cake."[9]

New Federalism, 1980–1985 **New federalism** was a phrase frequently applied to efforts to reverse the flow of power to Washington and to return responsibilities to states and communities. (The phrase originated in the administration of Richard M. Nixon, 1969–74, who used it to describe general revenue sharing—making federal grants to state and local governments with few strings attached.) New Federalism was popular early in the administration of President Ronald Reagan, who tried to reduce federal involvement in domestic programs and encourage states and cities to undertake greater policy responsibilities themselves. The result was that state and local governments were forced to rely more on their own sources of revenue and less on federal money. Still, centralizing tendencies in the American federal system continued. While the general public usually gave better marks to state and local governments than to the federal government, paradoxically that same public also favored greater federal involvement in policy areas traditionally thought to be state or local responsibilities (see *What Do You Think?* "Which Government Does the Best Job?" on page 94).

Representational Federalism, 1985–1995 Despite centralizing tendencies, it was still widely assumed prior to 1985 that the Congress could not directly legislate how state and local governments should go about performing their traditional functions. However, in its 1985 *Garcia v. San Antonio Metropolitan Transit Authority* decision, the U.S. Supreme Court appeared to remove all barriers to direct congressional legislation in matters traditionally reserved to the states. The case arose after Congress directly ordered state and local governments to pay minimum wages to their employees. The Court dismissed arguments that the nature of American federalism and the

centralized federalism
Model of federalism in which the national government assumes primary responsibility for determining national goals in all major policy areas and directs state and local government activity through conditions attached to money grants.

new federalism Attempts to return power and responsibility to the states and reduce the role of the national government in domestic affairs.

During the Great Depression of the 1930s, the massive public works projects sponsored by the federal government under President Franklin Roosevelt's New Deal reflected the emergence of cooperative federalism. Programs of the Work Progress Administration, like the one shown here, were responsible for the construction of buildings, bridges, highways, and airports throughout the country.

Medicare for the elderly was added to Social Security in 1965 as part of President Lyndon B. Johnson's Great Society program. Increasingly, health care has come to be viewed as a federal government responsibility. Today, both Democrats and Republicans support Medicare and promise to add prescription drugs to its benefits.

Reserved Powers Clause of the Tenth Amendment prevented Congress from directly legislating in state affairs. It said that the only protection for state powers was to be found in the states' role in electing U.S. senators, members of the U.S. House of Representatives, and the president. The court's ruling asserts a concept known as **representational federalism**: Federalism is defined by the role of the states in electing members of Congress and the president, not by any constitutional division of powers. The United States is said to retain a federal system because its national officials are selected from subunits of government—the president through the allocation of Electoral College votes to the states and the Congress through the allocation of two Senate seats per state and the apportionment of representatives based on state population. Whatever protection exists for state power and independence must be found in the national political process, in the influence of state and district voters on their senators and representatives. In a strongly worded dissenting opinion in *Garcia*, Justice Lewis Powell argued that if federalism is to be retained, the Constitution—not Congress—should divide powers. "The states' role in our system of government is a matter of constitutional law, not legislative grace. . . . [This decision] today rejects almost 200 years of the understanding of the constitutional status of federalism."[10]

FEDERALISM REVIVED?

In recent years federalism has experienced a modest revival. The U.S. Supreme Court today appears to be somewhat more respectful of the powers of states and somewhat less willing to see these powers trampled upon by the national government.[11]

In 1995 the U.S. Supreme Court issued its first opinion in more than sixty years that recognized a limit on Congress' power over interstate commerce and reaffirmed the Founders' notion of a national government with only the powers enumerated in the Constitution.[12] The Court found that the federal Gun Free School Zones Act was unconstitutional because it exceeded Congress's powers under the Interstate Commerce Clause. (See *Up Close:* "Can the Federal Government Outlaw Guns in Schools?" on page 107.) Chief Justice William H. Rehnquist, writing for the majority in a 5 to 4 decision in *U.S. vs. Lopez*, even cited James Madison with approval:

representational federalism
Assertion that no constitutional division of powers exists between the nation and the states but the states retain their constitutional role merely by selecting the president and members of Congress.

Former presidential press secretary, James Brady, was permanently disabled in the assassination attempt on President Reagan in 1981. Brady and his wife led the effort to pass the Brady Act, which, among other things, ordered state and local officials to conduct background checks on gun purchasers. The Supreme Court held that portion of the Act to be an unconstitutional violation of the principle of federalism.

"The powers delegated by the proposed Constitution to the federal government are few and defined. Those which are to remain in the state governments are numerous and indefinite" (*Federalist*, Number 45).

In another victory for federalism, the U.S. Supreme Court ruled in 1996 in *Seminole Tribe vs. Florida* that the Eleventh Amendment shields states from lawsuits by private parties that seek to force states to comply with federal laws enacted under the commerce power.[13] And in 1999 in *Alden vs. Maine*, the Supreme Court held that states were also shielded in their own courts from lawsuits in which private parties seek to enforce federal mandates. In an opinion that surveyed the history of American federalism, Justice Kennedy wrote: "Congress has vast power but not all power. . . . When Congress legislates in matters affecting the states it may not treat these sovereign entities as mere prefectures or corporations."[14]

In defense of federalism, the Supreme Court invalidated a provision of a very popular law of Congress—the Brady Handgun Violence Protection Act. The Court decided in 1997 that the law's command to local law enforcement officers to conduct background checks on gun purchasers violated "the very principle of separate state sovereignty." The Court affirmed that the federal government "may neither issue directives requiring the states to address particular problems, nor command the states' officers, or those of their political subdivisions, to administer or enforce the federal regulatory program." *Printz v. U.S.*, 521 U.S. 890 (1997).[15] And the Court held that in the Violence Against Women Act, Congress also invaded the reserved police power of the states.[16]

The Supreme Court's apparent revival of federalism has been greeted with cautious optimism. However, all of the recent Supreme Court rulings reaffirming federalism have come in narrow 5 to 4 decisions. The closeness of these votes, together with these decisions' contrast to more than a half-century of case law in support of national power, provide no guarantee that in the future the Supreme Court will continue to move in the direction of strengthening federalism.

Can the Federal Government Outlaw Guns in Schools?

Are there any limits at all to Congress's enumerated powers? Are there any areas of power truly *reserved* for the states only?

When a student, Alfonso Lopez, was apprehended at his Texas high school carrying a .38 caliber handgun, federal agents charged him with violating the federal Gun-Free School Zones Act of 1990. He was convicted and sentenced to six months in prison. His attorney appealed on the ground that it was beyond the constitutionally delegated powers of Congress to police local school zones; the Fifth Circuit Court agreed, and the case was appealed by the U.S. government to the Supreme Court in 1995.

After reviewing virtually all of the key Commerce Clause cases in its history, the Court determined that an activity must *substantially affect* interstate commerce in order to be regulated by Congress. "The Court has never declared that Congress may use a relatively trivial impact on commerce as an excuse for broad general resolution of state and private activities." The U.S. government argued that the Gun-Free School Zones Act was a constitutional exercise of its interstate commerce power:

> [P]ossession of a firearm in a school zone may result in violent crime and that violent crime can be

expected to affect the functioning of the national economy in two ways. First, the costs of violent crime are substantial, and, through the mechanism of insurance, those costs are spread throughout the population. Second, violent crime reduces the willingness of individuals to travel to areas within the country that are perceived to be unsafe.

The Court rejected these arguments, holding that such tenuous reasoning would remove virtually all limits to federal power. "If we were to accept the Government's arguments, we are hard-pressed to posit any activity by an individual that Congress is without power to regulate." Moreover, "To uphold the Government's contentions here, we would have to pile inference upon inference in a manner that would bid fair to convert congressional authority under the Commerce Clause to a general police power of the sort retained by the states."

Voting with the majority were Justices Rehnquist (appointed to the Court by President Richard Nixon in 1971 and made Chief Justice by Reagan in 1986), Anthony M. Kennedy (Reagan, 1988), Sandra Day O'Connor (Reagan, 1981), Antonin Scalia (Reagan, 1986), and Clarence Thomas (Bush, 1991). Justice Stephen G. Breyer (Clinton, 1994) wrote a dissenting opinion agreeing with the government's argument; he was joined by Justices John Paul Stevens (Ford, 1975), David Souter (Bush, 1990), and Ruth Bader Ginsburg (Clinton, 1993).

Source: *U.S. v. Lopez*, 514 U.S. 549 (1995).

MONEY AND POWER FLOW TO WASHINGTON

Over the years, power in the federal system has flowed to Washington because tax money has flowed to Washington. With its financial resources, the federal government has been able to offer assistance to state and local governments and thereby involve itself in just about every governmental function performed by these governments. Today the federal government is no longer one of *enumerated* or *delegated* powers. No activities are really *reserved* to the states. Through its power to tax and spend for the *general welfare*, the national government is now deeply involved in welfare, education, transportation, police protection, housing, hospitals, urban development, and other activities that were once the exclusive domain of state and local government (see *Up Close*: "How Congress Set a National Drinking Age" on page 109).

Today grant-in-aid programs are the single most important source of federal influence over state and local activity. A **grant-in-aid** is defined as "payment of funds by one level of government (national or state) to be expended by another level (state or local) for a specified purpose, usually on a matching-funds basis (the federal government puts up only as much as the state or locality) and in accordance with prescribed standards of requirements."[17] No state or local government is *required* to accept grants-in-aid. Participation in grant-in-aid programs is voluntary. So in theory, if conditions attached to the grant money are too oppressive, state and local governments can simply decline to participate and pass up these funds.

About one-quarter of all state and local government revenues currently come from federal grants. Federal grants are available in nearly every major category of state and local government activity. Over 500 separate grant programs are administered by various federal agencies. So numerous and diverse are these grants that state and local officials often lack information about their availability, purpose, and requirements. "Grantmanship"—knowing where and how to obtain federal grants—is highly valued in state and local government. Federal grants can be obtained to preserve historic buildings, develop minority-owned businesses, aid foreign refugees, drain abandoned mines, control riots, and subsidize school milk programs, and so on. However, welfare (including cash benefits and food stamps), health (including Medicaid for the poor), and highways account for more than three-fourths of federal aid money (see Figure 4-3).

Thus many of the special projects and ongoing programs carried out today by state and local governments are funded by grants from the federal government. These funds have generally been dispersed as either categorical grants or block grants.

- *Categorical Grant:* A grant for a specific, narrow project. The project must be approved by a federal administrative agency. About 90 percent of federal aid money is distributed in the form of categorical grants. Categorical grants can be distributed on a project basis or a formula basis. Grants made on a project basis are distributed by federal administrative agencies to state or local governments that compete for project funds in their applications. Federal agencies have a great deal of discretion in selecting specific projects for support, and they can exercise direct control over the projects. Most categorical grants are distributed to state

grants-in-aid Payments of funds from the national government to state or local governments or from a state government to local governments for specific purposes.

FIGURE 4-3 **Purposes of Federal Grants to State and Local Governments**

Over one-fifth of all state and local government revenues are derived from federal grants. Federal grants-in-aid to state and local governments are especially vital in the areas of health and welfare.

Source: *Budget of United States Government, 2000.*

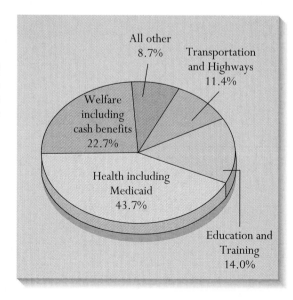

All other 8.7%

Transportation and Highways 11.4%

Welfare including cash benefits 22.7%

Health including Medicaid 43.7%

Education and Training 14.0%

How Congress Set a National Drinking Age

Traditionally the *reserved* powers of the states included protection of the health, safety, and well-being of their citizens. The *enumerated* powers of Congress in the Constitution did not include regulating the sale and consumption of alcoholic beverages. Every state determined its own minimum age for drinking.

When the Twenty-sixth Amendment to the Constitution was passed in 1971, guaranteeing eighteen-year-olds the right to vote, most states lowered their minimum drinking age to eighteen. But by the early 1980s, some states had raised their minimums back to twenty-one in response to reports of teenage drinking and driving. Indeed, the National Transportation Safety Board reported that teenagers were statistically more likely to be involved in alcohol-related deaths than nonteenagers. The National Student Association, restaurant owners, and the beverage industry claimed that the selection of *all* teenagers for restriction was age discrimination. Whatever the merits of the argument, the issue was widely considered to be a *state* concern.

But the minimum drinking age became a national issue as a result of emotional appeals by groups such as Mothers Against Drunk Driving (MADD). Tragic stories told at televised committee hearings by grieving relatives of dead teenagers swept away federalism arguments. A few Congress members tried to argue that a national drinking age infringed on the powers of the state in a matter traditionally under state control. However, the new law did not directly mandate a national drinking age. Instead, it ordered the withholding of 10 percent of all federal highway funds from any state that failed to raise its minimum drinking age to twenty-one. States retained the rights to ignore the national minimum and give up a portion of their highway funds. (Congress used this same approach in 1974 in establishing a national 55-mile-per-hour speed limit.) Opponents of this device labeled it federal blackmail and a federal intrusion into state responsibilities. For some state officials, then, the issue was not teen drinking but rather the preemption of state authority.

Proponents of the legislation cited the *national* interest in setting a uniform minimum drinking age. They argued that protecting the lives of young people outweighed the states' interest in preserving their authority. Moreover, teens were crossing state lines to drink in states with lower drinking ages. New York, for example, with a minimum drinking age of nineteen, was attracting teenagers from Pennsylvania and New Jersey, where the drinking age was twenty-one. Reports of "bloody borders" were used to justify national action to establish a uniform drinking age. Although the Reagan White House had pledged to return responsibility to the states, it did not wish to offend the nation's mothers on such an emotional issue. Despite initial reservations, President Ronald Reagan supported the bill and signed it into law in 1984.

From a purely constitutional perspective, Congress simply exercised its power to spend money for the general welfare; it did not *directly* legislate in an area *reserved* to the states. Technically, states remain free to set their own minimum drinking age. Despite heated arguments in many state legislatures, all of the states adopted the twenty-one-year-old minimum national drinking age by 1990.

Appeals by groups such as Mothers Against Drunk Driving (MADD) helped overcome concerns that legislation effectively setting a national drinking age would infringe on state authority.

or local governments according to a fixed formula set by Congress. Medicaid and Food Stamps (see Chapter 17) are the largest categorical grant programs.

- *Block Grant:* A grant for a general governmental function, such as health, social services, law enforcement, education, or community development. State and local governments have fairly wide discretion in deciding how to spend federal block grant money within a functional area. For example, cities receiving "community development" block grants can decide for themselves about specific neighborhood development projects, housing projects, community facilities, and so on. All block grants are distributed on a formula basis set by Congress. Federal administrative agencies may require reports and adherence to rules and guide-lines, but they do not choose which specific projects to fund. Only about 10 percent of federal grant-in-aid money is distributed in the form of block grants.

State and local government dependence on federal aid rose rapidly in the 1960s and 1970s (see Figure 4-4). This was a period of expansion of "Great Society" federal grant programs in welfare cash assistance, food stamps, and Medicaid—medical care for the poor (see Chapter 17, "Politics and Social Welfare"). In addition, a "General Revenue Sharing" program was begun in 1972; this program channeled federal money to state and local governments to use largely as they saw fit.

President Ronald Reagan temporarily reversed the trend toward greater federal support of state and local government during the 1980s. The Reagan Administration ended General Revenue Sharing altogether in 1986, arguing that local officials did not spend so-called free money from Washington with the same care that they exercised when spending money extracted from their own voter-taxpayers. The Reagan Admin-istration also replaced some categorical grant programs, notably in health services, social services, community development, mental health programs, and education, with block grants to support local efforts in these areas. Actually, the struggle in Congress between those who favored categorical grants (mostly liberals and Democrats) and those who wanted to consolidate them into block grants (Reagan and the Republicans) ended with most categorical grant programs remaining independent.

State and local government dependence on federal aid rose again during the Clin-ton Administration. Much of this rise is attributable to the rising costs of Medicaid. Health care is currently the fastest rising cost of state government. Today about one dollar in every four spent by state and local governments comes to them from federal grants-in-aid.

COERCIVE FEDERALISM: PREEMPTIONS AND MANDATES

Traditionally, Congress avoided issuing direct orders to state and local governments. Instead, it sought to influence them by offering grants of money with federal rules, regulations, or "guidelines" attached. In theory at least, states and communities were free to forgo the money and ignore the strings attached to it. But increasingly Congress has undertaken direct regulation of areas traditionally reserved to the states and restricted state authority to regulate these areas. And it has issued direct orders to state and local governments to perform various services and comply with federal law in the performance of these services.

preemption Total or partial federal assumption of power in a particular field, restricting the authority of the states.

Federal Preemptions   The supremacy of federal laws over those of the states, spelled out in the National Supremacy Clause of the Constitution, permits Congress to decide whether or not there is **preemption** of state laws in a particular field by

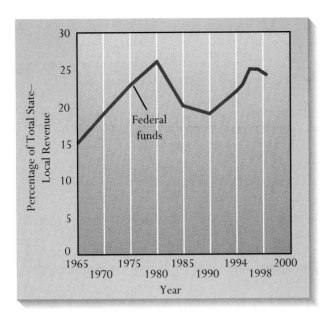

FIGURE 4-4 State and Local Government Reliance on Federal Money

Under the New Federalism of the 1980s, federal money as a percentage of state and local revenue fell significantly. State and local governments had to rely more heavily on their own sources of revenue than on federal funds. In recent years, however, state and local reliance on federal money has begun to creep upward again.

federal law. In **total preemption**, the federal government assumes all regulatory powers in a particular field—for example, copyrights, bankruptcy, railroads, and airlines. No state regulations in a totally preempted field are permitted. **Partial preemption** stipulates that a state law on the same subject is valid as long as it does not conflict with the federal law in the same area. For example, the Occupational Safety and Health Act of 1970 specifically permits state regulation of any occupational safety or health issue on which the federal Occupational Safety and Health Administration (OSHA) has *not* developed a standard; but once OSHA enacts a standard, all state standards are nullified. A specific form of partial preemption called **standard partial preemption** permits states to regulate activities in a field already regulated by the federal government, as long as state regulatory standards are at least as stringent as those of the federal government. Usually states must submit their regulations to the responsible federal agency for approval; the federal agency may revoke a state's regulating power if that state fails to enforce the approved standards. For example, the federal Environmental Protection Agency (EPA) permits state environmental regulations that meet or exceed EPA standards.

Federal Mandates Federal **mandates** are direct orders to state and local governments to perform a particular activity or service or to comply with federal laws in the performance of their functions. Federal mandates occur in a wide variety of areas, from civil rights to minimum-wage regulations. Their range is reflected in some recent examples of federal mandates to state and local governments:

- *Age Discrimination Act, 1986:* Outlaws mandatory retirement ages for public as well as private employees, including police, fire fighters, and state college and university faculty.
- *Asbestos Hazard Emergency Act, 1986:* Orders school districts to inspect for asbestos hazards and remove asbestos from school buildings when necessary.
- *Safe Drinking Water Act, 1986:* Establishes national requirements for municipal water supplies; regulates municipal waste treatment plants.
- *Clean Air Act, 1990:* Bans municipal incinerators and requires auto emission inspections in certain urban areas.

total preemption Federal government's assumption of all regulatory powers in a particular field.

partial preemption Federal government's assumption of some regulatory powers in a particular field, with the stipulation that a state law on the same subject as a federal law is valid if it does not conflict with the federal law in the same area.

standard partial preemption Form of partial preemption in which the states are permitted to regulate activities already regulated by the federal government if the state regulatory standards are at least as stringent as the federal government's.

mandates Direct federal orders to state and local governments requiring them to perform a service or to obey federal laws in the performance of their functions.

- *Americans with Disabilities Act, 1990:* Requires all state and local government buildings to promote handicapped access.
- *NationalVoter Registration Act, 1993:* Requires states to register voters at driver's license, welfare, and unemployment compensation offices.

State and local governments frequently complain that the costs imposed on them by complying with such federal mandates are seldom reimbursed by Washington.

"Unfunded" Mandates   Federal mandates often impose heavy costs on states and communities. When no federal monies are provided to cover these costs, the mandates are said to be **unfunded mandates**. Governors, mayors, and other state and local officials (including Bill Clinton, when he served as governor of Arkansas) have often urged Congress to stop imposing unfunded mandates on states and communities. Private industries have long voiced the same complaint. Regulations and mandates allow Congress to address problems while pushing the costs of doing so onto others. In 1995 Congress responded to these complaints by requiring that any bill imposing unfunded costs of $50 million or more on state and local governments (as determined by the Congressional Budget Office) would be subject to an additional procedural vote; a majority must vote to waive a prohibition against unfunded mandates before such a bill can come to the House or Senate floor. But this modest restraint has not proven to be very effective.

A DEVOLUTION REVOLUTION?

Controversy over federalism—what level of government should do what and who should pay for it—is as old as the nation itself (see *A ConflictingView:* "Liberals, Conservatives, and Federalism"). Beginning in 1995, with a new Republican majority in both houses of Congress and Republicans holding a majority of state governorships, debates over federalism were renewed. The new phrase was **devolution**—the passing down of responsibilities from the national government to the states.

Welfare Reform and Federalism   Welfare reform turned out to be the key to devolution. Bill Clinton once promised "to end welfare as we know it," but it was a Republican Congress in 1996 that did so. After President Clinton had twice vetoed welfare reform bills, he and Congress finally agreed to merge welfare reform with devolution. A new Temporary Assistance to Needy Families program (see Chapter 17) replaced direct federal cash aid welfare "entitlements." The new program:

- Establishes block grants with lump-sum allocations to the states for cash welfare payments.
- Grants the states broad flexibility in determining eligibility and benefit levels for persons receiving such aid.
- Limits the use of federally aided cash grants for most recipients to two continuing years and five years over their lifetime.
- Allows states to increase welfare spending if they choose to do so but penalizing states that reduce their spending for cash aid below 75 percent of their 1996 levels.
- Allows states to deny additional cash payments for children born to women already receiving welfare assistance and allowing states to deny cash payments to parents under eighteen who do not live with an adult and attend school.

unfunded mandates
Mandates that impose costs on state and local governments (and private industry) without reimbursement from the federal government.

devolution   Passing down of responsibilities from the national government to the states.

Liberals, Conservatives, and Federalism

From the earliest days of the Republic, American leaders and scholars have argued over federalism. Political interests that constitute a majority at the national level and control the national government generally praise the virtue of national supremacy. Political interests that do not control the national government but exercise controlling influence in one or more states generally see great merit in preserving the powers of the states.

In recent years, political conflict over federalism—over the division between national versus state and local responsibilities and finances—has tended to follow traditional "liberal" and "conservative" political cleavages. Generally, liberals seek to enhance the power of the *national* government because they believe people's lives can be changed—and bettered—by the exercise of national governmental power. The government in Washington has more power and resources than do state and local governments, which many liberals regard as too slow, cumbersome, weak, and unresponsive. Thus liberalism and centralization are closely related in American politics. The liberal argument for national authority can be summarized as follows:

- There is insufficient concern about social problems by state and local governments. The federal government must take the lead in civil rights, equal employment opportunities, care for the poor and aged, the provision of adequate medical care for all Americans, and the elimination of urban poverty and blight.

- It is difficult to achieve change when reform-minded citizens must deal with 50 state governments and more than 85,000 local governments. Change is more likely to be accomplished by a strong central government.

- State and local governments contribute to inequality in society by setting different levels of services in education, welfare, health, and other public functions. A strong national government can ensure uniformity of standards throughout the nation.

- A strong national government can unify the nation behind principles and ideals of social justice and economic progress. Extreme decentralization may favor local or regional "special" interests at the expense of the general "public" interest.

In contrast, conservatives generally seek to return power to *state and local* governments. Conservatives are skeptical about the "good" that government can do and believe that adding to the power of the national government is not an effective way of resolving society's problems. On the contrary, they argue that "government is the problem, not the solution." Excessive government regulation, burdensome taxation, and inflationary government spending combine to restrict individual freedom, penalize work and savings, and destroy incentives for economic growth. Government should be kept small, controllable, and close to the people. The conservative argument for state and local autonomy can be summarized as follows:

- Grass-roots government promotes a sense of self-responsibility and self-reliance.

- State and local governments can better adapt public programs to local needs and conditions.

- State and local governments promote participation in politics and civic responsibility by allowing more people to become involved in public questions.

- Competition between states and cities can result in improved public programs and services.

- The existence of multiple state and local governments encourages experimentation and innovation in public policy, from which the whole nation may gain.

There is no way to settle the argument over federalism once and for all. Debates about federalism are part of the fabric of American politics.

Jeb Bush: Leadership in the States

Florida's Jeb Bush never held elective office before winning the governorship of the nation's fourth largest state in 1998. But his family's name recognition and ability to raise campaign cash paved the way for the youngest son of the former president to the state capitol in Tallahassee. That same election year, his brother, George W. Bush, won re-election to the governorship of Texas. While this was not the first time that two brothers simultaneously occupied the governorship of different states (in the 1960s, Nelson Rockefeller served as governor of New York while his brother, Winthrope, served as governor of Arkansas), the success of the Bush brothers in state politics forecast the continuation of a Republican political dynasty.

After graduating from exclusive Phillips Academy in Andover Massachusetts, John Ellis Bush (who uses his initials as his first name) chose to attend the University of Texas rather than follow the family tradition of attending Yale University. (His father and older brother graduated from Yale and his grandfather, U.S. Senator Prescott Bush, served as chairman of the Yale Corporation board.) Young Jeb also surprised his family by traveling to Mexico, meeting and marrying a young Mexican girl, Columbia, and later converting to her Catholic faith. Characteristically impatient to move forward, he finished college in 2 1/2 years, majoring in Latin American Studies. His first job was with the large Texas Commerce Bank, where he headed up their Caracas, Venezuela, office. In 1980 he moved to Miami, formed a real estate partnership, and immersed himself in the Latin American culture of that city.

Despite his claimed desire to create his own civic profile, his name won him easy access to Republican circles in Florida. In the 1980s he served as chairman of the Miami-Dade County Republicans and as state campaign chairman for his father. He served briefly as state Secretary of Commerce under Republican Governor Bob Martinez. By 1994, Jeb Bush felt ready to challenge the popular incumbent Democratic governor, Lawton Chiles. Bush easily won the GOP primary, beating out seven other candidates, and used his campaign chest to finance an expensive television campaign against Chiles. His mother and father came to Florida to assist in fund-raising. Ahead in the early polls, Jeb emphasized conservative themes. But Chiles counterattacked vigorously, citing Bush's lack of experience and dependence on his father's name to get ahead. On election day, Chiles squeaked out the closest victory (51 percent) of his long political career.

Jeb Bush began campaigning for the 1998 Florida governor's race the day after his narrow 1994 defeat. He created a think tank, the Foundation for Florida's Future, to develop policy positions (and keep his campaign staff together). He also became a trustee of the influential, conservative, Washington think tank, the Heritage Foundation. He courted Florida's large Latin American population in fluent Spanish, and helped to open a charter school in Liberty City, an African-American neighborhood in Miami.

In his 1998 campaign for the governorship, he followed his brother's lead in adding "compassionate" to his self-described conservatism. He defeated the lackluster Democratic former lieutenant governor, winning 55 percent of the vote, including a large majority of Florida's Latino voters. In his first year as governor, he succeeded in getting virtually all of his policy proposals approved by a Republican legislature. His "A-Plus" school program calls for grading public schools and giving private school vouchers to pupils attending public schools that are found to be failing. His "10-20-Life" legislation requires criminals to be locked up for ten years if they display a gun while committing a violent crime, twenty if they fire the gun, and life if they cause a death or bodily injury. But he faced controversy over his "One Florida Initiative" to end racial preferences in state university admissions and to substitute a plan for admitting applicants from the top 20 percent of their high school graduation classes.

Bush's critics charge him with acting arrogantly, failing to consult with others, and steam rolling his programs through the compliant Republican legislature. But the tall (6 foot, 4 inch), youthful looking, articulate governor wins high approval ratings in polls of Floridians. And it can't hurt him to have his brother in the White House.

Twenty-First Century Directions

The historical trend of American federalism has been toward nationalization—the growth of power of the national government relative to the power of the states. The twenty-first century is not likely to see any permanent reversal of this trend. However, from time to time, federalism will be reasserted and state powers reaffirmed by the Supreme Court.

↑ **National Power** Power will continue to concentrate in Washington. Presidents, members of Congress, and candidates for these offices, will promise voters to solve virtually every problem that the nation faces, from drug use, guns in schools, domestic violence, to health costs, urban "sprawl," and the reading, writing, and arithmetic skills of schoolchildren. No elected federal official or candidate for federal office can respond to voters' concerns about any problem by saying it is not a federal responsibility. The result will be the continued growth of federal power.

↑ **State Dependence on Federal Money** Federal money in the form of grants-in-aid will continue to be the favored method by which Washington controls the activities of state and local governments. Money is power, and Washington can raise far more revenue than state or local governments. These governments will continue to face "bribery and blackmail" from Washington—"bribery" by the offer of federal money, and "blackmail" by the knowledge that this money will go to other states and cities if not accepted with all strings attached. The result will be an ever-growing dependence of state local governments on federal revenues.

↓ **Direct Federal Mandates to State and Local Governments** The Supreme Court may place restraints on direct federal mandates to the state and local governments. In recent years the Court has revived the original constitutional vision of a national government with only *enumerated* powers and state governments as sovereign entities. This recent judicial trend reverses nearly a century of Supreme Court tilt toward unrestrained federal power. But the Court appears ready to revive federalism, at least to the extent that it may block direct congressional orders to state and local officials regarding the performance of their traditional functions. The result will be that Congress will be careful to use the lure of federal money to influence state and local governments rather than issuing them direct orders.

Since Franklin D. Roosevelt's New Deal, with its federal guarantee of cash Aid to Families with Dependent Children (AFDC), low-income mothers and children had enjoyed a federal "entitlement" to welfare payments. But welfare reform, with its devolution of responsibility to the states, ended this 60-year-old federal entitlement. Note, however, that Congress continues to place "strings" on the use of federal welfare funds, including a two-year limit on continuing payments to beneficiaries in a five-year lifetime limit.

Federalism Impact Assessments President Ronald Reagan issued an "Executive Order on Federalism" in 1987 requiring federal executive agencies to prepare "federalism assessment" reports prior to issuing any new rules or regulations that might impact state powers, laws, or programs. But this Executive Order has been ignored by virtually all federal agencies,[18] including the Department of Health and Human Services and the Environmental Protection Agency, the agencies that produce the most federal rules (see Chapter 12, "The Bureaucracy: Bureaucratic Politics"). President Bill Clinton added more confusion to federalism assessment with his own Executive Order on Federalism in 1998. Clinton's order listed so many exceptions to the requirement that federal agencies respect federalism that the effect has been to eliminate this restraint on the federal bureaucracy.

Political Obstacles to Devolution and Federalism Politicians in Washington are fond of the rhetoric of federalism. They know that Americans generally prefer governments closer to home. Yet at the same time they confront strong political pressures to "DO SOMETHING!" about virtually every problem that confronts individuals, families, or communities, whether or not doing so may overstep the enumerated powers of the national government. Politicians gain very little by telling their constituents that a particular problem—violence in the schools, domestic abuse, physician-assisted suicide, and so on—is not a federal responsibility and should be dealt with at the state or local level of government.

Moreover, neither presidents nor members of Congress are inclined to restrain their own power. Both liberals and conservatives in Washington are motivated to tie their own strings to federal grant-in-aid money, issue their own federal mandates, and otherwise "correct" what they perceive to be errors or inadequacies of state policies.

SUMMARY NOTES

- The struggle for power between the national government and the states over two centuries has shaped American federalism today.

- Federalism is the division of power between two separate authorities, the nation and the state, each of which enforces its own laws directly on its citizens and neither of which can change the division of power without the consent of the other.

- American federalism was designed by the Founders as an additional protection for individual liberty by providing for the division and dispersal of power among multiple units of government.

- Federalism has also been defended as a means of increasing opportunities to hold public office, improving governmental efficiency, ensuring policy responsiveness, encouraging policy innovation, and managing conflict.

- However, federalism can also obstruct and frustrate national action. Narrow state interests can sometimes prevail over national interests or the interests of minorities within states. Segregation was long protected by theories of states' rights. Federalism also results in uneven levels of public services through the nation.

- Power has flowed to the national government over time, as the original state-centered division of power has evolved into a national-centered system of government. Among the most important historical influences on this shift in power toward Washington have been

the Supreme Court's broad interpretation of national power, the national government's victory over the secessionist states in the Civil War, the establishment of a national system of civil rights based on the Fourteenth Amendment, the growth of a national economy governed by Congress under its interstate commerce power, and the national government's accumulation of power through its greater financial resources.

- Federal grants to state and local governments have greatly expanded the national government's powers in areas previously regarded as *reserved* to the states. State and local governments have become increasingly dependent on federal money.

- Federal grants are available for most state and local government activities, but welfare, health, and highways account for about three-fourths of these grants.

- Although Congress has generally refrained from directly legislating in areas traditionally *reserved* to the states, federal power in local affairs has grown as a result of federal rules, regulations, and guidelines established as conditions for the receipt of federal funds.

- The Supreme Court in its *Garcia* decision in 1985 removed all constitutional barriers to direct congressional legislation in matters traditionally reserved to the states. Establishing the principle of representational federalism, the Court said that states could defend their own interests through their representation in the national government.

- Representational federalism focuses on the role of the states in electing national officials—the president through the allocation of Electoral College votes to the states, the Senate through the allocation of two seats for each state, and the House through the appointment of representatives based on the state's population.

- Recent efforts at the "devolution" of federal responsibilities for welfare resulted in an end to federal individual "entitlements" to cash welfare payments and their replacement with block grants for cash aid to the states. But Congress continues to place "strings" on the use of federal welfare grants to the states.

KEY TERMS

SELECTED READINGS

BEER, SAMUEL H. *To Make a Nation: The Rediscovery of American Federalism.* Cambridge, Mass.: Harvard University Press, 1993. A historical account of the development of both federalism and nationalism in American political philosophy.

DYE, THOMAS R. *American Federalism: Competition among Governments.* Lexington, Mass.: Lexington Books, 1990. A theory of "competitive federalism" arguing that rivalries among governments improve public services while lowering taxes, restrain the growth of government, promote innovation and experimentation in public policies, inspire greater responsiveness to the preferences of citizen-taxpayers, and encourage economic growth.

ELAZAR, DANIEL J. *The American Partnership.* Chicago: University of Chicago Press, 1962. A study of the historical evolution of federalism, stressing the nation-state sharing of policy concerns and financing, from the early days of the Republic, and the politics behind the gradual growth of national power.

GREVE, MICHAEL S. *Real Federalism.* Washington, D.C.: AEI Press, 1999. Why real "competitive" federalism matters and how it can be achieved in the current political environments.

OSTRUM, VINCENT. *The Meaning of American Federalism.* San Francisco: ICS Press, 1991. A theoretical examination of federalism, setting forth the conditions for a self-governing rather than a state-governed society and arguing that multiple, overlapping units of government, with various checks on one another's power, provide a viable democratic system of conflict resolution.

PETERSON, PAUL E. *The Price of Federalism.* Washington, D.C.: Brookings Institution, 1995. Historical, theoretical, and empirical perspectives merged into a new, timely model of federalism that would allocate social welfare functions to the national government and education and economic development to states and communities.

RIVLIN, ALICE M. *Reviving the American Dream.* Washington, D.C.: Brookings Institution, 1992. A comprehensive plan to restructure responsibilities between the national government and the states. The federal government would turn over to the states most of its programs in education, highways, economic development, and job training, along with common shared taxes to finance state and local efforts to revitalize the economy. The federal government would focus on welfare, Social Security, and health care, as well as international relations.

VAN HORN, CARL E. *The State of the States.* 3rd ed. Washington, D.C.: C.Q. Books, 1996. An assessment of the challenges facing state governments as a result of the devolution revolution.

Opinion and Participation

Thinking and Acting in Politics

ASK YOURSELF ABOUT POLITICS

1 Should political leaders pay attention to public opinion polls when making decisions for the country?
Yes ⬤   No ⬤

2 Do you believe that your representative in Congress cares about your personal opinion on important issues?
Yes ⬤   No ⬤

3 Can you name the two U.S. senators from your state?
Yes ⬤   No ⬤

4 Is our government really legitimate when only about half the people vote in presidential elections?
Yes ⬤   No ⬤

5 Do you identify yourself with the same political party as your family?
Yes ⬤   No ⬤

6 Is it appropriate for religious leaders to try to influence how people vote?
Yes ⬤   No ⬤

7 Have you ever personally called or written to your representative in Congress?
Yes ⬤   No ⬤

8 Do you think you will ever run for public office yourself?
Yes ⬤   No ⬤

By thinking about politics and acting on your political opinions—voting, talking to friends, writing letters, joining organizations, attending meetings and rallies, contributing money, marching in demonstrations, or running for office yourself—you are participating in politics.

POLITICS AND PUBLIC OPINION

For most Americans, politics is *not* as interesting as football or basketball, or the sex lives of celebrities, or prime-time television entertainment. Although politicians, pollsters, and commentators frequently assume that Americans have formed opinions on major public issues, in fact, most have not given them very much thought. Nevertheless, **public opinion** commands the attention of politicians, the news media, and political scientists.

Public opinion is given a lot of attention in democracies because democratic government rests on the consent of the governed. The question of whether public opinion *should* direct government policy has confounded political philosophers for centuries. Edmund Burke, writing in 1790, argued that democratic representatives should serve the *interests* of the people, but not necessarily conform to their *will*, in deciding questions of public policy. In contrast, other political philosophers have evaluated the success of democratic institutions by whether or not they produce policies that conform to popular opinion.

Major shifts in public opinion in the United States generally translate into policy change. Both the president and Congress appear to respond over time to *general* public preferences for "more" or "less" government regulation, "more" or "less" government spending, "getting tough on crime," "reforming welfare," and so on.[1] But public opinion is often weak, unstable, ill informed, or nonexistent on *specific* policy issues. Consequently, elected officials have greater flexibility in dealing with these issues—and, at the same time, there is an increase in the influence of lobbyists, interest groups, reporters, commentators, and others who have direct access to policy makers. Moreover, the absence of well-formed public opinion on an issue provides interest groups and the media with the opportunity to influence policy indirectly by shaping popular opinion.

Politicians read the opinion polls. And even though many elected representatives claim that they exercise independent judgment about what is best for the nation in their decision making, we can be reasonably sure their "independent judgment" is influenced at least in part by what they think their constituents want. Public opinion commands the attention of politicians because even if only a small number of voters cast their ballots on the basis of the candidates' policy positions, those votes are still important. The cynical stereotype of the politician who reads the opinion polls before taking stands on the issues is often embarrassingly accurate.

All this attention to public opinion has created a thriving industry in public opinion polling and **survey research**. Polls have become a fixture of American political life (see *Up Close:* "Can We Believe the Polls?" on page 122). But how much do Americans really think about politics? How informed, stable, and consistent is public opinion?

Knowledge Levels   Most Americans do not follow politics closely enough to develop well-informed opinions on many public issues (see Figure 5-1). Low levels of knowledge about government and public affairs make it difficult for people to form opinions on specific issues or policy proposals. Many opinion surveys ask

public opinion   Aggregate of attitudes and opinions of individuals on a significant issue.

survey research   Gathering of information about public opinion by questioning a representative sample of the population.

FIGURE 5-1   What Do Americans Know about Politics?

Politics is not the major interest of most Americans, and as a result, knowledge about the political system is limited. Less than one-third of the general public know the names of their representatives in Congress or their U.S. senators, and knowledge of specific foreign and domestic matters is even more limited.

Source: Data reported in Michael X. DelliCarpini and Scott Keeter, "The U.S. Public's Knowledge of Politics," *Public Opinion Quarterly* 55 (May 1991): 583–612. Reprinted by permission of University of Chicago Press.

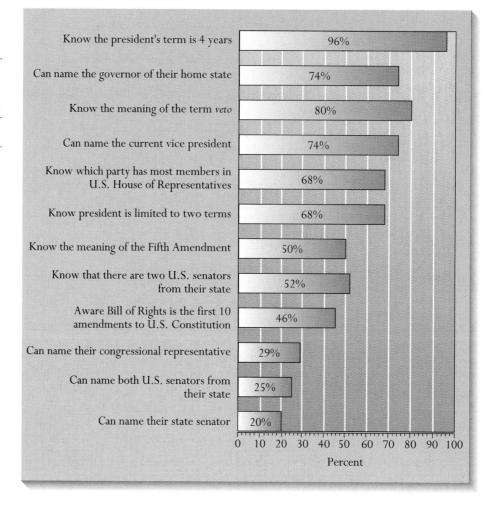

	Percent
Know the president's term is 4 years	96%
Can name the governor of their home state	74%
Know the meaning of the term *veto*	80%
Can name the current vice president	74%
Know which party has most members in U.S. House of Representatives	68%
Know president is limited to two terms	68%
Know the meaning of the Fifth Amendment	50%
Know that there are two U.S. senators from their state	52%
Aware Bill of Rights is the first 10 amendments to U.S. Constitution	46%
Can name their congressional representative	29%
Can name both U.S. senators from their state	25%
Can name their state senator	20%

questions about topics that people had not considered before being interviewed. Few respondents are willing to admit that they know nothing about the topic or have "no opinion." Respondents believe they should provide some sort of answer, even if their opinion was nonexistent before the question was asked. The result is that the polls themselves "create" opinions.[2]

The "Halo Effect"   Many respondents give "good citizen" or socially respectable answers, whether they are truthful or not, even to an anonymous interviewer. This **halo effect** leads to an *underestimation* of the true extent of prejudice, hatred, and bigotry. A very common example of the halo effect is the fact that people do not like to admit that they do not vote. Surveys regularly report higher percentages of people *saying* they voted in an election than the *actual* number of ballots cast (see Figure 5-2). Moreover, postelection surveys almost always produce higher percentages of people who say they voted for the winner than the actual vote tally for the winner. Apparently respondents do not like to admit that they backed the loser.

Inconsistencies   Because so many people hold no real opinion on political issues, the wording of a question frequently determines their response. People respond positively to positive phrases (for example, "helping poor people," "improving education," "cleaning up the environment") and negatively to negative phrases (for example, "raising taxes," "expanding governmental power," "restricting choice").

The wording of questions, combined with weak or nonexistent opinion, often produces inconsistent responses. For example, when asked whether they agreed or disagreed with the statement that "people should have the right to purchase a sexually explicit book, magazine, or movie, if that's what they want to do," an overwhelming 80 percent endorsed the statement. However, when the same respondents were also asked whether they agreed with the opposite statement that "community authorities should be able to prohibit the selling of magazines or movies they consider to be pornographic," 65 percent approved of this view as well.[3]

Instability   Many people answer survey questions impulsively without very serious consideration. They may hold fairly fixed attitudes—liberal or conservative, for example—but they do not bother to mentally consult their attitude when responding to a question. This lack of thought often results in an apparent instability of opinions—people giving contradictory responses to the same question when asked it at different times.[4]

Salience   People are likely to think about issues that receive a great deal of attention in the mass media—television, newspapers, magazines. **Salient issues** are

halo effect   Tendency of survey respondents to provide socially acceptable answers to questions.

salient issues   Issues about which most people have an opinion.

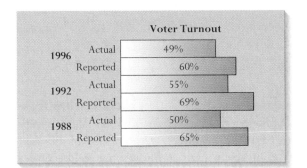

Voter Turnout		
1996	Actual	49%
	Reported	60%
1992	Actual	55%
	Reported	69%
1988	Actual	50%
	Reported	65%

FIGURE 5-2 Halo Effects in Reported Presidential Voting

The halo effect in survey research—the tendency of respondents to give answers that are socially acceptable—is easily observable in voter surveys. Many more people claim to have voted than actually did so.

Sources: General Social Surveys, 1994, 1996 (Chicago: National Opinion Research Center).

UP CLOSE

Can We Believe the Polls?

Survey research is a flourishing political enterprise. The national news media—notably CBS, NBC, ABC, and CNN television networks, the *New York Times* and the *Washington Post*, and *Time* and *Newsweek* magazines—regularly sponsor independent national surveys, especially during election campaigns. Major survey organizations—the American Institute of Public Opinion (Gallup), Louis Harris and Associates, National Opinion Research Center (NORC), the Roper Organization, National Election Studies (University of Michigan)—have been in business for a long time and have files of survey results going back many years. Political candidates also contract with private marketing and opinion research firms to conduct surveys in conjunction with their campaigns.

Public opinion surveys depend on the selection of a *random sample* of persons chosen in a way which ensures that every person in the *universe* of people about whom information is desired has an equal chance of being selected for interviewing. National samples, representative of all adults or all voters, usually include only about 1,000 persons. First, geographical areas (for example, counties or telephone area codes) that are representative of all such areas in the nation are chosen. Then residential telephone numbers are randomly selected within these areas. Once the numbers have been selected at random, the poll taker does not make substitutions but calls back several times if necessary to make contact so as not to bias the sample toward people who stay at home.

Even when random-selection procedures are closely followed, the sample may not be truly representative of the universe. But survey researchers can estimate the *sampling error* through the mathematics of probability. The sampling error is usually expressed as a percentage range—for example, plus or minus 3 percent—above and below the sample response within which there is a 95 percent likelihood that the universe response would be found if the entire universe were questioned. For example, if 65 percent of the survey respondents favor the death penalty and the sampling error is calculated at plus or minus 3 percent, then we can say there is a 95 percent probability that a survey of the whole population (the universe) would produce a response of between 62 and 68 percent in favor of the death penalty.

"Loaded" or "leading" questions are often used by unprofessional pollsters simply to produce results favorable to their side of an argument. Professional

those that people think about most—issues on which they hold stronger and more stable opinions. These are issues that people feel relate directly to their own lives, such as abortion (see *Up Close:* "Abortion: The 'Hot-Button' Issue" on page 124). Salient issues are, therefore, more important in politics.

Salient issues change over time. In general, during recessions the most salient issue is "Jobs, Jobs, Jobs!"—that is, unemployment and the economy. During inflationary periods, the issue is "the high cost of living." During wartime, the war itself becomes the public's principal concern. A gasoline shortage can turn public concern toward energy issues. The Gallup Opinion Organization regularly asks Americans what they think is "the most important problem facing America." The results are shown in Figure 5-3 on page 126. Over time, public interest has shifted from inflation, to drugs, to crime, to health care. These salient issues drive the political debate of the times.

SOCIALIZATION: THE ORIGINS OF POLITICAL OPINIONS

socialization Learning of values, beliefs, and opinions.

Where do people acquire their political opinions? Political **socialization** is the learning of political values, beliefs, and opinions (see *Compared to What?* "How 'Exceptional' Is Opinion in America?" on page 128 for a look at the results of different socialization patterns in other lands). It begins early in life when a child acquires

pollsters strive for questions that are clear and precise, easily understood by the respondents, and as neutral and unbiased as possible. Nevertheless, because all questions have a potential bias, it is often better to examine *changes over time* in response to identically worded questions. Perhaps the best-known continuing question in public opinion polling is the presidential approval rating: "Do you approve or disapprove of the way_____is handling his job as president?" Changes over time in public response to this question alert scholars, commentators, and presidents themselves to their public standing (see Chapter 11).

A survey can only measure opinions *at the time* it is taken. A few days later public opinion may change, especially if major events that receive heavy television coverage intervene. Some political pollsters conduct continuous surveys until election night in order to catch last-minute opinion changes.

A common test of the accuracy of survey research is the comparison of the actual vote in presidential elections to the predictions made by the polls (see figure). Discrepancies between the actual and predicted vote percentages are sometimes used as rough measures of the validity of surveys.

Gallup Forecasting Errors in Presidential Elections

	Final Poll Predictions		Actual Vote		Error
	%	winner	%	winner	%
1996	52.0	Clinton	49.2	Clinton	2.8
1992	49.0	Clinton	43.0	Clinton	6.0
1988	56.0	Bush	53.4	Bush	2.6
1984	59.0	Reagan	58.8	Reagan	0.2

images and attitudes toward public authority. Preschool children see "police officer" and "president" as powerful yet benevolent "helpers." These figures—police officer and president—are usually the first recognized sources of authority above the parents who must be obeyed. They are usually positive images of authority at these early ages:

Q: What does the policeman do?

A: He catches bad people.[5]

Even the American flag is recognized by most U.S. preschoolers, who pick it out when asked, "Which flag is your favorite?" These early positive perceptions about political figures and symbols may later provide *diffuse support* for the political system—a reservoir of goodwill toward governmental authority that lends legitimacy to the political order.

Family The family is the first agent of socialization, and some family influences appear to stay with people over a lifetime.[6] Children in the early school grades (3 to 5) begin to identify themselves as Republicans or Democrats. These childhood party identifications are almost always the same as those of the parents. Indeed, parent-child correspondence in party identification may last a lifetime.[7] The children who abandon the party of their parents tend to become independents rather

Abortion: The "Hot-Button" Issue

Although public opinion may be weak or nonexistent on many policy questions, there are a few "hot-button" issues in politics—issues on which virtually everyone has an opinion and many people feel very intensely about.

Abortion is one such highly sensitive issue. Both *pro-choice* proponents of legalized abortion and *pro-life* opponents claim to have public opinion on their side. *Interpretation* of the poll results becomes a political activity itself. Consider, for example, responses to the general question posed in the graph pictured here.

Pro-choice forces interpret these results as overwhelming support for legalized abortion; pro-life

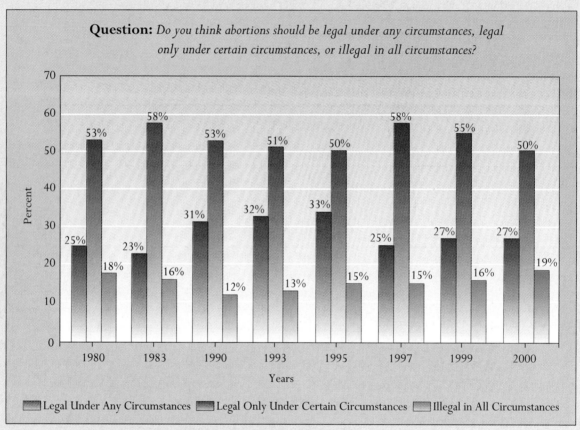

Question: *Do you think abortions should be legal under any circumstances, legal only under certain circumstances, or illegal in all circumstances?*

■ Legal Under Any Circumstances ■ Legal Only Under Certain Circumstances ■ Illegal in All Circumstances

Source: Gallup Organization and National Opinion Research Center, May 8, 2000.

than identify with the opposition party. However, party identification appears to be more easily passed on from parent to child than specific opinions on policy questions. Perhaps the reason is that parental party identifications are known to children, but few families conduct specific discussions of policy questions.

School Political revolutionaries once believed that the school was the key to molding political values and beliefs. After the communist revolutions in Russia in 1917 and China in 1949, the schools became the focus of political indoctrination

commentators interpret these results as majority support for restricting abortion. Indeed, public opinion appears to support *specific restrictions on* abortion (see below).

In short, most Americans appear to want to keep some abortions legal but they believe that government should place certain restrictions on the practice.

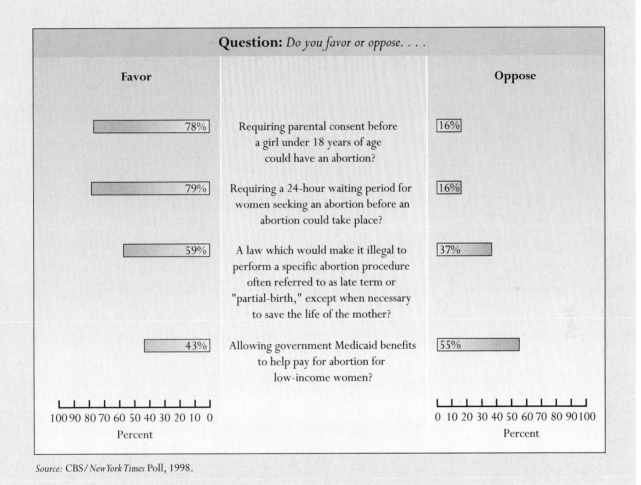

Question: *Do you favor or oppose. . . .*

Favor		Oppose
78%	Requiring parental consent before a girl under 18 years of age could have an abortion?	16%
79%	Requiring a 24-hour waiting period for women seeking an abortion before an abortion could take place?	16%
59%	A law which would make it illegal to perform a specific abortion procedure often referred to as late term or "partial-birth," except when necessary to save the life of the mother?	37%
43%	Allowing government Medicaid benefits to help pay for abortion for low-income women?	55%

100 90 80 70 60 50 40 30 20 10 0
Percent

0 10 20 30 40 50 60 70 80 90 100
Percent

Source: CBS/*New York Times* Poll, 1998.

of the population. Today political battles rage over textbooks, teaching methods, prayer in schools, and other manifestations of politics in the classroom. But no strong evidence indicates a causal relationship between what is taught in the schools and the political attitudes of students.

Certainly the schools provide the factual basis for understanding government—how the president is chosen, the three branches of government, how a law is passed. But even this elemental knowledge is likely to fade if not reinforced by additional education or exposure to the news media or discussion with family or peers.

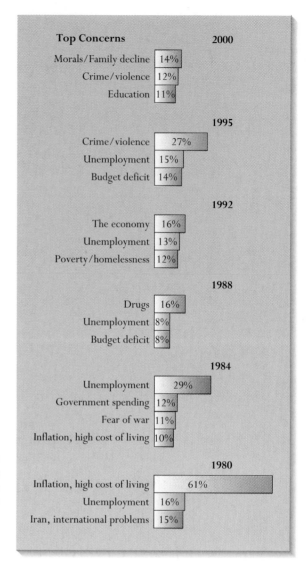

FIGURE 5-3 What's to Worry About?

Public concerns shift over time, as indicated by changing responses to the question, "What is the most important problem facing America?" In recent years, Americans have been alternately concerned about the economy, unemployment, drugs, and crime.

Source: Gallup opinion polls.

The schools *try* to inculcate "good citizenship" values, including support for democratic rules, tolerance toward others, the importance of voting, and the legitimacy (rightfulness) of government authority. Patriotic symbols and rituals abound in the classroom—the flag, the Pledge of Allegiance—and students are taught to respect the institutions of government. Generally the younger the student, the more positive the attitudes expressed toward political authority.[8] Yet despite the efforts of the schools to inspire support for the political system, distrust and cynicism creep in during the high school years. Although American youth retain a generally positive view of the political system, they share with adults increasing skepticism toward specific institutions and practices. During high school, students acquire some ability to think along liberal-conservative dimensions. The college experience appears to produce a "liberalizing" effect: College seniors tend to be more liberal than entering freshmen (see *What Do You Think?* "College Students' Opinions" on page 130). But over the years following graduation, liberal views tend to moderate.

Although no direct evidence indicates that the schools can inculcate democratic values, people with more education tend to be more tolerant than those with less

Source: PEANUTS reprinted by permission of UFS, Inc.

education and to be generally more supportive of the political system (see Table 5-1 on page 129). This pattern suggests that the effects of schooling are gradual and subtle.

Church   Religious beliefs and values may also shape political opinion. *Which* religion an individual identifies with (for example, Protestant, Catholic, Jewish) affects public opinion. So does *how important* religion is in the individual's life. It is difficult to explain exactly how religion affects political values, but we can observe differences in the opinions expressed by Protestants, Catholics, and Jews; by people who say their religious beliefs are strong versus those who say they are not; and between fundamentalists (those who believe in a literal interpretation of the Bible) and nonfundamentalists. Religion shapes political attitudes on a variety of issues, including abortion, drugs, the death penalty, homosexuality, and prayer in public schools[9] (see Table 5-2 on page 129). Religion also plays a measurable role in political ideology. Fundamentalists are more likely to describe themselves as conservatives than as moderates, and very few accept the liberal label.

Religion helps to shape politics and public opinion. Here Catholics protest a tax-supported New York museum's showing of an exhibit that included a feces-smeared painting of the Virgin Mary.

How "Exceptional" Is Opinion in America?

Do Americans differ much from Europeans in their social and political values? The American political culture places great value on individual liberty, limited government intervention in people's personal lives, equality of opportunity, and individual responsibility for one's own fate in life (see Chapter 2). The strong American commitment to these values has been labeled American "exceptionalism," suggesting that people in other nations, including the Western European democracies, are not as strongly committed to these values as are people in the United States.

The values of the political culture influence opinion on many specific issues. If the American political culture is truly "exceptional," Americans should differ significantly from Europeans on questions dealing with individual liberty, social mobility, and the role of government in society. And, indeed, cross-national survey research results do show significant differences between Americans and Europeans on these issues (see table).

Americans believe strongly in an "opportunity" society where people get ahead by their own efforts. Other peoples are more committed to a "security" society where the government assumes principal responsibility for their well-being. For example, Americans are much less likely to agree that the role of government is to reduce income differences between people or to "provide everyone with a guaranteed basic income." Americans are less likely than others (with the possible exception of the independent-minded Australians) to believe that government "should provide a job for everyone who wants one." Finally, Americans, more than other free peoples, believe in the possibility of upward social mobility— "improving our standard of living."

	"Government should reduce differences between high and low incomes"	"Government should provide everyone with a guaranteed basic income"	"Government should provide a job for everyone who wants one"	"In my country, people like me have a good chance of improving our standard of living"
United States	29%	21%	45%	72%
Australia	44	38	40	61
Switzerland	43	43	50	59
Great Britain	64	61	59	37
Netherlands	65	50	75	26
Germany	61	56	77	40
Austria	81	57	80	47
Italy	82	67	82	45
Hungary	80	79	92	33

Source: Surveys for the International Social Survey Program by National Opinion Research Center (United States); by Social and Community Planning Research, London (Great Britain); by Zentrum for Umfragen, Methoden, und Analysen, Mannheim (West Germany); by Ricerca Sociale e di Marketing, Milan (Italy); by Institute für Soziologie, Graz University (Austria); by Australian National Research School of Social Sciences. Reported in *American Enterprise* 1 (March/April 1990): 115–17.

Mixing Politics and Religion The United States is one of the most religious societies in the world, in terms of the proportion of the people who say they believe in God (96 percent), who say God has guided them in making decisions in their life (77 percent), who say they belong to an organized religion (70 percent), who say that

Table 5–1 Education and Tolerance

	Percentage Responding "Yes" (by highest degree completed)				
	No High School	High School	Junior College	College Degree	Total
If such a person wanted to make a speech in your community, should he be allowed to speak?					
Atheist	52%	73%	78%	86%	73%
Racist	47	61	60	73	61
Homosexual	59	79	84	91	79
Should such a person be allowed to teach in a college or university?					
Atheist	31%	50%	54%	68%	52%
Racist	33	41	45	52	42
Homosexual	47	71	79	83	71

Source: *General Social Survey, 1996* (Chicago: National Opinion Research Center, 1997).

religion is "very important" in their own life (60 percent), and who say they attend church at least once a month (58 percent). Most Americans believe religion should play an important role in addressing "all or most of today's problems" (64 percent), and they lament that religion is "losing its influence" in American life (69 percent).

At the same time, however, most Americans are concerned about religious leaders exercising influence in political life. Most respondents say it is "not appropriate for religious leaders to talk about their political beliefs as part of their religious activities (61 percent), "religious leaders should not try to influence how people vote in elections" (64 percent), and "religious groups should *not* advance their beliefs by being involved in politics and working to affect policy" (54 percent).[10]

Generational and Life-Cycle Effects   Age group differences in opinion occur on some important issues. This generation gap may be a product of **generational effects**—historical events that affect the views of those who lived

generational effects   Historical events that affect the views of those who lived through them.

Table 5–2 Religion and Public Opinion

Opinion	Affiliation			Faith		Belief That the Bible Is		
	Protestant	Catholic	Jew	Strong	Not Very Strong	Literal Word of God	Inspired by God	Book of Fables
Abortion for any reason should be legal	40%	33%	94%	28%	55%	29%	44%	74%
Legalize marijuana	19	21	41	13	29	12	22	43
Support death penalty	75	76	70	68	80	69	79	72
Remove book that favored homosexuality from library	34	22	6	36	23	43	20	17
Support prayer in public school	67	55	14	70	53	77	55	33

Source: *General Social Survey, 1996* (Chicago: National Opinion Research Center, 1997).

College Students' Opinions

College students' opinions today appear to be somewhat more conservative than they were a generation ago, although student opinion varies with the nature of the issue. Students today take a tougher line toward crime and drugs: They support the death penalty, believe the courts are too lenient with criminals, and oppose legalization of marijuana. The students of the 1970s confronted an unpopular war in Vietnam, faced a military draft, and were more likely to experiment with drugs and alternative lifestyles. Today's students confront greater economic competition and increased educational requirements for employment. They are more concerned with their financial future than students were a generation ago and are less interested in "developing a meaningful philosophy of life" (see graph).

However, college students remain somewhat more liberal than the general population. Moreover, college seniors and graduate students are more liberal than first-year students; students at prestigious Ivy League universities are more liberal than students at state universities and community colleges; and students in humanities and social sciences are more liberal than students in engineering, physical sciences, and business. Over the years following graduation, many of these liberal predispositions tend to moderate.

The "liberalizing" effect of college may come about because of exposure to liberal professors (see *Up Close:* "Ideology on the Campus: Students versus Professors" in Chapter 2). It may also be the result of greater exposure to the political culture. College students read more newspapers and magazines than nonstudents, watch more television news, and see and hear more political activity on campus. They become aware of various reform movements—for example, civil rights, the women's movement, environmentalism—that noncollege people of the same age have little knowledge of. This "enlightenment" may directly promote liberal views: Even students who do not identify themselves with these movements learn what is socially acceptable and currently fashionable in educated circles.

through them. For example, the "Depression generation"—those persons who grew up during the Great Depression of the 1930s—may give greater support to government income-security programs because of this experience. The "baby boomers"—those persons who were born in the high-birthrate years following World War II (1946–64)—experienced the civil rights movement, the war in Vietnam, and changes in sexual morality, all of which may affect their views on many social issues.

The large size of the baby-boom generation makes their views especially important in politics. On some issues it is possible to identify a distinctive baby-boom generational viewpoint. For example, with regard to abortion, baby boomers are generally more supportive of legal abortion under various circumstances than either younger or older persons. However, over time much of the distinctiveness of the

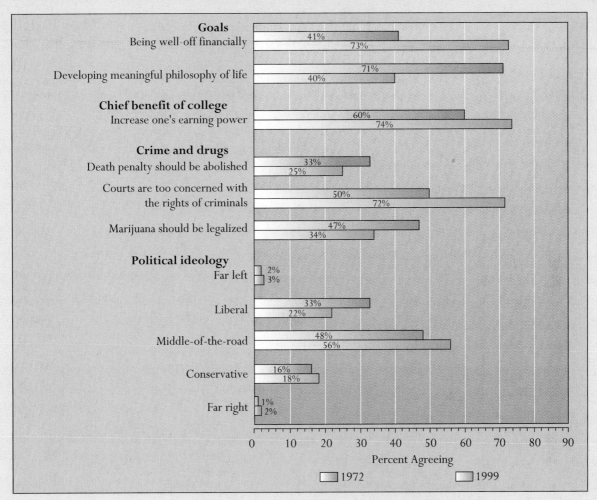

Goals
Being well-off financially — 41% / 73%

Developing meaningful philosophy of life — 71% / 40%

Chief benefit of college
Increase one's earning power — 60% / 74%

Crime and drugs
Death penalty should be abolished — 33% / 25%

Courts are too concerned with the rights of criminals — 50% / 72%

Marijuana should be legalized — 47% / 34%

Political ideology
Far left — 2% / 3%

Liberal — 33% / 22%

Middle-of-the-road — 48% / 56%

Conservative — 16% / 18%

Far right — 1% / 2%

Percent Agreeing — 0 10 20 30 40 50 60 70 80 90

☐ 1972   ☐ 1999

Source: From *The American Freshman: National Norms for Fall 1972, 1999* (American Council on Education & UCLA), as reported in the *Chronical of Higher Education,* January 2000. Copyright © 2000 The American Freshman. Reprinted by permission.

baby-boom generation has faded. As baby boomers have matured, their views have fitted more into common patterns of opinion.

A generation gap in opinion may also be a product of **life-cycle effects**— changes in life circumstances associated with age that affect one's views. Young people are expected to be idealistic. As they age and take on the responsibilities of raising children, holding a job, and paying a mortgage, they become more practical in outlook. The elderly are less amenable to social change, especially changes in morals. There is some limited evidence of life-cycle effects, but they are difficult to sort out from generational effects.[11]

Media Influence   Television is the major source of political information for Americans. More than two-thirds report that they receive "all or most" of their

life-cycle effects   Changes in life circumstances associated with age that affect one's views.

news from television, making newspapers, magazines, books, and radio secondary to television as a source of political information (see Chapter 6). Moreover, Americans rate television the "most believable" channel of communication.

But the effect of television on opinion is not really in persuading people to take one side of an issue or another. Instead, the principal effect is in *setting the agenda* for thinking and talking about politics. Television does not tell people *what* to think, but it does tell them what to think *about* (see Chapter 6, "Mass Media: Setting the Political Agenda"). Television coverage determines matters of general public concern. Without coverage, the general public would not know about, think about, or discuss most events, personalities, and issues. Media attention creates issues, and the amount of attention given an issue determines its importance.

The media can create new opinions more easily than they can change existing ones. The media can often suggest how we feel about new events or issues—those about which we have no prior feelings or experiences. And the media can reinforce values and attitudes we already hold. But there is very little evidence to indicate that the media can change existing values. (We return to the discussion of media power in Chapter 6.)

IDEOLOGY AND OPINION

Ideology helps to shape opinion. Many people, especially politically interested and active people, approach policy questions with a fairly consistent and integrated set of principles—that is, an *ideology* (see Chapter 2). Liberal and conservative ideas about the proper role of government in the economy, about the regulation of social conduct, about equality and the distribution of income, and about civil rights influence people's views on specific policy questions.

To what extent do self-described liberals and conservatives differ over specific issues? Can we predict people's stances on particular issues by knowing whether they call themselves liberal or conservative? Generally speaking, self-described liberals and conservatives do differ in their responses to specific policy questions, although some take policy positions inconsistent with their proclaimed ideology (see Table 5-3). People who describe themselves as liberal generally favor governmental efforts to reduce income inequalities and to improve the positions of African Americans, other minorities, and women. Overall, it appears that ideology and opinion are fairly well linked—that the liberal-conservative dimension is related to opinions on specific policy questions.[12]

Yet it is also true that substantial percentages of self-described conservatives take liberal policy positions, and self-described liberals take conservative positions. These inconsistencies may show that significant portions of the population do not consistently apply ideological principles when determining their position on specific issues. The consistent application of ideology to policy issues may be more characteristic of the interested and active few than of the mass of citizens. Or these apparent inconsistencies may arise because people are focusing on different dimensions of liberalism and conservatism when they label themselves. That is, some people who label themselves conservatives may hold traditional social views about abortion, homosexuality, prayer in the schools, crime, and pornography, but they want government to guarantee economic security. The term *populist* is sometimes applied to these social conservatives—economic liberals (see Chapter 2). Or these same people may label themselves liberal based on their view of the role of government in the

Table 5-3 Ideology and Opinion

	Percentage Agreeing			
	Liberals	Moderates	Conservatives	Total
Equality				
"Government should reduce income differences"	51%	41%	29%	39%
"Government should not concern itself with income differences"	31	32	51	38
Courts' treatment of criminals				
"Too harsh"	5	4	2	3
"Not harsh enough"	76	83	89	82
"About right"	13	8	6	9
Social issues				
Favor legalizing marijuana	34	22	15	23
Favor school prayer	43	60	67	58
Oppose busing for racial balance in public schools	52	63	71	63

Source: General Social Survey, 1996 (Chicago: National Opinion Research Center, 1997).

economy, even though they hold traditional views about social conduct. In short, a single liberal-conservative dimension may be inadequate for describing the ideology of Americans, and this inadequacy explains the apparent inconsistencies.

GENDER AND OPINION

A **gender gap** in public opinion—a difference of opinion between men and women—occurs on only a few issues. Interestingly, a gender gap does *not* appear on women's issues: abortion, the role of women in business and politics, whether one would vote for a qualified woman for president, or whether men are better suited for political office. On these issues, men and women do not differ significantly (see Figure 5-4 on page 134).

Instead, gender differences are more likely to appear on issues related to the use of force—for example, on gun control or the death penalty. Although majorities of both men and women support both gun control and the death penalty, men appear to give less support to gun control and more support to the death penalty than women do. The greater propensity of men to endorse the use of force has also been observed in international affairs. Small differences between men and women have also been reported on so-called compassion issues, with women more likely to favor protection for the vulnerable members of society, including children and aged, ill, and disabled people.

Politically, the most important gender gap is in party identification. Women are more likely to identify themselves as Democrats, and men more likely to identify themselves as Republicans. This difference emerged in the 1980s, when men were more likely than women to support Republican president Ronald Reagan. (Group differences in party identification are discussed at length in Chapter 7.)

gender gap Aggregate differences in political opinions of men and women.

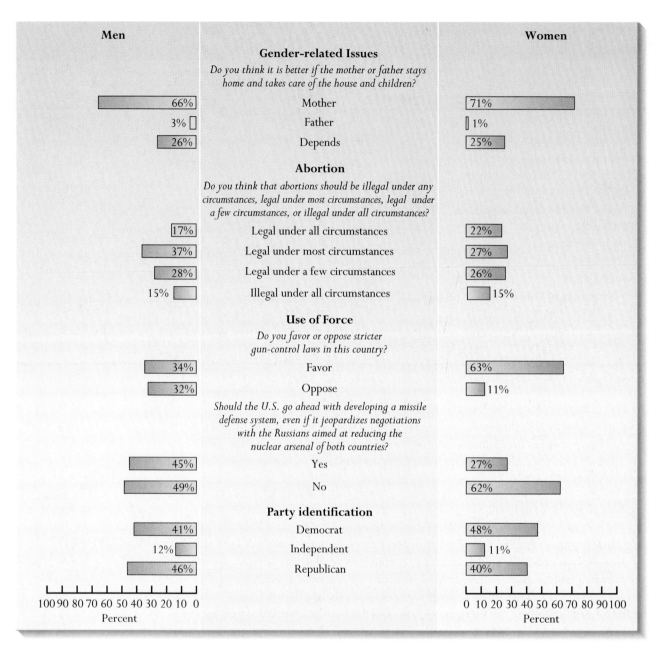

Men

Women

Gender-related Issues

Do you think it is better if the mother or father stays home and takes care of the house and children?

	Men		Women
Mother	66%		71%
Father	3%		1%
Depends	26%		25%

Abortion

Do you think that abortions should be illegal under any circumstances, legal under most circumstances, legal under a few circumstances, or illegal under all circumstances?

	Men		Women
Legal under all circumstances	17%		22%
Legal under most circumstances	37%		27%
Legal under a few circumstances	28%		26%
Illegal under all circumstances	15%		15%

Use of Force

Do you favor or oppose stricter gun-control laws in this country?

	Men		Women
Favor	34%		63%
Oppose	32%		11%

Should the U.S. go ahead with developing a missile defense system, even if it jeopardizes negotiations with the Russians aimed at reducing the nuclear arsenal of both countries?

	Men		Women
Yes	45%		27%
No	49%		62%

Party identification

	Men		Women
Democrat	41%		48%
Independent	12%		11%
Republican	46%		40%

100 90 80 70 60 50 40 30 20 10 0
Percent

0 10 20 30 40 50 60 70 80 90 100
Percent

FIGURE 5-4   Searching for the Gender Gap

Men and women do not differ significantly on gender-related issues such as abortion, but they do tend to hold different opinions on other issues and in party affiliation, suggesting the influence of gender (or at least of gender socialization) on political opinion.

Source: National opinion surveys, reported in *Public Agenda Online,* 1999.

RACE AND OPINION

Opinion over the extent of discrimination in the United States and over the causes of and remedies for racial inequality differs sharply across racial lines. Most whites believe there is very little discrimination toward African Americans

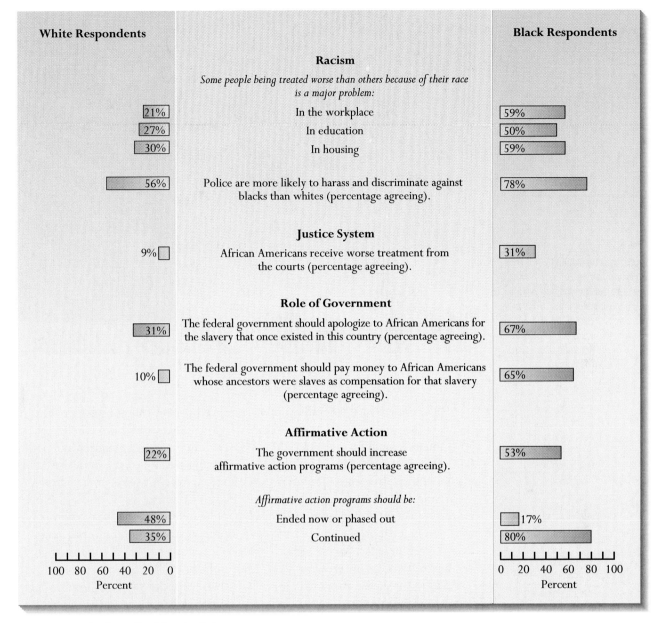

White Respondents   **Black Respondents**

Racism

Some people being treated worse than others because of their race is a major problem:

21%	In the workplace	59%
27%	In education	50%
30%	In housing	59%
56%	Police are more likely to harass and discriminate against blacks than whites (percentage agreeing).	78%

Justice System

9%	African Americans receive worse treatment from the courts (percentage agreeing).	31%

Role of Government

31%	The federal government should apologize to African Americans for the slavery that once existed in this country (percentage agreeing).	67%
10%	The federal government should pay money to African Americans whose ancestors were slaves as compensation for that slavery (percentage agreeing).	65%

Affirmative Action

22%	The government should increase affirmative action programs (percentage agreeing).	53%

Affirmative action programs should be:

48%	Ended now or phased out	17%
35%	Continued	80%

100 80 60 40 20 0   0 20 40 60 80 100
Percent   Percent

FIGURE 5-5 Black and White Opinions

Blacks and whites differ over the extent of racism in the United States as well as over what, if anything, should be done about it.

Source: National opinion surveys, reported in *Public Agenda Online*, 1999.

in jobs, housing, or education and that differences between whites and blacks in society occur as a result of a lack of motivation among black people. Most African Americans strongly disagree with these views and believe that discrimination continues in employment, housing, and education and that differences between whites and blacks in standards of living are "mainly due to discrimination" (see Figure 5-5).

Students at Augustana College react to the verdict in the O.J. Simpson case. The verdict focused national attention on the great differences between the beliefs of whites and African Americans about the role of racism in the criminal justice system.

African Americans generally support a more positive role for government in reducing inequality in society. Approximately two out of every three believe that government should do more to reduce income differences between rich and poor. Blacks favor busing to achieve racial balance in public schools, a view not shared by many whites. Given these preferences for a strong role for government, it is not surprising that more blacks than whites identify themselves as liberals. Note, however, that about one-quarter of black people identify themselves as conservative. And indeed, on certain social issues—crime, drugs, school prayers—majorities of black people take conservative positions. However, black support for the death penalty is significantly less than white support.

African Americans are much more likely than whites to support governmental actions and programs to improve the position of black people and other minorities. Levels of support for affirmative action depend on the wording of the question, but regardless of wording, blacks are more likely to support racial and minority preferences than whites. For example, both blacks and whites say they "favor affirmative action programs in business," with blacks more likely to do so than whites. However, if the question specifies "preferential treatment" for blacks and minorities, whites oppose affirmative action and blacks support it.

POLICY AND OPINION

Does public opinion determine government policy? It is widely assumed that in a democracy government policy will be heavily influenced by public opinion. Yet, as noted earlier, public opinion is weak or nonexistent on many policy questions; it is frequently inconsistent and unstable; and it is poorly informed about many policy issues. Under these circumstances, political leaders—presidents and

Should Government Leaders Pay More Attention to Public Opinion in Policy Making?

Over 200 years ago, the British parliamentarian Edmund Burke told his constituents: "Your representative owes you, not his industry only, but his judgment, and he betrays you instead of serving you, if he sacrifices it to your opinion." Since then "Burkian representation" has come to mean using one's own judgment in governmental decision making and paying little or no attention to public opinion polls. Indeed, many politicians boast of their own courage and independence and their willingness to ignore opinion polls on major issues.

But the American people believe that the country would be much better off if politicians paid *more* attention to public opinion.

Q.   *If the leaders of the nation followed the views of the public more closely, do you think that the nation would be better off, or worse off than it is today?*

Better	81%
Worse	10%

Indeed, most Americans believe that members of Congress should "read up on the polls" in order to "get a sense of the public's views."

Q.   *Please tell me which statement you agree with most. (A) When members of Congress are thinking about how vote to on an issue, they should read up on the polls, because this can help them get a sense of the public's views on the issue. (B) When members of Congress are thinking about how to vote on an issue, they should not read the polls, because this will distract them from thinking about what is right.*

Should read polls	67%
Should not read polls	26%

But fewer than one-third of the members of Congress believe that the American people know enough to form wise opinions on public issues. When Congress members themselves were questioned—"*Do you think the American public knows enough about the issues you face to form wise opinions about what should be done about these issues, or not?*"—the results (Yes—31 percent, No—47 percent, Maybe—17 percent) indicated that Congress members do not have a very high regard for the "wisdom of the people," no matter what they say in their political speeches.

Source: Center on Policy Alternatives, as reported in *The Polling Report*, February 15, 1999.

members of Congress, bureaucrats, judges, and other public officials—are relatively unconstrained by mass opinion in policy decisions (see *What Do You Think?* "Should Government Leaders Pay More Attention to Public Opinion in Policy Making?"). Moreover, in the absence of well-formed public opinion on an issue, other political actors—lobbyists and lawyers, interest group spokespersons, journalists and commentators, television reporters and executives—can influence public policy by communicating directly with government officials, claiming to represent the public. They can also influence public policy indirectly by molding and shaping public opinion.

The weakness of public opinion on many policy issues increases the influence of elites, that small group of people who are interested and active in public affairs; who call or write their elected representatives; who join organizations and contribute money to causes and candidates; who attend meetings, rallies, and demonstrations; and who hold strong opinions on a wide variety of public issues. According to political scientist V. O. Key, Jr., the linkage between ordinary citizens and democratic government depends heavily on "that thin stratum of persons referred to variously as the political elite, the political activists, the leadership echelons, or the influentials."[13] Thus political *participation* appears to be the essential link between opinion and policy.

INDIVIDUAL PARTICIPATION IN POLITICS

Democracies provide a variety of ways for individuals to participate in politics. People may run for, and win, public office; take part in marches, demonstrations, and protests; make financial contributions to political candidates or causes; attend political meetings, speeches, and rallies; write letters to public officials or to newspapers; wear a political button or place a bumper sticker on their car; belong to organizations that support or oppose particular candidates or take stands on public issues; attempt to influence friends while discussing candidates or issues; and vote in elections. Individuals may also participate in politics passively, by simply following political issues and campaigns in the media, acquiring knowledge, forming opinions about public affairs, and expressing their views to others. These forms of political participation can be ranked according to their order of frequency (see Figure 5-6). Only a little more than half of the voting-age population vote in presidential elections, and far fewer vote in state and local elections.

FIGURE 5-6 Political Participation

Only a small percentage of the American people are actively engaged in the political process, yet they receive most of the media attention. Less than 1 percent of the population runs for office at any level of government, and only about half of all voting-age Americans bother to go to the polls.

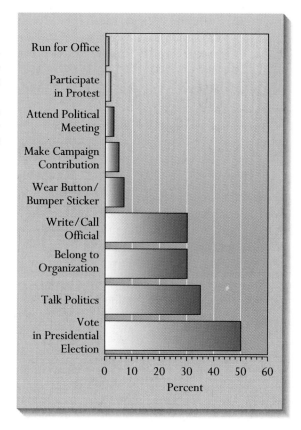

SECURING THE RIGHT TO VOTE

Popular participation in government is part of the very definition of democracy. The long history of struggle to secure the right to vote—**suffrage**—reflects the democratizing of the American political system.

The Elimination of Property Qualifications, 1800–1840 The Constitution of 1787 left it to the states to determine voter qualifications. The Founders generally believed that only men of property had a sufficient "stake in society" to exercise their vote in a "responsible" fashion. However, the Founders could not agree on the wording of property qualifications for insertion into the Constitution, so they left the issue to the states, feeling safe in the knowledge that at the time every state had property qualifications for voting. Yet over time, Jeffersonian and Jacksonian principles of democracy, including confidence in the judgment of ordinary citizens, spread rapidly in the new Republic. The states themselves eliminated most property qualifications by 1840. Thus before the Civil War (1861–65), the vote had been extended to virtually all *white males* over twenty-one years of age.

The Fifteenth Amendment, 1870 The first important limitation on state powers over voting came with the ratification of the Fifteenth Amendment: "The right of citizens of the United States to vote shall not be denied or abridged by the United States or by any state on account of race, color, or previous condition of servitude." The object of this amendment, passed by the Reconstruction Congress after the Civil War and ratified in 1870, was to extend the vote to former black slaves and prohibit voter discrimination on the basis of race. The Fifteenth Amendment also gave Congress the power to enforce black voting rights "by appropriate legislation." The states retain their right to determine voter qualifications, *as long as they do not practice racial discrimination*, and Congress has the power to pass legislation ensuring black voting rights.

Continued Denial of Voting Rights, 1870–1964 For almost 100 years after the adoption of the Fifteenth Amendment, white politicians in the southern states were able to defeat its purposes. Social and economic pressures and threats of violence were used to intimidate many thousands of would-be black voters.

There were also many "legal" methods of disenfranchisement, including a technique known as the **white primary**. So strong was the Democratic Party throughout the South that the Democratic nomination for public office was tantamount to election. Thus *primary elections* to choose the Democratic nominee were the only elections in which real choices were made. If black people were prevented from voting in Democratic primaries, they could be effectively disenfranchised. Therefore, southern state legislatures resorted to the simple device of declaring the Democratic Party in southern states a private club and ruling that only white people could participate in its elections—that is, in primary elections. Blacks were free to vote in "official" general elections, but all whites tacitly agreed to support the Democratic, or "white man's," Party in general elections, regardless of their differences in the primary. Not until 1944, in *Smith v. Allwright*, did the Supreme Court declare the white primary unconstitutional and bring primary elections under the purview of the Fifteenth Amendment.

suffrage Legal right to vote.

white primary Democratic Party primary elections in many southern counties in the early part of the twentieth century that excluded black people from voting.

Passage of the Voting Rights Act of 1965 opened the voting booth to millions of black voters formerly kept from the polls by a variety of discrimatory regulations in the South. Here African Americans in rural Alabama in 1966 line up at a local store to cast their votes in a primary that focused on an issue central to their existence—segregation.

From an estimated 5 percent of voting-age black people registered in southern states in the 1940s, black registration rose to an estimated 20 percent in 1952, 25 percent in 1956, 28 percent in 1960, and 39 percent in 1964. But this last figure was still only about half of the comparable figure for white registration in the South. Despite the Fifteenth Amendment, many local registrars in the South succeeded in barring black registration by an endless variety of obstacles, delays, and frustrations. Application forms for registration were lengthy and complicated; even a minor error, like underlining rather than circling in the "Mr.—Mrs.—Miss" set of choices, as instructed, would lead to rejection. **Literacy tests** were the most common form of disenfranchisement. Many a black college graduate failed to interpret "properly" the complex legal documents that were part of the test. White applicants for voter registration were seldom asked to go through these lengthy procedures.

The Civil Rights Act, the Twenty-fourth Amendment, and the Voting Rights Act, 1964–65

The Civil Rights Act of 1964 made it unlawful for registrars to apply unequal standards in registration procedures or to reject applications because of immaterial errors. It required that literacy tests be in writing and made a sixth-grade education a presumption of literacy. In 1970 Congress outlawed literacy tests altogether.

The Twenty-fourth Amendment to the Constitution, ratified in 1964, made **poll taxes**—taxes required of all voters—unconstitutional as a requirement for voting in national elections. In 1966 the Supreme Court declared poll taxes unconstitutional in state and local elections as well.[14]

In early 1965 civil rights organizations led by Martin Luther King, Jr., effectively demonstrated against local registrars in Selma, Alabama, who were still keeping large numbers of black people off the voting rolls. Registrars there closed their offices for all but a few hours every month, placed limits on the number of applications processed, went out to lunch when black applicants appeared, delayed months before processing black applications, and used a variety of other methods to keep blacks disenfranchised. In response to the Selma march, Congress enacted

literacy test Examination of a person's ability to read and write as a prerequisite to voter registration; outlawed by Voting Rights Act (1965) as discriminatory.

poll taxes Taxes imposed as a prerequisite to voting; prohibited by the Twenty-fourth Amendment.

The turn of the century saw the acceleration of the women's suffrage movement. Although Woodrow Wilson expressed support for granting the vote to women even before he took office in 1912, it took the activities of women "manning the homefront" during World War I to persuade the male electorate to pass the Nineteenth Amendment and give women access to the ballot box throughout the nation.

the strong Voting Rights Act in 1965. The U.S. attorney general, upon evidence of voter discrimination, was empowered to replace local registrars with federal registrars, abolish literacy tests, and register voters under simplified federal procedures. Southern counties that had previously discriminated in voting registration hurried to sign up black voters just to avoid the imposition of federal registrars. The Voting Rights Act of 1965 proved to be very effective, and Congress has voted to extend it over the years.

The Nineteenth Amendment, 1920 Following the Civil War, many of the women who had been active in the abolitionist movement to end slavery turned their attention to the condition of women in the United States. As abolitionists, they had learned to organize, conduct petition campaigns, and parade and demonstrate. Now they sought to improve the legal and political rights of women. In 1869 the Wyoming territory adopted women's suffrage; later, several other western states followed suit. But it was not until the Nineteenth Amendment was added to the U.S. Constitution in 1920 that women's right to vote in all elections was constitutionally guaranteed.

The Twenty-Sixth Amendment, 1971 The movement for eighteen-year-old voting received its original impetus during World War II. It was argued successfully in Georgia in 1944 that because eighteen-year-olds were being called upon to fight and die for their country, they deserved to have a voice in the conduct of government. However, this argument failed to convince adult voters in other states; qualifications for military service were not regarded as the same as qualifications for rational decision making in elections. In state after state, voters rejected state constitutional amendments designed to extend the vote to eighteen-year-olds.

Congress intervened on behalf of eighteen-year-old voting with the passage of the Twenty-sixth Amendment to the Constitution.[15] The states quickly ratified this amendment in 1971 during a period of national turbulence over the Vietnam War.

Many supporters of the amendment believed that protests on the campuses and streets would be reduced if youthful protesters were given the vote.

The National Voter Registration Act, 1993   The National Voter Registration Act of 1993 mandates that the states offer people the opportunity to register to vote when they apply for driver's licenses or apply for welfare services. States must also offer registration by mail, and they must accept a simplified registration form prepared by the Federal Elections Commission. Finally, it bars states from removing the names of people from registration lists for failure to vote. Turnout gains from the act, however, proved to be modest at best.[16]

WHY VOTE?

Deciding whether to cast a vote in an election is just as important as deciding which candidate to vote for. *About half of the voting-age population in the United States typically fails to vote even in presidential elections.* Voter **turnout**—the number of actual voters in relation to the number of people eligible to register and vote—is even lower in off-year congressional and state elections, when presidential elections are not held. Turnout in local elections (for example, city, county, school board) is even lower when these elections are held separately from national elections. Voter turnout in presidential elections steadily declined for several decades (see Figure 5-7). Only the three-way presidential race in 1992 temporarily reversed the downward trend. In the Clinton-Dole presidential contest in 1996, turnout fell below 50 percent for the first time in over a century. In the Bush-Gore race in 2000 turnout remained below 50 percent despite the closeness of the race.

Why vote? Usually, this question is asked in the negative: Why do so many people fail to register and vote? But greater insight into the question of voter participation can be obtained if we try to understand what motivates the people who do go to the polls.

The Rational Voter   From a purely "rational" perspective, an individual should vote only if the costs of voting (time spent in registering, informing oneself about the candidates, and going to the polls) are *less* than the expected value of having the preferred candidate win (the personal benefits gained from having one's candidate win), multiplied by the probability that one's own vote will be the deciding vote. Why vote when registering, following the political news, and getting to the polls take away time from work, family, or leisure activity? Why vote when the winner will not really change one's life for the better, or even do things much differently from what the loser would have done? Most important, why vote when the chance that one individual vote will determine who wins is very small? Thought of in this fashion, the wonder is that millions of Americans continue to vote.

The "rational" model can explain voter turnout only by adding "the intrinsic rewards of voting" to the equation. These rewards include the ethic of voting, patriotism, a sense of duty, and allegiance to democracy. People exercise their right to vote out of respect for that right rather than for any personal tangible benefit they expect to receive. They can look at the voting returns on television later in the evening, knowing they were part of an important national event. These psychological rewards do not depend on whether a single vote determines the outcome. Millions of people vote out of a sense of duty and commitment to democracy.

turnout   Number of voters who actually cast ballots in an election, as a percentage of people eligible to register and vote.

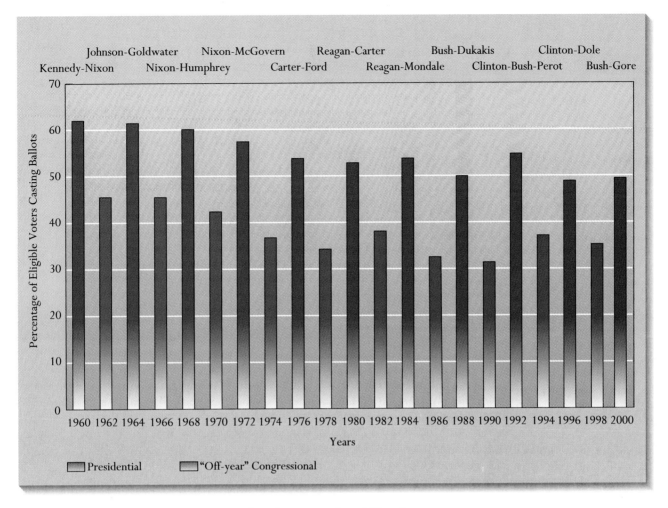

FIGURE 5-7 Voter Turnout in Presidential and Congressional Elections

Voter turnout is always higher in years with a presidential election. However, voter turnout has generally declined since 1960, even in presidential election years. The exception came in 1992, when intense interest in the contest between George Bush and Bill Clinton—spiced by the entry of independent Ross Perot—led to a higher-than-normal turnout. In 1996 fewer than half of voting-age Americans bothered to cast ballots. And despite the tightness of the Bush-Gore contest in 2000, voter turnout failed to rise above 50 percent.

The Burden of Registration   Voter **registration** is a major obstacle to voting. Not only must citizens care enough to go to the polls on election day; they must also expend time and energy, weeks before the election, to register. Registration usually occurs at a time when interest in the campaign is far from its peak. It may involve a trip to the county courthouse and a procedure more complicated than voting itself. The registration requirement reduces voter turnout significantly. Approximately 85 percent of *registered voters* turn out for a presidential election, but this figure represents only about 50 percent of the *voting-age population*. This discrepancy suggests that registration is a significant barrier to participation.

Registration is supposed to prevent fraud. Voters must identify themselves on Election Day and show they have previously registered in their districts as voters; once they have voted, their names are checked off and they cannot vote again. Registration was adopted by most states in the early twentieth century as a reform designed to reduce the fraudulent voting that was often encouraged and organized

registration Requirement that prospective voters establish their identity and place of residence prior to an election in order to be eligible to vote.

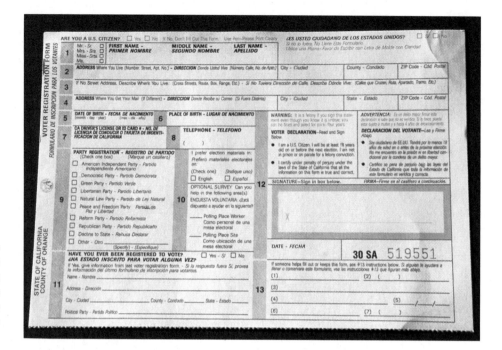

Voter registration is designed to prevent fraud but it also tends to discourage people from exercising their right to vote. Spanish language registration forms, where they are used, may ease the burden of registration for some.

by political machines. "Vote early and vote often" was the rallying cry of many party bosses, who sent their legions to the polls for repeated voting. (Registration did not end all voting fraud; some enterprising old party bosses continued to cast votes for registered persons who had died—"the tombstone vote"—or moved away.) But the trade-off for reducing fraud was to create an additional burden on the voter: registration.

THE POLITICS OF VOTER TURNOUT

Politics drives the debate over easing voter registration requirements. Democrats generally favor minimal requirements—for example, same-day registration, registration by mail, and registration at welfare and motor vehicle licensing offices. They know that nonvoters are heavily drawn from groups that typically support the Democratic Party, including the less-educated, lower-income, and minority groups. Republicans are often less enthusiastic about easing voting requirements, but it is politically embarrassing to appear to oppose increased participation. It is not surprising that the National Voter Registration Act of 1993, popularly known as the "Motor-Voter Act," was a product of a Democratic Congress and a Democratic president.

The Stimulus of Competition   The more lively the competition between parties or between candidates, the greater the interest of citizens and the larger the voter turnout. When parties and candidates compete vigorously, they make news and are given large play by the mass media. Consequently, a setting of competitive politics generates more political stimuli than does a setting with weak competition. People are also more likely to perceive that their votes count in a close contest, and thus they are more likely to cast them. Moreover, when parties or candidates are fighting in a close contest, their supporters tend to spend more time and energy campaigning and getting out the vote.

Political Alienation People who feel politics is irrelevant to their life—or who feel they cannot personally affect public affairs—are less likely to vote than people who feel they themselves can affect political outcomes and that these outcomes affect their life. Given the level of **political alienation** (two-thirds of respondents agree with the statement, "Most public officials are not really interested in the problems of people like me"),[17] it is surprising that so many people vote. Alienation is high among voters, and it is even higher among nonvoters.

Intensity Finally, as we might expect, people who feel strongly about politics and who hold strong opinions about political issues are more likely to vote than people who do not. For example, people who describe themselves as *extreme* liberals or *extreme* conservatives are more likely to vote than people who describe themselves as moderates.

Explaining Turnouts The general decline in U.S. voter turnout over the last several decades has generated a variety of explanations. This decline has occurred despite an easing of registration requirements and procedures over time. It may be a product of increasing distrust of government (see *What Do You Think?* "Can You Trust the Government?" in Chapter 1), which is related to political alienation. People who distrust the government are likely to feel they have little influence in politics. They are therefore less likely to go to the trouble of registering and voting. The focus of the media, particularly television, on corruption in government, sex scandals involving politicians, conflicts of interest, waste and inefficiency, and negative campaign advertising may add to popular feelings of alienation.

Another explanation focuses on the expansion of the electorate to include young people eighteen to twenty-one years of age. Young people do not vote in the same proportions as older people (see Figure 5-8). After the electorate was expanded by

political alienation Belief that politics is irrelevant to one's life and that one cannot personally affect public affairs.

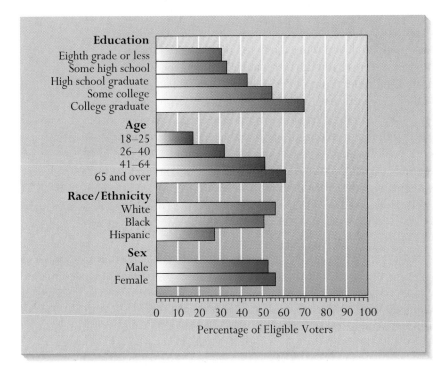

FIGURE 5-8 Voter Turnout by Social Groups

Although there is virtually no gender gap in who goes to the polls, voter turnout increases with education, age, and income. Major efforts to "get out the vote" in the African American community have raised voter turnout to nearly that of whites, but turnout among Hispanics continues to lag.

Source: U.S. Bureau of the Census, *Statistical Abstract of the United States, 1998.* Data for 1996 presidential election.

the Twenty-sixth Amendment to include persons eighteen years of age and over, voter turnout actually dropped, from 60.9 percent in the 1968 presidential election to 55.2 percent in the 1972 presidential election, the largest turnout decline in successive presidential elections.

Still another explanation focuses on the declining role of party organizations in the political system. Strong party organizations, or machines, that canvassed neighborhoods, took citizens to the courthouse to register them, contacted them personally during campaigns, and saw to it that they got to the polls on election day have largely disappeared (see Chapter 7).

Regardless of the explanations offered, it is interesting to note that most European democracies report higher voter turnout rates than the United States (see *Compared to What?* "Voter Turnout in Western Democracies").

VOTERS AND NONVOTERS

Who votes and who doesn't? The perceived benefits and costs of voting apparently do not fall evenly across all social groups. Nonvoting would generate less concern if voters were a representative cross section of nonvoters. But voters differ from nonvoters in politically important ways.

Voters are better educated than nonvoters. Education appears to be the most important determinant of voter turnout (see Figure 5-8). It may be that schooling promotes an interest in politics, instills the ethic of citizen participation, or gives people a better awareness of public affairs and an understanding of the role of elections in a democracy. Education is associated with a sense of confidence and political *efficacy*, the feeling that one can indeed have a personal impact on public affairs.

Age is another factor affecting voter participation. Perhaps because young people have more distractions, more demands on their time in school, work, or new family responsibilities, nonvoting is greatest among eighteen- to twenty-one-year-olds. In contrast, older Americans are politically influential in part because candidates know they turn out at the polls.

High-income people are more likely to vote than are low-income people. Most of this difference stems from the fact that high-income people are more likely to be well educated and older. But poor people may also feel alienated from the political system—they may lack a sense of political efficacy; they may feel they have little control over their own lives, let alone over public affairs. Or poor people may simply be so absorbed in the problems of life that they have little time or energy to spend on registering and voting.[18]

Income and education differences between participants and nonparticipants are even greater when other forms of political participation are considered. Higher-income, better-educated people are much more likely to be among those who make campaign contributions, who write or call their elected representatives, and who join and work in active political organizations.[19]

Historically, race was a major determinant of nonvoting. Black voter turnout, especially in the South, was markedly lower than white voter turnout. Black people continue today to have a slightly lower overall voter turnout than whites, but most of the remaining difference is attributable to differences between blacks and whites in educational and income levels. Blacks and whites at the same educational and income levels register and vote with the same frequency. Indeed, in cities where black people are well organized politically, black voter turnout may exceed white voter turnout.[20]

Voter Turnout in Western Democracies

Other Western democracies regularly report higher voter turnout rates than the United States (see figure). Yet in an apparent paradox, Americans seem to be more supportive of their political institutions, less alienated from their political system, and even more patriotic than citizens of Western European nations. Why, then, are voter turnouts in the United States so much lower than in these other democracies?

The answer to this question lies primarily in the legal and institutional differences between the United States and the other democracies. First of all, in Austria, Australia, Belgium, and Italy, voting is *mandatory*. Penalties and the level of enforcement vary within and across these countries. Moreover, registration laws in the United States make voting more difficult than in other countries. In Western Europe, all citizens are required to register with the government and obtain identification cards. These cards are then used for admission to the polls. In contrast, voter registration is entirely voluntary in the United States, and voters must reregister if they change residences. Nearly 50 percent of the U.S. population changes residence at least once in a five-year period, thus necessitating reregistration.

Parties in the United States are more loosely organized, less disciplined, and less able to mobilize voters than are European parties. Moreover, many elections in the United States, notably elections for Congress, are not very competitive. The United States organizes congressional elections by district with winner-take-all rules, whereas many European parliaments are selected by proportional representation, with seats allocated to parties based on national vote totals. Proportional representation means every vote counts toward seats in the legislative body. Thus greater competition and proportional representation may encourage higher voter turnout in European democracies.

But cultural differences may also contribute to differences in turnout. The American political culture, with its tradition of individualism and self-reliance and its reluctance to empower government (see Chapter 2), encourages Americans to resolve their problems through their own efforts rather than looking to government for solutions. Government is not as central to Americans as it is to Europeans, and therefore getting to the polls on election day is not seen as so important.

Voter turnout is substantially higher in most of the industrialized world than in the United States. In particular, nations such as Australia, where voting is mandatory, have very high turnouts. Ease of voter registration in most other nations also contributes to higher turnouts there.

United States
Australia*
Austria*
Belgium*
Canada
Denmark
Finland
France
Great Britain
Greece
Israel
Italy*
Japan
Netherlands
New Zealand
Norway
Portugal
Spain
Sweden
Switzerland
West Germany

0 10 20 30 40 50 60 70 80 90 100
Percentage Voting in
National Elections

* Voting is compulsory.

Source: Congressional Research Service, reported in *Congressional Quarterly Weekly Report*, April 2, 1988, p. 863.

The greatest racial disparity in voter turnout is between Hispanics and others. Low voter participation by Hispanics may be a product of language differences, lack of cultural assimilation, or noncitizenship status.

NONVOTING: WHAT DIFFERENCE DOES IT MAKE?

How concerned should we be about low levels of participation in American politics? Certainly the democratic ideal envisions an active, participating citizenry. Democratic government, asserts the Declaration of Independence, derives its "just powers from the consent of the governed." The legitimacy of democratic government can be more easily questioned when half of the people fail to vote. That is, it is easier to question whether the government truly represents "the people" when only half of the people vote even in a presidential election. Voting is an expression of good citizenship, and it reinforces attachment to the nation and to democratic government. Nonvoting suggests alienation from the political system.

However, the *right* to vote is more important to democratic government than voter turnout. The nineteenth-century English political philosopher John Stuart Mill wrote, "Men, as well as women, do not need political rights in order that they may govern, but in order that they may not be misgoverned."[21] As long as all adult Americans possess the right to vote, politicians must consider their interests. "Rulers and ruling classes are under a necessity of considering the interests of those who have the suffrage."[22] Democratic governments cannot really ignore the interests of anyone who can vote. People who have the right to vote, but who have voluntarily chosen not to exercise it in the past, can always change their minds, go to the polls, and "throw the rascals out."

Indeed, a huge army of nonvoters "hangs over the democratic process like a bomb ready to explode and change the course of history."[23] Some commentators view this latent "bomb" with alarm, but others view it as a potential resource in hard times. The last major surge in voting turnout occurred in 1932 in the midst of the Depression, when voters went to the polls in droves to oust incumbent Herbert Hoover and elect Franklin D. Roosevelt, who changed the role of government in the economy.

Voluntary nonvoting is not the same as being denied the suffrage. Politicians can indeed ignore the interests of people denied the vote by restrictive laws or practices or by intimidation or force. But when people choose not to exercise their right to vote, they may be saying that they do not believe their interests are really affected by government. The late Senator Sam Ervin is widely quoted on the topic of nonvoters:

> I'm not going to shed any crocodile tears if people don't care enough to vote. I don't believe in making it easy for apathetic lazy people. I'd be extremely happy if nobody in the United States voted except for the people who thought about the issues and made up their own minds and wanted to vote.[24]

But the class bias in voting presents another concern. It is frequently argued that greater overall turnout by better-educated, higher-income, older whites tilts the political system toward the interests of upper socioeconomic classes at the expense of poorer, less-educated, younger, black, and Hispanic people.[25] Thus the people we would expect to be most in need of government help are least represented among voters. This underrepresentation not only harms their policy interests but also contributes even further to their feelings of political alienation.

However, it is difficult to predict that major changes would occur in specific public policies if all socioeconomic groups voted with the same frequency. As we have already observed, rich and poor, black and white, often share the same opinions on policy issues or differ only in degree. The likely policy consequences of increased voter participation may be overestimated by scholars and commentators.[26]

PROTEST AS POLITICAL PARTICIPATION

Protests, marches, and demonstrations are important forms of political participation. Indeed, the First Amendment guarantees the right "peaceably to assemble, and to petition the government for a redress of grievances." A march to the steps of Congress, a demonstration in Lafayette Park across the street from the White House, a mass assembly of people on the Washington Mall with speakers, sign waving, and songs, and the presentation of petitions to government officials are all forms of participation protected by the First Amendment.

Protests **Protests** are generally designed to call attention to an issue and to motivate others to apply pressure on public officials. In fact, protests are usually directed at the news media rather than at public officials themselves. If protesters could persuade public officials directly in the fashion of lobbyists and interest groups, they would not need to protest. Protests are intended to generate attention and support among previously uncommitted people—enough so the ultimate targets of the protest, public officials, will be pressured to act to redress grievances.

Coverage by the news media, especially television, is vital to the success of protest activity. The media not only carry the protesters' message to the mass public but also inform public officials about what is taking place. Protests provide the media with "good visuals"—pictorial dramatizations of political issues. The media welcome opportunities to present political issues in a confrontational fashion because confrontation helps capture larger audiences. Thus protesters and the media use each other to advance their separate goals.

Protests are most commonly employed by groups that have little influence in electoral politics. They were a key device of the civil rights movement at a time when many African Americans were barred from voting. In the absence of protest, the majority white population—and the public officials they elected—were at best unconcerned with the plight of black people in a segregated society. Protests, including a dramatic march on Washington in 1963 at which Martin Luther King, Jr., delivered his inspirational "I Have a Dream" speech, called attention to the injustices of segregation and placed civil rights on the agenda of decision makers.

Protests can be effectively employed by groups that are relatively small in number but whose members feel very intensely about the issue. Often the protest is a means by which these groups can obtain bargaining power with decision makers. Protests may threaten to tarnish the reputations of government officials or private corporations, or may threaten to disrupt their daily activities or reduce their business through boycotts or pressure on customers. If the protest is successful, protest leaders can then offer to end the protest in exchange for concessions from their targets.

Civil Disobedience **Civil disobedience** is a form of protest that involves breaking what are perceived as "unjust" laws. The purpose is to call attention to the existence of injustice. In the words of Martin Luther King, Jr., civil disobedi-

protests Public marches or demonstrations designed to call attention to an issue and motivate others to apply pressure on public officials.

How to Run for Office

Many rewards come with elected office—the opportunity to help shape public policy, public attention and name recognition, and many business, professional, and social contacts. But there are many drawbacks as well—the absence of privacy, a microscopic review of one's past, constant calls, meetings, interviews and handshaking, and perhaps most onerous of all, the continual need to solicit campaign funds.

Before You Run—Getting Involved Get involved in various organizations in your community:

- Neighborhood associations.
- Chambers of commerce, business associations.
- Churches and synagogues (become an usher, if possible, for visibility).
- Political groups (Democratic or Republican clubs, League of Women Voters, and so on).
- Parent-Teacher Associations (PTAs).
- Service clubs (Rotary, Kiwanis, Civitan, Toastmasters).
- Recreation organizations (Little League, flag football, soccer leagues, running and walking clubs, for example, as participant, coach, or umpire).

Deciding to Run—Know What You're Doing In deciding to run, and choosing the office for which you wish to run, you should become thoroughly familiar with the issues, duties, and responsibilities.

- Attend council or commission meetings, state legislative sessions, and/or committee hearings.
- Become familiar with current issues and office-holders, and obtain a copy of and read the budget.
- Learn the demographics of your district (racial, ethnic, and age composition; occupational mix; average income; neighborhood differences). If you do not fit the prevailing racial, ethnic, or age composition, think about moving to another district.
- Memorize a brief (preferably less than seven seconds) answer to the question, "Why are you running?"

Getting in the Race Contact your county elections department to obtain the following:

- Qualifying forms and information.
- Campaign financing forms and regulations.

- District and street maps for your district.
- Recent election results in your district.
- Election-law book or pamphlet.
- Voter registration lists (usually sold as lists, or labels, or tapes).
- Contact your party's county chairperson for advice; convince the party's leaders that you can win. Ask for a list of their regular campaign contributors.

Raising Money The easiest way to finance a campaign is to be rich enough to provide your own funds. Failing that, you must:

- Establish a campaign fund, according to the laws of your state.
- Find a treasurer/campaign-finance chairperson who knows many wealthy, politically involved people.
- Invite wealthy, politically involved people to small coffees, cocktail parties, dinners; give a brief campaign speech and then have your finance chairperson solicit contributions.
- Follow up fund-raising events and meetings with personal phone calls.
- Be prepared to continue fund-raising activities throughout your campaign; file accurate financial disclosure statements as required by state law.

Getting Organized Professional campaign managers and management firms almost always outperform volunteers. If you cannot afford professional management, you must rely on yourself or trusted friends to perform the following:

- Draw up a budget based on reasonable expectations of campaign funding.
- Interview and select a professional campaign-management firm, or appoint a trusted campaign manager.
- Ask trusted friends from various clubs, activities, neighborhoods, churches, and so on, to meet and serve as a campaign committee. If your district is racially or ethnically diverse, make sure all groups are represented on your committee.
- Decide on a campaign theme; research issues important to your community; develop brief, well-articulated positions on these issues.
- Open a campaign headquarters with desks and telephones. Buy a cell phone; use call forwarding; stay in contact. Use your garage if you can't afford an office.

- Arrange to meet with newspaper editors, editorial boards, TV station executives, and political reporters. Be prepared for tough questions.

- Hire a media consultant or advertising agency, or appoint a volunteer media director who knows television, radio, and newspaper advertising.

- Arrange a press conference to announce your candidacy. Notify all media well in advance. Arrange for overflow crowd of supporters to cheer and applaud.

- Produce eyecatching, inspirational 15- or 30-second television and radio ads that present a favorable image of you and stress your campaign theme.

- Prepare and print attractive campaign brochures, signs, and bumper stickers.

- Hire a local survey-research firm to conduct telephone surveys of voters in your district, asking what they think are the most important issues, how they stand on them, whether they recognize your name and your theme, and how they plan to vote. Be prepared to change your theme and your position on issues if surveys show strong opposition to your views.

On the Campaign Trail   Campaigns themselves may be primarily *media centered* or primarily *door-to-door* ("retail") or some combination of both.

- Buy media time as early as possible from television and radio stations; insist on prime-time slots before, during, and after popular shows.

- Buy newspaper ads; insist on their placement in popular, well-read sections of the paper.

- Attend every community gathering possible, just to be seen, even if you do not give a speech. Keep all speeches short. Focus on one or two issues that your polls show are important to voters.

- Recruit paid or unpaid volunteers to hand out literature door-to-door. Record names and addresses of voters who say they support you.

- Canvass door-to-door with a brief (seven-second) self-introduction and statement of your reasons for running. Use registration lists to identify members of your own party, and try to address them by name. Also canvass offices, factories, coffee shops, shopping malls—anywhere you find a crowd.

- Organize a phone bank, either professional or volunteer. Prepare *brief* introduction and phone statements. Record names of people who say they support you.

- Know your opponent: Research his or her past affiliations, indiscretions if any, previous voting record, and public positions on issues.

- Be prepared to "define" your opponent in negative terms. Negative advertising works. But be fair: Base your comments on your opponent's public record. Emphasize his or her positions that clearly deviate from your district voters' known preferences.

Primary versus General Elections   Remember that you will usually have to campaign in two elections—your party's primary and the general election.

- Before the primary, identify potential opposition in your own party, try to dissuade them from running.

- Allocate your budget first to win the primary election. If you lose the primary, you won't need any funds for the general election.

- In general elections, you must broaden your appeal without distancing your own party supporters. Deemphasize your party affiliation unless your district regularly elects members of your party. In a close district or a district that regularly votes for the opposition party, stress your independence and your commitment to the *district's* interests.

On Election Day   Turning out your voters is the key to success. Election day is the busiest day of the campaign for you and your staff.

- Use your phone bank to place as many calls as possible to party members in your district (especially those who have indicated in previous calls and visits that they support you). Remind them to vote; make sure your phone workers can tell each voter where to go to cast his or her vote.

- Solicit volunteers to drive people to the polls.

- Assign workers to as many polling places as possible. Most state laws require that they stay a specified distance from the voting booths. But they should be in evidence with your signs and literature to buttonhole voters before they go into the booths.

- Show up at city or county election office on election night with prepared victory statement thanking supporters and pledging your service to the district. (Also draft a courteous concession statement pledging your support to the winner, in case you lose.)

- Attend victory party with your supporters; meet many "new" friends.

Cruelty or violence directed at peaceful protesters further dramatizes their cause. In Jackson, Mississippi in 1963, segregationists poured mustard, ketchup, and sugar over lunch counter sit-in protesters. But far more serious violence, including murder, was perpetrated against civil rights protesters in the 1960's.

ence "seeks so to dramatize the issue that it can no longer be ignored"[27] (see *A Conflicting View:* "Sometimes It's Right to Disobey the Law" in Chapter 1). Those truly engaging in civil disobedience do not attempt to evade punishment for breaking the law but instead willingly accept the penalty. By doing so, they demonstrate not only their sincerity and commitment but also the injustice of the law. Cruelty or violence directed at the protesters by police or others contributes further to the drama of injustice. Like other protest activity, the success of civil disobedience depends on the willingness of the mass media to carry the message to both the general public and the political leadership.

Violence   Violence can also be a form of political participation. Indeed, political violence—for example, assassinations, rioting, burning, looting—has been uncomfortably frequent in American politics over the years (see *A Conflicting View:* "American Politics as Violence" in Chapter 1). It is important to distinguish violence from protest. Peaceful protest is constitutionally protected. Often, organized protest activity harnesses frustrations and hostilities, directs them into constitutionally acceptable activities, and thus avoids violence. Likewise, civil disobedience should be distinguished from violence. Civil disobedience breaks only "unjust" laws, without violence, and willingly accepts punishment without trying to escape.

Effectiveness   How effective are protests? Protests can be effective in achieving some goals under some conditions. But protests are useless or even counterproductive in pursuit of other goals under other conditions. Here are some generalizations about the effectiveness of protests:

- Protests are more likely to be effective when directed at specific problems or laws rather than at general conditions that cannot readily be remedied by governmental action.

civil disobedience   Form of public protest involving the breaking of laws believed to be unjust.

Twenty-First Century Directions

Public opinion and political participation are highly praised in democratic societies. Over time major concerns of the American public are addressed by politicians, and changes in public opinion work their way into public policy. The *opportunity* to participate in politics gives legitimacy to democratic government, whether people choose to directly participate or not.

⬇ *Political Participation* Voter participation is likely to remain at or below 50 percent of the eligible population for the foreseeable future. Good economic times and the absence of a major war allow people to turn their attention to personal and family concerns and away from government and public affairs. Fewer people participate in protests and demonstrations, and fewer people make campaign contributions (even while larger contributions push up overall campaign spending). Fewer well-qualified Americans will choose to run for public office. Only a major national crisis would bring people back to the voting booth, or encourage a new wave of marches and demonstrations, or inspire the best-qualified people to get into the political arena.

⬆ *Polling and Opinion Making* Public-opinion polling and efforts to sway public opinion will continue to intensify. Survey research will become more and more sophisticated, for example, by better identifying people most likely to vote and most likely to contribute money. Politicians will place ever greater reliance on what pollsters tell them. Efforts to sway opinion will also become more sophisticated and more costly. We can expect to see more and better political advertising by candidates, officeholders, parties, and interest groups, in every medium from television to the Internet.

◀▶ *2020, Better or Worse?* Most Americans are generally optimistic about future. They believe that the quality of life in 2020 will be "better" (60 percent) rather than worse (36 percent). However, when asked their opinion about the future direction of *specific* conditions in country, the results are mixed.

Q. *Thinking about the future of the country, by the year 2020 do you think the country's _____ is/are more likely to get better or worse?*

	Better	Worse
Race relations	66%	30%
Quality of medical care	54	43
Environment	42	55
Moral Values	34	62

Americans are more concerned about a continuing decline in moral values than in any other problem confronting their country.

Source: Harris Poll, reported in *The Polling Report*, January 11, 1999.

- Protests are more likely to be effective when targeted toward public officials who are capable of granting the desired concession or resolving the specific problem. Protests with no specific targets and protests directed at officials who have no power to change things are generally unproductive.
- Protests are more likely to succeed when the goal is limited to gaining access or representation in decision making or to placing an issue on the agenda of decision makers.
- Protests are not always effective in actually getting laws changed and are even less effective in ensuring that the impact of the changes will really improve the conditions that led to the protest.

Public officials can defuse protest activity in a variety of ways. They may greet protesters with smiles and reassurances that they agree with their goals. They may disperse symbolic satisfaction without any tangible results. They may grant token concessions with great publicity, perhaps remedying a specific case of injustice while doing little to affect general conditions. Or public officials may claim to be constrained either legally or financially from doing anything—the "I-would-like-to-help-you-but-I-can't" strategy. Or public officials can directly confront the protesters by charging that they are unrepresentative of the groups they are trying to help.

Perhaps the most challenging and sometimes the most effective kind of protest is to run for public office (see *Up Close:* "How to Run for Office"). Whether at the local level, such as the school board, or at the state or national level, the participation of one individual as a candidate—even when not elected—can make a difference in public affairs.

SUMMARY NOTES

- Public opinion commands the attention of elected public officials in a democracy, yet many Americans are poorly informed and unconcerned about politics; their opinions on public issues are often changeable and inconsistent. Only a few highly salient issues generate strong and stable opinions.

- Political socialization—the learning of political values, beliefs, and opinions—starts at an early age. It is influenced by family, school, church, age group, and the media.

- Ideology also shapes opinion, especially among politically interested and active people who employ fairly consistent liberal or conservative ideas in forming their opinions on specific issues.

- Race and gender also influence public opinion. Blacks and whites differ over the extent of discrimination in the United States, as well as over its causes and remedies. Men and women tend to differ over issues involving the use of force. In recent years, women have tended to give greater support to the Democratic Party than men have.

- Individuals can exercise power in a democratic political system in a variety of ways. They can run for public office, take part in demonstrations and protests, make financial contributions to candidates, attend political events, write letters to newspapers or public officials, belong to political organizations, vote in elections, or simply hold and express opinions on public issues.

- Securing the right to vote for all Americans required nearly 200 years of political struggle. Key victories

included the elimination of property qualifications by 1840, the Fifteenth Amendment in 1870 (eliminating restrictions based on race), the Nineteenth Amendment in 1920 (eliminating restrictions based on gender), the Civil Rights Act of 1964 and Voting Rights Act of 1965 (eliminating racial obstacles), the Twenty-fourth Amendment in 1964 (eliminating poll taxes), and the Twenty-sixth Amendment in 1971 (extending the right to vote to eighteen-year-olds).

- About half of the voting-age population fails to vote even in presidential elections. Voter turnout has steadily declined in recent decades. Voter registration is a major obstacle to voting. Turnout is affected by competition as well as by feelings of political alienation and distrust of government. Young people have the poorest record of voter turnout of any age group.

- Voluntary nonvoting is not as serious a threat to democracy as denial of the right to vote. Nevertheless, the class bias in voting may tilt the political system toward the interests of higher-income, better-educated, older whites at the expense of lower-income, less-educated, younger minorities.

- Protest is an important form of participation in politics. Protests are more commonly employed by groups with little direct influence over public officials. The object is to generate attention and support from previously uncommitted people in order to bring new pressure on public officials to redress grievances. Media coverage is vital to the success of protests.

KEY TERMS

SELECTED READINGS

ASHER, HERBERT. *Polling and the Public: What Every Citizen Should Know.* 4th ed. Washington, D.C.: Congressional Quarterly Press, 1998. Explains methods of polling and how results can be influenced by wording, sampling, and interviewing techniques; also covers how polls are used by the media and in campaigns.

BARKER, LUCIUS J., MACK H. JONES, and KATHERINE TATE, *African Americans and the American Political System.* 4th ed. Englewood Cliffs, N.J.: Prentice Hall, 1998. An overview of African American political participation and the responsiveness of the presidency, Congress, courts, parties, and interest groups.

CONWAY, M. MARGARET. *Political Participation in the United States.* 2nd ed. Washington, D.C.: Congressional Quarterly Press, 1991. A comprehensive summary of who participates in politics and why.

CONWAY, M. MARGARET, GERTRUDE A. STEVERNAGEL, and DAVID AHERN. *Women and Political Participation.* Washington, D.C.: Congressional Quarterly Press, 1997. An examination of cultural change and women's participation in politics, including treatment of the gender gap in political attitudes and the impact of women's membership in the political elite.

ERIKSON, ROBERT S., and KENT L. TEDIN. *American Public Opinion.* 5th ed. Needham, Mass.: Allyn and Bacon, 1995. A comprehensive review of the forces influencing public opinion and an assessment of the influence of public opinion in American politics.

GREENSTEIN, FRED I. *Children and Politics.* New Haven, Conn.: Yale University Press, 1985. Early research on what children know about politics and how they learned it.

PAGE, BENJAMIN I., and ROBERT Y. SHAPIRO. *The Rational Public: Fifty Years of Trends in Americans' Policy Preferences.* Chicago: University of Chicago Press, 1992. An argument that government policies generally reflect public opinion.

STIMSON, JAMES A. *Public Opinion in America: Moods, Cycles, and Swings.* 2nd ed. Boulder, Colo.: Westview Press, 1998. A systematic analysis of swings and cycles in "policy moods" that roughly correspond to liberal and conservative views concerning the effectiveness of government in dealing with perceived problems.

WALD, KENNETH D. *Religion and Politics in the United States.* 3rd ed. Washington, D.C.: Congressional Quarterly Press, 1996. An explanation of the impact of religion on American political culture, the policy process, and voting behavior.

WALTON, HANES, and ROBERT C. SMITH. *African American Politics.* New York: Longman, 2000. A comprehensive American government textbook emphasizing the diversity of African American opinions and behavior.

ZALLER, JOHN R. *The Nature and Origins of Mass Opinion.* New York: Cambridge University Press, 1992. An effort to develop and test a conceptual model of how people form political preferences, how political views and arguments diffuse through the population, and how people evaluate this information and convert their reactions into public opinion.

Mass Media
Setting the Political Agenda

ASK YOURSELF ABOUT POLITICS

1 Are media professionals—
news reporters, editors,
anchors—the true voice of
the people in public affairs?
Yes ⬤   No ⬤

2 Do the media mirror what
is really news, rather than
deciding themselves
what's important and then
making it news?
Yes ⬤   No ⬤

3 Is television your most
important source of news?
Yes ⬤   No ⬤

4 Should the media report on
all aspects of the private
lives of public officials?
Yes ⬤   No ⬤

5 Do the media report
equally fairly on Democratic
and Republican candidates
for office?
Yes ⬤   No ⬤

6 Should the media be legally
required to be fair and
accurate in reporting political news?
Yes ⬤   No ⬤

7 Are you more alienated than
attracted by the media's
coverage of politics?
Yes ⬤   No ⬤

8 Is your choice of candidates in elections affected
by their advertising?
Yes ⬤   No ⬤

THE POWER OF THE MEDIA

Politics—the struggle over who gets what, when, and how—is largely carried out in the **mass media**. The arenas of political conflict are the various media of mass communication—television, newspapers, magazines, radio, books, recordings, motion pictures, the Internet (see *Up Close: "Media* Is a Plural Noun"). What we know about politics comes to us largely through these media. Unless we ourselves are admitted to the White House Oval Office or the committee rooms of Congress or dinner parties at foreign embassies, or unless we ourselves attend political rallies and demonstrations or travel to distant battlefields, we must rely on the mass media to tell us about politics. Furthermore, few of us ever have the opportunity to personally evaluate the character of presidential candidates or cabinet members or members of Congress, or to learn their views on public issues by talking with them face to face. Instead, we must learn about people as well as events from the mass media.

Great power derives from the control of information. *Who knows what* helps to determine *who gets what*. The media not only provide an arena for politics; they are themselves players in that arena. The media not only report on the struggles for power in society; they are themselves participants in those struggles. The media have long been referred to as America's "fourth branch" of government—and for good reason.

National News Media   Media power is concentrated in the leading television networks (ABC, CBS, NBC, Fox, and CNN), the nation's leading newspapers (*New York Times, Washington Post,*

Ask yourself how much of your knowledge about politics in America comes from television and newspapers and the radio. What you know about politics and how you participate are, in fact, largely determined by the power of the media to decide what they want you to know.

Wall Street Journal), and broad-circulation newsmagazines (*Newsweek*, *Time*, and *U.S. News and World Report*) (see Figure 6-1). The reporters, anchors, editors, and producers of these prestige news organizations constitute a relatively small group of people in whose hands rests the power to decide what we will know about people, events, and issues.

The Power of Television Television is the most powerful medium of communication. It is the first true *mass* communication medium. Virtually every home in the United States has a television set, and the average home has the set turned on for about seven hours a day. Television is regularly chosen over other news media by Americans as "the believable" news source (see Figure 6-2). The national network evening news shows (*NBC Nightly News*, *ABC World News Tonight*, *CBS Evening News*) have lost viewship in recent years (down from a combined average of 40 million in 1980 to 28 million today). But viewship of cable CNN and its headline companion HNN has risen, and viewship of local television news has remained strong. Indeed, today more people watch local news than national network news. Television weekly news and magazines, notably CBS's *60 Minutes* and ABC's *20/20*, are regularly listed among the most popular shows on television; and television "tabloids" (such as *Hardcopy* and *Inside Edition*) are also gaining viewers. The power of television derives not only from its large audiences but also from its ability to communicate emotions as well as information. Television's power is found in its visuals—angry faces in a rioting mob, police beating an African American motorist, wounded soldiers being unloaded from a helicopter—scenes that convey an emotional message. Moreover, television focuses on the faces of individuals as well as on their words, portraying honesty or deception, humility or arrogance, compassion or indifference, humor or meanness, and a host of other personal characteristics. Skillful politicians understand that *what* one says may not be as important as *how* one says it. Image triumphs over substance on television.

The Myth of the Mirror Media people themselves often deny that they exercise great power. They sometimes claim that they only "mirror" reality. They like

mass media All means of communication with the general public, including television, newspapers, magazines, radio, books, recordings, motion pictures, and the Internet.

FIGURE 6-1 The National News Media

A handful of media outlets in the United States serve as the major sources of news information for the American public. Television is by far the most influential source today, with most Americans getting their news primarily from TV. The growth of cable television in recent years has accelerated this trend, with CNN becoming the "crisis network," the place to turn to see a war, an earthquake, or any other major event.

Source: Television viewers reported by A. C. Nielsen and Company for 1996; newspaper circulation for 1997 as reported by Newspaper Association of America Information Resource Center; magazine circulation as reported by Magazine Publishers of America.

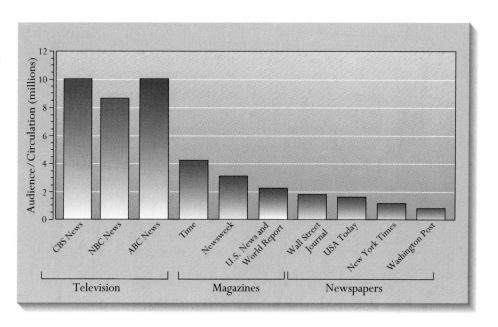

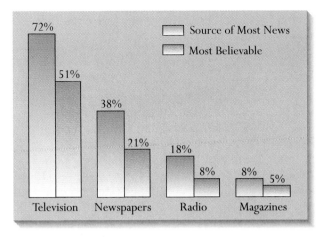

FIGURE 6-2 Where Americans Get Their News

Questions: First, I'd like to ask you where you usually get most of your news about what's going on in the world today—from the newspapers, or radio, or television, or magazines, or talking to people, or where?

If you got conflicting or different reports of the same news story from radio, television, the magazines, and the newspapers, which of the four versions would you be most inclined to believe—the one on radio or television or magazines or newspapers?

Note: Percentages (for sources of news) add up to 125 percent due to multiple responses. For trend line on these questions, see Harold W. Stanley and Richard G. Niemi, *Vital Statistics on American Politics, 1999–2000* (Washington, D.C.: Congressional Quarterly Press 1999). Between 1962 and 1964, television passed newspapers as a source of most news Between 1958 and 1960, television passed newspapers as the most believable medium.

to think of themselves as unbiased reporters who simply narrate happenings and transmit videotaped portrayals of people and events as they really are. Occasionally, editors or reporters or anchors will acknowledge that they make important decisions about what stories, people, events, or issues will be covered in the news, how much time or space they will be given, what visuals will be used, and what sources will be quoted. They may also occasionally acknowledge that they provide interpretations of the news and that their personal politics affect these interpretations. A few media people may even recognize that they can set the agenda for political decision making by focusing special attention on particular issues. But whether or not the editors, reporters, producers, or anchors acknowledge their own power, it is clear that they do more than passively mirror reality.

SOURCES OF MEDIA POWER

Government and the media are natural adversaries. (Thomas Jefferson once wrote that he would prefer newspapers without government to a government without newspapers. But after serving as president, he wrote that people who never read newspapers are better informed than those who do, because ignorance is closer to the truth than the falsehoods spread by newspapers.) Public officials have long been frustrated by the media. But the U.S. Constitution's First Amendment guarantee of a free press anticipates this conflict between government and the media. It prohibits government from resolving this conflict by silencing its critics.

Media professionals—television and newspaper reporters, editors, anchors, and producers—are not neutral observers of American politics but rather are active

Media Is a Plural Noun

For most of us, politics is a *mediated* experience. What we know about our political world comes to us not from personal experience but through the mass media. We can broaden our political knowledge by regularly monitoring all types of media.

Television   For many years, national television was dominated by three networks: American Broadcasting Company (ABC), Columbia Broadcasting System (CBS), and National Broadcasting Company (NBC). As late as 1970, they captured more than 90 percent of the television audiences; today they capture only about half. Technological developments, notably cable television and satellite broadcasting, destroyed the comfortable oligopoly of ABC, CBS, and NBC.

Today, more than two-thirds of the nation's homes have cable TV. Cable News Network (CNN), begun by independent entrepreneur Ted Turner, and its half-hourly Headline News, and MSNBC are major competitors in news broadcasting, with their around-the-clock coverage. C-SPAN regularly broadcasts congressional proceedings and other Washington events. Other cable channels offer viewers a wide choice of sports broadcasting (ESPN), music (MTV), court trials (Court TV), satellite "superstations" (Ted Turner's TNT), and pay television (HBO and Showtime).

Radio   The nation's 10,000 radio stations are about evenly divided between AM and FM band broadcasting. Most programming features music, but *talk radio* is growing in both listeners and political importance. Talk-show hosts take telephone calls that often signal popular concerns and emotions. Often the hosts themselves are highly opinionated (for example, conservative Rush Limbaugh) and enjoy a national following.

Newspapers   More than 70 percent of the adult population read one or another of the nation's 1,500 daily newspapers. The nation's *prestige* newspapers— the *New York Times*, *Washington Post*, and *Wall Street Journal*—are regularly read by government officials, corporate chiefs, interest-group leaders, and other media people.

Magazines   The leading weekly newsmagazines— *Time* (4.1 million), *Newsweek* (3.2 million), and *U.S. News and World Report* (2.3 million)—reach a smaller but more politically attentive audience than do newspapers. Magazines of political commentary—for example, the *Nation* (liberal), *New Republic* (liberal), *National Review* (conservative), *American Spectator* (conservative), *Public Interest* (neo-conservative), and *Washington Monthly* (neo-liberal, anti-establishment)— reach very small but politically active audiences. The newer *George*, founded by the late John F. Kennedy, Jr., offers light, breezy, people-oriented coverage of current politics.

Motion Pictures   Most of the 250 or so feature films produced and distributed in the United States each year are commercial ventures designed to attract theater-going (younger) audiences. Controversy over the effects of the sex and violence shown on the screen are almost as old as the movie industry itself. A system of industry self-regulation, with its *G*, *PG*, *R*, and *NC-17* (formerly *X*) ratings, was designed to deflect criticism and avoid government intervention.

A generation ago, the movie industry generally avoided movies with a social or political "message." As one wit at a major studio quipped, "If I want to send a message, I use Western Union." But independent producers broke the major studio monopoly, and today Hollywood regularly produces movies with liberal social and political themes.

Books and Recordings   About half of all Americans claim to have read a book in the past year. About half of the 62,000 books published each year are textbooks for elementary or secondary schools or colleges and universities. Most of the trade books marketed in shopping mall bookstores across the country have little political content. However, a few books each year capture the attention of politically minded readers and help shape debate among opinion leaders.

Most of the one billion recordings (tapes, CDs, etc.) sold each year, mainly to young people, feature romantic themes. But some popular recordings incorporate a political message. Folk music has a tradition of social protest; rap music often voices racial

The White House home page on the World Wide Web.

concerns; country music often reflects populist and patriotic themes.

The Internet   The newest of the media now in play in politics is the Internet. Its use is recent enough that formal studies of its effectiveness are just beginning. But people in public life—from the president, to members of Congress, to interest groups, to local party organizers—have taken advantage of its presence to establish Web home pages and bulletin boards, and all the major online services have chat groups for political exchange. Several large media companies have ventured onto the Internet with Web sites including ABC (www.abcnews.go.com), CNN (www.cnn.com), *Newsweek* (www.newsweek.com), *USA Today* (www.usatoday.com), and the Associated Press (www.newsday.com).

Source: U.S. Bureau of the Census, *Statistical Abstract of the United States, 1998*, Section 18.

Politicians have a love-hate relationship with the media. They crave the recognition and celebrity that the media can confer on them, but they also fear attack from the media.

participants. They not only report events but also discover events to report, assign them political meaning, and predict their consequences (see *People in Politics:* "Stars of the Network News: Rather, Jennings, and Brokaw"). They seek to challenge government officials, debate political candidates, and define the problems of society. They see their profession as a "sacred trust" and themselves as the true voice of the people in public affairs.

Newsmaking Deciding what is "news" and who is "newsworthy"—**newsmaking**—is the most important source of media power. It is only through the media that the general public comes to know about events, personalities, and issues. Media attention makes topics public, creates issues, and elevates personalities from obscurity to celebrity. Each day, editors, producers, and reporters must select from millions of events, topics, and people those that will be videotaped, written about, and talked about. The media can never be a "picture of the world" because the whole world cannot be squeezed into the picture. The media must decide what is and is not "news."

Decisions about what will be news both influence popular discussion and cue public officials about topics they must turn their attention to. Politicians cannot respond to reporters' questions by saying, "I don't know," or "That's not important," or "No comment." Media attention to a topic requires public officials to respond to it. Moreover, the media decide how important an issue or person or event is by their allocation of time and space. Topics given early placement on the newscast and several minutes of airtime or that receive front-page newspaper coverage with headlines and pictures are believed to be important by viewers and readers.

Politicians have a love-hate relationship with the media. They need media attention to promote themselves, their message, and their programs. They crave the exposure, the name recognition, and the celebrity status that the media can confer. At the same time, they fear attack by the media. They know the media are active players in the political game, not just passive spectators. The media seek sensational stories of sin, sexuality, corruption, and scandal in government to

newsmaking Deciding what events, topics, presentations, and issues will be given coverage in the news.

Stars of the Network News: Rather, Jennings, and Brokaw

From left to right: Network news anchors Peter Jennings, Tom Brokaw, and Dan Rather.

Television news strives for credibility. Anchors are chosen not only for their personal appearance but also for the credibility they can lend to the news. The recognized all-time champion of credibility was CBS's Walter Cronkite, who for many years was "the most trusted man in America," according to all of the national polls.

Each night about 28 million Americans watch one of three men: Dan Rather, Peter Jennings, or Tom Brokaw. No other individuals—not presidents, movie stars, or popes—have had such extensive contact with so many people. These network celebrities are recognized and heard by more people than anyone else on the planet. The networks demand that an anchor be the network's premier journalist, principal showman, top editor, star, symbol of news excellence, and single most important living logo.

Anchors, then, are both celebrities and newspeople. They are chosen for their mass appeal, but they must also bring journalistic expertise to their jobs. The anchors help select from thousands of hours of videotapes and hundreds of separate stories that will be squeezed into the twenty-two minutes of nightly network news (eight minutes are reserved for commercials). Each minute represents approximately 160 spoken words; the total number of words on the entire newscast is less than found on a single news-

paper page. These inherent restrictions of the medium give great power to the anchors and their executive producers through their selection of what Americans will see and hear about the world each night.

All three network anchors are middle-aged, Anglo-Saxon, male Protestants. All share liberal and reformist social values and political beliefs.

Dan Rather, who deliberately projects an image of emotional intensity, has created both strong attachments and heated animosities among his audiences. He is most despised by conservatives because of his undisguised and passionate liberal views. Rather worked his way up through the ranks of CBS news following graduation from Sam Houston State College. He was a reporter and news director for the CBS affiliate station in Houston, then chief of the CBS London Bureau, and later Vietnam correspondent. He came to national prominence in 1966 as a CBS White House correspondent and took over the anchor position from Walter Cronkite in 1981.

The Canadian-born Peter Jennings projects an image of thoughtful, urbane sophistication. He is widely traveled (his father was a journalist), but his formal education ended in the tenth grade. ABC's *World News Tonight with Peter Jennings* devotes slightly more time to international news than do its rival news shows.

Tom Brokaw offers a calm, unemotional delivery with occasional touches of wry humor. Brokaw graduated from the University of South Dakota and started his career at an Omaha television station. He anchored local news in Atlanta and Los Angeles before moving up to the post of NBC White House correspondent in 1973. He hosted the NBC *Today* show from 1976 to 1982, and his show biz and talk-show-host experience has served him well as anchor of the *NBC Nightly News* since then. He is less ideological than Rather or Jennings and can appear relaxed and friendly with Republicans as well as Democrats.

The ratings race among the anchors is very close. Indeed, the closeness of those ratings may be driving the shows toward even more sensational themes, violent confrontations, and dramatic hype. Although all current shows have commentators, they are used less often; and it is now almost mandatory to end the show with a crowd-pleasing human interest story.

Groups hoping for free media coverage of their cause can improve their chances by framing their protests in dramatic form. Here, members of an animal-rights group attract the press by getting arrested during a protest against the fur industry, in which they painted themselves with red paint and wore leghold traps.

attract viewers and readers, and thus the media pose a constant danger to politicians. Politicians understand the power of the media to make or break their careers.

Agenda Setting   **Agenda setting** is the power to decide what will be decided. It is the power to define society's "problems," to create political issues, and to set forth alternative solutions. Deciding which issues will be addressed by government may be even more important than deciding how the issues will be resolved. The distinguished political scientist E.E. Schattschneider once wrote, "He who determines what politics is about runs the country."[1]

The real power of the media lies in their ability to set the political agenda for the nation. This power grows out of their ability to decide what is news. Media coverage determines what both citizens and public officials regard as "crises" or "problems" or "issues" to be resolved. Conditions ignored by the media seldom get on the agenda of political leaders. Media attention forces public officials to speak on the topic, take positions, and respond to questions. Media inattention allows problems to be ignored by government. "TV is the Great Legitimator. TV confers reality. Nothing happens in America, practically everyone seems to agree, until it happens on television."[2]

Political issues do not just "happen." The media are crucial to their development. Organized interest groups, professional public relations firms, government bureaucracies, political candidates, and elected officials all try to solicit the assistance of the media in shaping the political agenda. Creating an issue, publicizing it, dramatizing it, turning it into a "crisis," getting people to talk about it, and ultimately forcing government to do something about it, are the tactics of agenda setting. The participation of the mass media is vital to their success.[3]

Interpreting   The media not only decide what will be news, they also interpret the news for us. Editors, reporters, and anchors provide each story with an *angle*, an interpretation that places the story in a context and speculates about its meaning and consequences. The interpretation tells us what to think about the news.

News is presented in "stories." Reporters do not report facts; they tell stories. The story structure gives meaning to various pieces of information. Some common angles or themes of news stories are these:

- *Good guys versus bad guys:* for example, corrupt officials, foreign dictators, corporate polluters, and other assorted villains versus honest citizens, exploited workers, endangered children, or other innocents.
- *Little guys versus big guys:* for example, big corporations, the military, or insensitive bureaucracies versus consumers, taxpayers, poor people, or the elderly.
- *Appearance versus reality:* for example, the public statements of government officials or corporate executives versus whatever contradicting facts hardworking investigative reporters can find.

News is also "pictures." A story without visuals is not likely to be selected as television news in the first place. The use of visuals reinforces the angle. A close-up shot can reveal hostility, insincerity, or anxiety on the face of villains or can show fear, concern, sincerity, or compassion on the face of innocents. To emphasize elements of a story, an editor can stop the action, use slow motion, zoom the

agenda setting   Deciding what will be decided; defining the problems and issues to be addressed by decision makers.

lens, add graphics, cut back and forth between antagonists, cut away for audience reaction, and so on. Videotaped interviews can be spliced to make the interviewees appear knowledgeable, informed, and sincere or, alternatively, ignorant, insensitive, and mean-spirited. The media jealously guard the right to edit interviews themselves, rejecting virtually all attempts by interviewees to review and edit their own interviews.

Socializing   The media have power to socialize audiences to the political culture. News, entertainment, and advertising all contribute to **socialization**—to the learning of political values. Socialization through television and motion pictures begins in early childhood and continues throughout life. Most of the political information people learn comes to them through television— specific facts as well as general values. Election coverage, for example, shows "how democracy works," encourages political participation, and legitimizes the winner's control of government. Advertising shows Americans desirable middle-class standards of living even while it encourages people to buy automobiles, detergent, and beer, and entertainment programming socializes them to "acceptable" ways of life. Political values such as racial tolerance, sexual equality, and support for law enforcement are reinforced in movies, situation comedies, and police shows. Realistic "docudramas" seize on specific political themes, from abortion, to homosexuality, to drug use, to child abuse, to AIDS. Entertainment news programming such as the highly popular *60 Minutes* is now regular prime-time fare. Thirty years ago, movies and television avoided political controversy. Today they thrive on it.

Persuading   The media, in both paid advertising and news and entertainment programming, engage in direct efforts to change our attitudes, opinions, and behavior. Newspaper editorials have traditionally been employed for direct persuasion. A great deal of the political commentary on television news and interview programs is aimed at persuading people to adopt the views of the commentators. Even many entertainment programs and movies are intended to promote specific political viewpoints. But most direct persuasion efforts come to us through paid advertising.

Corporations may use their advertising dollars not only to promote sales of their product but also to convey the message that they are good citizens—sensitive to the environment, concerned with worker and consumer safety, devoted to providing more and better jobs, goods, and services to America.

Political campaigning is now largely a media battle, with paid political advertisements as the weapons. Candidates rely on professional campaign-management firms, with their pollsters, public relations specialists, advertising-production people, and media consultants, to carry on the fight.

Governments and political leaders must rely on persuasion through the mass media to carry out their programs. Presidents can take their message directly to people in televised speeches, news conferences, and the yearly State of the Union message. Presidents by custom are accorded television time whenever they request it. In this way, they can go over the heads of Congress and even the media executives and reporters themselves to communicate directly with the people.

In short, persuasion is central to politics, and the media are the key to persuasion.

socialization   The learning of a culture and its values.

"Bad news" is far more likely to be seen on television than "good news." The 1999 shooting at Columbine High School in Colorado was one of the most widely covered news stories of the year.

THE POLITICS OF THE MEDIA

The politics of the media are shaped by (1) their *economic interest*, (2) their *professional environment*, and (3) their *ideological leanings*. The economic interests of the media are primarily to attract and hold readers and viewers. Over one-quarter of all prime-time television (8–11 P.M.) is devoted to commercial advertising. Americans get more than one minute of commercials for every three minutes of news and entertainment. Television networks and commercial stations charge advertisers on the basis of audience estimates made by the rating services. One rating service, A. C. Nielsen and Company, places electronic boxes in a national sample of television homes and calculates the proportion of these homes that watch a program (the rating), as well as the proportion of homes with their sets turned on that watch a particular program (the share). Newspapers' advertising revenue is based primarily on circulation figures. In short, the business of the media is to gather mass audiences to sell to advertisers.

Sensationalism The economic interest of the media—the need to capture and hold audience attention—creates a bias toward "hype" in the selection of news, its presentation, and its interpretation. To attract viewers and readers, the media bias the news toward violence, conflict, scandal, corruption, sex, scares of various sorts, and the personal lives of politicians and celebrities. News is selected primarily for its emotional impact on audiences; its social, economic, or political significance is secondary to the need to capture attention.

News must "touch" audiences personally, arouse emotions, and hold the interest of people with short attention spans. Scare stories—street crime, drug use, AIDS, nuclear power plant accidents, global warming, and a host of health alarms—make "good" news, for they cause viewers to fear for their personal safety (see *Up Close:* What the Public Watches On the News). The sex lives of politicians, once by custom off-limits to the press, are now public "affairs." Scandal and corruption among politicians, as well as selfishness and greed among business executives, are regular media themes.

Negativism The media are biased toward bad news. Bad news attracts larger audiences than good news. Television news displays a pervasive bias toward the negative in American life—in government, business, the military, politics, education, and everywhere else. Bad-news stories on television outnumber good-news stories by at least 3 to 1.[4]

Good news gets little attention. For example, television news watchers are not likely to know that illegal drug use is declining in the United States; that both the air and water are measurably cleaner today than in past decades; that the nuclear power industry has the best safety record of any major industry in the United States; and that the aged in America are wealthier and enjoy higher incomes than the nonaged. Television has generally failed to report these stories or, even worse, has implied that the opposite is true.[5] Good news—stories about improved health statistics, longer life spans, better safety records, higher educational levels, for example—seldom provides the dramatic element needed to capture audience attention. The result is an overwhelming bad-news bias, especially on television.

muckraking Journalistic exposés of corruption, wrong-doing, or mismanagement in government, business, and other institutions of society.

Muckraking The professional environment of reporters and editors predisposes them toward an activist style of journalism once dubbed **muckraking**. Reporters today view themselves as "watchdogs" of the public trust. They see themselves in

What the Public Watches on the News

Public pays relatively little attention to politics when they watch the news. The most closely watched stories are those dealing with disasters of various sorts. In the past fifteen years, only news about the Gulf War in 1991–92 and the outcome of the 1996 presidential election was followed "very closely" by even half of the American people. The explosion of the Space Shuttle Challenger was the single most watched news story.

The ordering of responses of the American public to the question of what stories were followed "very closely" is listed as follows:

Percent Followed Very Closely

- Explosion of the Space Shuttle Challenger (July 86)   80%
- Destruction Caused by the San Francisco Earthquake (Nov 89)   73%
- Verdict in Rodney King Case and Following Riots and Disturbances (May 92)   70%
- The Crash of a Paris-bound TWA Plane off the Coast of New York (July 96)   69%
- Little Girl in Texas Who Was Rescued after Falling into a Well (Oct 87)   69%
- The Shootings of Students and Teachers by Two Students at a Colorado High School (Late April 99)   68%
- War's End and the Homecoming of U.S. Forces from the Gulf (March 91)   67%
- Hurricane Andrew (Sept 92)   66%
- Iraq's Invasion of Kuwait and the Deployment of U.S. Forces to Saudi Arabia (Aug 90)   66%
- The Floods in the Midwest (Aug 93)   65%
- Earthquake in Southern California (Jan 94)   63%
- Iraq's Occupation of Kuwait and the Deployment of U.S. Forces to the Persian Gulf (Oct 90)   63%
- Iraq's Occupation of Kuwait and the Deployment of U.S. Forces to the Persian Gulf (Sept 90)   63%
- Iraq's Occupation of Kuwait and the Presence of U.S. Forces in the Persian Gulf (Nov 90)   62%

- Recent Increases in the Price of Gasoline (Oct 90)   62%
- Invasion of Panama (Jan 90)   60%
- Destruction Caused by Hurricane Hugo (Oct 89)   60%
- The Events Following the Shooting of Students and Teachers at a Colorado High School (May 99)   59%
- Iraq's Occupation of Kuwait and the Presence of U.S. Forces in the Persian Gulf (Jan 91)   59%
- The Oklahoma City Bombing (June 95)   58%
- U.S. Air Strikes Against Libya (July 86)   58%
- The Explosion of a Pipe-bomb at the Atlanta Olympics (July 96)   57%
- The Plight of the American Hostages and Other Westerners Detained in Iraq (Sept 90)   57%
- Recent Increase in the Price of Gasoline (Aug 90)   57%
- Recent Increases in the Price of Gasoline (Sept 90)   56%
- The Outcome of the 1996 Presidential Election (Dec 96)   55%
- The Death of John F. Kennedy, Jr., His Wife and Sister-in-Law in a Plane Crash Near Martha's Vineyard (Late July 99)   54%
- The Death of Princess Diana (Sept 97)   54%
- Crash of a United Airlines Dc-10 in Sioux City, Iowa (Aug 89)   53%
- Deployment of U.S. Forces to Somalia (Jan 93)   52%
- Alaska Oil Spill (May 89)   52%
- News about Cold Weather in Northeast and Midwest (Jan 94)   51%
- The Release of American Hostages and Other Westerners from Iraq and Kuwait (Jan 91)   51%
- Supreme Court Decision of Flag Burning (July 89)   51%
- Waco, Texas, Incident (May 93)   50%
- Opening of the Berlin Wall Between East and West Germany (Nov 89)   50%

Source: Pew Research Center for The People and The Press, 1999.

Hollywood celebrities are increasingly turning to (mostly liberal) politics. Actor Warren Beatty briefly considered running for president in 2000 as the Reform Party candidate.

noble terms—enemies of corruption, crusaders for justice, defenders of the disadvantaged. "The watchdog function, once considered remedial and subsidiary . . . [is now] paramount: the primary duty of the journalists is to focus attention on problems and deficits, failures and threats."[6] Their professional models are the crusading "investigative reporters" who expose wrongdoing in government, business, the military, and every other institution in society—except the media.

Many reporters go beyond the watchdog role and view themselves as adversaries of government. They see it as their job to expose politicians by unmasking their disguises, debunking their claims, and piercing their rhetoric. In short, until proven otherwise, political figures of any party or persuasion are presumed to be opponents. Even on entertainment shows, politicians are usually depicted as corrupt, hypocritical, and self-seeking, and business executives as crooked, greedy, and insensitive. Reporters are particularly proud of their work when it results in official investigations.

Liberalism in the Newsroom   The activist role that the media have taken upon themselves means that the personal values of reporters, editors, producers, and anchors are a very important element of American politics. The political values of the media are decidedly liberal and reformist. Political scientist Doris A. Graber writes about the politics of the media: "Economic and social liberalism prevails, as does a preference for an internationalist foreign policy, caution about military intervention, and some suspicion about the ethics of established large institutions, particularly government."[7] Most Americans agree that media news coverage is biased and the bias is in a liberal direction (see *What Do You Think?* "Are the Media Biased?").

The media elite—the executives, producers, reporters, editors, and anchors—are clearly liberal or left-leaning in their political news. One study of news executives reported that 63 percent described themselves as "left-leaning," only 27 percent as "middle-of-the-road," and 10 percent as "right-leaning." Newsmakers describe themselves as either "independent" (45 percent) or Democratic (44 percent); very few (9 percent) admit to being Republican.[8] A few conservative commentators are added to the liberal stew in order to add spice. Since controversy holds viewer attention, conservatives such as George Will, William F. Buckley, and Patrick Buchanan regularly play a confrontational role on news and talk shows.

Liberalism in Hollywood   With a few exceptions, Hollywood producers, directors, writers, studio executives, and actors are decidedly liberal in their political views, especially when compared with the general public. Of the Hollywood elite, more than 60 percent describe themselves as liberal and only 14 percent as conservative,[9] whereas in the general public, self-described conservatives outnumber liberals by a significant margin. Hollywood leaders are five time more likely to be Democrats than Republicans, and Hollywood is a major source of Democratic Party campaign funds. On both economic and social issues, the Hollywood elite is significantly more liberal than the nation's general public or college-educated public.

The question remains, however, how much political influence Hollywood exercises over its audiences. Many television shows and motion pictures have little political content; they are designed almost exclusively to entertain, to gather the largest audiences for advertisers, and to sell theater tickets. Even shows or movies with political themes or pronounced political biases may not influence audiences as much as Hollywood would wish.

Are the Media Biased?

Are the media biased, and if so in what direction—liberal or conservative? Arguments over media bias have grown in intensity as the media have come to play a central role in American politics.

Nearly three out of four Americans (74 percent) see "a fair amount" or "a great deal" of media bias in news coverage (see table below). And of those who see a bias, over twice as many see a liberal bias rather than a conservative bias. Indeed, even liberals see a liberal bias in the news; it is not a perception limited to conservatives, although they are more likely to see it. The liberal bias is much more likely to be seen by college graduates than by people who did not finish high school. It is also more likely to be seen by political activists than by those who engage in little or no political activity. However, African Americans are likely to see a conservative bias in the news, in contrast to the liberal bias perceived more often by whites.

Political bias is not Americans' only complaint about the national news media. Indeed, the most common complaint is that the media "ignore people's privacy" (80 percent). And majorities also complain about "one-sided coverage" (63 percent), "too negative" (61 percent), and "too much influence" (58 percent)—and they believe the media "abuse freedom of the press" (52 percent).

At the same time, Americans have high expectations of the role of the media in society: they expect the media to protect them from "abuse of power" by government, to hold public officials accountable, and to point out and help solve the problems of society.

Perceptions of Media Bias

	How Much Bias? "A Great Deal" or "Fair Amount" (%)	Direction of Bias	
		Liberal (%)	Conservative (%)
ALL	74	43	19
Race			
White	75	46	15
Black	64	24	40
Education			
Less than high school	56	29	33
High school graduate	75	42	19
College graduate	81	57	19
Ideology			
Liberal	70	41	22
Moderate	70	30	16
Conservative	81	57	19
Political Activism			
High	82	54	14
Low	76	42	22
None	65	34	22

Source: Data from *Media Monitor*, May/June, 1997, Center for Media and Public Affairs, Washington, D.C.

Hollywood Is Corrupting America

America's entertainment industry—its movie studios, TV-show producers, and record companies—are corrupting American culture with a deluge of graphic violence, mindless profanity, and irresponsible sex. That is the view of an increasing number of serious critics, not just religious "fanatics." National surveys regularly report that the vast majority of Americans believe that today's movies contain "too much violence" (82 percent), "too much profanity" (80 percent), and "too much sex" (72 percent). Most TV viewers believe that television shows "ridicule and make fun of religion" (72 percent) as well as "ridicule and make fun of traditional values such as marriage and motherhood" (64 percent). And the vast majority of Americans say that they are "concerned" with the amount of violence and sex in the popular media:

	Percent			Percent	
	Very Concerned	**Fairly Concerned**		**Not Very Concerned**	**Not at all Concerned**
How concerned are you about the amount of violence?	52%	25%		14%	9%
the amount of sex depicted in movies, television shows and popular music?	44	26		16	13

Source: Time/CNN national poll, reported in *Time*, June 12, 1995.

Hollywood produces relatively few uplifting movies (e.g., *Forrest Gump*, the *Lion King*, the *Little Princess*) compared to the number of sex-obsessed, profanity-ridden, and excessively violent films (e.g., *Natural Born Killers*, *Pulp Fiction*, *Fight Club*). Television shows have become increasingly controversial; they glamorize unmarried motherhood and celebrate homosexual life-styles. Records are released with lyrics that encourage cop-killing, rape, and suicide Critic Michael Medved writers:

> Our fellow citizens cherish the institution of marriage and consider religion an important priority in life; but the entertainment industry promotes every form of sexual adventurism and regularly ridicules religious believers as crooks or crazies. . . .

Conservatism on Talk Radio   Talk radio is the one medium where conservatism prevails. The single most listened-to talk radio show is the *Rush Limbaugh Show*, whose host regularly bashes "limousine liberals," "femi-Nazis," "environmental wackos," and "croissant people."[10] Talk radio might be portrayed as "call-in democracy." Callers respond almost immediately to reported news events. Call-in shows are the first to sense the public mood. Callers are not necessarily representative of the general public. Rather they are usually the most intense and outraged of citizens. But their complaints are early warning signs for wary politicians.

Nearly all parents want to convey to their children the importance of self-discipline, hard work, and decent manners; but the entertainment media celebrate vulgar behavior, contempt for all authority, and obscene language—which is inserted even in "family fare" where it is least expected.

Hollywood claims its movies simply reflect the sex, vulgarity, and violence already present in our culture, that restraints on movie makers would inhibit "creative oratory," and that censorship would violate "freedom of expression." They argue that politicians from Dan Quayle (who attacked *Murphy Brown* for glamorizing unmarried motherhood) to Bob Dole (who attacked Time-Warner for promoting "gangsta rap"), and Tipper Gore (for advocating warning labels on records), are merely pandering for the votes of religious conservatives. And they contend that the popularity of their movies, television shows, and records (judged in terms of money received from million's of movie-goers, viewers, and listeners) prove that Americans are entertained by the current Hollywood output, regardless of what socially approved responses they give to pollsters. "Movies drenched in gore, gangsta rap, even outright pornography are not some sort of alien interstellar dust malevolently drifting down on us, but products actively sought out and beloved by millions."*

Most Americans object to government censorship. Rather, they believe that the entertainment industry itself should exercise self-restraint.

Do you favor or oppose each of the following as a way to reduce the amount of sex and violence in popular entertainment?

	Percent	
	Favor	Oppose
Tighten parental supervision	93%	6%
Warning labels on records	83	15
Voluntary self-restraint by entertainment companies	81	15
Government censorship	27	69

Thus, a free society must rely on the virtue and social responsibility of the entertainment industry directors, as well as public pressure for moral sensitivity. Or as former U.S. Senator Bill Bradley put it: "The answer has got to be more citizenship in the boardroom, not censorship. The public has got to hold boards of directors, executives, and corporations accountable for making money out of trash."[†]

---

*Quoting Katha Pollitt, *Time* June 12, 1995, pp. 33–36.
[†]*Time* June 12, 1995, p. 34.

MEDIATED ELECTIONS

Political campaigning is largely a media activity, and the media, especially television, shape the nation's electoral politics.

The Media and Candidate-Voter Linkage   The media are the principal link between candidates and the voters. At one time, political party organizations performed this function, with city, ward, and precinct workers knocking on doors, distributing campaign literature, organizing rallies and candidate appearances, and getting out the vote on election day. But television has largely replaced party organizations and personal contact as the means by which candidates communicate with voters. Candidates come directly into the living room via television—on the nightly news, in broadcast debates and interviews, and in paid advertising (see Figure 6-3).

Media campaigning requires candidates to possess great skill in communications. Candidates must be able to project a favorable media *image*. The image is a composite of the candidate's words, mannerisms, appearance, personality, warmth, friendliness, humor, and ease in front of a camera. Policy positions have less to do with image than the candidate's ability to project personal qualities—leadership, compassion, strength, and character.

Television places an especially important emphasis on personal communication skills. Print media—newspapers and magazines—communicate only what is said. But *television communicates not only what is said but also how it is said*. For example, newspaper reports of Ronald Reagan's commonplace speeches and time-worn slogans failed to capture his true audience appeal, the folksy, warm, comfortable, reassuring manner, the humor and humility, and the likable personality that made Reagan "the Great Communicator." Reagan prevailed over hostile reporters, editors, and commentators because he was able to effectively communicate directly to mass audiences.

The Media and Candidate Selection   The media strongly influence the early selection of candidates. Media coverage creates *name recognition*, an essential quality for any candidate. Early media "mentions" of senators, governors, and other political figures as possible presidential contenders help to sort out the field even

FIGURE 6-3   Sources of Political Campaign Information

Source: The survey was conducted jointly by *The Washington Post*, Harvard University, and the Kaiser Family Foundation; reported in *The Polling Report*, December 9, 1996.

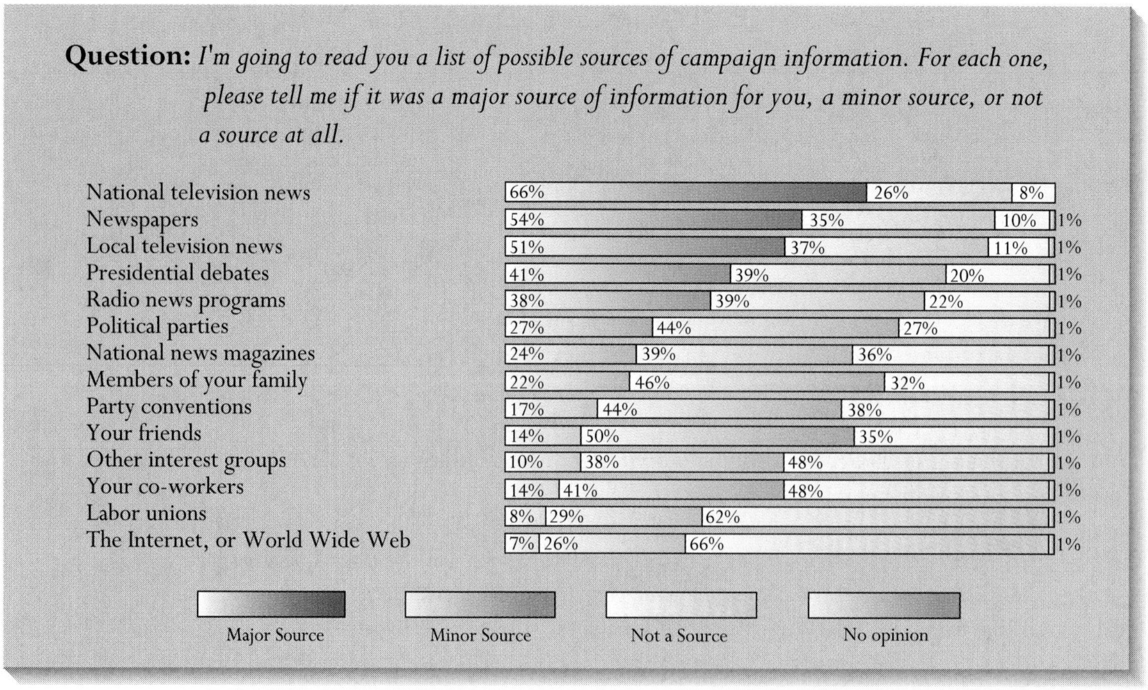

Question: *I'm going to read you a list of possible sources of campaign information. For each one, please tell me if it was a major source of information for you, a minor source, or not a source at all.*

Source	Major Source	Minor Source	Not a Source	No opinion
National television news	66%	26%	8%	
Newspapers	54%	35%	10%	1%
Local television news	51%	37%	11%	1%
Presidential debates	41%	39%	20%	1%
Radio news programs	38%	39%	22%	1%
Political parties	27%	44%	27%	1%
National news magazines	24%	39%	36%	1%
Members of your family	22%	46%	32%	1%
Party conventions	17%	44%	38%	1%
Your friends	14%	50%	35%	1%
Other interest groups	10%	38%	48%	1%
Your co-workers	14%	41%	48%	1%
Labor unions	8%	29%	62%	1%
The Internet, or World Wide Web	7%	26%	66%	1%

before the election year begins. Conversely, media inattention can condemn aspiring politicians to obscurity.

The media sort out the serious candidates early in a race. They even assign front-runner status, which may be either a blessing or a curse, depending on subsequent media coverage. In presidential primaries, the media play the *expectations game*, setting vote margins that the front-runner must meet in order to maintain *momentum*. If the front-runner does not win by a large enough margin, the media may declare the runner-up the "real" winner. This sorting out of candidates by the media influences not only voters, but—more important—financial contributors. The media-designated favorite is more likely to receive campaign contributions; financial backers do not like to waste money on losers. And as contributions roll in, the favorite can buy more television advertising, adding momentum to the campaign.

In presidential elections, the media sorting process places great emphasis on the early primary states, particularly New Hampshire, whose primary in early February is customarily the first contest in a presidential election year. Less than 1 percent of convention delegates are chosen by this small state, but media coverage is intense, and the winner quickly becomes the media-designated front-runner.[11]

The Media and the Horse Race   The media give election campaigns **horse-race coverage**: reporting on who is ahead or behind, what the candidates' strategies are, how much money they are spending, and, above all, what their current standing in the polls is. Such stories account for more than half of all television news coverage of an election. Additional stories are centered on *campaign* issues—controversies that arise on the campaign trail itself, including verbal blunders by the candidate—and *character* issues, such as the sex life of the candidate. In contrast, *policy* issues typically account for fewer than one-quarter of the television news stories on a presidential election campaign.

The Media as Campaign Watchdogs   The media's bad-news bias is evident in election campaigns as well as in general news reporting. Negative stories about all presidential candidates usually outnumber positive stories.[12] The media generally see their function in political campaigns as reporting on the weaknesses, blunders, and vulnerabilities of the candidates (see *What Do You Think?* "Should Media Report on the Private Lives of Public Officials?"). It might be argued that exposing the flaws of the candidates is an important function in a democracy. But the media's negative reporting about candidates and generally skeptical attitude toward their campaign speeches, promises, and advertisements may contribute to political alienation and cynicism among voters.

The media focus intense scrutiny on the personal lives of candidates—their marriages, sex lives, drug or alcohol use, personal finances, past friendships, military service, club memberships, and other potential sources of embarrassment. Virtually any past error in judgment or behavior by a candidate is given heavy coverage. But the media defend their attention to personal scandal on the ground that they are reporting on the "character issue." They argue that voters must have information on candidates' character as well as on their policy positions.

The Media and Political Bias   The media are very sensitive to charges of bias toward candidates or parties. Media people are overwhelmingly liberal and Democratic but generally try to deflect charges of political bias during an election campaign by giving almost equal coverage to both Democratic and Republican

horse-race coverage   Media coverage of electoral campaigns that concentrates on who is ahead and who is behind, and neglects the issues at stake.

Should the Media Report on the Private Lives of Public Officials?

Historically, reputable newspapers and magazines declined to carry stories about the sex lives of political figures. This unwritten ethic of journalism protected Presidents Franklin D. Roosevelt, Dwight D. Eisenhower, and John F. Kennedy during their political careers. But today, journalistic ethics (if there are any at all) do not limit reporting of sexual charges, rumors, or innuendoes or public questioning of candidates and appointees about whether they ever "cheated on their spouse," "smoked marijuana," or "watched pornographic movies."

The media's rationale is that these stories reflect on the *character* of a candidate and hence deserve reporting to the general public as information relevant to their choice for national leadership. (See *What Do You Think?* "Should We Judge Presidents on Private Character or Performance in Office" in Chapter 11.) Yet it seems clear that scandalous stories are pursued by the media primarily for their commercial value. Sex sells; it attracts viewers and readers. But the media's focus on sexual scandal and other misconduct obscures other issues. Politicians defending themselves from personal attack cannot get their political themes and messages across to voters. Moreover, otherwise qualified people may stay out of politics to avoid the embarrassment to themselves and their families that results from invasion of personal privacy.

Popular reaction to reports of President Clinton's sexual relationship with White House intern Monica Lewinsky suggests that most Americans separate private conduct from performance in office. Most believed that the affair was a "private matter":

Question: *(Feb. '98) Is this situation a private matter having to do with Clinton's personal life or a public matter having to do with Clinton's job as president?*

64%	29%	7%
Private	Public	No Answer

And, to the surprise of many media commentators, Clinton's job approval ratings *rose* markedly following the scandalous reports. Moreover, most Americans did *not* believe that Clinton should be impeached and removed from office as a result of the affair:

Question: *(Sept. '98) Do you think Clinton should resign now?*

35%	62%	3%
Yes	No	No Answer

Question: *(Sept. '98) Do you think President Clinton should be impeached and removed from office?*

31%	66%	3%
Yes	No	No Answer

Surveys of public opinion strongly suggest that Americans not only separate private conduct from performance in public office, but also oppose media reporting of private misconduct.

Sources: New York Times, February 24, 1998; CNN/USA Today poll, September 13, 1998.

candidates. Moreover, the media report negatively on both Republicans and Democrats, although some scholars count more negative stories about Republican candidates (see Figure 6-4).

The media are generally more critical of front-runners than of underdogs during a campaign. A horse race loses audience interest if one horse gets too far ahead, so the media tend to favor the underdog. "Frontrunners and incumbents consistently experienced the least balanced, least favorable news coverage."[13] During the presidential primary season, media attacks on an early favorite may result in gains for the underdog, who then becomes the new object of attack.

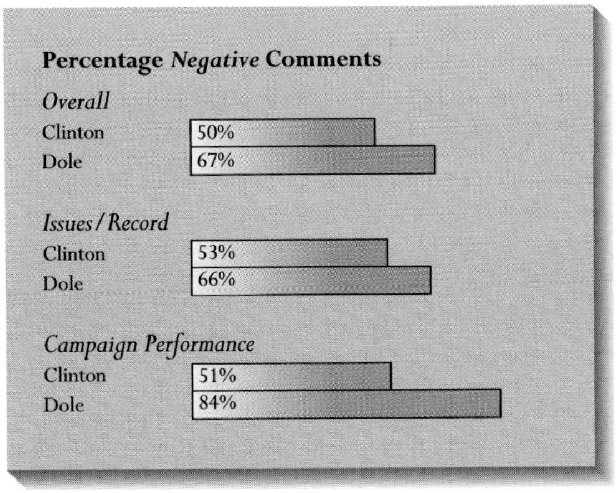

Percentage *Negative* Comments

Overall
Clinton | 50%
Dole | 67%

Issues / Record
Clinton | 53%
Dole | 66%

Campaign Performance
Clinton | 51%
Dole | 84%

FIGURE 6-4 Presidential Campaign Coverage by TV News in 1996

Source: Data from *Media Monitor*, December 1996, Center for Media and Public Affairs, Washington, D.C.

FREEDOM VERSUS FAIRNESS

Complaints about the fairness of media are as old as the printing press. Most early newspapers in the United States were allied with political parties; they were not expected to be fair in their coverage. It was only in the early 1900s that many large newspapers broke their ties with parties and proclaimed themselves independent. And it was not until the 1920s and 1930s that the norms of journalistic professionalism and accuracy gained widespread acceptance.

The Constitution protects the *freedom* of the press; it was not intended to guarantee *fairness*. The First Amendment's guarantee of freedom of the press was originally designed to protect the press from government attempts to silence criticism. Over the years, the U.S. Supreme Court has greatly expanded the meaning of the free-press guarantee.

No Prior Restraint   The Supreme Court has interpreted freedom of the press to mean that government may place no **prior restraint** on speech or publication (that is, before it is said or published). Originally, this doctrine was designed to prevent the government from closing down or seizing newspapers. Today, the doctrine prevents the government from censoring any news items. In the famous case of the Pentagon Papers, the *New York Times* and *Washington Post* undertook to publish secret information stolen from the files of the State Department and Defense Department regarding U.S. policy in Vietnam while the war was still going on.[14] No one disputed the fact that stealing the secret material was illegal. What was at issue was the ability of the government to prevent the publication of stolen documents in order to protect national security. The Supreme Court rejected the national security argument and reaffirmed that the government may place no prior restraint on publication. If the government wishes to keep military secrets, it must not let them fall into the hands of the American press.

Press versus Electronic Media   In the early days of radio, broadcast channels were limited, and anyone with a radio transmitter could broadcast on any frequency. As a result, interference was a common frustration of early broadcasters. The industry petitioned the federal government to regulate and license the assignment and use of broadcast frequencies.

prior restraint   Power of government to prevent publication or to require approval before publication; generally prohibited by the First Amendment.

The Federal Communications Commission (FCC) was established in 1934 to allocate broadcast frequencies and to license stations for "the public interest, convenience and necessity." The act clearly instructed the FCC: "Nothing in this Act shall be understood or construed to give the Commission the power of censorship." However, the FCC views a broadcast license and exclusive right to use a particular frequency as a *public trust*. Thus broadcasters, unlike newspapers and magazines, are licensed by a government agency and supposed to operate in the *public interest*.

The Equal-Time Requirement   The FCC requires radio and television stations that provide airtime to a political candidate to offer competing candidates the same amount of airtime at the same price. Stations are not required to give free time to candidates, but if stations choose to give free time to one candidate, they must do so for the candidate's opponents. But this **equal-time rule** does not apply to newscasts, news specials, or even long documentaries; nor does it apply to talk shows like *Larry King Live* (see *People in Politics:"Larry King Live"*). Nor does it apply to presidential press conferences or presidential addresses to the nation, although the networks now generally offer free time for a "Republican response" to a Democratic president, and vice versa. A biased news presentation does not require the network or station to grant equal time to opponents of its views. And it is important to note that newspapers, unlike radio and television, have never been required to provide equal time to opposing views (see *Compared to What?* "America's TV Culture in Perspective").

LIBEL AND SLANDER

Communications that wrongly damage an individual are known in law as **libel** (when written) and **slander** (when spoken). The injured party must prove in court that the communication caused actual damage and was either false or defamatory. A damaging falsehood or words or phrases that are defamatory (such as "Joe Jones is a rotten son of a bitch") are libelous and are not protected by the First Amendment from lawsuits seeking compensation.

Public Officials   Over the years, the media have sought to narrow the protection afforded public officials against libel and slander. In 1964 the U.S. Supreme Court ruled in the case of *New York Times v. Sullivan* that public officials did not have a right to recover damages for false statements unless they are made with "malicious intent."[15] The **Sullivan rule** requires public officials not only to show that the media published or broadcast false and damaging statements but also to prove they did so knowing that their statements were false and damaging or that they did so with "reckless disregard" for the truth or falsehood of their statements. The effect of the Sullivan rule is to free the media to say virtually anything about public officials. Indeed, the media have sought to expand the definition of "public officials" to "public figures"—that is, to include anyone they choose as the subject of a story.

"Absence of Malice"   The First Amendment protects the right of the media to be biased, unfair, negative, sensational, and even offensive. Indeed, even *damaging falsehoods* may be printed or broadcast as long as the media can show that the story was not deliberately fabricated by them with malicious intent, that is, if the media can show an "absence of malice."[14]

equal-time rule   Federal Communications Commission (FCC) requirement that broadcasters who sell time to any political candidate must make equal time available to opposing candidates at the same price.

libel   Writings that are false and malicious and are intended to damage an individual.

slander   Oral statements that are false and malicious and are intended to damage an individual.

Sullivan rule   Court guideline that false and malicious statements regarding public officials are protected by the First Amendment unless it can be proven they were known to be false at the time they were made or were made with "reckless disregard" for their truth or falsehood.

Larry King Live

Who turned presidential politics into talk-show entertainment? A strong argument can be made that Larry King was personally responsible for changing the nature of presidential campaigning. It was Larry King who nudged frequent talk-show guest Ross Perot into the presidential arena. And it was Larry King who demonstrated to the candidates that the talk-show format was a good way to reach out to the American people.

Larry King's supremacy in talk-show politics came late in life, after a half-century of hustling and hard knocks, no college education, bouts of gambling followed by bankruptcy, and multiple marriages. King has written five books about himself, describing his rise from Brooklyn neighborhoods; his friendships with Jackie Gleason, Frank Sinatra, and other celebrities; and his hardscrabble life. As he tells it, he hung around a New York radio station for five years before taking a bus to Miami to try his luck first as a disk jockey and later as a sports announcer. After a decade in Miami, he had his own TV interview show, a talk show on radio, and a newspaper column, and he was color commentator for the Miami Dolphins. He lived the fast life, running up huge debts and dealing in shady financial transactions. He was arrested in 1971 on grand larceny charges; they were dropped only because the statute of limitations had expired. He lost his TV and radio shows and his newspaper column. He ended up in Shreveport, Louisiana, doing play by play for the World Football League's Shreveport Steamers. In 1975 he was bankrupt but back in Miami doing radio. In 1978 he moved to Washington to launch his Mutual Network radio talk show. As radio talk shows gained popularity, so did King. When CNN started twenty-four-hour broadcasting in 1982, the new TV network turned to King to do an evening interview show, *Larry King Live*. At first, the show merely filled the space between the evening and the late news. A decade later, the show was making news itself.

King's success is directly attributable to his accommodating style. He actually listens to his guests; he lets them speak for themselves; he unashamedly plugs their books, records, and movies. He does *not* attack his guests; he does not assume the adversarial, abrasive style preferred by reporters like Sam Donaldson, Dan Rather, and Mike Wallace. An old-fashioned liberal himself, King appears comfortable interviewing politicians of every stripe. He lets guests talk about themselves. He tosses "softball" questions: "If I were to interview the president about an alleged sexual affair, I wouldn't ask if he'd had one, I'd ask him, 'How does it feel to read these things about yourself?' "

With his emphasis on feelings, emotions, and motives rather than on facts, it is little wonder that King's style attracts politicians . . . or that *Larry King Live* is the highest rated show on CNN.

Source: Time, October 5, 1992, p. 76.

Shielding Sources   The media argue that the First Amendment allows them to refuse to reveal the names of their sources, even when this information is required in criminal investigations and trials. Thus far, the U.S. Supreme Court has not given blanket protection to reporters to withhold information from court proceedings. However, a number of states have passed *shield laws* protecting reporters from being forced to reveal their sources.

POLITICS AND THE INTERNET

The development of any new media of communications invariably affects political life. Just as first, radio, and later television, reshaped politics in America, today the Internet is having its own unique impact on public affairs. The Internet provides a channel

America's TV Culture in Perspective

America is a TV culture. Americans rely more on television for news and entertainment than people in other advanced industrial nations do. Perhaps more important, Americans have greater confidence in the media than other peoples do. Consider, for example, the question "Would you say you have a great deal of confidence, only some confidence, hardly any confidence, or no confidence at all in the media—press, radio, and television?" When this question was asked of a national sample of Americans, 69 percent responded that they had a great deal or at least some confidence in the media. But majorities in four other countries—France, Great Britain, Germany, and Spain—said they had little or no confidence in the media (see "confidence in the media" figure).

How much do the media influence key decisions in society? A majority of people in both the United States and these same European nations believe the media exert a large influence on public opinion. Americans appear to be closer to unanimity on this point (88 percent) than are Europeans. When people are asked how much influence the media exerts on particular governing institutions—the executive, the legislature, and the judiciary—Americans are much more likely to perceive strong media influence than are Europeans (see "media influence" figure).

Source: Adapted from Lawrence Parisot, "Attitudes about the Media: A Five Country Study," *Public Opinion* 43 (January/February 1988): 18, 60.

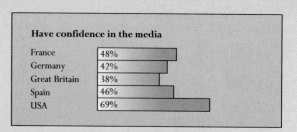

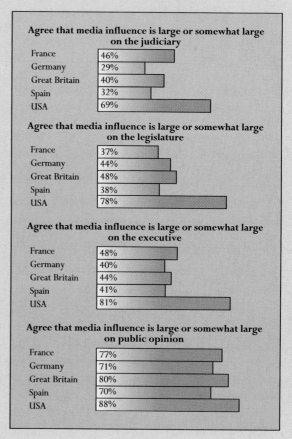

for *interactive mass participation* in politics. It is unruly and chaotic by design. It offers the promise of abundant and diverse information in the opportunity for increased political participation. It empowers anyone who can design the WebSite to spread their views, whether their views are profound and public-spirited or hateful and obscene.

Chaotic by Design   During the Cold War, the RAND Corporation, a technological research think tank, proposed the Internet as a communications network that might survive a nuclear attack. It was deliberately designed to operate without any central authority or organization. Should any part of the system be destroyed, messages would still find their way to their destinations. The later development of the World Wide Web language allowed any connected computer in the world to communicate with any other connected computer. And introduction of the World Wide Web in 1992 also meant that users no longer needed computer expertise to communicate. By 1995 Americans were buying more computers than television sets and sending more e-mail than "snail mail." Since then, Internet usage has continued to mushroom (see Figure 6-5).

Political WebSites Abound   The Internet is awash in political WebSites.[17] The simple query "politics" on a standard search program can return well over a million matches. Almost all federal agencies, including the White House, Congress, the federal judiciary, and executive departments and agencies, maintain WebSites. Individual elected officeholders, including all members of Congress, maintain sites that include personal biographies, committee assignments, legislative accomplishments, issue statements, and press releases. The home pages of the Democratic and Republican parties offer political news, issue positions, opportunities to become active in party affairs, and invitations to send them money. No serious candidate for major public office lacks a WebSite; these campaign sites usually including flattering biographies, press releases, and, of course, invitations to contribute financially to the candidates' campaigns. All major interest groups maintain WebSites—business, trade, and professional groups; labor unions; ideological and issue groups; women's, religious, environmental, and civil rights groups. Indeed, this virtual tidal wave of politics on the Internet may turn out to offer too much information in too fragmented a fashion, thereby simply adding to apathy and indifference.

Internet Uncensored   The Internet allows unrestricted freedom of expression, from scientific discourses on particle physics and information on the latest developments in medical science, to invitations to join in paramilitary "militia" and offers to exchange pornographic photos and messages. Commercial sex sites outnumber any other category on the Web.

Congress unsuccessfully attempted to outlaw "indecent" and "patently offensive" material on the Internet and its Communications Decency Act of 1996. But the U.S. Supreme Court gave the Internet First Amendment protection in 1997 in *Reno vs. American Civil Liberties Union*.[18] The Court recognized the Internet as an important form of popular expression protected by the Constitution. Congress had sought to make it a federal crime to send or display "indecent" material to persons under 18 years of age (material describing or displaying sexual activities or organs in

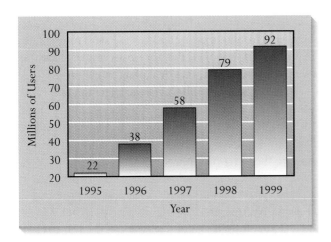

FIGURE 6-5   Growth of Internet Users

Source: CommerceNet/Nielsen Internet Demographic Survey, June 1999.

"patently offensive" fashion). But the Supreme Court reiterated its view that government may not limit the adult population to "only what is fit for children." The Court decision places the burden of filtering Internet messages on parents. Filtering software can be installed on home computers, but a First Amendment issue arises when it is installed on computers in public libraries.

The Privacy Problem   While the Internet facilitates the exercise of the right of free expression, it poses a problem for the right of privacy. Government and private industry have been collecting information on individuals for many years, from driving records to credit reports. But the Internet offers a vastly expanded and easily accessible source of data on individuals, including their earnings, purchases, hobbies, medical condition, reading habits, and more. Surfing the Internet may seem anonymous but it is not. WebSites can easily track visitors and may even send out "cookies"—files quietly stored in visitors' computers that continue to provide identification and information. Encryption (coding) programs are available, but the Federal Bureau of Investigation demands "recovery keys" from manufacturers in order to maintain surveillance.

MEDIA EFFECTS: SHAPING POLITICAL LIFE

What effects do the media have on public opinion and political behavior? Let us consider media effects on (1) information and agenda setting, (2) values and opinions, and (3) behavior. These categories of effects are ranked by the degree of influence the media are likely to have over us. The strongest effects of the media are on our information levels and societal concerns. The media also influence values and opinions, but the strength of media effects in these areas is diluted by many other influences. Finally, it is most difficult to establish the independent effect of the media on behavior.

Information and Agenda-Setting Effects   The media strongly influence what we know about our world and how we think and talk about it. Years ago, foreign-policy expert Bernard Cohen, in the first book to assess the effects of the media on foreign policy, put it this way: "The mass media may not be successful in telling people what to think, but the media are stunningly successful in telling their audience what to think about"[16] (see *Up Close:* "The Media Age" on page 182).

However, **information overload** diminishes the influence of the media in determining what we think about. So many communications are directed at us that we cannot possibly process them all. A person's ability to recall a media report depends on repeated exposure to it and reinforcement through personal experience. For example, an individual who has a brother in a trouble spot in the Middle East is more likely to be aware of reports from that area of the world. But too many voices with too many messages cause most viewers to block out a great deal of information.

Information overload may be especially heavy in political news. Television tells most viewers more about politics than they really want to know. Political scientist Austin Ranney writes, "The fact is that for most Americans politics is still far from being the most interesting and important thing in life. To them, politics is usually confusing, boring, repetitious, and above all irrelevant to the things that really matter in their lives."[17]

Effects on Values and Opinions   The media often tell us how we *should* feel about news events or issues, especially those about which we have no prior feelings or experiences. The media can reinforce values and attitudes we already

information overload   Situation in which individuals are subjected to so many communications that they cannot make sense of them.

hold. However, the media seldom *change* our preexisting values or opinions. Media influence over values and opinions is reduced by **selective perception**, mentally screening out information or opinions we disagree with. People tend to see and hear only what they want to see and hear. For example, television news concentration on scandal, abuse, and corruption in government has not always produced the liberal, reformist values among viewers that media people expected. On the contrary, the focus of network executives on governmental scandals—Watergate, the Iran-contra scandal, the sexual antics of politicians, congressional check kiting, and so on—has produced feelings of general political distrust and cynicism toward government and the political system. These feelings have been labeled **television malaise**, a combination of social distrust, political cynicism, feelings of powerlessness, and disaffection from parties and politics that seems to stem from television's emphasis on the negative aspects of American life.

The media do not *intend* to create television malaise; they are performing their self-declared watchdog role. They expect their stories to encourage liberal reform of our political institutions. But the result is often alienation rather than reform.

Direct Effects on Public Opinion　Can the media change public opinion, and if so, how? For many years, political scientists claimed that the media had only minimal effects on public opinions and behavior. This early view was based largely on the fact that newspaper editorial endorsements seldom affected people's votes. But serious research on the effects of television tells a different story.

In an extensive study of eighty policy issues over fifteen years, political scientists examined public opinion polls on various policy issues at a first point in time, then media content over a following interval of time, and finally public opinion on these same issues at the end of the interval. The purpose was to learn if media content—messages scored by their relevance to the issue, their salience in the broadcast, their pro/con direction, the credibility of the news source, and quality of the reporting—changed public opinion. Most people's opinions remained constant over time (opinion at the first time period is the best predictor of opinion at the second time period). However, when opinion did change, it changed in the direction supported by the media. "News variables alone account for nearly half the variance in opinion change." Other findings include the following:

- Anchors, reporters, and commentators have the greatest impact on opinion change. Television newscasters have high credibility and trust with the general public. Their opinions are crucial in shaping mass opinion.

- Independent experts interviewed by the media have a substantial impact on opinion, but not as great as newscasters themselves.

- A popular president can also shift public opinion somewhat. Unpopular presidents do not have much success as opinion movers, however.

- Interest groups on the whole have a slightly negative effect on public opinion. "In many instances they seem actually to have antagonized the public and created a genuine adverse effect"; such cases include Vietnam War protesters, nuclear freeze advocates, and other demonstrators and protesters, even peaceful ones.[20]

Effects on Behavior　Many studies have focused on the effects of the media on behavior: studies of the effects of TV violence, studies of the effects of television on children, and studies of the effects of obscenity and pornography.[21]

selective perception
Mentally screening out information or opinions with which one disagrees.

television malaise　Generalized feelings of distrust, cynicism, and powerlessness stemming from television's emphasis on the negative aspects of American life.

The Media Age

The print media—newspapers, magazines, and books—have played a major role in American politics since colonial times. But today the electronic media—radio, television, and cable television—dominate in political communication.

Radio was widely introduced into American homes in the 1920s and 1930s, allowing President Franklin D. Roosevelt to become the first "media president," directly communicating with the American people through radio "fireside chats." After World War II, the popularity of television spread quickly; between 1950 and 1960, the percentage of homes with TV sets grew from 9 to 87.

Some notable political media innovations over the years:

- **1952:** The first paid commercial TV ad in a presidential campaign appeared, on behalf of Dwight D. Eisenhower. The black-and-white ad began with a voice-over—"Eisenhower answers the nation!"—followed by citizens asking favorable questions and Eisenhower responding, and ending with a musical jingle: "I like Ike." Although crude by current standards, it nevertheless set a precedent in media campaigning.

- **1952:** The "Checkers speech" by Eisenhower's running mate, Richard M. Nixon, represented the first direct television appeal to the people over the heads of party leaders. Nixon was about to be dumped from the Republican ticket for hiding secret slush-fund money from campaign contributors. He went on national television with an emotional appeal, claiming that the only personal item he ever took from a campaign contributor was his daughters' little dog, Checkers. Thousands of viewers called and wired in sympathy. Ike kept Nixon on the ticket.

- **1960:** The first televised debate between presidential candidates featured a youthful, handsome John F. Kennedy against a shifty-eyed Richard M. Nixon with a pronounced "five o'clock shadow." Nixon doggedly scored debater points, but JFK presented a cool and confident image and spoke directly to the viewers. The debate swung the popular tide toward Kennedy, who won in a very tight contest. Nixon attributed his defeat to his failure to shave before the broadcast.

- **1964:** The first "negative" TV ad was the "Daisy Girl" commercial sponsored by the Lyndon Johnson campaign against Republican conservative Barry Goldwater. It implied that Goldwater would start a nuclear war. It showed a little girl picking petals off a daisy while an ominous voice counted down "10-9-8-7 . . ." to a nuclear explosion, followed by a statement that Lyndon Johnson could be trusted to keep the peace.

- **1976:** President Gerald Ford was the first incumbent president to agree to a televised debate. (No televised presidential debates were held in the Nixon-Humphrey race in 1968 or in the Nixon-McGovern race in 1972. Apparently Nixon had learned his lesson.) Ford stumbled badly, and Jimmy Carter went on to victory.

- **1982:** CNN (Cable News Network), introduced by the maverick media mogul Ted Turner, began twenty-four-hour broadcasting.

- **1991:** The Persian Gulf War was the first war to be fought live on television. (Although film and videotape reports of the Vietnam War had been

Although it is difficult to generalize from these studies, television appears more likely to reinforce behavioral tendencies than to change them. For example, televised violence may trigger violent behavior in children who are already predisposed to such behavior, but televised violence has little behavioral effect on average children.[22] Nevertheless, we know that television advertising sells products. And we know that political candidates spend millions to persuade audiences to go out and vote for them on election day. Both manufacturers and politicians create name recognition, employ product differentiation, try to associate with audiences, and use repetition to communicate their messages. These

The first televised presidential election debates were in 1960 between Senator John F. Kennedy and Vice President Richard Nixon. Nixon came armed with statistics, but his dour demeanor, "five o'clock shadow," and stiff presentation fared poorly in contrast to Kennedy's open, relaxed, confident air.

important molders of public opinion in America, the technology of that era did not allow live reporting. In the Gulf War, the Iraqi government permitted CNN to continue live broadcasts from Baghdad, including spectacular coverage of the first night's air raids on the city.

● **1992:** In the presidential election, television talk shows became a major focus of the campaign. Wealthy independent candidate Ross Perot actually conducted an all-media campaign, rejecting in-person appearances in favor of such media techniques as half-hour "infomercials."

● **1994–95:** The arrest and trial of celebrity O.J. Simpson on murder charges so dominated the national news that more television time was devoted to the O.J. story than to the actions of the president and Congress.

● **1996:** The presidential election was given less television time and newspaper space than previous elections. Clinton's large lead throughout the campaign, public boredom with Whitewater and other scandals, and Dole's lackluster performance frustrated reporters in search of drama. Network TV news gave Clinton twice as much positive coverage as Dole.

● **1997–98:** Sex scandals involving Bill Clinton dominated the news and talk shows, but public opinion polls gave the president the highest approval ratings of his two terms in office.

● **2000:** On election night, the networks prematurely called the presidential election, first for Gore and then for Bush, causing confusion among the public and embarrassment for the networks.

tactics are designed to affect our behavior both in the marketplace and in the election booth.

Political ads are more successful in motivating a candidate's supporters to go to the polls than they are in changing opponents into supporters. It is unlikely that voters who dislike a candidate will be persuaded by political advertising to change their votes. But many potential voters are undecided, and the support of many others is dubbed "soft." Going to the polls on election day requires effort—people have errands to do, it may be raining, they may be tired. Television advertising is more effective with the marginal voters.

Twenty-First Century Directions

Media power has influenced American politics since the earliest days of the Republic. *The Federalist*, published in New York newspapers in 1787–88, were the equivalent of today's "op-ed" (opinion-editorial) articles. But printed news and opinion was always easy to overlook. Television is really the first medium of *mass* communication. Virtually everyone watches television, and it is difficult to ignore political news. Thus, television has become, and will remain, the principal arena of American politics.

⬆ *Media Diversity* Technological advances in cable and satellite broadcasting and the Internet will continue to multiply channels of communication. Hundreds of separate broadcast channels will become available to most homes. While most viewers will choose movies, reruns, talk and entertainment shows, they will at least have the opportunity to view channels dealing with politics and public affairs. Parties, as well as religious, ideological, and public interest groups, will increasingly sponsor their own cable and satellite channels. And politics will flourish on the Internet. Political web sites will mushroom as increasing percentages of the population will gain access to the Internet. The net will provide increasing opportunities for minority, specialized, and fringe parties and candidates to reach selected audiences with customized messages.

Public demand to police the Internet will grow, but the technology of communication will outrace the technology of censorship.

⬇ *Media Civility and Fairness* The major television networks, confronting increased competition, will continue their descent into hype and sensationalism. Network news broadcasts will become ever more "tabloid" in appearance, featuring stories on sex, scandal, disaster, and corruption. The distinction between news and entertainment will fade. Impartial, analytical information about public affairs will become ever more scarce on network television.

"Attack journalism" will flourish. Conflict, strife, and discord will dominate political stories; indeed, reporters themselves will stage the fights. Scandal and corruption will dominate reporting from Washington. Politicians, both Democrats and Republicans and both liberals and conservatives, will suffer predominantly negative reporting.

⬆ *Television Malaise* The result of the media's bad-news bias will be continuing distrust and disillusionment among Americans with regard to their political leaders and institutions. People will remain "turned off" to politics; mass participation in politics, including voter turnout, will continue its downward trend. Disillusioned citizens will increasingly turn away from the Democratic and Republican parties and "politics as usual," and increasingly turn toward independent and "anti-Washington" candidates.

SUMMARY NOTES

- The mass media in America not only report on the struggle for power; they are participants themselves in that struggle.

- It is only through the media that the general public comes to know about political events, personalities, and issues. Newsmaking—deciding what is or is not "news"—is a major source of media power. Media coverage not only influences popular discussion but also forces public officials to respond.

- Media power also derives from the media's ability to set the agenda for public decision making—to determine what citizens and public officials will regard as "crises," "problems," or "issues" to be resolved by government.

- The media also exercise power in their interpretation of the news. News is presented in story form; pictures, words, sources, and story selection all contribute to interpretation.

- The media play a major role in socializing people to the political culture. Socialization occurs in news, entertainment, and advertising.

- The politics of the media are shaped by their economic interest in attracting readers and viewers. This interest largely accounts for the sensational and negative aspects of news reporting.
- The professional environment of newspeople encourages an activist, watchdog role in politics. The politics of most newspeople are liberal and Democratic.
- Political campaigning is largely a media activity. The media have replaced the parties as the principal linkage between candidates and voters. But the media tend to report the campaign as a horse race, at the expense of issue coverage, and to focus more on candidates' character than on their voting records or issue positions.
- The First Amendment guarantee of freedom of press protects the media from government efforts to silence or censor them and allows the media to be "unfair" when they choose to be. The Federal Communication Commission exercises some modest controls over the electronic media, since the rights to exclusive use of broadcast frequencies is a *public trust*.

- Public officials are afforded very little protection by libel and slander laws. The Supreme Court's Sullivan rule allows even damaging falsehoods to be written and broadcast as long as newspeople themselves do not deliberately fabricate lies with "malicious intent" or "reckless disregard."
- Media effects on political life can be observed in (1) information and agenda setting, (2) values and opinions, and (3) behavior—in that order of influence. The media strongly influence what we know about politics and what we talk about. The media are less effective in changing existing opinions, values, and beliefs than they are in creating new ones. Nevertheless, the media can change many people's opinions, based on the credibility of news anchors and reporters. Direct media effects on behavior are limited. Political ads are more important in motivating supporters to go to the polls, and in swinging undecided or "soft" voters, than in changing the minds of committed voters.

KEY TERMS

mass media 158	muckraking 166	libel 176	selective perception 181
newsmaking 162	horse-race coverage 173	slander 176	television malaise 181
agenda setting 164	prior restraint 175	Sullivan rule 176	
socialization 165	equal-time rule 176	information overload 180	

SELECTED READINGS

ANSOLABEHERE, STEPHEN, ROY BEHR, and SHANTO IYENGAR. *The Media Game: American Politics in the Television Age.* New York: Macmillan, 1993. A comprehensive text assessing the changes in the political system brought about by the rise of television since the 1950s.

FALLOWS, JAMES. *Breaking the News: How the Media Undermine American Democracy.* New York: Pantheon Books, 1996. An argument that today's arrogant, cynical, and scandal-minded news reporting is turning readers and viewers away and undermining support for democracy.

GRABER, DORIS A. *Mass Media and American Politics.* 5th ed. Washington, D.C.: Congressional Quarterly Press, 1997. A wide-ranging description of media effects on campaigns, parties, and elections, as well as on social values and public policies.

LICHTER, ROBERT S., STANLEY ROTHMAN, and LINDA S. LICHTER. *The Media Elite.* Bethesda, Md.: Adler and Adler,

1986. A thorough study of the social and political values of top leaders in the mass media, based on extensive interviews of key people in the most influential media outlets.

PATTERSON, THOMAS E. *Out of Order.* New York: Random House, 1994. The antipolitical bias of the media poisons national election campaigns; policy questions are ignored in favor of the personal characteristics of candidates, their campaign strategies, and their standing in the horse race.

PRINDLE, DAVID F. *Risky Business.* Boulder, Colo.: Westview Press, 1993. An examination of the politics of Hollywood, its liberalism, activism, self-indulgence, and celebrity egotism.

SABATO, LARRY J. *Feeding Frenzy: How Attack Journalism Has Transformed American Politics.* New York: Free Press, 1992. A strong argument that the media prefer "to employ titillation rather than scrutiny" and as a result produce "trivialization rather than enlightenment."

Political Parties
Organizing Politics

ASK YOURSELF ABOUT POLITICS

1 Generally speaking, how would you identify yourself: as a Republican, Democrat, independent, or something else?
Republican ⬤
Democrat ⬤
Independent ⬤
Other ⬤

2 Which major political party better represents the interests of people like yourself?
Republican ⬤
Democrat ⬤

3 Does the Republican Party favor the rich more than the middle class or poor?
Yes ⬤ No ⬤

4 Does the Democratic Party favor the poor more than the middle class or rich?
Yes ⬤ No ⬤

5 Which major party does a better job of protecting the Social Security system?
Republican ⬤
Democrat ⬤

6 Which major party does a better job of handling foreign affairs?
Republican ⬤
Democrat ⬤

7 Should elected officials be bound by their party's platform?
Yes ⬤ No ⬤

8 Do we need a third party to challenge the Republican and Democratic parties?
Yes ⬤ No ⬤

How much power do political parties really have to determine who gets what in America? We hear the terms *Republican* and *Democratic* linked to people and to policies, but do these parties have real power beyond that of organizing for elections?

THE POWER OF ORGANIZATION

In the struggle for power, organization grants advantage. Italian political scientist Gaetano Mosca once put it succinctly: "A hundred men acting uniformly in concert, with a common understanding, will triumph over a thousand men who are not in accord and can therefore be dealt with one by one."[1] Thus politics centers on organization—on organizing people to win office and to influence public policy.

Political organizations—parties and interest groups—function as intermediaries between individuals and government. They organize individuals to give them power in selecting government officials—who governs—and in determining public policy—for what ends. Generally, **political parties** are more concerned with winning public office in elections than with influencing policy, whereas *interest groups* are more directly concerned with public policy and involve themselves with elections only to advance their policy interests (see Figure 7-1 on page 188). In other words, parties and interest groups have an informal division of functions, with parties focusing on personnel and interest groups focusing on policy. Yet both organize individuals for more effective political action.

AMERICAN PARTIES: A HISTORICAL PERSPECTIVE

Parties are *not* mentioned in the Constitution. Indeed, the nation's Founders regarded both parties and interest groups as "factions," citizens united by "some common impulse of passion,

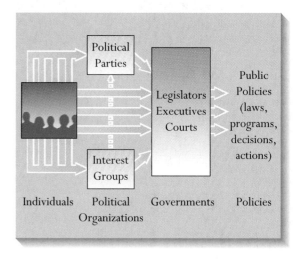

FIGURE 7-1 Political Organizations as Intermediaries

All political organizations function as intermediaries between individuals and government. Parties are concerned primarily with winning elected office; interest groups are concerned with influencing policy.

or of interest, adverse to the rights of other citizens, or to the permanent and aggregate interests of the community." The Founders viewed factions as "mischievous" and "dangerous."[2] Yet the emergence of parties was inevitable as people sought to organize themselves to exercise power over who governs (see Figure 7-2).

The Emergence of Parties: Federalists and Democratic-Republicans In his Farewell Address, George Washington warned the nation about political parties: "Let me . . . warn you in the most solemn manner against the baneful effects of the spirit of party generally."[3] As president, Washington stood above the factions that were coalescing around his secretary of treasury, Alexander Hamilton, and around his former secretary of state, Thomas Jefferson. Jefferson had resigned from Washington's cabinet in 1793 to protest the fiscal policies of Hamilton, notably his creation of a national bank and repayment of the state's Revolutionary War debts with federal funds. Washington had endorsed Hamilton's policies, but so great was the first president's prestige that Jefferson and his followers directed their fire not against Washington but against Hamilton, John Adams, and their supporters, who called themselves **Federalists** after their leaders' outspoken defense of the Constitution during the ratification process. By the 1790s, Jefferson and Madison, as well as many **Anti-Federalists** who had initially opposed the ratification of the Constitution, began calling themselves *Republicans* or *Democratic-Republicans*, terms that had become popular after the French Revolution in 1789.

Adams narrowly defeated Jefferson in the presidential election of 1796. This election was an important milestone in the development of the parties and the presidential election system. For the first time, two candidates campaigned as members of opposing parties, and candidates for presidential elector in each state pledged themselves as "Adams's men" or "Jefferson's men." By committing themselves in advance of the actual presidential vote, these pledged electors enabled voters in each state to determine the outcome of the presidential election.

Party activity intensified in anticipation of the election of 1800. Jefferson's Democratic-Republican Party first saw the importance of organizing voters, circulating literature, and rallying the masses to their causes. Many Federalists viewed this early party activity with disdain. Indeed, the Federalists even tried to outlaw public criticism of the federal government by means of the Alien and Sedition Acts of 1798, which among other things made it a crime to publish false or malicious writings

political organizations Parties and interest groups that function as intermediaries between individuals and government.

political parties Organizations that seek to achieve power by winning public office.

Federalists Those who supported the U.S. Constitution during the ratification process and who later formed a political party in support of John Adams's presidential candidacy.

Anti-Federalists Those who opposed the ratification of the U.S. Constitution and the creation of a strong national government.

FIGURE 7-2 Change and Continuity in the American Party System

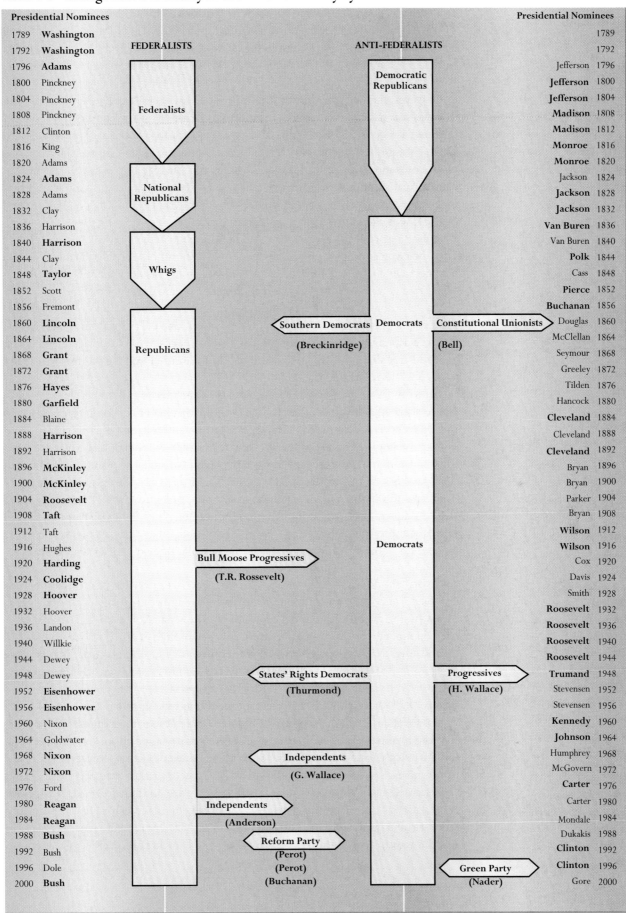

Presidential Nominees				Presidential Nominees
1789 Washington		FEDERALISTS	ANTI-FEDERALISTS	1789
1792 Washington				1792
1796 Adams			Democratic Republicans	Jefferson 1796
1800 Pinckney				Jefferson 1800
1804 Pinckney	Federalists			Jefferson 1804
1808 Pinckney				Madison 1808
1812 Clinton				Madison 1812
1816 King				Monroe 1816
1820 Adams				Monroe 1820
1824 Adams				Jackson 1824
1828 Adams	National Republicans			Jackson 1828
1832 Clay				Jackson 1832
1836 Harrison				Van Buren 1836
1840 Harrison				Van Buren 1840
1844 Clay	Whigs			Polk 1844
1848 Taylor				Cass 1848
1852 Scott				Pierce 1852
1856 Fremont				Buchanan 1856
1860 Lincoln		Southern Democrats Democrats Constitutional Unionists		Douglas 1860
1864 Lincoln		(Breckinridge) (Bell)		McClellan 1864
1868 Grant	Republicans			Seymour 1868
1872 Grant				Greeley 1872
1876 Hayes				Tilden 1876
1880 Garfield				Hancock 1880
1884 Blaine				Cleveland 1884
1888 Harrison				Cleveland 1888
1892 Harrison				Cleveland 1892
1896 McKinley				Bryan 1896
1900 McKinley				Bryan 1900
1904 Roosevelt				Parker 1904
1908 Taft				Bryan 1908
1912 Taft				Wilson 1912
1916 Hughes			Democrats	Wilson 1916
1920 Harding		Bull Moose Progressives		Cox 1920
1924 Coolidge		(T.R. Rossevelt)		Davis 1924
1928 Hoover				Smith 1928
1932 Hoover				Roosevelt 1932
1936 Landon				Roosevelt 1936
1940 Willkie				Roosevelt 1940
1944 Dewey				Roosevelt 1944
1948 Dewey		States' Rights Democrats Progressives		Trumand 1948
1952 Eisenhower		(Thurmond) (H. Wallace)		Stevensen 1952
1956 Eisenhower				Stevensen 1956
1960 Nixon				Kennedy 1960
1964 Goldwater				Johnson 1964
1968 Nixon		Independents		Humphrey 1968
1972 Nixon		(G. Wallace)		McGovern 1972
1976 Ford				Carter 1976
1980 Reagan		Independents		Carter 1980
1984 Reagan		(Anderson)		Mondale 1984
1988 Bush		Reform Party		Dukakis 1988
1992 Bush		(Perot)		Clinton 1992
1996 Dole		(Perot) Green Party		Clinton 1996
2000 Bush		(Buchanan) (Nader)		Gore 2000

against the (Federalist) Congress or president or to "stir up hatred" against them. These acts directly challenged the newly adopted First Amendment guarantees of freedom of speech and press. But in the election of 1800, the Federalists went down to defeat. Democratic-Republican electors won a **majority** (more than half the votes cast) in the Electoral College.

However, the original Constitution provided that each presidential elector could cast two votes; the person getting the most votes won the presidency and the runner-up won the vice presidency. If no one won a majority, the president would be elected by the House of Representatives. In 1800 each Democratic-Republican elector cast one of his votes for Jefferson and the other for Aaron Burr, Jefferson's vice presidential running mate. But the result was an unintended tie between Jefferson and Burr, throwing the election into the House of Representatives. (The Twelfth Amendment, ratified in 1804, remedied the problem by requiring electors to cast separate votes for president and vice president.) A few disgruntled Federalists in the House considered giving Burr their votes just to embarrass Jefferson, and the ambitious Burr encouraged this chicanery. But in the end, the House selected Jefferson. President Adams and the Federalists turned over the reins of government to Jefferson and the Democratic-Republicans.

The election of 1800 was a landmark in American democracy—the first time that control of government passed peacefully from one party to another on the basis of an election outcome. As commonplace as that may seem to Americans today, the peaceful transfer of power from one group to another remains a rarity in many political systems around the world.

Jefferson's Democratic-Republican Party—later to be called the Democrats— was so successful that the Federalist Party never regained the presidency or control of Congress. The Federalists tended to represent merchants, manufacturers, and shippers, who were concentrated in New York and New England. The Democratic-Republicans tended to represent agrarian interests, from large plantation owners to small farmers. In the mostly agrarian America of the early 1800s, the Democratic-Republican Party prevailed. Jefferson easily won reelection in 1804, and his allies, James Madison and James Monroe, overwhelmed their Federalist opponents in subsequent presidential elections. By 1820, the Federalist Party had ceased to exist. Indeed, for a few years, it seemed as if the new nation had ended party politics.

Jacksonian Democrats and Whigs Partisan politics soon reappeared, however. The Democratic-Republicans had already begun to fight among themselves by the 1824 presidential election. Andrew Jackson won a **plurality** (at least one more vote than anyone else in the race) but not a majority of the popular and Electoral College vote, but he then lost to John Quincy Adams in a close decision by the factionalized House of Representatives. Jackson led his supporters to found a new party, the **Democratic Party**, to organize popular support for his 1828 presidential bid, which succeeded in ousting Adams.

Jacksonian ideas both *democratized* and *nationalized* the party system. Under Jackson, the Democratic Party began to mobilize voters on behalf of the party and its candidates. It pressed the states to lower property qualifications for voting in order to recruit new Democratic Party voters. The electorate expanded from 365,000 voters in 1824 to well over a million in 1828 and over 2 million in 1840. The Democratic Party also pressed the states to choose presidential electors by popular vote rather than by state legislatures. Thus Jackson and his Democratic successor, Martin Van Buren, ran truly national campaigns directed at the voters in every state.

majority   Election by more than 50 percent of all votes cast in the contest.

plurality   Election by at least one vote more than any other candidate in the race.

Democratic Party One of the main parties in American politics; it traces its origins to Thomas Jefferson's Democratic-Republican Party, acquiring its current name under Andrew Jackson in 1828.

At the same time, Jackson's opponents formed the Whig Party, named after the British party of that name. Like the British Whigs, who opposed the power of the king, the American Whigs charged "King Andrew" with usurping the powers of Congress and the people. The Whigs quickly adopted the Democrats' tactics of national campaigning and popular organizing. By 1840, the Whigs were able to gain the White House, running William Henry Harrison—nicknamed "Old Tippecanoe" from his victory at Tippecanoe over Native Americans in 1811—and John Tyler and featuring the slogan "Tippecanoe and Tyler too."

Post–Civil War Republican Dominance   Whigs and Democrats continued to share national power until the slavery conflict that ignited the Civil War destroyed the old party system. The Republican Party had formed in 1854 to oppose the spread of slavery to the western territories. By the election of 1860, the slavery issue so divided the nation that four parties offered presidential candidates: Lincoln the Republican, Stephen A. Douglas the northern Democrat, John C. Breckinridge the southern Democrat, and John Bell the Constitutional Union Party candidate. No party came close to winning a majority of the popular vote, but Lincoln won in the Electoral College.

The new party system that emerged from the Civil War featured a victorious **Republican Party** that generally represented the northern industrial economy and a struggling Democratic Party that generally represented a southern agricultural economy. The Republican Party won every presidential election from 1860 to 1912 except for two victories by Democratic reformer and New York governor Grover Cleveland (see *Up Close:* "The Donkey and the Elephant" on page 192).

Yet the Democratic Party offered a serious challenge in the election of 1896 and realigned the party affiliations of the nation's voters. The Democratic Party nominated William Jennings Bryan, a talented orator and a religious fundamentalist. Bryan sought to rally the nation's white "have-nots" to the Democratic Party banner, particularly the debt-ridden farmers of the South and West. His plan was to stimulate inflation (and thus enable debtors to pay their debts with "cheaper," less valuable dollars) through using plentiful, western-mined "free silver," rather than gold, as the monetary standard. He defeated Cleveland's faction and the "Gold Democrats" in the 1896 Democratic Party convention with his famous Cross of Gold speech: "You shall not crucify mankind upon a cross of gold."

But the Republican Party rallied its forces in perhaps the most bitter presidential battle in history. It sought to convince the nation that high tariffs, protection for manufacturers, and a solid monetary standard would lead to prosperity for industrial workers as well as the new tycoons. The campaign, directed by Marcus Alonzo Hanna, attorney for John D. Rockefeller's Standard Oil Company, spent an unprecedented $16 million (an amount in inflation-adjusted dollars that has never been equaled) to elect Republican William McKinley, advertised as the candidate who would bring a "full dinner pail" to all. The battle also produced one of the largest voter turnouts in history. McKinley won in a landslide. Bryan ran twice again but lost by even larger margins. The Republican Party solidified the loyalty of industrial workers, small-business owners, bankers, and large manufacturers, as well as black voters, who respected "the party of Lincoln" and despised the segregationist practices of the southern Democratic Party.

So great was the Republican Party's dominance in national elections that only a split among Republicans enabled the Democrat Woodrow Wilson to capture the

Republican Party   One of the two main parties in American politics; it traces its origins to the antislavery and nationalist forces that united in the 1850s and nominated Abraham Lincoln for president in 1860.

The Donkey and the Elephant

The popular nineteenth-century cartoonist Thomas Nast is generally credited with giving the Democratic and Republican parties their current symbols: the donkey and the elephant. In *Harper's Weekly* cartoons in the 1870s, Nast critically portrayed the Democratic Party as a stubborn mule "without pride of ancestry nor hope of posterity." During this period of Republican Party dominance, Nast portrayed the Republican Party as an elephant, the biggest beast in the political jungle. Now both party symbols are used with pride.

"A LIVE JACKASS KICKING A DEAD LION."
And such a Lion! and such a Jackass!

In the 1870 cartoon on the left, published following the death of Lincoln's Secretary of War E.M. Stanton, Nast shows a donkey (labeled "Copperheads," a disparaging term for the mostly Democratic Northerners who were sympathetic to the South during the Civil War) kicking the dead Stanton, who is portrayed as a lion. The 1874 cartoon on the right features the elephant as the Republican Vote and the donkey masquerading as a lion.

presidency in 1912. Republican Theodore Roosevelt (who became president following McKinley's assassination and had won reelection in 1904) sought to recapture the presidency from his former protégé, Republican William Howard Taft. In the **GOP** convention ("Grand Old Party," as the Republicans began labeling themselves), party regulars rejected the unpredictable Roosevelt in favor of Taft, even though Roosevelt had won the few primary elections that had recently been initiated. An irate Teddy Roosevelt launched a third, progressive party, the "Bull Moose," which actually outpolled the Republican Party in the 1912 election—the only time a third party has surpassed one of the two major parties in U.S. history. But the result was a victory for the Democratic candidate, former Princeton political science professor Woodrow Wilson. Following Wilson's two terms, Republicans again reasserted their political dominance with victories by Warren G. Harding, Calvin Coolidge, and Herbert Hoover.

GOP "Grand Old Party"—a popular label for the Republican Party.

The New Deal Democratic Party   The promise of prosperity that empowered the Republican Party and held its membership together faded in the light of the Great Depression. The U.S. stock market crashed in 1929, and by the early

Franklin Roosevelt campaigning among coal miners in West Virginia during the presidential election campaign of 1932. Roosevelt's optimism and "can-do" attitude in the face of the Great Depression helped cement the New Deal Democratic coalition that won him the presidency.

1930s, one-quarter of the labor force was unemployed. Having lost confidence in the nation's business and political leadership, in 1932 American voters turned out incumbent Republican President Herbert Hoover in favor of Democrat Franklin D. Roosevelt, who promised the country a **New Deal**.

More than just bringing the Democrats to the White House, the Great Depression marked another party realignment. This time, traditionally Republican voting groups changed their affiliation and enabled the Democratic Party to dominate national politics for a generation. This realignment actually began in 1928, when Democratic presidential candidate Al Smith, a Catholic, won many northern, urban, ethnic voters away from the Republican Party. By 1932, a majority New Deal Democratic coalition had been formed in American politics. It consisted of the following groups:

- Working classes and union members, especially in large cities.
- White ethnic groups who had previously aligned themselves with Republican machines.
- Catholics and Jews.
- African Americans, who ended their historic affiliation with the party of Lincoln to pursue new economic and social goals.
- Poor people, who associated the New Deal with expanded welfare and Social Security programs.
- Southern whites, who had provided the most loyal block of Democratic voters since the Civil War.

To be sure, this majority coalition had many internal factions: southern "Dixiecrats" walked out of the Democratic Party convention in 1948 to protest a party platform that called for an end to racial discrimination in employment. But the promise of a New Deal—with its vast array of government supports for workers, elderly and disabled people, widows and children, and farmers—held this coalition together reasonably well. President Harry Truman's **Fair Deal** proved that the coalition could survive its founder, Franklin D. Roosevelt. Repub-

New Deal Policies of President Franklin D. Roosevelt during the depression of the 1930s that helped form a Democratic Party coalition of urban working-class, ethnic, Catholic, Jewish, poor, and southern voters.

Fair Deal Policies of President Harry Truman extending Roosevelt's New Deal and maintaining the Democratic Party's voter coalition.

lican Dwight D. Eisenhower made inroads into this coalition by virtue of his personal popularity and the Republican Party's acceptance of most New Deal programs. But John F. Kennedy's "New Frontier" demonstrated the continuing appeal of the Democratic Party tradition. Lyndon Johnson's **Great Society** went further than the programs of any of his predecessors in government intervention in the economic and social life of the nation. Indeed, it might be argued that the Great Society laid the foundation for a political reaction that eventually destroyed the old Democratic coalition and led to yet another new party alignment (see Figure 7-3).

A New Republican Majority   The American political system underwent massive convulsions in the late 1960s as a result of both the civil rights revolution at home and an unpopular war in Vietnam. Strains were felt in all of the nation's political institutions, from the courts to the Congress to the presidency. And when Lyndon Johnson announced his decision not to run for reelection in 1968, the Democratic Party erupted in a battle that ultimately destroyed its majority support among presidential voters.

At the 1968 Democratic Party convention in Chicago, Vice President Hubert Humphrey controlled a majority of the delegates inside the convention hall, but antiwar protesters dominated media coverage outside the hall. When Chicago police attacked unruly demonstrators with batons, the media broadcast to the world an image of the nation's turmoil. In the presidential campaign that followed, both candidates—Democrat Hubert Humphrey and Republican Richard Nixon— presented nearly identical positions supporting the U.S. military commitment in Vietnam while endorsing a negotiated, "honorable" settlement of the war. But the image of the Democratic Party became associated with the street protesters. Inside the convention hall, pressure from women and minorities led party leaders to adopt changes in the party's delegate-selection process for future conventions to assure better representation of these groups—at the expense of Democratic officeholders (see "Making Party Rules" later in this chapter for more details).

In 1972 the Democratic Party convention strongly reflected the views of antiwar protesters, civil rights advocates, feminist organizations, and liberal activists generally. The visibility of these activists, who appeared to be well to the left of both Democratic Party voters and the electorate in general, allowed the Republican Party to portray the Democratic presidential nominee, George McGovern, as an unpatriotic liberal, willing to "crawl to Hanoi" and to sacrifice the nation's honor for peace. It also allowed the Republicans to characterize the new Democratic Party as soft on crime, tolerant of disorder, and committed to racial and sexual quotas in American life. Richard Nixon, never very popular personally, was able to win in a landslide in 1972. The Watergate scandal and Nixon's forced resignation only temporarily stemmed the tide of "the new Republican majority." Democrat Jimmy Carter's narrow victory over Republican Gerald R. Ford in 1976 owed much to the latter's pardon of Nixon.

The Reagan Coalition   Under the leadership of Ronald Reagan, the Republican Party was able to assemble a majority coalition that dominated presidential elections in the 1980s, giving Reagan landslide victories in 1980 and 1984 and George Bush a convincing win in 1988. The **Reagan Coalition** consisted of the following groups:

Great Society   Policies of President Lyndon Johnson that promised to solve the nation's social and economic problems through government intervention.

Reagan Coalition   Combination of economic and social conservatives, religious fundamentalists, and defense-minded anticommunists who rallied behind Republican President Ronald Reagan.

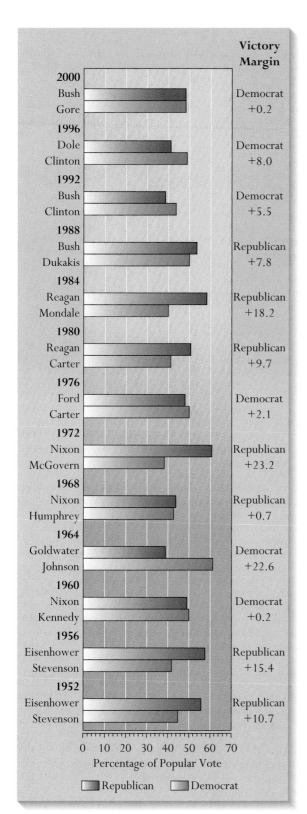

Victory
Margin

2000
Bush
Gore — Democrat +0.2

1996
Dole
Clinton — Democrat +8.0

1992
Bush
Clinton — Democrat +5.5

1988
Bush
Dukakis — Republican +7.8

1984
Reagan
Mondale — Republican +18.2

1980
Reagan
Carter — Republican +9.7

1976
Ford
Carter — Democrat +2.1

1972
Nixon
McGovern — Republican +23.2

1968
Nixon
Humphrey — Republican +0.7

1964
Goldwater
Johnson — Democrat +22.6

1960
Nixon
Kennedy — Democrat +0.2

1956
Eisenhower
Stevenson — Republican +15.4

1952
Eisenhower
Stevenson — Republican +10.7

0 10 20 30 40 50 60 70
Percentage of Popular Vote

■ Republican   □ Democrat

FIGURE 7-3 The Parties in Presidential Voting

Despite the dominance of the Democratic Party in terms of numbers of registered voters, Republicans have won more presidential elections since 1952, indicating that, at the presidential level, voters are not always loyal to their party. The popular vote divided almost evenly in 2000.

Battles between so-called hippie demonstrators and police in Chicago during the Democratic National Convention in 1968 bolstered Republicans' arguments that government by the Democrats had led to a breakdown in fundamental values and that the nation had to shift gears in order to restore "law and order."

- Economic conservatives concerned about high taxes and excessive government regulation, including business and professional voters who had traditionally supported the Republican Party.

- Social conservatives concerned about crime, drugs, and racial conflict, including many white ethnic voters and union members who had traditionally voted Democratic.

- Religious fundamentalists concerned about such issues as abortion and prayer in schools.

- Southern whites concerned about racial issues, including affirmative action programs.

- Internationalists and anticommunists who wanted the United States to maintain a strong military force and to confront Soviet-backed Marxist regimes around the world.

Reagan held this coalition together in large part through his personal popularity and his infectious optimism about the United States and its future. Although sometimes at odds with one another, economic conservatives, religious fundamentalists, and internationalists could unite behind the "Great Communicator." Reagan's presidential victory in 1980 helped to elect a Republican majority to the U.S. Senate and encouraged Democratic conservatives in the Democrat-controlled House of Representatives to frequently vote with Republicans. As a result, Reagan got most of what he asked of Congress in his first term: cuts in personal income taxes, increased spending for national defense, and slower growth of federal regulatory activity. With the assistance of the Federal Reserve Board, inflation was brought under control. But Reagan largely failed to cut government spending as he had promised, and the result was a series of huge federal deficits. Reagan appointed conservatives to the

Supreme Court and the federal judiciary (see Chapter 13), but no major decisions were reversed (including the *Roe v. Wade* decision, protecting abortion); social conservatives had to be content with the president's symbolic support.

During these years, the national Democratic Party was saddled with an unpopular image as the party of special-interest groups. As more middle-class and working-class voters deserted to the GOP, the key remaining loyal Democratic constituencies were African Americans and other minorities, government employees, union leaders, liberal intellectuals in the media and universities, feminist organizations, and environmentalists. Democratic presidential candidates Walter Mondale in 1984 and Michael Dukakis in 1988 were obliged to take liberal positions to win the support of these groups in the primary elections. Later, both candidates sought to move toward the center of the ideological battleground in the general election. But Republican Party strategists were able to "define" Mondale and Dukakis through negative campaign advertising (see Chapter 8) as liberal defenders of special-interest groups. The general conservative tilt of public opinion in the 1980s added to the effectiveness of the GOP strategy of branding Democratic presidential candidates with the "*L* word" (*liberal*).

Clinton and the "New" Democrats   Yet even while Democratic candidates fared poorly in presidential elections, Democrats continued to maintain control of the House of Representatives, to win back control of the U.S. Senate in 1986, and to hold more state governorships and state legislative seats than the Republicans. Thus the Democratic Party retained a strong leadership base on which to rebuild itself.

During the 1980s, Democratic leaders among governors and senators came together in the **Democratic Leadership Council** to create a "new" Democratic Party closer to the center of the political spectrum. The chair of the Democratic Leadership Council was the young, energetic, and successful governor of Arkansas, Bill Clinton. The concern of the council was that the Democratic Party's traditional support for social justice and social welfare programs was overshadowing its commitment to economic prosperity. Many council members argued that a healthy economy was a prerequisite to progress in social welfare. Not all Democrats agreed with the council agenda. African American leaders (including the Reverend Jesse Jackson), as well as liberal and environmental groups, feared that the priorities of the council would result in the sacrifice of traditional Democratic Party commitments to minorities, poor people, and the environment.

In the 1992 presidential election, Bill Clinton was in a strong position to take advantage of the faltering economy under George Bush, to stress the "new" Democratic Party's commitment to the middle class, and to avoid being labeled as a liberal defender of special interests. At the same time, he managed to rally the party's core activist groups—liberals, intellectuals, African Americans, feminists, and environmentalists. Many liberals in the party deliberately soft-pedaled their views during the 1992 election in order not to offend voters, hoping to win with Clinton and then fight for liberal programs later. Clinton won with 43 percent of the vote, to George Bush's 38 percent. Independent Ross Perot captured a surprising 19 percent of the popular vote, including many voters who were alienated from both the Democratic and the Republican parties. Once in office, Clinton appeared to revert to liberal policy directions rather than to pursue the more moderate line he had espoused as a "new" Democrat. As Clinton's ratings sagged, the opportunity arose for a Republican resurgence.

Democratic Leadership Council   Organization of party leaders who sought to create a "new" Democratic Party to appeal to middle-class, moderate voters.

J.C. Watts, Jr., Can the Republican Party Attract African Americans?

African Americans are the most loyal group of Democratic Party voters. Rarely do Republican candidates win more than 10 percent of the black vote. But J.C. Watts of Oklahoma, one of only two African American Republican members of Congress, argues: "Democrats just don't pay attention to African Americans because they are already the most loyal voting block in the ranks. And the Republicans have said, 'We don't have to pay attention because they vote Democrat.' I want to change all that."

Julius Caesar Watts, Jr., graduated from Eufaula High School in Oklahoma and won a football scholarship to the University of Oklahoma, where he quarterbacked the Sooners to two consecutive Big Eight championships. He twice defeated the Florida State Seminoles in Orange Bowl games in 1981 and 1982, and was named MVP of both games. He graduated with a degree in journalism and went on to play quarterback in the Canadian Football League for six years. Returning to Norman, Oklahoma, to work in real estate, he was soon recruited by the Republican Party to run for the state's elected

Corporation Commission. He became the first African American to be elected to statewide office in Oklahoma since Reconstruction.

"J.C.'s" name recognition and fame in Oklahoma football circles, and his strong commitment to Christian values, made him a favorite speaker at events across the state. He is a leader in the Fellowship of Christian Athletes and a frequent guest preacher in the Southern Baptist Church.

In 1994 Watts undertook a politically daunting challenge—running for Congress as an African American Republican in an overwhelmingly white Democratic district. He won the GOP primary in a five-candidate field and went on to face a liberal Democrat in the general election. Watts stood by his conservative beliefs, including opposition to homosexuals in the military, opposition to abortion except to save the life of the woman, support for a balanced budget, and support for a two-year limit on welfare benefits. He won a near-landslide 58 percent of the vote.

The national Republican Party has featured J.C. Watts in many of its key events in the hopes of attracting more conservative African Americans to the GOP. In 1997 Watts gave the Republican response to President Clinton's State of the Union Address on national television: "I didn't get my values from Washington. I got my values from a strong family, a strong church, and a strong neighborhood . . . I was taught, in the words of Dr. Martin Luther King Jr., to judge a man not by the color of his skin but by the content of his character. And I was taught that character is doing what's right, when nobody's looking."

Republican Resurgence A political earthquake shook Washington in the 1994 congressional elections, when the Republicans for the first time in forty years captured the House of Representatives (see "*People in Politics:* J. C. Watts, Jr., Can the Republican Party Attract African Americans?"), regained control of the Senate, and captured a majority of the nation's governorships. For the first time in history Republicans won more seats in the South than the Democrats. This southern swing to the Republicans in congressional elections seemed to confirm the realignment of southern voters that had begun earlier in presidential elections. Just two years after a Democratic president had been elected, the GOP won its biggest nationwide victory since the Great Depression.

Clinton Holds On Following the Republican victory, the Democratic Party appeared to be in temporary disarray. The new Republican House Speaker, Newt Gingrich, tried to seize national policy leadership; Clinton was widely viewed as a failed president. But the Republicans quickly squandered their political opportunity. They had made many promises in a well-publicized "Contract with America"—a balanced federal budget, congressional term limits, tax cuts, welfare reform, and more—but they delivered little. Majority Leader Bob Dole failed by one vote to pass the Balanced Budget Amendment in the Senate. President Clinton took an unexpectedly hard line toward GOP spending cuts and vetoed several budget bills. When the federal government officially "closed down" for lack of appropriated funds, the public appeared to blame Republicans. Polls showed a dramatic recovery in the president's approval ratings. Clinton skillfully portrayed GOP leaders, especially Newt Gingrich, as "extremists" and himself as a responsible moderate prepared to trim the budget, reduce the deficit, and reform welfare, "while still protecting Medicare, Medicaid, education, and the environment." By early 1996, Clinton had set the stage for his reelection campaign.

Bill Clinton is the first Democratic president to be reelected since Franklin D. Roosevelt. Clinton rode to victory on a robust economy. Voters put aside doubts about Clinton's character, and they ignored Republican Bob Dole's call for tax reductions. Clinton won with 49 percent of the popular vote to Dole's 41 percent and Perot's 8 percent. But Clinton's victory failed to rejuvenate the Democratic Party's fortunes across the country. The GOP retained its majorities in both houses of Congress.

2000—A Nation Divided The nation was more evenly divided in 2000 than perhaps any other time in the history of the Democratic and Republican parties. Not only was the presidential vote almost tied but both houses of Congress were split almost evenly between Democrats and Republicans. The Republican Party lost seats in the House of Representatives in 1998 and again in 2000. Yet the GOP still retained a razor-thin margin of control of that body. In the Senate, the 2000 election created a historic 50–50 tie between Democrats and Republicans. But the death or resignation of a single Senator could cause a change in party control of the Senate.

An evenly divided electorate produced a politically weakened president and a Congress so closely split that little significant legislation was expected for at least two years.

POLITICAL PARTIES AND DEMOCRATIC GOVERNMENT

"Political parties created democracy, and modern democracy is unthinkable save in terms of the parties."[4] Traditionally, political scientists have praised parties as indispensable to democratic government. They have argued that parties are essential for organizing popular majorities to exercise control over government. The development of political parties in all the democracies of the world testifies to the underlying importance of parties to democratic government. But political parties in the United States have lost their preeminent position as instruments of democracy. Other structures and organizations in society—interest groups, the mass media, independent campaign organizations, primary elections, social welfare agencies—now perform many of the functions traditionally regarded as prerogatives of political parties. Nevertheless, the

Democratic and Republican parties remain important organizing structures for politics in the United States.

"Responsible" Parties in Theory   In theory, political parties function in a democracy to organize majorities around broad principles of government in order to win public office and enact these principles into law. A "responsible" party should:

- Adopt a platform setting forth its principles and policy positions.
- Recruit candidates for public office who agree with the party's platform.
- Inform and educate the public about the platform.
- Organize and direct campaigns based on platform principles.
- Organize the legislature to ensure party control in policy making.
- Hold its elected officials responsible for enacting the party's platform.

If responsible, disciplined, policy-oriented parties competed for majority support, *if* they offered clear policy alternatives to the voters, and *if* the voters cast their ballots on the basis of these policy options, *then* the winning party would have a "policy mandate" from the people to guide the course of government. In that way, the democratic ideal of government by majority rule would be implemented.

Winning Wins over Principle   However, the **responsible party model** never accurately described the American party system. The major American parties have been loose coalitions of individuals and groups seeking to attract sufficient votes to gain control of government. *Winning has generally been more important than any principles or policies.* America's major parties must appeal to tens of millions of voters in every section of the nation and from all walks of life. If a major party is to acquire a majority capable of controlling the U.S. government, it cannot limit its appeal by relying on a single unifying principle. Instead, it must form coalitions of voters from as many sectors of the population as it can. Major American parties therefore usually do not emphasize particular principles or ideologies so much as try to find a common ground of agreement among many different people. This emphasis does not mean no policy differences exist between the American parties. On the contrary, each party tends to appeal to a distinctive coalition of interests, and therefore each party expresses somewhat distinctive policy views (see *What Do You Think?* "Popular Images of the Democratic and Republican Parties").

In their efforts to win, major American political parties strive to attract the support of the large numbers of people near the center of public opinion. Generally more votes are at the center of the ideological spectrum—the middle-of-the-road—than on the extreme liberal or conservative ends. Thus *no real incentive exists for vote-maximizing parties to take strong policy positions in opposition to each other.* As the Democratic and Republican policy positions approach the center, the parties seem to echo each other, and critics attack them as Tweedledee and Tweedledum (see Figure 7-4 on page 202).

The Erosion of Traditional Party Functions   Parties play only a limited role in campaign organization and finance. Campaigns are generally directed by professional campaign management firms or by the candidates' personal organizations, not by parties. Party organizations have largely been displaced in campaign activity by advertising firms, media consultants, pollsters, and others hired by the candidates themselves (see Chapter 8).

responsible party model
System in which competitive parties adopt a platform of principles, recruiting candidates and directing campaigns based on the platform, and holding their elected officials responsible for enacting it.

Popular Images of the Democratic and Republican Parties

What do Americans think of the Democratic and Republican parties? Generally speaking, the Democratic Party has been able to maintain an image of "the party of the common people," and the Republican Party has long been saddled with an image of "favoring the rich."

But when it comes to popular perceptions of each party's ability to deal with problems confronting the nation, the Democratic and Republican parties appear evenly matched. The Republican Party is trusted to "do a better job" in handling foreign affairs and maintaining a strong national defense. It also enjoys a reputation of being better at "holding down taxes."

The Democratic Party enjoys its greatest advantage on "compassion issues" like helping poor, elderly, and homeless people. And the Democrats have long enjoyed the support of the high-voter-turnout over-sixty-five age group because it is trusted to do a better job "protecting the Social Security system."

Source: As reported in *The Polling Report*, November 22, 1999.

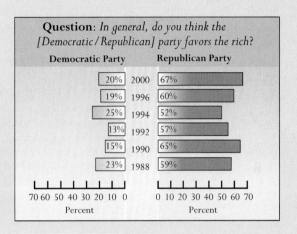

Question: *In general, do you think the [Democratic / Republican] party favors the rich?*

Democratic Party		Republican Party
20%	2000	67%
19%	1996	60%
25%	1994	52%
13%	1992	57%
15%	1990	65%
23%	1988	59%

Percent — 70 60 50 40 30 20 10 0 / 0 10 20 30 40 50 60 70 — Percent

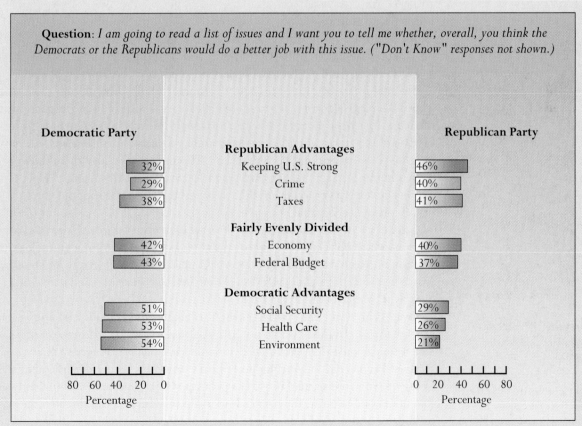

Question: *I am going to read a list of issues and I want you to tell me whether, overall, you think the Democrats or the Republicans would do a better job with this issue. ("Don't Know" responses not shown.)*

Democratic Party		Republican Party
Republican Advantages		
32%	Keeping U.S. Strong	46%
29%	Crime	40%
38%	Taxes	41%
Fairly Evenly Divided		
42%	Economy	40%
43%	Federal Budget	37%
Democratic Advantages		
51%	Social Security	29%
53%	Health Care	26%
54%	Environment	21%

Percentage — 80 60 40 20 0 / 0 20 40 60 80 — Percentage

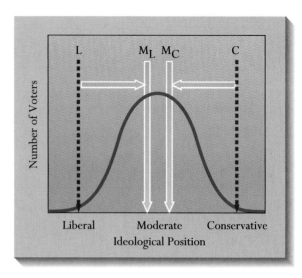

FIGURE 7-4 Winning versus Principle

Why don't we have a party system based on principles, with a liberal party and a conservative party, each offering the voters a real ideological choice? Let's assume that voters generally choose the party closest to their own ideological position. If the liberal party (L) took a strong ideological position to the left of most voters, the conservative party (C) would move toward the center, winning more moderate votes, even while retaining its conservative supporters, who would still prefer it to the more liberal opposition party. Likewise, if the conservative party took a strong ideological position to the right of most voters, the liberal party would move to the center and win. So both parties must abandon strong ideological positions and move to the center, becoming moderate in the fight for support of moderate voters.

American political parties also play only a limited role in recruiting candidates for elected office. *Most political candidates today are self-recruited.* People initiate their own candidacies, first contacting friends and financial supporters. Often in state and local races, candidates contact party officials only as a courtesy, if at all.

The major American political parties cannot really control who their **nominee**—the party's entry in a general election race—will be. Rather, party **nominations** for most elected offices are won in *primary elections*. In a **primary election**, registered voters select from among a party's members who meet minimum legal standards and choose to run. The primary winner then becomes the party's nominee. Party leaders may endorse a candidate in a primary election and may even work to try to ensure the victory of their favorite, but the voters in that party's primary select the nominee.

Candidates usually communicate directly with voters through the mass media. Television has replaced the party organization as the principal medium of communication between candidates and voters. Candidates no longer rely much on party workers to carry their message from door to door. Instead, candidates can come directly into the voters' living room via television.

Even if the American parties wanted to take stronger policy positions and to enact them into law, they would not have the means to do so. *American political parties have no way to bind their elected officials to the party platform or even to their campaign promises.* Parties have no strong disciplinary sanctions to use against members of Congress who vote against the party's policy position. The parties cannot deny them renomination. At most, the party's leadership in Congress can threaten the status, privileges, and pet bills of disloyal members (see Chapter 10). Party cohesion, where it exists, is more a product of like-mindedness than of party discipline.

nominee Political party's entry in a general election race.

nomination Political party's selection of its candidate for a public office.

primary elections Elections to choose party nominees for public office; may be open or closed.

Political parties as organizers of elections. (a) The Executive Committee of the Republican National Convention in Chicago in 1880. Conventions emerged as the main way for parties to select candidates in the nineteenth century. (b) Al Gore celebrates after winning the nation's first Republican primary in New Hampshire. Today, party candidates are determined by primary elections rather than by convention. (c) Parties also seek to attract voters through registration drives. (d) George W. Bush campaigning on his way to the Republican National Convention in Philadelphia. Parties provide the organizational structure for political campaigns.

Finally, American political parties no longer perform social welfare functions—trading off social services, patronage jobs, or petty favors in exchange for votes. Traditional party organizations, or **machines**, especially in large cities, once helped immigrants get settled in, found **patronage** jobs in government for party workers, and occasionally provided aid to impoverished but loyal party voters. But *government bureaucracies have replaced the political parties as providers of social services.* Government employment agencies, welfare agencies, civil service systems, and other bureaucracies now provide the social services once undertaken by political machines in search of votes.

PARTIES AS ORGANIZERS OF ELECTIONS

Despite the erosion of many of their functions, America's political parties survive as the principal institutions for organizing elections. Party nominations organize electoral choice by narrowing the field of aspiring office seekers to the Democratic

machine Tightly disciplined party organization, headed by a boss, that relies on material rewards—including patronage jobs—to control politics.

patronage Appointment to public office based on party loyalty.

and Republican candidates in most cases. Very few independents or third-party candidates are elected to high political office in the United States. Democratic or Republican Party nominations are sought by most serious aspirants for state and national office, often a year or two in advance of the actual election. **Nonpartisan elections**—elections in which there are no party nominations and all candidates run without an official party label—are common only in local elections, for city council, county commission, school board, judgeships, and so on. Only Nebraska has nonpartisan elections for its unicameral (one-house) state legislature. Party conventions are still held in many states in every presidential year, but these conventions seldom have the power to determine the parties' nominees for public office.

Party Conventions　Historically, party nominations were made by caucus or convention. The **caucus** was the earliest nominating process; party leaders (party chairs, elected officials, and "bosses") would simply meet several months before the election and decide on the party's nominee themselves. The early presidents— Thomas Jefferson, James Madison, James Monroe, and John Quincy Adams— were nominated by caucuses of Congress members. Complaints about the exclusion of people from this process led to nominations by convention—large meetings of delegates sent by local party organizations—starting in 1832. Andrew Jackson was the first president to be nominated by convention. The convention was considered more democratic than the caucus.

For nearly a century, party conventions were held at all levels of government— local, state, and national. City or county conventions included delegates from local **wards** and **precincts**, who nominated candidates for city or county office, for the state legislature, or even for the House of Representatives when a congressional district fell within the city or country. State conventions included delegates from counties, and they nominated governors, U.S. senators, and other statewide officers. State parties chose delegates to the Republican and Democratic national conventions every four years to nominate a president.

Party Primaries　Today, primary elections have largely replaced conventions as the means of selecting the Democratic and Republican nominees for public office.[5] Primary elections, introduced as part of the progressive reform movement of the early twentieth century, allow the party's *voters* to choose the party's nominee directly. The primary election was designed to bypass the power of party organizations and party leaders and to further democratize the nomination process. It generally succeeded in doing so, but it also had the effect of seriously weakening political parties, since candidates seeking a party nomination need only appeal to party *voters*—not *leaders*—for support in the primary election.[6]

Types of Primaries　There are some differences among the American states in how they conduct their primary elections.[7] **Closed primaries** allow only voters who have previously registered as Democrats or Republicans (or in some states voters who choose to register as Democrats or Republicans on primary election day) can cast a ballot in their chosen party's primary. Closed primaries tend to discourage people from officially registering as independents, even if they think of themselves as independent, because persons registered as independents cannot cast a ballot in either party's primary.

Open primaries allow voters to choose on election day which party primary they wish to participate in. Anyone, regardless of prior party affiliation, may choose to vote in either party's primary election. Voters simply request the ballot of one

nonpartisan elections
Elections in which candidates do not officially indicate their party affiliation; often used for city, county, school board, and judicial elections.

caucus　Nominating process in which party leaders select the party's nominee.

ward　Division of a city for electoral or administrative purposes or as a unit for organizing political parties.

precinct　Subdivision of a city, county, or ward for election purposes.

closed primaries　Primary elections in which voters must declare (or have previously declared) their party affiliation and can cast a ballot only in their own party's primary election.

open primaries　Primary elections in which a voter may cast a ballot in either party's primary election.

Voter turn-out among 18 to 21 year olds is lower than any other age group. Here, University of New Hampshire students register to vote in the 2000 election.

party or the other. Open primaries provide opportunities for voters to cross over party lines and vote in the primary of the party they usually do not support. Opponents of open primaries have argued that these types of primary elections allow for **raiding**—organized efforts by one party to get its members to cross over to the opposition party's primary and defeat an attractive candidate and thereby improve the raiding party's chances of winning the general election. But there is little evidence to show that large numbers of voters connive in such a fashion.

The U.S. Supreme Court declared that the *blanket primary* violated the First Amendment freedom of association right of political parties to choose their own candidates. California had adopted a primary system that gave all voters, regardless of party affiliation, ballots that included the names of *all* candidates in *both* parties. Candidates of each party who received the most votes were to become the nominees of those parties and move on to face each other in the general election. But in *California Democratic Party v. Jones* (2000), the U.S. Supreme Court held that the blanket primary forced the parties to open their candidate-selection process "to persons wholly unaffiliated with the party, who may have different views from the party" and therefore violated the First Amendment associational rights of parties. The decision directly affected the previously blanket primary states—California, Washington, and Alaska—and raised doubts about various forms of open primaries elsewhere.

Louisiana is unique in its nonpartisan primary elections. All candidates, regardless of their party affiliation, run in the same primary election. If a candidate gets over 50 percent of the vote, he or she wins the office, without appearing on the general election ballot. If no one receives over 50 percent of the primary election votes, then top two vote-getters, regardless of party, face each other in the general election.

Some states hold a **runoff primary** when no candidate receives a majority or a designated percentage of the vote in the party's first primary election. A runoff primary is limited to the two highest vote-getters in the first primary. Runoff elections are more common in the southern United States.[8] In most states, only a plurality of votes is needed to win a primary election.

General Elections Several months after the primaries and conventions, the **general election** (usually held in November, on the first Tuesday after the first

raiding Organized efforts by one party to get its members to cross over in a primary and defeat an attractive candidate in the opposition party's primary.

Blanket primary All candidates, regardless of party, run in the same primary election; the top vote-getter among Republicans and top vote-getter among Democrats go on to face each other in the general election.

runoff primary Additional primary held between the top two vote-getters in a primary where no candidate has received a majority of the vote.

general election Election to choose among candidates nominated by parties and/or independent candidates who gained access to the ballot by petition.

Monday for presidential and most state elections) determines who will occupy elective office. Winners of the Democratic and Republican primary elections must face each other—and any independent or third-party candidates—in the general election. Voters in the general election may choose any candidate, regardless of how they voted earlier in their party's primary or whether they voted in the primary at all.

Independent and minor-party candidates can get on the general election ballot, although the process is usually very difficult. Most states require independent candidates to file a petition with the signatures of several thousand registered voters. The number of signatures varies from state to state and office to office, but it may range up to 5 or 10 percent of *all* registered voters, a very large number that, in a big state especially, presents a difficult obstacle. The same petition requirements usually apply to minor parties, although some states automatically carry a minor party's nominee on the general election ballot if that party's candidate or candidates received a certain percentage (for example, 10 percent) of the vote in the previous general election.

WHERE'S THE PARTY?

The Democratic and Republican parties are found in different political arenas (see Figure 7-5). There is, first of all, the **party-in-the-electorate**—the voters who identify themselves as Democrats or Republicans and who tend to vote for the candidates of their party. The party-in-the-electorate appears to be in decline today. Party loyalties among voters are weakening. More people identify themselves as independents, and more **ticket splitters** divide their votes between candidates of different parties for different offices in the same general election, and more voters cast their ballots without regard to the party affiliation of the candidates than ever before.

The second locus of party activity is the **party-in-the-government**—officials who received their party's nomination and won the general election. The party-in-the-government includes members of Congress, state legislators and local government officials, and elected members of the executive branch, including the president and governors.

Party identification and loyalty among elected officeholders (the party-in-the-government) are generally stronger than party identification and loyalty among the party-in-the-electorate. Nevertheless, party loyalties among elected officials have also weakened over time. (We examine the role of parties in Congress in Chapter 9 and the president's party role in Chapter 10.)

Finally, there is the **party organization**—national and state party officials and workers, committee members, convention delegates, and others active in the party. The Democratic and Republican party organizations formally resemble the American federal system, with national committees, officers and staffs, and national conventions, 50 state committees, and more than 3,000 county committees with city, ward, and precinct levels under their supervision. State committees are not very responsive to the direction of the national committee; and in most states, city and county party organizations operate quite independently of the state committees. In other words, no real hierarchy of authority exists in American parties.

National Party Structure The Democratic and Republican national party conventions possess *formal* authority over the parties. They meet every four years not only to nominate candidates for president and vice president but also to adopt a party platform, choose party officers, and adopt rules for the party's operation.

party-in-the-electorate Voters who identify themselves with a party.

ticket splitter Person who votes for candidates of different parties for different offices in a general election.

party-in-the-government Public officials who were nominated by their party and who identify themselves in office with their party.

party organization National and state party officials and workers, committee members, convention delegates, and others active in the party.

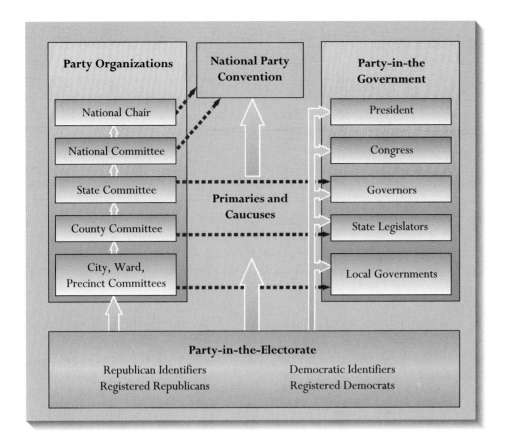

FIGURE 7-5 Where's the Party?

Even among Americans who strongly identify with a major party, there are differences among those who are strictly members of the party-in-the-electorate (voters), those who are members of the party-in-the-government (elected officials), and those who are members of the party organization (national and state party committee members).

Because the convention is a large body that meets for only three or four days, however, its real function is to ratify decisions made by national party leaders, as well as to formally nominate presidential and vice presidential candidates.

The Democratic and Republican national committees, made up of delegates from each state and territory, are supposed to govern party affairs *between* conventions. But the *real* work of the national party organizations is undertaken by the national party chairs and staff. The national chair is officially chosen by the national committee but is actually chosen by the party's presidential candidate. If the party wins the presidency, the national chair usually serves as a liaison with the president for party affairs. If the party loses, the chair may be replaced before the next national convention. The national chair is supposed to be neutral in the party's primary battles, but when an incumbent president is seeking reelection, the national chair and staff lean very heavily in the president's favor.

The power of the national chair and staff lies in their ability to raise campaign funds and assist the party's candidates in presidential and congressional elections. The staff of the Republican National Committee (RNC) took the lead in fund raising in the 1980s, devising sophisticated computerized mailing lists and a huge file of potential contributors. The RNC used these funds to assist Republican candidates in House and Senate races, commission polls, develop campaign themes, analyze voter trends, and promote the party as a whole in national advertising. The success of the RNC inspired the Democratic National Committee (DNC) to emulate these activities. By 1992, the DNC was able to match the RNC in fund raising.

State Party Organizations State party organizations consist of a state committee, a state chair who heads the committee, and a staff working at the state capital. Democratic and Republican state committees vary from state to state in composition, organization, and function. The state party chair is generally selected by the state committee, but this selection is often dictated by the party's candidate for governor. Membership on the state committee may range from about a dozen up to several hundred. The members may be chosen through party primaries or by state party conventions. Generally, representation on state committees is allocated by counties, but occasionally other units of government are recognized in state party organizations.

Most state party organizations maintain full-time staffs, including an executive director and public relations, fund-raising, and research people. These organizations help to raise campaign funds for their candidates, conduct registration drives, provide advice and services to their nominees, and even recruit candidates to run in election districts and for offices where the party would otherwise have no names on the ballot. Services to candidates may include advertising and media consulting, advice on election-law compliance, polling, research (including research on opponents), registration and voter identification, mailing lists, and even seminars on campaign techniques.

State committees are also supposed to direct the campaigns for important statewide elections—governors and U.S. senators. They are supposed to serve as central coordinating agencies for these election campaigns and as the party's principal fund-raising organization in the state. Today the role of the state committee is very often limited, however, because most candidates have their own campaign organizations.

Legislative Party Structures   The parties organize the U.S. Senate and House of Representatives, and they organize most state legislatures as well. The majority party in the House meets in caucus to select the speaker of the house as well as the House majority leader and whip (see "Organizing Congress: Party and Leadership" in Chapter 10). The minority party elects its own minority leader and whip. The majority party in the Senate elects the president pro tempore, who presides during the (frequent) absences of the vice president, as well as the Senate majority leader and whip. The minority party in the Senate elects its own minority leader and whip. Committee assignments in both the House and the Senate are allocated on a party basis; committee chairs are always majority-party members.

County Committees   The nation's 3,000 Republican and 3,000 Democratic county chairs probably constitute the most important building blocks in party organization in the nation. City and county party officers and committees are chosen in local primary elections; they cannot be removed by state or national party authorities.

NATIONAL PARTY CONVENTIONS

The Democratic and Republican parties are showcased every four years at the national party **convention**. The official purpose of these four-day fun-filled events is the nomination of the presidential candidates and their vice presidential running mates. Yet the presidential choices have usually already been made in the parties' **presidential primaries** and caucuses earlier in the year. By midsummer convention time, delegates pledged to cast their convention vote for one or another of the

convention Nominating process in which delegates from local party organizations select the party's nominees.

presidential primaries Primary elections in the states in which voters in each party can choose a presidential candidate for its party's nomination. Outcomes help determine the distribution of pledged delegates to each party's national nominating convention.

presidential candidates have already been selected. Not since 1952, when the Democrats took three convention ballots to select Adlai Stevenson as their presidential candidate, has convention voting gone beyond the first ballot.[9] The possibility exists that in some future presidential race no candidate will win a majority of delegates in the primaries and caucuses, and the result will be a *brokered* convention in which delegates will exercise independent power to select the party nominee. But this event is unlikely.

The Democratic and Republican national conventions are really televised party rallies, designed to showcase the presidential nominee, confirm the nominee's choice for a running mate, and inspire television viewers to support the party and its candidates in the forthcoming general election. Indeed, the national party conventions are largely media events, carefully staged to present an attractive image of the party and its nominees. Party luminaries jockey for key time slots at the podium, and the party prepares slick videotaped commercials touting its nominee for prime-time presentation.

Convention Delegates   Over time, the spread of presidential primary elections has taken the suspense out of the national party conventions. As late as 1968, fewer than half of the delegates were selected in primary elections. But today, the selection of more than 80 percent of pledged delegates by the party's primary voters has greatly diminished the role of party officials in presidential selection.

Both parties award **delegates** to each state in rough proportion to the number of party voters in the state. Democratic Party rules currently require that all popularly elected delegates from each state be awarded to the presidential candidates according to their proportion of that state's primary or caucus vote, after the candidates reach a 15 percent vote threshold. Republican Party rules allow states either to apportion their delegates according to the primary or caucus vote or to adopt a winner-take-all system of awarding all state delegates to the state's primary election victor.

Convention delegates are generally party activists, ideologically motivated and strongly committed to their presidential candidates.[10] Democratic delegates are much more *liberal* than Democratic voters, and Republican delegates are more *conservative* than Republican voters (see Figure 7-6). There is a slight tendency for Democratic and Republican delegates to differ in social backgrounds; usually more African Americans, women, and union members are found among Democratic delegates than among Republican delegates.

Making Party Rules   National party conventions make rules for the party, including rules governing the selection of delegates at the next party convention. Democrats are especially likely to focus on delegate selection rules. In 1972 the Democratic Party responded to charges that African Americans, women, and other minorities were underrepresented among the delegates by appointing a special commission chaired by Senator George McGovern to "reform" the party. The McGovern Commission took "affirmative steps" to ensure that the next convention would include "goals" for the representation of African Americans, women, and other minorities among the delegates in proportion to their presence in the Democratic electorate. The effect of these reforms was to reduce the influence of Democratic officeholders (members of Congress, governors, state legislators, and mayors) at the convention and to increase the influence of ideologically motivated activists. Later rule changes eliminated the *unit vote*, in which all delegates from a

delegates   Accredited voting members of a party's national presidential nominating convention.

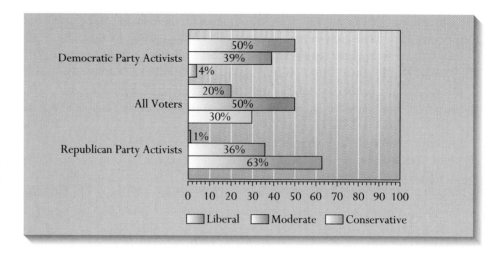

FIGURE 7-6 Ideologies of Voters versus Party Activists

Democratic and Republican party activists (convention delegates in 1996) are far more likely to hold divergent liberal and conservative views than voters generally.

Source: NBC News/*Wall Street Journal* Poll, as reported in *The Polling Report,* September 29, 1997.

state were required to vote with the majority of the state's delegation and which required that all delegates who were pledged to a candidate vote for that candidate unless *released* by the candidate.

Then, in the 1980s, the Democratic Leadership Council pressed the party to reserve some convention delegate seats for **superdelegates**—elected officials and party leaders not bound to one candidate—with the expectation that these delegates would be more moderate than the liberal party activists. The notion was that the superdelegates would inject more balanced, less ideological political judgments into convention deliberations, thus improving the party's chances of victory in the general elections. As a result, many Democratic senators, governors, and members of Congress now attend the convention as superdelegates. If presidential candidates ever fail to win a majority of delegates in the primaries, these superdelegates may some day control a nomination.

Party Platforms   National conventions also write party **platforms**, setting out the party's goals and policy positions. Because a party's platform is not binding on its nominees, platform *planks* are largely symbolic, although they often provide heated arguments and provide distinct differences between the parties to present to voters (see *Up Close:* "Democratic and Republican Platforms: Can You Tell the Difference?").

Selecting a Running Mate   Perhaps the only suspense remaining in national party conventions centers on the presidential nominee's choice of a vice presidential running mate. Even a presidential candidate who has decided on a running mate well in advance of the convention may choose to wait until the convention to announce the choice; otherwise there would be little real "news value" to the convention, and the television networks would give less coverage to it. By encouraging speculation about who the running mate will be, the candidate and the convention manager can sustain media interest. (For a discussion of various strategies in selecting a running mate, see "The Vice Presidential Waiting Game" in Chapter 11.)

The convention *always* accepts the presidential candidate's recommendation for a running mate. No formal rules require the convention to do so, but it would be politically unacceptable for the convention to override the first important decision of the

superdelegates Delegates to the Democratic Party national convention selected because of their position in the government or the party and not pledged to any candidate.

platform Statement of principles adopted by a political party at its national convention (specific portions of the platform are known as planks); a platform is not binding on the party's candidates.

Democratic and Republican Platforms: Can You Tell the Difference?

These statements from the Democratic and Republican platforms in 2000 differ in both tone and substance.

Can you guess which statements are taken from the Democratic platform and which from the Republican?

Medicare

A. We propose an unprecedented tax credit that will enable millions of individuals and families to purchase private health insurance that's right for them.

B. Instead of the guaranteed insured prescription drug benefit that [we] believe should be added to Medicare, [they] are proposing to leave to insurance companies the decisions about whether or where a drug benefit might be offered . . .

Social Security

A. Each of today's workers should be free to direct a portion of their payroll taxes to personal investments for their retirement future.

B. To build on the success of Social Security [we] propose the creation of a Retirement Savings Plus—voluntary tax-free personally-controlled savings accounts—that would let Americans save and invest on top of the foundation of Social Security's guaranteed benefit . . . . They have a far different plan—the scheme that would come not in addition to Social Security but at the expense of it.

Defense

A. America must deploy effective missile defenses at the earliest possible date.

B. We reject [their] plans . . . to construct an unproven, expensive and ill-conceived missile defense system that would plunge us into a new arms race.

Family

A. We support the traditional definition of "marriage" as the legal union of one man and one woman . . . . We do not believe sexual preference should be given special legal protection or standing in law.

B. We support the full inclusion of gay and lesbian families in the life of the nation.

Abortion

A. The unborn child has a fundamental right to life which cannot be infringed. We support a human life amendment to the Constitution and we endorse legislation to make clear that the 14th Amendment's protection applies to unborn children.

B. [We] stand behind the right of every woman to choose, consistent with *Roe v Wade*, and regardless of ability to pay.

Excerpts from Republican [A] and Democratic [B] party platforms, 2000.

party's presidential nominee. Convention delegates set aside any personal reservations they may have and unanimously endorse the presidential nominee's choice.

Campaign Kickoff   The final evening of the national conventions is really the kickoff for the general election campaign. The presidential nominee's acceptance speech tries to set the tone for the fall campaign. Party celebrities, including defeated presidential candidates, join hands at the podium as a symbol of party unity. Presidential and vice presidential candidates, spouses, and families assemble under balloons and streamers, amid the happy noise and hoopla, to signal the start of the general election campaign.[11]

THE PARTY VOTERS

Traditionally, the Democratic Party has been able to claim to be the majority party in the United States (see Figure 7-7). In opinion polls, those who "identified" with the Democratic Party generally outnumbered those who "identified" with the Republican Party. (**Party identification** is determined by response to the question, "Generally speaking, how would you identify yourself: as a Republican, Democrat, independent, or something else?") But the Democratic Party advantage among the voters has eroded over time, partly as a result of a gradual increase in the number of people who call themselves independents.

Dealignment   **Dealignment** describes the decline in attractiveness of the political parties to the voters, the growing reluctance of people to identify themselves with either party, and a decrease in reliance on a candidate's party affiliation in voter choice. Dealignment is evident not only in the growing numbers of self-described independents but also in the declining numbers of those who identify themselves as "strong" Democrats or Republicans. In short, the electorate is less partisan than it once was.

party identification   Self-described identification with a political party, usually in response to the question, "Generally speaking, how would you identify yourself: as a Republican, Democrat, independent, or something else?"

dealignment   Declining attractiveness of the parties to the voters, a reluctance to identify strongly with a party, and a decrease in reliance on party affiliation in voter choice.

FIGURE 7-7   Party Identification in the Electorate

For many years, the Democratic Party enjoyed a substantial lead in party identification among voters. This Democratic lead eroded somewhat following the election of Republican President Ronald Reagan in 1980. Independent identification over the years has risen, suggesting that many voters have become disillusioned with both parties. Relatively few people consider themselves "strong" Democrats or Republicans.

Source: Data from National Election Studies, University of Michigan.

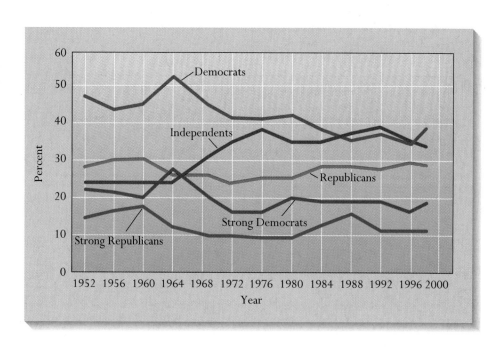

Party Loyalty in Voting   Despite the decline in partisan identification in the electorate, it is important to note that *party identification is a strong influence in voter choice in elections.* Most voters cast their ballot for the candidate of their party. This is true in presidential elections (see Figure 7-8) and even more true in congressional and state elections. Those who identify themselves as Democrats are somewhat more likely to vote for a Republican presidential candidate than those who identify themselves as Republicans are to vote for a Democratic presidential candidate. Republican Ronald Reagan was able to win more than one-quarter of self-identified Democrats in 1980 and 1984, earning these crossover voters the label "Reagan Democrats."[12]

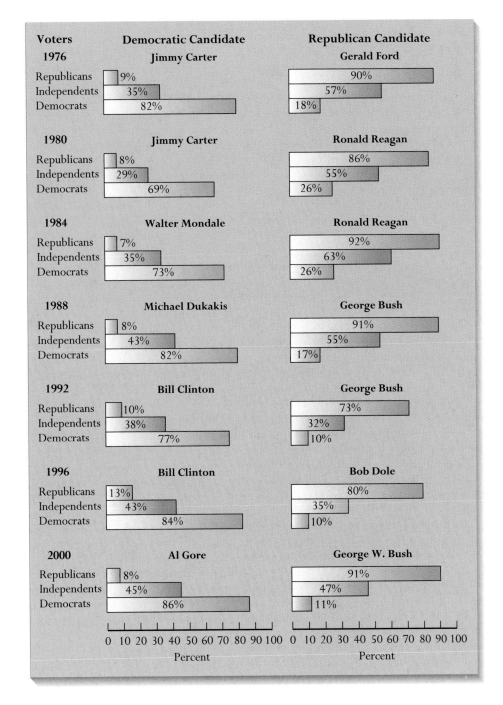

FIGURE 7-8   Republican, Democratic, and Independent Voters in Presidential Elections

As the percentages here indicate, in recent years registered Democrats have been more likely to "cross over" and vote for a Republican candidate for president than registered Republicans have been to vote for the Democratic presidential candidate.

Source: New York Times.

UP CLOSE

A Typology of Donkeys and Elephants

Among voters, the Democratic and Republican parties are loose coalitions of people with differing sets of values and beliefs. There are significant political and social differences *within* each of the parties as well as *across* the parties. Extensive surveys of voters prior to the 2000 presidential election produced the following types of voters:

REPUBLICANS

Staunch Conservatives (12% of registered voters)
Party Identification: 72% Republican; 24% Independent leaning Republican.

The most partisan Republican group; pro-business, pro-military, pro-life, patriotic, distrustful of government; predominantly white, male, Protestant, older, and financially secure; politically very active with high voter turnout; issue priorities: morality and taxes.

Moderate Republicans (12% of registered voters)
Party Identification: 76% Republican; 22% Independent leaning Republican.

Loyal Republicans, but more positive in their views toward government and politicians; pro-business, pro-military, patriotic, pro-environmental protection; predominantly white, well educated, and financially secure; politically attentive regular voters; issue priorities: Social Security and education.

Populist Republicans (9% of registered voters)
Party Identification: 72% Republican; 25% Independent leaning Republican.

Less affluent than other Republican groups; strong religious faith and conservative views on moral issues; favor government efforts to help the needy; predominantly white, female, less educated, evangelical Protestants; low political knowledge, average voter turnout; issue priorities: morality and Social Security.

INDEPENDENTS

New Prosperity Independents (11% of registered voters)
Party Identification: 69% Independent, 21% Republican, 5% Democrat.

Affluent and less religious; basically nonpartisan with a slight leaning toward the Republican Party; critical of government and favorable toward having a third major political party; pro-business, pro-environmental protection, and tolerant on social issues; predominantly well educated and young; politically knowledgeable but average in voter turnout; issue priorities: education and the economy.

The Disaffected (10% of registered voters)
Party Identification: 73% Independent, 8% Democrat, 6% Republican.

Dissatisfied with both parties and with the ability of politicians to help improve things; distrustful of government, politicians, and business corporations; anti-immigrant and intolerant of homosexuality; less educated and

Realignment?   Although Democratic Party loyalty has eroded over the last twenty years, it is not clear whether or not this erosion is a classic party **realignment**.[13] Most scholars agree that party realignments occurred in the presidential elections of 1824 (Jackson, Democrats), 1860 (Lincoln, Republicans), 1896 (Bryan, Democrats), and 1932 (Roosevelt, Democrats). This historical sequence gave rise to a theory that realigning elections occur every thirty-six years. According to this theory, the election of 1968 should have been a realigning one. It is true that Richard Nixon's 1968 victory marked the beginning of a 24-year Republican era in presidential election victories that was broken only by Jimmy Carter in 1976. But there was relatively little shifting of the party loyalties of major social groups, and the Democratic Party remained the dominant party in the electorate and in Congress.

The Democratic Party still receives *disproportionate* support from Catholics, Jews, African Americans, less educated and lower income groups, blue-collar workers,

realignment   Long-term shift in social-group support for various political parties that creates new coalitions in each party.

lower income; low political knowledge and low voter turnout; issue priorities; Social Security and health care.

DEMOCRATS

Liberal Democrats (10% of registered voters)

Party Identification: 56% Democrats; 41% Independent leaning Democrat.

Strong supporters of Democratic candidates, although many prefer to call themselves Independents; pro-choice, pro-civil rights, pro-gay rights, anti-business, and pro-environmental protection; well educated and least religious of all typology groups; most politically knowledgeable of all groups and above-average voter turnout; issue priorities: education and health care.

Socially Conservative Democrats (14% of registered voters)

Party Identification: 70% Democrat; 27% Independent leaning Democrat.

Describing themselves as working-class Democrats, this group differs from other Democratic groups in its conservative views on social issues; religious, patriotic, pro-military, anti-business, pro-labor union, less tolerant; slightly less educated, older, and married; average political knowledge and average voter turnout; issue priorities: Social Security and health care.

New Democrats (10% of registered voters)

Party Identification: 75% Democrat; 21% Independent leaning Democrat.

Favorable view of government, yet generally pro-business; concerned about environmental issues, but somewhat less concerned about the poor, black Americans, and immigrants than Liberal Democrats; well-educated, middle-income, women; average political knowledge and average voter turnout; issue priorities: Social Security and education.

Partisan Poor (11% of registered voters)

Party Identification: 85% Democrat; 12% Independent leaning Democrat.

Poorest of the ten groups and including the largest group of African Americans; religious, anti-business, strong supporters of civil rights; believe the government should do even more to help the poor; low-income, not well-educated, largest group of single mothers; average voter turnout; issue priorities: Social Security and poverty.

BYSTANDERS

Bystanders (0% of registered voters)

Party Identification: 54% Independent; 25% Democrat; 10% Republican.

Americans who choose not to participate in politics; do not bother to register or vote; somewhat sympathetic to the poor; young, less educated, working class; low political knowledge; no priority political issues.

Source: The Pew Research Center for the People and the Press, *Retro-politics, The Political Typology,* Version 3.0, 1999.

union members, and big-city residents. The Republican Party still receives *disproportionate* support from Protestants, whites, more educated and higher income groups, white-collar workers, nonunion workers, and suburban and small-town dwellers (see *Up Close:* "A Typology of Donkeys and Elephant"). Disproportionate support does not mean these groups *always* give a majority of their votes to the indicated party, but only that they give that party a larger percentage of their votes than the party receives from the general electorate. This pattern of social-group voting and party identification has remained relatively stable over the years, even though the GOP has made some gains among many of the traditionally Democratic groups (see Figure 7-9 on page 216). The only major *shift* in social-group support has occurred among southern whites. This group has shifted from heavily Democratic in party identification to a substantial Republican preference. Thus it is questionable whether a true party realignment has occurred[14] (see *Across the USA:* "Democratic and Republican Party Strength in the States" on page 217).

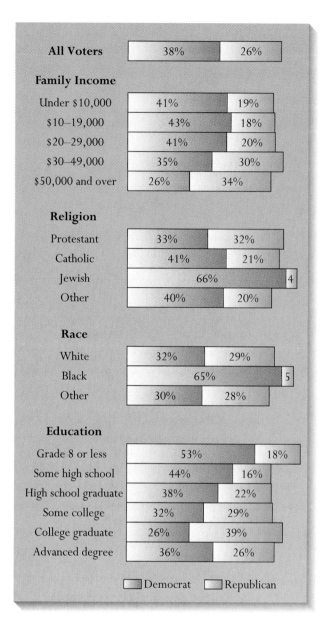

	Democrat	Republican
All Voters	38%	26%
Family Income		
Under $10,000	41%	19%
$10–19,000	43%	18%
$20–29,000	41%	20%
$30–49,000	35%	30%
$50,000 and over	26%	34%
Religion		
Protestant	33%	32%
Catholic	41%	21%
Jewish	66%	4
Other	40%	20%
Race		
White	32%	29%
Black	65%	5
Other	30%	28%
Education		
Grade 8 or less	53%	18%
Some high school	44%	16%
High school graduate	38%	22%
Some college	32%	29%
College graduate	26%	39%
Advanced degree	36%	26%

FIGURE 7-9 Social-Group Support for the Democratic and Republican Parties

The Democratic Party draws disproportionate support from low-income, less educated, Catholic, Jewish, and African American voters. The Republican Party relies more heavily on support from high-income, college-educated, white Protestant voters.

Source: Data from National Election Studies, University of Michigan.

THIRD PARTIES IN THE U.S. SYSTEM

Despite the cultural and electoral barriers to victory, **third parties**, more accurately called minor parties, are a common feature of American politics. These parties can be roughly classified by the role they play in the political system.

Ideological Parties   **Ideological parties** exist to promote an ideology rather than to win elections. They use the electoral process to express their views and to rally activists to their cause, and they measure success not by victory at the polls but by their ability to bring their name and their views to the attention of the American public. The socialist parties, which have run candidates in virtually every presidential election in this century, are prime examples of ideological parties in the United States (see also *Up Close:* "The Libertarian Party: A Dissenting Voice" on page 218).

third party Political party that challenges the two major parties in an election.

ideological party Third party that exists to promote an ideology rather than to win elections.

Democratic and Republican Party Strength in the States

The Democratic and Republican parties compete in every state. Indeed, party competition within states has increased as the once heavily Democratic states of the "Solid South" have developed stronger Republican Party ties. But some voters have favored candidates of one party in gubernatorial and congressional elections and the other in presidential elections in recent years.

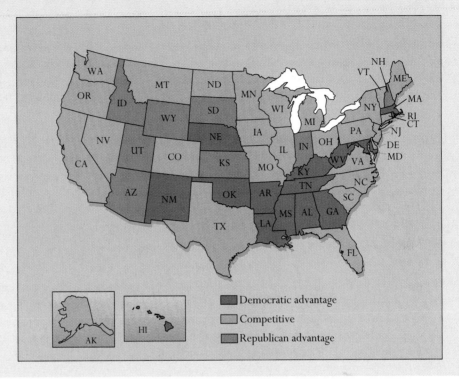

■ Democratic advantage
□ Competitive
■ Republican advantage

Protest Parties **Protest parties** arise around popular issues or concerns that the major parties have failed to address. An important historical example of a protest party is the Populist Party of the late 1800s. It arose as a protest by midwestern farmers against eastern railroads, "trusts" and monopolies, and the gold standard. The Populists threatened to capture the wave of popular support for railroad regulation, cheap money, and anti-monopoly legislation, and thus they endangered the established Democratic and Republican parties. But when the Democratic Party nominated William Jennings Bryan in 1896, the Populist Party officially endorsed Bryan and temporarily disappeared as a significant independent political organization. Populist ideas were set forth again in a new Progressive Party, which nominated Robert M. La Follette for president in 1924; the Democratic and Republican parties both nominated conservative candidates that year, helping La Follette to win almost 17 percent of the popular vote.

Not all major protest movements have been accompanied by the formation of third parties. Indeed, protest leaders have often argued that a third-party effort distracts the movement from a more effective strategy of capturing control of one or both of the major parties. The labor-union-organizing movement of the 1930s and the civil rights and antiwar movements of the 1960s did not spark a separate third party but instead worked largely *within* the dominant Democratic Party to advance their goals.

protest party   Third party that arises in response to issues of popular concern which have not been addressed by the major parties.

The Libertarian Party: A Dissenting Voice

Would you like to see the federal income tax repealed; the Internal Revenue Service abolished; foreign aid ended; all U.S. troops brought home from overseas; and individual choice "in all matters," from abortion to gun control to drug use? Would you like to eliminate government farm subsidies; end federal support for public broadcasting, science, and the arts; and "privatize" education and "charitize" welfare? These are the campaign promises of the Libertarian Party, whose presidential candidates' names appeared on the ballot in all fifty states in 1992 and 1996.

The Libertarian Party is unique in its uncompromising commitment to the classical liberal, eighteenth-century ideals of John Locke and Adam Smith. Libertarians oppose all interference by government in the private lives of citizens. They support unregulated free markets and the protection of private property rights. Thus they oppose environmental regulations, consumer protection laws, and laws that infringe on private property or "take" property for government use without just compensation to owners. They also oppose government efforts to regulate private morals—including laws outlawing drug use, prostitution, gambling, and pornography—believing these activities should be the exclusive choice of consenting individuals. Libertarians are strict noninterventionists in international affairs; they are opposed to the North Atlantic Treaty Organization (NATO) alliance, to foreign aid, to military involvements outside of U.S. territory, and to virtually all spending for national defense.

Although the Libertarian Party candidate for president regularly receives less than 1 percent of the popular vote, Libertarian ideas have entered the nation's policy debates and influenced both major parties. Republican candidates have frequently adopted Libertarian arguments on behalf of deregulation of market activities; Democratic candidates frequently use Libertarian arguments about individual "choice" in the areas of abortion, school prayer, and homosexual activity. And both the Democratic and the Republican parties have vocal "isolationist" wings that borrow Libertarian, noninterventionist arguments against foreign aid, international alliances, and military expenditures. Thus the Libertarian Party, like other ideological parties, functions to promote ideas rather than win elections.

Single-Issue Parties **Single-issue parties** have frequently formed around a particular cause. Single-issue parties are much like protest parties, although somewhat narrower in their policy focus. The Greenback Party of the late 1800s shared with the Populists a desire for cheap inflated currency in order to ease the burden of debt and mortgage payments by farmers. But the Greenback Party focused on a single remedy: an end to the gold standard and the issuance of cheap currency—"greenbacks."

Perhaps the most persistent of minor parties over the years has been the Prohibition Party. It achieved temporary success with the passage of the Eighteenth Amendment to the U.S. Constitution in 1919, which prohibited the manufacture, sale, or transportation of "intoxicating liquors," only to see its "noble experiment" fail and be repealed by the Twenty-first Amendment.

Today the Green Party provides an example of a single-issue party, with its primary emphasis on environmental protection. However, the Green Party itself contends that it is "part of the worldwide movement that promotes ecological wisdom, social justice, grassroots democracy and non-violence."

Splinter Parties Finally, many third parties in American politics are really **splinter parties**, parties formed by a dissatisfied faction of a major party. Splin-

single-issue party Third party formed around one particular cause.

splinter party Third party formed by a dissatisfied faction of a major party.

Ralph Nader, the nation's most visible interest-group entrepreneur, continues his fight against auto companies, speaking here to Toldeo residents unhappy with tax breaks given to Daimler-Chrysler to keep its plant in the city. In the 2000 presidential election, Nader was the Green Party's nominee.

ter parties may form around a particular individual, as did the Progressive (Bull Moose) Party of Theodore Roosevelt in 1912. As a popular former president, Teddy Roosevelt won more than 27 percent of the popular vote, outpolling Republican candidate William Howard Taft but allowing Democrat Woodrow Wilson to win the presidency.

Splinter parties also may emerge from an intense intraparty policy dispute. For example, in 1948 the States' Rights (Dixiecrat) Party formed in protest to the civil rights (fair employment practices) plan in the Democratic Party platform of that year and nominated Strom Thurmond for president. In 1968 George Wallace's American Independent Party won nearly 14 percent of the popular vote. Wallace attacked school desegregation and busing to achieve racial balance in schools, as well as crime in the streets, welfare "cheats," and meddling federal judges and bureaucrats. He abandoned his third-party organization in 1972 to run in the Democratic presidential primary elections. Following some Democratic primary victories, he was shot and disabled for life.

Third Party Prospects   In recent years, polls have reported that a majority of Americans favor the idea of a third party. But support for the *general* idea of a third party has never been matched by voter support for *specific* third-party or independent presidential candidates (see Table 7-1 on page 220). Moreover, it is very difficult for a third party or independent candidate to win electoral votes (see *Up Close:* Understanding the Electoral College in Chapter 8). Only Theodore Roosevelt, Robert M. La Follette, and George C. Wallace managed to win any electoral votes in the past century.

THE REFORM PARTY

There is widespread disillusionment in the United States with "politics as usual." This is reflected in the distrust expressed by Americans in their government (see *What Do You Think? Can You Trust the Government?* in Chapter 1), in their reluctance to believe that their government is really "of, by, and for the people" (see *What Do*

Table 7-1	Twentieth-Century Third-Party Presidential Votes	
Third-Party Presidential Candidates	**Popular Vote (percentage)**	**Electoral Votes (number)**
Theodore Roosevelt (1912), Progressive (Bull Moose) Party	27.4%	88
Robert M. La Follette (1924), Progressive Party	16.6	13
George C. Wallace (1968), American Independent party	13.5	46
John Anderson (1980), Independent	6.6	0
Ross Perot (1992), Independent	18.9	0
Ross Perot (1996), Reform Party	8.5	0
Ralph Nader (2000), Green Party	2.7	0

You Think? Is the American Government Of, By and For the People? in Chapter 1), and in their increasing dealignment from the Republican and Democratic parties. Can disgust with "politics as usual" be the catalyst for a new political party?

Creating a New Party While anyone with a WebSite can create a virtual political party, establishing a new *national* party with a place on the general election ballot in all fifty states is a monumental task. It requires $100 million or more and tens of thousands of working supporters throughout the nation. It is a task fit only for an eccentric, energetic, media-wise billionaire.

When the pint-sized Texas billionaire, Ross Perot, first announced on *Larry King Live* in 1992 that he intended to run fro President, he was not taken very seriously in Washington. But he quickly motivated tens of thousands of supporters in a grass-roots effort, "United We Stand," that succeeded in placing his name on ballot in all fifty states. He used his own money, nearly $100 million, to build a nationwide organization. Early in the campaign his poll numbers mushroomed to 35 percent, higher than any independent candidate's support in the history of modern polling. His twangy Texas quotes activated audiences. His political support came mostly from the center of the political spectrum—people who identified themselves as independent rather than as Democrats or Republicans. But "Perot mania" faded when he abruptly withdrew from the race in July immediately before the Democratic Party convention. His withdrawal gave Bill Clinton a giant leap in the polls. Perot reentered the race in September, participated in the first three-way presidential television debates, and won 19 percent of popular vote in the general election, the highest percentage won by a third party candidate since Teddy Roosevelt in 1912. But Perot's voters were spread across the nation and therefore he failed to win a single electoral vote.

But the temperamental tycoon proceeded to turn his independent "United We Stand" organization into a political party—the Reform Party. The Party not only

Jesse "The Body" Ventura

"Retaliate in '98" was his campaign slogan. Retaliate for what? Apparently Minnesotans were asked to retaliate against two-party politics-as-usual in their state. They did so in a colorful three-way race in which the Reform Party candidate Jesse "The Body" Ventura, former Navy Seal, pro wrestler, and talk show host, upended the more politically experienced Republican and Democratic candidates, St. Paul Mayor Norm Coleman and state attorney general Hubert Humphrey III. Ventura's victory stunned the nation's political establishment; even Ross Perot was notably silent about his party's first statewide win.

Although the six foot four inch, 250 pound, shaved-headed, former wrestler is a frequent target of late-night TV comedians, Ventura argues "I'm not some big dumb wrestler." He served a four-year term as mayor of Brooklyn Park, a medium-size city in Minnesota, and as a popular radio talk show host in the Twin Cities.

Born James Janos in blue-collar Minneapolis, he joined the Navy after high school and was trained as a Navy Seal. After six years of Navy service, which included a tour in Vietnam, he rode with a motorcycle club in California, worked as a bodyguard, and then took up professional wrestling under a new name, Jesse "The Body" Ventura. He was very successful in his new profession, becoming a regular opponent of top wrestling star Hulk Hogan.

Ventura was forced to retire from wrestling in 1984 with a pulmonary embolism. But he maintained his charismatic tough-guy image by playing roles in action movies, including Arnold Schwarzenegger's popular film *Predator*. Later his deep booming voice and straight talk served him well as a talk show host in his home-town of Minneapolis. He expressed generally populist political views on his show—opposing taxes and big government as well as corporate welfare, and favoring gay rights laws and the legalization of marijuana. He became especially popular with young people who turned out in surprising numbers to support him on election day.

Ventura himself acknowledges he must now learn on the job, get along with Democratic and Republican legislators, and perhaps hold in check his free-wheeling nature. But with characteristic bravado, he says "I can do the job. It's not like it's transplanting kidneys."

enjoyed ballot access in all of the states, but because of Perot's 1992 vote showing, the Reform Party qualified for federal campaign matching funds in 1996. Early that year Perot teased his followers about whether he would run again, and even recruited former Colorado Governor, Richard Lamm, to enter the race for the Reform Party nomination. But Perot later took control of his new party and had himself nominated in an awkward "electronic convention." However, his popular support in early polls languished at only 5 percent of likely voters, and he was given little chance of winning any state's electoral votes. He was excluded from the presidential debates; he accepted taxpayer-funded presidential campaign money this time; and in his television appearances, including *Larry King Live*, he often appeared prickly, irritating, and autocratic. On Election Day he won fewer than half of the votes (9 percent) that he had garnered four years earlier, and again failed to win any state's electoral votes.

Political Parties of the World

Party politics vary throughout the world, but some general patterns are apparent. Multiparty systems occur in nations with proportional representation, whereas two-party systems occur in nations with winner-take-all elections. France has a unique two-step electoral system: all parties run candidates in a first election, and the top two candidates in each district face off in a second election. In Germany, half of the Bundestag (national legislature) is chosen by proportional representation and half by winner-take-all district elections. Both the German and the French electoral systems support a multiparty system, although two-party coalitions dominate government. Small Communist parties are found in multiparty Western democracies, but wherever the Communist Party has taken power, it has established a one-party system. Most two-party systems have one party oriented more toward free markets and another party more toward a welfare state or democratic socialism.

Nation	System	Major Parties	Party Orientation
Australia	Two-party, winner-take-all elections	Liberal Party Labor Party	Free enterprise Democratic socialism
Austria	Multiparty, proportional representation	Austrian Socialist Party Austrian Peoples Party Austrian Freedom Party	Democratic socialism Christian democratic Free enterprise, anti-immigration
Canada	Multiparty, winner-take-all elections	Liberal Party Progressive Conservative Party Le Parti Québecois New Democratic Party	Free enterprise, social reform Conservative, preservation of Canada Political sovereignty for Quebec Democratic socialism
China, People's Republic of	One-party system	Communist Party of China	Revolutionary class struggle, "market socialism"
Cuba	One-party system	Communist Party of Cuba	Revolutionary class struggle, socialism

A Party Without a Platform? Aside from attacking "politics as usual," Perot had little to say about philosophy of his new party. He avoided taking clear policy positions, promising only to "fix things" and appealing to voters as a "can do" outside challenging the political "establishment." In 1992 he vigorously attacked deficit spending, and 1996 he denounced international trade agreements. But he avoided identification with either liberal or conservative ideological positions. His support came mostly from independents and middle-of-the-roaders who were generally disillusioned with the Democratic and Republican parties. The Reform Party is neither a "splinter" party, nor a "single-issue" party, nor an ideological party. Perhaps it can be categorized as a "protest" party, but it seems to be protesting party politics generally, rather than any specific condition in society.

Nation	System	Major Parties	Party Orientation
France	Multiparty, two elections, winner-take-all elections	Rally for the Republic Union for French Democracy Socialist Party Unified Socialist Party Communist Party National Front Greens	Nationalism, "Gaulist" Centrist, European outlook Democratic socialism Socialism Communist society Anti-immigration Environmentalism
Germany	Multiparty, half proportional representation, winner-take-all elections	Christian Democratic Union Social Democratic Party Free Democratic Party Greens	Christian conservative Democratic socialism Free enterprise Environmentalism
Japan	Multiparty with a single dominant party, mixture of proportional representation and winner-take-all elections	Liberal Democratic Japan Socialist Party Komeito Party Japan Communist Party	Free enterprise Democratic socialism "Clean government" "Scientific socialism"
Israel	Multiparty with two major alignments, proportional representation	Likud Alignment Labour Alignment Liberal Party National Religious Party Communist Party	Nationalism Democratic socialism Free enterprise Religious orthodoxy Marxism-Leninism
United Kingdom	Modified two-party winner-take-all, elections	Conservative Party Labour Party Liberal Party	Free enterprise Social welfare state Free enterprise, centrist

The Reform Party Implosion in 2000   The Reform Party imploded at a raucus midsummer 2000 convention with rival factions almost coming to blows over control of the microphone. Firebrand conservative commentator Pat Buchanan appeared to control a majority of the delegates. But Perot followers, as well as Minnesota Governor Jesse Ventura, viewed Buchanan's candidacy as a hostile takeover of the Reform Party. They walked out of the convention hall and nominated their own candidate, John Hagelin, a Ph.D. in physics and a devotee of transcenental meditation. The Federal Elections Commission recognized Buchanan as the official nominee and awarded him the $12.6 million due to the Reform Party based on Perot's vote total in 1996. But Buchanan's right-wing rhetoric attracted less than one percent of the voters. Ralph Nader outpolled the combattive commentator and the Reform Party was left in a shambles, its future in doubt.

WHY THE TWO-PARTY SYSTEM PERSISTS

The two-party system is deeply ingrained in American politics. Although third parties have often made appearances in presidential elections, no third-party candidate has ever won the Oval Office. (Lincoln's new Republican Party in 1860 might be counted as an exception, but it quickly became a major party.) Very few third-party candidates have won seats in Congress. Many other democracies have multiple-party systems, so the question arises as to why the United States has had a two-party system throughout its history.[15]

Cultural Consensus   One explanation of the nation's two-party system focuses on the broad consensus supporting the American political culture (see Chapter 2). The values of democracy, capitalism, free enterprise, individual liberty, religious freedom, and equality of opportunity are so widely shared that no party challenging these values has ever won much of a following. There is little support in the American political culture for avowedly fascist, communist, authoritarian, or other antidemocratic parties. Moreover, the American political culture includes a strong belief in the separation of church and state. Political parties with religious affiliations, common in European democracies, are absent from American politics. Socialist parties have frequently appeared on the scene under various labels—the Socialist Party, the Socialist Labor Party, and the Socialist Workers Party. But the largest popular vote ever garnered by a socialist candidate in a presidential election was the 6 percent won by Eugene V. Debs in 1912. In contrast, socialist parties have frequently won control of European governments.

On broad policy issues, most Americans cluster near the center. This general consensus tends to discourage multiple parties. There does not appear to be sufficient room for them to stake out a position on the ideological spectrum that would detach voters from the two major parties.

This cultural explanation blends with the influence of historical precedents. The American two-party system has gained acceptance through custom. The nation's first party system developed from two coalitions, Federalists and Anti-Federalists, and this dual pattern has been reinforced over two centuries.

Winner-Take-All Electoral System   Yet another explanation of the American two-party system focuses on the electoral system itself. Winners in presidential and congressional elections, as well as in state gubernatorial and legislative elections, are usually determined by a plurality, winner-take-all vote. Even in elections that require a majority of more than 50 percent to win—which may involve a runoff election—only one party's candidate wins in the end. Because of the winner-take-all nature of U.S. elections, parties and candidates have an overriding incentive to broaden their appeal to a plurality or majority of voters. Losers come away empty-handed. There is not much incentive in such a system for a party to form to represent the views of 5 or 10 percent of the electorate.

Americans are so accustomed to winner-take-all elections that they seldom consider alternatives. In some countries, legislative bodies are elected by **proportional representation**, whereby all voters cast a single ballot for the party of their choice and legislative seats are then apportioned to the parties in proportion to their total vote in the electorate (see *Compared to What?* "Political Parties of the World"). Minority parties are assured of legislative seats, perhaps with as little as

proportional representation   Electoral system that allocates seats in a legislature based on the proportion of votes each party receives in a national election.

Twenty-First Century Directions

The Democratic and Republican parties are here to stay. America's two-party system is entrenched in the nation's political culture and its electoral system. Anyone seriously wishing to capture a seat in Congress or the Oval Office of the White House must work within the Democratic or Republican parties.

⬅➡ *Democratic Versus Republican Party Success* The Democratic Party's claim to the title of majority party in America will be subject to serious challenge in the years ahead. A strong economy tends to focus voters' concerns away from bread-and-butter issues that generally help the Democratic Party, and toward issues on which the Republican Party enjoys an advantage—lower taxes, crimefighting, and public morality. An economic downturn will encourage Democratic voting, as will concerns that Social Security and Medicare may not be able to handle the aging of the large baby-boom generation. Providing adequate health care is another concern that may help inspire to Democratic victories. But unpopular wars, prolonged and victoryless military commitments, and weakened U.S. defenses, could refocus Americans on national security affairs and thereby strengthen the Republican Party.

⬅➡ *Voter Alignments* Group voter alignments have remained relatively stable since the 1930s, with the exception of Republican Party gains among Southern whites. The Republican hold on the South is likely to solidify, with Texas and Florida becoming bastions of GOP strength. The Democratic Party can continue to count on its core supporters—African Americans, union members, liberals, teachers, environmentalists, and feminists. Both parties will contend vigorously for the growing Hispanic vote. The GOP may see splits between its economic conservatives, on the one hand, and its social and religious conservatives on the other. And the GOP must worry about the continuing erosion of support among women voters.

⬇ *Reform Party Prospects* Americans have always complained about "politics as usual." They have always enjoyed critics and cartoonists who have lampooned the Democratic and Republican parties. And Americans have increasingly expressed support for the general idea of a new third party. But when presented with the opportunity to vote for independent or third-party candidates, Americans have overwhelmingly chosen to cast their ballots in the Democratic or Republican columns.

10 or 15 percent of the vote. If no party wins 50 percent of the votes and seats, the parties try to form a coalition of parties to establish control of the government. In these nations, party coalition building to form a governing majority occurs *after* the election rather than *before* the election, as it does in winner-take-all elections systems.

Legal Access to the Ballot Another factor in the American two-party system may be electoral system barriers to third parties. The Democratic and Republican nominees are automatically included on all general election ballots, but third-party and independent candidates face difficult obstacles in getting their names listed. In presidential elections, a third-party candidate must meet the varied requirements of fifty separate states to appear on their ballots along with the Democratic and Republican nominees. These requirements often include filing petitions signed by up to 5 or 10 percent of registered voters. In addition, states require third parties to win 5 or 10 percent of the vote in the last election in order to retain their position on the ballot in subsequent elections. In 1980 independent John Anderson gained access to the ballot in all fifty states, as did independent Ross Perot in 1992. But just doing so required a considerable expenditure of effort and money that the major parties were able to avoid.

SUMMARY NOTES

- Organization grants advantage in the struggle for power. Political parties organize individuals and groups to exercise power in democracies by winning elected office.

- Political parties are not mentioned in the U.S. Constitution, yet they have played a central role in American political history. Major party realignments have occurred at critical points in American history, as major social groups shifted their political loyalties.

- In theory, political parties are "responsible" organizations that adopt a principled platform, recruit candidates who support the platform, educate the public about it, direct an issue-oriented campaign, and then organize the legislature and ensure that their candidates enact the party's platform.

- But in the American two-party system, winning office by appealing to the large numbers of people at the center of the political spectrum becomes more important than promoting strong policy positions. American parties cannot bind elected officials to campaign promises anyway.

- American parties have lost many of their traditional functions over time. Party nominations are won by individual candidates in primary elections rather than through selection by party leaders. Most political candidates are self-selected; they organize their own campaigns. Television has replaced the party as the principal means of educating the public. And government bureaucracies, not party machines, provide social services.

- Party nominations are won in primary elections as earlier caucus and convention methods of nomination have largely disappeared. Party primary elections in the various states may be open or closed and may or may not require runoff primaries. The nominees selected in each party's primary election then battle each other in the general election.

- The parties battle in three major arenas. The *party-in-the electorate* refers to party identification among voters. The *party-in-the-government* refers to party identification and organization among elected officials. The *party organization* refers to party offices at the local, state, and national levels.

- The Democratic and Republican parties are structured to include national party conventions, national committees with chairs and staff, congressional party organizations, state committees, and county and local committees.

- Since presidential nominations are now generally decided in primary elections—with pledged delegates selected before the opening of the national conventions and with party platforms largely symbolic and wholly unenforceable on the candidates—the conventions have become largely media events designed to kick off the general election campaign.

- *Dealignment* refers to a decline in the attractiveness of the parties to the voters, a growing reluctance of people to identify strongly with either party, and greater voter willingness to cross party lines. Despite dealignment, party identification remains a strong influence in voter choice.

- Opinion polls indicate that most Americans support the general idea of a third party, but throughout the twentieth century no third-party presidential candidate won very many votes.

- In the United States, many aspects of the political system—including cultural consensus, the winner-take-all electoral system, and legal restrictions to ballot access—place major obstacles in the way of success for third parties and independent candidates. Although never successful at gaining federal office in significant numbers, ideological, protest, single-issue, and splinter third parties have often been effective at getting popular issues on the federal agenda.

KEY TERMS

SELECTED READINGS

BECK, PAUL ALLEN. *Party Politics in America.* 8th ed. New York: Longman, 1997. An authoritative text on the American party system—party organizations, the parties-in-government, and the parties-in-the-electorate.

DOWNS, ANTHONY. *An Economic Theory of Democracy.* New York: Harper & Row, 1957. The classic work describing rational choice winning strategies for political parties and explaining why there is no incentive for vote-maximizing parties in a two-party system to adopt widely separate policy positions.

KEEFE, WILLIAM J. *Parties, Politics, and Public Policy in America.* 8th ed. Washington, D.C.: CQ Press, 1997. A comprehensive survey of American political parties, from the nominating process to campaign finance and the changing affiliations of voters.

LOWI, THEODORE E., and JOSEPH ROMANGE. *Debating the Two Party System.* Boulder, Colo.: Rowman & Littlefield, 1997. Lowi argues that the two-party system is no longer adequate to represent the people of a diverse nation; Romange counters that two parties help unify the country and instruct Americans about the value of compromise.

ROSENSTONE, STEVEN J., ROY L. BEHR, and EDWARD H. LAZARUS. *Third Parties in America.* 2nd ed. Princeton, N.J.: Princeton University Press, 1996. A review of the history of third parties in American politics with an analysis of the various causes of third-party movements.

WATTENBERG, MARTIN P. *The Decline of American Political Parties, 1952–1992.* Cambridge, Mass.: Harvard University Press, 1994. An authoritative discussion of increasing negative attitudes toward the parties and the growing dealignment in the electorate.

ZEIGLER, HARMON. *Political Parties in Industrial Democracies.* Itasca, Ill.: Peacock, 1992. An insightful comparative analysis of parties and interest groups in Western European nations, Japan, and the United States.

Campaigns and Elections

Deciding Who Governs

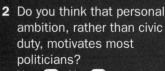

ASK YOURSELF ABOUT POLITICS

1 Should elected officials be bound by their campaign promises?
Yes ⬤ No ⬤

2 Do you think that personal ambition, rather than civic duty, motivates most politicians?
Yes ⬤ No ⬤

3 Do career politicians serve their constituents better than those who go into politics for just a short time?
Yes ⬤ No ⬤

4 Should people vote on the basis of a candidate's personal character rather than his or her policy positions?
Yes ⬤ No ⬤

5 Would you vote for a candidate who used negative ads to discredit an opponent?
Yes ⬤ No ⬤

6 Do political campaign contributions have too much influence on elections and government policy?
Yes ⬤ No ⬤

7 Are high campaign costs discouraging good people from becoming candidates?
Yes ⬤ No ⬤

8 Should presidents be elected by direct popular vote?
Yes ⬤ No ⬤

What real power do you have in a democracy? By casting ballots, citizens in a democracy have the power to determine who will represent them, who will make up the government under which they live. You, then, are an integral part of the democratic process every time you vote in an election.

ELECTIONS IN A DEMOCRACY

Democratic government is government by "the consent of the governed." Elections give practical meaning to this notion of "consent." Elections allow people to choose among competing candidates and parties and to decide who will occupy public office. Elections give people the opportunity to pass judgment on current officeholders, either by reelecting them (granting continued consent) or by throwing them out of office (withdrawing consent).

In a representative democracy, elections function primarily to choose personnel to occupy public office—to decide "who governs." But elections also have an indirect influence on public policy, allowing voters to influence policy directions by choosing between candidates or parties with different policy priorities. Thus elections indirectly influence "who gets what"—that is, the outcomes of the political process.

Elections as Mandates?   However, it is difficult to argue that elections serve as "policy mandates"—that is, that elections allow voters to direct the course of public policy. Frequently, election winners claim a **mandate**—overwhelming support from the people—for their policies and programs. But for elections to serve as policy mandates, four conditions have to be met:

1. Competing candidates have to offer clear policy alternatives.
2. The voters have to cast their ballots on the basis of these policy alternatives alone.

www.prenhall.com/dye

President George W. Bush campaigning in early 2000. Candidates regularly appear with the American flag in the background.

3. The election results have to clearly indicate the voters' policy preferences.

4. Elected officials have to be bound by their campaign promises.[1]

As we shall see, none of these conditions is fully met in American elections. Often candidates do not differ much on policy questions, or they deliberately obscure their policy positions to avoid offending groups of voters. Voters themselves frequently pay little attention to policy issues in elections but rather vote along traditional party lines or group affiliations, or on the basis of the candidate's character, personality, or media image.

Moreover, even in elections in which issues seem to dominate the campaign, the outcome may not clearly reflect policy preferences. Candidates take stands on a variety of issues. It is never certain on which issues the voters agreed with the winner and on which issues they disagreed yet voted for the candidate anyway.

Finally, candidates often fail to abide by their campaign promises once they are elected. Some simply ignore their promises, assuming voters have forgotten about the campaign. Others point to changes in circumstances or conditions as a justification for abandoning a campaign pledge.

Retrospective Voting   Voters can influence future policy directions through retrospective judgments about the performance of incumbents, by either reelecting them or throwing them out of office.[2] Voters may not know what politicians will do in the future, but they can evaluate how well politicians performed in the past. When incumbent officeholders are defeated, it is reasonable to assume that voters did not like their performance and that newly elected officials should change policy course if they do not want to meet a similar fate in the next election. But it is not always clear what the defeated incumbents did in office that led to their

mandate Perception of popular support for a program or policy based on the margin of electoral victory won by a candidate who proposed it during a campaign.

Even presidential candidates must "press the flesh" of individual voters. Breakfast diner stops have become a campaign tradition.

ouster by the voters. Nor, indeed, can incumbents who won reelection assume that all of their policies are approved of by a majority of voters. Nevertheless, **retrospective voting** provides an overall judgment of how voters evaluate performance in office.

Retrospective voting is probably more important in presidential elections than in congressional elections. And most speculation about retrospective voting centers on the economy. Incumbent presidents seeking reelection in hard economic times have been regularly defeated by voters, and congressional candidates of the party in power may suffer as well during an economic downturn.

Protection of Rights Elections also provide protection against official abuse. The long struggle for African American voting rights in the United States was premised on the belief that once black people acquired the right to vote, government would become more responsive to their concerns. In signing the Voting Rights Act of 1965, President Lyndon Johnson expressed this view: "The vote is the most powerful instrument ever devised by man for breaking down injustice and destroying the terrible walls which imprison men because they are different from other men."[3] The subsequent history of racial politics in America (see Chapter 15) suggests that the vote is more effective in eliminating discriminatory laws than it is in resolving social or economic inequities. Nevertheless, *without* the vote, we can be certain that government would have very little incentive to respond to popular needs.

POWER AND AMBITION

Personal ambition is a driving force in politics. Politics attracts people for whom *power*—the drive to shape the world according to one's own beliefs and values—and *celebrity*—the public attention, deference, name recognition, and social status that accompany public office—are more rewarding than money, leisure, or privacy. "Political office today flows to those who want it enough to spend the time and energy mastering its pursuit. It flows in the direction of ambition—and talent."[4]

retrospective voting
Voting for or against a candidate or party on the basis of past performance.

Political ambition is the most distinguishing characteristic of elected officeholders. The people who run for and win public office are not necessarily the most intelligent, best informed, wealthiest, or most successful business or professional people. At all levels of the political system—from presidential candidates and members of Congress, to governors and state legislators, to city council and school board members—it is the most politically ambitious people who are willing to sacrifice time, family and private life, and energy and effort for the power and celebrity that come with public office.

Most politicians publicly deny that personal ambition is their real motivation for seeking public office. Rather, they describe their motives in highly idealistic terms: "civic duty," "service to community," "reforming the government," "protecting the environment," "bringing about change." These responses reflect the norms of our political culture. People are not supposed to enter politics to satisfy *personal* ambitions but rather to achieve *public* purposes. Many politicians do not really recognize their own drive for power or how much they crave celebrity. But if there were no personal rewards in politics, no one would run for office.

To achieve their ambitions, politicians must meet certain basic requirements and possess several key talents and skills.

Constitutional Requirements for Office   The constitutional requirements for presidential and congressional candidates are very few:

- *President:* A natural-born citizen of the United States, a resident for at least fourteen years, and at least thirty-five years of age (Article II, Section 1). The Twenty-second Amendment to the U.S. Constitution, passed in 1951 after Franklin D. Roosevelt's unprecedented four elections to the presidency, imposes one more restriction: a person cannot be elected president more than twice, or more than once if having served more than two years of another president's term.
- *U.S. Senate:* A resident of the state from which elected, a citizen of the United States for at least nine years, and at least thirty years of age (Article I, Section 3).
- *U.S. House of Representatives:* A resident of the state from which elected, a citizen of the United States for at least seven years, and at least twenty-five years of age (Article I, Section 2).

Political Entrepreneurship   One talent required of all politicians is **political entrepreneurship**—the ability to sell themselves to others as candidates, to raise money from contributors, to organize people to work on their behalf, and to communicate and publicize themselves through the media. Political parties no longer recruit candidates; candidates recruit themselves. Nor do interest groups recruit candidates; candidates seek out interest groups to win their support.

Political Temperament   Perhaps the most important personal qualification is the willingness to work long and hard, to live, eat, and breathe politics every day. Occasionally people win high office who really do not like political campaigning; they view it as a torture they must endure in order to gain office and exercise power. But most successful politicians are people who really like politics—the meetings, appearances, speeches, interviews, handshaking—and really enjoy interacting with other people (see *People in Politics:* "Colin Powell, Saying No to Presidential Politics").

political entrepreneurship
Ability to sell oneself as a candidate for public office, including skills of organizing, fund raising, communicating, and publicizing.

Colin Powell, Saying No to Presidential Politics

Colin Powell became the first person in modern political history to opt out of a presidential race while leading all other candidates, including the incumbent president, in the opinion polls. Colin Powell embodies the American dream: "a black kid of no early promise from an immigrant family of limited means who was raised in the South Bronx and somehow rose to become the National Security Adviser to the President of the United States and then Chairman of the Joint Chiefs of Staff."* He also rose to be the American public's preferred choice for president of the United States, yet decided he did not have the "passion and commitment" for political life that he "felt every day of my thirty-five years as a soldier."

Born in Harlem to Jamaican immigrant parents, Powell recounts his youth as proof that "it is possible to rise above conditions." After graduation from Morris High School in the South Bronx, Powell enrolled at The City College of New York on a ROTC scholarship. In 1958 he graduated with a degree in geology at the top of his ROTC class and was commissioned a second lieutenant in the U.S. Army. Powell went to South Vietnam as a military adviser in 1962 and returned for a second tour of service in 1968. In Vietnam, he was awarded two Purple Hearts, a Bronze Star for Valor, and the Legion of Merit.

In 1972 Powell returned to the classroom to pursue a master's degree in business administration from George Washington University and accept an appointment to the prestigious White House Fellows Program.

As a White House Fellow, Powell was assigned to the Office of Management and Budget, where he worked under Caspar Weinberger, later secretary of defense in the Reagan Administration. Powell's career was on a fast track after his White House duty. Powell was recalled to Washington in 1983 by Defense Secretary Weinberger to become senior military adviser to the secretary.

President George Bush chose General Powell in 1989 to head the Joint Chiefs of Staff, the nation's highest military position. It was Powell who helped convince the president that if military force were to be used to oust Saddam Hussein from Kuwait, it must be an overwhelming and decisive force, not gradual, limited escalation, as in Vietnam. Powell's televised press briefings during the war assured the American people of the competence and effectiveness of the U.S. military. The Gulf War victory restored the morale of U.S. military forces and the confidence of the American people in its military leadership.

To a great many Americans, Powell seemed to offer the nation what it most needed: a decisive leader with integrity and character, a political outsider untarnished by "politics as usual," and an African American whose "American journey"* could serve as a model for all and ease the nation's racial divisions. He was frequently compared to Dwight D. Eisenhower, whose military leadership in World War II ushered him into the White House. Like Ike, Powell waited until after army retirement to declare himself a Republican, yet after "prayerful consideration," he announced that he would not be a candidate for president of the United States "or any elective office." In recent years Powell has devoted himself exclusively to volunteer activities, notably as chairman of a national campaign, "America's Promise—Alliance for Youth."

---

*Colin Powell, *My American Journey* (New York: Random House, 1995).

Communication Skills   Another important personal qualification is the ability to communicate with others. Politicians must know how to talk, and talk, and talk—to large audiences, in press conferences and interviews, on television, to reporters, to small groups of financial contributors, on the phone, at airports and commencements, to their staffs, on the floor of Congress or the state legislature. It matters less what politicians say than how they look and sound saying it. They must communicate sincerity, compassion, confidence, and good humor, as well as ideas.

Former President Clinton prepares for an interview with reporters from the television news show 60 Minutes. *Successful politicians are skilled communicators; most truly enjoy the hard work and constant interaction with other people their careers entail.*

Professionalism   Politics is becoming increasingly professionalized. "Citizen officeholders"—people with business or professional careers who get into politics part time or for short periods of time—are being driven out of political life by career politicians—people who enter politics early in life as a full-time occupation and expect to make it their career. Politics increasingly demands all of a politician's time and energy. At all levels of government, from city council to state legislatures to the U.S. Congress, political work is becoming full-time and year-round. It is not only more demanding to *hold* office than it was a generation ago but also far more demanding to *run* for office. Campaigning has become more time consuming, more technically sophisticated, and much more costly.

Careerism   Professional political careers begin at a relatively early age. Politically ambitious young people seek out internships and staff positions with members of Congress, with congressional committees, in state legislators' or governors' offices, in mayors' offices, or in council chambers. Others volunteer to work in political campaigns. Many find political mentors from whom they learn how to organize campaigns, contact financial contributors, and deal with the media. Soon they are ready to run for local office or the state legislature. Rather than challenge a strong incumbent, they may wait for an open seat to be created by retirement, by reapportionment, or by its holder seeking another office. Or they may make an initial attempt against a strong incumbent of the opposition party in order to gain experience and win the appreciation of their own party's supporters for a good effort. Over time, running for and holding elective office become their career. They work harder at it than anyone else, in part because they have no real private-sector career to return to in case of defeat.

Lawyers in Politics   The prevalence of lawyers in politics is an American tradition. Among the fifty-five delegates to the Constitutional Convention in 1787, some twenty-five were lawyers. The political dominance of lawyers continues today, with lawyers filling more than half of U.S. Senate seats and nearly half of the seats in the U.S. House of Representatives.

It is sometimes argued that lawyers dominate in politics because of the parallel skills required in law and politics. Lawyers represent clients, so they can apply their professional experience to represent constituents in Congress. Lawyers are trained to deal with statutory law, so they are assumed to be reasonably familiar with the United States Code (the codified laws of the U.S. government) when they arrive in Congress to make or amend these statutes.

But it is more likely that people attracted to politics decide to go to law school fully aware of the tradition of lawyers in American politics. Moreover, political officeholding at the state and local level as well as in the national government can help a struggling lawyer's private practice through free public advertising and opportunities to make contacts with potential clients. Finally, there are many special opportunities for lawyers to acquire public office in "lawyers only" posts as judges and prosecuting attorneys in federal, state, and local governments. Law school graduates who accept modest salaries as U.S. attorneys in the Justice Department or in state or county prosecuting offices can gain valuable experience for later use in either private law practice or politics.

Most of the lawyers in the Congress, however, have become professional politicians over time. They have left their legal practices behind.

THE ADVANTAGES OF INCUMBENCY

In theory, elections offer voters the opportunity to "throw the rascals out." But in practice, voters seldom do so. **Incumbents**, people already holding public office, have a strong advantage when they seek reelection. The reelection rates of incumbents for *all* elective offices—city council, mayor, state legislature, governor, and especially Congress—are very high. Since 1950, more than 90 percent of all members of the House of Representatives who have sought reelection have been successful. (In 1998, 98 percent of all House members seeking reelection won.) The success rate of U.S. Senate incumbents is not as great, but it is still impressive; since 1950, more than 70 percent of senators seeking reelection have been successful.

Why do incumbents win so often? This is a particularly vexing question, inasmuch as so many people are distrustful of government and hold politicians in low esteem. Congress itself is the focal point of public disapproval and even ridicule. Yet people seem to distinguish between Congress as an institution—which they distrust—and their own members of Congress—whom they reelect. The result is something of a contradiction: popular members of Congress serving in an unpopular Congress (see *What Do You Think:* "Why Do Voters Reelect Members of an Unpopular Congress?" in Chapter 10). Three major advantages tend to enhance incumbents' chances of winning: name recognition, campaign contributions, and the resources of office.

Name Recognition   One reason for incumbents' success is that they begin the campaign with greater *name recognition* than their challengers, simply because they are the incumbent and their name has become familiar to their constituents over the previous years. Much of the daily work of all elected officials, especially members of Congress, is really public relations. Name recognition is a strategic advantage at the ballot box, especially if voters have little knowledge of policy positions or voting records. Voters tend to cast ballots for recognizable names over

incumbent Candidate currently in office seeking reelection.

unknowns. Cynics have concluded that there is no such thing as bad publicity, only publicity. Even in cases of well-publicized scandals, incumbent members of Congress have won reelection; presumably voters preferred "the devil they knew" to the one they did not.

The somewhat lower rate of reelection of Senate versus House members may be a result of the fact that Senate challengers are more likely to have held high-visibility offices—for example, governor or member of Congress—before running for the Senate. Thus Senate challengers often enjoy some name recognition even before the campaign begins. Greater media attention to a statewide Senate race also helps to move the challenger closer to the incumbent in public recognition. In contrast, House challengers are likely to have held less visible local or state legislative offices or to be political novices, and House races attract considerably less media attention than Senate races do.

Campaign Contributions   Incumbents have a strong advantage in raising campaign funds, simply because individuals and groups seeking access to those already in office are inspired to make contributions. Challengers have no immediate favors to offer; they must convince a potential contributor that they will win office and also that they are devoted to the interests of their financial backers.[5]

Contributing individuals and interest groups show a strong preference for incumbents over challengers. They do not wish to offend incumbent officeholders by contributing to their challengers; doing so risks both immediate retribution and future "freezing out" in the likely event of the challengers' defeat. Thus only when an incumbent has been especially hostile to an organization's interest or in rare cases where an incumbent seems especially vulnerable will an interest group support a challenger. Yet challengers need even larger campaign war chests than incumbents to be successful. Challengers must overcome the greater name recognition of incumbents, their many office resources, and their records of constituency service. Thus even if incumbents and challengers had equal campaign treasuries, incumbents would enjoy the advantage.

Resources of Office   Successful politicians use their offices to keep their names and faces before the public in various ways—public appearances, interviews, speeches, and press releases. Congressional incumbents make full use of the **franking privilege** (free use of the U.S. mails) to send self-promotional newsletters to tens of thousands of households in their district at taxpayers' expense. They travel on weekends to their district virtually year-round, using tax-funded travel allowances, to make local appearances, speeches, and contacts.

Members of Congress have large staffs working every day over many years with the principal objective of ensuring the reelection of their members. Indeed, Congress is structured as an "incumbent-protection society" organized and staffed to help guarantee the reelection of its members (see "Home Style" in Chapter 10). Service to constituents occupies the energies of congressional office staffs both in Washington and in local district offices established for this purpose. Casework wins voters one at a time: tracing lost Social Security checks, ferreting out which federal loans voters qualify for and helping them with their applications, and performing countless other personal favors. These individual "retail-level" favors are supplemented by larger scale projects that experienced members of Congress can bring to their district or state (roads, dams, post offices, buildings, schools, grants, contracts), as well as undesirable projects (landfills, waste disposal sites, halfway houses) that they

franking privilege   Free use of the U.S. mails granted to members of Congress to promote communication with constituents.

can keep out of their district. The longer incumbents have occupied the office, the more favors they have performed and the larger their networks of grateful voters.

CAMPAIGN STRATEGIES

Campaigning is largely a media activity, especially in presidential and congressional campaigns. Media campaigns are highly professionalized, relying on public relations and advertising specialists, professional fund raisers, media consultants, and pollsters. Campaign management involves techniques that strongly resemble those employed in marketing commercial products. Professional media campaign management includes developing a **campaign strategy**: compiling computerized mailing lists and invitations for fund-raising events; selecting a campaign theme and coming up with a desirable candidate image; monitoring the progress of the campaign with continual polling of the voters; producing television tapes for commercials, newspaper advertisements, signs, bumper stickers, and radio spots; selecting clothing and hairstyles for the candidate; writing speeches and scheduling appearances; and even planning the victory party.

Selecting a Theme   Finding the right theme or "message" for a campaign is essential; this effort is not greatly different from that of launching an advertising campaign for a new detergent. A successful theme or "message" is one that characterizes the candidate or the electoral choice confronting the voters. A campaign theme need not be controversial; indeed, it need not even focus on a specific issue. It might be as simple as "a leader you can trust"—an attempt to "package" the candidate as competent and trustworthy.

campaign strategy   Plan for a political campaign, usually including a theme, an attempt to define the opponent or the issues, and an effort to coordinate images and messages in news broadcasts and paid advertising.

Campaigning in 2000, Al Gore shed his coat and tie in favor of open collar shirts in order to avoid type-casting as too formal.

Most media campaigns focus on candidates' personal qualities rather than on their stands on policy issues. Professional campaigns are based on the assumption that a candidate's "image" is the most important factor affecting voter choice. This image is largely devoid of issues, except in very general terms: for example, "tough on crime," "stands up to the special interests," "fights for the taxpayer," or "cares about you."

Negative Campaigning: "Defining" the Opponent   A media campaign also seeks to "define" the opponent in negative terms. The original negative TV ad is generally identified as the 1964 "Daisy Girl" commercial, aired by the Lyndon B. Johnson presidential campaign (see *Up Close:* "Dirty Politics"). Negative ads can serve a purpose in exposing the record of an opponent. But negative campaigns risk an opponent's counterattack charges of "mudslinging," "dirty tricks," and "sleaze."

Research into the opponent's public and personal background provides the data for negative campaigning. Previous speeches and writings can be mined for embarrassing or mean-spirited statements. The voting record of the opponent can be scrutinized for unpopular policy positions. Any evils that occurred during an opponent's term of office can be attributed to him or her, either directly ("She knew and conspired in it") or indirectly ("He should have known and done something about it"). Personal scandals or embarrassments can be developed as evidence of "character." If campaign managers fear that highly personal attacks on an opponent will backfire, they may choose to leak the information to reporters and try to avoid attribution of the story to themselves or their candidate.

Negative advertising is often blamed on television's dominant role in political campaigns. "The high cost of television means now that you have to go for the jugular."[6] A political consultant summarized the current rules of political engagement as follows:

1. Advertise early if you have the money. . . .
2. Go negative early, often, and right through election day, if necessary.
3. Appeal to the heart and gut, rather than to the head.
4. Define your opponent to the voters before he or she can define him/herself or you.
5. If attacked, hit back even harder.
6. It's easier to give voters a negative impression of your opponent than it is to improve their image of you.[7]

Does negative campaigning really work? Professional campaign managers and consultants are convinced that negative ads are effective—more effective than positive ads. Regarding ads praising one's own qualities, they say "save them for your tombstone." But political science researchers conclude that "there is simply no evidence in the research literature that negative political advertisements are any more effective than positive political ads."[8]

Using Focus Groups and Polling   Focus group techniques can help in selecting campaign themes and identifying negative characteristics in opponents. A **focus group** is a small group of people brought together to view videotapes, listen to specific campaign appeals, and respond to particular topics and issues. Media professionals then develop a campaign strategy around "hot-button" issues—issues

focus group   In a political context, a small number of people brought together in a comfortable setting to discuss and respond to themes and issues, allowing campaign managers to develop and analyze strategies.

Dirty Politics

Political campaigning frequently turns ugly with negative advertising that is vicious and personal. It is widely believed that television's focus on personal character and private lives—rather than on policy positions and governmental experience—encourages negative campaigning. But vicious personal attacks in political campaigns began long before television. They are nearly as old as the nation itself.

"If Jefferson is elected," proclaimed Yale's president in 1800, "the Bible will be burned and we will see our wives and daughters the victims of legal prostitution." In 1864 *Harper's Weekly* decried the "mudslinging" of the day, lamenting that President Abraham Lincoln was regularly referred to by his opponent as a "filthy storyteller, despot, liar, thief, braggart, buffoon, monster, Ignoramus Abe, robber, swindler, tyrant, fiend, butcher, and pirate."

Television's first memorable attack advertisement was the "Daisy Girl" commercial broadcast by Lyndon Johnson's presidential campaign in 1964 against his Republican opponent, Barry Goldwater. Although never mentioning Goldwater by name, the purpose of the ad was to "define" him as a warmonger who would plunge the world into a nuclear holocaust. The ad opens with a small, innocent girl standing in an open field plucking petals from a daisy and counting, "1, 2, 3 . . ." When she reaches 9, an ominous adult male voice begins a countdown: "10, 9, 8 . . ." as the camera closes in on the child's face. At "zero," a mushroom cloud appears, reflected in her eyes, and envelops the screen. Lyndon Johnson's voice is heard: "These are the stakes."

The infamous Willie Horton ad, broadcast by an independent organization supporting Republican George Bush in 1988, portrayed Democrat Michael Dukakis as weak on crime prevention. It featured a close-up mug shot of a very threatening convicted murderer, Willie Horton, with a voice proclaiming, "Dukakis not only opposes the death penalty, he allowed first-degree murderers to have weekend passes from prison. One was Willie Horton who murdered a boy in a robbery, stabbing him nineteen times. Despite a life sentence, Horton received ten weekend passes from prison." A final photo shows Dukakis, with a voice-over announcing, "Weekend prison passes, Dukakis weak on crime."

"Attack ads" have multiplied in recent elections at all levels of government. In the Bush-Gore 2000 race, most paid advertising was directed against each opponent's policy positions. Bush's tax plan was "a giveaway to the superrich"; Gore's spending plans meant "more big government." However, some Bush ads attacked Gore for his exaggerations—"I invented the Internet"—implying that the Vice President tended to distort the truth. A few days before the election, the press disclosed that Bush had been arrested for drunk driving in 1976; Gore campaign aides denied any role in the disclosure.

What are the effects of negative advertising? First of all, it works more often than not. Controlled experiments indicate that targets of attack ads are rated less positively by people who have watched these ads. But another effect of negative advertising is to make voters more cynical about politics and government in general. There is conflicting evidence about whether or not negative campaigning by opposing candidates reduces voter turnout.

What, if anything, can be done? Government regulation of political speech directly contravenes the First Amendment. American democracy has survived negative campaigning for a long time. Some reform proposals have called for candidates to appear in person on camera when delivering an attack statement, or for media monitoring and criticism of attack messages as well as correction of erroneous positive claims. But it is unlikely that these reforms would have much of an impact on negative campaigning.

Frames from Lyndon Johnson's 1964 "Daisy Girl" commercial.

Source: Kathleen Hall Jamieson, *Dirty Politics: Deception, Distraction, and Democracy* (New York: Oxford University Press, 1992); also Stephen Ansolabehere et al., "Does Attack Advertising Demobilize the Electorate?" *American Political Science Review* 88 (December 1994): 829–38; Kim Fridkin Kahn and Patrick J. Kenney, "Do Negative Campaigns Mobilize or Suppress Turnout?" *American Political Science Review* 93 (December, 1999): 877–89.

that generate strong responses by focus groups—and avoid themes or issues that fail to elicit much interest.

The results of focus group work can then be tested in wider polling. Polling is a central feature of professional campaigning. Serious candidates for national and statewide offices almost always employ their own private polling firms, distinct from the national survey organizations that supply the media with survey data. Initial polling is generally designed to determine candidates' **name recognition**—the extent to which the voters recognize the candidates—and whatever positive and negative images are already associated with their names. "High negatives" of potential opponents may suggest an "attack" strategy, exploiting the weaknesses of the opponents.

High negatives for the candidate suggest the need for a strategy to overcome these images. For example, if the candidate is seen as too rich or too upper class or too "out of touch" with common people, then the campaign will show the candidate in blue jeans hanging out with factory workers in beer and pizza places. If the candidate's private life is under suspicion, then the campaign will feature appearances with a loving spouse and family attending church services. If the candidate is perceived as "too liberal," then centrist themes will be stressed; if seen as "too conservative," then moderation, warmth, and compassion will be emphasized. Astute campaign managers try not to completely reverse a candidate's previous political stances in order to deflect charges of "flip-flopping" and to avoid unintended images of insincerity.

Campaign polling is highly professionalized, with telephone banks, trained interviewers, and computer-assisted-telephone-interviewing (CATI) software that records and tabulates responses instantly and sends the results to campaign managers. In well-financed campaigns, polling is continual throughout the campaign, so that managers can assess progress on a daily basis. Polls chart the candidate's progress and, perhaps more important, help assess the effectiveness of specific campaign themes. If the candidate appears to be gaining support, the campaign stays on course. But if the candidate appears to be falling in the polls, the campaign manager comes under intense pressure to change themes and strategies. As election day nears, the pressure increases on the trailing candidate to "go negative"—to launch even more scathing attacks on the opponent.

Incumbent versus Challenger Strategies   Campaign strategies vary by the offices being sought, the nature of the times, and the imagination and inventiveness of the candidates' managers. But incumbency is perhaps the most important factor affecting the choice of a strategy. The challenger must attack the record of the incumbent; deplore current conditions in the city, state, or nation; and stress the need for change. Challengers are usually freer to take the offensive; incumbents must defend their record in office and either boast of accomplishments during their term or blame the opposition for blocking them. Challengers frequently opt for the "outsider" strategy, capitalizing on distrust and cynicism toward government.

News Management   News management is the key to the media campaign. News coverage of the candidates is more credible in the eyes of viewers than paid advertisements. The campaign is planned to get the maximum favorable "free" exposure on the evening news as well as to saturate the media with paid commercial advertising. Each day a candidate must do something interesting and "news-

name recognition   The extent to which voters know a candidate's name.

worthy," that is, likely to be reported as news. Thus each day of the campaign is organized to win favorable coverage on the nightly television news and in the next day's newspapers. Pictures are as important as words. Candidates must provide good **photo ops** for the media—opportunities where they can be photographed in settings or backgrounds that emphasize their themes. For example, if the theme is patriotism, then the candidate appears with war veterans, at a military base, or at a flag factory. If the theme is education, the candidate appears at a school; if crime control, then with police officers; if environmentalism, then in a wilderness area; if the economy, then at a closed factory or unemployment line or soup kitchen for the homeless.

Themes must be stated in concise and catchy **sound bites** that will register in the viewers' minds. Candidates now understand that the news media will select only a few seconds of an entire day of speech making for broadcast. The average length of a network news sound bite has shrunk from forty-five to seven seconds over the last thirty years. Thus extended or serious discussion of issues during a campaign is sacrificed to the need for one-liners on the nightly news. Indeed, if a campaign theme cannot fit on a bumper sticker, it is too complex.

Consequently, each day's campaigning is a series of photo ops and sound bites, all prepared with the evening news in mind. Between events, candidates must scramble to various fund-raising events—dinners, parties, personal meetings with large contributors. Thus candidates balance their time between "getting out the message" and finding ways to pay for getting it out.

Paid Advertising　Television "spot" ads must be prepared prior to and during the campaign. They involve employing expensive television advertising and production firms well in advance of the campaign and keeping them busy revising and producing new ads throughout the campaign to respond to changing issues or opponents' attacks. Commercial advertising is the most expensive aspect of the campaign. Heavy costs are incurred in the production of the ads and in the purchase of broadcast time. The Federal Communications Commission (FCC) does not permit television networks or stations to charge more than standard commercial rates for political ads, but these rates are already high. Networks and stations are required to offer the same rates and times to all candidates, but if one candidate's campaign treasury is weak or exhausted, an opponent can saturate broadcast airtime.

Free Airtime　All candidates seek free airtime on news and talk shows, but the need to gain free exposure is much greater for underfunded candidates. They must go to extremes in devising media events, and they must encourage and participate in free televised debates. The debate format is particularly well suited for candidates who cannot match their opponents in paid commercial advertising. Thus well-funded and poorly funded candidates may jockey over the number and times of public debates.

Money and Message Win Elections　Professional campaign managers and consultants generally agree: The quality of the campaign theme, together with the money to communicate it, is what wins elections. Party and candidate are viewed as less important (See Table 8-1). They believe that making factually untrue statements is unethical, but they do *not* believe that negative ads are unethical. Professionals themselves are disproportionately white, male, and wealthy. Most are

photo ops　Staged opportunities for the media to photograph the candidate in a favorable setting.

sound bites　Concise and catchy phrases that attract media coverage.

Table 8-1 Professionals Identify the Keys to Winning Elections

	Percent Rating as . . .		
	Most Important	**Somewhat Important**	**Least Important**
Quality of the candidate's message	82	17	1
Amount of money available to campaign	74	25	1
Partisan makeup of a state or House district	52	44	2
Candidate's abilities as a campaigner	46	52	2

Source: Survey of 200 professional political consultants, reported by the Pew Research Center for the People and the Press, *TheViews of Political Consultants* (1999).

relatively young; they usually start their careers by managing local or state races, rather than congressional or presidential races.

HOW MUCH DOES IT COST TO GET ELECTED?

Getting elected to public office has never been more expensive. The professionalization of campaigning and the heavy costs of television advertising drive up the costs of running for office. Campaign costs are rising with each election cycle (see Figure 8-1). In the presidential election year 2000, campaign spending by *all* presidential and congressional candidates, the Democratic and Republican parties, and independent political organization is estimated to have topped *$3 billion* (see *What Do You Think?* "Does Money Buy Influence in Washington?").

Congressional Costs   The typical winning campaign for a seat in the House of Representatives costs nearly $700,000. House members seeking to retain their seats must raise this amount *every two years*. Even losers typically spend over $200,000 (see Table 8-2 on page 244). The typical winning campaign for a U.S. Senate seat costs over $5 million. But Senate campaign costs vary a great deal from state to state; Senate seats in the larger states may cost $10 or $20 million or more.

The upward spiral in congressional campaign spending continued through 2000 with almost $1 *billion* spent by all House and Senate candidates. New York's high-profile Senate race between Democrat Hillary Clinton and Republican Rick Lazio attracted a combined $85 million in contributions from across the nation. A new individual spending record was set by multi-millionaire Democrat Jon Corzine in his successful bid for a U.S. Senate seat from New Jersey; Corzine spent about $60 million of his *own* money.

Spending for House seats also varies a great deal from one race to another. (The spending record for a House seat is held by former Speaker Republican Newt Gingrich of Georgia, who spent more than $7.5 million awaiting reelection in 1998.) In nearly two-thirds of all House districts, one candidate (almost always the incumbent) outspends his or her opponent by a factor of ten to one or more. Only

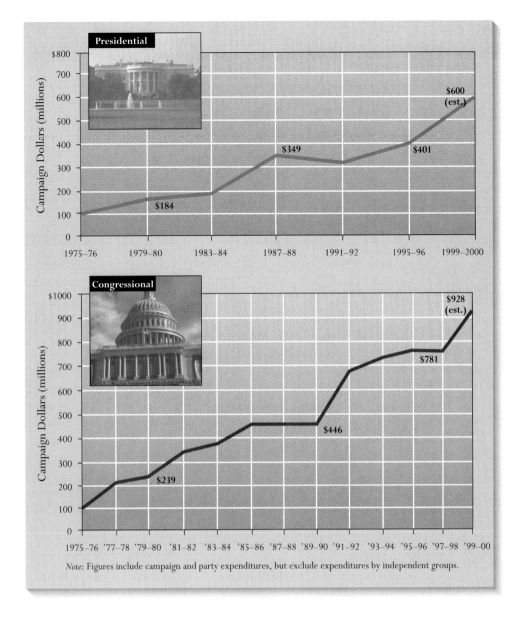

FIGURE 8-1 **The Growing Costs of Campaigns**

Source: Federal Elections Commission, as reported in *Congressional Quarterly Weekly Reports*, April 5, 1997, p. 772; updated from Federal Election Commission data. 1999 – 2000 from Federal Election Commission, November 2, 2000.

about 16 percent of House campaigns are financially competitive; that is, neither candidate spends more than twice as much as his or her opponent. In the remaining 84 percent of House campaigns, one candidate spends more than twice as much as his or her opponent.

Presidential Costs   More cash was spent in the 2000 presidential race than in any previous election. The closeness of the election seemed to inspire more contributions, an increase of about 50 percent over the Clinton-Dole race in 1996. Overall, more than $600 million was spent by presidential candidates in the primary and general elections. George W. Bush spent more than $100,000 million just to win the Republican presidential *nomination*. In the general election, Bush outspent Gore, but not by much. Nonetheless, Bush's overall spending set a new record in presidential races of more than $200 million.

Table 8-2　The Cost of Getting Elected to Congress

Senate	1998	2000
Average winner spent	$5,227,761	—
Average loser spent	$2,839,813	—
Most expensive campaign	$27,159,681 (Alfonse D'Amato, R-NY)	$60,000,000 (Jon Corzine, D-NJ)
House of Representatives	**1998**	**2000**
Average winner spent	$650,428	—
Average loser spent	$210,614	—
Most expensive campaign	$7,578,716 (Newt Gingrich, R-GA)	$6,200,000 (James E. Rogan, R-CA)

RAISING CAMPAIGN CASH

Fund raising to meet the high costs of campaigning is the most important hurdle for any candidate for public office. Campaign funds come from a wide range of sources—small donors, big donors, interest groups of every stripe, corporations, labor unions, even taxpayers. In some cases, candidates pay their own way (or most of it). More typically, however, candidates for high public office—particularly incumbents—have become adept at running their campaigns using other people's money, not their own. Sources of campaign cash for all congressional races in 1998 as well as the presidential race in 1996 and spending by the national parties are shown in Table 8-2.

Public Money　All taxpayers have the option of helping fund presidential elections through public money by checking off a box on their income tax returns that allocates $3 of their tax money for the Presidential Election Campaign Fund. In reality, only about 13 percent of taxpayers have checked that box in the last couple of years, and recently the fund has been in jeopardy of not having enough money to make its promised payments to the candidates. Public funds are also allocated to help the parties pay for their nominating conventions; the Democrats and Republicans each got about $13.5 million for that purpose in 2000.

Small Donations　Millions of Americans participate in campaign financing, either by giving directly to candidates or the parties, or by giving to political action committees, which then distribute their funds to candidates. For members of Congress, small donors typically make up about 20–25 percent of their campaign funds. The proportion is higher for presidential candidates and is highest of all in **hard money** contributions—money given directly to candidates' campaigns and subject to regulated limits. Beyond the total of dollars given, however, little is known about where all that money came from. Under federal law, donations under $200 need not be itemized, so contributors' names and addresses are recorded only by the candidates and parties, not passed along to the Federal Election Commission as part of the public record.

Large Individual Donors　A $1,000 check is the preferred entry fee for "fat-cat" contributors; many give substantially more. They are the donors whose names

hard money　Political contributions given directly to candidates' campaigns and subject to regulated limits.

Does Money Buy Influence in Washington?

Americans are clearly troubled by the role money plays in politics. About two-thirds believe excessive influence of political contributions on elections and government policy is a major problem with the system. A similar proportion feel this way about the conflicts of interest created when elected officials solicit or accept political contributions while they are making policy decisions. An even greater percentage believe the high cost of campaigns discourages good people from running for office.

Money is believed to obstruct good government in a variety of ways. At the very least, it is seen as distracting people's representatives from the jobs they were elected to do. A solid majority think elected officials in Washington spend too much time on political fund raising. But many see money's effects as much more pernicious than simply reducing the efficiency of the federal government. More than half of Americans believe political contributions often buy influence in Washington for one group by denying another group its fair say; as many as half think money often determines who gets elected and appointed to federal office. Nearly half see the influence of money in politics seriously undermining democratic ideals by often leading elected officials to support policies they don't personally believe are best for the country.

Major Problems with Political System	Percentage Responding "Yes"
"Political contributions have too much influence on elections and government policy"	66%
"Elected officials seek or receive political contributions while making decisions about issues of concern to those giving money"	65
"Elected officials spend too much of their time raising money for election campaigns"	63
"Good people are being discouraged from becoming candidates because of the high costs of campaigns"	71

How Frequently Does the Use of Money Buy Political Influence in Washington?	Percentage Responding "Often"
"Gives one group more influence by keeping another from having its fair say"	55%
"Determines election outcomes"	52
"Gets someone appointed to office who would not otherwise be considered"	50
"Keeps important legislation from being passed"	48
"Leads elected officials to support policies they don't think are best for the country"	45

Source: Princeton Survey Research Associates for the Center for Responsive Politics, *Money and Politics Survey, 1997.*

Campaign fund-raising has extended to the Internet. Candidate websites offer the opportunity to make direct contributions.

are on the candidates' Rolodexes. They are the ones in attendance when the president, the Speaker of the House, or other top political dignitaries travel around the country doing fund raisers. They are also the ones who are wined, dined, prodded, and cajoled in a seemingly ceaseless effort by the parties and the candidates to raise funds for the next election.

Political Action Committees **Political action committees (PACs)** are the most reliable source of money for reelection campaigns in Congress. Corporations and unions are not allowed to contribute directly to campaigns from corporate or union funds, but they may form PACs to seek contributions from managers and stockholders and their families, or union workers and their families. PACs are organized not only by corporations and unions but also by trade and professional associations, environmental groups, and liberal and conservative ideological groups. The wealthiest PACs are based in Washington, D.C. (see "PAC Power" in Chapter 9). PACs are very cautious; their job is to get a maximum return on their contributions, winning influence and goodwill with as many lawmakers as possible in Washington. There's no return on their investment if their recipients lose at the polls, therefore most PACs—particularly business PACs—give most of their dollars to incumbents seeking reelection.

Political Action Committee (PAC) Organization created by a corporation, union, or other interest group to collect and distribute campaign funds to candidates.

soft money Political contributions, not subject to regulated limits, given to a party for activities such as party building or voter registration, but not directly for campaigns.

Soft Money Under federal election law, hard money is contributed directly to candidates for federal office—for Congress and president and vice-president. These direct campaign contributions to candidates are limited by federal law to $1,000 per individual contributor (see "Regulating Campaign Finance" on page 252). **Soft money**, in contrast, can be raised by the Democratic and Republican parties with no restrictions on amount or who can give. Technically, soft money is supposed to be used for party building, get-out-the-vote drives, issues education, and general party participation. In reality, both parties undertake to raise as much soft money as possible, an effort that has a lot more to do with electing candidates than building the party.

Table 8-3   Sources of Campaign Cash

Source	Presidential Election Year 1996		Midterm Congressional Election Year 1998	
	$ Millions	%	$ Millions	%
Small Donations	734	30.6	351	23.5
Large Individual Donors	597	21.8	464	31.0
Political Action Committees (PACs)	243	10.1	269	18.0
Soft Money	262	10.8	225	15.0
Candidates	161	6.7	92	6.1
Public (Taxpayer) Financing	211	8.8	—	—
Other	200	8.2	95	6.4
TOTAL	$2,400	100.0	$1,496	100.0

Source: Center for Responsive Politics, from Federal Elections Commission data.

Soft money is the fastest growing source of campaign funds (see Figure 8-2). Nearly all soft money is raised in large contributions—indeed, the reason soft money has been so popular with the parties is that it allows big donors to give without having to abide by the limits imposed on direct campaign contributions. Another advantage is that corporations, labor unions, and other groups can give directly from their organization's treasury, which they cannot legally do in contributions to candidates. For both the Democrats and the Republicans, corporate donations are the biggest single source of soft money.

FIGURE 8-2   The Growth of "Soft Money"

Source: Center for Responsive Politics, based on Federal Election Commission data.

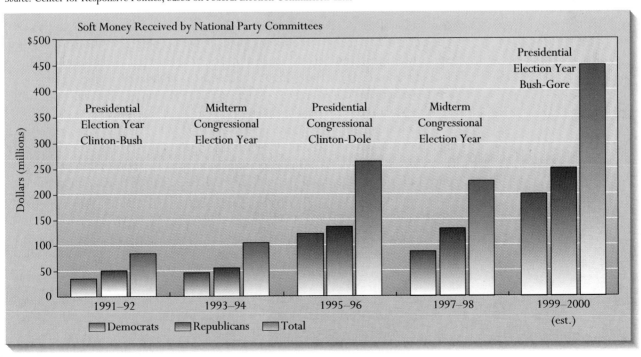

Confirming that politicians will willingly make fools of themselves, if necessary, to raise campaign cash, senators Trent Lott, Larry Craig, John Ashcroft, and James Jeffords appear as the "singing senators" during a Republican Party fund-raising event.

Candidate Self-Financing   Candidates for federal office also pump millions into their own campaigns. There are no federal restrictions on the amount of money individuals can spend on their own campaign. Leading the field in the last two presidential races was publishing magnate Steve Forbes, whose unsuccessful bids for the Republican nomination for president were largely funded with millions from his personal fortune. Senate and House candidates frequently put $50,000 to $100,000 or more of their own money into their campaigns, through either outright gifts or personal loans. (Candidates who loan themselves the money to run are able to pay themselves back later from outside contributions.)

Issue Ads   The costs of **issue ads** independently produced by interest groups are not officially reported to the Federal Elections Commission (or to anyone else) as a source of campaign funding. Issue ads advocate policy positions rather than explicitly advising voters cast their ballots for or against particular candidates. But most of these ads leave little doubt about which candidate is being supported or targeted. There are no federal restrictions on issue ads; any such restrictions would probably violate the First Amendment's guarantee of free speech.

Issue ads are multiplying rapidly in each election cycle. The AFL-CIO is the largest single sponsor of issue ads, all of which favor pro-union Democratic candidates. The National Rifle Association is close behind with its sponsorship of anti-gun-control ads that usually favor Republican candidates. The National Education Association (pro-Democratic) and the American Medical Association (pro-Republican) also sponsor millions of dollars of issue ads in each election cycle.

WHAT DO CONTRIBUTORS "BUY"?

Issue ads   Ads that advocate policy positions rather than explicitly supporting or opposing particular candidates.

What does money buy in politics? A cynic might say that money can buy anything—for example, special appropriations for public works directly benefiting the contributor, special tax breaks, special federal regulations. Scandals involving the direct (quid pro quo) purchase of special favors, privileges, exemptions, and treatments

BOTTOM LINERS

© 1999 Tribune Media Services, Inc.
All Rights Reserved.   11/23

"Ultimately, I want to get into political fund raising...I'm just here to make some contacts."

Source: © Tribune Media Services, Inc. All Rights Reserved.
Reprinted with permission.

have been common enough in the past, and they are likely to continue in the future. But campaign contributions are rarely made in the form of a direct trade-off for a favorable vote. Such an arrangement risks exposure as bribery and may be prosecuted under the law. Campaign contributions are more likely to be made without any *explicit* quid pro quo but rather with a general understanding that the contributor has confidence in the candidate's good judgment on issues directly affecting the contributor. The contributor expects the candidate to be smart enough to figure out how to vote in order to keep the contributions coming in the future.

The Big-Money Contributors Big-money contributors—businesses, unions, professional associations—pump millions into presidential and congressional elections. Figure 8-3 lists the top twenty-five contributors to candidates and parties in the 1996 election. Note that union contributions are heavily weighted toward Democrats, as are the contributions of the Association of Trial Lawyers. Businesses and business associations tend to split their contributions between the parties, but Republicans usually get the largest share.

Buying Access to Policy Makers Large contributors expect to be able to call or visit and present their views directly to "their" officeholders. At the presidential level, major contributors who cannot get a meeting with the president expect to meet at least with high-level White House staff or cabinet officials. At the congressional level, major contributors usually expect to meet or speak directly with their representative or senator. Members of Congress boast of responding to letters, calls, or visits by any constituent, but contributors can expect a more immediate and direct response than noncontributors can. Lobbyists for contributing organizations routinely expect and receive a hearing from members of Congress.

Vice President Al Gore with movie star Leonardo De Caprio. Politicians often seek the support of celebrities to boost their campaigns and help raise funds.

Rank	Contributor	Total Contributions	% Dem.	% Rep.	Rank	Contributor	Total Contributions	% Dem.	% Rep.
1.	AT&T	$4,321,339	38%	62%	24.	Enron Corp.	$1,904,947	25%	75%
2.	American Federation of State, County, and Muncipal Employees	$4,090,764	98%	2%	25.	BellSouth Corp.	$1,889,577	43%	57%
					26.	American Federation of Teachers	$1,873,700	99%	1%
3.	Service Employees International Union	$3,548,024	97%	3%	27.	Merrill Lynch	$1,865,107	25%	75%
4.	Microsoft Corp.	$3,454,594	46%	54%	28.	Joseph E. Seagram & Sons	$1,845,061	72%	28%
5.	Communications Workers of America	$3,135,014	99%	1%	29.	National Auto Dealers Assn.	$1,801,950	29%	71%
6.	Citigroup Inc.	$3,129,283	53%	47%	30.	National Assn. of Home Builders	$1,749,099	35%	65%
7.	International Brotherhood of Electrical Workers	$2,979,740	97%	2%	31.	National Beer Wholesalers Assn.	$1,722,761	18%	82%
8.	Verizon Communications	$2,762,118	37%	63%	32.	Blue Cross/Blue Shield	$1,705,352	27%	73%
9.	Goldman Sachs Group	$2,657,842	73%	27%	33.	Laborers Union	$1,705,325	92%	8%
10.	United Parcel Service	$2,582,464	23%	77%	34.	Pfizer Inc.	$1,703,242	16%	84%
11.	SBC Communications	$2,512,528	47%	53%	35.	National Education Assn.	$1,665,285	91%	9%
12.	Philip Morris	$2,469,575	21%	79%	36.	Bristol-Myers Squibb	$1,645,017	17%	83%
13.	National Assn. of Realtors	$2,445,511	41%	58%	37.	Freddie Mac	$1,643,239	36%	64%
14.	Assn. of Trial Lawyers of America	$2,365,400	86%	14%	38.	Carpenters & Joiners Union	$1,594,895	88%	12%
15.	United Food & Commercial Workers Union	$2,339,648	99%	1%	39.	Morgan Stanley, Dean Witter & Co.	$1,535,515	32%	68%
					40.	AFLAC Inc.	$1,492,135	47%	53%
16.	National Rifle Assn.	$2,311,212	7%	93%	41.	Union Pacific Corp.	$1,490,630	16%	83%
17.	Teamsters Union	$2,143,145	94%	6%	42.	Marine Engineers Union	$1,455,750	56%	44%
18.	Ernst & Young	$2,099,509	41%	59%	43.	United Auto Workers	$1,438,270	99%	1%
19.	Lockheed Martin	$2,003,617	39%	61%	44.	National Assn. of Letter Carriers	$1,430,000	87%	13%
20.	Machinists/Aerospace Workers Union	$1,981,638	99%	1%	45.	Emily's List	$1,406,665	100%	0%
21.	Sheet Metal Workers Union	$1,971,384	99%	1%	46.	General Electric	$1,399,089	37%	63%
					47.	Andersen Worldwide	$1,391,607	28%	72%
22.	MBNA America Bank	$1,951,975	19%	81%	48.	Deloitte & Touche	$1,365,011	29%	71%
23.	Federal Express Corp.	$1,909,478	35%	65%	49.	Boeing Co.	$1,356,220	44%	56%
					50.	Pricewaterhouse Coopers	$1,341,149	26%	74%

FIGURE 8-3 The Big-Money Contributors

Figures include all contributions made to candidates or political parties in the 1999–2000 election cycle by the listed organizations, their PACs, employees and immediate families. Included are direct contributions to candidates, as well as hard- and soft-money contributions to the political parties. Independent expenditures are not included, nor are expenditures on "issue ads" or other indirect or unreported election year expenses.

Source: Center for Responsive Politics, Washington, D.C. (Nov. 2000).

Buying Government Assistance   Many individual large contributors do business with government agencies. They expect any representative or senator they have supported to intervene on their behalf with these agencies, sometimes acting to cut red tape, ensure fairness, and expedite their cases, and other times pressuring the agencies for a favorable decision. Officials in the White House or the cabinet may also be expected to intervene on behalf of major contributors. There is little question raised when the intervention merely expedites consideration of a contributor's case, but pressure to bend rules or regulations to get favorable decisions raises ethical problems for officeholders (see "Congressional Ethics" in Chapter 10).

Individual Contributors   Those who contribute to presidential and/or congressional campaign funds do so for a variety of reasons. Some contributors are ideologically motivated. They make their contributions based on their perception of the ideological position of the candidate (or perhaps their perception of the candidate's opponent). They may make contributions to congressional candidates across the country who share their policy views. Liberal and conservative networks of contributors can be contacted through specialized mailing lists—for example, liberals through television producer Norman Lear's People for the American Way and conservatives through North Carolina Senator Jesse Helms's National Congressional Club. Feminists have been effective in soliciting individual contributions across the country and funneling them very early in a campaign to women candidates through EMILY's list. Ideological contributors may only get the satisfaction of knowing that they are financially backing their cause in the political process. Some contributors simply enjoy the opportunity to be near and to be seen with high-ranking politicians. Politicians pose for photos with contributors, who later frame the photos and hang them in their office to impress their friends, associates, and customers. About 7 to 10 percent of the population claims in national surveys to have contributed to candidates running for public office. Contributors are disproportionately high-income, older people with strong partisan views (see Figure 8-4).

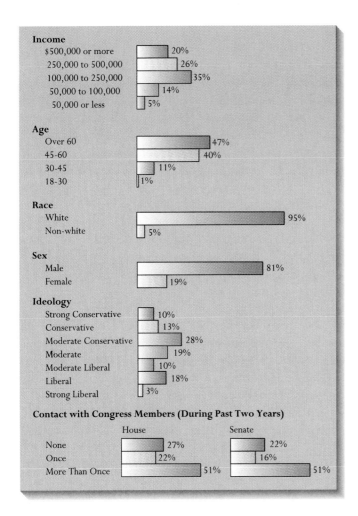

FIGURE 8-4   Characteristics of Individual Political Contributors

Contributors to political campaigns generally have been older, and have higher incomes than most Americans. Whites and males contribute more than blacks and females, and conservatives contribute more than liberals.

Source: John Green, Paul Herrnson, Lynda Powell, Clyde Wilcox, "Individual Congressional Campaign Contributions," press release, June 9, 1998. Center for Responsive Politics.

Fund-Raising Chores   Fund raising occupies more of a candidate's time than any other campaign activity. Candidates must personally contact as many individual contributors as possible. They work late into the evening on the telephone with potential contributors. Fund-raising dinners, cocktail parties, barbecues, fish frys, and so on, are scheduled nearly every day of a campaign. The candidate is expected to appear personally to "press the flesh" of big contributors. Movie and rock stars and other assorted celebrities may also be asked to appear at fund-raising affairs to generate attendance. Dinners may run $250 to $1,000 a plate in presidential affairs, although often less in Senate or House campaigns. Tickets may be "bundled" to well-heeled individual contributors or sold in blocks to organizations. Fund-raising techniques are limited only by the imagination of the campaign manager.

REGULATING CAMPAIGN FINANCE

The **Federal Election Commission (FEC)** is responsible for enforcing limits on individual and organizational contributions to all federal elections, administering the public funding of presidential campaigns, and requiring full disclosure of all campaign financial activity in presidential and congressional elections. Enforcement of these federal election and campaign finance laws lies in the hands of the six-member FEC. Appointed by the president to serve staggered six-year terms, commission members are traditionally split 3 to 3 between Republicans and Democrats.

Limits on Contributions   The FEC limits direct individual contributions to a candidate's campaign to $1,000 per election and organizational contributions to $5,000 per election. But there are many ways in which individuals and organizations can legally surmount these limits (see Table 8-4: "Rules and Loopholes: What You Can Do and Cannot Do in Federal Campaign Finance"). Contributors may give a candidate $1,000 for each member of their family in a primary election and then another $1,000 per member in the general election. Organizations may generate much more than the $5,000 limit by bundling (combining) $1,000 additional contributions from individual members. As noted earlier, both individuals and organizations can give unlimited amounts of soft money to the parties, as long as it is not spent directly on a particular candidate's campaign. Independent organizations can spend money beyond the FEC's limit for a presidential candidate or party in order to promote their political views, so long as these organizations do so "without cooperation or consultation with the candidate of his or her campaign." Finally, as noted, individuals may spend as much of their own money on their own campaigns as they wish.[9]

By law, every candidate for federal office must file periodic reports with the FEC detailing both the income and the expenditures of their campaign. Individual contributors who give an aggregate of $200 or more must be identified by name, address, occupation, and employer. All PAC and party contributions, no matter how large or small, must also be itemized. In addition, PACs themselves must file reports with the FEC at least four times a year, detailing both the contributions received by the PAC and the names of candidates and other groups that received the PAC's donations.

Federal Funding of Presidential Elections   Federal funding, financed by the $3 checkoff box on individual income tax returns, is available to presidential candidates in primary and general elections, as well as to major-party nominating conven-

Federal Election Commission (FEC)   Agency charged with enforcing federal election laws and disbursing public presidential campaign funds.

Table 8-4 Rules and Loopholes: What You Can Do and Cannot Do in Federal Campaign Finance

Rules

- As an individual you may give no more than $1,000 per election to a federal candidate's campaign. This limit applies separately to each election—primaries, runoffs, and the general election.
- You may give no more than $5,000 per calendar year to a PAC or state party committee.
- You may give no more than $20,000 per calendar year to a national party committee.
- You may give no more than $25,000 total per calendar year to candidates and parties.
- Your contributions exceeding $100 must be made by check. Contributions of more than $200 must be accompanied by a report of your name, address, occupation and employment, and the date and amount of the contribution.
- Your presidential campaign contributions up to $250 may be matched by federal funds.
- Any independent expenditures you may make (for example for your own advertisement in a newspaper or on television urging the public to vote for or against a candidate) must not be coordinated in any way with the candidate or the party and must include a notice stating who has paid for the communication and that is not authorized by the candidate or the party.

Loopholes

- *Soft money.* You may give as much as you wish to state and local political parties for voter registration drives, party mailings, and advertising.
- *Self financing.* You may use as much of your own money for your own campaign as you wish.
- *Family contributions.* You may multiply the size of individual contributions by the number of members of your family. (However, contributions from children under 18 must come from their own bank accounts or trust funds.)
- *Issue ads.* You may spend as much as you wish to advertise your own political views and your own support or opposition to candidates, so long as you do not coordinate your expenditures with a candidate or party.
- *Independent organizations.* You may give as much as you wish to organizations, including unions, environmental groups, ideological organizations, women's groups, etc., for them to use in their own independent issue advertisements.

tions. Candidates seeking the nomination in presidential primary elections can qualify for federal funds by raising $5,000 from private contributions no greater than $250 each in each of twenty states. In the general election, Democratic and Republican nominees are funded equally at levels determined by the FEC. In order to receive federal funding, presidential candidates must agree to FEC limits on their campaign spending in both primary and general elections. Until 1992, all presidential candidates agreed to the FEC limits and accepted federal funding; but independent Texas billionaire H. Ross Perot funded his own campaign that year, rejecting federal funds, and publishing mogul Steve Forbes rejected federal funds in 1996 and 2000 and paid for his own unsuccessful Republican presidential primary race.

With the largest campaign warchest ever assembled by a presidential candidate, George W. Bush decided early in 2000 to forgo federal funding and thus avoid the spending limits that such funding imposes as a condition of receipt.

Federal funding pays about one-third of the primary campaign costs of presidential candidates and all the *official* presidential campaign organization costs in the general election. The parties also receive federal funds for their nominating conventions. Should these regulations be changed? Reformers disagree sharply about how the limitations should be changed (see *A Conflicting View:* "Reforming Campaign Finance").

THE PRESIDENTIAL CAMPAIGN: THE PRIMARY RACE

The phrase *presidential fever* refers to the burning political ambition required to seek the presidency. The grueling presidential campaign is a test of strength, character, endurance, and determination. It is physically exhausting and mentally and emotionally draining. Every aspect of the candidates' lives—and the lives of their families—is subject to microscopic inspection by the news media. Most of this coverage is critical, and much of it is unfair. Yet candidates are expected to handle it all with grace and humor, from the earliest testing of the waters through a full-fledged campaign.

Media Mentions   Politicians with presidential ambitions may begin by promoting presidential *mentions* by media columnists and commentators. The media help to identify "presidential timber" years in advance of a presidential race simply by drawing up lists of potential candidates, commenting on their qualifications, and speculating about their intentions. Mentions are likely to come to prominent governors or senators who start making speeches outside of their state, who grab the media spotlight on a national issue, or who simply let it be known to the media "off the record" that they are considering a presidential race. Visiting New Hampshire and giving speeches there is viewed as "testing the waters" and a signal of presidential ambitions (see *Up Close:* "Presidential Primaries 2000" on page 256).

Presidential Credentials   Political experience as vice president, governor, U.S. senator, or member of Congress not only inspires presidential ambition but also provides vital experience in political campaigning. However, virtually all presidential candidates testify that the presidential arena is far more challenging than politics at any other level. The experience of running for and holding high public office appears to be a political requirement for the presidency. Some recent presidential aspirants (Independent Ross Perot, Republican Steve Forbes, and Republican Patrick Buchanan) have tried to make a virtue of their lack of previous political office holding, no doubt hoping to attract support from the many Americans who disdain "politics as usual." But in the twentieth century no major party nominee for president has not previously held office as vice president, governor, U.S. senator, or member of Congress except World War II hero General Dwight D. Eisenhower.

The Decision to Run   The decision to run for president involves complex personal and political calculations. Ambition to occupy the world's most powerful office must be weighed against the staggering costs—emotional as well as financial—of a presidential campaign.

Reforming Campaign Finance

Battles over campaign finance reform reflect conflict between the parties. Historically, Republicans enjoyed a greater ability to raise money from their more affluent loyalists. Democrats were usually more dependent on unions and political action committee (PAC) money. Political scientist Frank Sorauf writes, "Nothing colors the politics of regulating campaign finance as much as the central fact that the Congress is regulating its own electoral activity. . . . The members of Congress know campaign finance at first hand, and they know that even the slightest change in the structure of regulations may have considerable consequences for their own political careers."

Reform Goals Ideally, reform of campaign financing should minimize the opportunity for corruption, inspire voter confidence in the integrity of the political system, equalize influence between rich and poor, encourage competitive elections by giving challengers a fair chance against incumbents, and at the same time preserve free speech and the right of people to promote their views at election time. But it is not clear that any reform proposals could achieve all of these goals at once.

Eliminate PACs? Proposals to outlaw PACs and ban all contributions by corporations, unions, and interest groups raise constitutional questions about the right of groups to express their preferences and participate in the electoral process. The Supreme Court might strike down a congressional attempt to ban PACs as a violation of the First Amendment. Republicans might gain more from such a ban than Democrats; if PAC and union money were to be eliminated, individual contributions would become the only game in town, a situation that might favor Republicans.

Public Funding and Limits on Spending? It is frequently argued that congressional elections should be publicly funded and limits placed on congressional campaign spending, just as they are in presidential elec-

tions. Most members of Congress dislike the constant chore of asking people for money. Freeing them from obligations to contributors would presumably reduce the influence of well-heeled special interests in congressional decision making. Members of Congress would no longer be obliged to give special consideration to the requests of wealthy individual contributors and big-spending PACs. Perhaps the general public would be less cynical about Congress and more confident of the fairness of the system.

But public funding would entail limits on campaign spending for the candidates. Equal limits for congressional incumbents and challengers would grant a strong advantage to incumbents, who already have name recognition and years of constituent contacts and services working on their behalf. Indeed, skeptics charge that public funding with campaign limits is really an "incumbent protection" plan, and many taxpayers are offended by the very idea of politicians using tax dollars to run for public office. Indeed, most taxpayers refuse even to check off $3 of their taxes for presidential campaigns.

Banning Soft Money? Current laws allow unlimited contributions in soft money to political parties. Soft money allows big contributors to exercise disproportionate influence in party affairs. But this soft money also gives the parties what little direct influence they have over members of Congress. Cutting off party funding would further weaken the party system.

Curtailing Independent Spending? Independent spending on "issue ads" by organizations are currently allowed by law, so long as the independent persons or groups doing so do not coordinate with the candidate. But curtailing independent spending on political communication is likely to be an unconstitutional infringement on First Amendment—protected free speech. The Supreme Court ruled in *Buckley v. Valeo* (1976) that organizations and individuals may spend as much as they wish on political communications.

Source: Frank Sorauf, *Inside Campaign Finance* (New Haven, Conn.: Yale University Press, 1992), p. 191.

Presidential Primaries 2000

The 2000 presidential primary season ended very early. Indeed, the primaries were so "front-loaded" that George W. Bush and Al Gore sewed up their party's nominations in a scant five weeks, from New Hampshire's February 1st opening primary to the March 7th primaries in California, New York, Ohio, and eight other states. A majority of the nation's primary voters went to the polls *after* the nominations had been won.

Front-loading—the bunching of the primaries early in the election year—clearly helped each party's more established and well financed candidate. George W. Bush and Al Gore led all other Republicans and Democrats respectively at the beginning of the year in national polls and in campaign contributions. Indeed, George W. Bush set a new financial record, amassing nearly $70 million *before* the first primary. Nevertheless, both eventual nominees faced serious challengers early in their campaigns.

U.S. Senator John McCain rocked the Republican establishment with a surprise victory in New Hampshire. His impressive 49 to 31 percent win over Bush encouraged McCain supporters to believe an upset was in the making. McCain's life story as a former Navy pilot who spent five torturous years in a Vietnam prison is a compelling tale. McCain added to his voter appeal by positioning himself as an insurgent within his own party, blunt-talking and independent-minded, an advocate of campaign finance reform. His reputation as a maverick was not really appreciated by his colleagues in the Senate who viewed him as uncooperative, sanctimonious, and temperamental. His victory in Michigan's open primary confirmed McCain's support among independent voters, and his challenge to the GOP establishment was heralded by the national news media. But his victories in New Hampshire and Michigan turned out to be the high-water mark of his presidential bid.

George W. Bush was the pick of Republican Party regulars and heavy campaign contributors. Bush's advisers were aware that long weeks of "retail" campaigning by McCain might pay off for him among New Hampshire's independent-minded voters. But they also knew that the big state votes coming early on March 7th (California, New York, Ohio) and March 14th (Texas and Florida) would be decisive. Moreover, they knew that they had the money to buy expensive television advertising in these big states— money that McCain could not match. Bush's only worry was that media hoopla over McCain's early wins might ignite an anti-establishment firestorm, brand Bush as a loser, and send voters and contributors to the charismatic war hero. But Bush's victories in South Carolina (February 12) and Virginia (February 19) indicated that Republican party regulars were standing behind the Texas governor. Bush effectively won the nomination when he swept to victory in California, New York, and Ohio on March 7th; he did not even need his expected victories in his home state of Texas and his brother's home state of Florida the following week. He quickly turned his attention to pacifying McCain and his supporters and unifying the GOP against Al Gore.

Al Gore had an even easier task in brushing aside the challenge from former New Jersey Senator and one-time National Basketball Association star, Bill Bradley. Bradley had considered running for president in 1992, but the thoughtful, introverted, former athlete left the Democratic primaries to Bill Clinton that year. He later left the U.S. Senate, citing his frustration with the political process. The Gore campaign went on the attack early, comparing Al's praiseworthy "stay in Washington and fight" to Bill's "cut and run" decision to leave politics. When Gore won convincingly in New Hampshire's Democratic primary, despite that state's reputation for supporting underdogs, the Gore camp was reassured of victory. Bradley's last chance depended on winning New York; he hoped that his popular image as a star player for the New York Knicks would tip the scales in his favor. But New York Democrats stayed with their party's establishment choice. Bradley conceded after losing New York, and Gore was able to save campaign money for the fight against Bush in the general election.

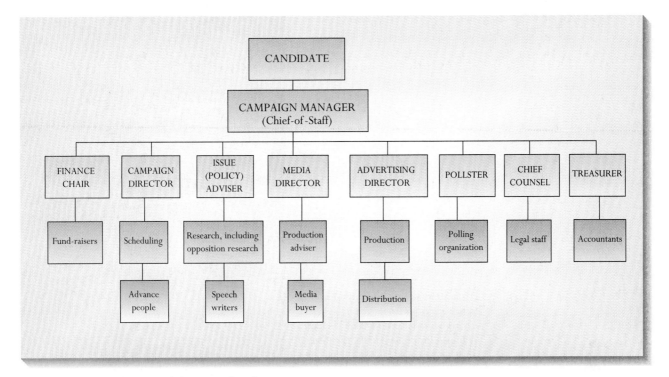

FIGURE 8-5 Typical Campaign Organization

Campaign organizations vary, but most assign someone to perform these tasks: funding, scheduling appearances, speech writing, media production and buying, polling, advertising, legal compliance, and check writing, even if, in local campaigns, all these tasks must be performed by the candidate or his or her family members.

Serious planning, organizing, and fund raising must begin at least two years before the general election. A staff must be assembled—campaign managers and strategists, fund raisers, media experts, pollsters, issues advisers and speech writers, lawyers and accountants—and supporters must be identified in key states throughout the nation. Paid and volunteer workers must be assembled (see Figure 8-5). Leaders among important interest groups must be contacted. A general campaign strategy must be developed, an organization put in place, and several millions of dollars in campaign contributions pledged in advance of the race. Often the decision to run hinges on whether initial pledges of campaign contributions appear adequate. The serious candidate must be able to anticipate contributions of $20 million or more for primary elections.

A Strategy for the Primaries The road to the White House consists of two separate races: the primary elections and caucuses leading to the Democratic and Republican party nominations, and the general election. Each of these races requires a separate strategy. The primary race requires an appeal to party activists and the more ideologically motivated primary voters in key states. The general election requires an appeal to the less partisan, less attentive, more ideologically moderate general election voters. Thus the campaign strategy developed to win the nomination must give way after the national conventions to a strategy to win the November general election.

The New Hampshire Primary The primary season begins in the winter snows of New Hampshire, traditionally the first state to hold a presidential primary election. New Hampshire is far more important *strategically* to a presidential

Presidential hopefuls multiply when the incumbent is forced to step down after serving two terms in office. Vice President Al Gore is the inside track for the Democratic nomination in 2000, but the Republican nomination has attracted a host of "wannabes."

campaign than it is in delegate strength. As a small state, New Hampshire supplies fewer than 1 percent of the delegates at the Democratic and Republican conventions. But the New Hampshire primary looms very large in media coverage and hence in overall campaign strategy. Although the popular Iowa party caucuses are held even earlier, New Hampshire is the nation's first primary, and the media begin speculating about its outcome and reporting early state-poll results months in advance.

The "expectations" game is played with a vengeance. Media polls and commentators set the candidates' expected vote percentages, and the candidates and their spokespersons try to deflate these expectations. On election night, the candidates' **spin doctors** sally forth among the crowds of television and newspaper reporters to give a favorable interpretation of the outcome. The candidates themselves appear at campaign headquarters (and, they hope, on national television) to give the same favorable spin to the election results. But the media itself—particularly the television network anchors and reporters and commentators—interpret the results for the American people, determining the early favorites in the presidential "horse race."

New Hampshire provides the initial *momentum* for the presidential candidates. "Momentum" is more than just a media catchword. The Democratic and Republican winners in New Hampshire have demonstrated their voter appeal, their "electability." Favorable New Hampshire results inspire more financial contributions and thus the resources needed to carry the fight into the next group of primary elections. Unfavorable New Hampshire results tend to dry up contributions; weak candidates may be forced into an early withdrawal.

spin doctor   Practitioner of the art of spin control, or manipulation of media reporting to favor one's own candidate.

The Front-End Strategy A **front-end strategy** places heavy emphasis on the results from New Hampshire and other early primary states. This strategy involves spending all or most of the candidate's available resources—time, energy, and money—on the early primary states, in the hopes that early victories will provide the momentum, in media attention and financial contributions, to continue the race. The front-end loading of the primary election schedule makes it especially important for candidates to raise "early money."

The front-end strategy became especially important in the 2000 presidential primaries after several key states, including California and New York, moved up the date of their primary elections to early March. State legislators in these states expressed frustration over the media attention given to tiny New Hampshire, and they sought to gain publicity and influence for their states in presidential nominating politics by selecting an earlier date for their primaries. (The New Hampshire Legislature responded by officially setting its primary date one week earlier than any other state's primary.) The result for the 2000 primary campaign was that the winning candidates—Democrat Al Gore and Republican George W. Bush—had already locked up their parties' nominations by the end of March.

This "front loading" of the 2000 presidential primary elections made the ability to raise *early* campaign money even more important. Indeed, the leading candidates of both parties—George W. Bush, Al Gore, Bill Bradley, Steve Forbes—had well in excess of $20 million in their campaign chests *before* the end of 1999. George W. Bush had collected an unprecedented $60 million. The battle for early money appeared to force several would-be candidates out of the race, including Elizabeth Dole who had been running second to George W. Bush in the polls (see *People in Politics:* Elizabeth Dole on page 262).

Big-State Strategy Presidential aspirants who begin the race with widespread support among party activists, heavy financial backing, and strong endorsements from the major interest groups can focus their attention on the big-state primaries. A **big-state strategy** generally requires more money, more workers, and better organization than a front-end strategy. But the big states—California, New York, Texas, Florida, Pennsylvania, Ohio, and Michigan—have the most delegates. The results of these primaries may determine the Democratic and Republican nominees, assuming that most or all of them are won by the same candidates. It is rare that more than two candidates in each party survive as credible candidates after the big states have made their selections. By this stage of the race, many uncommitted delegates begin to commit themselves and their convention votes to the leader.

Convention Showplace Once a presidential candidate has enough votes to assure nomination, this uncrowned winner must prepare for the party's convention. Organizing and orchestrating convention forces, dominating the platform and rules writing, enjoying the nominating speeches and the traditional roll call of the state delegations, mugging for the television camera when the nominating vote goes over the top, submitting the vice presidential nominee's name for convention approval, and preparing and delivering a rousing acceptance speech to begin the fall campaign are just a few of the many tasks awaiting the winner—and the winner's campaign team.

Presidential candidates usually submit their choice for vice president in the run-up to the party's national convention. George W. Bush's 2000 running mate, Dick Cheney, was viewed by some as having been chosen to lend an air of maturity to the Republican ticket. Cheney was Secretary of Defense in Bush's father's administration.

front-end strategy Presidential political campaign strategy in which a candidate focuses on winning early primaries to build momentum.

big-state strategy Presidential political campaign strategy in which a candidate focuses on winning primaries in large states because of their high delegate counts.

Too Close to Call

The 2000 presidential election turned out to be one of the most bitterly contested races in the nation's history, an election "too close to call."

Early Campaign Strategies   By traditional expectations, Democrat Al Gore's election should have been a "slam dunk." The nation was enjoying economic prosperity, low unemployment, low inflation, budget surpluses, and a relative peace. Traditionally under such conditions, Americans have kept the incumbent party in the White House.

But the campaign started off very badly for Al Gore. The vice president was perceived as a stiff, wooden prop for his boss, the flawed yet charismatic Bill Clinton. Gore trailed George W. Bush badly in opinion polls for the first eight months of the election year. He tried to "reinvent" himself several times—self-consciously projecting different images of himself at different times. His "image adviser" recommended that he give up formal suits and ties for more relaxed sweaters and open collar shirts and that he become an "Alpha male"—spirited and aggressive rather than subdued and wonkish. Yet throughout the spring he seemed unable to shed the image of a loyal, decent, yet colorless backup to the more magnetic Clinton.

George W. Bush's campaign rested largely on his personal appeal to voters—his warmth, good humor, and general likability. Early on, he settled on the theme of "*compassionate* conservatism," trying to appeal to independents, minorities, and especially women. Yet he knew that he was confronting an incumbent vice president who had held office during good economic times. Bush's only avenue of attack was that the Clinton/Gore administration had wasted opportunities—failing to save Social Security, to reform Medicare, to advance education, or to grant tax relief: "You had your chance." But Bush's running mate selection of Dick Cheney, former Secretary of Defense and close friend of Bush's father, seemed to confirm the suspicion that "Dubya" was not up to the job of president, that he needed his father's guidance.

The Race Narrows   Al Gore's fortunes changed dramatically at the Democratic convention in August. In a deliberate effort to overcome his image of formality, he planted a passionate kiss on his wife as he strode to the podium. He reinvented himself once again, this time as a populist fighting for "working people" against the powerful special interests—the oil companies, the insurance companies, the hated HMO's. His voice was stronger, his rhetoric more powerful, and even if his new persona seemed somewhat artificial, he struck a chord with the American people. Perhaps more importantly, Gore distanced himself from the scandals of the Clinton administration, even while simultaneously claiming credit for eight years of prosperity. His running mate selection, U.S. Senator Joseph Lieberman of Connecticut, the first Jew to appear on a major party ticket and an outspoken critic of Bill Clinton's scandalous behavior, was widely applauded. The selection seemed to affirm Al Gore's claim "I am my own man." Gore won a huge convention "bounce" in the polls.

Bush partially dispelled the notion that he lacked sufficient *gravitas* (wisdom and experience) in the televised presidential debates. Gore appeared overly aggressive, perhaps even rude, especially in the first debate. Bush retook the lead in the polls following the debates. But each day there seemed to be large gyrations in the polling figures.

Throughout most of the campaign, Bush and Gore attacked each other in speeches and television ads on the issues—for example, whether to allow young workers to invest part of their Social Security payments in the stockmarket (Bush) or whether this was "a dangerous idea" (Gore); whether prescription drugs for seniors should be provided directly through Medicare (Gore) or through subsidies for seniors to buy private insurance (Bush); whether to provide a large across-the-board tax cut (Bush) or a smaller "targeted" tax cut (Gore). Bush had long ago admitted to "youthful indiscretions," so when it was revealed late in the campaign that he had been arrested for drunk driving in 1976, few voters were swayed by this news. As the election neared, Bush's narrow lead fell within the margin of error in most polls.

Electoral Vote Strategies   The Bush campaign conceded New York, California, and most of the Northeastern states to Gore. The Gore campaign conceded Texas and most of the Southern and Mountain states to Bush. The battleground states were Pennsylvania, Ohio, Michigan, Illinois, Wisconsin, and especially Florida. Bush's younger brother, Jeb Bush, had been elected governor of Florida in 1998 and Republicans controlled both houses of the legislature.

Throughout election day, Democrats worked furiously to get out their vote. Vans shuttled voters to the polls from senior citizen homes, African American churches, and union halls. Early in the evening the television networks "called" all of the battleground states for Gore, in effect declaring him the winner. But by 9 p.m. Florida was yanked back into the undecided column; the electoral college vote looked like it was splitting down the middle. Around 1 a.m. Florida was "called" for Bush, and the networks pronounced him the next president of the United States. Gore telephoned Bush to concede and started toward downtown Nashville to give his concession speech. But his cell phones began to buzz and beep: the gap in Florida was closing fast. Gore withdrew his concession. For the second time, the television networks pulled Florida back into the "Too Close to Call" column. NBC anchor Tom Brokaw acknowledged "We don't have egg on our face. We have an omelet."

The Battle after the Bell The morning after election day, it was clear that Al Gore had won the nationwide popular vote. But the electoral college outcome depended on Florida's 25 electoral votes. Bush's lead in Florida, after several machine recounts and the count of absentee ballots, was 930 votes out of six million cast in that state.

Armies of lawyers descended on Florida. The Gore campaign demanded hand recounts of the votes in the state's three most populous and Democratic counties—Miami-Dade, Broward (Fort Lauderdale), and Palm Beach. Bush's lawyers argued that the hand counts in these counties were late, unreliable, subjective, and open to partisan bias. Gore's lawyers argued that the Palm Beach "butterfly" ballot was confusing (the Gore/Lieberman punch hole was positioned third instead of second under Bush/Cheney; Buchanan's punch hole was positioned second). They also argued that partially detached "chads" (small perforated squares in the punch cards that should fall out when the voter punches the ballot) should be inspected to ascertain the "intent" of the voter.

The Florida Supreme Court ordered that hand counts may continue, setting back the Florida legislature's enacted deadline for the receipt of county votes by more than a week to November 26, 2000. But the Court declined to give county canvassers (vote counters) specific instructions about counting chads, including "dimpled chads" where voters may have indented the punch cards but not broken through them.

Florida's Secretary of State (separately-elected Republican Katherine Harris) certified the state's vote

immediately after the Court's new deadline: Bush was declared the winner by 537 votes. Bush went on national television declaring that he was "honored and humbled" to have won Florida's vote and the presidency, and "respectfully" asked Gore to "reconsider" his pledge to contest the election. Gore went on national television vowing to fight on "until every vote is counted."

A President Chosen by the Supreme Court
Gore formally protested the Florida vote, expecting that his protest would eventually be decided by the Florida Supreme Court, with its seven Democratic-appointed justices. And, indeed, by a 4–3 vote the Florida high court agreed. It ordered a hand recount of all "undervotes" in the state—ballots that failed to register a presidential selection on machines—to determine the "intent" of the voter.

However, Bush appealed to the Supreme Court of the United States, arguing that the Florida Supreme Court had overreached its authority under the U.S. Constitution when it substituted its own deadline for the deadline enacted by the state's legislature. (Article II, Section 1, declares that "Each State shall appoint [presidential electors] in such Manner as the *Legislature* thereof may direct…") Bush's lawyers also argued that without specific standards to determine the "intent" of the voter, different vote-counters would use different standards (counting or not counting "dimpled," "pregnant," "indented," etc. chads). Without uniform rules, such a recount would violate the Equal Protection Clause of the 14th Amendment.

In *Bush v. Gore*, the U.S. Supreme Court agreed (by a 7–2 vote) that the Florida court had created "constitutional problems" involving the Equal Protection Clause, and the Court ordered (by a 5–4 vote) that the hand count be ended altogether. The effect of the decision was to reinstate the Florida Secretary of State's certification of Bush as the winner of Florida's 25 electoral votes and consequently the winner of the Electoral College vote for president by the narrowest of margins: 271–267.

For the first time in the nation's history, a presidential election was decided by the Supreme Court of the United States. Perhaps only the Supreme Court possesses sufficient legitimacy in the minds of the American public to bring about a resolution to the closest presidential electoral vote in history.

PEOPLE IN POLITICS

Elizabeth Dole

Elizabeth Dole dropped out of the race for the Republican presidential nomination well before the first primary ballot was cast. She did so despite the fact that she was running second to George W. Bush in the polls at the time. Her explanation: "The bottom line remains money. In fact, it's a kind of Catch 22. Inadequate funding . . . restricts your ability to communicate with voters. It places a ceiling on travel and travel staff. Over time, it becomes nearly impossible to sustain an effective campaign."

Elizabeth Dole is a Phi Beta Kappa graduate of Duke University who went on to receive both a master's degree in government from Harvard and a law degree from Harvard Law School. In 1971, she was appointed Assistant to the President for Consumer Affairs under Richard Nixon, and began a long career in appointed positions in the federal government. Although never *elected* to office, she served as a member of the Federal Trade Commission for six years, and was later appointed to President Ronald Reagan's Cabinet as Secretary of Transportation—the first woman to hold that position. When President George Bush assumed office in 1989, she switched cabinet positions, becoming Secretary of Labor.

She became president of the American Red Cross in 1991 and served in that post until her husband, Bob Dole, launched his unsuccessful presidential bid in 1996. She campaigned very effectively on behalf of her husband; she comfortably worked audiences "Oprah-style"—microphone in hand fielding questions with grace, charm, and wit. After his defeat she resumed her presidency of the American Red Cross, but she resigned in early 1999 to pursue her own presidential ambition.

She campaigned across the country for nine months and established herself as a serious contender for the Republican nomination. Indeed, polls suggested that she would defeat the probable Democratic nominee, Al Gore. But as she would later lament:

"At times I have felt as if there were two entirely separate campaigns under way. Outside the Beltway, real people by the thousands turned out to discuss their schools and health-care, tax cuts and the state of our defenses. . . . [But] I have learned that the current political calendar and election laws favor those who get an early start and can tap into huge private fortunes, or who have a pre-existing network of political supporters."

THE PRESIDENTIAL CAMPAIGN: THE GENERAL ELECTION BATTLE

Buoyed by the conventions—and often by postconvention bounces in the polls—the new nominees must now face the general electorate.

General Election Strategies   Strategies in the general election are as varied as the imaginations of campaign advisers, media consultants, pollsters, and the candidates themselves. As noted earlier, campaign strategies are affected by the nature of the times and the state of the economy; by the incumbent or challenger status of the candidate; by the issues, conditions, scandals, or events currently being spotlighted by the media; and by the dynamics of the campaign itself as the candidates attack and defend themselves.

Electoral College   The 538 presidential electors apportioned among the states according to their congressional representation (plus 3 for the District of Columbia) whose votes officially elect the president and vice president of the United States.

Presidential election campaigns must focus on the **Electoral College**. The president is not elected by the national popular vote total but rather by a majority of the *electoral* votes of the states. Electoral votes are won by plurality, winner-take-all popular voting in each of the states (see *Up Close:* "Understanding the Electoral College" on page264). Thus a narrow plurality win in a state delivers *all* of that state's electoral votes. Big-state victories, even by very narrow margins, can deliver big electoral prizes. The biggest prizes are California with 54 electoral votes, New York with 33, and Texas with 32. With a total of 538 electoral votes at stake, *the winner must garner victories in states that total a minimum of 270 electoral votes.*

Targeting the Swing States   In focusing on the most populous states, with their large electoral votes, candidates must decide which of these states are "winnable," then direct their time, energy, and money to these *swing states.* Candidates cannot afford to spend too much effort in states that already seem to be solidly in their column, although they must avoid the perception that they are ignoring these strong bases of support. Neither can candidates waste much effort on states that already appear to be solidly in their opponent's column. So the swing states receive most of the candidates' time, attention, and television advertising money.

Regional Alignments   A glance at the Electoral College vote results in recent elections (see *Across the USA:* "How the States Voted" on page 266) suggests that Republican candidates depend heavily on electoral votes from the South and the Mountain States. Florida and Texas are the keys to Republican presidential election strength. The Democratic presidential electoral base is found in the Northeast and upper Midwest. Even when Democratic candidates have lost in New York, Massachusetts, Pennsylvania, Illinois, Michigan, and Wisconsin, the vote margin in these states has been fairly close. California, with its prize of 54 electoral votes, is the most important swing state. California voters supported the Republican ticket in every election from 1968 to 1988; their swing to the Democratic ticket in 1992, 1996, and 2000 restored that party's presidential fortunes. Among the Republican "must-win" states, Dole held on to Texas in 1996 but lost Florida. Florida became the central focus of the nation in 2000 when its twenty-five electoral votes determined the eventual outcome of the election.

The Presidential Debates   The nationally televised presidential debates are the central feature of the general election campaign. These debates attract more viewers than any other campaign event. Moreover, they enable a candidate to reach undecided voters and the opponent's supporters, as well as the candidate's own partisans. Even people who usually pay little attention to politics may be drawn in by the drama of the confrontation (see *Up Close:* "The Presidential Debates" on page 268).

The debates allow viewers an opportunity to see and hear candidates together and to compare their responses to questions as they stand side by side. The debates give audiences a better view of the candidates than they can get from thirty-second commercial ads or seven-second news sound bites. Viewers can at least judge how the candidates react under pressure.

However, the debates emphasize candidate image over substantive policy issues. Candidates must appear presidential. They must appear confident, compassionate, concerned, and good humored. They must not appear uncertain or unsure of themselves, or aloof or out of touch with viewers, or easily upset by hostile questions. They must avoid verbal slips or gaffes or even unpolished or awkward gestures. They must remember that the debates are not really debates so much as joint press conferences in which the candidates respond to questions with rehearsed mini-speeches and practiced sound bites.[10]

Should We Scrap the Electoral College?

Americans were given a dramatic reminder in 2000 that the president of the United States is *not* elected by nationwide *popular* vote but rather by a majority of the *electoral votes* of the states.

How the Electoral College Works The Constitution grants each state a number of electors equal to the number of its congressional representatives and senators combined (see map). Because representatives are apportioned to the states on the basis of population, the electoral vote of the states is subject to change after each ten-year census. No state has fewer than three electoral votes, because the Constitution guarantees every state two U.S. senators and at least one representative. The Twenty-third Amendment granted three electoral votes to the District of Columbia even though it has no voting members of Congress. So winning the presidency requires winning in states with at least 270 of the 538 total electoral votes.

Voters in presidential elections are actually choosing a slate of presidential electors pledged to vote for their party's presidential and vice presidential candidates. The names of electors seldom appear on the ballot, only the names of the candidates and their parties. The slate that wins a *plurality* of the popular vote in a state (more than any other slate, not necessarily a majority) casts *all* of the state's vote in the Electoral College. (This "winner-take-all" system in the states is not mandated by the Constitution; a state legislature could allocate a state's electoral votes in proportion to the split in the popular vote.) The winner-take-all system in the states helps ensure that the Electoral College produces a majority for one candidate.

The Electoral College never meets at a single location; rather, electors meet at their respective state capitols to cast their ballots around December 15, following the general election on the first Tuesday after the first Monday of November. The results are sent to the presiding officer of the Senate, the vice president, who in January presides over their count in the presence of both houses of Congress and formally announces the results. These procedures are usually considered a formality, but the U.S. Constitution does not *require* that electors cast their vote for the winning presidential candidate in their state, and occasionally "faithless electors" disrupt the process, although none has ever changed the outcome.

If no candidate wins a majority of electoral votes, the House of Representatives chooses the president from among the three candidates with the largest number of electoral votes, with each state casting *one* vote. The Constitution does not specify how House delegations should determine their vote, but by House rules, the state's vote goes to the candidate receiving a majority vote in the delegation.

The Historical Record Only two presidential elections have ever been decided formally by the House of Representatives. In 1800 Thomas Jefferson and Aaron Burr tied in the Electoral College because the Twelfth Amendment had not yet been adopted to separate presidential from vice presidential voting; all the Democratic-Republican electors voted for both Jefferson and Burr, creating a tie. In 1824 Andrew Jackson won the popular vote and more electoral votes than anyone else but failed to get a majority. The House chose John Quincy Adams over Jackson, causing a popular uproar and ensuring Jackson's election in 1828.

In addition, in 1876, the Congress was called on to decide which electoral results from the southern states to validate; a Republican Congress chose to validate enough Republican electoral votes to allow Republican Rutherford B. Hayes to win, even though Democrat Samuel Tilden had won more popular votes. Hayes promised the Democratic southern states that in return for their acknowledgment of his presidential claim, he would end the military occupation of the South.

In 1888, the Electoral College vote failed to reflect the popular vote. Benjamin Harrison received 233 electoral votes to incumbent president Grover Cleveland's 168, even though Cleveland won about 90,000 more popular votes than Harrison. Harrison served a single lackluster term; Cleveland was elected for a second time in 1892, the only president to serve two nonconsecutive terms.

2000—"Too Close to Call" Al Gore eked out a close victory in the nationwide popular vote, receiving about 300,000 more votes (out of the more than 100 million ballots cast) than George W. Bush. But the vote in several states was extremely close. The key turned out to be Florida's 25 electoral votes. The Florida Secretary of State declared Bush the winner by a scant 537 votes out of six million cast in that state. The Gore campaign demanded *hand* recounts, especially in heavily Democratic counties in South Florida. The Bush campaign responded that hand counts are subjective, unreliable, and open to partisan bias. Eventually the U.S. Supreme Court decided that late hand recounts violated the state legislature's constitutionally enacted deadline and that subjective hand counts threatened to violate the Equal Protection Clause of the 14th Amendment.

What Would Replace the Electoral College?

Constitutional proposals to reform the Electoral College have circulated for nearly two hundred years, but none has won widespread support. These reform proposals have included (1) election of the president by direct national popular vote; (2) allocation of each state's electoral vote in proportion to the popular vote each candidate received in the state; (3) allocation of electoral votes to winners of each congressional district and two to the statewide winners.

But most reform proposals create as many problems as they resolve. If the president is to be elected by direct nationwide popular vote, should a plurality vote be sufficient to win? Or should a national runoff be held in the event that no one receives a majority in the first election? Would proportional allocation of electoral votes encourage third-party candidates to enter the race in order to deny the leading candidate a majority?

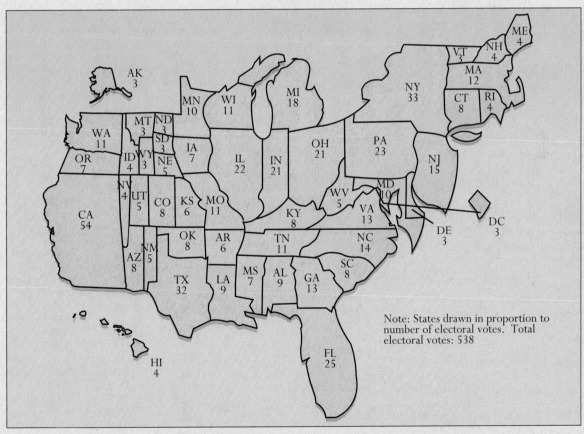

Note: States drawn in proportion to number of electoral votes. Total electoral votes: 538

In this map, each state is drawn in a size relative to the number of Electoral College votes it cast in the 2000 presidential election. It represents the apportionment following the 1990 census; a new apportionment following the 2000 census changes the number of electoral votes cast by several states.

Source: Holly Idelson, "Count Adds Seats in Eight States," *Congressional Quarterly Weekly Report* 48 (December 29, 1990), p. 4220.

How the States Voted

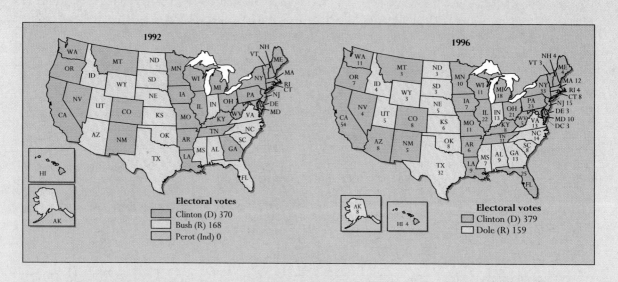

1992

Electoral votes
- Clinton (D) 370
- Bush (R) 168
- Perot (Ind) 0

1996

Electoral votes
- Clinton (D) 379
- Dole (R) 159

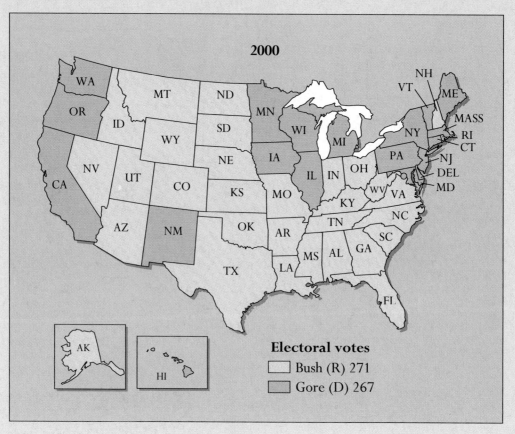

2000

Electoral votes
- Bush (R) 271
- Gore (D) 267

THE VOTER DECIDES

Understanding the reasons behind the voters' choice at the ballot box is a central concern of candidates, campaign strategists, commentators, and political scientists. Perhaps no other area of politics has been investigated so thoroughly as voting behavior. Survey data on voter choice have been collected for presidential elections for the past half century.[11] We know that voters cast ballots for and against candidates for a variety of reasons—party affiliation, group interests, characteristics and images of the candidates themselves, the economy, and policy issues. But forecasting election outcomes remains a risky business (see *Up Close:* "Tracking Campaigns" on page 270).

Party Affiliation   Although many people claim to vote for "the person, not the party," party identification remains a powerful influence in voter choice. Party ties among voters have weakened over time, with increasing proportions of voters labeling themselves as independents or only weak Democrats or Republicans, and more voters opting to split their tickets or cross party lines than did so a generation ago (see Chapter 7). Nevertheless, party identification remains one of the most important influences on voter choice. Party affiliation is more important in congressional than in presidential elections, but even in presidential elections the tendency to see the candidate of one's own party as "the best person" is very strong.

Consider the three presidential elections (see Figure 8-6 on page 272). Self-identified Republicans voted overwhelmingly for Bush in 1992, for Dole in 1996, and for George W. Bush in 2000. Self-identified Democrats voted overwhelmingly for Clinton in 1992 and 1996, and Gore in 2000.

Because Republican identifiers are outnumbered in the electorate by Democratic identifiers, Republican presidential candidates, and many Republican congressional candidates as well, *must* appeal to independent and Democratic crossover voters.

Group Voting   We already know that various social and economic groups give disproportionate support to the Democratic and Republican parties (see Chapter 7). So it comes as no surprise that recent Democratic presidential candidates have received disproportionate support from African Americans, Catholics, Jews, less-educated and lower-income voters, and union workers; Republican presidential candidates have fared better among whites, Protestants, and better-educated and higher-income voters (see Figure 8-7 on page 273). That is, these groups have given a larger percentage of their vote to the Democratic or Republican candidates than the candidate received from the total electorate.

Race and Gender Gaps   Among the more interesting group voting patterns is the serious *gender gap* affecting recent Republican candidates. Although Reagan won the women's vote in both 1980 and 1984, his vote percentages among men were considerably higher than among women. Bush lost the women's vote in both 1988 and 1992. In 1996 the gender gap widened, with a stunning 54 percent of women voting for Clinton as opposed to only 38 percent for Dole.[12] African Americans have long constituted the most loyal group of Democratic voters, regularly giving the Democratic presidential nominee 85 to 90 percent or more of their vote. The Hispanic vote is heavily Democratic, although a significant portion of Hispanics, notably Cuban Americans in Florida, are solidly Republican.

The Presidential Debates

Presidential debates attract more viewers than any other campaign activity. They produce vastly greater audiences than the candidates could garner by any other means. Most campaign activities—speeches, rallies, motorcades—reach only supporters. Such activities may inspire supporters to go to the polls, contribute money, and even work to get others to vote their way. But televised debates reach undecided voters as well as supporters, and they allow candidates to be seen by supporters of their opponent. Debates allow people to directly compare the responses of each candidate. Even if issues are not really discussed in depth, people see how presidential candidates react as human beings under pressure.

Kennedy-Nixon   Televised presidential debates began in 1960 when John F. Kennedy and Richard M. Nixon confronted each other on a bare stage before an America watching on black-and-white TV sets. Nixon was the vice president in the popular presidential administration of Dwight Eisenhower; he was also an accomplished college debate-team member. He prepared for the debates as if they were college debates, memorizing facts and arguments. But he failed to realize that image triumphs over substance on television. By contrast, Kennedy was handsome, cool, confident; whatever doubts the American people may have had regarding his youth and inexperience were dispelled by his polished manner. Radio listeners tended to think that Nixon won, and debate coaches scored him the winner. But television viewers preferred the glamorous young Kennedy. The polls shifted in Kennedy's direction after the debate, and he won in a very close general election.

Carter-Ford   President Lyndon Johnson avoided debating in 1964, and Nixon, having learned his lesson, declined to debate in 1968 and 1972. Thus televised presidential debates did not resume until 1976, when incumbent president Gerald Ford, perceiving he was behind in the polls, agreed to debate challenger Jimmy Carter. Ford made a series of verbal slips—saying, for example, that the nations of Eastern Europe were free

from Soviet domination. Carter was widely perceived as having won the debate, and he went on to victory in the general election.

Reagan-Carter and Reagan-Mondale   It was Ronald Reagan who demonstrated the true power of television. Reagan had lived his life in front of a camera. It was the principal tool of both of his trades—actor and politician. In 1980 incumbent president Jimmy Carter talked rapidly and seriously about programs, figures, and budgets. But Reagan was master of the stage; he was relaxed, confident, joking. He appeared to treat the president of the United States as an overly aggressive, impulsive younger man, regrettably given to exaggeration ("There you go again."). When it was all over, it was clear to most viewers that Carter had been bested by a true professional in media skills.

However, in the first of two televised debates with Walter Mondale in 1984, Reagan's skills of a lifetime seemed to desert him. He stumbled over statistics and groped for words. Reagan's poor performance raised the only issue that might conceivably defeat him—his age. The president had looked and sounded *old*. But in the second debate, Reagan laid the perfect trap for his questioners. When asked about his age and capacity to lead the nation, he responded with a serious deadpan expression to a hushed audience and waiting America: "I want you to know that I will not make age an issue in this campaign. I am not going to exploit for political purposes [pause] my opponent's youth and inexperience." The studio audience broke into uncontrolled laughter. Even Mondale had to laugh. With a classic one-liner, Reagan buried the age issue and won not only the debate but also the election.

Bush-Dukakis   In 1988 Michael Dukakis ensured his defeat with a cold, detached performance in the presidential debates, beginning with the very first question. When CNN anchor Bernard Shaw asked, "Governor, if Kitty Dukakis were raped and murdered, would you favor an irrevocable death penalty for the killer?" The question demanded an emotional reply. Instead, Dukakis responded with an impersonal recitation of his stock position on law enforcement. Bush seized the opportunity to establish a more personal relationship with the viewers: "I do believe some crimes are so heinous, so brutal, so outrageous . . . I do believe in the death penalty." Voters responded to Bush, electing him.

Clinton-Bush-Perot   The three-way presidential debates of 1992 drew the largest television audiences in the history of presidential debates. In the first debate, Ross Perot's Texas twang and down-home folksy style stole the show. Chided by his opponents for having no governmental experience, he shot back, "Well, they have a point. I don't have any experience in running up a $4 trillion dollar debt." But it was Bill Clinton's smooth performance in the second debate, with its talk-show format, that seemed to wrap up the election. Ahead in the polls, Clinton appeared at ease walking about the stage and responding to audience questions with sympathy and sincerity. By contrast, George Bush appeared stiff and formal, and somewhat ill at ease with the "unpresidential" format.

Clinton-Dole   A desperate Bob Dole, running 20 points behind, faced a newly "presidential" Bill Clinton in their two 1996 debates. (Perot's poor standing in the polls led to his exclusion.) Dole tried to counter his image as a grumpy old man in the first encounter; his humor actually won more laughs from the audience than Clinton. Dole injected more barbs in the second debate, complaining of "ethical problems in the White House." But Clinton remained cool and comfortable, ignoring the challenger and focusing on the nation's economic health. Viewers, most of whom were already in Clinton's court, judged him the winner of both debates.

Bush-Gore   Separate formats were agreed upon for three debates—the traditional podium, a conference table, and a town hall setting. Gore was assertive, almost to the point of rudeness, but both candidates focused on policy differences rather than on personal attacks. Viewers gave Gore the edge in these debates but they found Bush more likable. Bush appeared to benefit more in the post-debate polls. An estimated 47 million people watched the first debate; viewership fell to 36 million for the second and third debates. Most observers rated the single vice-presidential debate between Dick Cheney and Joe Lieberman as friendlier and more informative than the Bush-Gore encounters.

Tracking Campaigns

Voter swings in loyalty during presidential campaigns suggest that the outcome of elections is by no means certain at the outset (see graphs). Tracking polls during the 1992 campaign showed large swings in opinion in midsummer, the time of the Democratic and Republican nominating conventions. In contrast, tracking polls in 1996 showed uncommon stability in Clinton's large lead over Dole throughout the campaign.

At the start of his 1992 reelection bid, George Bush enjoyed a comfortable lead in the polls. But in late spring, the independent candidacy of Ross Perot eroded Bush's support. Bill Clinton was mired in third place. The Bush campaign launched a strong attack on Perot, calling him temperamentally unfit to be president and encouraging the press to delve into his financial dealings and penchant for investigating his opponents. Perot's support began to drop in the polls, and he abruptly announced his withdrawal from the race on July 16, the start of the Democratic convention. Perot supporters were set adrift at precisely the moment that Bill Clinton was benefiting from favorable television coverage of the Democratic convention. Clinton soared ahead in the polls. The race narrowed somewhat in the fall, but Clinton never lost his lead.

The "Horse Race": Tracking the Presidential Campaigns in the Polls (1992 and 1996)

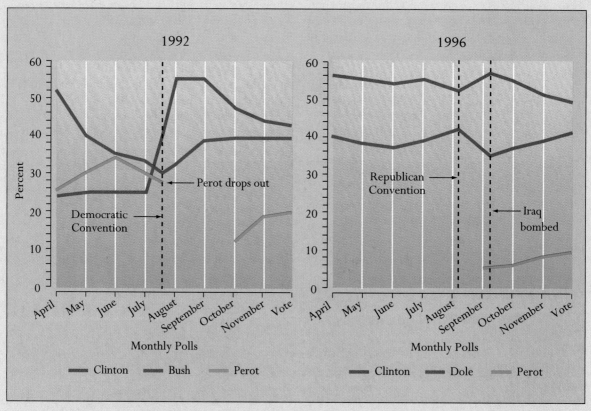

In contrast to the volatile 1992 campaign, the presidential campaign of 1996 was so stable that voters appeared to lose interest. Clinton maintained a comfortable lead all year, dipping only slightly during the GOP convention in August and peaking during the September bombing of Iraq. Perot never mounted a serious threat. Clinton's margin of victory, however, was somewhat narrower than the tracking polls had forecast.

As the November election drew near in 2000, the tracking polls became very volatile. Bush led comfortably throughout the spring and early summer, reaching his highest margin over Gore during the Republican National Convention. But Gore made a dramatic comeback during the Democratic Convention, closing the gap with Bush. By early September, Gore had crept ahead. The October presidential debates produced large gyrations in the polls. The day before the first debate, Gore was ahead by 10 points, but following the debates, Bush retook the lead. Viewers tended to see Gore as knowledgeable but overbearing, while Bush was judged to be weak on issues but generally likable. By November, most polls showed Bush slightly ahead but within the margin of error in polling. None of the polls forecast Gore's slim margin of victory in the nationwide popular vote.

The "Horse Race": Tracking the Presidential Campaigns in the Polls (2000)

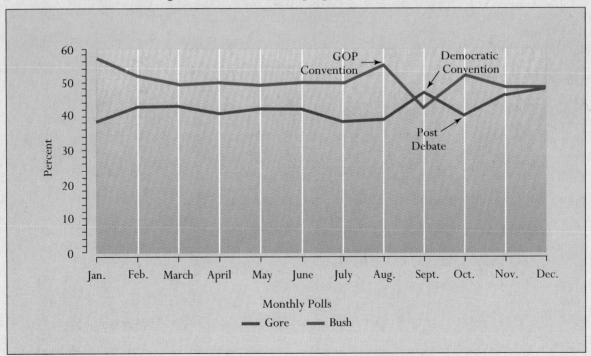

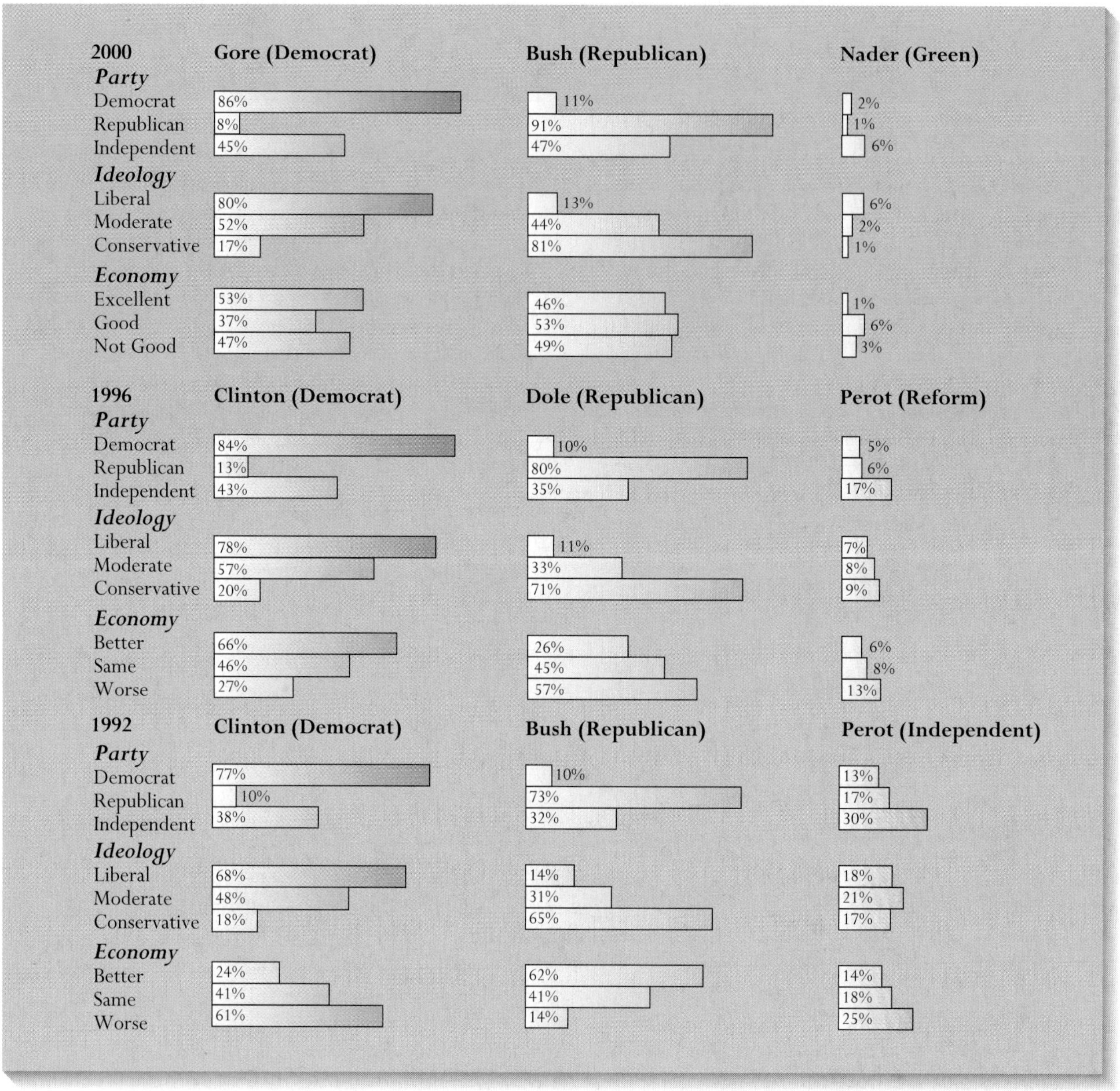

2000

	Gore (Democrat)	Bush (Republican)	Nader (Green)
Party			
Democrat	86%	11%	2%
Republican	8%	91%	1%
Independent	45%	47%	6%
Ideology			
Liberal	80%	13%	6%
Moderate	52%	44%	2%
Conservative	17%	81%	1%
Economy			
Excellent	53%	46%	1%
Good	37%	53%	6%
Not Good	47%	49%	3%

1996

	Clinton (Democrat)	Dole (Republican)	Perot (Reform)
Party			
Democrat	84%	10%	5%
Republican	13%	80%	6%
Independent	43%	35%	17%
Ideology			
Liberal	78%	11%	7%
Moderate	57%	33%	8%
Conservative	20%	71%	9%
Economy			
Better	66%	26%	6%
Same	46%	45%	8%
Worse	27%	57%	13%

1992

	Clinton (Democrat)	Bush (Republican)	Perot (Independent)
Party			
Democrat	77%	10%	13%
Republican	10%	73%	17%
Independent	38%	32%	30%
Ideology			
Liberal	68%	14%	18%
Moderate	48%	31%	21%
Conservative	18%	65%	17%
Economy			
Better	24%	62%	14%
Same	41%	41%	18%
Worse	61%	14%	25%

FIGURE 8-6 Party, Ideology, and Nature of the Times in Presidential Voting

Those who identify themselves as members of a major political party are highly likely to vote for the presidential candidates of their party. Likewise, those who identify themselves as liberals are more likely than average to vote for Democrats, and those who identify themselves as conservatives are more likely to vote for Republicans in presidential elections. In addition, voters who see the economic picture as better are more likely to vote for the incumbent; those who are concerned about the nation's economy are more likely to vote against the incumbent.

Source: Election exit polls, Voter News Service.

Approximately 52 percent of voters are women. The gender gap remained wide in 2000. According to exit polls, Gore won the women's vote 54 to 42, while Bush won the men's vote 53 to 43.

Candidate Image   In an age of direct communication between candidates and voters via television, the image of candidates and their ability to relate to audiences have emerged as important determinants of voter choice. As party and group iden-

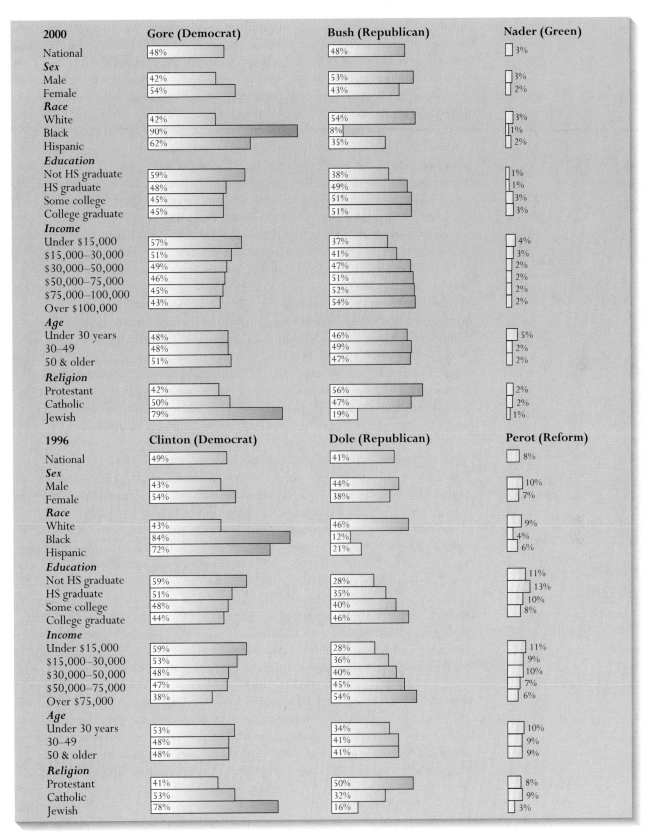

2000	Gore (Democrat)	Bush (Republican)	Nader (Green)
National	48%	48%	3%
Sex			
Male	42%	53%	3%
Female	54%	43%	2%
Race			
White	42%	54%	3%
Black	90%	8%	1%
Hispanic	62%	35%	2%
Education			
Not HS graduate	59%	38%	1%
HS graduate	48%	49%	1%
Some college	45%	51%	3%
College graduate	45%	51%	3%
Income			
Under $15,000	57%	37%	4%
$15,000–30,000	51%	41%	3%
$30,000–50,000	49%	47%	2%
$50,000–75,000	46%	51%	2%
$75,000–100,000	45%	52%	2%
Over $100,000	43%	54%	2%
Age			
Under 30 years	48%	46%	5%
30–49	48%	49%	2%
50 & older	51%	47%	2%
Religion			
Protestant	42%	56%	2%
Catholic	50%	47%	2%
Jewish	79%	19%	1%

1996	Clinton (Democrat)	Dole (Republican)	Perot (Reform)
National	49%	41%	8%
Sex			
Male	43%	44%	10%
Female	54%	38%	7%
Race			
White	43%	46%	9%
Black	84%	12%	4%
Hispanic	72%	21%	6%
Education			
Not HS graduate	59%	28%	11%
HS graduate	51%	35%	13%
Some college	48%	40%	10%
College graduate	44%	46%	8%
Income			
Under $15,000	59%	28%	11%
$15,000–30,000	53%	36%	9%
$30,000–50,000	48%	40%	10%
$50,000–75,000	47%	45%	7%
Over $75,000	38%	54%	6%
Age			
Under 30 years	53%	34%	10%
30–49	48%	41%	9%
50 & older	48%	41%	9%
Religion			
Protestant	41%	50%	8%
Catholic	53%	32%	9%
Jewish	78%	16%	3%

FIGURE 8-7 Group Voting in Presidential Elections

Democratic presidential candidates regularly do better among African American, Hispanic, Jewish, lower income, less educated voters. The gender gap—men tending to vote Republican and women Democratic—first emerged in the Reagan years and has widened in recent elections.

Source: Election exit polls, Voter News Service.

tifications have moderated and independent and middle-of-the-road identifications among voters have grown, the personal characteristics of candidates have become central to many voters. Indeed, the personal qualities of candidates are most important in the decision of less partisan, less ideological voters. Candidate image is most important in presidential contests, inasmuch as presidential candidates are personally more visible to the voter than candidates for lesser offices.[13]

It is difficult to identify exactly what personal qualities appeal most to voters. Warmth, compassion, strength, confidence, honesty, sincerity, good humor, appearance, and "character" all seem important. "Character" has become a central feature of media coverage of candidates (see Chapter 6). Reports of extramarital affairs, experimentation with drugs, draft dodging, cheating in college, shady financial dealings, conflicts of interest, or lying or misrepresenting facts receive heavy media coverage because they attract large audiences. But it is difficult to estimate how many voters are swayed by so-called character issues.

Attractive personal qualities can win support from opposition-party identifiers and people who disagree on the issues. John F. Kennedy's handsome and youthful appearance, charm, self-confidence, and disarming good humor defeated the heavy-jowled, shifty-eyed, defensive, and ill-humored Richard Nixon. Ronald Reagan's folksy mannerisms, warm humor, and comfortable rapport with television audiences justly earned him the title "The Great Communicator." Reagan disarmed his critics by laughing at his own personal flubs—falling asleep at meetings, forgetting names—and by telling his own age jokes. His personal appeal won more Democratic voters than any other Republican candidate has won in modern history, and he won the votes of many people who disagreed with him on the issues.

In the 2000 presidential election, exit polls indicated that Bush was rated higher than Gore on "leadership and personal qualities." But Gore was rated higher on his "positions on the issues." Most of the people who said leadership qualities were more important voted for Bush. Most of the people who said issues were more important voted for Gore. Finally, the Clinton scandals did not appear to hurt Gore very much.

An important reservation regarding image voting: although many voters cite favorable or unfavorable personal characteristics of the candidates as the reason for their vote, it turns out that Democratic voters usually perceive favorable attributes in Democratic candidates and unfavorable attributes in Republican candidates, and Republican voters see just the opposite. In other words, the voters' perceptions of the candidates' personal qualities are influenced by the voters' party identifications and perhaps by their group affiliations as well. Thus evaluations of the candidates' personal characteristics may not be a significant independent determinant of voter choice, especially for people who identify themselves as strong Democrats or Republicans.

The Economy Fairly accurate predictions of voting outcomes in presidential elections can be made from models of the American economy. Economic conditions at election time—recent growth or decline in personal income, the unemployment rate, consumer confidence, and so on—are related to the vote given the incumbent versus the challenger. Ever since the once-popular Republican incumbent Herbert Hoover was trounced by Franklin Roosevelt as the Great Depression of the 1930s deepened, politicians have understood that voters hold the incumbent party responsible for hard economic times.

Perhaps no other lesson has been as well learned by politicians: Hard economic times hurt incumbents and favor challengers. The economy may not be the only important factor in presidential voting, but it is certainly a factor of great impor-

Twenty-First Century Directions

The legendary football coach Vince Lombardi once put it very succinctly: "Winning isn't the most important thing. . . . It's the *only* thing." It is highly unlikely that winning elections will become any less important in the twenty-first century.

▲ The costs of campaigning and the importance of fund raising in electoral politics will continue to grow. The ability to raise funds will become the chief criterion for candidate selection in both parties. As a result, big-money contributors will become even more influential in determining the direction of American politics.

▼ Effective campaign finance reform will fail. Incumbents benefit most from the current system, and it is unlikely that they can be convinced to make any significant changes that might benefit challengers. Even if some reform legislation is passed by Congress, for example, limits on soft money contributions to parties, new channels of money will flow into electoral politics.

◀▶ As long as the economy remains strong, voters will cast their ballots based on traditional party affiliations and the images projected by candidates. Very few voters will be motivated by issues alone. Retrospective voting will occur only when the economy suffers a significant setback. Both Democratic and Republican candidates will portray themselves as moderates; they will endeavor to avoid identification with the extreme liberal or conservative wings of their parties.

▼ Reform of the electoral college system will continue to flounder. The consensus required to amend the Constitution to change the system will not develop, owing to differences on how to change it and to the entrenched position of both major parties under the current system.

tance. Some evidence indicates that it is not voters' *own* personal economic well-being that affects their vote but rather voter perception of *general* economic conditions. People who perceive the economy as getting worse are likely to vote against the incumbent party, whereas people who think the economy is getting better support the incumbent.[14] Thus voters who thought the economy was getting *worse* in 1992 supported challenger Bill Clinton over incumbent president George Bush. But the reverse was true in 1996; more people thought the economy was better, and the people who thought so voted heavily for incumbent Bill Clinton. In 2000, Gore won the votes of those who thought the economy was "excellent," but economic voting did not seem to be as influential as in previous presidential races.

Issue Voting   Casting one's vote exclusively on the basis of the policy positions of the candidates is rare. Most voters are unaware of the specific positions taken by candidates on the issues. Indeed, voters often believe that their preferred candidate agrees with them on the issues, even when this is not the case. In other words, voters project their own policy views onto their favorite candidate more often than they decide to vote for a candidate because of his or her position on the issues.

However, when asked specifically about issues, voters are willing to name those they care most about (see Table 8-5 on page 276). Voters do not always make their choices based on a candidate's stated policy positions, but voters *do* strongly favor candidates whose policy views they assume match their own. Only when a key issue

Table 8-5   Issues the Voters Cared about in 2000

Rank	Issue	Presidential Vote of Those Who Listed Issue as "Most Important"		
		Gore	Bush	Nader
1	Economy/jobs	59%	38%	2%
2	Education	52	44	3
3	Social Security	59	39	1
4	Taxes	17	80	2
5	World affairs	40	54	4
6	Health care	64	33	3
7	Medicare/prescription drugs	60	38	1

takes center stage do voters really become aware of what the candidates actually propose to do. In the 1992, 1996, and 2000 elections, the economy was the issue that voters cared about most. In all three elections, Clinton and Gore won the votes of the people most concerned about the economy (see Table 8-3). Clinton and Gore also won the strong support of people (especially senior citizens) concerned with Medicare and Social Security, as well as people concerned about education. Taxes and foreign policy were Bush's best issues.

SUMMARY NOTES

- In a democracy, elections decide "who governs." But they also indirectly affect public policy, influencing "who gets what."

- Although winning candidates often claim a mandate for their policy proposals, in reality few campaigns present clear policy alternatives to the voters, few voters cast their ballots on the basis of policy considerations, and the policy preferences of the electorate can seldom be determined from election outcomes.

- Nevertheless, voters can influence future policy directions through retrospective judgments about the performance of incumbents, returning them to office or turning them out. Most retrospective voting appears to center on the economy.

- Personal ambition for power and celebrity drives the decision to seek public office. Political entrepreneurship, professionalism, and careerism have come to dominate political recruitment; lawyers have traditionally dominated American politics.

- Incumbents begin campaigns with many advantages: name recognition, financial support, goodwill from services they perform for constituents, large-scale public projects they bring to their districts, and the other resources of office.

- Campaigning for office is largely a media activity, dominated by professional advertising specialists, fund raisers, media consultants, and pollsters.

- The professionalization of campaigning and the heavy costs of a media campaign drive up the costs of running for office. These huge costs make candidates heavily dependent on financial support from individuals and organizations. Fund raising occupies more of a candidate's time than any other campaign activity.

- Campaign contributions are made by politically active individuals and organizations, including political action committees. Many contributions are made in order to gain access to policy makers and assistance with government business. Some contributors are ideologically motivated; others merely seek to rub shoulders with powerful people.

- Presidential primary election strategies emphasize appeals to party activists and core supporters, including the more ideologically motivated primary voters.

- In the general election campaign, presidential candidates usually seek to broaden their appeal to moderate, centrist voters while holding on to their core supporters. Campaigns must focus on states where the candidate has the best chance of gaining the 270 electoral votes needed to win.

- Voter choice is influenced by party identification, group membership, perceived image of the candidates, economic conditions, and, to a lesser extent, ideology and issue preferences.

KEY TERMS

mandate   230

retrospective voting   231

political
   entrepreneurship   232

incumbent   235

franking privilege   236

campaign strategy   237

focus group   238

name recognition   240

photo ops   241

sound bites   241

hard money   244

Political Action Committee
   (PAC)   246

soft money   246

Issue ads   248

Federal Election Commission
   (FEC)   252

spin doctor   258

front-end strategy   259

big-state strategy   259

Electoral College   262

SELECTED READINGS

ABRAMSON, PAUL R., JOHN H. ALDRICH, and DAVID W. RHODE. *Change and Continuity in the 1996 Elections.* Washington: Congressional Quarterly Press, 1998. An in-depth analysis of the 1996 presidential and congressional elections assessing the impact of party loyalties, presidential performance, group memberships, and policy preferences on voter choice.

DiCLERICO, ROBERT. Ed. *Campaigns and Elections in America* Upper Saddle River, N.J.: Prentice Hall, 2000. Essays by leading scholars on the nominating process, campaign finance, media campaigning, turnout, voter choice, and the party system.

FIORINA, MORRIS P. *Retrospective Voting in American National Elections.* Princeton, N.J.: Princeton University Press, 1988. Argues that retrospective judgments guide voter choice in presidential elections.

FLANAGAN, WILLIAM H., and NANCY H. ZINGALE. *Political Behavior of the American Electorate.* 9th ed. Washington, D.C.: Congressional Quarterly Press, 1998. A brief but comprehensive summary of the extensive research literature on the effects of party identification, opinion, ideology, the media, and candidate image on voter choice and election outcomes.

IYENGAR, SHANTO, and Stephen ANSOLABEHERE. *Going Negative: How Political Advertisements Shrink and Polarize the Electorate.* New York: Free Press, 1996. The real problem with negative political ads is not that they sway voters to support one candidate over another, but that they reinforce the belief that all are dishonest and cynical.

MATALIN, MARY, and JAMES CARVILLE. *All's Fair: Love, War and Running for President.* New York: Random House and Simon & Schuster, 1994. Inside the presidential campaign of George Bush and Bill Clinton in 1992 by their respective campaign directors, who were romantically involved and were married after the campaign.

POLSBY, NELSON W., and AARON WILDAVSKY. *Presidential Elections: Strategies and Structures* 10th ed. New York: Chatham House 2000. Updated classic on presidential campaign strategies.

ROSENSTONE, STEVEN. *Forecasting Presidential Elections.* New Haven, Conn.: Yale University Press, 1985. A discussion of the models employed to forecast presidential election outcomes based on unemployment, inflation, and personal income statistics.

SABATO, LARRY J., and GLENN R. SIMPSON. *Dirty Little Secrets: The Persistence of Corruption in American Politics.* New York: Random House Times Books, 1996. A political scientist and a journalist combine to produce a lurid report on unethical and corrupt practices in campaigns and elections.

SORAUF, FRANK J. *Inside Campaign Finance.* New Haven, Conn.: Yale University Press, 1992. A comprehensive description of campaign financing in America, individual contributions, PACs, party funds, independent organizations, soft money, intermediaries and brokers, and so on, together with a balanced appraisal of the prospects and potential consequences of reform.

Interest Groups
Getting Their Share and More

INTEREST-GROUP POWER

Organization is a means to power—to determining who gets what in society. Interest groups are organizations that seek to influence government policy. Organization concentrates power, and concentrated power prevails over unorganized interests. The First Amendment to the Constitution recognizes "the right of the people peaceably to assemble, and to petition the government for a redress of grievances." Americans thus enjoy a fundamental right to organize themselves to influence government.

Electoral versus Interest-Group Systems The *electoral system* is organized to represent geographically defined constituencies—states and congressional districts in Congress. The *interest-group system* is organized to represent economic, professional, ideological, religious, racial, gender, and issue constituencies.[1] In other words, the interest-group system supplements the electoral system by providing people with another avenue of participation. Individuals may participate in politics by supporting candidates and parties in elections, and also by joining **interest groups**, organizations that pressure government to advance their interests.

Interest-group activity provides more direct representation of policy preferences than electoral politics. At best, individual voters can influence government policy only indirectly through elections (see Chapter 8). Elected politicians try to represent many different—and even occasionally conflicting—interests. But interest groups provide concentrated and direct representation of policy views in government.

1 Do special-interest groups in America obstruct the majority of citizens' wishes on public policy?
Yes ● No ●

2 Should people join an interest group such as the American Association of Retired Persons for its discounts, magazines, and travel guides even if they disagree with its policy goals?
Yes ● No ●

3 Should state and local governments use taxpayers' money to lobby Congress to get federal funds?
Yes ● No ●

4 Should former government officials be allowed to lobby their former colleagues?
Yes ● No ●

5 Should religious groups organize themselves to influence public policy?
Yes ● No ●

6 Should interest groups be prohibited from making large campaign contributions in their effort to influence public policy?
Yes ● No ●

7 If a lobbyist makes a campaign contribution to a Congress member, hoping to gain support for a bill, is this a form of bribery?
Yes ● No ●

8 Is organized interest-group activity a cause of government gridlock?
Yes ● No ●

What role do interest groups play in politics? Their organization, their money, and their influence in Washington raise the possibility that interest groups, rather than individuals, may in fact hold the real power in politics. They may be the "who" that determines the "what" that the rest of us get.

Checking Majoritarianism   The interest-group system gives voice to special interests, whereas parties and the electoral system cater to the majority interest. Indeed, interest groups are often defended as a check on **majoritarianism**, the tendency of democratic governments to allow the faint preferences of a majority to prevail over the intense feelings of minorities. However, the interest-group system is frequently attacked because it obstructs the majority from implementing its preferences in public policy.

Concentrating Benefits While Dispersing Costs   Interest groups seek special benefits, subsidies, privileges, and protections from the government. The costs of these *concentrated* benefits are usually *dispersed* to all taxpayers, none of whom individually bears enough added cost to merit spending time, energy, or money to organize a group to oppose the benefit. Thus the interest-group system concentrates benefits to the few and disperses costs to the many. The system favors small, well-organized, homogeneous interests that seek the expansion of government activity at the expense of larger but less well-organized citizen-taxpayers. Over long periods of time, the cumulative activities of many special-interest groups, each seeking concentrated benefits to themselves and dispersed costs to others, result in what has been termed **organizational sclerosis**, a society so encrusted with subsidies, benefits, regulations, protections, and special treatments for organized groups that work, productivity, and investment are discouraged and everyone's standard of living is lowered.

ORIGINS OF INTEREST GROUPS

James Madison viewed interest groups—which he called "factions"—as a necessary evil in politics. He defined a faction as "a number of citizens, whether amounting to a majority or a minority of the whole, who are united and actuated by some common impulse of passion, or of interest, adverse to the rights of other citizens, or to the permanent and aggregate interests of the community." He believed that interest groups not only conflict with each other but, more important, also conflict with the common good. Nevertheless, Madison believed that the origin of interest groups was to be found in human nature—"a zeal for different opinions concerning religion, concerning government, and many other points"—and therefore impossible to eliminate from politics.[2]

Protecting Economic Interests   Madison believed that "the most common and durable source of factions, has been the various and unequal distribution of property." With genuine insight, he identified *economic interests* as the most prevalent in politics: "a landed interest, a manufacturing interest, a mercantile interest, a moneyed interest, with many lesser interests." From Madison's era to the present, businesspeople and professionals, bankers and insurers, farmers and factory workers, merchants and shippers have organized themselves to press their demands on government (see *Up Close:* "Superlobby: The Business Roundtable" on page 282).

Advancing Social Movements   Major social movements in American history have spawned many interest groups. Abolitionist groups were formed before the Civil War to fight slavery. The National Association for the Advancement of Colored People (NAACP) emerged in 1909 to fight segregation laws and to rally public

interest groups   Organizations that seek to influence government policy.

majoritarianism   Tendency of democratic governments to allow the faint preferences of the majority to prevail over the intense feelings of minorities.

organizational sclerosis   Society encrusted with so many special benefits to interest groups that everyone's standard of living is lowered.

(a)   *(b)*

(c)   *(d)*

(e)   *(f)*

From (a) theWhiskey Rebellion of 1794 to (b) violent early union protests like the Haymarket Riot of 1886 to (c) Carrie Nation's battle to ban liquor and (d) the women's suffrage movement of the late nineteenth and early twentieth centuries to (e) the civil rights marches of the 1960s and (f) the gay rights marches of the 1990s, protest has had a long and strong history for interest groups in the United States. Some protests have been violent and others peaceful, but by addressing key issues of the time, all have prompted public debate and many have resulted in changes in public policy.

281

Superlobby:
The Business Roundtable

The Business Roundtable was established in 1972 "in the belief that business executives should take an increased role in the continuing debates about public policy." The organization is composed of the chief executives of the 200 largest corporations in America and is financed through corporate membership fees. For many years, the U.S. Chamber of Commerce, the National Association of Manufacturers, the Business Council, and hundreds of industry associations such as the powerful American Petroleum Institute had represented business in traditional interest-group fashion. Why did business create this superorganization? The Business Roundtable itself says:

> The answer is that business leaders believed there was a need that was not being filled, and they invented the Roundtable to fill it. They wanted an organization in which the chief executive officers of leading enterprises take positions and advocate those positions. . . . The Roundtable therefore was formed with two major goals:
>
> 1. to enable chief executives from different corporations to work together to analyze specific issues affecting the economy and business; and
> 2. to present government and the public with knowledgeable, timely information, and with practical, positive suggestions for action.*

In brief, traditional interest-group representation was inadequate for the nation's top corporate leadership. It wished to come together *itself* to decide on public policy and press its views in Washington.

The power of the Business Roundtable stems in part from its "firm rule" that a corporate chief executive officer (CEO) cannot send a substitute to its meetings. Moreover, corporate CEOs lobby the Congress in person rather than sending paid lobbyists. Members of Congress are impressed when the chair of IBM appears at a congressional hearing on business regulation or when the chair of GTE speaks to a congressional

committee about taxation, or when the chair of Prudential talks to Congress about Social Security, or when the head of B. F. Goodrich testifies before the Senate Judiciary Committee about antitrust policy. One congressional staff member explained, "If a corporation sends its Washington representative to our office, he's probably going to be shunted over to a legislative assistant. But the chairman of the board is going to get in to see the senator." Another aide echoed those sentiments: "Very few members of Congress would not meet with the president of a Business Roundtable corporation."[†]

The work of the Business Roundtable is organized by means of task forces on various issues of priority to its members. For example, there are task forces on education, the environment, government regulation, health, the federal budget, international trade, taxation, and welfare.

The Business Roundtable has experienced both victories and defeats in Congress. During the Ford and Carter administrations, the Roundtable successfully opposed the creation of a new federal consumer protection agency comparable to the Environmental Protection Agency. During the Reagan years, the Roundtable was at the forefront of "deregulation" and tax cutting. But the Roundtable lost a lengthy battle over mandated family leaves in 1993 when the Congress sent the Family Leave Act to President Bill Clinton to sign as his first major legislative victory. The Roundtable also was defeated in its opposition to the expansion of the Clean Air Act of 1990, which it believes imposes excessive compliance costs on industry and handicaps American corporations in global competition. And the Roundtable is regularly defeated in efforts to reform the nation's liability laws; its principal opponent in this struggle has been the Association of Trial Lawyers, some of whose members sit in the Congress itself. So even with all of its prestige and resources, the Business Roundtable does not win all of its battles.

---

*Quotations about the reasons for the establishment of the Business Roundtable from "The History of the Business Roundtable," 1998.

[†]*Time*, April 13, 1981, pp. 76–77.

support against lynching and other violence against African Americans. Farm organizations emerged from the populist movement of the late nineteenth century to press demands for railroad rate regulation and easier credit terms. The small trade unions that workers formed in the nineteenth century to improve their pay and working conditions gave way to large national unions in the 1930s as workers sought protection for the rights to organize, bargain collectively, and strike. The success of the women's suffrage movement led to the formation of the League of Women Voters in the early twentieth century, and a generation later the feminist movement inspired the National Organization for Women (NOW).

Seeking Government Benefits   As government expands its activities, it creates more interest groups. Wars create veterans' organizations. The first large veterans' group—the Grand Army of the Republic—formed after the Civil War and successfully lobbied for bonus payments to veterans over the years. Today the American Legion, the Veterans of Foreign Wars, and the Vietnam Veterans of America engage in lobbying the Congress and monitor the activities of the Department of Veterans Affairs. As the welfare state grew, so did organizations seeking to obtain benefits for their members, including the nation's largest interest group, the American Association of Retired Persons (AARP). Over time, organizations seeking to protect and expand welfare benefits for the poor also emerged (see *People in Politics:* "Marian Wright Edelman, Lobbying for the Poor"). Federal grant-in-aid programs to state and local governments inspired the development of governmental interest groups— the Council of State Governments, the National League of Cities, the National Governors Association, the U.S. Conference of Mayors, and so on—so that it is not uncommon today to see governments lobby other governments. Expanded government support for education led to political activity by the National Education Association, the American Federation of Teachers, the American Association of Land Grant Colleges and Universities, and other educational groups.

Responding to Government Regulation   As more businesses and professions came under government regulation in the twentieth century, more organizations formed to protect their interests, including such large and powerful groups as the American Medical Association (doctors), the American Bar Association (lawyers), and the National Association of Broadcasters (broadcasters). Indeed, the issue of regulation—whether of public utilities, interstate transportation, mine safety, medicines, or children's pajamas—always causes the formation of interest groups. Some form to demand regulation; others form to protect their members from regulatory burdens.

THE ORGANIZED INTERESTS IN WASHINGTON

The Washington, D.C., telephone directory lists hundreds of organizations with their own offices in the capital and hundreds of additional firms of paid lawyers and lobbyists. Trade and professional associations and corporations have the most lobbies in Washington, but unions, public-interest groups, farm groups, and organized interests representing minorities, women, and the elderly also recognize that they need to be "where the action is." There are more than one million nonprofit organizations in the United States, several thousand of which are officially registered in Washington as lobbyists.[3] Among this huge assortment of organizations, many of which are very influential in their highly specialized fields, are a number of well-known interest

Marian Wright Edelman, Lobbying for the Poor

As founder and president of the Children's Defense Fund, Marian Wright Edelman has become legendary in Washington as a persuasive and persistent lobbyist on behalf of civil rights and social welfare legislation. A close friend of the Kennedy family, Edelman regularly testifies at Senate committee hearings, providing rapid-fire statistics on the effects of poverty on African American children. Each year the Children's Defense Fund, with a staff of more than a hundred in its Washington headquarters, produces numerous reports on infant mortality, homelessness, prenatal care, child nutrition, drug use, child abuse, teenage pregnancy, and single-parent households.

Marian Wright grew up in segregated rural South Carolina, the academically gifted daughter of a Baptist minister with a strong commitment to social justice. At an early age, she worked at the Wright House for the Aged, which her father had established. She entered all-black Spelman College in Atlanta and studied abroad at the Sorbonne in Paris and the University of Geneva, intending to take up a career in the foreign service. But Wright changed her career plans when she became involved in the early civil rights struggles in Atlanta. After graduating from Spelman, she entered Yale Law School to prepare herself in civil rights law. Upon her graduation in 1963, she immediately went to work for the National Association for the Advancement of Colored People Legal Defense Fund and traveled to

Mississippi, where for four years she undertook the dangerous work of defending civil rights workers. In 1967 she met Peter Edelman, a Harvard Law School graduate and legislative aide to Senator Robert Kennedy; together they persuaded Kennedy to personally tour the most poverty-stricken areas of the Mississippi Delta, where the senator directly confronted hungry children living in miserable conditions.

The following year Wright and Edelman were married and settled in Washington, where she established the Washington Research Project, a public-interest research and lobbying organization on behalf of President Lyndon Johnson's War on Poverty. She maintained her Washington base even while directing the Harvard University Center for Law and Education during the several years that her husband served as vice president of the University of Massachusetts. In 1973 she organized the Children's Defense Fund in Washington with the support of private foundation grants and government grants and contracts. Part think tank and part lobbying organization, the Children's Defense Fund describes itself as an advocate for millions of "voiceless and voteless," neglected and abused, poor children. It was the principal lobbying group behind the Head Start program as well as federal child care and the Family Leave Act of 1993.

Marian Wright Edelman is especially effective as an advocate of social welfare programs with her lively style, sense of urgency, and wealth of information about children in poverty. "The real joy comes from achieving results, when you really see you've got a law that will protect children from being abused, that will provide them with proper health care and dental care. My greatest reward will be seeing thirteen million poor children lifted out of poverty."*

*New York Times, February 27, 1986, p. A10.

groups. Even a partial list of organized interest groups provides some idea of both the depth and the breadth of such associations in U.S. political life and of the complexities facing modern legislators in trying to please such vastly different groups (see Table 9-1).

Business and Trade Organizations   Traditionally, economic organizations have dominated interest-group politics in Washington. There is ample evidence that economic interests continue to play a major role in national policy making, despite the rapid growth over the last several decades of consumer and environ-

| Table 9–1 | Major Organized Interest Groups, by Type |

Business

Business Roundtable
National Association of Manufacturers
National Federation of Independent
  Businesses
National Small Business Association
U.S. Chamber of Commerce

Trade

American Bankers Association
American Gas Association
American Iron and Steel Institute
American Petroleum Institute
American Truckers Association
Automobile Dealers Association
Home Builders Association
Motion Picture Association of America
National Association of Broadcasters
National Association of Real Estate
  Boards

Professional

American Bar Association
American Medical Association
Association of Trial Lawyers
National Education Association

Union

AFL-CIO
American Federation of State,
  County, and Municipal Employees
American Federation of Teachers
International Brotherhood of Teamsters
International Ladies' Garment Work-
  ers Union
National Association of Letter Carriers
United Auto Workers
United Postal Workers
United Steel Workers

Agricultural

American Farm Bureau Federation
National Cattlemen's Association

National Farmers Union
National Grange
National Milk Producers Federation
Tobacco Institute

Women

League of Women Voters
National Organization for Women

Public Interest

Common Cause
Consumer Federation of America
Public Citizen
Public Interest Research Groups

Ideological

American Conservative Union
Americans for Constitutional Action
  (conservative)
Americans for Democratic Action
  (liberal)
People for the American Way
  (liberal)
National Conservative Political Action
  Committee (conservative)

Single Issue

Mothers against Drunk Driving
National Abortion Rights Action
  League
National Rifle Association
National Right-to-Life Committee
Planned Parenthood Federation of
  America
National Taxpayers Union

Environmental

Environmental Defense Fund
Greenpeace
National Wildlife Federation
Natural Resources Defense Council
Nature Conservancy
Sierra Club
Wilderness Society

Religious

American-Israeli Public Affairs
  Committee
Anti-Defamation League of B'nai B'rith
Christian Coalition
National Council of Churches
U.S. Catholic Conference

Civil Rights

American Civil Liberties Union
American Indian Movement
Mexican-American Legal Defense and
  Education Fund
National Association for the Advance-
  ment of Colored People
National Urban League
Rainbow Coalition
Southern Christian Leadership
  Conference

Age Related

American Association of Retired
  Persons
Children's Defense Fund

Veterans

American Legion
Veterans of Foreign Wars
Vietnam Veterans of America

Defense

Air Force Association
American Security Council
Army Association
Navy Association

Government

National Association of Counties
National Conference of State Legislators
National Governors Association
National League of Cities
U.S. Conference of Mayors

mental organizations. Certainly in terms of the sheer number of organizations with offices and representatives in Washington, business and professional groups and occupational and trade associations predominate. More than half of the organizations with offices in Washington are business or trade associations, and another 15 percent are professional associations.

Business interests are represented, first of all, by large inclusive organizations, such as the U.S. Chamber of Commerce, representing thousands of local chambers of commerce across the nation; the National Association of Manufacturers; the Business Roundtable, representing the nation's largest corporations; and the National Federation of Independent Businesses, representing small business. Specific business interests are also represented by thousands of **trade associations**. These associations can closely monitor the interests of their specialized memberships. Among the most powerful of these associations are the American Bankers Association, the American Gas Association, the American Iron and Steel Institute, the National Association of Real Estate Boards, the American Petroleum Institute, and the National Association of Broadcasters. In addition, many individual corporations and firms achieve representation in Washington by opening their own lobbying offices or by hiring experienced professional lobbying and law firms.

Professional Associations   Professional associations rival business and trade organizations in lobbying influence. The American Bar Association (ABA), the American Medical Association (AMA), and the National Education Association (NEA) are three of the most influential groups in Washington. For example, the American Bar Association, which includes virtually all of the nation's practicing attorneys, and its more specialized offspring, the American Association of Trial Lawyers, have successfully resisted efforts to reform the nation's tort laws (see "America Drowning in a Sea of Lawsuits," Chapter 13).

Many years ago, the AMA fought against national health insurance plans, arguing that socialized medicine would erode quality medical care. But when Medicare for the aged and Medicaid for the poor were pushed forward by President Lyndon Johnson in 1965, the AMA switched tactics, supporting the legislation as a means of bringing vast sums of tax money into the nation's health care system. Initially the strategy proved immensely profitable: Medicare and Medicaid spending grew rapidly in the federal budget. Government payments also now account for nearly one-third of the average doctor's income. However, the AMA eventually learned that government money is almost always accompanied by government efforts to regulate costs and practices. The AMA has been forced to accept government payment schedules for various procedures. The Medicare and Medicaid programs encourage beneficiaries to enroll in health maintenance organizations (HMOs) which in turn often check physicians' practices and procedures. The AMA remains vigorously opposed to any limits on physicians' decisions about care for their patients. But only about 32 percent of the nation's physicians are now members of the AMA, down from nearly 65 percent thirty years ago. Today many physicians believe they are better represented by more specialized medical groups (for example, the American College of Surgeons, the American Academy of Family Physicians, the American Society of Internal Medicine), especially in negotiations over government fee schedules for particular procedures.

Organized Labor   Labor organizations have declined in membership over the last several decades. The percentage of the nonagricultural work force belonging to unions has declined from about 35 percent in the 1950s to about 14 percent today. This decline has occurred primarily as a result of changes in the economy: rapid growth of professional, managerial, finance, technical, sales, and service

trade associations Interest groups composed of businesses in specific industries.

employment, where unions are weakest; and slower growth or stagnation of manufacture, mining, and construction employment, where unions are strongest. Yet even in manufacturing, union membership today is only about 20 percent of the work force.

Nevertheless, labor unions remain a major political influence in Congress and the Democratic Party. The AFL-CIO is a federation of sixty-eight separate unions with more than 13 million members. The AFL-CIO has long maintained a large and capable lobbying staff in Washington, and it provides both financial contributions and campaign services (registration, get-out-the-vote, information, endorsements) for members of Congress it favors. Many of the larger individual unions also maintain offices in Washington and offer campaign contributions and services.

Today union influence is greatest among government employees, including teachers. The American Federation of State, County, and Municipal Employees (AFSCME), the National Education Association (NEA), the American Federation of Teachers (AFT), and the Teamsters Union (which recruits public employees in sanitation and transportation) are among the few unions maintaining or growing in membership.

Labor union political campaign contributions (see "PAC Power" below) remain a major source of union influence in Washington. The AFSCME, NEA, Teamsters, United Auto Workers, United Steel Workers, Electrical Workers, Machinists, and Letter Carriers, as well as the AFL-CIO itself, are regularly ranked among the top contributors in congressional elections. Almost all union campaign contributions go to Democratic candidates.

Farm Organizations   Even though the farm population of the United States has declined from about 25 percent of the total population in the 1930s to less than 3 percent today, farmers—especially large agricultural producers—remain a very potent political force in Washington. Agricultural interests are organized both into large inclusive groups, such as the American Farm Bureau Federation and the National Grange, and into very effective specialized groups, such as the National Milk Producers and the National Cattlemen's Association. Small and low-income farmers are represented by the National Farmers Union.

Women's Organizations   Women's organizations date back to the antislavery societies in pre–Civil War America. The first generation of feminists—Lucretia Mott, Elizabeth Cady Stanton, Lucy Stone, and Susan B. Anthony—learned to organize, hold public meetings, and conduct petition campaigns as abolitionists. After the Civil War, women were successful in changing many state laws that abridged the rights of married women and otherwise treated them as "chattel" (property) of their husbands. Women were also prominent in the Anti-Saloon League, which succeeded in outlawing prostitution and gambling in every state except Nevada and provided a major source of support for the Eighteenth Amendment (Prohibition). In the early twentieth century, the feminist movement concentrated on obtaining the vote (suffrage) for women. Today the League of Women Voters—a broad-based organization that provides information to voters—backs registration and get-out-the-vote drives and generally supports measures seeking to ensure honesty and integrity in government.

Interest in feminist politics revived in the wake of the civil rights movement of the 1960s. New organizations sprang up to compete with the conventional activities of the League of Women Voters by taking a more activist stance toward women's issues. The largest of these organizations is the National Organization for Women (NOW), founded in 1966.

Religious Groups   Churches and religious groups have a long history of involvement in American politics—from the pre–Civil War antislavery crusades, to the prohibition effort in the early twentieth century, to the civil rights movement of the 1960s. The leadership for the historic Civil Rights Act of 1964 came from the Reverend Martin Luther King, Jr., and his Southern Christian Leadership Conference. Today religious groups span the political spectrum, from liberal organizations such as the National Council of Churches and Anti-Defamation League of B'nai B'rith, to conservative and fundamentalist organizations, such as the Christian Coalition, often referred to as the "religious right" (see *Up Close:* "The Christian Coalition: Organizing the Faithful").

The American-Israel Public Affairs Committee is regularly ranked as one of Washington's most powerful lobbies (see *Up Close:* "Washington's Most Powerful Lobbies" later in this chapter). It is actually a foreign-policy lobby rather than a religious lobby, although its support is concentrated in the American Jewish community. It lobbies on behalf of Israel's interests, including continuing substantial foreign aid.

Public-Interest Groups   **Public-interest groups** claim to represent broad classes of people—consumers, voters, reformers, or the public as a whole. Groups with lofty-sounding names, such as Common Cause, Public Citizen, and the Consumer Federation of America, perceive themselves as balancing the narrow, "selfish" interests of business organizations, trade associations, unions, and other "special" interests. Public-interest groups generally lobby for greater government regulation of consumer products, public safety, campaign finance, and so on. Their reform agenda, as well as their call for a larger regulatory role for government, makes them frequent allies of liberal ideological groups, civil rights organizations, and environmental groups.[4]

Many public interest groups were initially formed in the 1970s by "entrepreneurs" who saw an untapped "market" for the representation of these interests. Among the most influential public-interest groups are Common Cause, a self-styled "citizens' lobby," and the sprawling network of organizations created by consumer advocate Ralph Nader (see *People in Politics:* "Ralph Nader, People's Lobbyist" on page 290). Common Cause tends to focus on election-law reform, public financing of elections, and limitations on political contributions. The Nader organization began as a consumer protection group focusing on auto safety but soon spread to encompass a wide variety of causes.

Single-Issue Groups   Like public-interest groups, **single-issue groups** appeal to principle and belief. But as their name implies, single-issue groups concentrate their attention on a single cause. They attract the support of individuals with a strong commitment to that cause. Single-issue groups have little incentive to compromise their position. They exist for a single cause; no other issues really matter to them. They are by nature passionate and often shrill. Their attraction to members is the intensity of their beliefs.

Among the most vocal single-issue groups in recent years have been the organizations on both sides of the abortion issue. The National Abortion Rights Action League (NARAL) describes itself as "pro-choice" and opposes any restrictions on a woman's right to obtain an abortion. The National Right-to-Life Committee

public-interest groups
Interest groups that claim to represent broad classes of people or the public as a whole.

single-issue groups   Organizations formed to support or oppose government action on a specific issue.

The Christian Coalition: Organizing the Faithful

Christian fundamentalists, whose religious beliefs are based on a literal reading of the Bible, have become a more significant political force in the United States through effective organization. Perhaps the most influential Christian fundamentalist organization today is the Christian Coalition with nearly 2 million active members throughout the country.

Fundamentalist Christians are opposed to abortion, pornography, and homosexuality; they favor the recognition of religion in public life, including prayer in schools; and they despair at the decline of traditional family values in American culture, including motion pictures and television broadcasting. Historically fundamentalist Protestant churches avoided politics as profane and concentrated evangelical efforts on saving individual souls. Their few ventures into worldly politics—notably the prohibition movement in the early twentieth century—ended in defeat. Their strength tended to be in the southern, rural, and poorer regions of the country. They were widely ridiculed on the national media.

In the 1960s, television evangelism emerged as a religious force in the United States. The Reverend Pat Robertson founded the Christian Broadcasting Network (CBN) to air his popular *700 Club* and later purchased the Family Channel. But efforts by social conservatives to build a "moral majority" for political action largely failed, as did Robertson's presidential candidacy in 1988. Televangelists, including Jerry Falwell and Tammy Fay Baker, suffered popular disdain following some well-publicized scandals. As president, Ronald Reagan gave symbolic support to the political agenda of social and religious conservatives but concentrated instead on the concerns of economic conservatives (for deregulation and tax reduction) and anticommunist conservatives (for a military buildup and challenge to the Soviet Union). Robertson eventually turned over his embattled political organization, the Christian Coalition, to a young, energetic, professional political organizer, Ralph Reed.

Under Reed's direction, the Christian Coalition rose in political influence across the country—in local politics, school board elections, state legislative and governors' races, and congressional politics. Building from the grass roots, in local communities and churches, Reed made the Christian Coalition perhaps the most powerful religious-based lobby in the nation. Although officially nonpartisan, the coalition represents an important force in Republican politics; religious fundamentalists may constitute as much as one-third of the party's voter support. The Christian Coalition does not officially endorse candidates, but its voter guides clearly indicate which candidates reflect the coalition's position on major issues. The distribution of more than 33 million of these guides, mostly in churches on the weekend before the Tuesday election, was credited with helping Republicans capture control of Congress in 1994. The political influence of the Christian Coalition in Republican politics, and the "religious right" generally, ensures that most GOP candidates for public office publicly express support for a "profamily" agenda. This agenda includes a constitutional amendment allowing prayer in public schools; vouchers for parents to send their children to private, religious schools; tax credits to families with children; banning late-term abortions as well as banning the use of taxpayer funds to pay for abortions; restrictions on pornography on cable television and the Internet; and a requirement that criminals make restitution to their victims after release. In 1995, Reed boasted that fundamentalist Christians "have finally gained a place at the table, a sense of legitimacy, and a voice in the conversation we call democracy."*

However, some Christian activists, disheartened by President Clinton's continued popularity during the Lewinsky sex scandal, have become discouraged about working in the political arena. They worry that they have "lost the cultural war." They urge a redirection of fundamentalist Christian efforts toward local schools, neighborhoods, and communities. Ralph Reed resigned as president of the Christian Coalition in 1998, and Pat Robertson reassumed leadership of the organization.

Congressional Quarterly Weekly Report, May 20, 1995, p. 1449.

Ralph Nader, People's Lobbyist

Much of the credit for the growth of public-interest groups in recent decades goes to Ralph Nader, the self-appointed "people's lobbyist" who achieved national celebrity as an advocate of consumer protection laws. From seat belts and nonsmoking sections to nuclear power regulation, insurance rates, food and drug legislation, and worker safety, Nader's influence has been widely felt in American society.

The child of Lebanese immigrants who operated a small bakery in Winsted, Connecticut, Nader graduated from the Woodrow Wilson School of Public and International Affairs at Princeton University magna cum laude, then went on to Harvard Law School, where he earned an LL.B. with distinction in 1958. After a short stint in the army, Nader opened a private law practice in Hartford, Connecticut, but soon left to travel throughout the world, working as a free-lance journalist for the *Christian Science Monitor*.

An article that Nader wrote for the *Harvard Law Review* on auto design and safety brought him to the attention of then-Acting Secretary of Labor (now U.S. Senator from New York) Daniel Patrick Moynihan. Moynihan hired the young attorney as a staff consultant on highway safety. While employed at the Department of Labor, Nader wrote and published his book *Unsafe at Any Speed* (1965), which charged that General Motors Corporation preferred styling to safety. Nader was thrust further into the national spotlight when he sued General Motors for invading his privacy by hiring private detectives to investigate him. With his $16 million in settlement money (plus substantial royalty and speaking income), Nader began to construct an organizational colossus. In 1969 Nader founded his Washington-based Center for Study of Responsive Law and staffed it with aggressive young lawyers. These "Nader's Raiders" launched attacks against a number of federal regulatory agencies, charging them with lax enforcement.

In 1971 Nader started Public Citizen, Inc., to enlist members of the general public in a broad array of causes. Among these causes: *Congress Watch* which directly lobbies Congress on health, safety, and environmental issues, as well as campaign finance reform; *The Health Research Group* that lobbies the Food and Drug Administration for greater regulation, including tobacco restrictions; *The Litigation Group* which generates class-action suits against corporations and governments; *The Critical Mass Energy Project* which opposes nuclear energy and the oil and gas industry; *Global Trade Watch* which opposes free trade as a threat to the environment; and *Buyers Up*, a home heating-oil cooperative that also monitors quality of gasoline sold to consumers.

Nader's independence and altruism, his contempt for bureaucratic lethargy and incompetence, and his posture as David fighting the corporate Goliaths of the world appealed to idealistic young people at colleges and universities across the nation. Capitalizing on his campus popularity, Nader formed hundreds of Public Interest Research Groups (PIRGs) and overcame the "free-rider" problem by pressuring university administrators on many campuses to add PIRG dues to student activities fees.

Nader has resigned from direct participation in most of the organizations he founded, leaving them to be managed by a new generation of consumer advocates. Nader ran for president in 1996 as a Green Party (environmental protection) candidate. But he campaigned very little and refused to solicit contributions. In public appearances he often seemed argumentative and self-righteous. He ended up with less than 1 percent of the popular vote nationwide.

Nader's decision to actively campaign for the presidency in 2000 angered many of his liberal Democratic friends. They believed that most of his nearly three million votes nationwide (about 3 percent of the popular vote) would otherwise have gone to Democrat Al Gore. Nader argued that he was positioning the Green Party as a watchdog over a "corrupt" two-party system.

Source: "The Ralph Nader Trust," *Forbes*, September 17, 1990, pp. 120–21; quotation from *Newsmakers* (Detroit: Gale Research, 1989), p. 360.

describes itself as "pro-life" and opposes abortion for any reason other than to preserve the life of the mother. Other prominent single-issue groups include the National Rifle Association (opposed to gun control) and Mothers against Drunk Driving (MADD).

Ideological Groups   **Ideological organizations** pursue liberal or conservative agendas, often with great passion and considerable financial resources derived from true-believing contributors. The ideological groups rely heavily on computerized mailings to solicit funds from persons identified as holding liberal or conservative views. The oldest of the established ideological groups is the liberal Americans for Democratic Action (ADA), well known for its annual liberalism ratings of members of the Congress according to their support for or rejection of programs of concern. The American Conservative Union (ACU) also rates members of Congress each year. Overall, Democrats do better on the liberal list and Republicans on the conservative list, although both parties include some members whose policies frequently put them on the opposite side of the fence from the majority of their fellow party members (see Table 9-2 on page 292). Other interest groups, such as the AFL-CIO, the National Taxpayers Union, and the National Abortion Rights Action League, also rate members of Congress, but these groups have a narrower focus than the ADA and ACU. Yet another prominent ideological group, People for the American Way, was formed by television producer Norman Lear to coordinate the efforts of liberals in the entertainment industry as well as the general public, but it issues no ratings.

Government Lobbies   The federal government's grant-in-aid programs to state and local governments (see Chapter 4) have spawned a host of lobbying efforts by these governments in Washington, D.C. Thus state- and local-government taxpayers foot the bill to lobby Washington to transfer federal taxpayers' revenues to states and communities. The National Governors Association occupies a beautiful marble building, the Hall of the States, in Washington, along with representatives of the separate states and many major cities. The National League of Cities and the National Association of Counties also maintain large Washington offices, as does the U.S. Conference of Mayors. The National Conference of State Legislators sends its lobbyists to Washington from its Denver headquarters. These groups pursue a wide policy agenda and often confront internal disputes. But they are united in their support for increased federal transfers of tax revenues to states and cities.

LEADERS AND FOLLOWERS

Organizations require leadership. And over time leaders develop a perspective somewhat different from that of their organizations' membership. A key question in interest-group politics is how well organization leaders represent the views of their members.

Interest-Group Entrepreneurs   People who create organizations and build membership in those organizations—**interest-group entrepreneurs**—have played a major role in strengthening the interest-group system in recent decades. These entrepreneurs help overcome a major obstacle to the formation of strong interest groups—the *free-rider* problem.

ideological organizations
Interest groups that pursue ideologically based (liberal or conservative) agendas.

interest-group entrepreneurs   Leaders who create organizations and market memberships.

Table 9-2 Ideological Interest-Group Ratings for U.S. Senators

Most Liberal Senators	% Liberal
Paul Wellstone (D-Minn.)	100
Ron Wyden (D-Oreg.)	100
Barbara Boxer (D-Cal.)	95
Christopher Dodd (D-Conn.)	95
Tom Harkin (D-Iowa)	95
Paul Sarbanes (D-Md.)	95
Edward Kennedy (D-Mass.)	95
John Kerry (D-Mass.)	95
Bob Kerrey (D-Neb.)	95
Frank Lautenberg (D-N.J.)	95
Most Conservative Senators	
Jesse Helms (R-N.C.)	0
Phil Gramm (R-Tex.)	0
Strom Thurmond (R-S.C.)	0
Tom Cochran (R-Miss.)	0
Trent Lott (R-Miss.)	0
Don Nickles (R-Okla.)	0
Rick Santorum (R-Pa.)	0
Slade Gorton (R-Wash.)	0
Kay Hutchinson (R-Tex.)	0
Mitch McConnell (R-Ky.)	0
Most Liberal Republicans	
James Jeffords (R-Vt.)	55
Arlen Specter (R-Pa.)	45
John Chafee (R-R.I.)	45
Olympia Snowe (R-Me.)	35
Most Conservative Democrats	
Ernest Hollings (D-S.C.)	55
John Braux (D-La.)	75

Source: Americans for Democratic Action for 1998 Senate Voting Record. 1999.

Free-riders are people who benefit from the efforts of others but do not contribute to the costs of those efforts. Not everyone feels an obligation to support organizations that represent their interests or views. Some people feel that their own small contribution will not make a difference in the success or failure of the organization's goals and, moreover, that they will benefit from any successes even if they are not members. Indeed, most organizations enroll only a tiny fraction of the people they claim to represent. The task of the interest-group entrepreneur is to convince people to join the organization, either by appealing to their sense of obligation or by attracting them through tangible benefits.

free-riders People who do not belong to an organization or pay dues, yet nevertheless benefit from its activities.

Marketing Membership   Interest-group entrepreneurs make different appeals for membership depending on the nature of the organization. Some appeal to passion or purpose, as, for example, those who seek to create ideological (liberal or conservative) organizations, public-interest organizations committed to environmental or consumer protection or governmental reform, and single-issue organizations devoted to the support or opposition of a single policy issue (gun control, abortion, and so on). Entrepreneurs of these organizations appeal to people's sense of duty and commitment to the cause rather than to material rewards of membership. By using sophisticated computerized mailing lists, they can solicit support from sympathetic people.[5]

Business, trade, and professional organizations usually offer their members many tangible benefits in addition to lobbying on behalf of their economic interests. These benefits may include magazines, journals, and newsletters that provide access to business, trade, and professional information as well as national conventions and meetings that serve as social settings for the development of contacts, friendships, and business and professional relationships. Some organizations also offer discount travel and insurance, credit cards, and the like, that go only to dues-paying members.

It is generally easier to organize smaller, specialized economic interests than larger, general, noneconomic interests. People more easily recognize that their own membership is important to the success of a small organization, and economic interests are more readily calculated in dollar terms.

Large organizations with broad goals—such as advancing the interests of all veterans or all retired people or all automobile drivers—must rely even more heavily on tangible benefits to solicit members. Indeed, some organizations have succeeded in recruiting millions of members (for example, the AARP with 36 million members, the American Automobile Association with 28 million members), most of whom have very little knowledge about the policy positions or lobbying activities of the organization. These members joined to receive specific benefits—magazines, insurance, travel tips, discounts. Leaders of these organizations may claim to speak for millions of members, but it is unlikely that these millions all share the policy views expressed by the leaders.

Organizational Democracy and Leader/Member Agreement   Most organized interest groups are run by a small group of leaders and activists. Few interest groups are governed democratically; members may drop out if they do not like the direction their organization is taking but rarely do they have the opportunity to directly challenge or replace the organization's leadership. Relatively few members attend national meetings, vote in organizational elections, or try to exercise influence within their organization. Thus the leadership may not always reflect the views of the membership, especially in large organizations that rely heavily on tangible benefits to recruit members. Leaders of these organizations enjoy considerable freedom in adopting policy positions and negotiating, bargaining, and compromising in the political arena.

The exception to this rule is the single-issue group. Because the strength of these groups is in the intensity of their members' beliefs, the leaders of such groups are closely tied to their members' views. They cannot bargain or compromise these views or adopt policy positions at variance with those of their members.

Class Bias in Membership   Americans are joiners. A majority of the population belong to at least one organization, most often a church. Yet membership in organized interest groups is clearly linked to socioeconomic status. Membership is greatest among professional and managerial, college-educated, and high-income persons.[6]

THE WASHINGTON LOBBYISTS

Washington is a labyrinth of interest representatives—lawyers and law firms; independent consultants; public and governmental relations firms; business, professional, and trade associations; and advocates of special causes. It is estimated that more than 14,000 people in Washington fit the definition of **lobbyist**, a person working to influence government policies and actions. These figures suggest at least twenty-five lobbyists for every member of Congress.

Who Are the Lobbyists? Lobbyists in Washington, D.C., represent a broad array of concerns (see Table 9-3). They share a common goal—to influence the making and enforcing of laws—and common tactics to achieve this goal. Many lobbyists are the employees of interest-group organizations who devote all of their efforts to their sponsors.

Some lobbying organizations rely heavily on their campaign contributions to achieve lobbying power; others rely on large memberships, and still others on politically active members who concentrate their attention on a narrow range of issues (see *Up Close:* "Washington's Most Powerful Lobbies").

Other lobbyists are located in independent law, consulting, or public relations firms that take on clients for fees (see Table 9-4). Independent lobbyists, especially law firms, are often secretive about whom they represent, especially when they represent foreign governments. Lobbyists frequently prefer to label their activities as "government relations," "public affairs," "regulatory liaison," "legislative counseling," or merely "representation."

In reality, many independent lawyers and lobbyists in Washington are "fixers" who offer to influence government policies for a price. Many are former government officials—former Congress members, cabinet secretaries, White House aides, and the like—who "know their way around." Their personal connections help to "open doors" to allow their paying clients to "just get a chance to talk" with top officials.

Regulation of Lobbies The Constitution's First Amendment guarantee of the right "to petition the government for a redress of grievances" protects lobbying. But the government can and does regulate lobbying activities, primarily through disclosure laws. The Regulation of Lobbying Act requires lobbyists to register and to report how much they spend, but definitions of *lobbying* are unclear and enforce-

lobbyist Person working to influence government policies and actions.

Table 9-3	Types of Lobbyists	
Business, trade, and professional organization officers (approximately 2,200 organizations)		5,000
Representatives of individual corporations		1,500
Representatives of special causes		2,500
Lawyers registered as lobbyists		3,000
Public and governmental relations		2,500
Political action committee officers		200
Think tank officers		150

Source: Washington Representatives, 1995 (Washington, D.C.: Columbia Books, 1995).

UP CLOSE

Washington's Most Powerful Lobbies

Fortune magazine sponsored a survey of more than 2,000 Washington "insiders," including members of Congress, their staffs, and White House officials, asking them to rank the most powerful lobbyists in the capital. The results were as follows:

The "Power 25"

1. American Association of Retired Persons
2. American Israel Public Affairs Committee
3. AFL-CIO
4. National Federation of Independent Business
5. Association of Trial Lawyers of America
6. National Rifle Association of America
7. Christian Coalition
8. American Medical Association
9. National Education Association
10. National Right to Life Committee
11. National Association of Realtors
12. American Bankers Association
13. National Association of Manufacturers
14. American Federation of State, County, and Municipal Employees
15. Chamber of Commerce of the U.S.A.
16. Veterans of Foreign Wars of the United States
17. American Farm Bureau Federation
18. Motion Picture Association of America
19. National Association of Home Builders of the U.S.
20. National Association of Broadcasters
21. American Hospital Association
22. National Governors' Association
23. American Legion
24. National Restaurant Association
25. International Brotherhood of Teamsters

Source: *Fortune*, December 8, 1997.

ment is weak. Many large lobbying groups—for example, the National Association of Manufacturers, the American Bankers Association, and Americans for Constitutional Action—have never registered as lobbyists. These organizations claim that because lobbying is not their principal activity, they need not register under the law. In addition, financial reports of lobbyists grossly underestimate the extent of lobbying in Congress because the law requires reports of only money spent for direct lobbying before Congress, not money spent for public relations. Another weakness in the law is that it applies only to attempts to influence Congress; it does not regulate lobbying activities in administrative agencies or the executive branch.

Tax laws require nonprofit organizations to refrain from direct lobbying in order to retain their tax-free status. Under current tax law, individual contributions to nonprofit charitable and educational organizations are tax deductible, and the income of these organizations is tax free. But these organizations risk losing these tax preferences if a "substantial part" of their activities is "attempting to influence legislation." Thus, for example, Washington think tanks such as the Brookings Institution, the American Enterprise Institute, and the Heritage Foundation (see *Up Close:* "Think Tanks: The Battle of Ideas" in Chapter 2) refrain from direct lobbying even though they make policy recommendations. But the line between public affairs "education" and "lobbying" is very fuzzy.

Table 9-4	Washington's Top Independent Lobbying Firms (Ranked by Receipts from Lobbying)

Rank/Organization

1 Cassidy & Associates
2 Verner, Liipfert et al.
3 Patton Boggs LLP
4 Akin, Gump et al.
5 Preston, Gates et al.
6 Barbour, Griffith & Rogers
7 Washington Counsel
8 Williams & Jensen
9 Baker, Donelson et al.
10 Hogan & Hartson
11 PricewaterhouseCoopers
12 Van Scoyoc Associates
13 Timmons & Co.
14 Podesta.com
15 Alcalde & Fay
16 Arnold & Porter
17 Dutko Group
18 Black, Kelly et al.
19 Capitol Associates
20 Mayer, Brown & Platt
21 Boland & Madigan Inc.
22 Griffin, Johnson et al.
23 McDermott, Will & Emery
24 Arter & Hadden
25 Wexler Group

Source: Data from the Center for Responsive Politics.

THE FINE ART OF LOBBYING

Any activity directed at a government decision maker with the hope of influencing decisions is a form of **lobbying**. (The term arose from the practice of waiting in the lobbies of legislative chambers to meet and persuade legislators.) For organized interests, lobbying is continuous—in congressional committees, in congressional staff offices, at the White House, at executive agencies, at Washington cocktail parties. If a group loses a round in Congress, it continues the fight in the agency in charge of executing the policy, or it challenges the policy in the courts. The following year it resumes the struggle in Congress: It fights to repeal the offending legislation, to weaken amendments, or to reduce the agency's budget enough to cripple enforcement efforts.

Lobbying techniques are as varied as the imagination of interest-group leaders, but such activities generally fall into seven categories: (1) public relations; (2) access; (3) information; (4) grass-roots mobilization; (5) protests and demonstrations; (6) coalition building; and (7) campaign support. In the real world of Washington power

lobbying Activities directed at government officials with the hope of influencing their decisions.

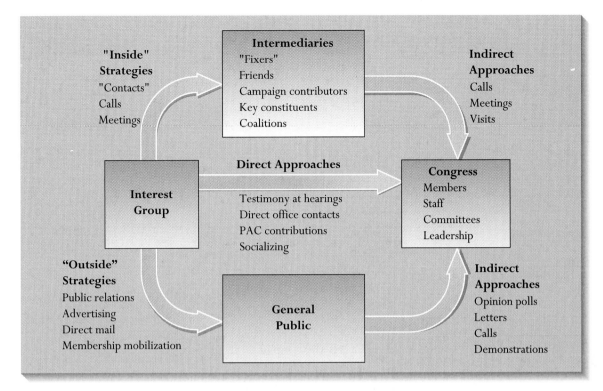

FIGURE 9-1 A Guide to the Fine Art of Lobbying

Interest groups seek to influence public policy both directly through lobbying and campaign contributions (inside strategy) and indirectly through public relations efforts to mold public opinion (outside strategy).

struggles, all these techniques may be applied simultaneously, or innovative techniques may be discovered and applied at any time (see Figure 9-1).

Public Relations Many interest groups actually spend more of their time, energy, and resources on **public relations**—developing and maintaining a favorable climate of opinion in the nation—than on direct lobbying of Congress. The mass media—television, magazines, newspapers—are saturated with expensive ads by oil companies, auto companies, chemical manufacturers, trade associations, teachers' unions, and many other groups, all seeking to create a favorable image for themselves with the general public. These ads are designed to go well beyond promoting the sale of particular products; they portray these organizations as patriotic citizens, protectors of the environment, providers of jobs, defenders of family values, and supporters of the American way of life. Generally, business interests have an advantage in the area of public relations because public relations and sales and marketing activities are synonymous. But paid advertising is less credible than news stories and media commentary. Hence interest groups generate a daily flood of press releases, media events, interviews, reports, and studies for the media. Media news stories appear to favor liberal public interest groups (Table 9-5 on page 298).

Access "Opening doors" is a major business in Washington. To influence decision makers, organized interests must first acquire **access** to them. Individuals who have personal contacts in Congress, the White House, or the bureaucracy

public relations Building and maintaining goodwill with the general public.

access Meeting and talking with decision makers, a prerequisite to direct persuasion.

Table 9-5   Television News Coverage of Interest Groups

Type of Interest Group	Percent of All Interest Group References
Citizen groups	45.6
Think tanks	4.3
Corporations	24.3
Trade associations	13.0
Professional associations	3.8
Labor unions	4.0
Other[a]	5.1
Total	100.1

Data from 295 newscasts during 1995, alternating among broadcasts by ABC, CBS, CNN *Headline News*, and NBC. There were 847 references to groups. These references were contained in 548 distinct stories.

[a]Veterans, nonprofits, churches, and other groups.

Source: Jeffrey M. Berry, *The New Liberalism*. (Washington, D.C.: Brookings Institution Press, 1999), p. 122.

(or who say they do) sell their services at high prices. Washington law firms, public relations agencies, and consultants—often former insiders—all offer their connections, along with their advice, to their clients. The personal prestige of the lobbyist, together with the group's perceived political influence, helps open doors in Washington.

Washington socializing is often an exercise in access—rubbing elbows with powerful people. Well-heeled lobbyists regularly pay hundreds, even thousands, of dollars per plate at fund-raising dinners for members of Congress. Lobbyists regularly provide dinners, drinks, travel, vacations, and other amenities to members of Congress, their families, and congressional staff, as well as to White House and other executive officials. (Until recently, *honoraria*—direct payments to members of Congress for speaking to an organization—were common, but congressional ethics legislation now prohibits honoraria for House members and limits annual honoraria income for senators to 27 percent of their salaries.) These favors are rarely provided on a direct quid pro quo basis in exchange for votes. Rather, they are designed to gain access—"just a chance to talk."

Information   Once lobbyists gain access, their knowledge and information become valuable resources to those they lobby. Members of Congress and their staffs look to lobbyists for *technical expertise* on the issue under debate as well as *political information* about the group's position on the issue. Members of Congress must vote on hundreds of questions each year, and it is impossible for them to be fully informed about the wide variety of bills and issues they face. Consequently many of them (and administrators in the executive branch as well) come to depend on trusted lobbyists.

Lobbyists also spend considerable time and effort keeping informed about bills affecting their interests. They must be thoroughly familiar with the "ins and outs" of the legislative process—the relevant committees and subcommittees, their schedules of meetings and hearings, their key staff members, the best moments to act, the precise language for proposed bills and amendments, the witnesses for hearings,

Table 9-6 Activities of Professional Lobbyists

Activity	Lobbyists Participating in Activity
Testifying at hearings	99%
Contacting government officials directly	98
Making informal contacts over meals, and so on	95
Presenting research results	92
Helping write legislation	85
Mounting grass-roots lobbying campaigns	80
Telling legislators the impact of legislation in their districts	75
Pursuing litigation	72
Publicizing candidates' voting records	44
Making in-kind (work, skill) contributions to campaigns	24
Endorsing candidates publicly	22
Engaging in protests or demonstrations	20

Source: From *Organized Interests and American Democracy* by Kay Lehman Schlozman and John T. Tierney. Copyright © 1986 by Kay Lehman Schlozman and John T. Tierney. Reprinted by permission of HarperCollins Publishers, Inc.

and the political strengths and weaknesses of the legislators themselves. In their campaign to win congressional and bureaucratic support for their programs, lobbyists engage in many different types of activities. Nearly all testify at congressional hearings and make direct contact with government officials on issues that affect them. In addition, lobbyists provide the technical reports and analyses used by congressional staffs in their legislative research. Engaging in protest demonstrations is a less common activity, in part because it involves a high risk of alienating some members of Congress (see Table 9-6).

Experienced lobbyists develop a reputation for accurate information. Most successful lobbyists do not supply faulty information; their success depends on maintaining the trust and confidence of decision makers. A reputation for honesty is as important as a reputation for influence.

Grass-Roots Mobilization Many organized interests lobby Congress from both the *outside* and the *inside*. From the outside, organizations seek to mobilize **grass-roots lobbying** of members of Congress by their constituents. Lobbyists frequently encourage letters and calls from "the folks back home." Larger organized interests often have local chapters throughout the nation and can mobilize these local affiliates to apply pressure when necessary. Lobbyists encourage influential local people to visit the office of a member of Congress personally or to make a personal phone call on behalf of the group's position. And, naturally, members are urged to vote for or against certain candidates, based on their policy stances (see *Up Close:* "AARP: The Nation's Most Powerful Interest Group" on page 300).

Experienced lawmakers recognize attempts by lobby groups to orchestrate "spontaneous" grass-roots outpourings of cards and letters. Pressure mail is often identical in wording and content. Nevertheless, members of Congress dare not ignore

grass-roots lobbying
Attempts to influence government decision making by inspiring constituents to contact their representatives.

AARP: The Nation's Most Powerful Interest Group

The American Association of Retired Persons (AARP) is the nation's largest and most powerful interest group, with more than 36 million members. The AARP's principal interests are the Social Security and Medicare system programs, the nation's largest and most expensive entitlements. It led the fight in Congress against the Balanced Budget Amendment to the Constitution.

Like many other interest groups, the AARP has grown in membership not only by appealing to the political interests of retired people but also by offering a wide array of material benefits. For an $8 annual fee, members are offered a variety of services, including discounted rates on home, auto, and life insurance; discounted mail-order drugs; tax advisory services; discounted rates on hotels, rental cars, and

Source: Reprinted, with permission, from the April 1997 issue of *Reason* Magazine. Copyright 1998 by the Reason Foundation, 3415 S. Sepulveda Blvd., Suite 400, Los Angeles, CA.

a flood of letters and telegrams from home, for the mail shows that constituents are aware of the issue and care enough to sign their names.

Another grass-roots tactic is to mobilize the press in the home district of a member of Congress. Lobbyists may provide news, analyses, and editorials to local newspapers and then clip favorable articles to send to lawmakers. Lobby groups may also buy advertisements in hometown newspapers.

Protests and Demonstrations   Interest groups occasionally employ protests and demonstrations to attract media attention to their concerns and thereby apply pressure on officials to take action. For these actions to succeed in getting issues on the agenda of decision makers in Congress, in the White House, and in executive agencies, participation by the media, especially television, is essential. The media

so on; a newsletter, *The AARP Bulletin*; and a semi-monthly magazine, *Modern Maturity*.

Senior citizens are the most politically powerful age group in the population. They constitute 28 percent of the voting-age population, but because of their high voter-turnout rates, they constitute more than one-third of the voters on election day. Persons over sixty-five average a 68 percent turnout rate in presidential elections and a 61 percent rate in congressional elections. In contrast, the turnout rate for those aged eighteen to twenty-one is 36 percent in presidential elections and 19 percent in congressional elections. In short, the voting power of senior citizens is twice that of young people. No elected official can afford to offend the seniors, and seniors strongly support generous Social Security and Medicare benefits.

The power of the "gray lobby" is clearly evident in the federal budget (see graph). The federal government invests relatively little in education, training, and social services for young people. Yet the federal government's most costly function is the support of the nation's senior citizens. Social Security, Medicare, and federal retirement programs now account for about 40 percent of all federal spending.

The political power of senior citizens is so great that prospects for limiting current or even future increases in government benefits for the elderly are slim. Social Security is said to be the "third rail of American politics—touch it and you're dead."

Critics of the AARP argue that its lobbyists in Washington do not fairly represent the views of the nation's senior citizens, that few of its members know

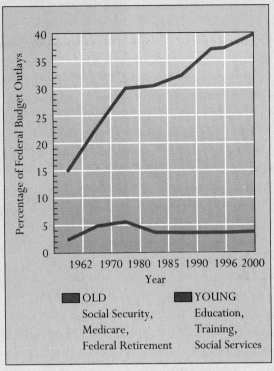

Young and Old in the Federal Budget

Source: Budget of the United States Government, 2000.

what its lobbying arm does at the nation's capital. AARP keeps its dues low, and consequently its membership high, through its business ties with insurance companies, its magazine advertising revenue, and commercial royalties revenues for endorsing products and services.

carry the message of the protest or demonstration both to the general public and directly to government officials (see "Protest as Political Participation" in Chapter 5).

Organized interest groups most often resort to protests and demonstrations when (1) they are frustrated in more traditional "inside" lobbying efforts; and/or (2) they wish to intensify pressure on officials at a specific point in time. Demonstrations typically attract media attention for a short time only. But media coverage of specific events can carry a clear message—for example, farmers driving tractors through Washington to protest farm conditions; motorcyclists conducting a giant "bike-in" to protest laws requiring helmets; cattle raisers driving steers down the Washington Mall to protest beef prices. The potential drawbacks to such activities are that the attention is short-lived and the group's reputation may be tarnished if the protest turns nasty or violent.

The Christian Coalition remains a major political force, especially within the Republican Party. Here, George W. Bush addresses the Coalition during the Republican presidential primaries in 2000.

Coalition Building   Interest groups frequently seek to build **coalitions** with other groups in order to increase their power. Coalitions tend to form among groups with parallel interests: for example, the National Organization for Women, the League of Women Voters, and the National Abortion Rights Action League on women's issues. Coalitions usually form temporarily around a single piece of legislation in a major effort to secure or prevent its passage.

Campaign Support   Perhaps the real key to success in lobbying is the campaign contribution. Interest-group contributions not only help lobbyists gain access and a favorable hearing but also help elect people friendly to the group's goals. As the costs of campaigning increase, legislators must depend more heavily on the contributions of organized interests.

Most experienced lobbyists avoid making electoral threats. Amateur lobbyists sometimes threaten legislators by vowing to defeat them at the next election, but this tactic usually produces a hostile reaction among members of Congress. Legislators are likely to respond to crude pressures by demonstrating their independence and voting against the threatening lobbyist. Moreover, experienced members of Congress know that such threats are empty; lobbyists can seldom deliver enough votes to influence the outcome of an election.

Experienced lobbyists also avoid offering a campaign contribution in exchange for a specific vote.[7] Crude "vote buying" (bribery) is illegal and risks repulsing politicians who refuse bribes. **Bribery**, when it occurs, is probably limited to very narrow and specific actions—payments to intervene in a particular case before an administrative agency; payments to insert a very specific break in a tax bill or a specific exemption in a trade bill; payments to obtain a specific contract with the government. Bribery on major issues is very unlikely; there is too much publicity and too many participants for bribery to be effective (but see *Up Close:* "The Cash Constituents of Congress" in Chapter 10).

coalition   A joining together of interest groups (or individuals) to achieve a common goal.

bribery   Giving or offering anything of value in an effort to influence government officials in the performance of their duties.

Instead of bribery, organized interests contribute to an incumbent member of Congress over a long period of time and leave it to the lawmaker to figure out how to retain their support. Only when a legislator consistently works against an organized interest will it consider contributing to that lawmaker's opponent in an election.

PAC POWER

Organized interest groups channel their campaign contributions through **political action committees (PACs)**. PACs are organized by corporations, labor unions, trade associations, ideological and issue-oriented groups, and cooperatives and nonprofit corporations to solicit campaign contributions and distribute them to political candidates.

Origins   The first PACs were created by organized labor to circumvent prohibitions against using union dues to finance elections. Corporations, like labor unions, had long been prohibited from making direct campaign contributions. Prior to passage of the Federal Election Campaign Act of 1974, which encouraged corporations to create their own PACs, PACs were relatively rare. But once begun, PACs mushroomed in number, not leveling off until the late 1980s (see Table 9-7). Today corporate PACs far outnumber labor PACs. Trade and professional associations quickly organized their own PACs. Soon entrepreneurs for ideological, environmental, and single-issue groups created PACs. Increasingly political candidates turned to PACs as a major source of campaign financing.

Regulation   PACs are regulated by the Federal Election Commission (FEC), which requires them to register and report their finances and political contributions periodically. A registered PAC that has received contributions from more than fifty people and has contributed to at least five campaigns is eligible to contribute $5,000 to any candidate (per election), $15,000 to a party's national committee, and $5,000 to any other PAC. These limits mean that PACs can give five times as much to candidates in each election as can individuals, who are limited to $1,000. Individuals may, however, give $5,000 to any PAC. Thus the 1974 reform act, although intended to reform campaign financing, actually encouraged the growth of PACs and PAC power.

political action committees (PACs)   Organizations that solicit and receive campaign contributions from corporations, unions, trade associations, and ideological and issue-oriented groups, and their members, then distribute these funds to political candidates.

Table 9-7	The Growth of PACs			
	1974	**1980**	**1988**	**1998**
Corporate	89	1,206	1,816	1,836
Labor	201	297	354	358
Trade and professional	318	576	786	896
Ideological issue	—	374	1,115	1,259
All other	—	98	197	179
Total	608	2,551	4,268	4,528

Source: Federal Elections Commission, 1998.

Distributing PAC Money   Because PAC contributions are in larger lumps than individual contributions, PAC contributions often attract more attention from members of Congress. PACs are also easier for politicians to deal with because there are far fewer PACs (about 4,000) than voters. The PACs listed in Table 9-8 give millions of dollars each year to finance the campaigns of their potential allies. The single largest distributor of PAC money to political candidates in 1996 was EMILY's List (see *Up Close:* "EMILY's List").

Most PACs use their campaign contributions to acquire access and influence with decision makers. Corporate, trade, and professional PAC contributions go overwhelmingly to incumbents, regardless of party (see Table 9-9 on page 306). Leaders of these PACs know that incumbents are rarely defeated, and they do not wish to antagonize even unsympathetic members of Congress by backing challengers. However, ideological and issue-oriented PACs are more likely to allocate funds according to the candidates' policy positions and voting records. Labor PACs give almost all of their contributions to Democrats. Ideological and issue-oriented PACs give money to challengers as well as incumbents; in recent years, these groups collectively favored Democrats as women's, environmental, abortion rights, and elderly groups proliferated.

The pattern of contributing to congressional incumbents resulted in a shift of contributions from Democrats to Republicans when the GOP took control of both houses of Congress after the 1994 election. PAC money is less important in the Senate than in the House. PAC contributions account for about 35 percent of House campaign contributions; they only account for about 20 percent of Senate campaign contributions. Actually PACs contribute more *dollars* to the average senator than to the average House member. But because Senate campaigns cost so much more than

Table 9-8   The Big-Money PACs

Corporate PACs

American Telephone and Telegraph Co. (AT&T PAC)
Federal Express Corporation PAC (FEPAC)
Team Ameritech (PAC)
Philip Morris (PHIL-PAC)
United Parcel Service (UPSPAC)
Lockheed Martin Employees PAC
Union Pacific Fund for Effective Government

Labor PACs

American Federation of State County & Municipal Employees (PEOPLE PAC)
United Automobile Workers (V-CAP)
Machinists Non-Partisan Political League

Teamsters PAC
International Brotherhood of Electrical Workers
United Food & Commercial Workers (Active Ballot Fund)
Communications Workers of America (CWA-COPE)
United Steel Workers of America
AFL-CIO Committee on Political Education (AFL-CIO COPE)
Letter Carriers PAC

Trade and Professional PACs

Association of Trial Lawyers
National Education Assn.
American Medical Assn.
National Auto Dealers Assn.
American Federation of Teachers
Realtors PAC

American Bankers Assn. (BANKPAC)
American Institute of CPAs
National Association of Life Underwriters
National Association of Home Builders (BUILDPAC)

Ideological and Issue PACs

EMILY's List
National Rifle Association
Political Victory Fund
Women's Campaign Fund
National Committee for an Effective Congress
National Committee to Preserve Social Security and Welfare
National Right to Life PAC
Hollywood Women's PAC

Source: Federal Elections Commission, 1999.

EMILY's List

Fund raising is the greatest obstacle to mounting a successful campaign against an incumbent. And the most difficult problem facing challengers is raising money *early* in the campaign, when they have little name recognition and little or no standing in the polls.

EMILY's List is a politically adroit and effective effort to support liberal Democratic women candidates by infusing *early money* into their campaigns. EMILY stands for Early Money Is Like Yeast, because "it makes the dough rise." Early contributions provide the initial credibility that a candidate, especially a challenger, needs in order to solicit additional funds from individuals and organizations. EMILY is a fund-raising network of thousands of contributors, each of whom pays $100 to join and pledges to give at least $100 to two women from a list of candidates prepared by EMILY's leaders. Most of the contributors are professional women who appreciate EMILY's screening of pro-choice, liberal women candidates around the country. In 1996 EMILY helped distribute more than $9 million among liberal Democratic women candidates for Congress.

EMILY's List was begun by a wealthy heir to a founder of IBM, Ellen Malcolm. Malcolm graduated from Hollins College in Virginia in 1969 and joined the liberal public-interest group Common Cause as a volunteer. She later joined the staff of the National Women's Political Caucus. In 1980 she established her own private foundation, Windom Fund, to channel money to women and minority groups. (She reportedly invented the Windom name to preserve her own anonymity as the benefactor.) She created EMILY's List in 1985.

Women challengers for congressional races traditionally faced frustration in fund raising. Incumbent male officeholders enjoyed a huge fund-raising advantage because contributors expected them to win and therefore opened their wallets to gain access and goodwill. Contributing to women challengers, even by people who supported their views, was often considered a waste of money. EMILY's List has helped to overcome defeatism among both women candidates and contributors.

EMILY's List claims success in electing liberal Democratic women to the U.S. Senate (including Barbara Boxer and Dianne Feinstein, both of California; Mary Landrieu, Louisiana; Blanche Lincoln, Arkansas; Patty Murray, Washington; and Barbara Milkulski, Maryland) as well as over 40 liberal Democratic women House members. EMILY's List was a heavy contributor to Hillary Clinton's campaign for New York's open U.S. Senate seat in 2000.

Senator Barbara Milkulski, Democrat of Maryland and a beneficiary of EMILY's List, at a news conference.

House campaigns, PAC contributions are *proportionally* less. Senators must rely more on individual contributions than House members do.

LOBBYING THE BUREAUCRACY

Lobbying does not cease after a law is passed. Rather, interest groups try to influence the implementation of the law. Interest groups know that bureaucrats exercise considerable discretion in policy implementation (see "Bureaucratic Power" in

Table 9-9 Distribution of PAC Contributions in Congressional Elections

	Percentage of PAC Contributions			
	1997–98	1995–96	1993–94	1989–90
All Candidates				
Incumbents	76%	67%	72%	74%
Challengers	10	15	10	12
Open Seats	14	18	18	14
Senate				
Democrats	40	35	50	57
Republicans	51	65	50	43
House				
Democrats	40	50	67	67
Republicans	51	50	33	33

Source: Federal Elections Commission, 1999.

Chapter 12). Thus many interests spend as much or more time and energy trying to influence executive agencies than Congress.

Lobbying the bureaucracy involves various types of activities, including monitoring regulatory agencies for notices of new rules and regulatory changes; providing reports, testimony, and evidence in administrative hearings; submitting contract and grant applications and lobbying for their acceptance; and monitoring the performance of executive agencies on behalf of group members. Groups may try to influence the creation of a new agency to carry out the law or influence the assignment of implementation to an existing "friendly" agency. They may try to influence the selection of personnel to head the implementing agency. They may lobby the agency to devote more money and personnel to enforcement of the law (or less, depending on a group's preference). They may argue for strict rules and regulations—or loose interpretations of the law—by the implementing agencies. Lobbyists frequently appear at administrative hearings to offer information. They often undertake to sponsor test cases of administrative regulations on behalf of affected members. In short, lobbying extends throughout the government.[8]

Iron Triangles   In general, interest groups strive to maintain close working relationships with the departments and agencies that serve their members or regulate their industries. Conversely, bureaucracies seek to nourish relationships with powerful "client" groups that are capable of pressuring Congress to expand their authority and increase their budgets. Both bureaucracies and interest groups seek close working relationships with the congressional committees that exercise jurisdictions over their policy function. Finally, members of Congress seek the political and financial support of powerful interest groups, and members also seek to influence bureaucrats to favor supportive interest groups.

The mutual interests of congressional committee members, organized groups, and bureaucratic agencies come together to form what has been labeled the "iron triangles" of American government. **Iron triangles** refer to stable relationships among interest groups, congressional committees, and administrative agencies functioning in the same policy area. Each of the three sides of these triangles depends

iron triangles   Mutually supportive relationships among interest groups, government agencies, and legislative committees with jurisdiction over a specific policy area.

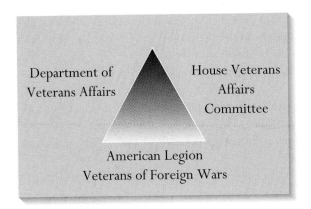

FIGURE 9-2 Iron Triangles

The iron triangle approach provides a convenient way to look at the interrelationship among interest groups, executive agencies, and congressional committees. As this example shows, veterans' interest groups work closely with both the Department of Veterans Affairs (executive agency) and the House Veterans Affairs Committee.

on the support of the other two; their cooperation serves their own interests (see Figure 9-2).

In an iron triangle, bureaucracies, interest groups, and congressional committees "scratch each other's back." Bureaucrats get political support from interest groups in their requests for expanded power and authority and increased budgetary allocations. Interest groups get favorable treatment of their members by the bureaucracy. Congressional committee members get political and financial support from interest groups, as well as favorable treatment for their constituents and contributors who are served or regulated by the bureaucracy.

Iron triangles are more likely to develop in specialized policy areas over which there is relatively little internal conflict.[9] However, conflict, rather than cooperation, is more likely to characterize bureaucratic–congressional–interest-group relationships when powerful, diverse interests are at stake. For example, the Occupational Safety and Health Administration is caught between the demands of labor unions and industry groups. The U.S. Forest Service is caught between the demands of environmental groups and the lumber industry. The Environmental Protection Agency is pressured by environmental groups as well as by industry and agriculture. These kinds of conflicts break open the iron triangles or prevent them from forming in the first place.

Policy Networks Generally, we think of American government in terms of the separate branches—Congress, the president and the bureaucracy, and the courts—with interest groups portrayed as external to government itself. But it is also possible to envision government as a series of **policy networks**—interactions in a common policy area among interest-group leaders and lobbyists, members of Congress and their staff personnel, executive agency officials, lawyers and consultants, foundation and think tank people, and even reporters and journalists assigned to the field. Policy networks develop among people who share some knowledge and interest in a policy field—for example, weapons procurement, housing, environment, transportation, or energy—and who regularly interact with each other in the policy arena. Policy networks may include people who differ strongly with each other as well as people who share similar views. What they have in common is their policy expertise and regular interaction. They can participate in negotiations and reach compromises as well as try to outwit and outmaneuver each other.

Revolving Doors It is not uncommon in Washington for people in a policy network to switch jobs, moving from a post in the government to a job in the

policy networks Interaction in a common policy area among lobbyists, elected officials, staff personnel, bureaucrats, journalists, and private-sector experts.

private sector, or vice versa, or moving to different posts within the government. In one example, an individual might move from a job in a corporation (Pillsbury or General Mills) to the staff of an interest group (American Farm Bureau Federation), and then to the executive agency charged with implementing policy in the field (U.S. Department of Agriculture) or to the staff of a House or Senate committee with jurisdiction over the field (House Agricultural Committee or Senate Agriculture, Nutrition, and Forestry Committee). The common currency of moves within a network is both policy expertise and contacts within the field.

The term **revolving doors** is often used to criticize people who move from a government post (where they acquired experience, knowledge, and personal contacts) to a job in the private sector as a consultant, lobbyist, or salesperson. Defense contractors may recruit high-ranking military officers or Defense Department officials to help sell weapons to their former employers. Trade associations may recruit congressional staffers, White House staffers, or high-ranking agency heads as lobbyists, or these people may leave government service to start their own lobbying firms. Attorneys from the Justice Department, the Internal Revenue Service, and federal regulatory agencies may be recruited by Washington law firms to represent clients in dealings with their former employers. Following retirement, many members of Congress turn to lobbying their former colleagues.

Concern about revolving doors centers not only on individuals cashing in on their knowledge, experience, and contacts obtained through government employment, but also on the possibility that some government officials will be tempted to tilt their decisions in favor of corporations, law firms, or interest groups that promise these officials well-paid jobs after they leave government employment (see *What Do You Think?* "Is It What You Know or Who You Know?").

The Ethics in Government Act limits postgovernment employment in an effort to reduce the potential for corruption. Former members of Congress are not permitted to lobby Congress for one year after leaving that body. Former employees of executive agencies are not permitted to lobby their agency for one year after leaving government service, and they are not permitted to lobby their agency for two years on any matter over which they had any responsibility while employed by the government.

LOBBYING THE COURTS

Interest groups play an important role in influencing federal courts. Many of the key cases brought to the federal courts are initiated by interest groups. Indeed, **litigation** is becoming a favored instrument of interest-group politics. Groups that oppose a new law or an agency's action often challenge it in court as unconstitutional or as violating the law. Interest groups bring issues to the courts by (1) supplying the attorneys for individuals who are parties to a case; (2) bringing suits to the courts on behalf of classes of citizens; or (3) filing companion **amicus curiae** (literally "friend of the court") arguments in cases in which they are interested.

The nation's most powerful interest groups all have legal divisions specializing in these techniques. The American Civil Liberties Union is one of the most active federal court litigants on behalf of criminal defendants (see *Up Close:* "Politics and the ACLU" in Chapter 14). The early civil rights strategy of the National Association for the Advancement of Colored People (NAACP) was directed by its Legal

revolving doors The movement of individuals from government positions to jobs in the private sector, using the experience, knowledge, and contacts they acquired in government employment.

litigation Legal dispute brought before a court.

amicus curiae Person or group other than the defendant or the plaintiff or the prosecution that submits an argument in a case for the court's consideration.

Is It What You Know or Who You Know?

A majority of paid lobbyists in Washington come to their jobs from government. The "revolving door" complaint is that these people exploit their government experience for private gain. A survey of Washington lobbyists revealed that 55 percent had held some government position before becoming a lobbyist. More had worked in the executive branch than in Congress, and a few had worked in both branches of government. Full-time staff lobbyists for interest groups had somewhat less government experience than independent lawyer lobbyists (78 percent of whom had government experience) and professional lobbying consultants (62 percent of whom had government experience).

How helpful is this experience, and, more important, is it "what you know" or "who you know" that counts most in lobbying? The "good old boy" theory of lobbying suggests that success depends mostly on contacts with officials, knowing them personally and maintaining warm relations with them, so that when they are asked to do something, they are most likely to respond favorably. But the knowledge theory of lobbying suggests that success is more a product of (1) knowledge about legislative and bureaucratic processes; and (2) substantive policy expertise.

When lobbyists themselves are asked questions on this topic, they acknowledge that government experience is important in lobbying (see table). Some 87 percent of lobbyists reported that their time in government was helpful in their present work; 80 percent said that it helped them to gain familiarity with the policy-making process; and 70 percent reported that it gave them familiarity with the issues. Government experience is also helpful in making contacts with decision makers. Contacts made through congressional experience appear to be more important than contacts made through executive branch experience. But, according to the lobbyists themselves, "what you know" is more important than "who you know."

Helpfulness of Government

	Responses by Lobbyists with Congressional Experience	Responses by Lobbyists with Executive Experience
Government experience provides:		
Issue familiarity	72%	72%
Knowledge of decision-making process	92	81
Contacts in administration	48	53
Contacts in Congress	87	49

Source: Derived from Robert H. Salisbury et al., "Who You Know versus What You Know: The Uses of Government Experience for Washington Lobbyists," *American Journal of Political Science* 33 (February 1989): 175–195.

Defense and Education Fund under the leadership of Thurgood Marshall (see *People in Politics:* "Thurgood Marshall" in Chapter 15). The NAACP chose to sponsor a suit by Linda Brown against the Board of Education in her hometown—Topeka, Kansas—in order to win the historic 1954 desegregation decision.[10] The National Abortion Rights Action League (NARAL) is active in sponsoring legal challenges to abortion restrictions. The Environmental Defense Fund and the Natural Resources Defense Council specialize in environmental litigation.

The special rules of judicial decision making preclude direct lobbying of judges by interest groups (see "The Special Rules of Judicial Decision Making" in Chapter 13). Directly contacting federal judges about a case, letter writing, telephoning, and demonstrating outside of federal courtrooms are all considered inappropriate conduct. They inspire more resentment than support among federal judges. However, interest groups have been very active in direct lobbying of Congress over judicial appointments. Key interest groups supporting abortion rights—the National Abortion Rights Action League, People for the American Way, the National Organization for Women, and so on—have played a central role in confirmation battles (see *Up Close:* "The Confirmation of Clarence Thomas" in Chapter 13).

POLITICS AS INTEREST-GROUP CONFLICT

Politics can be viewed as a struggle among interest groups over government policy. Interest groups, rather than individual citizens, can be viewed as the principal participants in American politics.

Pluralism as Democratic Politics Pluralism (see Chapter 2) is the idea that democracy can be preserved in a large, complex society through individual membership in interest groups that compete, bargain, and compromise over government policy. Individuals are influential in politics only when they act as part of, or on behalf of, groups. (Only leaders of organizations participate directly in policy making.) The group becomes the essential bridge between the individual and the government. Pluralists argue that interest-group politics is a natural extension of the democratic ideals of popular participation in government, freedom of association, and competition over public policy.

Pluralism portrays public policy at any given time as the equilibrium reached in the struggle among interest groups to influence policy (see Figure 9-3). This equilibrium is determined by the relative influence of interest groups. Changes in the relative influence of any interest group can be expected to result in changes in public policy; policy will move in the direction desired by the groups gaining in influence and away from the desires of groups losing influence.

According to this view of political life, government plays a passive role, merely "refereeing" group struggles. Public policy at any given moment represents the "equilibrium" point of the group pressures—the balance of competing interests. The job of politicians is to function as brokers of group interests, arranging compromises and balancing interests.

Balancing Group Power Pluralism assumes that compromises *can* be arranged and that interests *can* be balanced in relatively stable fashion. It assumes that no single interest will ever become so dominant that it can reject compromise and proceed to impose its will on the nation without regard for the interests of other people. This assumption is based on several beliefs. The first is that interest groups act as a check on each other and that a system of *countervailing power* will protect the interests of all. For example, the power of big business will be checked by the countervailing power of big labor and big government.

A second belief is that *overlapping group membership* will tend to moderate the demands of particular groups and lead to compromise. Because no group can command the undivided loyalty of all its members, its demands will be less drastic

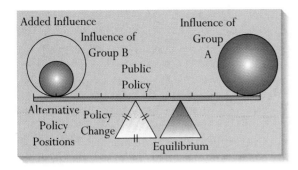

FIGURE 9-3 The Interest-Group Model

According to pluralist theorists, policy in a democracy is the result of various special-interest groups "reaching equilibrium"—arriving at a compromise position that requires all parties to give up something but gives all parties something they wanted.

and its leaders more amenable to compromise. If the leaders of any group go too far with their demands, those of its members who also belong to other groups endangered by these immoderate demands will balk.

A third belief is that radical programs and doctrinaire demands will be checked by the large, unorganized, but potentially significant *latent interest group* that is composed of all Americans who believe in toleration, compromise, and democratic processes.

Interest-Group Politics: How Democratic?   There are several problems with accepting pluralism as the legitimate heir to classic democratic theory. Democratic theory envisions public policy as the rational choice of individuals with equal influence who evaluate their needs and reach a majority decision with due regard for the rights of others. This traditional theory does not view public policy as a product of interest-group pressures. In fact, classic democratic theorists viewed interest groups and even political parties as intruders into an individualistic brand of citizenship and politics. Today critics of pluralism charge that interest groups dominate the political arena, monopolize access to governmental power, and thereby restrict individual participation rather than enhance it.

Pluralism contends that different groups of leaders make decisions about different issues, but critics charge that these leaders do not necessarily compete with each other. Rather, groups of leaders often allow other groups of leaders to govern their own spheres of influence without interference. Accommodation, rather than competition, may be the prevailing style of leadership interaction: "You scratch my back, and I'll scratch yours."

Another assumption of pluralism is that group membership enhances the individual's influence on policy. But only rarely are interest groups democratically governed. Individuals may provide the numerical strength for organizations, but interest groups are usually run by a small elite of officers and activists. Leaders of corporations, banks, labor unions, medical associations, and bar associations—whose views and agendas often differ from those of their membership—remain in control year after year. Very few people attend meetings, vote in organizational elections, or make their influence felt within their organization.

Finally, pluralists hope that the power of diverse institutions and organizations in society will roughly balance out and prevent the emergence of a power monopoly. Yet inequality of power among organizations is commonplace. Examples abound of narrow, organized interests achieving their goals at the expense of the broader, unorganized public. Furthermore, producer interests, bound together by economic ties, usually dominate less well-organized consumer groups and groups based on noneconomic interests. Special interests seeking governmental subsidies, payments,

Twenty-First Century Directions

As James Madison observed in 1787, "factions" arise from human nature—"a zeal for different opinions concerning religion, concerning government, and many other points"—and they will never be eliminated from politics in a democracy. And modern technology—from computerized targeting of citizens for mailings, to the proliferation of Internet "org" addresses—promises to multiply and empower "factions" throughout the twenty-first century.

⬆ The number and diversity of interest groups will continue to expand. Indeed, the Internet enables ever more specialized groups of people to form themselves into active organizations. Anyone who can build a WebSite has the potential to create an organization and press its demands upon government. Interest group entrepreneurs will vastly expand the number of dot-org addresses.

⬇ Technological developments are driving down the costs of communication and organization. Among the principal beneficiaries of these lowered costs will be *non*economic interest groups—ideological groups, public interest groups, single issue groups.

⬅➡ Nonetheless, economic interests will continue to play the dominant role in American politics. Corporations, trade associations, and labor unions (notably public employee unions) have more financial resources to support their lobbying efforts than noneconomic groups. PACs will continue to be a major source of campaign financing, although the more rapid growth of soft money may reduce the overall percentage of campaign funds coming from PACs.

⬇ Attempts to "reform" the interest group system may bring about marginal changes in tactics, but major reforms are doomed to failure. Even in the unlikely event that Congress would outlaw PACs, organized interests would find other ways to channel money into politics. Any effort to outlaw political participation, or even political campaign expenditures by interest groups, would run afoul of the Constitution's First Amendment guarantee of the right "to assemble and petition the government for redress of grievances."

⬇ Over time, the accumulation of special protections, privileges, subsidies, quotas, and treatments by the multitude of interest groups will prove costly to society. Interest groups supporting government regulation of various aspects of American life—on the job, at the store, in the home—will succeed in increasingly entangling people in red tape, wasted time, legal fees, and litigation. The inefficiencies created by this accumulation of special interest privileges and protections will prevent the American people from achieving the standard of living that they might otherwise enjoy. Their only comfort may come from knowing that things are worse in other countries.

and "entitlements" regularly prevail over the broader yet unorganized interests of taxpayers.

Interest-Group Politics: Gridlock and Paralysis Even if the pluralists are correct that the public interest is only the equilibrium of special-interest claims, some consensus among major interest groups is required if government is to function at all. Democracies require a sense of community and common purpose among the people. If the demands of special interests displace the public interest, government cannot function effectively. Uncompromising claims by conflicting special interests create policy *gridlock*. Yet if politicians try to placate every special interest, the result is confusing, contradictory, and muddled policy—or worse, no policy at all.

Interest-group paralysis and the resulting inability of government to act decisively to resolve national problems weaken popular confidence in government. "The function of government is to govern. A weak government, a government which lacks authority, fails to perform its function, is immoral in the same sense in which a corrupt judge, a cowardly soldier, or an ignorant teacher, is immoral."[11]

Over time, the continued buildup of special protections, privileges, and treatments in society results in "institutional sclerosis." Economist Mancur Olson argues that the accumulation of special interest subsidies, quotas, and protections leads to economic stagnation. Interest groups focus on gaining distributive advantages—a larger share of the pie for themselves—rather than on growth of the whole economy—a larger pie.[12] Major interest groups are more interested in winning income transfers to themselves through government action than in promoting the growth of national income. The more entrenched the interest-group system becomes, the slower the growth of the national economy.

SUMMARY NOTES

- Organizations concentrate power, and concentrated power prevails over diffused power. Interest groups are organizations that seek to influence government policy.

- The interest-group system supplements the electoral system as a form of representation. The electoral system is designed to respond to broad, majority preferences in geographically defined constituencies. The interest-group system represents narrower, minority interests in economic, professional, ideological, religious, racial, gender, and issue constituencies.

- Interest groups originated to protect economic interests, to advance social movements, to seek government benefits, and to respond to government activity. As government has expanded into more sectors of American life, more interest groups have formed to influence government policy.

- Washington lobbying groups represent a wide array of organized interests. But business, trade, and professional associations outnumber labor union, women's, public-interest, single-issue, and ideological groups.

- Interest-group formation has been aided in recent decades by entrepreneurs who create and build group memberships. They urge people to join organizations either by appealing to their sense of oblig-ation or by providing an array of direct tangible benefits.

- Most organized groups are dominated by small groups of leaders and activists. Few groups are governed democratically; members who oppose the direction of the organization usually drop out rather than challenge the leadership. Group membership and especially group leadership overrepresent educated, upper-middle-class segments of the population.

- Lobbying activities include advertising and public relations, obtaining access to government officials, providing them with technical and political information, mobilizing constituents, building coalitions, organizing demonstrations, and providing campaign support. Bribery is illegal, and most lobbyists avoid exacting specific vote promises in exchange for campaign contributions.

- Organized political action committees (PACs) proliferated following the 1974 "reform" of campaign finance laws. Most PAC money goes to incumbents; interest-group leaders know that incumbents are rarely defeated.

- The mutual interests of organized groups, congressional committees, and bureaucratic agencies sometimes come together to form "iron triangles" of mutual support and cooperation in specific policy areas. In many policy areas, loose "policy networks" emerge among people who share an interest and expertise—although not necessarily opinions—about a policy and are in regular contact with each other.

- The "revolving door" problem emerges when individuals use the knowledge, experience, and contacts obtained through government employment to secure high-paying jobs with corporations, law firms, lobbying and consulting firms, and interest groups doing business with their old agencies.

- Interest groups influence the nation's courts not only by providing financial and legal support for issues of concern to them but also by lobbying Congress over judicial appointments.

- Pluralism views interest-group activities as a form of democratic representation. According to the pluralists, public policy reflects the equilibrium of group influence and a reasonable approximation of society's preferences. Competition among groups, overlapping group memberships, and latent interest groups all combine to ensure that no single group dominates the system.

- Critics of pluralism warn that interest groups may monopolize power and restrict individual participation in politics rather than enhance it. They note that interest groups are not usually democratically governed, nor are their leaders or members representative of the general population. They warn that accommodation rather than competition may characterize group interaction and that narrow producer interests tend to achieve their goals at the expense of broader consumer (taxpayer) interests.

- The growing power of special interests, when combined with the declining power of parties and the fragmentation of government, may lead to gridlock and paralysis in policy making. The general public interest may be lost in the conflicting claims of special interests.

KEY TERMS

SELECTED READINGS

BERRY, JEFFREY M. *The Interest Group Society.* White Plains, N.Y.: Longman, 1997. An overview of lobbying in all three branches of government as well as grass-roots lobbying, within the context of democratic (Madisonian) theory.

BERRY, JEFFREY M. *The New Liberalism: The Rising Power of Citizen Groups.* Washington, D.C.: Brookings Institution Press, 1999. A description of the increasing number and activities of liberal interest groups in Washington and their success in defeating both business and conservative groups.

CIGLER, ALLAN J., and BURDETT A. LOOMIS, EDS. *Interest Group Politics.* 5th ed. Washington, D.C.: Congressional Quarterly Press, 1998. A collection of essays examining interest-group politics.

HREBENAR, RONALD J. *Interest Group Politics in America.* 3rd ed. New York: M. E. Sharpe, 1996. A concise, readable, and timely introduction to the study of group power.

LOWI, THEODORE J. *The End of Liberalism.* New York: Norton, 1969. The classic critique of "interest-group liberalism," describing how special interests contribute to the growth of government and the development of "clientism."

MAHOOD, H. R. *Interest Groups in American National Politics.* Upper Saddle River, N.J.: Prentice Hall, 2000. Comprehensive text covering the organization of interests, lobbying Congress, the executive, and the courts, PAC infulence, and pluralist theory.

OLSON, MANCUR. *The Logic of Collective Action.* Cambridge, Mass.: Harvard University Press, 1965. A highly theoretical inquiry into the benefits and costs to individuals of joining groups and the obstacles (including the free-rider problem) to forming organized interest groups.

OLSON, MANCUR. *The Rise and Decline of Nations.* New Haven, Conn.: Yale University Press, 1982. Argues that, over time, the development of powerful special-interest lobbies has led to institutional sclerosis, inefficiency, and slowed economic growth.

SCHLOZMAN, KAY LEHMANN, and JOHN T. TIERNEY. *Organized Interests and American Democracy.* New York: Harper & Row, 1986. Comprehensive examination of interest groups in American politics, with original survey data from Washington lobbyists.

WOLPE, BRUCE E., and BERTRAM J. LEVINE. *Lobbying Congress.* 2nd ed. Washington, D.C.: CQ Press, 1996. A practical guide to lobbying on Capitol Hill written by experienced lobbyists.

Congress
Politics on Capitol Hill

ASK YOURSELF ABOUT POLITICS

1 Should members of Congress be limited in the number of terms they can serve?
Yes ⬤   No ⬤

2 Should congressional districts be drawn to ensure that minorities win seats in Congress in rough proportion to their populations in the states?
Yes ⬤   No ⬤

3 Should a party's candidates for Congress across the country join together and pledge to support specific policy positions?
Yes ⬤   No ⬤

4 Would the nation be better served if the president and the majority Congress were from the same party?
Yes ⬤   No ⬤

5 Is it ethical for Congress members to pay special attention to requests for assistance by people who make large campaign contributions?
Yes ⬤   No ⬤

6 Are there too many lawyers in Congress?
Yes ⬤   No ⬤

7 Are members of Congress obliged to vote the way their constituents wish, even if they personally disagree?
Yes ⬤   No ⬤

THE POWERS OF CONGRESS

James Madison argued that the control of "faction" was "the principal task of modern legislation."[1] He meant that in enacting laws, legislators were really balancing interests, finding compromises, and resolving conflicts. Public policies—laws, regulations, and budgets—represent temporary balances of power among conflicting interests. As the relative power of these interests changes over time, new laws, amendments, and increases or decreases in funding will be enacted, reflecting new balances of power.

Constitutional Powers The Constitution gives very broad powers to Congress. "All legislative Powers herein granted shall be vested in a Congress of the United States, which shall consist of a Senate and House of Representatives." The nation's Founders envisioned Congress as the first and most powerful branch of government. They equated national powers with the powers of Congress and gave Congress the most clearly specified role in national government (see Table 10–1 on page 318).

Article I empowers Congress to levy taxes, borrow and spend money, regulate interstate commerce, establish a national money supply, establish a post office, declare war, raise and support an army and navy, establish a court system, and pass all laws "necessary and proper" to implement these powers. Congress may also propose amendments to the Constitution or call a convention to do so. Congress admits new states. In the event that no presidential candidate receives a majority of votes in the Electoral College, the House of Representatives selects the president. The

Who are the members of Congress? How did they get there, and how do they manage to stay there? How did Congress—the official institution for deciding who gets what in America—get its powers, and how does it use them?

Table 10-1 | Constitutional Powers of Congress

Powers of Both House and Senate	Powers of House Only	Powers of Senate Only
• Appropriate money • Authorize borrowing }"Power of the purse" • Levy taxes • Regulate currency and punish counterfeiting • Establish post office and post roads • Make bankruptcy laws • Regulate interstate and foreign commerce • Establish rules of naturalization • Fix weights and measures • Make patent and copyright law • Provide for government of District of Columbia • Admit new states • Establish lower federal courts • Propose amendments to the Constitution • Declare war • Raise and support military forces } War-making powers • Provide for militia • "Make all laws which shall be necessary and proper for carrying into Execution the foregoing Powers, and all other powers vested by this Constitution in the Government of the United States" } Implied powers	• Originate tax bills • Bring impeachment charges	• Advise and consent to (ratify) treaties • Confirm appointments to Supreme Court and federal judiciary, ambassador, cabinet, and other high executive posts • Try impeachments

Senate is called on for "advice and consent" to treaties and confirms presidential nominations to executive and judicial posts. The House has the power to impeach, and the Senate to try, any officer of the U.S. government, including the president. Each **congressional session** convenes on January 3 following congressional elections in November of even-numbered years.

Institutional Conflict   Over two centuries, the separate branches of the national government—the Congress, the presidency and the executive branch, and the Supreme Court and federal judiciary—have struggled for power and preeminence in governing. This struggle for power among the separate institutions is precisely what the Founders envisioned. In writing the Constitution, they sought to create "opposite and rival interests" among the separate branches of the national government. "The constant aim," explained Madison, "is to divide and arrange the several offices in such a manner as that each may be a check on the other"[2] (see Appendix, *Federalist Papers*, No. 51). From time to time, first the Congress, then the presidency, and occasionally the Supreme Court have appeared to become the most powerful branch of government.

Throughout much of the twentieth century, Congress ceded leadership in national policy making to the president and the executive branch. Congress largely responded to the policy initiatives and spending requests originating from the president, executive agencies, and interest groups. Congress did not merely ratify or "rubber-stamp"

congressional session   Each Congress elected in November of even-numbered years meets the following January 3 and remains in session for two years. Since the first Congress to meet under the Constitution in 1789, Congresses have been numbered by session (for example, 106th Congress 1999–2001, 107th Congress 2001–03, 108th Congress 2003–2005).

Henry Hyde, Chair of the Republican-controlled House Judiciary Committee, presides over the Clinton impeachment hearings in December 1998. Rep. John Conyers (right), the ranking Democrat on the Committee, disapproved of the Committee's party-line impeachment vote.

these initiatives and requests; it played an independent role in the policy-making process. But this role was essentially a deliberative one, in which Congress accepted, modified, amended, or rejected the policies and budget requests initiated by others.

It is easier for the Congress to obstruct the policy initiatives of the president than it is to assume policy leadership itself. Congress can defeat presidential policy proposals, deny presidential budget requests, delay or reject presidential appointments, investigate executive agencies, hold committee hearings to spotlight improprieties, and generally immobilize the executive branch. It can investigate and question nominees for the Supreme Court and the federal judiciary; it can legislate changes in the jurisdiction of the federal courts; and it can try to reverse court decisions by amending laws or the Constitution itself. The Congress can even threaten to impeach the president or federal judges. But these are largely reactive, obstructionist actions, usually accompanied by a great deal of oratory.

From time to time, however, Congress has attempted to reassert national leadership. This effort was especially obvious in the 104th Congress, elected in 1994 and controlled by Republicans for the first time in forty years. The House of Representatives, under former Speaker Newt Gingrich, undertook to set the nation's policy agenda in a "Contract with America" that included term limits for Congress members, a balanced budget amendment to the Constitution, tax cuts, and welfare reform. But most of the promises in this contract failed to pass and some were vetoed by the president. The important institutional lesson was that the Congress occasionally tries to seize the policy initiative, but, over the long term, national leadership and policy initiative remain with the president.

Dividing Congressional Power: House and Senate

Congress must not only share national power with the executive and judicial branches of government; it must share power within itself. The framers of the Constitution took the advice of the nation's eldest diplomat, Benjamin Franklin: "It is not enough that your legislature should be numerous; it should also be divided. . . . One division should watch over and control the other, supply its wants, correct its blunders, and cross its designs, should they be criminal or erroneous."[3] Accordingly, the U.S. Congress is **bicameral**—composed of two houses (see Figure 10–1).

bicameral Any legislative body that consists of two separate chambers or houses; in the United States, the Senate represents 50 statewide voter constituencies, and the House of Representatives represents voters in 435 separate districts.

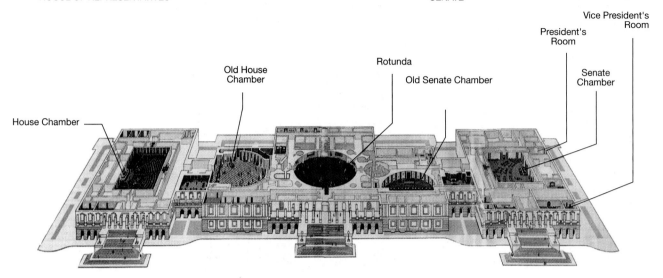

FIGURE 10–1   Corridors of Power in Congress

The architecture and floor plan of the Capitol Building in Washington reflect the bicameral division of Congress, with one wing for the House of Representatives and one for the Senate.

No law can be passed and no money can be spent unless both the House of Representatives and the Senate pass identical laws. Yet the House and the Senate have very different constituencies and terms. The House consists of 435 voting members, elected from districts within each state apportioned on the basis of equal population. (The average congressional district since the 1990 census has a population of 571,700; the House also includes nonvoting delegates from Puerto Rico, the District of Columbia, Guam, the Virgin Islands, and American Samoa.) All House members face election every two years. The Senate consists of 100 members serving six-year terms, elected by statewide constituencies. Senate terms are staggered so that one-third of senators are elected every two years (see Table 10–2).

The House of Representatives, with its two-year terms, was designed to be more responsive to the popular mood. Representatives are fond of referring to their chamber as "the people's House," and the Constitution requires that all revenue-raising bills originate in the House. The Senate was designed to be a smaller, more deliberative body, with its members serving six-year terms. Indeed, the Senate is the more prestigious body. House members frequently give up their seats to run for the Senate; the reverse has seldom occurred. Moreover, the Senate exercises certain powers not given to the House: the power to ratify treaties and the power to confirm federal judges, ambassadors, cabinet members, and other high executive officials.

Domestic versus Foreign and Defense Policy   Congress is more powerful in domestic than in foreign and military affairs. It is freer to reject presidential initiatives in domestic policy areas such as welfare, health, education, the environment, and taxation. But Congress usually follows presidential leadership in foreign and defense policy even though constitutionally the president and Congress share power in these arenas. The president is "Commander-in-Chief" of the armed forces, but only Congress can "declare war." The president appoints and receives ambassadors and "makes treaties," but the Senate must confirm appointments and

Table 10-2 Comparing the House and Senate

	House of Representatives	Senate
Terms	Two years	Six years
Members	435	100
Elections	All every two years	One-third every two years
Constituencies	Congressional districts	States
Unique powers	Originate tax bills Bring impeachment charges	Advise and consent to (ratify) treaties by two-thirds vote Confirm appointments Try impeachment charges
Debate on bills	Limited by Rules Committee	Unlimited, except by unanimous consent or vote of cloture (three-fifths)
Member prestige	Modest; smaller personal staffs, fewer committee assignments	High; larger personal staffs, more committee assignments, always addressed as "Senator"
Leadership	Hierarchical, with speaker, majority and minority leaders and whips, and committees, especially Rules, concentrating power	Less hierarchical, with each senator exercising more influence on leadership, committees, and floor votes
Committees	Twenty standing and select committees Each member on about five committees Difficult to bypass	Twenty standing and select committees Each member on about seven committees Easier to bypass

provide "advice and consent" to treaties. Historically presidents have led the nation in matters of war and peace. Presidents have sent U.S. troops beyond the borders of the United States in military actions on more than two hundred occasions. In contrast, Congress has formally declared war only five times: the War of 1812, the Mexican War in 1846, the Spanish-American War in 1898, World War I in 1917, and World War II in 1941. Congress did not declare war in the Korean War (1950–53), the Vietnam War (1965–73), or the Persian Gulf War (1991).

The Vietnam experience inspired Congress to try to reassert its powers over war and peace. Military embarrassment, prolonged and indecisive fighting, and accumulating casualties—all vividly displayed on national television—encouraged Congress to challenge presidential war-making power. The War Powers Act of 1973, passed over the veto of President Richard Nixon, who was weakened by the Watergate scandal, sought to curtail the president's power to commit U.S. military forces to combat (see "Commander-in-Chief" in Chapter 11). But this act has not proven effective, and both Republican and Democratic presidents have continued to exercise war-making powers.

The Power of the Purse Congress's real power in both domestic and foreign (defense) policy centers on its **power of the purse**—its power over federal taxing and spending. Only Congress can "lay and collect Taxes, Duties, Imposts and Excises" (Article I, Section 8), and only Congress can authorize spending: "No

power of the purse
Congress's exclusive, constitutional power to authorize expenditures by all agencies of the federal government.

Money shall be drawn from the Treasury, but in Consequence of Appropriations made by Law" (Article I, Section 9).

Congress jealously guards these powers. Presidents initiate taxing and spending policies by sending their budgets to the Congress each year (see "The Bureaucracy and the Budgetary Process" in Chapter 12 for details). But Congress has the last word on taxing and spending. The most important bills that Congress considers each year are usually the budget resolutions setting ceilings on various categories of expenditures and the later appropriations bills authorizing specific expenditures. It is often in these appropriations bills that Congress exercises its greatest influence over national policy. Thus, for example, the Congress's involvement in foreign affairs centers on its annual consideration of appropriations for foreign aid, its involvement in military affairs centers on its annual deliberations over the defense appropriations bill, and so on.

Oversight of the Bureaucracy Congressional **oversight** of the federal bureaucracy is a continuing process by which Congress reviews the activities of the executive branch. The *formal* rationale of oversight is to determine whether the purposes of laws passed by Congress are being achieved by executive agencies and whether appropriations established by Congress are being spent as intended. Often the *real* purpose is to influence executive branch decisions, secure favorable treatment for friends and constituents, embarrass presidential appointees, undercut political support for particular programs or agencies, lay the political groundwork for budgetary increases or decreases for an agency, or simply enhance the power of congressional committees and subcommittees and those who chair them.

Oversight is carried out primarily through congressional committees and subcommittees. Individual senators and representatives can engage in a form of oversight simply by writing or calling executive agencies, but committees and their staffs carry on the bulk of oversight activity. Because committees and subcommittees specialize in particular areas of policy making, each tends to focus its oversight activities on particular executive departments and agencies. Oversight is particularly intense during budget hearings. Subcommittees of both the House and the Senate Appropriations Committees are especially interested in how money is being spent by the agencies they oversee.

Oversight often begins when special-interest groups or constituents complain about bureaucratic performance. Minor complaints can be resolved by members of Congress or their staffs contacting the executive agency involved, but executive officials may also be called to a congressional committee or subcommittee hearing to explain and defend their actions. Sitting before a hostile congressional committee in the glare of television cameras and responding to unfriendly questions can be embarrassing and unpleasant. Thus, executive officials have a powerful motivation to comply with the wishes of a member of Congress and escape such treatment.

Agenda Setting and Media Attention **Congressional hearings** and investigations often involve agenda setting—bringing issues to the public's attention and placing them on the national agenda. For agenda-setting purposes, congressional committees or subcommittees need the assistance of the media. Televised hearings and investigations are perhaps the most effective means by which Congress can attract attention to issues as well as to itself and its members.

oversight Congressional monitoring of the activities of executive branch agencies to determine if the laws are being faithfully executed.

congressional hearings Congressional committee sessions in which members listen to witnesses who provide information and opinions on matters of interest to the committee, including pending legislation.

Hearings and investigations are similar in some ways, but hearings are usually held on a specific bill in order to build a record of both technical information (what is the problem and how legislation might be crafted to resolve it) and political information (who favors and who opposes various legislative options). In contrast, investigations are held on alleged misdeeds or scandals. Although the U.S. Supreme Court has held that there must be some "legislative purpose" behind a **congressional investigation**, that phrase has been interpreted very broadly indeed.[4]

The *formal* rationale for congressional investigations is that Congress is seeking information to assist in its lawmaking function. But from the earliest Congress to the present, the investigating powers of Congress have often been used for political purposes: to rally popular support for policies or programs favored by Congress; to attack the president, other high officials in the administration, or presidential policies or programs; to focus media attention and public debate on particular issues; or simply to win media coverage and popular recognition for members of Congress. Congressional investigators have the legal power to subpoena witnesses (force them to appear), administer oaths, compel testimony, and initiate criminal charges for contempt (refusing to cooperate) and perjury (lying). These powers can be exercised by Congress's regular committees and subcommittees and by committees appointed especially to conduct a particular investigation.

Congress cannot impose criminal punishments as a result of its investigations. (This would be a *bill of attainder* forbidden by Article I, Section 9 of the Constitution.) But the information uncovered in a congressional investigation can be turned over to the U.S. Department of Justice, which may proceed with its own criminal investigation and perhaps indictment and trial of alleged wrongdoers in federal courts.

Congressional investigations have long been used as an opportunity for Congress to expose wrongdoing on the part of executive branch officials. The first congressional investigation (1792) examined why General Arthur St. Clair had been defeated by the Indians in Ohio; the Crédit Mobilier investigations (1872–73) revealed scandals in the Grant Administration; the Select Committee on Campaign Practices, known universally as the "Watergate Committee," exposed the activities of President Richard Nixon's inner circle that led to impeachment charges and Nixon's forced resignation; a House and Senate Joint Select Committee conducted the Iran-contra investigation in the Reagan Administration; the Senate Special Whitewater Committee investigated matters related to Bill and Hillary Clinton's real estate investments in Arkansas.

Impeachment and Removal Potentially Congress's most formidable power is that of impeaching and removing from office the president, other officers of the United States, and federal judges, including Supreme Court justices. Congress can do so only for "Treason, Bribery or other High Crimes and Misdemeanors." The House of Representatives has the sole authority to bring charges of impeachment by a simple majority vote. Impeachment is analogous to a criminal indictment; it does not remove an officer but merely subjects him or her to trial by the Senate. Only the Senate, following a trial, can remove the federal official from office, and then only by a two-thirds vote.

Bill Clinton is the second president in the nation's history to be impeached by the U.S. House of Representative. (Andrew Johnson was the first in 1867; after a one-month trial in the Senate the "guilty" vote fell one short of two-thirds needed for

congressional investigation
Congressional committee hearings on alleged misdeeds or scandals.

removal. President Richard Nixon resigned just prior to an impending impeachment vote in 1974.) The 1998 House impeachment vote split along partisan lines, with Republicans voting "yes" and Democrats voting "no". Two Articles of Impeachment were passed, one for perjury before a grand jury, and one for obstruction of justice. In the subsequent Senate trial, only 45 Senators (less than a majority and far less than the needed two-thirds) voted to convict President Clinton on the first charge, and only 50 voted to convict on the second.

What constitutes "High Crimes and Misdemeanors"? The Constitution is silent on this question; most observers now conclude that an impeachable offense is anything that the House thinks is impeachable. But the constitutional words suggest that Congress is not to impeach presidents, federal judges, or any other officials, simply because Congress disagrees with their policies or decisions. Indeed, the phrase "High Crimes and Misdemeanors" implies *serious* criminal conduct, not *personal* wrongdoing or immorality. According to Alexander Hamilton, impeachment should deal with "the abuse or violation of some public trust" (*Federalist 65*). But as we shall see, impeachment is very political. (See "Sex, Lies, and Impeachment" in Chapter 11.)

Throughout the impeachment investigation, the House vote, and the Senate trial, public opinion weighed heavily in favor of President Clinton and against his removal from office. The Republican-controlled Congress appeared to ignore popular opinion and its own public disapproval ratings rose.

CONGRESSIONAL APPORTIONMENT AND REDISTRICTING

The Constitution states that "Representatives . . . shall be apportioned among the several states . . . according to their respective Numbers." It orders an "actual enumeration" (census) every ten years. And it provides that every state shall have at least one representative, in addition to two senators, regardless of population. But the Constitution is silent on the size of the House of Representatives. Congress itself determines its own size; for more than a century, it allowed itself to grow to accommodate new states and population growth. In 1910 it fixed the membership of the House at 435.

The effect of doing so has been to expand the population of House districts over the years. Following the 2000 census, House districts will have populations of about 635,000. It is sometimes argued that such large House constituencies prevent meaningful communication between citizens and their representatives. (The Framers originally envisioned House districts of no more than 30,000 people.) But expanding the size of the House would complicate its work, reduce the influence of individual members, require more procedural controls, and probably strengthen the power of party leaders.

apportionment The allocation of legislative seats to jurisdictions based on population. Seats in the U.S. House of Representatives are apportioned to the states on the basis of their population after every ten-year census.

Apportionment **Apportionment** refers to the allocation of House seats to the states after each ten-year census. The Constitution does not specify a mathematical method of apportionment; Congress adopted a complex "method of equal proportion" in 1929, which so far has withstood court challenges (see *Across the USA:* "Apportionment of House Seats, 1990–2000," which shows the current apportionment, together with the states that expect to gain and lose seats after the 2000 census).

Apportionment of House Seats, 2000–2010

When the number of seats in the House of Representatives stays constant, as it has at 435 seats since 1910, each census requires a reapportionment of seats among the states. Arizona, Florida, Texas, and Georgia, with rapid population growth, each gained two seats. New York and Pennsylvania, with slow population growth, each lost two seats. Changing population statistics do not affect Senate seats, however, since the Constitution stipulates that every state shall have two senators, elected by all voters in the state, regardless of the state's population.

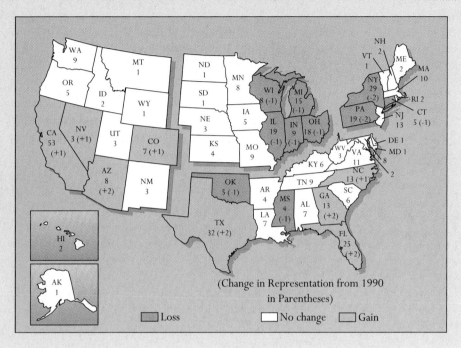

(Change in Representation from 1990 in Parentheses)

☐ Loss   ☐ No change   ☐ Gain

Malapportionment The Constitution does not determine how the states should apportion seats among their own citizens. State legislatures were long notorious for their **malapportionment**—congressional (and state legislative) districts with grossly unequal numbers of people. Some congressional districts had twice the average number of people per district, and others had only half as many. In 1962, for example, Georgia's congressional districts varied in size from a rural district of 272,154 to an Atlanta district of 823,860. In a district twice the size of the average district, the value of an individual's vote was heavily diluted. In a district half the size of the average, the value of an individual's vote was greatly magnified.

Enter the Supreme Court Prior to 1962, the Supreme Court refused to intervene in apportionment, holding that this question belonged to the state legislatures and that the federal courts should avoid this "political thicket." So the Supreme Court's decision in the landmark case *Baker v. Carr* (1962) came as a surprise. The Court ruled that inequalities in voters' influence resulting from different-size districts violated the Equal Protection Clause of the Fourteenth Amendment. The case dealt with a complaint about Tennessee's state legislative districts, but the Court soon extended its holding to congressional districts as well.[5] "The conception of political equality from the Declaration of Independence to Lincoln's Gettys-

malapportionment Unequal numbers of people in legislative districts resulting in inequality of voter representation.

burg Address, to the Fourteenth, Fifteenth, Seventeenth, and Nineteenth Amendments, can mean only one thing—one person, one vote."[6]

The shift in the Supreme Court's policy raised a new question: How equal must districts be in order to guarantee voters "equal protection of the law"? The courts have ruled that only official U.S. Bureau of the Census figures may be used: estimated changes since the last census may *not* be used. In recent years, the courts have insisted on nearly exact mathematical equality in congressional districts.

"Enumeration"　The U.S. Constitution is very specific in its wording: It calls for an "actual Enumeration" (Article I, Section 2) of the population in each ten-year census. However, the U.S. Bureau of the Census has considered the use of samples and estimates to correct what it perceives to be "undercounts." Undercounting is said to occur when certain populations are difficult to identify and count on an individual basis, populations such as recent non-English-speaking immigrants or residents of neighborhoods likely to mistake government census takers for law enforcement officers or other unwelcome government officials. Political leaders (usually Democrats) of states and cities with large immigrant and minority populations have favored the substitution of samples and estimates for actual head counts. However, the U.S. Supreme Court held in 1999 that the Census Act of 1976 prohibits sampling for purposes of apportioning House members among the states.[7] Congress may use sampling for determining the allocation of grant-in-aid funds if it wishes.

Redistricting　**Redistricting** refers to the drawing of boundary lines of congressional districts following the census. After each census, some states gain and others lose seats, depending on whether their populations have grown faster or slower than the nation's population. In addition, population shifts within a state may force districting changes. Congressional district boundaries are drawn by state legislatures in each state; a state's redistricting act must pass both houses of the state legislature and win the governor's signature (or be passed over a gubernatorial veto). The U.S. Justice Department and the federal judiciary are also deeply involved in redistricting issues, particularly questions of whether or not redistricting disadvantages African Americans or other minorities.

Gerrymandering　**Gerrymandering** is the drawing of district lines for political advantage (see Figure 10–2). The population of districts may be equal, yet the district boundaries are drawn in such a fashion as to grant advantage or disadvantage to specific groups of voters. Gerrymandering has long been used by parties in control of the state legislatures to maximize their seats in Congress and state legislatures.

Gerrymandering, with the aid of sophisticated computer-mapping programs and data on past voting records of precincts, is a highly technical task. But consider a simple example where a city is entitled to three representatives and the eastern third of the city is Republican but the western two-thirds is Democratic (see Figure 10–3 on page 328). If the Republicans could draw the district lines, they might draw them along a north-south direction to allow their party to win in one of the three districts. In contrast, if Democrats could draw the district lines, they might draw them along an east-west direction to allow their party to win all three districts by diluting the Republican vote. Such dividing up and diluting of a strong minority to deny it the power to elect a representative is called **splintering**. Often gerry-

redistricting　Drawing of legislative district boundary lines following each ten-year census.

gerrymandering　Drawing district boundary lines for political advantage.

splintering　Redistricting in which a strong minority is divided up and diluted to prevent it from electing a representative.

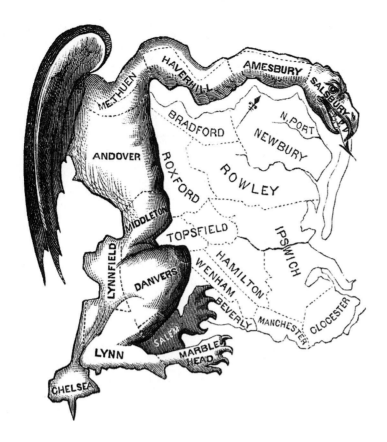

FIGURE 10–2 The Original Gerrymander

The term gerrymander immortalizes Governor Elbridge Gerry (1744–1814) of Massachusetts, who in 1811 redistricted the state legislature to favor Democrats over Federalists. A district north of Boston was designed to concentrate, and thus "waste," Federalist votes. This political cartoon from the Boston Gazette, March 26, 1812, depicted the new district lines as a salamander, dubbing the process the "gerrymander."

mandering is not as neat as our example; district lines may twist and turn, creating grotesque patterns in order to achieve the desired effects. Another gerrymandering strategy—**packing**—is the heavy concentration of one party's voters in a single district in order to "waste" their votes and allow modest majorities of the party doing the redistricting to win in other districts.

Partisan Gerrymandering   Generally, partisan gerrymandering does not violate federal court standards for "equal protection" under the Fourteenth Amendment. There is no constitutional obligation to allocate seats "to the contending parties in proportion to what their anticipated statewide vote will be."[8] However, the federal courts may intervene in political gerrymandering if it "consistently degrades a voter's or a group of voters' influence on the political process as a whole."[9] These vague standards set forth by the U.S. Supreme Court open the door to judicial intervention in particularly grievous cases of partisan gerrymandering.

Party control of state legislatures and governorships during post-census redistricting can tilt Congressional representation toward the majority party in a state. Democrats benefited from holding a majority of state legislative chambers and state governorships following the 1990 census. (Frustrated Republicans in some states championed efforts to create African-American districts, hoping to "pack" traditional Democratic minority voters into a few districts, and thereby improve Republican chances in the remaining "bleached" districts.) However, it is important to note that Republicans were still able to capture control of the House of Representatives in 1994 and retain control in 1996, 1998, and 2000.

packing Redistricting in which partisan voters are concentrated in a single district, "wasting" their majority vote and allowing the opposition to win by modest majorities in other districts.

FIGURE 10–3 Gerrymandering in Action

Depending on how an area is divided into districts, the result may benefit one party or the other. In this example, dividing the area so one district has virtually all the Republicans gives that party a victory in that district while ceding the other two districts to the Democrats. In contrast, Democrats benefit when Republican voters are divided among the three districts so that their votes are splintered.

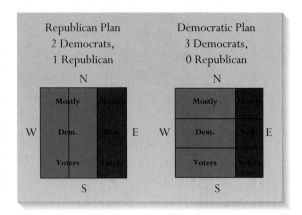

Divided government in the states (where one party controls one or both houses of the legislature and the other party controls the governorship) makes partisan gerrymandering more difficult. The 2000 elections produced divided government in over half of the states.

Racial Gerrymandering Racial gerrymandering to disadvantage African Americans and other minorities violates both the Equal Protection Clause of the Fourteenth Amendment and the Voting Rights Act of 1965. The Voting Rights Act specifies that redistricting in states with a history of voter discrimination or low voter participation must be "cleared" in advance with the U.S. Justice Department. The act extends special protection not only to African American voters but also to Hispanic, Native American, Alaska Native, and Asian voters.

In 1982 Congress strengthened the Voting Rights Act by outlawing any electoral arrangement that has the effect of weakening minority voting power. This *effects test* replaced the earlier *intent test*, under which redistricting was outlawed only if boundaries were intentionally drawn to dilute minority political influence. In *Thornburg v. Gingles* (1986), the Supreme Court interpreted the effects test to require state legislatures to redistrict their states in a way that maximizes minority representation in Congress and the state legislatures.[10] The effect of this ruling was to require **affirmative racial gerrymandering**—the creation of predominately African American and minority districts (labeled "majority-minority" districts) whenever possible. Following the 1990 census, redistricting in legislatures in states with large minority populations was closely scrutinized by the U.S. Justice Department and the federal courts. The result was a dramatic increase in African American and Hispanic representation in Congress.

Nevertheless, the Supreme Court has expressed constitutional doubts about bizarre-shaped districts based *solely* on racial composition. In a controversial 5 to 4 decision in *Shaw v. Reno* (1993), Justice Sandra Day O'Connor wrote, "Racial gerrymandering, even for remedial purposes, may balkanize us into competing racial factions. . . . A reapportionment plan that includes in one district individuals who have little in common with one another but the color of their skin bears an uncomfortable resemblance to political apartheid"[11] (see Figure 10–4). Later the Court held that the use of race as the "predominant factor" in dividing district lines is unconstitutional: "When the state assigns voters on the basis of race, it engages in the offensive and demeaning assumption that voters of a particular race, because of their race, think alike, share the same political interests and will prefer the same candidates at the polls."[12] But the Court stopped short of saying that *all* race-

affirmative racial gerrymandering Drawing district boundary lines to maximize minority representation.

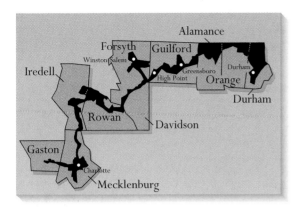

FIGURE 10–4 Affirmative Racial Gerrymandering

North Carolina's Twelfth Congressional District was drawn up to be a "majority-minority" district by combining African American communities over a wide region of the state. The U.S. Supreme Court in Shaw v. Reno (1993) ordered a court review of this district to determine whether it incorporated any common interest other than race. The North Carolina legislature redrew the district in 1997, lowering its black population from 57 to 46 percent, yet keeping its lengthy connection of black voters from Charlotte to Greensboro.

conscious districting is unconstitutional. Several states redrew the boundaries of majority-minority districts trying to conform to the Court's opinions. Incumbent African American Congress members managed to hold on to their seats in these states. Redistricting after the 2000 census will bring about further court involvement in racial gerrymandering. According to Justice Ruth Bader Ginsberg, "The Court has not yet spoken its final word."[13]

GETTING TO CAPITOL HILL

Members of Congress are independent political entrepreneurs—selling themselves, their services, and their personal policy views to the voters in 435 House districts and 50 states across the country. They initiate their own candidacies, raise most of their campaign funds from individual contributors, put together personal campaign organizations, and get themselves elected with relatively little help from their party. Their reelection campaigns depend on their ability to raise funds from individuals and interest groups and on the services and other benefits they provide to their constituents.

Who Runs for Congress?   Members of Congress come from a wide variety of backgrounds, ranging from acting and professional sports to medicine and the ministry. However, exceptionally high percentages of senators and representatives have prior experience in at least one of three fields—law, business, or public service (see Table 10–3). Members of Congress are increasingly career politicians, people who decided early in life to devote themselves to running for and occupying public office.[14] The many lawyers, by and large, are *not* practicing attorneys. Rather, the typical lawyer-legislator is a political activist with a law degree. These are people who graduated from law school and immediately sought public jobs—as federal or state prosecuting attorneys, as attorneys for federal or state agencies, or as staff assistants in congressional, state, or city offices. They used their early job experiences to make political contacts and learn how to organize a political campaign, find financial contributors, and deal with the media. Another group of Congress members are former businesspeople—not employees of large corporations, but people whose personal or family businesses brought them into close

| Table 10-3 | Backgrounds of Congress Members |

	House			Senate			Congress
	Democrat	Republican	Total	Democrat	Republican	Total	Total
Occupation							
Actor/Entertainer		1	1		1	1	2
Aeronautics		1	1				1
Agriculture	8	14	22	1	5	6	28
Artistic/Creative	1	1	2				2
Business/Banking	53	106	159	6	18	24	183
Clergy		1	1		1	1	2
Education	49	34	84*	5	8	13	97
Engineering	1	8	9				9
Health Care	2	1	3				3
Journalism	2	6	9*	2	6	8	17
Labor Organizing	1		1				1
Law	87	76	163	27	28	55	218
Law Enforcement	8	2	10				10
Medicine	5	10	15		2	2	17
Military		1	1		1	1	2
Professional Sports		2	2		1	1	3
Public Service/Politics	57	49	106	10	8	18	124
Real Estate	3	17	20	2	2	4	24
Technical/Trade	1	2	3				3
Miscellaneous	1	5	6				6
Religion							
Protestant Total	107	171	278	21	42	63	341
Baptist	34	28	62	1	7	8	70
Methodist	16	34	50	5	7	12	62
Presbyterian	15	26	41	1	6	7	48
Episcopalian	9	21	30	4	9	13	43
Lutheran	9	8	17	3	2	5	22
Mormon	2	10	12	1	4	5	17
Other Protestant	22	44	66	6	7	13	79
Jewish	21	1	21	10	1	11	34
Catholic	76	50	126	14	11	25	151
Other/Unspecified	7	0	7	0	1	1	8
Average Age	53.1	52.1	52.6	57.4	59.0	58.3	53.7

Because some members have more than one occupation, totals are higher than total memberships

*Includes Rep. Bernard Sanders, Independent-Vt.

Source: Congressional Quarterly Weekly Report, January 9, 1999, for 106th Congress, 1999–2001.

contact with government and their local community, in real estate, insurance, franchise dealerships, community banks, and so forth.

House members are generally younger than Senators. South Carolina Senator Strom Thurmond is the oldest person ever to serve in the Congress; he turned 98 in 2000 and served 45 years in the Senate. The average length of service of Senators is ten years, slightly less than two terms; the average length of service of Representative is eight years, or four terms. In religious affiliation, the majority of the members of both houses of Congress are Protestant; Baptist and Methodist are the largest denominations. Less than thirty percent are Catholic, and about six percent are Jewish.

Competition for Seats   Careerism in Congress is aided by the electoral advantages enjoyed by incumbents over challengers. Greater name recognition, advantages in raising campaign funds, and the resources of congressional offices all combine to limit competition for seats in Congress and to reelect the vast majority of incumbents (see "The Advantages of Incumbency" in Chapter 8). A congressional district in which the incumbent regularly wins by a large margin (55 to 60 percent or more of the vote) is regarded as a **safe seat**. More than two-thirds of the members of the House of Representatives sit comfortably in safe seats. Even incumbents elected by close margins enjoy many advantages over challengers. The result is an incumbent reelection percentage for House members that usually exceeds 90 percent. The average reelection rate for U.S. senators is more than 80 percent (see Figure 10–5).

Aspirants for congressional careers are well advised to wait for open seats. **Open seats** in the House of Representatives are created when incumbents retire or vacate the seat to run for higher office. These opportunities occur on average in about 10 percent of House seats in each election. But every ten years reapportionment creates many new opportunities to win election to Congress. Reapportionment creates

safe seat   Legislative district in which the incumbent regularly wins by a large margin of the vote.

open seat   Seat in a legislature for which no incumbent is running for reelection.

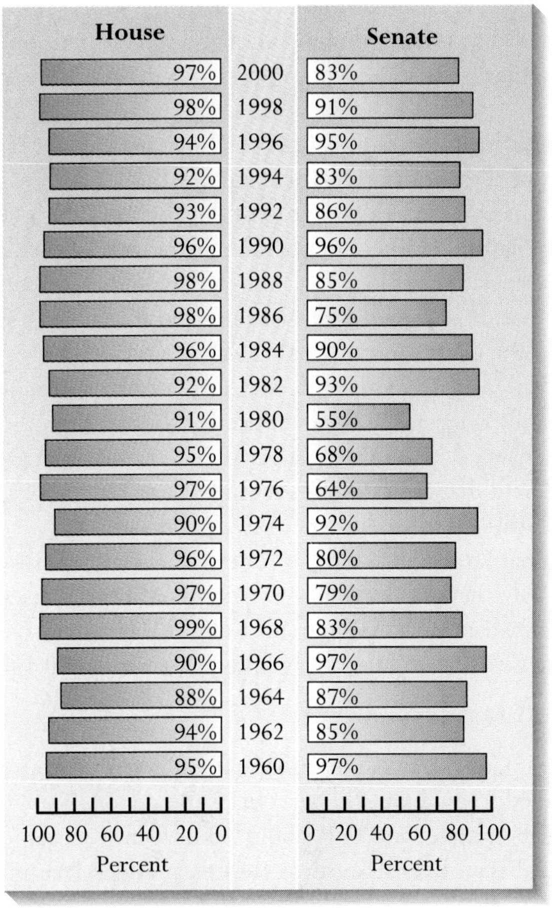

House		Senate
97%	2000	83%
98%	1998	91%
94%	1996	95%
92%	1994	83%
93%	1992	86%
96%	1990	96%
98%	1988	85%
98%	1986	75%
96%	1984	90%
92%	1982	93%
91%	1980	55%
95%	1978	68%
97%	1976	64%
90%	1974	92%
96%	1972	80%
97%	1970	79%
99%	1968	83%
90%	1966	97%
88%	1964	87%
94%	1962	85%
95%	1960	97%

100 80 60 40 20 0 Percent   0 20 40 60 80 100 Percent

FIGURE 10–5 Incumbent Advantage

Despite periodic movements to "throw the bums out," voters in most districts and states routinely reelect their members of Congress. Although incumbents do not always retain their seats, the odds are strongly in their favor. In recent decades, more than 90 percent of representatives and 80 percent of senators who have sought reelection have been returned to Congress by voters in their districts or states.

new seats in states gaining population, just as it forces out some incumbents in states losing population. Redistricting also threatens incumbents with new constituencies, where they have less name recognition, no history of casework, and perhaps no common racial or ethnic identification. Thus forced retirements and electoral defeats are more common in the first election following each ten-year reapportionment and redistricting of Congress.

Senate races are somewhat more competitive. Senate challengers are usually people who have political experience and name recognition as members of the House, governors, or other high state officials. Even so, most Senate incumbents seeking reelection are victorious over their challengers (see *What Do You Think?* "Why Do Voters Reelect Members of an Unpopular Congress?").

Turnover   Despite a high rate of reelection of incumbents in Congress, **turnover** of membership in recent years has been fairly high. Turnover occurs more frequently as a result of retirement, resignation (sometimes to run for higher office), or reapportionment (and the loss of an incumbent's seat) than it does as a result of an incumbent's defeat in a bid for reelection. Roughly 10 percent of Congress members voluntarily leave office when their term expires.[15]

Congressional Term Limits?   Public distrust of government helped to fuel a movement in the states to limit congressional terms. Several states attempted to limit their state's House members to four two-year terms and their Senators to two six-year terms. Proponents of congressional term limits argued that career politicians become isolated from the lives and concerns of average citizens, that they acquire an "inside the Beltway" (the circle of highways that surrounds Washington) mentality. They also argued that term limits would increase competition, creating "open-seat" races on a regular basis and encouraging more people to seek public office.

Opponents of congressional term limits argued that they infringe on the voters' freedom of choice. If voters are upset with the performance of their Congress members, they can limit their terms by not reelecting them. But if voters wish to keep popular and experienced legislators in office, they should be permitted to do so. Opponents also argued that inexperienced Congress members would be forced to rely more on the policy information supplied them by bureaucrats, lobbyists, and staff people—thus weakening the institution of Congress.

But the U.S. Supreme Court ruled in 1995 that the states themselves cannot limit the terms of their members of Congress. "If the qualifications set forth in the text of the Constitution are to be changed, that text must be amended." In a controversial 5 to 4 decision, the Court held that the Founders intended age, citizenship, and residency to be the *only* qualifications for members of Congress.

National polls regularly report that 70 percent or more Americans favor congressional term limits. But it is not likely that the necessary two-thirds of both houses of Congress will ever vote for a constitutional amendment to limit their own stay in office. Thus, the Supreme Court's decision effectively killed the movement for congressional term limits.

The Congressional Electorate   Congressional elections generally fail to arouse much interest among voters. Indeed, only about 60 percent of the general public can name one U.S. senator from their state, and only about 40 percent can name both of their U.S. senators. Members of the House of Representatives fare no

turnover   Replacement of members of Congress by retirement or resignation, by reapportionment, or (more rarely) by electoral defeat, usually expressed as a percentage of members newly elected.

Why Do Voters Reelect Members of an Unpopular Congress?

Congress is the least popular branch of government. Public approval of Congress is well below that of the presidency and the Supreme Court. What accounts for this lack of popularity? The belief that members of Congress "spend more time thinking about their own political futures than they do in passing legislation" may contribute to this sentiment. Well-publicized congressional scandals, pay raises, and perks offend taxpayers.

But public distrust of Congress may also arise from a misunderstanding of democratic government: "People do not wish to see uncertainty, conflicting options, long debate, competing interests, confusion, and compromised imperfect solutions. . . . They often see a patently unrealistic form of democracy."*

But in an apparent paradox, most voters *approve of their own* representative (see figure below), even while Congress itself is the object of popular distrust and ridicule. A majority of voters believe that their own representatives "deserve reelection."

This apparent contradiction is explained in part by differing expectations: Americans expect Congress to deal with national issues, but they expect their own representatives to deal with local concerns and even personal problems. Members of Congress understand this concern and consequently devote a great deal of their time to constituent service. Indeed, many members of Congress try to dissociate themselves from Congress, attacking Congress in their own campaigns and contributing to negative images of the institution. Finally, the national news media are highly critical of Congress, but local news media frequently portray local members of Congress in a more favorable light.

Q. "Do you approve of the way the U.S. Congress is handling its job?" "Do you approve or disapprove of the way the representative from your own congressional district is handling his/her job?"

---

*John R. Hibbing and Elizabeth Theiss-Morse, *Congress as Public Enemy* (Cambridge: Cambridge University Press, 1995), p. 147. Also cited by Roger H. Davidson and Walter J. Oleszak, *Congress and Its Members* (Washington, DC: CQ Press, 2000), p. 416.

Percentage of Those Expressing Approval of Their Representatives and Congress

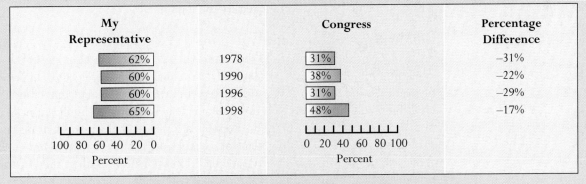

My Representative		Congress	Percentage Difference
62%	1978	31%	−31%
60%	1990	38%	−22%
60%	1996	31%	−29%
65%	1998	48%	−17%

Source: 1973 and 1990 surveys by the Gallup Organization, as reported in *American Enterprise*, January–February 1991, p. 83; 1996 and 1998 by the Gallup Organization.

---

better: less than half of the general public can name their representative.[16] But even constituents who know the names of their congressional delegation seldom know anything about the policy positions of these elected officials or about their votes on specific issues. Turnout in congressional *general elections* averages only about 35 percent in off-year (nonpresidential) elections. Turnout in congressional *primary*

During his tenure as Speaker of the House of Representatives, Newt Gingrich was a major player in the unsuccessful fight for congressional term limits.

elections seldom exceeds 15 to 20 percent of persons eligible to vote. This lack of public attentiveness to congressional elections gives a great advantage to candidates with high name recognition, generally the incumbents.

Independence of Congressional Voting   Congressional voting is largely independent of presidential voting. The same voters who elected Republican presidents in 1968, 1972, 1980, 1984, and 1988 simultaneously elected Democratic majorities to the House of Representatives. And while reelecting Democratic President Bill Clinton in 1996, voters simultaneously reelected Republican majorities in the House and Senate. In 2000, Republicans maintained a razor-thin margin in the House, despite Gore's popular vote victory. It is unlikely that voters deliberately seek to impose *divided party government* on the nation. Rather, they cast their presidential and congressional votes on the basis of differing expectations of presidents versus members of Congress.[17]

Congressional Campaign Financing   Raising the $700,000 it can take to win a House seat or the $5 million for a successful Senate campaign is a major job in and of itself (see "How Much Does It Cost to Get Elected?" in Chapter 8). Even incumbents who face little or no competition still work hard at fund raising, "banking" contributions against some future challenger. Large campaign chests, assembled well in advance of an election, can also be used to frighten off would-be challengers. Campaign funds can be used to build a strong personal organization

Table 10-4	Congressional Campaign Spending	
	House	**Senate**
Average incumbent	$628,064	$5,015,685
Average challenger	$301,289	$2,418,075
Average open-seat candidate	$638,571	$2,970,018

Source: Federal Elections Commission, 1998.

back home, finance picnics and other festivities for constituents, expand the margin of victory, and develop a reputation for invincibility that may someday protect against an unknown challenger.[18]

Incumbents in the House of Representatives raise and spend more than twice as much money as their challengers (see Table 10–4). Most individual contributors as well as business and corporate PACs are very pragmatic: they fund incumbents, regardless of party, in order to gain and maintain access to decision makers. Union PACs generally fund Democrats, based on the Democratic Party's perceived support for the goals of organized labor. Ideological PACs usually base their contributions on the perceived "correctness" of the voting records of members of Congress. Challengers thus must rely far more heavily on their own resources than do incumbents, although all candidates are free to spend as much of their own money as they wish.

Does money buy elections? In about 90 percent of all congressional races, the candidate who spends the most money wins. However, because most winning candidates are incumbents, the money probably reflects the expected political outcome rather than shapes it. But even in open-seat races, the candidate who spends the most money usually wins.

The Historic Democratic Party Dominance of Congress For forty years (1954–94) Democrats enjoyed an advantage in congressional races; in fact, the Democratic Party was said to have a "permanent majority" in the House of Representatives (see Figure 10–6 on page 336). Thus the Republican victory in the congressional election of 1994 was widely described as a political "earthquake." It gave the GOP control of the House for the first time in four decades, as well as control of the Senate.

The historic Democratic dominance of Congress was attributed to several factors. First, over those four decades more voters identified themselves with the Democratic Party than with the Republican Party (see Chapter 7). Party identification plays a significant role in congressional voting; it is estimated that 75 percent of those who identify themselves with a party cast their vote for the congressional candidate of their party.[19] Second, the Democratic advantage was buttressed by the fact that many voters considered local rather than national conditions when casting congressional votes. House campaigns were usually 435 separate local contests emphasizing personal qualities of the candidates and their ability to serve their district's constituents. Voters may have wanted to curtail overall federal spending in Washington (a traditional Republican promise), but they wanted a member of Congress who would "bring home the bacon." Although both Republican and Democratic congressional candidates usually promised to bring money and jobs to their districts, Democratic candidates appeared more creditable on such promises because

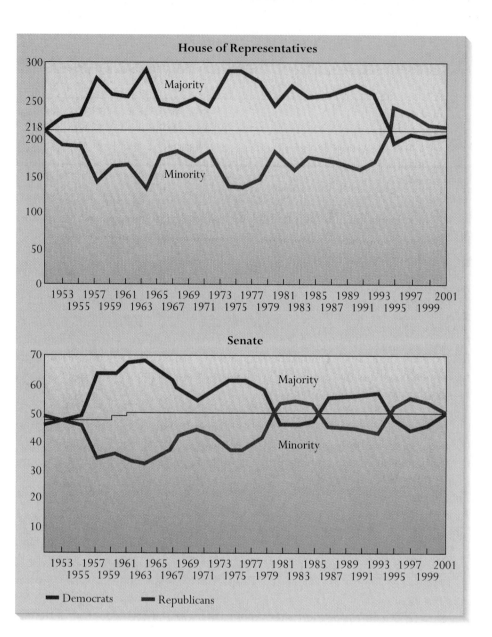

FIGURE 10–6   Party Control of the House and Senate

Except for two very brief periods, Democrats continuously controlled both the House of Representatives and the Senate for more than forty years. The Democratic Party's "permanent" control of Congress was ended in 1994, when Republicans won majorities in both houses. Republicans retained control of Congress despite President Clinton's victory in 1996, and retained control by a slim margin in the House in 1998 and 2000. And in 2000, the U.S. Senate split 50–50, with Republican Vice President Dick Cheney called upon to cast tie-breaking votes.

their party generally supported large domestic-spending programs. Finally, Democratic congressional candidates over those years enjoyed the many advantages of incumbency. It was thought that only death or retirement would dislodge many of them from their seats.

The Republican "Revolution"?   The sweeping Republican victory in 1994—especially the party's capturing control of the House of Representatives—surprised many analysts.[20] Just two years after a Democratic president won election and Democrats won substantial majorities in both houses of Congress, the GOP gained its most complete victory in many years. How did it happen?

First of all, the Republican congressional candidates, under the leadership of Newt Gingrich, largely succeeded in *nationalizing* the midterm congressional election. That is, Republican candidates sought to exploit the voters' general skepticism about government and disenchantment with its performance. Voters were often unfamiliar with specific Republican promises, but they correctly sensed that the Republicans favored "less government."

The Democratic advantage in bringing "pork"—lucrative federal projects—to their districts was turned against them. Indeed, the most powerful House Democratic incumbent, Speaker Thomas S. Foley of Washington, was unable to convince his constituents in 1994 that his thirty years of service to them and his impressive record of bringing pork to the district justified his reelection. Foley became the first Speaker of the House in more than one hundred years to suffer defeat in a bid for reelection.

The GOP's capture of control of both houses of Congress in 1994 for the first time in forty years raised conservatives' hopes of a "revolution" in public policy. The new Republican House Speaker, Newt Gingrich, was the acknowledged leader of the revolution, with Republican Senate Majority Leader Bob Dole in tow. But soon the revolution began to fizzle out. Two key Republican campaign promises failed to pass the Congress: the House failed to muster the necessary two-thirds majority for a constitutional amendment to impose congressional term limits, and the Senate failed to do so on behalf of a balanced budget amendment.

But worse was yet to come for the Republicans. Congress passed several budget resolutions aimed at balancing the federal budget in seven years, only to see them vetoed. Clinton positioned himself as the defender of popular programs—Medicare, Medicaid, education, and the environment—consistently referring to congressional efforts to reduce the rate of growth in these programs as "cuts." The failure of Congress and the president to agree on appropriations temporarily shut down the federal government in 1995. To the surprise of the Republican leadership, opinion polls reported that Americans blamed the GOP Congress for the gridlock. Clinton's approval ratings rose, and Newt Gingrich was portrayed as a mean-spirited "extremist." Eventually Congress and the president agreed on a compromise budget, a welfare reform bill, and health insurance portability (see Chapter 17).

The Democratic Revival Republicans succeeded in maintaining their control of Congress despite Clinton's reelection in 1996. Collectively, the voters seemed to say they preferred divided government, that they wanted a Republican Congress which would press for a balanced budget, but they also wanted a Democratic president who would defend popular middle-class entitlement programs. In short, voters seemed reluctant to allow either party to govern unchaperoned by the other.

Democrats gained house seats in both the 1996 and 1998 Congressional elections. Although the GOP retained a slim majority in the House of Representatives, the 1998 midterm election stunned Republicans. They had expected to benefit from Clinton's acknowledged sexual misconduct and the House impeachment investigation. But voters generally sided with Clinton. Some Democratic voters may even have turned out especially to defend the still-popular president. Republicans had expected major gains in both the House (where they lost seats) and in the Senate (where they merely maintained their 55–45 margin). Democrats were encouraged because historically the party controlling the White House had *lost* seats in midterm elections.

Congress Divided The congressional elections of 2000 reflected the close partisan division of the nation. Republicans barely held on to their majority in the House of Representatives. The election produced a historic 50–50 tie in the Senate; control of the Senate rests upon the tie-breaking vote of the vice president. The election of Hillary Rodham Clinton from New York to the Senate promised increased media attention to that body. The partisan cleavage in both houses does not bode well for the passage of any major legislation. Party leaders in both houses will be severely tested in their efforts to prevent defections on party line votes.

LIFE IN CONGRESS

"All politics is local," declared former House Speaker Thomas P. "Tip" O'Neill, himself once the master of both Boston ward politics and the U.S. House of Representatives. Attention to the local constituency is the key to survival and success in congressional politics. If Congress often fails to deal responsibly with national problems, the explanation lies in part with the design of the institution. House members must devote primary attention to their districts and Senate members to their states. Only *after* their constituencies are served can they turn their attention to national policy making.

The "Representativeness" of Congress   The Constitution requires only that members of the House of Representatives be (1) residents of the state they represent (they need not live in their congressional district, although virtually all do so); (2) U.S. citizens for at least seven years; and (3) at least twenty-five years old. Senators must also be residents of the state they represent, but they must be at least thirty years old and U.S. citizens for at least nine years.

African Americans were first elected to Congress following the Civil War—seven black representatives and one black senator served in 1875. But with the end of Reconstruction, black membership in Congress fell to a single seat in the House from 1891 to 1955. Following the Civil Rights Act of 1964 and the Voting Rights Act of 1965, black membership in Congress rose steadily. Redistricting following the 1990 census resulted in many new "majority-minority" congressional districts. After the 1992 elections, black membership in the House rose dramatically (see Figure 10–7), with most elected from predominately African American districts. As a result, although African Americans today make up a little more than 12 percent of the U.S.

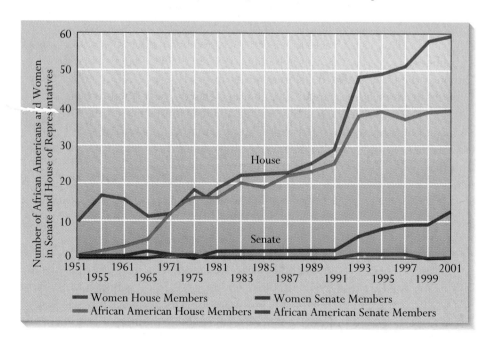

FIGURE 10–7   Women and African Americans in Congress, 1951–2001

Although the House of Representatives is still far short of "looking like America," in recent years the number of African American and female members has risen noticeably. Both groups made particularly impressive advances in the 1992 elections, as did Hispanics. More women now serve in the Senate than ever before. (The only African American woman to ever serve in that body, Democrat Carol Moseley-Braun of Illinois, lost her seat in 1998.)

population, they make up less than 9 percent of the House membership. Hispanics now account for 9 percent of the U.S. population but only about 4 percent of House membership. Only one Native American serves in Congress (see *People in Politics:* "Ben Nighthorse Campbell, Native American Voice in Congress" on page 340).

Women have made impressive gains in both the House and the Senate in the last decade. The "year of the woman" election in 1992 brought a significant increase in the number of women in the House of Representatives. In 2000, women's representation in the House continued upward; 59 women serve in the 107th Congress (2001–2003), divided between 41 Democrats and 18 Republicans. In the Senate, California is represented by two Democratic women, Diane Feinstein and Barbara Boxer. They are joined by 8 other Democratic women Senators, including former First Lady Hillary Rodham Clinton. Three Republican women serve in the Senate: Kay Hutchinson from Texas and Olympia Snowe and Susan Collins from Maine. Although this is the largest delegation of women ever to serve together in the U.S. Senate, it is still only 13 percent of that body.

Congresswoman Marge Roukema of New Jersey meets with a staff member at her offices in Washington, D.C. Congressional staff play a key role in the legislative process.

Congressional Staff Congress is composed of a great deal more than 535 elected senators and representatives. Congressional staff and other support personnel now total some 25,000 people. Each representative has a staff of twenty or more people, usually headed by a chief of staff or administrative assistant and including legislative assistants, communications specialists, constituent-service personnel, office managers, secretaries, and aides of various sorts. Senators frequently have staffs of thirty to fifty or more people. All representatives and senators are provided with offices both in Washington and in their home districts and states. In addition, representatives receive more than $500,000 apiece for office expenses, travel, and staff; and senators receive $2 million or more, depending on the size of their state's population. Overall, Congress spends more than *$2 billion* on itself each year.

Congressional staff people exercise great influence over legislation.[21] Many experienced "Hill rats" have worked for the same member of Congress for many years. Many senior aides earn more than $100,000 per year. They become very familiar with "their" member's political strengths and vulnerabilities and handle much of the member's contacts with interest groups and constituents. Staff people, more than members themselves, move the legislative process—scheduling committee hearings, writing bills and amendments, and tracking the progress of such proposals through committees and floor proceedings. By working with the staff of other members of Congress or the staff of committees and negotiating with interest-group representatives, congressional staff are often able to work out policy compromises, determine the wording of legislation, or even outline "deals" for their member's vote (all subject to later approval by their member). With multiple demands on their time, members of Congress come to depend on their staff not only for information about the content of legislation but also for political recommendations about what position to take regarding it. Indeed, staff have become so important in the internal operations of Congress that members have less direct contact with each other than in the past, a situation that often makes modern congressional relations impersonal.

In addition to the personal staffs of members of Congress, congressional committees have their own staffs, ranging in size from 25 to more than 200 persons. Committee staffs are generally beholden to the committee chair and are often replaced when a new chair is named. Minority committee members do control some committee staff positions, however.

Ben Nighthorse Campbell, Native American Voice in Congress

In an age of slick Ivy League career politicians, the colorful style of Ben Nighthorse Campbell is a welcome relief. Campbell is part Native American and official chief of the Northern Cheyenne nation. Growing up with an alcoholic father and a mother suffering from tuberculosis, he dropped out of high school and joined the Air Force, then later worked his way through the California State University at San Jose by driving a truck. Along the way, Campbell took up judo and won a spot on the U.S. Olympic team. His business skills in marketing Indian jewelry allowed him to go into cattle ranching and horse training in southwest Colorado and to win election to the House of Representatives in an upset in 1986. In 1988 and 1990, Colorado voters reelected him with more than 70 percent of the vote.

As a member of the House Agriculture Committee, Campbell was strongly supportive of ranching and mining interests, portraying himself as a social liberal and a fiscal conservative. When he announced his attention to run for the seat of retiring Democratic Senator Tim Wirth, environmental groups rushed to support his opponents, including former three-term governor Richard Lamm. But the witty and outspoken Campbell easily captured the Democratic nomination in a three-way race and entered the general election race with a wide lead over Republican state senator Terry Considine. The gap narrowed somewhat as Considine launched attack ads claiming Campbell was a pawn of the oil and mining companies, but Campbell, with his ponytail and trademark string tie, kept the confidence of Colorado voters and won a convincing 55 to 45 percent victory.

Campbell shocked his Democratic colleagues in the Senate in early 1995 when he announced his switch to the Republican Party. During his first two years in the Senate as a Democrat, he had given only lukewarm support to this party and President Bill Clinton, complaining that his moderate views were often out of sync with the Democratic leadership. Yet even while announcing his switch, he warned his new Republican colleagues that he would continue to support liberal positions on many social issues, including abortion.

Campbell's party change did not affect his popularity with Colorado voters. He won reelection as a Republican in 1998 with 62 percent of the vote. His Democratic opponent, Dottie Lamm, daughter of former governor Richard Lamm, failed to exact family retribution for her father's earlier loss to the charismatic Campbell. He can now boast that he has never lost an election in either party.

Support Agencies   In addition to the thousands of personal and committee staff who are supposed to assist members of Congress in research and analysis, four congressional support agencies provide Congress with information:

- The Library of Congress and its Congressional Research Service (CRS) are the oldest congressional support agencies. Members of Congress can turn to the Library of Congress for references and information. The CRS responds to direct requests of members for factual information on virtually any topic. It tracks major bills in Congress and produces summaries of each bill introduced. This information is available on computer terminals in members' offices.

- The General Accounting Office (GAO) has broad authority to oversee the operations and finances of executive agencies, to evaluate their programs, and to report its findings to Congress. Established as an arm of Congress in 1921, the GAO largely confined itself to financial auditing and management studies in its early years but expanded to more than five thousand employees in the

1970s and undertook a broad agenda of policy research and evaluation. Most GAO studies and reports are requested by members of Congress and congressional committees, but the GAO also undertakes some studies on its own initiative.

- The Congressional Budget Office (CBO) was created by the Congressional Budget and Impoundment Act of 1974 to strengthen Congress's role in the budgeting process. It was designed as a congressional counterweight to the president's Office of Management and Budget (see Chapter 14). The CBO supplies the House and Senate budget committees with its own budgetary analyses and economic forecasts, sometimes challenging those found in the president's annual budget.

- The Government Printing Office (GPO), created in 1860 as the publisher of the *Congressional Record*, now distributes over 20,000 different government publications in U.S. government bookstores throughout the nation.

Note that the CBO was created at a time when Congress was growing in power relative to a presidency weakened by Vietnam and Watergate. In these same years, Congress encouraged the GAO to undertake a more active and critical role relative to executive agencies. Thus, the growth of congressional staff and supporting agencies is tied to the struggle for power between the legislative and executive branches.

Workload   Members of Congress claim to work twelve- to fifteen-hour days: two to three hours in committee and subcommittee meetings; two to three hours on the floor of the chamber; three to four hours meeting with constituents, interest groups, other members, and staff in their offices; and two to three hours attending conferences, events, and meetings in Washington.[22] Members of Congress may introduce anywhere from ten to fifty bills in a session of Congress. (A "session" convenes in January following a congressional election and extends for two years, until after the next election.) Most bills are introduced merely to exhibit the member's commitment to a particular group or issue. Cosigning a popular bill is a common practice; particularly popular bills may have 100 or 200 cosigners in the House of Representatives. Although thousands of bills are introduced, only 400 to 800 are passed in a session.

Members of Congress resent the notion that they are overpaid, underworked, pampered, self-seeking, corrupt, and ineffective. They respond to the bell calling them to the floor for a recorded vote 900 to 1,000 times a session. Each representative is a member of at least two standing committees and four subcommittees, and each senator may be a member of four committees and many more subcommittees. Thousands of committee and subcommittee meetings are scheduled each session.

Pay and Perks   Taxpayers can relate directly to what members of Congress spend on themselves, even while millions—and even billions—of dollars spent on government programs remain relatively incomprehensible. Taxpayers thus were enraged when Congress, in a late-night session in 1991, raised its own pay from $89,500 to $129,000. Congress claimed the pay raise was a "reform," since it was coupled with a stipulation that members of Congress would no longer be allowed to accept honoraria from interest groups for their speeches and appearances, thus supposedly reducing members' dependence on outside income. Many angry taxpayers saw only a 44 percent pay raise, in the midst of a national recession, for a Congress that was doing little to remedy the nation's problems. By 2000 automatic cost-of-living increases, also enacted by Congress, had raised members' pay to $141,300.

As the pay-raise debate raged in Washington, several states resurrected a constitutional amendment originally proposed by James Madison. Although passed by the Congress in 1789, it had never been ratified by the necessary three-quarters of the states. The 203-year-old amendment, requiring a House election to intervene before a congressional pay raise can take effect, was added as the Twenty-seventh Amendment when ratified by four states (for a total of thirty-nine) in 1992.

Even more damaging to public confidence in Congress have been revelations about the "perks" (privileges) accorded its members. For example, Congress had long maintained its own "bank"—actually more like an employee credit union—where members deposited their pay and wrote checks. Overdrafts were common, because members regularly wrote checks in anticipation of pay deposits. Some members clearly abused the privilege, writing hundreds of overdrafts totaling tens of thousands of dollars. Technically, no government (taxpayer) funds were involved. But when the "check-kiting" scandal was reported by the media in 1992, most people believed that members of Congress were abusing their power. Other perks also came under fire—travel and office expenses, the free congressional health club, free medical clinic, free parking, free video studios for making self-promotional tapes, free mailing privileges, and a subsidized dining room, gift shop, and barbershop.

HOME STYLE

Members of Congress spend as much time politically cultivating their districts and states as they do legislating. **Home style** refers to the activities of senators and representatives in promoting their images among constituents and personally attending to constituents' problems and interests.[23] These activities include members' allocations of their personnel and staff resources to constituent services; members' personal appearances in the home district or state to demonstrate personal attention; and members' efforts to explain their Washington activities to the voters back home.

Casework **Casework** is really a form of "retail" politics. Members of Congress can win votes one at a time by helping constituents on a personal level. Casework can involve everything from tracing lost Social Security checks and Medicare claims to providing information about federal programs, solving problems with the Internal Revenue Service, and assisting with federal job applications. Over time, grateful voters accumulate, giving incumbents an advantage at election time. Congressional staff do much of the actual casework, but letters go out over the signature of the member of Congress. One estimate of staff work suggests that House members' offices process more than 100 cases a week on average, and senators' offices process more than 300.[24] Senators and representatives blame the growth of government for increasing casework, but it is also clear that members solicit casework, frequently reminding constituents to bring their problems to their member of Congress.

home style Activities of Congress members specifically directed at their home constituencies.

casework Services performed by legislators or their staff on behalf of individual constituents.

Former New Jersey Representative Robert Torricelli celebrates his 1996 election to the U.S. Senate, taking the seat vacated by Bill Bradley.

The downside to extensive casework is that it may detract from Congress members' ability to deal effectively with national issues. Former U.S. Senator and vice president Walter Mondale observed:

> Constituent service can . . . be a bottomless pit. The danger is that a member of Congress will end up as little more than an ombudsman between citizens and government agencies. As important as this work is, it takes precious time away from Congress's central responsibilities as both a deliberative and a lawmaking body.[25]

Pork Barrel　**Pork barreling** describes the efforts of senators and representatives to "bring home the bacon"—to bring federally funded projects, grants, and contracts that primarily benefit a single district or state to their home constituencies. Opportunities for pork barreling have never been greater: roads, dams, parks, and post offices are now overshadowed by redevelopment grants to city governments, research grants to universities, weapons contracts to local plants, "demonstration" projects of all kinds, and myriad other "goodies" tucked inside each year's annual appropriations bills. Members of Congress understand the importance of supporting each other's pork-barrel projects, cooperating in the "incumbent-protection society." Even though pork barreling adds to the public's negative image of Congress as an institution, individual members gain local popularity for the benefits they bring to home districts and states.

Pressing the Flesh　Senators and representatives spend a great deal of time in their home states and districts. Although congressional sessions last virtually all year, members of Congress find ways to spend more than a hundred days per year at home.[26] It is important to be seen at home—giving speeches and attending dinners, fund-raising events, civic occasions, and so on. To accommodate this aspect of home style, Congress usually follows a Tuesday-to-Thursday schedule of legisla-

pork barreling Legislation designed to make government benefits, including jobs and projects used as political patronage, flow to a particular district or state.

tive business, allowing members to spend longer weekends in their home districts. Congress also enjoys long recesses during the late summer and over holidays.

Puffing Images   To promote their images back home, members make generous use of their **franking privilege** (free mailing) to send their constituents newsletters, questionnaires, biographical material, and information about federal programs. Newsletters "puff" the accomplishments of the member; questionnaires are designed more to flatter voters than to assess opinions; and informational brochures tout federal services members claim credit for providing and defending. Congress's penchant for self-promotion has also kept pace with the media and electronic ages. Congress now provides its members with television studios and support for making videotapes to send to local stations in home districts, and all members have addresses on the Internet.

ORGANIZING CONGRESS: PARTY AND LEADERSHIP

Congress is composed of people who think of themselves as leaders, not followers. They got elected without much help from their party. Yet they realize that their chances of attaining their personal goals—getting reelected and influencing policy— are enhanced if they cooperate with each other.[27]

Party Organizations in Congress   The Democratic and Republican party organizations within the House of Representatives and the Senate are the principal bases for organizing Congress (see Figure 10–8). The leadership of each house of Congress, although nominally elected by the entire chamber, is actually chosen by secret ballot of the members of each party at a "conference" or caucus (see Table 10–5).

The parties and their leaders do not choose congressional candidates, nor can they deny them renomination; all members of Congress are responsible for their own primary and general election success. But party leadership in each chamber can help incumbents achieve their reelection goals. Each party in the House and Senate sponsors a campaign committee that channels some campaign funding to party

franking privilege   Free mail service afforded members of Congress.

Table 10-5	Leadership in Congress
Senate	
President Pro Tempore	Strom Thurmond (R-S.C.)
Majority Leader	Trent Lott (R-Miss.)
Majority Whip	Don Nickles (R-Okla.)
Minority Leader	Tom Daschle (D-S.D.)
House	
Speaker	Dennis Hastert (R-Ill.)
Majority Leader	Dick Armey (R-Tex.)
Majority Whip	Tom DeLay (R-Tex.)
Minority Leader	Richard Gephardt (D-Mo.)
Minority Whip	David Bonior (D-Mich.)

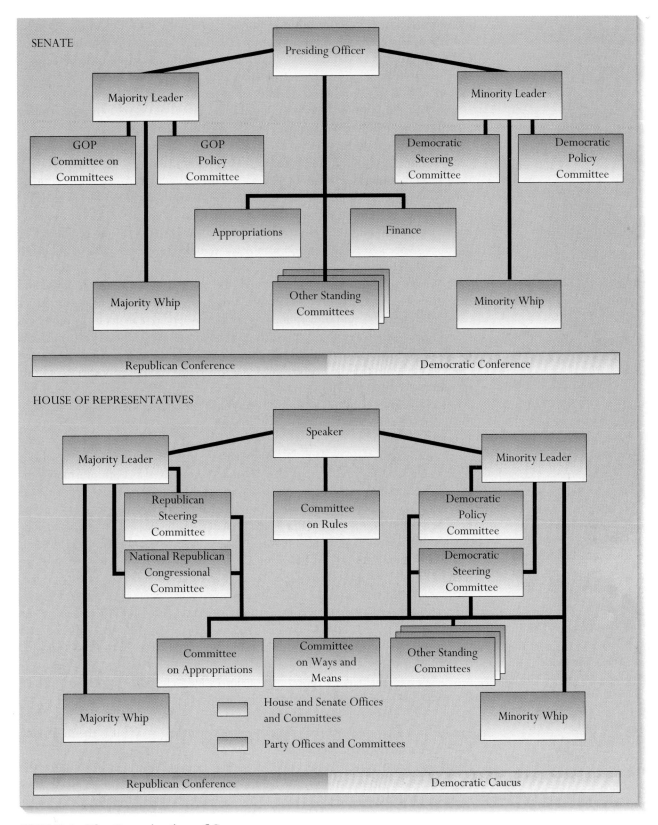

FIGURE 10–8 The Organization of Congress

Aside from naming the Speaker of the House as head of that body's operations and the vice president as overseer of Senate deliberations, the Constitution is silent on the organization of Congress. Political parties have filled this gap: both majority and minority parties have their own leadership, which governs the appointment of members to the various committees, where much of the work of Congress actually takes place.

members seeking reelection, although these Republican and Democratic congressional and senatorial campaign committees contribute less money than either PACs or individuals to the candidates.[28] Rather, good relations between members and their party's leadership are more important in the quest for power and influence in Washington.

Occasionally, congressional party leaders are urged to exercise more discipline over their members, to ensure that they support the party's position on key votes. Theoretically, party leaders in the House and Senate could do so by denying disloyal members appointment to preferred committees, by regularly burying their favorite bills, by cutting their pork-barrel projects from the budget, or by denying them party campaign funds. But except in very extreme cases, party leaders have been reluctant to employ these punishments. Members of Congress cherish their independence. They respect each other's need to get reelected. A member's vote lost today may be won next week if the member is not alienated by disciplinary action.

Majority status confers great power on the party that controls the House and the Senate. The majority party chooses the leadership in each body, selects the chairs of every committee, and insures that every committee has a majority of members from the majority party. In other words, if Republicans are in the majority in either the House or the Senate or both, Republicans will occupy all leadership positions, chair every committee, and constitute a majority of the members of every committee; and, of course, the Democrats enjoy the same advantages when they capture a majority of either body. Majority party members in each house even take in more campaign contributions than minority[29] members.

In the House: "Mr. Speaker"   In the House of Representatives, the key leadership figure is the **Speaker of the House**, who serves as both presiding officer of the chamber and leader of the majority party. In the House, the Speaker has many powers. The Speaker decides who shall be recognized to speak on the floor and rules on points of order (with advice from the parliamentarian), including whether a motion or amendment is germane (relevant) to the business at hand. The Speaker decides to which committees new bills will be assigned and can schedule or delay votes on a bill. The Speaker appoints members of select, special, and conference committees and names majority-party members to the Rules Committee. And the Speaker controls both patronage jobs and office space in the Capitol. Although the norm of fairness requires the Speaker to apply the rules of the House consistently, the Speaker is elected by the majority party and is expected to favor that party. However, the effectiveness and success of the Speaker really rest "less on formal rules than on personal prestige, sensitivity to member needs, ability to persuade and skill at mediating disputes"[30].

House Leaders and Whips   The Speaker's principal assistant is the **majority leader**. The majority leader formulates the party's legislative program in consultation with other party leaders and steers the program through the House. The majority leader also must persuade committee leaders to support the aims of party leaders in acting on legislation before their committees. Finally, the majority leader arranges the legislative schedule with the cooperation of key party members.

The minority party in the House selects a **minority leader** whose duties correspond to those of the majority leader, except that the minority leader has no author-

Speaker of the House
Presiding officer of the House of Representatives.

majority leader   In the House, the majority party leader and second in command to the Speaker; in the Senate, the leader of the majority party.

minority leader   In both the House and Senate, the leader of the opposition party.

Dick Gephardt, Minority Leader

House Minority Leader Richard A. Gephardt is frequently described as a "workaholic who combines a love of policy and a lust for politics." Recently he has also tried to combine his House Democratic leadership post with his personal ambition to be president of the United States. Indeed, this aspiration has led to clashes with his chief rival, Vice President Al Gore, as well as with President Clinton, whose support of Gore appears solid. The result is a House Democratic leader sometimes at odds with a Democratic White House.

Dick Gephardt has lived all of his life in St. Louis. He graduated from Northwestern University, where he was student body president, then attended the University of Michigan Law School. When he returned home, he served the powerful Democratic party in St. Louis as precinct captain and alderman. His party loyalty helped him win a seat in Congress in 1976. In 1984 he was elected chair of the House Democratic Caucus; in 1988, House Democratic leader (second only to the Democratic House Speaker); in 1994, minority leader, the top Democratic spot when Republicans gained control of the House.

But even as Gephardt was rising in the House Democratic Party hierarchy, he nurtured his ambition to occupy the White House. He briefly entered the 1988 race for the Democratic presidential nomination, easily won the Iowa caucus, but lost to Michael Dukakis in the New Hampshire primary and dropped out. President George Bush's popularity following victory in the Persian Gulf War led Gephardt and other prominent Democrats to sit out the 1992 presidential election, opening the way for Arkansas Governor Bill Clinton.

Early in his congressional career Gephardt compiled a moderate to conservative record, but as President Clinton moved to capture the Democratic Party's center, Gephardt assumed leadership of the party's liberal wing. He moved leftward in policy positions—supporting abortion rights, gun control, and health and welfare spending but opposing tax cuts, a balanced budget amendment, defense spending, and even Clinton's trade agreements, arguing that they undermined U.S. labor and environmental standards.

Gephardt contends that he is battling for "the heart and soul of the Democratic Party" and has the support of many of its core constituencies, including labor and environmental groups, who believe that Bill Clinton—and perhaps Al Gore—moved too far toward the center. In a now closely-divided House, Gephardt will exercise extraordinary power for a minority leader.

---

ity over the scheduling of legislation. The minority leader's principal duty has been to organize the forces of the minority party to counter the legislative program of the majority and to pass the minority party's bills. It is also the minority leader's duty to consult ranking minority members of House committees and to encourage them to adopt party positions and to follow the lead of the president if the minority party controls the White House (see *People in Politics:* "Dick Gephardt, Minority Leader").

In both parties, **whips** assist leaders in keeping track of the whereabouts of party members and in pressuring them to vote the party line. Whips are also responsible for ensuring the attendance of party members at important roll calls and for canvassing their colleagues on their likely support for or opposition to party-formulated legislation. Finally, whips are involved regularly in the formation of party policy and the scheduling of legislation.

whips In both the House and Senate, the principal assistants to the party leaders and next in command to those leaders.

Republican Speaker of the House Dennis Hastert leads a very slim Republican majority in the 107th Congress (2001–2003).

In the Senate: "Mr. President"   The Constitution declares the vice president of the United States to be the presiding officer of the Senate. But vice presidents seldom exercise this senatorial responsibility, largely because the presiding officer of the Senate has very little power. Having only 100 members, the Senate usually does not restrict debate and has fewer scheduling constraints than the House. The only significant power of the vice president is the right to cast a deciding vote in the event of a tie on a Senate roll call. In the usual absence of the vice president, the Senate is presided over by a *president pro tempore*. This honorific position is traditionally granted by the majority party to one of its senior stalwarts. The job of presiding over the Senate is so boring that neither the vice president nor the president pro tempore is found very often in the chamber. Junior senators are often asked to assume the chore. Nevertheless, speeches on the Senate floor begin with the salutation "Mr. President," referring to the president of the Senate, *not* the president of the United States.

Senate Majority and Minority Leaders   Senate leadership is actually in the hands of the Senate majority leader, but the Senate majority leader is not as powerful in that body as the Speaker is in the House. With fewer members, all of whom perceive themselves as powerful leaders, the Senate is less hierarchically organized than the House. The Senate majority leader's principal power is scheduling the business of the Senate and recognizing the first speaker in floor debate. To be effective in policy making, the majority leader must be skilled in interpersonal persuasion and communication. Moreover, in the media age, the Senate majority leader must also be a national spokesperson for the party, along with the Speaker of the House. Republican Senate Leader Trent Lott and Republican Speaker of the House Dennis Hastert are their party's leading congressional spokesmen. The minority party leader in the Senate, Democrat Tom Daschle, represents the opposition in negotiations with the majority leader over Senate business. With the majority leader, the minority party leader tends to dominate floor debate in the Senate.

Career Paths within Congress   Movement up the party hierarchy in each house is the most common way of achieving a leadership position. The traditional succession pattern in the House is from whip to majority leader to Speaker. In the Senate, Republicans and Democrats frequently resort to election contests in choosing their party leaders, yet both parties have increasingly adopted a two-step succession route from whip to leader. Once in office, leaders in both parties are rarely removed.[31]

IN COMMITTEE

Much of the real work of Congress is done in committee. The floor of Congress is often deserted; C-SPAN focuses on the podium, not the empty chamber. Members dash to the floor when the bell rings throughout the Capitol signaling a roll-call vote. Otherwise they are found in their offices or in the committee rooms, where the real work of Congress is done.

Standing Committees   The committee system provides for a division of labor in the Congress, assigning responsibility for work and allowing members to develop some expertise. The committee system is as old as the Congress itself: the very first Congress regularly assigned the task of wording bills to selected members who were believed to have a particular expertise. Soon a system of **standing**

committees—permanent committees that specialize in a particular area of legislation—emerged. House committees have thirty to forty members and Senate committees fifteen to twenty members each. The proportions of Democrats and Republicans on each committee reflect the proportions of Democrats and Republicans in the House and Senate as a whole. Thus the majority party has a majority of members on every committee; and every committee is chaired by a member of the majority party. The minority membership on each committee is led by the *ranking minority member*, the minority-party committee member with the most seniority.

The principal function of standing committees is the screening and drafting of legislation. With 8,000 to 10,000 or more bills introduced each session, the screening function is essential. The standing committees are the gatekeepers of Congress; less than 10 percent of the legislation introduced will pass the Congress. With rare exceptions, bills are not submitted to a vote by the full membership of the House or Senate without prior approval by the majority of a standing committee. Moreover, committees do not merely sort through bills assigned to them to find what they like. Rather, committees—or more often their subcommittees—draft (write) legislation themselves. Committees may amend, rewrite, or write their own bills. Committees are "little legislatures" within their own policy jurisdictions. Each committee guards its own policy jurisdiction jealously; jurisdictional squabbles between committees are common.

Decentralization and Subcommittees   Congressional subcommittees within each standing committee further decentralize the legislative process. At present, the House has about 90 subcommittees and the Senate about 70 subcommittees, each of which functions independently of its full committee (see Table 10–6 on page 350). Subcommittees have fixed jurisdictions (for example, the House International Relations Committee has subcommittees on Africa, Asia and the Pacific, International Economic Policy, International Operations and Human Rights, and the Western Hemisphere); they meet and schedule their own hearings; and they have their own staffs and budgets. However, bills recommended by a subcommittee still require full standing-committee endorsement before being reported to the floor of the House or Senate. Full committees usually, but not always, ratify the decisions of their subcommittees.

Subcommittees decentralize power in Congress. Interest groups no longer concentrate their attention on a few senior standing-committee chairs and party leaders. Rather, they concentrate on those subcommittees dealing most directly with their concerns. Likewise, executive agencies must respond to subcommittees with policy oversight. Both lobbyists and bureaucrats must seek out "their" subcommittee and try to win the support of the chair and perhaps the ranking minority member. (For example, agents of the postal workers' union, the U.S. Postal Service, and private competitors such as FedEx and United Parcel Service all converge on the Post Office and Civil Service Subcommittee of the Senate Governmental Affairs Committee.) The result has been hundreds of policy networks, each featuring subcommittee members and staff, lobbyists with an interest in the subcommittee's field, and bureaucrats in the executive branch charged with implementing congressional policy in that field.

Chairing a committee or subcommittee gives members of Congress the opportunity to exercise power, attract media attention, and thus improve their chances of

standing committee
Permanent committee of the House or Senate that deals with matters within a specified subject area.

Table 10-6 Standing Committees in Congress

Senate

Agriculture, Nutrition, and Forestry	Governmental Affairs
Appropriations	Indian Affairs
Armed Services	Judiciary
Banking, Housing, and Urban Affairs	Labor and Human Resources
Budget	Rules and Administration
Commerce, Science, and Transportation	Select Ethics
Energy and Natural Resources	Select Intelligence
Environment and Public Works	Small Business
Finance	Special Aging
Foreign Relations	Veterans' Affairs

House

Agriculture	National Security
Appropriations	Resources
Banking and Financial Services	Rules
Budget	Science
Commerce	Select Intelligence
Education and the Workforce	Small Business
Government Reform and Oversight	Standards of Official Conduct
House Oversight	Transportation and Infrastructure
International Relations	Veterans' Affairs
Judiciary	Ways and Means

reelection. Often committees have become "fiefdoms" over which their chairs exercise complete control and jealously guard their power. This situation allows a very small number of House and Senate members to block legislation. Many decisions are not really made by the whole Congress. Rather, they are made by subcommittee members with a special interest in the policy under consideration. Although the committee system may satisfy the desire of members to gain power, prestige, and reelection opportunities, it weakens responsible government in the Congress as a whole.

Committee Membership   Given the power of the committee system, it is not surprising that members of Congress have a very keen interest in their committee assignments. Members strive for assignments that will give them influence in Congress, allow them to exercise power in Washington, and ultimately improve their chances for reelection. For example, a member from a big city may seek a seat on Banking, Finance, and Urban Affairs, a member from a farm district may seek a seat on Agriculture, and a member from a district with a large military base may seek a seat on National Security or Veterans' Affairs. Everyone seeks a seat on Appropriations, because both the House and the Senate Appropriations committees have subcommittees in each area of federal spending.[32]

Party leadership in both the House and the Senate largely determines committee assignments. These assignments are given to new Democratic House members by the Democratic Steering and Policy Committee; new Democratic senators receive

Senate Foreign Relations Committee chair Jesse Helms (right) enraged fellow Republicans by quashing the nomination of Republican William Weld, governor of Massachusetts, to be ambassador to Mexico. Helms, a conservative, was displeased with Weld's moderate politics. In contrast, Republican Senator Richard Lugar (left) strongly supported Weld. Helms's success reflects the power of committee chairs.

their assignments from the Senate Democratic Steering Committee. New Republican members receive their committee assignments from the Republican Committee on Committees in both houses. The leadership generally tries to honor new members' requests and improve their chances for reelection, but because incumbent members of committees are seldom removed, openings on powerful committees are infrequent.

Seniority   Committee chairs are elected in the majority-party caucus. But the **seniority system** governs most movement into committee leadership positions. The seniority system ranks all committee members in each party according to the length of time they have served on the committee. If the majority-party chair exits the Congress or leaves the committee, that position is filled by the next *ranking majority-party member*. New members of a committee are initially added to the bottom of the ranking of their party; they climb the seniority ranking by remaining on the committee and accruing years of seniority. Members who stay in Congress but "hop" committees are usually placed at the bottom of their new committee's list.

The seniority system has a long tradition in the Congress. The advantage is that it tends to reduce conflict among members, who otherwise would be constantly engaged in running for committee posts. It also increases the stability of policy direction in committees over time. Critics of the system note, though, that the seniority system grants greater power to members from "safe" districts—districts that offer little electoral challenge to the incumbent. (Historically in the Democratic Party, these districts were in the conservative South, and opposition to the seniority system developed among liberal northern Democrats. But in recent years, many liberal Democrats gained seniority and the seniority system again became entrenched.) The seniority rule for selecting committee chairs has been violated on only a few notable occasions.

Committee Hearings   The decision of a congressional committee to hold public hearings on a bill or topic is an important one. It signals congressional interest in a particular policy matter and sets the agenda for congressional policy making. Ignoring an issue by refusing to hold hearings on it usually condemns it

seniority system   Custom whereby the member of Congress who has served the longest on the majority side of a committee becomes its chair and the member who has served the longest on the minority side becomes its ranking member.

"Ted" Kennedy: Keeping Liberalism Alive in the U.S. Senate

To the American public, Massachusetts Sen. Edward M. "Ted" Kennedy is largely a symbol of his family's legendary triumphs and tragedies. But in the U.S. Senate, Kennedy has established himself over the years as the recognized leader of liberal Democrats and a highly effective legislator.

Ted Kennedy's father, Joseph P. Kennedy, was a wealthy banker and stock market manipulator who provided key financial backing for the 1932 presidential campaign of Franklin D. Roosevelt. FDR later appointed "Old Joe" as Ambassador to England. The senior Kennedy fathered nine children, including Joseph P. Jr., who was killed in World War II; President John F. Kennedy who was assassinated in 1963; Sen. Robert F. Kennedy who was assassinated in 1968; and youngest, Edward M. "Ted" Kennedy.

Although born to great wealth (he received his first communion from the Pope), Ted Kennedy acquired the sense of competition fostered in the large Kennedy household. In 1951, suspended from Harvard for cheating on an examination, he joined the Army and served two years in Germany. He was later re-admitted to Harvard where he graduated in 1956. Rejected by Harvard Law School, he enrolled instead in the University of Virginia Law School and completed his law degree in 1959. When he was just 30 years old, the minimum age for a U.S. Senator, he announced his candidacy for the Massachusetts Senate seat formerly held by his brother, who was then president. His 1962 election to the U.S. Senate reflected the esteem that Massachusetts voters have always held for his family.

Kennedy performed better in the Senate than many had expected. He worked hard learning about national health problems and problems of the elderly. In 1969 he was elected Senate Democratic Whip by his colleagues. But his personal life was marred by accident, tragedy, and scandal. He nearly died in a 1964 plane crash in which he suffered a broken back. He was frequently the object of romantic gossip in Washington. In 1969, a young woman died when the car Kennedy was driving plunged off a narrow bridge on Chappaquiddick Island after a late-night party. Missing for ten hours after the accident, Kennedy later made a dramatic national television appearance claiming that the tragedy had been an accident that he had

to oblivion. Public hearings allow interest groups and government bureaucrats to present formal arguments to Congress. Testimony comes mostly from government officials, lobbyists, and occasional experts recommended by interest groups or committee staff members. Hearings are usually organized by the staff under the direction of the chair. Staff members contact favored lobbyists and bureaucrats and schedule their appearances. Committee hearings are regularly listed in the *Washington Post* and are open to the public. Indeed, the purpose of many hearings is not really to inform members of Congress but instead to rally public support behind an issue or a bill. The media are the real target audience of many public hearings, with committee members jockeying in front of the cameras for a "sound bite" on the evening news.

drafting a bill Actual writing of a bill in legal language.

markup Line-by-line revision of a bill in committee by editing each phrase and word.

Markup   Once hearings are completed, the committee's staff is usually assigned the task of writing a report and **drafting a bill**. The staff's bill generally reflects the chair's policy views. But the staff draft is subject to committee **markup**, a line-by-line consideration of the wording of the bill. Markup sessions are frequently closed to the public in order to expedite work. Lobbyists are forced to stand in the hallways, buttonholing members as they go into and out of committee rooms.

been too confused to report until the next day. He pled guilty to the minor charge of leaving the scene of the accident. Senate Democrats removed Kennedy from his position as majority party whip.

Kennedy deliberately avoided Democratic presidential battles in both 1972 and 1976, believing that the public's memory of Chappaquiddick was still too fresh. However, in late 1979, with President Jimmy Carter standing in a near all-time low for presidents in opinion polls, Kennedy announced his presidential candidacy. But shortly thereafter, Soviet troops invaded neighboring Afghanistan. Support for the president was equated with support for America, and Carter benefited from this "rally round the flag" effect. Carter defeated Kennedy in the Democratic primaries, but Kennedy polished his own charismatic image with a dramatic inspiring speech at the 1980 Democratic national convention.

Kennedy avoided subsequent presidential races, citing family affairs as his reason. And indeed, family problems continued to plague him. He was divorced from his first wife, Joan, and stories were published in women's magazines portraying her as a victim of his heavy drinking and "womanizing." At the same time, he felt responsible for the many "third-generation" offspring of his deceased brother Robert, as well as his own children. One nephew died a drug-related death in a Miami motel in 1984, and another was found not guilty of rape charges in a nationally televised trial in 1992. That same year Kennedy married an accomplished Washington attorney and undertook to change his personal lifestyle. He delivered a moving eulogy on national television at the funeral of his nephew John F. Kennedy, Jr. after a plane crash in 1999 that killed JFK Jr., his wife, and sister-in-law.

As the ranking Democrat on the Senate Health, Education, and Labor Committee, Kennedy has undertaken the lead in a variety of important legislative issues. He helped pass the Family Leave Act of 1993, the Kennedy-Kasselbaum Act of 1996 that mandated health insurance "portability" (see Chapter 17), and increases in the minimum wage. While conservatives have frequently targeted Kennedy for his liberal politics, he has proven adept at working with Republicans in the Senate to win compromises in legislation. According to the *Congressional Quarterly*, "Kennedy long ago understood what might be called the Iron Law of the Senate, which is that very little can be accomplished without the 60 votes needed to overcome filibusters."* In 2000 he was elected to his seventh full term as U.S. senator from Massachusetts.

---

*"50 Ways To Do the Job of Congress," *Congressional Quarterly*, October 30, 1999.

It is in markup that the detailed work of lawmaking takes place. Markup sessions require patience and skill in negotiation. Committee or subcommittee chairs may try to develop consensus on various parts of the bill, either within the whole committee or within the committee's majority. In marking up a bill, members of a subcommittee must always remember that the bill must pass both in the full committee and on the floor of the chamber. Although they have considerable freedom in writing their own policy preferences into law, especially on the details of the legislation, they must give some consideration to the views of these larger bodies. Consultations with party leadership are not infrequent.

Most bills die in committee. Some are voted down, but most are simply ignored. Bills introduced simply to reassure constituents or interest groups that a representative is committed to "doing something" for them generally die quietly. But House members who really want action on a bill can be frustrated by committee inaction. The only way to force a floor vote on a bill opposed by a committee is to get a majority (218) of House members to sign a **discharge petition**. Out of hundreds of discharge petition efforts, only a few dozen have succeeded. The Senate also can forcibly "discharge" a bill from committee by simple majority vote; but because senators can attach any amendment to any bill they wish, there is generally no need to go this route.

discharge petition Petition signed by at least 218 House members to force a vote on a bill within a committee that opposes it.

ON THE FLOOR

A favorable "report" by a standing committee of the House or Senate places a bill on the "calendar." The word "calendar" is misleading, because bills on the calendar are not considered in chronological order, and many die on the calendar without ever reaching the floor.

House Rules Committee   Even after a bill has been approved by a standing committee, getting it to the floor of the House of Representatives for a vote by the full membership requires favorable action by the Rules Committee. The Rules Committee acts as a powerful "traffic cop" for the House. In order to reach the floor, a bill must receive a rule from the Rules Committee. The Rules Committee can kill a bill simply by refusing to give it a rule. A **rule** determines when the bill will be considered by the House and how long the debate on the bill will last. More important, a rule determines whether amendments from the floor will be permitted and, if so, how many. A **closed rule** forbids House members from offering any amendments and speeds up consideration of the bill in the form submitted by the standing committee. A **restricted rule** allows certain specified amendments to be considered. An **open rule** permits unlimited amendments. Most key bills are brought to the floor of the House with fairly restrictive rules. In recent sessions, about three-quarters of all bills reaching the floor were restricted, and an additional 10 to 15 percent were fully closed. Only a few bills were open.

In both houses, when a bill reaches the floor, the debate can be baffling to the uninitiated because of the terminology and conventions of speech used by the speakers (see *Up Close:* "What Are They Talking About?" on page 356 for an explanation of selected terms used in congressional debates; see, also, the glossary items in the margins of this book).

Senate Floor Traditions   The Senate has no rules committee but relies instead on a **unanimous consent agreement** negotiated between the majority and minority leader to govern consideration of a bill. The unanimous consent agreement generally specifies when the bill will be debated, what amendments will be considered, and when the final vote will be taken. But as the name implies, a single senator can object to a unanimous consent agreement and thus hold up Senate consideration of a bill. Senators do not usually do so, because they know that a reputation for obstructionism will imperil their own favorite bills at a later date. Once accepted, a unanimous consent agreement is binding on the Senate and cannot be changed without another unanimous consent agreement. To get unanimous consent, Senate leaders must consult with all interested senators. Unanimous consent agreements have become more common in recent years as they have become more specific in their provisions.

The Senate cherishes its tradition of unrestricted floor debate. Senators may speak as long as they wish or even try to **filibuster** a bill to death by talking nonstop and tying up the Senate for so long that the leadership is forced to drop the bill in order to go on to other work. Senate rules also allow senators to place a "hold" on a bill, indicating their unwillingness to grant unanimous consent to its consideration. Debate may be ended only if sixty or more senators vote for **cloture**, a process of petition and voting that limits the debate. A cloture vote requires a petition signed

---

rule   Stipulation attached to a bill in the House of Representatives that governs its consideration on the floor, including when and for how long it can be debated and how many (if any) amendments may be appended to it.

closed rule   Rule that forbids adding any amendments to a bill under consideration by the House.

restricted rule   Rule that allows specified amendments to be added to a bill under consideration by the House.

open rule   Rule that permits unlimited amendments to a bill under consideration by the House.

unanimous consent agreement   Negotiated by the majority and minority leaders of the Senate, it specifies when a bill will be taken up on the floor, what amendments will be considered, and when a vote will be taken.

filibuster   Delaying tactic by a senator or group of senators, using the Senate's unlimited debate rule to prevent a vote on a bill.

cloture   Vote to end debate—that is, to end a filibuster—which requires a three-fifths vote of the entire membership of the Senate.

by sixteen senators; two days must elapse between the petition's introduction and the cloture vote. If cloture passes, then each senator is limited to one hour of debate on the bill. Despite the obstacles to cloture, in recent years it has been used with increasing frequency.

Senate floor procedures also permit unlimited amendments to be offered, even those that are not "germane" to the bill. A **rider** is an amendment to a bill that is not germane to the bill's purposes.

These Senate traditions of unlimited debate and unrestricted floor amendments give individual senators considerably more power over legislation than individual representatives enjoy.

Floor Voting   The key floor votes are usually on *amendments* to bills rather than on their final passage. Indeed, "killer amendments" are deliberately designed to defeat the original purpose of the bill. Other amendments may water down the bill so much that it will have little policy impact. Thus the true policy preferences of senators or representatives may be reflected more in their votes on amendments than their vote on final passage. Members may later claim to have supported legislation on the basis of their vote on final passage, even though they earlier voted for amendments designed to defeat the bill's purposes.

Members may also obscure their voting records by calling for a voice vote—simply shouting "aye" or "nay"—and avoiding recording of their individual votes. In contrast, a **roll-call vote** involves the casting of individual votes, which are reported in the *Congressional Record* and are available to the media and the general public. Electronic voting machines in the House allow members to insert their cards and record their votes automatically. The Senate, truer to tradition, uses no electronic counters.

Conference Committees   The Constitution requires that both houses of Congress pass a bill with identical wording. However, many major bills pass each house in different forms, not only with different wording but sometimes with wholly different provisions. Occasionally the House or the Senate will resolve these differences by reconsidering the matter and passing the other chamber's version of the bill. But about 15 percent of the time, serious differences arise and bills are assigned to **conference committees** to reach agreement on a single version for resubmission to both houses. Conference committees are temporary, with members appointed by the leadership in each house, usually from among the senior members of the committees that approved the bills.

Conference committees can be very powerful. Their final bill is usually (although not always) passed in both houses and sent to the president for approval. In resolving differences between the House and the Senate versions, the conference committee makes many final policy decisions. Although conference committees have considerable leeway in striking compromises, they focus on points of disagreement and usually do not change provisions already approved by both houses. Figure 10–9 on page 358 summarizes the lawmaking process.

DECISION MAKING IN CONGRESS

How do senators and representatives decide about how they will vote on legislation? From an almost limitless number of considerations that go into congressional decision making, a few factors recur across a range of voting decisions: party loyalty, pres-

rider Amendment to a bill that is not germane to the bill's purposes.

roll-call vote Vote of the full House or Senate on which all members' individual votes are recorded and made public.

conference committee Meeting between representatives of the House and Senate to reconcile differences over provisions of a bill passed by both houses.

What Are They Talking About?

Visitors to Congress and TV viewers of C-SPAN are often confused by the language used during debates. Here some common phrases heard in the U.S. Congress, as well as state legislatures, are briefly defined.

Act   Legislation that has passed both houses of Congress and been signed by or passed over the veto of the president, thus becoming law.

Bills   Legislative proposals before Congress—designated "HR" in the House or "S" in the Senate plus the number assigned when they are introduced during the two-year congressional term.

Calendar   A list of business awaiting possible action by each chamber. The Houses uses five legislative calendars (Corrections, Discharge, House, Private, and Union calendars). The Senate places all legislative matters reported from committee on one calendar.

Committee of the Whole   All House members sitting as a committee, with its own chair, not the Speaker. A measure is debated and amendments may be proposed, with votes on amendments as needed. The committee, however, cannot pass a bill. When the committee completes its work, members may demand a roll-call vote on any amendment adopted in the Committee of the Whole. The final vote is on passage of the legislation.

Congressional Record   The daily printed account of proceedings in both the House and Senate chambers, showing substantially verbatim debate, statements, and a record of floor action. Members are entitled to have their extraneous remarks printed in an appendix known as "Extension of Remarks."

Enacting Clause   Key phrase in bills beginning, "Be it enacted by the Senate and House of Repre-

sentatives. . . ." A successful motion to strike it from legislation kills the measure.

Five-Minute Rule   When the House sits as the Committee of the Whole, under the rule a member offering an amendment is allowed to speak five minutes in its favor and an opponent is allowed to speak five minutes in opposition.

Floor Manager   Member who has the task of steering legislation through floor debate and the amendment process to a final vote in the House or the Senate.

Germane   Pertaining to the subject matter of the measure at hand. All House amendments must be germane to the bill being considered. The Senate requires that amendments be germane when they are proposed to general appropriation bills, bills being considered once cloture has been adopted, or, frequently, when proceeding under a unanimous consent agreement placing a time limit on consideration of a bill.

Hopper   Box on House clerk's desk where members deposit bills and resolutions to introduce them.

Motion   In the House or Senate chamber, a request by a member to institute any one of a wide array of parliamentary actions.

Point of Order   Objection raised by a member that the chamber is departing from rules governing its conduct of business.

Questions of Privilege   Matters affecting members of Congress individually or collectively. Questions involving individual members are called questions of "personal privilege." A member rising to ask a question of personal privilege is given precedence over almost all other proceedings.

Quorum   Number of members whose presence is necessary for the transaction of business. In the Senate and House, it is a majority of the membership.

Reading of Bills   Traditional procedure required bills to be read three times before they were passed. This custom is of little modern significance. Normally a bill is considered to have its first reading when it is introduced and printed, by title, in the *Congressional Record*. The second reading comes when floor consideration begins. (This is the most likely point at which there is an actual reading of the bill, if there is any.) The third reading (again, usually by title) takes place when floor action has been completed on amendments.

Recommit to Committee   A motion, made on the floor after a bill has been debated, to return it to the committee that reported it. If approved, recommittal usually is considered a death blow to the bill.

Reconsider a Vote   A motion to reconsider the vote by which an action was taken can be made only by a member who voted on the prevailing side of the original question.

Report   Document that explains the action of a committee when it returns a bill referred to it to the parent chamber.

Resolution   A "simple" resolution, designated "H Res" or "S Res," deals with matters entirely within the prerogatives of one house or the other. It requires neither passage by the other chamber nor approval by the president, and it does not have the force of law. Resolutions are often used to express the sentiments of a house such as condolences to the family of a deceased member or to comment on foreign policy or executive business.

Standing Vote   Nonrecorded vote used in both the House and Senate. (A standing vote also is called a division vote.) Members in favor of a proposal stand and are counted by the presiding officer.

Strike from the Record   Remarks made on the House floor may offend some member, who moves that the offending words be expunged from the debate as published in the *Congressional Record*.

Substitute   A motion, amendment, or entire bill introduced in place of the pending legislative

business. Passage of a substitute measure kills the original measure by supplanting it.

Suspend the Rules   Often a time-saving procedure for passing bills in the House. The wording of the motion, which may be made by any member recognized by the Speaker, is: "I move to suspend the rules and pass the bill . . ." A favorable vote by two-thirds of those present is required for passage.

Table a Bill   Widely used parliamentary procedures used to block or kill amendments or other parliamentary questions. Motions to table are not debatable and require a simple majority vote. When approved, a tabling motion is considered the final disposition of that issue.

Unanimous Consent   Proceedings of the House or Senate and action on legislation often take place upon the unanimous consent of the chamber, whether or not a rule of the chamber is being violated. Unanimous consent is used to expedite floor action.

U.S. Code   A consolidation and codification of the general and permanent laws of the United States arranged by subject under 50 titles, the first 6 dealing with general or political subjects, and the other 44 alphabetically arranged from agriculture to war. The *U.S. Code* is updated annually, and a new set of bound volumes is published every six years.

Without Objection   Used in lieu of a vote on noncontroversial motions, amendments, or bills that may be passed in either the House or Senate if no member voices an objection.

Yeas and Nays   The Constitution requires that yea-and-nay votes be taken and recorded when requested by one-fifth of the members present.

Yielding   When a member has been recognized to speak, no other member may speak unless he or she obtains permission from the member recognized. This permission is called yielding and usually is requested in the form, "Will the gentleman yield to me?"

Bill Introduction

Subcommittee Hearings

Committee Action

Floor Action

Conference Action

Presidential Decision

HOUSE	SENATE
Bill is introduced and assigned to a committee, which refers it to the appropriate subcommittee.	Bill is introduced and assigned to a committee, which refers it to the appropriate subcommittee.

Subcommittee
Subcommittee holds hearings and "marks up" the bill. If the bill is approved in some form, it goes to the full committee.

Committee
Full committee considers the bill. If the bill is approved in some form, it is "reported" to the full House and placed on the House calendar.

Subcommittee
Subcommittee holds hearings, debates provisions and "marks up" the bill. If a bill is approved, it goes to the full committee.

Committee
Full committee considers the bill. If the bill is approved in some form, it is "reported" to the full Senate and placed on the Senate calendar.

Rules Committee
Rules Committee issues a rule to govern debate on the floor. Sends it to the full House.

Full House
Full House debates the bill and may amend it. If the bill passes and it is in a form different from the Senate version, it must go to a conference committee.

Leadership
Majority and minority leaders negotiate "unanimous consent" agreements scheduling full Senate debate and vote on the bill.

Full Senate
Full Senate debates the bill. Senate may amend it. If the bill passes and is in a form different from the House version, it must go to a conference committee.

Conference Committee
Conference committee of senators and representatives meets to reconcile differences between bills. When agreement is reached, a compromise bill is sent back to both the House and the Senate.

President
President signs or vetoes the bill. Congress can override a veto by a two-thirds majority vote in both the House and Senate.

LAW

FIGURE 10–9   How a Bill Becomes a Law

This diagram depicts the major hurdles a successful bill must overcome in order to be enacted into law. Few bills introduced travel this full path; less than 10 percent of bills introduced are passed by Congress and sent to the president for approval or veto. Bills fail at every step along the path, but most die in committees and subcommittees, usually from inaction rather than from being voted down.

identical support or opposition, constituency concerns, interest-group pressures, and the personal values and ideologies of members themselves.[33]

Party Voting   Party appears to be the most significant influence on congressional voting. **Party votes** are roll-call votes on which a majority of voting Democrats oppose a majority of voting Republicans. Traditionally, party votes occurred on roughly *half* of all roll-call votes in Congress. But partisanship in Congress, as reflected in the percentage of party votes, has *risen* in recent years to over 60 percent of all roll-call votes (see Figure 10–10).

Party unity is measured by the percentage of Democrats and Republicans who stick by their party on party votes. Republican Party unity has remained at fairly constant levels (75–85 percent) in both the House and the Senate over the past twenty years. Until recently, Democratic Party cohesion was weakened by the frequent defection of southern Democrats. But in the last several sessions, Democratic Party unity in the House has matched that of the Republican Party, with both parties holding the votes of over 80 percent of their members.

Rising Partisanship   Democrats and Republicans in Congress are voting along party lines more than ever before. What accounts for this rise in partisanship? First of all, the Democratic Party has become more liberal and the Republican Party has become more conservative in recent years. Conservative Democrats, once very common in Southern politics, are rapidly disappearing. The once prominent "conservative coalition" of Republicans and Southern Democrats is no longer an important voting block in today's Congress. Today Republicans outnumber Democrats among Southern Congress members. At the same time, the ranks of liberal Republicans, mostly from the Northeast, has thinned. Second, the decline in voter turnout, especially in primary elections, has added to the importance of well-organized and ideologically motivated groups. A reputation as a "moderate" is not much help in a low-voter-turnout primary election. In these elections

party vote   Majority of Democrats voting in opposition to a majority of Republicans.

party unity   Percentage of Democrats and Republicans who stick with their party on party votes.

FIGURE 10–10   Party Voting in Congress

Partisanship varies over time in Congress. For many years, between 30 and 40 percent of votes in the House and Senate were party votes—votes on which a majority of Democrats were in opposition to a majority of Republicans—but in recent years the percentage has risen, indicating an increasingly partisan environment in Congress.

Note: Data indicate the percentage of all recorded votes on which a majority of voting Democrats opposed a majority of voting Republicans.

Source: Based on data from *Congressional Quarterly Weekly Report*, December 11, 1999, p. 2994.

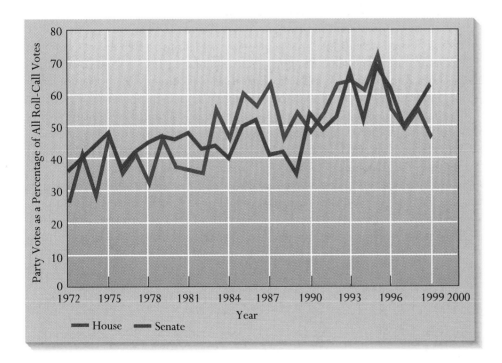

Republicans must be more concerned with pleasing conservative activists (e.g., the Christian Coalition, National Right-to-Life, National Rifle Association, etc.), and Democrats must be more concerned with pleasing liberal groups (National Education Association, National Association of State County and Municipal Employees, Emily's List, etc.). And third, the rising costs of campaigning make members ever more dependent upon the financial support of these interests.

Conflict between the parties occurs frequently on domestic social and economic issues—welfare, housing and urban affairs, health, business regulation, taxing, and spending. On civil rights issues, voting often follows party lines on amendments and other preliminary matters but then swings to **bipartisan** voting on a final bill. This pattern suggests that the parties tend to agree on the general goals of civil rights legislation but not on the means. Traditionally, bipartisanship was the goal of both presidents and congressional leaders on foreign and defense policy issues. Since the Vietnam War, however, Democrats in the House have been more critical of U.S. military involvements (and defense spending in general) than have Republicans, although many Democrats in the Senate have continued to support presidential initiatives.

Party may also influence congressional voting even when ideology is not a concern. Members of Congress run under party labels. (Only one Independent, Vermont's Bernard Sanders, serves in the House.) So there is some incentive for Democrats and Republicans in Congress to improve the image of their parties generally. The party leadership tries to appeal to party loyalty whenever it can. Members do have an interest in seeing their party win majority status in their chamber. Majority status means committee and subcommittee chairs, control over committee and subcommittee budgets and staff, and a better opportunity to get pork-barrel legislation passed. Finally, party leaders in the House and Senate do have modest favors to disperse. In short, party loyalty is not an insignificant factor in congressional voting.

Presidential Support or Opposition Presidential influence in congressional voting is closely tied to party. Presidents almost always receive their greatest support from members of their own party (see Figure 10–11). Indeed, the policy *gridlock* associated with *divided government*—in past decades, a Republican president and a Democratic-controlled Congress, but beginning in 1995 a Democratic president and a Republican-controlled Congress—arises directly from the tendency of the opposition party to obstruct the president's policy proposals.

The decentralization of power in the congressional committee system also limits the president's ability to influence voting. The president cannot simply negotiate with the leadership of the House and Senate but instead must deal with scores of committee and subcommittee chairs and ranking members. To win the support of so many members of Congress, presidents often must agree to insert pork into presidential bills, promise patronage jobs, or offer presidential assistance in campaign fund raising.

If negotiations break down, presidents can "go over the heads" of Congress, using the media to appeal directly to the people to support presidential programs and force Congress to act. The president has better access to the media than Congress has. But such threats and appeals can only be effective when (1) the president himself is popular with the public; and (2) the issue is one about which constituents can be made to feel intensely.

bipartisan Agreement by members of both the Democratic and the Republican parties.

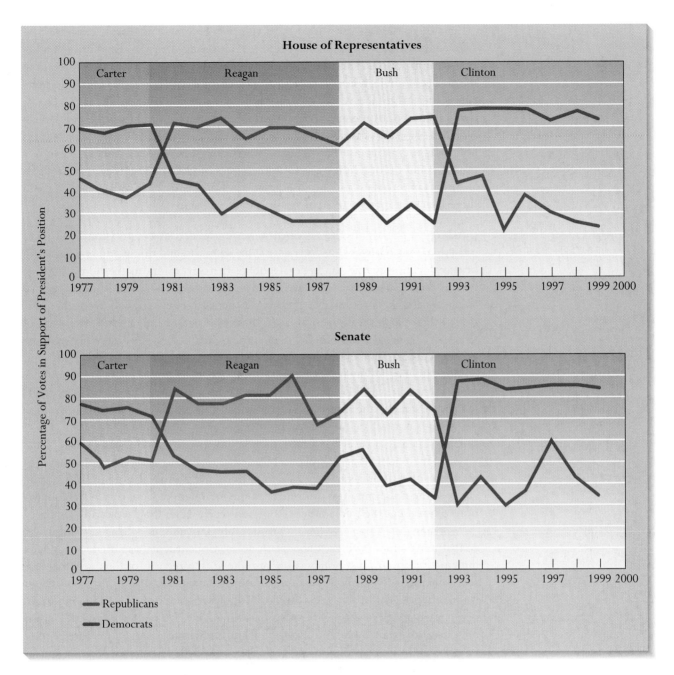

FIGURE 10-11 Congressional Voting in Support of the President

Presidents always receive more support in Congress from members of their own party. Democratic presidents Jimmy Carter and Bill Clinton could count on winning large majorities of Democratic members' votes; Republican presidents Ronald Reagan and George Bush won large majorities of GOP members' votes. Percentages indicate congressional votes supporting the president on votes on which the president took a position.

Source: Norman J. Ornstein, Thomas E. Mann, and Michael J. Malbin, *Vital Statistics on Congress 1999–2000* (Washington, D.C.: Congressional Quarterly Inc., 2000), pp. 254–255; and *Congressional Quarterly World Report*, December 11, 1999, p. 2987.

Finally, presidents can threaten to veto legislation. This threat, expressed or implied, confronts congressional leaders, committee chairs, and sponsors of a bill with several options. They must decide whether to (1) modify the bill to overcome the president's objections; (2) try to get two-thirds of both houses to commit to overriding the threatened veto; or (3) pass the bill and dare the president to veto it, then make a political issue out of the president's opposition. Historically, less than 5 percent of vetoes have been overridden by the Congress. Unless the president is politically very weak (as Richard Nixon was during the Watergate scandal), Congress cannot count on overriding a veto. If members of Congress truly want to address an important problem and not just define a political issue, they must negotiate with the White House to write a bill the president will sign.

Constituency Influence   Constituency influence in congressional voting is most apparent on issues that attract media attention and discussion and generate intense feelings among the general public. If many voters in the home state or district know about an issue and have intense feelings about it, members of Congress are likely to defer to their constituents' feelings, regardless of the position of their party's leadership or even their own personal feelings.[34] Members of Congress from *safe seats* seem to be just as attuned to the interests of their constituents as members from competitive seats.

Constituency influence is particularly important on economic issues. Members from districts heavily dependent on a particular industry are routinely found protecting and advancing the interests of that industry. This kind of constituency representation is not unlike pork-barrel politics.

Constituencies may also exercise a subtle influence by conditioning the personal views of members. Many members were born, were raised, and continue to live in the towns they represent; over a lifetime they have absorbed and internalized the views of their communities. Moreover, some members of Congress feel an obligation to represent their constituents' opinions even when they personally disagree.

Members of Congress have considerable latitude in voting against their constituents' opinions if they choose to do so. Constituents, as noted earlier, lack information about most policy issues and the voting records of their senators and representatives. Even when constituents know about an issue and feel strongly about it, members can afford to cast a "wrong" vote from time to time. A long record of home-style politics—casework, pork barreling, visits, public appearances, and so on—can isolate members of Congress from the wrath generated by their voting records. Only a long string of "wrong" votes on issues important to constituents is likely to jeopardize an incumbent.

Interest-Group Influence   Inside the Washington Beltway, the influence of interest groups, lobbyists, and fund raisers on members of Congress is well understood. This influence is seldom talked about back home or on the campaign trail, except perhaps by challengers. Lobbyists have their greatest effects on the *details* of public policy. Congressional decisions made in committee rooms, at markup sessions, and around conference tables can mean billions of dollars to industries and tens of millions to individual companies. Pressures from competing interest groups can be intense as lobbyists buttonhole lawmakers and try to win legislative amendments that can make or break business fortunes. One of the most potent tools in the lobbyist's arsenal is money. The prohibitive cost of modern campaigning has dictated that dollars are crucial to electoral victory, and virtually all members of Congress spend more time than they would like courting it, raising it, and stockpiling it for the next election.

Voters may be wrong when they think that all members of Congress are crooks, but they are not far off the mark when they worry that their own representatives may be listening to two competing sets of constituents—the real constituents back home in the district and the cash constituents who come calling in Washington, D.C. (see *Up Close:* The Cash Constituents of Congress on page 364.)[35]

Personal Values   It was the eighteenth-century English political philosopher Edmund Burke, himself a member of Parliament, who told his constituents: "You choose a member indeed; but when you have chosen him, he is not a member of Bristol, but he is a member of *Parliament.*" Burke defended the classic notion of representatives as **trustees** who feel obligated to use their own best judgment about what is good for the nation as a whole. In this theory, representatives are not obligated to vote the views of their constituents. This notion contrasts with the idea of representatives as **delegates** who feel obligated to vote according to the views of "the folks back home" regardless of their own personal viewpoint. Most legislators *claim* to be trustees, perhaps because of the halo effect generated by the independence implied in the term.

Democratic political philosophers have pondered the merits of trustee versus delegate representation over the centuries, but the question only rarely arises in actual congressional deliberations. In many cases, members' own personal views and those of their constituents are virtually identical. (However, there is some evidence that members themselves may exaggerate the knowledge and issue-oriented tendencies of voters, since those most likely to communicate directly with their members of Congress are among the most knowledgeable and issue-oriented people in the district.[36]) Even when legislators perceive conflicts between their own views and those of their constituents, most attempt to find a compromise between these competing demands rather than choose one role or another exclusively. The political independence of members of Congress—their independence from party, combined with the ignorance of their constituents about most policy issues—allows members to give great weight to their own personal ideologies in voting.

CUSTOMS AND NORMS

Over time, institutions develop customs and norms of behavior to assist in their functioning. These are not merely quaint and curious folkways; they promote the purposes of the institution. Congressional customs and norms are designed to help members work together, to reduce interpersonal conflict, to facilitate bargaining and promote compromise, and in general to make life in Congress a little more pleasant.

Civility   Traditionally members of Congress understood that uncivil behavior—expressions of anger, personal attacks on character, ugly confrontations, flaming rhetoric—undermined the lawmaking function. Indeed, civility was encouraged by the longstanding custom of members of Congress referring to each other in elaborately courteous terms: "my distinguished colleague from Ohio," "the honorable representative from Pennsylvania," and the like. By custom, even bitter partisan enemies in Congress were expected to avoid harsh personal attacks on each other. The purpose

trustees   Legislators who feel obligated to use their own best judgment in decision making.

delegates   Legislators who feel obligated to present the views of their home constituents.

The Cash Constituents of Congress

As the costs of campaigning spiral upward, the influence of big money contributors in Congress increases. Corporations, unions, trade associations, and lawyers are regularly found among the largest congressional campaign contributors. The voices of these cash constituents frequently rise above the voices of voting constituents back home, especially on issues that few voters know much about.

The list of top contributors changes slightly from election to election, depending in part on what issues are high on the congressional agenda. The table on page 365 lists the 25 largest contributors in the 1998 midterm congressional election; these amounts include direct campaign contributions, PAC contributions, and soft-money contributions to the parties. Philip Morris

tops the list in 1998, perhaps because anti-tobacco legislation was being considered by Congress. Unions, especially public employee unions (the American Federation of State County and Municipal Employees, National Education Association, and the Teamsters Union which now organizes among public employees), are almost always listed among the top contributors. Virtually all union contributions go to Democratic candidates.

The Association of Trial Lawyers is also regularly found among the top contributors; their strong support of Democratic candidates may be explained by the interest of lawyers in opposing tort reform—limits on damages that courts may award to consumers (and their lawyers) for faults in products and services.

Defense industry corporations remain among the top contributors, although their ranking has declined as defense spending has decreased over the years.

of this custom was to try to maintain an atmosphere in which people who hold very different opinions can nevertheless function with some degree of decorum. Unfortunately, many of these customs and norms of behavior are breaking down. Individual ambition and the drive for power and celebrity have led to a decline in courtesy, cooperation, and respect for traditional norms. One result is that it has become increasingly difficult for Congress to reach agreement on policy issues. Another result is that life in Congress is increasingly tedious, conflict filled, and unpleasant (see *A Conflicting View:* "Congress Can Act Responsibly on Occasion" on page 366).

In early 1997 concerned members of the House sponsored a weekend "Civility Retreat," inviting both members and their families in an effort to improve collegiality. Although more than two hundred members attended, just weeks later House members were heatedly arguing on the floor over calls for the impeachment of both President Clinton and Speaker Gingrich.

Congressional Election, 25 Largest Contributors, 1998

Rank	Contributor	Total	Democrat	Republican
1	Philip Morris	$2,596,260	22.9%	77.0%
2	Intl Brotherhood of Electrical Workers	$2,327,414	98.1%	1.8%
3	Assn of Trial Lawyers of America	$2,313,836	85.7%	13.9%
4	American Fedn of St/Cnty/Munic Employees	$2,097,164	97.4%	2.5%
5	AT&T	$1,772,585	40.6%	59.3%
6	Teamsters Union	$1,731,250	94.2%	5.5%
7	National Education Assn	$1,681,314	91.2%	8.7%
8	National Assn of Realtors	$1,651,104	39.7%	60.3%
9	National Assn of Home Builders	$1,632,240	31.9%	68.1%
10	Travelers Group	$1,631,316	44.1%	55.8%
11	United Food & Commercial Workers Union	$1,587,621	97.3%	2.0%
12	United Parcel Service	$1,578,181	21.7%	78.3%
13	American Medical Assn	$1,558,917	32.8%	67.0%
14	Communications Workers of America	$1,514,748	99.4%	0.5%
15	Amway	$1,469,291	0.0%	100.0%
16	United Auto Workers	$1,469,165	98.6%	1.1%
17	National Assn of Letter Carriers	$1,463,821	82.1%	17.6%
18	Bell Atlantic	$1,458,277	33.4%	66.3%
19	National Auto Dealers Assn	$1,445,905	32.7%	67.3%
20	BellSouth Corp	$1,375,028	44.5%	55.5%
21	Laborers Union	$1,372,474	90.7%	9.1%
22	Marine Engineers Union	$1,369,585	47.7%	52.3%
23	Machinists/Aerospace Workers Union	$1,356,100	99.0%	0.7%
24	Boeing Co	$1,349,008	37.2%	62.7%
25	Lockheed Martin	$1,327,386	36.3%	63.7%

Source: Center for Responsive Politics.

The Demise of the Apprenticeship Norm   Not too many years ago, "the first rule"[37] of congressional behavior was that new members were expected to be seen but not heard on the floor, to be studious in their committee work, and to be cooperative with party leaders. But the institutional norm of apprenticeship was swept aside in the 1970s as increasingly ambitious and independent senators and representatives arrived on Capitol Hill. Today new members of Congress feel free to grab the spotlight on the floor, in committee, and in front of television cameras. "The evidence is clear, unequivocal, and overwhelming: the [apprenticeship] norm is simply gone."[38] Nevertheless, experienced members are more active and influential in shaping legislation than are new members.[39]

Specialization and Deference   The committee system encourages members of Congress to specialize in particular policy areas. Even the most independent and

Congress Can Act Responsibly on Occasion

Congress is not always mired in partisanship, squabbling and gridlock. On occasion it acts responsibly in the national interest. Indeed, consider the following congressional landmarks in U.S. history:

Louisiana Purchase (1803)   President Thomas Jefferson offered to purchase from France nearly 830,000 square miles between the Mississippi and the Rockies for $15 million—about three cents an acre. There is no constitutional provision authorizing the federal government to buy foreign territory, but the Senate, accepting Jefferson's broad interpretation of the Constitution, approved the purchase. The House appropriated the money to consummate the deal. On December 29, 1803, the United States took possession of North America's heartland, doubling the nation's size with territory that would comprise 13 states.

Homestead Act (1862)   This Civil War-era legislation allowed any family head or adult male to claim 160 acres of prairie land for a $10 registration fee and a promise to live there continuously for five years. It opened up the midwestern United States for immediate settlement. The act drew thousands of English, Irish, Germans, Swedes, Danes, Norwegians, and Czechs to the United States, pushing settlement farther west.

Social Security Act (1935)   The act was designed to secure "the men, women, and children of the nation against certain hazards and vicissitudes of life," explained President Franklin Roosevelt. The act's best-known measure is the social insurance system that provides monthly checks to the elderly.

National Labor Relations Act (1935)   By declaring workers had a right to join unions and bargain collectively with employers for pay raises and improved working conditions, the act spurred the growth of the nation's major industrial unions. Labor's Magna Carta also provided workers with the legal weapons to improve plant conditions and protect themselves from employer harassment.

G.I. Bill of Rights (1944)   The G.I. Bill of Rights, known officially as the Servicemen's Readjustment Act of 1944, offered to pay tuition for college or trade education to ex-World War II servicemen. It also mandated that they receive up to $500 a year for tuition, books, and supplies. Nearly 8 million veterans who took advantage of this first G.I. Bill and American higher education expanded rapidly as a result. Veterans also made use of the bill's guaranteed mortgages and low interest rates to buy new homes in the suburbs, inspiring a development boom.

Truman Doctrine (1947) and NATO (1949)   The Truman Doctrine initiated U.S. resistance to expansion of the Soviet Union into Western Europe following World War II, and the NATO Treaty has provided the framework for European Security for half a century. Truman declared to a joint session of Congress, "I believe that it must be the policy of the United States to support free people who are resisting attempted subjugation by armed minorities or by outside pressures."

Federal Highway Act (1956)   President Dwight D. Eisenhower was right when he said "More than any single action by the government since the end of the war, this one would change the face of America." The most expensive public-works project in U.S. history, the highway act built the 41,000 mile nationwide interstate-highway system.

Civil Rights Act of 1964   Only Congress could end racial segregation in privately owned businesses and facilities. It did so by an overwhelming vote of both Houses in the Civil Rights Act of 1964. Injustices endure, but the end of segregated restaurants, theaters, and drinking fountains provided new opportunities for African-Americans and helped change white attitudes. In addition, Title VII of the act prohibits gender discrimination and serves as the legal bulwark for the women's rights.

Voting Rights Act of 1965   President Johnson signed this act in the same room in the Capitol where Abraham Lincoln had penned the Emancipation Proclamation. This legislation guaranteed all Americans the most fundamental of all rights—the right to vote. Between the 1964 and 1968 presidential elections, black voter registration increased 50 percent across the nation, even in the reluctant southern states, giving African Americans newfound political clout.

Medicare and Medicaid (1965)   Congress amended the Social Security Act of 1935 to provide for national health insurance for the aged (Medicare) and for the poor (Medicaid).

ambitious members can perceive the advantage of developing power and expertise in an area especially relevant to their constituents. Traditionally, members who developed a special expertise and accumulated years of service on a standing committee were deferred to in floor proceedings. These specialists were "cue givers" for party members when bills or amendments were being voted on. Members are still likely to defer to specialized committee members when the issues are technical or complicated, or when the issue is outside of their own area of policy specialization, but deference is increasingly rare on major public issues.

Bargaining   Bargaining is central to the legislative process. Little could be achieved if individual members were unwilling to bargain with each other for votes both in committees and on the floor. A willingness to bargain is a long-standing functional norm of Congress.

Members of Congress are not expected to violate their consciences in the bargaining process. On the contrary, members respect one another's issues of conscience and receive respect in return. On most issues, however, members can and do bargain their support. "Horse trading" is very common in committee work.[40] Members may bargain in their own personal interest, in the interests of constituents or groups, or even in the interests of their committee with members of other committees. Because most bargaining occurs in a committee setting, it is seldom a matter of public record. The success and reputation of committee chairs largely depend on their ability to work out bargains and compromises.

Bargaining can assume different forms. Explicit trade-offs such as "If you vote for my bill, I'll vote for yours" are the simplest form of bargaining, but implicit understandings may be more common. Members may help other members in anticipation of receiving reciprocal help at some future unspecified time. Moreover, representatives who refuse to cooperate on a regular basis may find little support for their own bills. Mutual "back scratching" allows members to develop a reservoir of IOUs for the future. Building credit is good business for most members; one can never tell when one will need help in the future.

Bargaining requires a certain kind of integrity. Members of Congress must stick to their agreements. They must not consistently ask too high a price for their cooperation. They must recognize and return favors. They must not renege on promises. They must be trustworthy.

Conference-committee bargaining is essential if legislation acceptable to both houses is to be written. Indeed, it is expected that conferees from each house will bargain and compromise their differences. "Every House-Senate conference is expected to proceed via the methods of 'give and take,' 'trading back and forth,' 'pulling and hauling,' 'horse-trading and compromise,' 'splitting the difference,' etc."[41]

Reciprocity   The norm of *reciprocity*—favors rendered should be repaid in kind—supports the bargaining process. Reciprocity may mean simply supporting a bill that is important to a colleague. But it may also extend to committees and subcommittees. In order to minimize intercommittee disputes over legislation, jurisdiction, or appropriations, "committees negotiate treaties of reciprocity ranging from 'I will stay out of your specialty if you will stay out of mine,' to 'I'll support your bill if you will support mine.'"[42]

The norm of reciprocity facilitates compromise and agreement and getting the work of Congress accomplished. Members who were willing to accept "half a loaf" traditionally accomplished more than those who insisted on a "whole loaf." But the norm of reciprocity may have weakened in recent years.

Logrolling   Perhaps the most celebrated and reviled form of reciprocity, **logrolling** is mutual agreement to support projects that primarily benefit individual members of Congress and their constituencies. Logrolling is closely associated with pork-barrel legislation. Yet it can occur in virtually any kind of legislation. Even interest-group lobbyists may logroll with each other, promising to support each other's legislative agendas.

Leader-Follower Relations   Because leaders have few means of disciplining members, they must rely heavily on their bargaining skills to solicit cooperation and get the work of Congress accomplished. Party leaders can appeal to members' concerns for their party image among the voters. Individual majority members want to keep their party in the majority—if for no other reason than to retain their committee and subcommittee chairs. Individual minority members would like their party to win control of their house in order to assume the power and privileges of committee and subcommittee chairs. Party leaders must appeal to more than partisanship to win cooperation, however.

To secure cooperation, leaders can grant—or withhold—some tangible benefits. A member of the House needs the Speaker's support to get recognition, to have a bill called up, to get a bill scheduled, to see to it that a bill gets assigned to a preferred committee, to get a good committee assignment, and to help a bill get out of the Rules Committee, for example.

Party leaders may also seek to gain support from their followers by doing favors that ease their lives in Washington, advance their legislative careers, and help them with their reelection. Favors from party leaders oblige members to respond to leaders' requests at a later time. Members themselves like to build up a reservoir of good feeling and friendship with the leadership, knowing that eventually they will need some favors from the leadership.

Gridlock   Congress is often criticized for legislative "gridlock"—the failure to enact laws, including appropriations acts, that are widely perceived to have merit. Indeed, much of the popular frustration with Congress relates to gridlock arising from policy and budgetary stalemates. Research has suggested that the following factors contribute to congressional gridlock:[43]

- Divided party control of the presidency and Congress
- Divided party control of the House and Senate
- Greater ideological polarization (liberal versus conservative) of the parties
- In the Senate, the willingness of members to filibuster against a bill, requiring 60 votes to overcome the opposition

In contrast, the factors that appear to lessen gridlock and encourage significant legislative accomplishment include:

- Unified party control of the presidency, House, and Senate
- Larger numbers of moderates among Democrats and Republicans in Congress (as opposed to larger numbers of strong liberals and strong conservatives)
- Overwhelming public support for new legislation

logrolling   Bargaining for agreement among legislators to support each other's favorite bills, especially projects that primarily benefit individual members and their constituents.

Note that the constitutional structure of American government—separation of powers and checks and balances, as well as bicameralism—plays a major role in gridlock, as does the American two-party system. Overcoming gridlock requires a willingness of members of both parties in both houses of Congress, as well as the White House, to bargain and compromise over legislation. And it requires strong public opinion in support of congressional action.

CONGRESSIONAL ETHICS

Although critics might consider the phrase *congressional ethics* to be an oxymoron, the moral climate of Congress today is probably better than in earlier eras of American history. Nevertheless, Congress as an institution has suffered from well-publicized scandals that continue to prompt calls for reform.

Initially selected by his Republican colleagues to be Speaker of the House of Representatives, Bob Livingston was forced to give up his speakership after rumors of an alleged extramarital affair.

Ethics Rules   Congress has an interest in maintaining the integrity of the institution itself and the trust of the people. Thus Congress has established its own rules of ethics. These rules include the following:

- *Financial disclosure:* All members must file personal financial statements each year.
- *Honoraria:* Members cannot accept fees for speeches or personal appearances.
- *Campaign funds:* Surplus campaign funds cannot be put to personal use. (A loophole allowed members elected before 1980 to keep such funds if they left office before January 1, 1993. A record number of House members resigned in 1992; many of them kept substantial amounts of campaign money.)
- *Gifts:* Members may not accept gifts worth more than $200 for representatives and $300 for senators (with annual increases in these amounts for inflation).
- *Free travel:* Members may not accept free travel from private corporations or individuals for more than four days of domestic travel and seven days of international travel per year. (Taxpayer-paid "junkets" to investigate problems at home or abroad or attend international meetings are not prohibited.)
- *Lobbying:* Former members may not lobby Congress for at least one year after retirement.

But these limited rules have not gone very far in restoring popular trust in Congress.

Gray Areas: Services and Contributions   Congress members are expected to perform services for their political contributors. However, a direct *quid pro quo*—receiving a financial contribution specifically for the performance of official duty—is illegal. Few Congress members would be so foolish as to openly state a price to a potential contributor for a specific service, and most contributors know not to state a dollar amount that would be forthcoming if the member performed a particular service for them. But what if the contribution and the service occur close together?

When banker Charles H. Keating contributed $1 million to U.S. Senator Alan Cranston (D-CA) in 1985 within days of Cranston's calls to the Federal Home Loan Bank Board urging the Board to allow Keating's shaky bank to remain open, the Board obliged. But eventually Keating's bank collapsed costing U.S. taxpayers $2 billion; Keating was later convicted on fraud charges. When Keating himself was asked whether his large campaign contributions bought him influence, he replied, "I certainly hope so." Senator Cranston claimed that he was just performing a service for a constituent. But the Senate Ethics Committee found that Cranston's "impermissible pattern of conduct violated established norms of behavior in the Senate . . . {and} was improper and repugnant."[44] Cranston announced his intention not seek reelection and the Senate took no further action. But the Ethics Committee offered little in the way of a future guidance in handling services for campaign contributors.

Expulsion   The Constitution gives Congress the power to discipline its own members. "Each House may . . . punish its Members for disorderly Behaviour, and, with the Concurrence of two thirds, expel a Member." But the Constitution fails to define *disorderly behavior*.

It seems reasonable to believe that criminal conduct falls within the constitutional definition of disorderly behavior. Bribery is a criminal act: it is illegal to solicit or receive anything of value in return for the performance of a government duty. During its notorious Abscam investigation in 1980, the Federal Bureau of Investigation set up a sting operation in which agents posing as wealthy Arabs offered bribe money to members of Congress while secretly videotaping the transactions. Six representatives and one senator were convicted. But criminal conviction does not automatically result in expulsion from Congress. In the Abscam case, only one defendant, Representative Michael Ozzie Myers (D-Pa.), was expelled, becoming the first member to be expelled since the Civil War. (Two other House members and the senator resigned rather than face expulsion, and the other three representatives were defeated for reelection. Perhaps the most interesting result of the Abscam investigation: only one member of Congress approached by the FBI, Democratic Senator Larry Presler of South Dakota, turned down the bribe.) The powerful chair of the House Ways and Means Committee, Democrat Dan Rostenkowski (Ill.), was indicted by a federal grand jury in 1994 for misuse of congressional office funds; he refused to resign from Congress, but his Chicago constituents voted him out of office. Democratic Representative Mel Reynolds (Ill.) resigned in 1995, following his criminal conviction on charges of sexual misconduct. (A special election to fill his vacated seat was won by Jesse Jackson, Jr., son of the popular preacher, commentator, and former Democratic presidential contender.) Republican Senator Robert Packwood (Oreg.) resigned in 1995 in order to avoid official expulsion following a Senate Ethics Committee report charging him with numerous counts of sexual harassment of female staff.

Censure   A lesser punishment in the Congress than expulsion is official **censure**. Censured members are obliged to "stand in the well" and listen to the charges read against them. It is supposed to be a humiliating experience and fatal to one's political career. In 1983 two members of Congress were censured for sexual misconduct with teenage congressional pages. Both were obliged to "stand in the well." Representative Daniel B. Crane (R-Ill.), who acknowledged a sexual relationship with a female page, was subsequently defeated for reelection. But Representative Gerry E. Studds (D-Mass.), who admitted to a homosexual relationship with a male teenage page, won reelection.

The threat of censure can be a potent one, though. In 1989, Speaker of the House Jim Wright (D-Tex.) was found to have circumvented ethics rules regarding outside

censure   Public reprimand for wrongdoing, given to a member standing in the chamber before Congress.

░ LOOKING AHEAD

Twenty-First Century Directions

Congress ceded policy leadership to the president early in the twentieth century. Periodic efforts by Congress to reassume a national leadership role have consistently foundered. There is no indication that the twenty-first century will see a resurgence of Congress.

⬇ Public confidence in Congress as an institution is not likely to improve. Congress remains the least trusted branch of American government. While popular approval of Congress may rise and fall somewhat with economic conditions, scandals, and crises, in general Congress will remain both misunderstood and unappreciated.

⬇ Congress will find it increasingly difficult to deal effectively with national problems. Increasingly leadership will come from the White House rather than the Capitol. At best, Congress may

serve as a check upon presidential policy initiatives. Congress may be able to obstruct change, but it cannot bring about change on its own.

⬆ However, individual Congress members may come to play an increasingly important role as intermediaries between their constituents and the vast federal bureaucracy. "Home style" politics will come to occupy most of the time and energy of most members of Congress. Citizens will tend to regard their own legislators as representatives of their personal and local interests. They will increasingly judge their Congress member on his or her personal service and service to the district.

⬇ Partisanship within the Congress will continue unabated. The Democratic and Republican parties in the Congress will continue to move apart ideologically. The resulting conflicts, bitterness, and even incivility in the halls of Congress will further erode public confidence in the institution.

financial payments to a member. He received heavy royalties on sales to interest groups of a book he authored. He also accepted large gifts from supporters, including the free use of an expensive condominium. He resigned the Speaker's post as well as his seat in Congress.

SUMMARY NOTES

- The Constitution places all of the delegated powers of the national government in the Congress. The Founders expected Congress to be the principal institution for resolving national conflicts, balancing interests, and deciding who gets what. Today, Congress is a central battleground in the struggle over national policy. Congress generally does not initiate but responds to policy initiatives and budget requests originating from the president, the bureaucracy, and interest groups. Over time, the president and the executive branch, together with the Supreme Court and federal judiciary, have come to dominate national policy making.

- The Congress represents local and state interests in policy making. The Senate's constituencies are the 50 states, and the House's constituencies are 435 separate districts. Both houses of Congress, but especially the House of Representatives, wield power in domestic and foreign affairs primarily through the "power of the purse."

- Congressional powers include oversight and investigation. These powers are exercised primarily through committees. Although Congress claims these powers are a necessary part of lawmaking, their real purpose is usually to influence agency decision making, to build political support for increases or decreases in agency funding, to lay the political foundation for new programs and policies, and to capture media attention and enhance the power of members of Congress.

- Congress is gradually becoming more "representative" of the general population in terms of race and gender. Redistricting, under federal court interpretations of the Voting Rights Act, has increased African American and Hispanic representation in Congress. And women have significantly increased their presence in Congress in recent years. Nevertheless, women and minorities do not occupy seats in Congress proportional to their share of the general population.

- Members of Congress are independent political entrepreneurs. They initiate their own candidacies, raise their own campaign funds, and get themselves elected with very little help from their party. Members of Congress are largely career politicians who skillfully use the advantages of incumbency to stay in office. Incumbents outspend challengers by large margins. Interest-group political action committees and individual contributors strongly favor incumbents. Congressional elections are seldom focused on great national issues but rather on local issues and personalities and the ability of candidates to "bring home the bacon" from Washington and serve their constituents.

- Congress as an institution is not very popular with the American people. Scandals, pay raises, perks, and privileges reported in the media have hurt the image of the institution. Nevertheless, individual members of Congress remain popular with their districts' voters.

- Members of Congress spend as much time on "home-style" activities—promoting their images back home and attending to constituents' problems—as they do legislating. Casework wins votes one at a time, gradually accumulating political support back home, and members often support each other's "pork-barrel" projects.

- Despite the independence of members, the Democratic and Republican party structures in the House and Senate remain the principal bases for organizing Congress. Party leaders in the House and Senate generally control the flow of business in each house, assigning bills to committees, scheduling or delaying votes, and appointing members to committees. But leaders must bargain for votes; they have few

formal disciplinary powers. They cannot deny renomination to recalcitrant members.

- The real legislative work of Congress is done in committees. Standing committees screen and draft legislation; with rare exceptions, bills do not reach the floor without approval by a majority of a standing committee. The committee and subcommittee system decentralizes power in Congress. The system satisfies the desires of members to gain power, prestige, and electoral advantage, but it weakens responsible government in the Congress as a whole. All congressional committees are chaired by members of the majority party. Seniority is still the major determinant of power in Congress.

- In order to become law, a bill must win committee approval and withstand debate in both houses of Congress. The rules attached to a bill's passage in the House can significantly help or hurt its chances. Bills passed with differences in the two houses must be reworked in a conference committee composed of members of both houses and then passed in identical form in both.

- In deciding how to vote on legislation, Congress members are influenced by party loyalty, presidential support or opposition, constituency concerns, interest-group pressures, and their own personal values and ideology. Party majorities oppose each other on roughly half of all roll-call votes in Congress. Presidents receive the greatest support in Congress from members of their own party.

- The customs and norms of Congress help reduce interpersonal conflict, facilitate bargaining and compromise, and make life more pleasant on Capitol Hill. They include the recognition of special competencies of members, a willingness to bargain and compromise, mutual "back scratching" and logrolling, reciprocity, and deference toward the leadership. But traditional customs and norms have weakened over time as more members have pursued independent political agendas. And partisanship and incivility in Congress have risen in recent years.

- Congress establishes its own rules of ethics. The Constitution empowers each house to expel its own members for "disorderly conduct" by a two-thirds vote, but expulsion has seldom occurred. Some members have resigned to avoid expulsion; others have been officially censured yet remained in Congress.

KEY TERMS

SELECTED READINGS

Congressional Quarterly. *How Congress Works* 3rd ed. Washington, DC: CQ Press, 1998. A description and explanation of the rules and procedures that govern the House and the Senate.

DAVIDSON, ROBERT H., and WALTER J. OLESZEK. *Congress and Its Members.* 7th ed. Washington, D.C.: Congressional Quarterly Press, 1999. Authoritative text on Congress covering the recruitment of members, elections, house styles and hill styles, leadership, decision making, and relations with interest groups, presidency, and courts. Emphasizes tension between lawmaking responsibilities and desire to be reelected.

FENNO, RICHARD F. *Home Style.* Boston: Little, Brown, 1978. The classic description of how attention to constituency by members of Congress enhances their reelection prospects. Home-style activities, including casework, pork barreling, travel and appearances back home, newsletters, and surveys, are described in detail.

FIORINA, MORRIS P. *Congress: Keystone to the Washington Establishment.* 2nd ed. New Haven, Conn.: Yale University Press, 1989. A lively description of members of Congress as independent political entrepreneurs serving themselves by serving local constituencies and ensuring their own reelection, often at the expense of the national interest.

GUIDEL, ROBERT K., DONALD A. GROSS, and TODD G. SHIELDS. *Money Matters: Consequences of Campaign Finance Reform in House Elections.* Lanham, MA: Rowen & Littlefield, 1999. An argument for congressional campaign finance reform.

KAPTOR, MARCY. *Women of Congress.* Washington, D.C.: Congressional Quarterly Press, 1996. An account of the progress of women toward longer tenure, greater seniority, and more influential committee appointments and how women in Congress still differ from men on these factors.

LELOUP, LANCE T., and STEVEN A. SHULL. *The President and Congress: Collaboration and Combat in National Policymaking.* New York: Longman, 1999. The identification of four patterns of national policymaking: presidential leadership, congressional leadership, consensus/cooperation, and deadlock/resolution.

ORNSTEIN, NORMAN J., THOMAS E. MANN, and MICHAEL J. MALBIN. *Vital Statistics on Congress.* Washington, D.C.: Congressional Quarterly Press, 2000. Published biennially. Excellent source of data on members of Congress, congressional elections, campaign finance, committees and staff, workload, and voting alignments.

SINCLAIR, BARBARA. *Unorthodox Lawmaking.* Washington, D.C.: Congressional Quarterly Press, 1997. A description of the various detours and shortcuts a major bill is likely to take in Congress, including five recent case studies.

The President

White House Politics

ASK YOURSELF ABOUT POLITICS

1 Do you approve of the way the president is handling his job?
Yes ⬤ No ⬤

2 Should presidents have the power to take actions not specifically authorized by law or the Constitution that they believe necessary for the nation's well-being?
Yes ⬤ No ⬤

3 Should the American people consider private moral conduct in evaluating presidential performance?
Yes ⬤ No ⬤

4 Should Congress rally to support a president's decision to send U.S. troops into action even if it disagrees with the decision?
Yes ⬤ No ⬤

5 Should the president be obliged to spend money appropriated by Congress for projects the president considers to be unnecessary or wasteful?
Yes ⬤ No ⬤

6 Should Congress have the authority to call home U.S. troops sent by the president to engage in military actions overseas?
Yes ⬤ No ⬤

7 Should Congress impeach and remove a president whose policy decisions damage the nation?
Yes ⬤ No ⬤

8 Is presidential performance more related to character and personality than to policy positions?
Yes ⬤ No ⬤

How much power does the president of the United States really have—over policies, over legislation, over the budget, over how this country is viewed by other nations, even over how it views itself?

PRESIDENTIAL POWER

Americans look to their president for "Greatness." The presidency embodies the popular "great man" view of history and public affairs—attributing progress in the world to the actions of particular individuals. Great presidents are those associated with great events: George Washington with the founding of the nation, Abraham Lincoln with the preservation of the Union, Franklin D. Roosevelt with the nation's emergence from economic depression and victory in World War II (see *What Do You Think?* "How Would You Rate the Presidents?" on page 377). People tend to believe that the president is responsible for "peace and prosperity" as well as for "change." They expect their president to present a "vision" of America's future and to symbolize the nation.

The Symbolic President The president personifies American government for most people. People expect the president to act decisively and effectively to deal with national problems. They expect the president to be "compassionate"—to show concern for problems confronting individual citizens.[1] The president, while playing these roles, is the focus of public attention and the nation's leading celebrity. Presidents receive more media coverage than any other person in the nation, for everything from their policy statements to their favorite foods to their dogs and cats.

Managing Crises In times of crisis, the American people look to their president to take action, to provide reassurance, and to protect the nation and its people. It is the president, not

⭐ www.prenhall.com/dye

The president and first lady personify government for many Americans. They become national celebrities and the focus of media attention.

the Congress or the courts, who is expected to speak on behalf of the American people in times of national triumph and tragedy.[2] The president gives expression to the nation's pride in victory. The nation's heroes are welcomed and its championship sports teams are feted in the White House Rose Garden.

The president also gives expression to the nation's sadness in tragedy and strives to help the nation go forward. When the *Challenger* spacecraft disintegrated before the eyes of millions of television viewers in 1986, President Ronald Reagan canceled his State of the Union Address and went on national television to give voice to the nation's feelings about the disaster and to explain it to children: "I want to say something to the schoolchildren of America who were watching the live coverage of the shuttle's takeoff. I know it is hard to understand, but sometimes painful things like this happen. It's part of the process of exploration and discovery. It's all part of taking a chance and expanding man's horizons. The future doesn't belong to the faint-hearted. It belongs to the brave."

Providing Policy Leadership   The president is expected to set policy priorities for the nation. Most policy initiatives originate in the White House and various departments and agencies of the executive branch, then are forwarded to Congress with the president's approval. Presidential programs are submitted to Congress in the form of messages, including the president's annual State of the Union Address, and in the Budget of the United States Government, which the president presents each year to Congress.

As a political leader, the president is expected to mobilize political support for policy proposals. It is not enough for the president to send policy proposals to Congress. The president must rally public opinion, lobby members of Congress, and win legislative battles. To avoid being perceived as weak or ineffective, presidents must get as much of their legislative programs through Congress as possible. Presidents use the threat of a veto to prevent Congress from passing bills they oppose; when forced to veto a bill, they fight to prevent an override of the veto. The president thus is responsible for "getting things done" in the policy arena.

How Would You Rate the Presidents?

From time to time, historians have been polled to rate U.S. presidents (see table). The survey ratings given the presidents have been remarkably consistent. Abraham Lincoln, George Washington, and Franklin Roosevelt are universally recognized as the greatest American presidents. It is more difficult for historians to rate recent presidents; the views of historians are influenced by their own (generally liberal and reformist) political views. Richard Nixon once commented, "History will treat me fairly. Historians probably won't."

Historians may tend to rank activist presidents who led the nation through war or economic crisis higher than passive presidents who guided the nation in peace and prosperity. Initially Dwight Eisenhower, who presided in the relatively calm 1950s, was ranked low by historians. But later, after comparing his performance with those who came after him, his steadiness and avoidance of war raised his ranking dramatically.

Arthur M. Schlesinger (1948)	Arthur M. Schlesinger, Jr. (1962)	Robert Murray (1982)	Arthur M. Schlesinger, Jr. (1996)	W. J. Ridings, S. B. McIver (1997)
Great	**Great**	**Presidential Rank**	**Great**	**Overall Ranking**
1. Lincoln	1. Lincoln	1. Lincoln	1. Lincoln	1. Lincoln
2. Washington	2. Washington	2. F. Roosevelt	2. Washington	2. F. Roosevelt
3. F. Roosevelt	3. F. Roosevelt	3. Washington	3. F. Roosevelt	3. Washington
4. Wilson	4. Wilson	4. Jefferson	**Near Great**	4. Jefferson
5. Jefferson	5. Jefferson	5. T. Roosevelt	4. Jefferson	5. T. Roosevelt
6. Jackson		6. Wilson	5. Jackson	6. Wilson
Near Great	**Near Great**	7. Jackson	6. T. Roosevelt	7. Truman
7. T. Roosevelt	6. Jackson	8. Truman	7. Wilson	8. Jackson
8. Cleveland	7. T. Roosevelt	9. J. Adams	8. Truman	9. Eisenhower
9. J. Adams	8. Polk	10. L. Johnson	9. Polk	10. Madison
10. Polk	Truman (tie)	11. Eisenhower	**High Average**	11. Polk
Average	10. J. Adams	12. Polk	10. Eisenhower	12. L. Johnson
11. J. Q. Adams	11. Cleveland	13. Kennedy	11. J. Adams	13. Monroe
12. Monroe		14. Madison	12. Kennedy	14. J. Adams
13. Hayes	**Average**	15. Monroe	13. Cleveland	15. Kennedy
14. Madison	12. Madison	16. J. Q. Adams	14. L. Johnson	16. Cleveland
15. Van Buren	13. J. Q. Adams	17. Cleveland	15. Monroe	17. McKinley
16. Taft	14. Hayes	18. McKinley	16. McKinley	18. J. Q. Adams
17. Arthur	15. McKinley	19. Taft	**Average**	19. Carter
18. McKinley	16. Taft	20. Van Buren	17. Madison	20. Taft
19. A. Johnson	17. Van Buren	21. Hoover	18. J. Q. Adams	21. Van Buren
20. Hoover	18. Monroe	22. Hayes	19. B. Harrison	22. Bush
21. B. Harrison	19. Hoover	23. Arthur	20. Clinton	23. Clinton
Below Average	20. B. Harrison	24. Ford	21. Van Buren	24. Hoover
22. Tyler	21. Arthur	25. Carter	22. Taft	25. Hayes
23. Coolidge	Eisenhower (tie)	26. B. Harrison	23. Hayes	26. Reagan
24. Fillmore	23. A. Johnson	27. Taylor	24. Bush	27. Ford
25. Taylor		28. Tyler	25. Reagan	28. Arthur
26. Buchanan	**Below Average**	29. Fillmore	26. Arthur	29. Taylor
27. Pierce	24. Taylor	30. Coolidge	27. Carter	30. Garfield
Failure	25. Tyler	31. Pierce	28. Ford	31. B. Harrison
28. Grant	26. Fillmore	32. A. Johnson	**Below Average**	32. Nixon
29. Harding	27. Coolidge	33. Buchanan	29. Taylor	33. Coolidge
	28. Pierce	34. Nixon	30. Coolidge	34. Tyler
	29. Buchanan	35. Grant	31. Fillmore	35. W. Harrison
		36. Harding	32. Tyler	36. Fillmore
	Failure		**Failure**	37. Pierce
	30. Grant		33. Pierce	38. Grant
	31. Harding		34. Grant	39. A. Johnson
			35. Hoover	40. Buchanan
			36. Nixon	41. Harding
			37. A. Johnson	
			38. Buchanan	
			39. Harding	

Note: These ratings result from surveys of scholars ranging in number from 55 to 950.

Sources: Arthur Murphy, "Evaluating the Presidents of the United States," *Presidential Studies Quarterly* 14 (1984): 117–26; Arthur M. Schlesinger, Jr., "Rating the Presidents: Washington to Clinton," *Political Science Quarterly* 112 (1997): 179–90; William J. Ridings and Stuart B. McIver, *Rating the Presidents* (Secaucus, N.J.: Citadel Press, 1997).

Managing the Economy   The American people hold the president responsible for maintaining a healthy economy. Presidents are blamed for economic downturns, whether or not governmental policies had anything to do with market conditions. The president is expected to "Do Something!" in the face of high unemployment, declining personal income, high mortgage rates, rising inflation, or even a stock market crash. Herbert Hoover in 1932, Gerald Ford in 1976, Jimmy Carter in 1980, and George Bush in 1992—all incumbent presidents defeated for reelection during recessions—learned the hard way that the general public holds the president responsible for hard economic times. Presidents must have an economic "game plan" to stimulate the economy—tax incentives to spur investments, spending proposals to create jobs, plans to lower interest rates (see Chapter 16).

Presidents themselves are partly responsible for these public expectations. Incumbent presidents have been quick to take credit for economic growth, low inflation, low interest rates, and low unemployment. And presidential candidates in recessionary times invariably promise "to get the economy moving again."

Managing the Government   As the chief executive of a mammoth federal bureaucracy with 2.8 million civilian employees, the president is responsible for implementing policy, that is, for achieving policy goals. Policy making does not end when a law is passed. Policy implementation involves issuing orders, creating organizations, recruiting and assigning personnel, disbursing funds, overseeing work, and evaluating results. It is true that the president cannot perform all of these tasks personally. But the ultimate responsibility for implementation—in the words of the Constitution, "to take Care that the Laws be faithfully executed"—rests with the president. Or as the sign on Harry Truman's desk put it: "THE BUCK STOPS HERE."

The Global President   Nations strive to speak with a single voice in international affairs; for the United States, the global voice is that of the president. As commander-in-chief of the armed forces of the United States, the president is a powerful voice in foreign affairs. Efforts by Congress to speak on behalf of the nation in foreign affairs and to limit the war-making power of the president have been generally unsuccessful. It is the president who orders American troops into combat. It is the president's finger that rests on the nuclear trigger.

CONSTITUTIONAL POWERS OF THE PRESIDENT

Popular expectations of presidential leadership far exceed the formal constitutional powers granted to the president. Compared with the Congress, the president has only modest constitutional powers (see Table 11–1). Nevertheless, presidents have pointed to a variety of clauses in Article II to support their rights to do everything from doubling the land area of the nation through purchase (Thomas Jefferson) to sending U.S. troops to keep the peace in Bosnia (Bill Clinton).

Who May Be President?   To become president, the Constitution specifies that a person must be a natural-born citizen at least thirty-five years of age and a resident of the United States for fourteen years.

Initially, the Constitution put no limit on how many terms a president could serve. George Washington set a precedent for a two-term maximum that endured until Franklin Roosevelt's decision to run for a third term in 1940 (and a fourth term

Table 11-1   The Constitutional Powers of the President

Chief Administrator

Implement policy: "take Care that the Laws be faithfully executed" (Article II, Section 3)

Supervise executive branch of government

Appoint and remove executive officials (Article II, Section 2)

Prepare executive budget for submission to Congress (by law of Congress)

Chief Legislator

Initiate policy: "give to the Congress Information of the State of the Union, and recommend to their Consideration such Measures as he shall judge necessary and expedient" (Article II, Section 3)

Veto legislation passed by Congress, subject to override by a two-thirds vote in both houses

Convene special session of Congress "on extraordinary Occasions" (Article II, Section 3)

Chief Diplomat

Make treaties "with the Advice and Consent of the Senate" (Article II, Section 2)

Exercise the power of diplomatic recognition: "receive Ambassadors" (Article II, Section 3)

Make executive agreements (by custom and international law)

Commander-in-Chief

Command U.S. armed forces: "The president shall be Commander-in-Chief of the Army and Navy" (Article II, Section 2)

Appoint military officers

Chief of State

"The executive Power shall be vested in a President" (Article II, Section 1)

Grant reprieves and pardons (Article II, Section 2)

Represent the nation as chief of state

Appoint federal court and Supreme Court judges (Article II, Section 2)

---

in 1944). In reaction to Roosevelt's lengthy tenure, in 1947 Congress proposed the Twenty-second Amendment (ratified in 1951), which officially restricts the president to two terms (or one full term if a vice president must complete more than two years of the previous president's term).

Presidential Succession   Until the adoption of the Twenty-fifth Amendment in 1967, the Constitution had said little about presidential succession, other than designating the vice president as successor to the president "in Case of the Removal, . . . Death, Resignation, or Inability" and giving Congress the power to decide "what Officer shall then act as President" if both the president and vice president are removed. The Constitution was silent on how to cope with serious presidential illnesses. It contained no provision for replacing a vice president. The incapacitation issue was more than theoretical: James A. Garfield lingered months after being shot in 1881; Woodrow Wilson was an invalid during his last years in office (1919–20); Dwight Eisenhower suffered major heart attacks in office; and Ronald Reagan was in serious condition following an assassination attempt in 1981.

The Twenty-fifth Amendment stipulates that when the vice president and a majority of the cabinet notify the Speaker of the House and the president pro tempore of the Senate in writing that the president "is unable to discharge the powers and duties of his office," then the vice president becomes *acting* president. To resume the powers of office, the president must then notify Congress in writing that "no inability exists." If the vice president and a majority of cabinet officers do not agree that the president is capable of resuming office, then the Congress "shall decide the issue" within twenty-one days. A two-thirds vote of both houses is required to replace the president with the vice president.

The disability provisions of the amendment have never been used, but the succession provisions have been. The Twenty-fifth Amendment provides for the selection of a new vice president by presidential nomination and confirmation by a majority vote of both houses of Congress. When Vice President Spiro Agnew resigned in the face of bribery charges in 1973, President Richard Nixon nominated the Republican leader of the House, Gerald Ford, as vice president; and when Nixon resigned in 1974, Ford assumed the presidency and made Nelson Rockefeller, governor of New York, his vice president. Thus Gerald Ford's two-year tenure in the White House marked the only time in history when the man serving as president had not been elected to either the presidency or the vice presidency. (If the offices of president and vice president are both vacated, then Congress by law has specified the next in line for the presidency as the Speaker of the House of Representatives, followed by the president pro tempore of the Senate, then the cabinet officers, beginning with the secretary of state.)

Impeachment   The Constitution grants Congress the power of **impeachment** over the president, vice president, and "all civil Officers of the United States" (Article II, Section 4). Technically, impeachment is a charge similar to a criminal indictment brought against an official. The power to bring charges of impeachment is given to the House of Representatives. The power to try all impeachments is given to the Senate, and "no Person shall be convicted without the Concurrence of two thirds of the Members present" (Article I, Section 3). Impeachment by the House and conviction by the Senate only remove an official from office; a subsequent criminal trial is required to inflict any other punishment.

The Constitution specifies that impeachment and conviction can only be for "Treason, Bribery, or other High Crimes and Misdemeanors." These words indicate that Congress is not to impeach presidents, federal judges, or any other officials simply because Congress disagrees with their decisions or policies. Indeed, the phrase implies that only serious criminal offenses, not political conflicts, can result in impeachment. Nevertheless, politics was at the root of the impeachment of President Andrew Johnson in 1867, and was a factor in the impeachment investigation opened by the House against President Clinton in 1998 (see *Up Close:* "Sex, Lies, Partisanship, and Impeachment" on page 380). Johnson was a southern Democrat who had remained loyal to the Union. Lincoln had chosen him as vice president in 1864 as a gesture of national unity. A Republican House impeached him on a party-line vote, but after a month-long trial in the Senate, the "guilty" vote fell one short of the two-thirds needed for removal.[3] In 1974, Richard Nixon resigned after the House Judiciary Committee recommended impeachment but before a vote by the full House (see *Up Close:* "Watergate and the Limits of Presidential Power").

Presidential Pardons   The Constitution grants the president the power to "grant Reprieves and Pardons." This power derives from the ancient right to appeal to the king to reverse errors of law or justice committed by the court system. It is absolute: the president may grant pardons to anyone for any reason. The most celebrated use of the presidential pardon was President Ford's blanket pardon of former President Nixon "for all offenses against the United States which he, Richard Nixon, has committed or may have committed or taken part in." Ford defended the pardon as necessary to end "the bitter controversy and divisive national debate," but his actions may have helped cause his defeat in the 1976 election.

impeachment   Equivalent of a criminal charge against an elected official; removal of the impeached official from office depends on the outcome of a trial.

Watergate and the Limits of Presidential Power

Richard Nixon was the only president ever to resign the office. He did so to escape certain impeachment by the House of Representatives and a certain guilty verdict in trial by the Senate. Yet Nixon's first term as president included a number of historic successes. He negotiated the first ever strategic nuclear arms limitation treaty, SALT I, with the Soviet Union. He changed the global balance of power in favor of the Western democracies by opening relations with the People's Republic of China and dividing the communist world. In his second term, he withdrew U.S. troops from Vietnam, negotiated a peace agreement, and ended one of America's longest and bloodiest wars. But his remarkable record is forever tarnished by his failure to understand the limits of presidential power.

On the night of June 17, 1972, five men with burglary tools and wiretapping devices were arrested in the offices of the Democratic National Committee in the Watergate Building in Washington. Also arrested were E. Howard Hunt, Jr., G. Gordon Liddy, and James W. McCord, Jr., all employed by the Committee to Reelect the President (CREEP). All pleaded guilty and were convicted, but U.S. District Court Judge John J. Sirica believed that the defendants were shielding whoever had ordered and paid for the operation.

Although there is no evidence that Nixon himself ordered or had prior knowledge of the break-in, he discussed with his chief of staff, H. R. Halderman, and White House advisers John Ehrlichman and John Dean the advisability of payoffs to buy the defendants' silence. Nixon hoped his landslide electoral victory in November 1972 would put the matter to rest.

But a series of sensational revelations in the *Washington Post* kept the story alive. Using an inside source known only as Deep Throat, Bob Woodward and Carl Bernstein, investigative reporters for the *Post*, alleged that key members of Nixon's reelection committee, including its chairman, former Attorney General John Mitchell, and White House staff were actively involved in the break-in and, more important, in the subsequent attempts at a cover-up.

In February 1973 the U.S. Senate formed a Special Select Committee on Campaign Activities—the "Watergate Committee"—to delve into Watergate and related activities. The committee's nationally televised hearings enthralled millions of viewers with lurid stories of "the White House horrors." John Dean broke with the White House and testified before the committee that he had earlier warned Nixon the cover-up was "a cancer growing on the presidency." Then, in a dramatic revelation, the committee—and the nation—learned that President Nixon maintained a secret tape-recording system in the Oval Office. Hoping that the tapes would prove or disprove charges of Nixon's involvement in the cover-up, the committee issued a subpoena to the White House. Nixon refused to comply, arguing that the constitutional separation of powers gave the president an "executive privilege" to withhold his private conversations from Congress. However the U.S. Supreme Court, voting 8 to 0 in *United States v. Richard M. Nixon*, ordered Nixon to turn over the tapes.

Despite the rambling nature of the tapes, committee members interpreted them as confirming Nixon's involvement in the payoffs and cover-up. Informed by congressional leaders of his own party that impeachment by a majority of the House and removal from office by two-thirds of the Senate were assured, on August 9, 1974, Richard Nixon resigned his office.

On September 8, 1974, new President Gerald R. Ford pardoned former President Nixon "for all offenses against the United States which he, Richard Nixon, has committed or may have committed or taken part in" during his presidency. Upon his death in 1994, Nixon was eulogized for his foreign policy successes.

Executive Power The Constitution declares that the "executive Power" shall be vested in the president, but it is unclear whether this statement grants the president any powers that are not specified later in the Constitution or given to the president by acts of Congress. In other words, does the grant of "executive Power" give presidents constitutional authority to act as they deem necessary *beyond* the

Sex, Lies, Partisanship, and Impeachment

Bill Clinton is the second president in the nation's history (following Andrew Johnson in 1867) to be impeached by the U.S. House of Representatives. (President Richard Nixon resigned just prior to an impeachment vote in 1974.)

Clinton's impeachment followed a report to the House by Independent Counsel Kenneth Starr in 1998 that accused the president of perjury, obstruction of justice, witness tampering, and "abuse of power." The Starr Report describes in graphic and lurid detail Clinton's sexual relationship with young White House intern Monica Lewinsky. It cites as impeachable offenses Clinton's lying about their relationship; his misleading testimony in a sworn statement in the Paula Jones case; and his evasive testimony before Starr's grand jury.

Does engaging in extramarital sex and lying about it meet the Constitution's standard for impeachment— "Treason, Bribery, or other High Crimes and Misdemeanors"? Perjury—knowingly giving false testimony in a sworn legal proceeding—is a criminal offense. But does the Constitution envision more serious misconduct? According to Alexander Hamilton in Federalist 65, impeachment should deal with "the abuse or violation of some public trust." Is Clinton's acknowledged "inappropriate behavior" a private affair or a violation of the public trust?

President Clinton greets well-wishers, including Monica Lewinsky, at a Democratic party event in January 1996. Clinton's acknowledged "inappropriate behavior" and his efforts to conceal his relationship with Lewinsky were the subjects of the impeachment investigation opened against him by the House in 1998.

How are such questions decided? Despite pious rhetoric in Congress about the "search for truth," "impartial investigation," and "unbiased constitutional judgment,"

actions specified elsewhere in the Constitution or specified in laws passed by Congress?

Contrasting views on this question have been offered over two centuries. President William Howard Taft provided the classic narrow interpretation of executive power:

> The true view of the executive function is, as I conceive it, that the president can exercise no power which cannot be fairly and reasonably traced to some specific grant of power or justly implied and included within such express grant as proper and necessary to its exercise. Such specific grants must be either in the federal constitution or in the pursuance thereof. There is no undefined residuum of power which can be exercised which seems to him to be in the public interest.[4]

Theodore Roosevelt, Taft's bitter opponent in a three-way race for the presidency in 1912, expressed the opposite view:

the impeachment process, whatever the merits of the charges against a president, is *political*, not judicial.

The House vote to impeach Clinton on December 19, 1998 (228 to 205) was largely along partisan lines, with all but five Republicans voting "yes" and all but five Democrats voting "no." And the vote in Clinton's Senate "trial" on February 12, 1999, was equally partisan. Even on the strongest charge—that Clinton had tried to obstruct justice—the Senate failed to find the president guilty. Removing Clinton failed to win even a majority of Senate votes, far less than the required two-thirds. All 45 Democrats were joined by five Republicans to create a 50–50 tie vote that left Clinton tarnished but still in office.

The Founders anticipated that impeachment would be a raucous, messy, and partisan process. Impeachable offenses, wrote Hamilton,

are of a nature which may with peculiar propriety be denominated POLITICAL, as they relate chiefly to injuries done immediately to the society itself. The prosecution of them, for this reason, will seldom fail to agitate the passions of the whole community, and to divide it into parties more or less friendly or inimical to the accused. In many cases it will connect itself with the pre-existing factions, and will enlist all their animosities, partialities, influence, and interest on one side or on the other; and in such cases there will always be the greatest danger that the decision will be regulated more by the comparative strength of parties, than by the real demonstrations of innocence or guilt.

Why then, is the impeachment of a president so rare, even during periods of divided government? Because in a democracy, the ultimate jury is the people—through elections—and Congress knows that.

The American people believed that the charges against Clinton were true—that he engaged in sexual misconduct and subsequently lied about it—but they did *not* believe that these charges should result in his impeachment and removal from office or even his resignation.*

QUESTION: *Do you approve or disapprove of the House decision to vote in favor of impeaching Clinton and sending the case to the Senate for trial? Yes—35% No—63%*

QUESTION: *Should the Senate vote in favor of convicting Clinton and removing him from office or vote against convicting? Vote to convict—29% Vote against convicting—68%*

QUESTION: *Do you think Bill Clinton should resign now and turn the presidency over to Al Gore? Yes—30% No—69%*

And Clinton's public approval rating reached a high point (68 percent) during the impeachment proceedings. By placing the power of impeachment and removal in the hands of Congress, the Founders insured that ultimately this power would be held accountable to the people.

---

*Gallup Poll, as reported in *USA Today*, December 21, 1998.

I decline to adopt the view that what was imperatively necessary for the nation could not be done by the president unless he could find some specific authorization to do it. My belief was that it was not only his right but his duty to do anything that the needs of the nation demanded, unless such action was forbidden by the Constitution or by the laws.[5]

Although the constitutional question has never been fully resolved, history has generally sided with those presidents who have taken an expansive view of their powers. John F. Kennedy expressed the modern view of the constitutional presidency:

The Constitution is a very wise document. It permits the president to assume just about as much power as he is capable of handling. . . . I believe that the president should use whatever power is necessary to do the job unless it is expressly forbidden by the Constitution.[6]

Some Historical Examples   U.S. history is filled with examples of presidents acting independently, beyond specific constitutional powers or laws of Congress. Among the most notable:

- George Washington issued a Proclamation of Neutrality during the war between France and Britain following the French Revolution, thereby establishing the president's power to make foreign policy.
- Thomas Jefferson, who prior to becoming president argued for a narrow interpretation of presidential powers, purchased the Louisiana Territory despite the fact that the Constitution contains no provision for the acquisition of territory, let alone authorizing presidential action to do so.
- Andrew Jackson ordered the removal of federal funds from the national bank and removed his secretary of the treasury from office, establishing the president's power to *remove* executive officials, a power not specifically mentioned in the Constitution.
- Abraham Lincoln, asking, "Was it possible to lose the nation yet preserve the Constitution?" established the precedent of vigorous presidential action in national emergencies: He blockaded southern ports, declared martial law in parts of the country, and issued the Emancipation Proclamation—all without constitutional or congressional authority.
- Franklin D. Roosevelt, battling the Great Depression during the 1930s, ordered the nation's banks to close temporarily. Following the Japanese attack on Pearl Harbor in 1941, he ordered the incarceration without trial of many thousands of Americans of Japanese ancestry living on the West Coast.

Checking Presidential Power   President Harry Truman believed that "the president has the right to keep the country from going to hell," and he was willing to use means beyond those specified in the Constitution or authorized by Congress. In 1952, while U.S. troops were fighting in Korea, steelworkers at home were threatening to strike. Rather than cross organized labor by forbidding the strike under the terms of the Taft-Hartley Act of 1947 (which he had opposed), Truman chose to seize the steel mills by executive order and continue their operations under U.S. government control. The U.S. Supreme Court ordered the steel mills returned to their owners, however, acknowledging that the president may have inherent powers to act in a national emergency but arguing that Congress had provided a legal remedy, however distasteful to the president. Thus the president can indeed act to keep the country from "going to hell," but if Congress has already acted to do so, the president must abide by the law.

Executive Privilege   Over the years, presidents and scholars have argued that the Constitution's establishment of a separate executive branch of government entitles the president to **executive privilege**—the right to keep confidential communications from other branches of government. Public exposure of internal executive communications would inhibit the president's ability to obtain candid advice from subordinates and would obstruct the president's ability to conduct negotiations with foreign governments or to command military operations.

But Congress has never recognized executive privilege. It has frequently tried to compel the testimony of executive officials at congressional hearings. Presidents have regularly refused to appear themselves at congressional hearings and have

executive privilege   Right of a president to withhold from other branches of government confidential communications within the executive branch; although posited by presidents, it has been upheld by the Supreme Court only in limited situations.

frequently refused to allow other executive officials to appear or divulge specific information, citing executive privilege. The federal courts have generally refrained from intervening in this dispute between the executive and legislative branches. However, the Supreme Court has ruled that the president is not immune from court orders when illegal acts are under investigation. In *United States v. Nixon* (1974), the U.S. Supreme Court acknowledged that although the president might legitimately claim executive privilege where military or diplomatic matters are involved, such a privilege cannot be invoked in a criminal investigation. The Court ordered President Nixon to surrender tape recordings of White House conversations between the president and his advisers during the Watergate scandal.

Presidential Impoundment   The Constitution states that "no Money shall be drawn from the Treasury, but in Consequence of appropriations made by Law" (Article I, Section 9). Clearly the president cannot spend money *not* appropriated by Congress. But the Constitution is silent on whether the president must spend all of the money appropriated by Congress for various purposes. Presidents from Thomas Jefferson onward frequently refused to spend money appropriated by Congress, an action referred to as **impoundment**. But taking advantage of a presidency weakened by the Watergate scandal, the Congress in 1974 passed the Budget and Impoundment Control Act, which requires the president to spend all appropriated funds. The act does provide, however, that presidents may send Congress a list of specific **deferrals**—items on which they wish to postpone spending—and **rescissions**—items they wish to cancel altogether. Congress by *resolution* (which cannot be vetoed by the president) may restore the deferrals and force the president to spend the money. Both houses of Congress must approve a rescission; otherwise the government must spend the money.

Congress tried to *strengthen* the president's control over spending in 1997. A Republican-controlled Congress, together with Democratic President Bill Clinton, agreed to a bill granting the president power to cancel any "item of new direct spending," as well as any "limited tax benefit" in an appropriations act, without vetoing the entire act. But the U.S. Supreme Court found this "line item veto" power unconstitutional (see "Line-Item Veto Power Denied" later in this chapter).

Responsibility to the Courts   The president is not "above the law"; that is, his conduct is not immune from judicial scrutiny. The president's official conduct must be lawful; federal courts may reverse presidential actions found to be unconstitutional or violative of laws of Congress. And presidents are not immune from criminal prosecution; they cannot ignore demands to provide information in criminal cases.[7] However, the Supreme Court has held that the president has "absolute immunity" from civil suits "arising out of the execution of official duties."[8] In other words, the president cannot be sued for damages caused by actions or decisions that are within his constitutional or legal authority.

But can the president be sued for *private* conduct beyond the scope of his official duties? In 1994 Paula Corbin Jones sued William Jefferson Clinton in federal district court in Arkansas, alleging that he made "abhorrent" sexual advances toward her in Little Rock in 1991 while he was governor and she was a state employee. Clinton's defense lawyers argued that the president should be immune from civil actions, especially those arising from events alleged to occur before he assumed office. They argued that the president's constitutional responsibilities are so important and

impoundment   Refusal by a president to spend monies appropriated by Congress; outlawed except with congressional consent by the Budget and Impoundment Control Act of 1974.

deferrals   Items on which a president wishes to postpone spending.

rescissions   Items on which a president wishes to cancel spending.

demanding that he must devote his undivided time and attention to them. He cannot be distracted by civil suits; otherwise a large volume of politically motivated frivolous litigation might undermine his ability to function effectively in office.

However, in 1997 the U.S. Supreme Court rejected the notion of presidential immunity from civil claims arising from actions outside of the president's official duties. Although advising lower courts to give "utmost deference to Presidential responsibilities" in handling the case, the Court held that "the doctrine of separation of powers does not require federal courts to stay all private actions against the president until he leaves office."[9] Clinton was obliged to settle the case with a financial payment to Jones.

The Constitution's Congressional Tilt   The Constitution, reflecting the Founders' view of the preeminence of the legislative branch, gives the last word to the Congress in disputes with the president:

- The Congress can override the president's veto of legislation if it can muster a two-thirds vote in both houses.
- The Congress can impeach and remove the president from office.
- Only the Congress can appropriate money.
- Major presidential appointments require Senate confirmation.
- The president is obliged by the Constitution to "take Care that the Laws be faithfully executed"—that is, the *laws of Congress*—regardless of any personal feelings about these laws.

Thus, Congress is *constitutionally* positioned to dominate American government. But it is the president who *politically* dominates the nation's public affairs.

POLITICAL RESOURCES OF THE PRESIDENT

The real sources of presidential power are not found in the Constitution. The president's power is the *power to persuade*. As Harry Truman put it, "I sit here all day trying to persuade people to do things they ought to have sense enough to do without my persuading them. . . . That's all the powers of the president amount to."[10]

The president's political resources are potentially very great. The nation looks to the president for leadership, for direction, for reassurance. The president is the focus of public and media attention. The president has the capacity to mobilize public opinion, to communicate directly with the American people, and to employ the symbols of office to advance policy initiatives in both foreign and domestic affairs.

The Reputation for Power   A reputation for power is itself a source of power. Presidents must strive to maintain the image of power in order to be effective. A president perceived as powerful can exercise great influence abroad with foreign governments and at home with the Congress, interest groups, and the executive bureaucracy. A president perceived as weak, unsteady, bumbling, or error prone will soon become unpopular and ineffective.

Presidential Popularity   Presidential popularity with the American people is a political resource. Popular presidents cannot always transfer their popularity into foreign policy successes or legislative victories, but popular presidents usually have more success than unpopular presidents.

Presidential popularity is regularly tracked in national opinion polls. For more than forty years, national surveys have asked the American public: "Do you approve or disapprove of the way _____ is handling his job as president?" (see Figures 11–1, 11–2 on 388). Analyses of variations over time in these poll results suggest some generalizations about presidential popularity.[11]

Presidential popularity is usually high at the beginning of a president's term of office, but this period can be very brief. The American public's high expectations for a new president can turn sour within a few months. A president's popularity will vary a great deal during a term in office, with sharp peaks and steep valleys in the ratings. But the general trend is downward.[12] Presidents usually recover some popularity at the end of their first term as they campaign for reelection.

Presidential popularity rises during crises. People "rally 'round the president" when the nation is confronted with an international threat or the president initiates a military action.[13] President George Bush, for example, registered the all-time high in presidential ratings during the Persian Gulf War. Likewise, the invasion of Grenada in 1983 and Panama in 1989 rallied support to the president. But prolonged warfare and stalemate erode popular support. In both the Korean and the Vietnam wars, initial public approval of the president and support for the war eroded over time as military operations stalemated and casualties mounted.[14]

FIGURE 11–1 Presidential Popularity over Time

Americans expect a great deal from their presidents and are quick to give these leaders the credit—and the blame—for major events in the nation's life. In general, public approval (as measured by response to the question "Do you approve or disapprove of the way _____ is handling the job of president?") is highest at the beginning of a new president's term in office and declines from that point. Major military confrontations generally raise presidential ratings initially but can (as in the case of Lyndon Johnson) cause dramatic decline if the conflict drags on. In addition, public approval of the president is closely linked to the nation's economic health. When the economy is in recession, Americans tend to take a negative view of the president.

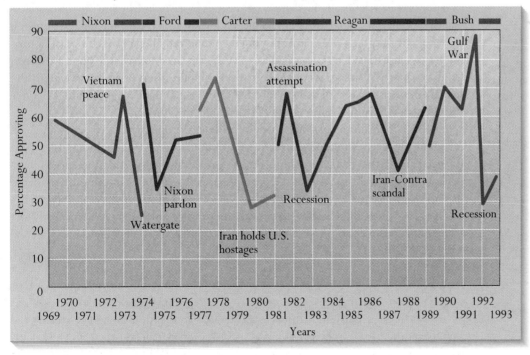

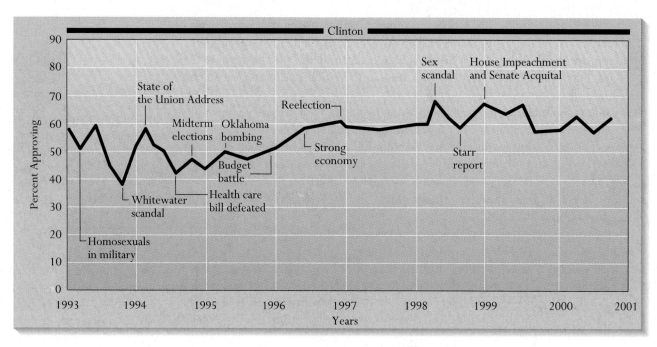

FIGURE 11-2 Bill Clinton's Popularity Ratings

During his first term, Bill Clinton experienced dips in popularity with his opening of military service to homosexuals, press coverage of the Whitewater scandal, and the defeat of his health care bill. But following the terrorist bombing of the Federal Building in Oklahoma City and his later battles with Congress over the budget, Clinton moved above the critical 50 percent approval level and maintained a positive rating throughout the 1996 presidential campaign. During his second term, the health of the nation's economy drove his approval over 60 percent, and, paradoxically, his ratings went up during a sex scandal.

Major scandals *may* also hurt presidential popularity and effectiveness. The Watergate scandal produced a low of 22 percent approval for Nixon just prior to his resignation. Reagan's generally high approval ratings were blemished by the Iran-contra scandal hearings in 1987, although he ultimately left office with the highest approval rating of any outgoing president. But highly publicized allegations of sexual improprieties against President Clinton in early 1998 appeared to have the opposite effect; Clinton's approval ratings went *up*. Perhaps the public differentiates between private sexual conduct and performance in office (see *What Do You Think? Should We Judge Presidents on Private Character or Performance in Office?*).

Finally, economic recessions erode presidential popularity. Every president in office during a recession has suffered loss of popular approval, including President Reagan during the 1982 recession. But no president suffered a more precipitous decline in approval ratings than George Bush, whose popularity plummeted from its Gulf War high of 89 percent to a low of 37 percent in only a year, largely as a result of recession. Bill Clinton's approval ratings were only mediocre during his first term, but robust economic growth pushed his popularity to new highs in his second term (see Figure 11–2).

Access to the Media   The president dominates the news more than any other single person. All major television networks, newspapers, and newsmagazines have reporters (usually their most experienced and skilled people) covering the "White House beat."[15] The presidential press secretary briefs these reporters daily, but the president also may appear in person in the White House press room at

Should We Judge Presidents on Private Character or Performance in Office?

In evaluating presidents, should we consider their private moral conduct or should we focus on how they perform their public duties? Can private morality be divorced from public trust? The sex scandals surrounding Bill Clinton, not only those alleged to have occurred before he was elected president, but also those alleged to have occurred in the Oval Office itself, brought these questions forcefully to the American people.

When allegations first emerged in January, 1998, that Clinton had had an affair with a twenty-one-year-old intern working at the White House, President Clinton himself emphatically denied the allegations, saying, "I did not have sexual relations with that woman, Ms. Lewinsky!" But a majority of the American people (62%) believed the allegations to be true.

Yet, while most Americans clearly believed the president had a sexual affair in the White House and subsequently lied about it, they also approved of the way Clinton was performing his job as president. Indeed, the public appeared to rally around the president following the allegations of sexual misconduct. Clinton's job rating, already a healthy 60 percent at the beginning of 1998, experienced a "Lewinsky bounce" following lurid news stories of the affair. Indeed, many people blamed the independent counsel Kenneth Starr for investigating the private life of the president (see *What Do You Think?* "Do We Need Special Prosecutors to Investigate Presidents?" in Chapter 13). And many people blamed the news media for focusing so much attention on the affair.

At the same time, opinion polls indicate most Americans felt that the president did not "share their values" (56%), did not "show good judgment" (56%), and was not "honest and trustworthy" (62%).

Various explanations have been offered for this apparent paradox—a public that believed the president had an affair in the White House and lied about it, that questioned his values and judgment, yet gave the president the highest approval ratings of his career. Many Americans believe that private sexual conduct is irrelevant to the performance of public duties. Private morality is viewed as a personal affair about which Americans should be nonjudgmental. Some people said, "If it's okay with Hillary, why should we worry?" Haven't we had adulterous presidents before, from Thomas Jefferson to John F. Kennedy, presidents who were ranked high in history? And many Americans believe that "they all do it." Indeed, in response to the question "Do you think most presidents have or have not had extramarital affairs while they were president?" some 59 percent say "most have," whereas only 33% percent say "most have not."

Others argue, nonetheless, that private character counts in presidential performance, indeed, that it is a prerequisite for public trust. The president, in this view, performs a symbolic role that requires dignity, honesty, and respect. A president publicly embarrassed by sexual scandal, diminished by jokes, and laughed at by late-night television audiences cannot perform this role. The acceptance of a president's adulterous behavior, according to one commentator, lowers society's standards of behavior. "The president's legacy . . . will be a further vulgarization and demoralization of society."*

---

*Gertrude Himmelfarb, "Private Lives, Public Morality," *New York Times*, February 9, 1998. Poll results reported in *The Polling Report*, February 9, 1998.

---

any time. Presidents regularly use this media access to advance their programs and priorities.[16]

Presidential press conferences can help mobilize popular support for presidential programs. Presidents often try to focus attention on particular legislative issues, and they generally open press conferences with a lengthy policy statement on these issues. But reporters' questions and subsequent reporting often refocus the press conference in other directions. The president cannot control the questions or limit the subject matter of press conferences. Indeed, the president cannot even ensure that the television networks—ABC, CBS, and NBC—will carry a

President Bush answers questions during a press conference. These meetings with the press can be a double-edged sword. They give the president an opportunity to present his point of view to the public, but they also allow the press to raise issues a president might rather avoid.

presidential press conference live, although CNN, with its all-news format, always does so.

Presidents may also use direct television addresses from the White House. President Reagan, who held relatively few press conferences, made heavy use of national prime-time television appeals to mobilize support for his programs. Reagan's appeals frequently resulted in a deluge of telephone calls, wires, and letters to Congress in support of the president. George Bush and Bill Clinton were far less successful in this approach. Presidents must also weigh the drawbacks of television addresses. The networks now routinely give opposition leaders television time to respond following the president's address.

Finally, presidents can try to mobilize popular support for a program by public appearances, addresses, and speeches. The national meetings or conventions of influential groups such as the American Newspaper Association, the American Legion, the National Association of Manufacturers, the U.S. Chamber of Commerce, and the National Association for the Advancement of Colored People can provide a forum. So can college and university commencements.

Party Leadership Presidents are leaders of their party, but this role is hardly a source of great strength. It is true that presidents select the national party chair, control the national committee and its Washington staff, and largely direct the national party convention. Incumbent presidents can use this power to help defeat challengers *within* their own parties. President Ford used this power to help defeat challenger Ronald Reagan in 1976; President Carter used it to help defeat challenger Ted Kennedy in 1980; and President Bush used it against challenger Pat Buchanan in 1992. But the role of party leader is of limited value to a president because the parties have few controls over their members (see Chapter 7).

Nevertheless, presidents enjoy much stronger support in Congress from members of their own party than from members of the opposition party. Some of the president's party support in Congress is a product of shared ideological values and policy positions. But Republican Congress members do have some stake in the success of a Republican president, as do Democratic members in the success of a Democratic president. Popular presidents may produce those few extra votes that make the difference for party candidates in close congressional districts.

CHIEF EXECUTIVE

The president is the chief executive of the nation's largest bureaucracy: 2.8 million civilian employees, 60 independent agencies, 14 departments, and the large Executive Office of the President. The formal organizational chart of the federal government places the president at the head of this giant structure (see Figure 12–1, "The Federal Bureaucracy," in Chapter 12). But the president cannot command this bureaucracy in the fashion of a military officer or a corporation president. When Harry Truman was preparing to turn over the White House to Dwight Eisenhower, he predicted that the general of the army would not understand the presidency: "He'll sit here and say 'Do this! Do that!' and nothing will happen. Poor Ike—it won't be a bit like the army. He'll find it very frustrating." Truman vastly underestimated the political skills of the former general, but the crusty Missourian clearly understood the frustrations confronting the nation's chief executive. The president does not command the executive branch of government but rather stands at its center—persuading, bargaining, negotiating, and compromising to achieve goals (see *People in Politics:* "Bill Clinton's Presidential Legacy" on page 392).

The Constitutional Executive   The Constitution is vague about the president's authority over the executive branch. It vests executive power in the presidency and grants the president authority to appoint principal officers of the government "by and with the Advice and Consent of the Senate." Under the Constitution, the president may also "require the Opinion, in writing, of the principal Officer in each of the executive Departments, upon any Subject relating to the Duties of their respective Offices." This awkward phrase presumably gives the president the power to oversee operations of the executive departments. Finally, and perhaps most important, the president is instructed to "take Care that the Laws be faithfully executed."

At the same time, Congress has substantial authority over the executive branch. Through its lawmaking abilities, Congress can establish or abolish executive departments and regulate their operations. Congress's "power of the purse" allows it to determine the budget of each department each year and thus to limit or broaden or even "micromanage" the activities of these departments. Moreover, Congress can pressure executive agencies by conducting investigations, calling administrators to task in public hearings, and directly contacting agencies with members' own complaints or those of their constituents.

Executive Orders   Presidents frequently use **executive orders** to implement their policies. Executive orders may direct specific federal agencies to carry out the president's wishes, or they may direct all federal agencies to pursue the president's preferred course of action. In any case, they must be based on either a president's constitutional powers or on powers delegated to the president by laws of Congress. Presidents regularly issue 50 to 100 executive orders each year, but some stand out. In 1942 President Franklin D. Roosevelt issued Executive Order

executive order   Formal regulation governing executive branch operations issued by the president.

Bill Clinton's Presidential Legacy

No one doubts that William Jefferson Clinton was one of the most intelligent men ever to occupy the Oval Office and that his knowledge of the details of government and public policy exceeded that of any other recent president. But with no fixed ideological compass, the Clinton presidency suffered "deep, near terminal ambivalence."*Throughout his first term he weighed conflicting advice from moderates and liberals with reference to a single overriding goal—reelection. In his second term, he became free to pursue a consistent course and establish a recognized legacy. But his overriding concern became that of avoiding impeachment and removal from office. His achievements, including eight years of relative peace and booming prosperity, will forever be marred by his personal misconduct in office.

Getting Started   Born Billy Blythe in rural Hope, Arkansas, three months after his father's death in an automobile accident (he assumed his stepfather's name of Clinton at age fifteen), young Bill learned that persistence and tenacity were the keys to success and acclaim. As a teenage delegate to Boys Nation, he won a handshake from President John F. Kennedy in 1963. He chose to attend Georgetown University in Washington to be near the nation's centers of power. As soon as he arrived in the capital he called on his state's senator, William J. Fulbright, chair of the Senate Foreign Relations Committee, and got a part-time job as a legislative aide. Clinton won a Rhodes Scholarship to Oxford University with the help of Senator Fulbright, himself a former Rhodes scholar. In London he helped organize anti-Vietnam War demonstrations, even while he worried that his antiwar activities might someday come back to haunt his political ambitions. When he received a draft notice, he promptly enrolled in the ROTC program at the University of Arkansas, making himself temporarily ineligible for the draft despite acknowledging that his real plans were to go to Yale Law School.

The Nation's Youngest Governor   Upon graduation from Yale, Clinton return to Arkansas. Trying to capitalize on the Watergate scandal, he challenged a veteran Republican member of Congress in 1974. As a young antiwar activist, he could have lost by a wide margin in conservative Arkansas. Instead, he came within a few votes of defeating a strong incumbent. In 1976 Clinton ran successfully for attorney general of Arkansas, and, in 1978, he jumped into the open gubernatorial contest and became the nation's youngest governor at age thirty-two.

Remolding His Image   As governor, Clinton first pushed a broad program of liberal reform for Arkansas, increasing taxes and expenditures. But he appeared to be an arrogant, crusading, liberal politician, out of touch with his conservative Arkansas constituency. He was defeated for reelection in 1980. His defeat "forever influenced the way he approached government and politics."† He proceeded to remold himself into a political moderate, calling for workfare to replace welfare, supporting the death penalty, and working to create a favorable business climate in Arkansas. He cut his long 1960's style hair, and his wife began using her married name Clinton (rather than Hillary Rodham) so as not to offend social conservatives. The moderate strategy proved successful; he was elected governor once again in 1982. By most accounts, Bill Clinton was a successful governor.

Clinton's view that only a moderate Democrat could win the presidency was reinforced by Michael Dukakis's disastrous defeat in 1988. Just as he had shaped his image to fit his Arkansas constituents, Clinton molded his national image as a moderate, pro-business, Democrat, capable of winning back the support of the white middle class.

First Term Flip-Flops   Bill Clinton won the White House in 1992 with only 43 percent of the popular vote, hardly a mandate for comprehensive policy change. His first major battle—to retain homosexuals in the military—proved a disaster. Military chiefs, led by the popular General Colin Powell, resisted, and Clinton was forced to retreat. He succeeded in getting the Democratic-controlled Congress to pass a large tax increase, raising the top marginal income tax rate from 31 to nearly 40 percent. But in his second year, he stumbled badly in his massive national health care program, and his approval ratings sagged.

The sweeping Republican congressional victory in 1994 appeared to foreshadow a one-term presidency for Clinton. But characteristically he mounted another political "comeback." He vetoed several Republican balanced budget plans; when the government temporarily "shut down," Clinton shifted the blame to the Republican Congress. He cast himself as the defender of "Medicare, Medicaid, education and the environment" against the mean-spirited Republican Speaker Newt Gingrich. Clinton's approval ratings began a long rise.

Shifting Toward Mini-Policies

Election year brought still more policy shifts. He announced, "The era of big government is over." He signed the Republican welfare bill that he had vetoed twice. Rather than champion large-scale change in the fashion of Roosevelt's New Deal, Clinton shifted to what might be labeled the "Small Deal"—an assembly of small changes easily understood by the American people—V-chips, school uniforms, gun control, time off for family emergencies, longer stays in maternity wards, for example. The strategy paid off among women voters at the polls: although men appeared to divide their votes evenly between Clinton and Dole, the president won women voters by a stunning 54 to 38 margin.

Second Term Drift?

At the start of his second term Clinton seemed to acknowledge that he had no mandate for new, large-scale government programs. He modestly observed in his election night victory speech: "Tonight we proclaim that the vital American center is alive and well." But even if he had sought to return to a liberal agenda, it is not likely that a Republican Congress would have allowed him to get very far. Critics of President Clinton describe his second term as "risk averse," adrift, and even aimless. Although he spoke on a multitude of policy proposals, he did not cite any single issue as his overriding priority.

The nation's booming economy in the 1990s kept Clinton's approval ratings high. It also provided a temporary solution to what had been the most vexing of all government problems: continuing deficit spending. Robust economic growth increased federal tax revenues enough to produce a balanced federal budget, a goal that had eluded presidents and Congresses for over a quarter-century. Clinton's call to use the surplus to "save Social Security first" (before tax cutting or new spending programs) reflected majority public opinion.

The Impeachment Legacy

Clinton's impeachment by the House of Representatives will color his legacy as president for all time, despite the partisan division of the vote and his acquittal by the Senate. The American public clearly separated his character flaws from his public performance as president. But with few specific policy achievements, it is likely that future descriptions of his presidency will focus on his sexual misconduct and open and public lying about it, and on his unprincipled instinct for political self-preservation. Moreover, his court battles with the hostile Independent Counsel weakened the institution of presidency; they established judicial precedents for allowing civil suits against a sitting president and even forcing Secret Service agents to testify against a president.

Presidential Greatness

Clinton himself seems aware that he will never be ranked among the great presidents. "Greatness," he believes, is as much a product of the times as the man. Clinton faced no really great national or international challenges during his presidency; an opposition-controlled Congress limited his policy options; and good economic times dampened the public's enthusiasm for new government programs.

It is not clear whether his policy centrism was pragmatic and skillful, or unprincipled and opportunistic. Perhaps he deserves praise for fiscal responsibility—initially raising taxes, presiding over economic growth with low inflation, and eventually presenting balanced federal budgets to the nation. On the other hand, perhaps his personal conduct contributed to the nation's cultural amoralism—its willingness to overlook character defects in its leadership as long as the good times roll on.

"The relevant question for the future is the impact of Clinton's character on his legacy. As the years go on and memory grows dim, the word 'impeached' is likely to be the sound bite that will define the Clinton presidency, at least for the lay public."[‡]

*Bob Woodward, *The Agenda* (New York: Simon & Schuster, 1994), p. 48.

†David Maranis, *First in His Class* (New York: Simon & Schuster, 1995), p. 400.

‡Bert A. Rockman, "Cutting With the Grain: Is There a Clinton Leadership Legacy?" in Colin Campbell and Bert A. Rockman, eds., *The Clinton Legacy* (New York: Chatham House, 2000), p. 288.

George W., in His Father's Footsteps

George W. Bush was born into his family's tradition of wealth, privilege, and public service. (Bush's grandfather, investment banker Prescott Bush, was a U.S. Senator from Connecticut and chairman of the Yale Corporation, the University's governing board.) He grew up in Midland, Texas, where his father had established himself in the oil business before going into politics—first as a Houston Congressman, then Republican National Chairman, Director of the CIA, Ambassador to China, and finally vice president and president of the United States. George W. followed in his father's footsteps to Yale University but he was not the scholar-athlete that his father had been. Rather, he was a friendly, likable, heavy-drinking president of his fraternity. Upon graduation in 1968, he joined the Texas Air National Guard, completed flight school, but never faced combat in Vietnam. He earned an MBA degree from the Harvard Business School and returned to Midland to enter the oil business himself. Later in his career he would acknowledge his "youthful indiscretions," including a drunk driving arrest in 1976.

Although his famous name attracted investors in a series of oil companies he managed, virtually all of them lost money (including the Harvard Management Company that invests that university's endowment funds). Even a deal with the government of oil rich Bahrain, negotiated while his father was president, failed to bail out Bush's Harken Energy Company. But Bush was able to sell off his oil interests and reinvest the money in the Texas Rangers baseball team; he eventually sold his interest in the Rangers in a deal that netted him over $15 million.

George W. Bush had never held public office before running for governor of Texas in 1994. But he had gained valuable political experience serving as an unofficial adviser to his father during his presidential campaigns. He went up against the sharp-tongued incumbent Democratic Governor Ann Richards, who ridiculed him as the "shrub" (little Bush). Bush heavily outspent Richards and won 54 percent of the vote, to become Texas's second Republican governor in modern times.

George W.'s political style fit comfortably with the Texas "good old boys" in both parties. Although the Texas legislature was controlled by Democrats, Bush won most of his early legislative battles. He supported legislation that gave law-abiding adult Texans the right to carry concealed handguns. A strong economy allowed him to improve public services yet keep Texas among the few states without an income tax. He supported educational reform by opposing the practice of "social promotion" and requiring third-, fifth-, and eighth-grade pupils to pass statewide tests before advancing to the next grade.

Bush's style was to meet frequently and privately with his Democratic opponents and to remain on friendly personal terms with them. He was willing to accept legislative compromises and tried to avoid controversies wherever possible. He helped to lead the gradual realignment of Texas away from its traditional Democratic roots and toward its current Republican coloration. (Currently Republicans hold not only the governorship but both U.S. Senate seats and all other statewide elected offices.) Bush was overwhelmingly reelected governor of Texas in 1998.

Reportedly, Bush was at first ambivalent about running for president, but a "pilgrimage" of senior Republican stalwarts came to Austin to urge him to run and to prep him on the issues. Bush denies that his father ever tried to influence his decision but many of his father's friends and political associates did, believing that only he could reclaim the White House for the GOP. They compared "Dubya" to Ronald Reagan—amiable, charming, and good-humored, even if a little vague on the details of public policy. His mother's 10,000-name Christmas card list of closest family friends helped in building a bankroll of more than $100 million *before* the campaign even began. And the GOP establishment stuck with him when he was challenged in the early primary elections by maverick Arizona Republican Senator and Vietnam war hero John McCain. Bush's father avoided public appearances with his son, not wishing to diminish the younger man's presidential stature. But George senior was a very effective fundraiser in the most expensive presidential campaign in the nation's history.

George W. Bush boasts of being a "uniter not a divider." His close, contested presidential election promises to test this boast. He is the first president to lose the popular vote yet win in the electoral college since Benjamin Harrison in 1888. Harrison's presidency was largely a failure, and the 1888 loser, Grover Cleveland, won the office four years later. It will require all of Bush's leadership abilities to avoid the same fate.

9066 for the internment of Japanese-Americans during World War II. In 1948 President Harry Truman issued Executive Order 9981 to desegregate the U.S. armed forces. In 1965 President Lyndon Johnson issued Executive Order 11246 to require that private firms with federal contracts institute affirmative action programs. A president can even declare a national emergency by executive order, a step that authorizes a broad range of unilateral actions.

Executive orders have legal force when they are based on the president's constitutional or statutory authority. And presidents typically take an expansive view of their own authority. (President George Washington issued an executive order declaring American neutrality in the war between France and England in 1793; while the Constitution gave the power to "declare war" to Congress, Washington assumed the authority to declare neutrality.) Federal courts have generally upheld presidential executive orders. However, the Supreme Court overturned an order by President Harry Truman in 1951 during the Korean War seizing the nation's steel mills.[17] Research on the frequency of executive orders suggests that: Democratic presidents issue more orders than Republican presidents; presidents may issue executive orders to circumvent Congress but only when they believe that Congress will not overturn their orders; and presidents issue more executive orders when they are running for re-election.[18]

Appointments   Presidential power over the executive branch derives in part from the president's authority to appoint and remove top officials. Presidents can shape policy by careful attention to top appointments—cabinet secretaries, assistant secretaries, agency heads, and White House staff. The key is to select people who share the president's policy views and who have the personal qualifications to do an effective job. However, in cabinet appointments political considerations weigh heavily: unifying various elements of the party; appealing for interest-group support; rewarding political loyalty; providing a temporary haven for unsuccessful party candidates; achieving a balance of racial, ethnic, and gender representation.[19] The appointment power gives the president only limited control over the executive branch of government. Of the executive branch's 2.8 million civilian employees, the president actually appoints only about 3,000. The vast majority of federal executive branch employees are civil servants—recruited, paid, and protected under civil service laws—and are not easily removed or punished by the president. Cabinet secretaries and heads of independent regulatory agencies require congressional confirmation, but presidents can choose their own White House staff without the approval of Congress.

Presidents have only limited power to remove the heads of independent regulatory agencies. By law, Congress sets the terms of these officials. Federal Communications Commission members are appointed for five years; Securities and Exchange Commission members for five years; and Federal Reserve Board members, responsible for the nation's money supply, enjoy the longest term of any executive officials—fourteen years. Congress's responsibility for term length for regulatory agencies is supposed to insulate those agencies, in particular their quasi-judicial responsibilities, from "political" influence.

Even having a presidential appointee at the helm of a department does not always guarantee the president control over that department. Many political appointees are stymied by the career bureaucrats in departments and agencies who have the knowledge, skills, and experience to function with little or no supervision from their nominal political chiefs. Rather than carrying out the president's policies, some appointees "go native": they yield to the career bureaucrats, adopt the prevailing customs and values of their agencies, and seek the support of the bureaucrats, interest groups, and congressional committees that determine the agencies' future.

Republican presidents have an especially difficult task controlling the bureaucracy because a majority of career bureaucrats are Democrats.[20] When President Nixon tried to deal with this problem by shifting power from executive departments to his White House staff, the unhappy result was that the White House staff itself became a large and powerful bureaucracy, frequently locked in conflict with executive departments. President Reagan instead tried appointing committed conservatives to head key agencies, only to see them isolated and undermined by angry bureaucrats. Some lower-level bureaucrats supplied the media and Congress with damaging reports about Reagan appointees' activities (see "Bureaucratic Politics" in Chapter 12).

Budget   Presidential authority also derives from the president's role in the budgetary process. The Constitution makes no mention of the president with regard to expenditures; rather, it grants the power of the purse to Congress. Indeed, for nearly 150 years, executive departments submitted their budget requests directly to the Congress without first submitting them to the president. But with the passage of the Budget and Accounting Act in 1921, Congress established the Office of Management and Budget (originally named the Bureau of the Budget) to assist the president in preparing an annual Budget of the United States Government for presentation to the Congress. The president's budget is simply a set of recommendations to the Congress. Congress must pass appropriations acts before the president or any executive department or agency may spend money. Congress can and frequently does alter the president's budget recommendations (see "The Politics of Budgeting" in Chapter 12).

The Cabinet   The **cabinet** is not mentioned in the U.S. Constitution; it has no formal powers. It consists of the secretaries of the executive departments and others the president may designate, including the vice president, the ambassador to the United Nations, the director of the Central Intelligence Agency, and the Special Trade Representative. According to custom, cabinet officials are ranked by the date their departments were created (see Table 11–2). Thus the Secretary of State is the senior cabinet officer, followed by the Secretary of the Treasury. They sit next to the president at Cabinet meetings; heads of the newest departments sit at the far ends of the table.

The cabinet rarely functions as a decision-making body. Cabinet officers in the United States are powerful because they head giant administrative organizations. The secretary of state, the secretary of defense, the secretary of the treasury, the attorney general, and, to a lesser extent, the other departmental secretaries are all people of power and prestige. But seldom does a strong president hold a cabinet meeting to decide important policy questions. More frequently, presidents know what they want and hold cabinet meetings only to help promote their views. Presidents who have tried to use the cabinet as a policy-making body have been disappointed. George Washington was frustrated by constant feuding between his secretary of the treasury, Alexander Hamilton, and his secretary of state, Thomas Jefferson. President Jimmy Carter promised "cabinet government" but soon found that meetings were little more than "adult show and tell." The cabinet is too large for serious discussion; its members are not necessarily familiar with issues beyond their own department's sphere of activity; they are preoccupied with managing

cabinet   The heads (secretaries) of the executive departments together with other top officials accorded Cabinet rank by the president; only occasionally does it meet as a body to advise and support the president.

Table 11-2 The Cabinet Departments

Department	Created
State	1789
Treasury	1789
Defense*	1947
Justice	1789
Interior	1849
Agriculture†	1889
Commerce	1913
Labor	1913
Health and Human Services‡	1953
Housing and Urban Development	1965
Transportation	1966
Energy	1977
Education	1979
Veterans' Affairs	1989

*Formerly the War and Navy Departments, created in 1789 and 1798, respectively.

†Agriculture Department created in 1862; made part of cabinet in 1889.

‡Originally Health, Education, and Welfare; reorganized in 1979, with the creation of a separate Department of Education.

large bureaucracies. Finally, cabinet members are frequently appointed not for policy guidance but to cement the president's relationships with interest groups—agriculture, veterans, labor, and so forth—or to provide the administration with racial, ethnic, and gender balance.

The Constitution requires that "Officers of the United States" be confirmed by the Senate. In the past, the Senate rarely rejected a presidential cabinet nomination; the traditional view was that presidents were entitled to pick their own people and even make their own mistakes. In recent years, however, the confirmation process has become more partisan and divisive, with the Senate conducting lengthy investigations and holding public hearings on presidential cabinet nominees. In 1989 the Senate rejected President Bush's nomination of John Tower as secretary of defense in a partisan battle featuring charges that the former Texas senator was a heavy drinker. In 1993 President Clinton was obliged to withdraw the nomination of Zoe Baird as attorney general following Senate hearings featuring the charge that she had employed an illegal alien as a babysitter and had failed to pay the woman's Social Security taxes. The intense public scrutiny and potential for partisan attacks, together with financial disclosure and conflict-of-interest laws, may be discouraging some well-qualified people from accepting cabinet posts.

The National Security Council The **National Security Council (NSC)** is really an "inner cabinet" created by law in 1947 to advise the president and coordinate foreign, defense, and intelligence activities. The president is chair, and the vice president, secretary of state, and secretary of defense are participating members. The chair of the Joint Chiefs of Staff and the director of the Central Intelligence Agency serve as advisers to the NSC, which is headed by the special assistant to the president

National Security Council (NSC) "Inner cabinet" that advises the president and coordinates foreign, defense, and intelligence activities.

for national security affairs. The purposes of the council are to advise and coordinate policy, but in the Iran-Contra scandal, a staff member of the NSC, Lt. Col. Oliver North, undertook to implement security policy. Various investigative committees strongly recommended that the NSC staff confine itself to an advisory role.

White House Staff   Today, presidents exercise their powers chiefly through the White House staff.[21] This staff includes the president's closest aides and advisers. Over the years, the White House staff has grown from Roosevelt's small "brain trust" of a dozen advisers to several hundred people, many with impressive titles, such as assistant to the president, deputy assistant to the president, special assistant to the president, and counsel to the president.

Senior White House staff members are trusted political advisers, often personal friends and long-time associates of the president. Some enjoy office space in the White House itself and daily contact with the president (see Figure 11–3). Appointed without Senate confirmation, they are loyal to the president alone, not to departments, agencies, or interest groups. Their many tasks include the following:

- Providing the president with sound advice on everything from national security to congressional affairs, policy development, and electoral politics.
- Monitoring the operations of executive departments and agencies and evaluating the performance of key executive officials.
- Setting the president's schedule, determining whom the president will see and call, where and when the president will travel, and where and to whom the president will make personal appearances and speeches.
- Above all, the staff must protect their boss, steering the president away from scandal, political blunders, and errors of judgment.

The senior White House staff normally includes a chief of staff, the national security adviser, a press secretary, the counsel to the president (an attorney), a director of personnel (patronage appointments), and assistants for political affairs, legislative liaison, management, and domestic policy. Staff organization depends on each president's personal taste. Some presidents have organized their staffs hierarchically, concentrating power in the chief of staff. Others have maintained direct contact with several staff members.

CHIEF LEGISLATOR AND LOBBYIST

The president has the principal responsibility for the initiation of national policy. Indeed, about 80 percent of the bills considered by Congress originate in the executive branch. Presidents have a strong incentive to fulfill this responsibility: the American people hold them responsible for anything that happens in the nation during their term of office, whether or not they have the authority or capacity to do anything about it.

Policy Initiation   The Founders understood that the president would be involved in policy initiation. The Constitution requires the president to "give to the Congress Information of the State of the Union," to "recommend to their Consideration such Measures as he shall judge necessary and expedient" (Article II, Section 3). "On extraordinary Occasions" the president may call a recessed Congress into special session. Each year the principal policy statement of the president comes in the State of the Union message to Congress. It is followed by the

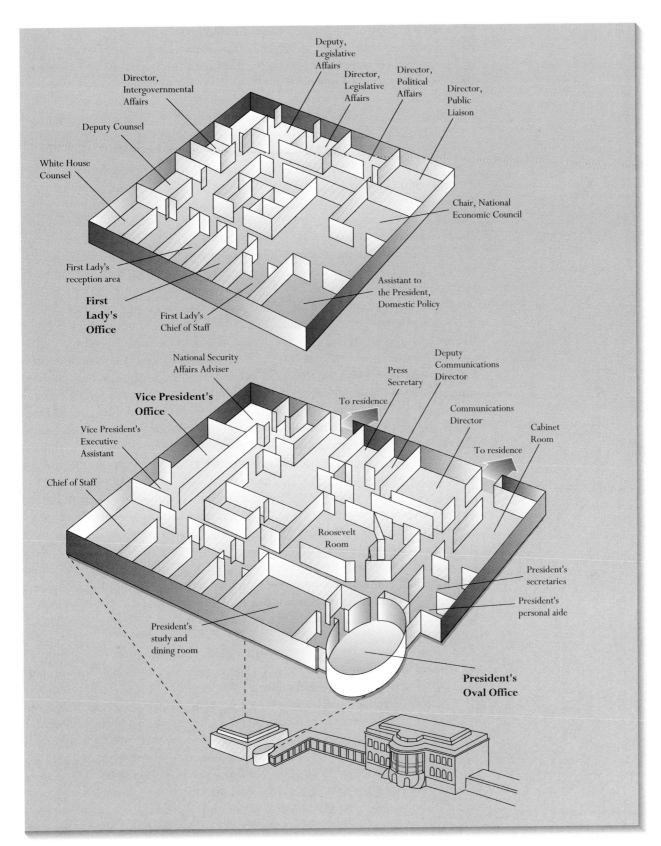

FIGURE 11–3 The White House Corridors of Power

Presidents allocate office space in the White House according to their own desires. An office located close to the president's is considered an indication of the power of the occupant. This diagram shows the office assignments during the Clinton Administration.

president's Budget of the United States Government, which sets forth the president's programs with price tags attached. Many other policy proposals are developed by executive departments and agencies, transmitted to the White House for the president's approval or "clearance," and then sent to Congress.

Congress may not accept all or even most of the president's proposals. Indeed, from time to time it may even try to develop its own legislative agenda in competition with the president's. But the president's legislative initiatives usually set the agenda of congressional decision making. As one experienced Washington lobbyist put it, "Obviously when the president sends up a bill, it takes first place in the queue. All other bills take second place."[22]

White House Lobbying   Presidents do not simply send their bills to Congress and then await the outcome. The president is also expected to be the chief lobbyist on behalf of the administration's bills as they make their way through the legislative labyrinth. The White House staff includes "legislative liaison" people—lobbyists for the president's programs. They organize the president's legislative proposals, track them through committee and floor proceedings, arrange committee appearances by executive department and agency representatives, count votes, and advise the president on when and how to "cut deals" and "twist arms."

Presidents are not without resources in lobbying Congress. They may exchange many favors, large and small, for the support of individual members. They can help direct "pork" to a member's district, promise White House support for a member's pet project, and assist in resolving a member's problems with the bureaucracy. Presidents also may issue or withhold invitations to the White House for prestigious ceremonies, dinners with visiting heads of state, and other glittering social occasions—an effective resource because most members of Congress value the prestige associated with close White House "connections."

The president may choose to "twist arms" individually—by telephoning and meeting with wavering members of Congress. Arm twisting is generally reserved for the president's most important legislative battles. There is seldom time for a president to contact individual members of Congress personally about many bills in various stages of the legislative process—in subcommittee, full committee, floor consideration, conference committee, and final passage—in both the House and the Senate. Instead, the president must rely on White House staff for most legislative contacts and use personal appeals sparingly.

The Honeymoon   The **honeymoon period** at the very start of a president's term offers the best opportunity to get the new administration's legislative proposals enacted into law. Presidential influence in Congress is generally highest at this time both because the president's personal popularity is typically at its height and because the president can claim the recent election results as a popular mandate for key programs. Sophisticated members of Congress know that votes cast for a presidential candidate are not necessarily votes cast for that candidate's policy position (see "The Voter Decides" in Chapter 8). But election results signal members of Congress, in a language they understand well, that the president is politically popular and that they must give the administration's programs careful consideration. President Lyndon Johnson succeeded in getting the bulk of his Great Society program enacted in the year following his landslide victory in 1964. Ronald Reagan pushed through the largest tax cut in American history in the year following his convincing electoral victory over incumbent president Jimmy Carter in 1980. Bill Clinton was

honeymoon period   Early months of a president's term in which his popularity with the public and influence with the Congress are generally high.

most successful with the Congress during his first year in office, in 1993, even winning approval for a major tax increase as part of a deficit-reduction package.

Presidential "Box Scores"   How successful are presidents in getting their legislation through Congress? *Congressional Quarterly* regularly compiles "box scores" of presidential success in Congress—percentages of presidential victories on congressional votes on which the president took a clear-cut position. The measure does not distinguish between bills that were important to the president and bills that may have been less significant. But viewed over time (see Figure 11–4), the presidential box scores provide interesting insights into the factors affecting the president's legislative success.

The most important determinant of presidential success in Congress is party control. Presidents are far more successful when they face a Congress controlled by their own party. Democratic presidents John F. Kennedy and Lyndon Johnson enjoyed the support of Democratic-controlled Congresses and posted average success scores over 80 percent. Jimmy Carter was hardly a popular president, but he enjoyed the support of a Democratic Congress and an average of 76.8 percent presidential support. Republican presidents Richard Nixon and Gerald Ford fared poorly with Democratic-controlled Congresses. Republican president Ronald Reagan was very successful in his first term when he faced a Democratic House and a Republican Senate, but after Democrats took over both houses of Congress, Reagan's success rate plum-

FIGURE 11–4   Presidential Success Scores in Congress

Presidential "box scores"—the percentage of times that a bill endorsed by the president is enacted by Congress—are closely linked to the strength of the president's party in Congress. For example, both Dwight D. Eisenhower and Ronald Reagan benefited from having a Republican majority in the Senate in their first terms and suffered when Democrats gained control of the Senate in their second terms. Democratic control of both houses of Congress resulted in significantly higher box scores for Democratic presidents John Kennedy, Lyndon Johnson, and Jimmy Carter than for Republicans Richard Nixon, Gerald Ford, and George Bush. Clinton was very successful in his first two years, when the Democrats controlled Congress, but when the Republicans won control following the 1994 midterm election, Clinton's box score plummeted.

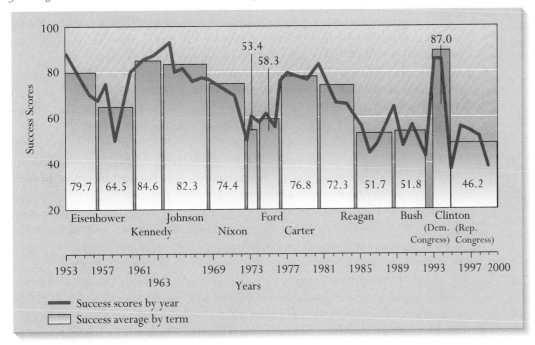

meted. During the Reagan and Bush presidencies, divided party control of government (Republicans in the White House and Democrats controlling one or both houses of Congress) was said to produce **gridlock**, the political inability of the government to act decisively on the nation's problems. President Bill Clinton's achievements when Democrats controlled the Congress (1993–94), contrasted with his dismal record in dealing with Republican-controlled Congresses (1995–99), provide a vivid illustration of the importance of party in determining a president's legislative success.

The Veto Power   The **veto** is the president's most powerful weapon in dealing with Congress. The veto is especially important to a president facing a Congress controlled by the opposition party. Even the *threat* of a veto enhances the president's bargaining power with Congress.[23] Confronted with such a threat, congressional leaders must calculate whether they can muster a two-thirds vote of both houses to override the veto.

To veto a bill passed by the Congress, the president sends to Congress a veto message specifying reasons for not signing it. If the president takes no action for ten days (excluding Sundays) after a bill has been passed by Congress, the bill becomes law without the president's signature. However, if Congress has adjourned within ten days of passing a bill and the president has not signed it, then the bill does not become law; this outcome is called a **pocket veto**.

A bill returned to Congress with a presidential veto message can be passed into law over the president's opposition by a two-thirds vote of houses. (A bill that has received a pocket veto cannot be overridden because the Congress is no longer in session.) In other words, the president needs only to hold the loyalty of more than one-third of *either* the House or the Senate to sustain a veto. If congressional leaders cannot count on the votes to **override**, they are forced to bargain with the president. "What will the president accept?" becomes a key legislative question.

The president's bargaining power with Congress has been enhanced over the years by a history of success in sustaining presidential vetoes.[24] From George Washington to Bill Clinton, more than 96 percent of all presidential vetoes have been sustained (see Table 11–3). For example, although Bush was unable to achieve much success in getting his own legislative proposals enacted by a Democratic Congress, he was extraordinarily successful in saying no. Of Bush's many vetoes, only one (regulation of cable TV) was overridden by Congress. Clinton did not veto any bills when Democrats controlled Congress, but he began a series of vetoes in his struggle with the Republican Congress elected in 1994. He was able to sustain almost all of his vetoes because Republicans did not have two-thirds of the seats in both houses and most Democratic Congress members stuck with their president.

Line-Item Veto Power Denied   For many years, presidents, both Democratic and Republican, petitioned Congress to give them the **line-item veto**, the ability to veto some provisions of a bill while accepting other provisions. The lack of presidential line-item veto power was especially frustrating when dealing with appropriations bills because the president could not veto specific pork-barrel provisions from major spending bills for defense, education, housing, welfare, and so on. Finally, in 1996 Congress granted the president authority to "cancel" spending items in any appropriation act and any limited tax benefit. Such cancellation would take effect immediately unless blocked by a special "disapproval bill" passed by Congress. The president could veto the disapproval bill, and a two-thirds vote of both houses would be required to override the veto.

gridlock   Political stalemate between the executive and legislative branches arising when one branch is controlled by one major political party and the other branch by the other party.

veto   Rejection of a legislative act by the executive branch; in the U.S. federal government, overriding of a veto requires a two-thirds majority in both houses of Congress.

pocket veto   Effective veto of a bill when Congress adjourns within ten days of passing it and the president fails to sign it.

override   Voting in Congress to enact legislation vetoed by the president; requires a two-thirds vote in both the House and Senate.

line-item veto   Power of the chief executive to reject some portions of a bill without rejecting all of it.

| | Table 11-3 | Presidential Vetoes |

President	Total Vetoes*	Vetoes Overridden	Percentage of Vetoes Sustained
F. Roosevelt	633	9	99%
Truman	250	12	95
Eisenhower	181	2	99
Kennedy	21	0	100
L. Johnson	30	0	100
Nixon	43	5	90
Ford	66	12	85
Carter	31	2	94
Reagan	78	8	91
Bush	46	1	98
Clinton (7 years)	30	2	93

*Regular vetoes plus pocket vetoes.

Source: Harold W. Stanley and Richard G. Niemi, *Vital Statistics on American Politics, 1999–2000* (Washington, D.C.: CQ Press, 2000), p. 256. Updated by author.

However, opponents of the line-item veto successfully challenged its constitutionality, arguing that it transfers legislative power—granted by the Constitution only to Congress—to the president. The U.S. Supreme Court agreed: "There is no provision in the Constitution that authorizes the president to enact or amend or repeal statutes." The line-item veto, the Court said, "authorizes the president himself to elect to repeal laws, for his own policy reasons" and therefore violates the law-making procedures set forth in Article I of the Constitution.[25]

GLOBAL LEADER

The president of the United States is the leader of the world's largest and most powerful democracy. During the Cold War, the president of the United States was seen as the leader of the "free world." The threat of Soviet expansionism, the huge military forces of the Warsaw Pact, and Soviet-backed guerrilla wars around the world all added to the global role of the American president as the defender of democratic values. In today's post–Cold War world, Western Europe and Japan are formidable economic competitors and no longer routinely defer to American political leadership. But if a new stable world order based on democracy and self-determination is to emerge, the president of the United States must provide the necessary leadership.

Global leadership is based on a president's powers of persuasion. Presidents are more persuasive when the American economy is strong, when American military forces are perceived as ready and capable, and when the president is seen as having the support of the American people and Congress. America's allies as well as its enemies perceive the president as the controlling force over U.S. foreign and military policy. Only occasionally do they seek to bypass the president and appeal to the Congress or to American public opinion.

Presidents sometimes prefer their global role to the much more contentious infighting of domestic politics. Abroad, presidents are treated with great dignity as head of the world's most powerful state. In contrast, at home presidents must confront hostile and insulting reporters, backbiting bureaucrats, demanding interest groups, and contentious members of Congress.

Foreign Policy   As the nation's chief diplomat, the president has the principal responsibility for formulating U.S. foreign policy. The president's constitutional powers in foreign affairs are relatively modest. Presidents have the power to make treaties with foreign nations "with the Advice and Consent of the Senate." Presidents may negotiate with nations separately or through international organizations such as the North Atlantic Treaty Organization (NATO) or the United Nations, where the president determines the U.S. position in that body's deliberations. The Constitution also empowers the president to "appoint Ambassadors, other public Ministers, and Consuls" and to "receive Ambassadors." This power of **diplomatic recognition** permits a president to grant legitimacy to or withhold it from ruling groups around the world (to declare or refuse to declare them "rightful"). Despite controversy, President Franklin Roosevelt officially recognized the communist regime in Russia in 1933, Richard Nixon recognized the communist government of the People's Republic of China in 1972, and Carter recognized the communist Sandinistas' regime in Nicaragua in 1979. To date, all presidents have withheld diplomatic recognition of Fidel Castro's government in Cuba.

Presidents have expanded on these modest constitutional powers to dominate American foreign policy making. In part, they have done so as a product of their role as commander-in-chief. Military force is the ultimate diplomatic language. During wartime, or when war is threatened, military and foreign policy become inseparable. The president must decide on the use of force and, equally important, when and under what conditions to order a cease-fire or an end to hostilities.

Presidents have also come to dominate foreign policy as a product of the customary international recognition of the head of state as the legitimate voice of a government. Although nations may also watch the words and actions of the American

diplomatic recognition

Power of the president to grant "legitimacy" to or withhold it from a government of another nation (to declare or refuse to declare it "rightful").

President Bill Clinton with Israeli Prime Minister Ehud Barak in 1999. U.S. presidents, acting as our nation's "Chief Diplomat," have worked continuously for Mideast peace for more than a half-century.

Congress, the president's statements are generally taken to represent the official position of the U.S. government.

Treaties Treaties the president makes "by and with the Advice and Consent of the Senate" are legally binding upon the United States. The Constitution specifies that "all Treaties made . . . under the Authority of the United States, shall be the supreme Law of the Land; and the Judges in every State shall be bound thereby" (Article VI). Thus treaty provisions are directly enforceable in federal courts.

Although presidents may or may not listen to "advice" from the Senate on foreign policy, no formal treaty is valid unless "two-thirds of the Senators present concur" to its ratification. Although the Senate has ratified the vast majority of treaties, presidents must be sensitive to Senate concerns. The Senate defeat of the Versailles Treaty in 1920, which formally ended World War I and established the League of Nations, prompted Presidents Roosevelt and Truman to include prominent Democratic and Republican members of the Senate Foreign Relations Committee in the delegation that drafted the United Nations Charter in 1945 and the NATO Treaty in 1949.

President Clinton was sharply reminded of the need to develop bipartisan support for treaties in the Senate in 1999 when that body rejected the Comprehensive Test Ban Treaty. This Treaty would have prohibited all signatory nations from conducting any tests of nuclear weapons. Most Western European nations had already signed and ratified the nuclear test ban, but North Korea, Iraq, Iran, India, and Pakistan, among other nations, had rejected it. China and Russia appeared to be waiting for the United States to act first. The president argued that the United States should take moral leadership in worldwide nonproliferation of nuclear weapons. His opponents in the Senate argued that too many rogue nations would ignore the treaty and continue their own nuclear testing. Despite the Senate's rejection of the treaty, Clinton continued by executive order his own moratorium on nuclear testing by the United States (see Chapter 18).

Executive Agreements Over the years, presidents have come to rely heavily on **executive agreements** with other governments rather than formal treaties. An executive agreement signed by the president of the United States has much the same effect in international relations as a treaty. However, an executive agreement does not require Senate ratification. Presidents have asserted that their constitutional power to execute the laws, command the armed services, and determine foreign policy gives them the authority to make agreements with other nations and heads of state without obtaining approval of the U.S. Senate. However, unlike treaties, executive agreements do not supersede laws of the United States or of the states with which they conflict, but they are otherwise binding on the United States.

The use of executive agreements in important foreign policy matters was developed by President Franklin Roosevelt. Prior to his administration, executive agreements had been limited to minor matters. But in 1940, Roosevelt agreed to trade fifty American destroyers to England in exchange for naval bases in Newfoundland and the Caribbean. Roosevelt was intent on helping the British in their struggle against Nazi Germany, but before the Japanese attack on Pearl Harbor in 1941, isolationist sentiment in the Senate was too strong to win a two-thirds ratifying vote for such an agreement. Toward the end of World War II, Roosevelt at the Yalta Conference and Truman at the Potsdam Conference negotiated secret executive agreements dividing the occupation of Germany between the Western Allies and the Soviet Union.

executive agreement
Agreement with another nation signed by the president of the United States but less formal (and hence potentially less binding) than a treaty because it does not require Senate confirmation.

Although still part of the "Big Three" along with Prime Minister Winston Churchill of Great Britain (right) and Marshal Josef Stalin of the Soviet Union (left), it was a gravely ill President Franklin Roosevelt (middle) who traveled to Yalta, a port on Russia's Crimean peninsula, and negotiated secret executive agreements dividing Germany among the Allies in 1945. Germany remained divided until 1989, when protesters tore down the Berlin Wall and the Soviet Union under Mikhail Gorbachev acquiesced in the unification of Germany under a democratic government.

Congress has sometimes objected to executive agreements as usurping its own powers. In the Case Act of 1972, Congress required the president to inform Congress of all executive agreements within sixty days, but the act does not limit the president's power to make agreements. It is easier for Congress to renege on executive agreements than on treaties that the Senate has ratified. In 1973 President Nixon signed an executive agreement with South Vietnamese President Nguyen Van Thieu pledging that the United States would "respond with full force" if North Vietnam violated the Paris Peace Agreement that ended American participation in the Vietnam War. But when North Vietnam reinvaded the south in 1975, Congress rejected President Gerald Ford's pleas for renewed military aid to the South Vietnamese government, and Ford knew that it had become politically impossible for the United States to respond with force.

Intelligence   The president is responsible for the intelligence activities of the United States. Presidents have undertaken intelligence activities since the founding of the nation. During the Revolutionary War, General George Washington nurtured small groups of patriots living behind British lines who supplied him with information on Redcoat troop movements.[26] Today, the director of central intelligence (DCI) is appointed by the president (subject to Senate confirmation) and reports directly to the president. The DCI coordinates the activities of the Central Intelligence Agency, the National Security Agency (which monitors electronic broadcasts around the world), and the secret National Reconnaissance Office (which obtains information from satellites), as well as the intelligence activities of the Department of Defense.

The Central Intelligence Agency (CIA) is directly supervised by the DCI. It is responsible for the analysis, preparation, and distribution of intelligence to the president and the National Security Council. It is also responsible for the collection of human intelligence—reports obtained from foreign sources by CIA caseworkers around the world. And the CIA is responsible for all **covert action**—activities in support of the national interest of the United States that would be ineffective or counterproductive if their sponsorship were to be made public. For example, one of the largest covert actions ever undertaken by the United States was the support, for nearly ten years, of the Afghan rebels fighting Soviet occupation of their country during the Afghanistan War (1978–88). Public acknowledgment of such aid would have assisted the Soviet-backed regime in Afghanistan to claim that the rebels were not true patriots but rather "puppets" of the United States. The rebels themselves did not wish to acknowledge U.S. aid publicly, even though they knew it was essential to the success of their cause. Hence Presidents Carter and Reagan aided the Afghan rebels through covert action.

Covert action is, by definition, secret. And secrecy spawns elaborate conspiracy theories and flamboyant tales of intrigue and deception. In fact, most covert actions consist of routine transfers of economic aid and military equipment to pro-U.S. forces that do not wish to acknowledge such aid publicly. Although most covert actions would have widespread support among the American public if they were done openly, secrecy opens the possibility that a president will undertake to do by covert action what would be opposed by Congress and the American people if they knew about it.

In the atmosphere of suspicion and distrust engendered by the Watergate scandal, Congress passed intelligence oversight legislation in 1974 requiring a written "presidential finding" for any covert action and requiring that members of the House and Senate Intelligence Committees be informed of all covert actions. The president does not have to obtain congressional approval for covert actions; but Congress can halt such actions if it chooses to do so. For example, in 1982, Congress passed the controversial Boland Amendment, which ordered the president and executive branch not to spend federal funds to assist the Contra rebel forces in Nicaragua in their efforts to overthrow the communist Sandinistas' regime. The Reagan Administration's efforts to get around the Boland Amendment led directly to the Iran-Contra scandal (see *Up Close:* "Iran-Contra and the White House Staff" on page 408).

COMMANDER-IN-CHIEF

Global power derives primarily from the president's role as commander-in-chief of the armed forces of the United States. Presidential command over the armed forces is not merely symbolic; presidents may issue direct military orders to troops in the field. As president, Washington personally led troops to end the Whiskey Rebellion in 1794; Abraham Lincoln issued direct orders to his generals in the Civil War; Lyndon Johnson personally chose bombing targets in Vietnam; and George Bush personally ordered the Gulf War cease-fire after 100 hours of ground fighting. All presidents, whether they are experienced in world affairs or not, soon learn after taking office that their influence throughout the world is heavily dependent upon the command of capable military forces.

War-Making Power Constitutionally, war-making power is divided between the Congress and the president. Article I, Section 8, says, "The Congress shall have Power . . . to . . . provide for the common Defence . . . to declare War . . . to raise and support Armies . . . to provide and maintain a Navy . . . to make Rules for the Government and Regulation of the land and naval forces." However, Article II, Section 2, says, "The President shall be Commander-in-Chief of the Army and

covert action Secret intelligence activity outside U.S. borders undertaken with specific authorization by the president; acknowledgment of U.S. sponsorship would defeat or compromise its purpose.

Iran-Contra and the White House Staff

Ronald Reagan entered the White House with a strong sense of mission: to restore American military strength and respect in world councils. But he seldom involved himself in the details of policy or its implementation. Instead, he relied heavily on the White House staff and key cabinet officers to guide his presidency.

President Reagan was strongly committed to the support of pro-Western resistance movements in communist-dominated nations. He believed that the Soviet "evil empire" should be rolled back, not merely contained, and that the United States should assist "freedom fighters" in Afghanistan, Angola, and Nicaragua. Although Congress supported these actions in Afghanistan and Angola, it voted in 1982 to cut off U.S. aid to the Contra rebel forces fighting the Soviet-backed Sandinista regime in Nicaragua. The Boland Amendment specifically prohibited all executive branch agencies from sending any more aid to the Contras. But Reagan clearly communicated to his White House staff (especially his national security advisers Robert McFarlane and later John Poindexter) his desire to find ways to keep the Contra movement supplied. A National Security Council staff officer, Marine Lt. Col. Oliver North, was especially active in soliciting assistance for the Contras from private sources and from friendly foreign governments in a deliberate effort to circumvent the congressional ban.

In November 1986 a Lebanese newspaper disclosed that the United States had been secretly shipping arms to Iran in an effort to secure the release of Americans held hostage in Lebanon by Iranian-backed terrorists. It was later revealed that national security adviser McFarlane and North had been directly involved in these arms-for-hostages dealings. President Reagan initially denied that the arms shipments were a ransom-for-hostages deal, but upon thorough investigation, the Tower Commission, an independent commission assigned to investigate the incident, reported: "Whatever the intent, almost from the beginning the initiative became a series of arms-for-hostages deals."[*]

But the worst news was yet to be revealed. At a nationally televised press conference, Attorney General Ed Meese revealed that money paid by the Iranians for the weapons shipments had been diverted to the Contras. The scheme to divert the "profits" from the arms deals to the contras had been concocted by North, with the knowledge of McFarlane and Poindexter, and perhaps CIA director William Casey (who became seriously ill and died before the investigation was complete). There is no direct evidence or testimony that Reagan himself knew of the scheme to direct profits from Iranian dealings to the Contras, but the president's strong support of the Contra cause led North to believe that the president approved of the diversion of arms-sales money.

Trading arms for hostages with the hated regime in Iran was enough to send President Reagan's approval ratings into a steep decline. His presidency was badly shaken; there were murmurs on Capitol Hill about beginning impeachment proceedings. It was the worst moment of the previously popular president's eight years in office. Congress held nationally televised hearings on what became known as the Iran-Contra scandal. His Marine Corps uniform covered with a chestful of medals, North acknowledged misleading the Congress, but his appearance captured the imagination and sympathy of many Americans. Thousands of telegrams poured into Congress attacking the investigators and praising the patriotism of the Marine. North was eventually convicted of having lied earlier to Congress about aid to the Contras, but his conviction was overturned on appeal.

Presidents have always dominated foreign policy and have traditionally withheld information from Congress. But the Reagan Administration was chastened even by the congressional committee's minority (Republican) report: "The Constitution gives important foreign policy powers to both Congress and the President. Neither can accomplish very much over the long term by trying to go it alone."[†]

---

[*]*The Tower Commission Report* (New York: Times Books, 1987), p. 80.

[†]Joel Brinkely, ed., *Report of the Congressional Committees Investigating the Iran-Contra Affair* (New York: Times Books, 1988).

Navy of the United States." In defending the newly written Constitution, the *Federalist Papers* construed the president's war powers narrowly, implying that the war-making power of the president was little more than the power to defend against imminent invasion when Congress was not in session.

In reality, however, presidents have exercised their powers as commander-in-chief to order U.S. forces into military action overseas on many occasions—from John Adams's ordering of U.S. naval forces to attack French ships (1789–99) to Harry Truman's decision to intervene in the Korean War (1951–53) to Lyndon Johnson's and Richard Nixon's conduct of the Vietnam War (1965–73), to George Bush's Operation Desert Storm (1991). The Supreme Court has consistently refused to hear cases involving the war powers of the president and Congress. Supreme Court Chief Justice William H. Rehnquist wrote before he was elevated to the Court,

> It has been recognized from the earliest days of the Republic, by the President, by Congress, and by the Supreme Court, that the United States may lawfully engage in armed hostilities with a foreign power without Congressional declaration of war. Our history is replete with instances of "undeclared wars" from the war with France in 1789–1800 to the Vietnamese War.[27]

Thus, although Congress retains the formal power to "declare war," in modern times wars are seldom "declared." Instead, they begin with direct military actions, and the president, as Commander-in-Chief of the armed forces, determines what those actions will be. Historically, Congress accepted the fact that only the president has the information-gathering facilities and the ability to act with the speed and secrecy required for military decisions during the periods of crisis. Not until the Vietnam War, and later during the Persian Gulf War, was there serious congressional debate over whether the president has the power to commit the nation to war.

War Powers Act   In the early days of the Vietnam War, the liberal leadership of the nation strongly supported Democratic President Lyndon Johnson's power to commit the nation to war. By 1969, however, many congressional leaders had withdrawn their support of the war. With a new Republican president, Richard Nixon, and a Democratic Congress, congressional attacks on presidential policy became much more partisan.

Antiwar members of Congress made several attempts to end the war by cutting off money for U.S. military activity in Southeast Asia. Such legislation only passed after President Nixon announced a peace agreement in 1973, however. It is important to note that Congress has *never* voted to cut off funds to support American armies while they were in the field.

Congress also passed the **War Powers Act**, designed to restrict presidential war-making powers, in 1973. (President Nixon vetoed the bill, but the Watergate affair undermined his support in Congress, which overrode his veto.) The act has four major provisions:

1. In the absence of a congressional declaration of war, the president can commit armed forces to hostilities or to "situations where imminent involvement in hostilities is clearly indicated by the circumstances" *only*:

    - To repel an armed attack on the United States or to forestall the "direct and imminent threat of such an attack."

War Powers Act   Bill passed in 1973 to limit presidential war-making powers; it restricts when, why, and for how long a president can commit U.S. forces and requires notification of and, in many cases, approval by Congress.

- To repel an armed attack against U.S. armed forces outside the United States or to forestall the threat of such attack.
- To protect and evacuate U.S. citizens and nationals in another country if their lives are threatened.

2. The president must report promptly to Congress the commitment of forces for such purposes.
3. Involvement of U.S. forces must be no longer than sixty days unless Congress authorizes their continued use by specific legislation.
4. Congress can end a presidential commitment by resolution, an action that does not require the president's signature.

Presidential Noncompliance The War Powers Act raises constitutional questions. A commander-in-chief clearly can order U.S. forces to go anywhere. Presumably, Congress cannot constitutionally command troops, yet that is what the act attempts to do by specifying that troops must come home if Congress orders them to do so or if Congress simply fails to endorse the president's decision to commit them. No president—Democrat or Republican—can allow Congress to usurp this presidential authority. Thus, since the passage of the War Powers Act, presidents have continued to undertake military actions, including the following:

- President Gerald Ford ordered U.S. forces to attack a Cambodian island in 1975 to free the U.S. merchant ship *Mayaguez*; forty-one marines died in the attack. Ford notified the Congress of his action only after the attack.
- President Jimmy Carter did not notify Congress before ordering U.S. military forces to attempt a rescue of American embassy personnel held hostage by Iran in 1980.
- After President Reagan had committed troops to "peacekeeping" in Lebanon in 1982, Congress invoked the War Powers Act and attempted to limit U.S. marines to an eighteen-month stay. The president maintained that the act was unconstitutional and made it clear that the administration would keep the troops there as long as it desired. Only the deaths of 241 marines in a suicidal attack by an Islamic faction persuaded President Reagan to withdraw U.S. troops from Lebanon in 1984.
- In 1983 U.S. troops invaded the tiny Caribbean island of Grenada in the wake of a procommunist coup there. Informed after the fact, Congress chose not to invoke the War Powers Act in view of the invasion's rapid success.
- President Bush ignored the provisions of the War Powers Act in ordering the invasion of Panama in 1989 and in sending U.S. forces to Saudi Arabia in August 1990, following Saddam Hussein's invasion of Kuwait.
- Bush also claimed he had the constitutional power to order U.S. military forces to liberate Kuwait from Iraqi occupation, whether or not Congress authorized the action. Bush ordered military preparations to begin, and despite misgivings Congress voted to authorize the use of force a few days before U.S. air attacks began. Rapid military victory in the ensuing Gulf War silenced congressional critics.
- President Clinton ordered U.S. troops into Bosnia as part of a NATO "peacekeeping" operations in 1995 and into Kosovo in 1999.

The War Powers Act is not only constitutionally questionable but also politically weak. The president almost always enjoys great popular support in the initial stages of an international conflict. At this point, members of Congress are likely to be swept along and to endorse the president's action rather than invoking the War Powers Act and appearing unsupportive of U.S. troops. Only if the fighting goes badly, becomes protracted, or fails to produce decisive results is the War Powers Act likely to be invoked by Congress. Thus the War Powers Act remains largely a symbolic reminder to presidents that if things go badly, the Congress will desert them.

Presidential Use of Military Force in Domestic Affairs Democracies are generally reluctant to use military force in domestic affairs. Yet the president has the constitutional authority to "take Care that the Laws be faithfully executed" and, as Commander-in-Chief of the armed forces, can send them across the nation as well as across the globe. The Constitution appears to limit presidential use of military forces in domestic affairs to protecting states "against domestic Violence" and only "on Application of the [state] Legislature or the [state] Executive (when the Legislature cannot be convened)" (Article IV, Section 4). Although this provision would seem to require states themselves to request federal troops before they can be sent to quell domestic violence, historically presidents have not waited for state requests to send troops when federal laws, federal court orders, or federal constitutional guarantees are being violated.

Relying on their constitutional duty to "faithfully execute" federal laws and their command over the nation's armed forces, presidents have used military force in domestic disputes since the earliest days of the Republic. Perhaps the most significant example of a president's use of military force in domestic affairs was Dwight Eisenhower's 1957 dispatch of U.S. troops to Little Rock, Arkansas, to enforce a federal court's desegregation order. In this case, the president acted directly *against* the expressed wishes of the state's governor, Orval Faubus, who had posted state units of the National Guard at the entrance of Central High

As Commander-in-Chief, President Clinton ordered missile strikes on the Serbian capital of Belgrade in 1999 to force Serbian troop withdrawal from Kosovo. The Serbian Interior ministry, responsible for national police, was a target.

Despite a Supreme Court ruling that segregation in education was illegal, many southern states continued to try to keep their schoolhouse doors closed to black students. Here Elizabeth Eckford, a fifteen-year-old resident of Little Rock, Arkansas, is denied entry to Central High School by a member of the National Guard under the orders of Governor Orval Faubus. Not until President Dwight Eisenhower sent the 101st Airborne Division to Little Rock were the high court's desegregation orders enforced.

School to prevent the admission of black students that had been ordered by the federal court. Eisenhower officially called Arkansas's National Guard units into federal service, took personal command of them, and then ordered them to leave the high school. Ike then replaced the Guard units with U.S. federal troops under orders to enforce desegregation. Eisenhower's action marked a turning point in the struggle over school desegregation. The Supreme Court's historic desegregation decision in *Brown v. Board of Education of Topeka* might have been rendered meaningless had not the president chosen to use military force to secure compliance.

THE VICE PRESIDENTIAL WAITING GAME

The principal responsibility of the vice president is to be prepared to assume the responsibilities of the president. The phrase describing the job as "a heartbeat away from the presidency" is historically relevant: eight vice presidents have become president following the death of their predecessor. But vice presidents have not always been well prepared; Harry Truman, who succeeded Franklin Roosevelt while World War II still raged, had never even been informed about the secret atomic bomb project.

Political Selection Process   The political process surrounding the initial choice of vice presidential candidates does not necessarily produce the persons best qualified to occupy the White House. It is, indeed, a "crap shoot"[28]; if it produces a person well qualified to be president, it is only by luck. Candidates may *claim* that they select running mates who are highly qualified to take over as president, but this claim is seldom true.

Vice presidential candidates are chosen to give political "balance" to the ticket, to attract voters who might otherwise desert the party or stay home. Traditionally,

Democratic presidential candidates sought to give ideological and geographical balance to the ticket. Northern liberal presidential candidates (Adlai Stevenson, John Kennedy) selected southern conservatives (John Sparkman, Estes Kefauver, Lyndon Johnson) as their running mates. Walter Mondale selected New York Congresswoman Geraldine Ferraro in a bold move to exploit the gender gap. Liberal Massachusetts Governor Michael Dukakis returned to the earlier Democratic tradition, choosing to run with conservative Texas Senator Lloyd Bentsen. Bill Clinton sought a different kind of balance: Al Gore's military service in Vietnam and his unimpeachable family life helped offset reservations about Clinton's avoidance of the draft and his past marital troubles.

Traditionally, Republican presidential candidates sought to accommodate either the conservative or moderate wing of their party in their vice presidential selections. Moderate Eisenhower chose conservative Nixon. Conservative Barry Goldwater's selection of William Miller, an unknown conservative member of the House, ensured his loss of moderate support in 1964. In 1980 conservative Reagan first asked his moderate predecessor, Gerald Ford, to join him on the ticket before turning to his moderate primary opponent George Bush, who in 1988 tapped conservative Senator Dan Quayle. In 1996 Bob Dole gambled big in choosing the popular and charismatic—but opinionated and unpredictable—Jack Kemp as his running mate. Far behind in the polls, Dole could not afford a "safe" choice. He needed the former star quarterback of the Buffalo Bills to add excitement to the ticket, even at the risk of seeing Kemp call plays not approved by the coach.

Running behind in the polls prior to the 2000 Democratic convention, Al Gore believed he needed a dramatic choice of a running mate to stir interest in his campaign. Connecticut Senator Joe Lieberman would make history as the first Jew to run on a

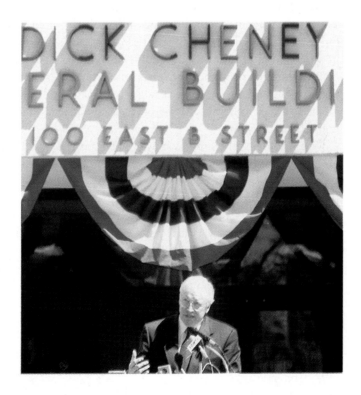

While the vice president has no official duties under the Constitution except to act as presiding officer of the Senate, vice presidents have often been called upon to share at least some of the ceremonial duties of the presidency and are sometimes able to use their position to further causes they support. Here, Vice President Dick Cheney speaks during a dedication ceremony after the federal building in Casper, Wyoming, was renamed the Dick Cheney Federal Building.

major party national ticket. Moreover, his moderate voting record balanced Gore's appeal to liberals. And perhaps most importantly, Lieberman's earlier public criticism of Clinton's behavior in office helped to distance Gore from his former boss's scandals.

Bush's dream running mate, General Colin Powell, turned down the offer. So Bush turned to Dick Cheney, Secretary of Defense in his father's administration during the Gulf War. It was hoped that Cheney would add *gravitas* (experience and wisdom) to the ticket. And Cheney's conservative voting record, as a former Congressman from Wyoming, helped reassure conservatives in the Republican Party that Bush was not overlooking them.

Vice Presidential Roles   Presidents determine what role their vice presidents will play in their administration. Constitutionally, the only role given the vice president is to preside over the Senate and to vote in case of a tie in that body. Presiding over the Senate is so tiresome that vice presidents perform it only on rare ceremonial occasions, but they have occasionally cast important tie-breaking votes. If the president chooses not to give the vice president much responsibility, the vice presidency becomes what its first occupant, John Adams, described as "the most insignificant office that ever the invention of man contrived or his imagination conceived." One of Franklin Roosevelt's three vice presidents, the salty Texan John Nance Garner, put it more pithily, saying that the job "ain't worth a bucket of warm spit" (reporters of that era may have substituted "spit" for Garner's actual wording).

The political functions of vice presidents are more significant than their governmental functions. Vice presidents are obliged to support their president and the administration's policies. But sometimes a president will use the vice president to launch strongly partisan political attacks on opponents while the president remains "above" the political squabbles and hence more "presidential." Richard Nixon served as a partisan "attack dog" for Eisenhower, then gave Spiro Agnew this task in his own administration. George Bush was a much more reserved vice president, but Dan Quayle renewed the tradition of the vice president as political "hit man." The attack role allows the vice president also to help cement political support for the president among highly partisan ideologues. Vice presidents are also useful in campaign fund raising. Large contributors expect a personal touch; the president cannot be everywhere at once, so the vice president is frequently a guest at political fund-raising events. Presidents also have traditionally sent their vice presidents to attend funerals of world leaders and placed them at the head of governmental commissions.

Vice presidents themselves strive to play a more significant policy-making role, often as senior presidential adviser and confidant. Recent presidents have encouraged the development of the vice presidency along these lines. Walter Mondale, the first modern vice president to perform this function, had an office in the White House next to the president's, had access to all important meetings and policy decisions, and was invited to lunch privately each week with President Carter. As vice president, George Bush claimed to have participated in every major decision of the Reagan Administration. Vice President Al Gore was routinely stationed behind President Clinton during major policy pronouncements. Clinton reportedly gave great weight to Gore's views on the environment, on cost savings in government, and on information technology. Gore also spoke out aggressively in defense of Clinton's policies. Thus the senior advisory role is becoming institutionalized over time.

Twenty-First Century Directions

The president personifies American government, not only for Americans but also for people around the world. The expectations placed on the president—from managing the nation's crises, insuring a strong economy, and providing policy direction and vision, to overseeing the vast federal bureaucracy—clearly exceed the president's formal authority. A president must rely on political skills and resources to be judged a successful president.

⬆ In global crises, the president's power will remain undiminished, indeed, and perhaps become even stronger as terrorists and rogue regimes threaten the security of Americans at home and abroad. Americans will demand action and Congress will defer to the president.

⬇ In domestic affairs, the president's power will continue to diminish; major national policy shifts, such as those initiated by 20th century presidents from Wilson to Roosevelt to Johnson to Reagan, are unlikely to occur in the foreseeable future. Both Congress and the judiciary have curbed presidential power. The Congress will search unceasingly for scandals large and small within the executive branch, and federal courts will continue to erode executive power.

⬅➡ If American voters continue to opt for divided government—a president of one party and a Congress controlled by the opposition party—the president's policy achievements will remain minimal. Inasmuch as partisanship in Washington is increasing, only a president whose party controls both houses of Congress can expect to bring about significant policy changes.

The Waiting Game   Politically, vice presidents are obliged to play a tortuous waiting game. They can use their time in office to build a network of contacts that can later be tapped for campaign contributions, workers, and support in their own race for the presidency, should they decide to run. But winning the presidency following retirement of their former boss requires a delicate balance. They must show loyalty to the president in order to win the president's endorsement and also to help ensure that the administration in which they participated is judged a success by voters. At the same time, vice presidents must demonstrate that they have independent leadership qualities and a policy agenda of their own to offer voters. This dilemma becomes more acute as their boss's term nears its end.

Historically, only a few sitting vice presidents have won election to the White House: John Adams (1797), Thomas Jefferson (1801), Martin Van Buren (1837), and George Bush (1988). In addition, four vice presidents won election in their own right after entering the Oval Office as a result of their predecessors' death: Theodore Roosevelt (1901), Calvin Coolidge (1923), Harry Truman (1945), and Lyndon Johnson (1963). Only one nonsitting former vice president has been elected president: Richard Nixon (1968, after losing to Kennedy in 1960). Thus, out of the forty-seven men who served the nation as vice president through 2000, only nine were ever elected to higher office.

SUMMARY NOTES

- The American presidency is potentially the most powerful office in the world. As head of state, the president symbolizes national unity and speaks on behalf of the American people to the world. And as commander-in-chief of the armed forces, the president has a powerful voice in national and international affairs. The president also symbolizes government for the American people, reassuring them in times of hardship and crises.

- As head of the government, the president is expected to set forth policy priorities for the nation, to manage the economy, to mobilize political support for the administration's programs in Congress, to manage the giant federal bureaucracy, and to recruit people for policy-making positions in both the executive and judicial branches of government.

- Popular expectations of presidential leadership far exceed the formal constitutional powers of the president: chief administrator, chief legislator, chief diplomat, commander-in-chief, and chief of state. The vague reference in the Constitution to "executive Power" has been used by presidents to justify actions beyond those specified elsewhere in the Constitution or in laws of Congress.

- It is the president's vast political resources that provide the true power base of the presidency. These include the president's reputation for power, personal popularity with the public, access to the media, and party leadership position.

- Presidential popularity and power are usually highest at the beginning of the term of office. Presidents are more likely to be successful in Congress during this honeymoon period. Presidents' popularity also rises during crises, especially during international threats and military actions. But prolonged indecision and stalemate erode popular support, as do scandals and economic recessions.

- As chief executive, the president oversees the huge federal bureaucracy. Presidential control of the executive branch is exercised through executive orders, appointments and removals, and budgetary recommendations to Congress. But the president's control of the executive branch is heavily circumscribed by Congress, which establishes executive departments and agencies, regulates their activities by law, and determines their budgets each year.

- Presidents are expected not only to initiate programs and policies but also to shepherd them through Congress. Presidential success scores in Congress indicate that presidents are more successful early in their term of office. Presidents who face a Congress controlled by the opposition party are far less successful in winning approval for their programs than presidents whose party holds a majority.

- The veto is the president's most powerful weapon in dealing with Congress. The president needs to hold the loyalty of only one more than one-third of either the House or the Senate to sustain a veto. Few vetoes are overridden. The threat of a veto enables the president to bargain in Congress for more acceptable legislation.

- During the long years of the Cold War, the president of the United States was the leader of the "free world." In the post–Cold War world, the president is still the leader of the world's most powerful democracy and is expected to exercise global leadership on behalf of a stable world order.

- Presidents have come to dominate foreign policy through treaty making, executive agreements, control of intelligence activities, and international recognition of their role as head of state. Above all, presidents have used their power as commander-in-chief of the armed forces to decide when to make war and when to seek peace.

- The global power of presidents derives primarily from this presidential role as Commander-in-Chief. Constitutionally, war-making power is divided between Congress and the president, but historically, it has been the president who has ordered U.S. military forces into action. In the War Powers Act, Congress tried to reassert its war-making power after the Vietnam War, but the act has failed to restrain presidents. Presidents have also used the armed forces in domestic affairs to "take Care that the Laws be faithfully executed."

- The principal responsibility of the vice president is to be prepared to assume the responsibilities of the president. However, the selection of the vice president is dominated more by political concerns than by consideration of presidential qualifications. Aside from officially presiding over the U.S. Senate, vice presidents perform whatever roles are assigned them by the president.

KEY TERMS

impeachment   380

executive privilege   384

impoundment   385

deferrals   385

rescissions   385

executive order   391

cabinet   396

National Security Council
  (NSC)   397

honeymoon period   400

gridlock   402

veto   402

pocket veto   402

override   402

line-item veto   402

diplomatic recognition   404

executive agreement   405

covert action   407

War Powers Act   409

SELECTED READINGS

BARBER, JAMES DAVID. *The Presidential Character: Predicting Performance in the White House*, 4th ed. Upper Saddle River, N.J.: Prentice Hall, 1992. An updated version of Barber's original thesis that a president's performance in office is largely a function of active/passive and positive/negative character; includes classifications of twentieth-century presidents through Reagan.

BRACE, PAUL, and BARBARA HINCKLEY. *Follow the Leader*. New York: Basic Books, 1992. The most marked increases in public approval of the president come on the heels of international crises, especially when the president responds with bold and decisive action.

BRODY, RICHARD A. *Assessing Presidents: The Media, Elite Opinion, and Public Support*. Stanford, Calif.: Stanford University Press, 1991. Develops the thesis that media and elite interpretations of presidential actions shape public evaluations of the president; includes analysis of the president's "honeymoon," "rally 'round the president" events, and the rise and fall of public approval ratings.

CAMPBELL, COLIN, and BERT A. ROCKMAN, eds., *The Clinton Legacy*. New York: Chatham House, 2000. Essays by presidential scholars evaluating the Clinton presidency, including his impact on the Democratic party, rhetoric, legislative record, and foreign policy.

DiCLERICO, ROBERT E. *The American President*. 5th ed. Upper Saddle River, N.J.: Prentice Hall, 2000. Comprehensive text on the presidency, focusing on selection, power, accountability, decision making, personality, and leadership.

EDWARDS, GEORGE C., III. *At the Margins: Presidential Leadership of Congress*. New Haven, Conn.: Yale University Press, 1989. A systematic examination of the factors affecting presidential success in Congress, including presidential popularity, party support, and lobbying efforts.

LOWI, THEODORE. *The Personal President*. Ithaca, N.Y.: Cornell University Press, 1987. An examination of the presidency from the perspective of the public and its reliance on the president for reassurance in crises.

MARANISS, DAVID. *First in His Class*. New York: Simon & Schuster, 1995. A biography of Bill Clinton, describing his overriding ambition, talent for politics, perseverance in the face of adversity, eagerness to please everyone, and tendency to shade the truth.

MILKUS, STANLEY, and MICHAEL NELSON. *The American Presidency: Origins and Development, 1776–1998*. 3rd ed. Washington, D.C.: CQ Press, 1999. A comprehensive history of the presidency which argues that the institution is best understood by examining its development over time; describes the significant presidential actions in the early days of the Republic that shaped the office, as well as the modern era in which the president has replaced Congress and the political parties as the leading instrument of popular rule.

NEUSTADT, RICHARD E. *Presidential Power*. New York: Wiley, 1960. The classic argument that the president's power is the power to persuade, that the formal constitutional powers of the presidency provide only a framework for the president's use of persuasion, public prestige, reputation for power, and other personal attributes to exercise real power.

SCHULTZ, JEFFREY D. *Presidential Scandals*. Washington, D.C.: CQ Press, 1999. An historical survey of scandals in presidential administrations, from George Washington to Bill Clinton.

**ASK YOURSELF
ABOUT POLITICS**

1 Do bureaucrats in Washington have too much power?
Yes ⬤ No ⬤

2 Do you believe the bureaucrats in Washington really believe in the value of the programs they administer?
Yes ⬤ No ⬤

3 Should the federal bureaucracy be managed by nonpartisan professionals rather than people politically loyal to the president?
Yes ⬤ No ⬤

4 Should the federal bureaucracy at all levels reflect the gender and minority ratios of the total civilian work force?
Yes ⬤ No ⬤

5 Do you believe the bureaucrats in Washington waste a lot of the money we pay in taxes?
Yes ⬤ No ⬤

6 Do you believe the federal government is spending more money but delivering less service?
Yes ⬤ No ⬤

7 Do you believe that the overall costs of federal regulatory activity are justified by the benefits?
Yes ⬤ No ⬤

8 Do you believe bureaucratic regulations of all kinds are hurting America's competitiveness in the global economy?
Yes ⬤ No ⬤

BUREAUCRATIC POWER

Political conflict does not end after a law has been passed by Congress and signed by the president. The arena for conflict merely shifts from Capitol Hill and the White House to the **bureaucracy**—to the myriad departments, agencies, and bureaus of the federal executive branch that implement the law. Despite the popular impression that policy is decided by the president and Congress and merely implemented by the federal bureaucracy, in fact policy is also made by the bureaucracy. Indeed, it is often remarked that "implementation is the continuation of policy making by other means." The Washington bureaucracy is a major base of power in the American system of government—independent of Congress, the president, the courts, and the people. Indeed, controlling the bureaucracy has become a major challenge of democratic government (see *What Do You Think?* "Do Bureaucrats in Washington Have Too Much Power?" on page 420).

The Nature of Bureaucracy "Bureaucracy" has become a negative term equated with red tape,[1] paper shuffling, duplication of effort, waste and inefficiency, impersonality, senseless regulations, and unresponsiveness to the needs of "real" people. But bureaucracy is really a form of social organization found not only in governments but also in corporations, armies, schools, and many other societal institutions. The German sociologist Max Weber described bureaucracy as a "rational" way for society to organize itself that has the following characteristics:

Power in Washington is not only exercised by the president, Congress, and courts, but also by 2.8 million federal bureaucrats—neither elected nor accountable to ordinary citizens—who determine in large measure who gets what in America.

 www.prenhall.com/dye

WHAT DO YOU THINK?

Do Bureaucrats in Washington Have Too Much Power?

Americans have always been suspicious of government power. Opinion polls regularly report that Americans believe "the federal government in Washington" has "too much power." A majority also believe that "major corporations" and "television news" have too much power.

But among federal government agencies, the tax-collecting Internal Revenue Service (IRS) is clearly the most feared. The power of the Central Intelligence

Agency (CIA) and the Bureau of Alcohol, Tobacco and Firearms (ATF) also appears to raise concerns among Americans, no doubt in part because of adverse publicity in recent years. (The CIA was deeply embarrassed by the revelation that a high officer, Aldrich Ames, had been paid millions of dollars by Russian agents to work secretly on their behalf; the ATF was strongly criticized for attacking the Branch Davidian compound in Waco, Texas, in 1993.)

In contrast, the U.S. military enjoys a favorable reputation among most Americans, 80 percent of whom believe it has "about the right amount of power" or "not enough." Local government in America and local police are also perceived as having about the right amount or not enough power.

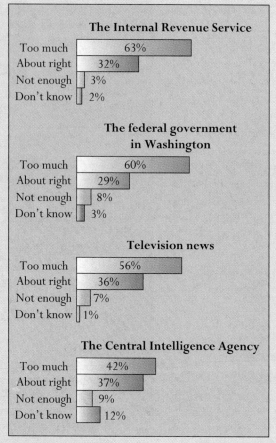

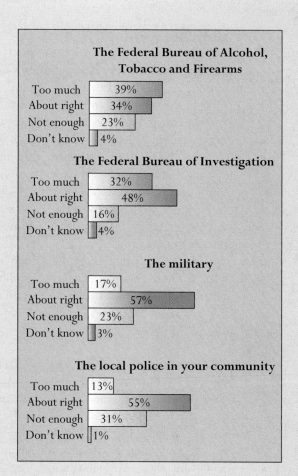

Source: Gallup Poll, 1995.

- **Chain of command**: Hierarchical structure of authority in which command flows downward.
- **Division of labor**: Work divided among many specialized workers in an effort to improve productivity.
- **Specification of authority**: Clear lines of responsibility with positions and units reporting to superiors.
- **Goal orientation**: Organizational goals determining structure, authority, and rules.
- **Impersonality**: All persons within the bureaucracy treated on "merit" principles, and all "clients" served by the bureaucracy treated equally according to rules; all activities undertaken according to rules; records maintained to assure rules are followed.[2]

Thus, according to Weber's definition, General Motors and IBM, the U.S. Marine Corps, the U.S. Department of Education, and all other institutions organized according to these principles are "bureaucracies."

The Growth of Bureaucratic Power Bureaucratic power has grown with advances in technology and increases in the size and complexity of society. The standard explanation for the growth of bureaucratic power in Washington is that Congress and the president do not have the time, energy, or expertise to handle the details of policy making. A related explanation is that the increasing complexity and sophistication of technology require technical experts ("technocrats") to actually carry out the intent of Congress and the president. Neither the president nor the 535 members of Congress can look after the myriad details involved in environmental protection, occupational safety, air traffic control, or thousands of other responsibilities of government. So the president and Congress create bureaucracies, appropriate money for them, and authorize them to draw up detailed rules, regulations, and "guidelines" that actually govern the nation. Bureaucratic agencies receive only vague and general directions from the president and Congress. Actual governance is in the hands of the Environmental Protection Agency, the Occupational Safety and Health Administration, the Federal Aviation Administration, and hundreds of similar agencies (see Figure 12–1 on page 422).

But there are also political explanations for the growth of bureaucratic power. Congress and the president often deliberately pass vague and ambiguous laws. These laws allow elected officials to show symbolically their concerns for environmental protection, occupational safety, and so on, yet avoid the controversies surrounding actual application of those lofty principles. Bureaucracies must then give practical meaning to these symbolic measures by developing specific rules and regulations. If the rules and regulations prove unpopular, Congress and the president can blame the bureaucrats and pretend that these unpopular decisions are a product of an "ungovernable" Washington bureaucracy.

Finally, as the bureaucracy itself has grown in size and influence, it has become its own source of power. Bureaucrats have a personal stake in expanding the size of their own agencies and budgets and adding to their own regulatory authority. They can mobilize their "client" groups (interest groups that directly benefit from the agency's programs, such as environmental groups on behalf of the Environmental Protection Agency, farm groups for the Department of Agriculture, the National Education Association for the Department of Education) in support of larger budgets and expanded authority.

bureaucracy Departments, agencies, bureaus, and offices that perform the functions of government.

chain of command Hierarchical structure of authority in which command flows downward; typical of a bureaucracy.

division of labor Division of work among many specialized workers in a bureaucracy.

specification of authority Clear lines of responsibility with positions and units reporting to superiors in a bureaucracy.

goal orientation Organizational goals that determine structure, authority, and rules in a bureaucracy.

impersonality Treatment of all persons within a bureaucracy on the basis of "merit" and of all "clients" served by the bureaucracy equally according to rule.

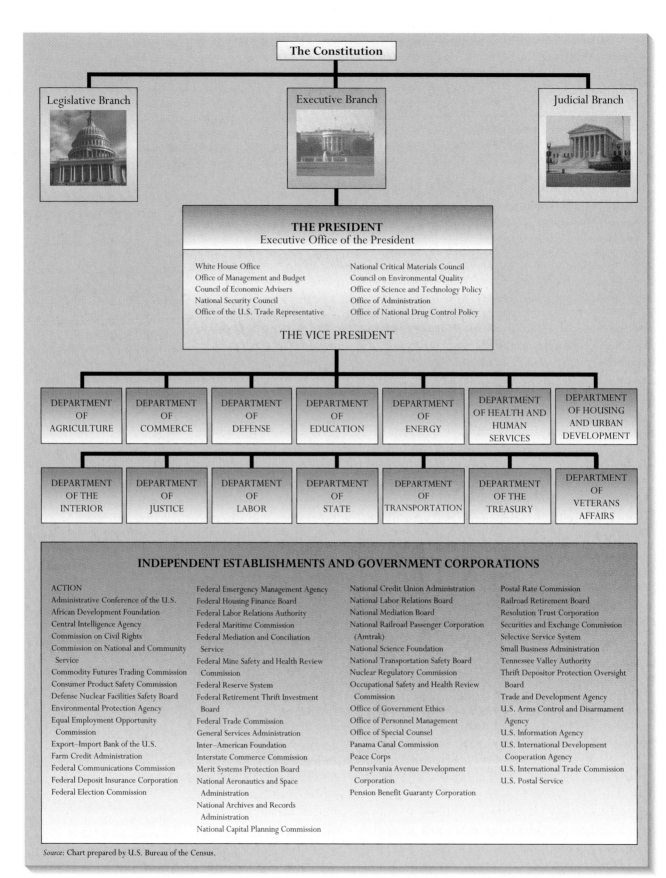

The Constitution

Legislative Branch

Executive Branch

Judicial Branch

THE PRESIDENT
Executive Office of the President

White House Office
Office of Management and Budget
Council of Economic Advisers
National Security Council
Office of the U.S. Trade Representative

National Critical Materials Council
Council on Environmental Quality
Office of Science and Technology Policy
Office of Administration
Office of National Drug Control Policy

THE VICE PRESIDENT

| DEPARTMENT OF AGRICULTURE | DEPARTMENT OF COMMERCE | DEPARTMENT OF DEFENSE | DEPARTMENT OF EDUCATION | DEPARTMENT OF ENERGY | DEPARTMENT OF HEALTH AND HUMAN SERVICES | DEPARTMENT OF HOUSING AND URBAN DEVELOPMENT |

| DEPARTMENT OF THE INTERIOR | DEPARTMENT OF JUSTICE | DEPARTMENT OF LABOR | DEPARTMENT OF STATE | DEPARTMENT OF TRANSPORTATION | DEPARTMENT OF THE TREASURY | DEPARTMENT OF VETERANS AFFAIRS |

INDEPENDENT ESTABLISHMENTS AND GOVERNMENT CORPORATIONS

ACTION
Administrative Conference of the U.S.
African Development Foundation
Central Intelligence Agency
Commission on Civil Rights
Commission on National and Community
  Service
Commodity Futures Trading Commission
Consumer Product Safety Commission
Defense Nuclear Facilities Safety Board
Environmental Protection Agency
Equal Employment Opportunity
  Commission
Export–Import Bank of the U.S.
Farm Credit Administration
Federal Communications Commission
Federal Deposit Insurance Corporation
Federal Election Commission

Federal Emergency Management Agency
Federal Housing Finance Board
Federal Labor Relations Authority
Federal Maritime Commission
Federal Mediation and Conciliation
  Service
Federal Mine Safety and Health Review
  Commission
Federal Reserve System
Federal Retirement Thrift Investment
  Board
Federal Trade Commission
General Services Administration
Inter–American Foundation
Interstate Commerce Commission
Merit Systems Protection Board
National Aeronautics and Space
  Administration
National Archives and Records
  Administration
National Capital Planning Commission

National Credit Union Administration
National Labor Relations Board
National Mediation Board
National Railroad Passenger Corporation
  (Amtrak)
National Science Foundation
National Transportation Safety Board
Nuclear Regulatory Commission
Occupational Safety and Health Review
  Commission
Office of Government Ethics
Office of Personnel Management
Office of Special Counsel
Panama Canal Commission
Peace Corps
Pennsylvania Avenue Development
  Corporation
Pension Benefit Guaranty Corporation

Postal Rate Commission
Railroad Retirement Board
Resolution Trust Corporation
Securities and Exchange Commission
Selective Service System
Small Business Administration
Tennessee Valley Authority
Thrift Depositor Protection Oversight
  Board
Trade and Development Agency
U.S. Arms Control and Disarmament
  Agency
U.S. Information Agency
U.S. International Development
  Cooperation Agency
U.S. International Trade Commission
U.S. Postal Service

Source: Chart prepared by U.S. Bureau of the Census.

FIGURE 12–1 The Federal Bureaucracy

Although the president has constitutional authority over the operation of the executive branch, Congress creates departments and agencies and appropriates their funds, and Senate approval is needed for presidential appointees to head departments.

Bureaucratic Power: Implementation   Bureaucracies are not *constitutionally* empowered to decide policy questions. But they do so, nevertheless, as they perform their tasks of implementation, regulation, and adjudication.

Implementation is the development of procedures and activities to carry out policies legislated by Congress. It may involve creating new agencies or bureaus or assigning new responsibilities to old agencies. It often requires bureaucracies to translate laws into operational rules and regulations and usually to allocate resources—money, personnel, offices, supplies—to the new function. All of these tasks involve decisions by bureaucrats, decisions that drive how the law will actually affect society. In some cases, bureaucrats delay the development of regulations based on a new law, assign enforcement responsibility to existing offices with other higher priority tasks, and allocate few people with limited resources to the task. In other cases, bureaucrats act forcefully in making new regulations, insist on strict enforcement, assign responsibilities to newly created aggressive offices with no other assignments, and allocate a great deal of staff time and agency resources to the task. Interested groups have a strong stake in these decisions, and they actively seek to influence the bureaucracy.

Bureaucratic Power: Regulation   **Regulation** involves the development of formal rules for implementing legislation. The federal bureaucracy publishes about 60,000 pages of rules in the *Federal Register* each year. The Environmental Protection Agency (EPA) is especially active in developing regulations governing the handling of virtually every substance in the air, water, or ground. The rule-making process for federal agencies is prescribed by an Administrative Procedures Act, first passed in 1946 and amended many times. Generally, agencies must:

1. Announce in the *Federal Register* that a new regulation is being considered.
2. Hold hearings to allow interested groups to present evidence and arguments regarding the proposed regulation.
3. Conduct research on the proposed regulation's economic and environmental impacts.
4. Solicit "public comments" (usually the arguments of interest groups).
5. Consult with higher officials, including the Office of Management and Budget.
6. Publish the new regulation in the *Federal Register*.

Regulatory battles are important because formal regulations that appear in the *Federal Register* have the effect of law. Congress can amend or repeal a regulation only by passing new legislation and obtaining the president's signature. Controversial bureaucratic regulations often remain in place because Congress is slow to act, because key committee members block corrective legislation, or because the president refuses to sign bills overturning the regulation.

Bureaucratic Power: Adjudication   **Adjudication** involves bureaucratic decisions about individual cases. Rule making resembles the legislative process, and adjudication resembles the judicial process. In adjudication, bureaucrats decide whether a person or firm is failing to comply with laws or regulations and, if so, what penalties or corrective actions are to be applied. Regulatory agencies and commissions—for example, the National Labor Relations Board, the Federal Communications Commission, the Equal Employment Opportunity Commission, the Federal Trade Commission, the Securities and Exchange Commission—are heavily engaged in adjudication. Their elaborate procedures and body of previous

implementation Development by the federal bureaucracy of procedures and activities to carry out policies legislated by Congress; it includes regulation as well as adjudication.

regulation Development by the federal bureaucracy of formal rules for implementing legislation.

adjudication Decision making by the federal bureaucracy as to whether or not an individual or organization has complied with or violated government laws and/or regulations.

decisions closely resemble the court system. Some agencies authorize specific hearing officers, administrative judges, or appellate divisions to accept evidence, hear arguments, and decide cases. Individuals and firms involved in these proceedings usually hire lawyers specializing in the field of regulation. Administrative hearings are somewhat less formal than a court trial, and the "judges" are employees of the agency itself. Losers may appeal to the federal courts, but the record of agency success in the federal courts discourages many appeals.

Bureaucratic Power: Administrative Discretion   Much of the work of bureaucrats is administrative routine—issuing Social Security checks, printing forms, delivering the mail. Routines are repetitive tasks performed according to established rules and procedures. Yet bureaucrats almost always have some discretion in performing even the most routine tasks. Discretion is greatest when cases do not exactly fit established rules, or when more than one rule might be applied to the same case, resulting in different outcomes. The Internal Revenue Service administers the hundreds of thousands of rules developed to implement the U.S. Tax Code, but each IRS auditing agent has wide discretion in deciding which rules to apply to a taxpayer's income, deductions, business expenses, and so on. Indeed, identical tax information submitted to different IRS offices almost always results in different estimates of tax liability. But even in more routine tasks, from processing Medicare applications to forwarding mail, individual bureaucrats can be friendly and helpful or hostile and obstructive.[3]

Bureaucratic Power and Budget Maximization   Bureaucrats generally believe strongly in the value of their programs and the importance of their tasks. Senior military officers and civilian officials of the Department of Defense believe in the importance of a strong national defense, and top officials in the Social Secu-

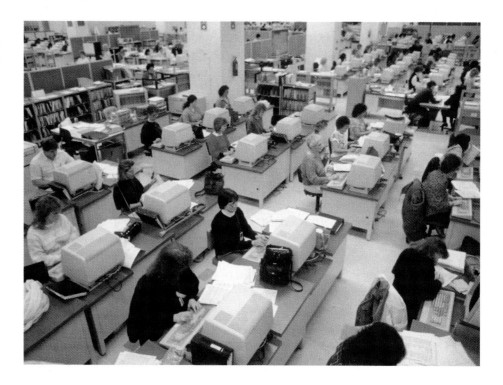

An Internal Revenue Service processing center. The IRS administers the nation's complex tax code, leaving wide discretion to its agents to determine how to apply the rules to individual taxpayers.

rity Administration are committed to maintaining the integrity of the retirement system and serving the nation's senior citizens. Beyond these public-spirited motives, bureaucrats, like everyone else, seek higher pay, greater job security, and added power and prestige for themselves.

These public and private motives converge to inspire bureaucrats to seek to expand the powers, functions, and budgets of their departments and agencies. Rarely do bureaucrats request a reduction in authority, the elimination of a program, or a decrease in their agency's budget. Rather, over time, **budget maximization**—expanding the agency's budget, staff, and authority as much as possible—becomes a driving force in government bureaucracies. This is especially true of discretionary funds. **Discretionary funds** are those that bureaucrats have flexibility in deciding how to spend, rather than money committed by law to specific purposes.[4] Thus, bureaucracies continually strive to add new functions, acquire more authority and responsibility, and increase their budgets and personnel. Bureaucratic expansion is just one of the reasons that government grows over time (see *Up Close:* "Why Government Grows, and Grows, and Grows" on page 426).

THE FEDERAL BUREAUCRACY

The federal bureaucracy—officially the executive branch of the U.S. government—consists of about 2.8 million civilian employees (plus 1.4 million persons in the armed forces) organized into 14 cabinet departments, 60 independent agencies, and a large Executive Office of the President (see Figure 12–1 on page 422 and Figure 12–2 on page 427). The expenditures of *all* governments in the United States—the federal government, the 50 state governments, and some 86,000 local governments—now amount to more than $2.7 *trillion* (roughly 30 percent of the U.S. gross domestic product, or GDP of $9.2 *trillion*). About two-thirds of this—about $1.8 *trillion* a year (about 20 percent of GDP)—is spent by the *federal* government. The healthy expansion of the U.S. economy in the 1990s, combined with slower growth in federal spending, actually *reduced* the governmental percentage of the GDP over the last decade (see Chapter 16). And government spending in the United States remains relatively modest compared to that of many nations (see *Compared to What:* "The Size of Government in Other Nations" on page 428).

Cabinet Departments   Cabinet departments employ about 60 percent of all federal workers. Each of the fourteen departments is headed by a secretary (with the exception of the Justice Department, which is headed by the attorney general) who is appointed by the president and must be confirmed by the Senate. Each department is hierarchically organized; each has its own organization chart. Although organizational patterns differ among departments, the chart for the Department of Health and Human Services shown in Figure 12–3 on page 429 is typical.

Government departments vary widely in the budgetary funds they control and in the number of personnel (see Table 12–1 on page 430). The largest budget belongs to the Department of Health and Human Services (HHS), primarily spent through its Social Security and Medicare and Medicaid outlays, which account for about 40 percent of all federal spending. The largest organization in the federal bureaucracy in terms of personnel is the Department of Defense (DOD), with nearly 1 million civilian employees in addition to 1.4 million military personnel. The Department of Defense is unique in that the civilian heads of the "Departments" of the Army,

budget maximization
Bureaucrats' tendencies to expand their agencies' budgets, staff, and authority.

discretionary funds
Budgeted funds not earmarked for specific purposes but available to be spent in accordance with the best judgment of a bureaucrat.

Why Government Grows, and Grows, and Grows

What accounts for the growth of government activity? Many theories offer explanations. The theories listed below are not mutually exclusive; indeed, probably all of the forces they identify contribute to government growth.

Societal Demands: Wagner's Law In the nineteenth century, economist Adolf Wagner proposed a "law of increasing state activity"—the notion that government activity increased faster than economic output in all developing societies.* He attributed this growth to a variety of factors including increasing demands in a developed society for social services such as education, welfare, and public health.

Wars and Crises Another theory is based on the fact that during periods of social upheaval, especially war or economic turmoil, people willingly accept higher-than-normal levels of taxation. During these periods, then, government grows. But after the stressful period is over, government size does not return to its previous levels. Instead, governments substitute new expenditures for those accepted during the crisis. Thus expenditures increase during crisis periods but never return to the precrisis levels after the crisis passes.

Fiscal "Illusion" This explanation assumes that government officials can increase revenues, and then expenditures, by altering tax-collecting devices so that voters do not realize how much money government is actually taking from them. The federal income tax grew very rapidly *after* the introduction of federal tax "withholding" in 1943. Since that time, wage earners have not received all of the money they earn and have come to perceive the missing portion as "belonging" to the federal government. This illusion is also aided by government-mandated withholding of Social Security taxes.

Bureaucratic Expansionism Bureaucrats and legislators have a personal interest in expanding government budgets. Bureaucrats want to increase the amount of money they can spend and the number of employees under their supervision. Legislators want to increase the resources over which they have jurisdiction and to enhance the government benefits bestowed on their constituents.

Interest-Group Pressures This explanation assumes that interest groups want to increase the size of government programs that benefit their own members. Benefits are visible and concentrated. Costs are invisible in many cases or are of less significance to those who will clearly benefit. As each interest group is motivated to act on behalf of its own members, largely ignoring the associated costs, government grows.

Politicians Seeking Votes Politicians in competitive elections frequently promise their constituents visible and exaggerated benefits while hiding or minimizing the costs to other voters. When these promises become policies, government grows.

Cumulative Unintended Consequences The current size of the government is the result of previous efforts to solve earlier problems. Once established, bureaucracies and programs live on, even when their original tasks no longer need doing. Over the years, the effects of all these decisions accumulate beyond what anyone originally intended.

Incrementalism Governments expand because decision making is incremental. Presidents and members of Congress focus on a narrow range of new policy proposals and *increases* or *decreases* in the budget. Old programs are never reviewed as a whole every year. The value of existing programs is seldom reconsidered.

---

*Adolf Wagner's major work is *Grundlegung der Politischen Ökonomie* (Leipzig, 1883). This work is discussed at length in Alan T. Peacock and Jack Wiseman, *The Growth of Public Expenditures in the United Kingdom* (Princeton, N.J.: Princeton University Press, 1961).

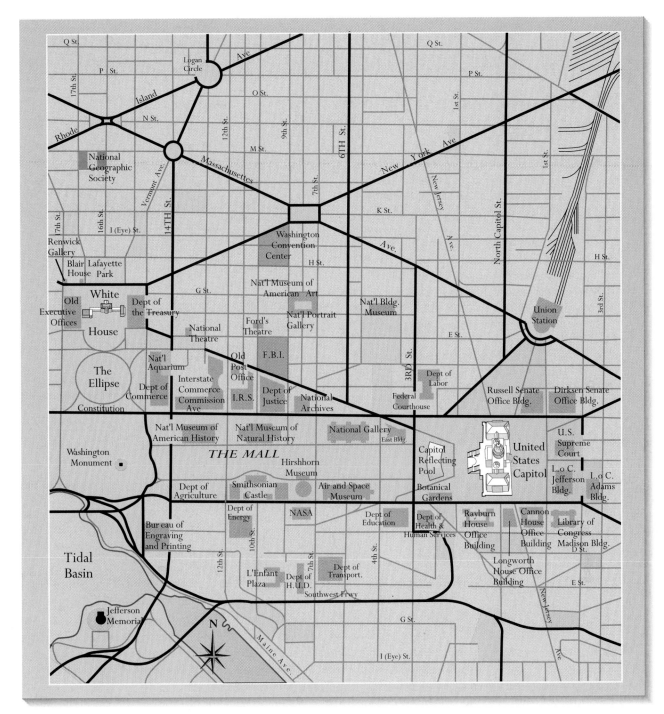

FIGURE 12–2   Corridors of Power in the Bureaucracy

This map shows the Capitol, the White House, and the major departments of the federal bureaucracy in Washington, D.C.

Navy, and Air Force are given the title "secretary" even though they really function as undersecretaries to the Secretary of Defense. This anomaly is a product of historical tradition: a secretary of war headed a separate War Department (created 1789) and the secretary of the navy headed a separate Department of the Navy (created 1798) until the creation of a unified Department of Defense in 1947.

The Size of Government in Other Nations

How does the size of the public sector in the United States compare with the size of the public sector in other economically-advanced, democratic countries? There is a great deal of variation in the size of government across countries. Government spending accounts for nearly two-thirds of the total output in Sweden. Government spending exceeds one-half of the total output of Denmark, Netherlands, Finland, Germany, Italy, Austria, Belgium, and France. The high level of government spending in these countries primarily reflects greater public-sector involvement in the provision of housing, health care, retirement insurance, and aid to the unemployed. The size of the public sectors in Australia, Japan, and Switzerland are only slightly higher than that of the United States.

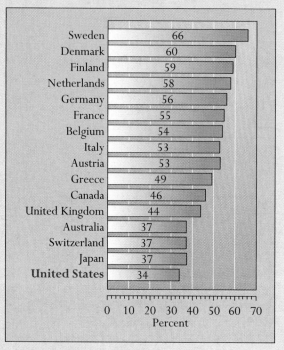

Governmental Percentage of Gross Domestic Product

Source: Joint Economic Committee of Congress, "The Size and Function of Government" (Washington, D.C.: 1998).

Cabinet status confers great legitimacy on a governmental function and prestige on the secretary, thus strengthening that individual's voice in the government. Therefore the elevation of an executive department to cabinet level often reflects political considerations as much as or more than national needs. Strong pressures from "client" interest groups (groups principally served by the department), as well as presidential and congressional desires to pose as defenders and promoters of particular interests, account for the establishment of all of the newer departments. President Woodrow Wilson appealed to the labor movement in 1913 when he separated out a Department of Labor from the earlier business-dominated Department of Commerce and Labor. In 1965 President Lyndon Johnson created the Department of Housing and Urban Development to demonstrate his concern for urban problems. Seeking support from teachers and educational administrators, President Jimmy Carter created a separate Department of Education in 1979 and changed the name of the former Department of Health, Education, and Welfare to the Department of Health and Human Services (perhaps finding the phrase "human services" more politically acceptable than "welfare"). President Ronald Reagan, tried and failed to "streamline" government by abolishing the Department of Education. But Reagan himself added a cabinet post, elevating the Veterans' Administration to the Depart-

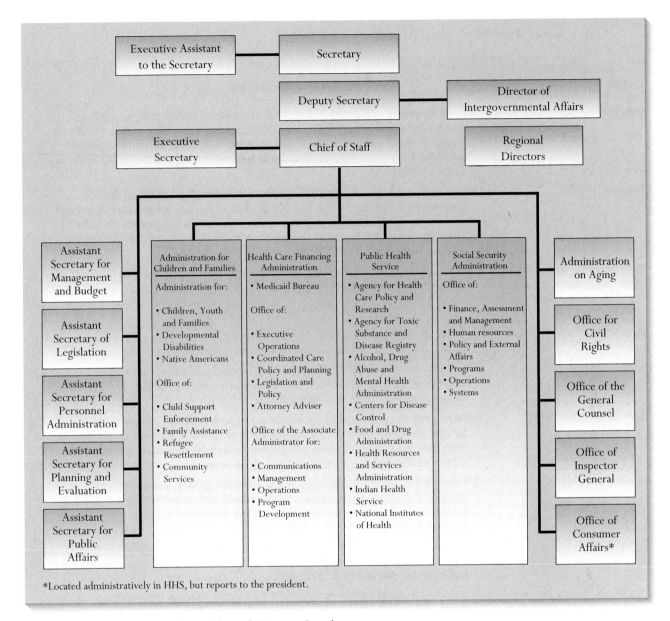

FIGURE 12–3 Department of Health and Human Services

The internal structures of various cabinet-level departments differ somewhat in specifics, but this chart of the Department of Health and Human Services (HHS) is typical of most. It includes secretary, deputy secretary, assistant secretaries, and multiple "administrations" (subdepartments), agencies, offices, and services.

ment of Veterans' Affairs in an attempt to ingratiate himself with veterans. President Clinton promised to elevate the Environmental Protection Agency (EPA) to a cabinet department, but his efforts stalled in the Republican-controlled Congress.

Cabinet Department Functions   The relative power and prestige of each cabinet-level department is a product not only of its size and budget but also of the importance of its function. By custom, the "pecking order" of departments—and therefore the prestige ranking of their secretaries—is determined by their years of origin. Thus the Departments of State, Treasury, Defense (War), and Justice, created by the First Congress in 1789, head the protocol list of depart-

Table 12-1 Cabinet Departments and Functions

Department and Date Created	Function
State (1789)	Advises the president on the formation and execution of foreign policy; negotiates treaties and agreements with foreign nations; represents the United States in the United Nations and in the more than fifty major international organizations and maintains U.S. embassies abroad; issues U.S. passports and, in foreign countries, visas to the United States.
Treasury (1789)	Serves as financial agent for the U.S. government; issues all payments of the U.S. government according to law; manages the debt of the U.S. government by issuing and recovering bonds and paying their interest; collects taxes owed to the U.S. government; collects taxes and enforces laws on alcohol, tobacco, and firearms and on customs duties; manufactures coins and currency.
Defense (1947; formerly the War Department, created in 1789, and the Navy Department, created 1798)	Provides the military forces needed to deter war and protect the national security interest; includes the Departments of the Army, Navy, and Air Force.
Justice (1789)	Enforces all federal laws, including consumer protection, antitrust, civil rights, drug, and immigration and naturalization; maintains federal prisons.
Interior (1849)	Has responsibility for public lands and natural resources, for American Indian reservations, and for people who live in island territories under U.S. administration; preserves national parks and historical sites.
Agriculture (1889)	Works to improve and maintain farm income and to develop and expand markets abroad for agricultural products; safeguards standards of quality in the food supply through inspection and grading services; administers rural development, credit, and conservation programs; administers food stamp program.
Commerce (1913)	Encourages the nation's international trade, economic growth, and technological advancement; conducts the census; provides social and economic statistics and analyses for business and government; maintains the merchant marine; grants patents and registers trademarks.
Labor (1913)	Oversees working conditions; administers federal labor laws; protects workers' pension rights; sponsors job training programs; keeps track of changes in employment, price, and other national economic indicators.
Health and Human Services (1953 as Health, Education, and Welfare; reorganized with Education as a separate department in 1979)	Administers to social welfare programs for the elderly, children, and youths; protects the health of the nation against impure and unsafe foods, drugs, and cosmetics; operates the Centers for Disease Control; funds the Medicare and Medicaid programs; and operates the Social Security system.
Housing and Urban Development (1965)	Is responsible for programs concerned with housing needs, fair housing opportunities, and the improvement and development of the nation's communities; administers mortgage insurance programs, rental subsidy programs, and neighborhood rehabilitation and preservation programs.
Transportation (1966)	Is responsible for the nation's highway planning, development, and construction; also urban mass transit, railroads, aviation, and the safety of waterways, ports, highways, and oil and gas pipelines.
Energy (1977)	Is responsible for the research, development, and demonstration of energy technology; marketing of federal electric power; energy conservation; the nuclear weapons program; regulation of energy production and use; and collection and analysis of energy data.
Education (1979)	Administers and coordinates most federal assistance to education.
Veterans' Affairs (1989)	Operates programs to benefit veterans and members of their families.

Source: The United States Government Manual 1996/97 (Washington, D.C.: Government Printing Office, 1997).

ments. Overall, the duties of the fourteen cabinet-level departments of the executive branch cover an enormous range—everything from providing mortgage insurance to overseeing the armed forces of the United States (see Table 12–1).

Cabinet Appointments   The Constitution requires that "Officers of the United States" be confirmed by the Senate. In the past, the Senate rarely rejected a presidential cabinet nomination; the traditional view was that presidents were entitled to pick their own people and even make their own mistakes. In recent years, however, the confirmation process has become more partisan and divisive, with the Senate conducting lengthy investigations and holding public hearings on presidential cabinet nominees. In 1989 the Senate rejected President Bush's nomination of John Tower as secretary of defense in a partisan battle featuring charges that the former Texas senator was a heavy drinker. In 1993 President Clinton was obliged to withdraw the nomination of Zoe Baird as attorney general following Senate hearings featuring the charge that she had employed an illegal alien as a babysitter and had failed to pay the woman's Social Security taxes. The intense public scrutiny and potential for partisan attacks, together with financial disclosure and conflict-of-interest laws, may be discouraging some well-qualified people from accepting cabinet posts.

Independent Regulatory Commissions   Independent regulatory commissions differ from cabinet departments in their function, organization, and accountability to the president. Their function is to *regulate* a sector of society—transportation, communications, banking, labor relations, and so on (see Table 12–2 on page 432). These commissions are empowered by Congress both to make and to enforce rules, and they thus function in a quasi-judicial fashion. To symbolize their impartiality, many of these organizations are headed by *commissions*, usually with five to ten members, rather than by a single secretary. Major policy decisions are made by majority vote of the commission. Finally, these agencies are more independent of the president than are cabinet departments. Their governing commissions are appointed by the president and confirmed by the Senate in the same fashion as cabinet secretaries, but their terms are fixed; they cannot be removed by the president.[5] These provisions are designed to insulate regulators from direct partisan or presidential pressures in their decision making.

A few powerful regulatory agencies remain inside cabinet departments. The most notable are the Food and Drug Administration (FDA), which remains in the Department of Health and Human Services and has broad authority to prevent the sale of drugs not deemed by the agency to be both "safe" and "effective"; the Occupational Health and Safety Administration (OSHA) in the Department of Labor, with authority to make rules governing any workplace in America; and the most powerful government agency of all, the Internal Revenue Service in the Treasury Department, with its broad authority to interpret the tax code, maintain records on every American, and investigate and punish alleged violations of the tax code.

Independent Agencies   Congress has created a number of independent agencies outside of any cabinet department. Like cabinet departments, these agencies are hierarchically organized with a single head—usually called an "administrator"—who is appointed by the president and confirmed by the Senate. Administrators have no fixed terms of office and can be dismissed by the president; thus they are independent only insofar as they report directly to the president rather

Table 12-2　Major Regulatory Bureaucracies

Commission	Date Created	Primary Functions
Federal Communications Commission (FCC)	1934	Regulates interstate and foreign communications by radio, television, wire, and cable.
Food and Drug Administration (FDA)	1930	Sets standards of safety and efficacy for foods, drugs, and medical devices.
Federal Home Loan Bank	1932	Regulates savings and loan associations that specialize in making home mortgage loans.
Federal Maritime Commission	1961	Regulates the waterborne foreign and domestic offshore commerce of the United States.
Federal Reserve Board (FRB)	1913	Regulates the nation's money supply by making monetary policy, which influences the lending and investing activities of commercial banks and the cost and availability of money and credit.
Federal Trade Commission (FTC)	1914	Regulates business to prohibit unfair methods of competition and unfair or deceptive acts or practices.
National Labor Relations Board (NLRB)	1935	Protects employees' rights to organize; prevents unfair labor practices.
Securities and Exchange Commission (SEC)	1934	Regulates the securities and financial markets (such as the stock market).
Occupational Safety and Health Administration (OSHA)	1970	Issues workplace regulations; investigates, cites, and penalizes for noncompliance.
Consumer Product Safety Commission (CPSC)	1972	Protects the public against product-related deaths, illnesses, and injuries.
Commodity Futures Trading Commission	1974	Regulates trading on the futures exchanges as well as the activities of commodity exchange members, public brokerage houses, commodity salespersons, trading advisers, and pool operators.
Nuclear Regulatory Commission (NRC)	1974	Regulates and licenses the users of nuclear energy.
Federal Energy Regulatory Commission (formerly Federal Power Commission)	1977	Regulates the transportation and sale of natural gas, the transmission and sale of electricity, the licensing of hydroelectric power projects, and the transportation of oil by pipeline.
Equal Employment Opportunity Commission (EEOC)	1964	Investigates and rules on charges of racial, gender, and age discrimination by employers and unions, in all aspects of employment.
Environmental Protection Agency (EPA)	1970	Issues and enforces pollution control standards regarding air, water, solid waste, pesticides, radiation, and toxic substances.

Source: The United States Government Manual 1996/97 (Washington, D.C.: Government Printing Office, 1997).

than through a cabinet secretary. Politically, this independence ensures that their interests and budgets will not be compromised by other concerns, as may occur in agencies located within departments. (For more on their operations, see "Regulatory Battles" later in this chapter.)

One of the most powerful independent agencies is the Environmental Protection Agency (EPA), which is responsible for implementing federal legislation dealing with clean air, safe drinking water, solid waste disposal, pesticides, radiation, and toxic substances. EPA establishes and enforces comprehensive and complex standards for thousands of substances in the environment. It enjoys the political support of influential environmental interest groups, including the Environmental Defense Fund, Friends of the Earth, National Audubon Society, National Wildlife Federation, Natural Resources Defense Council, Sierra Club, and the Wilderness Society.

The Federal Reserve System is most independent of all federal government agencies (see *Up Close:* "The Fed: America's Other Government" on page 434). The function of the Fed is to regulate the supply of money and thereby avoid both inflation and recession (see Chapter 16). The Federal Reserve System is independent of either the President or Congress. Its seven-member Board of Governors are appointed for *14-year terms.* Members are appointed by the President, with the consent of the Senate, but they may not be removed from the Board except for "cause." No member has ever been removed since the creation of the Board in 1913. The Chairman of the Board serves only a four-year term, but the Chairman's term overlaps that of president, so that new presidents cannot immediately name their own chair (see *People and Politics:* "Alan Greenspan, Inflation Fighter at the Fed" on page 436).

Government Corporations Government corporations are created by Congress to undertake independent commercial enterprises. They resemble private corporations in that they typically charge for their services. Like private corporations, too, they are usually governed by a chief executive officer and a board of directors, and they can buy and sell property and incur debts.

Presumably, government corporations perform a service that the private enterprise system has been unable to carry out adequately. The first government corporation was the Tennessee Valley Authority, created by President Franklin Roosevelt during the Depression to build dams and sell electricity at inexpensive rates to impoverished citizens in the mid-South. In 1970 Congress created Amtrak to restore railroad passenger service to the United States. The U.S. Post Office had originally been created as a cabinet-level department, but in 1971 it became the U.S. Postal Service, a government corporation with a mandate from Congress to break even. Nevertheless, when the Postal Service and other government corporations have run recurring deficits in their operations, Congress has provided subsidies to make up the difference.

Contractors and Consultants How has the federal government grown enormously in power and size, yet kept its number of employees at roughly the same level in recent years? The answer is found in the spectacular growth of private firms that live off federal contracting and consulting fees. Nearly one-fifth of all federal government spending flows through private contractors: for supplies, equipment, services, leases, and research and development. An army of scientists, economists, education specialists, management consultants, transportation experts, social scientists, and others are scattered across the country in universities, think tanks, consulting firms, and laboratories. Many are concentrated in the "beltway bandit" firms surrounding Washington, D.C.

The federal grant and contracting system is enormously complex; an estimated 150,000 federal contracting offices in nearly 500 agencies oversee thousands of outside contractors and consultants.[6] Although advertised bidding is sometimes

Cleaning up an oil spill on a California beach. The Environmental Protection Agency is perhaps the most powerful independent agency in the bureaucracy.

The "Fed": America's Other Government

The Federal Reserve System was created in 1913 to regulate the nation's monetary policy and credit conditions, to supervise and regulate all banking activity, and to provide various services to banks. Federal Reserve Banks are banks' banks (see figure). Only banks may open accounts at Federal Reserve Banks.

Banks create money—"demand deposits"—when they make loans. Currency (cash) in circulation, together with demand deposits, constitute the nation's money supply—"M1." But demand deposits far exceed currency; only about 5 percent of the money supply is in the form of currency. So banks really determine the money supply in their creation of demand deposits. However, the Fed requires that all banks maintain a reserve in deposits with a Federal Reserve Bank. If the Fed decides to set the "reserve ratio" at 20 percent, for example, then a bank may only create demand deposits up to five times the amount of its reserve. (If a bank has, for example, $100 million in reserve, its total demand deposits cannot exceed $500 million.) If the Fed decides that there is too much money in the economy (inflation), it can raise the reserve requirement, for example from 20 to 25 percent, reducing what a bank can create in demand deposits to only four times its reserve. (A bank that has $100 million in reserve can then only create $400 million in demand deposits.) Changing the "reserve ratio" is one way that the Fed can expand or contract the money supply.

The Fed can also expand or contract the money supply by changing the interest it charges member banks to borrow reserve. A bank can expand its demand deposits by borrowing reserve from the Fed, but it must pay the Fed an interest rate, called the "discount rate," in order to do so. By raising the discount rate the Fed can discourage banks from borrowing reserve and thereby contract the money supply; lowering the

Federal Reserve Chairman Alan Greenspan testifying before a House banking subcommittee on capital markets, securities, and government-sponsored enterprises.

discount rate encourages banks to expand the money supply. Interest rates generally—on loans to businesses, mortgages, car loans, etc.—rise and fall with rises and falls in the Fed's discount rate. Lowering rates encourages economic expansion; raising rates dampens inflation when it threatens the economy.

Finally, the Fed can also buy and sell U.S. Treasury bonds and notes in what is called "open market operations." The reserve of the Federal Reserve System consists of U.S. bonds and notes. If it sells more than it buys, it reduces its own reserve, and hence its ability to lend reserve to banks; this contracts the money supply. If it buys more than it sells, it adds to its own reserve, enabling it to lend reserve to banks and thereby expand the money supply.

These decisions, referred to as monetary policy (see Chapter 16), have a vital impact on the economy. Recessions can be countered by expanding the money supply, and inflation can be countered by contracting the money supply. These decisions by the Federal Reserve Board are made independently—they need

required by law, most contracts and grants are awarded without competition through negotiation with favored firms or "sole source contracts" with organizations believed by bureaucrats to be uniquely qualified. Even when federal agencies issue public requests for proposals (RFPs), often a favored contractor has been alerted and advised by bureaucrats within the agency about how to win the award.

not be ratified by president, the Congress, the courts, or any other governmental institution. Indeed, the Fed does not even depend on annual federal appropriations, but instead finances itself. This means that Congress does not even exercise its "power of the purse" over the Fed. Theoretically, Congress could amend or repeal the Federal Reserve Act of 1913, but to do so would be politically unthinkable. The only changes to the Act throughout the century have been to *add* to the powers of the Fed.

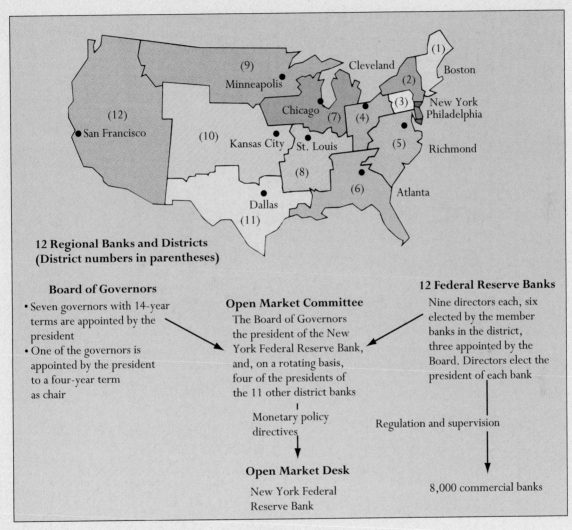

12 Regional Banks and Districts (District numbers in parentheses)

Board of Governors
- Seven governors with 14-year terms are appointed by the president
- One of the governors is appointed by the president to a four-year term as chair

Open Market Committee
The Board of Governors the president of the New York Federal Reserve Bank, and, on a rotating basis, four of the presidents of the 11 other district banks

Monetary policy directives

Open Market Desk
New York Federal Reserve Bank

12 Federal Reserve Banks
Nine directors each, six elected by the member banks in the district, three appointed by the Board. Directors elect the president of each bank

Regulation and supervision

8,000 commercial banks

The Structure of the Federal Reserve System

BUREAUCRACY AND DEMOCRACY

Traditionally, conflict over government employment centered on the question of partisanship versus competence. Should the federal bureaucracy be staffed by people politically loyal to the president, the president's party, or key members of Congress?

Alan Greenspan, Inflation Fighter at the Fed

Economist Alan Greenspan was first appointed chair of the Federal Reserve Board in 1987 by President Ronald Reagan. Greenspan has presided over the nation's longest period of economic growth in its history.

Born in New York City, Alan Greenspan studied music at the prestigious Julliard School and enjoyed a brief but successful career as a professional saxophone player in a big swing band before returning to the classroom at New York University. He received an M.A. in economics in 1950 under the tutelage of Arthur F. Burns, who served as chair of the Federal Reserve from 1970 to 1978. After graduation, Greenspan formed his own economic consulting company, Townsend-Greenspan, which provided economic forecasts for some of America's largest corporations. In his spare time, Greenspan completed his Ph.D. at New York University and became a fan of the social philosopher and writer Ayn Rand. Greenspan embraced Rand's vision of a society in which every person could realize his or her own potential in any chosen field without government interference or regulation.

Greenspan began his public service in the Nixon Administration, serving on commissions and task forces, including the Commission on an All-Volunteer Armed Force. In 1974 President Nixon appointed Greenspan to chair the Council of Economic Advisers, a position Greenspan continued to hold under President Gerald Ford. When the Carter Administration came to Washington in 1977, Greenspan returned to running his private company.

In the early 1980s, Fed chair Paul Volker instituted a tight money policy that ultimately brought down the high rates of inflation which had plagued the nation for most of the 1970s. The Reagan Administration eventually complained that Volker's stringent anti-inflationary policies were slowing economic growth. In August 1987 the Democrat Volker handed in his resignation and Reagan nominated Republican Greenspan to follow him.

Like Reagan, Greenspan opposed higher taxes, but what the president had hoped would be a loyal Republican soldier often acted independently and disagreed with the administration over expanding the money supply. Greenspan's management of the Fed has been widely praised by both Democrats and Republicans. He has earned credibility with his fellow economists by avoiding the Washington political game. He is credited for his quick reaction to the stock market crash on October 19, 1987, when he ensured that Federal Reserve Banks would have enough cash on hand to prevent panic following the record drop in stock prices. During the 1991 recession, Greenspan pushed interest rates down to a twenty-year low and cut required Federal Reserve funds in half in order to ease credit. As independent as the Fed itself, he has frequently criticized presidents and the Congress regarding the huge federal deficits. In 1999 President Clinton nominated Greenspan for a fourth term as Fed chairman.

Or should it be staffed by nonpartisan people selected on the basis of merit and protected from "political" influence?

The Spoils System Historically, government employment was allocated by the **spoils system**—selecting employees on the basis of party loyalty, electoral support, and political influence. Or as Senator William Marcy said in 1832, "They see nothing wrong in the rule that to the victors belong the spoils of the enemy."[7] The spoils system is most closely associated with President Andrew Jackson, who viewed it as a popular reform of the earlier tendency to appoint officials on the basis of kinship and class standing. Jackson sought to bring into government many of the common people who had supported him. Later in the nineteenth century, the bartering and sale of government jobs became so scandalous and time-consuming that presidents

spoils system Selection of employees for government agencies on the basis of party loyalty, electoral support, and political influence.

complained bitterly about the task. And when President James Garfield was shot and killed in 1881 by a disgruntled job seeker, the stage was set for reform.

The Merit System   The **merit system**—government employment based on competence, neutrality, and protection from partisanship—was introduced in the Pendleton Act of 1883. The act created the Civil Service Commission to establish a system for selecting government personnel based on merit, as determined by competitive examinations. In the beginning, "civil service" coverage included only about 10 percent of total federal employees. Over the years, however, more and more positions were placed under civil service, primarily at the behest of presidents who sought to "freeze in" their political appointees. By 1978 more than 90 percent of federal employees were covered by civil service or other merit systems.

The civil service system established a uniform General Schedule (GS) of job grades from GS 1 (lowest) to GS 15 (highest), with an Executive Schedule added later for top managers and pay ranges based on an individual's time in the grade. Each grade has specific educational requirements and examinations. College graduates generally begin at GS 5 or above; GS 9 through GS 12 are technical and supervisory positions; and GS 13, 14, and 15 are midlevel management and highly specialized positions. The Executive Schedule (the "supergrades") are reserved for positions of greatest responsibility. (In 1998 annual pay ranged from roughly $20,000 to $35,000 for Grades 5–8, up to $50,000 to $90,000 for Grades 13–15, and over $100,000 for some Executive Schedule positions.) When a position in a federal agency opens up, the agency is supposed to receive the names of the three people earning the highest examination scores for that position grade. The agency is supposed to hire one of the three, with the other two remaining at the top of the register for the next opening. But agencies often set highly specialized job qualifications that relatively few applicants possess, and special preferences abound in federal employment regulations.

About two-thirds of all federal civilian jobs come under the General Schedule system, with its written examinations and/or training, experience, and educational requirements. Most of the other one-third of federal civilian employees are part of the "excepted services"; they are employed by various agencies that have their own separate merit systems, such as the Federal Bureau of Investigation, the Central Intelligence Agency, the U.S. Postal Service, and the State Department Foreign Service. The military also has its own system of recruitment, promotion, and pay.

Political Involvement   Congress passed the Hatch Act in 1939, a law that prohibited federal employees from engaging in partisan political activity, including running for public office, soliciting campaign funds, or campaigning for or against a party or candidate. It also protected federal merit system employees from dismissal for partisan reasons. But over the years many federal employees came to believe that the Hatch Act infringed on their rights as citizens. (However, the Supreme Court upheld the Hatch Act against charges that it unconstitutionally denied federal employees their political rights.[8]) In 1993, a Democratic-controlled Congress repealed major portions of the Hatch Act, allowing civil servants to hold party positions and involve themselves in political fund raising and campaigning. They still may not be candidates for public office in partisan elections, or solicit contributions from subordinate employees or people who do business with—or have cases before—their agencies.

During the administration of Andrew Jackson, the spoils system was perhaps more overt than at any other time in the history of the U.S. federal government. Jackson claimed he was trying to involve more of the "common folk" in the government, but his selection of advisers on the basis of personal friendship rather than qualifications sometimes caused him difficulties.

merit system   Selection of employees for government agencies on the basis of competence, with no consideration of an individual's political stance and/or power.

The Problem of Responsiveness   The civil service system, like most "reforms," eventually created problems at least as troubling as those in the system it replaced. First of all, there is the problem of a *lack of responsiveness* to presidential direction. Civil servants, secure in their protected jobs, can be less than cooperative toward their presidentially appointed department or agency heads. They can slow or obstruct policy changes with which they personally disagree. Each bureau and agency develops its own "culture," usually in strong support of the governmental function or client group served by the organization. Changing the culture of an agency is extremely difficult, especially when a presidential administration is committed to reducing its resources, functions, or services. Bureaucrats' powers of policy obstruction are formidable: they can help mobilize interest group support against the president's policy; they can "leak" damaging information to sympathizers in Congress or the media to undermine the president's policy; they can delay and/or "sabotage" policies with which they disagree.

The Problem of Productivity   Perhaps the most troublesome problem in the federal bureaucracy has involved *productivity*—notably the inability to improve job performance because of the difficulties in rewarding or punishing civil servants. "Merit" salary rewards have generally proven ineffective in rewarding the performance of federal employees. More than 99 percent of federal workers regularly receive annual "merit" pay increases. Moreover, over time, federal employees have secured higher grade classifications and hence higher pay for most of the job positions in the General Schedule. This "inflation" in GS grades, combined with regular increases in salary and benefits, has resulted in many federal employees enjoying higher pay and benefits than employees in the private sector performing similar jobs.

At the same time, very poor performance often goes largely unpunished. Once hired and retained through a brief probationary period, a federal civil servant cannot be dismissed except for "cause." Severe obstacles to firing a civil servant result in a rate of dismissal of about one-tenth of 1 percent of all federal employees (see Table 12–3). It is doubtful that only such a tiny fraction are performing unsatisfactorily. A federal executive confronting a poorly performing or nonperforming employee must be prepared to spend more than a year in extended proceedings to secure a dismissal.

Table 12–3	Firing a Bureaucrat: What Federal Employees Require before They Can Be Dismissed

- Written notice at least thirty days in advance of a hearing to determine incompetence or misconduct.
- A statement of cause, indicating specific dates, places, and actions cited as incompetent or improper.
- The right to a hearing and decision by an impartial official, with the burden of proof falling on the agency that wishes to fire the employee.
- The right to have an attorney and to present witnesses in the employee's favor at the hearing.
- The right to appeal any adverse action to the Merit Systems Protection Board.
- The right to appeal any adverse action by the board to the U.S. Court of Appeals.
- The right to remain on the job and be paid until all appeals are exhausted.

Often costly substitute strategies are devised to work around or inspire the resignation of unsatisfactory federal employees—assigning them meaningless or boring tasks, denying them promotions, transferring them to distant or undesirable locations, removing secretaries or other supporting resources, and the like.

Civil Service Reform   Presidents routinely try to remedy some of the problems in the system (see *Up Close:* "Reinventing Government" on page 440). The Civil Service Reform Act of 1978 initiated by President Jimmy Carter, replaced the Civil Service Commission with the Office of Personnel Management (OPM) and made OPM responsible for recruiting, examining, training, and promoting federal employees. Unlike the Civil Service Commission, OPM is headed by a single director responsible to the president. The act also sought to (1) streamline procedures through which individuals could be disciplined for poor performance; (2) establish merit pay for middle-level managers; and (3) create a Senior Executive Service (SES) composed of about 8,000 top people designated for higher Executive Schedule grades and salaries who also might be given salary bonuses, transferred among agencies, or demoted, based on performance.

But like many reforms, this act failed to resolve the major problems—the responsiveness and productivity of the bureaucracy. No senior executives were fired, demoted, or involuntarily transferred. The bonus program proved difficult to implement: there are few recognized standards for judging meritorious work in the public service, and bonuses often reflect favoritism as much as merit.[9] Because the act creates a separate Merit Systems Protection Board to hear appeals by federal employees from dismissals, suspensions, and demotions, rates of dismissal for all grades have not changed substantially from earlier days.

Bureaucracy and Representation   In addition to the questions of responsiveness and productivity, there is also the question of the representativeness of the federal bureaucracy. Today, the federal bureaucracy *as a whole* reflects fairly well the gender and minority ratios of the U.S. population. Nearly 49 percent of the total civilian work force is female, 16.5 percent is black, and 5.2 is Hispanic. However, a close look at *top* bureaucratic positions reveals a somewhat different picture. As Table 12–4 on page 441 shows, only 9.1 percent of federal "executive" positions (levels GS 16–18) are filled by women, only 5.0 percent by blacks, and only 2.3 percent by Hispanics. Thus the federal bureaucracy, like other institutions in American society, is *un*representative of the general population in its top executive positions.

BUREAUCRATIC POLITICS

To whom is the federal bureaucracy really accountable? The president, Congress, or itself? Article II, Section 2, of the Constitution places the president at the head of the executive branch of government, with the power to "appoint Ambassadors, other public Ministers and Consuls, Judges of the Supreme Court, and all other Officers of the United States . . . which shall be established by Law." Appointment of these officials requires "the Advice and Consent of the Senate"—that is, a majority vote in the Senate. The Constitution also states that "the Congress may by Law vest the Appointment of such inferior Officers, as they think proper, in the President alone." If the bureaucracy is to be made accountable to the president, we would

"Reinventing" Government

How can we overcome "the bankruptcy of bureaucracy"—the waste, inefficiency, impersonality, and unresponsiveness of large government organizations? Solving the problem of bureaucracy is perceived as overcoming "the routine tendency to protect turf, to resist change, to build empires, to enlarge one's sphere of control, to protect projects and programs regardless of whether or not they are any longer needed."* The answer, according to current reformers, is to "reinvent government"—to focus on the needs of citizens, not bureaucrats, to inject competition into public service provision, to use market incentives whenever possible, to decentralize, and to encourage agencies to be mission-driven rather than rule-driven.

The notion of "reinventing government" gained popularity among centrist Democrats even before the Clinton Administration arrived in Washington. Some Democratic Party constituencies—notably government employees and their unions, teachers and their unions, and environmental groups—are concerned about the antibureaucratic thrust of many of the new reforms and fear the loss of government jobs to private contractors. But Clinton campaigned on the pledge to make government more efficient and responsive. Upon taking office, he assigned this task to Al Gore.

Vice presidents traditionally undertake symbolic roles in presidential administrations, but Al Gore responded to his assignment with considerable energy and enthusiasm, promptly producing a 168-page report of the National Performance Review, *Creating a Government That Works Better and Costs Less.*† The report includes 384 specific recommendations designed to put the "customer" (U.S. citizen) first, to "empower" government employees to get results, to cut red tape, to introduce competition and a market orientation wherever possible, and to decentralize government decision making. Many previous bureaucratic reform efforts had floundered, from Hoover Commission studies in the Truman and Eisenhower years to the Grace Commission in the Reagan Administration. But Bill Clinton boasted that the new effort would succeed because Vice President Gore was given the responsibility not just to devise recommendations but to oversee their implementation as well.

Making a point about red tape and bureaucratic inefficiency, President Clinton and Vice President Al Gore walk past two forklifts loaded with reams of federal rules and regulations before announcing their plans for "reinventing" government.

How successful was Al Gore at "reinventing" federal government? Periodically Gore published "status reports" on the implementation of his National Performance Review recommendations. As expected, these reports presented glowing accounts of "reinvention," bureaucratic "cultural change," "cutting red tape," and "putting customers first." But even after discounting for puffery, it seemed clear that some progress has been achieved. The most impressive evidence was the overall decline in federal employment, from 3.1 to 2.8 million civilian employees.‡

---

*David Osborne and Ted Gaebler, *Reinventing Government: How the Entrepreneurial Spirit Is Transforming the Public Sector* (New York: Addison-Wesley, 1992), pp. 23–24.

†Al Gore, *Creating a Government That Works Better and Costs Less* (Washington, D.C.: Government Printing Office, 1993).

‡*Statistical Abstract of the United States, 1999,* p. 363.

Table 12-4	Women and Minorities in the Federal Bureaucacy			
	Percentage Female	Percentage White, non-Hispanic	Percentage African American	Percentage Hispanic
Overall	48.7%	75.3%	17.8%	6.9%
By pay grade				
Lowest GS 1–4	74.8	60.8	30.1	9.1
GS 5–8	53.5	68.3	26.6	8.1
GS 9–12	32.9	88.0	8.3	3.7
GS 13–15	17.0	87.0	9.1	3.9
Executive	9.1	90.1	6.9	3.0
U.S. population (2000)	51.1	71.8	12.2	11.4

Table excludes American Indians, Alaska Natives, and Asian and Pacific Islanders.

Source: Statistical Abstract of the United States, 1999, p. 364.

expect the president to directly appoint *policy-making* executive officers. But it is difficult to determine exactly how many positions are truly "policy making."

Presidential "Plums"   The president retains direct control over about 3,000 federal jobs. Some 700 of these jobs are considered policy-making positions. They include presidential appointments authorized by law—cabinet and subcabinet officers, judges, U.S. marshals, U.S. attorneys, ambassadors, and members of various boards and commissions. The president also appoints a large number of "Schedule C" jobs throughout the bureaucracy, described as "confidential or policy-determining" in character. Each new administration goes through many months of high-powered lobbying and scrambling to fill these posts. Applicants with congressional sponsors, friends in the White House, or a record of loyal campaign work for the president compete for these "plums." Political loyalty must be weighed against administrative competence.

Rooms At The Top   The federal bureaucracy has "thickened" at the top, even as total federal employment declined. Over time, departments and agencies have added layers of administrators, variously titled "Deputy Secretary," "Under Secretary," "Assistant Secretary," "Deputy Assistant Secretary," etc. Table 12–5 on page 441 shows how cabinet departments have become top heavy with administrators; the same multiplication of layers of executive management has occurred in independent agencies as well.[10]

Whistle-Blowers   The question of bureaucratic responsiveness is complicated by the struggle between the president and Congress to control the bureaucracy. Congress expects federal agencies and employees to respond fully and promptly to its inquiries and to report candidly on policies, procedures, and expenditures. **Whistle-blowers** are federal employees (or employees of a firm supplying the government) who report government waste, mismanagement, or fraud to the media or to congressional committees or who "go public" with their policy disputes with their superiors. Congress generally encourages whistle-blowing as a means of getting information and controlling the bureaucracy, but the president and agency heads whose policies are under attack are often less kindly disposed toward whistle-blowers. In 1989 Congress passed the Whistleblower Protection Act, which

whistle-blower Employee of the federal government or of a firm supplying the government who reports waste, mismanagement, and/or fraud by a government agency or contractor.

Table 12-5	The "Thickening" of Bureaucracy: Growth in Number of Top Departmental Officials between 1962 and 1994	
	Kennedy Administration 1962	Clinton Administration 1994
Secretary	10	14
Deputy Secretary	6	21
Under Secretary	14	32
Assistant Secretary	81	212
Deputy Assistant Secretary	77	507
Deputy Administrator	52	190

established an independent agency to guarantee whistle-blowers protection against unjust dismissal, transfer, or demotion.

Agency Cultures   Over time, every bureaucracy tends to develop its own "culture"—beliefs about the values of the organization's programs and goals and close associations with the agency's client groups and political supporters. Many government agencies are dominated by people who have been in government service most of their lives, and most of these people have worked in the same functional field most of their lives. They believe their work is important, and they resist efforts by either the president or Congress to reduce the activities, size, or budget of their agency. Career bureaucrats tend to support enlargement of the public sector—to enhance education, welfare, housing, environmental and consumer protection, and so on.[11] Bureaucrats not only share a belief in the need for government expansion but also stand to benefit directly from increased authority, staffing, and funding as government takes on new and enlarged responsibilities.

Friends and Neighbors   Bureaucracies maintain their own cultures in part by staffing themselves. Informal practices in recruitment often circumvent civil service procedures. Very few people ever get hired by taking a federal civil service examination administered by OPM and then sitting and waiting to be called for an interview by an agency. Most bureaucratic hiring actually comes about through "networks" of personal friends and professional associates. People inside an agency contact their friends and associates when a position first becomes vacant; they then send their friends to OPM to formally qualify for the job. Thus inside candidates learn about an opening well before it appears on any list of vacant positions and can tailor their applications to the job description. Agencies may even send a "name request" to OPM, ensuring that the preselected person will appear on the list of qualified people. In this way, individuals sometimes move through many jobs within a specific policy network—for example, within environmental protection, within transportation, or within social welfare—shifting between the federal bureaucracy, state or local government, and private firms or interest groups in the same field. Network recruiting generally ensures that the people entering a bureaucracy will share the same values and attitudes of the people already there.

THE BUDGETARY PROCESS

The federal government's annual budget battles are the heart of political process. Budget battles decide who gets what and who pays the cost of government. The budget is the single most important policy statement of any government.

The president is responsible for submitting the annual Budget of the United States Government—with estimates of revenues and recommendations for expenditures—for consideration, amendment, and approval by the Congress. But the president's budget reflects the outcome of earlier bureaucratic battles over who gets what. Despite highly publicized wrangling between the president and Congress each year—and occasional declarations that the president's budget is "DOA" (dead on arrival)—final congressional appropriations rarely deviate by more than 2 or 3 percent from the original presidential budget. Thus the president and the Office of Management and Budget in the Executive Office of the President have real budgetary power.

The Office of Management and Budget The Office of Management and Budget (OMB) has the key responsibility for budget preparation. In addition to this major task, OMB has related responsibilities for improving the organization and management of the executive agencies, for coordinating the extensive statistical services of the federal government, and for analyzing and reviewing proposed legislation.

Preparation of the budget begins when OMB, after preliminary consultations with the executive agencies and in accord with presidential policy, develops targets or ceilings within which the agencies are encouraged to build their requests (see Figure 12–4 on page 444). Budget materials and instructions then go to the agencies, with the request that the forms be completed and returned to OMB. This request is followed by about three months of arduous work by agency budget officers, department heads, and the "grass-roots" bureaucracy in Washington, D.C., and out in the field. Budget officials at the bureau and departmental levels check requests from the smaller units, compare them with previous years' estimates, hold conferences, and make adjustments. The heads of agencies are expected to submit their completed requests to OMB by July or August. Although these requests usually remain within target levels, occasionally they include some "overceiling" items (requests above the suggested ceilings). With the requests of the spending agencies at hand, OMB begins its own budget review, including hearings at which top agency officials support their requests as convincingly as possible. Frequently OMB must say "no," that is, reduce agency requests. On rare occasions, dissatisfied agencies may ask the budget director to take their cases to the president.

The President's Budget In December, the president and the OMB director devote much time to the key document, *The Budget of the United States Government*, which by now is approaching its final stages of assembly. Each budget is named for the **fiscal year** in which it *ends*. The federal fiscal year begins on October 1 and ends the following September 30. (Thus the *Budget of the United States Government Fiscal Year 2002* begins October 1, 2001, and ends September 30, 2002.) Although the completed document includes a revenue plan with general estimates for taxes and other income, it is primarily an expenditure budget. (Revenue and tax policy staff work center in the Treasury Department, not in the Office of Management

fiscal year Yearly government accounting period, not necessarily the same as the calendar year. The federal government's fiscal year begins October 1 and ends September 30.

WHO	WHAT	WHEN
Presidential budget making		
President and OMB	OMB presents long-range forecasts for revenues and expenditures to the president. President and OMB develop general guidelines for all federal agencies. Agencies are sent guidelines and forms for their budget requests.	January February March
Executive agencies	Agencies prepare and submit budget requests to OMB.	April May June July
OMB and agencies	OMB reviews agency requests and holds hearings with agency officials.	August September October
OMB and president	OMB presents revised budget to president. President and OMB write budget message for Congress.	November December
President	President presents budget for the next fiscal year to Congress.	January
Congressional budget process		
CBO and congressional committees	CBO reviews taxing and spending proposals and reports to House and Senate budget committees.	February–May
Congress; House and Senate budget committees	Committees present first concurrent resolution, which sets overall total for budget outlays in major categories. Full House and Senate vote on resolution. Committees are instructed to stay within Budget Committee's resolution.	May June
Congress; House and Senate appropriations committees and budget committees	Appropriations committees and subcommittees draw up detailed appropriations bills and submit them to budget committees for second concurrent resolution. The full House and Senate vote on "reconciliations" and second (firm) concurrent resolution.	July August September
Congress and president	House and Senate pass various appropriations bills (nine to sixteen bills, by major functional category, such as "defense"). Each is sent to president for signature. (If successfully vetoed, a bill is revised and resubmitted to the president.)	September October
Executive budget implementation		
Congress and president	Fiscal year for all federal agencies begins October 1. If no appropriations bill for an agency has been passed by Congress and signed by the president, Congress must pass and the president sign a continuing resolution to allow the agency to spend at last years's level until a new appropriations bill is passed. If no continuing resolution is passed, the agency must officially cease spending government funds and must officially shut down.	After October 1

FIGURE 12–4   The Budget Process

Development, presentation, and approval of the federal budget for any fiscal year takes almost two full years. The executive branch spends more than a year on the process before Congress even begins its review and revision of the president's proposals. The problems of implementing the budgeted programs then fall to the federal bureaucracy.

and Budget.) In late January, the president presents Congress with the Budget of the United States Government for the fiscal year beginning October 1. After the budget is in legislative hands, the president may recommend further alterations as needs dictate.

House and Senate Budget Committees   The Constitution gives Congress the authority to decide how the government should spend its money: "No money shall be drawn from the Treasury, but in Consequence of Appropriations made by Law" (Article I, Section 9). The president's budget is sent initially to the House and Senate Budget Committees, which rely on their own bureaucracy, the Congressional Budget Office (CBO), to review the president's budget. Based on the CBO's assessment, these committees draft a first **budget resolution** (due May 15) setting forth target goals to guide congressional committees regarding specific appropriations and revenue measures. If proposed spending exceeds the targets in the budget resolution, the resolution comes back to the floor in a recon-ciliation measure. A second budget resolution (due September 15) sets binding budget figures for committees and subcommittees considering appropriations. In practice, however, these two budget resolutions are often folded into a single measure because Congress does not want to argue the same issues twice.

Congressional Appropriations Committees   Congressional approval of each year's spending is usually divided into thirteen separate appropriations bills (acts), each covering separate broad categories of spending (for example, defense, labor, human services and education, commerce, justice). These appropriations bills are drawn up by the House and Senate Appropriations Committees and their special-ized subcommittees, which function as overseers of agencies included in their appropriations bills. Committee work in the House of Representatives is usually more thorough than it is in the Senate; the committee in the Senate tends to be a "court of appeal" for agencies opposed to House action. Each committee, more-over, has about ten largely independent subcommittees, each reviewing the requests of a particular agency or a group of related functions. Specific appropri-ations bills are taken up by the subcommittees in hearings. Departmental officers answer questions on the conduct of their programs and defend their requests for the next fiscal year; lobbyists and other witnesses testify. Although committees and subcommittees have broad discretion in allocating funds to the agencies they monitor, they must stay within overall totals set forth in the second budget reso-lution adopted by Congress.

Appropriations Acts   In examining the interactions between Congress and the federal bureaucracy over spending, it is important to distinguish between appro-priations and authorization. An **authorization** is an act of Congress that estab-lishes a government program and defines the amount of money it may spend. Authorizations may be for one or several years. However, an authorization does not actually provide the money that has been authorized; only an **appropria-tions act** can do that. In fact, appropriations acts, which are usually for a single fiscal year, are almost always *less* than authorizations; deciding how much less is the real function of the Appropriations Committees and subcommittees. (By its own rules, Congress cannot appropriate money for programs it has not already authorized.) Appropriations acts include both obligational authority and outlays.

budget resolution
Congressional bill setting forth target budget figures for appro-priations to various government departments and agencies.

authorization   Act of Congress that establishes a government program and defines the amount of money it may spend.

appropriations act
Congressional bill that provides money for programs authorized by Congress.

Obligational authority permits a government agency to enter into contracts that will require the government to make payments beyond the fiscal years in question. **Outlays** must be spent in the fiscal year for which they are appropriated.

Continuing Resolutions and "Shutdowns"   All appropriations acts *should* be passed by both houses and signed by the president into law before October 1, the date of the start of the fiscal year. However, it is rare for Congress to meet this deadline, so the government usually finds itself beginning a new fiscal year without a budget. Constitutionally, any U.S. government agency for which Congress does not pass an appropriations act may not draw money from the Treasury and thus is obliged to shut down. To get around this problem, Congress usually adopts a **continuing resolution** that authorizes government agencies to keep spending money for a specified period at the same level as in the previous fiscal year.

A continuing resolution is supposed to grant additional time for Congress to pass, and the president to sign, appropriations acts. But occasionally this process has broken down in the heat of political combat over the budget: the time period specified in a continuing resolution has expired without agreement on appropriations acts or even on a new continuing resolution. Shutdowns occurred during the bitter battle between President Bill Clinton and the Republican-controlled Congress over the Fiscal Year 1996 budget. In theory, the absence of either appropriations acts or a continuing resolution should cause the entire federal government to "shut down," that is, to cease all operations and expenditures for lack of funds. But in practice, such shutdowns have been only partial, affecting only "nonessential" government employees and causing relatively little disruption.

THE POLITICS OF BUDGETING

Budgeting is very political. Being a good "bureaucratic politician" involves (1) cultivating a good base of support for requests among the public at large and among people served by the agency; (2) developing interest, enthusiasm, and support for one's program among top political figures and congressional leaders; (3) winning favorable coverage of agency activities in the media; and (4) following strategies that exploit opportunities[12] (see *Up Close:* "Bureaucratic Budget Strategies").

Budgeting Is "Incremental"   The most important factor determining the size and content of the budget each year is last year's budget. Decision makers generally use last year's expenditures as a *base*; active consideration of budget proposals generally focuses on new items and requested increases over last year's base. The budget of an agency is almost never reviewed as a whole. Agencies are seldom required to defend or explain budget requests that do *not* exceed current appropriations; but requested increases *do* require explanation and are most subject to reduction by OMB or Congress.

The result of **incremental budgeting** is that many programs, services, and expenditures continue long after there is any real justification for them. When new needs, services, and functions arise, they do not displace older ones but rather are *added* to the budget. Budget decisions are made incrementally because policy makers do not have the time, energy, or information to review every dollar of

---

obligational authority
Feature of some appropriations acts by which an agency is empowered to enter into contracts that will require the government to make payments beyond the fiscal year in question.

outlays   Actual dollar amounts to be spent by the federal government in a fiscal year.

continuing resolution
Congressional bill that authorizes government agencies to keep spending money for a specified period at the same level as in the previous fiscal year; passed when Congress is unable to enact final appropriations measures by October 1.

incremental budgeting
Method of budgeting that focuses on requested increases in funding for existing programs, accepting as legitimate their previous year's expenditures.

Bureaucratic Budget Strategies

How do bureaucrats go about "maximizing" their resources? Some of the most common budgetary strategies of bureaucrats are listed here. Remember that most bureaucrats believe strongly in the importance of their tasks; they pursue these strategies not only to increase their own power and prestige but also to better serve their client groups and the entire nation.

- *Spend it all:* Spend all of your current appropriation. Failure to use up an appropriation indicates the full amount was unnecessary in the first place, which in turn implies that your budget should be cut next year.

- *Ask for more:* Never request a sum less than your current appropriation. It is easier to find ways to spend up to current appropriation levels than it is to explain why you want a reduction. Besides, a reduction indicates your program is not growing, an embarrassing admission to most government administrators. Requesting an increase, at least enough to cover "inflation," demonstrates the continued importance of your program.

- *Put vital programs in the "base":* Put top priority programs into the basic budget—that is, that part of the budget within current appropriation

levels. The Office of Management and Budget (OMB) and legislative committees seldom challenge programs that appear to be part of existing operations.

- *Make new programs appear "incremental":* Requested increases should appear to be small and should appear to grow out of existing operations. Any appearance of a fundamental change in a budget should be avoided.

- *Give them something to cut:* Give the OMB and legislative committees something to cut. Normally it is desirable to submit requests for substantial increases in existing programs and many requests for new programs, in order to give higher political authorities something to cut. This approach enables authorities to "save" the public untold millions of dollars and justify their claim of promoting "economy" in government. Giving them something to cut also diverts attention from the basic budget with its vital programs.

- *Make cuts hurt:* If your agency is faced with a real budget cut—that is, a reduction from last year's appropriation—announce pending cuts in vital and popular programs in order to stir up opposition to the cut. For example, the National Park Service might announce the impending closing of the Washington Monument. Never acknowledge that cuts might be accommodated by your agency without reducing basic services.

every budget request every year. Nor do policy makers wish to refight every political battle over existing programs every year. So they generally accept last year's base spending level as legitimate and focus attention on proposed increases for each program.

Reformers have proposed "sunset" laws requiring bureaucrats to justify their programs every five to seven years or else the programs go out of existence, as well as **zero-based budgeting** that would force agencies to justify every penny requested—not just requested increases. In theory, sunset laws and zero-based budgeting would regularly prune unnecessary government programs, agencies, and expenditures and thus limit the growth of government and waste in government (see *What Do You Think?* "How Much Money Does the Government Waste?" on page 448). But in reality, sunset laws and zero-based budgeting require so much effort in justifying already accepted programs that executive agencies and legislative committees grow tired of the effort and return to incrementalism.

zero-based budgeting
Method of budgeting that demands justification for the entire budget request of an agency, not just its requested increase in funding.

How Much Money Does the Government Waste?

Bureaucracy is often associated in the public's mind with waste and inefficiency. But it is very difficult to determine objectively how much money government really wastes. People disagree on the value of various government programs. What is "waste" to one person may be a vital governmental function to another. One very conservative south Georgia farmer once explained politics to his son: "There's only three things that government should ever do—defend our country in war, keep the highways paved, and provide the peanut allotment." But even those who believe a government program is necessary may still believe some of the money going to that program is wasted by the bureaucracy.

Indeed, over the last twenty years, nearly two-thirds of Americans have described the government as wasting "a lot" of money rather than "some" or "not very much" (see graph). Belief in the wastefulness of government rose during the Vietnam War and Watergate years, just as confidence and trust in government declined.

Is public opinion correct in estimating that "a lot" of money is wasted? The General Accounting Office is an arm of Congress with broad authority to audit the operations and finances of federal agencies. GAO audits have frequently found fraud and mismanagement amounting to 10 percent or more of the spending of many agencies it has reviewed, which suggests that $180 *billion* of the overall federal budget of $1.8 trillion may be wasted.* Citizens' commissions studying the federal bureaucracy place an even higher figure on waste. The Grace Commission estimated waste at more than 20 percent of federal spending, more than enough to eliminate annual deficits.†

*General Accounting Office, *Federal Evaluation Issues* (Washington, D.C.: General Accounting Office, 1989).

†*President's Private Sector Survey on Cost Control* (Grace Commission Report) (Washington, D.C.: Government Printing Office, 1984).

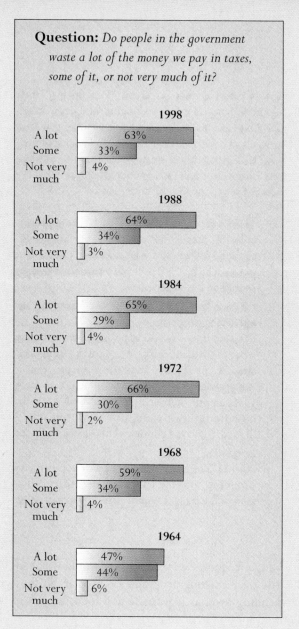

Question: *Do people in the government waste a lot of the money we pay in taxes, some of it, or not very much of it?*

1998
A lot — 63%
Some — 33%
Not very much — 4%

1988
A lot — 64%
Some — 34%
Not very much — 3%

1984
A lot — 65%
Some — 29%
Not very much — 4%

1972
A lot — 66%
Some — 30%
Not very much — 2%

1968
A lot — 59%
Some — 34%
Not very much — 4%

1964
A lot — 47%
Some — 44%
Not very much — 6%

Source: National Election Studies.

The "incremental" nature of budgetary politics helps reduce political conflicts and maintain stability in governmental programs. As bruising as budgetary battles are today, they would be much worse if the president or Congress undertook to review the value of *all* existing expenditures and programs each year. Comprehensive budgetary review would "overload the system" with political conflict by refighting every policy battle every year.[13]

Budgeting Is Nonprogrammatic Budgeting is *nonprogrammatic* in that an agency budget typically lists expenditures under ambiguous phrases: "personnel services," "contractual services," "travel," "supplies," "equipment." It is difficult to tell from such a listing exactly what programs the agency is spending its money on. Such a budget obscures policy decisions by hiding programs behind meaningless phrases. Even if these categories are broken down into line items (for example, under "personnel services," the line-item budget might say, "John Doaks, Assistant Administrator, $65,000"), it is still next to impossible to identify the costs of various programs.

For many years, reformers have called for budgeting by programs. **Program budgeting** would require agencies to present budgetary requests in terms of the end products they will produce or at least to allocate each expense to a specific program. However, bureaucrats are often unenthusiastic about program budgeting; it certainly adds to the time and energy devoted to budgeting, and many agencies are reluctant to describe precisely what it is they do and how much it really costs to do it. Moreover, some political functions are best served by *non*program budgeting. Agreement comes more easily when the items in dispute can be treated in dollars instead of programmatic differences. Congressional Appropriations Committees can focus on increases or decreases in overall dollar amounts for agencies rather than battle over even more contentious questions of which individual programs are worthy of support.

REGULATORY BATTLES

Bureaucracies regulate virtually every aspect of American life. Interest rates on loans are heavily influenced by the Federal Reserve Board. The National Labor Relations Board protects unions and prohibits "unfair labor practices." Safety in automobiles and buses is the responsibility of the National Transportation Safety Board. The Federal Deposit Insurance Corporation insures bank accounts. The Federal Trade Commission orders cigarette manufacturers to place a health warning on each pack. The Equal Employment Opportunity Commission investigates complaints about racial and sexual discrimination in jobs. The Consumer Product Safety Commission requires that toys be large enough that they cannot be swallowed by children. The Federal Communications Commission bans tobacco advertisements on television. The Environmental Protection Agency requires automobile companies to limit exhaust emissions. The Occupational Safety and Health Administration requires construction firms to place portable toilets at work sites. The Food and Drug Administration decides what drugs your doctor can prescribe. The list goes on and on. Indeed, it is difficult to find an activity in public or private life that is not regulated by the federal government (see *A Conflicting View*: "Bureaucratic Regulations Are Suffocating America" on page 450).

Federal regulatory bureaucracies are legislators, investigators, prosecutors, judges, and juries—all wrapped into one. They issue thousands of pages of rules and regulations each year; they investigate thousands of complaints and conduct thousands of inspections; they require businesses to submit hundreds of thousands of forms each year; they hold hearings, determine "compliance" and "noncompliance," issue corrective orders, and levy fines and penalties. Most economists agree that regulation adds to the cost of living, is an obstacle to innovation and produc-

program budgeting Identifying items in a budget according to the functions and programs they are to be spent on.

Bureaucratic Regulations Are Suffocating America

Today, bureaucratic regulations of all kinds—environmental controls, workplace safety rules, municipal building codes, government contracting guidelines—have become so numerous, detailed, and complex that they are stifling initiative, curtailing economic growth, wasting billions of dollars, and breeding popular contempt for law and government.

Consider, for example, the Environmental Protection Agency's rules and regulations, now *seventeen volumes* of fine print. Under one set of rules, before any land on which "toxic" waste was once used can be reused by anyone for any purpose, it must be cleaned to near perfect purity. The dirt must be made cleaner than soil that has never been used for anything. The result is that most new businesses choose to locate on virgin land rather than incur the enormous expense of cleaning dirt, and a great deal of land previously used by industry sits vacant while new land is developed.

These and similar examples of "the death of common sense" in bureaucratic regulations are set forth by critic Philip K. Howard, who argues, "We have constructed a system of regulatory law that basically outlaws common sense."* The result is that we direct our energy and wealth into defensive measures, designed not to improve our lives but to avoid tripping over senseless rules. People come to see government as their adversary and government regulations as obstacles in their lives.

The explosive growth in federal regulations in the last two decades has added heavy costs to the American economy. The costs of regulations do not appear in the federal budget: rather, they are paid for by businesses, employees, and consumers. Indeed, politicians prefer a regulatory approach to the environment, health, and safety precisely because it forces costs on the private sector—costs that are largely invisible to voters and taxpayers. Yet as the costs of regulation multiply for American businesses, the prices of their products rise in world markets.

How large is the regulatory bill? Proponents of a regulatory activity usually object to estimating its cost. Politicians who wish to develop an image as protectors of the environment, of consumers, of the disabled, and so on, do not want to call attention to the costs of their legislation. Only recently has the Office of Management and Budget (OMB) even attempted to estimate the costs of federal regulatory activity. Overall, regulatory activity costs Americans between $300 billion (OMB estimate) and $700 billion a year (estimate by Center for the Study of American Business), an amount equal to over one-third of the total federal budget. If the $700 billion estimate is correct, it means that each of America's 100 million households pays about $7,000 per year in the hidden costs of regulation. Paperwork requirements consume more than 5 billion hours of people's time, mostly to comply with the administration by the Internal Revenue Service of the tax laws. However, the costs of environmental controls, including the Environmental Protection Agency's enforcement of clean air and water and hazardous waste disposal regulations, are the fastest growing regulatory costs.

The real question is whether the *benefits* of this regulatory activity—for example, cleaner air and water, safer disposal of toxic wastes, safer consumer products, fewer workplace injuries, fewer highway deaths, protections against discrimination, improved access for disabled, and so on—are greater or less than the costs. But assessing the value of benefits is extraordinarily difficult. Many people object on ethical grounds to economic estimates of the value of a human life saved.

Regulation also places a heavy burden on innovations and productivity. The costs and delays in winning permission for a new product tend to discourage invention and to drive up prices. For example, new drugs are difficult to introduce in the United States because the Food and Drug Administration (FDA) typically requires up to ten years of testing. Western European nations are many years ahead in their number of life-saving drugs available; they speak of the "drug lag" in the United States. Critics charge that if aspirin were proposed for marketing today, it would not be approved by the FDA. Recently activists have succeeded in speeding up FDA approval of drugs to treat AIDS, but the agency has continued to delay the introduction of drugs to treat other diseases.

---

*Philip K. Howard, *The Death of Common Sense: How Law Is Suffocating America* (New York: Random House, 1995), pp. 10–11.

tivity, and hinders economic competition. Most regulatory commissions are independent; they are not under an executive department, and their members are appointed for long terms by a president who has little control over their activities.

Traditional Agencies: Capture Theory   The **capture theory of regulation** describes how some regulated industries come to benefit from government regulation and how some regulatory commissions come to represent the industries they are supposed to regulate rather than representing "the people." Historically, regulatory commissions have acted against only the most wayward members of an industry. By attacking those businesses that gave the industry bad publicity, the commissions actually helped improve the public's opinion of the industry as a whole. Regulatory commissions provided symbolic reassurance to the public that the behavior of the industry was proper. Among the traditional regulatory agencies that have been accused of becoming too close to their regulated industry are the Federal Communications Commission (FCC, the communications industry, including the television networks), the Securities and Exchange Commission (SEC, the securities industry and stock exchanges), the Federal Reserve Board (FRB, the banking industry), and National Labor Relations Board (NLRB, unions).

Commission members often come from the industry they are supposed to regulate, and after a few years in government, the "regulators" return to high-paying jobs in the industry, creating the *revolving door problem* described in Chapter 9. In addition, many regulatory commissions attract young attorneys fresh from law school to their staffs. Industry siphons off the "best and the brightest" of these, offering them much higher paying jobs as defenders against government regulation. Over the years, then, some industries have come to support their regulatory bureaucracies. Industries have often strongly opposed proposals to reduce government controls. Proposals to deregulate railroads, interstate trucking, and airlines have met with substantial opposition from both the regulatory bureaucracies and the regulated industries, working together.

The Newer Regulators: The Activists   In recent decades, Congress created several new "activist" regulatory agencies in response to the civil rights movement, the environmental movement, and the consumer protection movement. Unlike traditional regulatory agencies, the activist agencies do not regulate only a single industry; rather, they extend their jurisdiction to all industries. The Equal Employment Opportunity Commission (EEOC), the Environmental Protection Agency (EPA), and the Occupational Safety and Health Administration (OSHA) pose serious challenges to the business community. Many businesspeople argue that EEOC rules designed to prevent racial and sexual discrimination in employment and promotion (affirmative action guidelines) ignore the problems of their industry or their labor market and overlook the costs of training or the availability of qualified minorities. Likewise, many of OSHA's thousands of safety regulations appear costly and ridiculous to people in industry. The complaint about EPA is that it seldom considers the cost of its rulings to business or the consumer. Industry representatives contend that EPA should weigh the costs of its regulations against the benefits to the environment.

Deregulation   The demand to deregulate American life was politically very popular during President Ronald Reagan's administration in the 1980s. But **deregulation** made only limited progress in curtailing the power of the regulatory

capture theory of regulation   Theory describing how some regulated industries come to benefit from government regulation and how some regulatory commissions come to represent the industries they are supposed to regulate rather than representing "the people."

deregulation   Lifting of government rules and bureaucratic supervision from business and professional activity.

The deregulation of the airline industry contributed to the development of the hub-and-spoke system currently used by most airlines to reduce their costs. Here American Airlines aircraft congregate at the airline's hub in Dallas/Fort Worth. Although deregulation has caused fares to decrease on heavily competitive routes, critics charge that it has contributed to higher rates on non-competitive routes.

bureaucracies. Arguments for deregulation centered on the heavy costs of compliance with regulations, the burdens these costs imposed on innovation and productivity, and the adverse impact of regulatory activity on the global competitiveness of American industry. In 1978 Jimmy Carter succeeded in getting Congress to deregulate the airline industry. Against objections by the industry itself, which *wanted* continued regulation, the Civil Aeronautics Board was stripped of its powers to allocate airline routes to various carriers and to set rates. At the end of 1984, the board went out of existence, the first major regulatory agency ever to be abolished. With the airlines free to choose where to fly and what to charge, competition on heavily traveled routes (such as from New York to Los Angeles) reduced fares dramatically while prices rose on less traveled routes served by a single airline. Overall the cost of airline travel declined by 25 to 30 percent.[14] Competition caused airline profits to decline and financially weak airlines to declare bankruptcy. Also, during the 1980s the Interstate Commerce Commission (ICC), the first regulatory commission ever established by the federal government, dating from 1887, was stripped of most of its power to set railroad and trucking rates. The ICC itself was finally abolished in 1995. Prices to consumers of railroad and trucking services declined dramatically.[15]

Reregulation   Deregulation threatens to diminish politicians' power and to eliminate bureaucrats' jobs. It forces industries to become competitive and diminishes the role of interest group lobbyists. So in the absence of strong popular support for deregulation, pressures to continue and expand regulatory activity will always be strong in Washington.

Airline deregulation brought about a huge increase in airline travel. The airlines doubled their seating capacity and made more efficient use of their aircraft through the development of "hub-and-spoke" networks. Air safety continued to improve; fatalities per millions of miles flown declined; and by taking travelers away from far more dangerous highway travel, overall transportation safety was enhanced. But these favorable outcomes were overshadowed by complaints about congestion at major airports and increased flight delays, especially at peak hours. The major airports are publicly owned, and governments have been very slow in responding to increased air traffic. Congestion and delays are widely publicized, and politicians respond to complaints by calling for reregulation of airline travel.

The political incentives to create new regulatory agencies, grant additional powers to existing agencies, and add to the accumulation of federal regulations, are great. Politicians want to be seen "doing something" about any well-publicized problem in America. When the media reports accidents, health scares, environmental dangers, etc., politicians are interviewed for their response, and most feel obliged to call for new laws and regulations, with little regard to their likely costs or effectiveness.

REGULATING AMERICA

Federal regulatory agencies continually add more rules to American life. Roughly 5,000 new rules, all with the force of law, are issued by regulatory agencies each year. The Environmental Protection Agency (EPA) leads in making new rules, closely followed by the Internal Revenue Service (IRS) and the Federal Communications Commission (FCC).

Over 50 federal agencies have rule-making power. These agencies must publish proposed rules in the *Federal Register* and allow time for interested groups to "comment" on them. "Major rules," those estimated to cost Americans at least $100 or more per year in compliance, are sent to the Office of Management and Budget before being finalized. In the three-year period, 1996–1999, the General Accounting Office of Congress reported that 15,280 *new* final rules were issued. Some 222 of these new rules were listed as "major rules"; this means that, at a minimum, $22.2 billion of *new* costs of regulation were imposed on American society in just three years.[16]

Multiplying Regulations Inasmuch as proposed new regulations must be published in the *Federal Register*, the size of this publication is often used as an indicator of overall federal regulatory activity. In 1970, the *Federal Register* included roughly 20,000 pages; by 1980 it had expanded to over 73,000 pages. Only during the presidency of Ronald Reagan, who promised to reduce federal regulatory activity, did the size of the *Federal Register* decline somewhat (see Figure 12–5). But by 1998 it was again over 68,000 pages.

The accumulated regulations of federal government are published in the Code of Federal Regulations. The Code includes all regulations currently in effect. The Code has now expanded to over 135,000 pages in 200 volumes.

The Costs of Regulation Regulatory activity incurs costs for American businesses, employers, and consumers—costs which do not appear in federal budget. (The official budgets of all federal regulatory agencies combined add up to "only" about $15 billion.) Indeed, it is precisely because these costs do not appear in the federal budget that politicians prefer a regulatory approach to many of the nation's problems. Regulation shifts costs from the government itself onto the private sector, costs that are largely invisible to voters and taxpayers. Even when agencies themselves are supposed to calculate the costs of their regulations, their calcula-

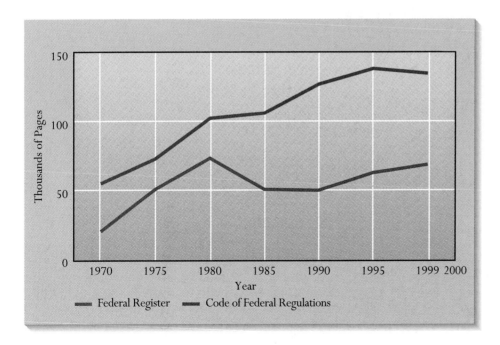

FIGURE 12–5
Regulating America

tions vary in quality and almost always underestimate the true costs. One independent estimate of the total costs of federal regulation sets the figure at $700 *billion*, or about 8 percent of the nation's Gross Domestic Product.[17]

Regulations impose costs on Americans in a variety of ways. First of all, there are the direct costs of compliance (those estimated in Figure 12–6). Direct costs include everything from adding pollution control devices and making businesses accessible to the disabled, to the overhead costs of paperwork, attorney and accounting fees, and staff time needed to negotiate the federal regulatory maze. Secondly, there are indirect economic costs—costs incurred by devoting resources to compliance that otherwise would be used to increase productivity. This loss economic output may amount to $1 *trillion* per year.[18] All of these costs, which typically are imposed on businesses, are ultimately passed onto American consumers in the form of higher prices.

CONGRESSIONAL CONSTRAINTS ON THE BUREAUCRACY

Bureaucracies are unelected hierarchical organizations, yet they must function within democratic government. To wed bureaucracy to democracy, ways must be found to ensure that bureaucracy is responsible to the people. Controlling the bureaucracy is a central concern of democratic government. The federal bureaucracy is responsible to all three branches of government—the president, the Congress, and the courts. Although the president is the nominal head of the executive agencies, Congress—through its power to create or eliminate and fund or fail to fund these agencies—exerts its full share of control. Most of the structure of the executive branch of government (see Figure 12–1) is determined by laws of Congress. Congress has the constitutional power to create or abolish executive departments and independent agencies, or to transfer their functions, as it wishes. Congress can by law expand or

FIGURE 12–6 The Costs of Federal Regulation

Source: Data from Thomas D. Hopkins, *Regulatory Costs in Profile* (Washington, D.C.: Center for the Study of Business, 1996). Estimates are in 1995 inflation adjusted dollars.

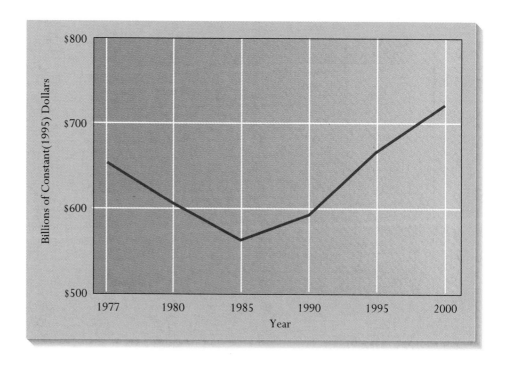

Former Attorney General Janet Reno and FBI director Louis Freeh testify before a Senate committee.

contract the discretionary authority of bureaucrats. It can grant broad authority to agencies in vaguely written language, thereby adding to the power of bureaucracies, which can then determine themselves how to define and implement their own authority. In contrast, narrow and detailed laws place constraints on the bureaucracy.

In addition to specific constraints on particular agencies, Congress has placed a number of general constraints on the entire federal bureaucracy. Among the more important laws governing bureaucratic behavior are these:

- *Administrative Procedures Act* (1946): Requires that agencies considering a new rule or policy give public notice in the *Federal Register*, solicit comments, and hold public hearings before adopting the new measures.
- *Freedom of Information Act* (1966): Requires agencies to allow citizens (and the media) to inspect all public records, with some exceptions for intelligence, current criminal investigations, and personnel actions.
- *Privacy Act* (1974): Requires agencies to keep confidential the personal records of individuals, notably their Social Security files and income tax records.

Senate Confirmation of Appointments   The U.S. Senate's power to confirm presidential appointments gives it some added influence over the bureaucracy.[19] It is true that once nominated and confirmed, cabinet secretaries and regulatory commission members can defy the Congress; only the president can remove them from office. Senators usually try to impress their own views on presidential appointees seeking confirmation, however. Senate committees holding confirmation hearings often subject appointees to lengthy lectures on how the members believe their departments or agencies should be run. In extreme cases, when presidential appointees do not sufficiently reflect the views of Senate leaders, their confirmation can be held up indefinitely or, in very rare cases, defeated in a floor vote on confirmation.

Congressional Oversight   Congressional oversight of the federal bureaucracy is a continuing activity.[20] Congress justifies its oversight activities on the ground that its lawmaking powers require it to determine whether the purposes of the laws it passed are being carried out. Congress has a legitimate interest in communicating legislative *intent* to bureaucrats charged with the responsibility of implementing laws of Congress. But often oversight activities are undertaken to influence bureaucratic decision making. Members of Congress may seek to secure favorable treatment for friends and constituents, try to lay the political groundwork for increases or decreases in agency appropriations, or simply strive to enhance their own power or the power of their committees or subcommittees over the bureaucracy.

Oversight is lodged primarily in congressional committees and subcommittees (see "In Committee" in Chapter 10) whose jurisdictions generally parallel those of executive departments and agencies. However, all too frequently, agencies are required to respond to multiple committee inquiries in both the House and the Senate. For example, the secretary of defense may be called to testify before both the House National Security and Senate Armed Forces committees, as well as the Defense Appropriations subcommittees of both the House and Senate Appropriations Committees, the Government Operations Committee of the House and the Senate Governmental Affairs Committee overseeing defense contracts, and the Senate Foreign Relations and House Foreign Affairs Committees. But the committee system in Congress often results in the development of close relationships between specific committees and subcommittees and their staffs and particular departments and agencies (see "Iron Triangles and Policy Networks" in Chapter 9).

Congressional Appropriations The congressional power to grant or to withhold the budget requests of bureaucracies and the president is perhaps Congress's most potent weapon in controlling the bureaucracy. Spending authorizations for executive agencies are determined by standing committees with jurisdiction in various policy areas, such as armed services, judiciary, education, and labor (see Table 10–4), and appropriations are determined by the House and Senate Appropriations Committees, and more specifically their subcommittees with particular jurisdictions. These committees and subcommittees exercise great power over executive agencies. The Defense Department, for example, must seek *authorizations* for new weapons systems from the House and Senate Armed Services Committees and *appropriations* to actually purchase these weapons from the House and Senate Appropriations Committees, especially their Defense Appropriations subcommittees.

Congress frequently undertakes to control the specific policies and actions of executive agencies through strings it attaches to appropriations measures. Congressional committees and subcommittees may write detailed instructions into appropriations acts about how money is to be spent, thus denying either the president or the bureaucracy any real discretion in implementing programs. For example, in some cases, the Defense Department has been forced to buy weapons it does not need or want simply because an influential member of Congress wrote a pork-barrel provision into the defense appropriations act.

Congressional Investigation Congressional investigations offer yet another tool for congressional oversight of the bureaucracy. Historically, congressional investigations have focused on scandal and wrongdoing in the executive branch (see "Oversight of the Bureaucracy" in Chapter 10). Occasionally, investigations even produce corrective legislation, although they more frequently produce changes in agency personnel, procedures, or policies. Investigations are more likely to follow media reports of waste, fraud, or scandal than to uncover previously unknown problems. In other words, investigations perform a political function for Congress—assuring voters that the Congress is taking action against bureaucratic abuses. Studies of routine bureaucratic performance are likely to be undertaken by the General Accounting Office (GAO), an arm of Congress and frequent critic of executive agencies. GAO may undertake studies of the operations of executive agencies on its own initiative but more often responds to requests for studies by specific members of Congress.

Casework   Perhaps the most frequent congressional oversight activities are calls, letters, and visits to the agencies by individual members of Congress seeking to influence particular actions on behalf of themselves or their constituents. A great deal of congressional **casework** involves intervening with executive agencies on behalf of constituents[21] (see Chapter 10). Executive departments and agencies generally try to deal with congressional requests and inquiries as favorably and rapidly as the law allows. Pressure from a congressional office will lead bureaucrats to speed up an application, correct an error, send information, review a case, or reinterpret a regulation to favor a client with congressional contacts. But bureaucrats become very uncomfortable when asked to violate established regulations on behalf of a favored person or firm. The line between serving constituents and unethical or illegal attempts to influence government agencies is sometimes very difficult to discern.

INTEREST GROUPS AND BUREAUCRATIC DECISION MAKING

Interest groups understand that great power is lodged in the bureaucracy. Indeed, interest groups exercise an even closer oversight of bureaucracy than do the president, Congress, and courts, largely because their interests are directly affected by day-to-day bureaucratic decisions. Interest groups focus their attention on the particular departments and agencies that serve or regulate their own members or that function in their chosen policy field. For example, the American Farm Bureau Federation monitors the actions of the Department of Agriculture; environmental lobbies—such as the National Wildlife Federation, the Sierra Club, and the Environmental Defense Fund—watch over the Environmental Protection Agency as well as the National Park Service; the American Legion, Veterans of Foreign Wars, and Vietnam Veterans "oversee" the Department of Veterans Affairs. Thus, specific groups come to have a proprietary interest in "their" specific departments and agencies. Departments and agencies understand that their "client" groups have a continuing interest in their activities.

Many bureaucracies owe their very existence to strong interest groups that successfully lobbied Congress to create them. The Environmental Protection Agency owes its existence to the environmental groups, just as the Equal Employment Opportunity Commission owes its existence to civil rights groups. Thus, many bureaucracies nourish interest groups' support to aid in expanding their authority and increasing their budgets (see "Iron Triangles and Policy Networks" in Chapter 9).

Interest groups can lobby bureaucracies directly by responding to notices of proposed regulations, testifying at public hearings, and providing information and commentary. Or interest groups can lobby Congress either in support of bureaucratic activity or to reverse a bureaucratic decision. Interest groups may also seek to "build fires" under bureaucrats by holding press conferences, undertaking advertising

Lobbying Washington can take many forms. Although most professional lobbyists operate quietly within the halls of the nation's capital, groups of private citizens often take to the streets to get their message across. Demonstrations may capture the attention of the media and thus may force bureaucrats and politicians at least to consider a group's cause, but the attention span of both media and Washington power brokers can be extremely short. Here people protest in front of the White House against President Clinton's decision to back NATO air attacks on Serbia.

casework Services performed by legislators and their staffs on behalf of individual constituents

Twenty-First Century Directions

The Washington bureaucracy may shrink in size, but its power and influence will continue to grow. Reform efforts have come and gone over the years—efforts to improve the efficiency, productivity, and responsiveness of the federal executive—but the Washington bureaucracy has remained relatively unchanged.

⬆ The power of the federal bureaucracy will continue to increase in response to both the increasing complexity of society and political demands to "do something" about virtually every problem confronting Americans. Bureaucratic agencies themselves, in conjunction with their networks of interest group supporters and congressional committees and subcommittees, will continue to press for additional authority, money, and personnel each year.

⬇ Efforts to streamline the federal bureaucracy—to reduce the number of cabinet departments and independent agencies—will fail. If anything, *new* departments, such as a Department of Environmental Protection, will be added to the federal government's already complex organization chart.

⬇ Civil service reform, including efforts to make the federal bureaucracy more productive and more responsive to presidential and congressional direction, will also fail. Each new era may bring new slogans and buzzwords to public administration, such as "reinventing government," but the bureaucracy will remain unchanged.

⬆ The Fed's success in the past decade in fighting inflation and avoiding recession will add even more to its power and independence. Only a major recession and/or excessively high interest rates would inspire congressional efforts to challenge the Fed's power. The Fed has successfully resisted efforts to curtail its independence in the past, and it will continue to do so in the future.

⬆ Federal regulatory activity will continue to expand, perhaps even accelerate, in the years ahead. The activist agencies—EPA, OSHA, EEOC—will lead the way in regulating America. Efforts by Congress to force regulatory agencies to accurately assess the economic costs of new rules against their expected benefits will fail. Bureaucrats will always find ways to overestimate the benefits and underestimate the costs of new regulations.

campaigns, and soliciting media support for agency actions. Or interest groups may even seek to influence bureaucracies through appeals to the federal courts.

JUDICIAL CONSTRAINTS ON THE BUREAUCRACY

Judicial oversight is another source of restraint on the bureaucracy. Bureaucratic decisions are subject to review by the federal courts. Federal courts can even issue *injunctions* (orders) to an executive agency *before* it issues or enforces a regulation or undertakes a particular action. Thus, the judiciary poses a check on bureaucratic power.

Judicial Standards for Bureaucratic Behavior Historically, the courts have stepped in when agency actions have violated laws passed by Congress, when agencies have exceeded the authority granted them under the laws, when the agency actions have been adjudged "arbitrary and unreasonable," and when agencies have failed in their legal duties under the law. The courts have also restrained the bureaucracy on procedural grounds—ensuring proper notice, fair hearings, rights of appeal, and so on. In short, appeal to the courts must cite failures of agencies to abide by substantive or procedural laws.

Judicial oversight tends to focus on (1) whether or not agencies are acting beyond the authority granted them by Congress; and (2) whether or not they are abiding by rules of procedural fairness. It is important to realize that the courts do not usually involve themselves in the *policy* decisions of bureaucracies. If policy decisions are made in accordance with the legal authority granted agencies by Congress, and if they are made with procedural fairness, the courts generally do not intervene.

Bureaucrats' Success in Court   Bureaucracies have been very successful in defending their actions in federal courts.[22] Individual citizens and interest groups seeking to restrain or reverse the actions or decisions of executive agencies have been largely *unsuccessful.* What accounts for this success? Bureaucracies have established elaborate administrative processes to protect their decisions from challenge on procedural grounds. Regulatory agencies have armies of attorneys, paid for out of tax monies, who specialize in these narrow fields of law. It is very expensive for individual citizens to challenge agency actions. Corporations and interest groups must weigh the costs of litigation against the costs of compliance before undertaking a legal challenge of the bureaucracy. Excessive delays in court proceedings, sometimes extending to several years, add to the time and expense of challenging bureaucratic decisions.

SUMMARY NOTES

- The Washington bureaucracy—the departments, agencies, and bureaus of the executive branch of the federal government—is a major base of power in American government. Political conflict does not end when a law is passed by Congress and signed by the president. The arena merely shifts to the bureaucracy.

- Bureaucratic power has grown with increases in the size of government, advances in technology, and the greater complexity of modern society. Congress and the president do not have the time, resources, or expertise to decide the details of policy across the wide range of social and economic activity in the nation. Bureaucracies must draw up the detailed rules and regulations that actually govern the nation. Often laws are passed for their symbolic value; bureaucrats must give practical meaning to these laws. And the bureaucracy itself is not sufficiently powerful to get laws passed adding to its authority, size, and budget.

- Policy implementation is the development of proce-

dures and activities and the allocation of money, personnel, and other resources to carry out the tasks mandated by law. Implementation includes regulation—the making of detailed rules based on the law—as well as adjudication—the application of laws and regulations to specific cases. Bureaucratic power increases with increases in administrative discretion.

- Bureaucracies usually seek to expand their own powers, functions, and budgets. Most bureaucrats believe strongly in the value of their own programs and the importance of their tasks. And bureaucrats, like everyone else, seek added power, pay, and prestige. Bureaucratic expansion contributes to the growth of government.

- The federal bureaucracy consists of 2.8 million civilian employees in 14 cabinet departments and more than 60 independent agencies, as well as a large Executive Office of the President. Federal employment is not growing, but federal spending, especially for entitlement programs, is growing rapidly.

Today federal spending amounts to more than 23 percent of GDP, and federal, state, and local government spending combined amounts to about 35 percent of GDP.

- Historically, political conflict over government employment centered on the question of partisanship versus competence. Over time, the "merit system" replaced the "spoils system" in federal employment, but the civil service system raised problems of responsiveness and productivity in the bureaucracy. Civil service reform efforts have not really resolved these problems.

- The president's control of the bureaucracy rests principally on the powers to appoint and remove policy-making officials, to recommend increases and decreases in agency budgets, and to recommend changes in agency structure and function.

- But the bureaucracy has developed various means to insulate itself from presidential influence. Bureaucrats have many ways to delay and obstruct policy decisions with which they disagree. Whistle-blowers may inform Congress or the media of waste, mismanagement, or fraud. A network of friends and professional associates among bureaucrats, congressional staffs, and client groups helps create a "culture" within each agency and department. The bureaucratic culture is highly resistant to change.

- Women and minorities are represented in overall federal employment in proportion to their percentages of the U.S. population. However, women and minorities are not proportionately represented in the higher levels of the bureaucracy.

- Budget battles over who gets what begin in the bureaucracy as departments and agencies send their budget requests forward to the president's Office of Management and Budget. OMB usually reduces agency requests in line with the president's priorities. The president submits spending recommendations to Congress early each year in the Budget of the United States Government. Congress is supposed to pass its appropriations acts prior to the beginning of the fiscal year, October 1, but frequently falls behind schedule.

- Budgeting is incremental, in that last year's agency expenditures are usually accepted as a base and attention is focused on proposed increases. Incrementalism saves time and effort and reduces political conflict by not requiring agencies to justify every dollar spent, only proposed increases each year. Nonprogrammatic budgeting also helps reduce conflict over the value of particular programs. The result, however, is that many established programs continue long after the need for them has disappeared.

- Bureaucracies regulate virtually every aspect of our lives. The costs of regulation are borne primarily by business and consumers; they do not appear in the federal budget. In part for this reason, a regulatory approach to national problems appeals to elected officials who seek to obscure the costs of government activity. It is difficult to calculate the true costs and benefits of much regulatory activity. After a brief period of deregulation in the 1980s, regulation has regained popular favor.

- Congress can exercise control over the bureaucracy in a variety of ways: by creating, abolishing, or reorganizing departments and agencies; by altering their authority and functions; by requiring bureaucrats to testify before congressional committees; by undertaking investigations and studies through the General Accounting Office; by intervening directly on behalf of constituents; by instructing presidential nominees in Senate confirmation hearings and occasionally delaying or defeating nominations; and especially by withholding or threatening to withhold agency appropriations or by writing very specific provisions into appropriations acts.

- Interest groups also influence bureaucratic decision making directly by testifying at public hearings and providing information and commentary, and indirectly by contacting the media, lobbying Congress, and initiating lawsuits.

- Judicial control of the bureaucracy is usually limited to determining whether agencies have exceeded the authority granted them by law or have abided by the rules of procedural fairness. Federal bureaucracies have a strong record of success in defending themselves in court.

KEY TERMS

bureaucracy 421

chain of command 421

division of labor 421

specification of
    authority 421

goal orientation 421

impersonality 421

implementation 423

regulation 423

adjudication 423

budget maximization 425

discretionary funds 425

spoils system 436

merit system 437

whistle-blower 441

fiscal year 443

budget resolution 445

authorization 445

appropriations act 445

obligational authority 446

outlays 446

continuing resolution 446

incremental budgeting 446

zero-based budgeting 447

program budgeting 449

capture theory of
    regulation 451

deregulation 451

casework 457

SELECTED READINGS

GORE, AL. *Creating a Government That Works Better and Costs Less.* Washington, D.C.: Government Printing Office, 1993. Specific recommendations for "reinventing" government by making citizens "customers," introducing competition, cutting red tape, and privatizing government services.

HENRY, NICHOLAS. *Public Administration and Public Affairs.* 7th ed. Upper Saddle River, N.J.: Prentice Hall, 1999. Authoritative introductory textbook on public organizations (bureaucracies), public management, and policy implementation.

HOWARD, PHILIP K. *The Death of Common Sense: How Law Is Suffocating America.* New York: Random House, 1995. Outrageous stories of bureaucratic senselessness coupled with a plea to allow bureaucrats flexibility in achieving the purposes of laws and holding them accountable for outcomes.

JOHNSON, RONALD N., and GARY D. LIBECAP. *The Federal Civil Service System and the Problem of Bureaucracy.* Chicago: University of Chicago Press, 1994. A convincing argument that civil service was not a product of a moral crusade by reformers against politicians but rather a result of presidents and Congresses competing to maximize their power.

KETTL, DONALD F. *Civil Service Reform.* Washington, D.C.: Brookings Institution, 1996. A brief introduction to the problems confronting government managers and some recommendations for reform.

MAXWELL, BRUCE. *CQ's Insider's Guide to Finding a Job in Washington.* Washington, DC: CQ Press, 2000. How to locate job vacancies, make contacts, "market" oneself, and build a career in the Washington bureaucracy.

OSBOURNE, DAVID, and TED GAEBLER. *Reinventing Government.* New York: Addison-Wesley, 1992. The respected manual of the "reinventing government" movement with recommendations to overcome the routine tendencies of bureaucracies and inject "the entrepreneurial spirit" in them.

SCHICK, ALLEN. *The Federal Budget: Politics, Policy, Process.* Washington, D.C.: Brookings Institution, 1995. A comprehensive explanation of the federal budgetary process.

WILSON, JAMES Q. *Bureaucracy: What Government Agencies Do and Why They Do It.* New York: Basic Books, 1989. In the author's words, "an effort to depict the essential features of bureaucratic life in the government agencies of the United States." Examining what really motivates middle-level public servants, Wilson argues that congressional attempts to "micromanage" government activities hamper the ability of bureaucrats to do their jobs.

Courts

Judicial Politics

ASK YOURSELF ABOUT POLITICS

1 Have the federal courts grown too powerful?
Yes ● No ●

2 Is it really democratic to allow federal court judges, who are appointed, not elected, and who serve for life, to overturn laws of an elected Congress and president?
Yes ● No ●

3 Should the Constitution be interpreted in terms of the original intentions of the Founders rather than the morality of society today?
Yes ● No ●

4 Are the costs of lawsuits in America becoming too burdensome on the economy?
Yes ● No ●

5 Should presidents appoint only judges who agree with their judicial philosophy?
Yes ● No ●

6 Should the Senate confirm Supreme Court appointees who oppose abortion?
Yes ● No ●

7 Should the Supreme Court overturn the law of Congress that prohibits federal funding of abortions for poor women?
Yes ● No ●

8 Is there a need to appoint special prosecutors to investigate presidents and other high officials?
Yes ● No ●

Do the Supreme Court and the federal judiciary in fact have the real power to shape public policies in the United States?

JUDICIAL POWER

"There is hardly a political question in the United States which does not sooner or later turn into a judicial one."[1] This observation by French diplomat and traveler Alexis de Tocqueville, although made in 1835, is even more accurate today. It is the Supreme Court and the federal judiciary, rather than the president or Congress, that has taken the lead in deciding many of the most heated issues of American politics. It has undertaken to:

- Eliminate racial segregation and decide about affirmative action.
- Ensure separation of church and state and decide about prayer in public schools.
- Determine the personal liberties of women and decide about abortion.
- Define the limits of free speech and free press and decide about obscenity, censorship, and pornography.
- Ensure equality of representation and require legislative districts to be equal in population.
- Define the rights of criminal defendants, prevent unlawful searches, limit the questioning of suspects, and prevent physical or mental intimidation of suspects.
- Decide the life-or-death issue of capital punishment.

Courts are "political" institutions. Like Congress, the president, and the bureaucracy, courts decide who gets what in American society. Judges do not merely "apply" the law to specific cases. Years ago, former Supreme Court Justice Felix Frankfurter

⭐ www.prenhall.com/dye

explained why this mechanistic theory of judicial objectivity fails to describe court decision making:

> The meaning of "due process" and the content of terms like "liberty" are not revealed by the Constitution. It is the Justices who make the meaning. They read into the neutral language of the Constitution their own economic and social views. . . . Let us face the fact that five Justices of the Supreme Court are the molders of policy rather than the impersonal vehicles of revealed truth.[2]

Constitutional Power of the Courts The Constitution grants "the judicial Power of the United States" to the Supreme Court and other "inferior Courts" that Congress may establish. The Constitution guarantees that the Supreme Court and federal judiciary will be politically independent: judges are appointed, not elected, and hold their appointments for life (barring commission of any impeachable offenses). It also guarantees that their salaries will not be reduced during their time in office. The Constitution goes on to list the kinds of cases and controversies that the federal courts may decide. The list is very broad; almost any issue can become a federal case. Federal judicial power extends to any case arising under the Constitution and federal laws and treaties, to cases in which officials of the federal government or of foreign governments are a party, and to cases between states or between citizens of different states.

Interpreting the Constitution: Judicial Review The Constitution is the "supreme Law of the Land" (Article VI). Judicial power is the power to decide cases and controversies and, in doing so, to decide what the Constitution and laws of Congress really mean. This authority—together with the guaranteed independence of judges—places great power in the Supreme Court and the federal judiciary. Indeed, because the Constitution takes precedence over laws of Congress as well as state constitutions and laws, it is the Supreme Court that ultimately decides whether Congress, the president, the states, and their local governments have acted constitutionally.

The power of **judicial review** is the power to invalidate laws of Congress or of the states that conflict with the U.S. Constitution. Judicial review is not specifically mentioned in the Constitution but has long been inferred from it. Even before the states had approved the Constitution, Alexander Hamilton wrote in 1787 that "limited government . . . can be preserved in practice no other way than through the medium of courts of justice, whose duty it is to declare all acts contrary to the manifest tenor of the Constitution void."[3] But it was the historic decision of *Marbury v. Madison* (1803)[4] that officially established judicial review as the most important judicial check on congressional power (see *People in Politics:* "John Marshall and Early Supreme Court Politics"). Writing for the majority, Chief Justice Marshall constructed a classic statement in judicial reasoning as he proceeded step by step to infer judicial review from the Constitution's Supremacy (Article VI) and Judicial Power (Article III, Section 1) Clauses:

- The Constitution is the supreme law of the land, binding on all branches of government: legislative, executive, and judicial.
- The Constitution deliberately establishes a government with limited powers.

judicial review Power of the courts, especially the Supreme Court, to declare laws of Congress, laws of the states, and actions of the president unconstitutional and invalid.

John Marshall and Early Supreme Court Politics

John Marshall was a dedicated Federalist. A prominent Virginia lawyer, he was elected a delegate to Virginia's Constitution-ratifying convention, where he was instrumental in winning his state's approval of the document in 1788. Later Marshall served as secretary of state in the administration of John Adams, where he came into conflict with Adams's vice president, Thomas Jefferson.

In the election of 1800, Jefferson's Democratic-Republicans crushed Adams's Federalist Party. But Adams, taking advantage of the fact that his term of office would not expire until the following March,* sought to pack the federal judiciary with Federalists. The lame duck Federalist majority in the Senate confirmed the appointments, and John Marshall was sworn in as Chief Justice of the Supreme Court on February 4, 1801. Many of these "midnight appointments" came at the very last hours of Adams's term of office.

At that time, a specified task of the secretary of state was to deliver judicial commissions to new judges. When Marshall left his position as secretary of state to become Chief Justice, several of these commissions were still undelivered. Jefferson and the Democratic-Republicans were enraged over this last-minute Federalist chicanery, so when Jefferson assumed office in March, he ordered his new secretary of state, James Madison, not to deliver the remaining commissions. William Marbury, one of the disappointed Federalist appointees, brought a lawsuit to the Supreme Court, asking it to issue a writ of mandamus ("we command") to James Madison, ordering him to do his duty and deliver the valid commission.

The Judiciary Act of 1789, which established the federal court system, had included a provision granting original jurisdiction to the Supreme Court to issue writs of mandamus. The case, therefore, came directly to new Chief Justice John Marshall, who had

failed to deliver the commission in the first place. (Today, we expect justices who are personally involved in a case to "recuse" themselves—that is, not to participate in that case, allowing the other justices to make the decision—but Marshall's actions were typical of his time.)

John Marshall realized that if he issued a direct order to Madison to deliver the commission, Madison would probably ignore it. The Court had no way to enforce such an order, and Madison had the support of President Jefferson. Issuing the writ would create a constitutional crisis in which the Supreme Court would most likely lose power. But if the Court failed to pronounce Madison's actions unlawful, it would lose legitimacy.

Marshall resolved his political dilemma with a brilliant judicial ploy. Writing for the majority in *Marbury v. Madison*, he announced that Madison was wrong to withhold the commission but that the Supreme Court could not issue a writ of mandamus because Section 13 of the Judiciary Act of 1789, which gave the Court *original* jurisdiction in the case, was unconstitutional. Giving the Supreme Court *original* jurisdiction conflicted with Article III, Section 2, of the Constitution, which gives the Supreme Court original jurisdiction only in cases affecting "Ambassadors, other public Ministers and Consuls, and those in which a State shall be a Party." "In all other Cases," the Constitution states that the Court shall have appellate jurisdiction. Thus Section 13 of the Judiciary Act was unconstitutional.

By declaring part of an act of Congress unconstitutional, Marshall accomplished multiple political objectives. He avoided a showdown with the executive branch that would undoubtedly have weakened the Court. He left Jefferson and Madison with no Court order to disobey. At the same time, Marshall forced Jefferson and the Democratic-Republicans to acknowledge the Supreme Court's power of judicial review—the power to declare an act of Congress unconstitutional. (To do otherwise would have meant acknowledging Marbury's claim.) Thus Marshall sacrificed Marbury's commission to a greater political goal, enhancing the Supreme Court's power.

---

*Not until the adoption of the Twentieth Amendment in 1933 was the president's inauguration moved up to January.

- Consequently, "an act of the legislature repugnant to the Constitution is void." If this were not true, the government would be unchecked and the Constitution would be an absurdity.
- Under the judicial power, "It is emphatically the province and duty of each of the judicial departments to say what the law is."
- "So if a law be in opposition to the Constitution . . . the court must determine which of these conflicting rules governs the case. This is the very essence of judicial duty."
- "If, then, the courts are to regard the Constitution, and the Constitution is superior to any ordinary act of the legislature, the Constitution, and not such ordinary act, must govern the case to which they both apply."
- Hence, if a law is repugnant to the Constitution, the judges are duty bound to declare that law void in order to uphold the supremacy of the Constitution.

Arguments over Judicial Review   The power of the federal courts to invalidate *state* laws and constitutions that conflict with federal laws or the federal Constitution is easily defended. Article VI states that the Constitution and federal laws and treaties are the supreme law of the land, "any Thing in the Constitution or Laws of any State to the Contrary notwithstanding." Indeed, the Constitution specifically obligates state judges to be "bound" by the Constitution and federal laws and to give these documents precedence over state constitutions and laws in rendering decisions. Federal court power over state decisions is probably essential to maintaining national unity: fifty different state interpretations of the meaning of the Constitution or of the laws and treaties of Congress would create unimaginable confusion. Thus the power of federal judicial review over state constitutions, laws, and court decisions is seldom questioned.

Today, the power of federal courts to invalidate laws of Congress and actions of the president is also widely accepted. No serious challenge to the power of judicial review has emerged in American politics. But we still might ask: Why should an appointed court's interpretation of the Constitution prevail over the views of an elected Congress and an elected president? Members of Congress and presidents swear to uphold the Constitution, and we can assume they do not pass laws they believe to be unconstitutional. Because both houses of Congress and the president must approve laws, why should federal courts be allowed to set aside these decisions? Is not judicial review, especially by unelected justices appointed for life, undemocratic?

Judicial Review of Laws of Congress   Judicial review is potentially the most powerful weapon in the hands of the Supreme Court. It enables the Court to assert its power over the Congress, the president, and the states and to substitute its own judgment for that of other branches of the federal government and the states. However, the Supreme Court has been fairly restrained in its use of judicial review to void acts of Congress. Prior to the Civil War, the Supreme Court invalidated very few laws of any kind. Since that time, however, the general trend has been for the U.S. Supreme Court to strike down more *state* laws as unconstitutional. In contrast, the Court has been relatively restrained in its rejection of *federal* laws; over two centuries the Court has struck down fewer than 150 of the more than 60,000 laws passed by Congress.

Nevertheless, some of the laws overturned by the Supreme Court have been very important. In 1857 the Court ruled in the case of *Dred Scott v. Sandford*[5] that the Missouri Compromise of 1820, which had restricted the expansion of slavery into U.S. territories, was invalid; this decision helped to bring about the Civil War. The Court overturned several important New Deal laws in the early 1930s in a direct effort to restrict the federal government's role in regulating the economy. The Court's frontal attack on President Franklin Roosevelt and the Democratic Congress created a constitutional crisis when Roosevelt responded with a proposal to "pack" the Court, to increase its traditional nine-member size to fifteen, so that his additional appointees—New Deal supporters—would dominate. (There is no constitutional provision specifying nine members; Congress could, if it chose to do so, change the number of justices on the Court.) The Court reversed its anti–New Deal stance in the late 1930s (inspiring the jibe "A switch in time saved nine") and began to interpret the federal government's powers much more broadly.[6] In *Buckley v. Valeo* (1976),[7] the Court struck down provisions of the Federal Election Campaign Act that had limited the amount individuals could spend to finance their own campaigns or express their own independent political views. In *United States v. Lopez* (1995), the Supreme Court struck down Congress's Gun-Free School Zones Act as an unconstitutional expansion of the interstate commerce power and an invasion of powers reserved to the states. Overall, however, the Supreme Court's use of judicial review against the Congress has been restrained.

Judicial Review of Presidential Actions   The Supreme Court has only rarely challenged presidential power. The Court has overturned presidential policies both on the grounds that they conflicted with laws of Congress and on the grounds that they conflicted with the Constitution. In *Ex parte Milligan* (1866),[8] for example, the Court held (somewhat belatedly) that President Abraham Lincoln could not suspend the writ of habeas corpus in rebellious states during the Civil War. In *Youngstown Sheet and Tube Co. v. Sawyer* in 1952,[9] it declared President Harry Truman's seizure of the nation's steel mills during the Korean War to be illegal. In 1974 it ordered President Richard Nixon to turn over taped White House conversations to the special Watergate prosecutor, leading to Nixon's forced resignation.[10] And in 1998 the Court held that President Bill Clinton was obliged to respond to a civil suit even while serving in office (see *Up Close:* "William Jefferson Clinton versus Paula Corbin Jones" in Chapter 11).

Judicial Review of State Laws   The Supreme Court has used its power of judicial review far more frequently to invalidate state laws. Some of these decisions had impact far beyond the individual states on trial. For example, the historic 1954 decision in *Brown v. Board of Education of Topeka*, declaring segregation of the races in public schools to be unconstitutional, struck down the laws of twenty-one states[11] (see Chapter 15). The 1973 *Roe v. Wade* decision, establishing the constitutional right to abortion, struck down anti-abortion laws in more than forty states.[12]

Interpreting Federal Laws   The power of the Supreme Court and the federal judiciary does not rest on judicial review alone. The courts also make policy in their interpretation of **statutory laws**—the laws of Congress. Frequently, Congress decides that an issue is too contentious to resolve. Members of Congress cannot themselves agree on specific language, so they write, sometimes

statutory laws   Laws made by act of Congress or the state legislatures, as opposed to constitutional law.

deliberately, vague, symbolic language into the law—words and phrases like "fairness," "equitableness," "good faith," "good cause," and "reasonableness"—effectively shifting policy making to the courts by giving courts the power to read meaning into these terms.

The Supreme Court's Policy Agenda   The Supreme Court, and federal courts generally, deal with a very wide range of policy issues. However, the overwhelming majority of cases decided by the Court involve disputes that arise out of government activity—disputes in which a government or a government agency is one party and an individual or firm is the contending party. The Supreme Court dominates policy making in the areas of (1) civil rights and the treatment of women and minorities; (2) the procedural rights of criminal defendants; and (3) freedom of speech, press, and religion. It is estimated that more than half of all the cases decided by the Supreme Court involve these three issue areas.[13] Some of these cases involve interpretations of statutory law, especially the Civil Rights Act of 1964, the Voting Rights Act of 1965, and later amendments of these acts by Congress. But in most civil rights and civil liberties cases, the Court must determine the meaning of the Constitution itself—the meaning of the First Amendment's freedom of speech and press and religion, the meaning of the Equal Protection Clause of the Fourteenth Amendment, and the meaning of the Due Process Clause of the Fifth and Fourteenth Amendments.

The Court is also active in determining the nature of American federalism (see Chapter 4), resolving disputes between states and the federal government. It has also played a key role in refereeing the struggle for power between Congress and the president. Finally, the Court devotes considerable attention to government regulatory activity—environmental protection, banking and securities regulation, labor-management relations. The Supreme Court is noticeably absent from the areas of national defense and international relations, leaving these issues to the president and Congress to resolve.

ACTIVISM VERSUS SELF-RESTRAINT

Supreme Court Justice Felix Frankfurter once wrote: "The only check upon our own exercise of power is our own sense of self-restraint. For the removal of unwise laws from the statute books, appeal lies not to the courts but to the ballot and to the processes of democratic government."[14]

Judicial Self-Restraint   The idea behind **judicial self-restraint** is that judges should not read their own philosophies into the Constitution and should avoid direct confrontations with Congress, the president, and the states whenever possible. The argument for judicial self-restraint is that federal judges are not elected by the people and therefore should not substitute their own views for the views of elected representatives. The courts should defer to the judgments of the other branches of government unless there is a clear violation of constitutional principle. The benefit of the doubt should be given to actions taken by elected officials. Courts should only impose remedies that are narrowly tailored to correct specific legal wrongs. As Justice Sandra Day O'Connor (see *People in Politics:* "Sandra Day O'Connor, Holding the Middle Ground") argued in her Senate confirmation hearings, "The courts should interpret the laws, not make them. . . . I do

judicial self-restraint Self-imposed limitation on judicial power by judges deferring to the policy judgments of elected branches of government.

Sandra Day O'Connor, Holding the Middle Ground

For nearly two hundred years, the U.S. Supreme Court was America's most exclusive all-male club. After 101 male justices, Sandra Day O'Connor was named to the Supreme Court by President Ronald Reagan in 1981. On the high court, O'Connor has succeeded in molding a moderate bloc of votes that holds the balance of power on the Supreme Court between liberal and conservative blocs. More important, perhaps, O'Connor has taken the lead in shaping Court policy on women's issues, including the most controversial issue of all—abortion.

Sandra Day grew up on her family's large Arizona ranch, graduated from Stanford with honors, and went on to Stanford Law School, where she finished near the top of her class (along with now Chief Justice of the Supreme Court William Rehnquist, who was first in the class). After graduation, she married John Jay O'Connor, a Phoenix attorney, and had three sons. She entered Arizona politics about the time her youngest son entered school. In 1969 she was appointed to fill a vacancy in the Arizona state senate and was later elected twice to that body, where she rose to become majority leader in 1973. She left the Arizona legislature in 1975 to become a Phoenix trial judge and in 1979 was appointed by a Democratic governor to the Arizona Court of Appeals, an intermediate court that does not hear major constitutional issues.

O'Connor had some business experience: she was formerly a director of the First National Bank of Arizona and Blue Cross/Blue Shield of Arizona. But until her appointment to the U.S. Supreme Court, she was an obscure state court judge. Her service as a Republican leader in the Arizona state senate qualified her as a moderately conservative party loyalist. However, it appears that her professional and political friendships had more to do with bringing her to President Ronald Reagan's attention than her record as a jurist. She had known both Justice Rehnquist and former Chief Justice Warren Burger for many years, and Barry Goldwater, Arizona's senior U.S. senator and Republican warhorse, had been her mentor in Arizona Republican politics. When Reagan's political advisers told him during the presidential campaign that he was not doing well among women voters (he opposed the Equal Rights Amendment), he responded by pledging to appoint a woman to the Supreme Court. Reagan's fulfillment of his campaign pledge was a politically popular decision. Feminist groups felt forced to support the appointment, even though O'Connor's record in Arizona was moderately conservative.

In her early Court deliberations, Justice O'Connor generally reflected the moderate conservatism of recent Republican appointees, but on gender questions she took an independent role from the beginning. Over time, her independent course has made her a swing vote on many key policy issues, from affirmative action to abortion. Indeed, her leadership of the Court on the abortion issue has preserved the constitutional right to abortion.

---

not believe it is a function of the Court to step in because times have changed or social mores have changed."[15]

Wisdom versus Constitutionality A law may be unwise, unjust, or even stupid and yet still be constitutional. One should not equate the wisdom of a law with its constitutionality, and the Court should decide only the constitutionality and not the wisdom of a law. Justice Oliver Wendell Holmes once lectured a younger colleague, sixty-one-year-old Justice Harlan Stone, on this point:

> Young man, about 75 years ago I learned that I was not God. And so, when the people . . . want to do something I can't find anything in the Constitution expressly forbidding them to do, I say, whether I like it or not, "Goddamn it, let 'em do it."[16]

However, the actual role of the Supreme Court in the nation's power struggles suggests that the Court indeed often equates wisdom with constitutionality. People frequently cite broad phrases in the Fifth and Fourteenth Amendments establishing constitutional standards of "due process of law" and "equal protection of the laws" when attacking laws they believe are unfair or unjust. Most Americans have come to believe that unwise laws must be unconstitutional. If so, then the courts must be the final arbiters of fairness and justice.

Original Intent   Should the Constitution be interpreted in terms of the intentions of the Founders or according to the morality of society today? Most jurists agree the Constitution is a living document, that it must be interpreted by each generation in the light of current conditions, and to do otherwise would soon render the document obsolete. But in interpreting the document, whose values should prevail—the values of the judges or the values of the Founders? The doctrine of **original intent** takes the values of the Founders as expressed in the text of the Constitution and attempts to apply these values to current conditions. Defenders of original intent argue that the words in the document must be given their historical meaning and that meaning must restrain the courts as well as the legislative and executive branches of government. That is, the Supreme Court should not set aside laws made by elected representatives unless they conflict with the original intent of the Founders. Judges who set aside laws that do not accord with their personal views of today's moral standards are simply substituting their own morality for that of elected bodies. Such decisions lack democratic legitimacy because there is no reason why judges' moral views should prevail over those of elected representatives.

Judicial Activism   However, the doctrine of original intent carries little weight with proponents of judicial activism. The idea behind **judicial activism** is that the Constitution is a living document whose strength lies in its flexibility, and judges should shape constitutional meaning to fit the needs of contemporary society. The argument for judicial activism is that viewing the Constitution as a broad and flexible document saves the nation from having to pass dozens of new constitutional amendments to accommodate changes in society. Instead, the courts need to give contemporary interpretations to constitutional phrases, particularly general phrases such as "due process of law" (Fifth Amendment), "equal protection of the laws" (Fourteenth Amendment), "establishment of religion" (First Amendment), and "cruel and unusual punishment" (Eighth Amendment). Courts have the responsibility to review the actions of other branches of government vigorously, to strike down unconstitutional acts, and to impose far-reaching remedies for legal wrongs whenever necessary.[17]

Stare Decisis   Conflicts between judicial activism and judicial self-restraint are underscored by questions of whether to let past decisions stand or to find constitutional support for overturning them. The principle of **stare decisis**, which means the issue has already been decided in earlier cases, is a fundamental notion in law. Reliance on **precedent** gives stability to the law; if every decision were new law, then no one would know what the law is from day to day. Yet the Supreme Court has discarded precedent in many of its most important decisions: *Brown v. Board of Education* (1954), which struck down laws segregating the races; *Baker v. Carr* (1962), which guaranteed equal representation in legislatures; *Roe v. Wade* (1973), which made abortion a constitutional right; and many other classic cases. Former Justice William O. Douglas, a defender of judicial activism, justified disregard of precedent as follows:

original intent   Judicial philosophy under which judges attempt to apply the values of the Founders to current issues.

judicial activism   Making of new law through judicial interpretations of the Constitution.

stare decisis   Judicial precept that the issue has already been decided in earlier cases and the earlier decision need only be applied in the specific case before the bench; the rule in most cases, it comes from the Latin for "the decision stands."

precedent   Legal principle that previous decisions should determine the outcome of current cases; the basis for stability in law.

The decisions of yesterday or of the last century are only the starting points. . . . A judge looking at a constitutional decision may have compulsions to revere the past history and accept what was once written. But he remembers above all else that it is the Constitution which he swore to support and defend, not the gloss which his predecessors may have put on it. So he comes to formulate his own laws, rejecting some earlier ones as false and embracing others. He cannot do otherwise unless he lets men long dead and unaware of the problems of the age in which he lives do his thinking for him.[18]

Rules of Restraint   Even an activist Supreme Court adheres to some general rules of judicial self-restraint, however, including the following:

- The Court will pass on the constitutionality of legislation only in an actual case; it will not advise the president or Congress on constitutional questions.
- The Court will not anticipate a question on constitutional law; it does not decide hypothetical cases.
- The Court will not formulate a rule of constitutional law broader than that required by the precise facts to which it must be applied.
- The Court will not decide on a constitutional question if some other ground exists on which it may dispose of the case.
- The Court will not decide on the validity of a law if the complainants fail to show that they have been injured by the law.
- When doubt exists about the constitutionality of a law, the Court will try to interpret the law so as to give it a constitutional meaning and avoid the necessity of declaring it unconstitutional.
- Complainants must have exhausted all remedies available in lower federal courts or state courts before the Supreme Court will accept review.
- The Court will invalidate a law only when a constitutional issue is crucial to the case and is substantial, not trivial.
- Occasionally the Court defers to Congress and the president, classifies an issue as a political question, and refuses to decide it. The Court has generally stayed out of foreign and military policy areas.
- If the Court holds a law unconstitutional, it will confine its decision to the particular section of the law that is unconstitutional; the rest of the statute stays intact.

STRUCTURE AND JURISDICTION OF FEDERAL COURTS

The federal court system consists of three levels of courts—the Supreme Court, the Courts of Appeals, and the district courts—together with various special courts (see Figure 13–1 on page 472). Only the Supreme Court is established by the Constitution, although the number of justices is determined by Congress. Article III authorizes Congress to establish such "inferior Courts" as it deems appropriate. Congress has designed a hierarchical system with a U.S. Court of Appeals divided into 12 regional circuit courts, a federal circuit, and 89 district courts in the fifty states and one each in Puerto Rico and the District of Columbia. Table 13–1 on page 473 describes their **jurisdiction** and distinguishes between **original jurisdiction**—where cases are begun, argued, and initially decided—and **appellate jurisdiction**—where cases begun in lower courts are argued and decided on **appeal**.

jurisdiction   Power of a court to hear a case in question.

original jurisdiction Refers to a particular court's power to serve as the place where a given case is initially argued and decided.

appellate jurisdiction Particular court's power to review a decision or action of a lower court.

appeal   In general, requests that a higher court review cases decided at a lower level. In the Supreme Court, certain cases are designated as appeals under federal law; formally, these must be heard by the Court.

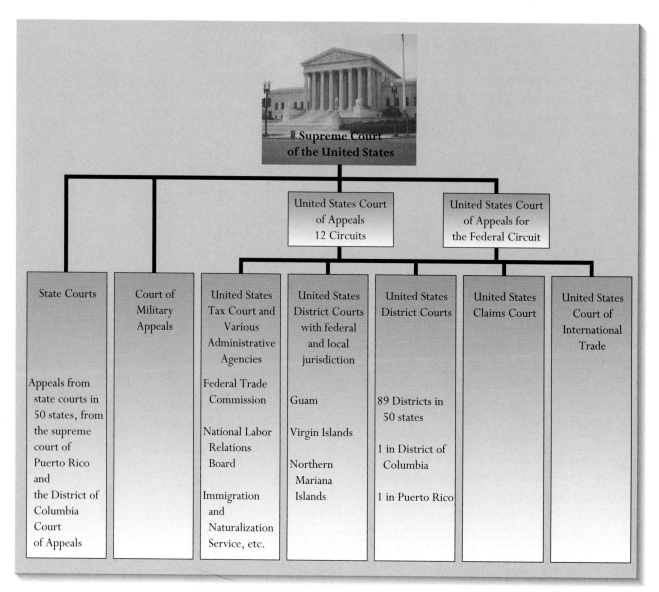

FIGURE 13-1 Structure of Federal Courts

The federal court system of the United States is divided into three levels: the courts of original jurisdiction (state courts, military courts, tax courts, district courts, claims courts, and international trade courts); U.S. Courts of Appeals (which hear appeals from all lower courts except state and military panels); and the U.S. Supreme Court, which can hear appeals from all sources.

The Supreme Court is the "court of last resort" in the United States, but it hears only a very small number of cases each year. In a handful of cases, the Supreme Court has original jurisdiction; these concern primarily disputes between states (or states and residents of other states), disputes between a state and the federal government, and disputes involving foreign dignitaries. However, most Supreme Court cases are appellate decisions involving cases from state supreme courts or cases tried first in a U.S. District Court.

district courts Original jurisdiction trial courts of the federal system.

District Courts **District courts** are the original jurisdiction trial courts of the federal system. Each state has at least one district court, and larger states have more (New York, for example, has four). There are more than six hundred federal

Table 13-1   Jurisdiction of Federal Courts

Supreme Court of the United States	United States Courts of Appeals	United States District Courts
Appellate jurisdiction (cases begin in a lower court); hears appeals, at its own discretion, from: 1. Lower federal courts 2. Highest state courts Original jurisdiction (cases begin in the Supreme Court) over cases involving: 1. Two or more states 2. The United States and a state 3. Foreign ambassadors and other diplomats 4. A state and a citizen of a different state (if begun by the state)	No original jurisdiction; hear only appeals from: 1. Federal district courts 2. U.S. regulatory commissions 3. Certain other federal courts	Original jurisdiction over cases involving: 1. Federal crimes 2. Civil suits under the federal law 3. Civil suits between citizens of states where the amount exceeds $50,000 4. Admiralty and maritime cases 5. Bankruptcy cases 6. Review of actions of certain federal administrative agencies 7. Other matters assigned to them by Congress

district judges, each appointed for life by the president and confirmed by the Senate. The president also appoints a U.S. marshall for each district to carry out orders of the court and maintain order in the courtroom. District courts hear criminal cases prosecuted by the Department of Justice as well as civil cases. As trial courts, the district courts make use of both **grand juries** (called to hear evidence and, if warranted, to indict a defendant by bringing formal criminal charges) and **petit (regular) juries** (which determine guilt or innocence). District courts may hear as many as 300,000 cases in a year, including 50,000 criminal cases.

Courts of Appeals   Federal **circuit courts** (see *Across the USA:* "Geographic Boundaries of Federal Courts" on page 474) are appellate courts. They do not hold trials or accept new evidence but consider only the records of the trial courts and oral or written arguments (**briefs**) submitted by attorneys. Federal law guarantees everyone the right to appeal, so the Court of Appeals has little discretion in this regard. Appellate judges themselves estimate that more than 80 percent of all appeals are frivolous—that is, without any real basis. There are more than a hundred circuit judges, each appointed for life by the president subject to confirmation by the Senate. Normally, these judges serve together on a panel to hear appeals. More than 90 percent of the cases decided by the Court of Appeals end at this level. Further appeal to the Supreme Court is not automatic; it must be approved by the Supreme Court itself. Because the Supreme Court hears very few cases, in most cases the decision of the circuit court becomes law.

Supreme Court   The Supreme Court of the United States is the final interpreter of all matters involving the Constitution and federal laws and treaties, whether the case began in a federal district court or in a state court. Appeals to the U.S. Supreme Court may come from a state court of last resort (usually a state's supreme court) or from lower federal courts. The Supreme Court determines whether to accept an appeal and consider a case. It may do so when there is a "substantial federal question" presented in a case or when there are "special and important reasons," or it may reject a case—with or without explaining why.

grand juries   Juries called to hear evidence and decide whether defendants should be indicted and tried.

petit (regular) juries   Juries called to determine guilt or innocence.

circuit courts   The twelve appellate courts that make up the middle level of the federal court system.

briefs   Documents submitted by an attorney to a court, setting out the facts of the case and the legal arguments in support of the party represented by the attorney.

Geographic Boundaries of Federal Courts

For administrative convenience, the U.S. District Courts are organized into twelve circuits (regions), plus the Federal Circuit (Washington, D.C.). Within each region, circuit court judges form panels to hear appeals from district courts. U.S. Circuit Courts of Appeal are numbered. U.S. District Courts are named for geographic regions of the states (East, West, North, South, Middle), for example, U.S. District Court for Northern California.

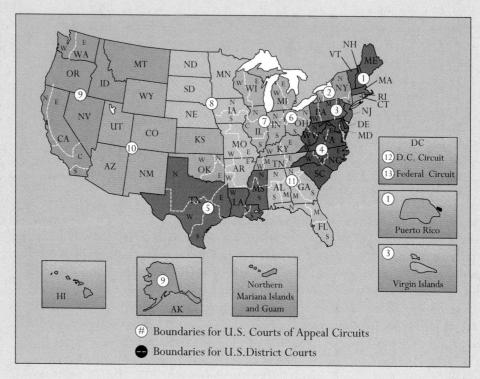

Boundaries for U.S. Courts of Appeal Circuits
Boundaries for U.S. District Courts

In the early days of the Republic, the size of the Supreme Court fluctuated, but since 1869 the membership has remained at nine: the Chief Justice and eight associate justices. The Supreme Court is in session each year from October through June, hearing oral arguments, accepting written briefs, conferring, and rendering opinions.

Appeals from State Courts   Each of the fifty states maintains its own courts. The federal courts are not necessarily superior to those courts; state and federal courts operate independently. State courts have original jurisdiction in most criminal and civil cases. Because the U.S. Supreme Court has appellate jurisdiction over state supreme courts as well as over lower federal courts, the Supreme Court oversees the nation's entire judicial system, but the great bulk of cases begin and end in the state court systems. The federal courts do not interfere once a case has been started in a state court except in very rare circumstances. And Congress has stipulated that legal disputes between citizens of different states must involve $50,000 or more to be heard in federal courts. Moreover, parties to cases in state courts must "exhaust their remedies"—that is, appeal their case all the way through the state court system—before the federal courts will hear an appeal. Appeals from state supreme courts go directly to the U.S. Supreme Court and not to a federal district or circuit court. Such appeals are usually made on the grounds that a federal question is involved in the case—that is, a question has arisen regarding the application of the Constitution or a federal law.

Federal Cases   Some 10 million civil and criminal cases are begun in the nation's courts each year (see *A Conflicting View:* "America Drowning Itself in a Sea of Lawsuits" on page 476). Fewer than 300,000 (3 percent) of the cases are begun in the federal courts. About 7,000 are appealed to the Supreme Court each year, but only about 100 of them are openly argued and decided by signed opinions. The Constitution "reserves" general police powers to the states. That is, civil disputes and most crimes—murder, robbery, assault, and rape—are normally state offenses rather than federal crimes and thus are tried in state and local courts.

Federal court caseloads have risen in recent years (see Figure 13–2 on page 477), in part because more civil disputes are being brought to federal courts. In addition, the U.S. Justice Department is prosecuting more criminal cases as federal law enforcement agencies—such as the Federal Bureau of Investigation (FBI), Drug Enforcement Administration (DEA), Internal Revenue Service (IRS), and Bureau of Alcohol, Tobacco and Firearms (ATF)—have stepped up their investigations. Most of this recent increase is attributable to enforcement of federal drug laws.

Traditionally, federal crimes were offenses directed against the U.S. government, its property, or its employees or were offenses involving the crossing of state lines. Over the years, however, Congress has greatly expanded the list of federal crimes so that federal and state criminal court jurisdictions often overlap, as they do, for example, in most drug violations.

Justices of the Supreme Court. Front row, from the left: Antonin Scalia, John Paul Stevens, Chief Justice William Rehnquist, Sandra Day O'Connor, and Anthony Kennedy. Back row, from the left: Ruth Bader Ginsburg, David Souter, Clarence Thomas, and Stephen Breyer.

America Is Drowning Itself in a Sea of Lawsuits

America is threatening to drown itself in a sea of lawsuits. Civil suits in the nation's courts exceed 10 *million* per year. There are more than 805,000 lawyers in the United States (compared to about 650,000 physicians). These lawyers are in business, and their business is litigation. Generating business means generating lawsuits. And just as businesses search for new products, lawyers search for new legal principles on which to bring lawsuits. They seek to expand legal liability for civil actions—that is, to expand the definition of civil wrongdoings, or torts.

Unquestionably, the threat of lawsuits is an important safeguard for society, compelling individuals, corporations, and government agencies to behave responsibly toward others. Because victims require compensation for *actual* damages incurred by the wrongdoing of others, liability laws protect all of us.

But we need to consider the social costs of frivolous lawsuits, especially those brought without any merit but initiated in the hope that individuals or firms will offer a settlement just to avoid the expenses of defending themselves. Legal expenses and excessive jury awards leveled against corporations increase insurance premiums for businesses and service providers. The Insurance Information Institute estimates that the overall costs of civil litigation in America is many times more than that of other industrial nations, perhaps amounting to over 2 percent of our nation's GDP. For example, the risk of lawsuits forces physicians to practice "defensive medicine," ordering expensive tests, multiple consultations with specialists, and expensive procedures, not because they are adjudged medically necessary, but rather to protect themselves from the possibility of a lawsuit.

Product Liability   The threat of lawsuits discourages new products from entering the marketplace. Virtually any accident involving a commercial product can inspire a product liability suit. An individual who gets cut opening a can of peas can sue the canning company. A woman who spills hot coffee on herself while driving sues the fast-food restaurant for making the coffee too hot. Hotels pay damages to persons raped in their rooms.

Third-Party Suits   Defendants in civil cases are not necessarily the parties directly responsible for damages to the plaintiff. Instead, wealthier third parties, who may indirectly contribute to an accident, are favorite targets of lawsuits. For example, if a drunk driver injures a pedestrian but the driver has only limited insurance and small personal wealth, a shrewd attorney will sue the bar that sold the driver the drinks instead of the driver. Insurance premiums have risen sharply for physicians seeking malpractice insurance, as have premiums for recreation facilities, nurseries and day-care centers, motels, and restaurants.

"Pain and Suffering" Awards   High jury awards in liability cases, sometimes running into tens of millions of dollars, cover much more than the doctor bills, lost wages, and cost of future care for injured parties. Most large damage awards are for *pain and suffering*. Pain and suffering awards are *added* compensation for the victim, beyond actual costs for medical care and lost wages.

"Joint and Severable" Liability   A legal rule known as *joint and severable liability* allows a plaintiff to collect the entire award from any party that contributed in any way to an accident if other defendants cannot pay. If, for example, a drunk driver crosses a median strip and crashes into another car, leaving its driver crippled, the victim may sue the city for not placing a guard railing in the median strip. The rule encourages trial lawyers to sue the party "with the deepest pockets," that is, the wealthiest party rather than the party most responsible for the accident.

Reform Politics   Reforming the nation's liability laws presents major challenges to the political system. The reform movement can count on support from some normally powerful interest groups—insurance companies, manufacturers, drug companies, hospitals, and physicians. But legal reform is an anathema to the legal profession itself, notably the powerful Association of Trial Lawyers. And lawyers compose the single largest occupational background of Congress members—indeed, of politicians generally.

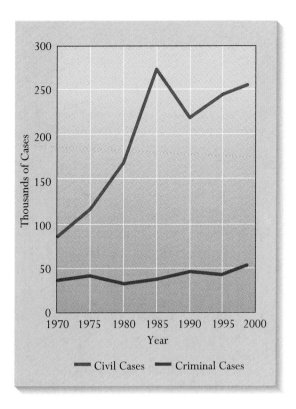

FIGURE 13-2 Caseloads in Federal Courts

Increasing caseloads in the federal courts have placed a heavy burden on prosecutors and judges. Although the increase in civil suits in the federal courts is the result of more plaintiffs insisting on taking their cases to the federal level both originally and on appeal, the increase in criminal cases is the result of Congress's decision to make more crimes—especially drug-related crimes—federal offenses and to pursue such criminals more vigorously.

THE SPECIAL RULES OF JUDICIAL DECISION MAKING

Courts are political institutions that resolve conflict and decide about public policy. But unlike Congress, the presidency, and the bureaucracy, the courts employ highly specialized rules in going about their work.

Cases and Controversies   One overriding characteristic of the way courts work is that they do not initiate policy but rather wait until a case or controversy is brought to them for resolution. A case must involve two disputing parties, one of which must have incurred some real damage as a result of the action or inaction of the other. Federal courts do *not* render "advisory" opinions about pending legislation or executive actions. They do *not* issue policy declarations or decide hypothetical cases. Federal courts do *not* render opinions about whether or not proposed laws of Congress are constitutional. Rather, the courts wait until disputing parties bring a case to them that requires them to interpret the meaning of a law or determine its constitutionality in order to resolve the case. Only then do courts render opinions.

The vast majority of cases do *not* involve important policy issues. Courts determine the guilt or innocence of criminal defendants. Courts enforce contracts and award damages to victims of negligence in **civil cases**. And courts render these decisions on the basis of established law. Only occasionally do courts make significant policy decisions.

Adversarial Proceedings   Underlying judicial decision making is the assumption that the best way to decide an issue is to allow two disputing parties to present arguments on each side. Judges in the United States do not investigate cases, ques-

civil cases Noncriminal court proceedings in which a plaintiff sues a defendant for damages in payment for harm inflicted.

tion witnesses, or develop arguments themselves (as they do in some European countries). This **adversarial system** depends on quality of argument on each side, which means it often depends on the capabilities of attorneys. There is no guarantee that the adversarial process will produce the best policy outcomes.

Standing   To bring an issue into court as a case, individuals or firms or interest groups must have **standing**; that is, they must be directly harmed by a law or action. People cannot "go to court" simply because they do not like what the government is doing. Merely being taxpayers does not entitle people to claim that they are damaged by government actions.[19] Individuals or firms automatically have standing when they are prosecuted by the government for violation of laws or regulations. Thus one way to gain standing in order to challenge the legality of a regulation or the constitutionality of a law is to violate the regulation or law and invite the government to prosecute.

To sue the government, plaintiffs must show they have suffered financial damages, loss of property, or physical or emotional harm as a direct result of the government's action. (The party initiating a suit and claiming damages is the **plaintiff**; the party against whom a suit is brought is the **defendant**.) The ancient legal doctrine of **sovereign immunity** means that one cannot sue the government without the government's consent. But by law, the U.S. government allows itself to be sued in a wide variety of contract and negligence cases. A citizen can also personally sue to force government officials to carry out acts that they are required by law to perform or for acting contrary to law. The government does not allow suits for damages as a result of military actions.

Class Action Suits   **Class action suits** are cases brought into court by individuals on behalf not only of themselves but also of all other persons "similarly situated." That is, the party bringing the case is acting on behalf of a "class" of people who have suffered the same damages from the same actions of the defendant. One of the most famous and far-reaching class action suits was *Brown v. Board of Education of Topeka* (1954). The plaintiff, Linda Brown of Topeka, Kansas, sued her local board of education on behalf of herself and all other black pupils who were forced to attend segregated schools, charging that such schools violated the Equal Protection Clause of the Fourteenth Amendment. When she won the case, the Court's ruling affected not only Linda Brown and the segregated public schools in Topeka but also all other black pupils similarly situated across the nation (see Chapter 15).

Since the *Brown* case, class action suits have grown in popularity. These suits have enabled attorneys and interest groups to bring multimillion-dollar suits against corporations and governments for damages to large numbers of people, even when none of them has individually suffered sufficient harm to merit bringing a case to court. For example, an individual overcharged by an electric utility would not want to incur the expense of suing for the return of a few dollars. But if attorneys sue the utility on behalf of a large number of customers similarly overcharged, the result may be a multimillion-dollar settlement from which the attorneys can deduct their hefty fees. In recent years, the courts have tightened the rules governing class action suits in order to stem the huge tide of suits generated by the legal profession. Today, federal courts generally require attorneys bringing class action suits to notify each member of the class on whose behalf the case is said to be brought.

adversarial system   Method of decision making in which an impartial judge or jury or decision maker hears arguments and reviews evidence presented by opposite sides.

standing   Requirement that the party who files a lawsuit have a legal stake in the outcome.

plaintiffs   Parties initiating suits and claiming damages. In criminal cases, the state acts as plaintiff on behalf of an injured society and requests fines and/or imprisonment as damages. In civil suits, the plaintiff is the injured party and seeks monetary damages.

defendants   Parties against whom a criminal or civil suit is brought.

sovereign immunity   Legal doctrine that individuals can sue the government only with the government's consent.

class action suits   Cases initiated by parties acting on behalf of themselves and all others similarly situated.

Class action suits initiated by attorneys or interest groups on behalf of large numbers of people are increasingly popular. Here an attorney announces a suit against the nation's tobacco companies on behalf of flight attendants previously subjected to smoke.

Legal Fees Going to court requires financial resources. Criminal defendants are guaranteed an attorney, without charge if they are poor, by the Sixth Amendment's guarantee of "Assistance of Counsel" (see Chapter 14).[20] However, persons who wish to bring a *civil* suit against governments or corporations must still arrange for the payment of legal fees. The most common arrangement is the **contingency fee**, in which plaintiffs agree to pay expenses and share one-third or more of the money damages with their lawyers if the case is won. If the case is lost, neither plaintiffs nor their lawyers receive anything for their labors. Lawyers do not usually participate in such arrangements unless the prospects for winning the case are good and the promised monetary reward is substantial. Civil suits against the government have increased since Congress enacted a law requiring governments to pay the attorneys' fees of citizens who successfully bring suit against public officials for violation of their constitutional rights.

Remedies and Relief Judicial power has vastly expanded through court determination of **remedies and relief**. These are the orders of a court following a decision that are designed to correct a wrong. In most cases, judges simply fine or sentence criminal defendants to jail or order losing defendants in civil suits to pay monetary damages to the winning plaintiffs. In recent years, however, federal district court judges have issued sweeping orders to governments to correct constitutional violations. For example, a federal district judge took over operation of the Boston public schools for more than ten years to remedy *de facto* (an existing, although not necessarily deliberate, pattern of) racial segregation. A federal district judge ordered the city of Yonkers, New York, to build public housing in white neighborhoods. A federal district judge took over the operation of the Alabama prison system to ensure proper prisoner treatment. A federal district judge ordered the Kansas City, Missouri, school board to increase taxes to pay for his desegregation plan. (This case reached the Supreme Court, which held that a federal court does have the power to levy taxes—a power reserved to the legislature in English-speaking countries for centuries—when necessary to implement a constitutional guarantee.)[21]

contingency fees Fees paid to attorneys to represent the plaintiff in a civil suit and receive in compensation an agreed-upon percentage of damages awarded (if any).

remedies and reliefs Orders of a court to correct a wrong, including a violation of the Constitution.

Appointments of Independent Counsels?   The Ethics in Government Act of 1978 granted federal courts the power, upon request of the attorney general, to appoint an independent counsel or "special prosecutor" to investigate and prosecute violations of federal law by the president and other high officials. Congress allowed the Act to expire in 1999 following the lengthy and expensive investigation of President Clinton by independent counsel Kenneth Starr (see *What Do You Think?* "Do We Need Special Prosecutors to Investigate Presidents?").

THE POLITICS OF SELECTING JUDGES

The Constitution specifies that all federal judges, including justices of the Supreme Court, shall be appointed by the president and confirmed by a majority vote of the Senate. Judicial recruitment is a political process: presidents almost always appoint members of their own party to the federal courts. More than 80 percent of federal judges have held some political office prior to their appointment to the court. More important, political philosophy now plays a major role in the selection of judges. Thus the appointment of federal judges has increasingly become an arena for conflict between presidents and their political opponents in the Senate.

The Politics of Presidential Selection   Presidents have a strong motivation to select judges who share their political philosophy. Judicial appointments are made for life. The Constitution stipulates that federal judges "shall hold their Offices during good Behaviour." Although a rather vague phrase, it has come to mean a virtually guaranteed life term. A president cannot remove a judge for any reason, and Congress cannot impeach judges just because it dislikes their decisions.

This independence of the judiciary has often frustrated presidents and Congresses. Presidents who have appointed people they thought were liberals or conservatives to the Supreme Court have sometimes been surprised by the decisions of their appointees. An estimated one-quarter of the justices of the Supreme Court have deviated from the political expectations of the presidents who appointed them.[22] For example, Chief Justice Earl Warren, perhaps the most liberal and activist chief justice in the Court's history, was appointed by Republican President Dwight Eisenhower. Previously the governor of California, Warren lacked judicial experience and received his appointment as a reward for swinging his state's delegation to Eisenhower at the 1952 Republican national convention. Eisenhower later complained that the Warren appointment was "the biggest damn mistake I ever made."

It is important to recognize that presidents' use of political criteria in selecting judges has a democratic influence on the courts. Presidents can campaign on the pledge to make the courts more liberal or conservative through their appointive powers, and voters are free to cast their ballots on the basis of this pledge.

litmus test   In political terms, a person's stand on a key issue that determines whether he or she will be appointed to public office or supported in electoral campaigns.

Political Litmus Test   Traditionally, presidents and senators have tried to discern where a Supreme Court candidate fits on the continuum of liberal activism versus conservative self-restraint. Democratic presidents and senators usually prefer liberal judges who express an activist philosophy. Republican presidents usually prefer conservative judges who express a philosophy of judicial self-restraint. Until very recently, both the president and the Senate denied using any political "litmus test" in judicial recruitment. A **litmus test** generally refers to recruitment based on a nominee's stand on a single issue. Since the Supreme Court

Do We Need Special Prosecutors to Investigate Presidents?

The Ethics in Government Act of 1978, passed in the wake of the Watergate scandal in the Nixon Administration, provided for the appointment of an independent counsel (special prosecutor) to investigate alleged crimes by the president and other high officials. The goal was to *take politics out of* the investigation of wrongdoing in high places. (Nixon had fired Attorney General Elliot Richardson and Justice Department prosecutor Archibald Cox in 1973 for investigating Watergate.) The act, generally referred to as the independent counsel law, obliged the attorney general "upon specific and credible evidence of federal crime" by a high government official to ask a three-judge federal panel to appoint an independent counsel from outside the Justice Department and to define the counsel's scope of investigation. The independent counsel was authorized to conduct the investigation, bring indictments, and prosecute cases in federal court.

The independent counsel law was challenged in the U.S. Supreme Court as a transferral of executive power ("to take care that the laws be faithfully executed"—Article II) to the judicial branch of government in violation of the separation of powers in the U.S. Constitution.* But the Court upheld the law, noting that the attorney general, an executive branch official appointed by the president, had to request the judiciary to appoint the independent counsel.

Whatever the original intent of the act, special prosecutors were often accused of *bringing politics into* the criminal justice system. Indeed, special prosecutor Kenneth Starr's dogged pursuit of Bill and Hillary Clinton was deemed a "witch-hunt" by friends of the president. The First Lady linked Starr to "a vast right-wing conspiracy" trying to reverse the outcome of two presidential elections.

Starr was appointed in 1994 with a mandate to investigate crimes stemming from the Clintons' relation with Whitewater Development Corporation, an Arkansas land development firm owned in part by the Clintons while Bill Clinton was governor. However, over the years, Starr successfully petitioned the three-judge federal oversight panel to expand his investiga-

tion to include the suicide of White House official Vince Foster, the firing of seven White House travel office employees, and the alleged misuse of FBI background files. And in early 1998, Starr's investigation was expanded again to include whether or not President Clinton committed perjury or asked others to do so in an effort to cover up sexual affairs. His investigatory methods included keeping former Clinton business partner Susan McDougal in jail for over a year, and threatening to bring perjury and obstruction of justice charges against Monica Lewinsky, her mother, and others to force them to testify against Clinton. His recommendation to the House to impeach President Clinton went well beyond anything originally envisioned by the authors of the Ethics in Government Act.

Congress allowed the independent counsel law to lapse in 1999. Democrats, infuriated by Starr's investigations, joined Republicans, who had earlier complained when Reagan and Bush administration officials were the targets of prosecution, in killing the Act. Most of the investigations by special counsels over the years had ended with no charges being filed against anyone. Many of those who were charged were *not* government officials but rather people only peripherally involved in the matters under investigation. Hundreds of innocent people had their bank accounts emptied defending themselves. With no limits on time or money to spend on investigations, special prosecutors frequently expanded their activities well beyond the original allegations into what critics call "witch hunts" or "fishing expeditions." As one observer complained: "If I have three FBI agents, three IRS agents, an unlimited amount of time, and an unlimited amount of money, I can indict anybody." Getting rid of the law, said its opponents, will help to "decriminalize" politics in Washington.

Any efforts to revive the independent counsel law will no doubt place limits on investigations, perhaps by reducing the number of officials covered to the president, vice president, and cabinet; or by limiting the time and money that can be spent; or by preventing special prosecutors from expanding investigations beyond the original allegations. But agreement on a new law is unlikely. Currently, the Attorney General has authority to appoint and remove special prosecutors and oversee their investigations.

Morrison v. Olson, 487 U.S. 654 (1988).

ruling on *Roe v. Wade* (1973), however, the single issue of abortion has come to dominate the politics of judicial recruitment. Although Presidents Ronald Reagan and George Bush denied applying a litmus test on this issue, many observers believe their nominees were selected with the expectation that they would help reverse *Roe v. Wade*. President Clinton was forthright in his pledge to nominate only justices who specifically support the *Roe v. Wade* decision.

Competence and Ethics   Although competence and ethics may be of lesser importance than party and political philosophy, they are serious considerations for the attorney general and Justice Department as they assist the president in screening nominees for federal judgeships. Given the close scrutiny to which the media and the Senate now subject nominees, even minor violations of laws or moral standards can lead to Senate rejection, especially when senators dislike a candidate's judicial philosophy. Questions of competence and ethics can seldom be separated from politics.

The Politics of Senate Confirmation   All presidential nominations for the federal judiciary, including the Supreme Court, are sent to the Senate for confirmation. The Senate refers them to its powerful Judiciary Committee, which holds hearings, votes on the nomination, and then reports to the full Senate, where floor debate may precede the final confirmation vote.

The Senate's involvement in federal district judgeships traditionally centered on the practice of **senatorial courtesy**. If senators from the president's party from the same state for which an appointment was being considered disapproved of a nominee, their Senate colleagues would defeat the nomination. But if the president and senators from that party agreed on the nomination, the full Senate, even if controlled by the opposition, customarily confirmed the nomination. During the Reagan-Bush years, however, partisan divisions between these Republican presidents and Senate Democrats eroded the tradition of senatorial courtesy.

Supreme Court nominations have always received close political scrutiny in the Senate. Over the last two centuries, the Senate has rejected or refused to confirm about 20 percent of presidential nominees to the high court, but only five nominees in this century (see Table 13–2). In the past, most senators believed that presidents deserved to appoint their own judges; the opposition party would get its own opportunity to appoint judges when it won the presidency. Only if the Senate found some personal disqualification in a nominee's background (for example, financial scandal, evidence of racial or religious bias, judicial incompetence) would a nominee likely be rejected. But publicity and partisanship over confirmation of Supreme Court nominees have increased markedly in recent years.[23]

The Bork Battle   The U.S. Senate's rejection of President Ronald Reagan's nomination of Judge Robert H. Bork in 1987 set a new precedent in Senate confirmation of Supreme Court nominees. The Senate rejected Bork because of his views, not because he lacked judicial qualifications. Bork had a reputation for "conservative activism"—a desire better to reflect the "original intent" of the Constitution's framers by rolling back some of the Supreme Court's broad interpretations of privacy rights, free speech, and equal protection of the law. Perhaps most controversial were his views on *Roe v. Wade*; he had labeled the Court's striking down of state laws prohibiting abortion as "wholly unjustifiable judicial usurpation of state legislative authority."

Unlike previous nominees, Bork was subjected by the Senate Judiciary Committee to extensive case-by-case questioning in nationally televised confirmation hear-

senatorial courtesy
Custom of the U.S. Senate with regard to presidential nominations to the judiciary to defer to the judgment of senators from the president's party from the same state as the nominee.

Table 13-2 Senate Confirmation Votes on Supreme Court Nominations since 1950

Nominee	President	Year	Vote
Earl Warren	Eisenhower	1954	NRV*
John Marshall Harlan	Eisenhower	1955	71–11
William J. Brennan	Eisenhower	1957	NRV
Charles Whittaker	Eisenhower	1957	NRV
Potter Stewart	Eisenhower	1959	70–17
Byron White	Kennedy	1962	NRV
Arthur Goldberg	Kennedy	1962	NRV
Abe Fortas	Johnson	1965	NRV
Thurgood Marshall	Johnson	1967	69–11
Abe Fortas[†]	Johnson	1968	Withdrawn[‡]
Homer Thornberry	Johnson	1968	No action
Warren Burger	Nixon	1969	74–3
Clement Haynsworth	Nixon	1969	Defeated 45–55
G. Harrold Carswell	Nixon	1970	Defeated 45–51
Harry Blackmun	Nixon	1970	94–0
Lewis Powell	Nixon	1971	89–1
William Rehnquist	Nixon	1971	68–26
John Paul Stevens	Nixon	1975	98–0
Sandra Day O'Connor	Reagan	1981	99–0
William Rehnquist[†]	Reagan	1986	65–33
Antonin Scalia	Reagan	1986	98–0
Robert Bork	Reagan	1987	Defeated 42–58
Douglas Ginsburg	Reagan	1987	Withdrawn
Anthony Kennedy	Reagan	1988	97–0
David Souter	Bush	1990	90–9
Clarence Thomas	Bush	1991	52–48
Ruth Bader Ginsburg	Clinton	1993	96–3
Stephen G. Breyer	Clinton	1994	87–9

*No recorded vote.

[†]Elevation to Chief Justice.

[‡]Nomination withdrawn after Senate vote failed to end filibuster against nomination; vote was 45 to 43 to end filibuster, and two-thirds majority was required.

Source: Congressional Quarterly, *The Supreme Court: Justice and the Law* (Washington, D.C.: Congressional Quarterly, 1983), p. 179; updated by the author.

ings, during which the bearded, scholarly Bork presented a poor TV image. The Democrat-controlled U.S. Senate rejected his nomination. Victory in the Bork battle encouraged liberal interest groups to closely scrutinize the personal lives and political views of subsequent nominees. Indeed, the Bork battle set the stage for an even more controversial political struggle—the confirmation of Justice Clarence Thomas (see *Up Close:* "The Confirmation of Clarence Thomas" on page 484).

WHO IS SELECTED?

What background and experiences are brought to the Supreme Court? Despite often holding very different views on the laws, the Constitution, and their interpretation, the justices of the U.S. Supreme Court tend to share a common back-

The Confirmation of Clarence Thomas

Television coverage of Senate confirmation hearings on Clarence Thomas's appointment to the Supreme Court in 1991 captivated a national audience. The conflict raised just about every "hot-button" issue in American politics, from abortion rights and affirmative action to sexual harassment.

Born to a teenage mother who earned $10 a week as a maid, Clarence Thomas and his brother lived in a dirt-floor shack in Pin Point, Georgia, where they were raised by strict, hardworking grandparents who taught young Clarence the value of education and sacrificed to send him to a Catholic school. He excelled academically and went on to mostly white Immaculate Conception Seminary College in Missouri to study for the Catholic priesthood. But when he overheard a fellow seminarian express satisfaction at the assassination of Dr. Martin Luther King, Jr., Thomas left the seminary in anger and enrolled at Holy Cross College, where he helped found the college's Black Student Union, and went on to graduate with honors and to win admission to Yale Law School.

Upon graduating from Yale, Thomas took a job as assistant attorney general in Missouri and later became a congressional aide to Republican Missouri Senator John Danforth. In 1981 he accepted the post as head of the Office of Civil Rights in the Department of Education. In 1982 he was named chair of the Equal Employment Opportunity Commission (EEOC), where he successfully eliminated much of that agency's financial mismanagement and aggressively pursued individual cases of discrimination. But at the same time, he spoke out against racial "quotas." In 1989 President Bush nominated him to the U.S. Court of Appeals, and he was easily confirmed by the Senate.

In tapping Thomas for the Supreme Court, the White House reasoned that the liberal groups who had blocked the earlier nomination of conservative Robert Bork would be reluctant to launch personal attacks on an African American. With the opposition fractured, the White House saw an opportunity to push a strong conservative nominee through the Democrat-dominated Senate Judiciary Committee and win confirmation by the full Senate.

But behind the scenes, liberal interest groups, including the National Abortion Rights Action League, People for the American Way, and the National Organization for Women, were searching for evidence to discredit Thomas. A University of Oklahoma law professor, Anita Hill, a former legal assistant to Thomas both at the Department of Education and later at the Equal Employment Opportunity Commission, charged, in a nationally televised press conference, that Thomas had sexually harassed her in both jobs. Thomas himself flatly denied the charges.

Democrats on the committee treated Hill with great deference, asking her to talk about her feelings and provide even more explicit details of Thomas's alleged misconduct. Given an opportunity to rebut Hill's charges, Thomas did so very emphatically: "This is a circus. It's a national disgrace. And from my standpoint as a black American, as far as I'm concerned, it is a high-tech lynching for uppity blacks who in any way deign to think for themselves."

In the end, there was no way to determine who was telling the truth, and "truth" in Washington is, at any rate, often determined by opinion polls. A majority of blacks as well as whites, and a majority of women as well as men, sided with the nominee.* In a fitting finale to the bitter and sleazy conflict, the final Senate confirmation vote was 52 to 48, the closest vote in the history of such confirmations. The best that can be said about the affair was that it placed the issue of sexual harassment on the national agenda.

---

*Gallup Opinion Reports, October 15, 1991, p. 209.

ground of education at the nation's most prestigious law schools and prior judicial experience.

Law Degrees   There is no constitutional requirement that Supreme Court justices be attorneys, but every person who has ever served on the High Court has been trained in law. Moreover, a majority of the justices have attended one or another of the nation's most prestigious law schools—Harvard, Yale, and Stanford (see Table 13–3).

Judicial Experience   Historically, about half of all Supreme Court justices have been federal or state court judges. Many justices have served some time as U.S. attorneys in the Department of Justice early in their legal careers. Relatively few have held elected political office; among today's justices, only Sandra Day O'Connor ever won an election (to the Arizona state legislature), but one chief justice—William Howard Taft—previously held the nation's highest elected post, the presidency.

Age   Most justices have been in their fifties when appointed to the Court. Presumably this is the age at which people acquire the necessary prominence and experience to bring themselves to the attention of the White House and Justice Department as potential candidates. At the same time, presidents seek to make a lasting imprint on the Court, and candidates in their fifties can be expected to serve on the Court for many more years than older candidates with the same credentials.

Race and Gender   No African American had ever served on the Supreme Court until President Lyndon Johnson's appointment of Thurgood Marshall in 1967. A Howard University Law School graduate, Marshall had served as counsel for the National Association for the Advancement of Colored People Legal Defense Fund and had personally argued the historic *Brown v. Board of Education* case before the Supreme Court in 1954. He served as solicitor general of the United States

Table 13-3	The Supreme Court				
Justice	Age at Appointment	President Who Appointed	Law School	Position at Time of Appointment	Years as a Judge before Appointment
William H. Rehnquist					
Original appointment	47	Nixon (1971)	Stanford	Asst. Attorney General	0
Chief Justice	61	Reagan (1986)			15
John Paul Stevens	50	Ford (1976)	Northwestern	U.S. Court of Appeals	5
Sandra Day O'Connor	51	Reagan (1981)	Stanford	State Court	6
Antonin Scalia	50	Reagan (1988)	Harvard	U.S. Court of Appeals	4
Anthony M. Kennedy	51	Reagan (1988)	Harvard	U.S. Court of Appeals	12
David H. Souter	50	Bush (1990)	Harvard	State Supreme Court	13
Clarence Thomas	43	Bush (1991)	Yale	U.S. Court of Appeals	2
Ruth Bader Ginsburg	60	Clinton (1993)	Columbia	U.S. Court of Appeals	13
Stephen G. Breyer	56	Clinton (1994)	Harvard	U.S. Court of Appeals	14

under President Lyndon Johnson before his elevation to the high court. Upon Marshall's retirement in 1991, President George Bush sought to retain minority representation on the Supreme Court, yet at the same time to reinforce conservative judicial views with, with his selection of Clarence Thomas.

No woman had served on the Supreme Court prior to the appointment of Sandra Day O'Connor by President Ronald Reagan in 1981. O'Connor was Reagan's first Supreme Court appointment. Although a relatively unknown Arizona state court judge, she had the powerful support of Arizona Republican Senator Barry Goldwater and Stanford classmate Justice William Rehnquist. The second woman to serve on the high court, Ruth Bader Ginsburg, had served as an attorney for the American Civil Liberties Union while teaching at Columbia Law School and had argued and won several important gender discrimination cases. President Jimmy Carter appointed her in 1980 to the U.S. Court of Appeals; President Bill Clinton elevated her to the Supreme Court in 1993.

SUPREME COURT DECISION MAKING

The Supreme Court sets its own agenda: it decides what it wants to decide. Of the more than 5,000 requests for hearing that come to its docket each year, the Court issues opinions on only about 200 cases. Another 150 or so cases are decided *summarily* (without opinion) by a Court order either affirming or reversing the lower court decision. The Supreme Court refuses to rule at all on the vast majority of cases that are submitted to it. Thus the rhetorical threat to "take this all the way to the Supreme Court" is usually an empty one. It is important, however, to realize that a refusal to rule also creates law by allowing the decision of the lower court to stand. That is why the U.S. Circuit Courts of Appeals are powerful bodies.

Setting the Agenda: Granting Certiorari   Most cases reach the Supreme Court when a party in a case appeals to the Court to issue a **writ of certiorari** (literally to "make more certain"), a decision by the Court to require a lower federal or state court to turn over its records on a case.[24] To "grant certiorari"— that is, to decide to hear arguments in a case and render a decision—the Supreme Court relies on its *rule of four*: four justices must agree to do so. Deciding which cases to hear takes up a great deal of the Court's time.

What criteria does the Supreme Court use in choosing its policy agenda—that is, in choosing the cases it wishes to decide? The Court rarely explains why it accepts or rejects cases, but there are some general patterns. First, the Court accepts cases involving issues that the justices are interested in. The justices are clearly interested in the area of First Amendment freedoms—speech, press, and religion. Members of the Court are also interested in civil rights issues under the Equal Protection Clause of the Fourteenth Amendment and the civil rights laws and in overseeing the criminal justice system and defining the Due Process Clauses of the Fifth and Fourteenth Amendments.

In addition, the Court seems to feel an obligation to accept cases involving questions that have been decided differently by different circuit courts of appeals. The Supreme Court generally tries to see to it that "the law" does not differ from one circuit to another. Likewise, the Supreme Court usually acts when lower courts have made decisions clearly at odds with Supreme Court interpretations in order

writ of certiorari   Writ issued by the Supreme Court, at its discretion, to order a lower court to prepare the record of a case and send it to the Supreme Court for review. Most cases come to the Court as petitions for writs of certiorari.

to maintain control of the federal judiciary. Finally, the Supreme Court is more likely to accept a case in which the U.S. government is a party and requests a review, especially when an issue appears to be one of overriding importance to the government. In fact, the U.S. government is a party in almost half of the cases decided by the Supreme Court.

Hearing Arguments   Once the Supreme Court places a case on its decision calendar, attorneys for both sides submit written briefs on the issues. The Supreme Court may also allow interest groups to submit **amicus curiae** (literally, "friend of the court") briefs. This process allows interest groups direct access to the Supreme Court. In the affirmative action case of *University of California Regents v. Bakke* (1978),[25] the Court accepted 59 amicus curiae briefs representing more than 100 interest groups. The U.S. government frequently submits amicus curiae arguments in cases in which it is not a party. The **solicitor general** of the United States is responsible for presenting the government's arguments both in cases in which the government is a party and in cases in which the government is merely an amicus curiae.

Oral arguments before the Supreme Court are a time-honored ritual of American government. They take place in the marble "temple"—the Supreme Court building across the street from the U.S. Capitol in Washington, D.C. (see Figure 13–3). The justices, clad in their black robes, sit behind a high "bench" and peer down at the attorneys presenting their arguments. Arguing a case before the Supreme Court is said to be an intimidating experience. Each side is usually limited to either a half-hour or an hour of argument, but justices frequently interrupt with their own pointed questioning. Court watchers sometimes try to predict the Court's decision from the tenor of the questioning. Oral argument is the most public phase of Supreme Court decision making, but no one really knows whether these arguments ever change the justices' minds.

amicus curiae   Literally, "friend of the court"; a person, private group or institution, or government agency that is not a party to a case but participates in the case (usually through submission of a brief) at the invitation of the court or on its own initiative.

solicitor general   Attorney in the Department of Justice who represents the U.S. government before the Supreme Court and any other courts.

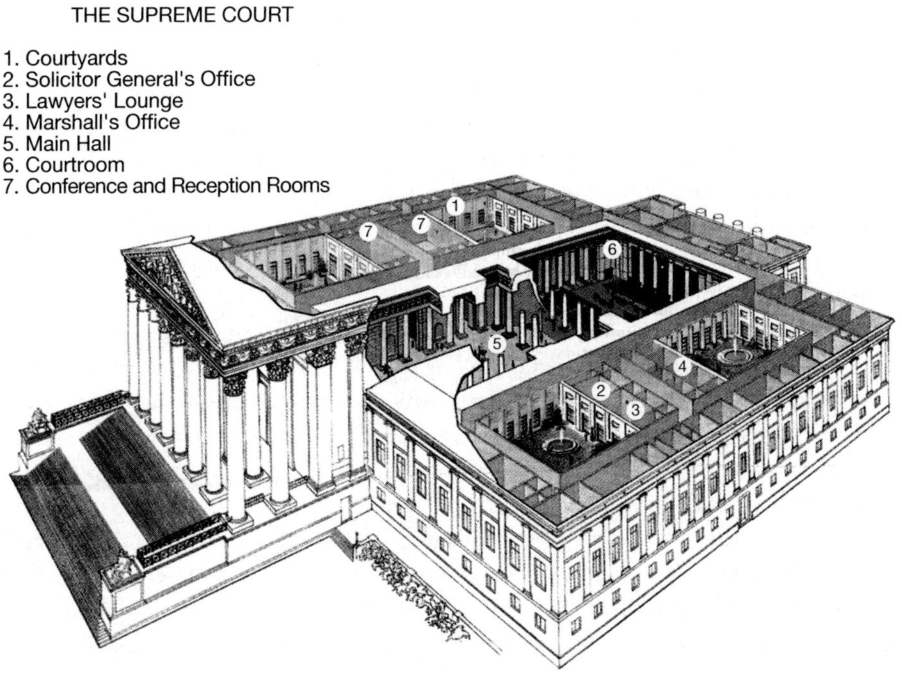

THE SUPREME COURT

1. Courtyards
2. Solicitor General's Office
3. Lawyers' Lounge
4. Marshall's Office
5. Main Hall
6. Courtroom
7. Conference and Reception Rooms

FIGURE 13–3   Corridors of Power in the Supreme Court

This cutaway shows the location of the principal offices and chambers of the Supreme Court building.

In Conference The actual decisions are made in private conferences among the justices. These conferences usually take place on Wednesdays and Fridays and cover the cases argued orally during the same week. The Chief Justice (currently William Rehnquist; see *People in Politics:* "William Rehnquist, Leading the Conservative Bloc") presides, and only justices (no law clerks) are present. It is customary for the Chief Justice to speak first on the issues, followed by each associate justice in order of seniority. A majority must decide which party wins or loses and whether a lower court's decision is to be affirmed or reversed.

Writing Opinions The *written* opinion determines the actual outcome of the case (votes in conference are not binding). When the decision is unanimous, the Chief Justice traditionally writes the opinion. In the case of a split decision, the Chief Justice may take on the task of writing the **majority opinion** or assign it to another justice in the majority. If the Chief Justice is in the minority, the senior justice in the majority makes the assignment. Writing the opinion of the Court is the central task in Supreme Court policy making. Broadly written opinions may effect sweeping policy changes; narrowly written opinions may decide a particular case but have very little policy impact. The reasons cited for the decision become binding law, to be applied by lower courts in future cases. Yet despite the crucial role of opinion writing in Court policy making, most opinions are actually written by law clerks who are only recent graduates of the nation's prestigious law schools. The justices themselves read, edit, correct, and sometimes rewrite drafts prepared by clerks, but clerks may have a strong influence over the position taken by justices on the issues.

In addition, the views of the legal profession itself—as reflected by the American Bar Association (ABA) as well as the numerous law reviews published by law schools—influence the Court in subtle yet important ways. Often new interpretations of laws or the Constitution first appear in prestigious law journals, then are borrowed by Supreme Court clerks preparing drafts of opinions by justices, and finally become law when incorporated into majority opinions.

A draft of the opinion is circulated among members of the majority. Any majority member who disagrees with the reasoning in the opinion, and thus disagrees with the policy that is proposed, may either negotiate changes in the opinion with others in the majority or write a concurring opinion. A **concurring opinion** agrees with the decision about which party wins the case but sets forth a different reason for the decision, proposing, in fact, a different policy position.

Justices in the minority often agree to present a **dissenting opinion**. The dissenting opinion sets forth the views of justices who disagree with both the decision and the majority reasoning. Dissenting opinions do not have the force of law. They are written both to express opposition to the majority view and to appeal to a future Court to someday modify or reverse the position of the majority. Occasionally, the Court is unable to agree on a clear policy position on particularly vexing questions. If the majority is strongly divided over the reasoning behind their decision and as many as four justices dissent altogether from the decision, lower courts will lack clear guidance and future cases will be decided on a case-by-case basis, depending on multiple factors occurring in each case (see, for example, "Affirmative Action in the Courts" in Chapter 15). The absence of a clear opinion of the Court, supported by a unified majority of the justices, invites additional cases, keeping the issue on the Court's agenda until such time (if any) as the Court establishes a clear policy on the issue.

majority opinion Opinion in a case that is subscribed to by a majority of the judges who participated in the decision.

concurring opinion Opinion by a member of a court that agrees with the result reached by the court in the case but disagrees with or departs from the court's rationale for the decision.

dissenting opinion Opinion by a member of a court that disagrees with the result reached by the court in the case.

William Rehnquist, Leading the Conservative Bloc

In the more than two hundred years of Supreme Court history, the Court has contained some of the finest legal minds of its time (as well as its share of less-than-brilliant legalists). Only three men, however, have been "promoted" from the post of associate justice to Chief Justice: Edward D. White (Chief Justice from 1910 to 1921), Harlan F. Stone (Chief Justice from 1941 to 1946), and the current Chief Justice, William H. Rehnquist.

Rehnquist grew up in the affluent Milwaukee suburb of Shorewood, where his mother was a civic activist and local Republican leader. After serving in the Army Air Corps during World War II as a weather observer in North Africa, he took advantage of the G.I. Bill to attend Stanford University, where he graduated Phi Beta Kappa with a degree in political science in 1948. He went on to graduate school at Harvard, earning a master's degree, then returned to Stanford to attend law school, finishing at the top of his class and winning the chance to serve as a clerk for the late Justice Robert H. Jackson, one of the Court's more conservative thinkers. When his internship at the Supreme Court ended, Rehnquist moved to Arizona to begin private practice. In Phoenix, he became active in the Arizona State Republican Party and worked on the presidential campaigns of Barry Goldwater in 1964 and Richard Nixon in 1968.

Following Nixon's election, Rehnquist went to Washington as assistant attorney general. On several occasions, Rehnquist publicly criticized the Supreme Court as having gone too far in protecting the rights of the accused.

When a seat on the Supreme Court became open in 1971, Nixon, who had pledged in his campaign to appoint "judicial conservatives" to the Court, nominated Rehnquist, anticipating that the relatively young conservative (age forty-seven) would serve for a long time. The nomination sparked a debate in the Senate over what Rehnquist's opponents labeled his "ultra-conservative" philosophy. Numerous civil rights groups and liberals spoke against him in the Senate Judiciary Committee's hearings, but Rehnquist successfully defended his positions, responding calmly and professionally to hostile questions by Senators Edward Kennedy and Birch Bayh. The Senate voted 68 to 26 in favor of confirming the nomination.

Rehnquist arrived at the Court just as it was beginning to reconcile years of judicial activism under recently retired Chief Justice Earl Warren with the more restrained approach of Chief Justice Warren Burger. But Burger never followed a true conservative or restraintist position; the Chief Justice frequently led the Court in upholding defendants' rights, court-ordered desegregation, and affirmative action plans. As a result, Rehnquist wrote so many "lone dissenting" opinions that his law clerks presented him with a Lone Ranger doll. In *Roe v. Wade* in 1973, Rehnquist wrote in his dissenting opinion (which only Justice Byron White joined) that "Abortion involves the purposeful termination of potential life" and is therefore "beyond the rubric of personal privacy."

Over time Rehnquist began to find additional support on the Court for his positions, not because he had changed but because the Court membership changed. In 1986, after fifteen years on the Court, Rehnquist was nominated by President Reagan to the position of Chief Justice upon Burger's retirement. At the same time, Reagan nominated another strong conservative, Antonin Scalia, to take Rehnquist's seat as associate justice. Again Rehnquist came under sharp attack in the Senate Judiciary Committee, but no one really doubted his brilliance in constitutional law. The Senate tradition of confirming presidential nominees (barring evidence of incompetence or lack of ethics) still held sway, and Rehnquist was confirmed.

With the appointment of this conservative leader to the most conservative Court in fifty years, many observers looked for major changes in the high court's decisions. Instead, Rehnquist has wound up the leader of only the most conservative members on the Court.

POLITICS AND THE SUPREME COURT

The political views of Supreme Court justices have an important influence on Court decisions. Justices are swayed primarily by their own ideological views; but public opinion, the president's position, and the arguments of interest groups, all contribute to the outcome of cases.

Liberal and Conservative Voting Blocs Although liberal and conservative voting blocs on the Court are visible over time, on any given case particular justices may deviate from their perceived ideological position. Many cases do not present a liberal-conservative dimension. Each case presents a separate set of facts, and even justices who share a general philosophy may perceive the central facts of a case differently. Moreover, the liberal-versus-conservative dimension sometimes clashes with the activist-versus-self-restraint dimension. Although we generally think of liberals as favoring activism and conservatives self-restraint, occasionally those who favor self-restraint are obliged to approve of legislation that violates their personal conservative beliefs because opposing it would substitute their judgment for that of elected officials. So ideological blocs are not always good predictors of voting outcomes on the Court.

Over time, the composition of the Supreme Court has changed, as has the power of its various liberal and conservative voting blocs (see Table 13–4). The liberal bloc, headed by Chief Justice Earl Warren, dominated Court decision making from the mid-1950s through the end of the 1960s. The liberal bloc gradually weakened following President Richard Nixon's appointment of Warren Burger as Chief Justice in 1969, but not all of Nixon's appointees joined the conservative bloc; Justice Harry Blackmun and Justice Lewis Powell frequently joined in voting with the liberal bloc. Among Nixon's appointees, only William Rehnquist has consistently adopted conservative positions. President Gerald Ford's only appointee to the Court, John Paul

Table 13–4	Liberal and Conservative Voting Blocs on the Supreme Court		
	The Warren Court	**The Burger Court**	**The Rehnquist Court**
	1968	1975	2000
Liberal	Earl Warren Hugo Black William O. Douglas Thurgood Marshall William J. Brennan Abe Fortas	William O. Douglas Thurgood Marshall William J. Brennan	John Paul Stevens Ruth Bader Ginsburg Stephen G. Breyer
Moderate	Potter Stewart Byron White	Potter Stewart Byron White Lewis Powell Harry Blackmun	Anthony Kennedy Sandra Day O'Connor David Souter
Conservative	John Marshall Harlan	Warren Burger William Rehnquist	William Rehnquist Antonin Scalia Clarence Thomas

Stevens, began as a moderate and drifted to the liberal bloc. As a result, the Burger Court, although generally not as activist as the Warren Court, still did not reverse any earlier liberal holdings.

President Ronald Reagan, who had campaigned on a pledge to restrain the liberal activism of the Court, tried to appoint conservatives. His first appointee, Sandra Day O'Connor, turned out to be less conservative than expected, especially on women's issues and abortion rights. When Chief Justice Burger retired in 1986, Reagan seized on the opportunity to strengthen the conservative bloc by elevating Rehnquist to Chief Justice (see *People in Politics:* William Rehnquist, Leading the Conservative Bloc). Reagan also appointed Antonin Scalia, another strong conservative, to the Court. Reagan added Anthony Kennedy to the Court in 1988, hoping to give Rehnquist and the conservative bloc the opportunity to form a majority. Had President Reagan succeeded in getting the powerful conservative voice of Robert Bork on the Court, it is possible that many earlier liberal decisions, including *Roe v. Wade*, would have been reversed. But the Senate rejected Bork; David Souter, the man ultimately confirmed, compiled a moderate record.

Liberals worried that the appointment of conservative Clarence Thomas as a replacement for the liberal Thurgood Marshall would give the conservative bloc a commanding voice in Supreme Court policy making. But no solid conservative majority emerged. Justices Rehnquist, Scalia, and Thomas are considered the core of the conservative bloc, but they must win over at least two of the more moderate justices in order to form a majority in a case. President Bill Clinton's appointees, Ruth Bader Ginsburg and Stephen G. Breyer, have consistently supported liberal views on the Supreme Court. On key questions, the moderate bloc has the deciding vote (see *Up Close:* "Privacy, Abortion, and the Constitution" on page 492).

While the moderate bloc currently holds the balance of power on the Court, the Court as a whole has moved in a conservative direction since the high watermark of judicial liberalism during the era of Chief Justice Earl Warren (1953–1968). Liberalism on the Court—as measured by pro-individual rights decisions against the government in civil liberties cases, pro-defendant decisions in criminal cases, and pro-women and minorities in civil rights cases—has declined significantly since the 1960s (see Table 13–5 on page 494).

If vacancies occur during the presidency of George W. Bush, he is likely to try to strengthen the conservative bloc. However, confirmations of his nominations will be closely fought in an evenly-divided, partisan Senate.

Public Opinion "By all arguable evidence of the modern Supreme Court, Court appears to reflect public opinion about as accurately as other policy makers."[26] And indeed, on the liberal-conservative dimension, it can be argued that Supreme Court decisions have generally followed shifts in American public opinion. However, the Court appears to lag behind public opinion. It is doubtful that the justices read opinion polls; their jobs do not depend on public approval ratings. Rather, it is more likely that the justices, whose nomination and confirmation depended on an elected president and Senate, generally share the views of those who put them on the bench. Thus, public opinion affects the Court only indirectly, through the nomination and confirmation process.

Presidential Influence Even after a president's initial appointment of a Justice to the High Court, a president may exercise some influence over judicial decision making. The Office of the U.S. Solicitor General is charged with the

Privacy, Abortion, and the Constitution

No other issue has generated more emotional, political, and legal controversy for the Supreme Court than abortion. Yet prior to the 1973 Court decision in *Roe v. Wade*, abortion was not a significant issue in American national politics. Since the 1800s, abortions for any purpose other than saving the life of the mother had been criminal offenses under most state laws. About a dozen states acted in the late 1960s to permit abortions in cases of rape or incest or to protect the physical (and, in some cases, mental) health of the mother. Relatively few abortions were performed under these laws, however, because of the red tape involved—review of each case by several concurring physicians, approval of a hospital board, and so forth. Then in 1970, New York, Alaska, Hawaii, and Washington enacted laws that in effect permitted abortion at the request of the woman involved and the concurrence of her physician.

The Right to Privacy Meanwhile, the Supreme Court was developing a new constitutional right—the right of privacy—partly in response to a case brought to it by Planned Parenthood in 1965. When Estelle Griswold opened a birth control clinic on behalf of the Planned Parenthood League of Connecticut, the state found her in violation of a Connecticut law prohibiting the use of contraceptives. She challenged the constitutionality of the statute, and in its ruling in *Griswold v. Connecticut* the Supreme Court struck down the law by a vote of 7 to 2.*

Although the majority agreed that a right to privacy could be found in the Constitution, members of the majority could not agree on where it was to be found. Justice Douglas found it in "the penumbras formed by emanations from" the First, Third, Fourth, Ninth, and Fifteenth Amendments. Justices Goldberg, Warren, and Brennan found it in the Ninth Amendment: "The enumeration of the Constitution of certain rights, shall not be contrived to deny or disparage others retained by the people." Justice Harlan found the right in the word "liberty" in the Fourteenth Amendment. The fact that Griswold dealt with reproduction gave encouragement to groups advocating abortion rights.

Roe v. Wade In 1969 Norma McCorvey sought an abortion in Texas, but the doctor refused, citing a state law prohibiting abortion except to save a woman's life. McCorvey challenged the Texas law in federal courts on a variety of constitutional grounds, including the right to privacy. McCorvey became "Jane Roe," and the case became one of the most controversial in the Court's history.†

The Supreme Court ruled that the constitutional right of privacy as well as the Fourteenth Amendment's guarantee of "liberty" included a woman's decision to bear or not to bear a child. The Court held that the word "person" in the Constitution did not include the unborn child; therefore, the Fifth and Fourteenth Amendments' guarantee of "life, liberty, or property" did not protect the "life" of the fetus. The Court also ruled that a state's power to protect the health and safety of the mother could not justify any restriction on abortion in the first three months of pregnancy. Between the third and sixth months of pregnancy, a state could set standards for abortion procedures in order to protect the health of women, but a state could not prohibit abortions. Only in the final three months could a state prohibit or regulate abortion to protect the unborn.

Rather than end the political controversy over abortion, *Roe v. Wade* set off a conflagration. Congress defeated efforts to pass a constitutional amendment restricting abortion or declaring that life begins at conception. However, when Congress banned the use of federal funds under Medicaid (medical care for the poor) for abortions except to protect the life of a woman, the Supreme Court upheld the ban, holding that there was no constitutional obligation for governments to pay for abortions.‡

Reaffirming Roe v. Wade Abortion has become such a polarizing issue that "pro-choice" and "pro-life" groups are generally unwilling to search out a middle ground. Yet the current Supreme Court appears to have chosen a policy of affirming a woman's right to abortion while upholding modest restrictions, as evidenced by the Court's ruling in *Planned Parenthood of Pennsylvania v. Casey* (1992).§

In this case, the Supreme Court considered a series of restrictions on abortion enacted by Pennsylvania: that physicians must inform women of risks and alter-

Pro-life and pro-choice activists confront each other outside the Supreme Court in 1992 after the justices issued their ruling in Planned Parenthood of Pennsylvania v. Casey.

natives; that women must wait twenty-four hours after requesting an abortion before having one; and that the parents of minors must be notified. It struck down a requirement that spouses be notified.

Justice Sandra Day O'Connor took the lead in forming a moderate, swing bloc on the Court, consisting of herself, Anthony Kennedy, and David Souter. (Harry A. Blackmun and John Paul Stevens voted to uphold *Roe v. Wade* with *no* restrictions, making the vote 5 to 4.) Her majority opinion strongly reaffirmed the fundamental right of abortion, both on the basis of the Fourteenth Amendment and on the principle of stare decisis. But the majority also upheld states' rights to protect any fetus that reached the point of "viability." The Court went on to establish a new standard for constitutionally evaluating restrictions: they must not impose an "undue burden" on women seeking abortion or place "substantial obstacles" in her path. All of Pennsylvania's restrictions met this standard and were upheld except spousal notification.

Despite outcries from both pro-choice and pro-life forces, the *Casey* decision puts the Supreme Court almost exactly where opinion polls suggest most Americans are: generally supporting a woman's right to choose an abortion early in pregnancy but also supporting many restrictions on the exercise of that right.

The "Partial Birth Abortion" Controversy A number of states have attempted to outlaw an abortion procedure known as "intact dilation and evacuation" or "partial birth" abortion. This procedure, which is used in less than one percent of all abortions, involves partial delivery of the fetus feet-first, then vacuuming out the brain and crushing the skull to ease complete removal. Congress also voted to ban this procedure several times, only to have President Clinton veto the bans. In a surprise 5 to 4 decision, with Justice O'Conner supporting the majority, the Supreme Court declared a Nebraska law prohibiting the procedure to be an unconstitutional "undue burden" on a woman's right to an abortion. The Nebraska law failed to make an exception in its prohibition of the procedure "for the preservation of the health of the mother."[||]

Griswold v. Connecticut, 381 U.S. 479 (1965).

[†]*Roe v. Wade*, 410 U.S. 113 (1973).

[‡]*Harris v. McRae*, 448 U.S. 297 (1980).

[§]*Planned Parenthood v. Casey*, 510 U.S. 110 (1992).

[||]*Stenberg v. Carhart*, June 28, 2000.

Table 13-5 Liberalism in the Supreme Court

Type of Case	Percent Liberal Decisions		
	Warren Court	Burger Court	Rehnquist Court
Civil Liberties	67.7	43.6	42.8
Civil Rights	76.3	51.8	55.3
Criminal Procedures	59.4	34.2	33.2
First Amendment	69.0	48.6	48.5

Note: First Amendment includes all First Amendment guarantees plus due process and privacy; Criminal Procedures includes rights of persons accused of crime except due process; Civil Rights includes non-First Amendment cases pertaining to race, sex, age, and other individual characteristics. Civil Liberties combines all three of these types of cases.

Source: Derived from Lee Epstein et. al., *The Supreme Court Court Compendium: Data, Decisions and Developments,* Washington, D.C.: Congressional Quarterly Press, 1994, p. 166.

Kweisi Mfume resigned from a Maryland congressional seat that he had held for ten years in order to assume the leadership of the NAACP, the nation's oldest and largest civil rights organization.

responsibility of presenting the government's (the president's) views in cases not only to which the U.S. government is a party, but also in cases in which the president and the Attorney General have a strong interest and present their arguments in amicus curiae briefs. The Solicitor General's Office, in both Democratic and Republican presidential administrations, has compiled an enviable record in Supreme Court cases. When representing federal agencies that are parties to cases, the Solicitor General has won two-thirds of their cases before the Supreme Court over the years. And in cases where the Solicitor General has offered an amicus curiae brief, it has won about three-quarters of its cases. In contrast, the states have won fewer than half of the cases before the Supreme Court in which a state has been a party.[27]

Interest Group Influence   Interest groups have become a major presence in Supreme Court cases. First of all, interest groups (for example, Planned Parenthood, National Association for the Advancement of Colored People, American Civil Liberties Union, etc.) sponsor many cases themselves. They find persons they believe to be directly damaged by a public policy, initiate litigation on their behalf, and provide the attorneys and money to pursue these cases all the way to the Supreme Court. Secondly, it is now a rare case that comes to the Court without multiple amicus curiae briefs filed by interest groups.

How influential are interest groups in Supreme Court decisions? Certainly interest groups have a significant influence in bringing issues before the Supreme Court through their sponsorship of cases. It is unlikely that the Court would have acted when it did on many key issues from racial segregation in 1954 (*Brown v. Board of Education* sponsored by the NAACP) to abortion in 1992 (*Planned Parenthood v. Casey* sponsored by Planned Parenthood) in the absence of interest-group activity. And interest group amicus curiea briefs are now mentioned (cited) in about two-thirds of the written decisions of the Court.[28] However, these briefs may not have much *independent* effect on decisions, that is, they may not have convinced the justices to decide a case one way or another. Several studies have found that interest-group briefs have had very little effect on Supreme Court decisions.[29]

CHECKING COURT POWER

Many people are concerned about the extent to which we now rely on a nonelected judiciary to decide key policy issues rather than depending on a democratically elected president or Congress.

Legitimacy as a Restraint in the Judiciary   Court authority derives from legitimacy rather than force. By that we mean that the courts depend on their authority being seen as rightful, on people perceiving an obligation to abide by court decisions whether they agree with them or not. The courts have no significant force at their direct command. Federal marshals, who carry out the orders of federal courts, number only a few thousand. Courts must rely primarily on the executive branch for enforcement of their decisions.

Today most Americans believe that Supreme Court decisions are authoritative statements about the Constitution and that people have an obligation to obey these decisions whether they agree with them or not. Thus public opinion constrains other public officials—from the president, to governors, to school superintendents, to law enforcement officials—to obey Supreme Court decisions. Their constituents do not hold them personally responsible for unpopular actions ordered by the Supreme Court or federal judges. On the contrary, their constituents generally expect them to comply with court decisions.

The institutional legitimacy of the federal courts was tested in the civil rights battles of the 1950s and 1960s. In 1957 Governor Orval Faubus of Arkansas used state National Guard troops to halt federal marshals from escorting black students into a segregated Little Rock high school pursuant to a federal court order. President Dwight Eisenhower had his personal doubts about the wisdom of federal court-ordered desegregation, but the governor's open defiance of a federal court order could not be tolerated by a president sworn "to preserve, protect, and defend the Constitution of the United States." Eisenhower ordered U.S. Army troops to Little Rock to enforce the federal court's order, a decision that proved a historic turning point in the civil rights movement. But Eisenhower's decision also greatly strengthened federal courts, ensuring that the full force of the federal government would be used to gain compliance with their decisions.

Widespread opposition to Supreme Court policy can obstruct and delay its implementation. For example, the Supreme Court's 1963 ruling that prayer and Bible-reading exercises in public schools violated the No Establishment Clause of the First Amendment was very unpopular (see Chapter 14). Many public school systems simply ignored the decision. Enforcement required individuals or groups in school districts throughout the country to bring separate suits in federal courts. In school districts where no one strongly objected to prayer or where objectors did not have the will or resources to bring suit against school officials, the practice continued. Congress did not feel disposed to cut off federal funds to schools that allowed prayer, and the president was not disposed to send federal troops into the schools to halt Bible reading. Only gradually were prayers and other religious observances deleted from public school exercises.

Compliance with Court Policy   Federal and state court judges must apply Supreme Court policies when ruling on cases in their own courts.[30] Occasionally lower courts express their disagreement with the Supreme Court in an opinion, even when they feel obliged to carry out the High Court's policy. At times, lower federal and state courts try to give a narrow interpretation to a Supreme Court decision with which they disagree. But judges who seek to defy the Supreme Court face the ultimate sanction of reversal on appeal by the losing party. Professional pride usually inspires judges to avoid reversals of their judgments by higher courts even though a long record of reversals is not grounds for impeachment or removal of a federal judge.

Public officials who defy Supreme Court rulings risk lawsuits and court orders mandating compliance. Persons injured by noncompliance are likely to file suit against noncomplying officials, as are interest groups that monitor official compliance with the policies they support. These suits are expensive, time consuming, and potentially embarrassing to government officials and agencies. Once a court order is issued, continued defiance can result in fines and penalties for contempt of court.

The president of the United States is subject to federal court orders. Historically, this notion has been challenged: early presidents believed they were separate and at least co-equal to the courts and that their own determination about the legality or constitutionality of their own acts could not be overturned by the courts. President Andrew Jackson could—and did—say: "John Marshall has made his decision. Now let him enforce it," expressing the view that the president was not obliged to enforce court decisions he disagreed with.[31] But in the course of 200 years, the courts—not the president—have gained in legitimacy as the final authority on the law and the Constitution. Today a president who openly defied the Supreme Court would lose any claims to legitimacy and would risk impeachment by Congress.

The case of Richard Nixon illustrates the weakness of a modern president who would even consider defying the Supreme Court. When Nixon sought to invoke executive privilege to withhold damaging tapes of White House conversations in the Watergate investigation (see *Up Close:* "Watergate and the Limits of Presidential Power" in Chapter 11), federal district judge John Sirica rejected his claim and ordered that the tapes be turned over to the special prosecutor in the case. In arguments before the Supreme Court, Nixon's lawyers contended that the president would not have to comply with a Supreme Court decision to turn over the tapes. Yet when the Court ruled unanimously against him, Nixon felt bound to comply and released tapes that were very damaging to his cause. But Nixon understood that refusal to abide by a Supreme Court decision would most assuredly have resulted in impeachment. Under the circumstances, compliance was the better of two unattractive choices.[32]

Presidential Influence on Court Policy The president and Congress can exercise some restraint over court power through the checks and balances built into the Constitution. Using the office's powers of appointment, presidents have effectively modified the direction of Supreme Court policy and influenced lower federal courts as well. Certainly presidents must await the death or retirement of Supreme Court justices and federal judges, and presidents are constrained by the need to secure Senate confirmation of their appointees. However, over time presidential influence on the courts can be significant. During their combined twelve years in the White House, Ronald Reagan and George Bush were able to fill 70 percent of federal district and appellate court judgeships and six of nine Supreme Court positions with their own appointees. As noted earlier, however, their appointees did not always reflect these presidents' philosophy of judicial self-restraint in rendering decisions. Nevertheless, the federal courts tilted in a somewhat more conservative direction. President Bill Clinton's appointments generally strengthened liberal, activist impulses throughout the federal judiciary.

Congressional Checks on the Judiciary The Constitution gives Congress control over the structure and jurisdiction of federal district and appellate courts, but congressional use of this control has been restrained. Only the Supreme Court is established by the Constitution; Article III gives Congress the power to "ordain and establish" "inferior" courts. In theory, Congress could try to limit court jurisdiction to hear cases that Congress did not wish it to decide. Congress has used this power to lighten the federal courts' workload; for example, Congress has limited the jurisdiction of federal courts in cases between citizens of different states by requiring that the dispute involve more than $50,000. But Congress has never used this power to change court policy—for example, by removing federal court jurisdiction over school prayer cases or desegregation cases. Indeed federal courts would probably declare unconstitutional any congressional attempt to limit their power to interpret the Constitution by limiting jurisdiction.

Likewise, although Congress could, in theory, expand membership on the Supreme Court, the custom of a nine-member Supreme Court is now so deeply ingrained in American government that "court packing" is politically unthinkable. Franklin Roosevelt's unsuccessful 1937 attempt to expand the Supreme Court was the last serious assault on its membership. However, President Jimmy Carter succeeded in getting Congress to add a large number of federal district judgeships, and he used these new posts to appoint more women and minorities to the federal judiciary.

A more common congressional constraint on the Supreme Court is amending statutory laws to reverse federal court interpretations of these laws that Congress believes are in error. Thus when the Supreme Court decided that civil rights laws did not mandate a cutoff of all federal funds to a college upon evidence of discrimination in a single program but only the funds for that program,[33] Congress amended its own laws to require the more sweeping remedy. Likewise, when the Supreme Court ruled that existing civil rights legislation put the burden of proof of discrimination on plaintiffs rather than employers, Congress passed the Civil Rights Act of 1991, which requires employers to show why tests and other recruitment practices are a "business necessity." Although members of Congress frequently berate the Court for what they see as misreading of the laws, all Congress needs to do to reverse a Court interpretation of those laws is to pass amendments to them.

Constitutional amendment is the only means by which the Congress and the states can reverse a Supreme Court interpretation of the Constitution itself. After the Civil War, the Thirteenth Amendment abolishing slavery reversed the Supreme Court's *Dred Scott* decision (1857) that slavery was constitutionally protected. The Sixteenth Amendment (1913) gave Congress the power to impose an income tax, thus reversing the Supreme Court's earlier decision in *Pollock v. Farmer's Loan*[34] holding income taxes illegal (1895). But recent attempts to reverse Supreme Court interpretations of the Constitution by passing constitutional amendments on the issues of prayer in public schools, busing, and abortion have all failed to win congressional approval. The barriers to a constitutional amendment are formidable: a two-thirds vote of both houses of Congress and ratification by three-quarters of the states. Thus, for all practical purposes, the Constitution is what the Supreme Court says it is.

LOOKING AHEAD

Twenty-First Century Directions

The most controversial issues in American politics are eventually decided by the U.S. Supreme Court. We depend upon nine justices, who are appointed, not elected, and who serve life terms, to decide about race and equality, sex and abortion, religion and prayer, police and law-enforcement, and the death penalty. The U.S. Supreme Court is the most trusted branch of the federal government.

⬆ *Judicial Power* Judicial power will continue to grow. Federal caseloads will expand as interest groups turn more and more toward the strategy of litigation and Congress defines war crimes as federal offenses. Despite rhetorical praise of restraint, the federal judiciary will move toward greater activism, reviewing both state and federal laws.

⬇ *Legal Reform* Efforts to reform the nation's legal system by limiting product liability, third-party suits, "pain and suffering" awards, class action suits, and lawyers' fees, will fail. The trial lawyers, with assistance from anti-corporate consumer and public interest groups, will defeat all efforts at reforming or simplifying the nation's tort laws.

⬅➡ *Judicial Selection* The federal judicial selection process will continue to be highly politicized, with presidential appointments and Senate confirmations heavily influenced by the political views of prospective jurists. The precedents set in the battles over the Supreme Court nominations of Robert Bork and Clarence Thomas insure that judicial competence will be overshadowed by political considerations, notably the liberal or conservative views of the nominees, their views on activism versus restraint in judicial decision making, and their views on abortion.

⬅➡ *Liberal–Conservative Balance* President George W. Bush will try to maintain or strengthen the conservative bloc on the Court if called upon to fill any vacancies. However, an evenly-divided Senate ensures a vigorous battle over confirmation.

Congress can impeach federal court judges, but only for "cause" (committing crimes), not for their decisions. Although impeachment is frequently cited as a constitutional check on the judiciary, it has no real influence over judicial policy making. Only five federal court judges have ever been impeached by the House, convicted by the Senate, and removed from office, although two others were impeached and another nine resigned to avoid impeachment. In 1989 Federal District Court Judge Alcee Hastings became the first sitting judge in more than fifty years to be impeached, tried, and found guilty by the Congress. He was convicted by the Senate of perjury and conspiracy to obtain a $150,000 bribe; but a federal district court judge later ruled that he should have been tried by the full Senate, not a special committee of the Senate. Hastings declared the ruling a vindication; in 1992 he won a congressional seat in Florida, becoming the first person ever to become a member of the House after being impeached by that same body. Even criminal convictions do not ensure removal from office, although judges have resigned under fire.

SUMMARY NOTES

- Great power is lodged in the Supreme Court of the United States and the federal judiciary. These courts have undertaken to resolve many of the most divisive conflicts in American society. The judicial power is the power to decide cases and controversies, and in so doing to decide the meaning of the Constitution and laws of Congress.

- The power of judicial review is the power to invalidate laws of Congress or of the states that the federal courts believe conflict with the U.S. Constitution. This power is not specifically mentioned in the Constitution but was derived by Chief Justice John Marshall from the Supremacy Clause and the meaning of judicial power in Article III.

- The Supreme Court has been fairly restrained in its use of judicial review with regard to laws of Congress and actions of presidents; it has more frequently overturned state laws. The federal courts also exercise great power in the interpretation of the laws of Congress, especially when statutory language is vague.

- Arguments over judicial power are reflected in the conflicting philosophies of judicial activism and judicial self-restraint. Advocates of judicial restraint argue that judges must not substitute their own views for those of elected representatives and the remedy for unwise laws lies in the legislature, not the courts. Advocates of judicial activism argue that the courts must view the Constitution as a living document and its meaning must fit the needs of a changing society.

- The federal judiciary consists of three levels of courts—the Supreme Court, the U.S. Courts of Appeals, and the U.S. District Courts. The district courts are trial courts that hear both civil and criminal cases. The courts of appeals are appellate courts and do not hold trials but consider only the record of trial courts and the arguments (briefs) of attorneys. More than 90 percent of federal cases end in appeals courts. The Supreme Court can hear appeals from state high courts as well as lower federal courts. The Supreme Court hears only about 200 cases a year.

- Courts function under general rules of restraint that do not bind the president or Congress. The Supreme Court does not decide hypothetical cases or render advisory opinions. The principle of stare decisis, or reliance on precedent, is not set aside lightly.

- In the wake of the Watergate scandal, Congress passed an Ethics in Government Act in 1978 authorizing federal courts, upon application by the attorney general, to appoint independent counsels (special prosecutors) to investigate allegations against the president or other high federal officials. The intent of the law was to take politics out of the investigation of the highest officials, but the record of special prosecutors suggests that politics nonetheless drives many investigations.

- The selection of Supreme Court justices and federal judges is based more on political considerations than legal qualifications. Presidents almost always appoint judges from their own party, and presidents increasingly have sought judges who share their ideological views. However, because of the independence of judges once they are appointed, presidents have sometimes been disappointed in the decisions of their appointees. In addition, Senate approval of nominees has become increasingly politicized, with problems most evident when different parties control the White House and the Senate.

- The Supreme Court sets its own agenda for policy making, usually by granting or withholding certiorari. Generally four justices must agree to grant certiorari for a case to be decided by the Supreme Court. The Supreme Court has been especially active in policy making in interpreting the meaning of the Fourteenth Amendment's guarantee of "equal protection of the laws," as well as of the civil rights and voting rights acts of Congress. It has also been active in defining the meaning of freedom of press, speech, and religion in the First Amendment and "due process of law" in the Fifth Amendment. The federal courts are active in overseeing government regulatory activity. But federal courts have generally left the areas of national security and international relations to the president and Congress. In addition, the Court tends to accept cases involving questions decided differently by different courts of appeal, cases in which lower courts have challenged Supreme Court interpretations, and cases in which the U.S. government is a party and it requests review.

- Liberal and conservative blocs on the Supreme Court can be discerned over time. Generally, liberals have been judicial activists and conservatives have been restraintists. Today a moderate bloc appears to hold the balance of power.

- Court power derives primarily from legitimacy rather than force. Most Americans believe that Supreme Court decisions are authoritative statements about the Constitution and people have an obligation to obey these decisions whether they agree with them or not. Although early presidents thought of themselves as constitutional co-equals with the Supreme Court and not necessarily bound by Court decisions, today it would be politically unthinkable for a president to ignore a court order.

- There are very few checks on Supreme Court power. Presidents may try to influence Court policy through judicial nominations, but once judges are confirmed by the Senate they can pursue their own impulses. Congress has never used its power to limit the jurisdiction of federal courts in order to influence judicial decisions.

- Only by amending the Constitution can Congress and the states reverse a Supreme Court interpretation of its meaning. Congress can impeach federal judges only for committing crimes, not for their decisions.

KEY TERMS

judicial review 464	appellate jurisdiction 471	standing 478	writ of certiorari 486
statutory laws 467	appeal 471	plaintiffs 478	amicus curiae 487
judicial self-restraint 468	district courts 472	defendants 478	solicitor general 487
original intent 470	grand juries 473	sovereign immunity 478	majority opinion 488
judicial activism 470	petit (regular) juries 473	class action suits 478	concurring opinion 488
stare decisis 470	circuit courts 473	contingency fees 479	dissenting opinion 488
precedent 470	briefs 473	remedies and reliefs 479	
jurisdiction 471	civil cases 477	litmus test 480	
original jurisdiction 471	adversarial system 478	senatorial courtesy 482	

SELECTED READINGS

ABRAHAM, HENRY J. *The Judicial Process.* 7th ed. New York: Oxford University Press, 1998. Comprehensive survey of judicial politics and processes in the United States, England, and France. Provides an introduction to the nature and sources of law, as well as the organization, functioning, and staffing of the courts.

BAUM, LAWRENCE. *The Supreme Court.* 6th ed. Washington, D.C.: CQ Press, 1997. Readable introduction to the Supreme Court as a political institution, covering the selection and confirmation of judges, the nature of the issues decided by courts, the process of judicial decision making, and the impact of Supreme Court decisions.

CARP, ROBERT A., and RONALD AIDHAM. *The Federal Courts.* 3rd ed. Washington, D.C.: CQ Press, 1998. Overview of the federal judicial system, arguing that federal judges and Supreme Court justices function as part of the political system and engage in policy making that influences all our lives.

EPSTEIN, LEE, and JACK KNIGHT. *The Choices Justices Make.* Washington, D.C.: CQ Press, 1998. Account of the U.S. Supreme Court's strategic political decision making based on both public records and the private papers of justices.

EPSTEIN, LEE, JEFFREY A. SEGAL, HAROLD J. SPAETH, and THOMAS G. WALKER. *The Supreme Court Compendium: Data, Decisions and Developments.* Washington, D.C.: CQ Press, 1994. A comprehensive collection of data on the Supreme Court, its justices, its decisions, and even the public's views of its decisions.

NAGEL, ROBERT F. *Judicial Power and American Character*. New York: Oxford University Press, 1994. Critique of judicial reasoning as a mask for the exercise of power.

SCHWARTZ, BERNARD. *A History of the Supreme Court*. New York: Oxford University Press, 1995. Comprehensive one-volume history of the nation's highest court and the influence the Court has had on American politics and society.

U.S. Supreme Court decisions are available at most public and university libraries as well as at law libraries in volumes of *United States Reports*. Court opinions are cited by the names of the parties, for example, *Brown v. Board of Education of Topeka*, followed by a reference number such as 347 U.S. 483 (1954). The first number in the citation (347) is the volume number; "U.S." refers to *United States Reports*; the subsequent number is the page on which the decision begins; the year the case was decided is in parentheses.

CHAPTER
14

Politics and Personal Liberty

CHAPTER OUTLINE

ASK YOURSELF ABOUT POLITICS

1 Do you think the government has become so large and powerful that it poses a threat to the rights and freedoms of ordinary citizens?
Yes ⬤ No ⬤

2 Do you believe that using tax funds to pay tuition at church-affiliated schools violates the separation of church and state?
Yes ⬤ No ⬤

3 Do we have a constitutional right to physician-assisted suicide?
Yes ⬤ No ⬤

4 Should we have the right to burn the American flag?
Yes ⬤ No ⬤

5 Should organizations like the Ku Klux Klan and the American Nazi Party be permitted to hold marches and rallies?
Yes ⬤ No ⬤

6 Do law-abiding citizens have a constitutional right to carry a handgun for self-protection?
Yes ⬤ No ⬤

7 Do you believe that the seizure of property believed by police to be used in drug trafficking, without a judicial hearing or trial, violates civil liberty?
Yes ⬤ No ⬤

8 Is the death penalty a "cruel and unusual" punishment?
Yes ⬤ No ⬤

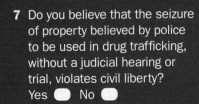

Government power defends your most basic rights to life, liberty, and the pursuit of happiness while at the same time ensuring that all other Americans have the same rights. The Founders guaranteed individual liberty in the earliest days of our nation through the first ten amendments to the Constitution—our Bill of Rights.

POWER AND INDIVIDUAL LIBERTY

To the authors of the Declaration of Independence, individual liberty was inherent in the human condition. It was not derived from governments or even from constitutions. Rather, governments and constitutions existed to make individual liberty more secure:

> We hold these truths to be self-evident, that all men are created equal, that they are endowed by their Creator with certain unalienable Rights, that among these are Life, Liberty and the pursuit of Happiness. That to secure these rights, Governments are instituted among Men, deriving their just powers from the consent of the governed.

The authors of the Bill of Rights (the first ten amendments to the Constitution) did *not* believe that they were creating individual rights, but rather that they were recognizing and guaranteeing rights that belonged to individuals by virtue of their humanity.

Authority and Liberty To avoid the brutal life of a lawless society, where the weak are at the mercy of the strong, people form governments and endow them with powers to secure peace and self-preservation. People voluntarily relinquish some of their individual freedom to establish a government that is capable of protecting them from their neighbors as well as from foreign aggressors. This government must be strong enough to maintain its own existence or it cannot defend the rights of its citizens.

But what happens when a government becomes too strong and infringes on the liberties of its citizens? How much liberty must individuals surrender to secure an orderly society? This is the classic dilemma of free government: people must create laws and governments to protect their freedom, but the laws and governments themselves restrict freedom.

Democracy and Personal Liberty   When democracy is defined only as a *decision-making process*—widespread popular participation and rule by majority—it offers little protection for individual liberty. Democracy must also be defined to include *substantive values*—a recognition of the dignity of all individuals and their equality under law. Otherwise, some people, particularly "the weaker party, or an obnoxious individual" would be vulnerable to deprivations of life, liberty, or property simply by decisions of majorities (see "The Paradox of Democracy" in Chapter 1). Indeed, the "great object" of the Constitution, according to James Madison, was to preserve popular government yet at the same time to protect individuals from "unjust" majorities.[1]

The purpose of the Constitution—and especially its Bill of Rights, passed by the First Congress in September 1789—is to limit governmental power over the individual, that is, to place personal liberty beyond the reach of government (see Table 14–1 on page 506). Each individual's rights to life, liberty, and property, due process of law, and equal protection of the law are not subject to majority vote. Or, as Supreme Court Justice Robert Jackson once declared,

> The very purpose of a Bill of Rights was to withdraw certain subjects from the vicissitudes of political controversy, to place them beyond the reach of majorities and officials, and to establish them as legal principles to be applied by the courts. One's right to life, liberty, and property, to free speech, a free press, freedom of worship and assembly, and other fundamental rights may not be submitted to vote: they depend on the outcome of no elections.[2]

Nationalizing the Bill of Rights   The Bill of Rights begins with the words "*Congress* shall make no law . . . ," indicating that it was originally intended to limit only the powers of the federal government. The Bill of Rights was added to the Constitution because of fear that the *federal* government might become too powerful and encroach on individual liberty. But what about encroachments by state and local governments and their officials? For more than one hundred years, the U.S. Supreme Court, reflecting what it saw as the intentions of the framers, refused to make the protections of the Bill of Rights binding on state and local governments. States had their own constitutions with many of the same rights, but state constitutions were enforceable only in state courts.[3]

With the addition of the Fourteenth Amendment to the Constitution following the Civil War, the question of the applicability of the Bill of Rights to the states arose anew. The Fourteenth Amendment includes the words "No State shall . . ."; its provisions are directed specifically at states. This amendment was designed to secure equality for newly freed slaves, but its provisions guaranteed that no one could be denied "the privileges or immunities of citizens," "life, liberty, or property," "due process of law," or "equal protection of the laws." Do these general phrases incorporate the protections of the Bill of Rights—make them applicable against *state* actions?

Initially, the U.S. Supreme Court rejected the argument that the Privileges or Immunities Clause[4] and the Due Process Clause[5] incorporated the Bill of Rights. But beginning in the 1920s, the Court handed down a long series of decisions that gradually brought about the **incorporation** of almost all of the protections of the Bill of Rights into the "liberty" guaranteed against state actions by the Due Process Clause of the Fourteenth Amendment. In *Gitlow v. New York* (1925), the Court ruled that "freedom of speech and of the press—which are protected by the First Amendment from abridgment by Congress—are among the fundamental personal rights and liberties protected by the due process clause of the Fourteenth Amendment from impairment by the states."[6] Over time, the Court applied the same reasoning in incorporating almost all provisions of the Bill of Rights into the Fourteenth Amendment's Due Process Clause (see Table 14–2 on page 508).

FREEDOM OF RELIGION

Americans are a very religious people. Belief in God and church attendance are more widespread in the United States than in any other advanced industrialized nation. Although many early American colonists came to the new land to escape religious persecution, they frequently established their own government-supported churches and imposed their own religious beliefs on others. Puritanism was the official faith of colonial Massachusetts, and Virginia officially established the Church of England. Only two colonies (Maryland and Rhode Island) provided for full religious freedom. In part to lessen the potential for conflict among the states, the framers of the Bill of Rights sought to prevent the new national government from establishing an official religion or interfering with religious exercises.[7] The very first words of the First Amendment set forth two separate prohibitions on government: "Congress shall make no law respecting an *establishment of religion*, or prohibiting the *free exercise* thereof." These two restrictions on government power—the Free Exercise Clause and the No Establishment Clause—guarantee separate religious freedoms.

Free Exercise of Religion The **Free Exercise Clause** prohibits government from restricting religious beliefs or practices. Although the wording of the First Amendment appears absolute ("Congress shall make no law . . ."), the U.S. Supreme Court has never interpreted the phrase to protect any conduct carried on in the name of religion. In the first major decision involving this clause, the Court ruled in 1879 that polygamy could be outlawed by Congress in Utah Territory even though some Mormons argued that it was part of their religious faith. The Court distinguished between belief and behavior, saying that "Congress was deprived of all legislative power over mere opinion [by the First Amendment], but was left free to reach actions which were in violation of social duties."[8] The Court also employed the Free Exercise Clause to strike down as unconstitutional an attempt by a state to prohibit private religious schools and force all children to attend public schools.[9] This decision protects the entire structure of private religious schools in the nation.

Later, the Supreme Court elaborated on its distinction between religious belief and religious practice. *Beliefs* are protected absolutely, but with regard to religious *practices*, the Court has generally upheld governmental restrictions when enacted for valid secular purposes.[10] Thus the government can outlaw religious practices that threaten health,

In 1990 the Supreme Court ruled against two Native Americans who had been fired from their jobs as drug counselors for taking peyote during religious ceremonies of the Native American Church. The Court maintained that the Free Exercise Clause does not exempt individuals from complying with valid laws regulating conduct. In this picture, a Native American holy man performs a ceremony outside the Court as it hears arguments on the case.

incorporation In constitutional law, the application of almost all of the Bill of Rights to the states through the Fourteenth Amendment.

Free Exercise Clause Clause in the First Amendment to the Constitution that prohibits the federal government from restricting religious beliefs and practices.

Table 14-1   **Constitutionally Protected Rights**

The Bill of Rights

The first ten amendments to the Constitution of the United States, passed by the First Congress of the United States in September 1789 and ratified by the states in December 1791.

Amendments	Protections
First Amendment: Religion, Speech, Press, Assembly, Petition	
Congress shall make no law respecting an establishment of religion, or prohibiting the free exercise thereof; or abridging the freedom of speech, or of the press; or the right of the people peaceably to assemble, and to petition the Government for a redress of grievances.	Prohibits government establishment of religion. Protects the free exercise of religion. Protects freedom of speech. Protects freedom of the press. Protects freedom of assembly. Protects the right to petition government "for a redress of grievances."
Second Amendment: Right to Bear Arms	
A well regulated Militia, being necessary to the security of a free State, the right of the people to keep and bear Arms, shall not be infringed.	Protects the right of people to bear arms and states to maintain militia (National Guard) units.
Third Amendment: Quartering of Soldiers	
No Soldier shall, in time of peace, be quartered in any house, without the consent of the Owner, nor in time of war, but in a manner to be prescribed by law.	Prohibits forcible quartering of soldiers in private homes in peacetime, or in war without congressional authorization.
Fourth Amendment: Searches and Seizures	
The right of the people to be secure in their persons, houses, papers, and effects, against unreasonable searches and seizures, shall not be violated, and no Warrants shall issue, but upon probable cause, supported by Oath or affirmation, and particularly describing the place to be searched, and the persons or things to be seized.	Protects against "unreasonable searches and seizures." Requires warrants for searches of homes and other places where there is a reasonable expectation of privacy. Judges may issue search warrants only with "probable cause"; and such warrants must be specific regarding the place to be searched and the things to be seized.
Fifth Amendment: Grand Juries, Double Jeopardy, Self-Incrimination, Due Process, Protection against Government Takings of Property	
No person shall be held to answer for a capital, or otherwise infamous crime, unless on a presentment or indictment of a Grand jury, except in cases arising in the land or naval forces, or in the Militia, when in actual service in time of war or public danger; nor shall any person be subject for the same offence to be twice put in jeopardy of life or limb; nor shall he be compelled in any criminal case to be a witness against himself, nor be deprived of life, liberty, or property, without due process of law; nor shall private property be taken for public use, without just compensation.	Requires that, before trial for a serious crime, a person (except military personnel) must be indicted by a grand jury. Prohibits double jeopardy (trial for the same offense a second time after being found innocent). Prohibits the government from forcing any person in a criminal case to be a witness against himself or herself. Prohibits the government from taking life, liberty, or property "without due process of law." Prohibits government from taking private property without paying "just compensation."
Sixth Amendment: Fair Trial	
In all criminal prosecutions, the accused shall enjoy the right to a speedy and public trial, by an impartial jury of the State and district wherein the crime shall have been committed, which district shall have been previously ascertained by law, and to be informed of the nature and cause of the accusation; to be confronted with the witnesses against him; to have compulsory process for obtaining witnesses in his favor, and to have the Assistance of Counsel for his defense.	Requires that the accused in a criminal case be given a speedy and public trial, and thus prohibits prolonged incarceration without trial or secret trials. Requires that trials be by jury and take place in the district where the crime was committed. Requires that the accused be informed of the charges, have the right to confront witnesses, have the right to force supporting witnesses to testify, and have the assistance of counsel.

(continued)

Table 14-1   **Constitutionally Protected Rights (continued)**

Amendments	Protections
Seventh Amendment: Trial by Jury in Civil Cases In Suits at common law, where the value in controversy shall exceed twenty dollars, the right of trial by jury shall be preserved, and no fact tried by a jury, shall be otherwise reexamined in any Court of the United States, than according to the rules of the common law.	Requires a jury trial in civil cases involving more than $20. Limits the degree to which factual questions decided by a jury may be reviewed by another court.
Eighth Amendment: Bail, Fines and Punishment Excessive bail shall not be required, nor excessive fines imposed, nor cruel and unusual punishments inflicted.	Prohibits excessive bail. Prohibits excessive fines. Prohibits cruel and unusual punishment.
Ninth Amendment: Unspecified Rights Retained by People The enumeration in the Constitution, of certain rights, shall not be construed to deny or disparage others retained by the people.	Protection of unspecified rights (including privacy) that are not listed in the Constitution. The Constitution shall not be interpreted to be a complete list of rights retained by the people.
Tenth Amendment: Rights Reserved to the States The powers not delegated to the United States by the Constitution, nor prohibited by it to the States, are reserved to the States respectively, or to the people.	States retain powers that are not granted by the Constitution to the national government or prohibited by it to the states.

Rights in the Text of the Constitution

Several rights were written into the text of the Constitution in 1787 and thus precede in time the adoption of the Bill of Rights.

Article I Section 9: Habeas Corpus, Bills of Attainder, and Ex Post Facto Laws The privilege of the Writ of Habeas Corpus shall not be suspended, unless when in Cases of Rebellion or Invasion the public Safety may require it. No Bill of Attainder or ex post facto Law shall be passed.	Habeas corpus prevents imprisonment without a judge's determination that a person is being lawfully detained. Prohibition of bills of attainder prevents Congress (and states) from deciding people guilty of a crime and imposing punishment without trial. Prohibition of ex post facto laws prevents Congress (and states) from declaring acts to be criminal that were committed before the passage of a law making them so.

Thirteenth and Fourteenth Amendments

The Bill of Rights begins with the words "Congress shall make no law . . ." indicating that it initially applied only to the *federal* government. Although states had their own constitutions that guarantee many of the same rights, for more than a century the Bill of Rights did not apply to state and local governments. Following the Civil War, the Thirteenth, Fourteenth, and Fifteenth (voting rights) Amendments were passed, restricting *state* governments and their local subdivisions. But not until many years later did the U.S. Supreme Court, in a long series of decisions, apply the Bill of Rights against the states.

Thirteenth Amendment Neither slavery nor involuntary servitude, except as a punishment for crime whereof the party shall have been duly convicted, shall exist within the United States, or any place subject to their jurisdiction.	Prohibits slavery or involuntary servitude except for punishment by law; applies to both governments and private citizens.
Fourteenth Amendment All persons born or naturalized in the United States, and subject to the jurisdiction thereof, are citizens of the United States and of the State wherein they reside. No State shall make or enforce any law which shall abridge the privileges or immunities of citizens of the United States; nor shall any State deprive any person of life, liberty, or property, without due process of law; nor deny to any person within its jurisdiction the equal protection of the laws.	Protects "privileges and immunities of citizenship." Prevents deprivation of life, liberty, or property "without due process of law"; this phrase incorporates virtually all of the rights specified in the Bill of Rights. Prevents denial of "equal protection of the laws" for all persons.

Table 14-2 The Nationalization of the Bill of Rights

Year	Amendment	Protection	Case
1925	First	Freedom of speech	*Gitlow v. New York*
1931	First	Freedom of press	*Near v. Minnesota*
1932	Sixth	Rights to counsel in capital cases	*Powell v. Alabama*
1937	First	Freedom of assembly	*DeJonge v. Oregon*
1940	First	Free exercise of religion	*Cantwell v. Connecticut*
1947	First	No establishment of religion	*Everson v. Board of Education*
1948	Sixth	Public trial	*In re Oliver*
1949	Fourth	No unreasonable searches and seizures	*Wolf v. Colorado*
1962	Eighth	No cruel and unusual punishments	*Robinson v. California*
1963	Sixth	Right to counsel in felony cases	*Gideon v. Wainwright*
1964	Fifth	Freedom from self-incrimination	*Malloy v. Hagan*
1967	Sixth	Speedy trial	*Klopfer v. North Carolina*
1968	Sixth	Jury trial in all criminal cases	*Duncan v. Louisiana*
1969	Fifth	No double jeopardy	*Benton v. Maryland*

safety, or welfare. The Free Exercise Clause does *not* confer the *right* to practice human sacrifice or even the ceremonial use of illegal drugs.[11] Individuals must comply with valid and neutral laws even if these laws restrict religious practices.

But the Supreme Court has continued to face many difficulties in applying its "valid secular test" to specific infringements of religious freedom. When some Amish parents refused to allow their children to attend any school beyond the eighth grade, the State of Wisconsin argued that its universal compulsory school attendance law had a valid purpose: the education of children. The Amish parents argued that high school exposed their children to worldly influences and values contrary to their religious beliefs. The Supreme Court sided with the Amish, deciding that their religious claims outweighed the legitimate interests of the state in education.[12] When a Florida city attempted to outlaw the Santeria (a mix of Catholicism and voodoo) practice of slaughtering animals in religious ceremonies, the Supreme Court held that the city's ordinance was "not neutral" and "targeted" a particular religious ceremony and was therefore unconstitutional.[13]

Yet the Supreme Court has upheld government actions that were challenged as infringements of religious freedom in several key cases. The Court approved of an Internal Revenue Service action revoking the tax-exempt status of Bob Jones University because of its rules against interracial dating or marriage among its students. The school argued that its rule was based on religious belief, but the Court held that the government had "an overriding interest in eradicating racial discrimination in education."[14] And the Court upheld an Oregon law that prohibited the possession of peyote (a hallucinogenic drug made from cactus plants) against the claims of a Native American church that its use was a religious sacrament.[15] The Court also upheld an Air Force dress code regulation that prevented Orthodox Jews from wearing a yarmulke while in uniform. The Court rejected the argument that the regulation violated the Free Exercise Clause, holding instead that "the mission of the military . . . [included fostering] obedience, unity, commitment and esprit de corps" overrides the individual freedom that would protect civilians from such a government regulation.[16]

No Establishment of Religion   Various meanings have been ascribed to the First Amendment prohibition against the "establishment" of religion. The first meaning—what the writers of the Bill of Rights had in mind—is that it merely prohibits the government from officially recognizing and supporting a national church, like the Church of England in that nation. A second meaning is somewhat broader: the government may not prefer one religion over another or demonstrate favoritism toward or discrimination against any particular religion, but it might recognize and encourage religious activities in general. The most expansive meaning is that the **No Establishment Clause** creates "a wall of separation between church and state" that prevents government from endorsing, aiding, sponsoring, or encouraging any or all religious activities. In 1947 Justice Hugo Black, writing for the Court majority, gave the following definition of this **wall-of-separation doctrine**:

> Neither a state nor the Federal Government can set up a church. Neither can pass laws which aid one religion, aid all religions, or prefer one religion over another. Neither can force nor influence a person to go to or to remain away from church . . . or force him to profess a belief or disbelief in any religion. . . . No tax in any amount, large or small, can be levied to support any religious activities or institutions, whatever they may be called, or whatever form they may adopt to teach or practice religion. Neither a state nor the Federal Government can, openly or secretly, participate in the affairs of any religious organizations or groups and vice versa. In the words of Jefferson, the clause against establishment of religion by law was intended to erect "a wall of separation between Church and State."[17]

Yet even while erecting this high rhetorical wall between church and state, the Court in this case upheld a state's provision of school bus service to parochial school pupils at public expense on the grounds that the buses did not directly aid religion but merely helped all children in the community proceed safely to and from school.[18] Although the Supreme Court has generally voiced its support for the wall-of-separation doctrine, on several occasions it has permitted cracks to develop in the wall. In allowing public schools to give pupils regular releases from school to attend religious instructions given outside of the school, Justice William O. Douglas wrote that the state and religion need not be "hostile, suspicious or even unfriendly."[19]

What Constitutes "Establishment"?   It has proven difficult for the Supreme Court to reconcile this wall-of-separation interpretation of the First Amendment with the fact that religion plays an important role in the life of most Americans. Public meetings, including sessions of the Congress, often begin with prayers;[20] coins are inscribed with the words "In God We Trust"; and the armed forces provide chaplains for U.S. soldiers.

The Supreme Court has set forth a three-part *Lemon test* for determining whether a particular state law constitutes "establishment" of religion and thus violates the First Amendment. To be constitutional, a law affecting religious activity:

1. Must have a secular purpose.
2. As its primary effect, must neither advance nor inhibit religion.
3. Must not foster "an excessive government entanglement with religion."[21]

Using this three-part test the Supreme Court held that it was unconstitutional for a state to pay the costs of teachers' salaries or instructional materials in parochial

No Establishment Clause
Clause in the First Amendment to the Constitution that is interpreted to require the separation of church and state.

wall-of-separation doctrine
The Supreme Court's interpretation of the No Establishment Clause that laws may not have as their purpose aid to one religion or aid to all religions.

schools. The justices argued that this practice would require excessive government controls and surveillance to ensure that funds were used only for secular instruction and thus involved "excessive entanglement between government and religion." However, the Court has upheld the use of tax funds to provide students attending church-related schools with nonreligious textbooks, lunches, transportation, sign-language interpreting, and special-education teachers. And the Court has upheld a state's granting of tax credits to parents whose children attend private schools, including religious schools.[22] The Court has also upheld government grants of money to church-related colleges and universities for secular purposes.[23] The Court has ruled that if public buildings are open to use for secular organizations, they must also be opened to use by religious organizations.[24] And the Court has held that a state institution (the University of Virginia) not only can but must grant student activity fees to religious organizations on the same basis as it grants these fees to secular organizations.[25]

The High Court has upheld tax exemptions for churches on the grounds that "the role of religious organizations as charitable associations, in furthering the secular objectives of the state, has become a fundamental concept in our society."[26] It held that schools must allow after-school meetings on school property by religious groups if such a privilege is extended to nonreligious groups.[27] Deductions on federal income tax returns for church contributions are also constitutional. The Supreme Court allows states to close stores on Sundays and otherwise set aside that day, as long as there is a secular purpose—such as "rest, repose, recreation and tranquility"—in doing so.[28]

But the Court has not always acted to "accommodate" religion. In a controversial case, the Court held that a Christmas nativity seen sitting alone on public property was an official "endorsement" of Christian belief and therefore violated the No Establishment Clause. However, if the Christian display was accompanied by a Menorah, a traditional Christmas tree, Santa Claus and reindeer, it would simply be "taking note of the season" and not an unconstitutional endorsement of religion.[29] And in another case, the Supreme Court held that a Louisiana law requiring the teaching

A Menorah lighting ceremony celebrating Chanukah on public property near the White House. The Supreme Court is divided over whether such public displays violate the No Establishment Clause of the First Amendment.

of "creationism" along with evolution in the public schools was an unconstitutional establishment of a religious belief.[30]

Prayer in the School   The Supreme Court's most controversial interpretation of the No Establishment Clause involved the question of prayer and Bible-reading ceremonies conducted by public schools. The practice of opening the school day with prayer and Bible-reading ceremonies was once widespread in American public schools. To avoid the denominational aspects of these ceremonies, New York State's Board of Regents substituted the following nondenominational prayer, which it required to be said aloud in each class in the presence of a teacher at the beginning of each school day: "Almighty God, we acknowledge our dependence upon Thee, and we beg Thy blessings upon us, our parents, our teachers, and our country." New York argued that this brief prayer did not violate the No Establishment Clause, because the prayer was denominationally neutral and because student participation in the prayer was voluntary. However, in *Engle v. Vitale* (1962), the Supreme Court stated that "the constitutional prohibition against laws respecting an establishment of a religion must at least mean in this country it is no part of the business of government to compose official prayers for any group of the American people to recite as part of a religious program carried on by government." The Court pointed out that making prayer voluntary did not free it from the prohibitions of the No Establishment Clause, and that clause prevented the *establishment* of a religious ceremony by a government agency regardless of whether the ceremony was voluntary.[31]

One year later, in the case of *Abington Township v. Schempp*, the Court considered the constitutionality of Bible-reading ceremonies in the public schools. Here again, even though the children were not required to participate, the Court found that Bible reading as an opening exercise in the schools was a religious ceremony. The justices went to some trouble in the majority opinion to point out that they were not "throwing the Bible out of the schools." They specifically stated that the *study* of the Bible or of religion, when presented objectively and as part of a secular program of education, did not violate the First Amendment; but religious *ceremonies* involving Bible reading or prayer established by a state or school did.[32]

State efforts to encourage "voluntary prayer" in public schools have also been struck down by the Supreme Court as unconstitutional. When the State of Alabama authorized a period of silence for "meditation or voluntary prayer" in public schools, the Court ruled that this action was an "establishment of religion." The Court said the law had no secular purpose, that it conveyed "a message of state endorsement and promotion of prayer," and that its real intent was to encourage prayer in public schools. In a stinging dissenting opinion, Justice William Rehnquist noted that the Supreme Court itself opened its session with a prayer and that both houses of Congress opened every session with prayers led by official chaplains paid by the government.

Justice Rehnquist went on to challenge the notion that it was not the Founders' intent to create "a wall-of-separation between church and state." He argued that the Court was misinterpreting Thomas Jefferson's phrase, that the Constitution does *not* "require the government to be strictly neutral between religion and irreligion," but only that the government must be nondiscriminatory among religions. "It would come as much of a shock to those who drafted the Bill of Rights as it will to a large number of thoughtful Americans today to learn that the Constitution, as construed by the majority, prohibits the [government] from endorsing prayer." But the major-

*Although the Supreme Court ruled in 1962 (*Engle v. Vitale*) that even voluntary prayer in public schools was an unconstitutional violation of the separation of church and state under the First Amendment, the question of prayer in the schools remains a heated one. Indeed, recent court rulings regarding nondenominational prayers at graduation ceremonies and sporting events have, if anything, further confused the issue.*

ity of the Supreme Court appears to be holding to the "wall-of-separation" doctrine. In 1992 the Court held that invocations and benedictions at public high school graduation ceremonies was an unconstitutional establishment of religion.[33]

Religious Freedom Restoration? Congress sought to intervene in government-religion disputes with a Religious Freedom Restoration Act in 1993. Traditionally, the Supreme Court had employed a "compelling interest" test to decide whether government could ban a religious practice; that is, the government had to prove a compelling public interest to justify even a nondiscriminatory law or regulation that infringed on the free exercise of religion.[34] But when the Court appeared to relax that test and to hold that religious beliefs cannot excuse persons from compliance with *any* otherwise valid law, Congress saw an opportunity to align itself with religion. It acted to exempt people from government laws or regulations that burden their religious freedom unless the government can prove that the burden is "the least restrictive means of furthering a compelling interest."[35] But the Supreme Court responded by declaring the act unconstitutional, asserting in *City of Boerne v. Flores* (1997) that only the courts can interpret the meaning of the Constitution and that Congress had overstepped it powers trying to do so itself.

FREEDOM OF SPEECH

Although the First Amendment is absolute in its wording ("Congress shall pass no law . . . abridging the freedom of speech"), the Supreme Court has never been willing to interpret this statement as a protection of *all* speech. What kinds of speech does the First Amendment protect from government control, and what kinds of speech may be constitutionally prohibited?

Clear and Present Danger Doctrine The classic example of speech that can be prohibited was given by Justice Oliver Wendell Holmes in 1919: "The most stringent protection of free speech would not protect a man in falsely shouting 'fire' in a theater and causing a panic."[36] Although Holmes recognized that the government may prevent speech that creates a serious and immediate danger to society, he objected to government attempts to stifle critics of its policies, such as the Espionage Act of 1917 and the Sedition Act of 1918. The Sedition Act prohibited, among other things, speech that was meant to discourage the sale of war bonds; "disloyal" speech about the government, the Constitution, the military forces, or the flag of the United States; and speech that urged the curtailment of war production. In the case of *Gitlow v. New York*, the majority supported the right of the government to curtail any speech that "tended to subvert or imperil the government," but Holmes dissented, arguing that "Every idea is an incitement. It offers itself for belief and if believed it is acted on unless some other belief outweighs it."[37] Unless the expression of an idea created a *serious and immediate danger*, Holmes argued that it should be tolerated and combated or defeated only by the expression of better ideas. This standard for determining the limits of free expression became known as the **clear and present danger doctrine**. Government should not curtail speech merely because it *might tend* to cause a future danger: "The question in every case is whether the words used are used in such circumstances and are of such a nature as to create a clear and present danger that they will bring about the substantive evils that Congress has a right to prevent."[38] Holmes's dissent inspired a long struggle in the courts to

clear and present danger doctrine Standard used by the courts to determine whether speech may be restricted; only speech that creates a serious and immediate danger to society may be restricted.

strengthen constitutional protections for speech and press (see *Up Close:* "The American Civil Liberties Union" on page 514).

Although Holmes was the first to use the phrase "clear and present danger," it was Justice Louis D. Brandeis who later developed the doctrine into a valuable constitutional principle that the Supreme Court gradually came to adopt. Brandeis explained that the doctrine involved two elements: (1) the clearness or seriousness of the expression; and (2) the immediacy of the danger flowing from the speech. With regard to immediacy he wrote,

> No danger flowing from speech can be deemed clear and present, unless the incidence of the evil apprehended is so imminent that it may befall before there is opportunity for full discussion. If there be time to expose through discussion the falsehood and fallacies, to avert the evil by the processes of education, the remedy to be applied is more speech, not enforced silence.

And with regard to seriousness he wrote,

> Moreover, even imminent danger cannot justify resort to prohibition [of speech] . . . unless the evil apprehended is relatively serious. Prohibition of free speech and assembly is a measure so stringent that it would be inappropriate as the means for averting a relatively trivial harm to society. . . . There must be the probability of serious injury to the State.[39]

Preferred Position Doctrine   Over the years, the Supreme Court has given the First Amendment freedom of speech, press, and assembly a special **preferred position** in constitutional law. These freedoms are especially important to the preservation of democracy. If speech, press, or assembly are prohibited by government, the people have no way to correct the government through democratic processes. Thus the burden of proof rests on the *government* to justify any restrictions on speech, writing, or assembly.[40] In other words, any speech or writing is presumed constitutional unless the government proves that a serious and immediate danger would ensue if the speech were allowed.

The Cold War Challenge   Despite the Supreme Court's endorsement of the clear and present danger and preferred position doctrines, in times of perceived national crisis the courts have been willing to permit some government restrictions of speech, press, and assembly. At the outbreak of World War II, just prior to U.S. entry into that world conflict, Congress passed the Smith Act, which stated,

> It shall be unlawful for any person to knowingly or willfully advocate, abet, advise, or teach the duty, necessity, desirability, or propriety of overthrowing or destroying any government in the United States by force or violence, or by the assassination of any officer of any such government.

Congress justified its action in terms of national security, initially as a protection against fascism during World War II, then later as a protection against communist revolution in the early days of the Cold War.

In 1949 the Department of Justice prosecuted Eugene V. Dennis and ten other top leaders of the Communist Party of the United States for violation of the Smith Act. A jury found them guilty of violating the act, and the party leaders were

preferred position   Refers to the tendency of the courts to give preference to the First Amendment rights to speech, press, and assembly when faced with conflicts.

The American Civil Liberties Union

The American Civil Liberties Union (ACLU) is one of the largest and most active interest groups devoted to litigation. Its Washington offices employ a staff of several hundred people; it counts on some five thousand volunteer lawyers across the country; and it has affiliates in every state and most large cities. The ACLU claims that its sole purpose is defense of civil liberty, that it has no other political agenda, that it defends the Communist Party and the Ku Klux Klan alike—not because it endorses their beliefs but because "the Bill of Rights is the ACLU's only client."* And indeed on occasion it has defended the liberties of Nazis, Klansmen, and other right-wing extremists to express their unpopular views. But most ACLU work has involved litigation on behalf of liberal causes, such as abortion rights, resistance to military service, support for affirmative action, and opposition to the death penalty.

The ACLU was founded in 1920 by Roger Baldwin, a wealthy radical activist who opposed both capitalism and war. Baldwin graduated from Harvard University and briefly taught sociology at Washington University in St. Louis. He refused to be drafted during World War I and served a year's imprisonment for draft violation. In prison, Baldwin joined the Industrial Workers of the World (IWW, or the "Wobblies"), a radical labor union that advocated violence to achieve its goals. In the early 1920s, the ACLU defended socialists, "Bolsheviks," labor organizers, and pacifists against government coercion, including those arrested in the "Red Scare" raids of Attorney General Alexander Mitchell Palmer.

Later the ACLU concentrated its efforts on the defense of First Amendment freedoms of speech, press, religion, and assembly. ACLU member Felix Frankfurter, later a Supreme Court justice, set the tone: "Civil liberty means liberty for those whom we do not like or even detest." In the famous "Monkey Trial" of 1925, the ACLU helped defend schoolteacher John Scopes for having taught the theory of evolution in violation of Tennessee state law. Later, it played a supporting role in the litigation efforts of the National Association for the Advancement of Colored People in the elimination of segregation; it defended Vietnam War protesters; it brought cases to court to ban prayer

In 1978 the ACLU defended the right of American Nazis to march in the Chicago suburb of Skokie, Illinois, home to many survivors of the Nazi holocaust in Europe.

and religious exercise in public schools; it has opposed the death penalty and fought for abortion rights; and it defended the rights of people to burn the American flag as a form of symbolic speech.

The ACLU's decision to defend the right of the American Nazi Party to march through Skokie, Illinois, a Chicago suburb with a large Jewish population, including some Holocaust survivors, created a crisis in the organization. The ACLU had defended Nazis and Klansmen before, but the Skokie case engendered more publicity than any earlier cases involving right-wing extremists. Many members quit the organization and financial contributions temporarily declined.

Today, the ACLU is racked by internal arguments over politically correct speech codes and over whether "hate crimes" (crimes committed with racist, sexist, antihomosexual, and similar motives) should invoke harsher sentences than the same crimes committed for other motives. "Pure" First Amendment defenders in the organization oppose speech codes and hate crime legislation, while many liberal members rationalize these penalties on speech and thought.

Former Supreme Court Chief Justice Earl Warren once said of the ACLU, "It is difficult to appreciate how far our freedoms might have eroded had it not been for the Union's valiant representation in the courts of the constitutional rights of people of all persuasions."[†]

---

*William A. Donohue, *The Politics of the American Civil Liberties Union* (New Brunswick: Transaction Books, 1985), p. 3.

[†]Quoted in *ACLU Annual Report*, 1977, cited in ibid., p. 2.

sentenced to jail terms ranging from one to five years. In 1951 the case of *Dennis v. United States* came to the Supreme Court on appeal. In upholding the conviction of the Communist Party leaders, the Court seemed to abandon Brandeis's idea that "present" meant "before there is opportunity for full discussion."[41] It seemed to substitute clear and *probable* for clear and *present*.

Since that time, however, the Supreme Court has returned to a policy closer to the original clear and present danger doctrine. As the Cold War progressed, Americans grew to view communism as a serious threat to democracy, but not a *present* danger. The overthrow of the American government advocated by communists was not an incitement to *immediate* action. A democracy must not itself become authoritarian to protect itself from authoritarianism. In later cases, the Supreme Court held that the mere advocacy of revolution, apart from unlawful action, is protected by the First Amendment.[42] It struck down federal laws requiring communist organizations to register with the government,[43] laws requiring individuals to sign "loyalty oaths,"[44] laws prohibiting communists from working in defense plants,[45] and laws stripping passports from Communist Party leaders.[46] In short, once the perceived Cold War crisis began to fade, the Supreme Court reasserted the First Amendment rights of individuals and groups.

Symbolic Speech   The First Amendment's guarantees of speech, press, and assembly are broadly interpreted to mean **freedom of expression**. Political expression encompasses more than just words. For example, when Mary Beth Tinker and her brothers were suspended for wearing black armbands to high school to protest the Vietnam War, they argued that the wearing of armbands constituted **symbolic speech** protected by the First Amendment. The Supreme Court agreed, noting that the school did not prohibit all wearing of symbols but instead singled out this particular expression for disciplinary action.[47] The Court also held that wearing Ku Klux Klan hoods and gathering together to burn a cross[48] and even burning the American flag (see *What Do You Think?:* "Do We Have a Constitutional Right to Burn the American Flag?" on page 516)[49] are protected expression. However, burning one's draft card does not constitute protected speech and exempt the burner from legal penalties for failure to carry such a card. The Court "cannot accept the view that an apparently limitless variety of conduct can be labeled 'speech.'"[50]

The Supreme Court continues to wrestle with the question of what kinds of conduct are symbolic speech protected by the First Amendment and what kinds of conduct are outside of this protection (see *What Do You Think?:* "Do We Have the Right to Die?" on page 517). Symbolic speech, like speech itself, cannot be banned just because it offends people. "If there is only one bedrock principle underlying the First Amendment, it is that the Government may not prohibit the expression of an idea simply because society finds the idea itself offensive or disagreeable."[51]

Speech and Public Order   The Supreme Court has wrestled with the question of whether speech can be prohibited when it stirs audiences to public disorder, not because the speaker urges lawless action but because the audience reacts to the speech with hostility. In short, can a speaker be arrested because of the *audience's* disorderly behavior? In an early case, the Supreme Court fashioned a *fighting words doctrine*, to the effect that words that "ordinary men know are likely to cause a fight" may be prohibited.[52] But later the Court seemed to realize that this doctrine, if broadly applied, could create a huge constitutional hole in the

The Supreme Court has ruled that Ku Klux Klan cross burnings constitute symbolic speech protected by the First Amendment.

freedom of expression
Collectively, the First Amendment rights to free speech, press, and assembly.

symbolic speech   Actions other than speech itself but protected by the First Amendment because they constitute political expression.

WHAT DO YOU THINK?

Do We Have a Constitutional Right to Burn the American Flag?

Flag waving is an American political tradition. The American flag symbolizes nationhood and national unity. Most states and the federal government have laws forbidding "desecration" of the flag.

Flag desecration is a physical act, but it also has symbolic meaning—for example, hatred of the United States or opposition to government policies. At the 1984 Republican national convention in Dallas, Gregory Lee Johnson joined a protest march against Reagan Administration policies, then doused an American flag with kerosene and set fire to it. As it burned, he and others chanted, "America, the red, white, and blue, we spit on you." Police arrested Johnson and charged him with violating a Texas law against flag desecration. The American Civil Liberties Union came to Johnson's defense, arguing that flag burning is "symbolic speech" protected by the First Amendment.

In the case of *Texas v. Johnson* (1989), a majority of Supreme Court justices argued that "Johnson's burning of the flag was conduct sufficiently imbued with elements of communication to implicate the First Amendment." They declared that when speech and conduct are combined in the same expressive act, the government must show that it has "a sufficiently important interest in regulating the non-speech element to justify incident limitations on First Amendment freedoms." In this case, "preserving the flag as a symbol of nationhood and national unity" was not deemed sufficiently important to justify limiting Johnson's freedom of expression.*

The Court's decision caused a political uproar. President George Bush immediately condemned it, and public opinion polls showed massive opposition to it. Congress quickly passed the Flag Protection Act of 1989, mandating a one-year jail sentence and $1,000 fine for anyone who "knowingly mutilates, defaces, physically defiles, burns, maintains on the floor or ground, or tramples upon, any flag of the United States." But just as promptly, the Supreme Court, by the same 5 to 4 vote, struck down the new federal law as unconstitutional, using the same reasoning as expressed in the *Johnson* case. Congress was not finished with the issue. Its next effort centered on the passage of a constitutional amendment:

"The Congress and the states shall have the power to prohibit physical desecration of the flag of the United States." Because Congress was controlled by the Democrats, Republicans were convinced that the failure to pass the amendment would hurt Democratic Party candidates in the next election. (A June 1990 Gallup Poll revealed that 68 percent of Americans supported a constitutional amendment protecting the flag.) But Democratic leaders argued that the proposed amendment would alter the Bill of Rights and that Republicans were trying to "politicize the flag." The Democratic leadership also called for a quick vote to forestall efforts to rally strong public support for the amendment. Republicans led the fight for the amendment, but the political appeal of supporting the flag pulled a large number of Democratic members of the House to their side. Supporters paid homage to the flag:

> Too many people have paid for it with their blood. Too many people have marched behind it. Too many kids and parents and widows have accepted this triangle as the last remembrance of their loved ones. Too many to have this ever demeaned.

Opponents frequently quoted the Supreme Court's majority opinion:

> The way to preserve the flag's special role is not to punish those who feel differently about these matters. It is to persuade them that they are wrong. . . . We can imagine no more appropriate response to burning a flag than waving one's own, no better way to counter a flag-burner's message than by saluting the flag that burns. . . . We do not consecrate the flag by punishing its desecration, for in doing so we dilute the freedom that this cherished emblem represents.†

In the end, the flag amendment was defeated when it garnered a majority of House votes but fewer than required to pass a constitutional amendment by the necessary two-thirds vote. Likewise, a majority of the Senate has voted several times in favor of the amendment, but it has always fallen short of the necessary two-thirds vote.

Texas v. Johnson, 491 U.S. 397 (1989).
†Quotations from *Congressional Quarterly*, June 23, 1990, p. 2004.

Do We Have the Right to Die?

In most states, for most of the nation's history, it has been a crime to assist another person to commit suicide. Michigan's prosecution of Dr. Jack Kevorkian for publicly participating in physician-assisted suicides launched a nationwide debate on the topic. More important, a group of physicians in Washington, along with their gravely ill patients, filed suit in federal court seeking a declaration that their state's law banning physician-assisted suicide violated the "liberty" guaranteed by the Fourteenth Amendment. They argued that mentally competent, terminally ill patients had the "right to die"; that is, they had a privacy right to request and receive aid in ending their life. They relied on the Supreme Court's previous rulings on abortion (see *Up Close*: "Privacy, Abortion, and the Constitution" in Chapter 13), contending that Washington's law placed an undue burden on the exercise of a privacy right. But the U.S. Supreme Court held that a law prohibiting "causing or aiding" a suicide did *not* violate the Fourteenth Amendment, that there is no *constitutional right* to physician-assisted suicide.* The Court implied that if the laws governing the practice are to be changed, they must be changed by legislatures, not by reinterpreting the Constitution. The Court observed that a number of states had recently reaffirmed their bans on physician-assisted suicide and that Congress specifically prohibits the use of federal funds for that purpose.

Nonetheless, public opinion generally favors physician-assisted suicide often referred to by supporters

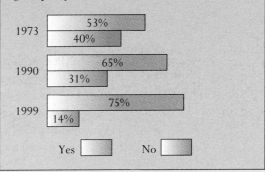

Question: *When a person has a disease that cannot be cured, do you think doctors should be allowed by law to end the patient's life by some painless means if the patient and his family request it?*

Source: Gallup Polls, reported in *The Polling Report*, July 28, 1997, p. 6, updated.

as "the right to die." Indeed support appears to have grown over the years:

The Supreme Court exercised "judicial restraint" in its (6 to 3) decision *not* to declare physician-assisted suicide a constitutionally protected liberty. It left the question to Congress and state legislatures. It is likely that "the right to die" will be hotly debated by the people and their elected representatives in the years ahead.

---

*Washington v. Glucksberg, 117 S.Ct. 2258 (1997).

First Amendment guarantee of free speech. Authorities could curtail speech simply because it met with audience hostility. The Court recognized that "speech is often provocative and challenging. It may . . . have profound unsettling effects. . . . That is why freedom of speech, while not absolute, is nevertheless protected against censorship."[53] The Court has also held that the First Amendment protects the use of four-letter words when used to express an idea: "One man's vulgarity may be another's lyric."[54] And the Court has consistently refused to allow government authorities to ban speech *before* it has occurred simply because they believe it *may* create a disturbance.

Many colleges and universities have undertaken to ban speech that is considered racist, sexist, homophobic, or otherwise "insensitive" to the feelings of women and minorities. Varieties of "speech codes," "hate codes," and sexual harassment regulations that prohibit verbal expressions raise serious constitutional questions, especially at state-supported colleges and universities. The First Amendment does not exclude insulting or offensive racist or sexist words or comments from its protection (see *Up Close:* "Political Correctness versus Free Speech on Campus"). Many of these college and university regulations would not withstand a judicial challenge if students or faculty undertook to oppose them in federal court.

Hate Speech and Hate Crimes "Hate" speech is usually defined as hostile or prejudicial attitudes expressed toward another person's or group's characteristics, notably sex, race, ethnicity, religion, or sexual orientation. Banning hate speech is now common at colleges and universities, in business employment and sports enterprises, on radio and television, and in the press. But do *government* prohibitions on hate speech violate the First Amendment?

Historically the Supreme Court viewed prohibitions on offensive speech as unconstitutional infringements of First Amendment freedoms. "The remedy to be applied is more speech, not enforced silence."[55]

The Supreme Court was called upon to review prohibitions on hate speech in 1992 when the City of St. Paul, Minnesota, enacted an ordinance prohibiting any communication that "arouses anger, alarm, or resentment among others on the basis of race, color, creed, religion, or gender." The ordinance defined such expressions as "disorderly conduct" and made them misdemeanors punishable by law. The city argued that it was protecting the community against "fighting words" that created a threat to public safety and order, and that such words should be placed outside the protection of the First Amendment in the same fashion as libel and slander.

But the Supreme Court, in a unanimous decision, struck down the city's effort to prohibit expressions only because they cause "hurt feelings, offense, or resentment." Speech expressing racial, gender, or religious intolerance is still speech, and it is protected by the First Amendment.[56]

However, the Supreme Court is willing to recognize that bias-motivated crimes—crimes intentionally directed at a victim because of his or her race, religion, disability, national origin, or sexual orientation—may be more heavily punished than the same crimes inspired by other motives. The Court held that a criminal defendant's "abstract beliefs, however obnoxious to most people, may not be taken into consideration by a sentencing judge."[57] But a defendant's *motive* for committing a particular criminal act has traditionally been a factor in sentencing, and a defendant's verbal statements can be used to determine motive.

Commercial Speech Do First Amendment freedoms of expression apply to commercial advertising? The Supreme Court has frequently asserted that **commercial speech** is protected by the First Amendment. The Court held that states cannot outlaw price advertising by pharmacists[58] or advertising for services by attorneys[59] and that cities cannot outlaw posting "For Sale" signs on property, even in the interests of halting white flight and promoting racially integrated neighborhoods. Advertising is the "dissemination of information" and is constitutionally protected.[60]

commercial speech Advertising communications given only partial protection under the First Amendment to the Constitution.

However, the Court has also been willing to weigh the First Amendment rights of commercial advertisers against the public interest served by regulation.[61] In other words, the Court seems to suspend its preferred position doctrine with regard to commercial advertising and to call for a "balancing of interests." Thus, the Supreme Court has allowed the Federal Communications Commission to regulate the contents

Political Correctness versus Free Speech on Campus

Universities have a very special responsibility to protect freedom of expression. The free and unfettered exchange of views is essential to the advancement of knowledge—the very purpose of universities. For centuries universities have fought to protect academic freedom from pressures arising from the world *outside* of the campus—governments, interest groups, financial contributors—arguing that the university must be a protected enclave for free expression of ideas. But today's threat to academic freedom arises from *within* universities—from efforts by administrations, faculty, and campus groups to suppress ideas, opinions, and language that are not "politically correct" (PC). PC activists seek to suppress opinions and expressions they consider to be racist, sexist, "homophobic," or otherwise "insensitive" to specified groups.*

Speech Codes The experience at the University of Michigan with its "Policy on Discrimination and Discriminatory Harassment" illustrates the battles occurring on many campuses over First Amendment rights. In 1988 a series of racial incidents on campus prompted the university to officially ban "any behavior verbal or physical" that "stigmatized" an individual "on the basis of race, ethnicity, religion, sex, sexual orientation, creed, national origin, ancestry, age, marital status, handicap, or Vietnam-era veteran status" or that created "an intimidating, hostile, or demeaning environment for educational pursuits." A published guide provided examples of banned activity, which included the following:

● A male student makes remarks in class like "women just aren't as good in this field as men."

● Jokes about gay men and lesbians.

● Commenting in a derogatory way about a particular person or group's physical appearance or sexual orientation, or their cultural origins, or religious beliefs.

Free Speech In 1989 "John Doe," a psychology graduate student studying gender differences in

personality traits and mental functions, filed suit in federal court requesting that the University of Michigan policy be declared a violation of the First Amendment. (He was permitted by the court to remain anonymous because of fear of retribution.) He was joined in his complaint against the university by the American Civil Liberties Union.

In its decision, the court acknowledged that the university had a legal responsibility to prevent racial or sexual discrimination or harassment. However, it did not have a right to

> establish an anti-discrimination policy which had the effect of prohibiting certain speech because it disagreed with ideas or messages sought to be conveyed. . . . Nor could the University proscribe speech simply because it was found to be offensive, even gravely so, by large numbers of people. . . . These principles acquire a special significance in the University setting, where the free and unfettered interplay of competing views is essential to the institution's educational mission. . . . While the Court is sympathetic to the University's obligation to ensure educational opportunities for all of its students, such efforts must not be at the expense of free speech.†

It seems ironic that students and faculty now must seek the protection of the federal courts from attempts by universities to limit speech. Traditionally, universities themselves fought to protect academic freedom. Academic freedom included the freedom of faculty and students to express themselves in the classroom, on the campus, and in writing, on controversial and sensitive topics, including race and gender. It was recognized that students often express ideas that are biased or ill informed, immature, or crudely expressed. But students were taught that the remedy for offensive language or off-color remarks or ill-chosen examples was more enlightened speech, not the suppression of speech.

---

*Dinesh D'Souza, *Illiberal Education: The Politics of Race and Sex on Campus* (New York: Vintage Books, 1992).

†*John Doe v. University of Michigan*, 721 F. Supp. 852 (1989).

of advertising on radio and television and even to ban advertising for cigarettes. The Federal Trade Commission enforces "truth" in advertising by requiring commercial packages and advertisers to prove all claims for their products.

Libel and Slander   Libel and slander have never been protected by the First Amendment against subsequent punishment (see "Libel and Slander" in Chapter 6). Once a communication is determined to be libelous or slanderous, it is outside of the protection of the First Amendment. The courts have traditionally defined "libel" as a "damaging falsehood." However, if plaintiffs are public officials they must prove that the statements made about them are not only false and damaging but also "made with actual malice"—that is, with knowledge that they are false or with "reckless disregard" of the truth—in order to prove libel.[62]

OBSCENITY AND THE LAW

Obscene materials of all kinds—words, publications, photos, videotapes, films—are also exempt from First Amendment protection. Most states ban the publication, sale, or possession of obscene material, and Congress bans its shipment in the mails. Because obscene material is not protected by the First Amendment, it can be banned without even an attempt to prove that it results in antisocial conduct. In other words, it is not necessary to show that obscene material would result in a clear and present danger to society, the test used to decide the legitimacy of *speech*. In order to ban obscene materials, the government need only prove that they are *obscene*.

Defining "obscenity" has confounded legislatures and the courts for years, however. State and federal laws often define pornography and obscenity in such terms as "lewd," "lascivious," "filthy," "indecent," "disgusting"—all equally as vague as "obscene." "Pornography" is simply a synonym for "obscenity." *Soft-core pornography* usually denotes nakedness and sexually suggestive poses; it is less likely to confront legal barriers. *Hard-core pornography* usually denotes explicit sexual activity. After many fruitless efforts by the Supreme Court to come up with a workable definition of "pornography" or "obscenity," a frustrated Justice Potter Stewart wrote in 1974, "I shall not today attempt further to define [hard-core pornography]. . . . But *I know it when I see it.*"[63]

Slackening Standards: Roth v. United States   The Court's first comprehensive effort to define "obscenity" came in *Roth v. United States* (1957). Although the Court upheld Roth's conviction for distributing pornographic magazines through the mails, it defined "obscenity" somewhat narrowly: "Whether to the average person applying contemporary community standards, the dominant theme of the material, taken as a whole, appeals to prurient interests."[64]

Note that the material must be obscene to the *average* person, not to children or particular groups of adults who might be especially offended by pornography. The standard is "contemporary," suggesting that what was once regarded as obscene might be acceptable today. Later, the *community standard* was clarified to mean the "society at large," not a particular state or local community.[65] The material must be "considered as a whole," meaning that even if a work includes some obscene material, it is still acceptable if its "dominant theme" is something other than "prurient."[66] The Court added that a work must be "utterly without redeeming social or literary merit" in order to be judged obscene.[67] The Court never really said what a "prurient" interest was but reassured everyone that "sex and obscenity are not synonymous."[68]

Tightening Standards: Miller v. California   The effect of the Roth decision, and the many and varied attempts by lower courts to apply its slippery standards, tended to limit law enforcement efforts to combat pornography during the 1960s and 1970s. The Supreme Court itself came under ridicule when it was learned that the justices had set up a movie room in the basement of the Supreme Court building to view films that had been brought before them in obscenity cases.[69]

So the Supreme Court tried again, in *Miller v. California* (1973), to give law enforcement officials some clearer standards in determining obscenity. Although the Court retained the "average person" and "contemporary" standards, it redefined "community" to mean the *local* community rather than the society at large. It also defined "prurient" as "patently offensive" representations or descriptions of "ultimate sex acts, normal or perverted, actual or simulated," as well as "masturbation, excretory functions, and lewd exhibition of the genitals." It rejected the earlier requirement that the work had to be "utterly without redeeming social value" in order to be judged obscene, and it substituted instead "lacks serious literary, artistic, political, or scientific value."[70]

The effect of the Supreme Court's *Miller* standards has been to increase the likelihood of conviction in obscenity-pornography cases.[71] It is easier to prove that a work lacks serious value than to prove that it is utterly without redeeming merit. Moreover, the *local community standard* allows prosecution of adult bookstores and X-rated video stores in some communities, while allowing the same stores to operate in other communities. The Supreme Court has also upheld local ordinances that ban nudity in public places, including bars and lounges. The Court rejected the argument that nude dancing was "expressive" conduct.[72]

Child Pornography   The Supreme Court has struck hard against child pornography—the "dissemination of material depicting children engaged in sexual conduct regardless of whether the material is obscene." Such conduct includes any visual depiction of children performing sexual acts or lewdly exhibiting their genitals. The Court held that safeguarding children used in films or photographs from sexual exploitation and abuse was "a government objective of overriding importance."[73] In such cases, the existence of the material itself is evidence that a crime has been committed. Thus the test for *child* pornography is much stricter than the *Miller* standards.

The Information Highway   New technologies continue to challenge courts in the application of First Amendment principles. Currently the Internet, the global computer communication network, allows users to gain access to information worldwide. Thousands of electronic bulletin boards give computer users with communication modems access to everything from bomb-making instructions and sex conversations to obscene photos and even child pornography. Many commercial access services ban obscene messages and exclude bulletin boards with racially or sexually offensive commentary. But can *government* try to ban such material from the Internet without violating First Amendment freedoms?

Congress tried unsuccessfully to ban "indecent" and "patently offensive" communications from the Internet in its Communications Decency Act of 1996. Proponents of the law cited the need to protect children from pornography. But in 1997 the

Despite public concerns about the ability of children to gain access to obscene materials on the Internet, the Supreme Court, calling it the "most participatory form of mass speech yet developed," ruled that Congress cannot limit the Internet's content to only what is fit for children.

Supreme Court held the act unconstitutional: "Notwithstanding the legitimacy and importance of the Congressional goal of protecting children from harmful materials, we agree that the statute abridges freedom of speech protected by the First Amendment." Government cannot limit Internet messages "to only what is fit for children." The Supreme Court agreed with the assertion that "as the most participatory form of mass speech yet developed [the Internet] deserves the highest protection from government intrusion."[74]

FREEDOM OF THE PRESS

Democracy depends on the free expression of ideas. Authoritarian regimes either monopolize the media or subject them to strict licensing and censorship of their content. The idea of a free and independent press is deeply rooted in the evolution of democratic government.

No Prior Restraint Doctrine   Long before the Bill of Rights was written, English law protected newspapers from government restrictions or licensing prior to publication—a practice called **prior restraint**. This protection, however, does not mean that publishers are exempt from *subsequent punishment* for libelous, obscene, or other illegal publications. Prior restraint is more dangerous to free expression because it allows the government to censor the work prior to publication and forces the defendants to *prove* that their material should *not* be censored. In contrast, subsequent punishment requires a trial in which the government must prove that the defendant's published materials are unlawful.

In *Near v. Minnesota* (1931), a muckraking publication that accused local officials of trafficking with gangsters was barred from publishing under a Minnesota law that prohibited the publication of a "malicious, scandalous or defamatory newspaper." The Supreme Court struck down the law as unconstitutional, affirming the *no-prior-restraint doctrine*. However, a close reading of the majority opinion reveals that the doctrine is not absolute. Chief Justice Charles Evans Hughes noted that

prior restraint   Government actions to restrict publication of a magazine, newspaper, or books on grounds of libel, obscenity, or other legal violations prior to actual publication of the work.

prior government censorship might be constitutional "if publication . . . threatened the country's safety in times of war."[75]

Yet the question of whether or not the government can restrain publication of stories that present a serious threat to national security remains unanswered. For example, can the government restrain the press from reporting in advance on the time and place of an impending U.S. military action, thereby warning an enemy and perhaps adding to American casualties? In the most important case on this question, *New York Times v. United States* (1971), the Supreme Court upheld the right of the newspaper to publish secret documents that had been stolen from State Department and Defense Department files. The material covered U.S. policy decisions in Vietnam, and it was published while the war was still being waged. But five separate (concurring) opinions were written by justices in the majority as well as two dissenting opinions. Only two justices argued that government can *never* restrain any publication regardless of the seriousness or immediacy of the harm. Others in the majority cited the government's failure to show proof in this case that publication "would surely result in direct, immediate, and irreparable damage to our nation or its people."[76] Presumably, if the government had produced such proof, the case might have been decided differently. The media interprets the decision as a blanket protection to publish anything it wishes regardless of harm to government or society.

Film Censorship   The no-prior-restraint doctrine was developed to protect the print media—books, magazines, newspapers. When the motion picture industry was in its infancy, the Supreme Court held that films were "business, pure and simple" and were not entitled to the protection of the First Amendment.[77] But as films grew in importance, the Court gradually extended First Amendment freedoms to cover motion pictures.[78] However, the Supreme Court has not given the film industry the same strong no-prior-restraint protection it has given the press. The Court has approved government requirements for prior submission of films to official censors, so long as (1) the burden of proof that the film is obscene rests with the censor; (2) a procedure exists for judicial determination of the issue; and (3) censors are required to act speedily.[79] To avoid government-imposed censorship the motion picture industry adopted its own system of rating films:

G: suitable for all audiences

PG: parental guidance suggested

PG-13: parental guidance strongly suggested for children under thirteen

R: restricted to those seventeen or older unless accompanied by a parent or guardian

NC-17: no one under seventeen admitted

Some city governments have sought to restrict showing of NC-17 films, and their restrictions have been upheld by the Courts.[80]

Radio and Television Censorship   The Federal Communications Commission was created in 1934 to allocate broadcast frequencies and to license stations. The exclusive right to use a particular frequency is a "public trust." Thus, broadcasters, unlike newspapers and magazines, are licensed by the government and subject to government rules. Although the First Amendment protects broadcasters, the Supreme Court has recognized the special obligations that may be imposed on them in exchange for the exclusive right to use a broadcast frequency. "No one

Television networks hope to avoid government-imposed censorship by offering warnings such as "viewer discretion advised."

has a First Amendment right to a license or to monopolize a radio frequency; to deny a station license because 'the public interest' requires it, is not a denial of free speech."[81] Thus the Court has upheld FCC-imposed "equal time" and "fairness" rules against broadcasters, even while striking down government attempts to impose the same rules on newspapers.[82]

Media Claims for Special Rights   The news media make various claims to special rights arising out of the First Amendment's guarantee of a free press. Reporters argue, for example, that they should be able to protect their news sources and are not obliged to give testimony in criminal cases when they have obtained evidence in confidence. However, the only witnesses the Constitution exempts from compulsory testimony are defendants themselves, who enjoy the Fifth Amendment's protection against "self-incrimination." The Supreme Court has flatly rejected reporters' claims to a privilege against compulsory testimony. "We cannot seriously entertain the notion that the First Amendment protects a newsman's agreement to conceal the criminal conduct of his source, or evidence thereof, on the theory that it is better to write about a crime than to do something about it."[83] The Court also has rejected the argument that media notes and records are confidential; instead, it sided with law enforcement officials who had used a valid warrant to search the *Stanford Daily*'s offices for photos showing demonstrators who had attacked police.[84]

Despite these rulings, reporters regularly boast of their willingness to go to jail to protect sources, and many have done so. But the media have also pressured the nation's legislatures for protection. Congress has passed the Privacy Protection Act, which sharply limits the ability of law enforcement officials to search press offices, and many states have passed **shield laws** specifically protecting reporters from giving testimony in criminal cases.

Conflicting "Rights"   The conflict between reporters' "rights" to protect their sources under shield laws and the constitutional right of individuals to face their accusers when on trial is just one example of the many conflicts over "rights" in American life. In the case of shield laws, the courts have ruled that "rights" granted by law are not equal to rights granted by the Constitution and have imprisoned those who try to hide behind these laws. Sometimes, however, conflict pits two constitutional rights against one another, as when a judge places a **gag order** on individuals involved in a case. In such cases, the court has essentially decreed that the First Amendment rights of free speech and freedom of the press must be postponed so that the right of an individual to receive a fair and impartial trial is not destroyed.

shield laws   Laws in some states that give reporters the right to refuse to name their sources or to release their notes in court cases; may be overturned by the courts when such refusals jeopardize a fair trial for a defendant.

gag order   Order by a judge banning discussion or reporting of a case in order to ensure a fair and impartial trial.

FREEDOM OF ASSEMBLY AND PETITION

The First Amendment guarantees "the right of the people peaceably to assemble, and to petition the government for redress of grievances." The right to organize political parties and interest groups derives from the right of assembly. And freedom of petition protects most lobbying activities.

The Right of Association   Freedom of assembly includes the right to form and join organizations and associations. In an important case during the early civil rights movement, the State of Alabama attempted to harass the National Association for the Advancement of Colored People by requiring it to turn over its membership lists to authorities. The Supreme Court held the state's action to be an unconstitutional infringement of the freedom of association.[85] In 1999 the Court struck down a Chicago city ordinance that prohibited street gangs from "loitering" in public places.[86]

The Supreme Court has also protected the right of students to form organizations. "First Amendment rights . . . are available to teachers and students. It can hardly be argued that either teachers or students shed their constitutional rights at the school house gate."[87] Attempts by a college or university to deny official recognition to a student organization based on its views violates the right of association.

Protests, Parades, and Demonstrations   Freedom of assembly includes the right to peacefully protest, parade, and demonstrate. Authorities may, within reasonable limits, enact restrictions regarding the "time, place, and manner" of an assembly so as to preserve public order, smooth traffic flow, freedom of movement, and even peace and quiet. But these regulations cannot be unevenly applied to groups with different views. Thus authorities may require a permit to parade, but they cannot deny a permit to a group because of the nature of their views or content of their message. For example, the Supreme Court held that city

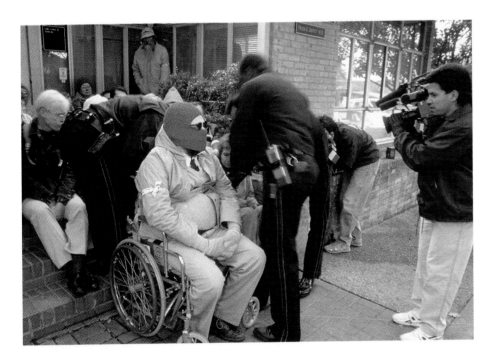

No rights are absolute. The freedom to assemble does not include the right to block public access to buildings. Congress reaffirmed this limitation in 1994 in a law guaranteeing access to abortion clinics.

authorities in Skokie, Illinois, acted unconstitutionally in prohibiting the American Nazi Party from holding a march in that city even though it was populated with large numbers of Jewish survivors of the Holocaust.[88]

Picketing Assemblies of people have a high potential for creating a public disturbance. Parades block traffic and litter the streets; loudspeakers assault the ears of local residents and bystanders; picket lines may block the free passage of others. Although the right of assembly is protected by the First Amendment, its exercise involves conduct as well as expression, and therefore it is usually subject to greater government regulation than expression alone. The Court has generally upheld reasonable use of public property for assembly, but it has not forced *private* property owners to accommodate speeches or assemblies. Airport terminals, shopping malls, and other open forums, which may or may not be publicly owned, have posed problems for the courts.

Freedom of assembly is currently being tested by opponents of abortion who picket abortion clinics, hoping to embarrass and dissuade women from entering them. Generally the courts have allowed limits on these demonstrations to ensure that people can move freely in and out of the clinics. Freedom of assembly does not include the right to block access to public or private buildings. And when abortion opponents demonstrated at the residence of a physician who performed abortions, the Supreme Court upheld a local ordinance barring assemblies in residential neighborhoods.[89] Physically obstructing access to buildings almost always violates state or local laws, as does the threat or use of force by picketers. The Supreme Court made a distinction between a "fixed buffer zone," prohibiting assembly around a building entrance, and a "floating buffer zone" (of 15 feet), prohibiting demonstrators from approaching individuals in public places. The "fixed" zone was held to be a constitutional limit on assembly, but the "floating" zone was held to be an *unconstitutional* limit on free speech.[90] In 1994 Congress passed a federal law guaranteeing access to abortion clinics, arguing that the federal government should act to guarantee a recognized constitutional right.

THE RIGHT TO BEAR ARMS

The Second Amendment to the U.S. Constitution states: "A well regulated Militia, being necessary to the security of a free State, the right of the people to keep and bear Arms, shall not be infringed."

Bearing Arms What is meant by the right of the people "to keep and bear arms"? One view is that the Second Amendment confers on Americans an *individual* constitutional right, like the First Amendment freedom of speech or press (see *Across the USA:* "Gun Control and the Second Amendment"). The history surrounding the adoption of the Second Amendment reveals the concern of colonists with attempts by despotic governments to confiscate the arms of citizens and render them helpless to resist tyranny. James Madison wrote in the *Federalist Papers*, No. 46 that "the advantage of being armed which the Americans possess over the people of almost every other nation, forms a barrier against the enterprise of [tyrannical] ambition."[91] The Second Amendment was adopted with little controversy; most state constitutions at the time, like Pennsylvania's, declared that "the people have a right to bear arms for the defense of themselves and the state." Early

Gun Control and the Second Amendment

One subject of contention in the debate over gun control is whether or not law-abiding citizens should be permitted to carry concealed handguns. Laws on this issue vary from state to state.

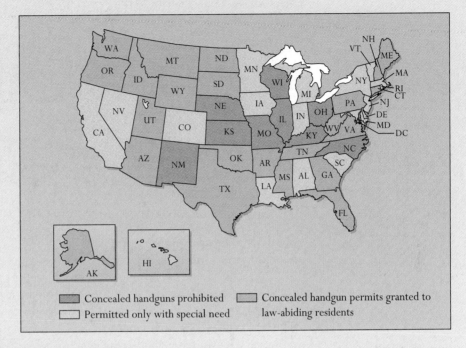

▢ Concealed handguns prohibited   ▢ Concealed handgun permits granted to
▢ Permitted only with special need   law-abiding residents

Attempts at gun control legislation frequently follow murders or assassination attempts on prominent figures. The Federal Gun Control Act of 1968 was a response to the assassinations of Senator Robert F. Kennedy and Martin Luther King, Jr., in that year. It banned mail-order sales of handguns and required that manufacturers place serial numbers on all firearms, that dealers record all sales, and that dealers be licensed by the Bureau of Alcohol, Tobacco and Firearms. In 1993 Congress passed the Brady Act, requiring a seven-day waiting period for the purchase of a handgun. The act is named for James S. Brady, former press secretary to President Ronald Reagan, who was severely wounded in the 1981 attempted assassination of the president. The Crime Control Act of 1994 banned the manufacture or sale of "assault weapons," generally defined to include both automatic and semiautomatic rifles and machine pistols. Opponents of these acts believe they are empty political gestures that erode the Second Amendment right to bear arms.

Proponents of gun control cite the U.S. Supreme Court decision in *United States v. Miller* (1939). In this case, the Court considered the constitutionality of the federal National Firearms Act of 1934, which, among other things, prohibited the transportation of sawed-off shotguns in interstate commerce. The defendant claimed that Congress could not infringe on his right to keep and bear arms. But the Court responded that a sawed-off shotgun had no "relationship to the preservation or efficiency of a well-regulated militia."* The clear implication of this decision is that the right to bear arms refers only to a state's right to maintain a militia. But even if an individual has a constitutional right to own a gun, the Supreme Court is likely to approve of reasonable restrictions on that right, including waiting periods for purchases, reporting, and registration. No constitutional right is viewed as absolute.

The Second Amendment does not necessarily include the right to carry a hidden gun. Currently about half of the states grant concealed weapons carrying permits to applicants who have never been convicted of a felony. (Generally a "concealed weapon" refers to a handgun carried on a person or within immediate reach in an automobile.) Nine states and the District of Columbia prohibit the carrying of concealed weapons altogether. Other states require applicants for permits to prove that they have a specific need to carry a weapon.

United States v. Miller, 307 U.S. 174 (1939).

The violent conclusion of the attempt by the Bureau of Alcohol, Tobacco and Firearms to enforce federal gun laws against the Branch Davidians in Waco, Texas. Members of citizen militia groups regard the ATF as a threat to their freedom to bear arms.

American political rhetoric was filled with praise for an armed citizenry able to protect its freedoms by force if necessary.

State Militias   But many constitutional scholars argue that the Second Amendment protects only the *collective* right of the states to form militias—that is, their right to maintain National Guard units. They focus on the qualifying phrase "a well-regulated Militia, being necessary to the security of a free State." The Second Amendment merely prevents Congress from denying the states the right to organize their own military units. If the Founders had wished to create an individual right to bear arms, they would not have inserted the phrase about a "well-regulated militia." (Opponents of this view argue that the original definition of a militia included all free males over eighteen.) Interpreted in this fashion, the Second Amendment does *not* protect private groups who form themselves into militias, nor does it guarantee citizens the right to own guns.

Citizen "Militias"   In recent years, self-styled citizen "militias" have cropped up across the nation. They are armed groups who more or less regularly get together dressed in camouflage to engage in military tactics and training. They generally view federal government agencies, and often the United Nations, as potential threats to their freedom. They view themselves as modern-day descendants of the American patriot militias who fought in the Revolutionary War. Indeed, the Militia Act of 1792 *required* "every free white male citizen of the respective states, resident therein, who is or shall be of the age of 18 years and under the age of 45 years" to be enrolled in the militia and equipped with "a good musket," a bayonet, and "24 rounds of ammunition." This law was not changed until 1912, when National Guard units replaced state militia.

Citizen militia groups frequently come into conflict with federal firearms regulations. Enforcement of these regulations is the responsibility of the Bureau of Alcohol, Tobacco and Firearms. It was the ATF's violent efforts to enforce federal gun laws that led to the deaths of more than seventy people at the Branch Davidian compound in Waco, Texas, in 1993. Radical militia groups have pledged to enforce their right to bear arms with violence if necessary.

RIGHTS OF CRIMINAL DEFENDANTS

While society needs the protection of the police, it is equally important to protect society from the police. Arbitrary searches and arrests, imprisonment without trial, forced confessions, beatings and torture, secret trials, tainted witnesses, excessive punishments, and other human rights violations are all too common throughout the world. The U.S. Constitution limits the powers of the police and protects the rights of the accused (see Table 14–3 on page 530).

The Guarantee of the Writ of Habeas Corpus　One of the oldest and most revered rights in English common law is the right to obtain a **writ of habeas corpus**, which is a court order directing public officials who are holding a person in custody to bring the prisoner into court and explain the reasons for confinement. If a judge finds that the prisoner is being unlawfully detained, or finds insufficient evidence that a crime has been committed or that the prisoner could have committed it, the judge must order the prisoner's release. Thus the writ of habeas corpus is a means to test the legality of any imprisonment.

The writ of habeas corpus was considered so fundamental to the framers of the Constitution that they included it in the original text of Article I: "The privilege of the Writ of Habeas Corpus shall not be suspended, unless when in Cases of Rebellion or Invasion the public Safety may require it." Despite the qualifying phrase, the Supreme Court has never sanctioned suspension of the writ of habeas corpus even during wartime. President Abraham Lincoln suspended the writ of habeas corpus in several areas during the Civil War, but in the case of *Ex parte Milligan* (1866), the Supreme Court ruled that the president had acted unconstitutionally.[92] (With the war over, however, the Court's decision had no practical effect.) Again, in 1946, the Supreme Court declared that the military had had no right to substitute military courts for ordinary courts in Hawaii during World War II, even though Hawaii was in an active theater of war.[93] State courts cannot issue writs of habeas corpus to federal officials, but federal judges may issue such writs to state officials whenever there is reason to believe that a person is being held in violation of the Constitution or laws of the United States.

The Prohibition of Bills of Attainder and Ex Post Facto Laws　Like the guarantee of habeas corpus, protection against bills of attainder and ex post facto laws was considered so fundamental to individual liberty that it was included in the original text of the Constitution. A **bill of attainder** is a legislative act inflicting punishment without judicial trial. An **ex post facto law** is a retroactive criminal law that works against the accused—for example, a law that makes an act criminal after the act is committed or a law that increases the punishment for a crime and applies it retroactively. Both the federal government and the states are prevented from passing such laws.

The fact that relatively few cases of bills of attainder or ex post facto laws have come to the federal courts does not diminish the importance of these protections. Rather, it testifies to the widespread appreciation of their importance in a free society.

writ of habeas corpus Court order directing public officials who are holding a person in custody to bring the prisoner into court and explain the reasons for confinement; the right to habeas corpus is protected by Article I of the Constitution.

bill of attainder Legislative act inflicting punishment without judicial trial; forbidden under Article I of the Constitution.

ex post facto law Retroactive criminal law that works against the accused; forbidden under Article I of the Constitution.

Table 14-3 **Individual Rights in the Criminal Justice Process**

Rights	Process
Fourth Amendment: Protection against unreasonable searches and seizures Warranted searches for sworn "probable cause." Exceptions: consent searches, safety searches, car searches, and searches incident to a valid arrest.	**Investigation by law enforcement officers** Expectation that police act lawfully.
Fifth Amendment: Protection against self-incrimination Miranda rules (see Figure 14–1)	**Arrest** Arrests based on warrants issued by judges and magistrates. Arrests based on crimes committed in the presence of law enforcement officials. Arrests for "probable cause."
Habeas corpus Police holding a person in custody must bring that person before a judge with cause to believe that a crime was committed and the prisoner committed it.	
Eighth Amendment: No excessive bail Defendant considered innocent until proven guilty; release on bail and amount of bail depends on seriousness of crime, trustworthiness of defendant, and safety of community.	**Hearing and bail** Preliminary hearing in which prosecutor presents testimony that a crime was committed and probable cause for charging the accused.
Fifth Amendment: Grand jury (federal) Federal prosecutors (but not necessarily state prosecutors) must convince a grand jury that a reasonable basis exists to believe the defendant committed a crime and he or she should be brought to trial.	**Indictment** Prosecutor, or a grand jury in federal cases, issues formal document naming the accused and specifying the charges.
Sixth Amendment: Right to Counsel Begins in investigation stage, when officials become "accusatory"; extends throughout criminal justice process. Free counsel for indigent defendants.	**Arraignment** Judge reads indictment to the accused and ensures that the accused understands charges and rights and has counsel. Judge asks defendant to choose a plea: Guilty, *nolo contendere* (no contest), or not guilty. If defendant pleads guilty or no contest, a trial is not necessary and defendant proceeds to sentencing.
Sixth Amendment: Right to a speedy and public trial Impartial jury. Right to confront witnesses. Right to compel favorable witnesses to testify.	**Trial** Impartial judge presides as prosecuting and defense attorneys present witnesses and evidence relevant to guilt or innocence of defendant and make arguments to the jury. Jury deliberates in secret and issues a verdict.
Fourth Amendment: Exclusionary rule Illegally obtained evidence cannot be used against defendant.	
Eighth Amendment: Protection against cruel and unusual punishments	**Sentencing** If the defendant is found not guilty, the process ends. Defendants who plead guilty or no contest and defendants found guilty by jury are sentenced by fine, imprisonment, or both by the judge. Sentences imposed must be commensurate to the crimes committed.
Fifth Amendment: Protection against double jeopardy Government cannot try a defendant again for the same offense.	**Appeal** Defendants found guilty may appeal to higher courts for reversal of verdict or a new trial based on errors made anywhere in the process.

Unreasonable Searches and Seizures   Individuals are protected by the Fourth Amendment from "unreasonable searches and seizures" of their private "persons, houses, papers, and effects." The Fourth Amendment lays out specific rules for searches and seizures of evidence: "No warrants shall issue, but upon probable cause, supported by Oath or affirmation, and particularly describing the place to be searched, and the persons or things to be seized." Judges cannot issue a **search warrant** just to let police see *if* an individual has committed a crime; there must be "probable cause" for such issuance. The indiscriminate searching of whole neighborhoods or groups of people is unconstitutional and is prevented by the Fourth Amendment's requirement that the place to be searched must be specifically described in the warrant. The requirement that the things to be seized must be described in the warrant is meant to prevent "fishing expeditions" into an individual's home and personal effects on the possibility that some evidence of unknown illegal activity might crop up. The only exception is if police, in the course of a valid search for a specified item, find other items whose very possession is a crime—for example, illicit drugs.

But the courts also permit police to undertake various other "reasonable" searches *without* a warrant: searches in connection with a valid arrest; searches to protect the safety of police officers; searches to obtain evidence in the immediate vicinity and in the suspect's control; searches to preserve evidence in danger of being immediately destroyed; and searches with the consent of a suspect. Indeed, most police searches today take place without warrant under one or another of these conditions. The Supreme Court has also allowed automobile searches and searches of open fields without warrants in many cases. The requirement of "probable cause" has been very loosely defined; even a "partially corroborated anonymous informant's tip" qualifies as "probable cause" to make a search, seizure, or arrest.[94] And if the police, while making a warranted search or otherwise lawfully on the premises, see evidence of a crime "in plain view," they may seize such evidence without further authorization.[95] However, the Court has held that merely stopping a car for a traffic violation does not give police excuse for a search of the car for drugs.[96]

Wiretapping and Electronic Surveillance   For many years the Supreme Court refused to view wiretapping as a search and seizure within the meaning of the Fourth Amendment.[97] However, over time as electronic surveillance techniques became more common and more sophisticated, the Court changed its position. The Court began to view wiretapping and electronic surveillance as a challenge to privacy rights implied by the Fourth Amendment; the Court held that such law enforcement techniques required "probable cause" and a warrant. The government may not undertake to eavesdrop where a person has "a reasonable expectation of privacy," without first showing probable cause and obtaining a warrant.[98] Congress has also enacted a law prohibiting federal agents from intercepting a wire, oral, or electronic communication without first obtaining a warrant. But the Court has upheld the wearing of a hidden body microphone and the recording of conversations between individuals and police or their agents, and the later use of such recordings as evidence in a criminal trial.[99]

Drug Testing   "Unreasonable" drug testing violates the Fourth Amendment. But the Supreme Court has held that it is reasonable to impose mandatory drug testing on railroad workers,[100] federal law enforcement agents,[101] and even students participating in athletics.[102] However, when the State of Georgia enacted

search warrant Court order permitting law enforcement officials to search a location in order to seize evidence of a crime; issued only for a specified location, in connection with a specific investigation, and on submission of proof that "probable cause" exists to warrant such a search.

New technologies continuously challenge the right of privacy implied by the Fourth Amendment. Here, a video camera monitors a Connecticut pre-school.

a law requiring drug testing for candidates for public office, the Court found it to be an "unreasonable" search in violation of the Fourth Amendment.[103] Apparently mandatory drug testing in occupations affecting public safety, and drug testing in schools to protect children, is reasonable, while suspicionless drug testing of the general public is not.

Arrests The Supreme Court has not applied the warrant requirement of the Fourth Amendment to arrests. Rather, the Court permits arrests without warrants (1) when a crime is committed in the presence of an officer; and (2) when an arrest is supported by "probable cause" to believe that a crime has been committed by the person apprehended.[104] However, the Court has held that police may not enter a home to arrest its occupant without either a warrant for the arrest or the consent of the owner.[105] And it has held that media "ride alongs" with police entering a suspect's home also violate the Fourth Amendment.[106]

Indictment The Fifth Amendment requires that an **indictment** be issued by a **grand jury** before a person may be brought to trial on a felony offense. This provision was designed as a protection against unreasonable and harassing prosecutions by the government. In principle, the grand jury is supposed to determine whether the evidence submitted to it by government prosecutors is sufficient to place a person on trial. In practice, however, grand juries spend very little time deliberating on the vast majority of cases. Neither defendants nor their attorneys are permitted to testify before grand juries without the prosecution's permission, which is rarely given. Thus the prosecutor controls the information submitted to grand juries and instructs them in their duties. In almost all cases, grand juries accept the prosecution's recommendations with little or no discussion. Thus grand juries, whose hearings are secret, do not provide much of a check on federal prosecutors, and their refusal to indict is very rare.

Self-Incrimination and the Right to Counsel Freedom from self-incrimination had its origin in English common law; it was originally designed to prevent persons from being tortured into confessions of guilt. It is also a logical

indictment Determination by a grand jury that sufficient evidence exists to warrant trial of an individual on a felony charge; necessary before an individual can be brought to trial.

grand jury Jury charged only with determining whether sufficient evidence exists to support indictment of an individual on a felony charge; the grand jury's decision to indict does not represent a conviction.

extension of the notion that individuals should not be forced to contribute to their own prosecution, that the burden of proof rests on the state. The Fifth Amendment protects people from both physical and psychological coercion.[107] It protects not only accused persons at their own trial but also witnesses testifying in trials of other persons, civil suits, congressional hearings, and so on. Thus "taking the Fifth" has become a standard phrase in our culture: "I refuse to answer that question on the grounds that it might tend to incriminate me." The protection also means that judges, prosecutors, and juries cannot use the refusal of people to take the stand at their own trial as evidence of guilt. Indeed, a judge or attorney is not even permitted to imply this to a jury, and a judge is obligated to instruct a jury *not* to infer guilt from a defendant's refusal to testify.

It is important to note that individuals may be forced to testify when they are not themselves the object of a criminal prosecution. Government officials may extend a **grant of immunity from prosecution** to a witness in order to compel testimony. Under a grant of immunity, the government agrees not to use any of the testimony against the witness; in return, the witness provides information that the government uses to prosecute others who are considered more dangerous or more important than the immune witness. Because such grants ensure that nothing the witnesses say can be used against them, immunized witnesses cannot refuse to answer under the Fifth Amendment.

The Supreme Court under Chief Justice Earl Warren greatly strengthened the Fifth Amendment protection against self-incrimination and the right to counsel in a series of rulings in the 1960s:

- *Gideon v. Wainwright* (1963): Equal protection under the Fourteenth Amendment requires that free legal counsel be appointed for all indigent defendants in all criminal cases.[108]

- *Escobedo v. Illinois* (1964): Suspects are entitled to confer with counsel as soon as police investigation focuses on them or once "the process shifts from investigatory to accusatory."[109]

- *Miranda v. Arizona* (1966): Before questioning suspects, a police officer must inform them of all their constitutional rights, including the right to counsel (appointed at no cost to the suspect if necessary) and the right to remain silent. Although suspects may knowingly waive these rights, the police cannot question anyone who at any point asks for a lawyer or declines "in any manner" to be questioned. If the police commit an error in these procedures, the accused goes free, regardless of the evidence of guilt.[110] Figure 14–1 on page 534 shows a typical "Miranda rights" card carried by police to ensure that they issue the proper warnings to those under arrest.

It is very difficult to determine the extent to which these decisions have really hampered efforts to halt the rise in crime in the United States. Studies of police behavior following these decisions show that at first police committed many procedural errors and guilty persons were freed, but after a year or so of adjustment to the new rules, successful prosecutions rose to the same level achieved before the decisions.[111]

The Exclusionary Rule Illegally obtained evidence and confessions may not be used in criminal trials. If police find evidence of a crime in an illegal search or if they elicit statements from suspects without informing them of their rights to

grant of immunity from prosecution Grant by the government to an individual of freedom from prosecution on a particular charge in return for testimony by that individual that might otherwise be self-incriminating.

METROPOLITAN POLICE DEPARTMENT	WAIVER
Warning As To Your Rights	

METROPOLITAN POLICE DEPARTMENT
Warning As To Your Rights

You are under arrest. Before we ask you any questions you must understand what your rights are.

You have the right to remain silent. You are not required to say anything to us at any time or to answer any questions. Anything you say can be used against you in court.

You have the right to talk to a lawyer for advice before we question you and to have him with you during questioning.

If you cannot afford a lawyer and want one, a lawyer will be provided for you.

If you want to answer questions now without a lawyer present, you will still have the right to stop answering at any time. You also have the right to stop answering at any time until you talk to a lawyer.

WAIVER

1. Have you read or had read to you the warning as to your rights?_____

2. Do you understand these rights? _____

3. Do you wish to answer any questions? _____

4. Are you willing to answer questions without having an attorney present? _____

5. Signature of defendant on line below.

_____

6. Time _____ Date _____

7. Signature of officer _____

8. Signature of witness _____

FIGURE 14-1   The Miranda Warning

Since the U.S. Supreme Court's ruling in the case of Miranda v. Arizona in 1966, law enforcement officials at all levels have routinely carried "Miranda rights" cards, which they read to accused individuals immediately after their arrest. This procedure has largely eliminated defendants' abilities to obtain dismissals and/or acquittals on the basis of ignorance of their rights or lack of proper counsel. The Supreme Court reaffirmed the Miranda rule in 2000.

remain silent or to have counsel, the evidence or statements produced are not admissible in a trial. This **exclusionary rule** is one of the more controversial procedural rights that the Supreme Court has extended to criminal defendants. The rule is also unique to the United States: in Great Britain evidence obtained illegally may be used against the accused, although the accused may bring charges against the police for damages.

The rule provides *enforcement* for the Fourth Amendment guarantee against unreasonable searches and seizures, as well as the Fifth Amendment guarantee against compulsory self-incrimination and the guarantee of counsel. Initially applied only in federal cases, in *Mapp v. Ohio* (1961) the Supreme Court extended the exclusionary rule to all criminal cases in the United States.[112] A *good faith exception* is made "when law enforcement officers have acted in objective good faith or their transgressions have been minor."[113] And police are *not* prohibited from tricking a suspect into giving them incriminating evidence.[114] But the exclusionary rule is frequently attacked for the high price it extracts from society—the release of guilty criminals. Why punish society because of the misconduct of police? Why not punish police directly, perhaps with disciplinary measures imposed by courts that discover errors, instead of letting guilty persons go free?

exclusionary rule   Rule of law that evidence found in an illegal search or resulting from an illegally obtained confession may not be admitted at trial.

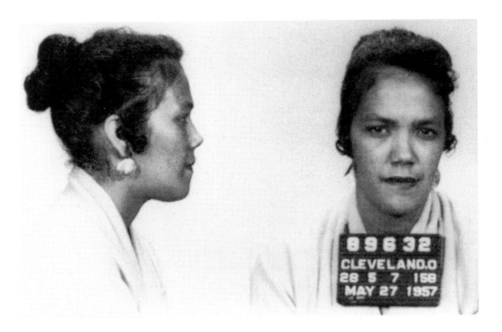

Dollree Mapp was arrested in 1957 but police seized vital evidence against her during an unwarranted, unconstitutional search. In Mapp v. Ohio *(1961), the U.S. Supreme Court held that evidence obtained illegally could not be used in a criminal trial.*

Bail Requirements   The Eighth Amendment says only that "*excessive* bail shall not be required." This clause does not say that pretrial release on bail will be available to all. The Supreme Court has held that "in our society liberty is the norm, and detention prior to trial or without trial is the carefully limited exception." Pretrial release on bail can be denied on the basis of the seriousness of the crime (bail is often denied in murder cases), the trustworthiness of the defendant (bail is often denied when the prosecution shows that the defendant is likely to flee before trial), or, in a more controversial exception, when release would threaten "the safety of any other person or the community."[115] If the court does not find any of these exceptions, it must set bail no higher than an amount reasonably calculated to ensure the defendant's later presence at trial.

Most criminal defendants cannot afford the bail money required for pretrial release. They must seek the services of a bail bondsman, who charges a heavy fee for filing the bail money with the court. The bail bondsman receives all of the bail money back when the defendant shows up for trial. But even if the defendant is found innocent, the bail bondsman retains the charge fee. (Thus the system is said to discriminate against poor defendants who cannot afford the bondsman's fee.) The failure of a criminal defendant to appear at his or her trial is itself a crime and subjects the defendant to immediate arrest as well as forfeiture of bail. Most states authorize bail bondsmen to find and arrest persons who have "jumped bail," return them to court, and thereby recover the bail money.

Fair Trial   The original text of the Constitution guaranteed jury trials in criminal cases, and the Sixth Amendment went on to correct weaknesses the framers saw in the English justice system at that time—closed proceedings, trials in absentia (where the defendant is not present), secret witnesses, long delays between arrest and trial, biased juries, and the absence of defense counsel. Specifically, the Sixth Amendment guarantees the following:

The War on Drugs Threatens Individual Liberty

Drug offenses currently account for over half of all prison sentences meted out by federal courts. The average federal sentence for drug crimes—possession, trafficking, or manufacturing of illegal substances—is seven years; the federal minimum sentence for possession of illegal drugs is five years. Nearly one million persons are arrested each year for drug violations.* The United States imprisons a larger proportion of its population than any other advanced nation.

The greatest threat arising from the "war on drugs," however, is the loss of personal liberty that has accompanied efforts to "take the profit out of crime." Congress passed a Racketeer Influenced and Corrupt Organizations Act (RICO) in 1970, following a 1968 presidential campaign in which President Richard Nixon made "getting tough on crime" a key issue. RICO authorizes federal agents to seize cash, bank accounts, homes, cars, boats, businesses, and other assets on "probable cause" to believe that they were used in criminal activity or were obtained with profits from criminal activity. People may be stopped in an airport terminal, a bus station, or on the street, on suspicion of drug trafficking, and have their cash and cars seized by law enforcement agencies. Boats and airplanes are also favored targets of seizure, but RICO also allows the seizure of bank accounts, homes, and businesses. Assets seized by federal law enforcement agencies—FBI, DEA, Customs Service, Treasury and Justice Departments—are usually retained by these agencies (or the profits of selling these assets at auction), and proceeds are often shared with state and local law-enforcement agencies that cooperated in the investigation. Thus, there is a strong bureaucratic incentive for agencies to concentrate on cases likely to result in forfeiture of these assets—primarily drug cases—and to overlook other law-enforcement activities.

RICO permits the government to seize property *before* any adjudication of guilt. Indeed a subsequent guilty verdict in a criminal trial is not necessary for the government to retain possession of the property seized. The only requirement is that government agents have "probable cause" to believe that the property was used in a crime or was purchased with the profits of crime. People whose property is seized under RICO must initiate a suit against the government. They have the burden of proving that they are innocent of any crime and, more importantly, that officers had no probable cause to seize their property. The proceedings are considered a civil suit by an individual against the government, not a criminal case by the government against the individual. The government, therefore, need not prove "beyond a reasonable doubt" that the person was involved in criminal activity or the property was used in commission of a crime. Rather, the person must prove his or her own innocence and the government's lack of probable cause to seize the property.

In a decision that seriously endangers personal liberty in America, the Supreme Court upheld RICO.† The Court ruled that the government's seizure of property is a civil and not a criminal punishment. This means that individuals whose property is seized are not afforded the constitutional rights of criminal defendants. They have no right to "due process of law" (Fifth Amendment), protection against double jeopardy (Fifth Amendment), or protection against "excessive fines" (Eighth Amendment).

Efforts in Congress to reform RICO have consistently failed. Members of Congress wish to avoid being labeled "soft on crime." And law-enforcement agencies—federal, state, and local—lobby heavily against reform.

Statistical Abstract of the United States 1999, p. 232.
†*U.S. v. Ursery*, 518 U.S. 267 (1996).

- The right to a speedy and public trial. ("Speedy" refers to the time between arrest and trial, not the time between the crime itself and trial,[116] but the Supreme Court has declined to set a specific time limit that defines speedy.[117])
- An impartial jury chosen from the state or district where the crime was committed.

- The right to confront (cross-examine) witnesses against the accused.
- The right of the accused to compel (subpoena) favorable witnesses to appear.
- The right of the accused to be represented by counsel.

Over the years the courts have elaborated on these elements of a fair trial so that today trial proceedings follow a rigidly structured format. First, attorneys make opening statements. The prosecution describes the crime and how it will prove beyond a reasonable doubt that the defendant committed it. The defense attorney argues either that the crime did not occur or that the defendant did not do it. Next, each side, again beginning with the prosecution, calls witnesses who first testify on "direct examination" for their side, then are cross-examined by the opposing attorney. Witnesses may be asked to verify evidence that is introduced as "exhibits." Defendants have a right to be present during their own trials (although an abusive and disruptive defendant may be considered to have waived his or her right to be present and be removed from the courtroom).[118] Prosecution witnesses must appear in the courtroom and submit to cross-examination (although special protection procedures, including videotaped testimony, may be used for children).[119] Prosecutors are obliged to disclose any information that might create a reasonable doubt about the defendant's guilt,[120] but the defendant may not be compelled to disclose incriminating information.

After all of the witnesses offered by both sides have been heard and cross-examined, prosecution and defense give their closing arguments. The burden of proof "beyond a reasonable doubt" rests with the prosecution; the defense does not need to prove that the accused is innocent, only that reasonable doubt exists regarding guilt.

Juries must be "impartial": they must not have prejudged the case or exhibit bias or prejudice or have a personal interest in the outcome. Judges can dismiss jurors for "cause." During jury selection, attorneys for the prosecution and defense are allowed a fixed number of "peremptory" challenges of jurors (although they cannot do so on the basis of race).[121] Jury selection is often regarded by attorneys as the key to the outcome of a case; both sides try to get presumed sympathetic people on the jury. In well-publicized cases, judges may "sequester" a jury (keep them in a hotel away from access to the mass media) in order to maintain impartiality. Judges may exclude press or television to prevent trials from becoming spectacles if they wish.[122] By tradition, English juries have had twelve members; however, the Supreme Court has allowed six-member juries in non-death-penalty cases.[123] Also by tradition, juries should arrive at a unanimous decision. If a jury cannot do so, judges declare a "hung" jury and the prosecutor may schedule a retrial. Only a "not guilty" prevents retrial of a defendant. Traditionally, it was believed that a lack of unanimity raised "reasonable doubt" about the defendant's guilt. But the Supreme Court has permitted nonunanimous verdicts in some cases.[124]

Plea Bargaining Few criminal cases actually go to trial. More than 90 percent of criminal cases are plea bargained.[125] In **plea bargaining**, the defendant agrees to plead guilty and waives the right to a jury trial in exchange for concessions made by the prosecutor, perhaps the dropping of more serious charges against the defendant or a pledge to seek a reduced sentence or fine. Some critics of plea bargaining view it as another form of leniency in the criminal justice system that reduces its deterrent effects. Other critics view plea bargaining as a violation of the

plea bargaining Practice of allowing defendants to plead guilty to lesser crimes than those with which they were originally charged in return for reduced sentences.

Constitution's protection against self-incrimination and guarantee of a fair jury trial. Prosecutors, they say, threaten defendants with serious charges and stiff penalties in order to force a guilty plea. Still other critics see plea bargaining as an "under-the-table" process that undermines respect for the criminal justice system.

Yet it is vital to the nation's court system that most defendants plead guilty. The court system would quickly break down from overload if any substantial proportion of defendants insisted on jury trials.

Double Jeopardy   The Constitution appears to bar multiple prosecutions for the same offense: "Nor shall any person be subject for the same offense to be twice put in jeopardy of life or lamb" (Amendment 5). But very early the Supreme Court held that this clause does not protect an individual from being tried a second time if jurors are deadlocked and cannot reach a verdict in the first trial (a "hung" jury).[126] Moreover, the Supreme Court has held that federal and state governments may separately try a person for the same offense if it violates both federal and state laws.[127] Thus, in the well-publicized Rodney King case in 1992, in which police officers were videotaped beating King, a California court found the officers not guilty of assault, but later the U.S. Justice Department won convictions against the officers in a federal court for violating King's civil rights. Finally, a verdict of guilt or innocence in a criminal trial does not preclude a civil trial in which plaintiffs (private citizens) sue for damages inflicted by the accused. Thus, O.J. Simpson was found not guilty of murder in a criminal trial but later found to be responsible for the deaths of two people in a civil trial. Civil courts, of course, can only impose monetary awards; they cannot impose criminal penalties.

THE DEATH PENALTY

Perhaps the most heated debate in criminal justice policy today concerns capital punishment. Opponents of the death penalty argue that it violates the prohibition against "cruel and unusual punishments" in the Eighth Amendment to the Constitution. They also argue that the death penalty is applied unequally. A large proportion of those executed have been poor, uneducated, and nonwhite. In contrast, many Americans feel that justice demands strong retribution for heinous crimes—a life for a life. A mere jail sentence for a multiple murderer or rapist-murderer seems unjust compared with the damage inflicted on society and the victims. In many cases, a life sentence means less than ten years in prison under the current early-release and parole policies in many states. Convicted murderers have been set free, and some have killed again.

Prohibition against Unfair Application   Prior to 1971, the death penalty was officially sanctioned by about half of the states. Federal law also retained the death penalty. However, no one had actually suffered the death penalty since 1967 because of numerous legal tangles and direct challenges to the constitutionality of capital punishment.

In *Furman v. Georgia* (1972), the Supreme Court ruled that capital punishment, as then imposed, violated the Eighth and Fourteenth Amendment prohibitions against cruel and unusual punishment and due process of law. The justices' reasoning in the case was very complex. Only Justices William J. Brennan and Thurgood Marshall declared that capital punishment itself is cruel and unusual. The other justices in the majority felt that death sentences had been applied unfairly; some individuals received the death penalty for crimes for which many others received much lighter sentences. These justices left open the possibility that capital punishment would be constitutional if it was specified for certain kinds of crime and applied uniformly.[128]

After this decision, a majority of states rewrote their death penalty laws to try to ensure fairness and uniformity of application. Generally, these laws mandate the death penalty for murders committed during rape, robbery, hijacking, or kidnapping; murder of prison guards; murder with torture; and multiple murders. They call for two trials to be held—one to determine guilt or innocence and another to determine the penalty. At the second trial, evidence of "aggravating" and "mitigating" factors must be presented; if there are aggravating factors but no mitigating factors, the death penalty is mandatory.

Death Penalty Reinstated   The revised death penalty laws were upheld in a series of cases that came before the Supreme Court in 1976. The Court concluded that "the punishment of death does *not* invariably violate the Constitution." The majority decision noted that the framers of the Bill of Rights had accepted death as a common penalty for crime. Although acknowledging that the Constitution and its amendments must be interpreted in a dynamic fashion, reflecting changing moral values, the Court's majority noted that most state legislatures have been willing to reenact the death penalty and hundreds of juries have been willing to impose that penalty. Thus "a large proportion of American society continues to regard it as an appropriate and necessary criminal sanction." Moreover, the Court held that the social purposes of retribution and deterrence justify the use of the death penalty; this ultimate sanction is "an expression of society's moral outrage at particularly offensive conduct."[129]

The Court reaffirmed that *Furman v. Georgia* struck down the death penalty only where it was invoked in "an arbitrary and capricious manner." A majority of the justices upheld the death penalty in states where the trial was a two-part proceeding, provided that during the second part the judge or jury was given relevant information and standards for deciding whether to impose the death penalty. The Court approved the consideration of "aggravating and mitigating circumstances." The Court also called for automatic review of all death sentences by state supreme courts to ensure that none is imposed under the influence of passion or prejudice, that aggravating factors are supported by the evidence, and that the sentence is not disproportionate to the crime. However, the court disapproved of state laws making the death penalty mandatory in all first-degree murder cases, holding that such laws were "unduly harsh and unworkably rigid."

Racial Bias   The death penalty has been challenged as a violation of the Equal Protection Clause of the Fourteenth Amendment because of racial bias in the application of the punishment. White murderers are just as likely to receive the death penalty as black murderers. However, some statistics show that if the *victim* is white there is a greater chance that the killer will be sentenced to death than if the victim is black. Nevertheless, the U.S. Supreme Court has ruled that statistical disparities in the race of victims by itself does not bar the use of the death penalty in all cases. There must be evidence of racial bias against a particular defendant in order for the Court to reverse a death sentence.[130]

Twenty-First Century Directions

The Founders understood that civil liberties do not enforce themselves, that a Bill of Rights is only a "parchment barrier" against tyranny, and that the preservation of liberty requires not only an independent judiciary but a vigilant citizenry. Threats to liberty in the twenty-first century will be as prevalent and as dangerous as any ever encountered in American history.

↑ ***Threats to the Liberty*** Freedom of expression is currently under heavy attack in American society. The attack on speech considered hurtful, insensitive, prejudiced, bigoted, or hateful is centered in the workplace, on college campuses, in sports and entertainment, and in the mass media. The drive to have government regulate such expression will succeed if Americans do not come to understand that the remedy for offensive speech is more speech, not suppression.

↓ ***Rights of Defendants*** The "war on drugs", and the fear that politicians have of the label "soft on crime," will continue to erode the rights of defendants in criminal cases. New "exceptions" to the Fourth Amendment protection against police searches and seizures will render this constitutional right virtually meaningless. Electronic and video surveillance, as well as drug testing, will become ever more pervasive in society.

←→ ***Freedom and the Internet*** Federal and state governments will continue to try to regulate expression on the Internet by attempting to ban pornography, prohibit anonymous communications, outlaw coding of messages, prevent sales of prescription drugs, and collect taxes from Internet sales. But Internet users and entrepreneurs will continue to find new ways to evade government regulations. The Internet will remain the freest form of mass communication.

Delays Once imposed, the death penalty is, of course, irreversible. It is the ultimate punishment, and it must not be imposed if there is any doubt whatsoever about the defendant's guilt. Yet how many opportunities should death row inmates have to challenge their convictions and sentences? The writ of habeas corpus is guaranteed in the Constitution, but how many habeas corpus petitions should federal courts allow a condemned prisoner to submit? Attorneys for prisoners often generate new claims for last-minute appeals, expecting that federal courts will delay executions for future hearings and adjudications. Sometimes these claims are repetitive and frivolous. Multiple appeals and writs by prisoners mean more than a decade between death sentence and execution.

In recent years, the Supreme Court has limited habeas corpus petitions of prisoners who have already exhausted their appeals and filed one claim in federal court and lost, and prisoners who failed to follow state rules of appeal. And the Congress, in its Antiterrorism Act of 1996, directed that claims raised in earlier habeas corpus petitions must be dismissed when raised again, unless they are accompanied by new evidence not knowable at the time of the earlier petition. The Supreme Court held this Act to be constitutional. So what if genuine new evidence is uncovered after all appeals have been exhausted? Prisoners must then rely on governors' pardons (or, in federal cases, a presidential pardon). Recently, some state governors have declared a moratorium (temporary halt) on all executions, fearing that some innocent persons may be put to death.

SUMMARY NOTES

- Laws and government are required to protect individual liberty. Yet laws and governments themselves restrict liberty. To resolve this dilemma, constitutions seek to limit governmental power over the individual. In the U.S. Constitution, the Bill of Rights is designed to place certain liberties beyond the reach of government.

- Initially the Bill of Rights applied against only the federal government, not state or local governments. But over time, the Bill of Rights was nationalized, as the Supreme Court applied the Due Process Clause of the Fourteenth Amendment to all governments in the United States.

- Freedom of religion encompasses two separate restrictions on government: government must not establish religion or prohibit its free exercise. Although the wording of the First Amendment is absolute ("Congress shall make no law . . .") the Supreme Court has allowed some restrictions on religious practices that threaten health, safety, or welfare.

- The Supreme Court's efforts to maintain "a wall of separation" between church and state have proven difficult and controversial. The Court's banning of prayer and religious ceremony in public schools more than thirty years ago remains politically unpopular today.

- The Supreme Court has never adopted the absolutist position that all speech is protected by the First Amendment. The Court's clear and present danger doctrine and its preferred position doctrine recognize the importance of free expression in a democracy, yet the Court has permitted some restrictions on expression, especially in times of perceived national crisis.

- The Supreme Court has placed obscenity outside of the protection of the First Amendment, but it has encountered considerable difficulty in defining "obscenity."

- Freedom of the press prevents government from imposing prior restraints (censorship) on the news media except periodically in wartime, when it has been argued that publication would result in serious harm or loss of life. The Supreme Court has allowed greater government authority over radio and television than over newspapers, on the grounds that radio and television are given exclusive rights to use specific broadcast frequencies.

- The First Amendment guarantee of the right of assembly and petition protects the organization of political parties and interest groups. It also protects the right of people to peacefully protest, parade, and demonstrate. Governments may, within reasonable limits, restrict these activities for valid reasons but may not apply different restrictions to different groups based on the nature of their views.

- The Second Amendment guarantees "the right of the people to keep and bear arms." However, it is frequently argued that this is not an individual right to possess a gun, but rather a collective right of the states to maintain National Guard units.

- Crime rates in the United States are currently declining. Yet a free society must balance any remedies to the crime problem against potential infringements of the rights of its citizens.

- The Constitution includes a number of important procedural guarantees in the criminal justice system: the writ of habeas corpus; prohibitions against bills of attainder and ex post facto laws; protection against unreasonable searches and seizures; protection against self-incrimination; guarantee of legal counsel; protection against excessive bail; guarantee of a fair public and speedy trial by an impartial jury; the right to confront witnesses and to compel favorable witnesses to testify; and protection against cruel or unusual punishment.

- The Supreme Court's exclusionary rule helps to enforce some of these procedural rights by excluding illegally obtained evidence and self-incriminating statements from criminal trials. In the 1960s, Court interpretations of the Fourth and Fifth Amendments strengthened the rights of criminal defendants. Police procedures adjusted quickly, and today there is little evidence that procedural rights greatly hamper law enforcement.

- Few criminal cases go to trial. Most are plea bargained, with the defendant pleading guilty in exchange for reduced charges and/or a lighter sentence. Although this practice is frequently criticized, without plea bargaining the nation's criminal court system would break down from case overload.

- The Supreme Court has ruled that the death penalty is not a "cruel and unusual punishment," but the Court has insisted on fairness and uniformity of application.

KEY TERMS

incorporation   505

Free Exercise Clause   505

No Establishment
    Clause   509

wall-of-separation
    doctrine   509

clear and present danger
    doctrine   512

preferred position   513

freedom of
    expression   515

symbolic speech   515

commercial
    speech   518

prior restraint   522

shield laws   524

gag order   524

writ of habeas
    corpus   529

bill of attainder   529

ex post facto
    law   529

search warrant   531

indictment   532

grand jury   532

grant of immunity from
    prosecution   533

exclusionary rule   534

plea bargaining   537

SELECTED READINGS

ELSHTAIN, JEAN BETHKE. *Democracy on Trial.* New York: Basic Books, 1995. "Communitarian" argument that America's emphasis on personal rights erodes the common good and subverts democracy.

EPSTEIN, LEE, and THOMAS G. WALKER. *Constitutional Law for a Changing America: Rights, Liberties and Justice.* 3rd ed. Washington, D.C.: CQ Press, 1998. An authoritative text on civil liberties and the rights of the criminally accused. It describes the political context of Supreme Court decisions and provides key excerpts from the most important decisions.

GARROW, DAVID. *Liberty and Sexuality: The Right to Privacy and the Making of Roe v. Wade.* New York: Macmillan, 1994. Historical account of the background and development of the right to sexual privacy.

HENTOFF, NAT. *Free Speech for Me—But Not for Thee.* New York: HarperCollins, 1992. Account of how both the right and the left in America try to suppress the opinions of those who disagree with them.

KOBYLKA, JOSEPH F. *The Politics of Obscenity.* Westport, Conn.: Greenwood Press, 1991. Comprehensive review of Supreme Court obscenity decisions, arguing that the *Miller* case in 1973 was a turning point away from a more permissive to a more restrictive approach toward sexually oriented material. It examines the litigation strategies of the American Civil Liberties Union and other groups in obscenity cases.

LEWIS, ANTHONY. *Gideon's Trumpet.* New York: Random House, 1964. The classic story of Clarence Gideon and how his handwritten habeas corpus plea made its way to the U.S. Supreme Court, resulting in the guarantee of free legal counsel for poor defendants in felony cases.

McClosky, Herbert, and Alida Brill. *Dimensions of Tolerance.* New York: Russell Sage Foundation, 1983. Using public opinion surveys, the authors assess popular and elite support for constitutional liberties; they conclude that intolerance is widespread in the mass public but that community and legal elites give greater support to constitutional principles.

Politics
and Civil Rights

ASK YOURSELF ABOUT POLITICS

1 Does the U.S. Constitution require the government to be color blind with respect to different races in all its laws and actions?
Yes ● No ●

2 If a city's schools are mostly black and the surrounding suburban schools are mostly white, should busing be used to achieve a better racial balance?
Yes ● No ●

3 Are differences between blacks and whites in average income mainly a product of discrimination?
Yes ● No ●

4 Do you generally favor affirmative action programs for women and minorities?
Yes ● No ●

5 Do you believe racial and sexual preferences in employment and education discriminate against white males?
Yes ● No ●

6 Should gender equality receive the same level of legal protection as racial equality?
Yes ● No ●

7 Do dirty jokes and foul language at work constitute sexual harassment?
Yes ● No ●

Equality has long been the central issue of American politics. What do we mean by equality? And what, if anything, should government do to achieve it?

THE POLITICS OF EQUALITY

Equality has been the central issue of American politics throughout the history of the nation. It is the issue that sparked the nation's only civil war, and it continues today to be the nation's most vexing political concern.

Conflict begins over the very definition of "equality" (see "Dilemmas of Equality" in Chapter 2). Although Americans agree in the abstract that everyone is equal, they disagree over what they mean by "equality." Traditionally, equality meant "equality of *opportunity*": an equal opportunity to develop individual talents and abilities and to be rewarded for work, initiative, merit, and achievement. Over time, the issue of equality has shifted to "equality of *results*": an equal sharing of income and material rewards. With this shift in definition has come political conflict over the question of what, if anything, government should do to narrow the gaps between rich and poor, men and women, blacks and whites, and all other groups in society. Achieving greater equality of results requires government policies that modify the effects of equality of opportunity—that is, policies leading to **redistribution** of income, wealth, jobs, promotions, admissions, and other benefits.

A related issue arises over whether "equality" is to be defined in individual or group terms. Traditionally, Americans thought of equality as the fair treatment of all *individuals*, rather than the treatment afforded particular *groups* such as racial and ethnic minorities, women, or disabled people. Inequality among groups takes on even greater political significance than inequality among individuals. Disparities between men and women, blacks and whites, and various ethnic groups spur political activity, as people in disadvantaged groups come to see their common plight and organize themselves for remedial political action.[1]

The nation's long struggle over equality has produced a number of constitutional and legal milestones in civil rights. These are summarized in Table 15–1. Much of the politics of civil rights centers on the development and interpretation of these guarantees of equality.

SLAVERY, SEGREGATION, AND THE CONSTITUTION

In penning the Declaration of Independence in 1776, Thomas Jefferson affirmed that "All men are created equal." Yet from 1619, when the first slaves were brought to Jamestown, Virginia, until 1865, when the Thirteenth Amendment to the Constitution outlawed the practice, slavery was a way of life in the United States. Africans were captured, enslaved, transported to America, bought and sold, and used as personal property.

Slavery and the Constitution   The Constitution of 1787 recognized and protected slavery in the United States. Article I stipulated that slaves were to be counted as three-fifths of a person for purposes of representation and taxation; it also prohibited any federal restriction on the importation of slaves until 1808. Article IV even guaranteed the return of escaped slaves to their owners. The Founders were aware that the practice of slavery contradicted their professed belief in "equality," and this contradiction caused them some embarrassment. Thus they avoided the word "slave" in favor of the euphemism "person held to Service or Labour" in writing the Constitution.

Supreme Court Chief Justice Roger Taney, ruling in the notorious case of *Dred Scott v. Sandford* in 1857, reflected the racism that prevailed in early America:

> They had for more than a century before been regarded as beings of an inferior order, and altogether unfit to associate with the white race, either in social or political relations; and so far inferior, that they had no rights which the white man was bound to respect; and that the negro might justly and lawfully be reduced to slavery for his benefit. He was bought and sold, and treated as an ordinary article of merchandise and traffic, whenever a profit could be made by it.

Taney's decision in this case interpreted the Constitution in terms of the *original intent* of the Founders. The ruling upheld slavery and the constitutional guarantee given slave owners for the return of slaves escaping to nonslave states.

redistribution Government policies meant to shift assets from one group to another.

abolition movement Social movement before the Civil War whose goal was to abolish slavery throughout the United States.

Emancipation and Reconstruction   A growing number of Americans, especially members of the **abolition movement**, disagreed with Taney. In 1860 internal party divisions over the slavery issue led to a four-way race for the presidency and the election of Abraham Lincoln. Although personally opposed to slavery, Lincoln had promised during the campaign not to push for abolition of slavery where it existed. Many southerners were unconvinced, however, and on December 20, 1860 (three months before Lincoln's inauguration), South Carolina became the first state to secede from the Union, touching off the Civil War.

Table 15-1   Guarantees of Civil Rights

Thirteenth Amendment (1865)

Neither slavery nor involuntary servitude, except as a punishment for crime whereof the party shall have been duly convicted, shall exist within the United States, or any place subject to their jurisdiction.

Fourteenth Amendment (1868)

No State shall make or enforce any law which shall abridge the privileges or immunities of citizens of the United States; nor shall any State deprive any person of life, liberty, or property, without due process of law; nor deny to any person within its jurisdiction the equal protection of the laws.

Fifteenth Amendment (1870)

The rights of the citizens of the United States to vote shall not be denied or abridged by the United States or by any State on account of race, color, or previous condition of servitude.

Nineteenth Amendment (1920)

The right of the citizens of the United States to vote shall not be denied or abridged by the United States or by any State on account of sex.

Civil Rights Acts of 1866, 1871, and 1875

Acts passed by the Reconstruction Congress following the Civil War. The Civil Rights Act of 1866 guaranteed newly freed persons the right to purchase, lease, and use real property. The Civil Rights Act of 1875 outlawed segregation in privately owned businesses and facilities, but in the Civil Rights Cases (1883), the Supreme Court declared the act an unconstitutional expansion of federal power, ruling that the Fourteenth Amendment limits only "State" actions. Other provisions of these acts were generally ignored for many decades. But the Civil Rights Act of 1871 has been revived in recent decades; the act makes it a federal crime for any person acting under the authority of state law to deprive another of rights protected by the Constitution.

Civil Rights Act of 1957

The first civil rights law passed by Congress since Reconstruction. It empowers the U.S. Justice Department to enforce voting rights, established the Civil Rights Division in the Justice Department, and created the Civil Rights Commission to study and report on civil rights in the United States.

Civil Rights Act of 1964

A comprehensive enactment designed to erase racial discrimination in both public and private sectors of American life. Major titles of the act: I. outlaws arbitrary discrimination in voter registration and expedites voting rights suits; II. bars discrimination in public accommodations, such as hotels and restaurants, that have a substantial relation to interstate commerce; III. and IV. authorize the national government to bring suits to desegregate public facilities and schools; V. extends the life and expands the power of the Civil Rights Commission; VI. provides for withholding federal funds from programs administered in a discriminatory manner; VII. establishes the right to equality in employment opportunities.

Civil Rights Act of 1968

Prohibits discrimination in the advertising, financing, sale, or rental of housing, based on race, religion, or national origin and, as of 1974, sex. A major amendment to the act in 1988 extended coverage to the handicapped and to families with children.

Voting Rights Act

Enacted by Congress in 1965 and renewed and expanded in 1970, 1975, and 1982, this law has sought to eliminate restrictions on voting that have been used to discriminate against blacks and other minority groups. Amendments in 1975 (1) required bilingual ballots in all states; (2) required approval by the Justice Department or a federal court of any election law changes in states covered by the act; (3) extended legal protection of voting rights to Hispanic Americans, Asian Americans, and Native Americans. The 1982 act provides that *intent* to discriminate need not be proven if the *results* demonstrate otherwise. Although the 1982 extension does not require racial quotas for city councils, school boards, or state legislatures, a judge may under the law redraw voting districts to give minorities maximum representation.

The Civil War was the nation's bloodiest war. (Combined deaths of Union and Confederate forces matched the nation's losses in World War II, even though the nation's population in 1860 was only 31 million compared to 140 million during World War II.) Very few families during the Civil War did not experience a direct loss from that conflict. As casualties mounted, northern Republicans joined

The Thirteenth, Fourteenth, and Fifteenth Amendments to the Constitution, as well as other legislation passed during Reconstruction, opened the ballot box and access to political office to the freedmen of the South. However, these gains were soon largely reversed by Jim Crow laws and segregation.

Jim Crow Second-class-citizen status conferred on blacks by southern segregation laws; derived from a nineteenth-century song-and-dance act (usually performed by a white man in blackface) that stereotyped blacks.

abolitionists in calling for emancipating, or freeing, the slaves simply to punish the Rebels. They knew that much of the South's power depended on slave labor. Lincoln also knew that if he proclaimed the war was being fought to free the slaves, military intervention by the British on behalf of the South was less likely. Accordingly, on September 22, 1862, Lincoln issued his Emancipation Proclamation. Claiming his right as Commander-in-Chief of the army and navy, he declared that, as of January 1, 1863, "all persons held as slaves within any State, or designated part of a State, the people whereof shall then be in rebellion against the United States, shall be then, thenceforward, and forever free." The Emancipation Proclamation did not come about as a result of demands by the people. It was a political and military action by the president intended to help preserve the Union.

The Emancipation Proclamation freed slaves in the seceding states, and the Thirteenth Amendment in 1865 abolished slavery everywhere in the nation. But freedom did not mean civil rights. The post–Civil War Republican Congress attempted to "reconstruct" southern society. The Fourteenth Amendment, ratified in 1868, made "equal protection of the laws" a command for every state to obey. The Fifteenth Amendment, passed in 1869 and ratified in 1870, prohibited federal and state governments from abridging the right to vote "on account of race, color, or previous condition of servitude." In addition, Congress passed a series of civil rights laws in the 1860s and 1870s guaranteeing the newly freed slaves protection in the exercise of their constitutional rights. Between 1865 and the early 1880s, the success of Reconstruction was evident in widespread black voting throughout the South, the presence of many blacks in federal and state offices, and the admission of blacks to theaters, restaurants, hotels, and public transportation.[2]

The Imposition of Segregation   But political support for Reconstruction policies soon began to erode. In the Compromise of 1877, the national government agreed to end military occupation of the South, give up its efforts to rearrange southern society, and lend tacit approval to white supremacy in that region. In return, the southern states pledged their support to the Union, accepted national supremacy, and agreed to permit the Republican presidential candidate, Rutherford B. Hayes, to assume the presidency, although the Democratic candidate, Samuel Tilden, had received more popular votes in the disputed election of 1876.

As white southerners regained political power and blacks lost the protection of federal forces, the Supreme Court moved to strike down Reconstruction laws. In the Civil Rights Cases of 1883, the Supreme Court declared federal civil rights laws preventing discrimination by private individuals to be unconstitutional.[3] By denying Congress the power to protect blacks from discrimination by businesses and individuals, the Court paved the way for the imposition of segregation as the prevailing social system of the South. In the 1880s and 1890s, white southerners imposed segregation in public accommodations, housing, education, employment, and almost every other sector of private and public life. By 1895 most southern states had passed laws *requiring* racial segregation in education and in public accommodations. At the time, more than 90 percent of the African American population of the United States lived in these states.

Segregation became the social instrument by which African Americans were "kept in their place"—that is, denied social, economic, educational, and political equality. In many states, **Jim Crow** followed them throughout life: birth in segregated hospital wards, education in segregated schools, residence in segregated housing, employment in segregated jobs, eating in segregated restaurants, and burial in segregated graveyards. Segregation was enforced by a variety of public and private sanctions, from lynch mobs to country club admission committees. But government was the principal instrument of segregation in both the southern and the border states of the nation. (For a look at the political reactions of African Americans to segregation, see *Up Close:* "African American Politics in Historical Perspective" on page 550).

Early Court Approval of Segregation Segregation was imposed despite the Fourteenth Amendment's guarantee of "equal protection of the laws." In the 1896 case of *Plessy v. Ferguson*, the Supreme Court upheld state laws requiring segregation. Although segregation laws involved state action, the Court held that segregation of the races did not violate the Equal Protection Clause of the Fourteenth Amendment so long as people in each race received equal treatment. Schools and other public facilities that were **separate but equal** were constitutional, the Court ruled.

> The object of the amendment was undoubtedly to enforce the absolute equality of the two races before the law, but in the nature of things it could not have been intended to abolish distinctions based upon color, or to enforce social, as distinguished from political, equality, or a commingling of the two races upon terms unsatisfactory to either. Laws permitting, and even requiring, their separation in places where they are liable to be brought into contact do not necessarily imply the inferiority of either race to the other, and have been generally, if not universally, recognized as within the competency of the state legislatures in the exercise of their police power.[4]

The effect of this decision was to give constitutional approval to segregation; the decision was not reversed until 1954.

EQUAL PROTECTION OF THE LAWS

The initial goal of the civil rights movement was to eliminate segregation laws, especially segregation in public education. Only after this battle was well under way could the civil rights movement turn to the fight against segregation and discrimination in all sectors of American life, *private* as well as *governmental*.

The NAACP and the Legal Battle The National Association for the Advancement of Colored People (NAACP) and its Legal Defense and Education Fund led the fight to abolish lawful segregation. As chief legal counsel to the fund, Thurgood Marshall (see *People in Politics:* "Thurgood Marshall, Advocate of Equal Protection") began a long legal campaign to ensure equal protection of the law for African Americans. Initially, the NAACP's strategy focused on achieving the "equal" portion of the separate-but-equal doctrine. Segregated facilities, including public schools, were seldom "equal," even with respect to physical conditions, teachers' salaries and qualifications, curricula, and other tangible factors. In other words, southern states failed to live up even to the segregationist doctrine of separate but equal. In a series of cases, Marshall and other NAACP lawyers convinced the Supreme Court to act when segregated facilities were clearly unequal. For example, the Court ordered the admission of individual blacks to white public universities where evidence indicated that separate black institutions were inferior or nonexistent.[5]

separate but equal Ruling of the Supreme Court in the case of *Plessy v. Ferguson* (1896) to the effect that segregated facilities were legal as long as the facilities were equal.

African American Politics in Historical Perspective

Many early histories of Reconstruction paid little attention to the political responses of African Americans to the imposition of segregation. But there were at least three distinct types of response: accommodation to segregation; the formation of a black protest movement and resort to legal action; and migration out of the South (to avoid some of the worst consequences of white supremacy) coupled with political mobilization of black voters in large northern cities.

Accommodation   The foremost African American advocate of accommodation to segregation was well-known educator Booker T. Washington (1856–1915). Washington enjoyed wide popularity among both white and black Americans. An adviser to two presidents (Theodore Roosevelt and William Howard Taft), he was highly respected by white philanthropists and government officials. In his famous Cotton States' Exposition speech in Atlanta in 1895, Washington assured whites that blacks were prepared to accept a separate position in society: "In all things that are purely social we can be as separate as the fingers, yet one as the hand in all things essential to mutual progress."*

Washington's hopes for black America lay in a program of self-help through education. He himself had attended Hampton Institute in Virginia, where the curriculum centered around practical trades for African Americans. Washington obtained some white philanthropic support in establishing his own Tuskegee Institute in Tuskegee, Alabama, in 1881. His first students helped build the school. Early curricula at Tuskegee emphasized immediately useful vocations, such as farming, teaching, and blacksmithing. One of Tuskegee's outstanding faculty members, George Washington Carver, researched and developed uses for southern crops. Washington urged his students to stay in the South, to acquire land, and to build homes, thereby helping to eliminate ignorance and poverty.

Protest   While Booker T. Washington was urging African Americans to make the best of segregation, a small group was organizing in support of a declaration of black resistance and protest that would later rewrite American public policy. The leader of this group was W.E.B. Du Bois (1868–1963), a historian and sociologist at Atlanta University. In 1905 Du Bois and a few other black intellectuals met in Niagara Falls, Canada, to draw up a platform intended to "assail the ears" and sear the consciences of white Americans. The Niagara Statement listed the major injustices perpetrated against African Americans since Reconstruction: the loss of voting rights, the imposition of Jim Crow laws and segregated public schools, the denial of equal job opportunities, the existence of inhumane conditions

Booker T. Washington

W.E.B. Du Bois

in southern prisons, the exclusion of blacks from West Point and Annapolis, and the federal government's failure to enforce the Fourteenth and Fifteenth Amendments. Out of the Niagara meeting came the idea of a nationwide organization dedicated to fighting for African Americans, and on February 12, 1909, the one hundredth anniversary of Abraham Lincoln's birth, the National Association for the Advancement of Colored People (NAACP) was founded.

Du Bois himself was on the original board of directors of the NAACP, although a majority of the early board members and financial contributors were white. Du Bois was also the NAACP's first director of research and the editor of its magazine, *Crisis*. The NAACP began a long and eventually successful campaign to establish black rights through legal action. Over the years, this organization brought hundreds of court cases at the local, state, and federal court levels on behalf of African Americans denied their constitutional rights.

Migration and Political Mobilization   World War I provided an opportunity for restive blacks in the South to escape the worst abuses of white supremacy by migrating en masse to northern cities. Between 1916 and 1918, an estimated half-million African Americans moved north to fill the labor shortage caused by the war effort. Most arrived in big northern cities only to find more poverty and segregation, but at least they could vote, and they did not encounter laws requiring segregation in public places.

The progressive "ghettoization" of African Americans—their migration from the rural South to the urban North and their increasing concentration in central cities—had profound political, as well as social, implications. The ghetto provided an environment conducive to political mobilization. As early as 1928, African Americans in Chicago were able to elect one of their own to the U.S. House of Representatives. The election of Oscar de Priest, the first black member of Congress from the North, signaled a new turn in American urban politics by announcing to white politicians that they would have to reckon with the black vote in northern cities. The black ghettos would soon provide an important element in a new political coalition that was about to take form: the Democratic Party of Franklin Delano Roosevelt.

The increasing concentration of African Americans in large, politically competitive, "swing" states provided black voters with new political power—not only to support the Democratic Party coalition in national politics but also to elect African Americans to local public office. Today African American mayors serve, or have served, in cities as diverse as New York, Chicago, Los Angeles, Detroit, Philadelphia, Atlanta, and New Orleans.

---

*Quoted in Henry Steele Commager, ed., *The Struggle for Racial Equality* (New York: Harper & Row, 1967), p. 19.

But Marshall's goal was to prove that segregation *itself* was inherently unequal whether or not facilities were equal in all tangible respects. In other words, Marshall sought a reversal of *Plessy v. Ferguson* and a ruling that separation of the races was unconstitutional. In 1952 Marshall led a team of NAACP lawyers in a suit to admit Linda Brown to the white public schools of Topeka, Kansas, one of the few segregated school systems where white and black schools were equal with respect to buildings, curricula, teachers' salaries, and other tangible factors. In choosing the *Brown* suit, the NAACP sought to prevent the Court from simply ordering the admission of black pupils because tangible facilities were not equal and to force the Court to review the doctrine of segregation itself.

Brown v. Board of Education of Topeka   On May 17, 1954, the Court rendered its historic decision in the case of *Brown v. Board of Education of Topeka:*

> Segregation of white and colored children in public schools has a detrimental effect upon the colored children. The impact is greater when it has the sanction of law, for the policy of separating the races is usually interpreted as denoting the inferiority of the Negro group. A sense of inferiority affects the motivation of a child to learn. Segregation with the sanction of law, therefore, has a tendency to retard the educational and mental development of Negro children and to deprive them of some of the benefits they would receive in a racially integrated school system. Whatever may have been the extent of psychological knowledge of the time of *Plessy v. Ferguson*, this finding is amply supported by modern authority. Any language in *Plessy v. Ferguson* contrary to this source is rejected. . . . We conclude that in the field of public education the doctrine of "separate but equal" has no place. Separate educational facilities are inherently unequal.[6]

The Supreme Court decision in *Brown* was symbolically very important. Although it would be many years before any significant number of black children would attend previously all-white schools in the South, the decision by the nation's highest court stimulated black hopes and expectations. Indeed, *Brown* started the modern civil rights movement. As the African American psychologist Kenneth Clark wrote, "This [civil rights] movement would probably not have existed at all were it not for the 1954 Supreme Court school desegregation decision, which provided a tremendous boost to the morale of blacks by its clear affirmation that color is irrelevant to the rights of American citizens."[7]

Enforcing Desegregation   The *Brown* ruling struck down the laws of twenty-one states as well as congressional laws segregating the schools of the District of Columbia.[8] Such a far-reaching exercise of judicial power was bound to meet with difficulties in enforcement, and the Supreme Court was careful not to risk its own authority. It did not order immediate national desegregation but rather required state and local authorities, under the supervision of federal district courts, to proceed with "all deliberate speed" in desegregation.[9] For more than fifteen years, state and school districts in the South waged a campaign of resistance to desegregation. Delays in implementing school desegregation continued until 1969, when the Supreme Court rejected a request by Mississippi officials for further delay, declaring that all school districts were obligated to end their dual school systems "at once" and "now and hereafter" to operate only integrated schools.[10]

Busing and Racial Balancing Federal district judges enjoy wide freedom in fashioning remedies for past or present discriminatory practices by governments. If a federal district court anywhere in the United States finds that any actions by governments or school officials have contributed to racial imbalances (for example, drawing school district attendance lines that separate black and white pupils), the judge may order the adoption of a desegregation plan to overcome racial imbalances produced by official action. A large number of cities have come under federal district court orders to improve racial balances in their schools through busing.

In the important case of *Swann v. Charlotte-Mecklenburg County Board of Education* (1971), the Supreme Court upheld the following:

- The use of racial balance requirements in schools and the assignment of pupils to schools based on race.
- "Close scrutiny" by judges of schools that are predominantly of one race.
- Gerrymandering of school attendance zones as well as "clustering" or "grouping" of schools to achieve racial balance.
- Court-ordered busing of pupils to achieve racial balance.[11]

The Court was careful to note, however, that racial imbalance in schools is not itself grounds for ordering these remedies unless it is also shown that some present or past governmental action contributed to the imbalance.

De Facto Segregation However, in the absence of any past or present governmental actions contributing to racial imbalance, states and school districts are not required by the Fourteenth Amendment to integrate their schools. For example, where central-city schools are predominantly black and suburban schools are predominantly white owing to residential patterns, cross-district busing is not required unless some official action brought about these racial imbalances. Thus in 1974 the Supreme Court threw out a lower federal court order for massive busing of students between Detroit and fifty-two suburban school districts.[12] Although Detroit city schools were 70 percent black and the suburban schools

Although the first conflicts over integration in the public schools erupted in the segregated southern states, northern cities later became the focus of unrest over school integration. When federal judges ordered the busing of schoolchildren outside their neighborhoods in order to achieve racial balances citywide, parents and politicians in some northern cities responded with a ferocity equal to earlier southern protests. In Boston, many parents initially boycotted a busing order in 1974, refusing to send their children to school at all or establishing private schools and even attacking busloads of minority children arriving at formerly white schools.

almost all white, none of the area school districts segregated students within their own boundaries. This important decision means that largely black central cities surrounded by largely white suburbs will remain segregated in practice because there are not enough white students living within the city boundaries to achieve integration.

De facto segregation is more common in the northern metropolitan areas than in the South. The states with the largest percentages of African American students attending schools that have 90 to 100 percent minority enrollments are Illinois (62 percent), Michigan (60 percent), New York (57 percent), and New Jersey (54 percent). The persistence of de facto segregation, together with a renewed interest in the quality of education, has caused many civil rights organizations to focus their attention on improving the quality of schools in urban areas rather than trying to desegregate these schools.

Many school districts in the South and elsewhere have operated under federal court supervision for many years. How long should court supervision continue, and what standards are to be used in determining when desegregation has been achieved once and for all? The Rehnquist-led Supreme Court in recent years has undertaken to free some school districts from direct federal court supervision. Where the last vestiges of state-sanctioned discrimination have been removed "as far as practicable," the Supreme Court has allowed lower federal courts to dissolve racial balancing plans even though imbalances due to residential patterns may continue to exist.[13]

THE CIVIL RIGHTS ACTS

The early goal of the civil rights movement was to eliminate discrimination and segregation practiced by *governments*, particularly states and school districts. When the civil rights movement turned to *private* discrimination—discrimination practiced by private owners of restaurants, hotels, motels, and stores; private employers, landlords, and real estate agents; and others who were not government officials— it had to take its fight to the Congress. The Constitution does not govern the activities of private individuals. Only Congress at the national level could outlaw discrimination in the private sector. Yet prior to 1964, Congress had been content to let the courts struggle with the question of civil rights. New political tactics and organizations were required to put the issue of equality on the agenda of Congress.

Martin Luther King, Jr., and Nonviolent Direct Action   Leadership in the struggle to eliminate discrimination and segregation from private life was provided by a young African American minister, Martin Luther King, Jr. (see *People in Politics:* "Martin Luther King, Jr., 'I Have a Dream'" on page 556). Under King, the civil rights movement developed and refined political techniques for use by American minorities, including **nonviolent direct action**. Nonviolent direct action is a form of protest that involves breaking "unjust" laws in an open, "loving," nonviolent fashion. The purpose of nonviolent direct action is to call attention—to "bear witness"— to the existence of injustice. In the words of Martin Luther King, Jr., such civil disobedience "seeks to dramatize the issue so that it can no longer be ignored"[14] (see also *A Conflicting View:* "Sometimes It's Right to Disobey the Law" in Chapter 1).

King formed the Southern Christian Leadership Conference (SCLC) in 1957 to develop and direct the growing nonviolent direct action movement. During the

de facto segregation   Racial imbalances not directly caused by official actions but rather by residential patterns.

nonviolent direct action   Strategy used by civil rights leaders such as Martin Luther King, Jr., in which protesters break "unjust" laws openly but in a "loving" fashion in order to bring the injustices of such laws to public attention.

In the civil rights march of 1963 more than 200,000 people marched peacefully on Washington, D.C., to end segregation. It was here that Martin Luther King, Jr., delivered his famous "I Have a Dream" speech.

next few years, the SCLC overshadowed the older NAACP in leading the fight against segregation. Where the NAACP had developed its strategy of court litigation to combat discrimination by *governments*, now the SCLC developed nonviolent direct action tactics to build widespread popular support and to pressure Congress to outlaw discrimination by *private businesses*.

The year 1963 was perhaps the most important for nonviolent direct action. The SCLC focused its efforts in Birmingham, Alabama, where King led thousands of marchers in a series of orderly and peaceful demonstrations. When police attacked the marchers with fire hoses, dogs, and cattle prods—in full view of national television cameras—millions of viewers around the country came to understand the injustices of segregation. The Birmingham action set off demonstrations in many parts of the country. The theme remained one of nonviolence, and it was usually whites rather than blacks who resorted to violence in these demonstrations. Responsible black leaders remained in control of the movement and won widespread support from the white community.

The culmination of King's nonviolent philosophy was a huge yet orderly march on Washington, D.C., held on August 28, 1963. More than 200,000 blacks and whites participated in the march, which was endorsed by many civic leaders, religious groups, and political figures. The march ended at the Lincoln Memorial, where Martin Luther King, Jr., delivered his most eloquent appeal, entitled "I Have a Dream." Congress passed the Civil Rights Act of 1964 by better than a two-thirds favorable vote in both houses; it won the overwhelming support of both Republican and Democratic members of Congress.

The Civil Rights Act of 1964 Signed into law on July 4, 1964, the Civil Rights Act of 1964 ranks with the Emancipation Proclamation, the Fourteenth Amendment, and the *Brown* case as one of the most important steps toward full equality for African Americans. Among its most important provisions are the following:

Martin Luther King, Jr., "I Have a Dream"

"If a man hasn't discovered something he will die for, he isn't fit to live."*

For Martin Luther King, Jr., (1929–1968), civil rights was something to die for, and before he died for the cause, he would shatter a century of southern segregation and set a new domestic agenda for the nation's leaders. King's contributions to the development of nonviolent direct action won him international acclaim and the Nobel Peace Prize.

King's father was the pastor of one of the South's largest and most influential African American congregations, the Ebenezer Baptist Church in Atlanta, Georgia. Young Martin was educated at Morehouse College in Atlanta and received a Ph.D. in religious studies at Boston University. Shortly after beginning his career as a Baptist minister in Montgomery, Alabama, in 1955, a black woman, Rosa Parks, refused to give up her seat to whites on a Montgomery bus, setting in motion a year-long bus boycott in that city. Only twenty-six years old, King was thrust into national prominence as the leader of that boycott, which ended in the elimination of segregation on the city's buses. In 1957 King founded the Southern Christian Leadership Conference (SCLC) to provide encouragement and leadership to the growing nonviolent protest movement against segregation.

Perhaps the most dramatic application of nonviolent direct action occurred in Birmingham, Alabama, in the spring of 1963. Under King's direction, the SCLC had chosen that city as a major site for demonstrations during the centennial year of the Emancipation Proclamation. By its own description the "Heart of Dixie," Birmingham was the most rigidly segregated large city in the United States at the time. King believed that if segregation could be successfully challenged in Birmingham, it might begin to crumble throughout the South. Thousands of African Americans, ranging from schoolchildren to senior citizens, staged protest marches in Birmingham from May 2 to May 7. Although the demonstrators conducted themselves in a nonviolent fashion, police and firefighters under the direction of Police Chief Eugene "Bull" Connor attacked the demonstrators with fire hoses, cattle prods, and police dogs, all in clear view of national television cameras. Thousands of demonstrators were dragged off to jail, including King. (It was at this time that King wrote his "Letter from Birmingham Jail," explaining and defending nonviolent direct action.) But Connor's "victory" was short-lived. Pictures of police brutality flashed throughout the nation and the world, touching the consciences of many white Americans.

King was also the driving force behind the most massive application of nonviolent direct action in U.S. history: the great "March on Washington" in August 1963, during which more than 200,000 black and white marchers converged on the nation's capital. The march ended at the Lincoln Memorial, where King delivered his most eloquent appeal, entitled "I Have a Dream."

> I still have a dream. It is a dream deeply rooted in the American dream. I have a dream that one day this nation will rise up and live out the true meaning of its creed: "We hold these truths to be self-evident, that all men are created equal."

Title II: It is unlawful to discriminate or segregate persons on the grounds of race, color, religion, or national origin in any public accommodation, including hotels, motels, restaurants, movies, theaters, sports arenas, entertainment houses, and other places that offer to serve the public. This prohibition extends to all business establishments whose operations affect interstate commerce or whose discriminatory practices are supported by state action.

I have a dream that one day on the red hills of Georgia, sons of former slaves and sons of former slave-owners will be able to sit down together at the table of brotherhood.

I have a dream that one day, even in the state of Mississippi, a state sweltering with the heat of injustice, sweltering with the heat of oppression, will be transformed into an oasis of freedom and justice.

I have a dream my four little children will one day live in a nation where they will not be judged by the color of their skin but by content of their character. . . .

And when this happens, and when we allow freedom to ring, when we let it ring from every village and hamlet, from every state and city, we will be able to speed up that day when all of God's children— black men and white men, Jews and Gentiles, Catholics and Protestants—will be able to join hands and to sing in the words of the old Negro spiritual, "Free at last, free at last; thank God Almighty, we are free at last."[†]

It was in the wake of the March on Washington that President John F. Kennedy sent to the Congress a strong civil rights bill that would be passed after his death—the Civil Rights Act of 1964. That same year, King received the Nobel Peace Prize.

Yet even after passage of this act, voting registrars in many southern counties continued to keep African Americans off of the voting rolls through a variety of discriminatory tactics. In 1965 King again took action. Selma, the county seat of Dallas County, Alabama, was chosen as the site to dramatize the voting rights problem. King organized a fifty-mile march from Selma to the state capitol in Montgomery. He didn't get very far. Acting on orders of Governor George Wallace to disband the marchers, state troopers did so with a vengeance—using tear gas, nightsticks, and whips. This time, however, the national government intervened: in his capacity as Commander-in-Chief of the armed forces, President Lyndon Johnson ordered the National Guard to protect the demonstrators, and the march continued. During the march, Johnson went on television to address a special joint session of Congress, urging passage of new legislation to assure African Americans the right to vote, and Congress responded with the Voting Rights Act of 1965.

White racial violence in the early 1960s, including murders and bombings of black and white civil rights workers, shocked and disgusted many whites in both the North and the South. In 1963 Medgar Evers, the NAACP's state chair for Mississippi, was shot to death by a sniper as he entered his Jackson home. That same year, a bomb killed four young black girls attending Sunday school in Birmingham. On the evening of April 3, 1968, King spoke to a crowd in Memphis, Tennessee, in eerily prophetic terms. "I just want to do God's will. And He's allowed me to go to the mountain. And I've looked over, and I've seen the promised land. I may not get there with you. But I want you to know tonight, that we, as a people will get to the promised land. So I'm happy tonight. I'm not worried about anything. I'm not fearing any man." On the night of April 4, 1968, the world's leading exponent of nonviolence was killed by an assassin's bullet.[‡]

---

[*]Martin Luther King, Jr., speech, June 23, 1963, Detroit, Michigan.

[†]Martin Luther King, Jr., "I Have a Dream" speech, August 28, 1963, at the Lincoln Memorial, Washington, D.C., printed in David J. Garrow, *Bearing the Cross: Martin Luther King, Jr., and the Southern Christian Leadership Conference* (New York: Vintage Books, 1988), pp. 283–84.

[‡]Martin Luther King, Jr., speech, April 3, 1968, Memphis, Tennessee, in ibid., p. 621.

Title VI: Each federal department and agency is to take action to end discrimination in all programs or activities receiving federal financial assistance in any form. This action may include termination of financial assistance to persistently discriminatory agencies.

Title VII: It is unlawful for any employer or labor union to discriminate against any individual in any fashion in employment because of the individual's race, color, religion, sex, or national origin. The Equal Employment Opportunity Commission is established to enforce this provision by investigation, conference, conciliation, persuasion, and, if need be, civil action in federal court.

The Civil Rights Act of 1968   For many years "fair housing" had been considered the most sensitive area of civil rights legislation. Discrimination in the sale and rental of housing was the last major civil rights problem on which Congress took action. Discrimination in housing had not been mentioned in the comprehensive Civil Rights Act of 1964. Prohibiting discrimination in the sale or rental of housing affected the constituencies of northern members of Congress; earlier public accommodations provisions had their greatest effect in the South.

Prospects for a fair housing law were poor at the beginning of 1968. However, when Martin Luther King, Jr., was assassinated on April 4, the mood of Congress and the nation changed dramatically. Congress passed a fair housing law as tribute to the slain civil rights leader. The Civil Rights Act of 1968 prohibited discrimination in the sale or rental of a dwelling to any person on the basis of race, color, religion, or national origin.

EQUALITY: OPPORTUNITY VERSUS RESULTS

Although the gains of the civil rights movement were immensely important, these gains were primarily in *opportunity* rather than in *results*. The civil rights movement of the 1960s did not bring about major changes in the conditions under which most African Americans lived in the United States. Racial politics today center around the *actual* inequalities between blacks and whites in incomes, jobs, housing, health, education, and other conditions of life.

Continuing Inequalities   The issue of inequality today is often posed as differences in the "life chances" of blacks and whites. Figures can reveal only the bare outline of an African American's "life chances" in this society (see Table 15–2). The average income of a black family is 61 percent of the average white family's income. Over 25 percent of all black families live below the recognized poverty line, whereas only 11 percent of white families do so. The black unemployment rate is more than twice as high as the white unemployment rate. Blacks are less likely to hold prestigious executive jobs in professional, managerial, clerical, or sales work. They do not hold many skilled craft jobs in industry but are concentrated in operative, service, and laboring positions. The civil rights movement opened up new opportunities for African Americans. But equality of *opportunity* is not the same as equality of *results*.

Explaining Inequalities   African American and Hispanic minorities have improved their economic condition in recent years. However, the income *disparity* between whites and minorities has remained about the same. Note that in 1970 black median family income was approximately 61 percent of white median family income, the same percentage as in 1998. This income gap remains despite a significant narrowing of differences in educational levels between whites and minorities.

Much, but certainly not all, of the disparity in income between whites and minorities disappears when educational levels are taken into account. Comparing the income of whites and minorities *at same educational levels* suggests that some discrimination may remain. Black college graduates on average earn about 77 percent of

Table 15-2 Minority Life Chances

	Median Income of Families				
	1970	**1975**	**1980**	**1985**	**1998**
White	$10,236	$14,268	$21,904	$29,152	$46,754
Black	6,279	8,779	12,674	16,786	28,602
Hispanic	—	9,551	14,716	19,027	28,142

	Percentage of Persons below Poverty Level			
	1975	**1980**	**1985**	**1998**
White	9.7%	10.2%	11.4%	11.0%
Black	31.3	32.5	31.3	26.5
Hispanic	26.9	25.7	29.0	29.1

	Unemployment Rate		
	1980	**1985**	**1998**
White	6.3%	6.2%	3.9%
Black	14.3	15.1	8.9
Hispanic	10.1	10.5	7.2

	Education: Percentage of Persons over Twenty-Five Completing High School				
	1960	**1970**	**1980**	**1990**	**1998**
White	43	55	69	79	84
Black	20	31	51	66	76
Hispanic	(NA)	32	44	51	56

	Education: Percentage of Persons over Twenty-Five Completing College				
	1960	**1970**	**1980**	**1990**	**1998**
White	8	11	17	22	25
Black	3	4	8	11	15
Hispanic	(NA)	4	8	9	11

Source: Statistical Abstract of the United States, 1999.

the income of white college graduates; black high school graduates earn about 80 percent of the income of white high school graduates. The average income of Hispanics is even closer to that of whites at the same educational levels. But neither African Americans nor Hispanics earn the same income as whites with the same educational background (see Table 15–3 on page 560).

When blacks and whites are asked in opinion polls to explain income inequality between the races, blacks attributed to discrimination (70 percent) while whites attributed to a lack of "motivation and willpower" (62 percent) among blacks.[15] But both blacks and whites agree that black progress depends more on "self-help" than on government programs.[16]

Policy Choices   What public policies should be pursued to achieve equality in America? Is it sufficient that government eliminate discrimination, guarantee equality of opportunity, and apply color-blind standards to both blacks and whites? Or

Harvard University's graduating class is racially diversified. The nation's most prestigious colleges and universities actively recruit quality minority students. While these graduates can look forward to high rewards, on average throughout the nation minority college graduates do not earn the same income as non-minority college graduates.

affirmative action Any program, whether enacted by a government or by a private organization, whose goal is to overcome the results of past unequal treatment of minorities and/or women by giving members of these groups preferential treatment in admissions, hiring, promotions, or other aspects of life.

quota Provision of some affirmative action programs in which specific numbers or percentages of positions are open only to minorities and/or women.

should government take **affirmative action** to overcome the results of past unequal treatment of blacks—preferential or compensatory treatment to assist black applications for university admissions and scholarships, job hiring and promotion, and other opportunities for advancement in life?

Shifting Goals in Civil Rights Policy For decades, the emphasis of government policy was on equal *opportunity*. This early nondiscrimination approach began with President Harry Truman's decision to desegregate the armed forces in 1948 and carried through to Title VI and Title VII of the Civil Rights Act of 1964, which eliminated discrimination in federally aided projects and private employment. Gradually, however, the goal of the civil rights movement shifted from the traditional aim of equality of opportunity through nondiscrimination alone to affirmative action involving the establishment of "goals and timetables" to achieve greater equality of results between blacks and whites. While avoiding the term **quota**, the notion of affirmative action tests the success of equal opportunity by observing whether blacks achieve admissions, jobs, and promotions in proportion to their numbers in the population.

Table 15-3	White and Minority Income by Educational Attainment

	Annual Mean Income, 1998				
	White	Black	Hispanic	Black/White Ratio	Hispanic/White Ratio
Graduate Degree	$52,475	$40,610	$46,556	77%	89%
Bachelor's Degree	41,439	32,062	33,465	77	81
High School Degree	23,618	18,930	19,558	80	83
No High School Degree	16,596	13,185	15,069	79	91

Source: U.S. Bureau of the Census, 2000. Data for 1998.

Affirmative Action   Affirmative action programs were initially developed in the federal bureaucracy. Federal executive agencies were authorized by the Civil Rights Act of 1964 to develop "rules and regulations" for desegregating any organization or business receiving federal funds. In 1965 President Lyndon B. Johnson signed Executive Order 11246, requiring all federal agencies and businesses contracting with the federal government to practice affirmative action. In 1972 the U.S. Office of Education issued guidelines that mandated "goals" for university admissions and faculty hiring of minorities and women. The Equal Employment Opportunity Commission (EEOC), established by the Civil Rights Act of 1964, is responsible for monitoring affirmative action programs in private employment.

Federal officials generally measure "progress" in affirmative action in terms of the number of disadvantaged group members admitted, employed, or promoted. The pressure to show "progress" can result in relaxation of traditional measures of qualifications, such as test scores and educational achievement. Advocates of affirmative action argue that these measures are not good predictors of performance on the job or in school and are biased in favor of white culture. State and local governments, schools, colleges and universities, and private employers are under pressure to drop these standards.

AFFIRMATIVE ACTION IN THE COURTS

The constitutional question posed by affirmative action programs is whether or not they discriminate against whites in violation of the Equal Protection Clause of the Fourteenth Amendment. A related question is whether or not affirmative action programs discriminate against whites in violation of the Civil Rights Act of 1964, which prohibits discrimination "on account of race," not just discrimination against blacks. Clearly, these are questions for the Supreme Court to resolve, but unfortunately the Court has failed to develop clear-cut answers.

The Bakke Case   In the absence of a history of racial discrimination, the Supreme Court has been willing to scrutinize affirmative action programs to ensure that they do not directly discriminate against whites. In *University of California Regents v. Bakke* (1978), the Supreme Court struck down a special admissions program for minorities at a state medical school on the grounds that it excluded a white applicant because of his race and violated his rights under the Equal Protection Clause.[17] Allan Bakke applied to the University of California Davis Medical School two consecutive years and was rejected; in both years, black applicants with significantly lower grade point averages and medical aptitude test scores were accepted through a special admissions program that reserved sixteen minority places in a class of one hundred.[18] The University of California did not deny that its admissions decisions were based on race. Instead, it argued that its racial classification was "benign," that is, designed to assist minorities. The special admissions program was designed to (1) "reduce the historical deficit of traditionally disfavored minorities in medical schools and the medical profession"; (2) "counter the effects of societal discrimination"; (3) "increase the number of physicians who will practice in communities currently underserved"; and (4) "obtain the educational benefits that flow from an ethnically diverse student body."

The Supreme Court held that these objectives were legitimate and that race and ethnic origin *may* be considered in reviewing applications to a state school without

Demonstrators at the Florida state capitol in Tallahassee chant "Shame on Bush" over Governor Jeb Bush's effort to ban racial preferences in university admissions and state contracting.

violating the Fourteenth Amendment's Equal Protection Clause. However, the Court also held that a separate admissions program for minorities with a specific quota of openings which were unavailable to white applicants *did* violate the Equal Protection Clause. The Court ordered the university to admit Bakke to its medical school and to eliminate the special admissions program. It recommended that California consider an admissions program developed at Harvard, which considers disadvantaged racial or ethnic background as a "plus" in an overall evaluation of an application but does not set numerical quotas or exclude any person from competing for all positions.

Reaction to the decision was predictable: supporters of affirmative action, particularly government officials from affirmative action programs, emphasized the Supreme Court's willingness to allow minority status to be considered a positive factor; opponents emphasized the Supreme Court's unwillingness to allow quotas that exclude whites from competing for some positions. Because Bakke had "won" the case, many observers felt that the Supreme Court was not going to permit racial quota systems.

Affirmative Action as a Remedy for Past Discrimination

The Supreme Court has continued to approve of affirmative action programs where there is evidence of past discriminatory practices. In *United Steelworkers of America v. Weber* (1979), the Supreme Court approved a plan developed by a private employer and a union to reserve 50 percent of higher paying, skilled jobs for minorities. The Court held that "employers and unions in the private sector [are] free to take such race-conscious steps to eliminate manifest racial imbalances in traditionally segregated job categories. We hold that Title VII does not prohibit such . . . affirmative action plans." According to the Court, it would be "ironic indeed" if the Civil Rights Act were used to prohibit voluntary private race-conscious efforts to overcome the past effects of discrimination.[19] In *United States v. Paradise* (1987), the Court upheld a rigid 50 percent black quota system for promotions in the Alabama Department of Safety, which had excluded blacks from the ranks of state troopers prior to 1972 and had not promoted any blacks higher than corporal prior to 1984. In a 5 to 4 decision, the majority stressed the long history of discrimination in the agency as a reason for upholding the quota system. Whatever burdens imposed on innocent parties were outweighed by the need to correct the effects of past discrimination.[20]

Cases Questioning Affirmative Action

However, the Supreme Court has continued to express concern about whites who are directly and adversely affected by government action solely because of their race. In *Firefighters Local Union 1784 v. Stotts* (1984), the Court ruled that a city could not lay off white firefighters in favor of black firefighters with less seniority.[21] In *City of Richmond v. Crosen Co.* (1989), the Supreme Court held that a minority **set-aside program** in Richmond, Virginia, which mandated that 30 percent of all city construction contracts must go to "blacks, Spanish-speaking, Orientals, Indians, Eskimos, or Aleuts," violated the Equal Protection Clause of the Fourteenth Amendment.[22]

Moreover, the Court has held that racial classifications in law must be subject to "strict scrutiny." This means that race-based actions by government—any disparate treatment of the races by federal, state, or local public agencies—must be found necessary to remedy past proven discrimination, or to further clearly identified, legitimate and "compelling" government interests. Moreover, race-based actions must be "narrowly tailored" and "least restrictive" so as to minimize adverse

set-aside program Program in which a specified number or percentage of contracts must go to designated minorities.

effects on rights of other individuals. In striking down a federal construction contract "set-aside" program for small businesses owned by racial minorities, the Court expressed skepticism about governmental racial classifications: "There is simply no way of determining what classifications are 'benign' and 'remedial' and what classifications are in fact motivated by illegitimate notions of racial inferiority or simple racial politics."[23]

The Court also held that achieving "racial diversity" in broadcasting was *not* a compelling governmental interest justifying the use of race in awarding broadcasting licenses by the Federal Communications Commission.[24]

Affirmative Action in Universities   Most colleges and universities in the United States—public as well as private—identify "diversity" as a goal, a term that presumably refers to racial and ethnic representation in the student body and faculty. But in an important U.S. Circuit Court of Appeals decision, *Hopwood v. Texas*,[25] the Fifth Circuit Court (covering Texas, Louisiana, and Mississippi) spoke out forcefully against the use of race and ethnicity to achieve "diversity" in the student body. The Circuit Court interpreted the Supreme Court's requirements of "strict scrutiny" and "compelling governmental interest" in approving racial classifications, as justifying only *remedial* efforts to overcome the effects of past discriminatory actions. The Circuit Court held that "achieving diversity" was *not* a "compelling governmental interest," and therefore the use of race or ethnicity in admissions merely to achieve diversity violated the Equal Protection Clause of the Fourteenth Amendment. The U.S. Supreme Court later affirmed this Court of Appeals decision, yet warned that it may not fully agree with its reasoning.[26] The *Hopwood* case has inspired the number of federal court challenges to university admissions policies across the country—challenges to the use of race and ethnicity in admissions to both undergraduate and graduate, law, and medical schools.

The Absence of a Clear Constitutional Principal   The Supreme Court's decisions on affirmative action have not yet established a clear and coherent interpretation of the Constitution. No clear rule of law or Constitutional principal tells us exactly what is permissible and what is prohibited in the way of racially conscious laws and practices. Nevertheless, over time some general tendencies in Supreme Court policy can be identified. Affirmative action programs are *more likely to be found constitutional* when:

- They are adopted in response to a past proven history of discrimination.
- They do not absolutely bar whites or ban them from competing or participating.
- They serve a clearly identified, legitimate, and "compelling governmental interest."
- They are "narrowly tailored" to achieve the government's compelling interest and represent the "least restrictive" means of doing so.

It is important to note that the Supreme Court has never adopted the color-blind doctrine, first espoused by Justice Harlan in his dissent from *Plessy v. Ferguson*, that "Our Constitution is colorblind, and neither knows nor tolerates classes among citizens." If the Equal Protection Clause required the laws of the United States and the states to be truly color blind, then no racial guidelines, goals, or quotas would be tolerated. Occasionally this view has been expressed in recent minority dissents.[27] (See A Conflicting View: "The Constitution Should Be Color-Blind" on page 564.)

The Constitution Should Be Color-Blind

In 1896 a single voice spoke out against *all* racial classifications—Supreme Court Justice John Harlan opposing segregation: "Our Constitution is color-blind and neither knows nor tolerates classes among the citizens." He was *dissenting* from the Supreme Court's majority opinion in the infamous case of *Plessy v. Ferguson*, which approved the segregationist doctrine of "separate but equal." Unfortunately, the ideal of a color-blind society remains almost as elusive today as it was more than a hundred years ago.

Martin Luther King, Jr., had a dream that "our children will one day live in a nation where they will not be judged by the color of their skin but by the content of their character." Can that dream be made a reality?

Over time, the civil rights movement shifted its focus from *individual rights to group benefits*. Affirmative action programs classify people by group membership, thereby challenging a belief widely held in the United States—that people be judged on individual attributes like character and achievement, rather than on race or gender. Racial and gender preferences are currently encountered in hiring and promotion practices in private and public employment and in college in university admissions, scholarships, and faculty recruitment. "New" groups—homosexuals, for example—seek to be classified among the preferred groups. The result has been increased intergroup tension in many arenas—on the job, in schools, and on college campuses.

Affirmative action programs divide Americans into two classes—those who enjoy legally mandated preferential treatment, and those who do not. Majority support for civil rights laws is weakening under growing resentment among those who are denied preferential treatment.

Some early supporters of affirmative action have come to view race-conscious programs as no longer necessary. They argue that disadvantages in society today are based more on class than on race. If prefer-

ences are to be granted at all, in their view, they should be based on economic disadvantage, not race.

Misgivings also have been expressed by a few African American scholars about the unfair stigmatizing of the supposed beneficiaries of affirmative action—a resulting negative stereotyping of blacks as unable to advance on merit alone. Race-conscious government policies, they argue, have done more harm than good. African American economist Glenn Loury claims that proponents of affirmative action have an inferiority complex: "When blacks say we have to have affirmative action, please don't take it away from us, it's almost like saying, you're right, we can't compete on merit. But I know that we can compete." Conservative columnist William Bennett says that "toxic" race relations, aggravated by affirmative action, have led to damaging forms of new segregation: "Affirmative action has not brought us what we want—a color-blind society. It has brought us an extremely color-conscious society. In our universities we have separate dorms, separate social centers. What's next—water fountains? That's not good and everybody knows it."

Many argue that affirmative action has caused the civil rights movement to lose widespread public support and instead become contentious and divisive. In fact, civil rights has become such a hot topic that most elected officials now prefer to avoid it. As one anonymous member of Congress put it, "The problem is political correctness—you can't talk openly." President Bill Clinton's sound bite on affirmative action—"Mend it, don't end it"—straddles the issue without resolving the controversy that surrounds it.

Many supporters of affirmative action would ideally prefer a color-blind society—the dream evoked by Martin Luther King, Jr., in his speech at the civil rights march. However, they see race-conscious policies as necessary to remedy the effects of both past and current discrimination: "If we abandon affirmative action we return to the old white boy network."

Source: Quotations reported in *Newsweek*, February 13, 1996.

BATTLES OVER AFFIRMATIVE ACTION

Political battles over affirmative action have been waged in the Congress and the states, as well as in the federal courts. Politicians are very much aware of survey results showing that most Americans favor affirmative action when it is expressed in the abstract. But they are equally aware that the poll results are much different when "preferences" or "quotas" are mentioned. Congress, ever mindful of the polls, has tried to find a way to advance affirmative action while avoiding direct reference to preferences or quotas.

Public Opinion and Affirmative Action   Most Americans agree that discrimination still exists in American society, even if they do not agree on what should be done about it. However, blacks and whites have come to hold very different opinions about the extent of discrimination today and about what, if anything, should be done about it (see *Up Close:* "Black and White Opinion on Affirmative Action" on page 566). Few Americans object to actions taken to remedy proven discrimination by private employers, public officials, or university administrations. But resentment among whites toward preferential treatment of minorities appears to be growing.

Affirmative Action in the Workplace   The Civil Rights Act of 1964, Title VII, bars racial or sexual discrimination in employment. But how can persons who feel they have been passed over for jobs or promotions go about the task of proving that discrimination was involved? Evidence of direct discrimination is often difficult to obtain. Can underrepresentation of minorities or women in a work force be used as evidence of discrimination in the absence of any evidence of direct discriminatory practices? If an employer uses a requirement or test that has a disparate effect on minorities or women, who has the burden of proof of showing that the requirement or test is relevant to effective job performance?

The Supreme Court responded to both of these questions in its interpretation of the Civil Rights Act in *Wards Cove Packing Co., Inc. v. Antonio* in 1989.[28] In a controversial 5 to 4 decision, the Court held that statistical imbalances in race or gender in the workplace were not sufficient evidence by themselves to prove discrimination. And the Court ruled it was up to plaintiffs to prove that an employer had no business reason for requirements or tests which had an adverse impact on minorities or women. This decision clearly made it more difficult to prove job discrimination.

Civil Rights and Women's Equity in Employment Act of 1991   Civil rights groups were highly critical of what they regarded as the Supreme Court's "narrowing" of the Civil Rights Act protections in employment. They turned to Congress to rewrite portions of the Civil Rights Act to "restore" these protections. Business lobbies, however, believed that accepting statistical imbalances as evidence of discrimination or that shifting the burden of proof to employers would result in hiring by "quotas" simply to avoid lawsuits. After nearly two years of negotiations on Capitol Hill and a reversal of President George Bush's initial opposition, Congress produced the Civil Rights and Women's Equity Act of 1991.[29] Among the more important provisions of the act were these:

- *Statistical imbalances:* The mere existence of statistical imbalance in an employer's work force is not, by itself, sufficient evidence to prove discrimination. However, statistical imbalances may be evidence of employment practices (rules, requirements, academic qualifications, tests) that have a "disparate impact" on minorities or women.

Black and White Opinion on Affirmative Action

Blacks and whites differ over the extent of discrimination in American society today and what, if anything, should be done about it. Blacks are far more likely than whites to believe that racial discrimination is the principal reason why blacks, on the average, have lower incomes and poorer housing than whites. Although 70 percent of blacks believe these differences are "mainly due to discrimination," only 47 percent of whites think so.

Affirmative Action   Given these different views on the extent of discrimination, it is not surprising that blacks and whites also differ on "affirmative action." There is widespread debate over the meaning of the term *affirmative action*. Insofar as it is interpreted to mean greater effort to make sure *opportunities* are equally open to all—that is, making sure schools and jobs are equally

available to all races and both sexes—there is little controversy over its desirability. But affirmative action becomes controversial when it is interpreted to mean equality of results in admissions, jobs, and promotions. And the proposed use of "preferences" and "quotas" to ensure equality of results among races and sexes produces polarization of opinion among Americans.

Levels of support for affirmative action often depend on the wording of the question. If the question is posed simply in terms of support for or opposition to "affirmative action," without specifying preferences or quotas, then whites as well as blacks favor it. Moreover, if affirmative action is defined in terms of "encouraging" minorities or providing job training or special education "to make them better qualified," most Americans, both black and white, are supportive. However, black and white opinion differs sharply over whether "diversity" is an important goal for colleges in universities, and whether "quotas" ought to be established for racial minorities.

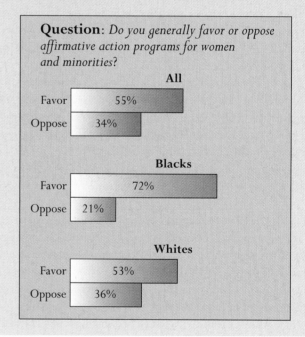

Question: *Do you feel that compared with whites, blacks...*

Blacks

Get equal pay for equal work in unskilled jobs	31%
Get equal pay for equal work in executive jobs	33%
Are promoted as rapidly to higher ranks of employment	13%
Have as good a chance of getting into skilled craft unions	41%

Whites

Get equal pay for equal work in unskilled jobs	72%
Get equal pay for equal work in executive jobs	78%
Are promoted as rapidly to higher ranks of employment	39%
Have as good a chance of getting into skilled craft unions	69%

Question: *Do you generally favor or oppose affirmative action programs for women and minorities?*

All

Favor	55%
Oppose	34%

Blacks

Favor	72%
Oppose	21%

Whites

Favor	53%
Oppose	36%

- *Disparate employment practices:* Employers bear the burden of proof that any practice which has a "disparate impact" is necessary and has "a significant and manifest relationship to the requirements for effective job performance."

Affirmative Action Battles in the States   National rethinking of affirmative action was inspired by a citizen's initiative placed on the ballot in California by

Question: *Do you favor or oppose providing job training for minorities and women to make them qualified for better jobs?*

All

Favor	82%
Oppose	17%

Blacks

Favor	94%
Oppose	6%

Whites

Favor	80%
Oppose	18%

Question: *Do you favor or oppose providing special educational classes for minorities and women to make them better qualified for college?*

All

Favor	75%
Oppose	22%

Blacks

Favor	90%
Oppose	9%

Whites

Favor	73%
Oppose	24%

Question: *In order to make up for past discrimination, do you favor or oppose programs which impose quotas for racial minorities?*

All

Favor	19%
Oppose	72%

Blacks

Favor	48%
Oppose	37%

Whites

Favor	15%
Oppose	78%

Question: *How important do you think it is for a college to have a racially diverse student body— that is, a mix of blacks, whites, Asians, Hispanics, and other minorities? Is it very important? Somewhat important? Or not very important at all?*

Very Important

All	43%
Blacks	76%
Whites	36%

Sources: Gallup poll, reported in *USA Today*, March 24, 1995; CBS News/*New York Times* poll, reported in *The Polling Report*, December 22, 1997.

popular petition and approved by 54 percent of the state's voters in 1996. The California Civil Rights Initiative added the following phrase to that state's constitution:

> Neither the state of California nor any of its political subdivisions or agents shall use race, sex, color, ethnicity or national origin as a criterion for either discriminating against, or granting preferential treatment to, any individual or group in

The Reverend Jesse Jackson leads a group of marchers protesting California's anti-affirmative action policies. Pictured alongside Jackson are radio personality Kasey Kasem and Delores Huerta, co-founder of the United Farm Workers' Union. Although many politicians claiming to speak for the American people indicate strong opposition to affirmative action policies, these policies actually garner widespread public support, as demonstrations such as this prove.

the operation of the State's system of public employment, public education or public contracting.

The key words are "or granting preferential treatment to . . ." Opponents argued that a constitutional ban on preferential treatment of minorities and women eliminates affirmative action programs in government, prevents governments from acting to correct historic racial or gender imbalances, and denies minorities and women the opportunity to seek legal protections in education and employment. Opponents challenged the California Civil Rights Initiative in federal courts arguing that by preventing minorities and women from seeking preferential treatment under law, the initiative violated the Equal Protection Clause of the Fourteenth Amendment. But a Circuit Court of Appeals held, and the U.S. Supreme Court affirmed, that "[A] ban on race or gender preferences, as a matter of law or logic, does not violate the Equal Protection Clause in any conventional sense. . . . Impediments to preferential treatment do not deny equal protection."[30] The Court reasoned that the Constitution allows some race-based preferences to correct past discrimination, but it does not prevent states from banning racial preferences altogether.

The California citizens initiative barring racial and gender preferences has inspired similar movements in other states. In 1998 voters in the state of Washington adopted a similarly worded state constitutional amendment by a large margin. In 2000 Florida's Governor Jeb Bush issued an executive order banning racial preferences in state contracting and university admissions. But in both Florida and Texas alternative plans were introduced to insure access to state universities by minorities. Both states now admit top academic students from every high school in the state regardless of their scores on standard achievement tests (e.g., SAT scores). Presumably this will allow students from schools with heavy minority enrollments to gain admission. It may also eventually improve academic competition among students within high schools. And it may turn out that banning racial preferences does not reduce the numbers of minorities attending state universities.

GENDER EQUALITY AND THE FOURTEENTH AMENDMENT

The historical context of the Fourteenth Amendment implies its intent to guarantee equality for newly freed slaves, but the wording of its Equal Protection Clause applies to "any person." Thus the text of the Fourteenth Amendment could be interpreted to bar any gender differences in the law, in the fashion of the once proposed yet never ratified Equal Rights Amendment. But the Supreme Court has not interpreted the Equal Protection Clause to give the same level of protection to gender equality as to racial equality. Indeed, in 1873 the Supreme Court specifically rejected arguments that this clause applied to women. The Court once upheld a state law banning women from practicing law, arguing that "The natural and proper timidity and delicacy which belongs to the female sex evidently unfits it for many of the occupations of civil life. . . . The paramount destiny and mission of women are to fulfill the noble and benign offices of wife and mother. This is the law of the Creator."[31]

Early Feminist Politics The earliest active feminist organizations grew out of the pre–Civil War antislavery movement. There the first generation of feminists—including Lucretia Mott, Elizabeth Cady Stanton, Lucy Stone, and Susan B. Anthony—learned to organize, hold public meetings, and conduct petition

Elizabeth Cady Stanton addresses a meeting. Stanton, with Lucretia Mott and others, organized one of the defining moments in feminist politics in the United States—the Seneca Falls convention of 1848. Participants at the convention approved a Declaration of Sentiments, modeled on the Declaration of Independence, that demanded legal and political rights for women, including the right to vote.

campaigns. After the Civil War, women were successful in changing many state laws that abridged the property rights of married women and otherwise treated them as "chattel" (property) of their husbands. By the early 1900s activists were also successful in winning some protections for women in the workplace, including state laws limiting women's hours of work, working conditions, and physical demands. At the time, these laws were regarded as "progressive."

The most successful feminist efforts of the 1800s centered on protection of women in families. The perceived threats to women's well-being were their husbands' drinking, gambling, and consorting with prostitutes. Women led the Anti-Saloon League, succeeded in outlawing gambling and prostitution in every state except Nevada, and provided the major source of moral support for the Eighteenth Amendment (Prohibition).

In the early twentieth century, the feminist movement concentrated on women's suffrage—the drive to guarantee women the right to vote. The early suffragists employed mass demonstrations, parades, picketing, and occasional disruption and civil disobedience—tactics similar to those of the civil rights movement of the 1960s. The culmination of their efforts was the 1920 passage of the Nineteenth Amendment to the Constitution: "The right of citizens of the United States to vote shall not be denied or abridged by the United States or by any State on account of sex." The suffrage movement spawned the League of Women Voters; in addition to women's right to vote, the League has sought protection of women in industry, child welfare laws, and honest election practices.

Judicial Scrutiny of Gender Classifications   In the 1970s, the Supreme Court became responsive to arguments that sex discrimination might violate the Equal Protection Clause of the Fourteenth Amendment. In *Reed v. Reed* (1971), it ruled that sexual classifications in the law "must be reasonable and not arbitrary, and must rest on some ground of difference having fair and substantial relation to . . . important governmental objectives."[32] This is a much more relaxed level of scrutiny than the Supreme Court gives to racial classification in the law. Since then, the Court has also made these rulings:

- A state can no longer set different ages for men and women to become legal adults[33] or purchase alcoholic beverages. [34]
- Women cannot be barred from police or firefighting jobs by arbitrary height and weight requirements. [35]
- Insurance and retirement plans for women must pay the same monthly benefits (even though women on the average live longer). [36]
- Schools must pay coaches in girls' sports the same as coaches in boys' sports. [37]

Continuing Gender Differences   The Supreme Court continues to wrestle with the question of whether some gender differences can be recognized in law. The question is most evident in laws dealing with sexual activity and reproduction. The Court has upheld statutory rape laws that make it a crime for an adult male to have sexual intercourse with a female under the age of eighteen, regardless of her consent. "We need not to be medical doctors to discern that young men and young women are not similarly situated with respect to the problems and the risks of sexual intercourse. Only women may become pregnant, and they suffer disproportionately the profound physical, emotional and psychological consequences of sexual activity."[38]

Women's participation in military service, particularly combat, raises even more controversial questions regarding permissible gender classifications. The Supreme Court appears to have bowed out of this particular controversy. In upholding Congress's draft registration law for men only, the Court ruled that "the constitutional power of Congress to raise and support armies and to make all laws necessary and proper to that end is broad and sweeping."[39] Congress and the Defense Department are responsible for determining assignments for women in the military. Women have won assignments to air and naval combat units but remain excluded from combat infantry, armor, artillery, special forces, and submarine duty.

Aims of the Equal Rights Amendment   The proposed Equal Rights Amendment to the U.S. Constitution, passed by Congress in 1972 but never ratified by the states, was worded very broadly: "Equality of rights under the law shall not be denied or abridged by the United States or any State on account of sex." Had it been ratified by the necessary thirty-eight states, it would have eliminated most, if not all, gender differences in the law. Without ERA, many important guarantees of equality for women rest on laws of Congress rather than on the Constitution.

GENDER EQUALITY IN THE ECONOMY

As cultural views of women's roles in society have changed and economic pressures on family budgets have increased, women's participation in the labor force has risen. The gap between women's and men's participation in the nation's work force is closing over time.[40] With the movement of women into the work force, feminist political activity has shifted toward economic concerns—gender equality in education, employment, pay, promotion, and credit.

Gender Equality in Civil Rights Laws   Title VII of the Civil Rights Act of 1964 prevents sexual (as well as racial) discrimination in hiring, pay, and promotions. The Equal Employment Opportunity Commission, the federal agency charged with eliminating discrimination in employment, has established guidelines barring stereotyped classifications of "men's jobs" and "women's jobs." The courts have repeatedly struck down state laws and employer practices that differentiate between men and women in hours, pay, retirement age, and so forth.

The Federal Equal Credit Opportunity Act of 1974 prohibits sex discrimination in credit transactions. Federal law prevents banks, credit unions, savings and loan associations, retail stores, and credit card companies from denying credit because of sex or marital status. However, these businesses may still deny credit for a poor or nonexistent credit rating, and some women who have always maintained accounts in their husband's name may still face credit problems if they apply in their own name.

Title IX of the Education Act Amendment of 1972 deals with sex discrimination in education. This federal law bars discrimination in admissions, housing, rules, financial aid, faculty and staff recruitment and pay, and—most troublesome of all—athletics. The latter problem has proven very difficult because men's football and basketball programs have traditionally brought in the money to finance all other sports, and men's football and basketball have received the largest share of school athletic budgets.

Employees of the Mitsubishi automobile plant in Normal, Illinois, demonstrated outside the offices of the Equal Employment Opportunity Commission in Chicago in April, 1996, in support of the company after it became the target of a sexual harassment investigation. The company provided transportation to the demonstration and paid the workers for the day.

The Earnings Gap   Despite protections under federal laws, women continue to earn substantially less than men do. Today women, on average, earn about 76 percent of what men do (see Figure 15–1 on 572). This earnings gap has been closing very slowly: In 1985 women earned an average 68 percent of men's earnings. The earnings gap is not primarily a product of **direct discrimination**; women in the same job with the same skills, qualifications, experience, and work record are not generally paid less than men. Such direct discrimination has been illegal since the Civil Rights Act of 1964. Rather, the earnings gap is primarily a product of a division in the labor market between traditionally male and female jobs, with lower salaries paid in traditionally female occupations.[41]

The Dual Labor Market and "Comparable Worth"   The existence of a "dual" labor market, with male-dominated "blue-collar" jobs distinguishable from female-dominated "pink-collar" jobs, continues to be a major obstacle to economic equality between men and women. These occupational differences result from cultural stereotyping, social conditioning, and training and education—all of which narrow the choices available to women. Although significant progress has been made in reducing occupational sex segregation (see Figure 15–2 on page 573), many observers nevertheless doubt that sexually differentiated occupations will be eliminated in the foreseeable future.

As a result of a growing recognition that the wage gap is more a result of occupational differentiation than direct discrimination, some feminist organizations have turned to a new approach—the demand that pay levels in various occupations be determined by **comparable worth** rather than by the labor market. Comparable worth goes beyond paying men and women equally for the same work and calls for paying the same wages for jobs of comparable value to the employer. Advocates of comparable worth argue that governmental agencies or the courts should evaluate

direct discrimination   Now illegal practice of differential pay for men versus women even when those individuals have equal qualifications and perform the same job.

comparable worth   Argument that pay levels for traditionally male and traditionally female jobs should be equalized by paying equally all jobs that are "worth about the same" to an employer.

FIGURE 15–1 The Earnings Gap: Median Weekly Earnings of Men and Women

The continuing "earnings gap" between men and women reflects a division in the labor market between traditionally male higher paying occupations and traditionally female lower paying positions.

Note: Figures in parentheses indicate the ratio of women's to men's median weekly earnings.

Source: *Statistical Abstract of the United States, 1999,* p. 445.

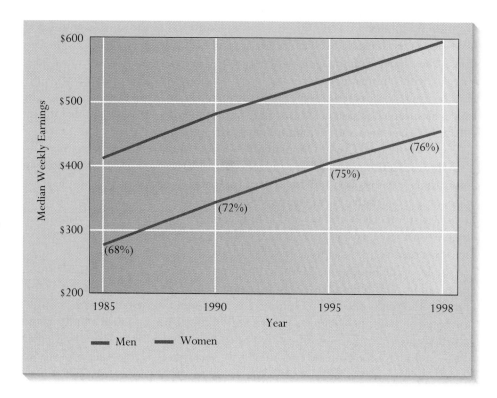

traditionally male and female jobs to determine their "worth" to the employer, perhaps by considering responsibilities, effort, knowledge, and skill requirements. Jobs adjudged to be "comparable" would be paid equal wages. Government agencies or the courts would replace the labor market in determining wage rates.

But comparable worth raises problems of implementation: Who would decide what wages should be for various jobs? What standards would be used to decide? EEOC has rejected the notion of comparable worth and declined to recommend wages for traditionally male and female jobs. And so far, the federal courts have refused to declare that differing wages in traditionally male and female occupations constitute evidence of sexual discrimination in violation of federal law. However, some state governments and private employers have undertaken to review their own pay scales to determine if traditionally female occupations are underpaid.

The "Glass Ceiling"   Few women have climbed the ladder to become president or chief executive officer or director of the nation's largest industrial corporations, banks, utilities, newspapers, or television networks.[42] Large numbers of women are entering the legal profession, but few are senior partners in the nation's largest and most prestigious law firms. Women are more likely to be found in the presidential cabinet than in the corporate boardroom.

The barriers to women's advancement to top positions are often very subtle, giving rise to the phrase **glass ceiling**. In explaining "why women aren't getting to the top," one observer argues that "At senior management levels competence is assumed. What you're looking for is someone who fits, someone who gets along, someone you trust. Now that's subtle stuff. How does a group of men feel that a woman is going to fit? I think it's very hard." Or, as a woman bank executive says, "The men just don't feel comfortable."[43]

glass ceiling   "Invisible" barriers to women rising to the highest positions in corporations and the professions.

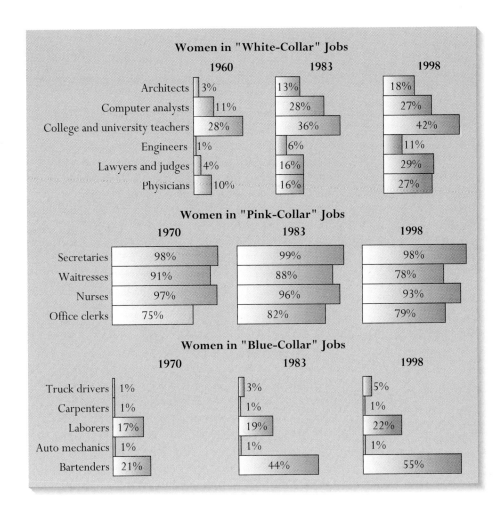

Women in "White-Collar" Jobs

	1960	1983	1998
Architects	3%	13%	18%
Computer analysts	11%	28%	27%
College and university teachers	28%	36%	42%
Engineers	1%	6%	11%
Lawyers and judges	4%	16%	29%
Physicians	10%	16%	27%

Women in "Pink-Collar" Jobs

	1970	1983	1998
Secretaries	98%	99%	98%
Waitresses	91%	88%	78%
Nurses	97%	96%	93%
Office clerks	75%	82%	79%

Women in "Blue-Collar" Jobs

	1970	1983	1998
Truck drivers	1%	3%	5%
Carpenters	1%	1%	1%
Laborers	17%	19%	22%
Auto mechanics	1%	1%	1%
Bartenders	21%	44%	55%

FIGURE 15–2 Gender Differentiation in the Labor Market

Most of the earnings gap between men and women in the U.S. labor force today is the result of the different job positions held by the two sexes. Although women are increasingly entering "white-collar" occupations long dominated by men, they continue to be disproportionately concentrated in "pink-collar" service positions. "Blue-collar" jobs have been the most resistant to change, remaining a male bastion, although women bartenders now outnumber men.

Sources: Statistical Abstract of the United States 1999, pp. 424–426.

There are many other explanations for the glass ceiling, all controversial: women choose staff assignments rather than fast-track, operating-head assignments. Women are cautious and unaggressive in corporate politics. Women have lower expectations about peak earnings and positions, and these expectations become self-fulfilling. Women bear children, and even during relatively short maternity absences they fall behind their male counterparts. Women are less likely to want to change locations than men, and immobile executives are worth less to a corporation than mobile ones. Women executives in sensitive positions come under even more pressure than men in similar posts. Women executives believe they get much more scrutiny than men and must work harder to succeed. And at all levels, increasing attention has been paid to sexual harassment (see *What Do You Think?* "What Constitutes Sexual Harassment?" on page 574). Finally, it is important to note that affirmative action efforts by governments—notably the EEOC—are directed primarily at entry-level positions rather than senior management posts.

HISPANICS IN AMERICA

Hispanics—a term the U.S. Census Bureau uses to refer to Mexican Americans, Puerto Ricans, Cubans, and others of Spanish-speaking ancestry and culture—now comprise over 11 percent of the U.S. population (see Table 15–4 on page

What Constitutes Sexual Harassment?

Various surveys report that up to one-third of female workers say they have experienced sexual harassment on the job.* But it is not always clear exactly what kind of behavior constitutes "sexual harassment."

The U.S. Supreme Court has provided some guidance in the development of sexual harassment definitions and prohibitions. Title VII of the Civil Rights Act of 1964 makes it "an unlawful employment practice to discriminate against any individual with respect to his [sic] compensation, terms, conditions or privileges of employment because of such individual's race, color, religion, sex, or national origin." In the employment context, the U.S. Supreme Court has approved the following definition of sexual harassment:

> Unwelcome sexual advances, requests for sexual favors, and other verbal or physical conduct of a sexual nature constitute sexual harassment when (1) submission to such conduct is made either explicitly or implicitly a term or condition of an individual's employment; (2) submission to or rejection of such conduct by an individual is used as the basis for employment decisions affecting such individual; or (3) such conduct has the purpose or effect of unreasonably interfering with an individual's work performance or creating an intimidating, hostile, or offensive working environment.[†]

There are no great difficulties in defining sexual harassment when jobs or promotions are conditioned on the granting of sexual favors. But several problems arise in defining a "hostile working environment." This phrase may include offensive utterances, sexual innuendoes, dirty jokes, the display of pornographic material, and unwanted proposals for dates. First, it would appear to include speech and hence raise First Amendment questions regarding how far speech may be curtailed by law in the workplace. Second, the definition depends more on the subjective feelings of the individual employee about what is "offensive" and "unwanted" than on an objective standard of behavior easily understood by all. Justice Sandra Day O'Connor wrestled with the definition of a "hostile work environment" in *Harris v. Forklift* in 1993. She held that a plaintiff need not show that the utterances caused psychological injury but that a "reasonable person," not just the plaintiff, must perceive the work environment to be hostile or abusive. Presumably a single incident would not constitute harassment; rather, courts should consider "the frequency of the discriminatory conduct," "its severity," and whether it "unreasonably interferes with an employee's work performance."[††]

What behaviors does a "reasonable person" believe to be sexual harassment? Some polls indicate that women are somewhat more likely to perceive sexual harassment in various behaviors than men (see figure). But neither women nor men are likely to perceive it to include repeated requests for a date, the telling of dirty jokes, or comments on attractiveness—even though these behaviors often inspire formal complaints.

Many university policies go well beyond both Supreme Court rulings and opinion polls in defining what constitutes sexual harassment, including the following:

576). The largest Hispanic subgroup is Mexican Americans. Some are descendants of citizens who lived in the Mexican territory annexed to the United States in 1848, but most have come to the United States in accelerating numbers in recent years. The largest Mexican American populations are found in Texas, Arizona, New Mexico, and California. Puerto Ricans constitute the second largest Hispanic subgroup. Many still retain ties to the commonwealth and move back and forth from Puerto Rico to New York. Cubans make up the third largest subgroup; most have fled from Fidel Castro's Cuba and live mainly in the Miami metropolitan area. Each of these Hispanic groups has encountered a different experience in American life. Indeed, some evidence indicates that these groups identify themselves separately, rather than as Hispanics.[44]

- "remarks about a person's clothing"
- "suggestive or insulting sounds"
- "leering at or ogling of a person's body"
- "nonsexual slurs about one's gender"
- "remarks that degrade another person or group on the basis of gender."

The National Association of Scholars worries that overly broad and vague definitions of sexual harassment can undermine academic freedom and inhibit classroom discussions of important yet sensitive topics including human sexuality, gender differences, sexual roles, and gender politics. Teaching and research on such topics, in their view, must not be constrained by the threat that the views expressed will be labeled "insensitive," "uncomfortable," or "incorrect"; faculty must feel free to provide their best academic and professional advice to students, collectively and individually, without fear that their comments will be officially labeled as "offensive" or "unwelcome"; and students must feel free to express themselves on matters of gender, whether or not their ideas are biased, immature, or crudely expressed.

*Washington Post National Weekly Edition, March 7, 1993.
†*Meritor Savings Bank v. Vinson*, 477 U.S. 57 (1986).
††*Harris v. Forklift Systems*, 126 L. Ed. 2d 295 (1993).

Question: *Here is a list of some different situations. We're interested in knowing whether you think they are forms of sexual harassment—not just inappropriate or in bad taste, but sexual harassment.*

Definitely is sexual harassment...

If a male boss makes it clear to a female employee that she must go to bed with him for a promotion
91%
92%

If a male boss asks very direct questions of a female employee about her personal sexual practices and preferences
59%
68%

If a female boss asks very direct questions of a male employee about his personal sexual practices and preferences
47%
57%

If a man once in a while asks a female employee of his to go out on dates, even though she has said no in the past
15%
21%

If a man once in a while tells dirty jokes in the presence of female employees
15%
16%

If a male boss tells a female employee that she looks very attractive today
3%
5%

☐ Men   ☐ Women

Source: Roper Organization as reported in American Enterprise, September/October, 1993, p. 93.

If all Hispanics are grouped together for statistical comparisons, their median family income level is well below that of whites (see Table 15–2). Hispanic poverty and unemployment rates are also higher than those of whites. The percentage of Hispanics completing high school and college education is well below that of both whites and blacks, suggesting language or other cultural obstacles in education. Yet within these overall racial comparisons, there are wide disparities among subgroups as well as among individuals.

Mexican Americans   The Mexican American population in the southwestern United States is growing very rapidly; it doubled in size between 1980 and 1990. For many years, agricultural business encouraged immigration of Mexican farm

Table 15-4	Minorities in America—2000	
	Number	**Percentage of Population**
African Americans	33,267,000	12.2
Hispanic Americans	30,393,000	11.4
Asian or Pacific Islander Americans	10,030,000	3.9
Native Americans, Eskimos, Aleuts	2,041,000	0.7
Total Population	271,237,000	100.0

Source: Statistical Abstract of the United States, 1999, p. 19.

laborers willing to endure harsh conditions for low pay. Many others came to the United States as *indocumentados*—undocumented, or illegal, aliens. In the Immigration Reform Act of 1986 Congress offered amnesty to all undocumented workers who had entered the United States prior to 1982.

Economic conditions in Mexico and elsewhere in Central America continue to fuel immigration, legal and illegal, to the United States. But with lower educational levels, average incomes of Mexican American families in the United States are lower and the poverty rate is higher than the general population. Although Mexican Americans have served as governors of Arizona and New Mexico and have won election to the U.S. Congress, their political power does not yet match their population percentages. Mexican American voter turnout is lower than other ethnic groups, perhaps because many are resident aliens or illegal immigrants not eligible to vote, or perhaps because of cultural factors that discourage political participation.[45]

Puerto Ricans   Residents of Puerto Rico are American citizens because Puerto Rico is a commonwealth of the United States. Puerto Rico's commonwealth government resembles that of a state, with a constitution and elected governor and legislature, but the island has no voting members of the U.S. Congress and no electoral votes for president. As citizens, Puerto Ricans can move anywhere in the United States; many have immigrated to New York City.

Median family income in Puerto Rico is higher than anywhere else in the Caribbean but only half that of the poorest state in the United States. Puerto Ricans have not fared as well economically as other Hispanic groups within the United States: Puerto Ricans have lower median family incomes and higher poverty percentages, in part perhaps because of lower work force participation. One explanation centers on the history of access to federal welfare programs on the island and the resulting social dependency it fostered among some Puerto Rican families.[46]

Puerto Ricans have long debated whether to remain a commonwealth of the United States, apply for statehood, or seek complete independence from the United States. As citizens of a commonwealth, Puerto Ricans pay no U.S. income tax (although their local taxes are substantial) while receiving all the benefits that U.S. citizens are entitled to—Social Security, welfare assistance, food stamps, Medicaid, Medicare, and so forth. If Puerto Rico chose to become a state, its voters could participate in presidential and congressional elections, but its taxpayers would not enjoy the same favorable cost-benefit ratio they enjoy under commonwealth status. Some Puerto Ricans also fear that statehood would dilute the island's cultural identity and force English on them as the national language.

As a state, Puerto Rico would have two U.S. senators and perhaps six U.S. representatives. The island's majority party, the Popular Democratic Party, is closely identified with the Democratic Party, so most of these new members would likely be Democrats. But the island's New Progressive Party, identified with the Republican Party, supports statehood, and many GOP leaders believe their party should appeal to Hispanic voters. If Puerto Ricans were to choose independence, a new constitution for the Republic of Puerto Rico would be drawn up by the islanders themselves.

Only Congress can admit a new state, but Congress is unlikely to act without the full support of Puerto Ricans themselves. Several non-binding referenda votes have been held in Puerto Rico over the years, the most recent in 1998. Opinion today appears to be closely divided, with commonwealth status edging out statehood by a small margin; independence has never received more than one percent of the vote.

Cuban Americans   Many Cuban Americans, especially those in the early waves of refugees from Castro's revolution in 1959, were skilled professionals and businesspeople, and they rapidly set about building Miami into a thriving economy. Although Cuban Americans are the smallest of the Hispanic subgroups, today they are better educated and enjoy higher incomes than the others. They are well organized politically, and they have succeeded in electing Cuban Americans to local office in Florida and to the U.S. Congress.

HISPANIC POLITICS

Mexican Americans constitute the largest portion, nearly three-quarters, of the nation's Hispanic population. Most reside in the Southwestern United States—California, Texas, Arizona, New Mexico, and Colorado. Puerto Ricans in New York, and Cubans and other Central and South Americans in Florida, constitute only about one-quarter of the Hispanic population. Thus, generalizations about Hispanic politics are heavily influenced by Mexican Americans.

Organizing for Political Activity   For many decades American agriculture encouraged Mexican American immigration, both legal and illegal, to labor in fields as *braceros*. Most of these migrant farm workers lived and worked under very difficult conditions; they were paid less than minimum wages for backbreaking labor. Farm workers were not covered by the federal National Labor Relations Act and therefore not protected in the right to organize labor unions. But civil rights activity among Hispanics, especially among farmworkers, grew during the 1960s under the leadership of Ceasar Chavez and his United Farm Workers union. Chavez organized a national boycott of grapes from California vineyards that refused to recognize the union or improve conditions. *LaRaza*, as the movement was called, finally ended in a union contract with the growers and later a California law protecting the right of farm workers to organize unions and bargain collectively with their employers. More importantly, the movement galvanized Mexican-Americans throughout the Southwest to engage in political activity.[47]

However, inasmuch as many Mexican American immigrants were noncitizens, and many were *indocumentados* (undocumented residents of the United States), the voting strength of Mexican Americans never matched their numbers in the population. The Immigration Reform and Control Act of 1986 granted amnesty to illegal aliens living in the United States in 1982. But the same Act also imposed penalties on employers who hired illegal aliens. The effect of these threatened penalties on many employers was to make them wary of hiring Hispanics, especially as permanent employees. At the same time, industries in need of cheap labor—agriculture, health and hospitals, restaurants, clothing manufacturers, etc.—continued to encourage legal and illegal immigration to fill minimum and even subminimum wage level jobs with few if any benefits.

Hispanic Political Power   Most Hispanics today believe that they confront less prejudice and discrimination than their parents (see Table 15–5). Nonetheless, in 1994 California voters approved a referendum, Proposition 187, that would have barred welfare and other benefits to persons living in the state illegally. Most Hispanics opposed the measure believing that it was motivated by prejudice. A federal court later declared major portions of Proposition 187 unconstitutional. And the U.S. Supreme Court has held that a state may not bar the children of illegal immigrants from attending public schools.[48]

Mexican American voter turnout remains weak. It is estimated in Texas, for example, that Hispanics surnames constitute about 25 percent of the state's voting age population. However, only about 15 percent of the state's registered voters are Hispanic, and the actual voter turnout of Hispanics is estimated at only 12 percent of the Texas electorate.[49]

Various explanations have been advanced for the lower voter participation of Mexican-Americans. Language barriers may still discourage some voters, even though ballots in many states are now available in Spanish language. Illegal immigrants, of course, cannot vote. Lower education and income levels are also associated with lower voter turnout. Nonetheless, Hispanic voting is on the increase throughout the nation and both Democratic and Republican candidates are increasingly aware of the importance of the Hispanic vote.

Overall, most Hispanics identify with the Democratic Party (see Table 15–5). Mexican Americans in the Southwestern states and Puerto Ricans in New York have traditionally supported Democratic candidates, while the strong anticommunist heritage among Cuban Americans has fostered a Republican voting tradition in Florida.

The Voting Rights Act of 1965, as later amended and as interpreted by the U.S. Supreme Court, extends voting rights protections to "language minorities," including Hispanics (see "Congressional Apportionment and Redistricting" in Chapter 10). Following redistricting after the 1990 census, Hispanic representation in Congress rose substantially; today there are nineteen Hispanic members of the House of Representatives—about 4 percent, still well below the 11 percent of the U.S. population which is Hispanic. Hispanics had been elected governors of Arizona, New Mexico, and Florida; and two big-city mayors, Federico Peña of Denver and Henry Cisneros of San Antonio, were elevated to cabinet positions in the Clinton administration.

NATIVE AMERICANS: TRAILS OF TEARS

Christopher Columbus, having erred in his estimate of the circumference of the globe, believed he had arrived in the Indian Ocean when he first came to the Caribbean. He mistook the Arawaks there for people of the East Indies, calling

Table 15-5 Hispanic Political Views, Young and Old

	All %	18–34 %	35 & Older %
"Which term do you prefer most for people who are of Spanish or Latin American descent: Hispanic or Latino?"			
Hispanic	55	57	53
Latino	22	24	20
No difference	21	18	24
Don't know	2	1	3
"Do you think the younger generation of Hispanic or Latino Americans faces more, less, or the same amount of prejudice and discrimination as their parents did when they were the same age?"			
More	23	23	23
Less	49	55	44
About the same	21	18	23
Don't know	7	4	10
Asked of registered voters: *"In politics today, do you consider yourself a Republican, Democrat or independent?"*			
Democrat	55	46	60
Independent	24	37	18
Republican	19	15	20
Other	2	2	2

Source: Princeton Survey Research for *Newsweek*, as reported in *The Polling Report*, July 5, 1999 (survey of Hispanic adults nationwide).

them *Indios*, and this Spanish word passed into English as "Indians"—a word that came to refer to all Native American peoples. But at the time of the first European contacts, these peoples had no common ethnic identity; hundreds of separate cultures and languages were thriving in the Americas. Although estimates vary, most historians believe 7 to 12 million people lived in the land that is now the United States and Canada; 25 million more lived in Mexico; and as many as 60 to 70 million in all lived in the Western Hemisphere, a number comparable to Europe's population at the time.

In the centuries that followed, the Native American population of the Western Hemisphere was devastated by warfare, by famine, and, most of all, by epidemic diseases brought from Europe. Overall, the Native population fell by 90 percent, the greatest known human disaster in world history. In the Europeans' conquest of the Americas, smallpox wreaked the greatest havoc, followed by measles, bubonic plague, influenza, typhus, diphtheria, and scarlet fever. Superior military technology, together with skill in exploiting hostilities between Native nations, gradually overcame the resistance of Native peoples. By 1910 only 210,000 Native Americans lived in the United States. Their population has slowly recovered to the current 2.2 million (less than 1 percent of the U.S. population). Many live on reservations and trust lands, the largest of which is the Navajo and Hopi enclave in the southwestern United States (see *Across the USA:* "Native American Peoples" on page 580).

The Trail of Broken Treaties In the Northwest Ordinance of 1787, Congress, in organizing the western territories of the new nation, declared, "The utmost good faith shall always be observed toward the Indians. Their lands and property

Native American Peoples

This map shows the locations of the principal Native American reservations in the United States. Tribal governments officially govern these reservations. (Alaska Natives, including Aleuts and Eskimos, live mostly in 200 villages widely scattered across rural Alaska; twelve regional Native American corporations administer property and mineral rights on behalf of Native peoples in that state.)

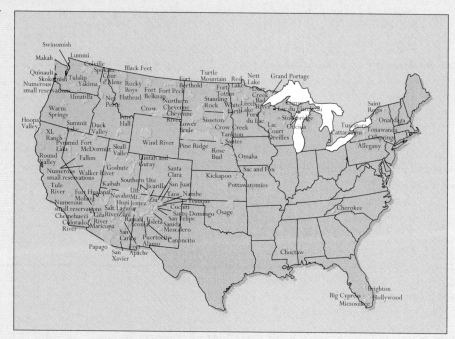

shall never be taken from them without their consent." And later, in the Intercourse Act of 1790, Congress declared that public treaties between the United States government and the independent Native nations would be the only legal means of obtaining "Indian" land.

As president, George Washington forged a treaty with the Creeks: in exchange for land concessions, the United States pledged to protect the boundaries of the Creek nation and to allow the Creeks themselves to punish all violators of their laws within these boundaries. This semblance of legality was reflected in hundreds of treaties that followed. (Indeed, in recent years some Native American nations have successfully sued in federal court for reparations and return of lands obtained in violation of the Intercourse Act of 1790 and subsequent treaties.) Yet Native lands were constantly invaded by whites. The resulting Native resistance typically led to wars that ultimately resulted in great loss of life among warriors and their families and the further loss of Native land. The cycle of invasion, resistance, military defeat, and further land concessions continued for a hundred years.

"Indian Territories" Following the purchase of the vast Louisiana Territory in 1803, President Thomas Jefferson sought to "civilize" the Natives by promoting farming in "reservations" that were located west of the Mississippi River. But soon, peoples who had been forced to move from Ohio to Missouri were forced to move again to survive the relentless white expansion. President James Monroe designated as "Indian territory" most of the Great Plains west of the Missouri River. Native peoples increasingly faced three unattractive choices: assimilation, removal, or extinction.

In 1814 the Creeks, encouraged by the British during the War of 1812 to attack American settlements, faced an army of Tennessee volunteer militia led by Andrew Jackson. At the Battle of Horseshoe Bend, Jackson's cannon fire decimated the Creek warriors. In the uneven Treaty of Fort Jackson, the Creeks, Choctaws, and Cherokees were forced to concede millions of acres of land.

By 1830 the "Five Civilized Tribes" of the southeastern United States (Cherokees, Chickasaws, Choctaws, Creeks, and Seminoles) had ceded most but not all of their lands. When gold was discovered on Cherokee land in northern Georgia in 1829, whites invaded their territory. Congress, at the heeding of the old "Indian fighter" President Andrew Jackson, passed the Removal Act, ordering the forcible relocation of the Natives to Oklahoma Indian Territory. The Cherokees tried to use the whites' law to defend their land, bringing their case to the U.S. Supreme Court. When Chief Justice John Marshall held the Cherokees were a "domestic dependent nation" that could not be forced to give up its land, President Jackson replied scornfully, "John Marshall has made his decision. Now let him enforce it." He sent a 7,000-strong army to pursue Seminoles into the huge Florida Everglades swamp and forced 16,000 Cherokees and other peoples on the infamous "Trail of Tears" march to Oklahoma in 1838.

Encroachment on the Indian Territory of the Great Plains was not long in coming. First, the territory was crossed by the Santa Fe and Oregon Trails, and a series of military forts were built to protect travelers. In 1854, under pressure from railroad interests, the U.S. government abolished much of the Indian Territory to create the Kansas and Nebraska territories, which were immediately opened to white settlers. The Native peoples in these lands—including Potawatomis, Kickapoos, Delawares, Shawnees, Miamis, Omahas, and Missouris—were forced to sign treaties accepting vastly reduced land reservations. But large, warlike buffalo-hunting nations remained in the northern Dakotas and western Great Plains: the Sioux, Cheyennes, Arapahoes, Comanches, and Kiowas. (Other smaller peoples inhabited the Rockies to California and the Pacific Northwest; the sedentary Pueblos, Hopis, and Pimas and the migrating Apaches and Navajos occupied the Southwest.) The Plains peoples took pride in their warrior status, often fighting among themselves.

"Indian Wars"   The "Indian Wars" were fought between the Plains nations and the U.S. Army between 1864 and 1890. Following the Civil War, the federal government began to assign boundaries to each nation and authorized the Bureau of Indian Affairs (BIA) to "assist and protect" Native peoples on their "reservations." But the reservations were repeatedly reduced in size until subsistence by hunting became impossible. Malnutrition and demoralization of the Native peoples were accelerated by the mass slaughter of the buffalo; vast herds, numbering perhaps as many as 70 million, were exterminated over the years. The most storied engagement of the long war occurred at the Little Bighorn River in Montana on June 25, 1876, where Civil War hero General George Armstrong Custer led elements of the U.S. Seventh Cavalry to destruction at the hands of Sioux and Cheyenne warriors led by Chief Crazy Horse, Sitting Bull, and Gall. But "Custer's last stand" inspired renewed army campaigns against the Plains peoples; the following year, Crazy Horse was forced to surrender. In 1881 destitute Sioux under Chief Sitting Bull returned from exile in Canada to surrender themselves to reservation life. Among the last peoples to hold

out were the Apaches, whose famous warrior Geronimo finally surrendered in 1886. Sporadic fighting continued until 1890, when a small malnourished band of Lakota Sioux were wiped out at Wounded Knee Creek.

The Attempted Destruction of Traditional Life   The Dawes Act of 1887 governed federal Native American policy for decades. The thrust of the policy was to break up Native lands, allotting acreage for individual homesteads in order to assimilate Natives into the white agricultural society. Farming was to replace hunting, and traditional Native customs were to be shed for English language and schooling. But this effort to destroy culture never really succeeded. Although Native peoples lost more than half of their 1877 reservation land, few lost their communal ties or accumulated much private property. Life on the reservations was often desperate. Natives suffered the worst poverty of any group in the United States, with high rates of infant mortality, alcoholism, and other diseases. The BIA, notoriously corrupt and mismanaged, encouraged dependency and regularly interfered with religious affairs and customs.

The New Deal   The New Deal under President Franklin D. Roosevelt came to Native Americans in the form of the Indian Reorganization Act of 1934. This act sought to restore Native tribal structures by recognizing these nations as instruments of the federal government. Land ownership was restored, and elected Native tribal councils were recognized as legal governments. Efforts to force assimilation were largely abandoned. The BIA became more sensitive to Native culture and began employing Native Americans in larger numbers.

Yet the BIA remained "paternalistic," frequently interfering in tribal "sovereignty." Moreover, in the 1950s Congress initiated a policy of "termination" of sovereignty rights for specific nations that consented to relinquish their lands in exchange for cash payments. Although only a few nations chose this course, the results were often calamitous: after the one-time cash payments were spent, Native peoples became dependent on state social welfare services and often slipped further into poverty and alcoholism.

The American Indian Movement   The civil rights movement of the 1960s inspired a new activism among Native American groups. The American Indian Movement (AIM) was founded in 1968 and attracted national headlines by occupying Alcatraz Island in San Francisco Bay. Violence flared in 1972 when AIM activists took over the site of the Wounded Knee battle and fought with FBI agents. Several Native nations succeeded in federal courts and Congress to win back lands and/or compensation for lands taken from them in treaty violations. Native culture was revitalized, and Vine Deloria's *Custer Died for Your Sins* (1969) and Dee Brown's *Bury My Heart at Wounded Knee* (1971) became national best-selling books.

Native Americans Today   The U.S. Constitution (Article I, Section 8) grants Congress the full power "to regulate Commerce . . . with the Indian Tribes." States are prevented from regulating or taxing Native peoples or extending their courts' jurisdiction over them unless authorized by Congress. The Supreme Court recognizes Native Americans "as members of quasi-sovereign tribal entities"[50] with powers to regulate their own internal affairs, establish their own courts, and enforce their own laws, all subject to congressional supervision. Thus, for example, many Native peoples chose to legalize gambling, including casino gambling, on reservations in states that otherwise prohibited the activity. As citizens, Native Americans have the right to vote

The Foxwoods Casino, on the Pequot Indian Reservation in Connecticut, has brought the tribe a new-found prosperity.

in state as well as national elections. Those living off of reservations have the same rights and responsibilities as other citizens. Ben Nighthorse Campbell, U.S. senator from Colorado, is the only tribal member (Northern Cheyenne) currently serving in Congress (see *People in Politics:* "Minority Faces in Congress" in Chapter 10).

The Bureau of Indian Affairs in the Department of the Interior continues to supervise reservation life, and Native Americans enrolled as members of nations and living on reservations are entitled to certain benefits established by law and treaty. Nevertheless, these peoples remain the poorest and least healthy in the United States, with high incidences of infant mortality, suicide, and alcoholism. Approximately half of all Native Americans live below the poverty line.

THE RIGHTS OF DISABLED AMERICANS

Disabled Americans were *not* among the classes of people protected by the landmark Civil Rights Act of 1964. Throughout most of the nation's history, little thought was given to making public or private buildings or facilities accessible to blind, deaf, or mobility-impaired people.[51] Not until the Education of Handicapped Children Act of 1975 did the federal government mandate that the nation's public schools provide free education to handicapped children.

The Americans with Disabilities Act (ADA) of 1990 is a sweeping law that prohibits discrimination against disabled people in private employment, government programs, public accommodations, and telecommunications. The act is vaguely worded in many of its provisions, requiring "reasonable accommodations" for disabled people that do not involve "undue hardship." This means disabled Americans do not have exactly the same standard of protection as minorities or women, who are protected from discrimination *regardless* of hardship or costs. (It also means that attorneys, consultants, and bureaucrats will make handsome incomes over the years interpreting the meaning of these phrases.) Specifically the ADA includes the following protections:

- *Employment:* Disabled people cannot be denied employment or promotion if, with "reasonable accommodation," they can perform the duties of the job. Reasonable accommodation need not be made if doing so would cause "undue hardship" on the employer.

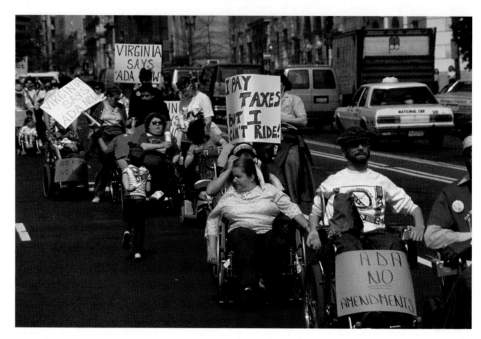

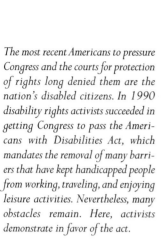

The most recent Americans to pressure Congress and the courts for protection of rights long denied them are the nation's disabled citizens. In 1990 disability rights activists succeeded in getting Congress to pass the Americans with Disabilities Act, which mandates the removal of many barriers that have kept handicapped people from working, traveling, and enjoying leisure activities. Nevertheless, many obstacles remain. Here, activists demonstrate in favor of the act.

- *Government programs:* Disabled people cannot be denied access to government programs or benefits. New buses, taxis, and trains must be accessible to disabled persons, including those in wheelchairs.

- *Public accommodations:* Disabled people must enjoy "full and equal" access to hotels, restaurants, stores, schools, parks, museums, auditoriums, and the like. To achieve equal access, owners of existing facilities must alter them "to the maximum extent feasible"; builders of new facilities must ensure that they are readily accessible to disabled persons unless doing so is structurally impossible.

- *Communications:* The Federal Communications Commission is directed to issue regulations that will ensure telecommunications devices for hearing- and speech-impaired people are available "to the extent possible and in the most efficient manner."

ADA has meant that many disabled persons have been able to have fuller, more productive lives. But ADA, as interpreted by the Equal Employment Opportunity Commission and federal courts, has begun to generate considerable controversy. Persons who are "learning disabled" have successfully sued colleges and universities, and even state bar associations, not only for admission but also to gain extra time and assistance in passing examinations. Persons claiming various mental disorders have successfully sued employers for being dismissed for chronic tardiness, inability to concentrate on the job, uncooperative and hostile attitudes toward supervisors, etc.[52]

INEQUALITY AND THE CONSTITUTION

Americans frequently claim "rights" that have no basis in the U.S. Constitution—for example, the "right" to an education, to medical care, to decent housing, to retirement benefits, to a job. The U.S. Constitution *limits* government; it protects individuals *from* government oppression. The U.S. Constitution does not mandate that governments act wisely or compassionately.

Constitutional versus Legal Rights   There is no requirement in the U.S. Constitution that governments establish education, welfare, or social security programs or provide housing, job training, or unemployment compensation. Whatever benefits individuals derive from these government programs, they do so as a matter of law, not as a constitutional right.

> The importance of a service performed by the State does not determine whether it must be regarded as fundamental for purposes of examination under the equal protection clause. . . . Education, of course, is not among the rights afforded explicit protection under our federal Constitution. Nor do we find any basis for saying it is implicitly so protected.[53]

"Reasonable" Classifications   Governments by law may classify people according to income, age, illness, disability, or any other "reasonable" standard in administering its programs. However, the Supreme Court has interpreted the Equal Protection Clause to mean only that governments may not practice "invidious" discrimination—that is, establish discriminatory classifications in the law which are "arbitrary and unreasonable" and have "no rational basis."[54] *Reasonable* classifications of individuals by law—those that serve a legitimate government purpose—are *not* unconstitutional. Yet the Equal Protection Clause obligates governments to treat equally all persons who are "similarly situated"—to treat every person who falls into a particular class in the same fashion as every other person in that class. Thus all persons who meet the eligibility requirements stated in the law must receive the same benefits. For example, if Congress establishes a public health care program for people sixty-five years of age and over (Medicare), then everyone in that age classification is entitled to the benefits of the program. Because the benefits of these programs are *legal* entitlements, not *constitutional* rights, however, Congress may choose to change the benefits or eligibility requirements at any time.

Protections for Poor Americans   The Constitution ensures that poor people are protected in their legal and political rights. Included among the specific protections given indigent persons are these:

- *Free legal counsel in criminal cases:* "From the very beginning, our state and national constitutions have laid great emphasis on procedures and substantial safeguards designed to assure fair trials before impartial tribunals in which every defendant stands equal before the law. This noble ideal cannot be realized if the poor man charged with a crime has to face his accusers without the lawyer to assist him."[55]

- *No tax or financial requirement for voting:* "A state violates the equal protection clause of the Fourteenth Amendment whenever it makes the affluence of the voter or payment of any fee an electoral standard."[56] This decision extended the Twenty-fourth Amendment's ban on poll taxes for national elections to state elections as well.

But the poor cannot demand government funding as a matter of constitutional right in order to exercise other recognized rights. For example, freedom of the press does not mean that the government must buy a printing press for anyone unable to afford one. Congress, in the controversial Hyde Amendment in 1977,

Twenty-First Century Directions

The civil rights movement has lost much of the moral support that energized Americans, both black and white, in the 1960s. Many whites believe that the removal of formal obstacles to equal opportunity—especially *Brown v. Board of Education* in 1954 and the Civil Rights Acts of 1964 in 1968—would lead to a color-blind society. But enduring inequalities in life chances between whites and minorities continue to inspire racial politics in America. Demands for equality of results, especially through preferential treatment in affirmative action programs, does not generate the same positive responses among whites as did earlier demands for equal opportunity.

↑ *Minority Political Participation* African American political participation, especially in Democratic Party politics, has already reached levels approximating the African American percentage of the U.S. population. And increasing numbers of black candidates are being elected to office in predominantly white constituencies. As Hispanic numbers rise, and younger Hispanics acculturated to American politics enter the political arena, larger numbers of Hispanics will win public office. Voter participation among Hispanics will rise. Within a few years, Hispanics will be America's largest and perhaps most influential minority.

↓ *Racial Preferences* While the U.S. Supreme Court is not likely to adopt a color-blind interpretation of the Constitution's Equal Protection Clause, the Court's "strict scrutiny" of racial preferences in state and federal laws and practices will gradually alter the thrust of affirmative action programs throughout the nation. And referenda barring racial preferences will succeed in more and more states. Educational institutions and employers will be obliged to turn to more open enrollment policies, more assistance to economically disadvantaged, more employment training and outreach in recruitment, to preserve equal opportunity for all Americans.

←→ *Continuing Racial and Gender Conflict* America is a litigious society. We have many more lawyers than physicians offering their services to us. The accumulation of civil rights laws with vaguely defined phrases—"hostile work environment," "sexual harassment," "reasonable accommodation for the disabled"—guarantees continuing court conflicts in virtually all areas of civil rights policy. Racial and gender conflict have driven American politics since the founding of the nation and will continue to do so throughout the 21st Century.

denied the use of Medicaid funds for poor women seeking abortions, and the Supreme Court rejected arguments that federal funding of abortions was required by the Constitution. Even though the Court reaffirmed that abortion was a constitutional right, "it simply does not follow that a woman's freedom of choice carries with it a constitutional entitlement to the financial means to avail herself of the protected choices. . . . Although the government may not place obstacles in the path of a woman's exercise of her freedom of choice, it need not remove those not of its own creation."[57]

Income Inequality Governments in the United States are not under any constitutional requirement to eliminate inequality of income or wealth. (The Founders believed that "dangerous leveling" was a violation of the right to property and to use and dispose of the fruits of one's own labors.) For example, representatives of poor, black, and Hispanic groups have charged that differences in public school spending per pupil among school districts in a state discriminate unconstitutionally against poor children. Although the state governments do not discriminate against the poor in their funding (on the contrary, most states have equalization programs written into state law giving more aid to schools serving poor students), it is argued that spending differences among local school districts violates the Equal Protection Clause of the Fourteenth Amendment. But the Supreme Court has ruled that disparities in school funding created by dependence on local property tax revenue and inequalities among districts in the value of property and amount of revenue raised does not violate the Equal Protection Clause. "We cannot say that such disparities are the product of a system that is so irrational as to be invidiously discriminatory."[58] Some *state* courts, however, have ruled that these same disparities violate *state* constitutional guarantees of equal protection.[59]

SUMMARY NOTES

- Equality has long been the central issue of American politics. Today, most Americans agree that all individuals should have an equal opportunity to make of their lives whatever they can without artificial barriers of race, class, gender, or ethnicity. Political conflict arises over what, if anything, government should do to achieve greater equality of results—the reduction of gaps between rich and poor, men and women, blacks and whites, and other groups in society.

- The original Constitution of 1787 recognized and protected slavery. Not until after the Civil War did the Thirteenth Amendment (1865) abolish slavery. But the Fourteenth Amendment's guarantee of "equal protection of the laws" and the Fifteenth Amendment's guarantee of voting rights were largely ignored in southern states after the federal government's Reconstruction efforts ended. Segregation was held constitutional by the U.S. Supreme Court in its "separate but equal" decision in *Plessy v. Ferguson* in 1896.

- The NAACP led the long legal battle in the federal courts to have segregation declared unconstitutional as a violation of the Equal Protection Clause of the Fourteenth Amendment. Under the leadership of Thurgood Marshall, a major victory was achieved in the case of *Brown v. Board of Education of Topeka* in 1954.

- The struggle over school desegregation continues even today. Federal courts are more likely to issue desegregation orders (including orders to bus pupils to achieve racial balance in schools) in school districts where present or past actions by government officials contributed to racial imbalances. Courts are less likely to order desegregation where racial imbalances are a product of residential patterns.

- The courts could eliminate *governmental* discrimination by enforcing the Fourteenth Amendment of the Constitution; but only Congress could end private discrimination through legislation. Martin Luther King, Jr.'s campaign of nonviolent direct action helped bring remaining racial injustices to the attention of Congress. Key legislation includes the Civil Rights Act of 1964, which bans discrimination in public accommodations, government-funded programs, and private employment; the Voting Rights Act of 1965, which authorizes strong federal action to protect voting rights; and the Civil Rights Act of 1968, which outlaws discrimination in housing.

- Today, racial politics center around continuing inequalities between blacks and whites in the areas of income, jobs, housing, health, education, and other conditions of life. Should the government concentrate on "equality of opportunity" and apply "color-blind" standards to both blacks and whites? Or should government take "affirmative action" to assist blacks and other minorities to overcome the results of past unequal treatment?

- Generally the Supreme Court is likely to approve of affirmative action programs when these programs have been adopted in response to a past proven history of discrimination, when they are narrowly tailored so as not to adversely affect the rights of individuals, when they do not absolutely bar whites from participating, and when they serve clearly identified, compelling, and legitimate government objectives.

- Congress is aware that public opinion generally supports affirmative action in the abstract but that white opinion rejects the specific notions of racial preferences and quotas. Recent battles in Congress have focused on whether statistical imbalances are evidence of discrimination and whether employers should bear the burden of proof that test requirements or practices with a disparate impact on minorities are related to job performance.

- The Equal Protection Clause of the Fourteenth Amendment applies to "any person," but traditionally the Supreme Court has recognized gender differences in laws. Nevertheless, in recent years the Court has struck down gender differences where they are unreasonable or arbitrary and unrelated to legitimate government objectives.

- Gender discrimination in employment has been illegal since the passage of the Civil Rights Act of 1964. Nevertheless, differences in average earnings of men and women persist, although these differences have narrowed somewhat over time. The earnings gap appears to be mainly a product of lower pay in occupations traditionally dominated by women and higher pay in traditionally male occupations. Although neither Congress nor the courts have mandated wages based on comparable worth of traditional men's and women's jobs in private employment, many governmental agencies and some private employers have undertaken to review wage rates to eliminate gender differences.

- Economic conditions in Mexico and other Spanish-speaking nations of the Western Hemisphere continue to fuel large-scale immigration, both legal and illegal, into the United States. But the political power of Mexican Americans, the nation's largest Hispanic group, does not yet match their population percentage. Their voter turnout remains lower than that of other ethnic groups in the United States.

- Since the arrival of the first Europeans on this continent, Native American peoples have experienced cycles of invasion, resistance, military defeat, and land concessions. Today Native American peoples collectively remain the poorest and least healthy of the nation's ethnic groups.

- The most recent major civil rights legislation is the Americans with Disabilities Act of 1990, which prohibits discrimination against disabled persons in private employment, government programs, public accommodations, and communications.

- The Equal Protection Clause does not bar government from treating persons in various income classes differently. However, governments must treat every individual in a class equally, and the classifications must not be "arbitrary" or "unreasonable." The poor cannot demand benefits or services as a matter of constitutional rights; but once government establishes a social welfare program by law, it must provide equal access to all persons "similarly situated."

KEY TERMS

redistribution   546
abolition movement   546
Jim Crow   548

separate but equal   549
de facto segregation   554
nonviolent direct action   554

affirmative action   560
quota   560
set-aside program   562

direct discrimination   571
comparable worth   571
glass ceiling   572

SELECTED READINGS

BARKER, LUCIUS J., and MACK H. JONES. *African Americans and the American Political System*, 4th ed. Upper Saddle River, N.J.: Prentice Hall, 1999. Comprehensive analysis of African American politics, examining access to the judicial arena, the interest-group process, political parties, Congress, and the White House.

BOWEN, WILLIAM G., and DEREK CURTIS BOK. *The Shape of the River*. Princeton, NJ.: Princeton University Press, 1999. An argument by two university presidents that preferential treatment of minorities in admissions to prestigious universities has led to the subsequent success in life by the beneficiaries of the preferences.

CONWAY, M. MARGARET, GERTRUDE A., STEURNAGEL, and DAVID W. AHERN. *Women and Political Participation*. Washington, D.C.: CQ Press, 1997. A wide-ranging review of changes in American political culture brought about by women's increasing political clout. Continuing gender differences in representation are explored.

FOX-GENOVESE, ELIZABETH. *Feminism Is Not the Story of My Life*. New York: Doubleday, 1995. Critique of radical feminism for failing to understand the central importance of marriage and motherhood in women's lives, and a discussion of how public policy could ease the clashing demands of work and family on women.

HACKER, ANDREW. *Two Nations*. New York: Charles Scribner's Sons, 1992. Argues that race is the principal political division in American society and racial separation, hostilities, and inequalities are at dangerous levels.

HERO, RODNEY E. *Latinos and the U.S. Political System*. Philadelphia: Temple University Press, 1992. General history of political participation of major Latino groups, arguing that different cultural behaviors limit their ability to participate in the interest-group system and policy-making process as currently structured.

KLUEGEL, JAMES R., and ELIOT R. SMITH. *Beliefs about Inequality*. New York: Aldine de Gruyter, 1986. Comprehensive description of Americans' beliefs and attitudes about inequality, based on extensive survey data, including evidence of changes in beliefs over time as well as inconsistencies and contradictions.

McGLEN, NANCY E., and KAREN O'CONNER. *Women, Politics, and American Society*. Upper Saddle River, N.J.: Prentice Hall, 1996. Comprehensive text contrasting women's rights and realities in politics, employment, education, reproduction, and family.

SIGELMAN, LEE, and SUSAN WELCH. *Black Americans' Views of Racial Inequality*. Cambridge, Mass.: Cambridge University Press, 1991. Analysis of survey research showing that black perceptions of racial inequality in America are considerably different from white perceptions. Although remaining optimistic about the future, blacks see discrimination as commonplace and are much more likely than whites to attribute black-white differences in education, occupation, and income to racism.

THERNSTROM, STEPHEN, and ABIGAIL THERNSTROM. *America in Black and White*. New York: Simon & Schuster, 1997. Information-rich analysis tracing social and economic progress of African Americans and arguing that gains in education and employment were greater *before* the introduction of affirmative action programs.

APPENDIX

THE DECLARATION OF INDEPENDENCE

Drafted mainly by Thomas Jefferson, this document adopted by the Second Continental Congress, and signed by John Hancock and fifty-five others, outlined the rights of man and the rights to rebellion and self-government. It declared the independence of the colonies from Great Britain, justified rebellion, and listed the grievances against George the III and his government. What is memorable about this famous document is not only that it declared the birth of a new nation, but that it set forth, with eloquence, our basic philosophy of liberty and representative democracy.

IN CONGRESS, JULY 4, 1776
(The unanimous Declaration of the Thirteen United States of America)

Preamble
When, in the course of human events, it becomes necessary for one people to dissolve the political bands which have connected them with another, and to assume, among the powers of the earth, the separate and equal station to which the laws of nature and of nature's God entitle them, a decent respect to the opinions of mankind requires that they should declare the causes which impel them to the separation.

New Principles of Government

We hold these truths to be self-evident; that all men are created equal, that they are endowed by their Creator with certain unalienable rights, that among these are life, liberty, and the pursuit of happiness.

That, to secure these rights, governments are instituted among men, deriving their just powers from the consent of the governed.

That whenever any form of government becomes destructive of these ends, it is the right of the people to alter or to abolish it, and to institute new government, laying its foundation on such principles, and organizing its powers in such form, as to them shall seem most likely to effect their safety and happiness. Prudence, indeed will dictate that governments long established should not be changed for light and transient causes; and accordingly all experience hath shown that mankind are more disposed to suffer while evils are sufferable, than to right themselves by abolishing the forms to which they are accustomed. But when a long train of abuses and usurpations, pursuing invariably the same object, evinces a design to reduce them under absolute despotism, it is their right, it is their duty, to throw off such government, and to provide new guards for their future security.

Reasons for Separation

Such has been the patient sufferance of these colonies; and such is now the necessity which constrains them to alter their former systems of government. The history of the present king of Great Britain is a history of repeated injuries and usurpations, all having in direct object the establishment of an absolute tyranny over these states. To prove this, let facts be submitted to a candid world.

He has refused his assent to laws, the most wholesome and necessary for the public good.

He has forbidden his governors to pass laws of immediate and pressing importance unless suspended in their operation till his assent should be obtained; and when so suspended, he has utterly neglected to attend to them.

He has refused to pass other laws for the accommodation of large districts of people, unless those people would relinquish the right of representation in the legislature, a right inestimable to them, and formidable to tyrants only.

He has called together legislative bodies at places unusual, uncomfortable, and distant for the depository of their public records, for the sole purpose of fatiguing them into compliance with his measures.

He has dissolved representative houses repeatedly, for opposing, with manly firmness, his invasions on the rights of people.

He has refused, for a long time after such dissolutions, to cause others to be elected; whereby the legislative powers incapable of annihilation, have returned to the people at large for their exercise; the state remaining, in the meantime, exposed to all the dangers of invasion from without and convulsions within.

He has endeavored to prevent the population of these states; for that purpose obstructing the laws of naturalization of foreigners, refusing to pass others to encourage their migration hither, and raising the conditions of new appropriations of lands.

He has obstructed the administration of justice, by refusing his assent to laws for establishing judiciary powers.

He has made judges dependent on his will alone for the tenure of their offices, and the amount and payment of their salaries.

He has erected a multitude of new offices, and sent hither swarms of officers to harass our people and eat out their substance.

He has kept among us, in times of peace, standing armies, without the consent of our legislature.

He has affected to render the military independent of, and superior to, the civil power.

He has combined with others to subject us to jurisdiction foreign to our constitution and unacknowledged by our laws, giving his assent to their acts of pretended legislation:

For quartering large bodies of armed troops among us;

For protecting them, by a mock trial, from punishment for any murders which they should commit on the inhabitants of these states;

For cutting off our trade with all parts of the world;

For imposing taxes on us without our consent;

For depriving us, in many cases, of the benefits of trial by jury;

For transporting us beyond seas, to be tried for pretended offenses;

For abolishing the free system of English laws in a neighboring province, establishing therein an arbitrary government, and enlarging its boundaries, so as to render it at once an example and fit instrument for introducing the same absolute rule into these colonies;

For taking away our charters, abolishing our most valuable laws, and altering, fundamentally, the forms of our governments;

For suspending our own legislatures, and declaring themselves invented with power to legislate for us in all cases whatsoever.

He has abdicated government here, by declaring us out of his protection and waging war against us.

He has plundered our seas, ravaged our coasts, burned our towns, and destroyed the lives of our people.

He is at this time transporting large armies of foreign mercenaries to complete the works of death, desolation, and tyranny already begun with circumstances of cruelty and perfidy scarcely paralleled in the most barbarous ages and totally unworthy of the head of a civilized nation.

He has constrained our fellow-citizens, taken captive on the high seas, to bear arms against their country, to become the executioners of their friends and brethren, or to fall themselves by their hands.

He has excited domestic insurrections among us, and has endeavored to bring on the inhabitants of our frontiers the merciless Indian savages, whose known rule of warfare is an undistinguished destruction of all ages, sexes, and conditions.

In every stage of these oppressions we have petitioned for redress in the most humble terms; our repeated petitions have been answered only by repeated injury. A prince whose character is thus marked by every act which may define a tyrant is unfit to be the ruler of a free people.

Nor have we been wanting in attention to our British brethren. We have warned them, from time to time, of attempts by their legislature to extend an unwarrantable jurisdiction over us. We have reminded them of the circumstances of our emigration and settlement here. We have appealed to their native justice and magnanimity; and we have conjured them, by the ties of our common kindred, to disavow these usurpations, which would inevitably interrupt our connections and correspondence. They, too, have been deaf to the voice of justice and of consanguinity. We must, therefore, acquiesce in the necessity which denounces our separation, and hold them, as we hold the rest of mankind, enemies in war, in peace, friends.

We, therefore, the representatives of the United States of America, in General Congress assembled, appealing to the Supreme Judge of the world for the rectitude of our intentions, do, in the name and by authority of the good people of these colonies, solemnly publish and declare, that these united colonies are, and of right ought to be, free and independent states; that they are absolved from all allegiance to the British crown, and that all political connection between them and the state of Great Britain is, and ought to be, totally dissolved; and that, as free and independent states, they have full power to levy war, conclude peace, contract alliances, establish commerce, and do all other acts and things which independent states may of a right do. And, for the support of this declaration, with a firm reliance on the protection of Divine Providence, we mutually pledge to each other our lives, our fortunes, and our sacred honor.

THE FEDERALIST, NO. 10, JAMES MADISON

To the People of the State of New York: Among the numerous advantages promised by a well-constructed union, none deserves to be more accurately developed than its tendency to break and control the violence of faction. The friend of popular governments, never finds himself so much alarmed for their character and fate, as when he contemplates their propensity to this dangerous vice. He will not fail, therefore, to set a due value on any plan which, without violating the principles to which he is attached, provides a proper cure for it. The instability, injustice, and confusion introduced into the public councils, have, in truth, been the mortal diseases under which popular governments have everywhere perished; as they continue to be the favourite and fruitful topics from which the adversaries to liberty derive their most specious declamations. The valuable improvements made by the American constitutions on the popular models, both ancient and modern, cannot certainly be too much admired; but it would be an unwarrantable partiality, to contend that they have as effectually obviated the danger on this side, as was wished and expected. Complaints are everywhere heard from our most considerate and virtuous citizens, equally the friends of public and private faith, and of public and personal liberty, that our governments are too unstable; that the public good is disregarded in the conflicts of rival parties; and that measures are too often decided, not according to the rules of justice, and the rights of the minor party, but by the superior force of an interested and overbearing majority. However anxiously we may wish that these complaints had no foundation, the evidence of known facts will not permit us to deny that they are in some degree true. It will be found, indeed, on a candid review of our situation, that some of the distresses under which we labour have been erroneously charged on the operation of our governments; but it will be found, at the same time, that other causes will not alone account for many of our heaviest misfortunes; and, particularly, for that prevailing and increasing distrust of public engagements, and alarm for private rights, which are echoed from one end of the continent to the other. These must be chiefly, if not wholly, effects of the unsteadiness and injustice, with which a factious spirit has tainted our public administrations.

By a faction, I understand a number of citizens, whether amounting to a majority or minority of the whole, who are united and actuated by some common impulse of passion, or of interest, adverse to the rights of other citizens, or to the permanent and aggregate interests of the community.

There are two methods of curing the mischiefs of faction: the one, by removing its causes; the other, by controlling its effects.

There are again two methods of removing the causes of faction: the one, by destroying the liberty which is essential to its existence; the other, by giving to every citizen the same opinions, the same passions, and the same interests.

It could never be more truly said, than of the first remedy, that it was worse than the disease. Liberty is to faction what air is to fire, an aliment without which it instantly expires. But it could not be a less folly to abolish liberty, which is essential to political life, because it nourishes faction, than it would be to wish the annihilation of air, which is essential to animal life, because it imparts to fire its destructive agency.

The second expedient is as impracticable, as the first would be unwise. As long as the reason of man continues fallible, and he is at liberty to exercise it, different opinions will be formed. As long as the connection subsists between his reason and his self-love, his opinions and his passions will have a reciprocal influence on each other; and the former will be objects to which the latter will attach themselves. The diversity in the faculties of men, from which the rights of property originate, is not less an insuperable obstacle to an uniformity of interests. The protection of these faculties is the first object of government. From the protection of different and unequal faculties of acquiring property, the possession of different degrees and kinds of property immediately results; and from the influence of these on the sentiments and views of the respective proprietors, ensues a division of the society into different interests and parties.

The latent causes of faction are thus sown in the nature of man; and we see them everywhere brought into different degrees of activity, according to the different circumstances of civil society. A zeal for different opinions concerning religion, concerning government, and many other points, as well of speculation as of practice; an attachment to different leaders ambitiously contending for preeminence and power; or to persons of other descriptions whose fortunes have been interesting to the human passions, have, in turn, divided mankind into parties, inflamed them with mutual animosity, and rendered them much more disposed to vex and oppress each other, than to cooperate for their common good. So strong is this propensity of mankind, to fall into mutual animosities, that where no substantial occasion presents itself, the most frivolous and fanciful distinctions have been sufficient to kindle their unfriendly passions and excite their most violent conflicts. But the most common and durable source of factions, has been the various and unequal distribution of property. Those who hold, and those who are without property, have ever formed distinct interests in society. Those who are creditors, and those who are debtors, fall under a like discrimination. A landed interest, a manufacturing interest, a mercantile interest, a moneyed interest, with many lesser interests, grow up of necessity in civilized nations, and divide them into different classes, actuated by different sentiments and views. The regulation of these various and interfering interests forms the principal task of modern legislation, and involves the spirit of the party and faction in the necessary and ordinary operations of the government.

No man is allowed to be a judge in his own cause; because his interest will certainly bias his judgment, and, not improbably, corrupt his integrity. With equal, nay, with greater reason, a body of men are unfit to be both judges and parties at the same time; yet what are many of the most important acts of legislation, but so many judicial determinations, not indeed concerning the right of single persons, but concerning the rights of large bodies of citizens? And what are the different classes of legislators, but advocates and parties to the causes which they determine? Is a law proposed concerning private debts? It is a question to which the creditors are parties on one side, and the debtors on the other. Justice ought to hold the balance between them. Yet the parties are, and must be, themselves the judges; and the most numerous party, or, in other words, the most powerful faction, must be expected to prevail. Shall domestic manufacturers be encouraged, and in what degree, by restrictions on foreign manufacturers are questions which would be differently decided by the landed and the manufacturing classes; and probably by neither with a sole regard to justice and the public good. The apportionment of taxes, on the various descriptions of property, is an act which seems to require the most exact impartiality; yet there is, perhaps, no legislative act, in which greater opportunity and temptation are given to a predominant party to trample on the rules of justice. Every shilling, with which they overburden the inferior number, is a shilling saved to their own pockets.

It is in vain to say, that enlightened statesmen will be able to adjust these clashing interests, and render them all subservient to the public good. Enlightened statesmen will not always be at the helm; nor, in many cases, can such an adjustment be made at all, without taking into view indirect and remote considerations, which will rarely prevail over the immediate interest which one party may find in disregarding the rights of another, or the good of the whole.

The inference to which we are brought is, that the *causes* of faction cannot be removed; and that relief is only to be sought in the means of controlling its *effects*.

If a faction consists of less than a majority, relief is supplied by the republican principle, which enables the majority to defeat its sinister views, by regular vote. It may clog the administration, it may convulse the society; but it will be unable to execute and mask its violence under the forms of the Constitution. When a majority is included in a faction, the form of popular government, on the other hand, enables it to sacrifice to its ruling passion or interest, both the public good and the rights of other citizens. To secure the public good, and private rights, against the danger of such a faction, and at the same time to preserve the spirit and the form of popular government, is then the great object to which our inquiries are directed. Let me add, that it is the great desideratum, by which alone this form of government can be rescued from the opprobrium under which it has so long laboured, and be recommended to the esteem and adoption of mankind.

By what means is this object attainable? Evidently by one of two only. Either the existence of the same passion or interest in a majority, at the same time, must be prevented; or the majority, having such coexistent passion or interest, must be rendered, by their number and local situation, unable to concert and carry into effect schemes of oppression. If the impulse and the opportunity be suffered to coincide, we well know that neither moral nor religious motives can be relied on as an adequate control. They are not found to be such on the injustice and violence of individuals, and lose their efficacy in proportion to the number combined together; that is, in proportion as their efficacy becomes needful.

From this view of the subject, it may be concluded, that a pure democracy, by which I mean a society consisting of a small number of citizens, who assemble and administer the government in person, can admit of no cure for the mischiefs of faction. A common passion or interest will, in almost every case, be felt by a majority of the whole; a communication and concert, results from the form of government itself; and there is nothing to check the inducements to sacrifice the weaker party, or an obnoxious individual. Hence, it is, that such democracies have ever been spectacles of turbulence and contention; have ever been found incompatible with personal security, or the rights of property; and have in general been as short in their lives, as they have been violent in their deaths. Theoretic politicians, who have patronized this species of government, have erroneously supposed, that by reducing mankind to a perfect equality in their political rights, they would, at the same time, be perfectly equalized and assimilated in their possessions, their opinions, and their passions.

A republic, by which I mean a government in which the scheme of representation takes place, opens a different prospect, and promises the cure for which we are seeking. Let us examine the points in which it varies from pure democracy, and we shall comprehend both the nature of the cure and the efficacy which it must derive from the union.

The two great points of difference, between a democracy and a republic, are, first, the delegation of the government, in the latter, to a small number of citizens, elected by the rest; secondly, the greater number of citizens, and greater sphere of country, over which the latter may be extended.

The effect of the first difference is, on the one hand, to refine and enlarge the public views, by passing them through the medium of a chosen body of citizens, whose wisdom may best discern the true interest of their country, and whose patriotism and love of justice, will be least likely to sacrifice it to temporary or partial considerations. Under such a regulation, it may well happen, that the public voice, pronounced by the representatives of the people, will be more consonant to the public good, than if pronounced by the people themselves, convened for the purpose. On the other hand the effect may be inverted. Men of factious tempers, of local prejudices, or of sinister designs, may by intrigue, by corruption, or by other means, first obtain the suffrages, and then betray the interest of the people. The question resulting is, whether small or extensive republics are most favourable to the election of proper guardians of the public weal; and it is clearly decided in favour of the latter by two obvious considerations.

In the first place, it is to be remarked that, however small the republic may be, the representatives must be raised to a certain number, in order to guard against the cabals of a few; and that however large it may be, they must be limited to a certain number, in order to guard against the confusion of a multitude. Hence, the number of representatives in the two cases not being in proportion to that of the constituents, and being proportionally greatest in the small republic, it follows, that if the proportion of fit characters be not less in the large than in the small republic, the former will present a greater option, and consequently a greater probability of a fit choice.

In the next place, as each representative will be chosen by a greater number of citizens in the large than in the small republic, it will be more difficult for unworthy candidates to practice with success the vicious arts, by which elections are too often carried; and the suffrages of the people being more free, will be more likely to centre in men who possess the most attractive merit, and the most diffusive and established characters.

It must be confessed, that in this, as in most other cases, there is a mean, on both sides of which inconveniences will be found to lie. By enlarging too much the number of electors, you render the representatives too little acquainted with all their local circumstances and lesser interests; as by reducing it too much, you render him unduly attached to these, and too little fit to comprehend and pursue great and national objects. The federal constitution forms a happy combination in this respect; the great and aggregate interests being referred to the national, the local and particular to the state legislatures.

The other point of difference is, the greater number of citizens, and extent of territory, which may be brought within the compass of republican, than of democratic government; and it is this circumstance principally which renders factious combinations less to be dreaded in the former, than in the latter. The smaller the society, the fewer probably will be the distinct parties and interests composing it; the fewer the distinct parties and interests, the more frequently will a majority be found of the same party; and the smaller the number of individuals composing a majority, and the smaller the compass within which they are placed, the more easily will they concert and execute their plans of oppression. Extend the sphere, and you take in a greater variety of parties and interests; you make it less probable that a majority of the whole will have a common motive to invade the rights of other citizens; or if such a common motive exists, it will be more difficult for all who feel it to discover their own strength, and to act in unison with each other. Besides other impediments, it may be remarked, that where there is a consciousness of unjust or dishonourable purposes, communication is always checked by distrust, in proportion to the number whose concurrence is necessary.

Hence, it clearly appears, that the same advantage, which a republic has over a democracy, in controlling the effects of faction, is enjoyed by a large

over a small republic—is enjoyed by the union over the states composing it. Does this advantage consist in the substitution of representatives, whose enlightened views and virtuous sentiments render them superior to local prejudices, and to schemes of injustice? It will not be denied that the representation of the union will be most likely to possess these requisite endowments. Does it consist in the greater security afforded by a greater variety of parties, against the event of any one party being able to outnumber and oppress the rest? In an equal degree does the increased variety of parties, comprised within the union, increase the security? Does it, in fine, consist in the greater obstacles opposed to the concert and accomplishment of the secret wishes of an unjust and interested majority? Here, again, the extent of the union gives it the most palpable advantage.

The influence of factious leaders may kindle a flame within their particular states, but will be unable to spread a general conflagration through the other states; a religious sect may degenerate into a political faction in a part of the confederacy; but the variety of sects dispersed over the entire face of it, must secure the national councils against any danger from that source; a rage for paper money, for an abolition of debts, for an equal division of property, or for any other improper or wicked project, will be less apt to pervade the whole body of the union than a particular member of it; in the same proportion as such a malady is more likely to taint a particular county or district, than an entire state.

In the extent and proper structure of the union, therefore, we behold a republican remedy for the diseases most incident to republican government. And according to the degree of pleasure and pride we feel in being republicans, ought to be our zeal in cherishing the spirit, and supporting the character of federalists.

THE FEDERALIST, NO. 51, JAMES MADISON

To what expedient, then, shall we finally resort, for maintaining in practice the necessary partition of power among the several departments as laid down in the Constitution? The only answer that can be given is that as all these exterior provisions are found to be inadequate the defect must be supplied, by so contriving the interior structure of the government as that its several constituent parts may, by their mutual relations, be the means of keeping each other in their proper places. Without presuming to undertake a full development of this important idea I will hazard a few general observations which may perhaps place it in a clearer light, and enable us to form a more correct judgment of the principles and structure of the government planned by the convention.

In order to lay a due foundation for that separate and distinct exercise of the different powers of government, which to a certain extent is admitted on all hands to be essential to the preservation of liberty, it is evident that each department should have a will of its own; and consequently should be so constituted that the members of each should have as little agency as possible in the appointment of the members of the others. Were this principle rigorously adhered to, it would require that all the appointments for the supreme executive, legislative, and judiciary magistracies should be drawn from the same fountain of authority, the people, through channels having no communication whatever with one another. Perhaps such a plan of constructing the several departments would be less difficult in practice than it may in contemplation appear. Some difficulties, however, and some additional expense would attend the execution of it. Some deviations, therefore, from the principle must be admitted. In the constitution of the judiciary department in particular, it might be inexpedient to insist rigorously on the principle: first, because peculiar qualifications being essential in the members, the primary consideration ought to be to select that mode of choice which best secures these qualifications; second, because the permanent tenure by which the appointments are held in that department must soon destroy all sense of dependence on the authority conferring them.

It is equally evident that the members of each department should be as little dependent as possible on those of the others for the emoluments annexed to their offices. Were the executive magistrate, or the judges, not independent of the legislature in this particular, their independence in every other would be merely nominal.

But the great security against a gradual concentration of the several powers in the same department consists in giving to those who administer each department the necessary constitutional means and personal motives to resist encroachments of the others. The provision for defense must in this, as in all other cases, be made commensurate to the danger of attack. Ambition must be made to counteract ambition. The interest of the man must be connected with the constitutional rights of the place. It may be a reflection on human nature that such devices should be necessary to control the abuses of government. But what is government itself but the greatest of all reflections on human nature? If men were angels, no government would be necessary. If angels were to govern men, neither external nor internal controls on government would be necessary. In framing a government which is to be administered by men over men, the great difficulty lies in this: you must first enable the government to control the governed; and in the next place oblige it to control itself. A dependence on the people is, no doubt, the primary control on the government; but experience has taught mankind the necessity of auxiliary precautions.

This policy of supplying, by opposite and rival interests, the defect of better motives, might be traced through the whole system of human affairs, private as well as public. We see it particularly displayed in all the subordinate distributions of power, where the constant aim is to divide and arrange the several offices in such a manner as that each may be a check on the other—that the private interest of every individual may be a sentinel over the public rights. These inventions of prudence cannot be less requisite in the distribution of the supreme powers of the State.

But it is not possible to give to each department an equal power of self-defense. In republican government, the legislative authority necessarily predominates. The remedy for this inconveniency is to divide the legislature into different branches; and to render them, by modes of election and different principles of action, as little connected with each other as the nature of their common functions and their common dependence on the society will admit. It may even be necessary to guard against dangerous encroachments by still further precautions. As the weight of the legislative authority requires that it should be thus divided, the weakness of the executive may require, on the other hand, that it should be fortified. An absolute negative on the legislature appears, at first view, to be the natural defense with which the executive magistrate should be armed. But perhaps it would be neither altogether safe nor alone sufficient. On ordinary occasions it might not be exerted with the requisite firmness, and on extraordinary occasions it might be perfidiously abused. May not this defect of an absolute negative be supplied by some qualified connection between this weaker department and the weaker branch of the stronger department, by which the latter may be led to support the constitutional rights of the former, without being too much detached from the rights of its own department?

If the principles on which these observations are founded be just, as I persuade myself they are, and they be applied as a criterion to the several State constitutions, and to the federal Constitution, it will be found that if the latter does not perfectly correspond with them, the former are infinitely less able to bear such a test.

There are, moreover, two considerations particularly applicable to the federal system of America, which place that system in a very interesting point of view.

First. In a single republic, all the power surrendered by the people is submitted to the administration of a single government; and the usurpations are guarded against by a division of the government into distinct and separate departments. In the compound republic of America, the power surrendered by the people is first divided between two distinct governments, and then the portion allotted to each subdivided among distinct and separate departments. Hence a double security arises to the rights of the people. The different governments will control each other, at the same time that each will be controlled by itself.

Second. It is of great importance in a republic not only to guard the society against the oppression of its rulers, but to guard one part of the society against the injustice of the other part. Different interests necessarily exist in different classes of citizens. If a majority be united by a common interest, the rights of the minority will be insecure. There are but two methods of providing against this evil: the one by creating a will in the community independent of the majority—that is, of the society itself; the other, by comprehending in the society so many separate descriptions of citizens as will render an unjust combination of a majority of the whole very improba-

ble, if not impracticable. The first method prevails in all governments possessing an hereditary or self-appointed authority. This, at best, is but a precarious security; because a power independent of the society may as well espouse the unjust views of the major as the rightful interests of the minor party, and may possibly be turned against both parties. The second method will be exemplified in the federal republic of the United States. Whilst all authority in it will be derived from and dependent on the society, the society itself will be broken into so many parts, interests and classes of citizens, that the rights of individuals, or of the minority, will be in little danger from interested combinations of the majority. In a free government the security for civil rights must be the same as that for religious rights. It consists in the one case in the multiplicity of interests, and in the other in the multiplicity of sects. The degree of security in both cases will depend on the number of interests and sects; and this may be presumed to depend on the extent of country and number of people comprehended under the same government. This view of the subject must particularly recommend a proper federal system to all the sincere and considerate friends of republican government, since it shows that in exact proportion as the territory of the Union may be formed into more circumscribed Confederacies, or States, oppressive combinations of a majority will be facilitated; the best security, under the republican forms, for the rights of every class of citizen, will be diminished; and consequently the stability and independence of some member of the government, the only other security, must be proportionally increased. Justice is the end of government. It is the end of civil society. It ever has been and ever will be pursued until it be obtained, or until liberty be lost in the pursuit. In a society under the forms of which the stronger faction can readily unite and

oppress the weaker, anarchy may as truly be said to reign as in a state of nature, where the weaker individual is not secured against the violence of the stronger; and as, in the latter state, even the stronger individuals are prompted, by the uncertainty of their condition, to submit to a government which may protect the weak as well as themselves; so, in the former state, will the more powerful factions or parties be gradually induced, by a like motive, to wish for a government which will protect all parties, the weaker as well as the more powerful. It can be little doubted that if the State of Rhode Island was separated from the Confederacy and left to itself, the insecurity of rights under the popular form of government within such narrow limits would be displayed by such reiterated oppressions of factious majorities that some power altogether independent of the people would soon be called for by the voice of the very factions whose misrule had proved the necessity of it. In the extended republic of the United States, and among the great variety of interests, parties, and sects which it embraces, a coalition of a majority of the whole society could seldom take place on any other principles than those of justice and the general good; whilst there being thus less danger to a minor from the will of a major party, there must be less pretext, also, to provide for the security of the former, by introducing into the government a will not dependent on the latter, or, in other words, a will independent of the society itself. It is no less certain that it is important, notwithstanding the contrary opinions which have been entertained that the larger the society, provided it lie within a practicable sphere, the more duly capable it will be of self-government. And happily for the *republican cause,* the practicable sphere may be carried to a very great extent by a judicious modification and mixture of the *federal principle.*

PRESIDENTIAL VOTING

Year	Candidates	Party	Electoral Vote	Popular Vote Percentage
1789	**George Washington**	Federalist	69	—
	John Adams	Federalist	34	
	Others		35	
1792	**George Washington**	Federalist	132	—
	John Adams	Federalist	77	
	Others		55	
1796	**John Adams**	Federalist	71	—
	Thomas Jefferson	Democratic-Republican	68	
	Thomas Pinckney	Federalist	59	
	Aaron Burr	Anti-Federalist	30	
	Others		48	
1800	**Thomas Jefferson**	Democratic-Republican	73	—
	Aaron Burr	Democratic-Republican	73	
	John Adams	Federalist	65	
	C. C. Pinckney	Federalist	64	
	John Jay	Federalist	1	
1804	**Thomas Jefferson**	Democratic-Republican	162	—
	C. C. Pinckney	Federalist	14	
1808	**James Madison**	Democratic-Republican	122	—
	C. C. Pinckney	Federalist	47	
	George Clinton	Independent-Republican	6	
1812	**James Madison**	Democratic-Republican	128	—
	De Witt Clinton	Fusion	89	
1816	**James Monroe**	Democratic-Republican	183	—
	Rufus King	Federalist	34	
1820	**James Monroe**	Democratic-Republican	231	—
	John Q. Adams	Independent-Republican	1	
1824	**John Q. Adams**	National Republican	84	—
	Andrew Jackson	Democratic	99	
	Henry Clay	Democratic-Republican	37	
	W. H. Crawford	Democratic-Republican	41	
1828	**Andrew Jackson**	Democratic	178	56.1
	John Q. Adams	National Republican	83	43.6
1832	**Andrew Jackson**	Democratic	219	54.2
	Henry Clay	National Republican	49	37.4
	William Wirt	Anti-Masonic	7	
	John Floyd	Nullifiers	11	
1836	**Martin Van Buren**	Democratic	170	50.8
	William H. Harrison	Whig	73	36.6
	Hugh L. White	Whig	26	
	Daniel Webster	Whig	14	
1840	**William H. Harrison**	Whig	234	52.9
	Martin Van Buren	Democratic	60	46.8
	(John Tyler, 1841)			
1844	**James K. Polk**	Democratic	170	49.5
	Henry Clay	Whig	105	48.1
1848	**Zachary Taylor**	Whig	163	47.3
	Lewis Cass	Democratic	127	42.5
	(Millard Fillmore, 1850)			

(continued on page 598)

Year	Candidates	Party	Electoral Vote	Popular Vote Percentage
1852	**Franklin Pierce**	Democratic	254	50.8
	Winfield Scott	Whig	42	43.9
1856	**James Buchanan**	Democratic	174	45.3
	John C. Fremont	Republican	114	33.1
	Millard Fillmore	American	8	
1860	**Abraham Lincoln**	Republican	180	39.8
	J. C. Breckinridge	Democratic	72	29.5
	Stephen A. Douglas	Democratic	12	
	John Bell	Constitutional Union	39	
1864	**Abraham Lincoln**	Republican	212	55.0
	George B. McClellan	Democratic	21	45.0
	(**Andrew Johnson,** 1865)			
1868	**Ulysses S. Grant**	Republican	214	52.7
	Horatio Seymour	Democratic	80	47.3
1872	**Ulysses S. Grant**	Republican	286	55.6
	Horace Greeley	Democratic	**	43.8
1876	**Rutherford B. Hayes**	Republican	185	47.9
	Samuel J. Tilden	Democratic	184	51.0
1880	**James A. Garfield**	Republican	214	48.3
	Winfield S. Hancock	Democratic	155	48.2
	(**Chester A. Arthur,** 1881)			
1884	**Grover Cleveland**	Democratic	219	48.5
	James G. Blaine	Republican	182	48.2
1888	**Benjamin Harrison**	Republican	233	48.6
	Grover Cleveland	Democratic	168	47.8
1892	**Grover Cleveland**	Democratic	277	46.1
	Benjamin Harrison	Republican	145	43.0
	James B. Weaver	People's	22	
1896	**William McKinley**	Republican	271	51.0
	William J. Bryan	Democratic	176	46.7
1900	**William McKinley**	Republican	292	51.7
	William J. Bryan	Democratic	155	45.5
	(**Theodore Roosevelt,** 1901)			
1904	**Theodore Roosevelt**	Republican	336	56.4
	Alton B. Parker	Democratic	140	37.6
1908	**William H. Taft**	Republican	321	51.6
	William J. Bryan	Democratic	162	43.0
1912	**Woodrow Wilson**	Democratic	435	41.8
	Theodore Roosevelt	Progressive	88	23.2
	William H. Taft	Republican	8	23.2
1916	**Woodrow Wilson**	Democratic	277	49.2
	Charles E. Hughes	Republican	254	46.1
1920	**Warren G. Harding**	Republican	404	60.3
	James M. Cox	Democratic	127	34.2
	(**Calvin Coolidge,** 1923)			
1924	**Calvin Coolidge**	Republican	382	54.1
	John W. Davis	Democratic	136	28.8
	Robert M. LaFollette	Progressive	13	

Year	Candidates	Party	Electoral Vote	Popular Vote Percentage
1928	**Herbert C. Hoover**	Republican	444	58.2
	Alfred E. Smith	Democratic	87	40.8
1932	**Franklin D. Roosevelt**	Democratic	472	57.4
	Herbert C. Hoover	Republican	59	39.6
1936	**Franklin D. Roosevelt**	Democratic	523	60.8
	Alfred M. Landon	Republican	8	36.5
1940	**Franklin D. Roosevelt**	Democratic	449	54.7
	Wendell L. Willkie	Republican	82	44.8
1944	**Franklin D. Roosevelt**	Democratic	432	53.4
	Thomas E. Dewey	Republican	99	45.9
	(Harry S Truman, 1945)			
1948	**Harry S Truman**	Democratic	303	49.5
	Thomas E. Dewey	Republican	189	45.1
	J. Strom Thurmond	States' Rights	39	
1952	**Dwight D. Eisenhower**	Republican	442	55.1
	Adlai E. Stevenson	Democratic	89	44.4
1956	**Dwight D. Eisenhower**	Republican	457	57.4
	Adlai E. Stevenson	Democratic	73	42.0
1960	**John F. Kennedy**	Democratic	303	49.7
	Richard M. Nixon	Republican	219	49.5
	(Lyndon B. Johnson, 1963)			
1964	**Lyndon B. Johnson**	Democratic	486	61.0
	Barry M. Goldwater	Republican	52	38.5
1968	**Richard M. Nixon**	Republican	301	43.4
	Hubert H. Humphrey	Democratic	191	42.7
	George C. Wallace	American Independent	46	
1972	**Richard M. Nixon**	Republican	520	60.7
	George S. McGovern	Democratic	17	37.5
	(Gerald R. Ford, 1974)			
1976	**Jimmy Carter**	Democratic	297	50.1
	Gerald R. Ford	Republican	240	48.0
1980	**Ronald Reagan**	Republican	489	50.7
	Jimmy Carter	Democratic	49	41.0
	John Anderson	Independent	—	
1984	**Ronald Reagan**	Republican	525	58.8
	Walter Mondale	Democratic	13	40.6
1988	**George Bush**	Republican	426	53.4
	Michael Dukakis	Democratic	112	45.6
1992	**Bill Clinton**	Democratic	370	43.2
	George Bush	Republican	168	37.7
	Ross Perot	Independent	0	19.0
1996	**Bill Clinton**	Democratic	379	49
	Robert Dole	Republican	159	41
	Ross Perot	Reform	0	8
2000	**George W. Bush**	Republican	271	48.0
	Al Gore	Democratic	267	48.0
	Ralph Nader	Green	—	3.0
	Pat Buchanan	Reform	—	—

PARTY CONTROL OF CONGRESS

Congress	Years	Party and President	Senate			House		
			DEM.	REP.	OTHER	DEM.	REP.	OTHER
57th	1901–03	R T. Roosevelt	29	*56*	3	153	*198*	5
58th	1903–05	R T. Roosevelt	32	*58*	—	178	*207*	—
59th	1905–07	R T. Roosevelt	32	*58*	—	136	*250*	—
60th	1907–09	R T. Roosevelt	29	*61*	—	164	*222*	—
61st	1909–11	R Taft	32	*59*	—	172	*219*	—
62d	1911–13	R Taft	42	*49*	—	*228*	162	1
63d	1913–15	D Wilson	*51*	44	1	*290*	127	18
64th	1915–17	D Wilson	*56*	39	1	*230*	193	8
65th	1917–19	D Wilson	*53*	42	1	200	*216*	9
66th	1919–21	D Wilson	48	*48*	1	191	*237*	7
67th	1921–23	R Harding	37	*59*	—	132	*300*	1
68th	1923–25	R Coolidge	43	*51*	2	207	*225*	3
69th	1925–27	R Coolidge	40	*54*	1	183	*247*	5
70th	1927–29	R Coolidge	47	*48*	1	195	*237*	3
71st	1929–31	R Hoover	39	*56*	1	163	*267*	1
72d	1931–33	R Hoover	47	*48*	1	216	*218*	1
73d	1933–35	D F. Roosevelt	*59*	36	1	*313*	117	5
74th	1935–37	D F. Roosevelt	*69*	25	2	*322*	103	10
75th	1937–39	D F. Roosevelt	*75*	17	4	*333*	89	13
76th	1939–41	D F. Roosevelt	*69*	23	4	*262*	169	4
77th	1941–43	D F. Roosevelt	*66*	28	2	*267*	162	6
78th	1943–45	D F. Roosevelt	*57*	38	1	*222*	209	4
79th	1945–47	D Truman	*57*	38	1	*243*	190	2
80th	1947–49	D Truman	45	*51*	—	188	*246*	1
81st	1949–51	D Truman	*54*	42	—	*263*	171	1
82d	1951–53	D Truman	*48*	47	1	*234*	199	2
83d	1953–55	R Eisenhower	47	*48*	1	213	*221*	1
84th	1955–57	R Eisenhower	*48*	47	1	*232*	203	—
85th	1957–59	R Eisenhower	*49*	47	—	*234*	201	—
86th	1959–61	R Eisenhower	*64*	34	—	*283*	154	—
87th	1961–63	D Kennedy	*64*	36	—	*263*	174	—
88th	1963–65	D { Kennedy / Johnson	*67*	33	—	*258*	176	—
89th	1965–67	D Johnson	*68*	32	—	*295*	140	—
90th	1967–69	D Johnson	*64*	36	—	*248*	187	—
91st	1969–71	R Nixon	*58*	42	—	*243*	192	—
92d	1971–73	R Nixon	*55*	45	—	*255*	180	—
93d	1973–75	R { Nixon / Ford	*57*	43	—	*243*	192	—
94th	1975–77	R Ford	*61*	38	—	*291*	144	—
95th	1977–79	D Carter	*62*	38	—	*292*	143	—
96th	1979–81	D Carter	*59*	41	—	*277*	158	—
97th	1981–83	R Reagan	47	*53*	—	*243*	192	—
98th	1983–85	R Reagan	46	*54*	—	*269*	166	—
99th	1985–87	R Reagan	47	*53*	—	*253*	182	—
100th	1987–89	R Reagan	*55*	45	—	*258*	177	—
101st	1989–91	R Bush	*55*	45	—	*260*	175	—
102d	1991–93	R Bush	*57*	43	—	*267*	167	1
103d	1993–95	D Clinton	*59*	43	—	*258*	176	1
104th	1995–97	D Clinton	46	*54*	—	204	*230*	1
105th	1997–99	D Clinton	45	*55*	—	207	*227*	1
106th	1999–2001	D Clinton	45	*55*	—	211	*223*	1
107th	2001–2003	R Bush	50	50	—	212	*221*	2

NOTES

CHAPTER ONE

1. For a discussion of various aspects of legitimacy and its measurement in public opinion polls, see M. Stephen Weatherford, "Measuring Political Legitimacy," *American Political Science Review* 86 (March 1992): 140–55.
2. Thomas Hobbes, *Leviathan* (1651).
3. For an explanation of the worldwide growth of democracy, see John Mueller, "Democracy and Ralph's Pretty Good Grocery Store," *American Journal of Political Science* 36 (November 1992): 983–1003.
4. John Locke, *Treatise on Government* (1688).
5. See Barbara S. Gamble, "Putting Civil Rights to a Popular Vote," *American Journal of Political Science*, 41 (January 1997): 245–269.
6. James Madison, Alexander Hamilton, and John Jay, *The Federalist Papers* (New York: Mentor Books, 1961), No. 10, p. 81. Madison's *Federalist Papers*, No. 10 and No. 51, are reprinted in the Appendix.
7. E. E. Shattschneider, *Two Hundred Million Americans in Search of a Government* (New York: Holt, Rinehart and Winston, 1969), p. 63.
8. Harold Lasswell and Daniel Lerner, *The Comparative Study of Elites* (Stanford, Calif.: Stanford University Press, 1952), p. 7.
9. C. Wright Mills's classic study, *The Power Elite* (New York: Oxford University Press, 1956), is widely cited by Marxist critics of American democracy, but it can be read profitably by anyone concerned with the effects of large bureaucracies—corporate, governmental, or military—on democratic government.
10. In *Who Rules America?* (New York: Prentice-Hall, 1967) and its sequel, *Who Rules America Now?* (New York: Prentice-Hall, 1983), sociologist G. William Domhoff argues that America is ruled by an "upper class" who attend the same prestigious private schools, intermarry among themselves, and join the same exclusive clubs. In *Who's Running America?* (New York: Prentice-Hall, 1976) and *Who's Running America? The Clinton Years* (New York: Prentice-Hall, 1995), political scientist Thomas R. Dye documents the concentration of power and the control of assets in the hands of officers and directors of the nation's largest corporations, banks, law firms, networks, foundations, and so forth. Dye argues, however, that most of these "institutional elites" were not born into the upper class but instead climbed the ladder to success.
11. Yale political scientist Robert A. Dahl is an important contributor to the development of pluralist theory, beginning with his *Preface to Democratic Theory* (Chicago: University of Chicago Press, 1956). He often refers to a pluralist system as a *polyarchy*—literally, a system with many centers of power. See his *Polyarchy* (New Haven, Conn.: Yale University Press, 1971); and for a revised defense of pluralism, see his *Democracy and Its Critics* (New Haven, Conn.: Yale University Press, 1989).

CHAPTER TWO

1. Gunnar Myrdal, *An American Dilemma* (New York: Harper, 1944).
2. See Martin Luther King, Jr., "Letter from Birmingham City Jail," April 16, 1963.
3. For a discussion of the sources and consequences of intolerance in the general public, see James L. Gibson, "The Political Consequences of Intolerance: Cultural Conformity and Political Freedom," *American Political Science Review* 86 (June 1992): 338–52.
4. Quoted in *The Idea of Equality*, ed. George Abernathy (Richmond, Va.: John Knox Press, 1959), p. 185; also in Herbert McClosky and John Zaller, *The American Ethos: Public Attitudes toward Capitalism and Democracy* (Cambridge, Mass.: Harvard University Press, 1984), p. 72.
5. Quoted in Richard Hofstadter, *The American Political Tradition* (New York: Knopf, 1948), p. 45. Historian Hofstadter describes the thinking of American political leaders from Jefferson and the Founders to Franklin D. Roosevelt.
6. For a discussion of how people balance the values of individualism and opposition to big government with humanitarianism and the desire to help others, see Stanley Feldman and John Zaller, "The Political Culture of Ambivalence: Ideological Responses to the Welfare State," *American Journal of Political Science* 36 (February 1992): 268–307.
7. Robert E. Lane, "Market Justice, Political Justice," *American Political Science Review* 80 (June 1986): 383–402.
8. Greg J. Duncan, *Years of Poverty, Years of Plenty* (Ann Arbor: University of Michigan Press, 1984).
9. *New York Times*/CBS News polls, reported in *New York Times*, February 15, 1993. Copyright © 1993 by The New York Times Company.
10. American Security Council, *The Illegal Immigration Crisis* (Washington, D.C.: ASC, 1994).
11. *Sale v. Haitian Centers Council*, 125 L. Ed. 2d 128 (1993).
12. See Stephen Earl Bennett, "Americans' Knowledge of Ideology, 1980–92," *American Politics Quarterly* 23 (July 1995): 259–78.
13. For evidence that ideological consistency increases with educational level, see William G. Jacoby, "Ideological Identification and Issue Attitude," *American Journal of Political Science* 35 (February 1991): 178–205.
14. Richard Hofstadter, *The Paranoid Style in American Politics* (New York: Knopf, 1965).
15. Francis Fukuyama, *The End of History and the Last Man* (New York: Free Press, 1992).
16. See Robert Kimball, *Tenured Radicals* (New York: Harper & Row, 1990).
17. Herbert Marcuse, *One-Dimensional Man* (Boston: Beacon Press, 1964).
18. Allan Bloom, *The Closing of the American Mind* (New York: Simon & Schuster, 1987), p. 15.

CHAPTER THREE

1. In *Federalist Papers*, No. 53, James Madison distinguishes a "constitution" from a law: a constitution is "established by the people and unalterable by the government, and a law established by the government and alterable by the government."
2. Another important decision on opening day of the Constitutional Convention was to keep the proceedings secret. James Madison made his own notes on the convention proceedings, and they were published many years later. See Max Ferrand, ed., *The Records of the Federal Convention of 1787* (New Haven, Conn.: Yale University Press, 1911).
3. See Edward Millican, *One United People: The Federalist Papers and the National Idea* (Lexington: University Press of Kentucky, 1990).
4. Charles A. Beard, *An Economic Interpretation of the Constitution* (New York: Macmillan, 1913).
5. Robert E. Brown, *Charles Beard and the Constitution* (Princeton, N.J.: Princeton University Press, 1956).
6. James Madison, *Federalist Papers*, No. 10; reprinted in the Appendix.
7. Alexander Hamilton, *Federalist Papers*, No. 78.

CHAPTER FOUR

1. The states are listed in the order in which their legislatures voted to secede. While occupied by Confederate troops, secessionist legislators in Missouri and Kentucky also voted to secede, but Unionist representatives from these states remained in Congress.
2. *Texas v. White*, 7 Wallace 700 (1869).
3. James Madison, *Federalist Papers*, No. 51, reprinted in the Appendix.
4. Ibid.
5. The arguments for "competitive federalism" are developed at length in Thomas R. Dye, *American Federalism: Competition among Governments* (Lexington, Mass.: Lexington Books, 1990).
6. David Osborne, *Laboratories of Democracy* (Cambridge, Mass.: Harvard Business School, 1988).
7. Morton Grodzins, *The American System* (Chicago: Rand McNally, 1966), pp. 8–9.
8. Ibid., p. 265.
9. Charles Press, *State and Community Governments in the Federal System* (New York: Wiley, 1979), p. 78.
10. *Garcia v. San Antonio Metropolitan Transit Authority*, 469 U.S. 528 (1985).
11. See Michael S. Greve, *Real Federalism: Why It Matters, How It Could Happen* (Washington, D.C.: AEI Press, 1999).
12. *U.S. v. Lopez*, 514 U.S. 549 (1995).
13. *Seminole Tribe of Florida v. Florida*, 517 U.S. 44 (1996).
14. *Alden v. Maine*, 67 U.S.L.W. 1401 (1999).
15. *Printz v. U.S.* 521 U.S. 890 (1997).
16. *Brzonkala v. Morrison* (2000).
17. *Federal-State-Local Relations: Federal Grants in Aid*, House Committee on Government Operations, 85th Cong., 2d sess., p. 7.
18. State Legislatures September 1999, p. 24.

CHAPTER FIVE

1. See James A. Stimson, Michael B. Mackuen, and Robert S. Erikson, "Dynamic Representation," *American Political Science Review* 89 (September 1995); 543–61.
2. Robert S. Erikson, Norman R. Luttbeg, and Kent L. Tedin, *American Public Opinion*, 3rd ed. (New York: Macmillan, 1988).
3. *Public Opinion* 9 (September/October 1986): 32, also cited by Erikson et al., *American Public Opinion*, p. 55.
4. For a summary of recent literature on public opinion, see James Stimson, "Opinion and Representation," *American Political Science Review* 89 (March 1995): 179–83.
5. Sandra K. Schwartz, "Preschoolers and Politics," in *New Directions in Political Socialization*, eds. David C. Schwartz and Sandra K. Schwartz (New York: Free Press, 1975), p. 242.
6. M. Kent Jennings and Richard G. Niemi, *The Political Character of Adolescence* (Princeton, N.J.: Princeton University Press, 1974), p. 41.
7. David O. Sears, and Carolyn Funk, "Evidence of the Long-Term Persistence of Adults' Political Predispositions" *Journal of Politics* 61 (February 1999): 1–28.
8. Robert D. Hess and Judith V. Torney, *The Development of Political Attitudes in Children* (Chicago: Aldine, 1977), p. 42.
9. See also Ted G. Jelen, "The Political Consequences of Religious Group Attitudes," *Journal of Politics* 55 (February 1993): 178–90.
10. See John C. Green, "The Christian Right in the 1994 Elections," *P.S.: Political Science and Politics* 28 (March 1995): 5–23.
11. See M. Kent Jennings, "Residues of a Movement: The Aging of the American Protest Generation," *American Political Science Review* 81 (June 1987): 370–72; M. Kent Jennings and Richard G. Niemi, *Generational Politics* (Princeton, N.J.: Princeton University Press, 1982).
12. See also James A. Stimson, *Public Opinion in America: Moods, Cycles, and Swings* (Boulder, Colo.: Westview Press, 1991).
13. V. O. Key, Jr., *Public Opinion and American Democracy* (New York: Knopf, 1967), p. 536.
14. *Harper v. Virginia State Board of Elections*, 383 U.S. 663 (1966).
15. Congress had earlier passed the Voting Rights Act of 1970, which (1) extended the vote to eighteen-year-olds regardless of state law; (2) abolished residency requirements in excess of thirty days; and (3) prohibited literacy tests. However, there was some constitutional debate about the power of Congress to change state laws on voting age. Although Congress could end racial discrimination, extending the vote to eighteen-year-olds was a different matter. All previous extensions of the vote had come by constitutional amendment. Hence Congress quickly passed the Twenty-sixth Amendment.
16. Staci L. Rhine, "Registration Reform and Turnout," *American Politics Quarterly* 23 (October 1995): 409–26: Stephen Knack, "Does 'Motor Voter' Work?" *Journal of Politics* 57 (August 1995): 796–811.
17. *General Social Survey, 1998* (Chicago: National Opinion Research Center, 1999).
18. John E. Filer, Lawrence W. Kenny, and Rebecca B. Morton, "Redistribution, Income, and Voting," *American Journal of Political Science* 37 (February 1993): 63–87.
19. Sidney Verba, Kay Schlozman, Henry Brady, and Norman Nie, "Citizen Activity: Who Participates? What Do They Say?" *American Political Science Review* 87 (June 1993): 303–18.
20. See Katherine Tate, "Black Political Participation in the 1984 and 1988 Presidential Elections," *American Political Science Review* 85 (December 1991): 1159–76.
21. John Stuart Mill, *Considerations on Representative Government* (Chicago: Regnery, Gateway, 1962; original publication 1859), p. 144.
22. Ibid., p. 130.
23. Attributed to Arthur Hadley by Austin Ranney in "Non-Voting Is Not a Social Disease," *Public Opinion* 6 (November/December 1983): 17.
24. Quoted in ibid., p. 18.
25. Francis Fox Piven and Richard Cloward, *Why Americans Don't Vote* (New York: Pantheon, 1987).
26. Verba et al., "Citizen Activity."
27. Martin Luther King, Jr., "Letter from Birmingham City Jail," April 16, 1963.

CHAPTER SIX

1. E. E. Schattschneider, *The Semisovereign People* (New York: Holt, Rinehart & Winston, 1961), p. 68.
2. William A. Henry, "News as Entertainment," in *What's News*, ed. Elie Abel (San Francisco: Institute for Contemporary Studies, 1981), p. 133.
3. Shanto Iyengar, *Is Anyone Responsible? How Television Frames Political Issues* (Chicago: University of Chicago Press, 1991).
4. Michael Jay Robinson, "Just How Liberal Is the News?" *Public Opinion* 38 (February/March 1983): 55–60.
5. Ben J. Wattenberg, *The Good News Is the Bad News Is Wrong* (New York: Simon & Schuster, 1984).
6. Ted Smith, "The Watchdog's Bite," *American Enterprise* 2 (January/February 1990): 66.
7. Doris A. Graber, *Mass Media and American Politics* (Washington, D.C.: Congressional Quarterly Press, 1980), p. 49.
8. S. Robert Lichter, Stanley Rothman, and Linda S. Lichter, *The Media Elite* (Bethesda, Md.: Adler and Adler, 1986).
9. David Prindle, "Hollywood Liberalism" *Social Science Quarterly* 71 (March 1993): 121.
10. David C. Barker, "Rushed Decisions: Political Talk Radio and Vote Choice," *Journal of Politics* 61 (May 1999): 527–539.

11. See David S. Castle, "Media Coverage of Presidential Primaries," *American Politics Quarterly* 19 (January 1991): 13–42; Christine F. Ridout, "The Role of Media Coverage of Iowa and New Hampshire," *American Politics Quarterly* 19 (January 1991): 43–58.

12. Michael Robinson and Margaret Sheehan, *Over the Wire and on TV* (New York: Sage, 1983). See also S. Robert Lichter, Daniel Amundson, and Richard Noyes, *The Video Campaign* (Washington, D.C.: American Enterprise Institute, 1988).

13. Ribonson and Sheehan, *Over the Wire and on TV*, p. 138.

14. *New York Times v. U.S.*, 376 U.S. 713 (1971).

15. *New York Times v. Sullivan*, 376 U.S. 254 (1964).

16. Bernard Cohen, *The Press and Foreign Policy* (Princeton, N.J.: Princeton University Press, 1963), p. 16.

17. Austin Ranney, *Channels of Power* (New York: Basic Books, 1983), p. 81.

18. *Reno v. American Civil Liberties Union* 117 S.Ct. 2329 (1997).

19. Glenn W. Richardson, *American Government* on the Internet (Fort Worth: Harcourt Brace, 1999).

20. Benjamin I. Page, Robert Y. Shapiro, and Glen R. Dempsey, "What Moves Public Opinion," *American Political Science Review* 81 (March 1987): 23–43.

21. National Institute of Mental Health, *Television and Behavior* (Washington, D.C.: Government Printing Office, 1982).

22. Brandon Centerwall, "Exposure to Television as a Risk Factor for Violence," *American Journal of Epidemiology* 129 (April 1989): 643–52.

CHAPTER SEVEN

1. Gaetano Mosca, *The Ruling Class* (New York: McGraw-Hill, 1939), p. 51.

2. James Madison, *Federalist Papers*, No. 10, reprinted in the Appendix.

3. George Washington, Farewell Address, September 17, 1796, in *Documents on American History*, 10th ed., eds. Henry Steele Commager and Milton Cantor, Upper Saddle River, N.J.: Prentice Hall, 1988), 1: 172.

4. E. E. Schattschneider, *Party Government* (New York: Holt, Rinehart, and Winston, 1942), p. 1.

5. Conventions continue to play a modest role in nominations in some states:

   ● Colorado: Parties may hold a preprimary convention to designate a candidate to be listed first on the primary ballot. All candidates receiving at least 30 percent of the delegate vote will be listed on the primary ballot.

   ● Connecticut: Party conventions are held to endorse candidates. If no one challenges the endorsed candidate, no primary election is held. If a challenger receives 20 percent of the delegate vote, a primary election will be held to determine the party's nominee in the general election.

   ● New York: Party conventions choose the party's "designated" candidate in primary elections. Anyone receiving 25 percent of the delegates also appears on the ballot.

   ● Utah: Party conventions select party's nominees.

   ● Illinois, Indiana, Michigan, and South Carolina: Party conventions nominate candidates for some minor state offices.

6. For an argument that primary elections force parties to be more responsive to voters, see John G. Geer and Mark E. Shere, "Party Competition and the Prisoner's Dilemma: An Argument for the Direct Primary," *Journal of Politics* 54 (August 1992): 365–74.

7. For an up-to-date listing of state primaries and relevant information about them, see *The Book of the States*, published biannually by the Council of State Governments, Lexington, Kentucky.

8. Louisiana is unique in its nonpartisan statewide primary and general elections. All candidates, regardless of party affiliation, run in the same primary election. If a candidate gets more than 50 percent of the vote, he or she wins the office outright; otherwise the top two vote-getters, regardless of party affiliation, face off in the second election.

9. Congressional Quarterly, *National Party Conventions 1831–1996* (Washington, D.C.: CQ Press, 1997).

10. See John M. Bruce, John A. Clark, and John H. Kessel, "Advocacy Politics in Presidential Parties," *American Political Science Review* 85 (December 1991): 1115–25.

11. For evidence that the national party conventions raise the poll standings of their presidential nominees, see James E. Campbell, Lynna L. Cherry, and Kenneth A. Wink, "The Convention Bump," *American Politics Quarterly* 20 (July 1992): 287–307.

12. See John A. Clark, John M. Bruce, John H. Kessel, and William G. Jacoby, "I'd Rather Switch Than Fight: Lifelong Democrats and Converts to Republicanism among Campaign Activists," *American Journal of Political Science* 35 (August 1991): 577–97.

13. For a scholarly debate over realignment, see Byron E. Schafer, ed., *The End of Realignment: Interpreting American Election Eras* (Madison: University of Wisconsin Press, 1991).

14. See Harold W. Stanley and Richard G. Niemi, "Partisanship and Group Support, 1952–1988," *American Politics Quarterly* 19 (April 1991): 189–210; Patricia Hurley, "Partisan Realignment in the 1980's," *Journal of Politics* 53 (February 1991): 55–63.

15. See Theodore J. Lowi and Joseph Romance, *A Republic of Parties: Debating the Two-Party System* (Lanham, MD: Rowman and Littlefield, 1998).

CHAPTER EIGHT

1. Gerald Pomper, *Elections in America* (New York: Dodd, Mead, 1968).

2. Morris P. Fiorina, *Retrospective Voting in American National Elections* (New Haven, Conn.: Yale University Press, 1988).

3. Quoted in *Congressional Quarterly Almanac, 1965* (Washington, D.C.: Congressional Quarterly, Inc., 1966), p. 267.

4. Alan Ehrenhalt, *The United States of Ambition: Politicians, Power and the Pursuit of Office* (New York: Random House, 1991), p. 22.

5. Alan I. Abramowitz, "Incumbency, Campaign Spending, and the Decline of Competition in U.S. House Elections," *Journal of Politics* 53 (February 1991): 55–70.

6. Herbert Alexander as quoted in Richard R. Lau, et al., "The Effects of Negative Political Advertisements," *American Political Science Review* 93 (December 1999): 851–875.

7. Quotation from Richard R. Lau, *op. cit.* p. 851.

8. *Op. cit.*, p. 857.

9. In the important U.S. Supreme Court decision in *Buckley v. Valeo* in 1976, James L. Buckley, former U.S. senator from New York, and his brother, William F. Buckley, the well-known conservative commentator, argued successfully that the laws limiting an individual's right to participate in political campaigns—financially or otherwise—violated First Amendment freedoms. Specifically, the U.S. Supreme Court held that no government could limit individuals' rights to spend money or publish or broadcast their own views on issues or elections. Candidates can spend as much of their own money as they wish on their own campaigns. Private individuals can spend as much as they wish to circulate their own views on an election, although their contributions to candidates and parties can still be limited. The Court, however, permitted governmental limitations on parties and campaign organizations and allowed the use of federal funds for financing campaigns. *Buckley v. Valeo*, 424 U.S. 1 (1976).

10. David J. Lanoue and Peter R. Schrott, *The*

Joint Press Conference: History, Impact, and Prospects of American Presidential Debates (Westport, Conn.: Greenwood Press, 1991).

11. University-based political scientists rely heavily on a series of National Election Studies, originated at the Survey Research Center at the University of Michigan, which have surveyed the voting-age population in every presidential election and most congressional elections since 1952.

12. For an assessment of gender issues in Clinton's victory, see Marian Lief Palley, "Elections 1992 and the Thomas Appointment," *P. S.: Political Science and Politics* 26 (March 1993): 28–31.

13. See Martin P. Wattenberg, *The Rise of Candidate-Centered Politics* (Cambridge, Mass.: Harvard University Press, 1991).

14. For an argument that voters look ahead to the economic future and reward or punish the president based on rational expectations, see Michael B. MacKuen, Robert S. Erickson, and James A. Stimson, "Peasants or Bankers? The American Electorate and the U.S. Economy," *American Political Science Review* 86 (September 1992): 680–95.

CHAPTER NINE

1. Political scientist David Truman defined an interest group as "any group that is based on one or more shared attitudes and makes certain demands upon other groups or organizations in society." See *The Governmental Process* (New York: Knopf, 1971), p. 33.

2. James Madison, *Federalist Papers*, No. 10, reprinted in the Appendix.

3. Gale Research Company, *Encyclopedia of Associations*. 29th ed. (Detroit: Gale Research, 1995).

4. Jeffrey M. Berry, *The New Liberalism: The Rising Power of Citizen Groups*. Washington, D.C.: Brookings Institution Press, 1999).

5. For both theory and survey data on the sources of interest-group mobilization, see Jack L. Walker, *Mobilizing Interest Groups in America: Patrons, Professions, and Social Movements* (Ann Arbor: University of Michigan Press, 1991).

6. Kay Lehmann Scholzman, "What Accent the Heavenly Chorus? Political Equality and the American Pressure System," *Journal of Politics* 46 (November 1984): 1006–32; see also Jeffrey M. Berry, Kent E. Portney, and Ken Thomson, *The Case for Participatory Democracy* (Washington, D.C.: Brookings, 1994).

7. For evidence that vote buying on congressional roll calls is rare, see Janet M. Grenzke, "Shopping in the Congressional Supermarket: The Currency Is Complex," *American Journal of Political Science* 33 (February 1989): 1–24. But for evidence that committee participation by members of Congress is influenced by political action committee money, see Richard L. Hall and Frank W. Wayman, "Buying Time: Moneyed Interests and the Mobilization of Bias in Congressional Committees," *American Political Science Review* 84 (September 1990): 797–819.

8. See, for example, Mark E. Patterson, "The Presidency and Organized Interests: White House Patterns of Interest Group Liaison," *American Political Science Review* 86 (September 1992): 612–22.

9. Paul Starobin, "Merchant Marine: Too Close to Its Clients," *National Journal*, June 11, 1988.

10. *Brown v. Board of Education of Topeka*, 349 U.S. 294 (1955).

11. Samuel Huntington, *Political Order in Changing Societies* (New Haven, Conn.: Yale University Press, 1965), p. 28.

12. Mancur Olson, *The Rise and Decline of Nations* (New Haven, Conn.: Yale University Press, 1982).

CHAPTER TEN

1. James Madison, *Federalist Papers*, No. 10, reprinted in the Appendix.

2. Ibid.

3. Quoted in Jay M. Schafritz, *The HarperCollins Dictionary of American Government and Politics* (New York: HarperCollins, 1992), p. 56.

4. *McGrain v. Dougherty*, 273 U.S. 13J (1927).

5. *Baker v. Carr*, 369 U.S. 186 (1962); *Wesberry v. Sanders*, 370 U.S. 1 (1964).

6. *Gray v. Sanders*, 322 U.S. 368 (1963).

7. *Department of Commerce v. U.S. House of Representatives* (1999).

8. *Gaffney v. Cummings*, 412 U.S. 763 (1973).

9. *Davis v. Bandemer*, 478 U.S. 109 (1986).

10. *Thornburg v. Gingles*, 478 U.S. 30 (1986).

11. *Shaw v. Reno*, 125 L Ed 2d 511 (1993).

12. *Miller v. Johnson*, June 29, 1995.

13. *Congressional Quarterly Weekly Report*, Oct. 7, 1995, p. 3065.

14. For an in-depth analysis of who decides to run for Congress and who does not, see Linda L. Fowler and Robert D. McClure, *Political Ambition: Who Decides to Run for Congress* (New Haven, Conn.: Yale University Press, 1990).

15. See Michael K. Moore and John R. Hibbing, "Situational Dissatisfaction in Congress: Explaining Voluntary Departures." *Journal of Politics* 60 (November 1998), 1088–1107.

16. See Robert A. Bernstein, *Elections, Representation, and Congressional Voting Behavior* (Upper Saddle River, N.J.: Prentice Hall, 1989).

17. See Gary Jacobson, *The Politics of Congressional Elections*, 3rd ed. (New York: HarperCollins, 1992).

18. See David Epstein and Peter Zemsky, "Money Talks: Deterring Quality Challengers in Congressional Elections," *American Political Science Review* 89 (June 1995): 295–322.

19. See Thomas E. Mann and Raymond Wolfinger, "Candidates and Parties in Congressional Elections," *American Political Science Review* 84 (September 1990): 545–64.

20. See Mary T. Hanna, "Political Science Caught Flat-Footed by Midterm Elections," *Chronicle of Higher Education*, November 30, 1994, pp. B1–2.

21. See Michael Malbin, *Unelected Representatives* (New York: Basic Books, 1980).

22. U.S. House of Representatives, Commission on Administrative Review, *Administrative Reorganization and Legislative Management*, 95th Cong., 1st sess., H. Doc. 95-232, pp. 17–19.

23. Richard F. Fenno, *Home Style* (Boston: Little, Brown, 1978).

24. John R. Johannes, "Casework in the House," in *The House at Work*, ed. Joseph Cooper (Austin: University of Texas Press, 1981).

25. Roger H. Davidson and Walter J. Oleszak, *Congress and Its Members* (Washington, DC: CQ Press, 2000), p. 419.

26. Glenn R. Parker, *Characteristics of Congress* (Upper Saddle River, N.J.: Prentice Hall, 1989), p. 30.

27. See David W. Rohde, *Parties and Leaders in the Postreform House* (Chicago: University of Chicago Press, 1991).

28. Barbara Sinclair, "The Emergence of Strong Leadership in the House of Representatives," *Journal of Politics* 54 (August 1992): 657–84.

29. Gary W. Cox and Eric Magar, "How Much Is Majority Status in the U.S. Congress Worth?" *American Political Science Review* 93 (June 1999): 299–310.

30. Roger H. Davidson and Walter J. Oleszek, *Congress and Its Members* (Washington, D.C.: CQ Press, 1981), p. 170.

31. John R. Hibbing, *Congressional Careers* (Chapel Hill: University of North Carolina Press, 1991).

32. See Charles Stewart and Tim Groseclose, "The Value of Committee Seats in the United States Senate," *American Journal of Political Science* 43 (July 1999): 963–973.

33. See John W. Kingdon, *Congressmen's Voting Decisions*, 3rd ed. (Ann Arbor: University of Michigan Press, 1989).

34. Ibid., p. 41.

35. Larry Markinson, *The Cash Constituents of Congress* (Washington, D.C.: CQ Press, 1992).

36. Kingdon, *Congressmen's Voting Decisions*, pp. 31–32.

37. Donald Matthews, *U.S. Senators and Their World* (New York: Vintage Books, 1960).

38. David Rohde, Norman J. Ornstein, and Robert L. Peabody, "Political Change and Legislative Norms," in *Studies of Congress*, ed.

Glenn R. Parker (Washington, D.C.: CQ Press, 1985), p. 175.

39. See John R. Hibbing, "Contours of the Modern Congressional Career," *American Political Science Review* 85 (June 1991): 405–28.

40. Parker, *Characteristics of Congress*, p. 12.

41. Richard Fenno, *Power of the Purse* (Boston: Little, Brown, 1965), p. 620.

42. Ibid., p. 73.

43. See David R. Mayhew, *Divided We Govern* (New Haven, CT: Yale University Press, 1991); Sarah A. Binder, "The Dynamics of Legislative Gridlock," *American Political Science Review* 93 (September 1999): 519–533.

44. *Congressional Quarterly Weekly Report*, November 23, 1991, p. 3437.

CHAPTER ELEVEN

1. For an argument that presidents encourage people to think of them as "the single head of government and moral leader of the nation who speaks for all of the people," see Barbara Hinckley, *The Symbolic Presidency: How Presidents Portray Themselves* (New York: Routledge, 1991).

2. See Theodore Lowi, *The Personal President* (Ithaca, N.Y.: Cornell University Press, 1987).

3. See Michael Less Benedict, *The Impeachment and Trial of Andrew Johnson* (New York: Norton, 1973).

4. William Howard Taft, *Our Chief Magistrate and His Powers* (New York: Columbia University Press, 1938), p. 138, reprinted in *The Presidency*, ed. John P. Roche (New York: Harcourt Brace Jovanovich, 1964), p. 23.

5. Quoted in Arthur B. Tourtellot, *Presidents on the Presidency* (New York: Doubleday, 1964), pp. 55–56.

6. Quoted in James MacGregor Burns, *John Kennedy: A Political Profile* (New York: Harcourt Brace, 1959), p. 275.

7. *United States v. Nixon* 418 U.S. 683 (1974).

8. *Nixon v. Fitzgerald* 457 U.S. 731 (1982).

9. *Clinton v. Jones* 520 U.S. 681 (1997).

10. Quoted in Richard Neustadt, *Presidential Power* (New York: Wiley, 1960), p. 9.

11. See George C. Edwards, *The Public Presidency* (New York: St. Martin's Press, 1983). See also Richard A. Brody, *Assessing Presidents: The Media, Elite Opinion, and Public Support* (Stanford, Calif.: Stanford University Press, 1991).

12. See Paul Brace and Barbara Hinckley, "The Structure of Presidential Approval," *Journal of Politics* 53 (November 1991): 993–1017.

13. See Charles Ostrom and Dennis Simon, "The President's Public," *American Journal of Political Science* 32 (November 1988): 1096–1119; and Ostrow and Simon, "The President and the Political Use of Force," *American Political Science Review* 80 (June 1986): 541–66.

14. John Mueller, *War, Presidents, and Public Opinion* (New York: Wiley, 1973).

15. For an irreverent description of White House reporting, see Sam Donaldson, *Hold On, Mr. President* (New York: Random House, 1987).

16. See George C. Edwards and B. Dan Wood, "Who Influences Whom," *American Political Science Review* 93 (June 1999): 327–344.

17. *Youngstown Sheet and Tube v. Sawyer*, 343 U.S. 579 (1951).

18. Kenneth R. Mayer, "Executive Orders and Presidential Power," *Journal of Politics*, 61 (May, 1999), 445–466; Christopher J. Deering and Forrest Maltzman, "The Politics of Executive Orders," *Political Research Quarterly*, 52 (December 1999), 767–783.

19. See also Jeffrey E. Cohen, *The Politics of the U.S. Cabinet* (Pittsburgh: University of Pittsburgh Press, 1988).

20. See Stanley Rothman and S. Robert Lichter, "How Liberal Are Bureaucrats?" *Regulation*, November–December 1983, pp. 16–22, for survey data on the voting behavior and political ideology of federal bureaucrats.

Earlier studies asserted that the party identification of bureaucrats reflected that of the general public; see Steven Thomas Seitz, *Bureaucracy, Policy and the Public* (St. Louis: Mosby, 1978).

21. See Bradley H. Patterson, Jr., *The Ring of Power* (New York: Basic Books, 1988).

22. John Kingdon, *Agenda, Alternatives, and Public Policies* (Boston: Little, Brown, 1984), p. 25.

23. See Daniel E. Ingberman and Dennis A. Yao, "Presidential Commitment and the Veto," *American Journal of Political Science* 35 (May 1991): 357–89; and Samuel B. Hoff, "Saying No," *American Politics Quarterly* 19 (July 1991): 310–23.

24. For a discussion of the factors affecting the use of the presidential veto, see John T. Woolley, "Institutions, the Election Cycle, and the Presidential Veto," *American Journal of Political Science* 35 (May 1991): 279–304.

25. *Clinton v. City of New York* 524 U.S. 417 (1998).

26. G. J. A. O'Toole, *Honorable Treachery: A History of U.S. Intelligence from the American Revolution to the CIA* (New York: Atlantic Monthly Press, 1991).

27. *Mora v. McNamara*, 389 U.S. 934 (1964); *Massachusetts v. Laird*, 400 U.S. 886 (1970). The Court specifically refused to intervene in the conduct of the Vietnam War by Presidents Johnson and Nixon.

28. Jules Witcover, *Crap Shoot: Rolling the Dice on the Vice Presidency* (New York: Crow Publishing, 1992).

CHAPTER TWELVE

1. "Red tape" derives its meaning from the use of reddish tape by seventeenth-century English courts to bind legal documents. Unwrapping court orders entangled one in "red tape." See Herbert Kaufman, *Red Tape: Its Uses and Abuses* (Washington, D.C.: Brookings Institution, 1977).

2. H. H. Gerth and C. Wright Mills, *From Max Weber* (New York: Oxford Press, 1958).

3. James Q. Wilson, *Bureaucracy: What Government Agencies Do and Why They Do It* (New York: Basic Books, 1989).

4. William Niskanen, *Bureaucracy and Representative Government* (Chicago: Aldine, 1971).

5. The constitutional question of whether

Congress can establish an executive branch commission and protect its members from dismissal by the president was settled in *Humphrey's Executor v. United States* (1935). Franklin Roosevelt fired Humphrey from the Federal Trade Commission despite a fixed term set by Congress. Humphrey died shortly afterward, and when the executors of his estate sued for his back pay, the Supreme Court ruled that his firing was illegal.

6. See Nicholas Henry, *Public Administration and Public Affairs*, 7th ed. (Upper Saddle River, N.J.: Prentice Hall, 1999), Chapter 11.

7. Quoted in U.S. Civil Service Commission, *Biography of an Ideal: A History of the Civil*

Service System (Washington, D.C.: Government Printing Office, 1973), p. 16.

8. *U.S. Civil Service Commission v. Letter Carriers* (1973).

9. See U.S. House of Representatives Committee on Post Office and Civil Service, *The Senior Executive Service* (Washington, D.C.: Government Printing Office, 1984).

10. Paul C. Light, *Thickening Government: Federal Hierarchy and the Diffusion of Accountability* (Washington, D.C.: Brookings Institution, 1995).

11. See Stanley Rothman and S. Robert Lichter, "How Liberal Are the Bureaucrats?" *Regulation*, November–December 1983.

12. Aaron Wildavsky, *The New Politics of the Budgetary Process* (Glenview, Ill.: Scott, Foresman, 1988), p. 8.

13. See also Lance T. LeLoup, *Budgetary Politics*, 4th ed. (Brunswick, Ohio: Kings Court, 1988).

14. Robert Crandell and Jerry Ellig, *Economic Deregulation and Consumer Choice* (Fairfax, VA: Center for Market Processes, 1997).

15. *Ibid.*

16. General Accounting Office, *Regulatory Enforcement Fairness Act Report*, 1999.

17. Thomas D. Hopkins, *Regulatory Costs in Profile*, Washington: Center for the Study of American Business, 1996.

18. Richard K. Vedder, "Federal Regulation's Impact on the Productivity Slowdown: A Trillion Dollar Drag," *Policy Study*, Center for the Study of American Business, July, 1996.

19. For research suggesting that the appointive power is a more important instrument of political control of the bureaucracy than budgets or legislation, see B. Dan Wood and Richard W. Waterman, "The Dynamics of Political Control of the Bureaucracy," *American Political Science Review* 83 (September 1991): 801–28.

20. See Joel D. Aberbach, *Keeping a Watchful Eye: The Politics of Congressional Oversight* (Washington, D.C.: Brookings Institution, 1990).

21. Evidence of the effectiveness of interventions by members of Congress in local offices of federal agencies is provided by John T. Scholz, Jim Twombly, and Barbara Headrick, "Street-Level Political Controls over Federal Bureaucracy," *American Political Science Review* 85 (September 1991): 829–50.

22. Bradley Cannon and Michael Giles, "Recurring Litigants: Federal Agencies before the Supreme Court," *Western Political Quarterly* 15 (September 1972): 183–91; Reginald S. Sheehan, "Federal Agencies and the Supreme Court," *American Politics Quarterly* 20 (October 1992): 478–500.

CHAPTER THIRTEEN

1. Alexis de Tocqueville, *Democracy in America* (1835; New York: Mentor Books, 1956), p. 75.

2. Felix Frankfurter, "The Supreme Court and the Public," *Forum* 83 (June 1930): 332.

3. Alexander Hamilton, *Federalist Papers*, No. 78 (New York: Modern Library, 1937), p. 505.

4. *Marbury v. Madison*, 1 Cranch 137 (1803).

5. *Dred Scott v. Sandford*, 19 Howard 393 (1857).

6. *National Labor Relations Board v. Jones and Laughlin Steel Corp.*, 301 U.S. 1 (1937).

7. *Buckley v. Valeo*, 424 U.S. 1 (1976).

8. *Ex parte Milligan*, 4 Wallace 2 (1866).

9. *Youngstown Sheet and Tube Co. v. Sawyer*, 343 U.S. 579 (1952).

10. *United States v. Nixon*, 418 U.S. 683 (1974).

11. *Brown v. Board of Education of Topeka*, 347 U.S. 483 (1954).

12. *Roe v. Wade*, 410 U.S. 113 (1973).

13. Lawrence Baum, *The Supreme Court*, 4th ed. (Washington, D.C.: CQ Press, 1992).

14. *West Virginia Board of Education v. Barnette*, 319 U.S. 624 (1943).

15. Quoted in Henry J. Abraham, *Justices and Presidents*, 3rd ed. (New York: Oxford University Press, 1992), p. 7.

16. Quoted in Charles P. Curtis, *Lions under the Throne* (Boston: Houghton Mifflin, 1947), p. 281.

17. Lee Epstein and Thomas G. Walker, *Constitutional Law for a Changing America*, 3rd ed., Washington, D.C.: CQ Press, 1998, pp. 33–34.

18. William O. Douglas, "Stare Decisis," *Record*, April 1947, cited in Henry J. Abraham, *The Judicial Process* (New York: Oxford University Press, 1968), p. 58.

19. *Flast v. Cohen*, 392 U.S. 83 (1968).

20. *Gideon v. Wainwright*, 372 U.S. 335 (1963).

21. *Missouri v. Jenkins*, 110 S. C. 1651 (1990).

22. Robert Scigliano, *The Supreme Court and the Presidency* (New York: Free Press, 1971), pp. 147–48.

23. See Bryon J. Moraski and Charles R. Shipan. "The Politics of Supreme Court Nominations," *American Journal of Political Science*, Vol. 43 (October, 1999) 1069–1095.

24. At one time the U.S. Supreme Court was legally required to accept certain "writs of appeal," but today very few cases come to the Court in this fashion.

25. *University of California Regents v. Bakke*, 438 U.S. 265 (1978).

26. Thomas Marshall, *Public Opinion and the Supreme Court*, New York: Unwin Hyman, 1989, p. 97.

27. *Compendium, op. cit.*, p. 572, 573.

28. *Compendium, op. cit.*, p. 582.

29. Lee Epstein and C. K. Rowland, "Debunking the Myth of Interest Group Invincibility," *American Political Science Review*, Vol. 85, (1991): 205–217.

30. *Abington School District v. Schempp*, 374 U.S. 203 (1963).

31. President Andrew Jackson's comments came in response to the Court's ruling in the case of *Cherokee Nation v. Georgia* (1831) and *Worcester v. Georgia* (1832), which forbade the federal or state governments from seizing Native American lands and forcing the people to move. Refusal by Jackson, an old "Indian fighter," to enforce the Court's decisions resulted in the infamous "Trail of Tears," the forced march of the Georgia Cherokees that left one-quarter of them dead along the path west.

32. See Baum, *Supreme Court*, p. 233.

33. *Grove City College v. Bell*, 465 U.S. 555 (1984).

34. *Pollock v. Farmer's Loan*, 158 U.S. 601 (1895).

CHAPTER FOURTEEN

1. James Madison, *Federalist Papers*, No. 10, reprinted in the Appendix.

2. *West Virginia Board of Education v. Barnette*, 319 U.S. 624 (1943).

3. *Barron v. Baltimore*, 7 Peters 243 (1833).

4. *Slaughter-House Cases*, 16 Wallace 36 (1873).

5. *Hurtado v. California*, 110 U.S. 516 (1884).

6. *Gitlow v. New York*, 268 U.S. 652 (1925).

7. For an argument that Madison and some other framers not only were concerned with lessening religious conflict but also were hostile to religion generally, see Thomas Lindsay, "James Madison on Religion and Politics," *American Political Science Review* 85 (December 1991): 1051–65.

8. *Reynolds v. United States*, 98 U.S. 145 (1879).

9. *Pierce v. Society of Sisters*, 268 U.S. 510 (1925).

10. *Cantwell v. Connecticut*, 310 U.S. 296 (1940).

11. *Employment Division v. Smith*, 494 U.S. 872 (1990).

12. *Wisconsin v. Yoder*, 406 U.S. 295 (1972).

13. *Church of Lukumi Babalu Aye v. City of Hialeah* 508 U.S. 520 (1993).

14. *Bob Jones University v. United States*, 461 U.S. 574 (1983).

15. *Employment Division of Oregon v. Smith*, 494 U.S. 872 (1990).

16. *Goldman v. Weinberger*, 475 U.S. 503 (1986).

17. *Everson v. Board of Education*, 330 U.S. 1, 15, 16 (1947).

18. Ibid.

19. *Zorach v. Clausen*, 343 U.S. 306 (1952).

20. Opening public meetings with prayer was ruled constitutional as "a tolerable acknowledgment of beliefs widely held among the people of this country." *Marsh v. Chambers*, 463 U.S. 783 (1983).

21. *Lemon v. Kurtzman*, 403 U.S. 602 (1971).

22. *Muebler v. Adams*, 463 U.S. 388 (1983).

23. *Tilton v. Richardson*, 403 U.S. 672 (1971).

24. *Lambs Chapel v. Center Moriches Union Free School District*, 508 U.S. 384 (1993).

25. *Rosenberger v. University of Virginia*, 515 U.S. 819 (1995).

26. *Walz v. Tax Commission*, 397 U.S. 664 (1970).

27. *Board of Education v. Mergens*, 497 U.S. 111 (1990).

28. *McGowan v. Maryland*, 366 U.S. 429 (1961), and *Braunfeld v. Brown*, 366 U.S. 599 (1961).

29. *County of Allegheny v. ACLU*, 492 U.S. 573 (1989).

30. *Edwards v. Aguillard*, 482 U.S. 578 (1987).

31. *Engle v. Vitale*, 370 U.S. 421 (1962).

32. *Abington School District v. Schempp*, 374 U.S. 203 (1963).

33. *Lee v. Weisman*, 505 U.S. 577 (1992).

34. *Wisconsin v. Yoder*, 406 U.S. 295 (1972).

35. *Employment Division v. Smith*, 494 U.S. 872 (1990).

36. *Schenck v. United States*, 249 U.S. 47 (1919).

37. *Gitlow v. New York*, 268 U.S. 652 (1925).

38. *Schenck v. United States*, 249 U.S. 47, 52 (1919).

39. *Whitney v. California*, 274 U.S. 357, 377 (1927), concurring opinion.

40. *Thomas v. Collins*, 323 U.S. 516 (1945).

41. *Dennis v. United States*, 341 U.S. 494 (1951).

42. *Yates v. United States*, 354 U.S. 298 (1957).

43. *Albertson v. Subversive Activities Control Board*, 382 U.S. 70 (1965).

44. *Whitehill v. Elkins*, 389 U.S. 54 (1967).

45. *United States v. Robel*, 389 U.S. 258 (1967).

46. *Aptheker v. Secretary of State*, 378 U.S. 500 (1964).

47. *Tinker v. Des Moines Independent Community School District*, 393 U.S. 503 (1969).

48. *Brandenburg v. Ohio*, 395 U.S. 444 (1969).

49. *Texas v. Johnson*, 491 U.S. 397 (1989).

50. *United States v. O'Brien*, 391 U.S. 367 (1968).

51. *Texas v. Johnson*, 491 U.S. 397 (1989).

52. *Chaplinsky v. New Hampshire*, 315 U.S. 568 (1942).

53. *Terminiello v. Chicago*, 337 U.S. 1 (1949).

54. *Cohen v. California*, 403 U.S. 15 (1971).

55. Justice Louis D. Brandeis opinion in *Whitney v. California*, 274 U.S. 357 (1927).

56. *R.A.V. v. City of St. Paul, Minnesota*, 505 U.S. 377 (1992).

57. *Wisconsin v. Mitchell*, 508 U.S. 476 (1993).

58. *Virginia State Board of Pharmacy v. Virginia Consumer Council, Inc.*, 425 U.S. 748 (1976).

59. *Bates v. Arizona State Bar*, 433 U.S. 350 (1977).

60. *Linmark Associates, Inc. v. Township of Willingboro*, 431 U.S. 85 (1977).

61. *Bigelow v. Virginia*, 421 U.S. 809 (1975).

62. *New York Times v. Sullivan*, 376 U.S. 254 (1964).

63. *Gertz v. Robert Welch, Inc.*, 418 U.S. 323 (1974).

64. *Roth v. United States*, 354 U.S. 476 (1957).

65. *Jacobellis v. Ohio*, 378 U.S. 184 (1964).

66. *Roth v. United States*, 354 U.S. 476 (1957).

67. *Jacobellis v. Ohio*, 378 U.S. 184 (1964).

68. *Roth v. United States*, 354 U.S. 476 (1957).

69. Bob Woodward and Scott Armstrong, *The Brethren* (New York: Avon, 1979), p. 233.

70. *Miller v. California*, 5413 U.S. 15 (1973).

71. Joseph F. Kobylka, *The Politics of Obscenity* (Westport, Conn.: Greenwood Press, 1991).

72. *Barnes v. Glenn Theatre*, 501 U.S. 560 (1991).

73. *New York v. Ferber*, 458 U.S. 747 (1982).

74. *Reno v. American Civil Liberties Union*, 117 S.Ct. 2329 (1997).

75. *Near v. Minnesota*, 283 U.S. 697 (1931).

76. *New York Times v. United States*, 403 U.S. 713 (1971).

77. *Mutual Film Corp. v. Industrial Commission*, 236 U.S. 230 (1915).

78. *Times Film Corporation v. Chicago*, 365 U.S. 43 (1961).

79. *Freedman v. Maryland*, 380 U.S. 51 (1965).

80. *Young v. American Mini Theaters, Inc.*, 427 U.S. 50 (1976).

81. *Red Lion Broadcasting Co. v. Federal Communications Commission*, 395 U.S. 367 (1969).

82. *Miami Herald Publishing Co. v. Tornillo*, 418 U.S. 241 (1974).

83. *Branzburg v. Hayes*, 408 U.S. 665 (1972).

84. *Zurcher v. Stanford Daily*, 436 U.S. 547 (1978).

85. *NAACP v. Alabama ex rel. Patterson*, 357 U.S. 449 (1958).

86. *City of Chicago v. Morales*, 527 U.S. 41 (1999).

87. *Healy v. James*, 408 U.S. 169 (1972).

88. *National Socialist Party of America v. Skokie*, 432 U.S. 43 (1977).

89. *Frisby v. Schultz*, 487 U.S. 474 (1988).

90. *Schenck v. Pro Choice Network of Western New York*, 519 U.S. 357 (1997).

91. James Madison, *Federalist Papers*, No. 46.

92. *Ex parte Milligan*, 4 Wallace 2 (1866).

93. *Duncan v. Kahanamosby*, 327 U.S. 304 (1946).

94. *Illinois v. Gates*, 462 U.S. 213 (1983).

95. *Arizona v. Hicks*, 480 U.S. 321 (1987).

96. *Knowles v. Iowa*, 525 U.S. 113 (1998).

97. *Olmstead v. U.S.*, 277 U.S. 438 (1928).

98. *Katz v. U.S.*, 309 U.S. 347 (1967).

99. *U.S. v. White*, 401 U.S. 745 (1971).

100. *Skinner v. Railway Labor Executive Association*, 489 U.S. 602 (1989).

101. *National Treasury Employees Union v. Von Rabb*, 489 U.S. 656 (1989).

102. *Veronia School District v. Acton*, 515 U.S. 646 (1995).

103. *Chandler v. Miller*, 520 U.S. 305 (1997).

104. *United States v. Watson*, 423 U.S. 411 (1976).

105. *Payton v. New York*, 445 U.S. 573 (1980).

106. *Wilson v. Layne*, 526 U.S. 603 (1999).

107. *Spano v. New York*, 360 U.S. 315 (1959).

108. *Gideon v. Wainwright*, 372 U.S. 335 (1963).

109. *Escobedo v. Illinois*, 378 U.S. 478 (1964).

110. *Miranda v. Arizona*, 384 U.S. 436 (1966).

111. Stephen Wasby, *The Impact of the United States Supreme Court* (Homewood, Ill.: Dorsey Press, 1970).

112. *Mapp v. Ohio*, 367 U.S. 643 (1961).

113. *United States v. Leon*, 468 U.S. 897 (1984).

114. *Illinois v. Perkins*, 497 U.S. 177 (1990).

115. *United States v. Salerno*, 481 U.S. 739 (1987).

116. *U.S. v. Marion*, 404 U.S. 307 (1971).

117. *Barker v. Wingo*, 407 U.S. 514 (1972).

118. *Illinois v. Allen*, 397 U.S. 337 (1970).

119. *Maryland v. Craig*, 497 U.S. 1 (1990).

120. *Brady v. Maryland*, 373 U.S. 83 (1963).

121. *Batson v. Kentucky*, 476 U.S. 79 (1986).

122. *Sheppard v. Maxwell*, 384 U.S. 333 (1966).

123. *Williams v. Florida*, 399 U.S. 78 (1970).

124. *Johnson v. Louisiana*, 406 U.S. 356 (1972); *Apodaca v. Oregon*, 406 U.S. 404 (1972).

125. U.S. Department of Justice, *The Prevalence of Guilty Pleas* (Washington, D.C.: Government Printing Office, 1984).

126. *U.S. v. Perez*, 9 Wheat. 579 (1824).

127. *Heath v. Alabama*, 474 U.S. 82 (1985).

128. *Furman v. Georgia*, 408 U.S. 238 (1972).

129. *Gregg v. Georgia*, 428 U.S. 153 (1976); *Proffitt v. Florida*, 428 U.S. 242 (1976); *Jurek v. Texas*, 428 U.S. 262 (1976).

130. *McCleskey v. Kemp*, 481 U.S. 279 (1987).

131. *Felker v. Turpin*, 518 U.S. 1051 (1996).

CHAPTER FIFTEEN

1. See Sidney Verba and Gary R. Orren, *Equality in America* (Cambridge, Mass.: Harvard University Press, 1985).

2. See C. Vann Woodward, *Reunion and Reaction* (Boston: Little, Brown, 1951), and Woodward, *The Strange Career of Jim Crow* (New York: Oxford University Press, 1957).

3. *Civil Rights Cases*, 100 U.S. 3 (1883).

4. *Plessy v. Ferguson*, 163 U.S. 537 (1896).

5. *Sweatt v. Painter*, 339 U.S. 629 (1950).

6. *Brown v. Board of Education of Topeka*, 347 U.S. 483 (1954).

7. Kenneth Clark, *Dark Ghetto* (New York: Harper & Row, 1965), p. 75.

8. The Supreme Court ruled that Congress was bound to respect the Equal Protection Clause of the Fourteenth Amendment even though the amendment is directed at states, because equal protection is a liberty guaranteed by the Fifth Amendment. *Bolling v. Sharpe*, 347 U.S. 497 (1954).

9. *Brown v. Board of Education of Topeka* (II), 349 U.S. 294 (1955).

10. *Alexander v. Holmes Board of Education*, 396 U.S. 19 (1969).

11. *Swann v. Charlotte-Mecklenburg County Board of Education*, 402 U.S. (1971).

12. *Milliken v. Bradley*, 418 U.S. 717 (1974).

13. *Board of Education v. Dowell*, 498 U.S. 550 (1991).

14. Martin Luther King, Jr., "Letter fro Birmingham City Jail," April 16, 1963.

15. General Social Survey, 1998.

16. Princeton Survey Research/*Newsweek*, April 1999. As reported in *The Polling Report*, June 7, 1999.

17. *University of California Regents v. Bakke*, 438 U.S. 265 (1978).

18. Bakke's overall grade point average was 3.46, and the average for special admissions students was 2.62. Bakke's MCAT scores were verbal, 96; quantitative, 94; science, 97; general information, 72. The average MCAT scores for special admissions students were verbal, 34; quantitative, 30; science, 37; general information, 18.

19. *United Steelworkers of America v. Weber*, 443 U.S. 193 (1979).

20. *United States v. Paradise*, 480 U.S. 149 (1987).

21. *Firefighters Local Union 1784 v. Stotts*, 467 U.S. 561 (1984).

22. *City of Richmond v. Crosen Co.*, 488 U.S. 469 (1989).

23. *Adarand Construction v. Pena*, 132 L Ed 2d 158 (1995).

24. *Metro Broadcasting v. F.C.C.*, 497 U.S. 547 (1990).

25. *Hopwood v. Texas*, 78 F. 3d 932 (1996).

26. *Hopwood v. Texas*, 116 S. Ct. 2581 (1996).

27. See Justice Antonin Scalia's dissenting opinion in *Johnson v. Transportation Agency of Santa Clara County*, 480 U.S. 616 (1987).

28. *Wards Cove Packing Co., Inc., v. Antonio*, 490 U.S. 642 (1989).

29. *Congressional Quarterly Weekly Report, June 8, 1991*, p. 1501.

30. *Coalition for Economic Equity v. Pete Wilson*, Ninth Circuit Court of Appeals, April 1997.

31. *Bradwell v. Illinois*, 16 Wall 130 (1873).

32. *Reed v. Reed*, 404 U.S. 71 (1971).

33. *Stanton v. Stanton*, 421 U.S. 7 (1975).

34. *Craig v. Boren*, 429 U.S. 190 (1976).

35. *Dothard v. Rawlinson*, 433 U.S. 321 (1977).

36. *Arizona v. Norris*, 103 S. Ct. 3492 (1983).

37. *EEOC v. Madison Community School District*, 55 U.S.L.W. 2644 (1987).

38. *Michael M. v. Superior Court of Sonoma County*, 450 U.S. 464 (1981).

39. *Rostker v. Goldberg*, 453 U.S. 57 (1981).

40. *Statistical Abstract of the United States, 1995*, p. 403.

41. National Research Council, National Academy of Sciences, *Women's Work, Men's Work* (Washington, D.C.: National Academy Press, 1985).

42. See Thomas R. Dye, *Who's Running America?* 6th ed. (Englewood Cliffs, N.J.: Prentice Hall, 1994).

43. Susan Fraker, "Why Women Aren't Getting to the Top," *Fortune*, April 16, 1984, pp. 40–45.

44. Rudolpho O. dela Garza et al., *Latino Voices: Mexican, Puerto Rican, and Cuban Perspectives on American Politics* (Boulder, Colo.: Westview Press, 1992).

45. See F. Luis Garcia, *Latinos in the Political System* (Notre Dame, Ind.: Notre Dame University Press, 1988).

46. Linda Chavez, "Tequila Sunrise: The Slow But Steady Progress of Hispanic Immigrants," *Policy Review* (Spring 1989): 64–67.

47. Peter Mathiessen, *Sal Si Puedes: Ceasar Chavez and the New American Revolution*. New York: Random House, 1969.

48. *Plyer v. Doe*, 457 U.S. 202 (1982).

49. Southwest Voter Research Institute, San Antonio, Texas, 1995.

50. *Morton v. Mancari*, 417 U.S. 535 (1974).

51. See Joseph P. Shapiro, *No Pity: People with Disabilities Forging a New Civil Rights Movement* (New York: Times Books/Random House, 1993).

52. *U.S. News and World Report*, Feb. 9, 1998.

53. *San Antonio Independent School District v. Rodriquez*, 411 U.S. 1 (1973).

54. *Williamson v. Lee Optical of Oklahoma*, 348 U.S. 483 (1955).

55. *Gideon v. Wainwright*, 372 U.S. 335 (1963).

56. *Harper v. Virginia State Board of Elections*, 383 U.S. 663 (1966).

57. *Harris v. McRae*, 448 U.S. 297 (1980).

58. *Rodriguez v. San Antonio Independent School District*, 411 U.S. 1 (1973).

59. *Serrano v. Priest*, 5 Cal. 3d 584 (1971).

PHOTO CREDITS

Chapter 1: Nick Ut/AP/Wide World Photos, 1; Trippet/SIPA Press, 2 (top left); Brad Markel/Liaison Agency, Inc., 2 (top right); Richard Sheinwald/AP/Wide World Photos, 2 (bottom left); UPI/Corbis, 2 (bottom right); The White House Photo Office, 5 (Johnson, Nixon, Carter); Gerald R. Ford Library, 9 (Ford); Michael Evans/The White House Photo Office, 9 (Reagan); Susan Biddle/The White House Photo Office, 9 (Bush); AP/Wide World Photos, 9 (Clinton); Copyright Flip Schulke, 8; W. Wellstood/Library of Congress, 14; Corbis, 15; Reuters/Corbis, 16; Don Hebib/Concord Monitor/Impact Visuals Photo & Graphics, Inc., 17.

Chapter 2: Frank Weise/AP/Wide World Photos, 24; Fred Prousaer/Reuters/Archive Photos, 27 (left); Rose Prouser/Reuters/Archive Photos, 27 (right); Smith/Monkmeyer Press, 32 (left); Rob Crandall/Stock Boston, 32 (right); Spencer Grant/Liaison Agency, Inc., 37 (top); Allan Tannenbaum/Corbis Sygma, 37 (bottom); Jon Levy/Liaison Agency, Inc., 43; Stephen Ferry/Liaison Agency, Inc., 44 (left); Nina Berman/SIPA Press, 44 (right); United States Senate, 45; Henry Abrams/UPI/Corbis, 50 (left); M. Richards/PhotoEdit, 50 (right).

Chapter 3: The Granger Collection, 54; The Granger Collection, 57; The Granger Collection, 59; Library of Congress, 62; London Illustrated News/Library of Congress, 65; Corbis, 68; J. Scott Applewhite/AP/Wide World Photos, 69; Stan Wakefield/Pearson Education/PH College, 73 (left and center); Irene Springer/Pearson Education/PH College 73 (right); John van der Lyn/White House Historical Association, 78; Stan Wakefield/Pearson Education/PH College, 82.

Chapter 4: Paul Vathis/AP/Wide World Photos, 88; Stan Wakefield/Pearson Education/PH College, 91 (top); Reuters/Vincent Kessler/Archive Photos, 91 (center); Dave Gaywood/SIPA Press, 91 (bottom); AP/Wide World Photos,

97; Thomas C. Roche/Library of Congress, 103; AP/Wide World Photos, 104; Toby Talbot/AP/Wide World Photos, 105; R. Ellis/Corbis Sygma, 106; Stephen Ferry/Liaison Agency, Inc., 109; David Woo/Dallas Morning News/Corbis/Sygma, 114.

Chapter 5: Steve Liss/Liaison Agency, Inc., 118; Dian Bondareff/AP/Wide World Photos, 127 (bottom); Larry Fisher/Quad-City Times/AP/Wide World Photos, 136; UPI/Corbis, 140; Corbis, 141; Tony Freeman/PhotoEdit, 144; Fred Blackwell/Jackson Daily News/AP/Wide World Photos, 152.

Chapter 6: Reuters/Jim Bourg/Archive Photos, 156; Tom Prettyman/PhotoEdit, 161; Jim Cole/AP/Wide World Photos, 162; Marty Lederhandler/AP/Wide World Photos, 163; Peter Morgan/Reuters/Archive Photos, 164; Andy King/Corbis Sygma, 166; Brooks Kraft/Corbis Sygma, 168; AP Wide World Photos, 177; UPI/Corbis, 183.

Chapter 7: Regina Celania/The Ottumwa Courier/AP/Wide World Photos, 186; The Granger Collection, 193 (left and right); UPI/Corbis, 193; UPI/Corbis, 196; Senator's Office, Oklahoma, 198; Culver Pictures, Inc., 203 (top left); Ira Wyman/Corbis/Sygma, 203 (top right); Jean-Marc Giboux/Liaison Agency, Inc., 203 (bottom left); Charlie Neibergall/AP/Wide World Photos, 203 (bottom right); Joel Page/AP/Wide World Photos, 205; Daniel Miller/AP/Wide World Photos, 219; Kevin Moloney/Liaison Agency, Inc., 221.

Chapter 8: Reuters/Rick Wilking/Archive Photos, 228; Eric Gay/AP/Wide World Photos, 230; Reuters/Mike Segar/Archive Photos, 231; AP/Wide World Photos, 233; Consolidated News Pictures/Archive Photos, 234; Ira Wyman/Corbis/Sygma, 237; Lyn-don Baines Johnson Library Collection, 239 (all photos); Stan Wakefield/Pearson Education/PH College, 243 (top and bottom); Reuters/Mike Segar/Archive Photos, 246; Alden Pellett/

AP/Wide World Photos, 248; Doug Mills/AP/Wide World Photos, 249; Jeffrey Macmillan/U.S. News & World Report, 258; Eric Draper/AP/Wide World Photos, 259; Damon Kiesow/Liaison Agency, Inc., 262; Ron Edmonds/AP/Wide World Photos, 269.

Chapter 9: Nina Berman/SIPA Press, 278; Culver Pictures, Inc., 281 (a); Stock Montage, Inc./Historical Pictures Collection, 281 (b); UPI/Corbis, 281 (c); Corbis, 281 (d); UPI/Corbis, 281 (e); LeDuc/Monkmeyer/AP/Wide World Photos, 281 (f); UPI Corbis, 284; AP/Wide World Photos, 290; Najlah Feanny/SABA Press Photos, Inc., 302; Dennis Cook/AP/Wide World Photos, 305.

Chapter 10: Martin Simon/SABA Press Photos, Inc., 316; Doug Mills/AP/Wide World Photos, 319; David Hume Kennerly/Corbis/Sygma, 334; Jeff Greenberg/The Image Works, 339; Ron Edmonds/AP/Wide World Photos, 340; Mike Derer/AP/Wide World Photos, 343; Rick Reinhard/Impact Visuals Photo & Graphics, Inc., 347; Joe Marquette/AP/Wide World Photos, 348; Reuters/Mark Wilson/Archive Photos, 351; Shana Raah/Corbis/Sygma, 352; Justin Lane/Liaison Agency, Inc., 369.

Chapter 11: Dennis Cook/AP/Wide World Photos, 374; Reuters/Jeff Mitchell/Archive Photos, 376; Mookie/Liaison Agency, Inc., 382; Wilfredo Lee/AP/Wide World Photos, 390; Mark Wilson/Liaison Agency, Inc., 392; Liaison Agency, Inc., 394; Greg Gibson/AP/Wide World Photos, 404; U.S. Army Photograph, 406; Yannis Kontos/Corbis/Sygma, 411; AP/Wide World Photos, 412; AP/Wide World Photos, 413.

Chapter 12: Stephen Marks/The Image Bank, 418; Stan Wakefield/Pearson Education/PH College, 422 (left and center); Irene Springer/Pearson Education/PH College 422 (right); Louie Psihoyos/Matrix International, Inc., 424; David Young-Wolff/PhotoEdit,

433; Reuters/Mike Theiler/Archive Photos, 436; Corbis, 437; J. Scott Applewhite/AP/Wide World Photos, 440; Stan Wakefield/Pearson Education/PH College, 444 (top and bottom); Bob Daemmrich/Stock Boston, 452 Robert Trippett/SIPA Press, 455; Richard Ellis/Corbis/Sygma, 457.

Chapter 13: Kenneth Lambert/Washington Times/Liaison Agency, Inc., 462; Cobis, 465; Reuters/Gary Hershorn/Archive Photos, 469; Irene Springer/Pearson Education/PH College, 472; J. Scott Applewhite/AP/Wide World Photos, 475; Colin Braley/Liaison Agency, Inc., 479; Reuters/Rick Wilking/Corbis, 484 (left and right); Rex Banner/Liaison Agency, Inc., 489; Marcy Nighswander/AP/Wide World Photos, 493; AP/Wide World Photos, 494.

Chapter 14: Chuck Nacke/Woodfin Camp & Associates, 502; Rick Bowmer/AP/Wide World Photos, 505; Kamenko Pajic/AP/Wide World Photos, 510; AP/Wide World Photos, 511; Jeff Lowenthal/Woodfin Camp & Associates, 514; Pat Sullivan/AP/Wide World Photos, 515; T. Crosby/Liaison Agency, Inc., 522; Tom Pantages, 494 (left and right); L. Kolvoord/The Image Works, 525; Rod Aydelotte/Waco Tribune Herald/Corbis/Sygma, 528; Steve Miller/AP/Wide World Photos, 532; AP/Wide World Photos, 535.

Chapter 15: Todd Bigelow/Black Star, 544; Culver Pictures, Inc., 548; Library of Congress, 550; The New York Public Library, Schomburg Center for Research in Black Culture, 551; AP/Wide World Photos, 553; Flip Schulke/Black Star, 555; Mike Smith/FPG International LLC, 556; Ira Wyman/Corbis/Sygma, 560; Michael Burchfield/AP/Wide World Photos, 562; Eric Risberg/AP/Wide World Photos, 568; Corbis, 569; Reuters/Ogrocki/Archive Photos, 571; Bob Child/AP/Wide World Photos, 583; Cynthia Johnson/Liaison Agency, Inc., 584.

INDEX

Elections (*continued*)
  See also Congressional elections;
    Presidential election
Electoral College:
  amendment related to, 83
  Democratic base, 263, 266
  first election, 63
  majority, 190
  operation of, 85, 264–65
  and presidential campaign,
    262–63
  reform proposals, 265
  Republican base, 263, 266
  votes per state, 265
Electronic surveillance, 531
Eleventh Amendment, 83, 106
Elitism, 18–20
  defined, 18
  and democratic society, 19–20
  power elite concept, 20
Emancipation Proclamation, 384,
  546–48
EMILY's list, 251
  organization/activities of, 305
End of history concept, elements
  of, 49–50
Engels, Frederick, 47
Engle v. Vitale, 511
Enumerated powers:
  defined, 76, 96
  and federal system, 96
  listing of, 98, 99–100
Environmental Defense Fund,
  309, 433, 457
Environmental interest groups,
  285, 433, 457
Environmental Protection Agency
  (EPA), 429
  functions of, 432–33, 449, 451
Equal Employment Opportunity
  Commission (EEOC), 423
  functions of, 432, 449, 561, 571
  origin of, 557–58
Equal protection:
  amendments related to, 83, 547,
    548
  and *Brown* case, 478
  and death penalty, 539–40
  and federal system, 97
Equal Rights Amendment (ERA),
  570
  ratification issue, 81–82
Equal-time rule, meaning of, 176
Equality, 28–30
  and democracy, 12
  and fairness, 29–30
  of opportunity, 28–29
  political equality, 28
  of results, 29
  See also Inequality
Erlichman, John, 381
Ervin, Sam, on nonvoters, 148
Escobedo v. Illinois, 533
Espionage Act of 1917, 512

no establishment clause, 509–11
  Lemon test, 509
Ethical rules, Congress, 369
Ethics in Government Act of 1978,
  308, 480, 481
European Union, as confederation,
  92
Evers, Medgar, 557
Ex parte Milligan, 467, 529
Ex post facto law, 529
Exclusionary rule, 533–34
Executive agreements, 405–6
Executive branch:
  Cabinet, 396–97
  checks and balances on, 72–73
  and Congress, 391
  Executive Office of the President,
    422
  National Security Council
    (NSC), 397–98
  presidential power over, 391,
    395–98
  White House staff, 398
Executive Office of the President,
  422
Executive orders, 391, 395
Executive power, 83–84, 381–84
Executive privilege, 384–85
Externalities, defined, 9
Extremism, views of, 47

F

Factions, Madison on, 78–79, 280,
  317
Fair Deal, defined, 193
Fairness, as American value, 29–30
Falwell, Jerry, 289
Family, and political socialization,
  123–24
Family Medical Leave Act, 45
Farm organizations, 283, 285, 287
Fascism, elements of, 47
Faubus, Orval, 103, 495
Federal budget, 443–49
  and Congress, 322, 391,
    445–46, 456
  example fiscal year, overview of,
    444
  incremental budgeting, 446–47
  and Office of Management and
    Budget (OMB), 443, 444
  politics of, 446–49
  and president, 396, 443–45
  program budgeting, 449
  types of strategies, 447
  zero-based budgeting, 447–48
Federal Bureau of Investigation
  (FBI), 101, 437
Federal Communications Commission (FCC), 423
  charges for political ads, 241
  equal-time rule, 176

functions of, 176, 432, 449,
  451, 523–24
Federal courts, 471–76
  appeals from state courts,
    474–75
  caseload, rise of, 475, 476
  courts of appeal, 473
  district courts, 472–73
  geographic boundaries of, 474
  structure/organization of, 472
  See also Supreme Court
Federal Deposit Insurance Corporation, functions of, 449
Federal Election Campaign Act of
  1974, 303, 467
Federal Election Commission
  (FEC):
  campaign financing rules,
    252–54
  and political action committees
    (PACs), 303
Federal employees:
  dismissal of, 438
  General Schedule (GS), 437, 438
  See also Bureaucracy
Federal Energy Regulatory
  Commission, functions of, 432
Federal Equal Credit Opportunity
  Act of 1974, 571
Federal funding, political
  campaigns, 252–54
Federal grants:
  block grants, 110
  categorical grants, 108, 110
  grant-in-aid, 108
Federal Gun Control Act of 1968,
  527
Federal Highway Act of 1916, 103,
  366
Federal Home Loan Bank, func-
  tions of, 432
Federal Maritime Commission,
  functions of, 432
Federal offenses, scope of,
  100–101
Federal Register, regulatory
  announcements, 423, 453
Federal Reserve Act of 1913, 435
Federal Reserve Banks, 434, 435
Federal Reserve Board (FRB),
  functions of, 432, 449
Federal Reserve System:
  appointments to, 433
  functions of, 434–35
  structure of, 435
Federal spending:
  and Congress, 321–22
  government waste, 448
Federal Trade Commission, 423
  functions of, 432, 449, 520
Federalism, 90–116
  centralized federalism, 101, 104
  conservative view of, 113
  and Constitution, 70, 96, 98–99

cooperative federalism, 100–101
cross-cultural view, 92
defined, 89–90
and devolution revolution, 112,
  115–16
dual federalism, 99–100
federalism assessment reports,
  115–16
historical events related to,
  102–3
liberal view of, 113
limitations of, 95, 97
modern revival of, 105–6
new federalism, 104
representational federalism,
  104–5
state-centered federalism, 99
strengths of, 93, 95
and welfare reform, 112, 115
See also States and national
  government
Federalist Papers:
  authors of, 74
  on direct democracy, 15
  and ratification of Constitution,
    74–75
  on right to bear arms, 526
  on war powers, 409
Federalists:
  and 1796 election, 85
  on Bill of Rights, 76–77
  party development, 188, 190
  on Supreme Court, 465
Feinstein, Diane, 339
Ferraro, Geraldine, 413
Fifteenth Amendment:
  enforcement of, 97
  rights of, 83, 102, 547, 548
Fifth Amendment, rights of, 81,
  100, 470, 506, 530
Fighting words doctrine, 515, 517
Filibuster, 354
Film censorship, 523
Fireside chats, 182
First Amendment:
  freedom of assembly and peti-
    tion, 81, 279, 294, 525–26
  freedom of press, 81, 159,
    175–77
  freedom of the press, 522–24
  freedom of religion, 16, 508–12
  freedom of speech, 512–22
  and Internet, 179–80
Fiscal year, defined, 443
Fitzgerald, Peter, 337
Flag burning issue, 516
Flag Protection Act of 1989, 516
Focus groups, and political
  campaigns, 238, 240
Foley, Thomas S., 337
Food and Drug Administration:
  approval of drugs, time frame,
    450
  functions of, 431, 432

Forbes, Steve, 253, 259
Ford, Gerald R.:
    and Congress, 401
    Mayzguez attack, 410
    and media, 182
    Nixon pardon, 380, 381
    presidential debate, 268
    Supreme Court appointment, 490–91
    terms of office, 194, 380
Foreign policy:
    Constitution on, 69–70
    and president, 404–7
Foreign Service, 437
Fourteenth Amendment:
    due process clause, 504–5, 547
    enforcement of, 97
    and right to die, 517
    rights of, 83, 102, 103, 470, 504, 517
Fourth Amendment, rights of, 81, 506, 530
Frankfurter, Felix, 463–64
    on judicial self-restraint, 468
Franking privilege, 344
    and incumbents, 236
Franklin, Benjamin, and Constitutional Convention, 66
Free exercise clause, 505, 508
Free market, and good and services, 9
Free-rider problem, 291–92
    defined, 292
Freedom of Access to Clinics Act, 45
Freedom of assembly and petition, 81, 279, 294, 525–26
    picketing, 526
    protests/demonstrations/parades, 525–26
    right of association, 525
Freedom of expression, 515
Freedom House, 12
Freedom of Information Act, 455
Freedom of the press, 81, 159, 175–77, 522–24
    absence of malice concept, 176
    censorship issue, 171
    and electronic media, 175–76
    film censorship, 523
    gag order, 524
    no prior restraint, 175, 522–23
    radio and television censorship, 523–24
    shielding of sources, 177, 524
    special rights issue, 524
    See also Mass media
Freedom of religion, 16, 81, 505, 508–12
    free exercise clause, 505, 508
    no establishment clause, 509–11
    prayer in school issue, 511–12
    religious freedom restoration issue, 512

Freedom of speech, 81, 512–22
    clear and present danger doctrine, 512–13
    commercial speech, 518, 520
    fighting words doctrine, 515, 517
    flag burning issue, 516
    freedom of expression, 515
    hate speech, 518
    libel and slander, 520
    obscenity, 520–22
    preferred position doctrine, 513
    symbolic speech, 515
    wartime restrictions of, 513, 515
Friends of the Earth, 433
Front-end strategy, presidential primaries, 259
Furman v. Georgia, 538–39

G

Gag order, 524
Garcia v. San Antonio Metropolitan Transit Authority, 104
Garfield, James A., 6, 379
Garner, John Nance, 414
Gays in military, 392
Gender gap:
    defined, 133
    and public opinion, 133
    and voting, 267
Gender inequality, 568–73
    civil rights law protections, 571
    earnings gap, 571–72
    and gender classifications, 569–70
    glass ceiling, 572–73
General Accounting Office (GAO), 340–41, 448, 457
General election, and political parties, 205–6
General Schedule (GS), federal employees, 437, 438
Generational effects, political socialization, 129–31
George Bush, in presidential election, 194
Gephardt, Dick, biographical information, 347
Geronimo, 582
Gerrymandering, 326–29
    affirmative gerrymandering, 328
    packing, 326
    partisan gerrymandering, 327–28
    racial gerrymandering, 328–29
    splintering, 326
Gettysburg Address, 16
G.I. Bill of Rights, 366
Gideon v. Wainwright, 533
Gingrich, Newt, 198, 336–37
Ginsberg, Ruth Bader, 329
    as chief justice, 486
    liberalism of, 491
Gitlow v. New York, 505

Glass ceiling, 572–73
Global leadership, of president, 378, 403–7
Glorious Revolution, 56
Goal orientation, defined, 421
Goldwater, Barry, 413
    and media, 182, 239
Goods and services:
    and free market, 9
    public goods, 7
GOP (Grand Old Party), 192
Gore, Al:
    campaign financing, 243
    and media, 183, 239
    party nomination of, 259
    presidential debate, 269
    reinventing government, 440
    as vice president, 413, 414
Gore, Tipper, 171
Government:
    defined, 2–3
    functions of, 7–9
    institutions of, 3
    legitimacy of, 5
    outcomes/goals of, 3
    participants in, 3
    processes related to, 3
    public confidence/trust issue, 4–5
    See also National government
Government corporations:
    functions of, 433
    listing of, 422
Government Printing Office (GPO), 341
Government spending:
    decline in relation to economy, 10–11
    extent of, 425
    largest outlays, 11
Governmental interest groups, 283, 285, 291
Governmental organizations, and Constitution, 98
Governmental systems:
    confederation, 90–91
    federalism, 90–116
    unitary system, 90–91
Grand Army of the Republic, 283
Grand jury:
    indictment by, 532
    role of, 473
Grant of immunity, 533
Grant-in-aid, defined, 108
Grants. *See* Federal grants
Grass-roots lobbying, 299–300
Great Compromise, provisions of, 64
Great Depression:
    and cooperative federalism, 100–101
    generation of, 130
    stock market crash of 1929, 192–93

Great Society, 10, 400
    defined, 194
    programs of, 101, 104, 110
Green Party, 218
Greenback Party, 218
Greenspan, Alan, biographical information, 436
Grenada, 410
Gridlock, 368–69, 402
Griswold v. Connecticut, 492
Gross domestic product (GDP):
    amount of, 9, 10
    defined, 9
Gun control:
    and Gun Free School Zones Act, 105, 106, 107
    and right to bear arms, 526–28
Gun Free School Zones Act, 105, 107, 467

H

Halderman, H.R., 381
Halo effect, public opinion polls, 121
Hamilton, Alexander:
    and Constitutional Convention, 60, 72
    and *Federalist Papers*, 74–75
    on impeachment, 324, 382
    on judicial system, 464
    national bank proposal, 102, 188
    as secretary of treasury, 66, 396
Hancock, John, 57
Hanna, Marcus Alonzo, 191
Hard money, campaign contributions, 244
Harding, Warren G., 192
Harlan, John, on segregation, 563, 564
Harris v. Forklift, 574
Harrison, Benjamin, 264
Harrison, William Henry, in presidential election, 191
Hastert, Dennis, 348
Hastings, Alcee, 498
Hatch Act of 1939, 437
Hate crimes, 514
Hate speech, 517–18
Hayes, Rutherford B., in presidential election, 264
Health care, American Medical Association (AMA) position on, 286
Health vs. Alabama, 100
Helms, Jesse, 251
Henry, Patrick, at Constitutional Convention, 75
Heritage Foundation, 114, 295
Herrnstein, Richard J., 34
Hill, Anita, 484
Hispanic Americans, 573–78
    Cuban Americans, 574, 577

Marshall, John (*continued*)
  and *Marbury v. Madison*, 72, 464–65
  and Native Americans, 581
Marshall, Thurgood, 309
  and *Brown* decision, 485, 549, 552
  as chief justice, 485–86
  and death penalty, 538–39
Marx, Karl, 47
Marxism, elements of, 47, 49
Mason, George, opposition to Constitution, 80
Mass media:
  agenda-setting, 164, 180
  bad news bias, 166
  books and recordings, 160–61
  censorship, 523–24
  conservatism of, 169, 170
  defined, 158
  effects on behavior, 181–83
  effects on values and opinions, 180–81
  and elections. *See* Mass media and elections
  Federal Communication Commission (FCC), 176
  freedom of press, 81, 159, 175–77
  and information overload, 180
  Internet, 161–62, 177–80
  interpretation of news by, 164–65
  libel and slander, 176–77
  liberalism of, 168, 169
  magazines, 160
  motion pictures, 160
  muckraking, 166, 168
  national news media, 157–58
  newsmaking, 162
  newspapers, 160
  persuasive power of, 165
  political media innovations, 182
  and political socialization, 131–32, 165
  and president, 388–90
  public attention to, 167
  and public opinion, 181
  public opinion of, 169, 178
  and sensationalism, 166
  talk radio, 160, 170
  television, 158, 160
Mass media and elections:
  campaign watchdog role of media, 173
  and candidate selection, 172–73
  candidate-voter linkage, 171–72
  equal-time rule, 176
  free airtime, 241
  historical view, 182–83
  horserace coverage, 173
  image of candidates, 272, 274

negative campaigning, 238, 239
news management, 240–41
paid advertising, 241
persuasion and media, 165
photo ops, 241
political bias, 173–74
privacy of candidate issue, 173, 174
sound bites, 241
spin doctors, role of, 258
Mayaguez, 410
Mayflower Compact, 56
Media. *See* Mass media
Medicaid, 366
Medicare, 9, 11, 366
Meese, Ed, 408
Merit system, 437
Mexican Americans, 36, 574, 575–76
Mikulski, Barbara, 339
Military forces:
  and Constitution, 68–69, 98
  in domestic disputes, 411–12
  War Powers Act, 410–11
Militia Act of 1792, 528
Militia movements, 6, 528–29
Mill, John Stuart, 148
  and gun laws, 528–29
Miller v. California, 521
Miller, William, 413
Mills, C. Wright, 20
Minorities. *See* Race and ethnicity; specific minority groups
Minority leader:
  House of Representatives, 346–47
  Senate, 348
Minutemen, 56–57
Miranda rights, 533, 534
Miranda v. Arizona, 533
Missouri Compromise, 467
Mitchell, John, 381
Moderates, public opinion of, 132–33
Mondale, Walter, 197
  presidential debate, 268
  as vice president, 414
Monetary policy, and Federal Reserve System, 434–35
Montpelier, 78, 79
Mormons, and polygamy, 505
Morrill Land Grant Act of 1862, 103
Moseley-Brown, Carol, 337
Mothers Against Drunk Driving (MADD), 109, 291
Mott, Lucretia, 287, 568
Mount Vernon, 62
Muckraking, 166, 168
Murray, Charles, 34
Murry, Patty, 339
Mussolini, Benito, 47
Myers, Michael Ozzie, 370

N

Nader, Ralph, 288
  biographical information, 290
Name recognition, of political candidates, 240
Nast, Thomas, 192
National Abortion Rights Action League (NARAL), 288, 291, 302, 309, 310
National Association for the Advancement of Colored People (NAACP), 21
  and *Brown* decision, 552
  Legal Defense Fund, 308–9, 485
  origin of, 280, 283, 551
National Association of Broadcasters, 285, 286
National Association of Counties, 291
National Association of Manufacturers, 285, 286, 295
National Association of Real Estate Boards, 285, 286
National Audubon Society, 433
National Conference of State Legislators, 291
National Congressional Club, 251
National Council of Churches, 288
National Education Association, 283, 286, 287
  and campaign finance, 248
National Farmers Union, 287
National Federation of Independent Businesses, 286
National Firearms Act of 1934, 527
National government:
  checks and balances, 72–73
  concurrent powers, 96, 98
  enumerated powers, 76–77, 96, 98
  as federal system, 90–116
  implied powers, 96, 98
  national supremacy, 96
  powers denied by Constitution, 98, 99
  reserved powers, 96
  separation of powers, 72–74
  and states. *See* States and national government
  structure defined by Constitution, 70–71
National Governors Association, 283, 291
National Grange, 287
National Labor Relations Act, 366
National Labor Relations Board, 423
  functions of, 432, 449
National League of Cities, 283, 291
National Organization for Women (NOW), 283, 288, 302, 310

National Park Service, 457
National party convention, 208–12, 259
  delegates, 209
  kickoff, 212
  party rules, 209–10
  platforms, 210
  running mate selection, 210, 212
  superdelegates, 210
National Performance Review, 440
National Reconnaissance Office, 406
National Resources Defense Council, 433
National Rifle Association (NRA), 21, 291
  and campaign finance, 248
National Right-to-Life Committee, 288, 291
National Security Agency, 406
National Security Council (NSC), 397–98, 406
National supremacy, and Constitution, 70
National Supremacy Clause, 110
  defined, 96
National Taxpayers Union, 291
National Transportation Safety Board, 449
National Voter Registration Act of 1993, 142, 144
  provisions of, 111
National Wildlife Federation, 433, 457
Nationalism:
  defined, 61
  Founder's belief in, 61
Native Americans, 578–83
  American Indian Movement (AIM), 582
  in Congress, 340
  destruction of population, 579
  Indian Wars, 581–82
  loss of land, 580–81
  and New Deal, 582
  reservations, 580–81
  violence toward, 6
Natural Resources Defense Council, 309
Near v. Minnesota, 522
Necessary and Proper Clause:
  defined, 96
  and *McCulloch v. Maryland*, 102
Negative campaigning, 238
New Deal, 10
  as cooperative federalism, 100–101
  defined, 193
  and Native Americans, 582
  New Deal Democratic coalition, 193
New federalism, 104
New Frontier, 194

Progressive Party. *See* Bull Moose
Party
Prohibition, amendments related
to, 83, 218, 569
Prohibition Party, 218
Property qualifications, and voting
rights, 139
Proportional representation,
meaning of, 224–25
Protest parties, 216
Protests, 149, 152–54
civil disobedience, 149, 152
defined, 149
effectiveness of, 152–54
freedom of assembly, 525–26
and organized interest groups,
300–301
as political participation, 149
violence, 152
Public Citizen, 288, 290
Public goods, defined, 7
Public-interest groups, 285, 288
Public Interest Research Groups
(PIRGs), 290
Public opinion:
on abortion, 124–25
on affirmative action, 136,
566–67
of bureaucracy, 420
of college students, 130
on confidence in media, 178
of Congressional representatives,
333
cross-cultural view, 128
defined, 120
and gender gap, 133
and ideology, 132–33
mass media influence, 181
of media bias, 169
on money in politics, 245
and policy making, 136–38
and political socialization,
122–32
and politics, 119–20
and race, 134–36
of state versus national government, 94
and Supreme Court decisions,
491
trust in branches of government,
74
Public opinion polls:
accuracy issue, 122–23
halo effect, 121
impulsive answering of, 121
and knowledge level of Americans, 120–21
random selection of participants,
122
and salient issues, 121–22
wording of questions, effects of,
121
Public relations, of interest
groups, 297
Publius, *Federalist Papers*, 74–75

Puerto Ricans, 36, 574, 576–77
Puerto Rico:
as commonwealth, 576
statehood issue, 577
Putin, Vladimir, 92

Q

Quayle, Dan, 171
as vice president, 413, 414
Quota, affirmative action, 560

R

Race and ethnicity, 35–36
African Americans, 35–36
in federal bureaucracy, 441
Hispanic Americans, 36, 573–78
and life chances, 559
Native Americans, 578–83
and public opinion, 134–36
and voting participation, 146–47
and voting pattern, 267
Racial gerrymandering, 328–29
Racial inequality:
and affirmative action, 560–68
and civil rights legislation,
555–58
and civil rights movement,
549–54
and death penalty, 539–40
income inequality, 558–59
segregation, 548–49
slavery, 546–48
Racketeer Influenced and Corrupt
Practices Act (RICO), 536
Radicalism:
academic radicalism, 50–52
and United States Constitution,
59
views of, 47
Radio:
censorship issue, 523–24
talk-radio, 160, 170
Raiding, primary elections, 205
Randolph, Edmund, and Constitutional Convention, 63
Random sample, for public opinion polls, 122
Rather, Dan, 163
Ratification:
of Constitution, 74–75
defined, 74
Reagan, Ronald:
and Bork nomination, 482–83,
491
and Congress, 401–2
and deregulation, 451–52
and federal aid, 110
federalism assessment reports,
115–16
as Great Communicator, 172,
196, 274

Iran-Conta affair, 408
presidential debate, 268
in presidential election, 194,
196
Reagan Coalition, 194, 196
Supreme Court appointments,
489, 491
tax cuts, 400
troops in Lebanon, 410
Realignment:
elections of, 214
party voters, 214–15
Reciprocity norm, lawmaking
process, 367–68
Redistricting:
meaning of, 326
splintering, 326–27
Reed, Ralph, 289
Reed v. Reed, 569–70
Referenda, defined, 71
Reform Party, 219–23
and Ross Perot, 220–22
Regulation, 449–54
activist regulators, 451, 452
capture theory of regulation,
451
cost of, 453–54
deregulation, 451–52
independent regulatory commissions, 431, 432
pros and cons of, 450
publication of new rules, 453
reregulation, 452
rule-making process, 423
and Supreme Court, 468
Regulation of Lobbying Act, 294
Rehnquist, William H., 486
biographical information, 489
and conservative bloc, 490, 491,
494
on prayer in schools, 511
and *U.S. vs. Lopez*, 105–6
on war powers, 409
Religious Freedom Restoration
Act, 512
Religious freedom. *See* Freedom of
religion
Religious interest groups, 285,
288
Religious orientation:
of Americans, statistics on,
128–29
and political socialization,
127–29
Remedies and relief, court decision, 479
Removal Act, 581
Reno vs. American Civil Liberties,
179
Representational federalism,
104–5
Representative democracy, meaning of, 17–18
Republican National Committee,
207

Republican Party:
and African Americans, 198
and Christian Coalition, 289
in Congress (Clinton administration), 199, 336–37, 402
Contract with America, 198
delegates, profile of, 209
electoral base, 263, 266
elephant as symbol, 192
as GOP (Grand Old Party), 192
largest contributors to, 250
liberal/conservative senators,
292
men versus women members,
133
party development, 191–92,
194, 196–97
party strength, regional view,
217
platform of, 211
popular image of, 201
presidential nominees/presi-
dents (1789–2000), 189
Republican National Committee, 207
and vice presidential candidate,
413
voter profile, 214–16, 267
Republicanism:
and Constitution, 61, 70–71
defined, 61
Rescission, defined, 385
Reservations, Native Americans,
580–81
Reserved powers:
defined, 96
and federal system, 96
listing of, 98, 109
Reserved Powers Clause, 105
Responsible party model, meaning
of, 200
Restricted rule, 354
Results, equality of, 29
Retrospective voting, 230–31
Revolutionary War, 6, 56–57
and Washington, 62–63
Revolving doors, 307–8
Reynolds, Mel, 370
Richardson, Elliot, 481
Rider, to bill, 355
Right to bear arms, 81, 506,
526–29
and gun control, 526–27
and militias, 528–29
Right to die, 517
Right ideology, defined, 47
Rights of criminal defendants,
529–40
amendments related to, 81, 530
bail requirements, 535
bill of attainder, prohibition of,
529
and death penalty, 538–40
double jeopardy, 538
drug testing, 531–32

Subculture, defined, 25
Suffrage:
  defined, 139
  women's suffrage movement, 283
  See also Voting rights
Sullivan rule, defined, 176
Superdelegates, defined, 210
Supreme Court:
  acceptance of cases, 486–87
  and amendment process, 82–83
  appeals to, 473–74
  and checks and balances, 72–73
  in conference, 488
  and Congress, 497–98
  and Constitution, 71, 464–66
  hearing arguments, 487
  and interest groups, 494
  interpretation of statutory laws, 467–68
  judicial activism of, 470
  judicial review, 72, 82–83, 464–65
  judicial self-restraint of, 468–69, 471
  jurisdiction, 472
  liberal/conservative voting blocs, 490–91, 494
  opinions, types of, 488
  and original intent of Constitution, 470
  packing of, 465, 467, 497
  and policymaking, 486–87
  presidential influence, 491, 494, 496–97
  restraints on, 495–98
  session, time period, 474
  stare decisis, 470–71
  writ of certiorari, 486
Supreme Court judges:
  background/experience of, 485–86
  selection of, 480, 482–86
Survey research:
  defined, 120
  See also Public opinion polls
Swann v. Charlotte-Mecklenburg County Board of Education, 553
Symbolic speech, 515

T

Taft-Hartley Act of 1947, 384
Taft, William Howard, 192, 219
  as chief justice, 485
  on executive power, 382
Talk-radio, 160
  conservatism of, 170
Taney, Roger, on racism, 546
Tariffs:
  and Constitution, 68
  defined, 68
Taxation:
  amendment related to, 83

and Congress, 321–22
and Constitution, 66, 67, 68
Teamsters Union, 287
Television:
  cable TV, 160
  censorship issue, 523–24
  historical political events on, 182–83
  leading news anchors, 163
  leading news programs, 158
  power of, 158
  and public opinion, 131–32
  See also Mass media; Mass media and elections
Television malaise, defined, 181
Temporary Assistance to Needy Families program, provisions of, 112, 115
Tennessee Valley Authority, 433
Tenth Amendment, rights of, 81, 96, 105, 507
Term limits, legislators, 332
Texas, electoral votes, 263
Texas v. Johnson, 516
Third Amendment:
  enforcement of, 97
  rights of, 81, 506
Third parties, 216–19
  ideological parties, 216
  presidential candidates, 219–20
  protest parties, 216
  single-issue parties, 218
  splinter parties, 218–19
Thirteenth Amendment, rights of, 83, 102, 507, 547
Thomas, Clarence:
  biographical information, 484
  conservatism of, 484, 491
Thornburg v. Gingles, 328
Three-fifths Compromise, 65
Thurmond, Strom, 219, 330
Tilden, Samuel, 264
Tippecanoe, 191
Tocqueville, Alexis de, 463
Total preemption, defined, 111
Totalitarianism, defined, 15
Tower Commission, 408
Tower, John, 397, 431
Trade associations:
  interest groups, 285, 286
  political action committees (PACs), 304
Treatise on Civil Government (Locke), 14
Treaty making, of president, 405
Truman Doctrine, 366
Truman, Harry, 391, 415
  desegregation of armed forces, 395, 560
  and Fair Deal, 193
  Korean War, 409
Trust in government, 4
Trustees, legislators as, 363
Turner, Ted, 160, 182

Twelfth Amendment, 83, 190
Twentieth Amendment, 83
Twenty-first Amendment, 79, 83, 218
Twenty-second Amendment, 83, 379
Twenty-third Amendment, 83, 264
Twenty-fourth Amendment, 83, 140
Twenty-fifth Amendment, 83, 346, 379–80
Twenty-sixth Amendment, 83, 109, 141–42, 146
Twenty-seventh Amendment, 83
Tyler, John, 191

U

Unanimous consent agreement, 354
Unfunded mandates, 112
Unions. *See* Labor organizations
Unitary system, 90–91
  elements of, 90
United Farm Workers, 577
United Nations Treaty, 405
United States v. Lopez, 467
United States v. Miller, 527
United States v. Nixon, 381, 385
United States v. Paradise, 562
United Steelworkers of America v. Weber, 562
University of California Regents v. Bakke, 487, 561–62
Unreasonable search and seizure, 531
Urban League for African Americans, 21
U.S. Chamber of Commerce, 285, 286
U.S. Conference of Mayors, 283
U.S. Postal Service, 433, 437
U.S. Tax Code, 424
U.S. vs. Lopez, 105–6, 107

V

Values, defined, 25
Van Buren, Martin:
  in presidential election, 190
  as vice president, 415
Ventura, Jesse, biographical information, 221
Veterans of Foreign Wars, 21, 283, 457
Veterans' interest groups, 283, 285
Veto, 362, 402–3
  line-item veto, 402–3
  override by Congress, 362, 402
  pocket veto, 402

Vice president, 412–15
  in presidency position, 415
  roles/functions of, 414
  as running mate, selection of, 210, 212
  selection of, 412–14
  senatorial role, 348
  succession of president, 379–80
Vietnam Veterans of America, 283
Vietnam War, 407, 409
  and Democratic Party, 194
Vigilantism, 6
Violence:
  and American politics, 6
  as political participation, 152
Virginia and Kentucky Resolutions, and states' rights, 97
Virginia Plan, 60, 64
Volker, Paul, 436
Voter registration, 143–44
  defined, 143
  Motor Voter Act, 142, 144
  purpose of, 143
Voter turnout, 142–49
  Congressional elections, 333–34
  cross-cultural view, 147
  decline, reasons for, 145–46
  defined, 142
  effects of nonvoting, 148–49
  nonvoters, profile of, 146–47
  nonvoting, reasons for, 142–45
  politics of, 144–46
  voters, profile of, 146
Voting:
  decision-making in presidential election, 267, 272, 274
  and direct democracy, 76
  group voting, 267, 272–73
  and party loyalty, 213
  race and gender gap, 267
  retrospective voting, 230–31
  voter profiles by party, 214–16, 267
Voting rights, 139–42
  African Americans, 139–40, 231
  and age, 146
  amendments related to, 83
  Civil Rights Act of 1964, 140
  as Constitutional Convention issue, 66
  disenfranchisement, forms of, 139–40
  Fifteenth Amendment, 139
  National Voter Registration Act of 1993, 142
  Nineteenth Amendment, 141
  property qualifications, removal of, 139
  Twenty-fourth Amendment, 140
  Twenty-sixth Amendment, 141–42
  Voting Rights Act of 1965, 141
  women, 141